COMPUTING FUNDAMENTALS AND PROGRAMMING IN C

Other titles by the same author

➲ **HANDBOOK OF COMPUTER FUNDAMENTALS**
ISBN : 978-93-82609-67-4
Pages : 400

➲ **SOFTWARE ENGINEERING**
ISBN : 978-81-90611-63-3
Pages : 656

COMPUTING FUNDAMENTALS AND PROGRAMMING IN C

Dr. Nasib Singh Gill
FIETE, PDS(Brunel, UK), Ph.D.(Computer Sc.), MBA
Professor & Head
Department of Computer Science & Applications and
Director, University Computer Centre
M.D. University, Rohtak–124001
Haryana, India

KHANNA BOOK PUBLISHING CO. (P) LTD.
Publisher of Engineering and Computer Books
4C/4344, Ansari Road, Darya Ganj, New Delhi-110002
Phone : 011-23244447-48 **Mobile:** +91-9910909320
E-mail : contact@khannabooks.com
Website : www.khannabooks.com

Dear Readers,

To prevent the piracy, this book is secured with HIGH SECURITY HOLOGRAM on the front title cover. In case you don't find the hologram on the front cover title, please write us to at contact@khannabooks.com or whatsapp us at +91-99109 09320 and avail special gift voucher for yourself.

Specimen of Hologram on front Cover title:

Moreover, there is a SPECIAL DISCOUNT COUPON for you with EVERY HOLOGRAM.

How to avail this SPECIAL DISCOUNT:

Step 1: Scratch the hologram
Step 2: Under the scratch area, your "coupon code" is available
Step 3: Logon to www.khannabooks.com
Step 4: Use your "coupon code" in the shopping cart and get your copy at a special discount
Step 5: Enjoy your reading!

Price: ₹ 625.00

ISBN: 978-93-81068-50-2

Computing Fundamentals and Programming in C
by Nasib S. Gill

First Edition: 2014
Reprint Edition: 2025

To view complete list of books, Please scan the QR Code:

Published by:
Khanna Book Publishing Co. (P) Ltd.
CIN: U22110DL1998PTC095547

Visit us at: **www.khannabooks.com**
Write us at: **contact@khannabooks.com**

Printed in Bharat.

DEDICATION

This book is dedicated to all

My Family Members,

My Relatives,

My Friends,

My Students,

&

All Beloved Readers.

"If someone says 'can't,' that shows you what to do."

— John Cage

"Power comes not from knowledge kept, but from knowledge shared."

— Bill Gates

"A ship in port is safe, but that is not what ships are for. Sail out to sea and do new things."

— Admiral Grace Hopper, Computer Pioneer

PREFACE

Computing Fundamentals and Programming in C is designed to serve as a unique book for an introductory core course on computers and programming in C. Written in a clear and lucid style, the book encourages self-study and motivates the student towards independent problem solving.

Computers play a pivotal role in our everyday lives. If you are curious about computers, if you want to know how they work and what they can do for you, and if we wonder what a computerized world of the future would be like, this book will help you - whatever your education and background.

We may use a computer as a medium to get more information, as a tool to perform certain activities, or as an integral part of another component.

The fundamentals of computers are the stepping stones to computer science. Nowadays, all courses, related and unrelated to computer science, require using a computer. Knowledge of the basics of computers has become a fundamental requirement, in whatever area we choose to study or follow professionally.

Today there is an ever-increasing awareness and curiosity about computers among people in all walks of life. In today's information age, knowledge of computer is a must. We feel mildly threatened by this new technology that is spreading fast, and have an inner urge to learn something about this new technology. Parents want their children to choose computer science as a subject in schools, youngsters enroll in large numbers in numerous computer professional classes and adults look for appreciation courses and books on computers.

While books on computer fundamentals and programming are plenty in number, there are not many which give broad introduction starting from computer evolution, its development, operation, applications, and implications and up till programming concepts in detail. This book is meant to fill this gap and is aimed at professionals, students and laymen who want to understand computers, network concepts, programming awareness and becoming proficient in C programming. While the presentation is kept simple, the coverage is wide.

The book begins with an introduction to the history of computing, basics of computer, number systems and data representation, codes, input/output devices, memory and secondary storage devices, software and basic concepts of operating systems. A major part of the book provides a detailed coverage of both computing fundamental related aspects as well as programming in C so that reader may to acquire the skills starting from grasping the basic knowledge of computers to writing programs in C. Concepts such as compilers, linkers, loaders, data types, functions, arrays, strings, pointers, and file management have been explained exhaustively. The book also includes case studies demonstrating the use of C in solving mathematical as well as real-life problems. Memory models, command-line arguments, and bitwise operators have been included to demonstrate the variety of problems that C can address. Interspersed with numerous solved examples based on daily life, the theory is also well supported by plenty of exercises at the end of each chapter.

This book fully meets the requirements of the students of undergraduate engineering courses as well as undergraduate and postgraduate students of computer applications. In other words, the book serves the purpose for almost all courses having subject on Computer Fundaments and C Programming including B.E./B.Tech., B.Sc. (Pass Course), B.Sc.(Computer Science), B.Sc.(IT), BCA, BCAII, MCA, MCAII, M.Sc.(Computer Science), M.Sc.(IT), M.Tech.(CSE/IT), MBA and so on.

When readers enjoy what they read, they remember it. The text's friendly style encourages students to read and increase their comprehension.

I would like to point out in advance that this book has been written based on the work done by many people who have provided information directly or indirectly through their books, publications or lectures. However, references have been provided at the end of the book, from where the author has drawn material for use.

I would appreciate if the readers notify me of any errors or omissions in the book. Also if you would like to suggest improvements or to contribute exercises, I would be glad to hear from you. I will do my utmost to ensure that they are corrected and serve your purpose most appropriately.

Key Features of the Book:

- *The complete spectrum of computing fundamentals starting from abc of computers to Internet usage has been well covered in simple and readers loving style.*
- *The language used in the book is lucid, is easy to understand, and facilitates easy grasping of concepts.*
- *The chapters have been logically arranged in sequence.*
- *The book is written in a reader-friendly manner both for the students and the teachers.*
- *Most of the contents presented in the book are in the form of bullets, organized sequentially. This form of presentation, rather than in a paragraph form, facilitates the reader to view, understand and remember the points better.*
- *The explanation is supported by diagrams, pictures and images wherever required.*
- *Sufficient exercises have been included for practice in addition to the solved examples in every chapter related to C programming.*
- *Pedagogy followed for sequencing the contents on C programming supported by adequate programming examples is likely to help the reader to become proficient very soon.*
- *Concepts of Pointers, Structures, Union and File Management have been extensively detailed to help advance learners.*
- *Adequate exercises have been given at the end of the every chapter.*
- *200 Problems on C Programming & their solutions.*
- *250 Additional descriptive questions on C programming.*

Contents

— NASIB SINGH GILL

ACKNOWLEDGEMENTS

It is my pleasure to take this opportunity to thank all those who helped me directly or indirectly in preparation of this book. The writing of a book of this nature would not have been possible without consulting the writings of many other learned writers and I am really indebted to all of them.

It took me almost three years to write this book. During my journey of book writing, I have been helped and supported by my family, friends and colleagues. I express my gratitude to one and all for their extensive support in this endeavor.

My special thanks go to all my students, who have always been eager to inform me the expectations of the students of a book. Their suggestions and feedback have helped me write this kind of simple book.

I am grateful to all my colleagues (Prof. Rajender Singh, Mrs. Pooja Mittal, Mrs. Preeti Gulia, Dr. Balkishan, Mr. Sandeep Dalal, Mr. Gopal Singh, Mrs. Pooja Singh, Prem Parkash, Dr. Priti, Mr. Ajay Sharma, Mr. Sushil Kumar, Mr. Ranbir, Mr. Surjeet and Mr. Subhash) in the Department of Computer Science & Applications and all well-wishers in the University for encouraging me directly or indirectly to write a simple and useful book on the subject. I thank them for their valuable advice and for their encouragement to disseminate information. I also thank them for continually inspiring me to write a good book.

Thanks to my publishers especially Mr Mukul Seth and Mr Puneet Khanna of Khanna Book Publishing Company (P) Ltd, New Delhi for their extensive support by providing their copyrighted needed stuff as well as bearing the delay in bringing this book in this form due to my existing overburdening responsibilities in the University.

I express my deep regards and love to my mother Mrs. Parmeshwari Devi, my wife Kamla Gill, my both sisters Saroj & Rajni, and Jijashri Sh. I.S. Balaine. Their affection makes me feel special, and I thank them both for guiding me through life and internal boosting to keep doing something new. My thanks are due, in memory of my father Late Sh Karam Singh Gill and my grandmother Late Manbhari Devi, who always loved and supported me. I also thank Prof. M.S. Punia, Mrs. Urmil, Asha, Sarla, Ashu, Vijay, and naughty Er. Vijender Singh and Er. Anand Dagar.

My special thanks to my lovely sons, Sahil and Sanket, my lovely nephews and nieces, namely, Amit, Neelam, Preeti, Akanksha, Jasmeet, Kannu, Vineet, Sakshi, Sarthak, Chulbul, Digvijay, Youvraj and Kartikey, for continually refreshing me as and when met, and making me ready for further long seating in accomplishing their expectation of me to achieve this piece of work.

Since this is not the first book on this topic, I thank the authors of other books on similar topic, whose books have been a source of ideas for me.

I thank the Almighty without whose grace it would have been impossible for me to accomplish this task.

–Nasib Singh Gill

CONTENTS

History of Computing

1.1 INTRODUCTION

In this chapter we will discuss the history of computing because it will give us the basic idea about the technological development trends in the past and its projection in the time to come. If we are interested to know about computers completely then we must start from the history of computers and look into the details of various technological advancements.

Man has developed from time to time various instruments to assist him in day-to-day calculation and for his data-processing needs. Depending upon the type of instruments used, the span of period has been split into following three ages:

- **Dark Age (5000 B.C. - 1890 A.D.)**
- **Middle Age (1890 - 1944)**
- **Modern Age (Since 1944)**

1.2 DARK AGE (5000 B.C. - 1890 A.D.)

In this age all the computing devices were manual-mechanical in nature and all the earliest data processing equipment were all manual-mechanical devices. We refer to the era when these machines were used exclusively as the Dark Ages of data processing. This age introduced the following devices.

1.2.1 Fingers

Perhaps the simplest calculating device which we can think of is our own fingers, which are certainly very easier and more portable. Even right now, children are taught by making use of fingers to add and subtract. This method of finger reckoning was widely used until a few centuries ago.

1.2.2 Abacus (5000 B.C)

Historian start the history of calculations with the Abacus and it was one of the simplest and earliest devices to aid arithmetic. Abacus was developed in China and was used by Greeks, Romans and Chinese. Abacus is nothing but a frame with beads strung on wires or rods. Abacus is shown in *Fig. 1.1.*

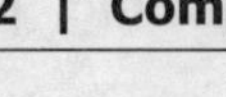

Fig. 1.1: Abacus

Arithmetic calculations are performed by manipulating the beads strung on different wires. The abacus is still used world-wide. A skilled abacus operator can calculate even faster than a clerk using a desk calculator. It is still in use in India and some Western countries.

1.2.3 Napier's Bones (1617)

John Napier (1550-1617), a Scottish mathematician, brought about the next great step towards today's computers. Napier is known for something called Napier's Bones. His ***"bones"*** are a set of eleven rods with numbers marked on them in such a way that by simply placing the rods side by side products and quotients of large numbers can be obtained. Napier is also best known for the invention of logarithms, which in turn led to the slide rule. It has also been claimed that, Napier also introduced the decimal point into common usage and eliminated the use of notation to indicate fractional position.

1.2.4 Oughtred's Slide Rule (1632)

Although the slide rule appeared in various forms in Europe during the 17th century, its invention is attributed to the English mathematician William Oughtred. He is credited for two discoveries, both of which were forms of a slide rule. He introduced the circular slide rule and the rectangular slide rule. Basically a slide rule consists of two movable rulers placed side by side. Each ruler is marked off in such a way that the actual distances from the beginning of the ruler are proportional to the logarithms of the numbers printed on the ruler. By sliding the rulers one can quickly multiply and divide. Each of these instruments had a common accuracy of three digits.

1.2.5 Schickard's Calculator (1623)

Wilhelm Schickard, a professor at the University of Tubingen, Germany, built the first mechanical calculator in 1623. It could work with six digits, and carried digits across columns. It worked, but never made beyond the prototype stage.

1.2.6 Pascal's Calculator

Blaise Pascal (1623-1662) was a great French mathematician and was also the son of a mathematician and tax collector, Etienne Pascal. Blaise Pascal ***(Fig. 1.2)*** is most remembered among Computer Scientists as the inventor of the calculator.

Fig. 1.2 : Blaise Pascal

In 1642, he presented this calculator his father to assist him. This calculator, called Pascaline, resembled the mechanical calculators used in 1940's. Pascal's Calculator is shown in ***Fig. 1.3.***

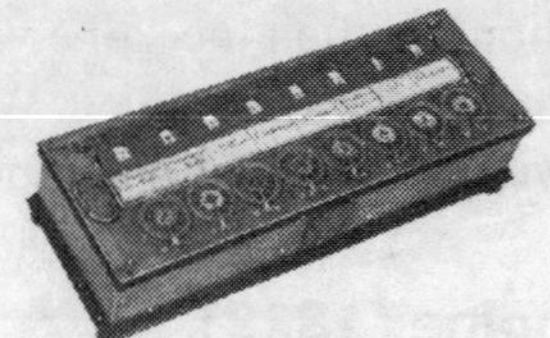

Fig. 1.3 : Pascal's Calculator

It didn't end the contributions by Pascal. He also invented the syringe, the hydraulic press, and Pascal's law of pressure. Pascal built Pascaline based on the design described by Hero of Alexandria to add up the distance travelled by a carriage. The basic principle of his calculator is still used today in Water Meters and modern-day Odometers.

The automobile odometer is an example of a device that still uses a series of cogwheels to calculate data. Pascal's machine was improved by the philosopher and mathematician Leibnitz, whose "Wheel" could also perform multiplication and division. Leibnitz Wheel is shown in *Fig. 1.4.*

Fig. 1.4 : Leibnitz Wheel

1.2.7 Leibnitz's Steppard Reckoner

Leibnitz (1646-1716) was born in Saxony (now Germany). He was most associated with his contributions to Integral Calculus. In 1694, he invented the Steppard Reckoner. This was another calculator similar to that of Pascaline, except that this device used stepped cylinders, like a music box, rather than gears. Based on the decimal system this device could multiply and divide as well as add and subtract. Unfortunately, both this and the Pascaline were simple too complicated for mass production and so they remained one-of-a-kind.

1.2.8 Jacquard's Loom (1801)

Joseph Marie Jacquard (1752-1834) was born in Lyon, France. He was a stone mason and later a weaver. He introduced the Punched Card Loom in 1801. This device was a new type of loom for weaving cloth. Punched cards controlled its operation. Needles could pull threads through cards where there were holes and not where were no holes. Thus pattern were stored on punched-cards. The pattern woven by the loom was determined by the placement of holes in a control card - only those threads whose guiding hook encountered a hole in the card could enter the pattern.

Fig. 1.5 :Jacquard's Loom

1.2.9 Colmar's Arithmometer (1820)

Thomas de Colmar (1785-1870) invented his first Arithmometer in 1820. This was the first mass produced calculator. It did multiplication in much the same way as Stepped Reckoner but at the size of about a desktop was much smaller and easier to produce. With some assistance from the user could do division as well. This device was widely used, but the importance of it was the inspirations that it later caused.

1.2.10 Babbage's Difference Engine (1823)

Charles Babbage (1792-1871) realized in 1812 that many long computations consisted of operations that were regularly repeated. Following this, he designed a calculating machine called Difference Engine. Difference Engine is shown in ***Fig. 1.6.***

Fig. 1.6 : Babbage's Difference Engine

It is based on the principal that, for certain formulas, the difference between certain values is constant. A machine of this type was later adopted by insurance companies for computing life tables.

1.2.11 Babbage's Analytical Engine (1833)

Charles Babbage (1792-1871) followed the difference engine with a much deeper and more general conception. This machine, never realized owing to the limited technology of the time, would have contained many features of present-day computers, including punched-card input, storage unit, arithmetic unit, printing unit, and control by a sequential program.

1.3 MIDDLE AGE (1890-1944)

In the Middle Age, all computing devices were electro-mechanical in nature. In other words, these worked mechanically with the help of electricity.

1.3.1 Hollerith's Tabulating Machine

The Middle Ages of data processing are said to have begun when Dr. Hollerith ***(Fig. 1.7),*** a statistician with the U.S. Bureau of the Census, completed a set of machines to help process the results of the 1890 census. Using 3 by 5 inch punched cards to record the data, he consulted a box to sort the data and a manually fed, electromagnetic counting machine to tabulate the data. The 1890 census was processed in ¼ th time needed for the 1880 census. Hollerith left the Census Bureau to build and sell his own tabulating machines. His company was the forerunner of IBM Corporation. His successor at the Census Bureau, Dr. James Powers, also left to form his own company, which ultimately became Sperry Rand Corporation.

Fig. 1.7 : Dr. Herman Hollerith

In 1908, Powers patented a 20-column punching machine. In the same year Hollerith developed a horizontal sorter whose rate was almost 275 cards per minute.

The speed and capabilities of punched-card machines continued to improve. Verifiers were invented to check that the right data were entered into the cards. Collators were invented to merge several sorted decks of cards into a single sorted deck. Electromechanical accounting machines were developed which could read cards containing both alphabetical and numerical data, perform simple arithmetic operations, and print the results.

1.3.2 Atanasoff Berry Computer (ABC)

In 1939, Dr. John Vincent Atanasoff ***(Fig. 1.8),*** Professor of Iowa State University, and his student Mr. Berry assembled a prototype of the ABC to perform faster calculations.

Fig. 1.8 : Dr. John Vincent Atanasoff

A working model was launched by them in 1942.

1.4 MODERN AGE (SINCE 1944)

Computers changed over time; they improved in speed, power and efficiency. Those changes are recognized as a progression of generations of discoveries, each characterized by specific developments.

1.4.1 Mark I (1944)

Howard H. Aiken of Harvard University in 1937 designed a machine that could automatically perform a sequence of arithmetic operations and it was completed in 1944. It was named Mark I. It was an electromechanical (relay) device, like the calculators which preceded it. It contained 72 adding accumulators and 60 sets of switches for setting constants and was operated by means of switches, buttons, wire plugboards and punched tape. Information was represented by patterns of open and closed mechanical relays. It is, interesting to note that it measured 15 meter long, 2.4 meter high and 0.6 meter wide.

The average multiplication and division times were about 4 and 11 seconds respectively. The results were printed at the rate of one result per 5 seconds. The input and output were by punched cards and paper tapes. It is interesting to note that Dr. Aiken did not learn of Babbage's work until Mark I was completed.

1.5 COMPUTER GENERATIONS

The history of computer development is often referred to in reference to the different generations of computing devices. A generation refers to the state of improvement in the product development process. This term is also used in the different advancements of new computer technology. With each new generation, the circuitry has gotten smaller and more advanced than the previous generation before it. As a result of the miniaturization, speed, power, and computer memory has proportionally increased. New discoveries are constantly being developed that affect the way we live, work and play.

Each generation of computers is characterized by major technological development that fundamentally changed the way computers operate, resulting in increasingly smaller, cheaper, and more powerful and more efficient and reliable devices. Read about each generation and the developments that led to the current devices that we use today.

The tem generation indicates the type of technology used in the computer construction. As new technology was emerging, it was being used in the making of computer. The new technology improved the speed, accuracy and storage capacity of the computers. Different technologies have been used for computers in different times.

Therefore, computers can be divided into five generations depending upon the technologies used. **These are:**

1. First Generation (1946 – 1959)
2. Second Generation (1959 – 1965)
3. Third Generation (1965 – 1971)
4. Fourth Generation (1971 – 1985)
5. Fifth Generation (1985 onwards)

1.5.1 FIRST GENERATION (1946-1959)

All subsequent computers after Mark I were all electronic. The early first-generation computers were powered by thousands of vacuum tubes. The first computers used vacuum tubes for circuitry and magnetic drums for memory, and were often enormous, taking up entire rooms. A magnetic drum, also referred to as drum, is a metal cylinder coated with magnetic iron-oxide material on which data and programs can be stored. Magnetic drums were once use as a primary storage device but have since been implemented as auxiliary storage devices.

The tracks on a magnetic drum are assigned to channels located around the circumference of the drum, forming adjacent circular bands that wind around the drum. A single drum can have up to 200 tracks. As the drum rotates at a speed of up to 3,000 rpm, the device's read/write heads deposit magnetized spots on the drum during the write operation and sense these spots during a read operation. This action is similar to that of a magnetic tape or disk drive.

Figure 1.9: Vacuum Tubes

They were very expensive to operate and in addition to using a great deal of electricity, generated a lot of heat, which was often the cause of malfunctions. First generation computers relied on machine language to perform operations, and they could only solve one problem at a time. Machine languages are the only languages understood by computers. While easily understood by computers, machine languages are almost impossible for humans to use because they consist entirely of numbers. Computer Programmers, therefore, use either **high level programming languages** or an assembly language programming. An assembly language contains the same instructions as a machine language, but the instructions and variables have names instead of being just numbers.

Programs written in high **level programming languages** retranslated into assembly language or machine language by a compiler. Assembly language program retranslated into machine language by a program called an assembler (assembly language compiler).

Every CPU has its own unique machine language. Programs must be rewritten or recompiled, therefore, to run on different types of computers. Input was based on punch card and paper tapes, and output was displayed on printouts.

ENIAC

In 1946 John Mauchley and Presper Eckert developed Electronic Numerical Integrator and Calculator (ENIAC) at the Moore School of Electrical Engineering at the University of Pennsylvania. It was the first electronic calculator. It occupied a room measuring 9 meter x 15 meter and contained 18,000 vacuum tubes, 1500 relays and weighed 30 tons. Programs were loaded into the machine by a system of changing wired plugboards and using a series of manual switches. ENIAC performed 5000 additions per second. Credit for inventions relating to the electronic implementations of the ENIAC computer was disputed till 1974. A US Court later ruled that Mr. John Vincent Atanasoff, a former Professor of Iowa State College was the originator of the important new concepts that led to the design of ENIAC. The Court concluded that Dr. Mauchley visited Mr. Atanasoff and visited the computer which he assembled in 1942 and got important ideas for the design of ENIAC.

EDVAC

The Moore School and Ballistics Research Laboratory of US Army built the computer Electronic Discrete Variable Automatic Computer (EDVAC) which was based on John Von Neumann's (Fig. 1.10) ideas. Neumann was the first to introduce in mid-1940s the 'Stored Program Concept' in the computer. EDVAC's storage capacity was 1024 words each of 44 bits each.

Fig. 1.10 : John Von Numann

There was also an auxiliary storage of 20,000 words. The access time of primary storage varied between 0.48 to 384 s. In the EDVAC, the computer program was fed into the storage unit by means of punched paper tape. The first program for EDVAC was written by John Von Neumann, which was a routine to arrange numbers in ascending order. Thus he showed that computers can be used for non-scientific computations.

EDSAC

Another computer using internal storage, called Electronic Delay Storage Automatic Computer (EDSAC) was developed in 1949 at the University of Manchester (UK). EDSAC was of some significance since it was the first computer to contain a changeable program of instructions within its own memory.

UNIVAC I

UNIVAC I and other similar computers were large because of the massive number of tubes required to operate the machines. The tubes themselves were large; they required a lot of energy and generated a great deal of heat. The computer's memory was stored on magnetic storage devices primarily magnetic tapes and magnetic drums. UNIVAC I is shown in ***Fig. 1.11.***

Fig. 1.11 : UNIVAC I

Most of the data were entered into the computer on punched cards similar to Jacquard's loom process. Output consisted of punched cards on paper, and machine and assembly languages were used to program the computers. however, a human operator physically had to reset relay switches and wiring before a program could be run.

Characteristics of First Generation

- Vacuum tubes
- Magnetic tape and magnetic drum for external storage
- Punched cards for input
- Punched cards and paper for output
- Machine and assembly languages
- Human operators to set switches
- *Examples :* UNIVAC I, UNIVAC II, Datamatic 100, EDSAC, Burrough 2202, etc.

Advantages

The main advantages of first-generation computers were:

1. These computers were the fastest of their time.
2. They were programmed using machine language.
3. The electronic digital computers were introduced due to the vacuum tube technology.

Disadvantages

The main disadvantages of first-generation computers were:

1. Very big in size
2. Not reliable
3. Consumed large amount of energy
4. Constant maintenance required
5. More heat generated and air-conditioning was required
6. More costly
7. Very slow in speed (data processing)
8. It was difficult to programmed, because they used only machine language
9. Non-portable
10. Limited commercial use

1.5.2 SECOND GENERATION (1959-1965)

Transistors replaced vacuum tubes and ushered in the second generation computer. Transistor is a device composed of semiconductor material that amplifies a signal or opens or closes a circuit. Invented in 1947 at Bell Labs, transistors have become the key ingredient of all digital circuits, including computers. Today's **latest microprocessor** contains tens of millions of microscopic transistors.

Prior to the invention of transistors, digital circuits were composed of vacuum tubes, which had many disadvantages. They were much larger, required more energy, dissipated more heat, and were more prone to failures. It's safe to say that without the invention of transistors, computing as we know it today would not be possible.

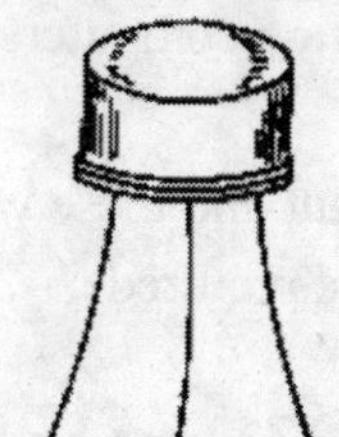

Figure 1.12: Transistors

The transistor was invented in 1947 but did not see widespread use in computers until the late 50s. The transistor was far superior to the vacuum tube, allowing computers to become smaller, faster, cheaper, more energy-efficient and more reliable than their first-generation predecessors. Though the transistor still generated a great deal of heat that subjected the computer to damage, it was a vast improvement over the vacuum tube. Second-generation computers still relied on punched cards for input and printouts for output.

Second-generation computers moved from cryptic binary machine language to symbolic, or assembly, languages, which allowed programmers to specify instructions in words. High-level programming languages were also being developed at this time, such as early versions of COBOL and FORTRAN. These were also the first computers that stored their instructions in their memory, which moved from a magnetic drum to magnetic core technology.

The first computers of this generation were developed for the atomic energy industry.

Characteristics of Second Generation

- Transistors
- Magnetic-core storage
- Magnetic tape and magnetic disk for external storage
- Punched cards and magnetic tape for input
- Punched cards and paper for output
- High-level languages- FORTRAN, COBOL, PL/I, BASIC and others
- Human operators to handle cards
- ***Examples :*** Honeywell 200-, 400-, 800-series, IBM 7070/7080, CDC 1604, Burrough B5000 series, etc.

Advantages

The main advantages of second-generation computers as compared to first-generation computers are:

1. Low in cost
2. Smaller in size
3. Fast in speed
4. Less heat generated More reliable and accurate in calculations

5. Consume low power etc.
6. Used for commercial purposes
7. Portable
8. Assembly language was introduced. This language is easy to write program than machine language

Disadvantages

The main disadvantages of this generation computers were:

1. Air-conditioning required
2. Commercial production was difficult and these were very costly
3. Constant (or frequent) maintenance required
4. Only used for special purposes

1.5.3 THIRD GENERATION (1965-1971)

During this time integrated circuits with transistors, resistors, and capacitors were etched onto a piece of silicon. This reduced the price and size of computers, adding to a general trend in the computer industry of miniaturization. The development of the integrated circuit was the hallmark of the third generation of computers. Transistors were miniaturized and placed on silicon chips, called semiconductors, which drastically increased the speed and efficiency of computers.

A non-metallic chemical element in the carbon family of elements, Silicon-atomic symbol "Si" - is the second most abundant element in the earth's crust, surpassed only by oxygen. Silicon does not occur un-combined in nature. Sand and almost all rocks contain silicon combined with oxygen, forming silica. When silicon combines with other elements, such as iron, aluminium or potassium, a silicate is formed. Compounds of silicon also occur in the atmosphere, natural waters, and many plants and in the bodies of some animals.

Silicon is the basic material used to make computer chips, transistors, silicon diodes and other electronic circuits and switching devices because its atomic structure makes the element an ideal semiconductor. Silicon is commonly doped, or mixed, with other elements, such as boron, phosphorous and arsenic, to alter its conductive properties.

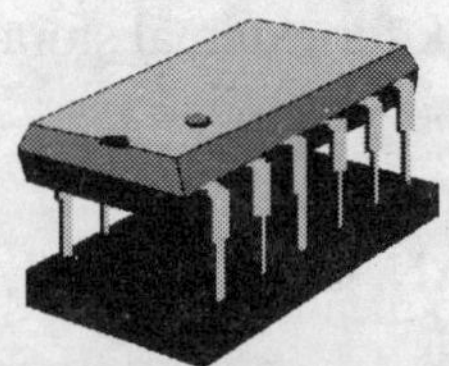

Figure 1.13: Integrated Circuits

A chip is a small piece of semi conducting material (usually silicon) on which an integrated circuit is embedded. A typical chip is less than ¼-square inches and can contain millions of electronic components (transistors). Computers consist of many chips placed on electronic boards called printed circuit boards. There are different types of chips. For example, CPU chips (also called microprocessors) contain an entire processing unit, whereas memory chips contain blank memory.

Semiconductor is a material that is neither a good conductor of electricity (like copper) nor a good insulator (like rubber). The most common semiconductor materials are silicon and germanium. These materials are then doped to create an excess or lack of electrons.

Computer chips, both for CPU and memory, are composed of semiconductor materials. Semiconductors make it possible to miniaturize electronic components, such as transistors. Not only does miniaturization mean that the components take up less space, it also means that they are faster and require less energy.

Digital Equipment Corporation (DEC) introduced the Programmed Data Processor- 1 (PDP-1), which can be called the first minicomputer due to its relatively small size. It is classified as a third generation computer because of the way it was built, even though it was made before 1965. The PDP-1 was also the computer that ran the very first video game, called Spacewar.

The software industry came into existence in the mid 1970?s as companies formed to write programs that would satisfy the increasing number of computer users. Computers were being used everywhere in business, government, military, and education environments. Because of the target market, the first software companies mostly offered accounting and statistical programs. This time period also had the first set of computing standards created for compatibility between systems.

E-mail originated sometime between 1961 and 1966, allowing computer users to send messages to each other as long as they were connected through a network. This is closely tied to the work that was being done on Advanced Research Projects Agency Network (ARPANET), networking technology and innovation that would one day bring the internet.

Fig. 1.14 : 3rd Generation Computer (DEC's Program Data Processor)

Characteristics of Third Generation

- Integrated circuits
- Improved disk storage
- Monitors and keyboards for input and output
- More high-level languages, including RPG and Pascal
- First complete operating system meant less involvement for human operators
- Family of computers introduced allowing compatibility
- Minicomputers used commercially
- ***Examples:*** IBM System/360, IBM System/370, Burrough 5700/6700, PDP-8 Series, PDP-11 Series, etc.

Advantages

The main advantages of third-generation as compared to previous generations of computers were:

1. Smaller in size
2. Production cost was low
3. Very fast in computational power

4. More reliable
5. Low power consumption
6. Maintenance cost was low because failure rate of hardware was very low
7. Magnetic disk, used for external storage
8. More storage capacity
9. Easily portable
10. Easy to operate
11. Upgraded easily
12. Widely used for various commercial applications all over the world
13. Lower heat generated
14. High-level languages were commonly used
15. Many input/output devices were introduced such as mouse and keyboard etc.

Disadvantages

The main disadvantages of third-generation computers were:

1. Air-conditioning required
2. Highly sophisticated technology required for the manufacturer chips

Distinct Feature

Instead of punched cards and printouts, users interacted with third generation computers through keyboards and monitors and interfaced with an operating system, which allowed the device to run many different applications at one time with a central program that monitored the memory. Computers for the first time became accessible to a mass audience because they were smaller and cheaper than their predecessors.

1.5.4 FOURTH GENERATION (1971-1985)

The microprocessor brought the fourth generation of computers, as thousands of integrated circuits we rebuilt onto a single silicon chip. A silicon chip contained a CPU. In the world of personal computers, the terms microprocessor and CPU are used interchangeably. At the heart of all personal computers and most workstations sits a microprocessor.

Figure 1.15: Microprocessor

Microprocessors also control the logic of almost all digital devices, from clock radios to fuel-injection systems for automobiles.

Three basic characteristics differentiate microprocessors:

- **Instruction Set:** The set of instructions that the microprocessor can execute.
- **Bandwidth:** The number of bits processed in a single instruction.
- **Clock Speed:** Given in megahertz (MHz), the clock speed determines how many instructions per second the processor can execute.

In both cases, the higher the value, the more powerful the CPU. For example, a 32-bit microprocessor that runs at 50MHz is more powerful than a 16-bitmicroprocessor that runs at 25MHz. What in the first generation filled an entire room could now fit in the palm of the hand. The Intel

4004chip, developed in 1971, located all the components of the computer - from the central processing unit and memory to input/output controls - on a single chip.

Abbreviation of central processing unit, and pronounced as separate letters. The CPU is the brains of the computer. Sometimes referred to simply as the processor or central processor, the CPU is where most calculations take place. In terms of computing power, the CPU is the most important element of a computer system.

On large machines, CPUs require one or more printed circuit boards. On personal computers and small workstations, the CPU is housed in a single chip called a microprocessor.

Two typical components of a CPU are:

- The arithmetic logic unit (ALU), which performs arithmetic and logical operations.
- The control unit, which extracts instructions from memory and decodes and executes them, calling on the ALU when necessary.

In 1981 IBM introduced its first computer for the home user, and in 1984 Apple introduced the Macintosh. Microprocessors also moved out of the realm of desktop computers and into many areas of life as more and more everyday products began to use microprocessors.

Computer technology had advanced so rapidly that computers could fit in something the size of a typewriter. These were called microcomputers, the first one being the Altair 8800. Many people acknowledge the Altair 8800 as the computer that sparked the modern computer revolution, especially since Bill Gates and Paul Allen founded Microsoft with a programming language called Altair BASIC-made specifically for the 8800.

A small company called Apple Computer, Inc. was established in 1976 and single handedly changed the industry forever. Steve Wozniak and Steve Jobs began to sell their Apple 1 computer that same year, and it quickly gained popularity. It came with a keyboard and only required a monitor to be plugged into the back of the system, which was a novel idea for computers at that time. The Apple II was released the next year and was the first mass produced microcomputer to be commercially sold, and also ushered in the era of personal computing.

In 1981, Microsoft Disk Operating System (MS-DOS) was released to run on the Intel 8086 microprocessor. Over the next few years MS-DOS became the most popular operating system in the world, eventually leading to Microsoft Windows 1.0 being released in 1985. In 1984 Apple introduced their Mac OS, which was the first operating system to be completely graphical. Both Mac OS and Windows used pull-down menus, icons, and windows to make computing more user-friendly. Computers were now being controlled with a mouse as well as keyboard. The first mouse was developed in 1981 by Xerox.

Software became much more common and diverse during this period with the development of spreadsheets, databases, and drawing programs. Computer networks and e-mail became much more prevalent as well.

The first truly portable computer, called the Osborne 1, was released in 1981. Portable computers like the TRS-80 Model 100 / 102 and IBM 5155 followed afterward.

Not all the computers of the time were small, of course. There were still being supercomputers built with the aim of being as fast as possible. These supercomputers were sold to companies, universities, and the military. An example of one such supercomputer is the Cray-1, which was released in 1976 by Cray Research. It became one of the best known and most successful supercomputers ever for its unique design and fast speed of 250 MFLOPS.

This generation was also important for the development of embedded systems. These are special systems, usually very tiny, that have computers inside to control their operation. These embedded systems were put into things like cars, thermostats, microwave ovens, wristwatches, and more.

As these small computers became more powerful, they could be linked together to form networks, which eventually led to the development of the Internet. Fourth generation computers also saw the development of GUI's, the mouse and handheld devices.

Characteristics of Fourth Generation

- LSI and VLSI
- Magnetic disk most common external storage
- Introduction of microcomputers
- Fourth-generation languages (4GLs) emerged and application software for microcomputers became popular
- Microcomputers used - Compaq Deskpro 386
- ***Typical examples:*** Burroughs B7700 and HP 3000 minicomputers

Advantages

The advantages of fourth-generation as compared to previous generation computers are:

1. Smaller in size
2. Production cost is very low
3. Very reliable
4. Hardware failure is negligible
5. Easily portable because of their small size
6. Totally general purpose
7. Air conditioning is not compulsory
8. Very high processing speed
9. Very large internal and external storage capacity
10. Used advanced input & output devices such as optical readers, laser printers, CD-ROM/DVD-ROM drives etc.

Disadvantages

The main disadvantage of fourth-generation computers is:

1. Highly sophisticated technology required for the manufacturer of microprocessor chips.

1.5.5 FIFTH GENERATION (Beyond 1985 and till-date)

The changes that have occurred since 1985 are plentiful. Computers have got tinier, more reliable, and many times faster. Computers are mostly built using components from many different corporations. For this reason, it is easier to focus on specific component advancements. Intel and AMD are the main computer processor companies in the world today and are constant rivals. There are many different personal computer companies that usually sell their hardware with a Microsoft Windows operating system preinstalled. Apple has a wide line of hardware and software as well. Computer graphics have got very powerful and are able to display full three dimensional graphics at high resolution. Nvidia and ATI are two companies in constant battle with one another to be the computer graphics hardware king.

Fig. 1.16: 5th Generation Computer (Powerful Laptop)

The software industry has grown a lot as well, offering all kinds of programs for almost anything you can think of. Microsoft Windows still dominates the operating system scene. In 1995 Microsoft released Windows 95, an operating system that catapulted them to a new level of dominance. In 1999 Apple revamped its operating system with the release of Mac OS X. In 1991 Linus Torvalds wrote the Linux kernel that has since spawned countless open source operating systems and open source software.

Computers have become more and more online orientated in modern times, especially with the development of the World Wide Web. Popular companies like Google and Yahoo! were started because of the internet.

In 2008 the IBM Roadrunner was introduced as the fastest computer in the world at 1.026 PFLOPS. Fast supercomputers aid in the production of movie special effects and the making of computer animated movies.

Fifth generation computing devices, based on artificial intelligence, are still in development, though there are some applications, such as voice recognition, that are being used today. Artificial Intelligence is the branch of computer science concerned with making computers behave like humans. The term was coined in 1956 by John McCarthy at the Massachusetts Institute of Technology.

Artificial intelligence includes:

- **Games Playing:** programming computers to play games such as chess and checkers.
- **Expert Systems:** programming computers to make decisions in real-life situations (for example, some expert systems help doctors diagnose diseases based on symptoms).
- **Natural Language:** programming computers to understand natural human languages.
- **Neural Networks:** Systems that simulate intelligence by attempting to reproduce the types of physical connections that occur in animal brains.
- **Robotics:** programming computers to see and hear and react to other sensory stimuli.

Characteristics of Fifth Generation

- Development of true artificial intelligence
- Development of Natural Language Processing
- Advancement in Parallel Processing
- Advancement in Superconductor Technology

Currently, no computers exhibit full artificial intelligence (that is, are able to simulate human behaviour). The greatest advances have occurred in the field of games playing. The best computer chess programs are now capable of beating humans. In May, 1997, an IBM super-computer called Deep Blue defeated world chess champion Gary Kasparov in a chess match.

Figure 1.17: Artificial Intelligence

In the area of robotics, computers are now widely used in assembly plants, but they are capable only of very limited tasks. Robots have great difficulty identifying objects based on appearance or feel, and they still move and handle objects clumsily.

Natural-language processing offers the greatest potential rewards because it would allow people to interact with computers without needing any specialized knowledge. You could simply walk up to a computer and talk to it. Unfortunately, programming computers to understand natural languages has proved to be more difficult than originally thought. Some rudimentary translation systems that translate from one human language to another are in existence, but they are not nearly as good as human translators.

There are also voice recognition systems that can convert spoken sounds into written words, but they do not understand what they are writing; they simply take dictation. Even these systems are quite limited -- you must speak slowly and distinctly.

In the early 1980s, expert systems were believed to represent the future of artificial intelligence and of computers in general. To date, however, they have not lived up to expectations. Many expert systems help human experts in such fields as medicine and engineering, but they are very expensive to produce and are helpful only in special situations.

Today, the hottest area of artificial intelligence is neural networks, which are proving successful in a number of disciplines such as voice recognition and natural-language processing.

There are several programming languages that are known as AI languages because they are used almost exclusively for AI applications. The two most common are LISP and Prolog.

Few major projects of 5th generation computers include the following:

- **ICOT Project in Japan:** The Japanese ICOT project is regarded as a critical element in Japan's industrial performance. A central institute ICOT has been set up where basic research takes place. Advances in architecture are intended to lead to the development of parallel inference computers for the next phase of the research.
- **MCC Project in USA:** In order to keep up with the Japanese program, a group of IT corporations in the USA have set up the MCC (Microelectronic and Computer Technology Corporation). The MCC carries out research and advanced product development, and makes the results available to sponsor corporations for implementation. The sponsors include Digital Equipment Corporation (DEC), National Cash Register (NCR) and chip manufacturers Motorola and National Semiconductor.

- **DARPA Project in USA:** Much of the 5th generation research and development is being co-ordinated by the Defence Advanced Research Project Agency (DARPA). This agency allocates US Government funds to IT projects with the actual or potential military applications.
- **Espirit Initiative EC:** The Espirit program is the EC's response to the Japanese 5th generation initiative. It has a small central directorate, which sponsors projects carried out by consortia of corporations and universities in EC countries. The Espirit program is likely to merge into the wider EUREKA initiative, which aims to co-ordinate research and development in a number of high-technology fields.
- **Alvey Program in Britain:** The Alvey is the advanced Information Technology (IT) program in UK and has a central directorate which allocates state funds covering up to 50 % of the cost of approved projects. The program is centred on four key enabling technologies :
  - *Software Engineering*
  - *VLSI Chip Architecture*
  - *Intelligent Knowledge Based Systems*
  - *Intelligent User Interfaces.*

Fifth generation computers are supposed to be the ideal computers. The scientists are working to design such computers that will have the following features.

1. Having their own thinking power
2. Making decisions themselves
3. Having capabilities of learning
4. Having capabilities of reasoning
5. Having large capacity of internal storage
6. Having extra high processing speed
7. Having capabilities of parallel processing

In these computers following technologies will be used:

- ULSIC (Ultra Large Scale Integrated Circuits) technology
- Artificial Intelligence (AI) technology also called the knowledge Processor. The AI means automatic programs that let the machines to think and decide themselves. The programming languages LISP (List Processor) and PROLOG (Programming with Logic) are used for artificial intelligence. The scientists at ICOT in Japan use the PROLOG to develop the Artificial Intelligence software.

1.6 EVOLUTION OF COMPUTING SYSTEMS

Computers have evolved from the fundamental principles of mathematical calculation and language processing. The computing systems of today are an outcome of the efforts and intellect of mathematicians, logicians, linguists and technologists from all over the world. Computer history comprises the evolutionary journey of computing systems, the timeline of operating systems as well as the history behind the development of a wide variety of computer software and hardware.

Here is a brief overview of the progress of computing technology from early days right up to the modern-day digital portable computers.

TABLE 1.1: 1940s Computing Systems

1939 | Hewlett-Packard is founded in California
Their first product was the popular HP 200A Audio Oscillator, used as sound effects generators for Walt Disney Pictures movie "Fantasia."

1940 | Complex Number Calculator (CNC)
Designed by researcher George Stibitz and completed by Bell Telephone Laboratories.

1941 | Z3 computer / Bombe
The Z3 was built by German engineer Konrad Zuse in complete isolation from developments elsewhere.
The Bombe was used to decrypt Nazi Military communications

1942 | Atanasoff-Berry Computer (ABC)
The ABC was designed and built by Professor John Vincent Atanasoff and graduate student Cliff Berry at Iowa State College

1943 | Project Whirlwind / Relay Interpolator
Project Whirlwind was a simulator to train bomber crews.
The Relay Interceptor assisted in testing its M-9 Gun Director.

1944 | Harvard Mark-1 / Colossus
The Harvard Mark-1 was a room-sized, relay-based calculator.
The Colossus was designed to break the complex Lorenz ciphers used by the Nazis during WWII.

1945 | "First Draft of a Report on the EDVAC"
Outlined the architecture of a stored-program computer, which would lead to the mainstream computers we know today.

1946 | ENIAC / AVIDAC
The ENIAC improved by 1,000 times on the speed of its contemporaries.

1948 | IBM SSEC
The Selective Sequence Electronic Calculator produced the moon-position tables used for plotting the course of the 1969 Apollo flight to the moon.

1949 | EDSAC / Manchester Mark I
The first practical stored-program computer.
The Manchester Mark I computer functioned as a complete system using the Williams tube for memory.

TABLE 1.2: 1950s Computing Systems

1960 | DEC PDP-1

The precursor to the minicomputer.

1961 | IBM 1401

The 1401 mainframe replaced the vacuum tube with smaller, more reliable transistors and used a magnetic core memory.

1962 | LINC (Laboratory Instrumentation Computer)

The first real time laboratory data processing machine.

1964 | IBM System 360

A family of six mutually compatible computers and 40 peripherals that could work together.

1964 | CDC 6600

The fastest computer of its time performed up to 3 million instructions per second - three times faster than the IBM Stretch.

1965 | DEC PDP-8

The first commercially successful minicomputer.

1966 | ILLIAC IV

The first large-scale array computer.

1966 | HP-2115

Hewlett-Packard entered the general purpose computer business with its HP-2115.

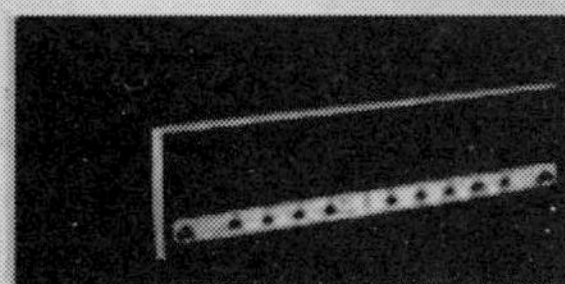

1968 | Nova

The Nova is introduced, with 32 kilobytes of memory, for $8,000.

1968 | Apollo Guidance Computer

The Apollo Guidance Computer made its debut orbiting the Earth on Apollo 7.

TABLE 1.3: 1960s Computing Systems

1960 | DEC PDP-1
The precursor to the minicomputer.

1961 | IBM 1401
The 1401 mainframe replaced the vacuum tube with smaller, more reliable transistors and used a magnetic core memory.

1962 | LINC (Laboratory Instrumentation Computer)
The first real time laboratory data processing machine.

1964 | IBM System 360
A family of six mutually compatible computers and 40 peripherals that could work together.

1964 | CDC 6600
The fastest computer of its time performed up to 3 million instructions per second - three times faster than the IBM Stretch.

1965 | DEC PDP-8
The first commercially successful minicomputer.

1966 | ILLIAC IV
The first large-scale array computer.

1966 | HP-2115
Hewlett-Packard entered the general purpose computer business with its HP-2115.

1968 | Nova
The Nova is introduced, with 32 kilobytes of memory, for $8,000.

1968 | Apollo Guidance Computer
The Apollo Guidance Computer made its debut orbiting the Earth on Apollo 7.

TABLE 1.4: 1970s Computing Systems

1971 | Kenback 1

The first personal computer, advertised for $750 in Scientific American.

1972 | HP-35

The HP-35 was a fast, extremely accurate electronic slide rule with a solid-state memory similar to that of a computer.

1973 | TV Typewriter / Micral

The first display of alphanumeric text on an ordinary television set. The Micral was the earliest commercial, non-kit personal computer based on a micro-processor.

1974 | Xerox Alto / Scelbi 8H

The first work station with a built-in mouse for input. The first commercially advertised U.S. computer based on a microprocessor

1975 | MITS Altair / Tandem-16

The Altair was based on Intel's 8080 microprocessor, and ran on BASIC. The Tandem was the first fault-tolerant computer, for online transaction processing.

1976 | Apple I / Cray I

Steve Wozniak designed the Apple I, later selling it with Steve Jobs. The Cray I was the first commercially successful vector processor.

1977 | Commodore PET

The Commodore Personal Electronic Transactor was the first of several personal computers released in 1977.

1977 | Apple II / TRS-80

The Apple II became an instant success when released in 1977. The TRS-80 was Tandy Radio Shack's first desktop computer.

1978 | VAX 11/780

The VAX 11/780 had the ability to address up to 4.3 gigabytes of virtual memory, 100 times the capacity of most minicomputers.

1979 | Atari 400 and 800

Atari introduces the Model 400 and 800 Computers with gaming abilities.

TABLE 1.5: 1980s Computing Systems

TABLE 1.6: 1990s Computing Systems

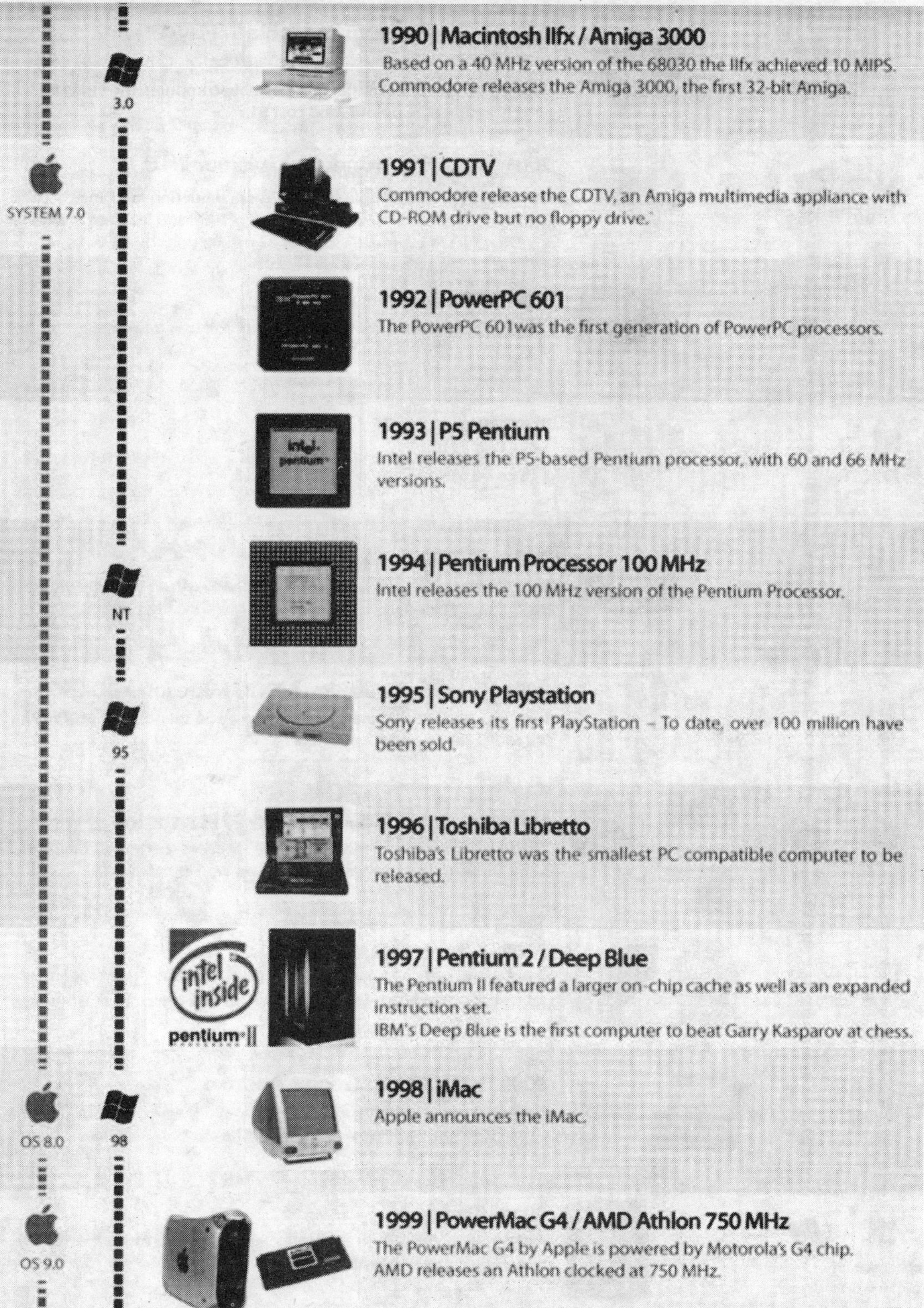

TABLE 1.7: 2000s Computing Systems

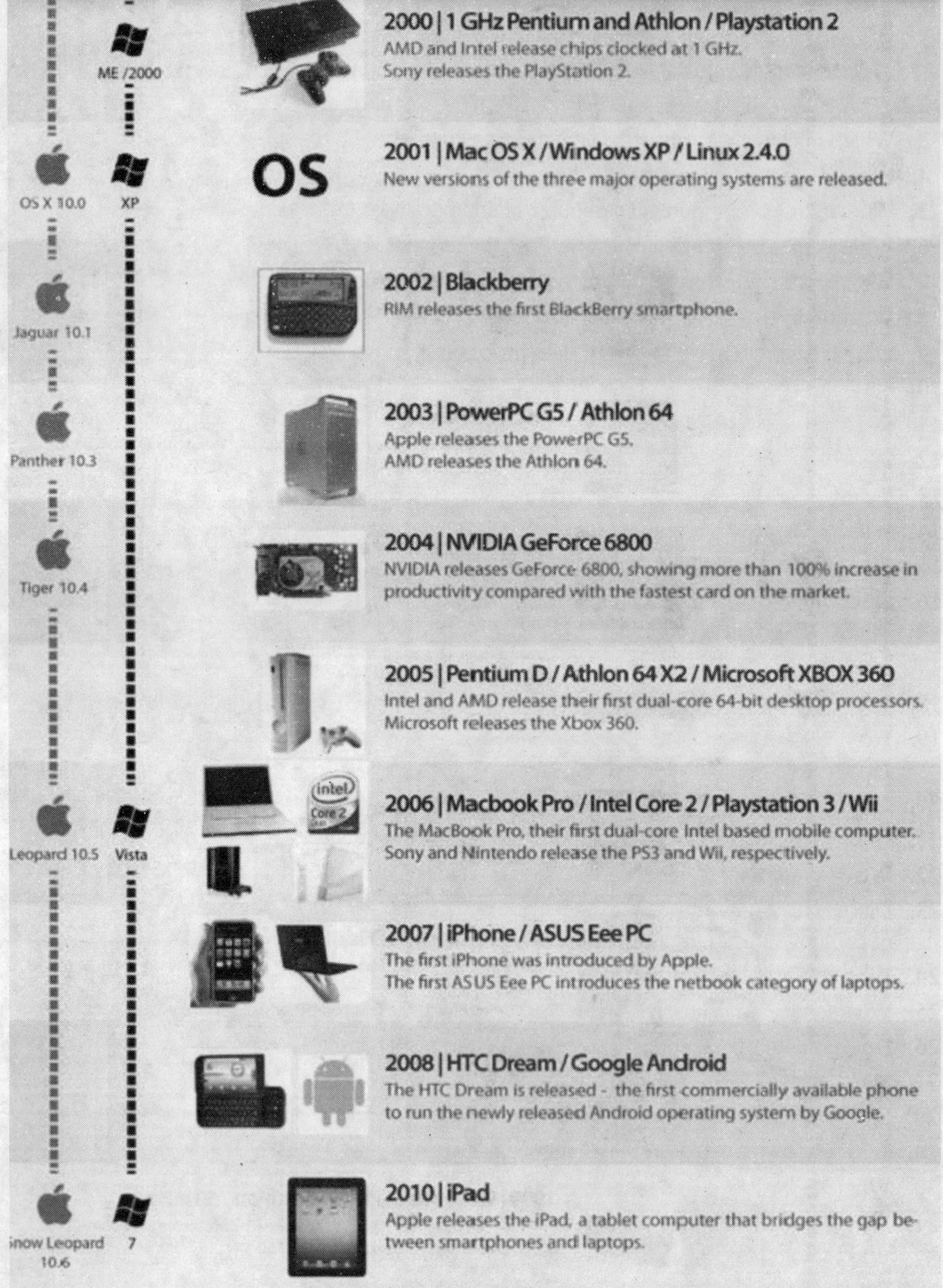

EXERCISES

1. Discuss the important features of various generations of computers. Also give some examples of computers belonging to each generation.
2. What is the stored program concept ? Why is it important ?
3. What is the contribution of John Napier to computing ?
4. What is an Abacus and what is its use ?
5. Why are microcomputers so popular in comparison to other computers ?
6. What is the contribution of Blaise Pascal and what is Pascaline ?
7. What are the latest trends in microprocessor technology ? Explain.
8. What do ENIAC, EDSAC, EDVAC and UNIVAC stand for ?
9. State the evolutionary stages of data processing.
10. State the contribution(s) due to John Von Neumann.
11. Differentiate the principles of Analytical and Differential Engine.
12. State the significance of Jacquard Loom ?
13. Detail out the description of Mark I electromechanical computer.
14. What is the contribution due to Charles Babbage ? Explain.
15. What are the limitations of human processing ? How these can be removed ?
16. Discuss the basis on which one divides the history of data processing into the Dark Ages, the Middle Ages and the Modern Ages.
17. Explain, how human-beings can act as information processor ?
18. Give the time period and the basic characteristic of the Middle Ages of data processing.
19. What are the implications for information systems design of the statement that humans are serial rather than parallel processors ?
20. Compare computer and human-beings.
21. Give three major innovations of 1st – , 2nd –, 3rd –, 4th – and 5th –generation computers.
22. What is the difference between a microcomputer and a microprocessor ?
23. Discuss the important features of various generations of computers. Also give some examples of computers belonging to each generation.
24. What is the stored program concept ? Why is it important ?
25. What is the contribution of John Napier to computing ?
26. How do analog computers differ digital computers ?
27. State the criteria for classification of digital computers.
28. Is digital computer more accurate than analog computer ? Justify your answer.
29. What are the operations that a computer is able to perform ?
30. What is an Abacus and what is its use ?
31. Why are microcomputers so popular in comparison to other computers ?
32. What is a digital computer ? Provide its anatomy and explain the functioning of such a computer through its block diagram.

33. What is the contribution of Blaise Pascal and what is Pascaline ?
34. What are the latest trends in microprocessor technology ? Explain.
35. What do ENIAC, EDSAC, EDVAC and UNIVAC stand for ?
36. State the evolutionary stages of data processing.
37. State the contribution(s) due to John Von Neumann.
38. Differentiate the principles of Analytical and Differential Engine.
39. State the significance of Jacquard Loom ?
40. Why should we go for computers ?
41. Detail out the description of Mark I electromechanical computer.
42. What is the contribution due to Charles Babbage ? Explain.
43. Comment on how computers are changing our traditional patterns of recreation.
44. What are different types of portable computers ?
45. In terms of physical size, how are PCs categorised ?
46. What is the difference between a microcomputer and minicomputer ?
47. What are the limitations of human processing ? How these can be removed ?
48. Discuss the basis on which one divides the history of data processing into the Dark Ages, the Middle Ages and the Modern Ages.
49. Give the time period and the basic characteristic of the Middle Ages of data processing.
50. What are the implications for information systems design of the statement that humans are serial rather than parallel processors ?
51. Compare computer and human-beings.
52. Give three major innovations of 1st –, 2nd –, 3rd –, 4th – and 5th –generation computers.

Basic Elements of Computer and Applications

2.1 INTRODUCTION

Let us begin with the word 'compute', which means 'to calculate'. We all are familiar with calculations in our day to day life. We apply mathematical operations like addition, subtraction, multiplication, etc. and many other formulae for calculations. Simpler calculations take less time but complex calculations take much longer time. Another factor is accuracy in calculations. So man explored the idea to develop a machine which can perform this type of arithmetic calculation faster and with full accuracy. This gave birth to a device or machine called **'computer'**.

2.2 COMPUTER

The ***computer*** we see today is quite different from the one made in the beginning. The number of applications of a computer has increased, the speed and accuracy of calculation has increased. You must appreciate the impact of computers in our day to day life. Reservation of tickets in Air Lines and Railways, payment of telephone and electricity bills, deposits and withdrawals of money from banks, business data processing, medical diagnosis, weather forecasting, etc. are some of the areas where computer has become extremely useful.

However, there is one limitation of the computer. Human beings do calculations on their own. But computer is a dumb machine and it has to be given proper instructions to carry out its calculation. This is why we should know how a computer works.

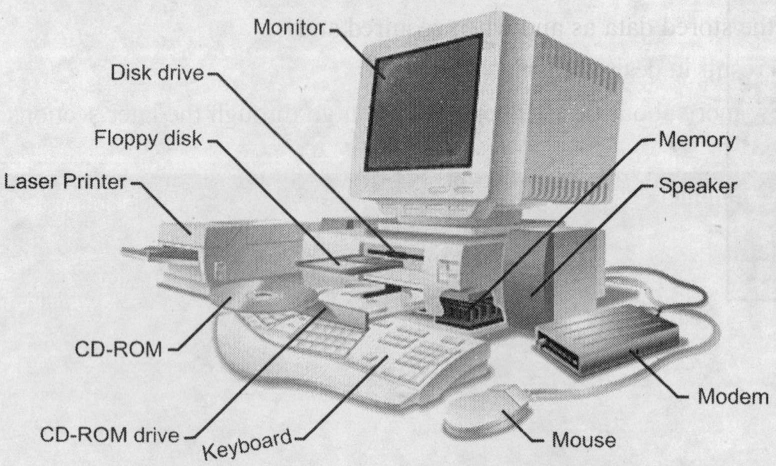

Figure 2.1 Components of a computer

Definition:

"A computer is an electronic machine that operates under the control of instructions, that accepts the input data, processes or manipulates the given data according to the predefined instructions and stores the result for future use".

It can also retrieve the stored results as and when required again. Now-a-days, data is processed with the help of computer. This modern technique to process data is known as Electronic Data Processing (EDP). Computer is also known as Electronic Data Processing machine.

The term data processing means:

- Arithmetic and logical operations on data to get required results.
- To send and receive information from one location to another.
- Arranging data into a specific order etc.

A computer can store, process and retrieve data as and when desired. The computer processes data with very high speed. In addition to being very fast, computer is also very accurate in calculations. These are the main capabilities of the computer.

Computer is an electronic device. As mentioned in the introduction it can do arithmetic calculations faster. But as you will see later it does much more than that. It can be compared to a magic box, which serves different purpose to different people. For a common man computer is simply a calculator, which works automatic and quite fast. For a person who knows much about it, computer is a machine capable of solving problems and manipulating data. It accepts data, processes the data by doing some mathematical and logical operations and gives us the desired output.

Therefore, we may define computer as a device that transforms data. Data can be anything like marks obtained by you in various subjects. It can also be name, age, sex, weight, height, etc. of all the students in your class or income, savings, investments, etc., of a country. Computer can be defined in terms of its functions. It can

- accept data
- store data
- process data as desired, and

- retrieve the stored data as and when required and
- print the result in desired format.

You will know more about these functions as you go through the later sections.

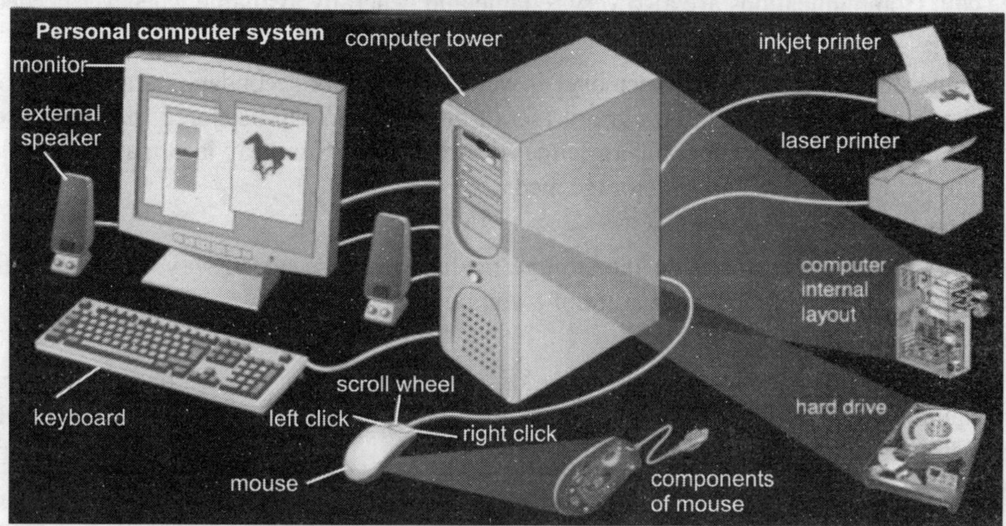

Figure 2.2: Basic Components of a Computer

2.3 CHARACTERISTICS OF A COMPUTER

Now-a-days computer is playing a main role in everyday life it has become the need of people just like television, telephone or other electronic devices at home. It solves the human problems very quickly as well as accurately. The important characteristics of a computer are described below:

1. Speed

The computer is a very high speed electronic device. The operations on the data inside the computer are performed through electronic circuits according to the given instructions. The data and instructions flow along these circuits with high speed that is close to the speed of light. Computer can perform million of billion of operations on the data in one second. The computer generates signals during the operation process therefore the speed of computer is usually measure in mega hertz (MHz) or gega hertz (GHz). It means million cycles units of frequency is hertz per second. Different computers have different speed.

2. Arithmetical and Logical Operations

A computer can perform arithmetical and logical operations. In arithmetic operations, it performs the addition, subtraction, multiplication and division on the numeric data. In logical operation it compares the numerical data as well as alphabetical data.

3. Accuracy

In addition to being very fast, computer is also very accurate device. it gives accurate output result provided that the correct input data and set of instructions are given to the computer. It means that output is totally depended on the given instructions and input data. If input data is in-correct then the resulting output will be in-correct. In computer terminology it is known as garbage-in garbage-out.

4. Reliability

The electronic components in modern computer have very low failure rate. The modern computer can perform very complicated calculations without creating any problem and produces consistent (reliable) results. In general, computers are very reliable. Many personal computers have never needed a service call. Communications are also very reliable and generally available whenever needed.

5. Storage

A computer has internal storage (memory) as well as external or secondary storage. In secondary storage, a large amount of data and programs (set of instructions) can be stored for future use. The stored data and programs are available any time for processing. Similarly information downloaded from the internet can be saved on the storage media.

6. Retrieving data and programs

The data and program stored on the storage media can be retrieved very quickly for further processing. It is also very important feature of a computer.

7. Automation

A computer can automatically perform operations without interfering the user during the operations. It controls automatically different devices attached with the computer. It executes automatically the program instructions one by one.

8. Versatility

Versatile means flexible. Modern computer can perform different kind of tasks one by one of simultaneously. It is the most important feature of computer. At one moment your are playing game on computer, the next moment you are composing and sending emails etc. In colleges and universities computers are use to deliver lectures to the students. The talent of computer is dependent on the software.

9. Communications

Today computer is mostly used to exchange messages or data through computer networks all over the world. For example the information can be received or send through the internet with the help of computer. It is most important feature of the modern information technology.

10. Diligence

A computer can continually work for hours without creating any error. It does not get tired while working after hours of work it performs the operations with the same accuracy as well as speed as the first one.

11. No Feelings

Computer is an electronic machine. It has no feelings. It detects objects on the basis of instructions given to it. Based on our feelings, taste, knowledge and experience: we can make certain decisions and judgments in our daily life. On the other hand, computer can not make such judgments on their own. Their judgments are totally based on instructions given to them.

12. Consistency

People often have difficulty to repeat their instructions again and again. For example, a lecturer feels difficulty to repeat a same lecture in a class room again and again. Computer can repeat actions consistently (again and again) without loosing its concentration:

- To run a spell checker (built into a word processor) for checking spellings in a document.
- To play multimedia animations for training purposes.
- To deliver a lecture through computer in a class room etc.

A computer will carry out the activity with the same way every time. You can listen a lecture or perform any action again and again.

13. Precision

Computers are not only fast and consistent but they also perform operations very accurately and precisely. For example, in manual calculations and rounding fractional values (That is value with decimal point can change the actual result). In computer however, you can keep the accuracy and precision upto the level, you desire. The length calculations remain always accurate.

2.4 CLASSIFICATION OF COMPUTERS

Though in general we use digital computers, however, present day computers may be classified into three categories:

- Analog
- Digital
- Hybrid

2.4.1 Analog Computers

Analog computers are computers which work on the basis of continuous measurement of physical quantities, e.g. pressure, voltage, current, temperature, current, length, etc. We can quote a number of instruments that work on the principles of an analog computers.

Limitations of Analog Computers

- These don't have logical facilities afforded by programming
- Don't have the ability to store data in large quantities
- Cost of implementation of computation is very high

Examples : Thermometer, Speedometer, Wall-clock, Voltmeter, Ammeter, etc.

2.4.2 Digital Computers

Digital computers are computers which represent data in terms of discrete number and processes data using the standard arithmetic operations. These computers directly operate on numbers and produce precise results. These are used in a unlimited number of applications. The basic differences between analog and digital computers are listed in **Table No. 2.1.**

We will be concerned with digital computers only because of the following reasons:

- The tasks that can be done on analog computers can also be done on digital computers while the reverse is not true.
- To understand the calculations made by an analog computer, some mathematical background is necessary, whereas digital computer can be used and understood without much mathematical background.
- The digital computer is used extensively in many areas of application.

2.4.3 Hybrid Computers

Design features of Analog and Digital computers can be combined to create a Hybrid Computer. Such computers are used for special applications only. Examples of such computers include:

- Chemical Process Control
- Patient Monitoring System
- Electronic Calculating Scale

- Missile Guidance Computer
- Flight Simulators For Training Air-plane Pilots
- Petroleum Distillation Monitoring Systems

2.4.4 Difference between Analog and Digital Computers

Table 2.1 : Analog Vs. Digital Computer

S.No.	Analog Computers	Digital Computers
1.	Represent continuous measurement of physical quantities e.g. rotation, voltage, temperature, etc.	Represent numbers by discrete coded patterns
2.	Accuracy is quite limited	Unlimited accuracy
3.	Represent physical or mathematical quantities	Represent numbers, letters and other symbols
4.	Data-storage scattered in various non-interchangeable devices	Data-storage concentrated in space, interchangeable and unlimited in duration
5.	Distinct elements used for each operation	Identical elements used in sequence
6.	Sets up analogy of problem	Breaks down problem into arithmetic operations
7.	Best-suited to represent measurable quantities and simulate response of physical systems by mathematical analogies	Best suited to handle discrete random processes, statistical data, and numerical problems of business and scientific nature
8.	Serves as model and mirrors relations of actual system	Digital computer compounds arithmetic data, unrelated to system it represents
9.	Operations usually carried out in real-time of physical system	Time of operations usually does not correspond to real-time.
10.	Relatively few devices used and easier programming	Many devices needed and difficult programming
11.	Basic operation performed by relatively few 'single-purpose' devices (integrators, multipliers, magnitude-comparators, etc.	Operation performed by relatively many interchangeable arithmetic devices such as adders, registers, accumulators, etc.

2.5 BASIC ANATOMY OF DIGITAL COMPUTER

Modern computer systems are available in numerous physical shapes and sizes, and truly speaking there is no end to it. Few of the shapes and sizes of computer system are given in ***Fig. 2.3*** and few others have already been discussed in the earlier portion of this chapter.

In Computer System, different parts of a computer are organized in such a way that, it helps to perform various operations to complete the given specific task. A computer is a sort of electric brain, which capable to solve mathematical problems with in movements or produce desired information or a controlling order.

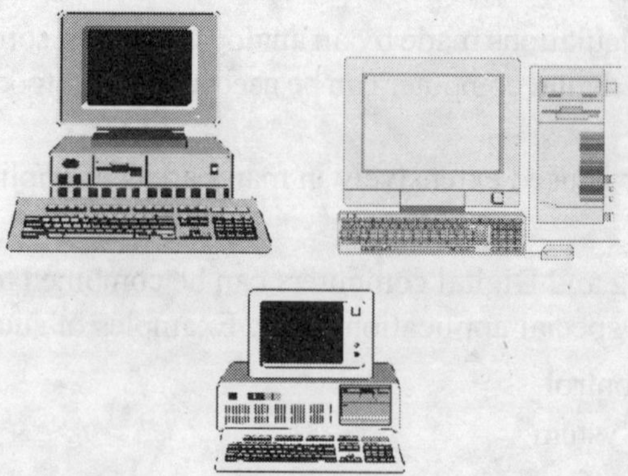

Fig. 2.3: Computer Systems

All the Modern electronic computer consists of three main components. These are indicated in the block diagram *(Fig. 2.4).*

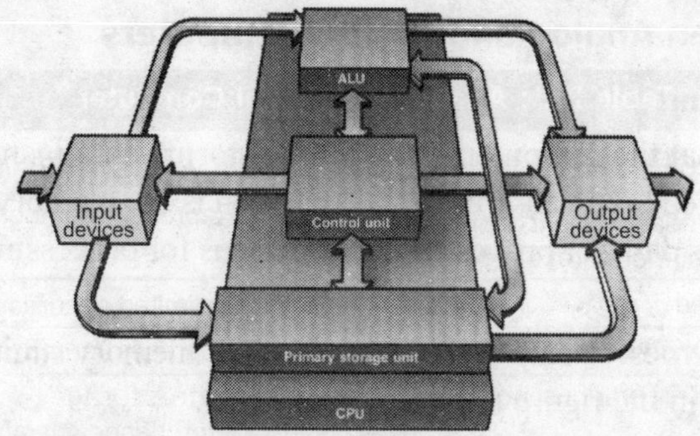

Fig. 2.4: Block Diagram of a Computer

Let us now study the organisation and function of each unit in detail.

I. INPUT UNIT

A unit provided to supply data to the computer is called **Input Unit.** This unit is also called Input Devices Unit and uses devices like mouse, lightpen, keyboard etc. to transfer data/information to the computer directly or may collect data on magnetic disks and tapes and later transfer it to the system.

Peripherals is the term applied to all devices that are connected to the CPU but are not part of the CPU. These include the Input/Output (I/O) and mass storage devices and other computer devices such as analog-to-digital converters. The collection of all peripheral equipments is called the computer configuration.

There are two types of peripherals given as under:

(i) Off-line Peripheral and

(ii) On-line Peripheral.

Auxiliary devices that are not directly connected to the CPU, such as keypunches, card sorters, and so on. These are called off-line devices. The term on-line devices refers to equipment that is connected to the CPU.

II. Central Processing Unit (CPU)

This unit is called the brain or heart and soul of the computer system. It comes in different shapes viz. Vertical CPU, Mid-Tower, Horizontal CPU, etc. Few popular CPU types are shown in **Fig. 2.5.**

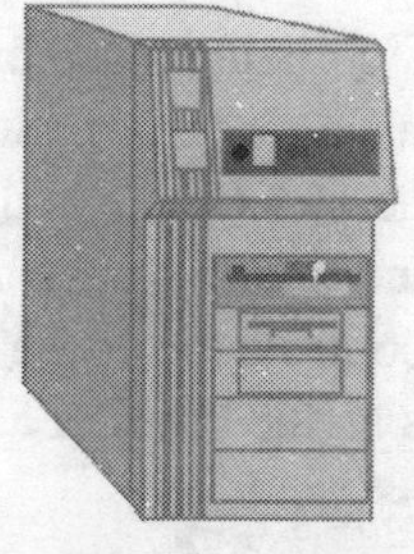

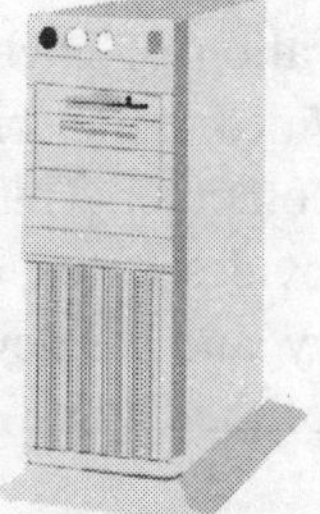

(a) Mid Tower CPU **(b) Vertical CPU**

Fig. 2.5: Few Popular CPU Shapes

It has the following three sub-units :

(i) Primary Storage Unit (or Memory Unit)

(ii) Arithmetic & Logic Unit (ALU)

(iii) Control Unit

(a) Primary Storage Unit

We are already aware that the computer is capable of storing data/instruction/information into it. Where does the data get stored? The answer to this question is the memory unit. Memory is a part of the microcomputer that holds data for processing, instructions for processing the data and information i.e. processed data.

As we have different types of data to be stored, this memory unit has four major logical areas, which are not shown in the figure to avoid complexity.

(i) Input Storage Area

The input data does not straight away go to the processor. It is first stored in this area till the processor asks for it.

(ii) Working Storage Area

'Working storage area' is like a sheet of scratch paper. When the data is being processed, there are some intermediate results that are not required as output but are required to obtain the output. Such results are stored in ***working storage area.***

(iii) Output Storage Area

The final output is not taken by the output devices immediately but is stored in memory till the output device is ready to receive it. Thus an ***'output storage area'*** holds the finished results of the processing operations until they are released on the output device.

(iv) Program Storage Area

In addition to above, the primary storage also contains a ***'program storage area'.*** The instructions for data manipulation are stored in this area.

(b) Arithmetic & Logic Unit (ALU)

This unit is capable of performing arithmetic operations and logical operations on the data stored in storage area. The basic arithmetic and logical operations include addition, subtraction, multiplication, division, ORing, ANDing, NOT (complementing), increment, decrement, shifting, clearing operations, etc. The data is transferred to ALU for processing and the intermediate results and final results are transferred to the storage area.

(c) Control Unit

This unit controls the operation of each unit of computer system by issuing control signals on the basis of instructions provided to the computer as a program. So this unit can be called the central nervous system of the computer. This unit generates timing and control signals necessary for execution of instructions. It provides status, control and timing signals necessary for the operation of other parts of the CPU, memory, and I/O devices. It controls the entire operation of the computer. It is actually the control section of the CPU, which acts as the brain of a computer.

III. Output Unit

The result generated by CPU is either transferred directly or from the output area of the memory to the output devices like visual display units (VDU) or printers, etc.

Mass Storage Devices

The primary storage area of the computer is limited in size and is expensive. Only, the frequently required instructions are stored in it. To supplement this limited memory, we use auxiliary or secondary storage devices like magnetic tapes and disks. The data can be transferred to/from these devices by the processor at a very fast speed. But as compared to primary storage, secondary storage is slow. But the advantage of secondary storage devices is that apart from being cheap, they are transferable which primary storage is not. There is no limit to secondary storage memory. This can be compared to human beings who use a note-book or pocket-diary to store the notes to supplement the brain.

2.6 WORKING OF DIGITAL COMPUTER

In order to carry out the operations mentioned in the previous section the computer allocates the task between its various functional units. The computer system is divided into three separate units for its operation. They are 1) arithmetic logical unit, 2) control unit, and 3) central processing unit.

2.6.1 ARITHMETIC LOGICAL UNIT (ALU)

Arithmetic logic unit is that part of the computer which performs the different logic operations and arithmetic calculations like addition, subtraction, multiplication and division. It is the high speed digital circuit that solves calculations and does comparisons.

After you enter data through the input device it is stored in the primary storage unit. The actual processing of the data and instruction are performed by Arithmetic Logical Unit. The major operations performed by the ALU are addition, subtraction, multiplication, division, logic and comparison. Data is transferred to ALU from storage unit when required. After processing the output is returned back to storage unit for further processing or getting stored.

Functions of Arithmetic Logic Unit

- Almost all the actions of the computer are done by it. It gets its data from a certain computer memory called **processor register.** After the data gets processed, its results get stored in output registers of the **arithmetic logic unit.**
- The **arithmetic logic unit** can perform integer arithmetic operations like addition, subtraction, etc.
- It can also perform bitwise logic operations like AND, OR, XOR, etc.
- The **arithmetic logic** unit performs bit-shifting operations like rotating or shifting a certain word to either the left or the right by a given number of bits. These can also be represented as divisions by 2 and also multiplications by 2. These are the simple operations carried out by the **arithmetic logic unit.**

2.6.2 CONTROL UNIT (CU)

The next component of computer is the Control Unit, which acts like the supervisor seeing that things are done in proper fashion. The control unit determines the sequence in which computer programs and instructions are executed. Things like processing of programs stored in the main memory, interpretation of the instructions and issuing of signals for other units of the computer to execute them. It also acts as a switch board operator when several users access the computer simultaneously. Thereby it coordinates the activities of computer's peripheral equipment as they perform the input and output. Therefore it is the manager of all operations mentioned in the previous section.

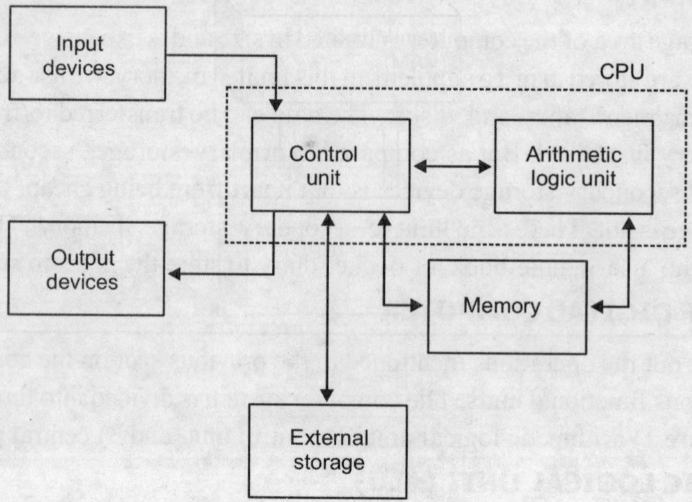

Figure 2.6: Control Unit

Control Unit and Micro-program

There was a time when the manufacturing of **control units** was a difficult process, especially in designing it. But today the scenario has changed. A **control unit** is executed in the form of micro-programs which remain in control stores. There is a micro sequencer which chooses the words and certain portions of those words which directly manage the various computer parts. These parts are arithmetic and logic units, buses, instruction registers, registers and input/output. Today the latest computers may possess subsidiary controllers for every subsystem, which would be supervised by the main **control unit.**

Functions of Control Unit

A **control unit** can be described as a sort of circuitry that supervises and controls the path of information that runs over the processor and organizes the various activities of those units that lie inside it.

- It carries out many tasks such as decoding, fetching, handling the execution and finally storing the results.
- It controls the execution of instructions in a sequential order.
- It guides the flow of data through the different parts of the computer.
- It interprets the instructions.
- It regulates the time controls of the processor.
- It sends and receives control signals from various peripheral devices.

A **control unit** is a major computer part which helps in the functioning of the central processing unit and in turn runs the whole computer.

2.6.3 CENTRAL PROCESSING UNIT (CPU)

The ALU and the CU of a computer system are jointly known as the central processing unit. You may call CPU as the brain of any computer system. It is just like brain that takes all major decisions, makes all sorts of calculations and directs different parts of the computer functions by activating and controlling the operations.

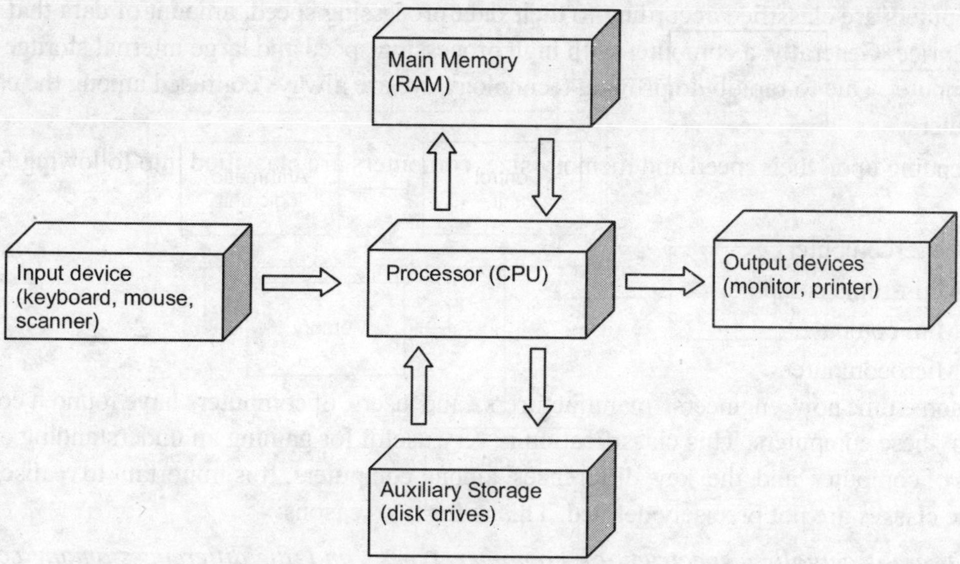

Figure 2.7: Computer Architecture

The CPU is Also Known As: processor, microprocessor, central processor, "the brains of the computer".

Central processing unit (CPU), principal part of any digital computer system, generally composed of the main memory, control unit, and arithmetic-logic unit. It constitutes the physical heart of the entire computer system; to it is linked various peripheral equipment, including input/output devices and auxiliary storage units.

The central processing unit (CPU) is the portion of a computer system that carries out the instructions of a computer program, and is the primary element carrying out the computer's functions. The central processing unit carries out each instruction of the program in sequence, to perform the basic arithmetical, logical, and input/output operations of the system. This term has been in use in the computer industry at least since the early 1960s. The form, design and implementation of CPUs have changed dramatically since the earliest examples, but their fundamental operation remains much the same.

Early CPUs were custom-designed as a part of a larger, sometimes one-of-a-kind, computer. However, this costly method of designing custom CPUs for a particular application has largely given way to the development of mass-produced processors that are made for one or many purposes. This standardization trend generally began in the era of discrete transistor mainframes and minicomputers and has rapidly accelerated with the popularization of the integrated circuit (IC). The IC has allowed increasingly complex CPUs to be designed and manufactured to tolerances on the order of nanometers. Both the miniaturization and standardization of CPUs have increased the presence of these digital devices in modern life far beyond the limited application of dedicated computing machines. Modern microprocessors appear in everything from automobiles to cell phones and children's toys.

2.7 CLASSIFICATION OF DIGITAL COMPUTERS

There is a wide variety of computers in the market today which differ in terms of physical size, price, capacity, and performance. The variety is so wide that it is sometimes difficult to see those elements that are shared by many computers and those elements that tend to differ among computers.

Computers are classified according to their data processing speed, amount of data that they can hold and price. Generally, a computer with high processing speed and large internal storage is called a big computer. Due to rapidly improving technology, we are always confused among the categories of computers.

Depending upon their speed and memory size, computers are classified into following four main groups.

1. Supercomputer
2. Mainframe computer
3. Mini computer
4. Microcomputer

For some time now, engineers, manufacturers, and users of computers have found it convenient to group these computers. This classification is very useful for gaining an understanding of the key elements of computer and the key differences among computers. It is important to realise, though, that these classes are not precisely defined. This is for two reasons:

- *There is actually a spectrum of computer types, and the differences among computers within each of three classes are as great as the differences between neighbouring classes.*
- *Computer technology is evolving rapidly, so that the microcomputer of today is as powerful as the minicomputer of a few years ago, and the minicomputer of today is as powerful as the mainframe of a few years ago.*

This classification implies differences between classes between in one or more characteristics. In the 1960s, before the microcomputer, there was a clear-cut distinction between minicomputers and mainframes. The most important characteristics that could be used to differentiate the two types of computers were:

- Speed
- Instruction sizes
- Number of CPU registers
- Word Length
- Main Memory Size
- Complexity of I/O modules
- Operating System Complexity
- Physical size
- Cost
- Virtual address space
- Secondary Memory Size
- Degree of Multiprogramming

2.7.1 SUPERCOMPUTER

Supercomputer is the most powerful and fastest, and also very expensive. It was developed in 1980s. It is used to process large amount of data and to solve the complicated scientific problems. It can perform more than one trillions calculations per second. It has large number of processors connected parallel. So parallel processing is done in this computer. In a single supercomputer thousands of users can be connected at the same time and the supercomputer handles the work of each user separately.

Supercomputers are mainly used for:

- Weather forecasting.
- Nuclear energy research.
- Aircraft design.
- Automotive design.
- To control industrial units.

The supercomputers are used in large organizations, research laboratories, aerospace centers, large industrial units etc. Nuclear scientists use supercomputers to create and analyze models of nuclear fission and fusions, predicting the actions and reactions of millions of atoms as they interact.

A supercomputer is shown in ***Fig.2.8.***

Fig. 2.8: Super Computer

There is a need for computers to solve mathematical problems of real processes, such as occur in disciplines including :

- Seismology
- Meteorology
- Atomic Physics
- Aerodynamics
- Plasma Physics
- Fluid-dynamics
- Nuclear Physics

Typically, these problems are characterised by the need for high precision and a program that repetitively performs floating-point arithmetic operations on large arrays of numbers. Most of these problem into the category known as continuous-field simulation.

The supercomputer has limited use and because of its price tag has a limited market. Only a few dozen of these machines are operational, mostly at research centres and some government agencies with scientific or engineering functions. As in some current applications in aerodynamics and nuclear physics, absorbing more than two days of computing time on a contemporary supercomputer, are needed for a single problem. Thus the technology and performance of the supercomputer continues to evolve.

Supercomputers are specially designed to maximise the number of FLOPS. Seymour Cray ***(Fig.2.9),*** owner of Cray Research is known as the ***'Father of Supercomputers'.***

Fig. 2.9: Seymour Cray

Today's supercomputers are not fast enough to simulate the airflow around an entire aircraft. Therefore, designers and builders of new air-planes simulate the airflow around separate parts of a plane. Thereafter, they combine the results to obtain an effective aerodynamic design. Thus the technology and performance of the supercomputer must continue to evolve.

Examples :

- CRAY X-MP/14, X-MP/24, X-MP/48
- CRAY Y-MP, Y-MPC
- CRAY 2
- CRAY 3
- ETA (EDC-ETA 10, ETA 20)
- C-DAC's PARAM
- NEC (NEC SX-3)
- IBM 3090 (with vector)
- Fujitsu (VP Series)
- Hitachi (HITAC S-300)
- PARAM,

  etc.

2.7.2 MAINFRAME COMPUTERS

The mainframe remains a distinct class of computers and are very powerful large general purpose computers. Large organisations use mainframe computer (shown in ***Fig.2.10***). Some of the key differences between the high end of mainframe class and the high end of the minicomputer class are there. One of the most dramatic differences is the speed of the two classes.

Fig. 2.10 : Mainframe Computer

Mainframe computers are also large-scale computers but supercomputers are larger than mainframe. These are also very expensive. The mainframe computer specially requires a very large clean room with air-conditioner. This makes it very expensive to buy and operate. It can support a large number of various equipments. It also has multiple processors. Large mainframe systems can handle the input and output requirements of several thousand of users. For example, IBM, S/390 mainframe can support 50,000 users simultaneously. The users often access then mainframe with terminals or personal computers.

A common measure of speed is millions of instructions per second (MIPS); this is the rate at which machine instructions are executed. However, the instruction sets of mainframes and super-minis are comparable , and so this is a fair comparison. Another dramatic area of difference is price.

Examples:

- DEC's VAX-8350, -8650
- HP 9000 Model 870S/400, Model 870S/300
- IBM 4300 Series (small to medium-size models)
- IBM 308X Series (large models)
- Latest model IBM 3090 Series (IBM 3090/600 installed in 1988)
- IBM Enterprise System/9000 Series
- ICL Series
- MEDHA Series
- Sperry Series; etc.

There are basically two types of terminals used with mainframe systems.

These are:

(i) Dumb Terminal: Dumb terminal does not have its own CPU and storage devices. This type of terminal uses the CPU and storage devices of mainframe system. Typically, a dumb terminal consists of monitor and a keyboard (or mouse).

(ii) Intelligent Terminal: Intelligent terminal has its own processor and can perform some processing operations. Usually, this type of terminal does not have its own storage. Typically, personal computers are used as intelligent terminals. A personal computer as an intelligent terminal gives facility to access data and other services from mainframe system. It also enables to store and process data locally.

The mainframe computers are specially used as servers on the World Wide Web. The mainframe computers are used in large organizations such as Banks, Airlines and Universities etc. where many people (users) need frequent access to the same data, which is usually organized into one or more huge databases. IBM is the major manufacturer of mainframe computers. The examples of mainframes are IBM S/390, Control Data CYBER 176 and Amdahl 580 etc.

2.7.3 MINICOMPUTERS

Minicomputers are faster and more powerful than microcomputers. The word-length of these computers is usually 32-bits or more. By the early 1960s, economic and technical factors combined to make small, inexpensive computers attractive for many applications. Many computing tasks could be accomplished with the less power than was then available on contemporary mainframe computers. For example, computers could be used to control some industrial or data acquisition process, such as checkout of the electronic system of a product on an assembly line. This type of task could be economically performed by a mainframe, but a small, relatively inexpensive computer could be used. While mainframe machines were run by staffs of operators, such costs could not be justified for the inexpensive minicomputer. Thus, direct interaction between the minicomputer and the user was required.

As the speed, instruction size, memory-size, and other characteristics of minicomputers increased with advancement in technology, its role changed. Many of the stand-alone or dedicated applications began to be performed by microcomputers. The minicomputer became a multi-user, or shared, system. Throughout the 1960s and 1970s, advances in technology led to the increasing functionality of the minicomputer. Instruction sets were enhanced to include operations on floating point numbers for scientific processing and on character strings for commercial applications. The availability of low-cost memory allowed a dramatic increase in the size of main memory attached to the minicomputer. The speed of instruction execution increased.

A minicomputer can support up to 64 or even 100 terminals. Minicomputers can support a greater variety of fast peripheral devices. Minicomputers are extensively used for multi-user and interactive applications in colleges, universities, research organisations, government organisations, industries and so on. These are also used for sophisticated real-time Industrial controls and interactive engineering design work.

Examples:

- Wipro S-68030V and S-68033V built around Motorola 68030 CPU
- HP 9000 series 800 (a Supermini) built around HP's VLSI RISC Processor
- HCL Magnum built around 68030 and 68040 CPUs
- IBM AS/400/B60 (installed in 1988)
- DEC's VAX 8842 (installed in 1988)
- Wipro LandMark 860 (a Supermini) built around Intel's 64-bit RISC processor i860 CPU, and so on.

The capabilities of a minicomputer are between mainframe and personal computer. These computers are also known as midrange computers.

The minicomputers are used in business, education and many other government departments. Although some minicomputers are designed for a single user but most are designed to handle multiple terminals. Minicomputers are commonly used as servers in network environment and hundreds of personal computers can be connected to the network with a minicomputer acting as server like mainframes, minicomputers are used as web servers. Single user minicomputers are used for sophisticated design tasks.

The first minicomputer was introduced in the mid-1960s by Digital Equipment Corporation (DEC). After this IBM Corporation (AS/400 computers) Data General Corporation and Prime Computer also designed the mini computers.

2.7.4 MICROCOMPUTER

The microcomputers are also known as personal computers or simply PCs. Microprocessor is used in this type of computer. These are very small in size and cost. The IBM's first microcomputer was designed in 1981 and was named as IBM-PC. After this many computer hardware companies copied the design of IBM-PC. The term "PC-compatible" refers any personal computer based on the original IBM personal computer design.

The most popular types of personal computers are the PC and the Apple. PC and PC-compatible computers have processors with different architectures than processors in Apple computers. These two types of computers also use different operating systems. PC and PC-compatible computers use the Windows operating system while Apple computers use the Macintosh operating system (MacOS). The majority of microcomputers sold today are part of IBM-compatible. However the Apple computer is neither an IBM nor a compatible. It is another family of computers made by Apple computer.

It is low-cost small digital computer. This type of computer contains a microprocessor as its CPU, a memory unit, input and output device(s). The word-length of these computers lie between 8 to 32-bits. These have a wide range of applications.

The microcomputer has become such a common part of everyday life that little need be said about it here. Home computers and personal office computers have proliferated, bringing computing power and literacy to more and more people.

On the basis of cost and performance, personal computers can be classified as :

- Personal Computer (PC)
- Personal Computer with Extended Technology (PC/XT)
- Personal Computer with Advanced Technology (PC/AT)
- Super AT or Super Micro

2.7.4.1 Personal Computer (PC)

PC is the simplest and cheapest type of personal computer. It uses Intel 8086/8088 as CPU, 640 KB RAM, 8KB ROM and normally two floppy disk drives. One of the drives is normally meant for holding bootable floppy diskette and the second one is used for holding the application package as well as for secondary storage. This type of computer does not contain any hard-disk. It is a single-user system. Its ROM can be extended from 8KB to 64 KB. It uses MS-DOS operation system. It may also employ 8087 math co-processor.

2.7.4.2 PC/XT

This type of computer contains hard-disk(s) as well as floppy disk drive i.e. 360 KB/1.2 MB. Its cost is obviously more than the PC due to additional components. It is also a single-user system. Its ROM can also be extended up to 64 KB. It also normally uses MS-DOS operation system. It may also employ 8087 math co-processor.

2.7.4.3 PC/AT

It contains 80286 as CPU, 640 KB RAM (can be expanded to 4 MB), 64 KB ROM (can be expanded to 128 KB), hard-disk drive and floppy-disk drive (360 KB/1.2 MB). Microprocessor 80286 is more powerful than the microprocessors of PC and PC/XTs. Up to 4 terminals can be connected to PC/AT to make it multi-user system by using XENIX as an operating system. Hard-disk capacity may lie in the range 20-80 MB. It uses 80287 math co-processor. Processing speed of PC, PC/XT and PC/AT lies in the range 1-5 MIPS.

2.7.4.4 Super AT (or Super micros)

These computers use a 32-bit CPU such as Intel 80386 or 80486. The processing speed of 80386 and 80496 may range from 3 to 5 MIPS and 12 MIPS at 25 MHz respectively. RAM size of these lie in the range 2-8 MB. In case of 80386 microprocessor, it can be extended up to 32 MB and in case of 80486 up to 64 MB. Hard-disk capacity of these lies in the range 200 MB-780 MB. Normally, UNIX is used as a multi-user operating system on these systems. 80386 CPU offers the connectivity up to 8-12 terminals whereas 80486 offers the connectivity up to 16-64 terminals.

Personal computers are available in two models. These are:

1. Desktop PCs
2. Tower PCs

A desktop personal computer is most popular model of personal computer. The system unit of the desktop personal computer can lie flat on the desk or table. In desktop personal computer, the monitor is usually placed on the system unit.

Another model of the personal computer is known as tower personal computer. The system unit of the tower PC is vertically placed on the desk of table. Usually the system unit of the tower model is placed on the floor to make desk space free and user can place other devices such as printer, scanner etc. on the desktop. Today computer tables are available which are specially designed for this purpose. The tower models are mostly used at homes and offices.

Microcomputers are further divided into following categories.

1. Laptop computer
2. Workstation
3. Network computer
4. Handheld computer

2.7.4.5 Laptop computer

Laptop computer is also known as notebook computer. It is small size (85-by-11 inch notebook computer and can fit inside a briefcase. The laptop computer is operated on a special battery and it does not have to be plugged in like desktop computer. The laptop computer is portable and fully functional microcomputer. It is mostly used during journey. It can be used on your lap in an airplane. It is because it is referred to as laptop computer.

The memory and storage capacity of laptop computer is almost equivalent to the PC or desktop computer. It also has the hard dist, floppy disk drive, Zip disk drive, CD-ROM drive, CD-writer etc. it has built-in keyboard and built-in trackball as pointing device. Laptop computer is also available with the same processing speed as the most powerful personal computer. It means that laptop computer has same features as personal computer. Laptop computers are more expensive than desktop computers. Normally these computers are frequently used in business travelers.

2.7.4.6 Workstations

Workstations are special single user computers having the same features as personal computer but have the processing speed equivalent to minicomputer or mainframe computer. A workstation computer can be fitted on a desktop. Scientists, engineers, architects and graphic designers mostly use these computers.

Workstation is an expensive and a very powerful machine used by engineers, scientists and other professionals such as artists, etc. who need to process a lot of data. People who need to execute complicated programs and display both work in progress and outputs graphically also make use of workstations.

These have advanced processors, more RAM and storage capacity than personal computers. These are usually used as single-user applications but these are used as servers on computer network and web servers as well.

Workstations use sophisticated display screens featuring high-resolution color graphics and operating systems such as UNIX, Windows NT, 95, 98 those permitted multitasking. Workstations also use powerful networking links to other computers.

Most significant feature of workstations is the powerful processor which churn out results much faster than the PCs.

Examples : Sun-, Apollo-, Hewlett-Packard-, NeXT- and IBM-workstations.

2.7.4.7 Network computers

Network computers are also version of personal computers having less processing power, memory and storage. These are specially designed as terminals for network environment. Some types of network computers have no storage. The network computers are designed for network, Internet or Intranet for data entry or to access data on the network. The network computers depend upon the network's server for data storage and to use software. These computers also use the network's server to perform some processing tasks.

In the mid-1990s the concept of network computers became popular among some PC manufacturers. As a result several variations of the network computers quickly became available. In business, variations of the network computer are Windows terminals, NetPCs and diskless workstations. Some network computers are designed to access only the Internet or to an Intranet. These devices are sometimes called Internet PCs, Internet boxes etc. In home some network computers do not include monitor. These are connected to home television, which serves as the output devices. A popular example of a home-based network computer is Web TV, which enables the user to connect a television to the Internet. The Web TV has a special set-top box used to connect to the Internet and also provides a set of simple controls which enable the user to navigate the Internet, send and receive e-mails and to perform other tasks on the network while watching television. Network computers are cheaper to purchase and to maintain than personal computers.

2.7.4.8 Handheld Computer

In the mid 1990s, many new types of small personal computing devices have been introduced and these are referred to as handheld computers. These computers are also referred to as Palmtop Computers. The handheld computers sometimes called Mini-Notebook Computers. The type of computer is named as handheld computer because it can fit in one hand while you can operate it with the other hand. Because of its reduced size, the screen of handheld computer is quite small. Similarly it also has small keyboard. The handheld computers are preferred by business traveler. Some handheld computers have a specialized keyboard. These computers are used by mobile employees, such as meter readers and parcel delivery people, whose jobs require them to move from place to place.

The examples of handheld computers are:

1. Personal Digital Assistance
2. Cellular telephones
3. H/PC Pro devices

2.7.4.9 Personal Digital Assistants (PDAs)

The PDA is one of the more popular lightweight mobile devices in use today. A PDA provides special functions such as taking notes, organizing telephone numbers and addresses. Most PDAs also offer a variety of other application software such as word processing, spreadsheet and games etc. Some PDAs include electronic books that enable users to read a book on the PDA's screen.

Many PDAs are web-based and users can send/receive e-mails and access the Internet. Similarly, some PDAs also provide telephone capabilities.

The primary input device of a PDA is the stylus. A stylus is an electronic pen and looks like a small ballpoint pen. This input device is used to write notes and store in the PDA by touching the screen. Some PDAs also support voice input.

2.7.4.10 Cellular phones

A cellular phone is a web-based telephone having features of analog and digital devices. It is also referred to as Smart Phone. In addition to basic phone capabilities, a cellular phone also provides the functions to receive and send e-mails & faxes and to access the Internet.

2.7.4.11 H/PC Pro Devices

H/PC Pro dive is new development in handheld technology. These systems are larger than PDAs but they are not quite as large as typical notebook PCs. These devices have features between PDAs and notebook PCs. The H/PC Pro device includes a full-size keyboard but it does not include disk. These systems also have RAM with very low storage capacity and slow speed of processor.

2.8 REASONS OF POPULARITY OF MICROCOMPUTERS

The microcomputers are very popular due to the following reasons:

(i) Useful: They are very useful. By using microcomputers, individuals and small businesses can increase productivity or accomplish tasks that would ordinarily take too much time or too much effort to even attempt manually.

(ii) Something For Everyone: Computers can be useful to a variety of people for a variety of tasks. they can be used to play games, teach children math, create new musical sounds, predict stck market trends, or serve as a handy reference resource.

(iii) Inexpensive: They are very inexpensive. Families or home businesses can afford to buy a small system to use at home.

(iv) Easy To Use: Microcomputers are relatively easy to use. Typically, people don't need to know how a computer actually operates internally to use one. Some computers are easy to use because many of the ready-to-use software packages have instructions that appear on the computer screen to guide you through the task at hand.

2.9 FUNCTIONAL SIMILARITIES OF COMPUTER SYSTEMS AND HUMAN BEINGS

We have already gone through the anatomy of a digital computer and functioning of a computer system using its various components. Besides, we are also well versed and aware with the functioning of human-beings using its various organs.

Processing of data by hand is satisfactory only when the amount of data to be processed is small and also the manual data processing is slow, monotonous and often subject to error. Human-beings utilises past experiences and intuitions for decision making whereas computer follows an algorithmic procedure. Human-beings as a decision maker utilises heuristic. Society will benefit most if complementary strengths of human beings and computers are utilised. Definitely, computers today have more intelligence than in the past and the strides are being made to increase machine capabilities.

The Newell-Simon model suggests that there are limitations on the ability of human as information processors :

- One set of limits concerns the processing of data and is directly related to short-term memory
- Another set of limits is the ability of humans to detect differences
- Humans are also limited in their ability to generate, integrate, and interpret probabilistic data.

Functional similarities of a computer system with human being is in the following **Table 2.2.**

Table 2.2 :Computer Vs. Human-being (Similarities)

S.No.	Comuter Element	Purpose	Human-being
1.	Input	Used to receive data and instructions in computer-compatible form	Input to the system is through ears, eyes, mouth or nose
2.	Main Storage	Used to hold input data and instructions temporarily before it is processed	Data and instructions are stored in brain and can be recalled whenever needed
3.	Secondary Storage	Used as an extension to main storage and the contents stored in it are retained permanently	Use pocket-diaries, notebooks, etc. to store contents for permanent use.
4.	ALU	Used to carry out arithmetic and logical computations desired in an instruction execution	Portion of our brain is used to carry out comparisons and calculations for helping out in logical judgements
5.	Control Unit	Used to receive stored instructions in serial fashion and one at a time.	Our brain controls our mental or body actions on the basis of calculations and comparisons.
		Interpret each instruction and prompt its execution by one of the units like input, output, storage or ALU.	Before taking any action, the old results stored in brain are also referred to and thus brain acts as a CPU.
6.	Output	Used to give out results via a suitable device e.g. VDU, printer, plotter, etc.	Output is either in the form of a speech using mouth or some action e.g. writing, gesture, body language, etc.

2.10 APPLICATIONS OF COMPUTERS

Computer is playing very important role in every field of life. Computers are everywhere such as at home, at school. In daily life a large number of activities are dependent on computers. The main fields where computer is playing very important role are:

2.10.1 Education

Education is the process of developing knowledge through instructions. The instructions are received from people such as parents, teachers etc. and from printed material such as books, journals etc. Today, the modern technique to get knowledge is by using computers.

All schools use computers in classrooms and labs to teach students. Many educators prefer to deliver their lectures by computer-based presentations. In schools, colleges and universities, students use software packages to complete their assignments.

The computer-based training (CBT) or presentation is also called computer aided instruction (CAI). In this method, computer is used as an aid to teach the students in the classroom. The instructions of particular subject are received from the instructions that use a program presented by a computer as learning medium. The web-based training (WBT) is another type of CBT that uses internet technology. It means that many websites provides online education. A lot of material of different topics is available on these websites. They also provide online lectures and tutorials for the students. The CBT and WBT are used in business education centers to educate people. People can get knowledge at very low cost as well as in very short period of time. Most of the WBT is free of cost.

Edutainment is another type of CBT. It is a type of educational software that combines the education with entertainment. This software is available on CD-ROMs and DVD-ROMs and teaches children in a fun and in exciting way. Similarly type in is learnt through these types of software.

2.10.2 Entertainment

Computer has also played a very important role for the entertainment of humans. Computer has become need of humans for entertainment at their home. Form example, to play video games at home, different game software is available to play games. Similarly, software is available to see movie films and to listen music. Today the movie files and famous songs are mostly available on CDs or on the web at very low cost. You can listen music while you work on the computer.

On the web, you can view fine art images in online museums and galleries. Some artists sell their works online and others display them for your viewing pleasure.

2.10.3 E-Commerce

E-commerce (electronic commerce) of e-trade or e-business is a financial business transaction conducted electronically between business partners over computer network (such as on Internet). With e-commerce, transactions can occur instantaneously and globally. This saves time for participants on both ends. The users can buy, sell and exchange of products or services via computer network. Today, many mobile computers can also access the internet on wireless.

There are many applications of e-commerce such as home banking, buying stocks, collaborating electronically with business partners around the globe, marketing and advertising products, providing services to the customers etc. There are several types of e-commerce like collaborative commerce business-to-commerce, consumer-to-consumer, mobile commerce etc.

The following services are mostly used in e-commerce or e-business:

(i) E-Mail: It is the most popular service through which we can electronically send and receive messages anywhere in the world. The spoken messages are sent and received through voice mail.

(ii) Video Conferencing: A video conference is a meeting between two or more people residing at various places. They can watch and talk with each other. They use a network (i.e. Internet). To participate in a video conference, you need a video camera, a microphone, speaker and software (special video conferencing software). Video conferencing also need a computer with a large memory and fast processor.

Video conferencing provides a complete simulation of a normal meeting environment, enabling both parties to see, hear and present material, just as if they are in the same room.

(iii) Electronic Shopping (E-Shopping): Many businesses now have websites that allow internet users to buy goods or services. Shopping can take place using a computer at home, or at a cybercafe. The e-shop can be anywhere in the world and it remains open 24 hours a day. You can purchase any goods such as books, software, movies, computers, cars, airline tickets etc. on the web.

(iv) Electronic Banking: One of the most popular uses of e-commerce is electronic banking. An electronic banking is also known as cyber-banking. It includes various banking activities conducted from home, a business, or on the road instead of a physical bank location. In all over the world, about 95 percent banks are online.

2.10.4 Traveling

Computer is also playing very important role in traveling by car or airplane to arrive easily and safely at your destination. Today many vehicles manufactured use special electronic equipments in the car that controls various activities of the car. These cars have GPS (Global Positioning System) receiver that reports your vehicle's location. These cars also have ***"Onboard Navigation Systems"*** that have the following features.

- Track the vehicle if it is stolen
- Provide emergency services
- Provide directions
- Provide roadside assistance
- Perform remote diagnostics if a warning light appears on the dashboard
- To make hotel and restaurant reservations

Today many vehicles also include options such as screens with e-mail and internet access, printers, fax capability etc. Airlines also provide online access. The passengers can connect their notebook or hand held computer to the web during their flights. Some airlines also provide web surfing devices to their passenger during their flights.

Computers are also used in cars to monitor fluid levels, temperatures, electrical systems etc. It is also used to monitor the air traffic etc.

2.10.5 Government

A government runs the country by making policies and provides citizens with up-to-date information. Most of the government departments have their own websites. The computers are used in all government departments have their own websites. The computers are used in all government offices to perform various activities. The government agencies use computers as part of their daily routine.

2.10.6 Home

Like other electronic devices used in home such as T.V. set, washing machine etc. computer has also become the need of every person at home. It is used at home as an educational tool for children. But it is also used at home to keep records, write letters, prepare budgets, connect with others to send and get information on the internet, to watch films and to listen music or other entertainment etc.

2.10.7 Health Care

Nearly every area of the medical field uses computers, such as laboratories, researches, scanning, monitoring, pharmacy etc., which are helping the doctors to diagnose diseases and many other purposes.

The main uses of computer in medical field are described below:

(i) Maintaining Patient History and Other Records: The complete bio-data as well as medical history of patient is recorded into the computer before check up of patient. The complete medical history (current and previous) is delivered to the related doctor for the check up of patient. In this way, much of the doctor's time is saved.

In addition to patient history, other information about doctors, medicines, chemicals and equipments is also maintained. It is very easy and efficient way to organize records than paper-based records. Any information about patients, doctors, equipments etc. can be retrieved very easily and quickly. In hospitals, mostly all the medical wards are interconnected through network. For example, if a patient is allocated a specific ward but being examined by a consultant and receiving treatment in other areas (wards) of the hospital, his detail can be viewed and updated at any terminal on the hospital's LAN network.

(ii) Patient Monitoring: The electronic scanning units (medical equipments) used in hospital can also be attached to computers. These are very expensive and are used to monitor the patient continuously. Thus computers are normally used in the following medical units of hospitals.

- ICU (Intensive Care Unit)
- Operation Theater
- Recovery Room
- Medical Ward
- EGG (Electrocardiograph)

The medical equipment with sensors attached to the patient that detects changes of heart rate, pulse rate, blood pressure, breathing and brain activity. If any unbalancing situation occurs, computer activates the alarming device, which creates sound and alerts the medical staff. The data is also logged and used to analyze the change in a patient's condition over a period of time.

(iii) Diagnosis of Diseases: Computer is also used in hospital for diagnosis. For example, laboratory tests on blood and tissue chemistry have become dependent on computer analysis.

One common use of computer is hospital is to scan the body of patient. A special scanner is used for this purpose. A scanner sends electromagnetic rays through a patient body and sensors detect that how much patient body have affects to any type of cancer (or disease). For example, the CAT (Computerized Axial Topography) scanner passes rays over the patient. A CAT scanner takes many X-rays around the body. It displays an image that enables physicians to look beneath the patient's skin. As the scanner passes over the patient, it displays and image of bone and tissue structure of patient on a computer screen.

(iv) Telemedicine: Another improvement in the medical field is the telemedicine. In telemedicine, you can access medical care centers using computers videoconferencing.

(v) Computer-Aided Surgery (CAS): Many surgeons also use computer aided surgery while they are in training. It is used to learn surgical techniques. The physicians and dentists also use the computer aided learning (CAL) program.

Many websites also provide up-to-date medical, fitness, etc. information. These websites also maintain databases about various problems and their solutions. There are also medical chat rooms on the internet.

2.10.8 Science

Computer is used in all branches of science to collect and analyze data. The scientists also use internet to collect the latest information around the world. Today, it is impossible to carry out scientific researches without use of computers. In all branches of science, it is mainly used to get accurate experimental results, for example to get accurate forecasting of weather etc.

2.10.9 Energy

Energy companies use computers to locate or search oil, coal, natural gas and uranium. Similarly electric power companies use computers to monitor the power networks. In addition, meter readers use hand held computers to record the units consumed in homes and business.

2.10.10 Industry

In industry, computers are used to control the manufacturing system and continuous running of the machinery. These also help in monitoring temperature [pressure, check the quality and accuracy and measurement needed in the manufacturing process.

In industry, robots are used to perform most of the activities as mentioned above. A robot is an automatic programmable machine that moves and performs mechanical tasks. It means that a robot acts like human beings. Robot can work in environment that is dangerous for human being such as opening chemical packages and packages believed to contain bombs. It can perform repetitive tasks continuously without any break, at very high accuracy than human. Robots can also be used in hundreds of applications such as:

- Assembling & spray-painting cars
- Lifting of heavy equipments, power cables etc.
- Testing blood samples
- Performing experiments in artificial satellites and radioactive environment etc.

2.10.11 Publishing

In the field of publishing, computer is playing very important role such as to publish the books, magazines and newspapers etc. The publishers use computer and word processors and graphics software to design pages of the books or magazines. Many writes and publishers use Internet to collect information that is used for compiling a new book of magazine. Some websites allow you to download and entire book, called an electronic book (e-book). The journalists also use the notebook computers and digital cameras to capture and record news.

2.10.12 Agriculture

In agriculture field also, computer is playing very important role. The agricultural scientists are computer for analyzing the agricultural data. The students of agriculture also uses computer to get latest information about agriculture on the internet. The farmers also use computer to get information about crops and to calculate bills and cost per acre as well as to get information about crops market prices.

EXERCISES

1. Discuss the important features of micro, mini, mainframes and super-computers.
2. What is a Computer ? What capabilities does a computer possess ?
3. What is the stored program concept ? Why is it important ?
4. How do analog computers differ digital computers ?
5. State the criteria for classification of digital computers.
6. Is digital computer more accurate than analog computer ? Justify your answer.
7. What are the operations that a computer is able to perform ?
8. What are the fundamental components of a computer system ? Which component of a computer system executes the program ?
9. Why are microcomputers so popular in comparison to other computers ?
10. What is a digital computer ? Provide its anatomy and explain the functioning of such a computer through its block diagram.
11. What are the latest trends in microprocessor technology ? Explain.
12. State the evolutionary stages of data processing.
13. What are the advantages and disadvantages of pen-based computing used by PDAs ? For what type of applications would you use a PDA ?
14. Why should we go for computers ?
15. Detail out the description of Mark I electromechanical computer.

16. What are the applications for supercomputers and embedded computers which are affecting our lives ?
17. How is a PC different from a Workstation ?
18. Comment on how computers are changing our traditional patterns of personal communication.
19. What is the difference between a Laptop and a Sub-notebook Computer ?
20. What is the Y2K problem ?
21. What are the characteristics of a computer ?
22. Do you think there is a continuing need to increase computer speed ? Can you think of examples in which more speed would be desirable ?
23. What is hybrid-computer? State its significance along with few important applications.
24. Why do embedded computers make tools more flexible ?
25. Identify at least 3 examples of computer systems you have seen or used.
26. Is a computer more intelligent than human-beings ? Justify your answer.
27. What is a PDA and for whom is it preferred ?
28. Elucidate difference between micro-computers and mainframes.
29. The computer has had far-reaching effects on our lives. How has the computer affected your life ?
30. What is a mainframe and what are its typical applications ?
31. Identify two types of portable microcomputers and explain how they differ from each other ?
32. What are supercomputers and where are they used ?
33. Comment on how computers are changing our traditional patterns of recreation.
34. What are different types of portable computers ?
35. In terms of physical size, how are PCs categorised ?
36. What is the difference between a microcomputer and minicomputer ?
37. What are the limitations of human processing ? How these can be removed ?
38. What are the implications for information systems design of the statement that humans are serial rather than parallel processors ?
39. Compare computer and human-beings.
40. What is the difference between a microcomputer and a microprocessor?
41. What are Cellular Phones? Are these different from PDAs? Justify your answer.
42. What are hybrid computers? Give some examples.
43. What makes microcomputers popular?
44. What are laptop computers? What are its specific characteristics?
45. How do you compare human beings and computers?
46. What are workstations?
47. What are network computers? What characterises network computer?
48. How computers are useful in publishing?
49. What are uses of computers in health care?
50. How computers help in the field of education?
51. What are limitations of computers?
52. What are the main capabilities of computers?
53. What are the important characteristics of computers?
54. How computers may help in travelling?
55. How computers can help in business? Name some business applications.
56. How computers can be helpful in science and arts? Discuss.

Number Systems and Data Represention

3.1 INTRODUCTION

A digital computer is an electronic machine that accepts a stream of symbols, stores them, processes them according to precise rules and produces meaningful output. Computers are used in scientific calculations, commercial and business data processing, air traffic control, space guidance, the educational field, and many other areas. The most important characteristic of a digital computer is its generality. It can follow a sequence of instructions, called a program that operates on given data.

In this Chapter we will discuss the Number Systems and representation of data in digital systems. There are two main categories of data:

(i) Numbers, and

(ii) Characters.

As mentioned earlier that internally in a digital system all data is represented by sequence of symbols where each symbol, called a bit, is either a 0 or a 1. The general properties of number systems, methods of their inter-conversions, complements and other data representation techniques are also discussed in this Chapter.

3.2 BASIC FEATURES OF DIGITAL SYSTEMS

Few basic features which are common to all digital systems are as under:

All streams of input symbols to a digital system are encoded with two distinct symbols 0 (zero) and 1 (one), known as binary digits or bits. Bits can be stored and manipulated reliably and inexpensively using electronic circuits.

The instructions for manipulating the symbols are to be properly specified so that a machine can be built to execute these. The instructions for manipulation are also encoded using bits.

A digital computer has a storage unit which stores the symbols to be manipulated and the encoded instructions for manipulation of the symbols.

Bit manipulation instructions are realized by electronic circuits.

3.3 NUMBER SYSTEMS

Number systems are very important to understand because the design and organisation of a computer depends on the number systems. The modern civilization is familiar with Decimal ***Number System,*** in which ten digits, namely 0 to 9 are used to represent any number. Now the decimal number system is used frequently in the field of Science and Technology. Once the famous Mathematician Laplace stated, "It is India that gave us the ingenious method of expressing all numbers by means of ten symbols, each symbol receiving a value of position as well as an absolute value, a profound and important idea which appears so simple to us now that we ignore its true merit."

Thus, the importance of a number system does not lie in the number of symbols used in it but what is important in it is the concept of face value (absolute value) and the place value (value of position) of a symbol. However, if instead of decimal system the binary number system, using two digits namely, 0 and 1, had been popular everywhere, the understanding of computer working would have been much easier. The binary number system is the one which is used in computers and is based on the fundamental concept of decimal number system. Various other number systems such as Octal System and Hexadecimal System (popularly known as Hex system) also use the fundamental concept of face value and place value.

The knowledge of number systems is essential for understanding of computers. The useful number systems discussed are:

- Binary Number System
- Decimal Number System
- Octal Number System
- Hexadecimal Number System.

3.3.1 Binary Number System

The **Binary Number System,** as the name suggests, consists of two digits namely, 0 and 1. These binary digits are called BITS. Thus, the word **BIT** stands for either of the binary digits, namely 0 or 1. Since this system uses two digits only, it has the **base** or **radix 2.** It may be noted that the base digit namely 2, is not the fundamental or basic digit of the system.Thus, all the numbers in binary system are written with the help of these two digits namely, 0 and 1. The positional value or place value of each digit in a binary number is twice the positional value of the digit on its right. This number system is identical to decimal number system with the base replaced by 2. The binary numbers are usually written with the base indicated as a subscript on the least significant digit (LSD). For example,

$$(101101.1011)_2$$

It can be represented as shown in Figure 3.1 :

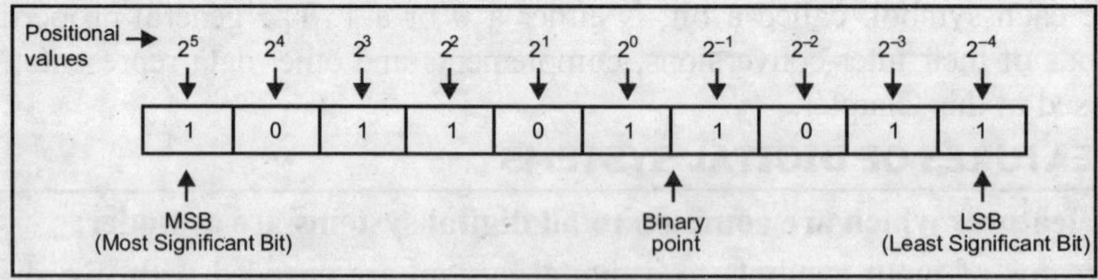

Fig. 3.1 Binary number shown with positional values.

Here, the places to the left of the binary point are positive powers of 2 and places to the right are negative powers of 2.

The commonly used terms in coding of data in computer terminology are :

BIT (BInary digiT): A binary digit is logical 0 or 1.

Nibble: A group of four bits (binary digits) is called a Nibble. It is useful in coding the numeric data to hexadecimal form.

Byte: A group of 8 bits make a byte. A byte is the smallest unit which can represent a data item or a character.

Computer Word: A computer word, like a byte, is a group of fixed number of bits which varies from computer to computer but is fixed for each computer. The number of bits in a computer word is known as the **word size** or **word length.**

Why is Binary Number System used in Computers?

(i) The circuits and switches in a computer have only two states, either on or off, which are represented by 1 and 0.

(ii) Handling of two digits, that is, 1 and 0 is simpler, cheaper and more reliable.

(iii) Every operation or activity that can be performed by decimal number system can also be done using binary number system, so it does not create any problem.

3.3.2. Octal Number System

This number system has **base** or **radix** 8. The basic digits of this system are 0, 1, 2, 3, 4, 5, 6 and 7. It may be noted that the base 8 is not the basic digit of the system. It is commonly used as a shorthand way of expressing binary quantities. Also the numbers represented in octal number system can be used directly for input and output operations.

The Octal Number System is also a positional value system, wherein each octal digit has its own value or weight expressed as a power of 8. For example,

$$(157246.3174)_8$$

It can be represented as shown in Figure 3.2 :

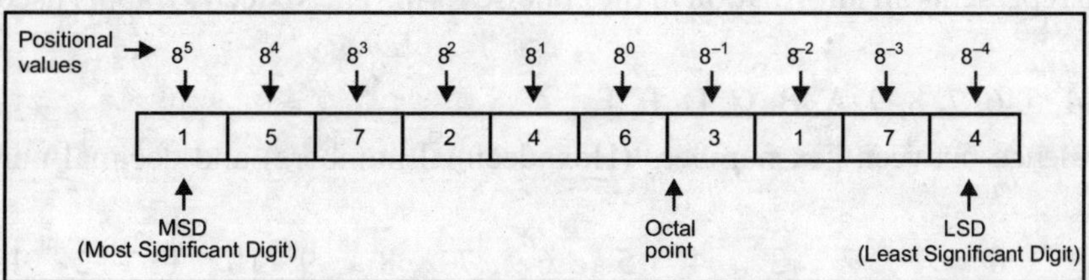

Fig. 3.2 Octal number shown with positional values.

Here, the places to the left of the octal point are positive powers of 8 and places to the right are negative powers of 8.

3.3.3 Decimal Number System

The decimal number system consists of 10 digits namely 0 to 9. A number written using these digits is called a decimal number. For example, the numbers 12876, –1024, 58.74, +768 are decimal numbers. Apart from these digits, the decimal point and ± signs may also be used in writing decimal numbers. The **base** or **radix** of the number system is the number of digits used in it. Since the decimal number system consists of 10 digits, the base of this system is 10. In a number system the base is not the fundamental digit of the system because fundamental digits in this system are 0, 1, 2, 3, 4, 5, 6, 7, 8, 9. The value of each digit in a number depends upon the following :

(i) The face value of the digit, that is, the digit itself.

(ii) The base of the system.

(iii) The position of the digit in the number.

Thus, the magnitude of a number depends upon the digits of which it is made, position of the digits and base of the system. For example,

$$351479.8265$$

Since no base is mentioned, the base is taken as 10.

It can be represented as shown in Figure 3.3 :

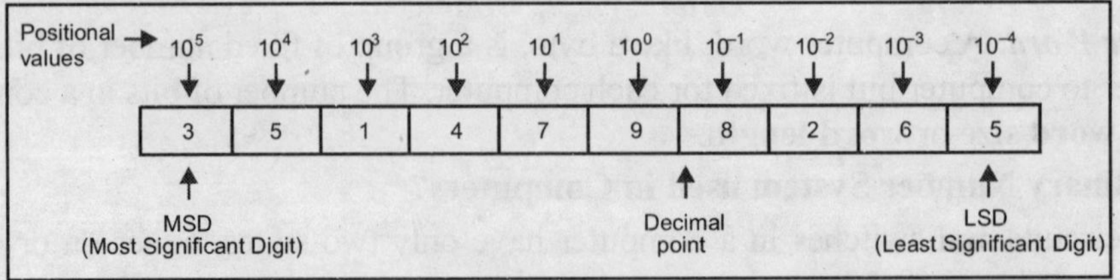

Fig. 3.3 Decimal number shown with positional values.

Here, the places to the left of the decimal point are positive powers of 10 and places to the right are negative powers of 10.

In a decimal number as we move from right to left (starting with the digit before decimal point) the positional or place value of each digit is 10 times the positional value of the digit to its right and as we move from left to right (starting with the digit after decimal point) the positional value of each digit becomes one-tenth of the positional value of the previous digit. The part of the number before the decimal point is called **integral part** and the one after the decimal point is called the **fractional part.**

3.3.4 Hexadecimal Number System

The Hexadecimal Number System, popularly known as Hex System, has sixteen symbols and therefore has the **base** or **radix** as 16 or H. It is very well suited for big computers. The hexadecimal number system represents an information in the concise form. The sixteen symbols used in this system are :

0, 1, 2, 3, 4, 5, 6, 7, 8, 9, A, B, C, D, E, F

The equivalence between hex-numbers (Hexadecimal numbers) and decimal numbers is given below:

Decimal	0	1	2	3	4	5	6	7	8	9	10	11	12	13	14	15
Hexadecimal	0	1	2	3	4	5	6	7	8	9	A	B	C	D	E	F

Hexadecimal number system is also a positional value system, wherein each hexadecimal digit/letter has its own value or weight expressed as a power of 16. For example,

$$(6A9E83.C5BD)_{16}$$

It can be represented as shown in Figure 3.4 :

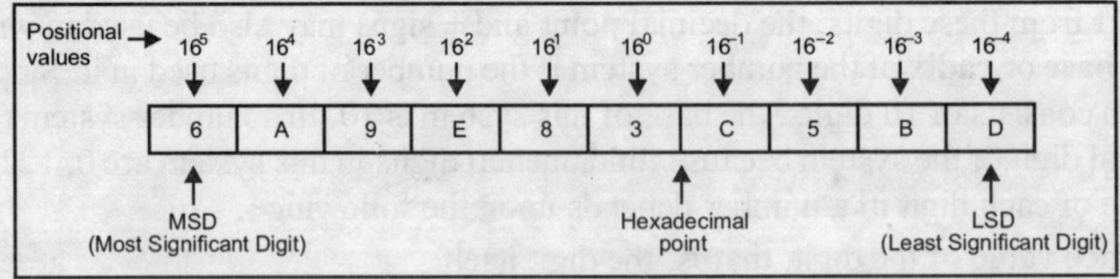

Fig. 3.4 Hexadecimal number shown with positional values.

Here, the places to the left of hexadecimal point are positive powers of 16 and places to the right are negative powers of 16.

The Table 3.1 illustrates the relation between binary, octal, decimal and hexadecimal number systems:

Table 3.1 Numbers with Different Bases

Binary (base 2)	*Octal* (base 8)	*Decimal* (base 10)	*Hexadecimal* (base 16)
0000	0	0	0
0001	1	1	1
0010	2	2	2
0011	3	3	3
0100	4	4	4
0101	5	5	5
0110	6	6	6
0111	7	7	7
1000	10	8	8
1001	11	9	9
1010	12	10	A
1011	13	11	B
1100	14	12	C
1101	15	13	D
1110	16	14	E
1111	17	15	F

3.4 INTERCONVERSION OF NUMBER SYSTEMS

The decimal number system is known as **International System** of numbers. This base (base 10) was used initially perhaps for the reason that man has 10 fingers. However, this system is unsuitable for computers because a computer uses electrical and electronic components which can exist only in two states. Hence, for computers the binary number system is required. But, the binary number system at the moment is indispensable for computers as it suffers from the defect of expansion. For example, a number in decimal system requiring only one digit for its representation may require more than one bits in binary form.

To overcome this problem various other number systems such as Octal (base 8) and Hexadecimal (base 16 or H) were developed. A base greater than 10 is preferred because it will require even lesser number of digits. The choices of bases 8 and 16 are useful because of their being multiple of two.

3.4.1 Binary to Decimal

A binary number can be converted to its decimal equivalent by adding the weights of the various positions in it which have a 1.

Example 1. *Find the decimal equivalent of the following binary numbers :*
(i) 10110 *(ii)* 101011 *(iii)* 11011100.

Solution.

(i)
$$(10110)_2 = 1 \times 2^4 + 0 \times 2^3 + 1 \times 2^2 + 1 \times 2^1 + 0 \times 2^0$$
$$= 16 + 0 + 4 + 2 + 0$$
$$= (22)_{10}.$$

It must be noted that the binary number 10110 has five digits in all. The most significant digit (MSD) has the fifth position (starting from rightmost digit) so it is multiplied by 2^4 and each digit on its right will be half of it in its positional value, so these are multiplied by 2^3, 2^2, 2^1, 2^0 respectively and the products so obtained are added to get the required decimal equivalent.

(ii) $(101011)_2 = 1 \times 2^5 + 0 \times 2^4 + 1 \times 2^3 + 0 \times 2^2 + 1 \times 2^1 + 1 \times 2^0$
$= 32 + 0 + 8 + 0 + 2 + 1$
$= (43)_{10}$
$= 43.$

(iii) $(11011100)_2 = 1 \times 2^7 + 1 \times 2^6 + 0 \times 2^5 + 1 \times 2^4 + 1 \times 2^3 + 1 \times 2^2 + 0 \times 2^1 + 0 \times 2^0$
$= 128 + 64 + 0 + 16 + 8 + 4 + 0 + 0$
$= (220)_{10}$
$= 220.$

Example 2. *Convert the following binary fractions to their decimal equivalents :*
(i) $(0.111)_2$ *(ii)* $(0.1010111)_2$ *(iii)* $(0.1011)_2$.

Solution.

(i) $(0.111)_2 = 1 \times 2^{-1} + 1 \times 2^{-2} + 1 \times 2^{-3}$
$= 1/2 + 1/4 + 1/8$
$= 0.5 + 0.25 + 0.125$
$= (0.875)_{10}$
$= 0.875$

$\therefore$ $(0.111)_2 = (0.875)_{10}$

(ii) $(0.1010111)_2 = 1 \times 2^{-1} + 0 \times 2^{-2} + 1 \times 2^{-3} + 0 \times 2^{-4} + 1 \times 2^{-5} + 1 \times 2^{-6} + 1 \times 2^{-7}$
$= 1/2 + 0 + 1/8 + 0 + 1/32 + 1/64 + 1/128$
$= 0.5 + .125 + 0.03125 + 0.015625 + 0.0078125$
$= (0.6796875)_{10}$
$= 0.6796875$

$\therefore$ $(0.1010111)_2 = (0.6796875)_{10}$

(iii) $(0.1011)_2 = 1 \times 2^{-1} + 0 \times 2^{-2} + 1 \times 2^{-3} + 1 \times 2^{-4}$
$= 1/2 + 0 + 1/8 + 1/16$
$= 0.5 + 0.125 + 0.0625$
$= (0.6875)_{10}$
$= 0.6875$

$(0.1011)_2 = (0.6875)_{10}$

Example 3. Find the decimal equivalent of the following binary numbers:
(i) $(110010.1011)_2$ (ii) $(1110.1001)_2$.

Solution.

(i) $(110010.1011)_2 = (1 \times 2^5) + (1 \times 2^4) + (0 \times 2^3) + (0 \times 2^2) + (1 \times 2^1) + (0 \times 2^0) + (1 \times 2^{-1}) + (0 \times 2^{-2}) + (1 \times 2^{-3}) + (1 \times 2^{-4})$
$= 32 + 16 + 0 + 0 + 2 + 0 + 0.5 + 0 + 0.125 + 0.0625$
$= (50.6875)_{10}$
$= 50.6875$

$(110010.1011)_2 = (50.6875)_{10}.$

(ii) $(1110.1001)_2 = 1 \times 2^3 + 1 \times 2^2 + 1 \times 2^1 + 0 \times 2^0 + 1 \times 2^{-1} + 0 \times 2^{-2}$

$+ 0 \times 2^{-3} + 1 \times 2^{-4}$

$= 8 + 4 + 2 + 0 + 1/2 + 0 + 0 + 1/16$

$= 14 + 0.5 + 0.0625$

$= 14.5625.$

Example 4. Provide the missing number $(11001.1101)_2 = (..........)_{10}$.

Solution. Let us find the decimal equivalent of the binary number.

$(11001.1101)_2 = 1 \times 2^4 + 1 \times 2^3 + 0 \times 2^2 + 0 \times 2^1 + 1 \times 2^0 + 1 \times 2^{-1}$

$+ 1 \times 2^{-2} + 0 \times 2^{-3} + 1 \times 2^{-4}$

$= 16 + 8 + 0 + 0 + 1 + 1/2 + 1/4 + 0 + 1/16$

$= 25 + 0.5 + 0.25 + 0.0625$

$= (25.8125)_{10}$

$= 25.8125$

Hence, the missing number is 25.8125.

3.4.2 Decimal to Binary

A positive decimal integer can be converted to binary form by successive division by 2. The procedure is given below:

Divide the given number N by 2 and let the quotient be q_1 and the remainder be R_1. Again divide the quotient q_1 by 2 and let the remainder be R_2. Continue the procedure of division till the quotient becomes 0 and in this case let the remainder be R_n.

Then, the binary representation by N is given as

$$N = R_n R_{n-1} ......R_3 R_2 R_1,$$

where each of the R's is either 0 or 1.

Example. Convert the following decimal integers into their binary equivalents:

(i) 25 *(ii)* 283 *(iii)* 5280.

Solution. (i) Start dividing 25 by 2 and continue the procedure till the quotient is 0. The procedure is shown below :

2	25	
2	12 – 1	$(= R_1)$ ↑
2	6 – 0	$(= R_2)$
2	3 – 0	$(= R_3)$
2	1 – 1	$(= R_4)$
	0 – 1	$(= R_5)$

The required number in the binary number system

$= R_5 R_4 R_3 R_2 R_1$

$= 11001$

Thus, $(25)_{10} = (11001)_2$

(ii) Start dividing 283 by 2 and continue the procedure till the quotient becomes 0.

2	283	
2	141 – 1	(= R_1) ↑
2	70 – 1	(= R_2)
2	35 – 0	(= R_3)
2	17 – 1	(= R_4)
2	8 – 1	(= R_5)
2	4 – 0	(= R_6)
2	2 – 0	(= R_7)
2	1 – 0	(= R_8)
	0 – 1	(= R_9)

The required binary equivalent of 283

$$= R_9\, R_8\, R_7\, R_6\, R_5\, R_4\, R_3\, R_2\, R_1$$

$$= (100011011)_2$$

Thus, $(283)_{10} = (100011011)_2$

(iii) Start dividing 5280 by 2 and continue the procedure till the quotient becomes 0.

2	5280	
2	2640 – 0	(= R_1) ↑
2	1320– 0	(= R_2)
2	660 – 0	(= R_3)
2	330 – 0	(= R_4)
2	165 – 0	(= R_5)
2	82 – 1	(= R_6)
2	41 – 0	(= R_7)
2	20 – 1	(= R_8)
2	10 – 0	(= R_9)
2	5 – 0	(= R_{10})
2	2 – 1	(= R_{11})
2	1 – 0	(= R_{12})
	0 1	(= R_{13})

The required binary equivalent of 5280

$$= R_{13}\, R_{12}\, R_{11}\, R_{10}\, R_9\, R_8\, R_7\, R_6\, R_5\, R_4\, R_3\, R_2\, R_1$$

$$= (1010010100000)_2$$

Thus, $(5280)_{10} = (1010010100000)_2$

The decimal digits and their binary equivalents are given below:

Decimal Digit	**Binary Equivalent**	
0	0	(0×2^0)
1	1	(1×2^0)
2	10	$(1 \times 2^1 + 0 \times 2^0)$
3	11	$(1 \times 2^1 + 1 \times 2^0)$
4	100	$(1 \times 2^2 + 0 \times 2^1 + 0 \times 2^0)$
5	101	$(1 \times 2^2 + 0 \times 2^1 + 1 \times 2^0)$
6	110	$(1 \times 2^2 + 1 \times 2^1 + 0 \times 2^0)$

7	111	$(1 \times 2^2 + 1 \times 2^1 + 1 \times 2^0)$
8	1000	$(1 \times 2^3 + 0 \times 2^2 + 0 \times 2^1 + 0 \times 2^0)$
9	1001	$(1 \times 2^3 + 0 \times 2^2 + 0 \times 2^1 + 1 \times 2^0)$

3.4.3 Decimal Fractions to Binary Fractions

While converting decimal fractions to binary fractions, instead of dividing by 2, multiply successively by 2 and instead of noting the remainders as in case of integers, keep track of the overflow. If overflow digits are $f_1, f_2, f_3, ...,$ fn then the equivalent binary fraction is

$$0 . f_1 f_2 f_3 ..... f_n$$

while multiplying by 2, it must be noted that every time only fractional part is to be multiplied and not the integral part. The following examples illustrate the procedure.

Example 1. Convert the decimal fractional number 0.8125 into its binary equivalent.

Solution.

```
          0.8125
        ×      2
f1    ←[1]. 6250
        ×      2      (Multiply only the fraction part)
f2    ←[1]. 2500
        ×      2
f3    ←[0]. 5000
        ×      2
f4    ←[1]. 0000
```

Further multiplication gives only zero digits as overflow.

Thus, $(0.8125)_{10} = 0. f_1 f_2 f_3 f_4$

$= (0.1101)_2$

Example 2. Convert 0.33 into its binary equivalent.

Solution.

```
          0.33
        ×    2
f1    ←[0]. 66
        ×    2
f2    ←[1]. 32
        ×    2      (Multiply only the fraction part)
f3    ←[0]. 64
        ×    2
f4    ←[1]. 28
        ×    2
f5    ←[0]. 56
        ×    2
f6    ←[1]. 12      and so on.
```

Thus, $(0.33)10 = 0.f_1 f_2 f_3 f_4 f_5 f_6......$

$= (0.010101...)_2$

3.4.4 Mixed Decimal Numbers to Binary

A mixed number consists of an integral part as well as a fractional part. For example, 38.625 is a mixed number. A mixed number in decimal system can be converted to its binary equivalent by converting the integral and fractional parts separately into their binary equivalent.

The following example illustrates this concept:

Example. Convert the decimal number 38.625 into its binary equivalent.

Solution. The given decimal number has two parts, namely an integral part 38 and a fractional part 0.625. These are to be converted into their binary equivalents separately, as given below:

2	38	
2	19 – 0	$(=R_1)$ ↑
2	9 – 1	$(=R_2)$
2	4 – 1	$(=R_3)$
2	2 – 0	$(=R_4)$
2	1 – 0	$(=R_5)$
	0 – 1	$(=R_6)$

Thus, the binary equivalent of $(38)_{10} = R_6\ R_5\ R_4\ R_3\ R_2\ R_1$

$= (100110)_2$

```
        0.625
          × 2
 f1   ←[1]. 250
          × 2        (Multiply only the fraction part)
 f2   ←[1]. 500
          × 2
 ↓f3  ←[1]. 000
```

Also

Further multiplication gives only zero digits as overflow.

Thus, $(0.625)_{10} = 0.f_1 f_2 f_3$

$= (0.101)_2$

Hence, $(38.625)_{10} = (100110.101)_2$

3.4.5 Decimal Numbers to Octal Numbers

For converting integer decimal numbers into their equivalent octal numbers, divide the given number repeatedly by 8 till the quotient obtained is zero. The following example illustrates this concept:

Example 1. Convert the following Decimal numbers into their Octal equivalents:
(i) 759 *(ii)* 1598.

Solution. *(i)* Start dividing 759 by 8 and continue the procedure till the quotient is 0. The procedure is shown below:

8	759	
8	94 – 7	↑ LSD
8	11 – 6	
8	1 – 3	
	0 – 1	MSD

Thus, $(759)_{10} = (1367)_8$

(ii)

8	1598	
8	199 – 6	↑ LSD
8	24 – 7	
8	3 – 0	
	0 – 3	MSD

Thus, $(1598)_{10} = (3076)_8$

For converting decimal fractions into their equivalent octal fractions, multiply the fractional part repeatedly by 8 and keep track of the overflow. The process of multiplication continues till the fractional part becomes zero or upto required number of digits.

The following example illustrates this concept:

Example 2. Convert the following decimal fractions to their equivalent octal fractions:

(i) $(0.125)_{10}$ *(ii)* $(0.175)_{10}$.

Solution. *(i)*

Thus, $(0.125)_{10} = (0.1)_8$

0.125
× 8
[1]. 000

(ii)

0.175
× 8
f_1 ← [1]. 400
× 8 (Multiply only the fraction part)
f_2 ← [3]. 200
× 8
f_3 ← [1]. 600
× 8
f_4 ← [4]. 800
× 8
f_5 ← [6]. 400
× 8
f_6 ← [3]. 200
× 8
f_7 ← [1]. 600
× 8
f_8 ← [4]. 800
× 8
f_9 ← [6]. 400 and so on.

Thus, $(0.175)_{10} = (0.1\ )_8$ recurrence

Here, the bar shows that these digits will be repeated infinitely.

For converting the decimal mixed numbers into their equivalent octal, integral and fractional parts are treated separately. Each part is converted to octal separately.

The following example illustrates this concept :

Example 3. Convert the following mixed decimal numbers to their equivalent Octal:

(i) 22.21875 *(ii)* 79.4375.

Solution. *(i)* $(22.21875)_{10}$

Integral part

8	22	
8	2 – 6	↑ LSD
	0 – 2	MSD

Fractional part

0.21875
× 8
[1]. 75000
× 8 (Multiply only the fraction part)
[6]. 00000

Thus, $(22)_{10} = (26)_8$ Thus, $(0.21875)_{10} = (0.16)_8$

Hence, $(22.21875)_{10} = (26.16)_8$

(ii) $(79.4375)_{10}$

Integral part

8	79	
8	9 – 7	↑ LSD
8	1 – 1	
	0 – 1	MSD

Fractional part

0.4375
× 8
[3]. 5000
× 8 (Multiply only the fraction part)
[4]. 0000

Thus, $(79)_{10} = (117)_8$ Thus, $(0.4375)_{10} = (0.34)_8$

Hence, $(79.4375)_{10} = (117.34)_8$

Note. *It may be noticed that when a decimal number is converted to its binary equivalent, a long string of binary digits, namely 0 and 1 is obtained. On the other hand, if the same decimal number is converted to its octal equivalent, the number so obtained contains less number of digits compared to binary. In fact, this was the reason for the development of Octal Number System. It must be remembered that computers still work in binary and all these number systems (except binary) are for users' convenience.*

3.4.6 Octal Numbers to Decimal Numbers

A mixed octal number can be converted to decimal number by the formula given below:

$$M = d_{n+1}8^n + d_n8^{n-1} + d_{n-1}8^{n-2} + \ldots\ldots d_3 8^2 + d_2 8^1 + d_1 8^0 + d_{-1}8^{-1} + d_{-2}8^{-2} + d_{-3}8^{-3} + \ldots + d_{-n}8^{-n}$$

Here, M is the mixed number

d_{n+1} is the digit in the $(n + 1)$th position of the integral part

d_{-1} is the digit immediately after the octal point.

The following examples illustrate this concept :

Example 1. Convert the following octal numbers into their decimal equivalents:

(i) $(47)_8$ *(ii)* $(564)_8$.

Solution. *(i)* $(47)_8 = 4 \times 8^1 + 7 \times 8^0$

$= 32 + 7 = 39$

Thus, $(47)_8 = (39)_{10}$

(ii) $(564)_8 = 5 \times 8^2 + 6 \times 8^1 + 4 \times 8^0$

$= 5 \times 64 + 6 \times 8 + 4 \times 1$

$= 320 + 48 + 4$

$= 372$

Thus, $(564)_8 = (372)_{10}$

Example 2. Convert the following octal fractions to their decimal equivalents:

(i) $(0.34)_8$ *(ii)* $(0.542)_8$.

Solution. *(i)* $(0.34)_8 = 3 \times 8^{-1} + 4 \times 8^{-2}$

$= 3 \times 1/8 + 4 \times 1/64$

$= 3 \times 0.125 + 4 \times 0.015625$

$= 0.375 + .062500$

$= (0.4375)10$

(ii) $(0.542)_8 = 5 \times 8^{-1} + 4 \times 8^{-2} + 2 \times 8^{-3}$

$= 5 \times 0.125 + 4 \times .015625 + 2 \times .001953125$

$= 0.625 + 0.062500 + .003906250$

$= (0.691406250)_{10}$

3.4.7 Octal to Binary

The Octal number system is widely used as a shorthand way of expressing binary values. The octal number system groups three binary bits together into one digit (0 to 7) as given below:

Octal	*Binary Equivalent*
0	000
1	001
2	010
3	011
4	100
5	101
6	110
7	111

To convert an octal number to its binary equivalent, each digit of the octal number is converted to its 3 bits binary equivalent.

The following examples illustrate this concept :

Example 1. Convert the following octal numbers into their binary equivalent:

(i) $(746)_8$ *(ii)* $(5043)_8$.

Solution. *(i)* $(746)_8 = \frac{111\ 100\ 110}{7\quad 4\quad 6}$

(Replace each octal digit by its 3 bits binary equivalent)

$= (111100110)_2$

Thus, $(746)_8 = (111100110)_2$

(ii) $(5043)_8 = \frac{101}{5}\frac{000}{0}\frac{100}{4}\frac{011}{3}$

$= (101000100011)_2$

Thus, $(5043)_8 = (101000100011)_2$

Example 2. Convert the following octal numbers into their binary equivalents:
(i) $(35.216)_8$ *(ii)* $(417.25)_8$.

Solution. *(i)* $(35.216)_8 = \frac{011}{3}\frac{101}{5}.\frac{010}{2}\frac{001}{1}\frac{110}{6}$

$= (11101.01000111)_2$

(Discarding the leftmost and right most zero)

Thus, $(35.216)_8 = (11101.01000111)_2$

(ii) $(417.25)_8 = \frac{100}{4}\frac{001}{1}\frac{111}{7}.\frac{010}{2}\frac{101}{5}$

$= (100001111.010101)_2$

Thus, $(417.25)_8 = (100001111.010101)_2$

3.4.8 Binary to Octal

For converting a binary number into its octal equivalent the following steps are followed:

(i) Divide the given binary number before the binary point into groups of three bits each (from right to left) and after the binary point into groups of three bits each (from left to right) by adding 0 bits for completing the groups (if needed).

(ii) Replace each group by its octal equivalent.

The following examples illustrate this concept:

Example 1. Convert the following Binary numbers into their Octal equivalents:
(i) $(11101)_2$ *(ii)* $(101010011011.10100011)_2$.

Solution. *(i)* $(11101)_2 = \overleftarrow{\frac{011}{3}\frac{101}{5}}$ (Replacing each group by its octal equivalent, 0 added on leftmost position for completing the group)

Thus, $(11101)_2 = (35)_8$

(ii) $(101010011011.10100011)_2 = \overleftarrow{\frac{101}{5}\frac{010}{2}\frac{011}{3}\frac{011}{3}}.\overrightarrow{\frac{101}{5}\frac{000}{0}\frac{110}{6}}$

(Replacing each group by its octal equivalent, 0 added on rightmost position for completing the group).

Thus, $(101010011011.10100011)_2 = (5233.506)_8$

Example 2. Convert the following Binary numbers into their Octal equivalents:
(i) $(10110101.11001)_2$ *(ii)* $(11110011.0001)_2$.

Solution. *(i)* $(10110101.11001)_2 = \underbrace{010}_{2}\ \underbrace{110}_{6}\ \underbrace{101}_{5}\ .\ \underbrace{110}_{6}\ \underbrace{010}_{2}$

Replacing each group by its equivalent, 0 added on leftmost and rightmost position for completing the group).

Thus, $(10110101.11001)_2 = (265.62)_8$

(ii) $(11110011.0001)_2 = \underbrace{011}_{3}\ \underbrace{110}_{6}\ \underbrace{011}_{3}\ .\ \underbrace{000}_{0}\ \underbrace{100}_{4}$

(Replacing each group by its equivalent, 0 added on leftmost and two 0's added on rightmost position for completing the group).

Thus, $(11110011.0001)_2 = (363.04)_8$

3.4.9 Decimal Numbers to Hexadecimal Numbers

For converting integer decimal numbers into their equivalent hexadecimal numbers, divide the given number repeatedly by 16 (if the remainder is greater than or equal to 10 then write its symbol, that is, A to F, otherwise the digit 0 to 9) till the quotient obtained is zero.

The following example illustrates this concept :

Example 1. Convert the following Decimal numbers into their Hexadecimal equivalents :

(i) $(28)_{10}$ *(ii)* $(1795)_{10}$.

Solution. *(i)* Start dividing 28 by 16 and continue the procedure till the quotient is 0. The procedure is given below:

16	28
16	1 – C
	0 – 1

Thus, $(28)_{10} = (1C)_{16}$

(ii)

16	1795
16	112 – 3
16	7 – 0
	0 – 7

Thus, $(1795)_{10} = (703)_{16}$

For converting decimal fractions into their equivalent hexadecimal fractions, multiply the fractional part repeatedly by 16 and keep track of the overflow. If the overflow is greater than equal to 10 then write its symbol, that is, A to F, otherwise the digit 0 to 9. The process of multiplication continues till the fractional part becomes zero or upto required number of digits.

The following example illustrates this concept :

Example 2. Convert the following decimal functions to their equivalent hexadecimal fractions:

(i) $(0.875)_{10}$ *(ii)* $(0.28125)_{10}$.

Solution. *(i)*

```
   0.875
  × 16
[14]. 000
   = E
```

Thus, $(0.875)_{10} = (0.E)_{16}$

(ii)

```
      0.28125
       × 16
|  [4]. 50000
|       × 16   (Multiply only the fractional part)
↓  [8]. 00000
```

Thus, $(0.28125)_{10} = (0.48)_{16}$

For converting a mixed decimal number to its hexadecimal equivalent, the integral and fractional parts are converted separately into their hexadecimal equivalents.

The following example illustrates this concept:

Example 3. Convert the following mixed decimal numbers to their equivalent hexadecimals:

(i) $(47.375)_{10}$ *(ii)* $(835.390625)_{10}$.

Solution. *(i)* $(47.375)_{10}$

```
Integral part                     Fractional part
16 | 47                              0.375
16 | 2 – 15   = F   ↑                × 16
   | 0 – 2          |             [6]. 000
Thus, (47)10 = (2F)16             Thus, (0.375)10 = (0.6)16
```

Hence, $(47.375)_{10} = (2F.6)_{16}$

(ii) $(835.390625)_{10}$

```
Integral part                     Fractional part
16 | 835                             0.390625
16 | 52 – 3   ↑                       × 16
16 | 3 – 4    |               |  [6]. 250000
   | 0 – 3    |               |        × 16
                              ↓  [4]. 000000
Thus, (835)10 = (343)16          Thus, (0.390625)10 = (0.64)16
```

Hence, $(835.390625)_{10} = (343.64)_{10}$

3.4.10 Hexadecimal Numbers to their Decimal Equivalents

The conversion of hexadecimal numbers to their decimal equivalents is performed by using the concept of the positional value of each digit in the number, whether it is an integer, a fraction or a mixed number. The following examples illustrate this concept:

Example 1. Convert the following hexadecimal numbers to their decimal equivalents:

(i) $(9D)_{16}$ *(ii)* $(517)_{16}$.

Solution. *(i)* $(9D)_{16} = 9 \times 16^1 + D \times 16^0$
$= 144 + 13 \times 1$ (D = 13)
$= 144 + 13$
$= 157$

Hence, $(9D)_{16} = (157)_{10}$

(ii) $(517)_{16} = 5 \times 16^2 + 1 \times 16^1 + 7 \times 16^0$
$= 5 \times 256 + 1 \times 16 + 7 \times 1$
$= 1280 + 16 + 7$
$= 1303$

Hence, $(517)_{16} = (1303)_{10}$

Example 2. Convert the following hexadecimal fractions into their decimal equivalents:
(i) $(0.48)_{16}$ *(ii)* $(0.125)_{16}$.

Solution. *(i)* $(0.48)_{16} = 4 \times 16^{-1} + 8 \times 16^{-2}$
$= 4 \times 1/16 + 8 \times 1/16^2$
$= 4 \times .0625 + 8 \times 0.00390625$
$= 0.2500 + .03125000$
$= 0.28125000$

Hence, $(0.48)_{16} = (0.28125)_{10}$

(ii) $(0.125)_{16} = 1 \times 16^{-1} + 2 \times 16^{-2} + 5 \times 16^{-3}$
$= 1 \times 0.0625 + 2 \times 0.00390625 + 5 \times 0.00024414$
$= 0.0625 + 0.00781250 + 0.00122070$
$= 0.07153320$

Hence, $(0.125)_{16} = (0.0715332)_{10}$

3.4.11 Hexadecimal to Binary

For converting a hexadecimal number to its binary equivalent, each digit of the hexadecimal number is converted to its 4-bits binary equivalent. For reading convenience, usually each nibble (4-bit binary equivalent) is written with a little space in between. The following examples illustrate this concept:

Example 1. Convert the following hexadecimal numbers into their binary equivalents:
(i) $(B9F)_{16}$ *(ii)* $(8796)_{16}$.

Solution. *(i)* $(59F)_{16} = \dfrac{0101}{5}\ \dfrac{1001}{9}\ \dfrac{1111}{F}$

(Replace each hexadecimal digit by its 4 bits binary equivalent)
$= (0101\ 1001\ 1111)_2$

Thus $(59F)_{16} = (0101\ 1001\ 1111)_2$

(ii) $(8796)_{16} = \dfrac{1111}{F}\ \dfrac{0011}{3}\ \dfrac{1010}{A} . \dfrac{1100}{C}\ \dfrac{1011}{B}$

(Replace each hexadecimal digit by its 4 bits binary equivalent)
$= (1000\ 0111\ 1001\ 0110)_2$

Thus, $(8796)_{16} = (1000\ 0111\ 1001\ 0110)_2$

Example 2. Convert the following hexadecimal numbers into their binary equivalents:
(i) $(F3A.CB)_{16}$ *(ii)* $(5D.8F)_{16}$.

Solution. *(i)* $(F3A.CB)_{16} = \underbrace{1111}_{F}\,\underbrace{0011}_{3}\,\underbrace{1010}_{A}\,.\,\underbrace{1100}_{C}\,\underbrace{1011}_{B}$

(Replace each hexadecimal digit by its 4 bits binary equivalent)

$= (1111\ 0011\ 1010\ .\ 1100\ 1011)_2$

Thus, $(F3A.CB)_{16} = (1111\ 0011\ 1010\ .\ 1100\ 1011)_2$

(ii) $(5D.8F)_{16} = \underbrace{0101}_{5}\,\underbrace{1101}_{D}\,.\,\underbrace{1000}_{8}\,\underbrace{1111}_{F}$

(Replace each hexadecimal digit by its 4 bits binary equivalent)

$= (0101\ 1101\ .\ 1000\ 1111)_2$

Thus, $(5D.8F)_{16} = (0101\ 1101\ .\ 1000\ 1111)_2$

Note. *It must be remembered that whatever number system one may use, the information stored in the computer memory is always in terms of binary digits. It is only for our convenience that we use octal or hexadecimal numbers.*

3.5 CONCEPT OF COMPLEMENTS

Complements are used in digital computers for simplifying the subtraction operation and for logical manipulations. There are two types of complements for each number system of base-*r*: the *r's* complement and the $(r - 1)$'s complement. When we deal with binary system the value of *r* is 2 and hence the complements are 2's and 1's complements. Similarly for decimal system the value of *r* is 10 and we get 10's and 9's complements. With 'the' same logic if the number system is octal we get 8's and 7's complement, while it is 16's and 15's complements for hexadecimal system.

3.5.1 The r's Complement

If a positive number *N* is given in base *r* with an integer part of *n* digits, the *r's* complement of *N* is given as $r^n - N$ for $N \neq 0$ and 0 for $N = 0$. The following examples will clarify the definition.

The 10's complement of $(23450)_{10}$ is $10^5 - 23450 = 76550$.

The number of digits in the number is $n = 5$.

The 10's complement of $(0.3245)_{10}$ is $100 - 0.3245 = 0.6755$.

Since the number of digits in the integer part of the number is $n = 0$, we have $10^0 = 1$.

The 10's complement of $(23.324)_{10}$ is $10^2 - 23.324 = 76.676$.

The number of digits in the integer part of the number is $n = 2$.

Now if we consider binary system, then $r = 2$.

The 2's complement of $(10110)_2$ is $(2^5)_{10} - (10110)_2 = (100000 - 10110)_2 = 01010$.

The 2's complement of $(0.1011)_2$ is $(2^0)_{10} - (0.1011)_2 = (1 - 0.1011)_2 = 0.0101$

Now if we consider octal system, then $r = 8$.

The 8's complement of $(2450)_8$ is $(8^4)_{10} - (2450)_8$

$= (4096_{10} - 2450_8)$

$= (4096_{10} - 1320_{10})$

$= 2776_{10}$.

$= 5330_8$.

Now if we consider hexadecimal system, then $r = 16$.

The 16's complement of $(4A30)_{16}$ is $(16^4)_{10} - (4A30)_{16}$

$= (65536_{10} - 4A30_{16})$

$= (65536_{10} - 18992_{10})$

$= 46544_{10}$

$= B5D0_{16}$.

From the above examples, it is clear that to find the 10's complement of a decimal number all of the bits till the first significant 0 are left unchanged and the first non-zero least significant digit is subtracted from 10 and the rest of the higher significant digits are subtracted from 9. With a similar reasoning the 2's complement of a binary number can be obtained by leaving all of the least significant zeros and the first non-zero digit unchanged, and then replacing 1's by 0's and 0's by 1's. Similarly the 8's complement of an octal number can be obtained by keeping all the bits till the first significant 0 unchanged, and the first non-zero least significant digit is subtracted from 8 and the rest of the higher significant digits are subtracted from 7. Similarly the 16's complement of a hexadecimal number can be obtained by keeping all the bits till the first significant 0 unchanged, and the first non-zero least significant digit is subtracted from 16 and the rest of the higher significant digits are subtracted from 15.

Since r's complement is a general term, hence r can take any value e.g., $r = 11$. Then we will have 11's complement for r's complement case and 10's complement for $(r - 1)$'s complement case.

3.5.2 The (*r* – 1)'s Complement

If a positive number N is given in base r with an integer part of n digits and a fraction part of m digits, then the $(r - 1)$'s complement of N is given as $(r^n - r^{-m} - N)$ for $N \neq 0$ and 0 for $N = 0$. The following examples will clarify the definition.

The 9's complement of $(23450)_{10}$ is $10^5 - 10^0 - 23450 = 76549$.

Since there is no fraction part, so $10^{-m} = 10^0 = 1$.

The 9's complement of $(0.3245)_{10}$ is $100 - 10^{-4} - 0.3245 = 0.6754$.

Since there is no integer part, so $10^n = 10^0 = 1$.

The 9's complement of $(23.324)_{10}$ is $10^2 - 10^{-3} - 23.324 = 76.675$.

Now if we consider binary system, then $r = 2$, i.e., $(r - 1) = 1$.

The 1's complement of $(10110)_2$ is $(2^5 - 1)_{10} - (10110)_2 = 01001$.

The 1's complement of $(0.1011)_2$ is $(1 - 2^{-4})_{10} - (0.1011)_2 = 0.0100$

Now if we consider octal system, then $r = 8$, i.e., $(r - 1) = 7$.

The 7's complement of $(2350)_8$ is $8^4 - 8^0 - 2350_8$

$= 4095_{10} - 1256_{10}$

$= 2839_{10}$

$= 5427_8$

The 15's complement of $(A3E4)_{16}$ is $16^4 - 16^0 - A3E4_{16}$

$= 65535_{10} - 41956_{10}$

$= 23579_{10}$

$= 5C1B_{16}$

From the above examples, it is clear that to find the 9's complement of a decimal number each of the digits can be separately subtracted from 9. The 1's complement of a binary number can be obtained by changing 1's into 0's and 0's into 1's. Similarly to find the 7's complement of a decimal number each of the digits can be separately subtracted from 7. Again to find the 15's complement of a decimal number each of the digits can be separately subtracted from 15.

Example. Find out the 11's and 10's complement of the number $(576)_{11}$.

Solution. The number in base is 11. So to find 11's complement we have to follow the r's complement rule and in order to get 10's complement the $(r - 1)$'s complement rule is to be followed.

11' complement :

$$r^n - N = 11^3 - 576_{11}$$
$$= (1331)_{10} - (576)_{11}$$

Now, $576_{11} = 5 \times 11^2 + 7 \times 11^1 + 6 \times 11^0$

$$= 605 + 77 + 6$$
$$= 688_{10}$$

Therefore, 11's complement is $1331_{10} - 688_{10} = 643_{10}$

Now, the decimal number has to be changed in the number system of base 11.

11	643
11	58 – 5
11	5 – 3
	0 – 5

Hence the 11's complement number is $(535)_{11}$

10' complement :

$$r^n - r^{-m} - N = 11^3 - 11^0 - 576_{11}$$
$$= (1331)_{10} - (1)_{10} - (576)_{11}$$

Therefore, 10's complement is $1331_{10} - 1_{10} - 688_{10} = 642_{10}$

Now, the decimal number has to be changed in the number system of base 11.

11	642
11	58 – 4
11	5 – 3
	0 – 5

Hence the 10's complement number is $(534)_{11}$.

3.6 REPRESENTATION OF DATA

We are familiar about different types of number systems. In order to talk to computers one has to convert the information, numeric or non-numeric, into binary form. Therefore, one must know how the information is stored in computer memory.

3.6.1 Binary Representation of Integers

The different ways of integer representation in computer memory are:

(i) Sign and Magnitude representation

(ii) One's complement representation

(iii) Two's complement representation

(i) Sign and Magnitude Representation: It is the conventional form for number representation. Every integer has a sign (+ or –) and a string of digits representing the magnitude.

For example,

+ 241 or 745 are positive integers (+ sign may be omitted)

– 127, – 82 are negative integers

The sign of a number is represented by the MSB (Most Significant Bit). If it stores value 0, the sign is +, and if stores 1, the sign is –.

Let us assume that the word size of the computer is 16 bits, then +93 will be represented as given below:

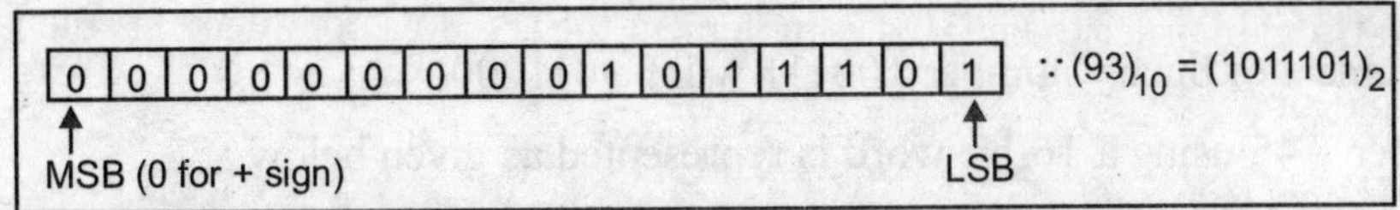

Fig. 3.5 Representation of Integer Number in binary form.

Since, bit pattern of 93 consists of 7 bits, it is expanded to 15 bits by adding the required number of zeros to the left as 000000001011101.

– 33 will be represented as given below:

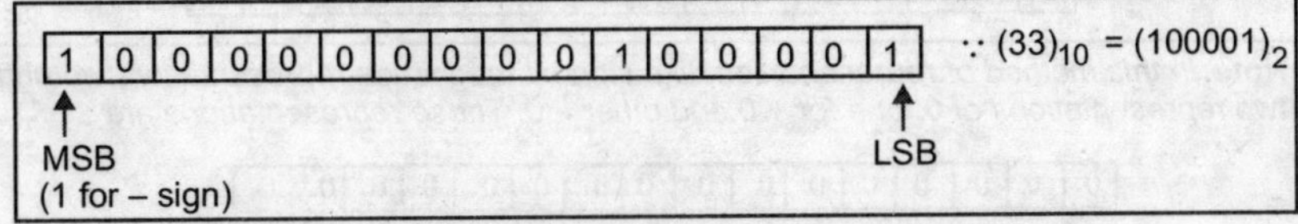

Fig. 3.6 Number in binary form.

Since bit pattern of 33 consists of 6 binary digits, it is expanded to 15 bits by adding the required number of zeros to the left as 000000000100001.

Integer Range for n bit Word. The range for integer numbers using sign and magnitude representation is given by the formula :

$$-2^{n-1} \quad \text{to} \quad 2^{n-1}-1$$

as 1 bit is used for sign notation so $(n–1)$ bits represent the magnitude.

For $n = 16$, the range is

	-2^{16-1}	to	$2^{16-1}-1$
that is	-2^{15}	to	$2^{15}-1$
or	– 32768	to	32767

Note. In this method of representation, we obtain two representations for 0, one for + 0 and other for – 0.

The number + 0 is represented as given below:

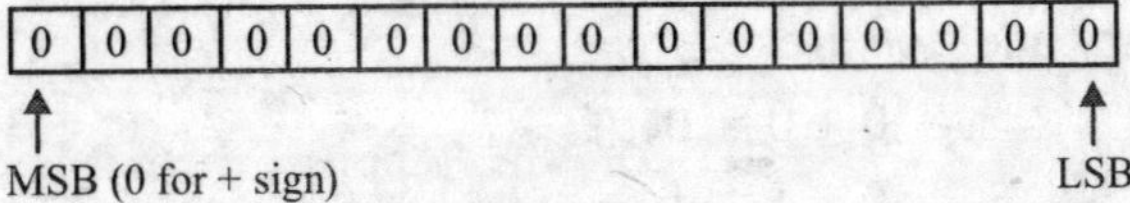

The number – 0 is represented as given below:

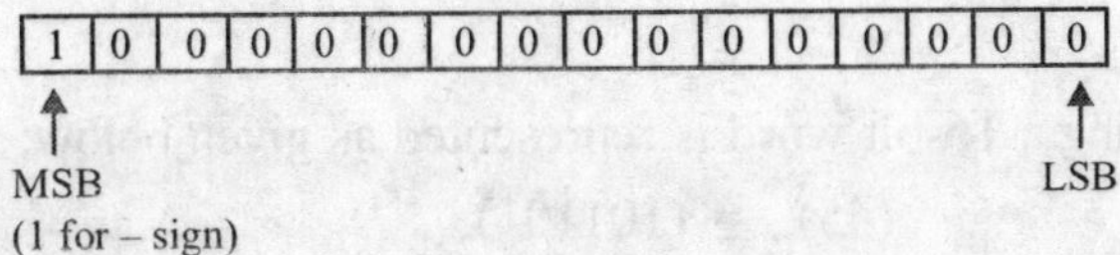

(ii) One's Complement Representation: Using one's complement positive numbers are represented by their binary equivalents (also known as true forms) and negative numbers by their 1's complements (also known as 1's complement forms). For an n-bit number, the maximum positive number which can be represented in 1's complement form is and the minimum negative number is $-(2^{n-1}-1)$.

1's complement of a binary number is found by replacing every 0 with 1 and every 1 with 0.

For example,

1's complement of binary number 100111 will be 011000

The number – 45 using a 16-bit word is represented as given below :

$\therefore \quad (45)_{10} = (101101)_2$

Now the 16-bit pattern is 0000000000101101

1's complement of the above pattern is 1111111111010010, which is stored as:

1	1	1	1	1	1	1	1	1	1	0	1	0	0	1	0

Note. *In this method of representation, like sign bit magnitude representation, we obtain two representations of 0, one for + 0 and other – 0. These representations are :*

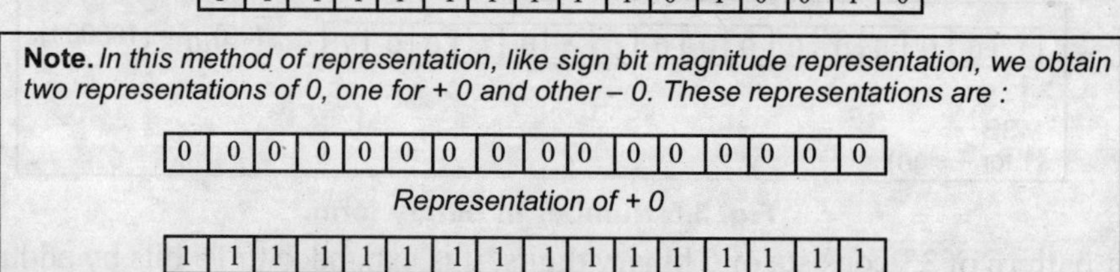

0	0	0	0	0	0	0	0	0	0	0	0	0	0	0	0

Representation of + 0

1	1	1	1	1	1	1	1	1	1	1	1	1	1	1	1

1's complement representation of – 0

(ii) Two's Complement Representation: Using two's complement positive numbers are represented by their binary equivalents (also known as true forms) and negative numbers by their 2's complement form. For an n-bit number, the maximum positive number which can be represented in 2's complement form is and the minimum negative number is -2^{n-1}.

2's complement of a number is found by adding 1 to its 1's complement.

or

For finding the 2's complement of a number, start from the LSB and write the bits as it is till the first 1 appears (**do not** change the first 1 to 0), then write the 1's complement of the remaining bits to the left side of it.

For example, 2's complement of binary number 1110001 will be calculated as given below:

1's complement of 1110001	= 0001110
	+1
2's complement of 1110001	= 0001111

Note. Rules for binary addition are :

$$0 + 0 = 0$$
$$0 + 1 = 1$$
$$1 + 0 = 1$$
$$1 + 1 = 10$$

The number - 45 using a 16-bit word is represented as given below:

$\therefore \quad (45)_{10} = (101101)_2$

Now the 16-bit pattern is 0000000000101101

1's complement of the bit pattern is 1111111111010010

The 2's complement is obtained as under:

1's complement is 1111111111010010

+1

2's complement is 1111111111010011

The above shown pattern is stored as:

1	1	1	1	1	1	1	1	1	1	0	1	0	0	1	1

Note. *Unlike sign-bit magnitude and 1's complement representation, both + 0 and – 0 have the same representation under 2's complement method.*

In general, the negative numbers are stored in the computer memory in 2's complement form and positive numbers in sign and magnitude form.

Comparison between 1's and 2's Complements

A comparison between 1's and 2's complements reveals the advantages and disadvantages of each.

(i) The 1's complement has the advantage of being easier to implement by digital components (viz. inverter) since the only thing to be done is to change the 1's to 0's and vice versa. To implement 2's complement we can follow two ways : (1) by finding out the 1's complement of the number and then adding 1 to the LSB of the 1's complement, and (2) by leaving all leading 0's in the LSB positions and the first 1 unchanged, and only then changing all 1's to 0's and vice versa.

(ii) During subtraction of two numbers by complement method, the 2's complement is advantageous since only one arithmetic addition is required. The 1's complement requires two arithmetic additions when an end-around carry occurs.

(iii) The 1's complement has an additional disadvantage of having two arithmetic zeros: one with all 0's and one with all 1's. The 2's complement has only one arithmetic zero. The fact is illustrated below :

We consider the subtraction of two equal binary numbers 1010 – 1010.

Using 1's complement :

1010

+ 0101 (1's complement of 1010)

+ 1111 (negative zero)

We complement again to obtain (–0000) (positive zero).

Using 2's complement:

1010

+ 0110 (2's complement of 1010)

(Carry over) 1 0000

After dropping the carry over, the result is +0000.

In this 2's complement method no question of negative or positive zero arises.

3.6.2 Fixed-point Representation of Numbers

In a fixed-point system of number representation all numbers are represented as integers or fraction. Signed integer or BCD numbers are known as fixed-point numbers because they contain no information about the binary point or decimal point. The binary or decimal point is assumed at the extreme right or left of the number. If the binary or decimal point is at the extreme right or left of the computer word, all numbers are positive or negative numbers. If the radix point is assumed to be at the extreme left, all numbers are positive or negative fraction. Suppose one has to multiply 7.35 × 80.64. This will be represented as 735 × 8064. The result will be 5927040. The decimal point has to be placed by the programmer to get the correct result, that is 592.7040. Thus in fixed-point of representation the user has to keep the track of radix point which is a tedious (very difficult) job.

In scientific applications of computers fractions are frequently used. So a system of representation which automatically keeps track of the position of the binary or decimal point is needed. Such a system of representation is known as floating point representation of numbers. It is discussed in the next section. Many computers and all electronic calculators use floating-point arithmetic operations. The computers which do not have internal circuitry for floating-point operations can solve the scientific problems involving fractions with the help of floating-point software.

3.6.3 Binary Representation of Real (Floating Point) Numbers

A number having both integer part as well as a fractional part is called real number or floating point number. It may be either positive or negative. For example, 975.88, 0.586, - 0.866 represent real decimal numbers and 1101.001, 0.0101, – 100.1001 represent binary real numbers.

Real numbers are represented in the memory of the computer by their **mantissa** and **exponent.** In the general form,

$$N = M \times R^e$$

The mantissa M and the exponent *e* are actually stored in a register of a computer. But, the base or radix R and the radix-point (decimal or binary point) are not present in the register. An assumption is made about these and the electronic circuitry taking these things into account performs the computation and manipulation.

Let us assume a 16-bit word for a computer having two parts : a 10-bit mantissa and a 6-bit exponent. The mantissa is in two's complement form ; the left most bit represents a sign bit. The binary point is assumed to be to the right of the sign bit.

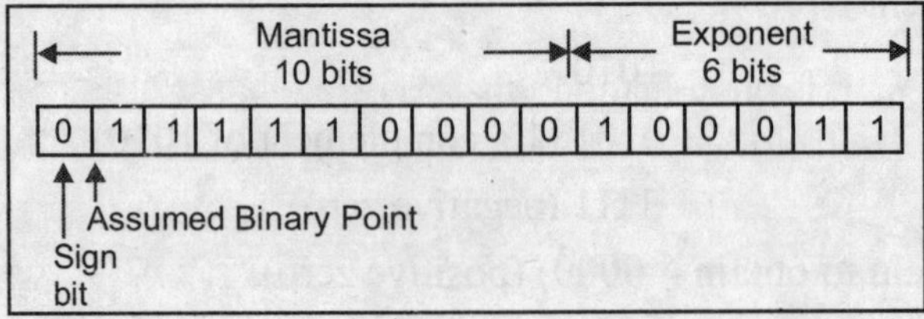

Fig. 3.7 Floating point format.

The 6 bits of the word store the exponent without any sign. The reason for not having the place for storage of the sign of exponent is that the exponent is represented in biased form.

Now, let us understand the meaning of biased form of the exponent.

The minimum number represented by 6 bits is (-2^5), that is, –32. While representing align the floating point numbers, this number 32 is added to the actual exponent, thus leaving no space for negative exponent. The new exponent (after adding 32 to the actual exponent) is called **Biased Exponent.** This code for floating point representation is called as the base 2 excess 32 code.

Some examples of this system for exponent part are given in Table 3.2 given below :

Table 3.2 Illustration of Biased Exponents

Actual Exponent	*Binary Representation (Biased Exponent)*
–32	0 0 0 0 0 0
–2	0 1 1 1 1 0
0	1 0 0 0 0 0
+5	1 0 0 1 0 1
+31	1 1 1 1 1 1

Now, using the above definitions, the floating point number in Figure 3.7 is :

Mantissa part is + 0.111110000

Exponent part is 100011

Subtracting 100000 from exponent

($\because$ $(100000)_2 = (32)_{10}$ was added to it)

The value of the number is

$$N = +(0.11111)_2 \times 2^3 \quad (N = M \times R^e)$$
$$= (111.11)_2$$
$$= 7.75$$

There are many formats of storage of floating point numbers on different computers. Some use two words for the mantissa and one for the exponent; others use one and one-half word for the mantissa and one-half word for the exponent. Few systems even allow selecting a format out of many, depending on the accuracy desired. Some use excess-n notation for the exponent; some use 2's complement. Some even use signed magnitude for both the mantissa and the exponent.

Floating point numbers are used to express very large and very small numbers. Using above mentioned system of storage for numbers, we can have 9-bit accuracy (1 bit allowed for sign of mantissa). The exponent bits add nothing to accuracy, only to magnitude. The accuracy of fixed point 2's complement numbers expressed in 16 bits is of 15 bits. So, the floating points are less accurate than an equivalent length fixed point number.

For achieving the full 10 bits of accuracy in the floating point number, the most significant bit of the mantissa is made non-zero and the number so obtained is said to be in the **normalized** (or standard) form. The process of shifting of mantissa left to make the most significant bit non-zero is called **normalization.**

POINTS TO REMEMBER

Numbers are represented by a string of digit symbols.

The binary number system has the base or radix 2, the octal 8 and hexadecimal 16.

Division remainder method is the most commonly used method for converting from decimal system to other systems. The following steps are carried out for integral part.

(i) Divide the given number of decimal system by the base or radix R of the desired system. By doing so, we get a quotient Q_1 and a remainder R_1.

(ii) Divided the quotient Q_1 by the radix R again to get quotient R_2 and a remainder R_2.

(iii) Repeat the above process till the quotient is 0 (zero) and a remainder R_n (say).

(iv) Write the converted number as $R_n R_{n-1} \ldots R_2 R_1$ for the integral part.

For converting decimal fractions to other fractions, instead of dividing by the radix R, multiply successively by R and instead of noting the remainders as in case of integers, keep track of the overflow. Stop when fractional part becomes zero or recurrence takes place. If overflow digits are $f_1, f_2, f_3, \ldots$ fn then he equivalent binary fraction is $0.f_1 f_2 \ldots f_n$. (Remember that while multiplying by R, every time fractional part is to be multiplied and not the integral part.)

Complements are used in digital systems for simplifying the subtraction operation and for logical manipulations.

Codes are used to represent information, error detection and error correction.

Integers can be represented in computer memory using sign and magnitude, 1's complement and 2's complement forms.

In general, the negative numbers are stored in the computer memory in 2's complement form and positive numbers in sign and magnitude form.

EXERCISES

1. What is a Number System ? State the utility of Number Systems.
2. Why do digital computers use binary numbers for their operation?
3. Convert the following binary numbers to equivalent decimal numbers:
   (i) 11011 (ii) 10011010
4. Convert the following decimal numbers to equivalent binary numbers:
   (i) 44 (ii) 155
5. Convert the following real binary numbers to equivalent decimal numbers:
   (i) 1101.11 (ii) 101001.1101
6. Convert the following decimal numbers to equivalent binary numbers:
   (i) 18.71875 (ii) 75.6875
7. Convert the following octal numbers to equivalent binary numbers:
   (i) 534 (ii) 647
8. Convert the following binary numbers to equivalent octal numbers:
   (i) 1100110 (ii) 10111101
9. Convert the following hexadecimal numbers to equivalent binary numbers:
   (i) 6BC (ii) 4C3F
10. Convert the following binary numbers to equivalent hexadecimal numbers:
    (i) 10110110111 (ii) 1101001100
11. Convert the binary number 101101.101101 into octal and hexadecimal number system.
12. The roots of the quadratic equation $x^2 - 12x + 37 = 0$ are 5 and 8. Find the base in which this equation is written.
13. Write short notes on the following:

(i) Binary representation of integers

(ii) Fixed-point representation of numbers.

(iii) Binary representation of floating point numbers.

14. Compare the 1's and 2's complements.
15. What is normalized floating point representation for real numbers?
16. Fill in the blanks :

    (i) $(94.00625)_{10} = (\ldots\ldots\ldots\ldots\ldots\ldots\ldots\ldots\ldots)_2$

    (ii) $(11011.0101)_2 = (\ldots\ldots\ldots\ldots\ldots\ldots\ldots\ldots\ldots)_{10} = (\ldots\ldots\ldots\ldots\ldots\ldots\ldots\ldots\ldots)_8$
17. What is the advantage of using hexadecimal numbers ?
18. Find the 1' and 2's complement of the following binary numbers :

    (i) 11001 (ii) 11110

ANSWERS

REVIEW QUESTIONS AND EXERCISES

3. (i) 27 (ii) 154
4. (i) 101100 (ii) 10011011
5. (i) 13.75 (ii) 41.8125
6. (i) 10010.10111 (ii) 1001011.1011
7. (i) 101011100 (ii) 110100111
8. (i) 146 (ii) 275
9. (i) 11010111100 (ii) 100110000111111
10. (i) 5B7 (ii) 34C
11. $(55.55)_8$, $(2D.B4)_{16}$
12. 11

SELF ASSESSMENT QUESTIONS

1. Fill in the blanks :

   (i) $(94.00625)_{10} = (\ldots\ldots\ldots\ldots\ldots\ldots\ldots\ldots\ldots)_2$

   (ii) $(11011.0101)_2 = (\ldots\ldots\ldots\ldots\ldots\ldots\ldots\ldots\ldots)_{10} = (\ldots\ldots\ldots\ldots\ldots\ldots\ldots\ldots\ldots)_8$

   (iii) ASCII stands for ....
2. What is the advantage of using hexadecimal numbers ?
3. Find the 1' and 2's complement of the following binary numbers :

   (i) 11001 (ii) 11110
4. Perform the following

   (i) $11100_2 - 11011_2$ (ii) $1111_2 - 100011_2$

   (iii) $101.101_2 - 11.011_2$ (iv) $1100.01_2 - 1001.10_2$ (v) $1001.1_2 - 101.11_2$
6. Write the 1's complement of the binary numbers given below:

   (i) 1100_2 (ii) 1101_2 (iii) 001 (iv) 010.11 (v) 01.111

Computer Codes

4.1 INTRODUCTION

Digital systems are built using binary devices. Coding is a technique by which a set of objects is represented in a machine by a set of binary numbers called codes. Computers and other digital circuits process data in binary format. To achieve this, a process of coding is required where each alphabet, special character or numeral is coded in a unique combination of 0 s and 1 s using a coding scheme known as code. Various binary codes are used to represent data which may be numeric, alphabets or special characters. Codes are also used for error detection and error correction in digital systems. Although, in digital systems in every code used, the information is represented in binary form, but the interpretation of the data is only possible if the code in which the data is being represented is known.

The full form of BCD is 'Binary-Coded Decimal'. Since this is coding scheme relating decimal and binary numbers, hence four bits are required to code each decimal number. For example, (35)10 is represented as 0011 0101 using BCD code, rather than (100011)2. From the example it is clear that it requires more number of bits to code a decimal number using BCD code than using the straight binary code. However, inspite of this disadvantage it is convenient to use BCD code for input and output operations in digital systems. For example, the binary number 1000011 represents 67 (decimal) in straight binary, 43 (decimal) in BCD and alphabet C in ASCII code. Hence while interpreting the data one must be very careful regarding the code used.

4.2 CODES

Codes can be broadly classified into following five groups:

(i) Weighted Binary Codes,
(ii) Non-weighted Codes,
(iii) Alphanumeric Codes,
(iv) Error-detecting Codes and
(v) Error-correcting Codes.

The commonly used codes are discussed below.

4.3 WEIGHTED BINARY CODES

If each position of a number represents a specific weight then the coding scheme is called weighted binary code. In such coding the bits are multiplied by their corresponding individual weight, and then the sum of these weighted bits gives the equivalent decimal digit.

4.3.1 NBCD Code

Natural Binary Coded Decimal (NBCD) code is also known as 8421 code. It is because 8, 4, 2 and 1 are the weights of the four bits of the BCD code. The weight of the LSB is 2^0 or 1, that of the next higher order bit is 2^1 or 2, that of the next higher order bit is 2^2 or 4, and that of the MSB is 2^3 or 8. Therefore, this is a weighted code and arithmetic operations can be performed using this code which will be discussed later on. The bit assignment 0101, for example, can be interpreted by the weights to represent the decimal digit 5 because $0 \times 8 + 1 \times 4 + 0 \times 2 + 1 \times 1 = 5$. Since four binary bits are used hence the maximum decimal equivalent that may be coded is 15_{10} (i.e., 1111_2). But the maximum decimal digit available is 910. Hence the binary codes 1010, 1011, 1100, 1101, 1110, 1111 representing 10, 11, 12, 13, 14 and 15 in decimal are never being used in BCD code. So these six codes are called forbidden codes and the group of these codes is called forbidden group in BCD code. BCD code for decimal digits 0 to 9 is shown in Table 4.1.

Table 4.1 Illustration of BCD Code of Decimal Digits

Decimal Digits	BCD Representation
0	0000
1	0001
2	0010
3	0011
4	0100
5	0101
6	0110
7	0111
8	1000
9	1001

The following examples illustrate the BCD encoding:

Example 1. *Give the BCD equivalent for the decimal number 509.*

Solution. The decimal number is 509

BCD code is 0101 0000 1001

Hence, $(509)_{10} = (010100001001)_{BCD}$

Example 2. *Give the BCD equivalent for the decimal number 49.27.*

Solution. The decimal number 4 9 2 7

BCD code 0100 1001 0010 0111

Hence, $(49.27)_{10} = (01001001.00100111)_{BCD}$

Here, we must distinguish carefully between encoding and conversion. For example, 14 when converted to binary would be 1 1 1 0. On the other hand, when it is encoded each digit must be represented by a 4-bit code and an encoding is 00010100. As mentioned earlier *encoding* requires more bits compared to conversion. On the average $\log_2 10 = 3.32$ bits are required when decimal numbers are converted to binary; as compared with this 4 bits per digit are needed in encoding. The ratio (4/3.3) = 1.2 is a measure of the extra bits (and consequently extra storage) needed if an encoding is used. On the other hand, conversion of decimal to binary is slower compared to encoding. It is due to the fact that an algorithm involving successive division is required for conversion whereas encoding is by straightforward table look-up. The slowness of conversion is not a major problem in computations having small volume of input/output. In business computers, where input/output dominates, it is necessary to examine BCD representation. In smaller digital system such as desk calculators, digital clocks, etc., it is uneconomical to incorporate complex electronic circuits to convert decimal to binary and vice versa. Thus BCD representation should be preferred.

4.3.2 $84\bar{2}\bar{1}$ Code

It is also possible to assign negative weights to decimal code, as shown by the $84\bar{2}\bar{1}$ code. In this case the bit combination 0101 is interpreted as the decimal digit 3, as obtained from $0 \times 8 + 1 \times 4 + 0 \times (-2) + 1 \times (-1) = 3$. This is a self-complementary code, that is, the 9's complement of the decimal number is obtained just by changing the 1's to 0's and 0's to 1's, or in effect by getting the 1's complement of the corresponding number. For example, if we change the 1's to 0's and 0's to 1's in the previous example we have 1010 which is interpreted as decimal 6, as obtained from $1 \times 8 + 0 \times 4 + 1 \times (-2) + 0 \times (-1) = 6$. And 6 is the 9's complement of 3. This property is useful when arithmetic operations are done internally with decimal numbers (in a binary code) and subtraction is calculated by means of 9's complement.

Table 4.2: Binary Codes for Decimal Digits

Decimal	(NBCD)			
Digit	8421	$84\bar{2}\bar{1}$	2421	Excess-3
0	0000	0000	0000	0011
1	0001	0111	0001	0100
2	0010	0110	0010	0101
3	0011	0101	0011	0110
4	0100	0100	0100	0111
5	0101	1011	1011	1000
6	0110	1010	1100	1001
7	0111	1001	1101	1010
8	1000	1000	1110	1011
9	1001	1111	1111	1100

4.3.3 2421 Code

Another weighted code is 2421 code. The weights assigned to the four digits are 2, 4, 2 and 1. The 2421 code is same as that in BCD from 0 to 4; however it varies from 5 to 9. For example, in this case the bit combination 0100 represents decimal 4; whereas the bit combination 1101 is interpreted as the decimal 7, as obtained from $2 \times 1 + 1 \times 4 + 0 \times 2 + 1 \times 1 = 7$. This is also a self-complementary code, that is, the 9's complement of the decimal number is obtained by changing the 1's to 0's and 0's to 1's. The 2421 codes for decimal number 0 through 9 are shown in Table 4.2.

4.4 NON-WEIGHTED BINARY CODES

These codes are not positionally weighted. It basically means that each position of the binary number is not assigned a fixed value. Excess-3 codes and Gray codes are such non-weighted codes.

4.4.1 Excess-3 Code

A decimal code that has been used in some old computers is excess-3 code. This is an unweighted code. This code assignment is obtained from the corresponding value of 4 bit binary code after adding 3 to the given decimal digit. Here the maximum value may be 11002 since the maximum decimal digit is 9 hence we have to add 3 to 9 and then get the BCD equivalent. Like 84-2-1 and 2421 codes excess-3 is also a self-complementary code, that is, the 9's complement of the decimal number is obtained by changing the 1's to 0's and 0's to 1's. This self-complementary property of the code helps considerably in performing subtraction operation in digital systems.

The following examples illustrate the Excess-3 code encoding:

Example 1. Convert $(359)_{10}$ into its Excess-3 code.

Solution.

The decimal number is	3	5	9
Add 3 to each bit	+3	+3	+3
Sum	6	8	12

Converting the above each sum into 4 bit binary equivalent, we have

4 bit binary equivalent	0110	1000	1100

Hence, the Excess-3 code for $(359)_{10}$ = 0110 1000 1100

Example 2. Convert $(58.43)_{10}$ into its Excess-3 code.

Solution.

The decimal number is	5	8	4	3
Add 3 to each bit	+3	+3	+3	+3
Sum	8	11	7	6

Converting the above each sum into 4 bit binary equivalent, we have

4 bit binary equivalent	1000	1011	0111	0110

Hence, the Excess-3 code for $(58.43)_{10}$ = 10001011.01110110

4.4.2 Gray Code

Gray code (or Cyclic Code or Reflected Code) belongs to a class of code known as minimum change code, in which a number changes by only one bit as it proceeds from one number to the next. Hence this code is not useful for arithmetic operations. This code finds extensive use for shaft encoders, in some types of analog-to-digital converters etc. Gray code is reflected code and is shown in Table 4.3. The Gray code may contain any number of bits. Here we take the example of four bit Gray Code. The code shown in Table 4.3 is only one of many possible such codes. To obtain a different **reflected code,** one can start with any bit combination and proceed to obtain the next bit combination by changing only one bit from 0 to 1 or 1 to 0 in any desired random fashion, as long as two numbers do not have identical code assignments. The Gray code is not a weighted code.

Table 4.3 Four-bit Reflected Code

Reflected Code	*Decimal Equivalent*
m4 0000	0
m3 0001	1
0011	2
m2 0010	3
0110	4
0111	5
0101	6

m1 0100	7
1100	8
1101	9
1111	10
m5 1110	11
1010	12
m6 1011	13
m7 1001	14
1000	15

Now we try to analyze the name **"Reflected Code"**. If we look at Table 4.3, we can consider seven virtual mirrors m1, m2, m3, m4, m5, m6 and m7 placed. Now for mirror m1 if we consider the MSB as the refractive index of the input and output medium then leaving out the MSB we can see that all of the eight combinations of three bits each, have its corresponding reflected counterparts. Similarly for mirrors m2 and m5 if we now leave the actual MSB we can consider the combination of three bits where now we consider the third bit as the new MSB. And similar arguments follow as for mirror m1. Similarly we may analyze the cases for mirrors m3, m4, m6 and m7.

Table 4.4 Binary and Gray Codes

Decimal Numbers	Binary Code	Gray Code
0	0000	0000
1	0001	0001
2	0010	0011
3	0011	0010
4	0100	0110
5	0101	0111
6	0110	0101
7	0111	0100
8	1000	1100
9	1001	1101
10	1010	1111
11	1011	1110
12	1100	1010
13	1101	1011
14	1110	1001
15	1111	1000

The Hamming distance (named after its inventor R.W. Hamming) between two equal length binary numbers is the number of positions in which they differ. For example, if A = 0111 and B = 1011, the Hamming distance between A and B is two as they differ in their first and second positions counting from left. The Hamming distance between two successive code groups in a cyclic code is unity, i.e., each code group is adjacent to the next in sequence. Following map (See Fig. 4.1) is coded to ensure that each square is at a unit distance from its adjacent square and each square in this map has four neighbours (adjacent squares).

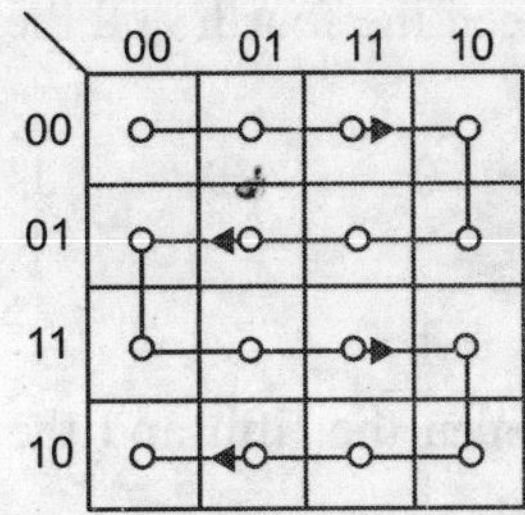

Fig. 4.1 A chart depicting a cyclic code.

The map shown in Figure 4.1 is called Karnaugh map and can be used to construct a large number of cyclic codes. One such code is shown in Table 4.4. Start assigning the code and proceed as shown by the arrow and the mark 'o' in Figure 4.1.

Conversion of a Binary Number into Gray Code

Any binary number can be converted into equivalent Gray code by following the steps:

(i) The MSB of the Gray code is same as the MSB of the binary number;

(ii) The second bit next to MSB of the Gray code equals the Ex-OR of the MSB and second bit of the binary number; it will be 0 if there are same binary bits or it will be 1 for different binary bits;

(iii) The third bit for Gray code equals the exclusive-OR of the second and third bits of the binary number, and similarly all the next lower order bits follow the same mechanism.

The following examples illustrate the conversion of binary numbers to Gray code:

Example 1. Convert $(101011)_2$ into Gray code.

Solution. Step 1. The MSB of the Gray code is same as the MSB of the binary number.

```
1   0   1   0   1   1   Binary
↓
1                       Gray
```

Step 2. Perform the Ex-OR between the MSB and the second bits of the binary. The result is 1 which is the second bit of the Gray code.

```
1  ⊕  0   1   0   1   1   Binary
   ↓
1  1                      Gray
```

Step 3. Perform the Ex-OR between the second and the third bits of the binary. The result is 1 which is the third bit of the Gray code.

```
1   0  ⊕  1   0   1   1   Binary
          ↓
1   1     1               Gray
```

Step 4. Perform the Ex-OR between the third and the fourth bits of the binary. The result is 1 which is the fourth bit of the Gray code.

```
1   0   1  ⊕  0   1   1   Binary
              ↓
1   1   1     1           Gray
```

Step 5. Perform the Ex-OR between the fourth and the fifth bits of the binary. The result is 1 which is the fifth bit of the Gray code.

1	0	1	0 ⊕	1	1		Binary
				↓			
1	1	1	1	1			Gray

Step 6. Perform the Ex-OR between the fifth and the sixth bits of the binary. The result is 0 which is the last bit of the Gray code.

1	0	1	0	1 ⊕	1	Binary
					↓	
1	1	1	1	1	0	Gray

After completing the conversion the Gray code of binary 101011 is 111110.

Example 2. *Convert* $(564)_{10}$ *into Gray code.*

Solution. Step 1. Convert the decimal 564 into equivalent binary.

Decimal number 564

Binary number 1000110100

Step 2. Convert the binary number into equivalent Gray code

1 ⊕ 0 ⊕ 0 ⊕ 0 ⊕ 1 ⊕ 1 ⊕ 0 ⊕ 1 ⊕ 0 ⊕ 0 Binary

↓ → ↓ → ↓ → ↓ → ↓ → ↓ → ↓ → ↓ → ↓ → ↓

1 1 0 0 1 0 1 1 1 0 Gray

Conversion of Gray Code into a Binary Number

Any Gray code can be converted into equivalent Binary number by following the steps:

(i) The MSB of the binary number is same as the MSB of the Gray code ;

(ii) The second bit next to MSB of the binary number equals the Ex-OR of the MSB of the binary number and second bit of the Gray code ; it will be 0 if there are same binary bits or it will be 1 for different binary bits ;

(iii) The third bit for binary number equals the exclusive-OR of the second bit of the binary number and third bit of the Gray code, and similarly all the next lower order bits follow the same mechanism.

Following example illustrate the conversion of Gray code into binary number:

Example. Convert the Gray code 101101 into a binary number.

Solution. Step 1. The MSB of the binary number is same as the MSB of the Gray code.

1	0	1	1	0	1	Gray
↓						
1						Binary

Step 2. Perform the Ex-OR between the MSB of the binary number and the second bit of the Gray code. The result is 1 which is the second bit of the binary number.

1	0	1	1	0	1	Gray
	↓					
1 →	1					Binary

Step 3. Perform the Ex-OR between the second bit of the binary number and the third bit of the Gray code. The result is 0 which is the third bit of the binary number.

Step 4. Perform the Ex-OR between the third bit of the binary number and the fourth bit of the Gray code. The result is 1 which is the fourth bit of the binary number.

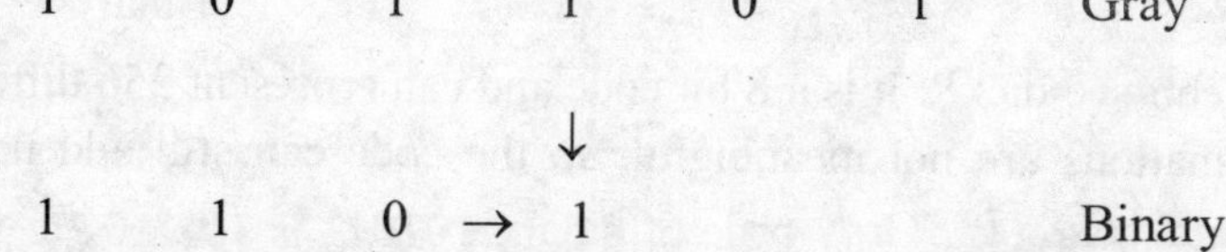

Step 5. Perform the Ex-OR between the fourth bit of the binary number and the fifth bit of the Gray code. The result is 1 which is the fifth bit of the binary number.

1 0 1 1 0 1 Gray
↓
1 1 0 1 → 1 Binary

Step 6. Perform the Ex-OR between the fifth bit of the binary number and the sixth bit of the Gray code. The result is 0 which is the last bit of the binary number.

1 0 1 1 0 1 Gray
↓
1 1 0 1 1 → 0 Binary

After completing the conversion the binary number of the Gray code 101101 is 110110.

4.5 ALPHANUMERIC CODES

Many applications of computer require not only of handling numbers, but also of letters. To represent alphabet it is necessary to have a binary code for the alphabet. In addition the same binary code must represent the decimal numbers and some other special characters. An alphanumeric code is a binary code of a group of elements consisting of ten decimal digits, the 26 letters of the alphabet (both in upper-case and lower-case), and a certain number of special symbols such as #, /, &, %, etc. The total number of elements in an alphanumeric code is greater than 36. Therefore it must be coded with a minimum number of 6 bits ($2^6 = 64$, but $2^5 = 32$ is insufficient). One possible six bit alphanumeric code is given in Table 2.5. It is used in many computers to represent alphanumeric characters and symbols internally and therefore can be called *"internal code"*. Frequently there is a need to represent more than 64 characters including the lower case letters and special control characters. For this reason the following two codes are normally used.

4.5.1 ASCII

The full form of ASCII (pronounced "as-kee") is "American Standard Code for Information Interchange", used in most microcomputers. It is actually a seven bit code, where a character is represented with seven bits. The character is stored as one byte with one bit remaining unused. But often the extra bit is used to extend the ASCII to represent an additional 128 characters. Some of the codes are shown in Table 4.5.

Now let us represent the word CODES in ASCII-7 code:

1000011	1001111	1000100	1000101	1010011
C	O	D	E	S

The same word CODES in ASCII-8 code can be represented as given below :

10100011	10101111	10100100	10100101	10110011
C	O	D	E	S

4.5.2 EBCDIC

It is pronounced as ''ebb-see-dick''. It is a 8 bit code and can represent 256 different characters. All of the 256 bit combinations are not meaningful, so the code can still add new characters if required.

The full form of EBCDIC is "Extended Binary Coded Decimal Interchange Code". It is also an alphanumeric code generally used in IBM equipments and in large computers for communicating alphanumeric data. For the different alphanumeric characters the code grouping in this code is different from the ASCII code. It is actually an eight bit code and a ninth bit is added as the parity bit. Out of the 8 bits, the first 4 bits are known as zero bits and the remainder 4 bits represent digit values.

Now let us represent the word CODES in EBCDIC Code :

11000011	11010110	11000100	11000101	11100010
C	O	D	E	S

Table 4.5 Partial List of Alphanumeric Codes

Character	*6-bit Internal Code*	*7-bit ASCII Code*	*8-bit EBCDIC Code*	*12-bit Hollerith Code*
A	010001	1000001	11000001	12,1
B	010010	1000010	11000010	12,2
C	010011	1000011	11000011	12,3
D	010100	1000100	11000100	12,4
E	010101	1000101	11000101	12,5
F	010110	1000110	11000110	12,6
G	010111	1000111	11000111	12,7
H	011000	1001000	11001000	12,8
I	011001	1001001	11001001	12,9
J	100001	1001010	11010001	11,1
K	100010	1001011	11010010	11,2
L	100011	1001100	11010011	11,3
M	100100	1001101	11010100	11,4
N	100101	1001110	11010101	11,5
O	100110	1001111	11010110	11,6
P	100111	1010000	11010111	11,7
Q	101000	1010001	11011000	11,8
R	101001	1010010	11011001	11,9
S	110010	1010011	11100010	0,2

T	110011	1010100	11100011	0,3
U	110100	1010101	11100100	0,4
V	110101	1010110	11100101	0,5
W	110110	1010111	11100110	0,6
X	110111	1011000	11100111	0,7
Y	111000	1011001	11101000	0,8
Z	111001	1011010	11101001	0,9
0	000000	0110000	11110000	0
1	000001	0110001	11110001	1
2	000010	0110010	11110010	2
3	000011	0110011	11110011	3
4	000100	0110100	11110100	4
5	000101	0110101	11110101	5
6	000110	0110110	11110110	6
7	000111	0110111	11110111	7
8	001000	0111000	11111000	8
9	001001	0111001	11111001	9
Blank	110000	0100000	01000000	No punch
.	011011	0101110	01001011	12,3,8
(	111100	0101000	01001101	12,5,8
+	010000	0101011	01001110	12,6,8
*	101100	0101010	01011100	11,4,8
$	101011	0100100	01011011	11,3,8
)	011100	0101001	01011101	11,5,8
/	110001	0101111	01100001	0,1
,	111011	0111100	01101011	0,3,8
=	001011	0111101	01111110	6,8
-	100000	0101101	01100000	11

4.5.3 Hollerith Code

Generally this code is used in punched cards. A punched card consists of 12 rows and 80 columns. An alphanumeric character is represented by each column of 12 bits each by punching holes in the appropriate rows. The presence of a hole represents a 1 and its absence indicates 0. The 12 rows are marked starting from the top, as 12, 11, 0, 1, 2, 3, 4, 5, 6, 7, 8, and 9. The first three rows are called the zone punch and the last nine are called the numeric punch. The code used here is called the Hollerith code. The alphabets are represented as two holes in a column, one in zone punch and the other in numeric punch; decimal digits are represented as a single hole in a numeric punch. Special characters are represented as one, two, or three holes in a column; while the zone is always used, the other two holes, if used, are in a numeric punch with the 8-th punch being commonly used. The Hollerith code is BCD and hence the transmission from EBCDIC is simple. The Hollerith code is used in the card readers and punches of large computers, while EBCDIC may be used within the computer.

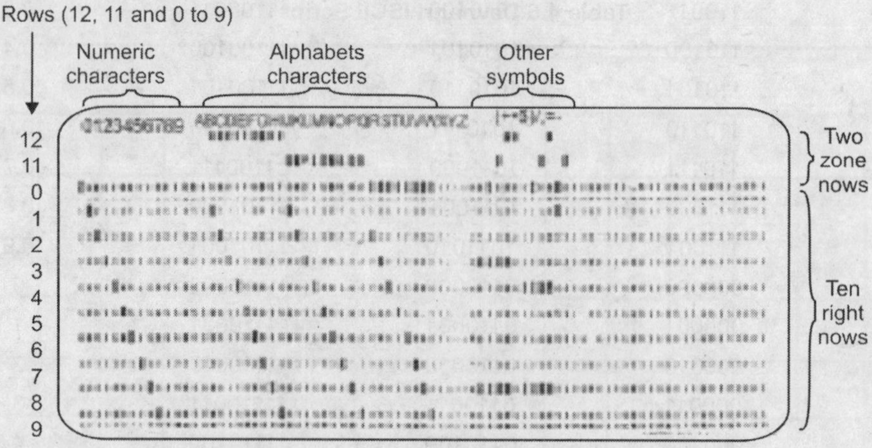

Fig. 4.2

A modern Hollerith card can handle a maximum of 80 alphanumeric characters. As this sample shown, numbers are coded by making a single punch in the appropriate card column; letters and special characters are coded by using double or triple punches. Note that the upper left-hand corner is missing from the card. This helps the machine operators make sure all the cards are turned the same way and that the deck itself has the proper orientation.

4.5.4 ISCII

ISCII stands for Indian Standard Code for Information Interchange. There are 18 scheduled languages in India as of today. These are in approximate order of usage: Hindi, Bengali, Telugu, Marathi, Tamil, Urdu, Gujarati, Kannada, Malayalam, Oriya, Punjabi, Assamese, Kashmiri, Sindhi, Konkani, Nepali, Manipuri and Sanskrit.

With the advent of computerization considerable work has been undertaken to facilitate the use of Indian languages on computers. These activities were generally limited to specific languages and were independent exercises of various organizations. Thus making data-interchange impossible. In such a scenario, it was important to have a common standard for coding Indian scripts. GIST (**G**raphics and **I**ntelligence based **S**cript **T**echnology) has played an important role in establishment of Indian standards.

In 1991, the Bureau of Indian Standards (BIS) adopted the Indian Standard Code for Information Interchange (ISCII), the ISCII standard that was evolved by a standardization committee, of which C-DAC was a member, under Department of Electronics during 1986-88. It is an 8 bit code which allows English and Indian Script alphabets to be used simultaneously. It retains the standard ASCII code for English. A common code for all Indian languages is feasible as all Indian scripts have a common origin from the Brahmi script. All GIST products are based on ISCII. Other than this, it has been used by IBM for PC-DOS, Apple for ILK, and several companies are developing products and solutions based on this representation. This has been made mandatory for the data being collected by organizations like the Election Commission, and for projects as Land Records Project etc.

Characters coded in ISCII need 8 bits for each character. This standard does not only apply to the Devnagri script, but also to Gujarati, Bengali, Gurumukhi, Assamese, Telugu, Kannada, Tamil and Malayalam script. Any software which allows ISCII codes, can be used in any Indian script, enhancing its commercial viability. Table 4.6 provides ISCII versions of Devnagri script:

Table 4.6 Devnagri ISCII Script

	0	1	2	3	4	5	6	7	10	11	12	13	14	15	16	17
240		ँ	ं	ः	अ	आ	इ	ई	उ	ऊ	ऋ		ए	ऐ	ऍ	
260	ओ	औ	ऑ	क	ख	ग	घ	ङ	च	छ	ज	झ	ञ	ट	ठ	ड
300	ढ	ण	त	थ	द	ध	न		प	फ	ब	भ	म	य		र
320	र	ल	ळ		व	श	ष	स	ह	INV	ा	ि	ी	ु	ू	ृ
340		े	ै	ॅ		ो	ौ	ॉ	्	़	।					ATR
360	EXT	०	१	२	३	४	५	६	७	८	९					

4.5.5 UNICODE

The UNICODE is the new universal coding standard being adopted by all newer platforms. The **Unicode Consortium** is a non-profit organization to develop, extend and promote use of the Unicode Standard, which specifies the representation of text in modern software products and standards. Formally,

Unicode provides a unique number for every character,
no matter what the platform,
no matter what the program,
no matter what the language.

Every computer works with numbers. The letters and other characters are stored by assigning a number for each one. Before Unicode was invented, there were hundreds of different encoding systems for assigning these numbers. No single encoding could contain enough characters, for example, the European Union alone requires several encodings to cover all its languages. Even for a single language like English no single encoding was adequate for all the letters, punctuation, and technical symbols in the common use.

These encoding systems also conflict with one another, that is, two encoding can use the same number for two different characters, or use different numbers for the same character. Any system (especially servers) needs to support many different encodings; yet whenever data is passed between different encodings or platforms, that data may be corrupted.

Utility of UNICODE

The Unicode Standard has been adopted by leading computer companies like Apple, IBM, Microsoft, Oracle and many others. Unicode is required by modern standards like such as JAVA, CORBA 3.0 etc. and is the official way to implement ISO. It is supported in many operating systems, all modern browsers and many other products. The emergence of the Unicode Standard, and the availability of tools supporting it, are among the most significant recent global software technology trends.

Unicode's significance is quite clear from the following points:

(i) Incorporating Unicode into client-server or multi-tiered applications and websites offers significant cost savings over the use of legacy character sets.

(ii) Unicode enables a single software product or a single website to be targeted across multiple platforms, languages and countries without re-engineering.

(iii) It allows data to be transported through many different systems without corruption.

The first version of the Unicode Standard, that is, Unicode 1.0.0 was released in October, 1991. Version numbers for the Unicode Standard consist of three fields: the major version, the minor version and the update version. For historical reasons the numbering within each of these fields is not necessarily consecutive. The latest Unicode Version is Unicode 4.0.0 which is in use from April, 2003. Unicode Version 3.2 represented 95,221 characters, whereas Unicode Version 4.0.0 has added many more characters.

4.6 ERROR DETECTING CODES

Binary information may be transmitted through some form of communication medium such as wires or radio waves or fibre optic cables etc. Any external noise introduced into a physical communication medium changes bit values from 0 to 1 or vice versa. An error detection code can be used to detect errors during transmission. The detected error cannot be corrected, but its presence may be indicated.

4.6.1 Parity Bit Coding Technique

A parity bit is an extra bit included with a message to make the total number of 1's either odd or even. A message of four bits and a parity bit, P, are shown in Table 4.7. In (a), P is chosen so that the sum of all 1's is odd (including the parity bit). In (b), P is chosen so that the sum of all 1's is even (including the parity bit). In the sending end, the message (in this case the first four bits) is applied to a "parity generation" circuit where the required P bit is generated. The message, including the parity bit, is transferred to its destination. In the receiving end, all the incoming bits (in this case five) are applied to a "parity check" circuit to check the proper parity adopted. An error is detected if the checked parity does not correspond to the adopted one. The parity method detects the presence of one, three, five, or any odd combination of errors. An even combination of errors is undetectable since even number of errors will not change the parity of the bits. The parity bit may be included with the message bits either on the MSB or on the LSB side. Hence in such cases some other coding scheme is to be adopted. Such a coding technique is Check Sums, which is discussed in next section.

Table 4.7 Parity Bit

(a) Message	*P (Odd)*	*(b) Message*	*P (Even)*
0000	1	0000	0
0001	0	0001	1
0010	0	0010	1
0011	1	0011	0
0100	0	0100	1
0101	1	0101	0
0110	1	0110	0
0111	0	0111	1
1000	0	1000	1
1001	1	1001	0
1010	1	1010	0
1011	0	1011	1
1100	1	1100	0
1101	0	1101	1
1110	0	1110	1
1111	1	1111	0

4.6.2 Check Sums Technique

As we have discussed above the parity bit technique fails for double error, hence we use the Check Sums method in such case. Initially any word A 10010011 is transmitted; next another word B 01110110 is transmitted. The binary digits in the two words are added and the sum obtained is retained in the transmitter. Then any other word C is transmitted and added to the previous sum retained in the transmitter and the new sum is now retained. In the similar manner, each word is added to the previous sum already been retained; after transmitting all the words, the final sum which is called the Check Sum is also transmitted. The same operation is done at the receiving end and the final sum which has been obtained here is being checked against the transmitted Check Sum. There is no error, if the two sums are equal.

4.7 ERROR CORRECTING CODES

We have already discussed two coding techniques, which may be used in data transmission to detect errors. But unfortunately the above discussed techniques are not capable of correcting the errors. For correction of errors now we will discuss a code called Hamming code.

Hamming Code

This coding had been developed by R. W. Hamming where one or more parity bits are added to a data character methodically in order to detect and correct errors. The number of bits changed from one code word to another is known as Hamming distance.

Let us consider A_i and A_j to be any two code words in any particular block code. Now the Hamming distance d_{ij} between the two vectors A_i and A_j is defined by the number of components in which they differ. Assuming that d_{ij} is determined for each pair of code words, the minimum value of d_{ij} is called the minimum Hamming distance, d_{min}.

For example,

A_i	1	0	0	1	0	1	1
	↓		↓			↓	
A_j	0	0	1	1	0	0	1

Here, these code words differ in the MSB and in the third and sixth bit positions from the left. Hence, d_{ij} is 3.

From Hamming's analysis of code distances, some important properties have been derived :

(i) For detection of single error d_{min} should be at least two.

(ii) For single error correction, d_{min} should be at least three, since the number of errors, $E \leq (d_{min} - 1)/2$.

(iii) Greater values of d_{min} will provide detection and/or correction of more number of errors.

The 7-bit Hamming (7, 4) code word $h_1\ h_2\ h_3\ h_4\ h_5\ h_6\ h_7$ associated with a 4-bit binary number $b_3\ b_2\ b_1\ b_0$ is:

$$h_1 = b_3 \oplus b_2 \oplus b_0$$
$$h_2 = b_3 \oplus b_1 \oplus b_0$$
$$h_4 = b_2 \oplus b_1 \oplus b_0$$
$$h_3 = b_3$$
$$h_5 = b_2$$
$$h_6 = b_1$$
$$h_7 = b_0$$

Bits h_1, h_2 and h_4 produce even parity bits for the bit fields $b_3\, b_2\, b_0$, $b_3\, b_1\, b_0$ and $b_2\, b_1\, b_0$ respectively. Generally the parity bits (h_1, h_2, h_4, h_8, h_{16}...) are located in the positions corresponding to ascending powers of two (i.e., $2^0, 2^1, 2^2, 2^3, 2^4... = 1, 2, 4, 8, 16...$).

The h_1 parity bit has a 1 in the LSB position of its binary representation. Therefore it can check all the bit positions, including it, which have 1's in the LSB position in the binary representation (i.e., h_1, h_3, h_5 and h_7). The binary representation of h_2 has a 1 in the middle bit position. Therefore it can check all the bit positions, including it, which have 1's in the middle bit position in the binary representation (i.e., h_2, h_3, h_6 and h_7). The h_4 parity bit has a 1 in the MSB position of its binary representation. Therefore it can check all the bit positions, including it, which have 1's in the MSB position in the binary representation (i.e., h_4, h_5, h_6 and h_7).

To decode a Hamming code, checking is to be done for odd parity over the bit fields in which even parity were previously established. For example, a single bit error is indicated by a non-zero parity word $a_4\, a_2\, a_1$, where

$$a_1 = h_1 \oplus h_3 \oplus h_5 \oplus h_7$$

$$a_2 = h_2 \oplus h_3 \oplus h_6 \oplus h_7$$

$$a_4 = h_4 \oplus h_5 \oplus h_6 \oplus h_7$$

If $a_4\, a_2\, a_1 = 000$, we conclude there is no error in Hamming code. On the other hand, if it has a non-zero value, it indicates the bit position in error. For example, if $a_4\, a_2\, a_1 = 110$, then bit 6 is in error. To correct this error, bit 6 has to be complemented.

Example 1. Encode data bits 0110 into a 7-bit even parity Hamming code.

Solution. Given $b_3\, b_2\, b_1\, b_0 = 0\,1\,1\,0$

Therefore,

$$h_1 = b_3 \oplus b_2 \oplus b_0 = 0 \oplus 1 \oplus 0 = 1$$

$$h_2 = b_3 \oplus b_1 \oplus b_0 = 0 \oplus 1 \oplus 0 = 1$$

$$h_4 = b_2 \oplus b_1 \oplus b_0 = 1 \oplus 1 \oplus 0 = 0$$

$$h_3 = b_3 = 0$$

$$h_5 = b_2 = 1$$

$$h_6 = b_1 = 1$$

$$h_7 = b_0 = 0$$

h_1	h_2	h_3	h_4	h_5	h_6	h_7
1	1	0	0	1	1	0

Example 2. A 7-bit Hamming code is received as 0110110. What is its correct code ?

Solution.

h_1	h_2	h_3	h_4	h_5	h_6	h_7
0	1	1	0	1	1	0

Now, to find the error,

Thus, $a_4\, a_2\, a_1 = 010$. Therefore, bit 2 is in error and the corrected code can be obtained by complementing the second bit in the received as 00 10110.

EXERCISES

1. What are BCD codes ?
2. Write a short note on the following:
   (i) Character codes
   (ii) Error detecting codes
   (iii) Error correcting codes
3. Differentiate between ASCII and EBCDIC character codes. Why is EBCDIC code used ?
4. What are the advantages of Grey codes ? Discuss their areas of applications.
5. Write a short note on the following :
   (i) ISCII (ii) UNICODE
6. Write the 4-bit BCD code for the following numbers :
   (i) 2710 (ii) 13510 (iii) 8610 (iv) 103410
7. Using binary notation, show the BCD coding for the following words :
   (i) CODES (ii) COMPUTER (iii) OLYMPICS (iv) PROGRAM
8. Why was BCD code extended to EBCDIC ?
   (i) EARTH (ii) LION (iii) FOX (iv) PROCESS
   How many bytes are needed for each of these representations ?
9. Using binary notation, write the ASCII-7 and ASCII-8 codes coding for the following words
   (i) LONG (ii) SHORT (iii) MEDAL (iv) EXAM
   How many bytes are needed for each of these representations ?
10. Perform the following additions using binary number system only.
   (i) $1011_2 + 11_2$ (ii) $111_2 + 0101_2$
   (iii) $1010_2 + 10_2$ (iv) $110011_2 + 1100_2$
   (v) $11001_2 + 111000_2$ (vi) $111111_2 + 110000_2$
   (vii) $101.011_2 + 10.110_2$ (viii) $1011.1010_2 + 1000.001_2$
   (ix) $11001.1011_2 + 10011.0110_2$
11. Evaluate:
   (i) $1100_2 - 101_2$ (ii) $1101_2 - 1011_2$
   (iii) $1010_2 - 111_2$ (iv) $11100_2 - 111_2$
   (v) $11100_2 - 11011_2$ (vi) $1111_2 - 100011_2$
   (vii) $101.101_2 - 11.011_2$ (viii) $1100.01_2 - 1001.10_2$
   (ix) $1001.1_2 - 101.11_2$
12. Find the difference using 1's and 2's complements methods :
   (i) $10001_2 - 01010_2$ (ii) $10_2 - 10011_2$
   (iii) $1101_2 - 1001_2$ (iv) $0.11_2 - 0.101_2$
13. Perform the following multiplications:
   (i) $1100_2 \times 10_2$ (ii) $1110_2 \times 111_2$

(iii) $10101_2 \times 101_2$ (iv) $1010.101_2 \times 1.01_2$
(v) $1100.001_2 \times 110.1_2$ (vi) $01011_2 \times 1001_2$
(vii) $1101112 \times 111_2$ (viii) $1100_2 \times 1001_2$

14. Divide the following binary numbers:
(i) $1100_2/10_2$ (ii) $11000_2/110_2$
(iii) $1110011_2/101_2$ (iv) $1100010_2/111_2$
(v) $11110_2/101_2$ (vi) $111011_2/111_2$

15. Why are subtractions using 2's complements used in modern computers? What are the difficulties with BCD or simple binary subtractions ?

16. Give the advantages and disadvantages of performing the various arithmetic operations by additive method in the digital computer.

17. Explain Booths multiplication with an example.

18. Subtract $(1010)_2$ from $(1101)_2$ using the 1's and 2's complement methods.

19. ASCII stands for ....

20. Write the Booth coded number for the following binary numbers in 2's complement form :
(i) 11101101 (ii) 11000110

ANSWERS

Review Questions and Exercises

6. (i) 00100111 (ii) 000100110101 (iii) 10000110
(iv) 0001000000110100

10. (i) 1110 (ii) 1100 (iii) 1100
(iv) 111111 (v) 1010001 (vi) 1101111
(vii) 1000.001 (viii) 10011.1100 (ix) 101101.0001

11. (i) 111 (ii) 10 (iii) 101
(iv) 10101 (v) 1 (vi) -10100
(vii) 10.010 (viii) 10.11 (ix) 11.11

12. (i) 00111 (ii) -10001 (iii) 0100
(iv) 0.001

13. (i) 11000 (ii) 1100010 (iii) 1101001
(iv) 1101.01001 (v) 1001110.1101 (vi) 1100011
(vii) 110000001 (viii) 1101100

14. (i) 110 (ii) 100 (iii) 10111
(iv) 1110 (v) 110 (vi) Quotient 1000, Remainder 11

Input and Output Devices

5.1 INTRODUCTION

A ***computer peripheral*** is any external device that provides input and output for the computer. For example, a keyboard and mouse are input peripherals, while a monitor and printer are output peripherals. Computer peripherals, or peripheral devices, are sometimes called "I/O devices" because they provide input and output for the computer. Some peripherals, such as external hard drives, provide both input and output for the computer.

5.2 INPUT CONCEPTS

Input is the process of entering and translating incoming data into machine-readable form so that they can be processed by a computer. The data to be entered are also often referred to as input. But before discussing concepts involving input, let's recall the meanings of some terms. Hardware is all the physical components of a computer system.

Any hardware item that is attached to the main unit of a computer houses the CPU is referred to as a peripheral device. An input device is a peripheral device through which data are entered and transformed into machine-readable form.

Three important things to be concerned with during the input process are:

The method of data preparation (transcriptive or source)

The type of processing to be used (batch or transaction)

The accuracy of the data being entered.

5.3 INPUT DEVICES

An **input device** is any hardware device that sends data to the computer, without any input devices, a computer would only be a display device and not allow users to interact with it, much like a TV. Following continuing research in the field of computer hardware, we have a large number of input devices. Recall that before data can be processed by the computer, they must be translated into machine-readable form and entered into the computer by an input device.

Many input devices can be classified according to:

- Modality of input (e.g. mechanical motion, audio, visual, etc.)
- The input is discrete (e.g. key presses) or continuous (e.g. a mouse's position, though digitized into a discrete quantity, is fast enough to be considered continuous)
- The number of degrees of freedom involved (e.g. two-dimensional traditional mice, or three-dimensional navigators designed for CAD applications)

Pointing devices, which are input devices used to specify a position in space, can further be classified according to:

- Whether the input is direct or indirect. With direct input, the input space coincides with the display space, i.e. pointing is done in the space where visual feedback or the cursor appears. Touch Screens and light pens involve direct input. Examples involving indirect input include the mouse and trackball.
- Whether the positional information is absolute (e.g. on a touch screen) or relative (e.g. with a mouse that can be lifted and repositioned)

Note that direct input is almost necessarily absolute, but indirect input may be either absolute or relative. For example, digitizing Graphics tablets that do not have an embedded screen involve indirect input and sense absolute positions and are often run in an absolute input mode, but they may also be setup to simulate a relative input mode where the stylus or puck can be lifted and repositioned.

Here, we list a variety of input devices:

- Punched Cards and Card Readers
- Keyboards
- Joysticks
- Trackballs
- Mouse
- Touch Screens
- Light Pens
- Touch Pad
- Digitizer
- Voice Recognition
- Key to Magnetic Media
- Financial Transaction Terminals
- Machine Vision Systems
- Source Data Input
- Magnetic-ink Character Recognition (MICR)
- Magnetic Strips
- Optical Recognition
- Point-of-Sale Terminals
- Barcode reader
- Digital camera
- Microphone
- MIDI keyboard
- Mouse (pointing device)
- Remote
- Scanner
- Webcam

5.3.1 Punched Cards and Card Readers

"Punched Card" was the one of the most commonly used media for communicating data and instructions to the computer in India before 1980. A punched card is a rigid piece of paper containing rows and columns of numbers. IBM card is called a standardized card which has 80 columns and is of the size 7 ½ inches x 3 ¼ inches x 0.007 inch. The columns are numbered 1-80 from left to right. One of its corner is usually trimmed to help to maintain proper positioning during processing. The top row in a card is called the 12-punch row; next is called 11th row and then next 10 rows are numbered consecutively from '0' to '9'. The top 2 rows are called as Zone Punch Rows and the bottom 10 rows are called as Digit Punch Rows.

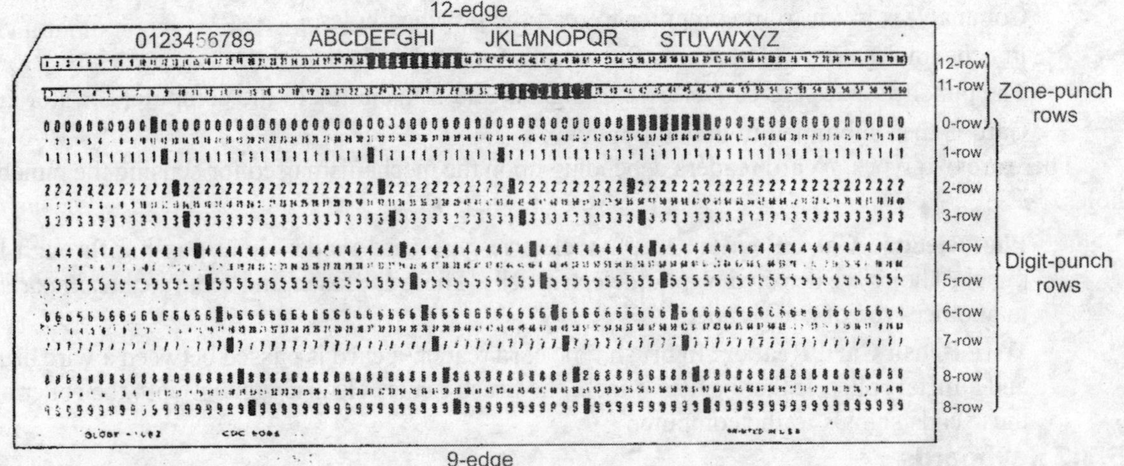

Fig. 5.1 : Punched Card

These cards are put into a keypunch machine. As the operator keys in the data to be stored, the keypunch machine places holes in the card to represent the data. The pattern of punched holes used to represent characters on the card is called the Hollerith code, named after its inventor, Herman Hollerith.

Each column of the punched card can record a single character as a set of holes punched in the vertical column. Thus a single can hold a maximum of 80 characters. The holes punched in the cards are interpreted by a card reader that translates the punched information into a machine-readable code, then sends it to the CPU for processing.

The punched-card system was one of the first methods used to input data. It has been almost totally replaced by newer, more efficient input devices.

Key Punching Machine

Punching of data on the card is called Key Punch and key punching is accomplished by means of a key punching machine which looks like a Typewriter. The most common type of key punch machines were IBM 026 and IBM 029. These machines have the following components :

Keyboard
Card hopper
Punching station
Card stacker
Column indicator

Back-space key
Program control unit
Program drum
Reading section
Switches
Printing mechanism, etc.

Card Reader

Card Reader was used as the primary input device in most of the early day computers. A card reader is connected to the computer and is required to initiate the following steps:

Put the punched cards in the read hopper of the card reader.

Command is given from computer to read the punched holes.

Punched holes are read at points for verification of data being read.

The punched holes are converted into signals and transmitted to the computer for storage.

Card is then submitted in the output stack.

There are two types of card readers depending upon the mechanism used for sensing the punched holes:

Photoelectric Card Reader: In photoelectric type card reader, light passing through the punched holes are detected by photoelectric cells. These are faster and accurate in comparison to another type of card reader.

Wire Brush Card Reader: In brush type card reader, a card is passed between a wire brush and a metal roller. If there exists punch, the brush makes electric contact with the roller and thus sends signals to the computer.

5.3.2 Keyboards

A keyboard is one of the today's most common and familiar input device. A keyboard's primary function is to act as an **input device.** The computer **keyboard** is used to enter text information into the computer, as when you type the contents of a report. Using a keyboard, a person can type a document, use keystroke shortcuts, access menus, play games and perform a variety of other tasks. Keyboards can have different keys depending on the manufacturer, the operating system they're designed for, and whether they are attached to a desktop computer or part of a laptop. But for the most part, these keys, also called **keycaps,** are the same size and shape from keyboard to keyboard. They're also placed at a similar distance from one another in a similar pattern, no matter what language or alphabet the keys represent.

Figure 5.2: Keyboards

The traditional QWERTY (so called because the first six letters on the top row are Q, W, E, R, T, and Y) typewriter keyboard compromises the basic portion of today's computer keyboard.

A typical computer keyboard contains all the letters, numbers, and symbols of a regular typewriter, plus a variety of other keys. The other keys include:

(i) A numeric keypad that looks and functions lime a calculator;

(ii) Function keys whose operation can be determined by the user or preprogrammed by the software being used; and

(iii) Special keys such as those used to control the movement of the cursor on the computer screen.

Description: A keyboard consists of rows of electronic switches ('keys') encased in a plastic surround. Each switch has a graphic on it that describes its function e.g. the switch with the letter 'B' on it will input the 'B' character into the computer. To input data, you need to depress the key. Key strokes are also combined to modify the input e.g. Holding the Shift key at the same time as depressing the 'A' key will cause a capital 'A' to be input rather than a lower case 'a'. Along-side the usual letters and special characters such as :@~()!"$% etc, there are a set if 'F' keys along the top that can be assigned special functions by the software you are running. For example F1 often brings up a help screen (but not always!).

Most keyboards have between 80 and 110 keys, including:

Alphanumeric keys

Numeric keypad

Function keys

Cursor movement keys

Alphanumeric keys: The Alphanumeric keys include the letters of the alphabet, generally laid out in the same pattern used for typewriters. According to legend, this layout, known as QWERTY for its first six letters, helped keep mechanical typewriters' metal arms from colliding and jamming as people typed. Some people question this story -- whether it's true or not, the QWERTY pattern had long been a standard by the time computer keyboards came around.

Keyboards can also use a variety of other typing key arrangements. The most widely known is **Dvorak,** named for its creator, August Dvorak. The Dvorak layout places all of the vowels on the left side of the keyboard and the most common consonants on the right. The most commonly used letters are all found along the home row. The **home row** is the main row where you place your fingers when you begin typing. People who prefer the Dvorak layout say it increases their typing speed and reduces fatigue. Other layouts include **ABCDE, XPeRT, QWERTZ** and **AZERTY.** Each is named for the first keys in the pattern. The QWERTZ and AZERTY arrangements are commonly used in Europe.

Numeric keys: To perform mathematical functions, use the numeric keypad as you would a keypad calculator. To activate the numeric keypad, press the NUM LOCK key. If you do not press the NUM LOCK key, the numeric keypad will function as cursor control keys.

Function keys: Function keys are special-purpose keys, numbered F1 through F10, used to communicate specific fictions to the operating system. These keys simplify tasks that might otherwise require several key strokes. These keys can also be used with other keys to increase the number of functions available. The software program in operation defines the function of these keys. Be sure to read the software owner/user manual to understand the purpose of these keys. These keys are generally located at the top of the keyboard.

Cursor movement keys: Cursor control keys move the cursor from one place to another on the display screen. The cursor is the indicator on the display screen that lets the user know where the next entry will be made. Cursor control keys have an arrowhead printed on them pointing in the direction that the key will move. Some keyboards have a separate set of keys for cursor movement; others have the cursor movement keys incorporated into the numeric keyboard. As long as the NUM LOCK key is OFF, the cursor movement keys function. Some software packages use the cursor control keys in combination with each other or with other keys to increase the number of ways and the speed with which you can move the cursor. Another cursor movement key - the SCROLL LOCK/ BREAK key - controls screen scrolling. When in the BREAK mode and used in conjunction with the CTRL key, the SCROLL LOCK key will interrupt program execution.

Advantages

The most efficient way of entering numbers, text and commands into the computer, as each key has a specific function.

Inexpensive, as virtually every computer needs one.

Disadvantages

You have to learn to type!

There are 'arrow keys' but they are not as good as a mouse for controlling the screen cursor.

May cause sore wrists and arms

5.3.3 Mouse

Mouse is a pointing device and it has been around us for more than 20 years. Douglas Engelbart of Stanford Research Center developed the mouse in 1963 as an alternative to the keyboard in the 1960s. Mouse was pioneered by Xerox in 1970s. Mouse is one of the biggest breakthroughs in Computer Ergonomics because it frees the user to a large extent from using the keyboard.

The mouse usually contains one to three buttons; as the user rolls it on a flat surface, the mouse controls cursor movement on the screen. When the user presses one of the buttons, the mouse either marks a place on the screen or makes selections from data on the screen.

Different types of mouse are shown in ***Fig. 5.3.***

(a) Simple Mouse (b) Cordless Mouse (c) Ball-point Mouse

Fig. 5.3 : Different Types of Mouse

Types of Mouse

There are three basic types of Mouse :

Mechanical Mouse

Optomechanical Mouse

Optical Mouse

Mechanical Mouse

A mechanical mouse has a rubber or metal ball on its underside that can roll in all directions. Mechanical sensors within the mouse detect the direction of the rolling ball and make a movement of the screen pointer accordingly.

Optomechanical Mouse

Optomechanical mouse is also similar to a mechanical mouse except that it uses optical sensors to detect the movement of the ball on the Mouse Pad.

Optical Mouse

Optical mouse uses a laser beam to detect the movement of mouse on specially designed Mouse Pad. We must move the mouse along a special mat with a grid so that optical mechanism has a frame of reference. This type of mouse has no mechanical moving parts. Optical mouse respond more quickly and precisely than any other mouse. These are very expensive.

A mouse can be used for many applications ranging from games to designing products with graphics. It provides an alternative for people who are uncomfortable with a keyboard, or it can be used in combination with a keyboard to enhance input operations.

The mouse is also used to draw sketches , diagram etc. on the CRT screen. It is also moved on graphic tablet for drawing work and the same is also used to edit text. For editing text on the screen the cursor is quickly moved to the desired point of the screen by moving the mouse.

Advantages

It is simple device and very easy to use.

It is not that very expensive.

It moves the cursor faster than the arrow keys of keyboard do.

Disadvantages

The movement of the cursor is not very sensitive to movement of mouse.

If the contact between wheels and mouse pad is lost, the cursor does not move.

5.3.4 Joysticks

A joystick is also a pointing device. It is used to move the cursor position on a CRT screen. Its function is similar to a mouse, except that with a mouse the cursor stops moving as soon as you stop moving the mouse. A joystick is a stick which has spherical ball at its lower end as well as at its upper end. A joystick uses a lever to control the position of the cursor. It internally translates the lever position and speed with which the joystick is moved into digital signals that are sent to the computer to control the cursor movement. Most joysticks include two buttons called triggers.

Fig. 5.4 : Joystick

Joysticks are used for Computer games but they are also used occasionally for CAD/CAM systems and other applications.

5.3.5 Trackballs

Trackball is another pointing device. A trackball is a mouse lying on its back. A trackball uses a hard sphere to control cursor movement. The ball can be rotated by hand in any direction. The associated electronic circuitry detects the direction and speed of spin. The trackball translates the sphere's direction and speed of rotation into digital signal used to control the cursor. The information is sent to the CPU for initiating further necessary action.

Different types of Trackball are shown in ***Fig. 5.5.***

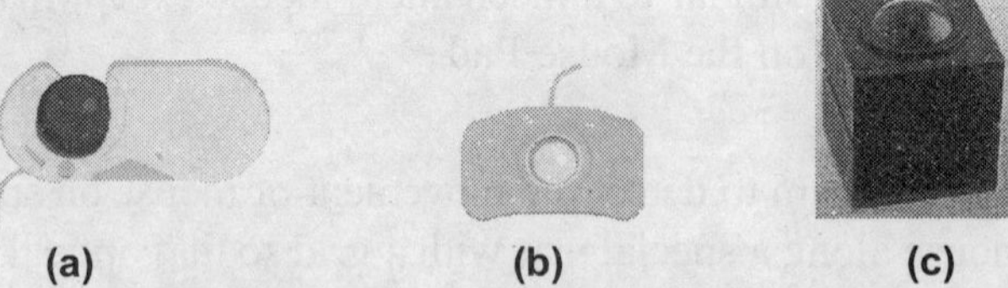

(a) (b) (c)

Fig. 5.5 : Various Types of Trackballs

Advantages

1. The benefit of using trackball over mouse is that trackball is stationary so it does not require much space to use it.
2. We can place a trackball on any type of surface, including our palm or lap.
3. Their compact size make them most suitable for portable computers.

5.3.6 Touch Screens

A touch screen is basically a display screen which can identify the occurrence and position of a touch inside the display region. The word normally refers to a touch or tap to the display of the gadget by a finger or hand. Touch screens can also identify added inactive objects, such as a stylus. However, if the object identified is active, as with a light pen, the phrase touch screen is normally irrelevant. The facility to interact directly with a display normally specifies the existence of a touch screen.

Figure 5.6: Touch Screen Monitor

Such touch screen displays can be connected to computers, laptops, PDAs, cell phones etc. They also project an important function in the blueprint of digital.

Touch screen is a type of display screen that has a touch-sensitive transparent panel covering the screen. A touch screen registers input when a finger or other object comes in contact with the screen. Two touch-screen techniques involve infrared beams and ultrasonic acoustic waves. Infrared beams crisscross the surface of the screen, and when a light beam is broken, that location is recorded.

The other technique involves ultrasonic acoustic waves that pass over the surface of the screen. When the wave signals are interrupted by some contact with the screen, that location is recorded. Because the acoustic waves bend with the curved surface of the screen, they are closer to the screen, thus giving more precision when locating the point of contact.

Touch screens have long been used in military applications. Today, because they have become less expensive, touch screens are found in many other applications. Touch screens have provided information and directions at EPCOT Center at Walt Disney World since 1982.

Visitors simply touch the items on the screen that would like more information about, and the computer displays a screen that supplies them with the details.

Automated lottery machines that use touch screens are becoming popular in supermarkets, carry outs, and retail stores. By touching the screen, selections, such as the type of game and the numbers to play are made. The computer registers the choice, then generates and prints the lottery ticket. Hewlett-Packard is one of the computer company that offers a series of microcomputers that have touch-screen capabilities.

5.3.7 Light Pens

A light pen is similar to a mouse, except that with a light pen we can move the pointer and select objects on the display screen by directly pointing to the object with the pen. It is a pen like device which is connected to the machine by a cable. Light pen consists photocells placed in its small tube. When it is brought to the screen, it detects the light emitted from the screen. The photocells are activated and electrical pulses send data to computer which identifies the menu option that activated the photo cell. A light pen can make selections, place objects, or indicate dimensions by simply touching the screen. A light pen does not emit light rather, it reacts to light through a photosensitive detector as its base.

Light pens are shown in ***Fig. 5.7.***

Fig. 5.7 : Light Pens

A light pen can also be used for graphical work. A user can draw directly on the CRT screen with the light pen if the computer system is provided with CAD package. It can be used to modify the graphs or drawings, identify color or thickness of the objects on the screen.

5.3.8 Touch Pad

A small, touch-sensitive pad is used as a pointing device on some portable computers. By moving a finger or other object along the pad, we can move the pointer on the display screen. The touch pad is related to the touch screen, but activated by different means. The touch pad uses pressure-sensitive materials to record data at the point where the pad is touched. Many appliances around the home, such as microwave ovens, use touch pads for programming time or temperature.

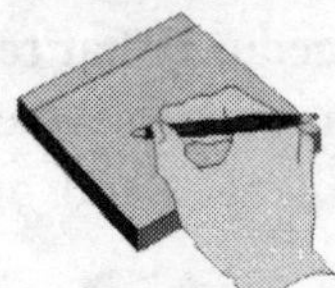

Fig. 5.8 : Touch Pad Using a Point-device

5.3.9 Digitizer

A digitizer, or graphics tablet, is similar to a light pen; however, instead of drawing on the screen, a separate tablet is used on which a special stylus is moved. Input tablets or digitizer tablets or graphical tablets are typically found in CAD terminals or engineering workstations, etc. These tablets are work surfaces that contain hundreds of copper wires in the form of a grid, which are connected to the computer. Each copper wire receives electric pulses. A stylus or pen, which is sensitive to these pulses send signals to the computer to form drawings. By selecting commands on the digitizer, objects can be drawn or erased, and coordinates can be marked on the screen. Light pens and digitizers are often used in the mechanical and architectural fields for drawing. The drawings are not made on the tablets directly but normally a sketch of drawing is traced on a paper kept on tablet by this pen, to transmit to the computer.

Digitizers are also called Digitizing Tablets, Graphics Tablets, Touch Tablets, or simply Tablets. Top-view of digitizer along with tablet is shown in **Fig. 5.9.**

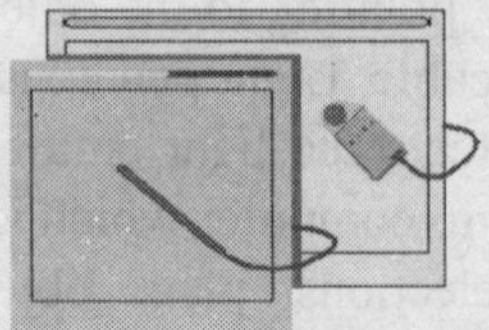

Fig. 5.9 : Digitizer With Tablet

Advantages

The sketches displayed on the screen are neater and more precise than that on paper.

Digitizers provide a capability of interactive graphics.

The drawings can easily be changed and their effects can quickly be analyzed, thus saving user time.

Disadvantages

They are costly.

They are suitable for applications which require high resolution graphics only.

5.3.10 Voice Recognition

Audio input provides direct and "user friendly" means of inputting data and instructions to the computer. Recently, a number of Voice Data Entry (VDE) systems have been developed. Voice recognition is one of the newest, most complex input techniques used to interact with the computer. The user inputs data by speaking into a microphone. The simplest form of voice recognition is a one-word command spoken by one person. Each command is isolated with pauses between the words.

With a voice-recognition device, a doctor can ask the computer for information about a patient and not interrupt a surgical operation. Some quality-control inspections can be performed more productively if inspectors can verbally list defects into the microphone of the computer instead of stopping to write them down. Any procedure that requires using both hands and recording data simultaneously can benefit from voice input. Voice recognition also opens up the world of computers to people who are physically challenged and are unable to use traditional types of input devices.

Voice-recognition systems can recognize a few hundred words; however, regional accents and words that sound alike but have different meanings, such as "their" and "there" are difficult to decipher and, thus, cause the system problems. Although research continues in this area, computer voice recognition of continuous speech or normal conversation is not currently available for widespread use.

Apart from Voice Data Entry Systems, some computers and even some calculators have been designed to generate spoken words. Here again the vocabulary is limited thus allowing their use only to limited application areas.

Types of Voice Systems

There are two types of voice recognition systems:

Continuous Speech

Discrete Word

Continuous Speech

Continuous speech recognition systems are used to control a microcomputer's operations and to issue commands to special application programs. For example, rather than using the keyword to shutdown the system, the user could simply say "Shutdown".

Examples

Apple Computer's PlainTalk System

IBM's Continuous Speech Series System

Discrete Word

A common activity in business is preparing memos and other written documents. Discrete-word recognition systems allow users to dictate directly into a microcomputer using microphone. The microcomputer stores the memo in a word processing file where it can be revised later or directly printed out.

Example : IBM Voice Type Simply Speaking is a popular system

Advantages

Easier to use and much efficient system

Unwanted inputs or unauthorized speakers can be identified and therefore unwanted access be traced and avoided.

Computer can be used very effectively by blind or handicapped people.

Disadvantages

Computer can have very limited vocabulary i.e., words which can be understood by it.

The accents or voice of different operators can't be distinguished and the computer will not be able to recognize words which are in its vocabulary.

5.3.11 Key to Magnetic Media

In earlier computer systems punched cards were the most common form of input but today the emphasis has switched to magnetic media. In office and business organizations, where traditionally data preparation is a major part of the work, keying information directly to magnetic tape or disk is now standard practice, superseding the use of the traditional punched card. Three methods are distinguishable :

(i) Key-to-tape

(ii) Key-to-cartridge/cassette

(iii) key-to-disk/diskette

Key-to-tape

A Key-to-tape device, sometimes referred to as a magnetic tape recorder, permits the recording information directly on the magnetic tape. An operator, copying from documents, keys the data electronically using a typewriter like keyboard. The data is stored temporarily by the device and typically displayed on a CRT for visual checking before being transferred to magnetic tape.

Key-to-cartridge/cassette

Information can also be keyed direct to small magnetic cassette tapes or cartridges and later transferred to standard magnetic tape for processing. A cassette, typically two and half inches by four inches in size, is capable of storing around 200,000 characters of information. A typical cartridge is smaller in capacity, averaging around 30,000 characters. These key input devices are easy to use and compact.

Key-to-disk/diskette

As with key-to-tape systems, information is entered via a keyboard and a copy displayed on a CRT to allow a visual check. A key-to-disk/diskette system normally comprises a mini computer, a number of key stations and a disk drive. The minicomputer is required to control the input from various stations, enabling the data to be held temporarily for verification and editing before allocation to the disk store. The process of keying to disk or diskette is more efficient and cost effective than punching data on cards for card input.

Advantages

- The key to magnetic media obviates the need of interposed media such as punched card.
- It is cost effective over a period of time.
- Large amount of data can be stored on the magnetic media which occupies much smaller space than the punched cards.
- The data on magnetic media does not get damaged easily as it does on punched cards.

Disadvantages

- Main drawback is its high initial cost. But, now-a-days even this cost has reduced substantially.
- This type of system depends on the processor. A breakdown results in all work being stalled.

5.3.12 Financial Transaction Terminals

These input devices are mainly for the financial transaction and are used mostly by banks and other finances institutions. Most of you must have seen the Automated Teller Machine (ATM). This machine works on its own. The ATMs are mainly owned by banks. Banks issue cards to the customer. Each card has the account number of the customer and credit limit stored on it magnetically. When the card is inserted in the machine, after checking the account number for validity, the user specific keys of the terminal, instructions can be given. After carrying out specific checks, the machine provides you with the required amount of money and updates your balance.

Advantages

- The machine works automatically without any human control
- Customers do not have to travel long distances and stand in long queues to carry out the transaction.

Disadvantages

- Fraud cases come across sometimes when people withdraw more money than the credit limit.

5.3.13 Machine Vision Systems

Usually robots have cameras fitted in them which act as eyes for them. These cameras grasp the image, scan it and decide the next action. Such machines are said to have vision. Robots with vision are used to identify manufacturing superficial defects in objects, assemble various parts of a system, etc.

Vision-input system is the science and technology of machines that see, where see in this case means that the machine is able to extract information from an image that is necessary to solve some task. As a scientific discipline, computer vision is concerned with the theory behind artificial systems that extract information from images. The image data can take many forms, such as video sequences, views from multiple cameras, or multi-dimensional data from a medical scanner.

A vision-input system allows a computer to accept by seeing an object. Input data in this case is normally an object's shape and features in the form of an image. The idea is to simulate the capability of a human vision system in a limited sense.

A computer with a vision-input device consists of a digital camera. Digital Camera is an input device used to take pictures and to store directly in computer in digital form. It operates on the same basic principle as a traditional or conventional camera but digital camera sends images directly inside the PC in digital form instead of storing it on a conventional film.

Figure 5.10: Vision input system

When a picture is taken with digital camera, the electric image of the picture is stored in digital form on the floppy disk or CD-R attached with the camera. The stored picture can be loaded into the computer from the disk for editing. As a technological discipline, vision-input system seeks to apply its theories and models to the construction of computer vision systems.

Examples of applications of Vision-input system include systems for:

Controlling processes (e.g., an industrial robot or an autonomous vehicle).

Detecting events (e.g., for visual surveillance or people counting).

Organizing information (e.g., for indexing databases of images and image sequences).

Modeling objects or environments (e.g., industrial inspection, medical image analysis or topographical modeling).

Interaction (e.g., as the input to a device for computer-human interaction).

Vision-input system is closely related to the study of biological vision. The field of biological vision studies and models the physiological processes behind visual perception in humans and other animals. Vision-input system, on the other hand, studies and describes the processes implemented in software and hardware behind artificial vision systems. Interdisciplinary exchange between biological and computer vision has proven fruitful for both fields. Vision-input system is, in some ways, the inverse of computer graphics. While computer graphics produces image data from 3D models, computer vision often produces 3D models from image data. There is also a trend towards a combination of the two disciplines, e.g., as explored in augmented reality. Sub-domains of vision-input system include scene reconstruction, event detection, video tracking, object recognition, learning, indexing, motion estimation, and image restoration.

Advantages

Machine vision systems are able to identify objects and carry out required operations on them.

No human intervention is required.

Disadvantages

A slight change in the shape of the object seen by the machine does not allow the specific operation to be carried out.

5.3.14 Source Data Input

Recall that data entered directly into a computer system without a transcription process is referred to as source data. Methods of source data input include magnetic-ink character recognition, magnetic strips, and optical recognition.

5.3.15 Magnetic-ink Character Recognition (MICR)

MICR is interpretation by a computer of a line of characters written in a special magnetic ink. These characters can be read by humans as well. You may have noticed a line of numbers and some odd-shaped characters on the bottom of your personal cheques. These magnetic ink characters are bank processing symbols representing the cheque number, customer account number, and bank identification number. When the bank receives the cheque, the amount of the cheque is also printed in magnetic ink. The cheques are sent through a MICR reader to interpret the information, update the appropriate accounts and, in some case, sort the cheques afterwards.

Magnetic ink is used on documents such as bank cheques and credit card slips because a MICR device can easily distinguish the appropriate magnetic characters no matter how much a user might have written over them

5.3.16 Magnetic Strips

Magnetic strips are thin bands of magnetically encoded data that are found on the backs of many credit cards and automated teller cards. The data stored on the card vary from one application to another, but they include account numbers or special access codes. Magnetic strip cards can also be used to limit access to high security areas. To enter a security area, a person inserts the card into a computerized "read" device; if the card contains the right code, the door automatically opens. Because data cannot be seen or interpreted by simply looking at the card, the stored data can be highly sensitive or personal.

5.3.17 Optical Recognition

Optical recognition occurs when a device scans a printed surface and translates the image the scanner sees into a machine-readable format that is understandable by the computer.

The three types of optical recognition described here are :

(i) Optical Mark Recognition (OMR)

(ii) Optical Bar Recognition (OBR)

(iii) Optical Character Recognition (OCR)

Optical mark recognition (OMR): It employs mark sensing, one of the simplest forms of optical recognition, to scan and translate, based on its location, a series of pen or pencil marks into computer-readable form. A computerized optical mark reader scores the tests by identifying the position of the mark, not its shape.

Optical bar recognition (OBR): It is a slightly more sophisticated type of optical recognition. An optical bar reader recognizes and interprets a pattern of lines that form a bar code. Bar codes, also called product codes, appear on products as a series of thick and thin black bars and spaces that are arranged to represent data, such as name of the manufacturer and the type of product. Interpretation of the code is based on the width of the lines rather than the location of the bar code. The bar code does not contain the price of the item. Prices are stored in the computer where the amount can be easily reprogrammed to reflect sale or special offers. The bar code is read by a scanner, and the price and products are then matched by the computer. The price may be displayed at a checkout counter by a point-of-sale (POS) terminal.

Optical character recognition (OCR): It is the most sophisticated type of optical recognition. An optical character reader works in much the same way as the human eye. It does not rely on the magnetic quality of the character such as MICR does; rather, it recognizes specially-shaped alphabetic and numeric characters. Capital and lower case letters, as well as a variety of different optical-character typesets, can be read.

5.3.18 Scanners

Scanner is a kind of input device that can read text or printed paper and translates the information in a convenient form to be understood by the computer. A scanner works on the principle of digitizing an image in the form of bit-matrix called 'bit-map'. The bit-map can be stored in a file, displayed on the screen, and can easily be manipulated by relevant packages/programs.

All kinds of scanned documents using an optical scanner gets converted in the form of bit-map and thus it does not distinguish between text or graphics. In order to edit text read by an optical scanner, we need an OCR system to translate the image into ASCII format. Almost all optical scanners sold today come along with OCR packages.

There are six distinct types of scanners:

- handheld
- flatbed
- sheetfed
- photo drum, and
- slide.

Each of these styles has its own practical applications and limitations. Theoretically, you could also include digital cameras as a type of scanner.

Flatbed (or simple) and Hand-held scanners are the most popular scanners in maximum use. These are shown in ***Fig. 5.11 (a)*** and ***(b)*** respectively.

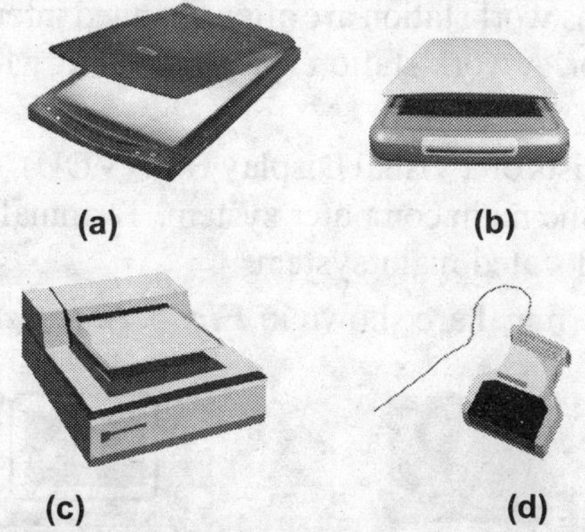

(a) to (c) Flatbed Scanners (d) Hand-held Scanner

Fig. 5.11: Types of Scanners

Scanners can be classified on the basis of following:

Scanning Technology
Bit-depth
Resolution
Size and Shape

Different applications require the use of different types of scanners and each type of scanner has unique features and comes in a different price range.

Description: The picture to be input is laid flat, face down on the surface of the scanner and the lid lowered to avoid stray light creeping in.

The scanner sweeps its sensors along the picture. As it does so, an image is built up as a series of 'pixels'. Each pixel represents a tiny part of the picture.

A scanner can

(1) Create a black and white image- handy for line drawings and text.

(2) Create a full colour image- excellent for inputting photographs.

The number of pixels can be adjusted to suit the image being taken. For example if a small file is required, then a low-resolution (75 dots per inch) black and white image may be adequate. This will result in an A4 sized image being only a few hundred kilobytes at most.

On the other hand if the highest quality is required then a high resolution (300 dots per inch+) full colour image is taken. This will result in a huge file, easily several Megabytes in size.

How Scanners Work?

Scanners work a lot like copy machines. But instead of immediately outputting an exact copy of the image, scanners send the information about the original to an electronic storage device connected to a host computer. Most scanners shine a bright light on to an original document or image and then measure the information that is reflected back into the scanner.

These electronic sensors respond to even the slightest variations in light intensity. Some of these sensors are sensitized to various colours; they use filters to block certain colours, which allow other colours to be measured more easily. Or they use prisms to separate the light into colours. Those that use prisms are known as **beam splitters** and are generally regarded as superior

5.3.19 Terminals

It is a device usually equipped with a keyboard and a display device, capable of sending and receiving information. The terms workstation are often changed interchangeably. However, a terminal may not have a human operator. A work station is a terminal at which human operator performs an application.

The terminal typically consists of a Visual Display Unit (VDU), a keyboard, and a communication link to hook the terminal with the main computer system. Terminal is used for inputting data to and retrieving data from remotely located main system.

Monitor (or VDU) and Terminal are shown in ***Fig. 5.12 (a) and (b)*** respectively.

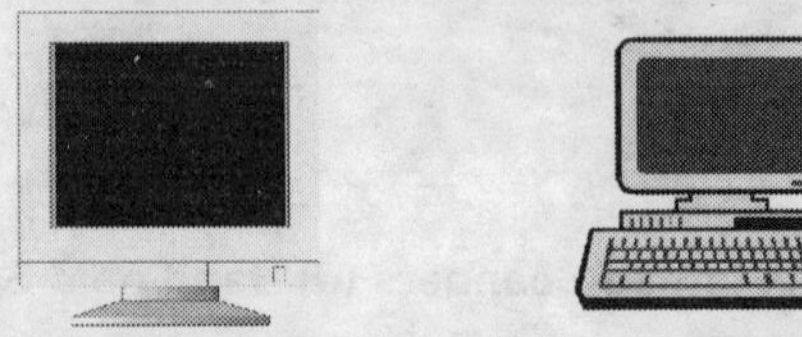

Fig. 5.12 : (a) Monitors (b) Terminal

VDUs are most common form of terminal i.e. a place where the information is displayed on the screen as it is typed.

Terminals fall into the following categories:

Dumb Terminals

Smart Terminals

Intelligent Terminals

5.3.19.1 Dumb Terminals

It is a terminal which can do nothing except communicate to and from a CPU. It is also called as a fixed function terminal or non-programmable terminal.

So a dumb terminal can't do any processing of its own and is used only for data input and retrieval. For example, railway reservation clerk might use a dumb terminal at customer counter for booking or canceling tickets.

5.3.19.2 Smart Terminals

These terminals can input and retrieve data and can perform limited processing of its own viz., editing or verifying the data. A smart terminal can not be used for programming. They are designed with a microprocessor chip that contains the circuit needed to perform arithmetic logic and control functions.

5.3.19.3 Intelligent Terminals

There terminals have built-in microprocessors that are user-programmable. They can process small jobs without the need to interact with the mainframe. In addition to keyboard, monitor and communication link, it also includes a processing unit, storage capabilities and software.

5.3.20 VOICE/SPEECH RECOGNITION SYSTEM

Voice recognition technology is prospering with its application being extended to different fields. With most reliable devices fabricated with the help of this technology, you can accomplish the task of installing security effectively.

5.3.21 SPEECH RECOGNITION

Computer technology that enables a device to recognize and understand spoken words, by digitizing the sound and matching its pattern against the stored patterns. Currently available devices are largely speaker-dependent (recognize speech of only one or two persons) and can recognize discrete speech (speech with pauses between words) better than the normal (continuous) speech. Their major applications are in assistive technology for helping people in working around their disabilities. Not to be confused with voice recognition which is used mainly in security devices?

Figure 5.13: Voice Systems

Voice recognition or speech recognition is a type of behavioural biometric technology, which is used to identify a user, with the help of pre-stored voice templates in the biometric device. Every individual has a distinct voice structure, which is based upon a number of characteristics. With the help of voice recognition technology, a number of devices have been manufactured to provide security at homes as well as offices. It is impossible for intruders and housebreakers to tamper with this technology and thus, you can rely upon voice recognition systems for maintaining high-level security.

Speech recognition (also known as **automatic speech recognition** or **computer speech recognition)** converts spoken words to text. The term "voice recognition" is sometimes used to refer to recognition systems that must be trained to a particular speaker-as is the case for most desktop recognition software. Recognizing the speaker can simplify the task of translating speech.

Speech recognition is a broader solution which refers to technology that can recognize speech without being targeted at single speaker-such as a call center system that can recognize arbitrary voices.

Speech recognition has various applications. It can be used in automated phone systems that allow the users to input choices and browse through menus without pressing any keys. Speech recognition systems are also used in businesses and homes to allow users to dictate to their computers and have their words transcribed into their word processing applications. They are currently being used for legal, medical or other transcription needs.

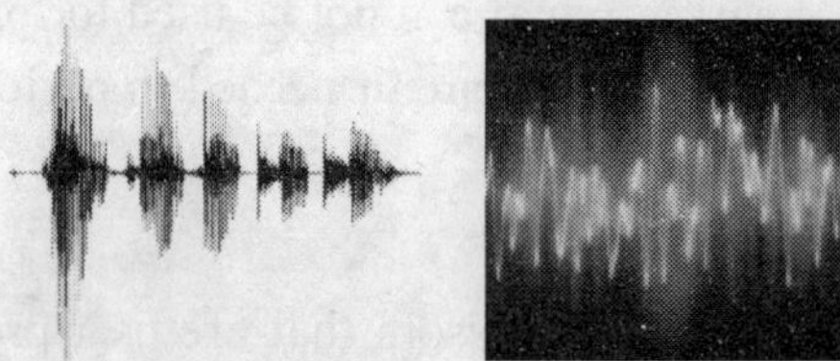

Figure 5.14: Speech Recognition

Speech recognition also offers a method for giving computer commands. With voice instructions, users can command their computers to browse through folders, look for a specific file or open and execute a specific program. Speech recognition software is also being used by differently able persons when they make use of their computers.

Features of Voice Recognition

1. Voice recognition is facilitated by microphones, which record the voice samples and store them for future use.
2. Voice recognition technology is the only form of biometrics, which make use of physical traits (like shape of the vocal trait) as well as behavioural traits (like voice texture, pronunciation and others).
3. Automatic recognition and verification processes are facilitated by this technology.
4. Devices designed using this technology offers voice recorder, voice alerting system and emergency power supports.

Applications of Voice Recognition

Voice recognition systems (speech recognition systems) are installed on those devices, which have no other alternative of biometric analysis than the voice. Here are few applications of this technology used at various places:

1. Modern cell phones are installed with voice recognition components, to control the access of unfamiliar callers.

2. ATM cards are also making use of this technology to ensure that authorized users use their cards to withdraw money from ATM terminals.
3. Door locks are designed with voice recognition technology to ensure that strangers are not allowed to pose threat to the security of your house and family.
4. Automobile locks and garage locks are also designed with this technology to ensure safety to cars.
5. Computer access is restricted to authorized users with the help pf devices based on this technology.

5.3.22 Point-of-Sale Terminal

A point-of-sale (POS) terminal is a device that reads data at the source of a transaction and immediately turns them into usable information. These terminals record data found on bar codes or MICR price tags on each product, calculate cost, and provide the consumer with a detailed receipt of the transaction. Some of these also directly update inventory files.

There are various bar-coding schemes in use; however, the most common is the Universal Product Code (UPC). Department and grocery stores have long used OBR, but other types of stores, factories, and manufacturing operations are starting to use bar codes to provide more efficient, cost-effective control of inventory.

5.4 OUTPUT CONCEPTS

The output devices receive results and other information from the computer and provides it to the users. Output is the process of translating data in machine-readable form into a form understandable to humans or readable by other machines. The information that is the result of processing is also often referred to as output. An output device is a peripheral device that allows a computer to communicate information to humans or another machine by accepting data from the computer and transforming them into usable forms.

Output is divided into two general categories:

Output that can be readily understood and used by humans

Output to secondary storage devices that hold the data to be used as input for further processing by a computer or for use by another machine.

In today's information society, people require clear, legible and output. Output that can be understood by humans can be categorized as :

Hard copy

Soft copy

Hard copy is the output, such as paper, that can be read immediately or stored and read later. It is relatively stable and permanent form of output. ***Soft copy*** is usually a screen-displayed output. It is transient form of output and is lost when the computer is turned off. But if the data needed to create the soft copy have been saved on disk or tapes, the soft copy can be reproduced on the screen anytime.

5.5 HARD COPY DEVICES

Graphics and text material can be produced with a wide selection of printers and plotters. A printer produces output, usually in the form of text, on paper; however, some printers produce graphics. A plotter produces graphic images on paper. The speed of the devices and the quality of the hard copy are the main features that determine the various prices of printers and plotters.

Print Quality

The quality available from hard-copy can vary considerably. You may have heard the terms :

Near-typeset quality
Letter-quality
Near-letter quality
Standard-quality
Draft-quality

Now, what do these terms mean ?

Near-typeset quality

Near-typeset quality print is similar in quality to what is produced by a typeset machine, such as the print found in a magazine.

Letter-quality

Letter-quality print is the equivalent of good typewriter print. This print is made using solid-line (fully-formed) characters as opposed to characters made up of dots or lines. Letter-quality print is used traditionally in business letters and in formal correspondence.

Near-letter quality

Printers that don't produce the fully-formed characters can still print high-quality documents using a near-letter quality print. On some printers this is done when the print head makes multiple passes over the same letters, filling in the spaces between the dots or lines.

Standard-quality

Standard-quality print is produced when characters composed of dots or lines are formed by a single pass of the print head. Generally, standard quality is suitable for most informal applications.

Draft-quality

At the low end of the quality scale is **draft-quality** print, sometimes called compressed print. This print is sometimes used for rough drafts, informal correspondence, or computer program listings. The characters are formed with a minimum number of dots or lines and are smaller than the standard quality characters.

The quality of type that a printer produces is determined by its printing mechanism :

(i) Impact and
(ii) Non-impact

5.6 SOFT-COPY DEVICES

Usually, a user prefers to see what the output looks like before making a permanent copy of it. Viewing the work allows corrections or rearrangement of material to suit specific needs. While most soft-copy output is seen on a display device, voice synthesis devices let us hear it as well.

Monitors

The most popular and certainly the most viewed form of output is found on the monitor. Monitor is another term for display screen. The term however usually refers to the entire box whereas display screen can mean just the screen. A monitor is a television-like device used to display data or information. Just like other output devices, monitors come in many styles and price ranges. Monitors allow users to view the results of processing, but they can be combined with keyboards so that input data can be viewed and checked as they are entered. This combination of keyboard and monitor is often called a terminal or workstation.

Monitor quality is often judged in terms of resolution, a measure of number of picture elements, or pixels, that a screen contains. A pixel is the smallest increment of a display screen that can be controlled individually - the more pixels, the clearer and sharper the image.

There are two kinds of viewing screens used for monitors :

Cathode-Ray Tube (CRT)

Flat-Panel Display

5.7 OUTPUT DEVICES

Any peripheral that receives or displays output from a computer. An inkjet printer is a good example of an **output device** that can make a hard copy of anything on a computer. Below is a listing of all the different computer output devices found on a computer.

Flat panel

Monitor

Printer

Projector

Sound card

Speakers

Video card

5.8 TYPES OF OUTPUT DEVICES

In the world of computers, input/output (I/O) refers to the communication between a computer and the user. Input is the data sent to the system, whereas output is the data sent by the system to the outside world. Computer output devices are computer hardware equipment that is used to communicate the results of data processing carried out by a computer to the user. There are a number of devices, which produce data in different forms, which includes audio, video or hard copy. Output device of computer are types of peripheral hardware connected that is connected to the computer, either using cables or over a wireless network. Immaterial whether you have desktop computers, laptop computers, supercomputers, etc., you will require at least one computer output device.

An **output device** is any piece of computer hardware equipment used to communicate the results of data processing carried out by an information processing system (such as a computer) to the outside world.

After the computer has processed your data, you often need to produce output of the results. This output could be a display on the computer screen, hardcopy on printed pages, or even the audio playback of music you composed on the computer.

Examples of output devices:

Monitors

Printers

Plotters

Speakers

Headphones

Voice Response Systems

Most of the computer output devices are common to home as well as office environments. At the same time, there are some devices, which are not as commonly available. Having said that, let's take a look at computer output devices list.

5.9 MONITORS

A computer display is also called a display screen or video display terminal (VDT). A monitor is a screen used to display the output. Images are represented on monitors by individual dots called pixels. A pixel is the smallest unit on the screen that can be turned on and off or made different shades. The density of the dots determines the clarity of the images, the resolution.

5.10 TYPES OF COMPUTER MONITORS

The computer **monitor** (also know as a **VDU** or **V**isual **D**isplay **U**nit) is the most common computer output device. For desktop computers, cathode ray monitors (**CRT**) are gradually being replaced by flat-screen monitors such as the Liquid Crystal Displays (**LCD**) and Thin Film Transistor (**TFT**) displays used with laptop computers because they use less power and take up less space.

5.10.1 CRT MONITOR

The traditional output device of a personal computer has been the **CRT** (Cathode Ray Tube) monitor. Just like a television set (an older one, anyway) the CRT monitor contains a large cathode ray tube that uses an electron beam of varying strength to "paint" a picture onto the color phosphorescent dots on the inside of the screen. CRT monitors are heavy and use more electrical power than flat panel displays, but they are preferred by some graphic artists for their accurate color rendition, and preferred by some gamers for faster response to rapidly changing graphics.

Figure 5.15: CRT monitor

5.10.2 FLAT PANEL DISPLAYS

Portable computers such as a laptop use flat panel displays, because they are more compact and consume less power than CRTs. Portable computers use several kinds of flat panel screens:

5.10.2.1 LCD (LIQUID CRYSTAL DISPLAY) MONITORS

Liquid crystal display, also known as liquid crystal diode, is one of the most advanced technologies available at present. Typically, an LCD monitor consists of a layer of color or monochrome pixels arranged schematically between a couple of transparent electrodes and two polarizing filters. Optical effect is achieved by polarizing the light in varied amounts and making it pass through the liquid crystal layer. At present, there are two different types of LCD technology available. These include the active matrix or TFT, and a passive matrix technology. Among these, TFT technology is much secure, reliable and generates better picture quality. On the other hand, passive matrix has a slow response time and is slowly becoming outdated.

Figure 5.16: Flat panel display (LCD)

Other types of flat panel technology exist (such as **plasma displays**) but LCDs are most commonly used in computers, especially laptops.

Flat panel displays are much lighter and less bulky than CRT monitors, and they consume much less power. They have been more expensive than CRTs in the past, but the price gap is narrowing. You will see many more flat panels in the future.

5.10.2.2 TFT MONITOR

A TFT monitor is a LCD display that uses thin-film transistor technology. Flat panel displays are quickly becoming the dominant display of choice and are replacing cathode ray tubes. These days, nearly all of the LCD monitors that are designed and developed use TFT technology to provide the picture. They were developed because, in the past, there was a reliance on the passive matrix LCD display.

Figure 5.17: TFT monitor

Since a typical 17-inch TFT monitor has upward of 1.3 million pixels that mean that there would be 1.3 million transistors. However, because the transistors are so small, they don't need very much charge to run. What this guarantees is that the image can be re-drawn very quickly. Therefore, if a mouse is moved across the screen, the pixels would light up as it moved instead of just disappearing.

5.10.2.3 PLASMA DISPLAY PANEL

A **plasma display** panel (PDP) is a type of flat panel display common to large TV displays (80 cm/30 in or larger). They are called "plasma" displays because the technology utilizes small cells containing electrically charged ionized gases, or what are in essence chambers more commonly known as fluorescent lamps.

Figure 5.17: A typical modern plasma screen television

Plasma Display Panels are flat monitors use the light emitted by ionized gas to display images. The two set of electrodes are arranged on a grid, to which a charge is applied. The display electrode releases the charge to ionize of gas, which in turn, releases the ultraviolet photons that collide with the phosphor coated cell walls and release the light photons. These light photons are then projected on the screen as image.

5.11 Classification of Monitors on the Basis of Signals

On the basis of the type of signal monitors accept, monitors can be classified in the following two categories :

Digital Monitors

Analog Monitors

5.11.1 Digital Monitors

A digital monitor accepts digital signals rather than analog signals. All monitors except flat-panel displays use CRT technology which is definitely analog. The term digital, therefore, refers only to the type of input received from the video adapter. A digital monitor then translates the digital signals into analog signals that control the actual display.

Although digital monitors are fast and produce clear images, they can't display variable colors continuously. Consequently, only low-quality video standards such as MDA, CGA, and EGA, specify digital signals. On the other hand, VGA and SVGA require an analog monitor. Some monitors are capable of accepting either type of analog or digital signals.

5.11.2 Analog Computers

This is the traditional type of color display screen that has been used years in TVs. In reality, all monitors based on CRT technology (except Flat-Panel Displays) are analog. Some monitors are called digital monitors because they accept digital signals from the video adapter.

For example, EGA monitors must be digital because the EGA standard specifies digital signals. Digital monitors must nevertheless translate the signals into an analog form before displaying images. Some monitors can accept both digital and analog signals.

Low-cost digital monitors are often called TTL monitors. Most monitors accept analog signals, which are required by the VGA, SVGA, 8514/A, and other high-resolution color standards.

Some monitors have fixed frequency, which means that they accept input at only one frequency. Another type of monitor, called a multi-scanning monitor, automatically adjusts to the frequency of the signals being sent to it. This means that it can accept input from different types of video adapters. Like fixed-frequency monitors, multi-scanning monitors accept TTL, analog, or both types of input.

5.12 Features of Monitors

Following are the major features of monitors which characterizes them.

Size
Resolution
Bandwidth
Refresh Rate
Interlacing/Non-interlacing
Phosphor Pitch or Dot Pitch
Convergence

Size

Size of the screen is one of the most important features. Like TVs, screen size is measured diagonally i.e. the distance from one corner to the opposite corner diagonally. A typical size for small VGA monitors is 14 inches. Screens of size 16 or more are called full-page monitors. In addition to their size, monitors can be either portrait or landscape.

The screen size is sometimes misleading because there is always an area around the edge of the screen that can't be used. Therefore, monitor manufacturers must now also state the viewable area i.e. the area of screen that is actually used.

Resolution

The resolution of monitor indicates how densely the pixels are packed. Pixel stands for Picture Element. A pixel is a single point in a graphic image. Graphic monitors display pictures by dividing the display screen into thousand or millions of pixels, arranged in rows and columns. The pixels are so close together that they appear connected. The number of bits used to represent each pixel determines how many colors or shades of gray can be displayed. For example, an 8-bit color monitor uses 8-bits for each pixel making it possible to display 2^8 (=256) different colors or shades of gray.

In color monitors, each pixel is composed of three dots : red, blue and green. Ideally the three dots should all converge at the same point failing which color pixels appear fuzzy.

In general, the more number of pixels, the sharper the image. Most modern monitors can display 1024x768 pixels which is the resolution of SVGA standard. Some high-end models can display 1280x1024 or even 1600 x 1200.

Bandwidth

The amount of data that can be transmitted in a fixed amount of time is called bandwidth. For digital devices, the bandwidth is usually expressed in bits per second (bps). For analog devices, the bandwidth is expressed in cycles per second or Hertz (Hz).

Refresh Rate

Display monitors must be refreshed many times per second. The refresh rate determines how many times per second the screen is to be refreshed. The refresh rate for a monitor is measured in Hertz (Hz) and is also called the vertical frequency or vertical refresh rate. The old standard for monitor refresh rates was 60 Hz, but a new standard developed by VESA sets the refresh rate at 75 Hz for VGA and SVGA monitors. The faster the refresher rate, the lesser the flickering on monitors.

Interlacing/Non-interlacing

Interlacing is a display technique that enables a monitor to provide more resolution inexpensively. With interlacing monitors, the electron guns draw only half the horizontal lines with each pass (e.g. all odd lines on one pass and all even lines on the next pass). Because an interlacing monitor refreshes only half the lines at one time, it can display twice as many lines per refresh cycle, giving it greater resolution. Another way of looking at it is that interlacing provides the same resolution as non-interlacing, but less expensively.

A shortcoming of interlacing is that the reaction time is slower, so programs that depend on quick refresh rates (e.g. animation, video, etc.), may experience flickering or streaking. If we are given two monitors that offer the same resolution, the non-interlacing one will generally be better.

Phosphor Pitch or Dot Pitch

The dot pitch is one of the principal characteristics that determine the quality of display monitors. Another term for dot-pitch is phosphor pitch. It is measurement that indicates the vertical distance between each pixel on a display screen. It is measured in inches. The lower the dot-pitch, the crisper the image. The dot pitch of color monitors for personal computers ranges from about 0.15 mm to 0.30 mm.

Convergence

Convergence refers to how sharply an individual color pixel on a monitor appears. Each pixel is composed of three dots : red, blue and green. If the dots are badly mis-converged, the pixel will appear blurred one. All monitors have some convergence errors, but they differ in degree.

5.13 Video Standards

There are a variety of vide standards that define resolution and colors for displays. Support for a graphics standard is determined by both the monitor and the video adapter. The monitor must be able to show the resolution and colors defined by the standard, and the video adapter must be capable of transmitting the appropriate signals to the monitor.

Following are some popular video standards for PCs :

Video Graphics Array (VGA)
Super VGA (SVGA)
8514/A
XGA
TI 34010

Video Graphics Array (VGA)

VGA video standard was developed by IBM for personal computers. It has become a de facto standard for PCs. In graphics mode, the resolution is either 640 x 480 or 320 x 200 with 16 colors and 256 colors respectively. In text mode, VGA systems provide a resolution of 720 x 400 pixels. The total palette of colors is 2,62,144.

Unlike earlier graphics standards for PCs - MDA (Monochrome Display Adapter), CGA (Color/Graphics Adapter) and EGA (Enhanced Graphics Adapter), VGA uses analog signals rather than digital signals. Consequently, a monitor designed for one of the older standards will not be able to use VGA. Since its introduction in 1987, several other standards have been developed that offer greater resolution and more colors, but VGA remains the lowest common denominator. All PCs made today support VGA, and possibly some other more advanced standards.

Super VGA (SVGA)

SVGA is a set of graphics standard designed to offer greater resolution than VGA. There are several varieties of SVGA, each providing following different resolutions :

800 × 600 pixels
1024 × 768 pixels
1280 ×1024 pixels
1600 × 1200 pixels

All SVGA standards support a palette of 16 million colors, but the number of colors that can be displayed simultaneously is limited by the amount of video memory installed in a system. One SVGA system might display only 16 simultaneous colors while another displays the entire palette of 16 million colors. SVGA video standards are developed by a consortium of monitors and graphics manufacturers called **Video Electronics Standard Association (VESA).**

8514/A

The 8514/A video standard provides a resolution of 1024 × 768 pixels, which gives about 2.5 times resolution of VGA having 640 × 480 pixels. Like VGA, 8514/A provides a palette of 2,62,000 colors, of which 256 can be displayed at one time. On monochrome displays, 8514/A provides 64 shades of gray. Original version of 8514/A relied on interlacing technique that makes it possible provide resolution at low cost. Interlacing, however, carries a performance penalty, so many manufacturers produce non-interlaced 8514/A clones.

XGA

XGA stands for extended graphics array. It is a very high resolution graphics standard introduced by IBM in 1990. It was designed to replace the older 8514/A video standards. It provides the same resolutions i.e. 640 × 480 or 1024 × 768 pixels, but supports more simultaneous colors i.e. 65,000 rather than 256 colors. Additionally, XGA allows monitors to be non-interlaced.

TI 34010

TI 34010 is a video standard from Texas Instruments that supports a resolution of 1024 × 768. TI 34010 conforms to TI's Graphics Architecture (TIGA). Unlike IBM's 8514/A, which supports the same resolution, TI 34010 is non-interlaced.

5.14 Sound Cards and Speakers

An expansion board that enables a computer to manipulate and output sounds. Sound cards are necessary for nearly all CD-ROMs and have become a common place on modern PCs. Sound Cards enable the computer to output sound through speakers connected to the board, to record sound input from a microphone connected to the computer, and manipulate sound stored on a disk.

Nearly all sound cards support **MIDI (Musical Instrument Digital Interface)** and most sound cards are Sound Blaster compatible. Sound cards use two basic methods to translate digital data into analog sounds.

Frequency Modulation Synthesis mimics different musical instruments according to built-in formulas.

Wave-table Synthesis relies on recordings of actual instruments to produce sound. It produces more accurate sound but is a more expensive technique.

5.15 PRINTERS

A **printer** is a peripheral which produces a text and/or graphics of documents stored in electronic form, usually on physical print media such as paper or transparencies. Many printers are primarily used as local peripherals, and are attached by a printer cable or, in most new printers, a USB cable to a computer which serves as a document source. Some printers, commonly known as **network printers,** have built-in network interfaces, typically wireless and/or Ethernet based, and can serve as a hard copy device for any user on the network. Individual printers are often designed to support both local and network connected users at the same time. There are several printer technologies, the most common of which are:

the daisy wheel printer

the dot-matrix printer (also called impact matrix printer)

the inkjet printer and the bubble jet printer

the laser printer

Today, daisy wheel printers and matrix printers are hardly ever used.

5.16 CATEGORIES OF PRINTERS

A printer is an output device that produces a hard copy of data. The resolution of printer output is expressed as DPI. Printers can be classified into different types in several ways.

First, the printers can be divided into three categories by the way they print.

Serial Printers: Also called a character printer. Print a single character at a time. They are usually inexpensive and slow.

Line Printers: Print a line at a time. They are expensive and very fast. Line printers use a band, a chain, etc.

Page Printers: Also called a laser printer. Print a page at a time. They usually use a laser to produce page images. Quality is best. This is a little bit expensive, but the price of the personal laser printer is decreasing. The price range of the personal laser printer is around $400, today.

Second, printers can be classified into two forms according to the use of a hammer.

Impact Printers: Hammer hits ribbons, papers or print head. Dot-matrix and daisy-wheel printers are the example. Noisy.

Nonimpact Printers: They do not have the hammer and do not hit. An example is an ink-jet and laser printer.

So, let's take a closer look at the various types of printers.

5.16.1 CHARACTER PRINTERS

They are used to print only one character at a time. A typewriter is an example of a character printer. Some of character printers are described below.

5.16.1.1 DAISY-WHEEL PRINTER

Daisy-Wheel is a printer mechanism that uses any kind of hub (wheel) having a set of spokes at the margin of the hub. The wheel can be removed to use a different character set. The end of each spoke is a raised image of a type character. When the wheel is turned and the required character is aligned to the print hammer, the character is then struck into a ribbon and onto a paper with the hammer. Daisy-Wheel Printer prints typewriter-like very high quality characters. However, they are slower and less reliable than dot-matrix printers. Microcomputer users seldom use this printer, because the better dot-matrix printers and inexpensive laser printers are available today. The speeds of daisy-wheel printers range from 30 to 60 characters per second (cps).

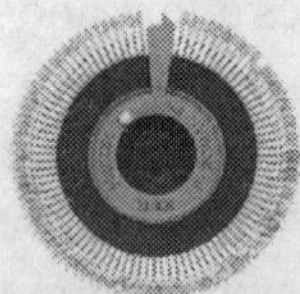

Figure 5.18: A daisy-wheel print wheel

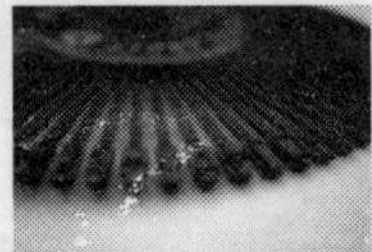

Figure 5.19: Plastic Daisy Wheel

5.16.1.2 DOT-MATRIX PRINTER

The **dot-matrix** printer allows you to print documents on paper thanks to the "back and forth" motion of a carriage housing a print head.

It has a print head containing a rectangular array of protruding wire pins,with the number of pins depending in the quality of the printer. Individual characters or graphics patterns are obtained by retracting certain pins so that the remaining pins form the pattern to the printed.

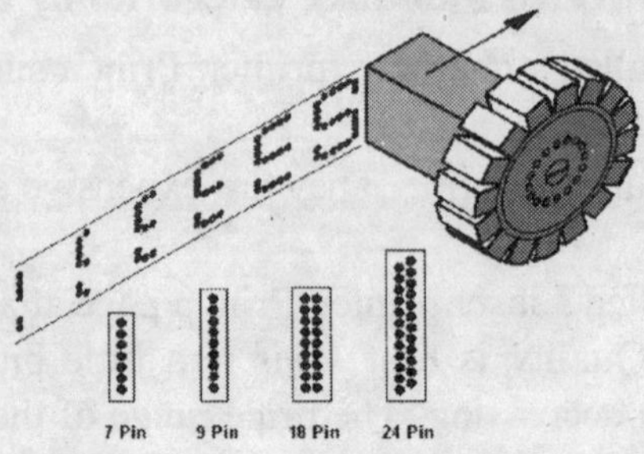

Figure 5.20: Dot Matrix Printer

Dot-matrix printers are printers that write characters and form graphic images using one or two columns of tiny dots on a print head. The dot hammer moving serially across the paper strikes an inked-ribbon and creates images on paper.

The print head travels from side to side across the paper and is made up of numerous pins which are pushed out to form the shape of each character.

The pins hit an ink ribbon against the paper so the characters are printed out.

The paper is usually continuous with holes down each side and perforations so the pages can be easily separated by tearing.

Because the pins make an impact against the paper the characters can be printed through several layers of self-carbonating paper to produce duplicate copies.

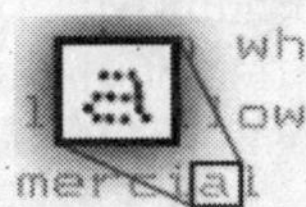

Figure 5.21: Dot Matrix Pins

An animation showing how head of a 21 pin dot-matrix printer moves across the paper, firing the pins that strike the ink against the paper.

5.16.1.3 CHARACTER MATRIX PRINTER

Character matrix printers are a category of computer printers (typically impact printers) that place characters from a fixed character set anywhere onto a fixed grid of possible locations on the page. Examples of these are daisy wheel printers, golf ball printers, chain printers, and band printers. A character printer prints one character at a time.

5.16.2 LINE PRINTERS

Line printers, as the name implies, print an entire line of text at a time. The **line printer** is a form of high speed impact printer in which one line of type is printed at a time. They are mostly associated with the early days of computing, but the technology is still in use. Print speeds of 600 to 1200 lines-per-minute (approximately 10 to 20 pages per minute) were common.

Figure 5.22: IBM 1403 line printer

Designs

Four principal designs existed:

Drum printers

Chain (train) printers

Band Printers

5.16.2.1 DRUM PRINTER

In a typical **drum printer** design, a fixed font character set is engraved onto the periphery of a number of print wheels, the number matching the number of columns (letters in a line) the printer could print. The wheels, joined to form a large drum (cylinder), spin at high speed and paper and an inked ribbon is stepped (moved) past the print position. As the desired character for each column passes the print position, a hammer strikes the paper from the rear and presses the paper against the ribbon and the drum, causing the desired character to be recorded on the continuous paper. Because the drum carrying the letterforms (characters) remains in constant motion, the strike-and-retreat action of the hammers had to be very fast. Typically, they were driven by voice coils mounted on the moving part of the hammer.

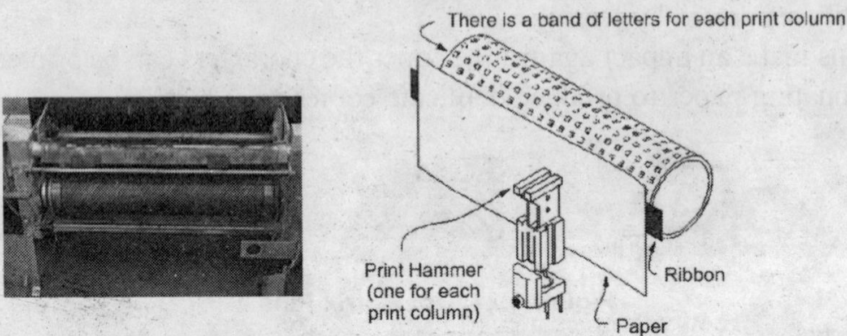

Figure 5.23: Drum printer

5.16.2.2 CHAIN PRINTER

A **chain printer** (also known as **train printers**) uses a printing mechanism that uses character typefaces linked together in a chain. The chain spins horizontally around a set of hammers aligned with each position. When the required character is in front of the selected print position, hammer in that position hits the paper into the ribbon against the character in the chain.

This printer is not commonly found around microcomputers, because it is a very expensive, high-speed machine designed originally for mainframes and minicomputers. Chain printers are very reliable and can speed up to 3000 lines per minute.

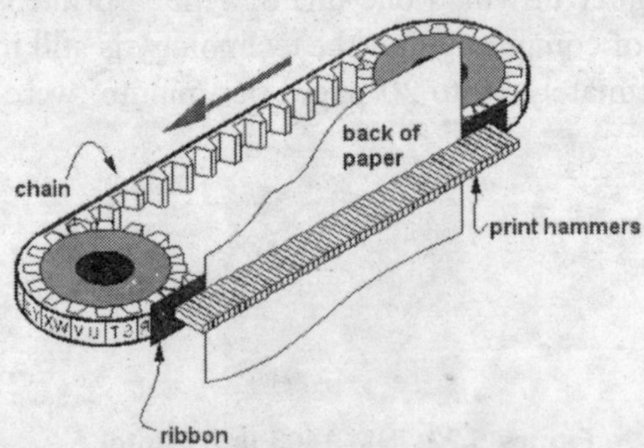

Figure 5.24: Chain printer

Character printers and line printers are called impact printers because they use electro-mechanical mechanism, which causes the character shape to strike against the paper and leave an image of the character on the paper.

5.16.2.3 BAND PRINTER

A band printer operates in a similar way except it uses a band instead of a chain and has fewer hammers. The hammers on a band printer are mounted on a carriage that moves across the paper to the appropriate print positions. Characters are rotated into place and struck by the hammers. Font styles can easily be changed by replacing a band or chain.

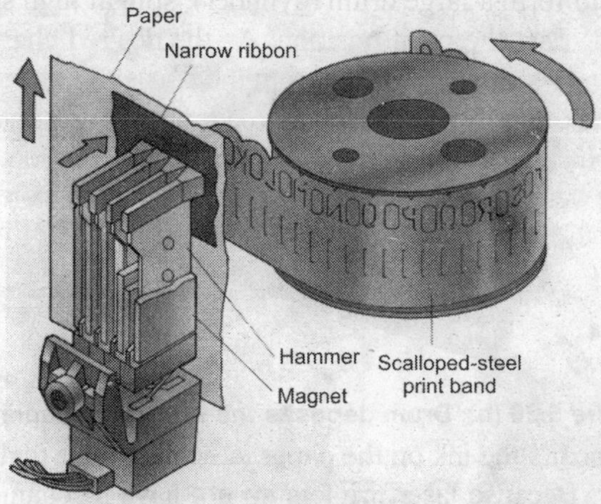

Fig. 5.25: Band Printer

(Paper sandwiched between Steel Band and Bank of Hammers)

5.16.3 PAGE PRINTERS

These are the very high speed non impact printers. They can produce documents at speeds of over 20,000 lines per minute. Electronics, xerography, lasers, and other technologies have made these high-volume systems possible. These techniques called electro-photographic techniques have developed from the paper copier technology. Page printers can produce pages of output at a rate equal to a photo copier.

5.16.3.1 LASER PRINTER

Laser printers are page printers that print one page at a time. It is a non-impact printer. A laser printer is a printer that uses the electro-photographic method used in a copy machine. A **laser printer** is a common type of computer printer that rapidly produces high quality text and graphics on plain paper.

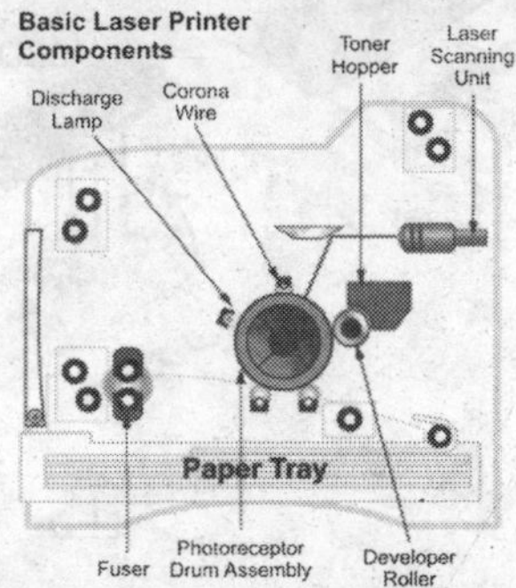

Figure 5.26 (a): The basic components of a laser printer

The **laser printers** produce quality print-outs inexpensively at a high print speed. However, these printers are mostly used in professional and semi-professional settings because of their high cost.

Laser printers use a technology that is close to that used by photocopiers. A laser printer is mainly made up of an elecrostatically charge photosensitive drum that attracts the ink in order to make a shape that will be deposited on the sheet of paper.

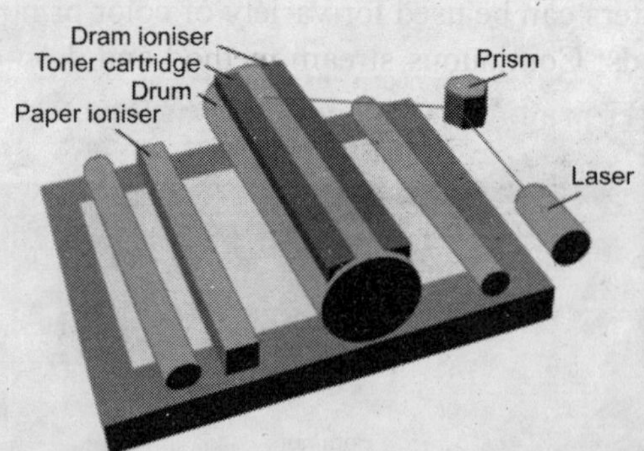

Figure 5.26 (b): Drum deposits the ink on the paper.

By turning, the drum deposits the ink on the paper. A heating wire (called a corona wire) finally attaches the ink to the paper. Because laser printers do not have mechanical heads, they are quick and quiet. Laser printers are faster than ink jet printers. Their speed is rated in **pages per minute (ppm).** Laser printers are more expensive than ink jets, but they are cheaper to run in the long term if you just need good quality black and white pages.

5.16.3.2 LED PRINTER

Another printer technology competes with laser printers: **LED** (*Light Emitting Diode*) technology. With this technology, an electroluminescent diode printhead polarises the drum with a very fine light ray, making very small dots. This technology is particularly well adapted for obtaining high resolutions (600, 1,200 or 2,400 dpi).

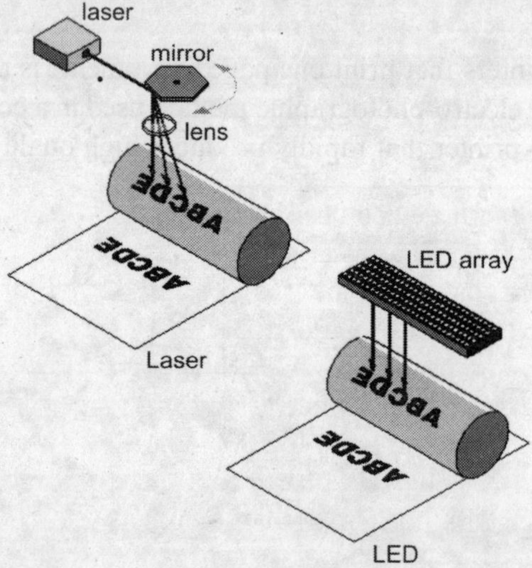

Figure 5.27: LED printer

Given that each diode is makes one point, print speed hardly affects resolution. Moreover, this technology lacks moving parts, which translates into less-expensive and more solid and reliable printers.

5.16.3.3 INKJET PRINTER

Ink-jet is a printer mechanism that sprays one or more color of ink at high speed onto the paper and produces high-quality printing. This printer also produces color printing as well as high-quality image. That is, ink-jet printers can be used for variety of color printing at a relatively low cost. Ink-jet printing has two methods: Continuous stream method and drop-on-demand method.

Inkjet printing, like laser printing, is a non-impact method.

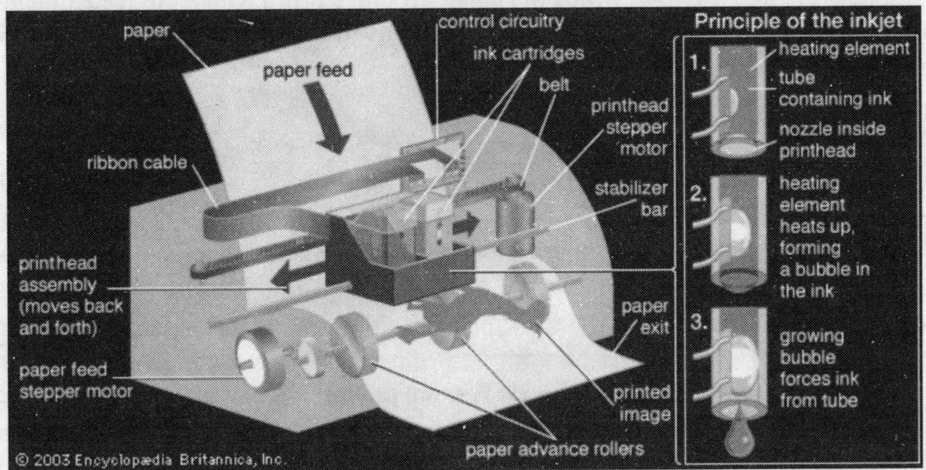

Figure 5.28: Ink Jet Printer

An **inkjet** printer is any printer that places extremely small droplets of ink onto paper to create an image. If you ever look at a piece of paper that has come out of an inkjet printer, you know that:

The dots are extremely small (usually between 50 and 60 microns in diameter), so small that they are tinier than the diameter of a human hair (70 microns)!

The dots are positioned very precisely, with resolutions of up to 1440x720 dots per inch (dpi).

The dots can have different colors combined together to create photo-quality images.

5.17 PLOTTER

A plotter is a special output device used to produce hardcopies of graphs and designs on the paper. A plotter is typically used to print large-format graphs or maps such as construction maps, engineering drawings and big posters. A plotter is a printer that interprets commands from a computer to make line drawings on paper with one or more automated pens. Unlike a regular printer, the plotter can draw continuous point-to-point lines directly from vector graphics files or commands. There are a number of different types of plotters: a drum plotter draws on paper wrapped around a drum which turns to produce one direction of the plot, while the pens move to provide the other direction; a flatbed plotter draws on paper placed on a flat surface; and an electrostatic plotter draws on negatively charged paper with positively charged toner.

Plotters were the first type of printer that could print with color and render graphics and full-size engineering drawings. As a rule, plotters are much more expensive than printers. They are most frequently used for CAE (computer-aided engineering) applications, such as CAD (computer-aided design) and CAM (computer-aided manufacturing). Hewlett-Packard is the leading vendor of plotters worldwide.

Plotters are divided into four types:

1. Drum plotters
2. Flatbed plotters

3. Inkjet plotters
4. LED plotters

5.17.1 DRUM PLOTTER

A drum plotter is pen plotter that wraps the paper around a drum with a pin feed attachment. The drum then rotates the paper as pens move across it and draw the image. It was the first output device used to print graphics and large engineering drawings.

Figure 5.29: A drum plotter

A drum plotter is also known as Roller Plotter. It consists of a drum or roller on which a paper is placed and the drum rotates back and forth to produce the graph on the paper. It also consists of mechanical device known as Robotic Drawing Arm that holds a set of colored ink pens or pencils. The Robotic Drawing Arm moves side to side as the paper are rolled back and forth through the roller. In this way, a perfect graph or map is created on the paper. This work is done under the control of computer. Drum Plotters are used to produce continuous output, such as plotting earthquake activity.

5.17.2 FLATBED PLOTTER

A flat-bed plotter is a mechanical drafting device used with many CAD programs for designers. The paper remains stationary on a flat surface while a pen moves across it horizontally and vertically. A flatbed plotter is also known as Table Plotter. It plots on paper that is spread and fixed over a rectangular flatbed table. The flatbed plotter uses two robotic drawing arms, each of which holds a set of colored ink pens or pencils. The drawing arms move over the stationary paper and draw the graph on the paper. Typically, the plot size is equal to the area of a bed. The plot size may be 20- by-50 feet. It is used in the design of cars, ships, aircrafts, buildings, highways etc. Flatbed plotter is very slow in drawing or printing graphs. The large and complicated drawing can take several hours to print. The main reason of the slow printing is due to the movement mechanical devices.

Figure 5.30: Flatbed Plotter

5.17.3 THE INKJET PLOTTER

This is the third kind of Plotter which is called as the Inkjet plotter. The inkjet plotter creates an image by spraying small droplets of ink onto a piece of paper. A popular choice for advertising agencies and graphic designers, inkjet plotters are used generally for large outputs, such as banners and billboards and large signs often seen on roadsides. They are available in thermal or piezoelectric models. Thermal inkjet plotters use heat to apply droplets of ink, while piezoelectric plotters use charged crystals to apply the ink. Inkjet plotters tend to produce better quality graphics than other types of plotters.

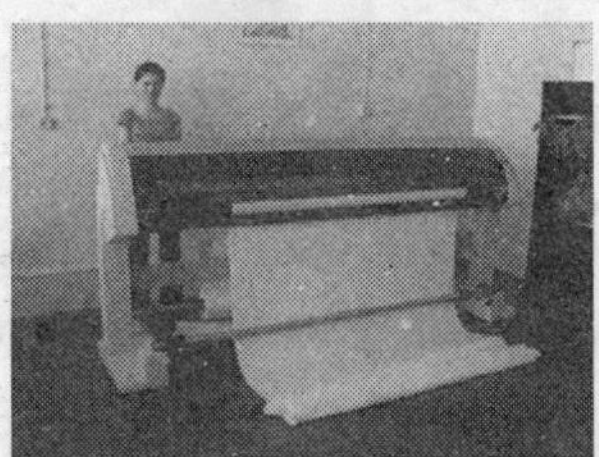

Figure 5.31: Inkjet plotter

In Today's world, virtually all inkjets create color. Low-end inkjets make the most of the three ink colors (cyan, magenta and yellow), but finally create a complex black that is often mud-spattered. Four-color inkjets make use of the black ink created for pure black printing alone.

5.17.4 LED PLOTTER

LED plotters are also called as Electrostatic plotters. It works similar to Laser Printers except that it uses LED as the heat source instead of Laser.

Figure 5.32: LED plotter

5.18 PROJECTOR

Projectors are display devices that project a computer created image. The computer sends the image data to the video card which then sends the video image to the projector. They are typically used for presentations or for viewing videos.

An output device that can take the display of a computer screen and project a large version of it onto a flat surface. **Projectors** are often used in meetings and presentations so that everyone in the room can view the presentation. In the picture to the right, are a ViewSonic projector and an example of what a projector may look like. Projectors used with computers are small devices that are rarely much larger than a toaster and typically weigh a few pounds.

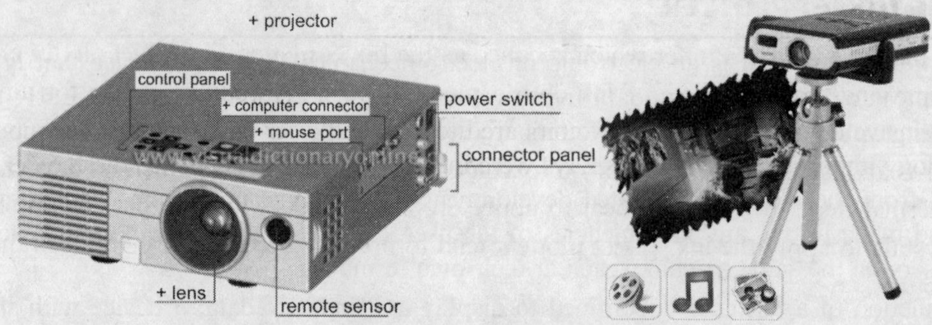

Figure 5.33: Projector

5.18.1 Multimedia Projector

Multimedia Projector is a hardware device, with which an image, such as the computer screen, is projected onto a flat screen. Image data is sent to the video card, by computer, which is then translated into a video image and sent to the projector. A projector is often used in meetings or to make presentations, because they allow for a large image to be shown, with which the display is available for a large audience.

Figure 5.34: Multimedia Projector

You may not have all kinds of output devices, but one multimedia projector is certainly necessary for you. For instance, the multimedia projector is really necessary for office. All computers might not have all the computer output devices, but it certainly does have one of the visual output devices, namely either a monitor or projector.

5.18.2 HANDHELD PROJECTOR

A **Handheld projector** (also known as a **pocket projector** or **mobile projector** or **pico projector)** is an emerging technology that applies the use of an image projector in a handheld device. It is a response to the emergence of compact portable devices such as mobile phones, personal digital assistants, and digital cameras, which have sufficient storage capacity to handle presentation materials but little space to accommodate an attached display screen. An important design characteristic of a handheld projector is the ability to project a clear image, regardless of the physical characteristics of the viewing surface.

5.19 TERMINALS

A **computer terminal** is an electronic or electromechanical hardware device that is used for entering data into, and displaying data from, a computer or a computing system. Early terminals were inexpensive devices but very slow compared to punched cards or paper tape for input, but as the technology improved and video displays were introduced, terminals pushed these older forms of interaction from the industry. A related development was timesharing systems, which evolved in parallel and made up for any inefficiencies of the user's typing ability with the ability to support multiple users on the same machine, each at their own terminal.

The function of a terminal is confined to display and input of data; a device with significant local programmable data processing capability may be called a "smart terminal" or fat client. A terminal that depends on the host computer for its processing power is called a dumb terminal or thin client. A personal computer can run software that emulates the function of a terminal, sometimes allowing concurrent use of local programs and access to a distant terminal host system.

5.19.1 SMART TERMINAL OR FAT CLIENT

A **fat client** (also called **heavy, rich,** or **thick client**) is a computer (client) in client-server architecture or networks that typically provides rich functionality independent of the central server. Originally known as just a 'client' or 'thick client', the name is contrasted to thin client, which describes a computer heavily dependent on a server's applications.

A fat client still requires at least periodic connection to a network or central server, but is often characterised by the ability to perform many functions without that connection. In contrast, a thin client generally does as little processing as possible and relies on accessing the server each time input data needs to be processed or validated.

5.19.2 DUMB TERMINAL OR THIN CLIENT

A **thin client** (sometimes also called a **lean** or **slim client**) is a computer or a computer program which depends heavily on some other computer (its server) to fulfill its traditional computational roles. This stands in contrast to the traditional fat client, a computer designed to take on these roles by itself. The exact roles assumed by the server may vary, from providing data persistence (for example, for diskless nodes) to actual information processing on the client's behalf.

Thin clients occur as components of a broader computer infrastructure, where many clients share their computations with the same server. As such, thin client infrastructures can be viewed as the amortization of some computing service across several user-interfaces. This is desirable in contexts where individual fat clients have much more functionality or power than the infrastructure either requires or uses.

The most common type of modern thin client is a low-end computer terminal which concentrates solely on providing a graphical user interface to the end-user. The remaining functionality, in particular the operating system, is provided by the server.

5.20 AUDIO

3D audio is a technique for giving more depth to traditional stereo sound. Typically, 3D sound or 3D audio is produced by placing a device in a room with Stereo Speakers. The device dynamically analyses the sound coming from the speakers and sends feedback to the sound system so that it can readjust the sound to give the impression that the speakers are further apart.

3D audio devices are particularly popular for improving computer audio where the speakers tend to be small and close together. There are a number of 3D audio devices that attach to a computer's sound card.

5.21 VOICE SYNTHESIS

Another emerging technology is voice synthesis and the computers that produce it. Voice synthesis is the process of electronically reproducing the human voice in recognizable patterns. Producing these patterns is an easy task. The English language and its rules of syntax are enough to confuse many humans. The voice response system usually is considered for applications requiring low-speed human-machine interaction. Audio response system is inexpensive. Such systems can be used with PCs. The TI **(Texas Instruments Company)** has developed a **"Speak and Spell"** system to teach children to spell and pronounce over 200 elementary words.

5.22 INPUT-OUTPUT PORTS

Input-output ports are material elements on the computer, allowing the system to communicate with exterior elements, in other words to exchange data, hence the name input-output interface (sometimes known as I/O interface).

5.22.1 SERIAL PORT

Serial ports (also called **RS-232,** after the name of the standard they refer to) represent the first interfaces to allow computers to exchange information with the "outside world". The term serial refers to data sent via a single wire: the bits are sent one after the other (refer to section on data transmission for a presentation on transmission modes).

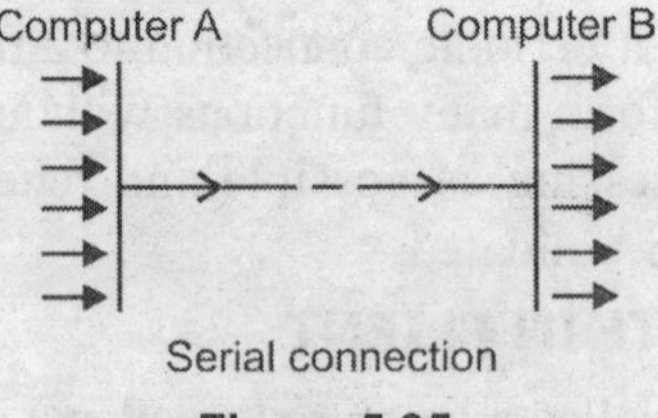

Figure 5.35

Serial ports were originally able to only send data and not receive it, hence two-way ports were developed (the ports on current computers are two-way); two-way serial ports therefore need two wires for communication.

Serial communication takes place asynchronously, meaning that no synchronisation signal (or clock) is required: the data may be sent at random intervals. In return, the peripheral must be able to distinguish the characters (one character is 8 bits in length) among the succession of bits which is sent. This is why, in this type of transmission, each character is preceded by a START bit and followed by a STOP bit. These control bits, which are needed for serial transmission, waste 20% of the bandwidth (for 10 bits sent, 8 are used to code the character and 2 are used for reception).

Serial ports are generally built into the mother board, which is why the connectors behind the casing and connected to the mother board by a wire cable can be used to connect an exterior element. Serial connectors generally have 9 or 25 pins and take the following form (DB9 and DB25 connectors respectively):

Figure 5.36

A personal computer generally has between one and four serial ports.

5.22.2 PARALLEL PORT

Parallel data transmission involves sending data simultaneously on several channels (wires). The parallel ports on personal computers can be used to send 8 bits (one octet) simultaneously via 8 wires.

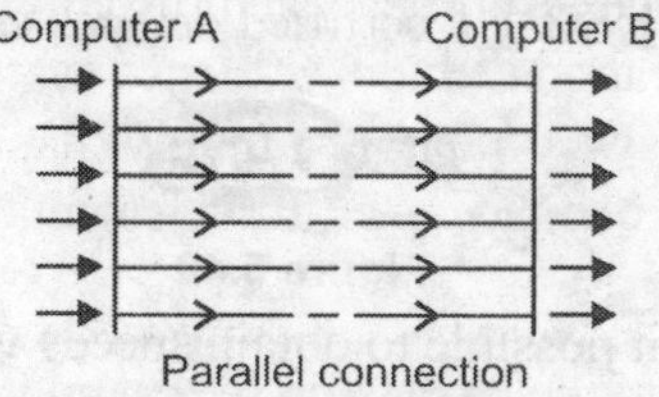

Figure 5.37

The first two-way parallel ports allowed for speeds of 2.4Mb/s. Enhanced parallel ports have been developed however to achieve higher speeds:

The EPP (Enhanced Parallel Port) achieves speeds of 8 to 16 Mbps

The ECP (Enhanced Capabilities Port), developed by Hewlett Packard and Microsoft. It has the same characteristics as the EPP with in addition a Plug and Play feature, allowing the computer to recognise the connected peripherals.

Parallel ports, like serial ports, are built into the mother board. DB25 connectors allow connection to an exterior element (e.g. a printer).

Figure 5.38

5.22.3 USB PORT

USB, or Universal Serial Bus, is a hardware bus standard that allows users to plug a peripheral device into a USB port and have it automatically configured and ready to use. It is one of the success stories of the personal computer. It not only works well, but also makes the life of the average computer user easier.

Figure 5.39

USB (Universal Serial Bus) is as its name suggests, based on serial type architecture. However, it is an input-output interface much quicker than standard serial ports. Serial architecture was used for this type of port for two main reasons:

Serial architecture gives the user a much higher clock rate than a parallel interface because a parallel interface does not support too high frequencies (in a high speed architecture, bits circulating on each wire arrive with lag, causing errors);

Serial cables are much cheaper than parallel cables.

5.22.3.1 USB STANDARDS

So, from 1995, the USB standard has been developed for connecting a wide range of devices.

The **USB 1.0** standard offers two modes of communication:

12 Mb/s in high speed mode,

1.5 Mb/s in low speed.

The **USB 1.1** standard provides several clarifications for USB device manufacturers but does not change anything in the speed. USB 1.1 certified devices carry the following logo:

Figure 5.40

The **USB 2.0** standard makes it possible to obtain speeds which can reach 480 Mbit/s/ USB 2.0 certified devices carry the following logo:

Figure 5.41

If there is no logo, the best way of determining if something is a low or high speed USB is to consult the product documentation insofar as the connectors are the same.

Compatibility between USB 1.0, 1.1 and 2.0 is assured. However, the use of a USB 2.0 device in a low speed USB port (i.e. 1.0 or 1.1) will limit the speed to 12Mbit/s maximum. Furthermore, the operating system is likely to display a message explaining that the speed will be restricted.

5.22.3.2 TYPES OF CONNECTORS

There are two types of USB connectors:

Connectors known as **type A,** where the shape is rectangular and generally used for less bandwidth intensive devices (keyboard, mouse, webcam, etc.);

Connectors known as **type B,** where the shape is square and mainly used for high speed devices (external hard disks, etc.);

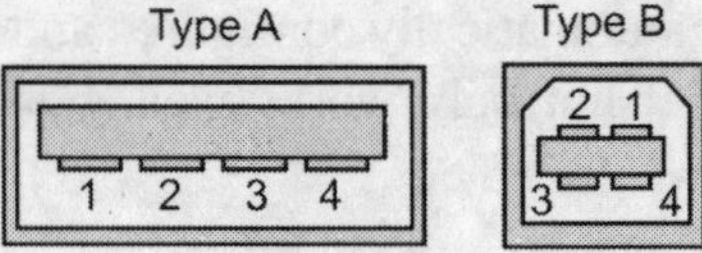

Figure 5.42

1. Power supply +5V (VBUS) 100mA maximum
2. Data (D–)
3. Data (D+)
4. Mass (GND)

5.22.3.3 OPERATION OF THE USB

One characteristic of USB architecture is that it can supply electricity to devices to which it connects, with a limit of 15 W maximum per device. To do so, it uses a cable made up of four wires (the GND mass, the BUS supply and two data wires called D– and D+).

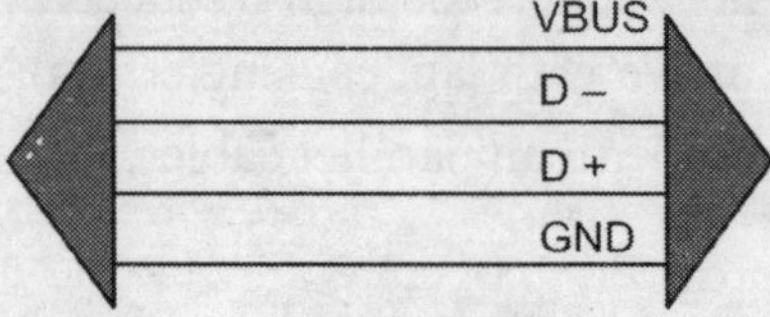

Figure 5.43

The USB standard allows devices to be chained by using a bus or star topology. So, devices can either be connected one to another or branched.

Branching is done using boxes called **"hubs"** comprising of a single input and several outputs. Some are active (supplying electric energy), others passive (power supplied by the computer).

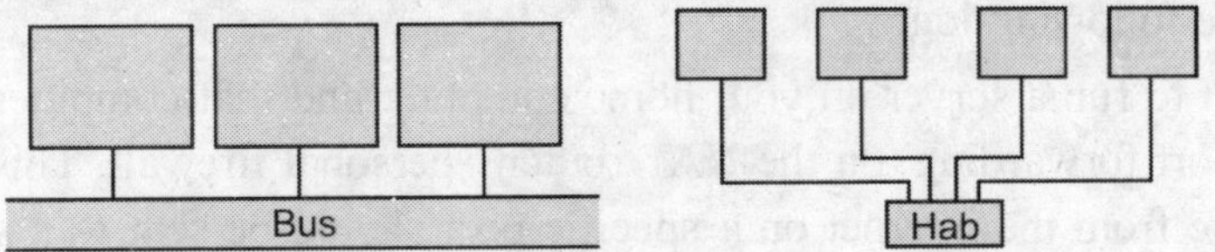

Figure 5.44

Communication between the host (computer) and devices is carried out according to a protocol (communication language) based on the token ring principle. This means that bandwidth is temporarily shared between all connected devices. The host (computer) issues a signal to begin the sequence every millisecond (ms), the time interval during which it will simultaneously give each device the opportunity to "speak". When the host wants to communicate with a device, it transmits a token (a data packet, containing the address of the device coded over 7 bits) designating a device, so it is the host that decides to "talk" with the devices. If the device recognises its address in the token, it sends a data packet (between 8 and 255 bytes) in response, if not it passes the packet to the other connected devices. Data is exchanged in this way is coded according to NRZI coding.

Since the address is coded over 7 bits, 128 devices (2^7) can simultaneously be connected to a port of this type. In reality, it is advisable to reduce this number to 127 because the 0 address is a reserved address.

Due to the maximum length of the cable between two devices of 5 metres and a maximum number of 5 hubs (supplied), it is possible to create a chain 25 meters in length.

USB ports support **hot plug and play.** So, devices can be connected without turning off the computer **(hot plug)**. When a device is connected to the host it detects the addition of a new item thanks to a change in the tension between the D+ and D- wires. At this time, the computer sends an initialisation signal to the device for 10ms, then it supplies the current using the GND and VBUS wires (up to 100mA). The device is then supplied with electric current and temporarily takes over the default address (0 address). The following stage consists of supplying it with its definitive address (this is the listing procedure). To do so, the computer interrogates devices already connected to know their addresses and allocates a new one, which identifies it by return. The host, having all the necessary characteristics is then able to load the appropriate driver.

5.22.4 FIREWALL PORT

To understand a firewall port, we must first understand IP Ports.

If the internet were radio, IP would be the radio waves and IP Ports would be the channels or frequencies. Every computer program that uses the internet runs on a port. One of the most common ports is 80. This port is used for the web. All browsers and web servers use this port to communicate together. Email uses a different port, mostly port 25.

A **firewall port,** directly relates to an IP port. Sometimes you will need to 'open a port' in your firewall protection or router for a program to operate. Most programmers these days are aware that people use firewalls and routers so they try to make their software fully compatible with them. There are occasionally still programs that need some manual configuration. This is most often the case when you try to run a 'server' on your home network. Some of the most common servers that people like to run are game servers. FireWire connectors and cables can be easily spotted thanks to their shape as well as the following logo:

When you want to run a server on your home computer and that computer is behind a firewall you must enable 'port forwarding' on the NAT router / personal firewall. This tells the router that any incoming traffic from the internet on a specific port should be sent to a specific computer on your network.

You will need three items of information to enable port forwarding.

(1) What port does the program use?

(2) What is the IP address of the local computer that is running the program?

(3) What is the IP address your internet connection?

Let's say you wanted to run a Rainbow 6 game server. Rainbow 6 uses port 2346. On the computer that runs the rainbow 6 server go to a command prompt and type IPCONFIG. This will show the IP address. It should be something like 192.168.0.3. Lastly, log into the administration screen of your NAT router/firewall. On one of the status screens it should show you the WAN IP address or Internet IP address.

Now, go to the 'port forwarding' or 'server' area of your router administration. It will be different on every brand router so you will need to find it. Next set up port 2346 to foreword to 192.168.0.3. Now you can tell your friends to contact your server at the WAN IP address you got from your router.

Now if you were to run a port scan of your WAN IP address you would find that 2346 is no longer blocked.

5.22.5 FIREWIRE BUS (IEEE 1394)

The **IEEE 1394** bus (name of the standard to which it makes reference) was developed at the end of 1995 in order to provide an interconnection system that allows data to circulate at a high speed and in real time. The company Apple gave it the commercial name **"FireWire"**, which is how it is most commonly known. Sony also gave it commercial name, **i.Link.** Texas Instruments preferred to call it Lynx.

FireWire is a port that exists on some computers that allows you to connect peripherals (particularly digital cameras) at a very high bandwidth. There are expansion boards (generally in PCI or PC Card / PCMCIA format) that allow you to equip a computer with FireWire connectors. FireWire connectors and cables can be easily spotted thanks to their shape as well as the following logo:

Fire Wire
Figure 5.45

5.22.5.1 FIREWIRE STANDARDS

There are different FireWire standards that allow you to obtain the following bandwidths:

Standard	Theoretical Bandwidth
IEEE 1394a	
IEEE 1394a-S100	100 Mbit/s
IEEE 1394a-S200	200 Mbit/s
IEEE 1394a-S400	400 Mbit/s
IEEE 1394b	
IEEE 1394b-S800	800 Mbit/s
IEEE 1394b-S1200	1,200 Mbit/s
IEEE 1394b-S1600	1,600 Mbit/s
IEEE 1394b-S3200	3,200 Mbit/s

The **IEEE 1394b** standard is also called **FireWire 2** or **FireWire Gigabit.**

5.22.5.2 FIREWIRE CONNECTORS

There are different FireWire connectors for each of the IEEE 1394 standards.

The IEEE 1394a standard specifies two connectors:

Connectors 1394a-1995:

Connectors 1394a-2000, called **mini-DV** because they are used on Digital Video (DV) cameras:

The IEEE 1394b standard specifies two types of connectors that are designed so that 1394b-Beta cables can be plugged into Beta and Bilingual connectors, but 1394b Bilingual cables can only be plugged into Bilingual connectors:

1394b Beta connectors:

1394b Bilingual connectors:

5.22.5.3 HOW THE FIREWIRE BUS WORKS

The IEEE 1394 bus has about the same structure as the USB bus except that it is a cable made up of six wires (2 pairs for the data and the clock and 2 wires for the power supply) that allow it to reach a bandwidth of 800 Mb/s (soon it should be able to reach 1.6 Gb/s, or even 3.2 Gb/s down the road). The two wires for the clock is the major difference between the USB bus and the IEEE 1394 bus, i.e. the possibility to operate in two transfer modes:

Asynchronous transfer mode: this mode is based on a transmission of packets at variable time intervals. This means that the host sends a data packet and waits to receive a receipt notification from the peripheral. If the host receives a receipt notification, it sends the next data packet. Otherwise, the first packet is resent after a certain period of time.

Synchronous mode: this mode allows data packets of specific sizes to be sent in regular intervals. A node called Cycle Master is in charge of sending a synchronisation packet (called a Cycle Start packet) every 125 microseconds. This way, no receipt notification is necessary, which guarantees a set bandwidth. Moreover, given that no receipt notification is necessary, the method of addressing a peripheral is simplified and the saved bandwidth allows you to gain throughput.

Another innovation of the IEEE 1394 standard: bridges (systems that allow you to link buses to other buses) can be used. Peripheral addresses are set with a node (i.e. peripheral) identifier encoded on 16 bits. This identifier is divided into two fields: a 10-bit field that identifies the bridge and a 6-bit field that specifies the node. Therefore, it is possible to connect 1,023 bridges (or $2^{10} - 1$) on which there can be 63 nodes (or $2^6 - 1$), which means it is possible to address 65,535 peripherals! The IEEE 1394 standard allows hot swapping. While the USB bus is intended for peripherals that do not require a lot of resources (e.g. a mouse or a keyboard), the IEEE 1394 bandwidth is larger and is intended to be used for new, unknown multimedia (video acquisition, etc.).

EXERCISES

1. What are input devices?
2. What do you mean by keyboard?
3. Explain the concept of mouse?
4. Explain the speech recognition system in detail?
5. What do you mean by digital camera?
6. Explain the working of scanners?
7. What do you mean by output devices?
8. What are printers? Explain the various types of printers in detail?
9. Explain the various types of plotters?
10. What do you mean by monitor?
11. Explain the various types of monitors?
12. What do you mean by projector?
13. State the necessities of Input and Output devices.
14. What are the reasons for the visual display unit to be more popular than punched card reader?
15. What is a Keyboard ? How does a simple keyboard differ from an ergonomically designed keyboard.
16. How does VDU act as input as well as output device ?
17. Differentiate between 'hardcopy' and 'softcopy' devices.
18. Name any two devices that can be used to output graphs and pictures.
19. What are the most extensively used input devices ?
20. Why punched card devices are not used extensively nowadays ?
21. Compare the advantages and limitations of a mouse and a keyboard as data input devices ?
22. In what circumstances line printers are preferred over dot matrix printers ?
23. What is meant by OMR ? Explain its functioning.
24. What are the most extensively used output devices ?

25. How do sound cards and speakers work as output devices ?
26. What are the advantages and disadvantages of MICR technology ?
27. How computer accept input from the keyboard ? Explain.
28. What is a plotter ? State their types and explain the functioning of each.
29. What are two pointing devices used for data input, and how do they work ?
30. How does analog monitor differ from digital monitors ?
31. What are the two types of printers that are popularly used ?
32. What is the relationship between a joystick and a graphic cursor ?
33. How do point-of-sale (POS) terminals work ?
34. What are the different types of printers ?
35. Describe an application for voice-recognizer.
36. What is the criteria for classification of printers ?
37. What is a plotter and how does it work ?
38. How can the quality of a DMP be controlled ?
39. How do Financial Transaction Terminals work ? Also state their merits and demerits.
40. What are voice-synthesizers ? State their importance.
41. Discuss relative merits and demerits of DMP, Daisywheel printer and Line printers.
42. What are thermal printers and how do they work ?
43. What is the difference between a laser printer and a LED printer ?
44. What is COM ? Also give its advantages and disadvantages.
45. Distinguish among character, line and page printers.
46. What do you understand by 3D audio ?
47. What is the difference between an impact and an non-impact printer ?
48. What does MICR stand for ? State the functioning of MICR input devices.
49. What is a monitor and how does it work ?
50. What is a mouse ? How does it point on to the screen ? Explain its working.
51. Which devices can provide us with graphical output ?
52. What are RGB monitors ? Explain their working.
53. What are the major characteristics of monitors ?
54. What is a joystick ? Where is it used ? Explain.
55. What is meant interlacing ? How does it affect the quality of display systems ?
56. What is an output device ? What are the major output devices for a computer ?
57. Is video camera an input device ? Justify your answer.
58. What are the effects of folding or stapling a MICR cheque ? How does it effect the data stored?
59. What is refresh rate ? What will happen if the refresh rate is not uniformly controlled ?
60. What are the different video standards ?
61. What do you mean by imaging ? Where is it beneficial ?
62. Identify the different types of printers and give a brief description of each.
63. What are scanners ? Where are they used ? Describe different types of scanners.
64. What does VESA stand for ? State its contribution in developing video standards.
65. What do you mean by VGA, SVGA, 5814/A, XGA and TI 34010 ?
66. What are the similarities and dissimilarities between a light pen and touch screen ?

67. What are the two most common output devices used with computers ? For what is each of them used ?
68. What do the bars on a data carrier represent ?
69. What is the difference between a Chain and band line-printers ?
70. What is a laser printer ? Explain its working.
71. What are bar codes ? Give two applications of bar codes.
72. Name an impact printer that prints fully formed characters.
73. List the following in order of their increasing resolution : SVGA, CGA, EGA, VGA.
74. How can you control the quality of a laser printer ? Explain.
75. What is OCR ? Explain its working.
76. Which output device generates graphs with the greatest precision, a pen plotter or a dot-matrix printer ?
77. How does a touch-screen works, and where could it be used ?
78. What are the pros and cons of using a plotter for output ?
79. What is a digitizer ? State its types.
80. Name a device that other than monitor that produces soft-copy output ?
81. Which kind of printer can produce near-typeset quality output ?
82. What are Touch Screens ? How do they differ from Touch Pads ?
83. What characterizes printer ?
84. List some relative advantages and disadvantages of CRT and flat panel monitors.
85. What are Vision Systems ? State their importance.
86. Explain how MICR cheques are useful in banks ?
87. What is the purpose of a point-of-sale terminals and financial-transaction terminals ?

Computer Memory and Secondary Storage

6.1 INTRODUCTION

Memory is that portion of a computer system that is used for the storage and subsequent retrieval of data and instructions. Memory is a quite essential component of digital computer. Computer memory exhibits perhaps the widest range of type, technology, organization, performance, and cost of any feature of a computer system.

6.2 CHARACTERISTICS OF MEMORY SYSTEMS

The complex subject of computer memory is made more manageable if we classify memory systems according to their key characteristics. The most important of these are listed in **Table 6.1**

Table 6.1 : Key Characteristics of Computer Memory Systems

(a) Location
- CPU
- Internal (main)
- External (secondary)

(b) Capacity
- Word size
- Number of words

(c) Unit of transfer
- Word
- Block

(d) **Access Method**
– Sequential access
– Direct access
– Random access
– Associative access

(e) **Performance**
– Access time
– Cycle time
– Transfer rate

(f) **Physical type**
– Semiconductor
– Magnetic

(g) **Physical Characteristics**
– Volatile/Nonvolatile
– Erasable/Non-erasable

(h) **Organization**

Location

Let us begin with the location of the memory. There is memory both internal and external to the computer. Internal memory is often its main memory. but there are other forms of internal memory. The CPU requires its own local memory, in the form registers. External memory consists of peripheral storage devices, such as disk and tape, that are accessible to the CPU via I/O controllers.

Capacity

Next characteristic of memory is its capacity. For internal memory, this is typically expressed in terms of bytes or words. External memory capacity is typically expressed in terms of bytes or Kbytes (KB) or Mbytes (MB). The storage capacity can be expressed in terms of Bytes. Few higher storage units are given below :

1 KB (Kilo Byte)	= 1024 Bytes	= 2^{10} Bytes
1 MB (Mega Byte)	= 1024 KB	= 2^{20} Bytes
1 GB (Giga Byte)	= 1024 MB	= 2^{30} Bytes
1 TB (Tera Byte)	= 1024 GB	= 2^{40} Bytes
1 PB (Peta Byte)	= 1024 TB	= 2^{50} Bytes
1 EB (Exa Byte)	= 1024 PB	= 2^{60} Bytes
1 ZB (Zetta Byte)	= 1024 EB	= 2^{70} Bytes
1 YB (Yetta Byte)	= 1024 ZB	= 2^{80} Bytes

Unit of Transfer

A related concept is the unit of transfer. For internal memory, the unit of transfer is equal to the number of data lines into and out of the memory module. This is often equal to the word length, but sometimes may not be. For main memory, this is the number of bits read out into memory at a time. For external memory, data are often transferred in much larger units than a word, and these are referred to as blocks.

Access Method

One of the sharpest distinctions among memory types is method of accessing units of data. Four types may be distinguished :

Sequential Access: Memory is organized into units of data, called records. access must be made in a specific linear sequence. Stored addressing information is used to separate records and assist in the retrieval process. A shared read/write mechanism is used, and this must be moved from its current location to the desired location, passing and rejecting each intermediate record.

Thus the time to access an arbitrary record is highly variable. Tape units are sequential access.

Direct Access: As with sequential access, direct access involves a shared read/write mechanism. however, individual blocks or records have a unique address based on physical location. access is accomplished by direct access to reach a general vicinity plus sequential searching, counting, or waiting to reach the final location. Again, access time is variable. Disk units are direct access.

Random Access: Each addressable location in memory has a unique, physically wired-in addressing mechanism. the time to access a given location is independent of the sequence of prior accesses and is constant. Thus any location can be selected at random and directly addressed and accessed. Main memory systems are random access.

Associative: This is a random-access type of memory that enables one to make a comparison of desired bit locations within a word for a specified match, and to do this for all words simultaneously. Thus a word is retrieved based on a portion of its contents rather than its address. As with ordinary random-access memory, each location has its own addressing mechanism, and retrieval time is constant independent of location or prior access patterns. Cache memories may employ associative access.

Performance

From user's point of view, the two most important characteristics of memory are capacity and performance. Three performance parameters are used :

Access Time: For random-access memory, this is the time it takes to perform a read or write operation, i.e., the time from the instant that an address is presented to the memory to the instant that data have been stored or make available for use. For non-random-access memory, access time is the time it takes to position the read-write mechanism at desired location.

Memory Cycle Time: This concept is primarily applied to random-access memory and consists of the access time plus any additional time required before a second access can commence. This additional time may be required for transients to die out on signal lines or to regenerate data if they are read destructively.

Transfer Rate: This is the rate at which data can be transferred into or out of a memory unit. For random access memory, it is equal to 1/(Cycle Time). For a non-random-access memory, the following relationship holds :

$$T_N = T_A + N/R$$

where

T_N = Average time to read or write N bits

T_A = Average access time
N = Number of bits
R = Transfer rate in bits per second (bps)

Physical Type

A variety of physical types of memory have been employed. The two most common types today are semiconductor memory and magnetic memory.

Physical Characteristic

Several physical characteristics of data storage are important. In a volatile memory, information decays naturally or is lost when electrical power is switched off. In a non-volatile memory, information once recorded remains without deterioration until deliberately changed; no electrical power is needed to retain information. Magnetic memories are non-volatile whereas semiconductor memory may either be volatile or non-volatile.

Non-erasable memory can not be altered, except by destroying the storage unit. Semiconductor memory of this type is known as read-only memory (ROM). A practical non-erasable memory must also be non-volatile.

Organization

For random-access memory, the organization is a key design issue. By organization is meant the physical arrangement of bits to form words. The obvious arrangement is not always used.

6.3 MEMORY HIERARCHY

The design constraints on a computer's memory can be summed up by three questions:

How Much ?
How Fast ?
How Expensive ?

How Much ?

The question of how much is open-ended. If the capacity is there, applications will likely be developed to use it.

How Fast ?

The question of how fast is, in a sense, easier to answer. To achieve greatest performance, the memory must be able to keep up with the CPU. That is, as the CPU is executing instructions, we would not want it to have to pause waiting for instructions or operands.

How Expensive ?

The final question must also be considered. For a practical system, the cost of memory must be reasonable in relationship to other components.

As might be expected, there is trade-off among the three key characteristics of memory, namely, cost, capacity, and access time. At any given time, a variety of technologies are used to implement memory systems. Across this spectrum of technologies, the following relationship holds :

Smaller access time, greater cost per bit
Greater capacity, smaller cost per bit
Greater capacity, greater access time

The dilemma facing the designer is clear. The designer would like to use memory technologies that provide for large-capacity memory, both because the capacity is needed and because the cost per bit is low. However, to meet performance requirements, the designer needs to use expensive, relatively lower-capacity memories with fast access time.

The way out of this dilemma is not to rely on a single memory component or technology, but to employ a memory hierarchy. A typical memory hierarchy is illustrated in **Fig. 6.1.**

As one goes down the hierarchy, the following occur:

(a) Decreasing cost per bit
(b) Increasing capacity
(c) Increasing access time
(d) Decreasing frequency of access of the memory by the CPU

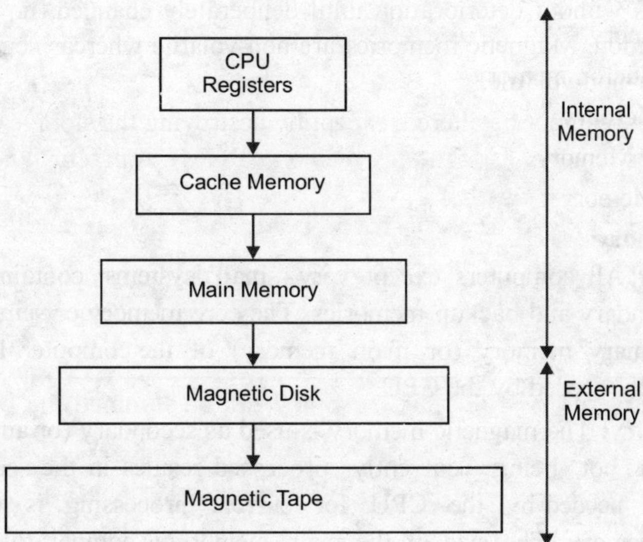

Fig 6.1 : The Memory Hierarchy

Thus smaller, more expensive, faster memories are supplemented by larger, cheaper, slower memories. The key to success of this organization is the decreasing frequency of access.

Main memory is the principal internal memory system of the computer. Each location in the main memory has a unique address and most instructions refer to a main memory address. Main memory is sometimes extended with a higher speed, smaller cache which is not visible to the programmer or to the CPU. The main memory and its extensions are typically volatile.

Data are stored more permanently on external mass storage devices. These are used to storage program and data files and are usually visible to the programmer only in terms of files and records rather than individual bytes or words. Magnetic disk and tape are the most commonly used external mass storage devices. Magnetic disk is also used to provide an extension to main memory known as virtual storage or virtual memory.

6.4 DESIRABLE CHARACTERISTICS OF MEMORY UNIT

The structure of the memory unit is perhaps the most important characteristic of a computer system. Some desirable features of the smallest constituent of the memory unit, i.e., binary cell are as :

It must be very fast.

It must be very compact in size.

It must have two stable states.

It must be capable of switching infinite number of times between these stable states.

Cost should be very low.

Time taken for reading and writing onto the binary cell should be very less.

Power consumption must be as small as possible.

6.5 TYPES OF MEMORY

At present the following three kinds of memory are commonly used in modern computers :

(a) Primary Memory

Core Memory

Semiconductor memory

(b) Secondary Memory

Magnetic Memory

Optical Memory

(c) Backup Memory

Primary Memory: All computers except very small systems contain all types of memory, namely, primary, secondary and backup memories. The core memory or semiconductor memory is employed as the primary memory (or main memory) of the computer. It stores programs and data which are currently needed by the CPU.

Secondary Memory: The magnetic memory is used as secondary (or auxiliary) memory. The information which is not being currently processed resides in the secondary memory. The information which is needed by the CPU for current processing is transferred from the secondary to main memory. The size of the main memory is comparatively much smaller than that of the secondary memory because of its high cost. The CPU communicates directly with the memory. As the CPU employs semiconductor technology and has very high speed, its matching memory must be very fast. Only semiconductor devices can provide the matching speed. Thus the main memory also must employ semiconductor technology. RAM and ROM ICs are used as the main memory of the computer. RAMs are volatile, i.e., their contents are erased when power goes off.

The auxiliary memory is employed for mass storage of programs, data and other information. Auxiliary memory has much larger capacity than main memory and is used to store system software, assemblers, compilers, useful packages, large data files etc. Auxiliary memory should not be of volatile nature but rather must be capable of storing information permanently. Magnetic memory has this property and thus retains the information once it is stored onto it. The magnetic memories such as hard disks and floppy disks are the most common secondary memories used in computers.

Backup Memory: Backup memory is used to store the copy of the important programs such as operating system, compilers etc. Floppy disks and magnetic tapes can be employed as backup storage. These programs are generally available in the secondary memory but their copies are also kept in the backup memory so that they can be reloaded into the secondary memory in case the programs stored in the secondary memory are lost accidentally or due to any other reason.

6.6 CORE MEMORY

This type of memory was introduced in the year 1955. It consists of tiny cores of doughnut-shaped objects called cores. The cores are made of ferromagnetic material. The individual cores are strung on wires to form a core plane. Several core planes are stacked one over the other to form a core stack.

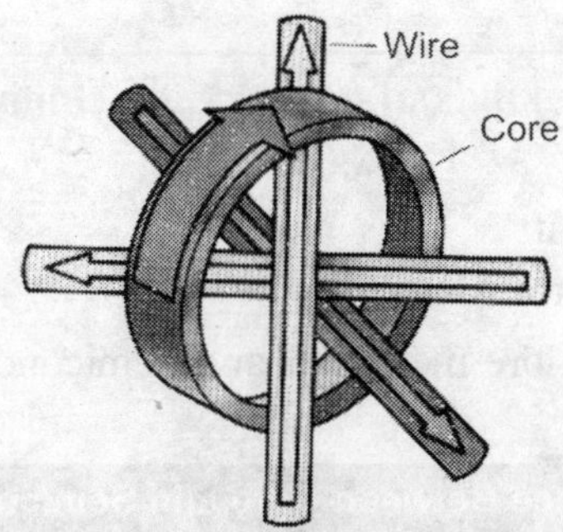

Fig. 6.2: Core Memory (One Core Cell)

The number of planes upon will depend upon the number of bits in a word. Thus, a 16-bit word will have a series of 17 planes including one plane for parity-checking. The actual number of elements in each plane will depend upon the memory size of the computer.

A basic principle of physics states that if a core is threaded by a wire carrying an electric current, the core will be magnetized in a certain direction, called its polarity, which depends upon the direction of the current through the wire.

The core can be put into one of two states. Furthermore, once the core is magnetized, it will keep its ***polarity*** even when the current is removed. It will change its polarity only when a current is sent through the wire in the opposite direction.

Now, one wants to be able to magnetize one core at a time; but it would be extremely inefficient to have one wire for each core. Therefore, cores are threaded by a grid of wires such that each core is threaded by two of the wires which are perpendicular to each other. Then, if currents of half the required strength are sent through the two wires threading a certain core, only that core is magnetized.

Reading the polarity of a given bit requires two additional wires, a sense wire and an inhibit wire, passing through the core. First, the computer will polarize the core in some given direction, say 0; then the computer will polarize the core in the opposite direction, 1. If initially the core was 0, then no change in the polarity of the core takes place in the first step; in particular, no current flows through the sense wire, which informs the computer that that core is 0. In the second step, in this case, the computer will simultaneously put a current through the inhibit wire while it attempts to write a 1. This will prevent a change in polarity of the core, so that it remains 0 after it is read. On the other hand, if the core was initially was initially 1, the first step will change the polarity of the core to 0. This will send a current through the sense wire, informing the computer that the core initially contained a 1. The second step restores the core to 1. The magnetic cores are stacked in parallel planes for the actual storage of data.

6.7 SEMICONDUCTOR MEMORY

The complete memory unit may be constructed from either bipolar or field-effect transistors on a single silicon chip, which may be referred to as Semi-conductor Memory. These were introduced by IBM in 1971. The semiconductor storage operates on the principle of a flip-flop in which the switch is set to a 0 and 1 position by a Write command which sets or restores the flip-flop.

The semiconductor memory is :

Faster
Compact
Lighter
Consumes less power
Static device
Having no rotating part in it

Core Memory Vs Semiconductor Memory

The main difference between Core memories and Semiconductor Memories are enumerated in Table 6.2:

Table 6.2 : Difference Between Core and Semiconductor Memories

S.NO	CORE MEMORY	SEMICONDUCTOR MEMORY
1.	Non-volatile	Generally Volatile
2.	Destructive readout	Non-destructive readout
3.	Limited range of read & write cycle times	Wide range of read & write cycle times
4.	Moderately priced	Low to moderately priced
5.	High power consumption	Low power consumption
6.	Best for large memories	Best for small or medium-sized memories
7.	Relatively large access time	Short access time
8.	Available only in large blocks	Available in wide variety of sizes
9.	Relatively large and heavy	Relatively small and light

6.8 TYPES OF SEMICONDUCTOR MEMORIES

Semiconductor memories are of two types :

(i) RAM (random access memory) and

(ii) ROM (read only memory)

6.8.1 Random Access Memory (RAM)

It is a type of computer memory that can be accessed randomly; that is, any byte of memory can be accessed without touching the preceding bytes. RAM is the most common type of memory found in computers and other devices, such as printers.

This type of memory is pronounced as **'ramm'** and can be used both for reading as well as writing and that is why RAM is also known as Read/Write memory. It is accessible to users. The user enters his program and data into RAM. It possesses random access property. The access time is same for each memory location. RAM is a volatile memory. The information stored into it is retained in it as long as the power supply is on. As soon as the power supply goes off (or interrupted) its stored information is lost. The programmer has to load his program and data into the RAM when the power is resumed.

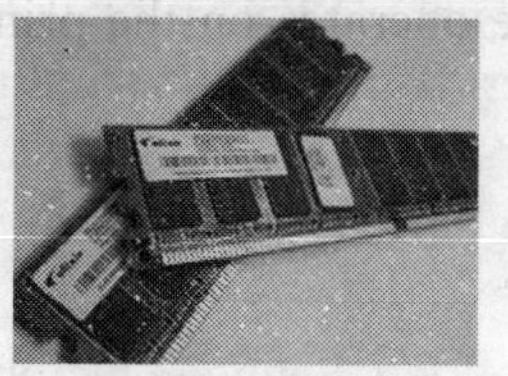

Figure 6.3: Random-Access Memory

It is the same as the main memory of computer system. RAM is not the correct name of R/W memory because both RAM and ROM possess random access property. But R/W memory has been called RAM since long and in practice it has become an established name. Thus R/W memory is commonly called RAM.

There are two basic types of RAM:

(a) Static RAM (SRAM) and

(b) Dynamic RAM (DRAM)

6.8.1.1 Static RAM (SRAM) Vs Dynamic RAM (DRAM)

Static RAMs retain stored information only as long as the power supply is on whereas a dynamic RAM loses its stored information in a very short time (in milli seconds) even though the power supply is on. In a dynamic RAM a binary state is stored on the gate to source to stray capacitor of a transistor of the MOS memory circuit. The presence of charge on the stray capacitor represents 1, and the absence of charge on the stray capacitor represents 0. The charge on these capacitors leak away as a result of normal leakage in a few milliseconds (msec). Therefore, dynamic RAMs have to be refreshed periodically, generally every 2 msec. The dynamic RAMs are cheaper and have high packing density and moderate speed. They consume less power. They are used where large capacity of memory is needed. Static RAMs are costlier and consume more power. They do not need refreshing circuitry. They have higher speed than dynamic RAMs.

In the table below we summarize the main differences between dynamic RAM (DRAM) and static RAM (SRAM).

Table 6.3: SRAM Vs DRAM

Feature	Dynamic RAM (DRAM)	Static RAM (SRAM)
Storage circuit	Capacitor	Flip-flop
Transfer speed	Slower than CPU	Same as CPU
Latency	High	Low
Density	High	Low
Power Consumption	Low	High
Cost	Cheap	Expensive

Even though static RAM is faster than dynamic RAM, its disadvantages prevent it from being used as the main RAM circuit.

Examples of SRAMs are :

Hitachi HM 6116, 2 K × 8

HM 6264, 8 K × 8

HM 6287, 64 K × 1;

NEC µPD43256, 32 k × 8; etc.

The refreshing and control circuitry for a dynamic RAM may be either on the chip itself or on a separate IC called dynamic RAM controller. If the DRAM and its refresh and control circuitry are on the same IC, it is called iRAM (integrated RAM). In other words the iRAM integrates a dynamic RAM and its control and refreshing circuitry into a single IC. iRAM is also known as quasi-static RAM or pseudo-static RAM.

Static and dynamic RAMs use MOS technology. Semiconductor memories (RAMs and ROMs) are implemented with NMOS. Semiconductor memories using CMOS technology are produced nowadays. They consume very low power. They are at present costly.

SRAMs hold information in a flip-flop circuit consisting of two cross-coupled inverters. In a RAM the memory cell must be associated with read and write facility. Six transistors are needed per memory cell in a static RAM.

DRAMs require less number of transistors per memory cells because information is stored on stray capacitors. Only one transistor is needed to form a memory cell of the DRAM. This results in high packing density of the DRAM compared to SRAM. The capacity of memory chips are given in the form of m × n bits.

For example, the capacity of Hitachi SRAM, HM 6287 is 64 K × 1 bits. The capacity of NEC SRAM µPD43256 is 32 K × 8 bits. A memory chip may be bit-, nibble-, or byte-oriented. The capacity written in the form 64 K × 1 bit means that one bit at a time can be read from or written into the memory. Such memories are bit-oriented. If the capacity is written as 32 K × 8, it means that 8 bits can be read from or written into the memory at a time. This type of memories are byte-oriented.

Examples of DRAMs are :

Toshiba DRAM TC 51100 of 1 M × 1 bits

TC 514256 of 256 K × 4 bits, etc.

Intel 21019 is a 1 MB × 9 bit DRAM. 4 MB × 9 bit DRAMs are also available. The ninth bit is for parity checking.

Advantages of RAMs

These are available in larger sizes than ROMs

They serve as temporary data storage

They can be updated and corrected

No special programming mechanism like ROMs are required

These do not require lead time like ROM

6.8.2 Read Only Memory (ROM)

Read Only Memory, commonly known as ROM, is a memory which is permanently programmed and can only be read. It also possesses random access property. RAMs are much cheaper compared to RAMs when produced in large volumes to defray the cost of making the mask. The stored information can only be read from ROMs at the time of operation. Information can not be written into a ROM by the users. In other words ROMs are not accessible to users. The contents of ROMs are decided by the manufacturers. The contents are permanently stored in a ROM at the time of manufacturer. From programming mode point of view the ROMs are placed in broad categories:

Masked-programmed ROMs and

User-programmed ROMs.

ROMs in which contents are written at the time of IC manufacturing are called mask-programmed RAMs. The following are user-programmable ROMs:

PROM

EPROM (or UVPROM)

E^2PROM

Non-volatile Flash memory

ROMs store information which is not subject to change. They store fixed programs. In microprocessor-based system which are used for industrial controls, ROMs store monitor, assembler, debugging package, function tables such as sine, cosine, square root and code-conversion tables, etc. An example of a ROM is Toshiba Mask ROM, TCS 534000, 512 k × 8 bits.

Figure 6.4: Read Only Memory

6.8.2.1 PROM

A version of ROM that can not be changed during normal operation but can be programmed under special conditions is Programmable Read Only Memory (PROM). Its contents are decided by the user. The user can store permanent programs, data or any other kind of information in a PROM. A special equipment called PROM programmer is available for the programming of PROMs. With the help of PROM programmer the user stores his programs in a PROM. PROMs are once programmable, i.e., the user can write his information in a PROM only once. PROMs are more cost effective if small number of chips are to be produced to store certain fixed programs. An example of PROM is 74S287.

6.8.2.2 EPROM or UVEPROM

Many MOS PROMs can be programmed more than once. One variety of such a PROM is the Erasable PROM or EPROM. The stored data in EPROMs can be erased by exposing it to high intensity short wave ultraviolet light for about 18-22 minutes. That's why it may also be called Ultra Violet Erasable PROM. An UV source of 2537 A^O wavelength can be used for the purpose. The technique of erasing contents is not easy and convenient because the EPROM IC has to be removed from the computer for the exposure to the UV light. When an EPROM is exposed to UV light the entire data is erased.

The user can not erase the contents of certain selected memory locations. EPROMs are cheap, reliable and hence they are widely used. These are used to store programs which are permanent but requires updation. Permanent programs which are at the research and development stage also need to be stored in EPROM because they are modified several times.

Wherever updation or modification in the programs at the development stages are required, EPROMs are more economical than PROMs because of their reusability. EPROM employ MOS technology and thus store 1 or 0 as the charge or no charge on the insulated floating-gate of the transistor. The UV light causes the stored charge to leak off. Thus the data are erased and it allows the user to reprogram the EPROM. For programming it requires high voltage, 30 V or more. But its operating voltage, i.e, the voltage for read operation is only 5V.

Examples of EPROMs are :

(i) Intel's 87C257, 256K (32K × 8) CHMOS EPROM
(ii) Intel's 27C040, 4M (512K × 8) CHMOS EPROM
(iii) Intel's 27C240, 4M (256K × 16) CHMOS EPROM
(iv) Intel's 27C010, 1M (128K × 8) Byte-wide high speed CHMOS EPROM
(v) Toshiba, TC571000, 1M (128K × 8) EPROM

6.8.2.3 EEPROM (or E2PROM or EAPROM)

Another variety in which we can change a particular location, without removing the memory from circuit board is called Electrically Alterable PROM (EAPROM) or Electrically Erasable PROM (EEPROM). The chip can be erased and reprogrammed on the board easily on a byte by byte basis. Either a single byte or the entire chip can be erased in one operation. It requires much shorter time, a few milli-seconds for erasing as compared to 10-20 minutes for EPROM. There is a limit on the number of times the EEPROMs can be reprogrammed, usually 10,000 times. It need not be removed from the computer's board for erasing. Compared to RAMs, EEPROM take much longer time for both writing and erasing a byte. But the access time for reading RAMs, ROMs, PROMs and EEPROMs are comparable, a few hundred nanoseconds.

Intel 2816 is a 16K (2K × 8) EEPROM. The access time for its various versions lies in the range of 220 ns - 400 ns. Any byte can be erased in 9 milliseconds without affecting the data in any other byte. The Intel's 2817A is also an 16K (2K × 8) EEPROM. It possesses automatic byte-erasing facility before write operation. It takes 20 ms for a combined erase/write operation.

Advantages of ROMs

They are non-volatile in nature
ROMs are easier to interface than RAMs
ROMs can not be accidentally changed
ROMs are cheaper than ROMs
ROMs are easy to test
These are more reliable than RAMs due to their reduced complexity
These are static and do not require refreshing
Its contents are always known and can be verified

6.8.2.4 Non-Volatile Flash Memory

Flash memory is a special type of EEPROM that can be erased and reprogrammed Non-volatile flash memories are also electrically erasable and re-programmable nonvolatile memories. They possess the feature of quick-pulse programming, a typical time is 100 μs for byte-program and 4 sec for chip-program.

EEPROM is similar to flash memory i.e. flash EEPROM. The main difference between EEPROM and flash EEPROM is that the first requires data to be written or erased one byte at a time whereas flash EEPROM chip allows data to be written or erased in blocks and the same makes it faster. The chip is flash erasable and programmable. The whole device is erased in one operation. A typical electrical flash erase time for the chip is 1 second. The access time for read-operation is 150-170 ns. It can be used in place of EPROM.

These are suitable for firmware storage whereas conventional E2PROMs are suitable for parameter storage. When codes are to be updated the entire codes are written to avoid errors. For updation of firmware codes, flash memories are very fast and economical as compared to EPROMs. In case of parameter updation, they need to be rewritten individually byte by byte while system is on-line, in normal operation. Hence, EEPROM are best suited for such applications.

This type of memory is very costly and also they have the limit on the number of times they can be reprogrammed usually 10,000 erase/write operations. But the failure rate is less compared to EEPROMs.

Examples of flash-memories are :

(i) Intel 28F512, 512K (64K × 8) bit CMOS Flash Memory

(ii) Intel 28F020, 2048K (256 × 8) bit CMOS Flash Memory

6.8.3 Applications of ROMs

1. **Code Converter :** This application is the most obvious use of a ROM. In general a ROM with an N-bit Memory Address Register (MAR) and M-bit Memory Buffer Register (MBR) can realise any N-input M-output combinational circuit.
2. **Character Generator :** Character displays in dot matrix form use ROMs for decoding and activating the display.
3. **Function Generators :** Tables for commonly used functions such as Cosine, Sine, Tangent etc may be stored in ROMs. The arguments are entered in MAR and the function values appear in the output register.
4. Control Unit Design : ROMs are used in the design of control units of present day computers.

6.8.4 Non-volatile RAM (NVRAM)

A Non-volatile RAM is nothing but a very high speed static RAM and EEPROM packed into a single IC. This type of RAM operates quite similar to RAM and in case of power failure the entire contents of the RAM are transferred automatically in parallel in the EEPROM.

Xicor Inc. has developed a nonvolatile RAM X2201 of 1K capacity. It contains a 1KB RAM and 1KB EEPROM. The entire contents of the RAM are transferred to the EEPROM in 4 ms. Intel 2004 is also a nonvolatile RAM of 512 × 8 bits capacity. It takes 10 ms to transfer the data from RAM to EEPROM. The data from EEPROM are transferred back into RAM when power is resumed. A STORE signal is used to save the contents of the RAM. A signal known as RECALL is used to get the contents back into the RAM from EEPROM.

Advantages of NVRAM

The advantage of the NVRAM is that a battery backup is not needed to save the working data in the event of the power failure. A typical example is the buffer storage for a communication system.

The NVRAM can be employed for buffer storage for data being transmitted or received over a communication line.

In the event of power failure, a single microprocessor instruction causes NVRAM to save all the buffered data.

6.8.5 Thin Film Memory

Thin-film memory consists of spots of a nickel-iron alloy deposited on a very thin plate of glass or plastic. The spots are connected by very thin copper wires etched into the plate. Each spot operates like a core, and the plate of spots is like a plane of cores. Thin-film memory is much more compact than core memory; each plane of spots is smaller than a single core. It is also faster and is just as stable. Although production costs were at first rather high, new production methods have brought thin-film units within a practical price range. In this type of memory, reading is non-destructive.

6.8.6 Magnetic Bubble Memory

This technology of magnetic bubble memory is based on tiny magnetic domains or "bubbles" that appear in certain kinds of crystalline materials under the control of magnetic and electrical fields. The presence of a bubble signifies a 1-bit and the absence a 0-bit. A train of bubbles can be shifted from cell to cell in a shift register to read the storage. Storage density is very high. The bubbles are similar to magnetic cores in that they retain their magnetism indefinitely. High cost and difficulty of production limited wide industry and user acceptance of bubble memories.

6.8.7 Holographic Memory

Two forms of holographic storage are available:

Mechanical and

Optical.

In the mechanical type of storage, data bits are stored by a laser beam which permanently records the information by "burning" the coating on tape or film. By this way 13 million bits can be stored per square inch. These spots can be read by a laser beam of lesser power.

In the optical holographic memory, a laser beam is passed through an array of light valves to produce binary pattern of darkness and light. This is stored on light sensitive material such as thermoplastics. The data thus stored is read by another laser beam.

6.9 MAGNETIC DISKS

A disk is a circular platter constructed of metal or of plastic coated with a magnetizable material. Data are recorded on and later retrieved from the disk via a conducting coil named the head. During a read or write operation, the head is stationary while the platter rotates beneath it.

The write mechanism is based on the fact that electricity flowing through a coil produces a magnetic field. Pulses are sent to the head, and magnetic patterns are recorded on the surface below, with different patterns for positive and negative currents. The read mechanism is based on the fact that a magnetic field moving relative to a coil produces an electrical current in the coil. When the surface of the disk passes under the head, it generates a current of the same polarity as the one recorded.

6.9.1 Disk Organization and Formatting

A disk must be prepared for use before data or programs can be stored on it. Each disk, regardless of size, is divided into concentric circles called ***tracks*** where data are stored. The disk is also divided into pie-shaped wedges called ***sectors,*** which further specify data storage locations on the disk. The number of tracks and sectors is usually determined by the computer's operating system during a formatting operation. The operating system labels each sector of each track with an address so that the computer can go directly to a specific area.

The head is relatively a small device capable of reading to or writing from a portion of the platter rotating beneath it. This gives rise to the organization of data on the platter in a concentric tracks. Each track has the same width as the head. Adjacent tracks are separated by gaps. This prevents, or at least minimizes, errors due to misalignment of the head or simply interference of magnetic fields. To simplify the electronics, the same number of bits are typically stored on each track. Thus the density, in bits per linear inch, increases as we move from the outermost track to the innermost track.

Data are transferred to and from the disk in terms of blocks. Typically, the block is smaller than the capacity of a track. Accordingly, data are stored in block-size regions called sectors. There are typically between 10 and 100 sectors per track, and these may be either fixed or variable length. To avoid imposing unreasonable precision requirements on the system, adjacent sectors are separated by intra-track (or inter-record) gaps.

How are sector positions within a track identified?

Clearly, there must be some starting point on the track and a way of identifying the start and end of each sector. These requirements are handled by means of control data recorded on the disk. Thus, the disk is formatted with some extra data used only by the disk drive and not accessible to the user.

Data Storage on Disks

Data is stored on disks using either of the following two methods :

(i) Sector Method

(ii) Cylinder Method

6.9.2 Sector Method

The diskette is divided into at least eight equal portions called sectors. In other words, each track has partitions called sectors. When the data is stored on the disk using sector method, the address of the data has three parts :

- Surface number
- Track number
- Sector number

For example, the address 015603 means that the required resides on the first surface. The track number is 56 and the sector number is 03. When the address is read by the computer, the read/write head is positioned on the particular track of the specified surface. Then the disk is rotated. R/W head reads the data of the track starting from sector 1. When the required data passes under it, it gets transmitted to the processor. The index hole of the disk indicates the first sector.

6.9.3 Cylinder Method

When we have a pack of disks, we prefer to use cylinder method. The number of access arms is equal to the number of disks. each arm has got its own read/write head. The address of the record consists of the cylinder number, surface number and record number. A cylinder is made up of the tracks with the same track number from all the surfaces.

The advantage of using cylinder method is that the read/write heads are all positioned together on the same cylinder but on different surfaces.

6.9.4 Characteristics of Magnetic Disk Systems

A magnetic disk system is a mylar or metallic platter on which electronic data can be stored. Although disk resemble phonograph records, they do not have the characteristic spiraling groove, however, data is accessed in much the same was as an individual song is selected on a record. Data files on the disk can be read sequentially or directly.

Table 6.4 lists the major characteristics that differentiate among the various types of disk systems.

Table 6.4: Characteristics of Disk Systems

1. Head Motion
   - Fixed-Head
   - Movable-Head
2. Disk Portability
   - Non-removable Disk
   - Removable Disk
3. Sides
   - Single-sided
   - Double-sided
4. Platters
   - Single-platter
   - Multiple-platter
5. Head Mechanism
   - Contact (floppy)
   - Fixed gap
   - Aerodynamic gap (Winchester)
6. Disk Access Time

Head Motion

First, the head may either be fixed or movable with respect to the radial direction of the platter. In a fixed-head disk, there is one read/write head per track. all the heads are mounted on a rigid arm that extends across all tracks. In a movable-head disk, there is one read/write head. As before, the head is mounted on an arm. since the head must be able to be positioned above any track, the arm can be extended or retracted for this purpose.

The disk itself is mounted in a disk drive, which consists of the arm, a shaft rotates the disk, and the electronics needed for input and output of binary data.

Disk Portability

A non-removable disk is permanently mounted in the disk drive. The removable disk can be removed and replaced with another disk. The advantage of the second type is that unlimited amounts of data are available with a limited number of disk systems. Furthermore, a disk may be moved from one computer system to another.

Sides

For most disks, the magnetizable coating is both applied both sides of the platter, which is then referred to as double-sided. Some less expensive disk systems use single-sided disks.

Platters

Some disk drives accommodates multiple platters stacked vertically about an inch apart. Multiple arms are provided. The platters come as a unit known as disk pack.

Head Mechanism

Finally, the head mechanism provides a clear classification of disks into three types. Traditionally, the read/write head has been positioned a fixed distance above the platter, allowing an air gap. At the other extreme is a head mechanism that actually comes into physical contact with the medium during a read or write operation. This mechanism is used with the floppy disk, which is a small, flexible platter and the least expensive type of disk.

To understand the third type of disk, we need to comment on the relationship between data density and the size of the air gap. The head must generate or sense an electromagnetic field of sufficient magnitude to write and read properly. The narrower the head is, the closer it must be to the platter surface to function. Since a narrower head means narrower tracks and therefore greater data density, this is desirable. However, the closer the head is to the disk, the greater the risk of error from impurities or imperfections. To push the technology further, the Winchester disk was developed. Winchester heads are used in sealed drive assemblies that are almost free of contaminants. They are designed to operate closer to the disks surface than conventional rigid disk heads, thus allowing greater data density. The head is in the shape of an aerodynamic foil which rests lightly on the platter's surface when the disk is motionless. The air pressure generated by the spinning disk is enough to make the foil rise above surface. The resulting no-contact system can be engineered to use narrower heads that operate closer to the platter surface than conventional rigid disk heads.

As a matter of historical interest, the term Winchester was originally used by IBM as a code name for their 3340 disk model prior to announcement. The 3340 was a removable disk pack with the heads sealed within the pack. The term is now applied to any sealed-unit disk drive with aerodynamic head design.

Disk Access Time

When the disk drive is operating, the disk is rotating at a constant speed. To read or write, the head must be positioned at the desired track and the beginning of the desired sector on that track. Track selection involves moving the head in a movable-head system or electronically selecting one head on a fixed-head system.

Seek Time

On a movable-head system, the time it takes to position the head on the track is known as seek-time. In either case, once the track is selected, the system waits until the appropriate sector rotates to line up with the head.

Latency Time

The time required by a sector to reach below the head is known as latency time. On an average it is half of the time taken for a rotation by the disk.

Access Time

The time taken to read or write from/into a desired location on the disk is called Access Time of the disk. In other words, access time is the sum of the seek time, if any, and the latency time. Once the head is in position, the read or write operation is then performed as the sector moves under the head.

Mathematically it is written as:

Access time = Average Seek Time + Rotational Latency + Transfer Time

6.9.5 Classification of Magnetic Disks

Depending upon the aforesaid characteristics, magnetic disks can be classified in the following manner:

Floppy Disk

- 8 inch
- 5.25 inch
- 3.5 inch

Hard Disk

Fixed Disk

Removable Cartridge

Disk Pack

Magnetic Drum

Magnetic Cards and Strips

Zip Disk

Jaz Disk

SuperDisk

Floppy Disks

A floppy diskette, also called simply a diskette or disk, is a small flexible disk. Floppy disks are commonly used as secondary and backup memory in personal computers. These disks are very thin and flexible and hence, they are called floppy. It has been around since the early 1970s.

Floppy disks are made of Mylar with a coating of magnetic material (iron oxide) on it. They are small, convenient and inexpensive. They are removable disks. A floppy disk is inserted into the computer when needed. If the same disk is to be used again and again, it can be kept inserted in the system. It is kept in a square protective cover made of thin plastic. The disk rotates freely in the protective jacket.

Disk surface and its organisation is shown in ***Fig. 6.4.***

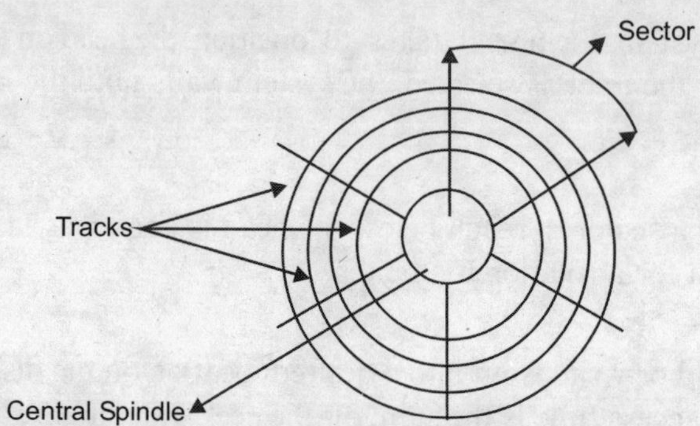

Fig. 6.5: Disk Surface and Its Organization

The different sizes of floppy disk are:

8 inch

5 ¼ inch

3 ½ inch

Floppy disk has been around us since early 1970s and was originally 8 inches in diameter. Today, the most popular sizes are : **5 ¼ inches square and 3 ½ inches square.** Size of 8 inches square is not that popular. 5¼ was the common size and was very popular before 1987. This type of floppy is generally capable of storing between 100 KB and 1.2 MB of data. The most common storage capacities of this size is 360 KB and 1.2MB.

5 ¼ inch and 3 ½ inch floppies are shown in **Fig. 6.6** and **Fig 6.7** respectively.

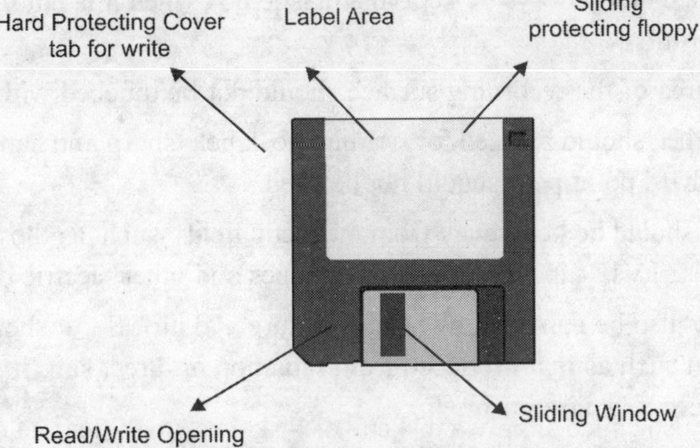

Fig. 6.6: 3 ½ Inch (1.44 MB) Floppy

The protective cover of a 3.5 inch disk is hard plastic whereas that of a 5.25 inch disk is thin vinyl. A 5.25 inch disk is also called mini-floppy whereas a 3.5 inch disk is called microfloppy. A disk has semi-random property. Track to track movement of the read/write head is random. The movement on the track while reading or writing data is serial. The most common sizes for PCs are 720 KB (Double Density) and 1.44 MB (High Density). Macintosh supports such disks of 400KB, 800 KB and 1.2 MB.

The average access time is 150-250 ms. It is about a million time slower than semiconductor memory. The access time for the data stored on the disk depends on the following :

(i) The seek-time

(ii) The search or latency time

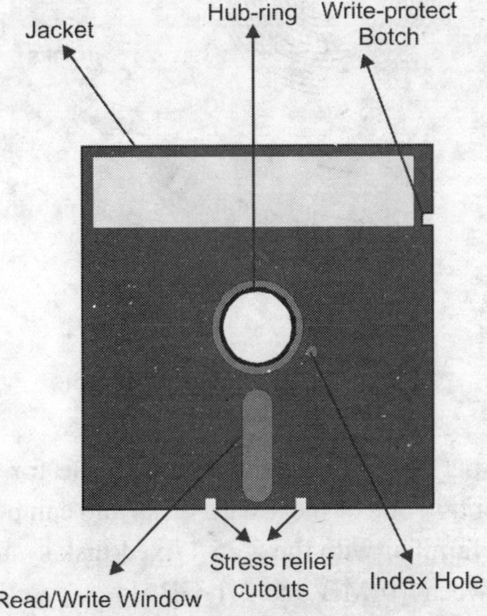

Fig. 6.7: 5 ¼ Inch Floppy

Cautions in Handling Floppy Disks

(a) A floppy disk should always be kept in a plastic box when it is not in use. It should be kept in vertical position.

(b) Its exposed area of the recording surface should not be touched with fingers.

(c) A felt-tipped pen should be used for writing the label. sharp and hard point such as dot pen or any other hard point pen should not be used.

(d) Floppy disks should be kept away from magnetic fields such as those generated by electric motors, radios, TVs, tape recorders, telephones and other electric devices.

(e) The disk may also be damaged by heat, moisture and dirt. So it should be kept away from excessive heat such as that produced from radiation or direct sun. It should be kept in dust and moisture free environment.

(f) The disk should not be removed while drive is running.

(g) The disk should not be bent.

Hard Disk

A hard disk is just that - hard and inflexible. The hard disk is made from materials such as aluminium instead of mylar. The I/O device used to transfer data to and from a hard disk is called a hard-disk drive. The read/write head of a hard-disk drive floats above the surface of the disk at a height of about 50 millionth of an inch (0.00005 inches). In comparison, a human hair is a hundred times larger in diameter.

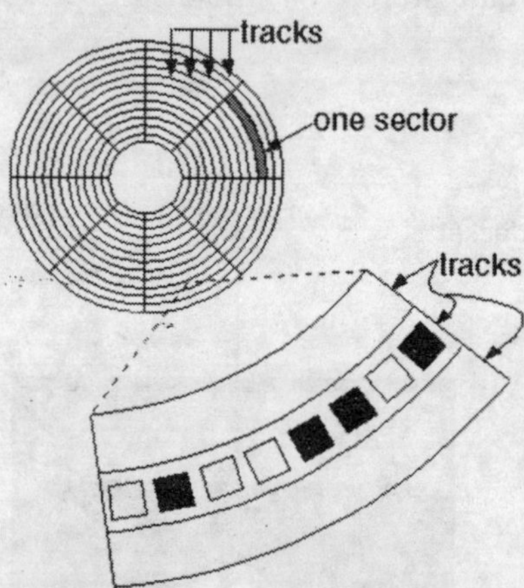

Figure 6.7: Tracks and Sectors

Fixed Disk

A fixed disk is enclosed permanently inside a sealed case for protection from environmental factors. Fixed-disk systems contain one or more hard disks and can be used in all types of computers. Home computer users may be familiar with the 5.25 " fixed-disk systems used with desktops, having typical storage capacities between 10 MB and 2.1 GB. In large computers, the fixed-disk system provides storage capacities in Giga-bytes (GB) or Tera-bytes (TB).

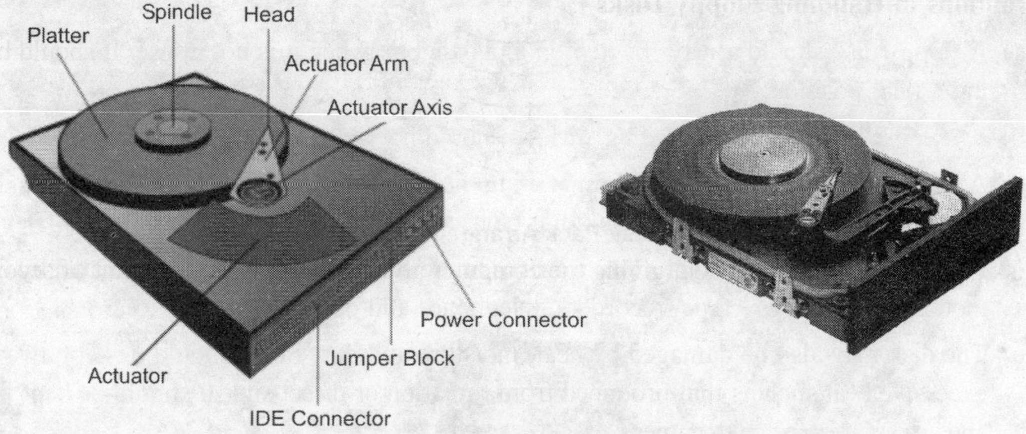

Fig. 6.8: Fixed Hard-disk(s) With Removed Outer Jacket

Winchester Disk

According to one of the authors, the term Winchester comes from an early type of disk drive developed by IBM that stored 30 MB and had 30 ms access time, so its inventor named it a Winchester in honour of the Winchester .30-caliber rifle.

According to another author, in the evolution of hard disk systems, IBM developed smaller rigid disk drives with one fixed and one removable disk pack. Each held about 30 MB of data and hence the model was named as 3030, which soon became ***"Winchester"*** (as in 30 caliber Winchester rifles). The dual-drive systems became obsolete, but the name is still used.

The Winchester hard disk, which is used in personal computers, has the following characteristics:

The head mechanism is enclosed in a sealed environment in which air is continuously filtered and circulated.

The disk rotates at high speed (about 3600 rpm) and the heads do not touch the surface of the disk

The disk surface is lubricated so that the heads may rest on the disk without scratches.

There is a very thin magnetic coating on the disk.

The recent developments in disks include the development of 20 MB-2.1GB storage disks, achieved by vertical recording instead of the present horizontal media surface recording.

Removable Cartridge

A storage system using Removable Cartridges has the same speed and capacity as a hard disk. These cartridges usually contain only one or two disks. Many hard-disk drives used with small computers are designed to use removable cartridges.

The advantage of this type of disk is that it may be removed at any time and a new or different cartridge may be inserted. For example, a user can have a separate cartridge for each application.

Disk Pack

A disk pack is another removable storage media in which several hard-disks are packed into a single plastic case. The disk-pack drives are designed for large systems that require larger storage capacities. Because a disk pack is susceptible to damage by scratching, the top of the first disk and the bottom of the last disk are generally not used.

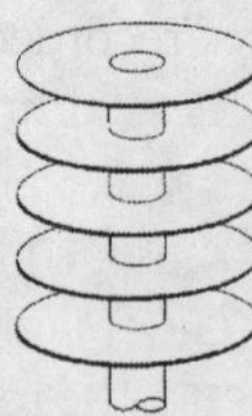

Fig. 6.9: Disk Pack Arranged on a Spindle

Disk packs can be interchanged, giving the computer a virtually unlimited amount of secondary storage.

Fig. 6.10: Disk Pack

Advantages of Magnetic Disks

(i) The data can be accessed sequentially as well as directly.
(ii) The access time is smaller, which results in efficient storage.
(iii) When a transaction is made, data can be updated immediately. There is no need to maintain a transaction file.
(iv) Software allows files to be altered simultaneously.
(v) Disk storage is much more durable and is less likely to be lost because of mishandling or a poor storage environment.
(vi) Inquiries can be answered quickly on the spot.

Disadvantages of Magnetic Disks

(i) They are more expensive than magnetic tapes.
(ii) Requires complex programming to gain access to files.
(iii) These are more heavier (particularly disk packs) and more difficult to replace than a magnetic tape.
(iv) Easily transported disks may pose security problems.
(v) Requires backup files to be prevent data from being lost during alterations.
(vi) When the data in master file is updated in case of a transaction, the old data is lost. Whereas in tapes, a new master-file is formed which has the updated data. The old master file is also retained for the desired time.

6.10 MAGNETIC DRUM

A magnetic drum is similar in a concept to a fixed stack magnetic disk, except that the information is stored on the outer surface of a drum, rotating at a high speed as opposed to the surface of a disk. a drum, as the name suggests, is cylindrical in shape, typically about 3 feet in length. The outer surface of the drum is coated in ferro-oxide, enabling the storage of information in coded form as magnetized or non-magnetized spots. The surface is divided into a number of tracks, each having one or more fixed read and record heads.

As in the case of magnetic disk, data are recorded serially along the tracks, from where any particular item can be directly accesses. Magnetic drums are used in places where very fast access and fast transfer speed are required.

A typical drum can store between 100,000 and 10,000,000 characters of information, transfer more than 1.5 million characters per second (CPS) with an appropriate access time of 6 to 29 ms (million seconds). Unlike a disk pack it can not bc rcmoved from a unit and replaced and is more expensive than disk. Magnetic drums are not used in our present day computers.

6.11 MAGNETIC CARDS AND STRIPS

A magnetic strip is a flexible plastic material of size 2 × 12 inches, on which data are magnetically recorded. Ten such strips put together is called as a sub-cell and twenty sub-cells are placed in a data cell drive. Like disk packs they can be removed. Cards and strips have high storage facility and slow access speed. They are much cheaper than disk packs, can accommodate reasonably large amount of data and the data stored are erasable.

6.12 ZIP DISK

These are high-capacity floppy disk drives developed by the Iomega Corporation. Zip disks are slightly larger than the conventional floppy disks, and are about twice as thick. These can store 100 MB of data. As they are relatively inexpensive and durable, so they have become a popular media for backing up hard disks and for transporting large files.

6.13 JAZ DISK

These are removable disk drives developed by the Iomega Corporation. The Jaz drive has a 12 ms average seek-time and a transfer rate of 5.5 MB per second. The removable cartridges hold 1 GB of data. The fast data rates and large storage capacity make it a viable alternative for backup storage as well as everyday use.

6.14 SuperDisk

This is a new disk storage technology developed by the Imation Corporation that supports very high-density diskettes. SuperDisk diskettes are etched with a servo pattern at the factory. This pattern then read by the SuperDisk drive to precisely align the read/write head. The result is that a SuperDisk diskette can have 2490 tracks, as opposed to the 135 tracks that conventional 3 ½ inch 1.44 MB diskettes use. This higher density translates into 120 MB capacity per diskette.

Unlike the other removable disk storage solutions, such as the Zip Drive, SuperDisk is backward compatible with older diskettes. This means that you can use the SuperDisk drive to read and write to older 1.44 MB diskettes as well as the new 120 MB SuperDisk diskettes. Imation's current SuperDisk drive is called the LS-120.

6.15 OPTICAL DISKS

In 1983, one of the most successful consumer products of all time was introduced : the Compact Disk (CD) digital audio system. The CD is a non-erasable disk that can store more than 60 minutes audio information on one side. The huge commercial success of the CD enabled the development of low-cost Optical Storage Technology that now promise to revolutionize data storage.

Information is written to or read from an optical disk using laser beam. An optical disk has very high storing capacity. Only one surface of an optical disk is used to store data. An optical disk is relatively inexpensive, and has a long life of at least 25 years. Its drives are inherently simple and inexpensive. As the read/write head does not touch the disk surface, there is no disk wear and no problem of head crash. Elaborate error checking codes can be used as there is no problem of space because the disks have very high storage capacity.

The greatest drawback of the optical disk system is its slow average seek time of the drive. In case of a hard disk the read/write head is a tiny magnet whereas in optical system the drive has to move on sizable optical assembly across the disk surface. This increases the seek time. In future it is expected that the access time will be reduced using fibre-optic system.

CD-ROM Drive with Optical Disk is shown in ***Fig. 6.11.***

Fig. 6.11: CD-ROM Drive With Optical Disk

Portable CD-ROM Drive is shown in ***Fig. 6.12.***

Fig. 6.12: Portable CD-ROM Drive

There are mainly following types of optical disk products :

I. Compact Disk (CD)
II. CD-ROM (Compact Disk Read-Only-Memory)
III. Compact Disk Interactive (CD-I)
IV. Digital Video Interface (DVI)
V. WORM (Write-Once-Read-Many)
VI. CD-R (Compact Disk-Recordable) Drive
VII. Erasable Optical Disk or CD-RW (ReWritable) Disk
VIII. Optical Card
IX. Optical Tape

Optical disk(s) are shown in ***Fig. 6.13 (a), Fig. 6.13 (b) and Fig. 6.13(c).***

(a) A CD-ROM Drive

(b) A CD-ROM Drive (without case)

(c)The optical lens of a CD Drive

Figure 6.13

Compact Disk (CD)

Compact Disk (CD) is a non-erasable disk that stores digitized audio information. The standard system uses 12 cm disks and can record more than 60 minutes of uninterrupted playing time.

CD-ROM

CD-ROM is an optical Compact Disk ROM. Prerecorded data can be read out. The manufacturer writes data on CD-ROMs. The disk is made up of resin, such as poly-carbonate. It is coated with a material which will change when a high intensity laser beam is focused on it. The coating material is highly reflective, usually aluminum. The high intensity laser beam forms a tiny pit along a trace to represent 1. For reading the data laser beam of less intensity is employed.

In some cases separate laser beams are employed : **one for writing and the other for reading.** The reflected laser is sensed by photodiode to read data. The intensity of the reflected light of laser changes as it encounters pit. A pit spreads the light so that the photodiode receives little reflected light. But the surface without pit reflects sufficient light to the photodiode. Thus the change in reflected light is sensed and converted into electrical signals for data reading purpose.

If the coating of the special material on the optical disk is thin film, a hole is formed when the laser beam falls on it. If the layer is a thick film a pit is formed. In some process of thick film, a bubble is formed instead of a pit. The unaltered areas between the pits are known as **lands.**

First of all, a master disk is prepared. By moulding a special plastic to the master disk, CD-ROMs are produced on mass scale. The plastic copy of the data is then covered with a clear plastic layer and backed with a reflecting coating.

CD-ROMs use long spiral tracks to store data serially. The track is divided into blocks of the same size. A CD-ROM disk rotates at a variable speed so that the pits are read by the laser at a constant linear speed. The speed of the disk is adjusted in such a manner that the track passes under the read/write head at a constant linear velocity (CLV). CD-ROM uses CLV or CAV (constant angular velocity) technology. The reported speeds of players that use CAV are generally not accurate because they refer only to the access speed for outer tracks and inner tracks are accessed more slowly.

CD-ROM is appropriate for the distribution of large amounts of data to a large number of users. Because of the expense of the initial writing process, it is not appropriate for individualized applications.

Advantages of CD-ROM

The information-storage capacity is much greater on the optical disk.

Mass replication of CD-ROMs is inexpensive and very fast.

These are removable and thus may be used suitably for archival storage.

Disadvantages of CD-ROM

It is read-only and can not be updated.

It has an access time much longer than that of a magnetic disk drive.

Compact Disk Interactive (CD-I)

Compact Disk Interactive (CDI) optical disk is a specification based on the use of CD-ROM. It describes methods for providing audio, video, graphics, text, and machine-executable code on CD-ROM.

Digital Video Interface (DVI)

Digital Video Interface (DVI) optical disk is a technology for producing digitized, compressed, representation of video information. The representation can be stored on CD or disk media. Current systems use CDs and can store about 20 minutes of video on one disk.

WORM (Write Once Read Many)

To accommodate applications in which only one or small number of copies of a set of data is needed, the write-once read many (WORM) type optical disk has been developed. For WORM, a disk has been prepared in such a way that it can be subsequently written once with a laser beam of modest intensity. Thus, with a somewhat more expensive disk controller than for CD-ROM, the customer can write once as well as read the disk. To provide for rapid access, the WORM uses constant angular velocity, at the sacrifice of some capacity.

A typical technique for preparing the disk is to use high-power laser to produce a series of blisters on the disk. when the preformatted medium is placed in a WORM drive, a low-powered laser can produce just enough heat to burst the prerecorded blisters. During a disk-read operation, a laser in the WORM drive illuminates the disk's surface. Since the burst blisters provide higher contrast than the surrounding area, these are easily recognized by simple electronics.

The WORM optical disk is attractive for archival storage of documents and files. It provides a permanent record of large volumes of user data.

Advantages

(i) High capacity
(ii) Better reliability
(iii) Longer life

Disadvantages

(i) Greater access time as compared to that of hard disk.

CD-R Drive

It is a special type of disk-drive that can create CD-ROMs and audio CDs. This allows the users to master a CD-ROM or audio CD for publishing. Until recently, CD-R drives were quite expensive, but prices have tremendously come down.

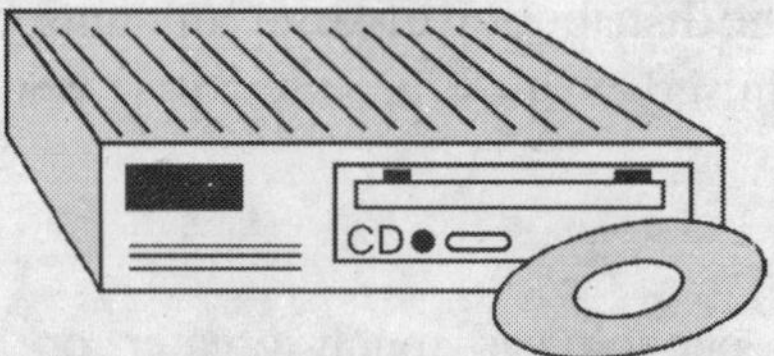

Fig. 6.14: CD-R Drive

Multi-session recording feature of many CD-R drives enables us to keep adding data to a CD-ROM over a period of time. This feature is extremely important if we want to use the CD-R drive to prepare backup CD-ROMs. For the purpose of creating CD-ROMs and audio CDs, CD-R software package will also be required besides CD-R drive. These drives can also read CD-ROMs and play audio CDs.

Erasable Optical Disk or CD-RW Disk

The most recent development in computer optical disks is the erasable optical disk. This disk can be repeatedly written and overwritten, as with any magnetic disk. Although a number of approaches have been tried, the only technology that has proved commercially feasible is the magneto-optical system. In this system, the energy of laser beam is used together with a magnetic field to record and erase information by reversing the magnetic poles in a small area of a disk coated with a magnetic material. The laser beam heats a specific spot while its temperature is elevated. As the polarization process does not cause a physical change in the disk, the process can be repeated many times. For reading, the direction of magnetism can be polarized by laser light. Polarized light reflected from a particular spot will change its degree of rotation depending on the magnetic field's orientation.

The erasable optical disk has the obvious advantages over CD-ROM and WORM that it can rewritten and thus used as true secondary storage. As such, it competes with magnetic disks.

Advantages of erasable optical disk over magnetic disk

High capacity : A 5.25-inch optical disk hold about 650 MB of data. The most advanced Winchester disks carry less than half that amount.

Portability : The optical disk can be removed from drive.

Semi-random Access : Erasable optical disk also uses format that makes semi-random access feasible.

Reliability : The engineering tolerance for optical disk are much less than for high-capacity magnetic disks. Thus, they exhibit higher reliability and longer life.

Drawback

Access time : The erasable disk has longer access time as compared to that of hard disk.

Optical Card

The optical or laser card is the of the size as a credit card and has an optical laser-encoded strip that can store approximately 2 MB of data. These cards have many potential uses, most notably for storing credit records or medical histories. Some people predict that these cards may one day lead to a cash-less and cheque-less.

Optical cards have the potential to store an individual's entire financial history, adding to or subtracting from appropriate accounts as a person makes, saves, or spends money. These cards may also supply a hospital with the holder's complete medical history. If emergency treatment is required, this information could expedite care.

Optical Tape

Continuing developments and refinements in optical technology include Optical Tape. Optical Tape is similar in appearance to magnetic tape, but data are stored by optical-laser techniques. Optical tapes which are in cassette form can store over 8 GB each, and the tape drives can hold 128 cassettes, providing a total storage of about 1 TB (1024 GB). Like other optical methods of data storage, optical is read-only. As optical technology develops, higher densities and expanded uses will result.

Magneto-Optical Drives

This is a type of disk drive that combines magnetic disk technologies with CD-ROM technologies. Like magnetic disks, these can be read as well written to and like floppy disks, they are also removable. These are faster than floppy and CD-ROM drives but not comparable to hard-disk drives. However, their storage capacity can be more than 200 MBs which is an enormous storage capacity in comparison to floppy disks.

6.16 MAGNETIC TAPES

A magnetic tape is usually a 0.5 inch wide plastic tape with a coating of magnetic material on one side. The length is generally 2400 feet. Records are stored on the tape one after the other in the order of the key field. The records have gaps between them called inter-record gaps (IRG). These gaps are created automatically at the time of writing the data on the tape. A record is read from the tape, then comes the IRG. The tape movement stops. During this time, the record is transferred to the computer. After the transmission the tape movement again starts and next record is read. But if the records are too small then having IRG after each record results in wastage of tape and also slows down the speed of access. So a number of records are grouped together to form a block. Record storage with IRG is shown in Fig. 6.15.

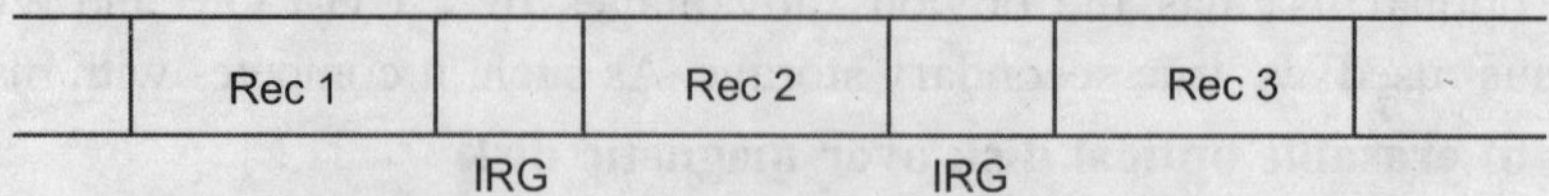

Fig 6.15: Record Storage With IRG

There is a gap between two consecutive blocks called the inter-block gap (IBG). The whole block is read by the access mechanism at one time. Storage with IBG is shown in Fig. 6.16.

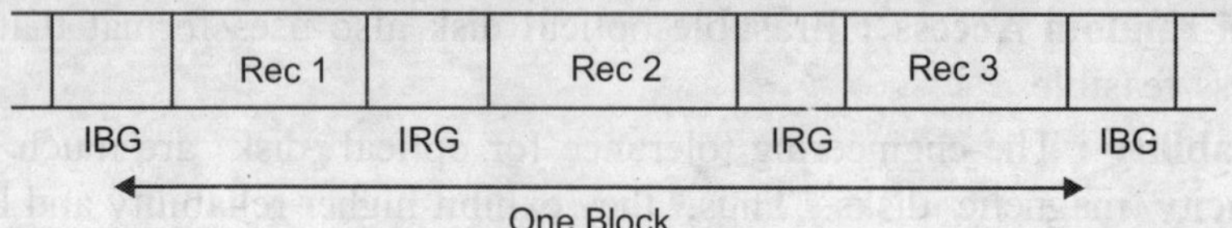

Fig 6.16: Storage with IBG

Every tape has a header and trailer label. The header label is at the beginning of the tape and stores the name of file, date of last updation and any other relevant information. The trailer label has the same information as header label. It may be possible that a number of files are stored in a tape.

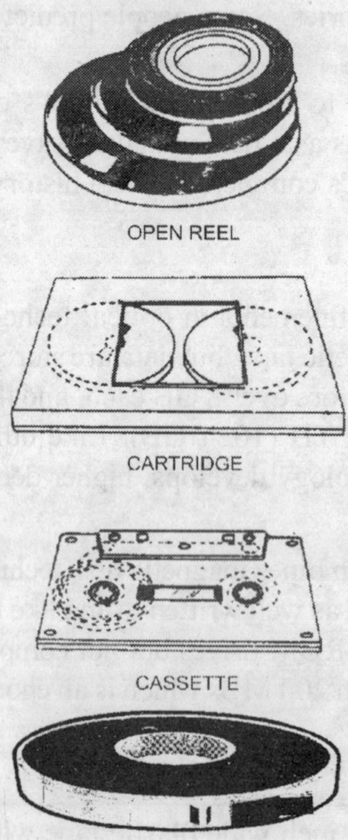

Fig. 6.17: Various Types of Magnetic Tapes

Main Characteristics of Magnetic Tapes

Some major characteristics of magnetic tapes are given as under

Tape Density

Character Set Used

Parity Check

Blocks : Fixed Length or Variable Length

Block Size

Labels

Mechanical Interlock

Headers and trailers

Length of tape

Drive mechanism

IRG and IBG

Blocking/Unblocking Storage

Tape densities are measured in bits per inch (bpi). Standard densities for 7 track tapes are 200 bpi, 556 bpi and 800 bpi. Standard densities for 9 track tapes are 800, 1600 and 6250 bpi.

Three **character sets** are used on magnetic tapes :

EBCDIC (8-bit code)

ASCII (7-bit code)

BCD (6-bit code)

Parity check is a method in which a parity bit is added to each word during write operation such that total number of bits in each word is either even (even parity) or odd (odd parity). During the read operation a check is made to ensure that the mode of parity is maintained.

Data is normally stored on the tape in blocks. On some tapes the block is of **fixed length** whereas on others it may be **variable in length.** The lengths are separated by a record gap and/or block gap.

Block size indicates how many records are grouped together, and is usually given in bytes.

Labels are used to identify the information that follows on the tape and these are system dependent. The following rule may be followed while deciding labels:

"Label if storing information, no label if transporting".

Mechanical interlock is provided on every computer tape to prevent accidental overwriting of information. A small plastic ring must be inserted before a tape may be written on. Thus removal of the ring prevents writing.

The amount of the data that can be held depends on the length of the tape, the number of IRGs, and the density of the tape. Density refers to how tightly the data can be packed and stored on a storage media. Here it is a measure of the number of characters or bytes of data that can be recorded on 1 inch of tape. Data transfer rate - the number of characters or bytes per second that can be transferred from the tape drive to the media or vice-versa - also varies.

Magnetic Tape Drive And Its Types

A tape drive performs the operation of writing onto the tape and also reading information from the tape. The tape is loaded onto the tape drive in the same way that a movie projector is threaded.

Fig. 6.18: Mounting of Magnetic Tape on Drive

There are two types of magnetic tape drive mechanisms. These are :

Using Vacuum Columns

Using Tension Arms

Tape Drive Using Vacuum Columns

In the tape drive using vacuum columns, tape is fed from a supply reel, then passing through a set read/write heads on to a take-up reel. The tape passes through two vacuum chambers, on either side of the read/write heads. This arrangement is required to prevent it from snapping when the tape speed varies. A servo mechanism maintains the correct length of tape between reel and capstan drive. Each track is provided with a read and write head.

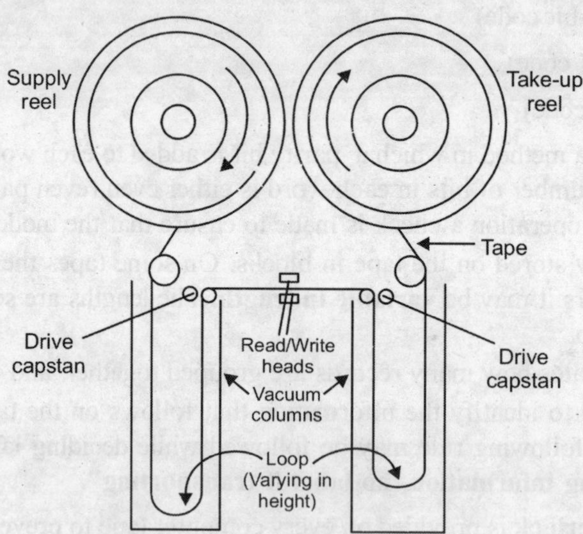

Fig. 6.19: Tape Drive Using Vacuum Columns

Tape Drive Using Tension Arms

In this type of drive, the tape is laced around a set of tension arms. The upper and lower arms are movable. When the tape is suddenly driven past the heads by the capstan, the mechanism provides a buffering supply of tape. Sufficient tape is maintained between the capstan and the tape reels by a servo mechanism, by driving upper and lower reels.

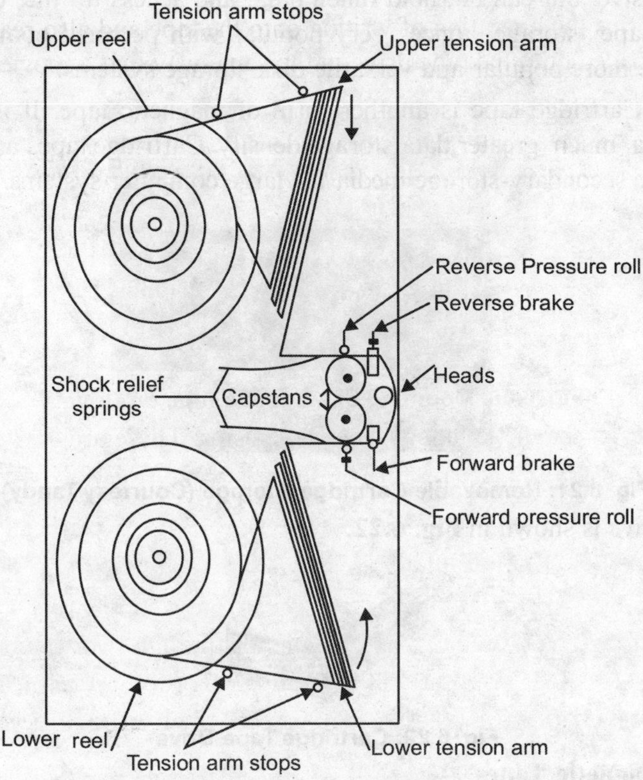

Fig. 6.20: Tape Drive Using Tension Arms

Brakes are also provided for fast stopping. Tension arm tape drives are available in tape speeds of 12.5 ips (inches per second) to 45 ips while vacuum column tape drives are available from 45 ips to 200 ips.

Types of Magnetic Tapes

There are three forms of magnetic tape :

(a) Reel-to-reel Tape

(b) Cassette Tape

(c) Cartridge Tape

Reel-to-reel Tape: A reel-to-reel tape is magnetic tape placed on reels about 10.5 inches in diameter. A typical tape is about 2400 feet long, 0.5 inch wide, and holds about 40 MB of data. Data transfer rates vary from approximately 5000 bytes per second to over million bytes per second. The more common tape drives have rates of 60,000 bytes per second. These tapes usually store data at a density of 1600 bytes per inch, but it can range from 800 to 6250 bytes per inch. Reel-to-reel tapes are relatively inexpensive, durable, and can hold a large quantity of data. They are used mainly with large-computer systems.

Cassette Tape: Cassette tape are similar to those used in audio tape players/recorders. Such types of tape are employed with small computers. The tape is about 0.25 inch wide, enclosed in a plastic case, and that's why suitable for mainly small computers. The major difference between the audio and digital tape cassettes is that the tape cassettes are used for storing data with higher quality and high density digital recording tapes.

They are inexpensive, but can not hold much data, and access to the data stored on them is fairly slow. Cassette tape storage, once very popular with personal computer users, has been largely replaced by the more popular and versatile disk storage systems.

Cartridge Tape: Cartridge tape is another form of magnetic tape. It is packaged similar to cassette tape but has a much greater data storage density. Cartridge tapes and reel-to-reel systems are very popular as the secondary-storage media for large computer systems.

Fig. 6.21: Removable Cartridge Storage (Courtesy Tandy)

Cartridge Tape Drive is shown in **Fig. 6.22.**

Fig. 6.22: Cartridge Tape Drive

Advantages of Magnetic Tapes

1. It is the cheapest storage medium for sequential access.
2. The storage capacity is very high.
3. A tape is erasable and reusable.
4. It is a low-cost backup
5. They require less space to be stored as compared to other storage devices.
6. Magnetic tapes are less prone to errors
7. Stores large amounts of data in a small space in comparison to punched cards.
8. It is the most suitable backup media for voluminous storage.
9. Transfers data between tape and the CPU rapidly.

Disadvantages of Magnetic Tapes

1. It is not a very reliable and durable media for storage as when a tape tears, some data is certainly lost.
2. Magnetic tapes require proper labels for content verification.
3. Only sequential access is possible and time required to access depends upon the location of the record on the tape.
4. Tapes are not easily distinguishable superficially.
5. Data can not be inserted in a tape. Each time an updation is to be made, a new copy of tape is made.
6. Environmental factors can distort data stored on magnetic tapes.
7. A tape can be read only by a machine, whereas punched cards can be read visually by an operator.

6.17 MAGNETIC TAPE Vs MAGNETIC DISK

Magnetic tape and disk have evolved together since the 1950s, filling different data storage needs for computer users. Tape drives store and archive large amounts of data economically. Disk drives access the data with great speed.

1. Random Access: Any data on a disk can be accessed in a few thousandths of a second. This is called random access---you don't need to search every file to find something.

2. Serial Access: A magnetic tape drive must search through all the files leading up to the one you want. This is serial access, reading one file after another.

3. Speed: For everyday file access, magnetic disk is faster because of its random access feature. For archiving files, tape and disk are about the same speed.

4. Archiving: Magnetic tape is less expensive to store large amounts of data for archiving. Data centers also use disks for archiving, though to a lesser extent.

5. Size: In 2009, the smallest magnetic disks are the size of a matchbox. The smallest tape drives are about the size of a small book.

6.18 VIRTUAL MEMORY

The concept of virtual memory was implemented in 1959 but it was extensively used only after 1970s. Virtual memory is a scheme implemented by hardware or software or both which appears to increase the memory of computer. In this system only that portion of the program and data that are being processed are kept in the primary storage. Information no longer required and needed is swapped between the primary and secondary storage. The swapping is transparent to the user. This process extends memory to the size of secondary storage units plus primary memory storage size and increases processing time and I/O operations.

A virtual memory system offers the following benefits:

- It frees the user from the chore of dividing a large program into modules and managing the transfer of modules between the disk and the main memory.
- It allows efficient sharing of memory space among different users of a timesharing/multiprogramming systems.
- It helps to develop programs that are independent of the configuration and capacity of memory systems

6.19 HIGH SPEED MEMORY

We are aware that the access time of main memories is slower than the speed of the processor. Since each instruction require several memory accesses, therefore, faster memories will be of great help in increasing the overall performance of a computer system. The following may be the four serious possibilities to enhance the speed of memory:

- Inserting Cache memory, known as a high speed memory, between the main memory and processor.
- Employing associative addressing in place of random access using which information can be retrieved at a very high speed on the basis of the portion of its contents as an address.
- Employing a faster but expensive technology for main memory having a very smaller access time and the same become available in the time to come due to technological advancement in memories.
- By employing Memory Interleaving using which more words are accessed in a single memory access cycle rather than accessing one word. This is termed as memory interleaving.

6.20 CACHE MEMORY

A very high speed small capacity memory introduced as a buffer between the CPU and the main memory is called a Cache Memory. Due to very high cost, small cache memories are intended to provide fast speed of memory retrieval. Only small sizes such as 8KB, 64 K, 128K, 256 KB, 512 KB etc. are normally provided in microcomputers whereas they can have 640 KB to 64 MB RAMs or even more Parts of the current program are copied from the main memory into the high speed cache.

The design of cache memory is such that it is not **"visible"** to a programmer. The CPU cycle time in a computer is normally much faster than the memory cycle time. Thus every time information is to be read from the memory to be used by CPU, this speed mismatch would make the CPU wait. Employing cache is an attempt to minimize this mismatch.

When the CPU refers to an instruction (or data), it is fetched from the cache if it is already there. This is called a hit. If it is not available, then it is called a miss and in this case the same is read from the main memory.

The hit ratio (h) is defined as follows :

$$h = \frac{\textbf{Number of times the time is found in cache}}{\textbf{Total number of addresses feferenced}}$$

The hit ratio is a fraction less than unity and is expressed as %age and (1-h) is often called miss ratio. If T_c and T_m are the cycle times of the cache and the main memory respectively, effective memory cycle time is given as :

$$T = h\,T_c + (1 - h)\,T_m$$

Example 1

If hit ratio h = 75 % , cache cycle-time T_c = 200 ns, memory cycle-time T_m = 800 ns, then what will be the effective memory cycle-time ?

Solution

Putting value of h = 0.75, T_c = 200 ns and T_m = 800 in the above given expression, we get the effective memory cycle-time,

$$\begin{aligned} T &= 0.75 \times 200 + 0.25 \times 800 \\ &= 150 + 200 \\ &= 350 \text{ ns.} \end{aligned}$$

Example 2

If memory read cycle takes 200 ns and a cache read cycle takes 50 ns, then what will be total time taken to read out the contents in 5 continuous memory references :

(i) with cache memory and

(ii) without cache memory

whereas first reference brings the main memory contents to cache and next four references from cache memory.

Solution

(i) Time taken with cache $= (200 + 50) + 50 \times 4$

$= 250 + 200 = 450$ ns

(ii) Time taken without cache $= 200 \times 5 = 1000$ ns

EXERCISES

1. What are disk systems ? Outline their typical characteristics.
2. What is meant by Memory Hierarchy ? State its importance.
3. State the function of memory in a computer ?
4. What do SRAM and DRAM stand for ? Discuss their merits and demerits.
5. What is a hard-disk and how does it work ?
6. Differentiate between Core and Semi-conductor memory.
7. What are high speed memories ? Explain their usage.
8. What are the advantages and disadvantages of magnetic tapes ?
9. What are the different types of memory ? Explain their merits and demerits.
10. What is the difference between seek-time and latency-time ?
11. Why is magnetic medium more appropriate as a storage medium than a semiconductor medium?
12. Describe the physical characteristics of magnetic tape.
13. What is magnetic strip ? Explain its working.
14. How does a random access device differ from a sequential access device ?
15. What are various types of semi-conductor memories ? State its types and applications.
16. What are the major secondary storage devices ?
17. When is magnetic tape storage used ?
18. What is a magnetic drum ? State its applications.
19. Why is it necessary to have a hierarchy of memory devices in a computer system ?
20. What does ROM stand for ? Enumerate the applications of ROM.
21. Why do we need secondary storage devices ? What are the characteristics of secondary storage?
22. What are the access times of semiconductor memory, hard-disks, and floppy-disks ?
23. What is a magnetic tape ? State its major characteristics.
24. Explain the working of magnetic media.
25. What are optical disks and how do they work ?
26. Why a floppy diskette is named so ? How is it different from a hard-disk ?
27. Explain the difference between Zip-Disk, Jaz-Disk and SuperDisk.
28. State the applications of ROM and RAM.
29. What are main-, secondary-, and backup-memories ? Explain the importance of each.
30. What are the various type of mechanisms used in magnetic tapes ?
31. What is virtual memory ? State its importance.
32. What does a core-memory mean ?
33. What is the role of Cache Memory ? Also explain the terms 'hit' and 'miss'.
34. Describe ROM, PROM and EEPROM with their merits and demerits.
35. What are different types of magnetic memory ? Outline each of these.
36. What are the traditional approaches to data manipulation and retrieval ?
37. What do you mean by buffering ? How buffering is helpful in data storage ?

38. What would happen if a hard disk drive's read/write head touches the disk while the disk was spinning ?
39. Is the distance between a hard disk drive's read/write head and the hard disk smaller than, greater than, or the same as the width of a human hair ?
40. State the advantages of magnetic disks over magnetic tapes.
41. What is meant by tape density ? How is it measured ?
42. Distinguish between the fixed-head and moving-head magnetic disk.
43. Under what circumstances is a new master file created in sequential processing ?
44. Outline the advantages of hard-disks over floppy-disks.
45. Which of the file organisation method would you choose and why ?
46. How do you protect a fixed hard disk from a head crash ?
47. What precautions are to be taken in handling floppy disks ?
48. Why don't heads on tape drives experience "crashes" ?
49. If a floppy can be used to boot a computer system, what is the need to have a separate ROM for the system ?
50. What characteristic of a disk drive determines the worst case latency time ?
51. What type of problem does error checking detects ?
52. How are physical and logical records related in a magnetic tape ?
53. How you can take care of your floppy disks ?
54. How data are represented on magnetic tape ?
55. Describe the file organisation format on the magnetic tape.
56. What are the two distinguishing features of diskette ? Give an example of each feature.
57. What is the purpose of inter-block gap ? What information is contained on a magnetic tape header label ? What is the purpose of an end-of-file marker ?
58. What is magnetic-bubble memory ? Explain its working and applications.
59. What is meant by destructive and non-destructive read out ?
60. Explain the components as well as working of a floppy-diskette.
61. Compare various types of optical-disks along with their respective areas of application.
62. Why are magnetic disks the most commonly used storage media ?
63. How are data represented on disks ?
64. What is flash-memory ? Explain its usage.
65. What is blocking ?
66. Explain data can be accessed on a magnetic disk using index.
67. Discuss seek-time and latency time in relation to fixed-head and moving-head disk systems.
68. What are magnetic cards and where are these used ?
69. How are Winchester disks superior to conventional hard disk systems ? What is the typical storage capacity of such disks ?
70. What is the main difference between the way data is stored in the tape and disk ?
71. What types of environmental hazards can damage a magnetic disk or accidentally erase data?
72. What is meant by formatting of a magnetic disk.
73. Differentiate between volatile-memory and non-volatile memory.

74. What factors decide the transfer rate of a disk system ?
75. Which are the two basic techniques used for addressing the data records that are stored on a disk ?
76. What are the three methods of accessing files in secondary storage ? Explain with an example each of them.
77. Briefly describe the term "sequential access".
78. How does block factor effect on the time required to access the tape ?
79. What is meant by magneto-optical disk ? Explain its working.
80. Fixed-head disk systems reduce total access time by avoiding either seek time or latency ? Which one is neglected and why ?
81. What are various types of magnetic-tapes ? Compare them with respect to their storage capacities.
82. What do you understand by volatility ?
83. The data transfer rate is faster in disk than in a magnetic tape. Why ?
84. What do you understand by disk-organisation ? Explain.
85. Explain the terms "disk pack" and "cylinder" in a hard-disk.
86. What do you mean by storage?
87. Explain the various primary and secondary storage devices?
88. What do you mean by random access memory? Explain the difference types of random access memory?
89. Difference between dynamic and static RAM.
90. What do you mean by read only memory?
91. What do you mean by essential start-up?
92. Explain the various types of read only memory in detail?
93. What do you mean by magnetic tape?
94. Explain various advantages and disadvantages of magnetic tape?
95. Explain the concept of magnetic disk?
96. Difference between magnetic tape and magnetic disk?
97. What do you mean by hard disk drive? Explain the performance of hard disk drive.
98. What do you mean by optical disk? Explain various optical storage devices.
99. What are the advantages and disadvantages of optical disk?
100. What do you mean by optical disk drive?

Data Communication, Computer Networks and Internet

7.1 INTRODUCTION

Data communication is the process of electronically sending data from one point to another. Linking one computer to another permits the power and resources of that computer to be tapped. It also makes possible the sharing and updating of data at different locations.

Computers that are physically located close to each other, either in the same room or building, can communicate data through a direct-cable link. Computers located far apart use a special form of data communication - telecommunication.

The process of using communication facilities such as telephone system and microwave relays to send data between computers is a form of data communication sometimes referred to as telecommunication, or teleprocessing.

7.2 DATA COMMUNICATION

We all are acquainted with some sorts of communication in our day to day life. For communication of information and messages we use telephone and postal communication systems. Similarly data and information from one computer system can be transmitted to other systems across geographical areas. Thus data transmission is the movement of information using some standard methods. These methods include electrical signals carried along a conductor, optical signals along an optical fibers and electromagnetic areas.

"Data Communications is the transfer of data or information between a source and a receiver. The source transmits the data and the receiver receives it."

Suppose a manager has to write several letters to various clients. First he has to use his PC and Word Processing package to prepare his letter. If the PC is connected to the entire client's PCs through networking, he can send the letters to all the clients within minutes. Thus irrespective of geographical areas, if PCs are connected through communication channel, the data and information, computer files and any other program can be transmitted to other computer systems within seconds.

The modern form of communication like e-mail and Internet is possible only because of computer networking.

The effectiveness of data communication depends upon these three fundamental characteristics.

1. **Delivery:** The system must deliver the data to the correct destination. The data must be received by the device or user to whom it was sent.
2. **Accuracy:** The system must deliver data accurately. Data that have been altered in transmission and left uncorrected are unusable.
3. **Timeliness:** The system must deliver data in a timely manner. Data delivered late are useless. In real time transmission data must be delivered without significant delay as in case of audio and video data.

Data communication consists of five basic components:

1. **Message:** The message is the information or data to be communicated. i can be text, numbers, pictures, sound or video or combination of these.
2. **Sender:** The sender is the device that sends the message. It can be a computer, work station, camera etc.
3. **Receiver:** The receiver is the device that receives the message. It can be a computer, work station, television etc.
4. **Medium:** The transmission medium is the path by which message travels from sender to receiver. It can be a wire, coaxial cable, fibre optics, laser or radio waves etc.
5. **Protocol:** A protocol is a set of rules that governs the data communication. It represents the agreement of communicating devices. Without a protocol devices can not communicate to each other.

7.3 FORMS OF DATA TRANSMISSION

There are two forms of data transmission :

Analog Data Transmission

Digital Data Transmission

Analog data transmission is the transmission of data in a continuous waveform. The telephone system is an example of a system designed for analog data transmission.

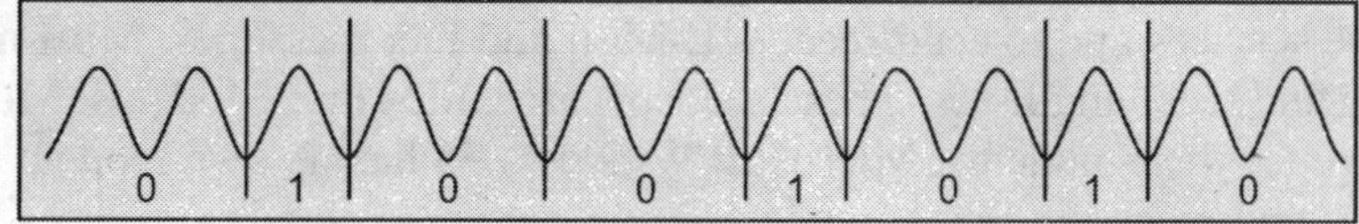

Fig 7.1 : Analog Signal (Waveform)

Digital data transmission is the transmission of data using distinct on and off electrical states. Recall that data in digital form are represented as either on (1) or off (0). Because the data communication is faster and more efficient than analog, it would seem that all data communication between computers would be in digital form, however, that is not the case. Totally digital is possible; however, the telephone system, an analog system, is used for a great percentage of data communication because it is the largest and most widely used communication system in place. Because of the expense involved in converting to a digital system in place. Because of the expense involved in converting to a digital system or running a duplicate digital system, a method was devised allowing the digital data to be transmitted over telephone lines. The process is called modulation-demodulation.

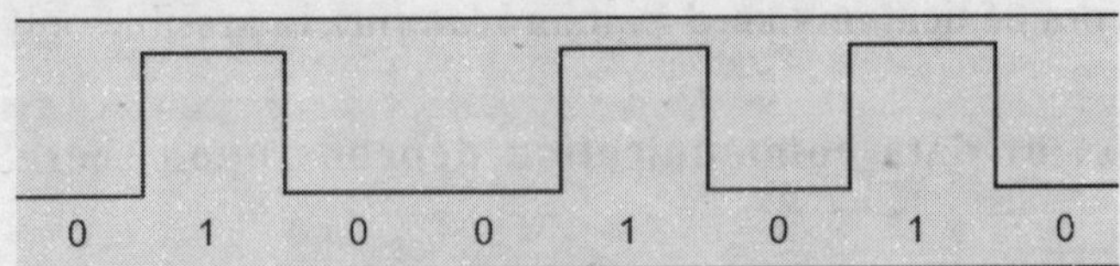

Fig. 7.2 : Digital Signal

Benefits of Digital Data Transmission

The following are the benefits gained by transmitting data in digital form :

- Ability to achieve extremely low error rates on digital circuits
- Properly designed digital circuits are less susceptible to distortion and interference
- Regeneration of digital signals to extend length of the link without accumulating additional noise and distortion as would be the case with analog repeaters
- Digital multiplexing is much simpler than frequency division multiplexing on analog lines
- Digital components and circuits are less expensive and more reliable than analog ones.
- Various forms of digital signals can be integrated and transmitted together e.g. data, digitized voice, digitized TV and FAX
- Complicated and complex functions such as statistical multiplexing and digital switching may be implemented on digital systems at low cost because the signals do not require expensive modems for conversion into digital form before they may be processed.

7.4 MODEM AND ITS TYPES

The word Modem stands for **M**odulator-**Dem**odulator. Data in computer is formatted as digital signals. However, because telephone lines were designed to transmit the human voice, they format data as analog signals. For communication between computers to take place over a telephone line, the digital signal must be converted to an analog signal before it is transmitted. After its journey over the telephone lines, the analog signal must then be reconverted back to a digital signal so that it can be used by the receiving computer.

The process of converting a digital signal to an analog signal is called modulation. Demodulation is the process of reconverting the analog signal back to a digital signal. The device that accomplishes both of these processes is called a modem.

When all the telephone lines become digital carrier, the modem will no longer be required. Till then you need a modem to connect to Internet, dial-into the bulletin board systems (BBSs) and other commercial on-line services and to send/receive E-Mail and Fax messages. Most modems today are capable of sending and receiving faxes. These modems are called Fax-Modems. Most manufacturers supply the software for their modems. Microsoft Windows 95 has its own modem utilities including utilities for sending and receiving faxes.

The speed at which modems can transfer data is measured in bits per second (bps). The modems that usually uses for connecting to the Internet have transfer rates in the range of 14,4 Kbps. But modems with transfer rates of 28.8 Kbps, 33.6 Kbps and 56 Kbps are now available in the market. If we intend to use a modem to explore the WWW and download a lot of files we should buy a faster modem of 28.8 Kbps or 33.6 Kbps.

Different types are Modems are shown in **Fig. 7.3.**

Fig. 7.3: Modems

The three basic types of modems used in microcomputers are :

(a) Acoustic Modem
(b) External Direct-connect Modem
(c) Internal Direct-connect Modem

7.4.1 Acoustic Modem

The acoustic modem, or acoustic coupler as it is sometimes called, has two cups into which the handset of your telephone is placed. The acoustic modem sends data through the mouthpiece and receives data through the ear-piece of the handset. This type of modem is not used very often today because :

(i) The signal is much more susceptible to distortion than with other types of modems; and
(ii) The carbon microphones used in a telephone handset limit the rate of data transmission.

7.4.2 External Direct-connect Modem

An external direct-connect modem is external to the computer and connects directly to the telephone line with a modular phone jack. The direct connection greatly reduces the signal's distortion and permits faster data transfer rates. A popular external direct-connect modems have 'a' variety of features not found on acoustic modems, including the ability to :

Check the operating status using status lights and speakers
Change the speed at which data are transmitted
Dial and answer the phone automatically
Respond to commands from a communication program
Self-test to verify the modem's ability to correctly transmit data

Because the specialised circuitry in these modems allows them to perform these and other functions, they often called **smart or intelligent** devices.

7.4.3 Internal Direct-connect Modem

An internal direct-connect modem has all the needed communication circuitry on a plug-in board that fits into one of the expansion slots inside the computer. A separate communication board or serial port with RS-232 interface is not needed. Internal direct-connect modems also link directly to the telephone line with a modular phone jack. These modems have many of the same special features as the external direct-connect modems. In addition, they take no desk space and are ideal for use in portable computers.

Internal Direct-connect Modem vs. External Direct-connect Modem

Both of these can be compared in **Table 7.1.**

Table 7.1

S.No.	Internal Direct-connect Modem	External Direct-connect Modem
1.	Very difficult to install and configure	Easy to install and configure
2.	Has its own built-in serial port and is thus unaffected by the UART chip problem.	It may require a new serial port if machine is old and the modem is faster.
3.	It doesn't require a serial cable or additional power socket.	It requires an additional electrical socket and cable
4.	It doesn't require additional desk space	It will need desk space.
5.	When modem gets stuck, we need to turn off the machine and then turn it on, which results in wastage of time	When it gets stuck, getting it back to work is as easy as flipping a switch
6.	It may require changes in hardware settings.	It hardly requires any change in hardware settings

7.5 COMMUNICATION CHANNELS

A communication channel is a medium through which data is transmitted among devices. It provides a way for data to be exchanged between remote sites and a computer or among multiple computer. The main providers of communication channels for computer users are the telephone companies and long distance carriers. It is also possible for an organisation to set up its own wires, cables, or electronic links to establish a private a communication capability. With either of these approaches, the primary types of channels available for transmission of data include the following :

Wire cable
Microwave
Fibre optics
Communication Satellites
Laser beams
RADAR

7.5.1 Wire Cable

Wire cable it is the most common type of data communication channel in use. It includes telegraph lines, telephone lines, and coaxial cables. These are the most popular channels. It can be classified in the following two categories :

Telegraph Cable
Telephone Cables
Twisted-pair Cable
Co-axial Cable

Telegraph Cable: A telegraph line usually consists of a single strand of wire connecting two points. The name telegraph ties this kind of channel to the days when transmissions took place on strands of wire that usually ran beside railroad tracks. Signals were initiated at telegraph keys that served as switches to make or break connections. Communication occurred when trained operators decoded the series of clicks that made up Morse Code.

This type of channel is simple and inexpensive. On telegraph lines, communication takes place in one direction at a time. Services available on telegraph lines are Simplex and Half-duplex transmissions.

Telephone Cables: One-way-at-a-time transmission would not work foe telephone calls. People want to be able to talk whenever they feel they have something to say. Therefore, telephone lines use two carriers, or a pair of wires to make it possible to send and receive signals at the same time. This kind of transmission is called full-duplex service. Under full-duplex transmission, two people can talk at once or two data transmission points can be sending and receiving at the same time.

Telephone Lines are shown in **Fig. 7.4**

Fig. 7.4: Telephone Lines

Telephone lines also make possible one-way transmission of greater information volumes than telegraph lines. This is because two wires have a far greater transmission capacity, or bandwidth, than one. Thus, while single telegraph lines carry about 60 words per minute, a single pair of wires that make up a telephone line can carry 1200 or more words per minute, depending on the line quality and signal generation methods.

Twisted-pair Cable: It is the oldest and still most common transmission line. It consists of copper wires twisted into pairs. These lines are used in established communication networks throughout the world for both voice as well as data transmission.

Co-axial Cable: It consists of a sturdy copper or aluminium wire wrapped with spacers to insulate and protect it. The insulation minimises the interference and distortion of the signals the cable carries. Groups of coaxial cables may be bundled together in a big cable for ease of installation. High-quality co-axial cables can be placed underground and laid on the floors of lakes and oceans. They allow high-speed data transmission.

Coaxial cables are used on mainframe computers to link the processor to secondary storage units and other high-speed peripherals. These are also used to transmit TV signals from cameras to broadcast transmitters or across the country for broadcast into different regions. Data transmission capabilities of coaxial cable channels run into the millions of bits per second tom provide broadband service.

Advantages

Easier to use

Cheaper to use the extensive wire-cable networks that already exists.

Reduced compatibility problems due to standardised technology used to transmit data over wire cables

Disadvantages

As data is transmitted in analog form while using wire cable, so digital data must be converted to an analog signal before they reach the wire cable.

Conversion from digital data to analog signal requires special hardware

Digital to analog form and then back to digital form conversion slows down the transmission of data.

Wire cable is subject to electrical interference making it less reliable than other types of communication channels.

Difficult to create physical links needed where users are separated by large distances or natural barriers such as mountains or seas.

7.5.2 Microwave

Another type of analog communication channel is microwave. Microwave signals are transmitted through the atmosphere as radio and television signals are transmitted rather than through wire cables. A microwave system consists of towers located at intervals of 25 to 30 miles on which dish-like antennas are mounted. Microwave signals must be transmitted in a straight line as they do not bend around corners or around the curve of the earth. Transmitter stations redirect and boost the signals. Satellites are also used to direct microwaves over geographically dispersed large areas.

Microwave systems have the capacity to carry large quantities of data i.e. both digital and analog at high rates of speed. They are used for the transmission of TV and telephonic signals.

Microwave tower and Radio Tower are shown in **Fig. 7.5.**

Fig. 7.5: (a) Microwave Tower (b) Radio Tower

Advantages

Microwave has a much lower error rate thus making it more reliable as compared to wire-cable.

Communication links can be made over large distances and rough terrains as there are no physical links between the sending and receiving systems.

Disadvantages

Very high cost of ground stations and satellites to support a microwave communication channels.

7.5.3 Fiber Optics

Third type of communication channel is fibre optics. Unlike wire cable and microwave, a fibre-optic channel transmits data in digital form. It uses light impulses that travel through clear flexible tubing. The tubing is thinner than a human hair and hundreds of them can fit in the same amount of space required for one wire cable. Technical developments continue to drive down the costs of installing, using and manufacturing fibre optics which will help to make it competitive with traditional cabling.

The 'core' of a fibre-optic cable is a very thin strand of highly refined cylindrical glass. The glass core of the cable may have a diameter as small as 4.5 m or as large as 400 m. A second layer of glass is called the clad which surrounds the core. The clad is fused directly to the core so that it is very difficult to see the boundary between the two with naked eyes.

Advantages

Transmission losses of fibre-optic cables are much lower than that of wire cables.

Fibre optics are very reliable communication channels.

Photons of light rather than an electrical signal move through the optical fibre and thus there are no chances of any sparking, which results into a safer system.

Provide substantial size and weight reduction as well as increased speed and greater carrying capacity.

Data can be transmitted at very high speeds with few or no errors.

Glass is immune to corrosive and oxide degradation and thus will stand up well in hostile environments.

Unlike wire cables, fibre-optic cables are not subject to electrical interference.

As the fibre-optic system carries no electrical current, the energy transmitted through the fibre can't radiate radio frequency interference and nor can it be contaminated by any external noise or radio frequency fields.

Disadvantages

Require repeaters to read and boost the signal strength because light pulses will lose signal strength over long distances.

It is limited to fixed point-to-point ground installations and can't leave the ground nor be associated with a mobile communication station.

Ways in which the light source can be modulated are limited.

Higher-power devices required as light-emitting sources are very costly.

7.5.4 Communication Satellites

The availability of communication satellites has made it possible to transmit microwave signals over thousands of miles. Satellites have now become an integral part of the world-wide communication system. Communication satellites in space orbiting 22,000 miles above the earth, are also used as microwave relay stations because they rotate at the precise point and speed above the equator that makes them appear stationary to microwave transmitters on the ground. The satellite is nothing more than a radio-relay station but they have one potential i.e. the capability of a direct line-of-sight path to 98 % of the earth's surface.

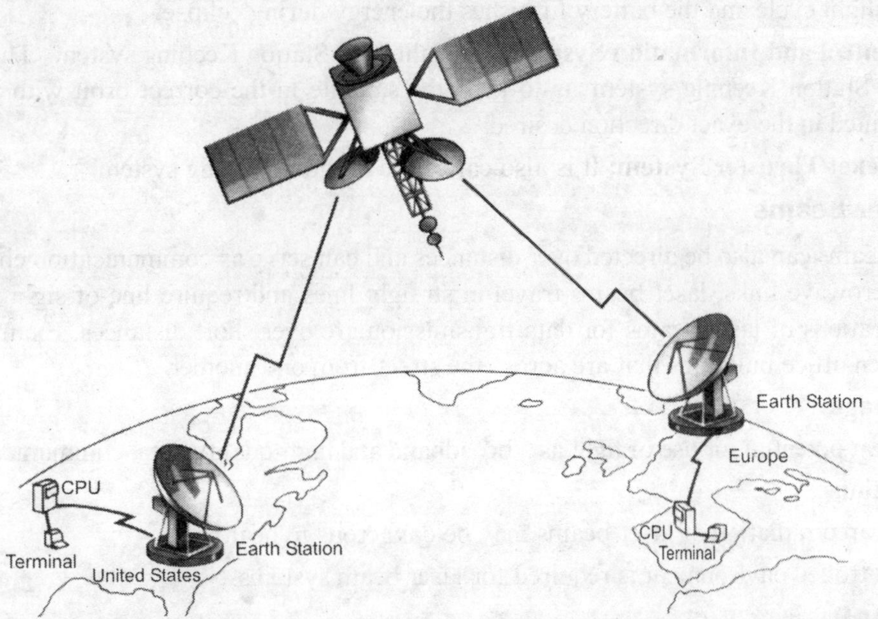

Fig. 7.6: Communication over geographical locations using Communication Satellites

Among the dozens of satellites now orbiting the earth and handling voice, video and data communications are those launched by INTELSAT (International Telecommunication Satellite Consortium). INTELSAT began with the Early Bird satellite in 1965 and now forms a world-wide communication system for over 100 countries. It accounts for most long-distance international communications.

Parts of communication satellite are shown in **Fig. 7.7.**

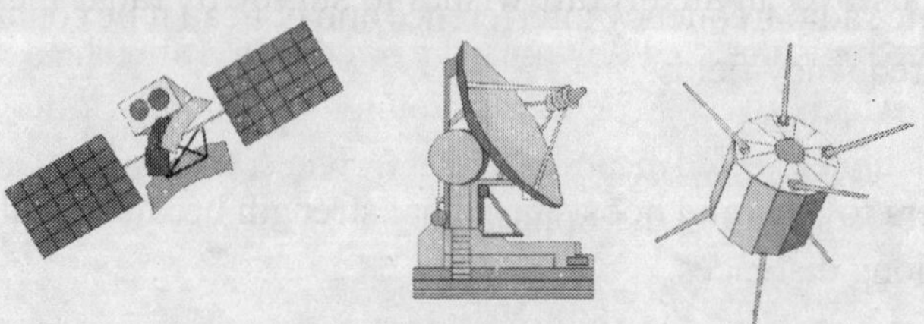

(a) Satellite With Panels (b) Satellite Antenna System (c) Satellite Complex

Fig. 7.7: Parts of Communication Satellite

Satellite Components

The following are five major components in a satellite:

Transponder: It is a high frequency radio receiver, a frequency down-converter and a power amplifier, which is used to transmit the down-link signal.

Antenna System: The antenna system contains the antennas and mechanisms to position them correctly. Once properly in place, they will generally function trouble-free for the life of the satellite.

Power Package: Power package is nothing but the power supply to the satellite. The satellite must be powered either from a battery or solar energy system. In the case of communication satellites in the Clarke orbit, a combination of battery power and solar energy is used. A solar cell system supplies the power to run the electronics and charge the batteries during the sunlight cycle and the battery furnishes the energy during eclipse.

Control and Information System: It is called the Station Keeping system. The function of the Station Keeping system is to keep the satellite in the correct orbit with the antennas pointed in the exact direction desired.

Rocket Thruster System: It is also called the Station Keeping system

7.5.5 Laser Beams

Laser beams can also be directed over distances and can serve as communication channels. As is true for microwave links, laser beams travel in straight lines and require line-of-sight relay points. Most applications of laser beams for data transmission are over short distances. Examples include links between office buildings that are across the street from one another.

Advantages

Great potential for use of light as a broadband and high-quality data communication carrier.

Limitations

Infrared radiation of laser beams may be dangerous to health.

Controlled environment is required for laser beam systems.

7.5.6 RADAR

The name **'RADAR'** is an acronym of Radio Detecting And Ranging. It denotes the method of scanning the surrounding space by means of high frequency radio waves, which are sent out from a powerful transmitter and are reflected by any objects, which they encounter. The reflected beam is picked up by a receiver and its strength and direction gives information on the size, distance, altitude, etc. of the object.

If for example, an observer in an aircraft wishes to survey by radar the terrain over which he is flying, a rotating radar beam is directed downward from the aircraft. The beam scans a circular area in the form of a sector, which sweeps round and round. Depending on the nature of the reflecting objects, the intensity of the reflected beam will vary. The transmission and reception of the high frequency waves are effected in the radar apparatus.

Fig. 7.8: RADAR System

The radar waves are generated in the transmitter, which is equipped with radio tubes of special designs. The transmitting antenna usually also functions as the receiving antenna. The process is called 'periodic changeover'. The receiver picks up the reflected beam and the corresponding electronic circuits are used to deflect an electron beam in a CRT (cathode ray tube). The beam is so deflected that it scans the luminescent screen from the center to the edge while it rotates at the same speed as the antenna.

RADAR Screen is shown in **Fig. 7.9.**

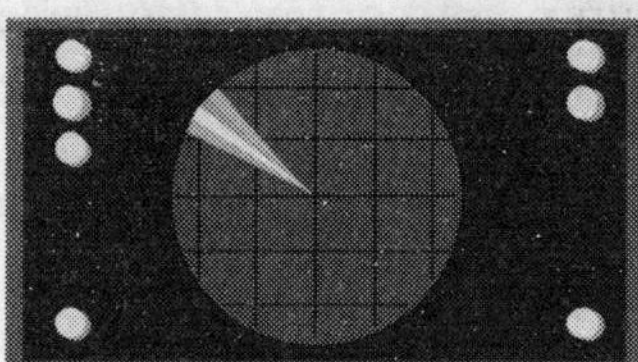

Fig. 7.9: RADAR Screen

Most radar sets employ pulse radar. This is so called because the transmitter sends out short intense bursts or pulses of energy with a relatively long interval between the pulses. The receiver is active during this interval. When sufficient time has elapsed to permit the reception of echoes from the most distant objects of interest, the transmitter sends another short pulse and the cycle is repeated.

7.6 DATA TRANSMISSION MODES

There are three ways for transmitting data from one point to another:

1. **Simplex:** In simplex mode the communication can take place in one direction. The receiver receives the signal from the transmitting device. In this mode the flow of information is Uni.-directional. Hence it is rarely used for data communication.
2. **Half-duplex:** In half-duplex mode the communication channel is used in both directions, but only in one direction at a time. Thus a half-duplex line can alternately send and receive data.
3. **Full-duplex:** In full duplex the communication channel is used in both directions at the same time. Use of full-duplex line improves the efficiency as the line turn-around time required in half-duplex arrangement is eliminated. Example of this mode of transmission is the telephone line.

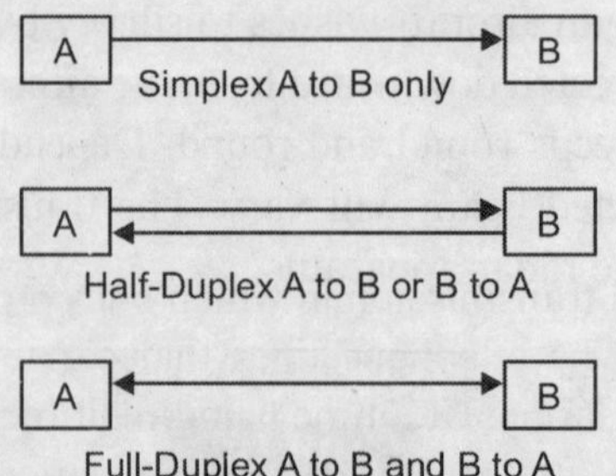

Figure 7.10: Data Transmission modes

7.7 COMMUNICATION CHANNEL CONFIGURATIONS

The following two are the principal communication channel configurations :

Point-to-point

Multi-point

7.7.1 Point-to-point Configuration

In a point-to-point channel configuration, a device (e.g., a terminal or computer) is connected directly to another device by a dedicated communication channel, giving those devices sole use of that channel. Point-to-point channel can be an inefficient and costly configuration if a terminal is not active enough to keep the line busy.

7.7.2 Multi-point Configuration

Another configuration is multi-point channel configuration in which three or more devices are connected to the same line. The multi-point configuration uses the communication channel more efficiently and reduces the amount of inter-cabling needed, which ultimately lower its cost.

Two methods are used to determine which device gets access to a channel :

Polling and

Contention.

Polling: In polling, the computer checks each device, one at a time, to see if the device has a message to send. If the device has a message ready, transmission begins; if not, the computer moves on to the next device to poll it. After all devices have been individually polled, the process begins again.

Limitation: A disadvantage to polling is that if there are no messages to be sent by the device being polled, the computer's processor will be idle, wasting expensive processor time.

Contention: Contention method puts the devices in control, i.e., each device monitors the communication channel to see if the channel is free. If the channel is free, the device will send its message. If the communication channel is being used, the device will wait for a pre-determined amount of time and will try again. This process is repeated until the channel is free.

Limitation: A problem with this approach is that although the processor is not idle, one device can tie up the communication channel for long periods of time.

7.8 CHANNEL SHARING

The purpose of channel sharing is to increase the efficiency of use of a communication channel. The following are three methods used to regulate the flow of data from communication channels into a computer :

Multiplexing
Concentration
Controlling

7.8.1 MULTIPLEXING

Multiplexing is a form of data transmission in which one communication channel carries several transmissions at the same time. The telephone lines that carry our daily conversations can carry thousands or even more of conversations at a time using multiplexing concept. The exact number of simultaneous transmission depends on the type of communication channel and the data transmission rate. Accordingly, the communication channel is shared in such a way as to maximum the utilization of the channel capacity. Thus the method of dividing a single channel into many channels so that a number of independent signals may be transmitted on it is known as Multiplexing.

Multiplexing schemes can be divided into three basic categories:

1. Frequency Division Multiplexing (FDM)
2. Time Division Multiplexing (TDM)
3. Wave Division Multiplexing (FDM)

7.8.1.1 Frequency Division Multiplexing (FDM)

FDM is the technique used to divide the bandwidth available in a physical medium into a number of smaller independent logical channels with each channel having a small bandwidth. The method of using a number of carrier frequencies each of which is modulated by an independent speech signal is in fact frequency division multiplexing.

Three voice-grade telephone channels are multiplexing using FDM. When many channels are multiplexed together, 400Hz is allocated to each channel to keep them well separated. First the voice channels are raised in frequency, each by a different amount. Then they can be combined, because no two channels how occupy the same portion of the spectrum. Notice that even though there are gaps (guard bands) between the channels, there is some overlap between adjacent channels, because the filters do not have sharp edges. This overlap means that a strong spike at the edge of one channel will be felt in the adjacent one as non-thermal noise.

Frequency-division multiplexing works best with low-speed devices. The frequency division multiplexing schemes used around the world is to some degree standardized. A wide spread standard is 12 400-Hz each voice channels (300Hz for user, plus two guard bands of 500Hz each) multiplexed into the 60 to 108 KHz band. Many carriers offer a 48 to 56 kbps leased line service to customers, based on the group. Other standards upto 230000 voice channels also exist.

Example: The allocated spectrum is about 1 MHz, roughly 500 to 1500 KHz. Different (stations, each operating in a portion of the spectrum. With the interchannel separation great enough to prevent interference. This system is an example of frequency division multiplexing.

Advantages of FDM

1. Here user can be added to the system by simply adding another pair of transmitter modulator and receiver demodulators.
2. FDM system support full duplex information flow which is required by most of application.
3. Noise problem for analog communication has lesser effect.

Disadvantages of FDM

1. In FDM system, the initial cost is high. This may include the cable between the two ends and the associated connectors for the cable.

2. In FDM system, a problem for one user can sometimes affect others.
3. In FDM system, each user requires a precise carrier frequency.

7.8.1.2 Time Division Multiplexing (TDM)

TDM is another popular method of utilizing the capacity of a physical channel effectively. Each user of the channel is allotted a small time interval during which is may transmit a message. Thus the total time available in the channel is divided and each user is allocated a time slice. In TDM, user send message sequentially one after another. Each user can, however, use the full channel bandwidth during the period he has control over the channel. The channel capacity is fully utilized in TDM by interleaving a number of messages belonging to different users into one long message. This message sent through the physical channel must be separated at the receiving end. Individual chunks of message sent by each user should be reassembled into a full message.

Unfortunately, TDM can only be used for digital data multiplexing. Since local loops produce analog signals, a conversion is needed from analog to digital in the end office. Where all the individual local loops come together to be combined onto outgoing trucks.

Example: In some countries, the individual stations have two logical sub channels: music and advertising. These two alternate in time on the same frequency first a burst of music, then a burst of advertising, then more music and so on. This situation is time division multiplexing.

Advantages of TDM

1. It uses a single links.
2. It does not require precise carrier matching at both end of the links.
3. Use of capacity is high.
4. Each to expand the number of users on a system at a low cost.
5. There is no need to include identification of the traffic stream on each packet.

Disadvantages of TDM

1. The sensitivity to other user problem is high.
2. Initial cost is high.
3. Technical complexity is more.
4. The noise problem for analog communication has greater effect.

7.8.1.3 Wave Division Multiplexing (WDM)

Wave or **Wavelength Division Multiplexing (WDM)** is used with fibre optic cables. WDM is a technology that closely resembles frequency division multiplexing, but is specifically used to combine lots of Optical Carrier signals into a single optical fibre.

The WDM technique relies on a laser that is designed to emit single colours of light. Each of the signals that are to be transmitted is then attached to a laser that will emit a different coloured light beam. All these individual light beams are then sent at the same time. At the receiving end, a device splits the combined colours back into the original individual colours again.

7.8.2 CONCENTRATION

Frequently, it is necessary to connect more devices to a computer than the communication channel can handle at once. Concentration is the process of connecting and serving these devices. A concentrator, often a minicomputer, is the hardware that provides concentration. When the number of devices transmitting exceeds the capability of the communication channel, the data are stored in a buffer for later transmission. Many multiplexers also provide concentration.

7.8.3 CONTROLLING

Controllers or cluster controllers, link groups of terminals or other devices to a communication channels. The controller polls the status of each terminal and transfers data from a terminal to the host computer when necessary.

7.9 FRONT-END PROCESSORS

A front-end processor is a processor that handles all the data-communication control functions. While the CPU in the front-end processor handles all the communication tasks, the CPU of the main computer is free to work on other tasks. The two processors interact only when data need to be passed between them. A typical front-end processor might control scores of communication channels of varying types and speeds coming from a number of diverse remote terminals.

Indeed, front-end processors are computers i.e. they have some identical circuitry and perform many of the operations that a data processing equipment performs. These can be programmed to perform a variety of functions such as concentration, error control, code conversion, buffering, and other functions related to data and message control.

7.10 DATA TRANSMISSION

In the present Information Technology (IT) scenario, speed of data transmission has a significant role to play. Every information enthusiast wants to be able to make the data transmission speeds even more faster. Information that once took days to receive now seems to be available on the very next moment of pressing the key.

What is Baud Rate?

The rate at which data is transferred is called the baud rate. In fact, baud rate is the number of times per second the signal being transmitted modulates or demodulates. Baud rate is measured in terms of bits per second (bps). Although higher speeds are possible, typical data transmission speeds are 300, 1200, 2400, 4800, 9600, 14,400 bps. There are two factors that determine the rate at which data can be transmitted over communication channels :

Channel bandwidth

Method of data transmission

7.10.1 Channel Bandwidths

The bandwidth, or grade, of a communication channel determines the rate, or speed, at which data can be transmitted over a channel. The term **"bandwidth"** is often shortened to **"band".** There are three bands for communication channels :

Narrow-band

Voice-band

Broad-band

The slowest of these is **the narrow-band channel,** which transmits data at rates between 40 and 100 bps. A telegraph line is a narrow-band channel.

Voice-band channel can transmit data at rates between 110 and 9,600 bps. Telephone lines are voice-band channels.

The fastest of these is the **broad-band channel,** which can transmit data at rates up to several mega-bits per second (mbps). Advancement in technology continues to improve to allow data to be transmitted on some types of broad-band channels in the range of billions-of-bits-per-second (bbps). Microwaves, coaxial cables, and fibre optics are all broad-band channels.

7.10.2 Methods of Data Transmission

There are two methods of transmission :

Asynchronous Transmission
Synchronous Transmissions

7.10.2.1 Asynchronous Transmission

It is a transmission method in which one character is sent at a time and the transfer of data is controlled by start bits and stop bits. Each character is surrounded by bits that signal the beginning and end of the character. These characters allow the receiving terminal to synchronise itself with the receipt of data on a character-by-character basis.

Asynchronous transmission is the least expensive of the two methods. It is often used in low-speed transmission of data in conjunction with narrow-band and some lower speed voice-band channels where the transmitting device operates manually or at irregular intervals.

7.10.2.2 Synchronous Transmission

In this type of transmission method, blocks of characters are transmitted in timed sequences. Rather than using start and stop bits around each character, each block of characters is marked with synchronisation characters. The receiving device accepts data until it detects a special ending character or a predetermined number of characters at which time the device knows the message has come to an end.

Protocols: A set of traffic rules and procedures framed for data transmission are called data-transmission protocols. The same protocols must be followed by all devices participating in the communication session. These rules may vary from one device to another.

Handshaking: Prearranged signals defining the protocol to be followed when transmitting and receiving data are sent between computers in an exchange called handshaking.

7.11 COMPUTER NETWORK

A computer network is an interconnection of various computer systems located at different places. In computer network two or more computers are linked together with a medium and data communication devices for the purpose of communicating data and sharing resources. The computer that provides resources to other computers on a network is known as server. In the network the individual computers, which access shared network resources, are known as workstations or nodes.

Fig. 7.11: Computer Network

7.11.1 Need of Computer Network

The need of a computer network arose due to:

Limited resources
Desire to share the resources
Cost Reduction

Today, that's a limiting view, because the most important resource is information. Network lets us share information and the same is achieved by **Resource Sharing.**

Resource Sharing: The purpose of many computer networks is to permit a far-flung community of users to share computer resources. Many such users now have their own microcomputers, so the shared resources have to be interesting enough to warrant access via a network. The facilities accessible by networks are in fact becoming more interesting at a rapid rate.

The remote computer may contain software which a user needs to employ. It may be proprietary software kept at one location. It may require a larger machine than any at the user's location. The distant computer may provide access to data which is stored and maintained at its location. Sometimes the remote machine controls a large or special printing facility. Sometimes the remote machine compiles programs which are used on smaller peripheral machines.

The resource sharing will automatically result in **Cost Reduction.**

Cost Reduction: There are various aspects of technology which are likely to force the price of terminal usage drastically lower. This is important because almost all aspects of telecommunications are characterised by high price elasticity. In other words, when the price comes down, the usage goes up.

7.11.2 Key Issues in a Computer Network

The following are the major key issues to be thrashed out very carefully before we go for a computer network :

Nature of Nodes : Whether participating nodes are homogeneous or heterogeneous in nature?

Topology : Which of the computer topology has to be followed ? Computer topology accounts for the physical arrangement of participating computers in the network.

Interconnection Type : Whether interconnection type is point-to-point, multi-point, or broadcast type ?

Reliability : How reliable our network is? Reliability aspect includes error rate, redundancy and recovery procedures.

Channel Capacity Allocation : Whether allocation of channel capacity is time-division or frequency division?

Routing Techniques : Whether message between nodes are to be routed through : Deterministic, Stochastic, and Distributed routing techniques?

Models : Which of the models i.e. Analytical models, Queuing models, Simulation models, Measurement and Validation models are applicable?

Channel Capacity : What are the channel capacities of the communication lines connecting nodes?

Access : Whether computer access in the network is direct-access or through a sub-network?

Protocols : What levels, standards and formats are to be followed while establishing communication between participating nodes ?

Performance : How is higher performance of computer network achieved ? Response time, time to connect, resource utilisation, etc. contribute towards performance of computer network.

Control : Whether centralised control, distributed control or hierarchical control of participating nodes of computer network is suitable ?

7.12 TYPES OF COMPUTER NETWORK

The following are different types of networks:

1. Local Area Network (LAN)
2. Wireless Local Area Network (WLAN)
3. Wide Area Network (WAN)
4. Metropolitan Area Network (MAN)
5. Storage Area Network (SAN)
6. Campus Area Network (CAN)
7. Personal Area Network (PAN)
8. Desk Area Network (DAN)

Criteria for Classification of Computer Networks

The following are the characteristics used to classify different types of computer networks :

Topology

Topology is nothing but the geometric arrangement of positioning computer systems to involve them in the form of a network. For example, Star topology, Bus topology, etc.

Protocol

The protocols are nothing but the set of rules and signals that are used for communication in the network. For example, 'Ethernet' is one of the most popular protocols for LANs.

Architecture

Networks can usually be classified in the following two types :

(i) Peer-to-peer architecture

(ii) Client-Server architecture

All of the above have been described next in this chapter.

7.12.1 Local Area Network (LAN)

A local area network (LAN) is two or more computers directly linked within a small well-defined area such as a room, building, or group of closely placed buildings. A LAN may be made up of only microcomputers or any combination of microcomputers and large systems.

LANs is shown in **Fig. 7.12.**

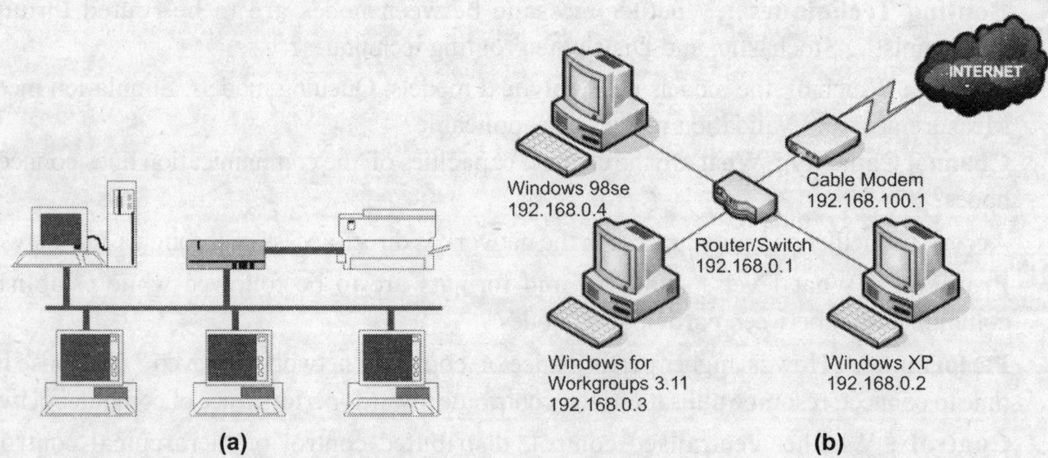

Fig. 7.12: Local Area Network(s)

The computer network which connect the computers in the different parts of the same big city like metropolitan city may be referred to as Metropolitan Area Network (MAN).

Interest in local area networks is constantly growing due to following two developments :

Development of powerful and user-friendly micro-computers

Developments in communication technology

The difference between a LAN and a multi-user system is that a LAN is made up of stand-alone computers whereas a multi-user system typically has one computer that is shared among two or more terminals.

A LAN usually consists of the following :

(i) Two or more computers

(ii) Peripheral devices such as printers and hard-disk drives

(iii) Software to control the operation of the computers or other devices connected to the LAN

(iv) Special cables, usually coaxial or fibre optic, to connect the computers and other devices

(v) A plug-in board to handle the data transmissions.

A benefit of a LAN is the reduction of hardware costs because several computers and users can share peripheral devices such as laser printers, hard-disk drives, color plotters, and modems. Another advantage is the users can share data.

Ensuring the security and privacy of data are two concerns of LAN users. The LAN must get the data to its destination, transmit the data correctly, and prevent unauthorised users from gaining access to that data. These tasks are accomplished through both the hardware and LAN software.

They vary in the type and number of computers that can be connected, the speed at which data can be transferred, and the type of the software used to control the network. Some LANs require that all the computers be of a certain brand, while others allow a variety of brands to be connected. The number of computers in a LAN varies widely from smaller LANs that typically connect 2 to 25 computers, to large LANs that can connect as many as 10,000 computers.

The length of the cable connecting a computer to a LAN also varies depending on the LAN. Most LANs allow cables of about 1000 feet, but some allow cables of several miles to be used. The data transfer speeds range from several thousand bits per second to around 10 million bits per second. The programs that control the LANs also vary in the features they offer. Some programs allow the use of more than one operating system; others allow only one. On some LANs, file access is limited to one user at a time; on others, more than one user can access a file simultaneously.

Hardware Requirements for LAN

The following are major hardware components/devices required for establishing LAN :

Transmission Channel

Network Interface Unit (NIU)

Servers

Workstations

Transmission Channel for LAN

Generally four types of channels are used for data transmission in a LAN. These are:

Twisted Pair Cable

Coaxial Cable

Fibre-Optic Cables

Radio Waves

Network Interface Unit: Network interface units connect each devices in the LAN network to shared transmission device. It contain the rules or logic to access the LAN. NIU is also used to implement LAN protocols and for device attachments. Its function depends on the type of topology used in LAN.

Servers & Workstations: One of the major benefits of implementation of LAN is sharing expensive resources such as storage devices, printers etc. This is achieved through providing servers on the LAN. It is dedicated computer that controls one or more resources. This contains both hardware and software interface for LAN. Three major categories of services used in LANs are :

File Server
Printer Server
Modem Server

In networking, file server is used to share storage space for files. Besides providing storage space for files in a LAN environment, it is used for taking periodical backup, and also to provide gateway to other servers within and between LANs.

Similarly printer server is used to handle printing works of all workstation connected in the network.

In LAN environment also modem is required to get connected to other network or simply to use a telephone. A modem server is used to share this expensive resource by all connected workstations in a network ring.

LAN Software

LAN operating system is required to operate on the LAN system. It has basically two aspects :

Server Software
Workstation Software

LAN operating system facilitates :

- Sharing of expensive resources e.g. printer, storage space etc.
- Security for data
- Connection to other network.

There are various types of LAN operating system. Some popular LAN operating systems are :

Novel Netware
Ethernet
Corvus
ArcNet
LAN Server
Omni Net
PC Net
IBM PC LAN
Etherlik Plus, etc.

7.12.2 Wireless LAN (WLAN)

WLANs provide wireless network communication over short distances using radio or infrared signals instead of traditional network cabling.

A WLAN typically extends an existing wired local area network. WLANs are built by attaching a device called the access point (AP) to the edge of the wired network. Clients communicate with the AP using a wireless network adapter similar in function to a traditional Ethernet adapter.

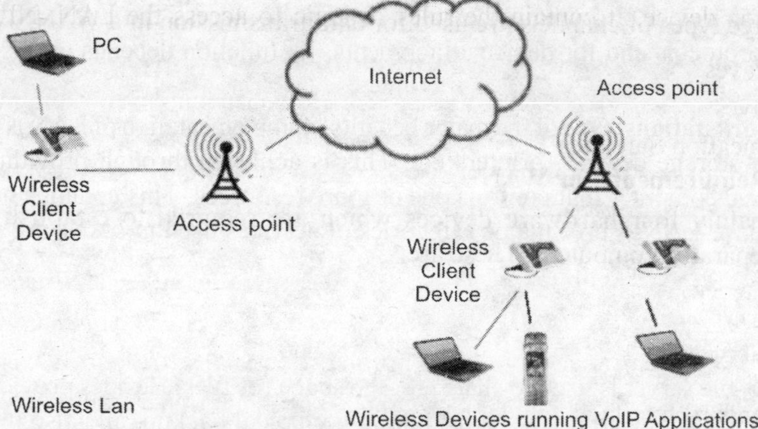

Fig. 7.13: Wireless Local Area Network (WLAN)

Network security remains an important issue for WLANs. Random wireless clients must usually be prohibited from joining the WLAN. Technologies like WEP raise the level of security on wireless networks to rival that of traditional wired networks.

7.12.3 Wide Area Networks (WAN)

A wide area network (WAN) is two or more computers that are geographically dispersed, linked by communication facilities such as telephone system or microwave relays. This type of network is usually limited to use by large corporations and government agencies because of the high costs involved in building and maintaining them.

A WAN is a network that links separate geographical locations and this network can be a public system or any of the various packet switched services provided by the public telecommunication agencies.

The main difference between a WAN and LAN is that, the LAN is under the complete control of the owner, whereas the WAN needs the involvement of another authority like telecom department. LANs are successful and capable of handling very high data transfer rates at low cost because of the small area covered. Besides LANs have a lower error rate than WANs.

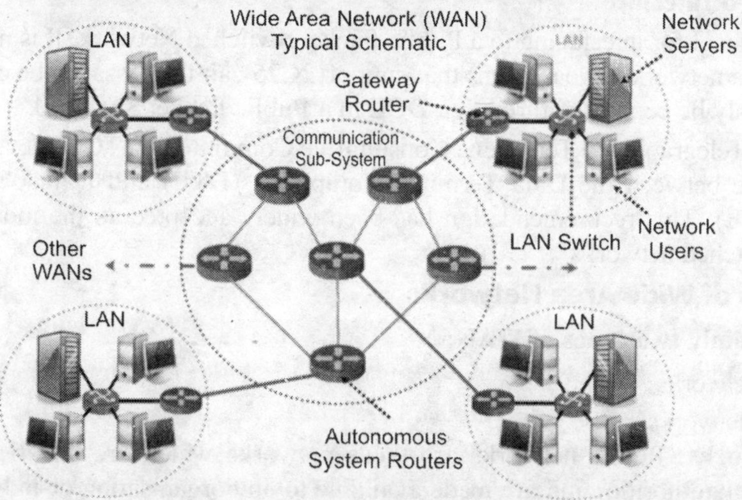

Fig. 7.14: Wide Area Network (WAN)

Transmission Channel for WAN

Generally three types of channels are used for data transmission in a WAN. These are:

Radio Waves

Microwaves

Communication Satellites

Hardware Requirements for WAN

There are mainly four hardware devices which are required to establish linkage between geographically separated computers. These are:

Bridges

Routers

Gateways

X.25 Standard Interface

Bridges: Bridges are used to connect two LANs that use the identical LAN protocols over a wide area. The bridge acts as an address filter which picks up packets from one LAN that are intended for a destination on another LAN and passes these packets on the network. The amount of processing required at the bridge is minimal because all the devices use the same protocols. In case the distance between two LANs is very large then the user is required to employ two identical bridges at either end of the communication link.

Routers: Router is a special type of device that can be used to connect networks that may not be similar. Such type of devices provide connectivity between two LANs or two WANs over large geographical distances. These devices operate at the Network Layer of the OSI model. These devices participate in a routing protocol to access the network topology, and on the basis of this information routers compute the best route from a sender to the receiver.

Gateways: Gateways are used to connect two dissimilar LANs. The terms Gateways and Routers are used interchangeably, though there is discriminating difference between the two. A router operates at the network layer whereas a gateway operates on the application layer of the OSI model.

A gateway is required to convert data packets from one protocol format to another before forwarding it, as it connects two dissimilar networks.

X.25 Standard Interface

X.25 is a protocol for interfacing to a Public Packet Switched Network. It is not a protocol used for implementing a network. Two systems that support X.25 can't necessarily be connected back-to-back. They can only be connected through a DCE in a Public Packet Switched.

International Telegraph and Telephone Consultative Committee (ITTCC) developed X.25 as the standard interface between the Data Terminal Equipment (DTE) and Data Circuit Terminating Equipment (DCTE). This recommendation has been widely accepted as the industry standard for public packet switched networks.

7.12.3.1 Types of Wide Area Networks

There are mainly two types of WAN:

Public Networks

Private Networks

Public Networks: Public networks are those networks which are installed and run by the telecommunication authorities and are made available to any organisation or individual who go for their subscription.

Private Networks: The basic technique used in all forms of private WAN is to use private circuits to link the locations to be served by the network. Between these fixed points the owner of the network has complete freedom to use the circuits in any way they want. They can use the circuits to carry large quantities of data or for high speed transmissions. Private wide area networks can be built using whatever standard technology is available.

7.12.4 Metropolitan Area Network (MAN)

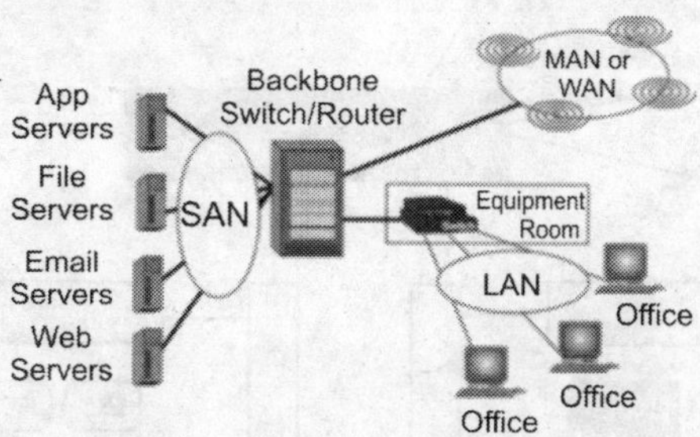

Fig. 7.15: Metropolitan Area Network (MAN)

A metropolitan area network (MAN) is a network that interconnects users with computer resources in a geographic area or region larger than that covered by even a large local area network (LAN) but smaller than the area covered by a wide area network (WAN). The term is applied to the interconnection of networks in a city into a single larger network (which may then also offer efficient connection to a wide area network). It is also used to mean the interconnection of several local area networks by bridging them with backbone lines. The latter usage is also sometimes referred to as a campus network.

7.12.5 Storage Area Network (SAN)

It is also known by the names like System Area Network, Server Area Network, or sometimes Small Area Network.

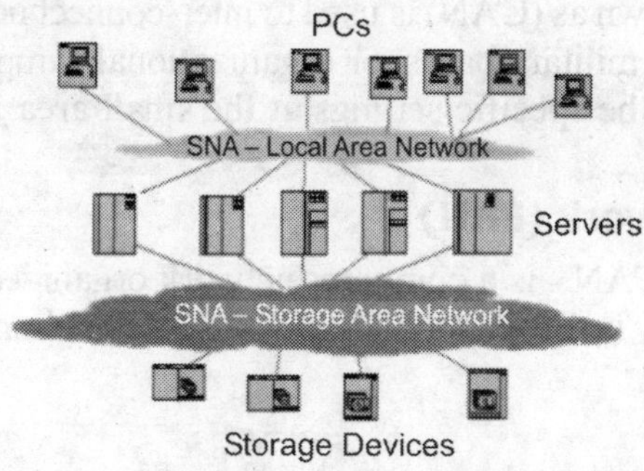

Fig. 7.16: Storage Area Network (SAN)

A storage area network (SAN) is a type of local area network (LAN) designed to handle large data transfers. A SAN typically supports data storage, retrieval and replication on business networks using high-end servers, multiple disk arrays and Fiber Channel interconnection technology.

SAN technology is similar but distinct from network attached storage (NAS) technology. While SANs traditionally employ low-level network protocols for transfering disk blocks, a NAS device typically works over TCP/IP and can be integrated fairly easily into home computer networks.

The term SAN can sometimes refer to system area networks instead of a storage area network. System area networks are clusters of high performance computers used for distributed processing applications requiring fast local network performance. Storage area networks, on the other, are designed specifically for data management.

7.12.6 Campus Area Network (CAN)

It is also known by the names like Controller Area Network, and often Cluster Area Network.

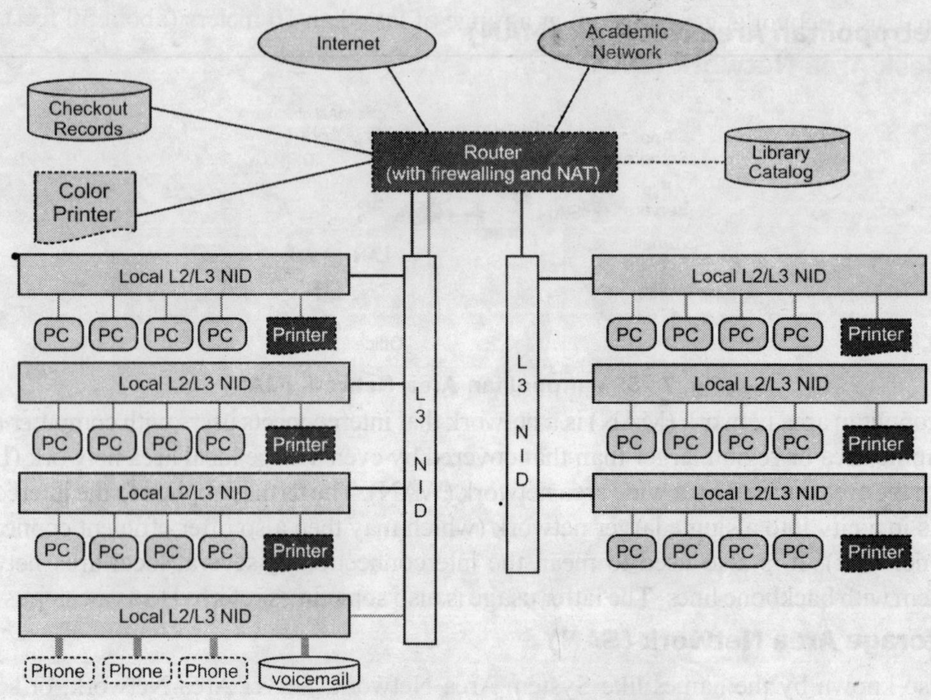

Fig. 7.17: Campus Area Network (CAN)

A campus area network known as (CAN) is used to inter-connect networks in limited geographical locality like university campus, military bases, or organizational campuses etc. It can be taken as the metropolitan network that has the specific settings at the small area just like a computer lab in the university.

7.12.7 Personal Area Network (PAN)

A personal area network - PAN - is a computer network organized around an individual person. Personal area networks typically involve a mobile computer, a cell phone and/or a handheld computing device such as a PDA.

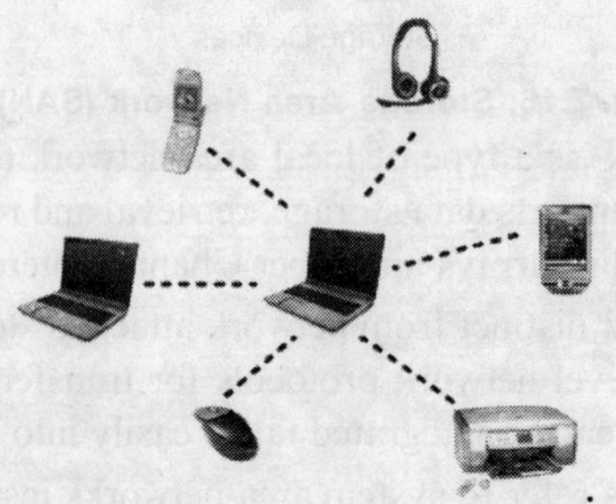

Fig. 7.18: Personal Area Network (PAN)

You can use these networks to transfer files including email and calendar appointments, digital photos and music.

Personal area networks can be constructed with cables or wirelessly. USB and FireWire technologies often link together a wired PAN while wireless PANs typically use Bluetooth or sometimes infrared connections. Bluetooth PANs are also called pico-nets.

Personal area networks generally cover a range of less than 10 meters (about 30 feet).

7.12.8 Desk Area Network (DAN)

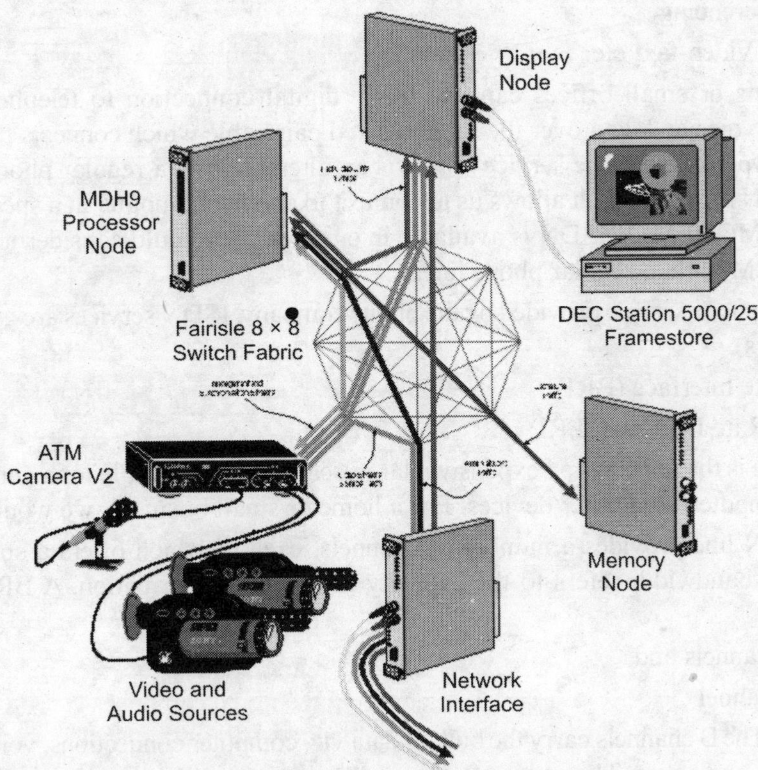

Fig. 7.19: Desk Area Network (DAN)

DAN (Desk Area Network) is an interconnection of computer devices around the ATM (Asynchronous Transfer Mode). This exchange of information between various peripherals and CPU is based on the transfer of ATM (Asynchronous Transfer Mode) cells mainly. DAN (Desk Area Network) enables the network to share resources over the network. It also provides the access to foreign devices. This system enables to form A/V connection. DAN (Desk Area Network) consists of A/V software. This software has four main layers. This software is intelligent enough to guide and support the A/V devices. It works on a simple process, when we on a VCR. And put a cassette into it, it is automatically connected to the monitor. VCR and other related devices are often connected to the network in order to built DAN (Desk Area Network).

7.13 INTEGRATED SERVICES DIGITAL NETWORK (ISDN)

- The ISDN is a networking concept providing for the integration of voice, video and data services using digital transmission media combining both circuit and packet switching techniques. ISDN was first launched in Singapore in 1990. ISDN is a type of telephone service which is an alternative to a regular phone line. The great advantage of ISDN for us is that it allows us connect to another computer at a speed which is faster than even fastest Modem. If ISDN is available in our area, we should consider it as an alternative to using a Modem with a regular phone line.

ISDN has following features :

Processing of various types of voice, video, data etc.

Transmission and processing of digital data

E-mail box

Tele-conferencing

Tele-fax, Video-fax, etc.

Users in shops or small offices can use their digital connection to telephone company for transmitting both voice and data over the same twisted pair cable which connects their telephone. In fact, ISDN is a type of telephone service which is an alternative to a regular phone line. The great advantage of ISDN for us is that it allows us to connect to another computer at a speed which is faster than even fastest MODEM. If ISDN is available in our area, we should consider it as an alternative to using a MODEM with a regular phone line.

ISDN is a telephone service provided by the phone company. ISDN services are generally delivered in one of two ways :

Basic Rate Interface (BRI)

Primary Rate Interface (PRI)

The difference is that a PRI is an expensive, large-scale service suitable for a company needing to connect many computers and other devices. For a home or small business, we would require a BRI.

A single ISDN line provides a number of channels, each of which offers a specific amount of bandwidth. Here, bandwidth refers to the capacity to transmit information. A BRI provides three channels :

Two B channels and

One D channel

B Channels: The B channels carry the bulk of data viz. computer connections, voice conversations, fax transmissions, and so on. The name **"B channel"** is short for **"bearer channel",** because the B channels bear most of the load.

D Channel: The D channel is used for the control of ISDN itself. It is used for sending the set-up and signalling information back and forth between the telephone system and our devices. The name **"D channel"** stands for **"data channel".** This is an unfortunate name, as it implies that the D channel transports our computer data, Actually, the D channel carries the internal ISDN data. Our data is actually carried on the B channels.

Within a standard BRI, each of the two B channels offers a bandwidth of 64 Kbps. We can use these B channels in two ways.

First, we can combine them into a single large channel and connect it to our computer. This effectively gives you up to 128 Kbps.

Secondly, you can use one B channel for our computer and another for a telephone. This means that we would have only 64 Kbps in bandwidth for the computer but we would not have to pay for a separate phone line. Moreover, we can use the computer and talk on the phone at the same time and they won't interfere with one another.

The D channel has 16 Kbps, however, it is used by ISDN itself and so it is not available for use with a computer or a telephone.

ISDN is a very important mean for very fast and accurate data transmission, and ISDN truly represents the next generation of the world's telephone service for all forms of telecommunications, including voice.

7.14 PUBLIC SWITCHED TELEPHONE NETWORK (PSTN)

Following are the main features of PSTN:

Low speed

Analog nature of transmission

Restricted bandwidth

Widespread availability

As PSTN is designed for telephones so modems are required when it is used for data communication. The PSTN is most useful in wide area data communications systems as an adjunct to other mechanisms. PSTN connections are usually easy to obtain at short notice, and are widely available and cover almost every location where people live and work. PSTN is most useful for occasional user or as backup to private circuits. It is also used for FAX machines.

7.15 PUBLIC SWITCHED DATA NETWORK (PSDN)

The major features of all PSDNs are:

High level of reliability

High quality of connections

PSDNs can support both low and high speeds at appropriate costs. Like PSTN, a PSDN is very useful and adjunct to a private network for backup and occasional access purposes. It can also be used to link computer systems and networks of one organisation to several other organisations. PSDN is very popular for connecting public and private mail systems to implement E-mail services with other companies.

I-Net is the first Public Switched Data Network owned by Department of Telecommunication (DOT). This network offers the following services :

Permitting subscribers to form private network within I-Net

Communication units across major cities of the country

Connection provision to other international network

7.16 VALUE ADDED NETWORKS

A value added carrier leases communication facilities from conventional common carriers and uses them in conjunction with computers to build a network which offers new types of communication services and tariffs.

In Value Added Services, the provider of such services must process, store and manipulate the data that is carried on the network i.e. add value to it. The technique can be used in specific types of business in which it is advantageous to be able to share information with other companies in the same line.

Electronic Data Interchange is one area for Value Added Services in which two trading partners exchange trading documents such as purchase orders, invoices, transportation etc. using electronic means. In India, VSNL (Videsh Sanchar Nigam Limited) is a service provider.

7.17 NETWORK TOPOLOGIES

In networking, the term topology is the way of connecting computers or nodes on a network. There are many ways in which computers are connected together in a computer network. Therefore network topology is defined as: the schemes of joining a number of computers in the form of a network are called Network Topologies.

We know that two or more devices are connected to a link for data communication. Similarly, two or more links form a topology. The topology of a network is the geometric representation of the relationship of all the links and the nodes (communication devices) to one another.

A network can be arranged in one of four different topologies:

Star Topology
Ring Topology
Bus Topology
Mesh Topology
Tree Topology
Hybrid Topology
Fully-connected Topology
Multi-drop Topology
Collapsed-Star Topology

Criteria for Selection of Network Topology

The main considerations in selecting a particular topology are :

The availability and cost of physical communication lines between nodes and line bandwidth
Throughput
The capability of a node to route information to other nodes
Delays due to routing of information
Maximum distance
Vulnerability to link or equipment failure
Maximum number of stations
Cost
Reliability of communication between nodes when there is a breakdown of a line or a node
Strategy of controlling communication between nodes in the network centralised or distributed

7.17.1 STAR TOPOLOGY

In a star network, each node (computer or other device) is directly connected to the central computer or Hub that provides connection points for nodes on the network. The star topology is the most common topology in use today. In star network, information or data is communicated from one computer to another through Hub. This form of network configuration looks like a star as shown in figure below.

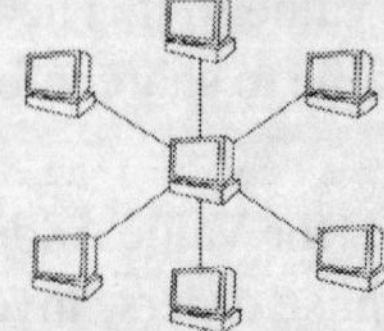

Figure 7.20: Star Topology

Advantages:

The main advantages of star topology are:

It is easy to install and to maintain.

You can easily add and remove nodes to and from the network without affecting the network.

If any node fails, other nodes are not affected.

Disadvantages:

The main disadvantages of star topology are:

This type of network depends upon the central Hub. If Hub fails the entire network is failed.

Each computer is directly connected to the Hub through a cable, so it becomes more costly.

7.17.2 RING TOPOLOGY

In ring network, each node is connected to two adjacent nodes in the form a closed ring or loop. In ring topology, the last node connects to the first node to complete the ring. In ring topology, each node has a dedicated point-to-point connection only with the two devices on either side of it.

In this network, data is communicated in one direction from node to node around the entire ring. When a computer in ring network sends message to another computer on the network, the message travels to each node or computer until it reaches its destination. The ring network configuration is shown in figure below.

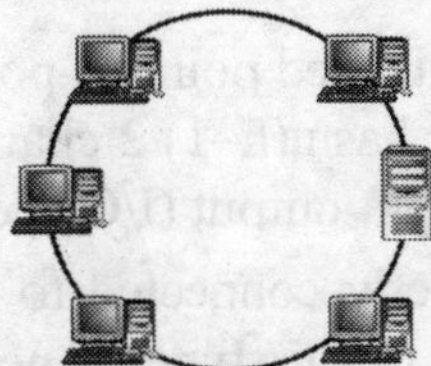

Figure 7.21: Ring Topology

Advantages:

The main advantages of ring topology are:

It is less expensive than star topology.

Nodes can be easily added or removed.

Disadvantages:

The main disadvantages of ring topology are:

It is more difficult to install and maintain.

If a node fails, it affects the entire network.

7.17.3 BUS TOPOLOGY

In bus network, all nodes are connected to a common communication medium or central cable. The central physical cable that connects the nodes is called Bus. The data is communicated between nodes in both directions through bus. A bus topology uses the multipoint connection. The central single cable (or bus) acts as backbone to link all the devices to the network.

In bus network, when a computer sends a message to another computer it also attaches the address of the destination computer. In bus topology, a special device called a terminator is attached at the cable's start and end points. A terminator stops the network signals.

In LAN, bus topology is mostly used. In this topology, each computer is assigned a unique address. The bus network configuration is given in figure image.

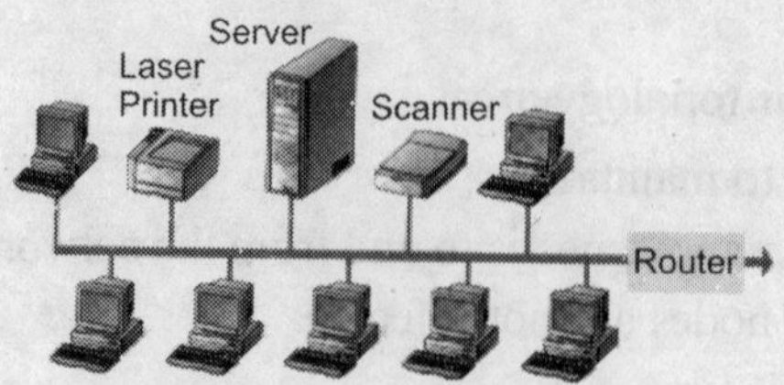

Figure 7.22: Bus Topology

Advantages:

The main advantages of bus topology are:

It is less expensive and easy to install and maintain.

When nodes are added and removed to and from the network, the network is not affected.

If one node fails other nodes are not affected.

Disadvantages:

The main disadvantages of bus topology are:

It supports only a small number of nodes.

Entire network fails if there is any problem in the central cable.

7.17.4 MESH TOPOLOY

In this topology, every node has a dedicated point-to-point connection to every other node on the network. A fully connected mesh network has n(n–1)/2 channels to link 'n' devices. Therefore, every device on the network must have 'n-1' input/output (I/O) ports.

In mesh network, each node is directly connected to all nodes on the network. This type of network involves the concept of routes. In this type of network, each node may send message to destination through multiple paths. It means that each node of mesh network has several possible paths to send (or to receive) message, but in Bus, Star, Ring and Tree topologies each node has only one path.

Advantages:

Mesh topology has the following advantages:

It has multiple links, so if one route is blocked then other routes can be used for data communication.

Each connection can have its own data load, so the traffic problem is eliminated.

It ensures the data privacy or security, because every message travels along a dedicated link.

Troubleshooting of this topology is easy as compared to other networks.

Its performance is not affected with heavy load of data transmission.

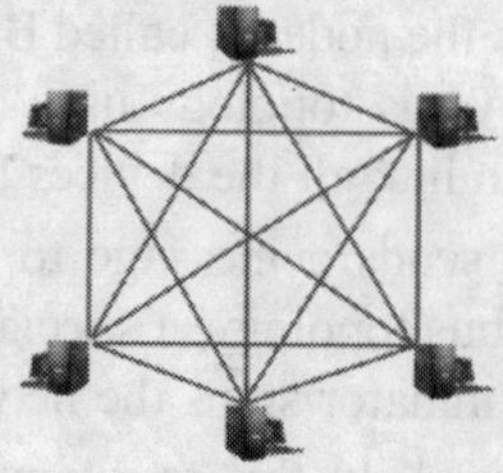

Figure 7.23: Mesh Topology

Disadvantages:

Mesh topology has the following disadvantages:

It becomes very expensive because a large number of cabling and 110 ports are required.

It is difficult to install.

7.17.5 TREE TOPOLOGY

In tree network, the nodes are connected to each other in such a way that forms a tree like structure. Typically to form a tree network, multiple star topologies are combined together. This type of network has combined features of bus and star topology.

On tree topology the hubs of each star topology are connected to the central hub that controls the entire network. However, some nodes can be directly connected to the central hub. The tree topology configuration is shown in figure below.

The central Hub in the tree network is an active hub. It contains a repeater (a hardware device), which re-generates the received bit patterns. The secondary hubs usually are passive hubs. The passive hub controls the nodes directly connected to it and exchange data to other devices connected to the other secondary hubs (or same hub) through the central hub. The secondary hub may also be active hub if another secondary hub is directly connected to it. The cable TV network is an example of tree topology, where main cable is divided into, branches and each branch is further divided into smaller branches and so on. The hub is used when a branch is created.

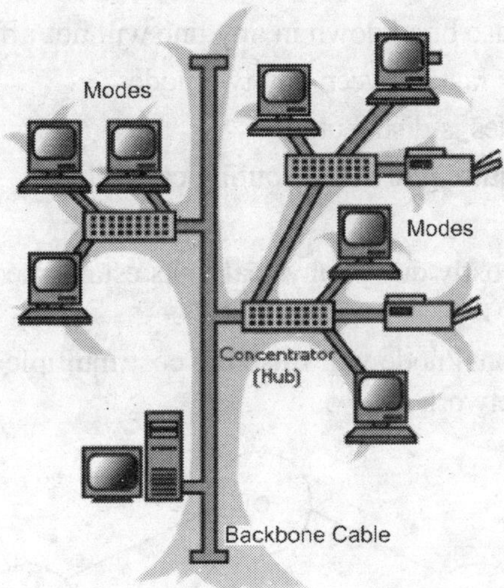

Figure 7.24: Tree Topology

Advantages:

The tree topology has the same advantages as star topology but it has some additional advantages. These are.

It allows more devices to be connected to the central Hub.

Disadvantages:

The tree topology also has the same disadvantages as star topology built has some additional disadvantages such as:

It because more expansive because more hubs are required to install the network.

7.17.6 HYBRID TOPOLOGY

Hybrid network is the combination of different topologies such as star, Ring, Mesh, Bus etc. For example, if a department uses a Bus network, second department uses the ring network, third department uses the Mesh network and fourth department uses the star network. All the networks of different types (of four departments) can be connected together through a central hub (in the form of star network) as shown in the figure below.

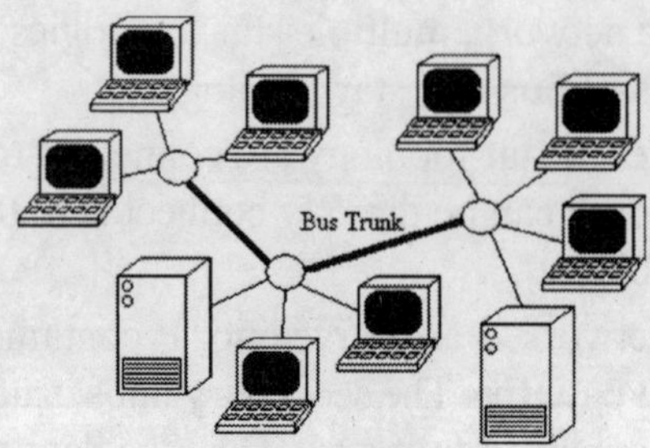

Figure 7.25: Hybrid Topology

7.17.7 FULLY-INTERCONNECTED NETWORK

A fully-connected topology has a separate physical links for connecting each node to any other node in the network.

Advantages

It is very reliable because breakdown in any line will not affect other links

Communication is very fast between any two nodes

The control among nodes is distributed

Each node does not require individual routing capability

Disadvantages

This topology is very costly due to physical links established from each node to every other node in the network

Addition of any additional node will raise the cost multiple times depending upon the total existing nodes in the network

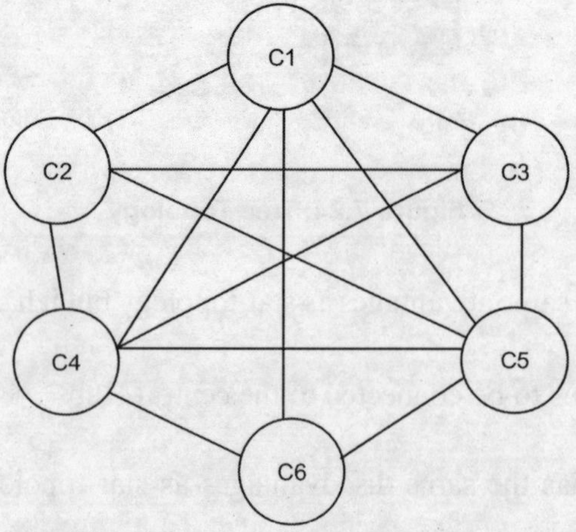

Fig. 7.26: Fully Inter-Connected Network

7.17.8 MULTI-DROP NETWORK

In this topology only one line is shared by all nodes. Whenever a message is transmitted, sender and destination addresses are associated as Tags and message rides on this single line. Receiver receives it and acknowledges the message through the same line.

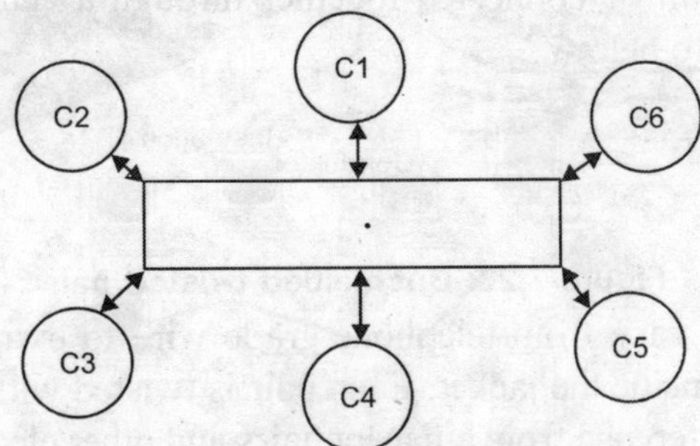

Fig. 7.27: Multi-Drop Network

Advantages

Cheaper due to reduction in total physical lines

Relatively higher reliability

Easier addition of nodes in the existing network

Disadvantages

Complete system fails if the single line gets disconnected

7.17.9 COLLAPSED-STAR NETWORK

In this topology the multiple ring networks are interconnected. Here, a central backbone is constructed, to which various other ring networks are connected. In this case, each ring is connected to the central ring via a high-speed bridge. High-speed bridge is a device that enables data to be routed from one network to another.

7.18 NETWORK CABLING

Cable is the medium through which information usually moves from one network device to another. There are several types of cable which are commonly used with LANs. In some cases, a network will utilize only one type of cable, other networks will use a variety of cable types. The type of cable chosen for a network is related to the network's topology, protocol, and size. Understanding the characteristics of different types of cable and how they relate to other aspects of a network is necessary for the development of a successful network.

The following sections discuss the types of cables used in networks and other related topics.

Unshielded Twisted Pair (UTP) Cable

Shielded Twisted Pair (STP) Cable

Coaxial Cable

Fiber Optic Cable

7.18.1 UNSHIELDED TWISTED PAIR (UTP) CABLE

Twisted pair cabling comes in two varieties: shielded and unshielded. Unshielded twisted pair (UTP) is the most popular and is generally the best option for school networks.

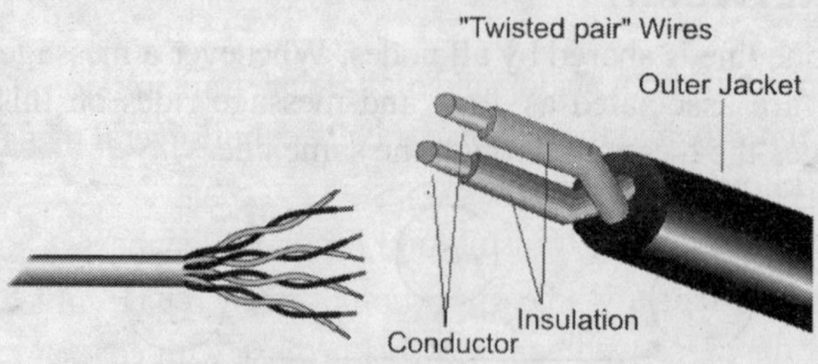

Figure 7.28: Unshielded twisted pair

The quality of UTP may vary from telephone-grade wire to extremely high-speed cable. The cable has four pairs of wires inside the jacket. Each pair is twisted with a different number of twists per inch to help eliminate interference from adjacent pairs and other electrical devices. The tighter the twisting, the higher the supported transmission rate and the greater the cost per foot. The EIA/TIA (Electronic Industry Association/Telecommunication Industry Association) has established standards of UTP and rated six categories of wire (additional categories are emerging).

7.18.2 UNSHIELDED TWISTED PAIR CONNECTOR

The standard connector for unshielded twisted pair cabling is an RJ-45 connector. This is a plastic connector that looks like a large telephone-style connector. A slot allows the RJ-45 to be inserted only one way. RJ stands for Registered Jack, implying that the connector follows a standard borrowed from the telephone industry. This standard designates which wire goes with each pin inside the connector.

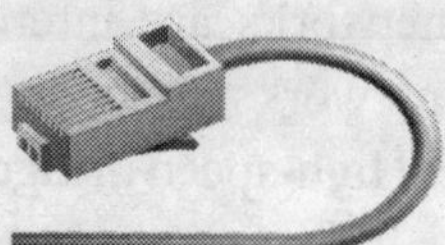

Figure 7.29: RJ-45 connector

7.18.3 SHIELDED TWISTED PAIR (STP) CABLE

Although UTP cable is the least expensive cable, it may be susceptible to radio and electrical frequency interference (it should not be too close to electric motors, fluorescent lights, etc.). If you must place cable in environments with lots of potential interference, or if you must place cable in extremely sensitive environments that may be susceptible to the electrical current in the UTP, shielded twisted pair may be the solution. Shielded cables can also help to extend the maximum distance of the cables.

Shielded twisted pair cable is available in three different configurations:

1. Each pair of wires is individually shielded with foil.
2. There is a foil or braid shield inside the jacket covering all wires (as a group).
3. There is a shield around each individual pair, as well as around the entire group of wires (referred to as double shield twisted pair).

Advantages:

– As the oldest method of data transmission, trained man power to repair and service this media of communications are easily available.

- In telephone system, signals can travel several kilometres without amplification when twisted pair wires are used.
- This media can be used for both analog and digital data transmission. The bandwidth depends on the thickness of the wire and the distance travelled, but several megabits per second can be achieved for a few kilometres in many cases.
- It is the least expensive media of transmission for short distances.
- The effect on the network as a whole, if portion of twisted pair cable is damaged; the entire network is not shut down, as well as it may be the case with coaxial cable.

Disadvantages:

- Easily pickup noise signals which results in higher error rates when the line length exceeds 100 meters.
- Being thin in size, they are likely to break easily.

7.18.4 COAXIAL CABLE

Coaxial cabling has a single copper conductor at its center. A plastic layer provides insulation between the center conductor and a braided metal shield. The metal shield helps to block any outside interference from

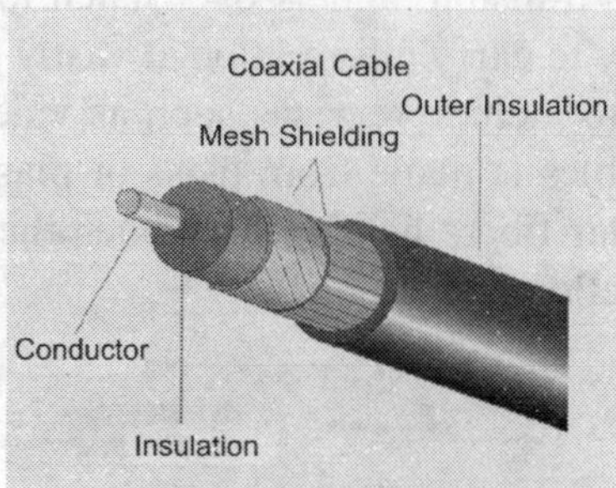

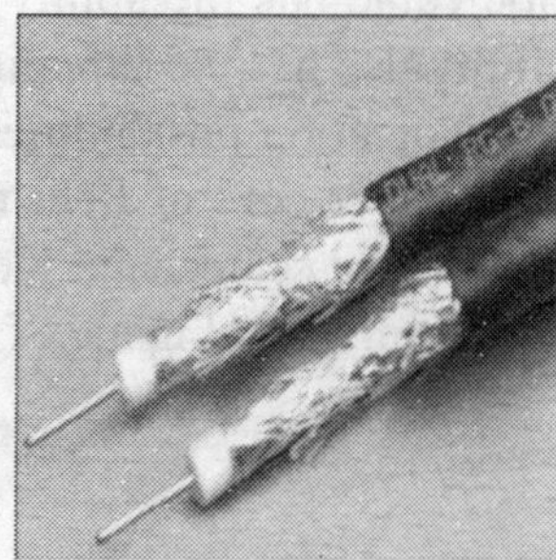

Figure 7.30: Coaxial cable

Although coaxial cabling is difficult to install, it is highly resistant to signal interference. In addition, it can support greater cable lengths between network devices than twisted pair cable. The two types of coaxial

Thin coaxial cable is also referred to as thinnet. 10Base2 refers to the specifications for thin coaxial cable carrying Ethernet signals. The 2 refers to the approximate maximum segment length being 200 meters. In actual fact the maximum segment length is 185 meters. Thin coaxial cable has been popular in

Thick coaxial cable is also referred to as thicknet. 10Base5 refers to the specifications for thick coaxial cable carrying Ethernet signals. The 5 refers to the maximum segment length being 500 meters. Thick coaxial cable has an extra protective plastic cover that helps keep moisture away from the center conductor. This makes thick coaxial a great choice when running longer lengths in a linear bus network. One disadvantage of thick coaxial is that it does

Advantages:

- It has better shielding than twisted pair, so it can span longer distances at higher data bps.
- It can be used for both Analog data transmission as well as digital transmission.
- Coaxial cable has higher bandwidth and excellent noise immunity.
- It is relatively inexpensive as compared to optic cables and easy to handle.

Disadvantages:

- Coaxial cable is more expensive than twisted pair.
- Coaxial cable emits less radiation which may cause interference with the communication equipment as compared to twisted pair.

7.18.5 COAXIAL CABLE CONNECTORS

The most common type of connector used with coaxial cables is the Bayone-Neill-Concelman (BNC) connector. Different types of adapters are available for BNC connectors, including a T-connector, barrel connector, and terminator. Connectors on the cable are the weakest points in any network.

Figure 7.31: BNC connector

7.18.6 FIBER OPTIC CABLE

Fiber optic cabling consists of a center glass core surrounded by several layers of protective materials. It transmits light rather than electronic signals eliminating the problem of electrical interference. This makes it ideal for certain environments that contain a large amount of electrical interference. Fiber optic cable has the ability to transmit signals over much longer distances than coaxial and twisted pair. It also has the capability to carry information at vastly greater speeds. This capacity broadens communication possibilities to include services such as video conferencing and interactive services. The center core of fiber cables is made from glass or plastic fibers. A plastic coating then cushions the fiber center, and Kevlar fibers help to strengthen the cables and prevent breakage. The outer insulating jacket made of Teflon or PVC.

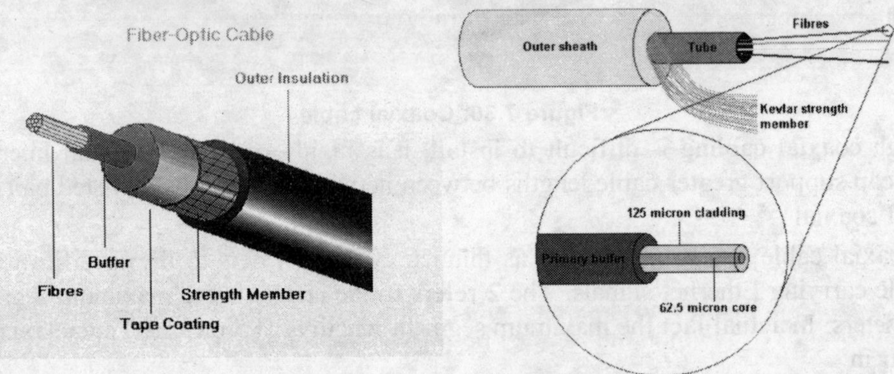

Figure 7.32: Fiber optic cable

There are two common types of fiber cables - single mode and multimode. Multimode cable has a larger diameter; however, both cables provide high bandwidth at high speeds. Single mode can provide more distance, but it is more expensive.

Advantages:

- It can handle much higher band widths.
- Fibers are not being affected by power surges, electromagnetic interference, or failures.
- Fiber is lighter than other transmission mediums.
- Fibers do not leak light and are quite difficult to tap. This gives excellent security.

Disadvantages:

- Fiber is an unfamiliar technology, so requires special skills.
- Since optical transmission is inherently unidirectional, two way communications requires either two fibers or two frequency bands on the fiber.
- Fiber interfaces cost more than electrical interfaces.

7.18.7 WIRELESS TRANSMISSION MEDIA

In wireless transmission media, communication devices communicate with each other and data is communicated through the air or space using broadcast radio signals, microwave signals and infrared signals. This transmission medium is used when it is impossible to install the cables. The data can be transmitted all over the world through this medium. The commonly used wireless transmission media are discussed below.

7.18.7.1 RADIO TRANSMISSION

Radio Waves are easy to generate, can travel long distances, and penetrate building easily, so they are widely used for communications, both indoors and outdoors. They are also omni-directional, so the transmitter and receiver do not have to be aligned physically. This feature is sometimes good, but sometimes bad.

The properties of radio waves are frequency dependent. At low frequencies they pass through obstacles well, but the power falls off sharply with distance from the source. At high frequencies, radio waves tend to travel in straight lines and bounce off obstacles. They are also absorbed by rain. At all frequencies, they are subject to interference from motors and other electrical equipment.

Due to radio's ability to travel long distances, interference between users is a problem. For this reasons, all governments license the use user of radio transmitters.

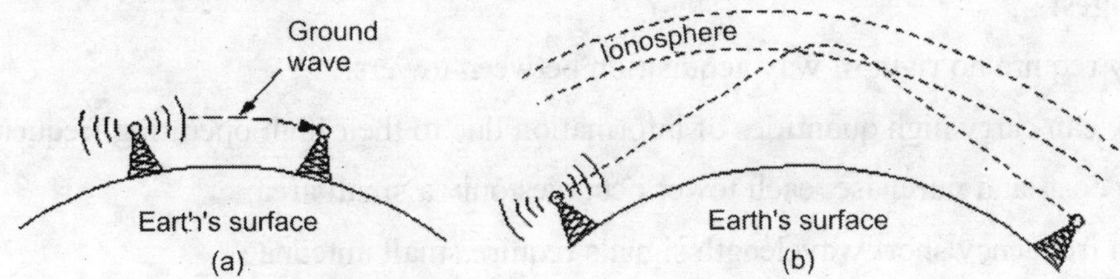

Figure 7.33: (a) In the VLF, VF, and MF bands, radio waves follow the curvature of the earth. (b) In the HF they bounce off the ionosphere.

In the VLF, LF, and MF bands, radio waves follow the ground (Figure 7.31(a)) and can be detected for about 1000 km at the lower frequencies, less at the higher ones. The main problem with using these bands for data communication is relatively low bandwidth they offer.

In the HF and VHF bands, the ground waves tend to be absorbed by the earth, but if they reach the ionosphere (a layer of charged particles circling the earth at a height of 100 to 500 km) are refracted (Figure 7.31(b)) by it and sent back to earth. Amateur radio operators use these bands to talk long distance.

i Broadcast Radio

It is a wireless transmission medium that is used to communicate information through radio signals in air, over long distance such as between cities and countries. In this medium, a transmitter is required to send messages (signals) and receiver is required to receive them. To receive the broadcast radio signal, the receiver has an antenna that is located in the range of signal. Some networks use a special device called transceiver used to send and to receive messages in the form of radio signals. The data transmission speed of broadcast radio is up to 54Mbps.

ii. Cellular Radio

Cellular radio is a form of broadcast radio that is used for mobile communications such as cellular telephones and wireless modems. A cellular telephone is a telephone device that uses high frequency radio waves to transmit voice and digital messages. Some mobile users connect their laptop computer or other mobile device to a cellular telephone to access the Web, send and receive e-mail etc. while away from a standard telephone line.

7.18.7.2 MICROWAVES TRANSMISSION

Microwave transmission is line of sight transmission. The transmit station must be in visible contact with the receive station. This sets a limit on the distance between stations depending on the local geography. Typically the line of sight due to the Earth's curvature is only 50 km to the horizon! Repeater stations must be placed so the data signal can hop, skip and jump across the country.

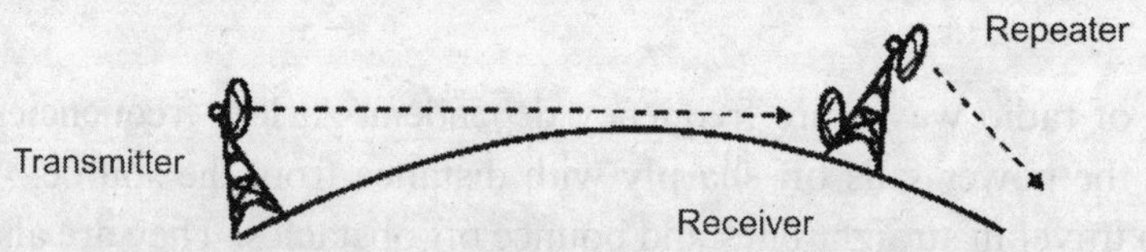

Figure 7.34: Microwaves Transmission

Microwaves operate at high operating frequencies of 3 to 10 GHz. This allows them to carry large quantities of data due to their large bandwidth.

Advantages:

a. They require no right of way acquisition between towers.

b. They can carry high quantities of information due to their high operating frequencies.

c. Low cost land purchase: each tower occupies only a small area.

d. High frequency/short wavelength signals require small antennae.

Disadvantages:

a. Attenuation by solid objects: birds, rain, snow and fog.

b. Reflected from flat surfaces like water and metal.

c. Diffracted (split) around solid objects.

d. Refracted by atmosphere, thus causing beam to be projected away from receiver.

7.18.7.3 COMMUNICATION SATELLITE

A communication satellite is a space station that receives microwave signals from earth microwave station (earth based station). The earth based stations often are microwave stations. Other devices, such as PDAs and OPS receivers, also functions as earth based stations. Transmitting a signal from ground or earth station to a satellite station in space is called up-linking and the reverse is called the down- linking.

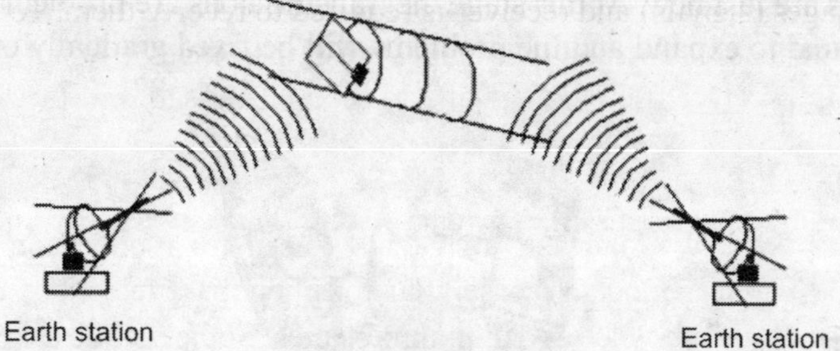

Figure 7.35: Communication Satellite Transmission System

Now-a-days, television & radio broadcast, global positioning systems and Internet also use the communication satellites. The communication satellite is launched about 22300 miles (or more) above the earth into space. The communication satellite consists of solar powered, transceiver that receives and sends signals. The signals are transmitted from one earth station to the satellite. The satellite receives and amplifies the signals and sends them to another earth station. This entire process takes only a few seconds. To communicate information from one country to another country more than one satellites are required. The data transmission speed of communication satellite is very high such as up to 1 Gbps.

7.18.8 OTHER TECHNOLOGIES

Infra- red: Infra-red has a wavelength just beyond the visible spectrum. It is invisible to the human eye and is heat sensitive. Infra red cameras can show an image in a totally dark room. New network systems are built around infra red connections.

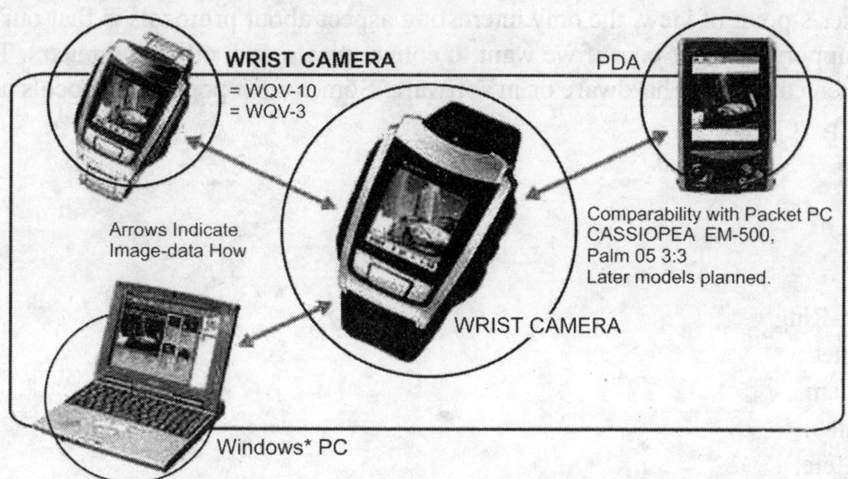

Figure 7.36: Infra-red Technologies

WAP: This is the mobile phone technology which can also access the internet and faxes. Been around for a few years now.

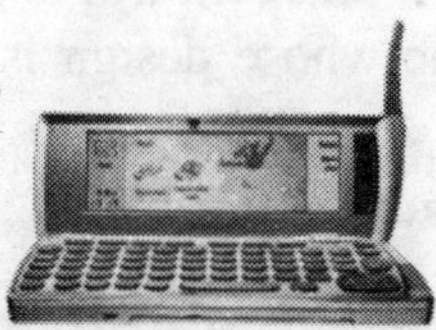

Figure 7.37: WAP

3G Video phones are just new. At this stage the transmissions are problematic and unreliable but the technology is bound to expand and the problems will be fixed gradually over the next couple of years.

Figure 7.38: 3G Technology

7.19 NETWORK PROTOCOLS

A protocol is an agreed upon format for transmitting data between two devices. The protocol determines the following:

- What type of error checking is to be used ?
- What data compression technique, if any, to be used ?
- How the sending device will indicate that it has finished sending a message ?
- How the receiving device will indicate that it has received a message ?

There are a variety of standard protocols from which programmers can choose. Each has its own particular advantages and disadvantages e.g. some are simpler than the others, some are more reliable, and some are faster.

From a user's point of view, the only interesting aspect about protocols is that our computer or device must support the right ones if we want to communicate with other computers. The protocols can be implemented either in hardware or in software. Some of the popular protocols are:

- TCP/IP
- HTTP
- FTP
- SMTP
- POP
- Token-Ring
- Ethernet
- Xmodem
- Kermit
- MNP, etc.

Computer Network Architecture

The best architecture ever possible is an Open-Architecture which allows the system to be connected easily to other devices, computers and programs made available by other manufacturers. Such architectures use off-the-shelf components and conform to approved standards. On the other hand, a system with a closed architecture is one whose design is proprietary which makes it difficult to connect the system to others.

Network architectures can be broadly classified as :

- Peer-to-peer
- Client-Server

Peer-to-peer Network Architecture

It is a type of network architecture in which each workstation (or node) has the same capabilities and responsibilities, meaning that none of these nodes is superior over other nodes.

Advantages

Simpler architecture

Less expensive

Disadvantage

Offer less performance under heavy loads

Client-Server Network Architecture

It is such a network architecture in which each computer or process on the network is either a client or a server. Here, server is having a superiority over other nodes and that's why other nodes will be clients and are likely to be served by the server. Servers must be powerful computers or processors dedicated to managing disk drives (file-servers), printers (print-servers), or network traffic (network-servers) whereas on the other hand clients may be lesser powerful PCs or workstations on which users can run applications. In such network architectures, clients completely rely on servers for resources viz. files, devices, etc.

7.20 APPLICATIONS OF COMPUTER NETWORKS

There is a long list of application areas which can be benefited by establishing Computer Networks. Few of the potential applications of Computer Networks are :

Information retrieval systems which search for books, technical reports, papers and articles on particular topics

News access machines which can search past news, stories or abstracts with given search criteria

Airline reservation, hotel-booking, railway-reservation, car-rental, etc.

A writer's aid : a dictionary, thesaurus, phrase generator, indexed dictionary of quotations, and encyclopaedia

Stock market information systems which allow searches for stocks that meet certain criteria, performance comparisons, moving averages, and various forecasting techniques

Electronic Financial Transactions (EFT) between banks and via cheque clearing house

Games of the type that grow or change with various enthusiasts adding to the complexity or diversity

Electronic Mail Messages Systems (EMMS)

Corporate information systems such as marketing information system, customer information system, product information system, personnel information system, etc.

Corporate systems of different systems such as Order-Entry System, Centralized Purchasing, Distributed Inventory Control, etc.

On-line systems for Investment Advice and Management, Tax Minimization, etc.

Resources of interest to a home user

Sports results

Theatre, movies, and community events information

Shopping information, prices, advertisements

Restaurants; good food guide
Household magazine, recipes, book reviews, film reviews
Holidays, hotels, travel booking
Radio and TV programmes
Medical assistance service
Insurance information
Computer Assisted Instruction (CAI)
School homework, quizzes, tests
Message sending service
Directories
Consumer reports
Employment directories and Job opportunities
Tax information and Tax assistance
Journey planning assistance viz. Train, bus, plane etc.
Catalogue of Open University and Virtual University courses

7.21 INTERNET

The word Internet is derived from two words 'Interconnection' and 'Network'. 'Network' is a set of two or more interconnected computers that are connected through a set of hardware devices to share information. When a large number of such 'Networks' are 'Interconnected' together to exchange information, using same set of rules and regulations, they constitute the Internet. A user of Internet may feel as if the interaction is carried with single large computer network, but actually it is a Network of Networks.

There are several ways to describe the Internet:

From a social point of view. The Internet can be thought of as millions of people communicating, sharing ideas and information. Any individual on the Internet can communicate with anyone else on the Internet. The Internet is a platform where people can communicate with others no matter where they are, their status, or their expertise. People communicate on the internet in a variety of ways: E-mail, Usenet etc.

From commercial point of view. The Internet is a vast collection of information that can be searched and retrieved electronically. This collection includes advice on all sorts of topics, data, electronic texts, images, software, commercial activities, and almost anything that a user may need.

Almost all of this information is shared free of charge, except what one pays to access the Internet, because sharing information and resources is at the basis of the Internet. One of the fastest growing sectors of work on the Internet is in the area of commercial applications. As the Internet use becomes more available and common, it's being viewed as a viable means of doing business and marketing.

One can access the information or communicate with others on the Internet by using a collection of tools and services that give access to people, information, and resources. There are three basic services: Telnet, FTP, WWW etc.

From technical point of view. As discussed earlier, the Internet is a Network of Networks. Every network and every computer on these networks exchange information according to some set rules and regulations which are called protocols. The computers that make up the network may be designed be different technologies or by different companies, but when they all use same protocols they can exchange data or information as a part of same network. Two most commonly used protocols for working with the Internet are Internet Protocol (IP) or Transmission Control Protocol (TCP).

Each computer system as well as each network on the Internet has a unique Internet address called an IP address. These IP addresses are numeric, like 122.35.65.221. Such numeric are difficult to be memorized by humans, so each numeric address corresponds to a name called domain name or host name, such as google.co.in. This address is used to exchange information with, send e-mail to, or use an Internet service that involves another computer system.

Internet is thus one of the greatest inventions of our time. It has given new dimensions to the way of communication. Any amount of data can be accessed and retrieved from any computer on the Internet within no time. Internet has become an inseparable part of not only the computer society but almost every individual nowadays. It brings a wealth of information to us just by a click of mouse.

7.22 EVOLUTION OF THE INTERNET

The Internet consists of a network of interconnected computers that transmit data using standard internet protocol (IP). Most people believe that the internet began in the mid-1990s, but in reality, it began much earlier than that.

In 1958 AT&T introduced the first commercial modem. It converted digital computer data into analog signals for transmission across its long distance network. This invention allowed computers to communicate over normal telephone circuits used for standard voice phone calls.

By the end of the 1960s, the Department of Defense constructed one of the first physical networks of computers by linking nodes at the University of California at Los Angeles, SRI (in Stanford), University of California at Santa Barbara, and University of Utah. This was known as the Advanced Research Projects Agency Network (ARPANET), and it grew quickly in the early 1970's, reaching 57 interconnected nodes in the network by July, 1975.

It was only a couple years after ARPANET began that the first e-mail program for the network was created by Ray Tomlinson in 1971. Tomlinson is also credited as the one who decided to use the @ symbol in email addresses. He sent the first email that same year. Five years later, in 1976, the Queen of England sent her first e-mail from a British Army base as a part of a demonstration of networking technology.

It wasn't until 1974 that the term "internet" was first used. The first documentation of the term was in a paper by Vinton "Vint" Cerf and Bob Kahn on Transmission Control Protocol (TCP). TCP is a fundamental protocol for Internet communications, allowing networked computers to create connections to one another, which can then be used to exchange data. These days people sometimes refer to the Internet as cyberspace, and the term "cyberspace" was coined in 1984 by William Gibson in his book, Neuromancer.

Many people think that the World Wide Web (WWW) is synonymous with the Internet, but the WWW is actually just a service that runs on the Internet. Other commonly known services operating over the Internet include email and FTP (File Transfer Protocol), but there are others such as Gopher and Usenet, which are not very popular or well known these days.

The World Wide Web was invented in 1990 by Tim Berners-Lee, in an effort to link scientific research. At the time he was a scientist at CERN, the European Organization for Nuclear Research. As part of the WWW he developed the HyperText Markup Language, better known as HTML, which is the language used to create web pages. In addition to HTML, other specifications such as Uniform Resource Locator (URL) and HyperText Transfer Protocol (HTTP) had to be developed to allow the Internet to expand to handle WWW communications.

In order to view Web pages, computers need programs which have become known as Web browsers. They send a signal to a server requesting a page, and the server responds by sending the necessary data for the web page, which the browser decodes and displays on the computer screen. Naturally, Berners-Lee is the person that created the first Web browser, so that the first web pages could be viewed. This first browser was originally called the WorldWideWeb, but the name was later changed to Nexus in order to be more distinct and avoid confusing it with the World Wide Web.

The first Web site was "info.cern.ch", and it was also built by Berners-Lee. It is worth noting that its address did not begin with the "www" prefix. In fact, there is no technical reason for a website to begin with www. The "www" prefix is a result of the common Internet convention used at the time the Web was developed of giving hostnames that correspond to the protocol they serve. Another peculiarity is that the term World Wide Web is longer to say when it is abbreviated. The acronym WWW actually contains more syllables than any other three-letter acronym in the English language.

It was on August 6, 1991 that the Web became an Internet service that was available to the public.

This was the date that Berners-Lee posted about the World Wide Web project to the alt.hypertext newsgroup on Usenet.

In 1993, the Mosaic web browser was released. Although it wasn't the first Web browser program, it was the first to become really popular due to its incorporation of graphics and the ability to run on the dominant mainstream operating system, Microsoft's Windows. Mosaic was originally designed for a UNIX system running X-windows, but was available for several other operating systems such as the Mac OS and Windows within a year. Almost as soon as graphics became available, the first banner ads began to appear-in 1994 to be exact. Also in 1994, Pizza Hut began to offer pizza ordering on its Web page.

Yahoo!, which was originally named "Jerry and David's Guide to the World Wide Web," was started in February 1994. It was not the first internet directory, but it was the first to become widely popular. By the fall of 1994 it had hit 1 million hits in a single day, with almost 100 thousand unique visitors. During its initial public offering in 1996, it sold 2.6 million shares-33.8 million dollars worth-at $13 each.

As of 2006, according to Internet World Stats, around 70% of the population in the United States is on the internet. Throughout the world, there are almost 1.1 billion users of the Internet as of 2006 and half of them reside in Europe and Asia. Worldwide Internet usage increased over 200% in thesix years from 2000 to 2006, yet there is still plenty of room for expansion considering that less than 1/6 of the world population is online. It is expected that US and world Internet usage will continue to grow.

This growth is often attributed to the lack of central administration, which allows organic growth of the network, as well as the non-proprietary open nature of the Internet protocols, which encourages vendor interoperability and prevents any one company from exerting too much control over the network. The estimated population of Internet users is 1.97 billion as of 30 June 2010.

From 2009 onward, the Internet is expected to grow significantly in Brazil, Russia, India, China, and Indonesia (BRICI countries). These countries have large populations and moderate to high economic growth, but still low Internet penetration rates. In 2009, the BRICI countries represented about 45 percent of the world's population and had approximately 610 million Internet users, but by 2015, Internet users in BRICI countries will double to 1.2 billion, and will triple in Indonesia.

7.23 APPLICATIONS OF THE INTERNET

The wide variety of applications provided by Internet can be categorized into following categories according to their behavior:

1. Information Retrieval Services

The Internet has enabled individuals and organizations to publish ideas and information to a large audience online at minimal charges and no time delay. Those ideas can be published in one of the following forms:

a) **Webpages:** Internet provides a pool of information through the webpages available on almost every topic. Publishing a webpage involves little initial cost and provides many attractive cost-free services. These websites can be referenced with Uniform Resource Locators (URL's) which allow providers to symbolically identify services and clients to locate websites and access them using Hypertext Transfer Protocol (HTTP). HTTP is a request/response protocol in which client sends a request to the server and the server responds with the requested webpage.
Webpages are designed using Hypertext Markup Language (HTML) which is a special formatting language that defines the placement and format of text and other objects on the webpage.

b) **Blogs:** Web logs or blogs are used as updateable online diaries as journals. Readers can post comments on each journal entry. The blogs are usually arranged in chronological order from the most recent post or entry at the top of main page to the older entries towards the bottom of the page.

c) **Advertisements:** The companies and organizations advertise their products via banners on popular websites. Banners are advertisements in the form of graphical images that runs across a webpage. The websites limit the size of the banner to a certain number of bytes so that it displays quickly. The advantage of such advertising is that the marketer can approach the user personally, thus a one-to-one approach between the company marketers and consumers can be established.

2. Communication Services

Internet provides its users one of the most attractive services to communicate over long distances. This communication can be carried out in one of the many forms mentioned here:

a) **Email:** Email is a basic communication service provided by the Internet. This is a way of sending electronic text messages between sender and receiver. Images, documents and other files can also be sent as mail attachments.

b) **Voice-over-Internet Protocol:** VoIP is a method of transmitting audio over the Internet by encoding analog audio in a digital form, transmitting it over the Internet, and decoding it back to analog form for listening. It carries the voice traffic over the Internet. VoIP can be free of cost or much less cost than a telephone, especially over long distances.

c) **Internet Relay Chat (IRC):** IRC enables people all over the world to talk over the Internet in real-time sessions. One can connect to an IRC Server across the Internet through an IRC client application and join a network to participate in world-wide conversations. One can then join any public chat room running on that server. Every message sent in a given chat room is sent by the IRC client application to the IRC server which then gets transmitted to all users connected to that chat room.

3. Data Transfer Services

Retrieving the information is only a first step in the overall transfer of information. Actual data is transferred using specific protocols used in transferring files over Internet. Various protocols used in data transfer are listed below:

a) **File Transfer:** File Transfer Protocol (FTP) is the protocol used for exchanging files over the Internet. FTP works in the same way as HTTP for transferring webpages from a server to a user's web browser. It is commonly used to download a file from a FTP server using the Internet or to upload a file to a FTP server.

b) **Gopher:** Gopher is a menu based document delivery system. An individual uses Gopher to access various types of information such as files, documents, and images. Gopher also allows access to ftp, telnet, and searchable databases. All of this is done by selecting items from menus.

7.24 GETTING CONNECTED TO THE INTERNET

An Internet Service Provider (ISP) is an organization that provides user access to the Internet and related services. There are many ISP's available depending upon the area they serve. They can be large national or multinational companies covering large number of cities or small companies serving only limited regions. Like any company, ISP's charge money in exchange of their Internet connection. Besides the standard Internet connection, an ISP provides services like domain hosting, web space, e-mail, instant messaging etc.

In order to access the Internet, one can connect to an ISP using different types of connections available such as dial-up phone, DSL, ISDN, Cable, Satellite and Wireless Internet Connections. Each of them differs in their speed and cost. An ISP provides each user with a username and password and a phone number to enable them to connect to the Internet.

There are many types of ISP's. Some are local ISP's operating at a local level, some are national ISP's operating at National level and some are global ISP's operating at International level. In India, there are total 183 ISP's that are operating at national level. Some of them are BSNL, Sify, Bharti Infotel, Tata Internet services, Reliance etc.

A user can connect to the Internet either by dialing into an ISP's computer or by directly connecting to an ISP. A dial up connection is initiated by dialing into a modem over the telephone link whereas a direct connection is a continuous connection to an ISP through a dedicated phone line. The various types of Internet connections available nowadays are:

1. Dial-up connection

Dial-up connection is the most widely used type of computer connection to the Internet. It connects a computer to the Internet using an analog modem as the interface. Dialing up with a modem is the cheapest and most widely available way to connect to the Internet, but because it offers comparatively slower connection speeds, graphics-intensive websites can take a long time to load. The maximum speed at which one can download data is limited by the telephone system's analog bandwidth, the line quality, and the Internet traffic load.

Dial-up customers usually need to enter a user name and password, as well as the ISP's phone number into a dialog box. The dial-up networking software uses this information to make the connection with the ISP. At the ISP's end, a computer checks the user name and password against a database of active customers. Once the ISP authenticates the information, the user is free to surf, check and send e-mails, download files, and so on. Typical dial-up connection speeds range from 2400 bps to 56 Kbps.

2. ISDN

Integrated Services Digital Network is a system of digital phone connections that has been designed for sending voice, video and data simultaneously over digital or ordinary phone lines, with a much faster speed and higher quality than an analog system can provide. ISDN is the international communication standard for data transmission along telephone lines and has transmission speeds up to 64 Kbps per channel.

ISDN uses two channels for communication which are the Bearer Channel or the B channel and the Delta Channel or the D channel. The B channel is used for data transmission and the D channel is used for signaling and control, though data can be transmitted through the D channel as well.

ISDN has two access options:

i) Basic Rate Interface

BRI is made up of two B channels with a bandwidth of 64 Kbit/s and a D channel with a bandwidth of 16 Kbit/s. It is also known as 2B+D.

ii) Primary Rate Interface

PRI has a greater number of B channels, which varies from nation to nation, and a D channel with a bandwidth of 64 Kbit/s.

3. DSL

Digital Subscriber Line (DSL) is a technology that allows high speed Internet connections over regular phone lines. In addition to offering significantly better download and upload speed than the traditional modems, DSL offers the benefit of always being on and one does not have to dial up the Internet Service Provider every time one has to get on the Internet. And unlike Cable modems, DSL connections are dedicated, so one does not have to share bandwidth with other users.

This broadband connection requires special equipment setup at both ends. At the user end, a DSL modem modulates digital information from the computer to send it along phone lines. These signals are then translated by a Multiplexer located at the phone company's nearest central office. The Multiplexer separates the voice from data signals, sending the latter to an ISP and from there to the Internet.

There are three main categories of DSL:

i) ADSL

Asymmetric Digital Subscriber Line supports data rates from 1.5 to 9 Mbps for downloading and 16 to 640 Kbps for uploading data. ADSL requires special ADSL modem.

ii) SDSL

Symmetric Digital Subscriber Line allows more data to be sent over existing copper telephone lines. SDSL supports data rates up to 3 Mbps. SDSL require special SDSL modem. SDSL is called symmetric because it supports the same data rates for uploading and downloading.

iii) VDSL

Very High DSL is a DSL technology that offers fast data rates over relatively short distances. The shorter the distance the faster the connection rate is. VDSL connection speed ranges from 128 Kbps to 8 Mbps.

DSL has one significant disadvantage that the farther the user is from the central office, the slower the connection is.

4. Cable TV Internet Connections

Through the use of cable modem one can have a broadband Internet connection that is designed to operate over cable TV lines. Cable TV Internet connection works by using TV channel space for data transmission, with certain channels used for downstream transmission and other channels for upstream transmission. Because the coaxial cable used by cable TV provides much greater bandwidth than telephone lines, a cable TV Internet connection can be used to achieve extremely fast access to the Internet. The speed ranges from 512 Kbps to 20 Mbps.

5. Satellite Internet Connections

Satellite Internet Connections allow a user to access the Internet via a satellite that orbits the earth. A satellite is placed at a static point above the earth's surface, in a fixed position. Because of enormous distances, signals must travel from the earth up to the satellite and back again so these connections are slightly slower than high speed terrestrial connections over copper wires. Such connections have a connection speed average around 492 up to 512 Kbps.

6. Wireless Internet Connections

Wireless Internet Connections are one of the newest Internet connection types. Instead of using telephone or cable lines for the Internet connection, the radio frequency bands are used. Wireless Internet connection provides an always-on connection which can be accessed from anywhere as long as one is within a network coverage area. It is typically more expensive and mainly available in metropolitan cities.

7.25 ELECTRONIC-MAIL

E-mail stands for electronic mail. It is the most popular service or facility provided by the Internet through which we can electronically send and receive messages anywhere in the world. E-mail is a fast and efficient method of communication. It is almost free of cost. The e-mail reaches to the destination in a few seconds. You can also send documents, pictures, audio and video files via e-mail by attaching the file with e-mail. It is also possible to send or receive e-mail messages through a mobile phone.

E-mail is a fast and efficient method of communication. You can also send your important data files or information to your own mail account and download these when required.

7.25.1 E-mail Address

E-mail -is sent and received with the reference of e-mail address. Therefore, each Internet user must have a unique e-mail account on an e-mail server, to send and receive e-mails. E-mail address consists of username and his address on the Internet. All ISP companies also provide the - e-mail address when theft membership is obtained.

The general format of an e-mail address is:

username@domain_name

Where

username: Specifies the name of user or organization. **Domain_name;** Specifies the name of server or ISP of which the user is member. For example, **"nasib.gill@mdurohtak.ac.in"** is e-mail address in which, "nasib.gill" is the name of user and "mdurohtak.ac.in" is the name of server.

You must type the correct e-mail address to send an e-mail, otherwise it is returned back. When some one sends e-mail to your e-mail address, it is stored in your mailbox. When you login to your account, you will usually be informed if you have new mail. Some mail systems will make sounds and tell you that you have new mail.

7.25.2 E-Mail Attachment

Attachment is a powerful feature of e-mail, which enables you to send additional files with your e-mail message. In this way, you can send and receive messages as well as document or program files. You can send documents, pictures or images, and audio & video files via e-mail, anywhere over the network. Attachment size varies from one e-mail service provider to the other.

7.25.3 HOW DOES E-MAIL WORK?

To create, send and receive e-mail, you need e-mail program, also called "email client". Once you send the message, your computer connects to your e-mail server and transmits a copy of your message. E-mail Server is a host computer on the Internet, which keeps track of information about millions of e-mail account holders. The server checks the address you have typed and finds out where the recipient e-mail server is. It connects to that server and transmits another copy of the message. Once the receiving e-mail server has received the message, the recipient is able to retrieve the message when connected to the server.

Most e-mail clients allow you to attach files to the e-mail message. In this way you can send and receive data as well as program files.

7.25.4 ADVANTAGES OF E-MAIL

There are several advantages of the e-mail facility available on the Internet. The main advantages of e-mail are:

1. It is extremely fast and reaches to the destination in a few minutes or even in few seconds. Typically, it takes 1 to 5 minutes to reach a destination in Europe (USA, England etc.) from Pakistan.
2. Its cost is very low. It is almost free.
3. One message can be sent to many persons with a single e-mail.
4. It is available round the clock and round the globe.
5. You can send and receive e-mail from anywhere in the world.
6. You can attach and send any type of files.
7. It is also possible to send or receive e-mail messages through a mobile phone.

7.25.5 LIMITATIONS OF E-MAIL

Although e-mail, provides the fast and efficient way to send and messages. It also has some limitations. These are described below.

1. Email is not necessarily private. Your confidential message read by someone such as network administrator.
2. Some email systems can send or receive text files only.
3. It is difficult to express emotions using email.
4. You can receive too much or unwanted emails.
5. You may not know about the person with whom you are communicating.

7.25.6 FREE E-MAIL ACCOUNT

Although you are provided with the e-mail account when you join any local ISP company. There are also some websites that provide facility to Internet users to create their own e-mail account, free of cost. The most popular websites are:

http://www.gmail.com

http://www.yahoo.com

http: //www.hotrnail.com

To create new e-mail account on the Hotmail, follow these steps.

Open the Hotmail website.

Click the Sign-up link for an E-mail account, a registration form will be displayed.

Fill the form correctly and send to the Hotmail server, your e-mail account is created.

After creation of your e-mail account, you are allotted a. username and password. You can check 'your e-mail account by entering the correct username and password. You can also compose and send the e-mail from your free e-mail account as well as you can manage your mails.

7.26 SEARCH ENGINE

Internet is a large source of information and contains almost millions of WebPages related to almost every topic that can be thought of. Initially to search for any relevant item of information, user needed to browse from an initial starting address of a known website, and then begin searching for links from one webpage to another, hoping to reach to the required information. This technique called **browsing** is a common, sequential way of getting the information. But it is very time consuming and tiring job these days when the internet connections are paid, and time needs to be saved. So many searching tools were developed for the searchers to get the relevant information in minimum time possible with accurate results.

A search engine is a program that searches documents for specified keywords and returns a list of the web pages where the keywords were found. A search engine is actually a huge database that contains references to thousands of web pages on the Internet. The searchers interact with these databases by proving some keywords. On the basis of these keywords, the databases return a list of availabie web pages along with their titles, URL, several first sentences etc. From these received results, user can choose the webpage whichever seems relevant.

Typically, a search engine works by sending out a spider to fetch as many documents as possible. A spider is a program that automatically fetches Web pages. Spiders are used to feed pages to search engines. It's called a spider because it crawls over the Web. Another term for these programs is WebCrawler. Because most Web pages contain links to other pages, a spider can start almost anywhere. As soon as it sees a link to another page, it goes off and fetches it. Large search engines, like Google, have many spiders working in parallel. Another program, called an indexer, then reads these documents and creates an index based on the words contained in each document. Each search engine uses a proprietary algorithm to create its indices such that only meaningful results are returned for each query.

The information that is received from a database is ranked according to various factors such as location and frequency of keywords in the web page, number of visits to the web page, or some other relevant factors. Redundant references are also removed from the results by most of the search engines.

Although search engine is really a general class of programs, the term is often used to specifically describe systems like **Google** (http://www.google.com), **Yahoo** (http://www.yahoo.com), **MSN Search** (http://search.msn.com), **Alta** Vista (http://altavista.com), **AOL Search** (http://search.aol.com) that enable users to search for documents on the World Wide Web.

Hence on the Internet, a search engine is a coordinated set of programs that includes:

A **spider** (also called a "crawler" or a "bot") that goes to every page or representative pages on every Web site that wants to be searchable and reads it, using hypertext links on each page to discover and read a site's other pages.

A program that creates a huge **index** (sometimes called a "catalog") from the pages that have been read.

A program that receives the search request, compares it to the entries in the index, and **returns results** to the user.

7.26.1 COMPONENTS OF SEARCH ENGINES

There are four main components to a search engine which will affect the results of the search.

1. WEB CRAWLER

This is the part of the search engine which goes through the pages on the internet and gathers the information for the search engine. Variable features which can affect any search results include:

Included pages: Most search engines will find information by beginning at one page and then following all of the links on that page. It will then follow all of the links on these new pages, and so on. Therefore, if a page is not linked to from another page, it may never be found by a search engine. Authors can include unlinked pages in a search engine by submitting them to each specific search engine.

Excluded pages: Some web administrators may choose to exclude their pages from search engines because they are internal pages or Intranets. Many web pages are also excluded because their content is dynamically generated from a database and a search engine cannot find it.

Documents types: Different search engines will search different document types. All will search HTML documents, but some will also search PDF, PowerPoint, Word, Excel, and more.

Frequency of crawling: An important part of a web crawler is how frequently it retrieves information from pages. Some sites it will visit more often than others.

2. DATABASE

The search engine's database is what searcher is actually searching. All of the information that a web crawler retrieves is stored in a database. Every time one uses a search engine, it is this database that is being searched, not the live internet. Variable features which can affect the search results include:

Size of the database: Some search engines will have extremely large databases (~5 billion pages) for one to search, while others will have comparatively small ones (~150 million pages). A small database is not necessarily worse, however, since it may offer more focused and higher quality results than a larger database.

Freshness of the database: The freshness of the database is a direct result of how frequently the web crawler retrieves new information. If the information in the database is fairly old, then the search results will suffer.

3. SEARCH ALGORITHM

Each search engine interprets the terms entered into the search box in different ways. Variable features which can affect the search results include:

Operators: Most search engines allow the use of operators such as AND, OR, and NOT in order to create complex search statements. The terms may need to be entered in upper case. Most of them also use the plus (+) sign to signal that a term must be included in the search results and a minus (-) sign to signal that a term must be excluded from the results.

Phrase Searching: Search engines will generally search for words as phrases when quotation marks are placed around the phrase. Some search engines may use a drop down menu which offers the option of searching the terms as a phrase.

Truncation: Some search engines will automatically truncate the terms you enter. This means that the search engine will not only search for the term exactly as you spelled it, but will also search on that term with alternate endings and as a plural. Some search engines will only search for variable endings on certain common words.

4. RANKING ALGORITHM

How a search engine ranks the results of the search is possibly the most important component of a search engine. Most searches will retrieve thousands of results. Since one probably will only look through the first 1-2 pages of results only, one needs the most relevant results to appear first. Variable features which can affect your search results include:

Location and Frequency: All search engines look at the location and frequency of words in a page. If a term appears near the top of a web page, such as in the title or in the first few paragraphs of text, it is assumed that the page is more relevant than if the term is used at the bottom of the page. Pages where the words appear more frequently in relation to the other words on the page also qualifies the page as being more relevant than other web pages.

Link Analysis: This feature analyzes how pages link to each other and then uses this information to determine the "importance" of each page. If a page is linked to from a large number of other pages, then it is ranked more highly.

Clickthrough measurement: Some search engines also use clickthrough analysis. This means that a search engine might watch what results someone selects from a particular search, and then eventually drop high-ranking pages that aren't attracting clicks, while promoting lower-ranking pages that do pull in visitors.

7.26.2 FINDING INFORMATION USING SEARCH ENGINE

A user opens a search engine webpage and types the keyword or a criterion that describes the information that is needed. Some search engines allow the use of some Boolean terms such as AND, OR, NOT to further restrict or widen the search results. The user can view the results of search in a search engine by going through the following process:

1. Here we use a Google as a search engine for our example. To open the Google webpage, http://www.google.com is typed in the address bar of the browser. Following home page which is the Google search engine appears:

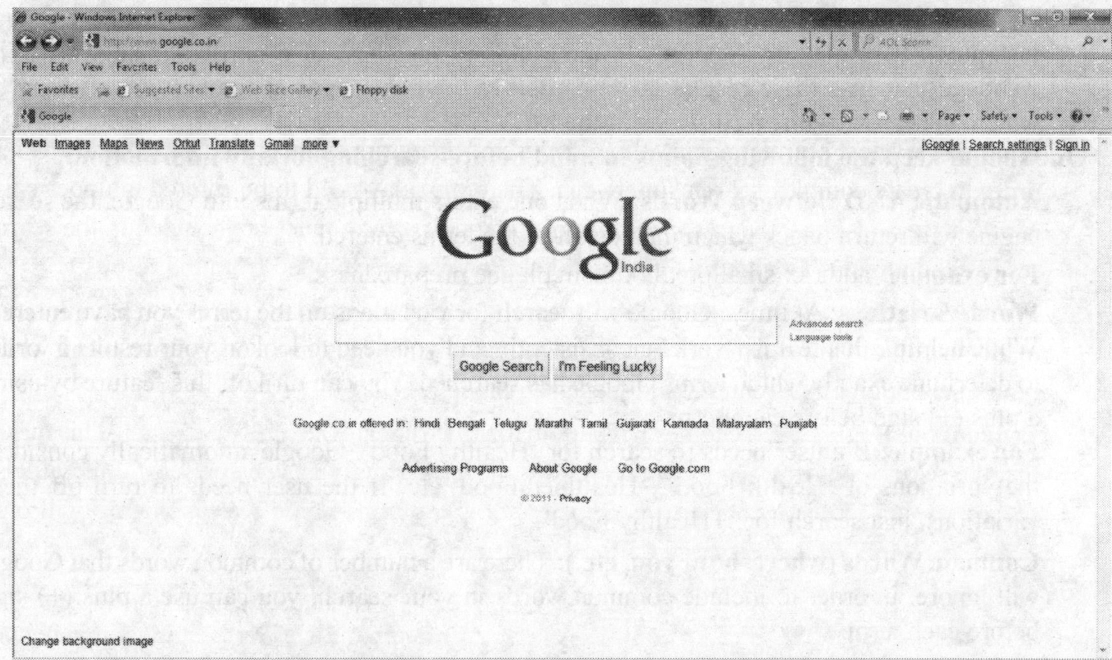

Figure 7.39

2. In the Search textbox, the keyword or search criteria that the user wants are typed. Suppose one needs to find information on **Taj Mahal.** When Search button is clicked, a new webpage lists all the available WebPages relating to the searched keyword along with a short description about the web site and it's URL.

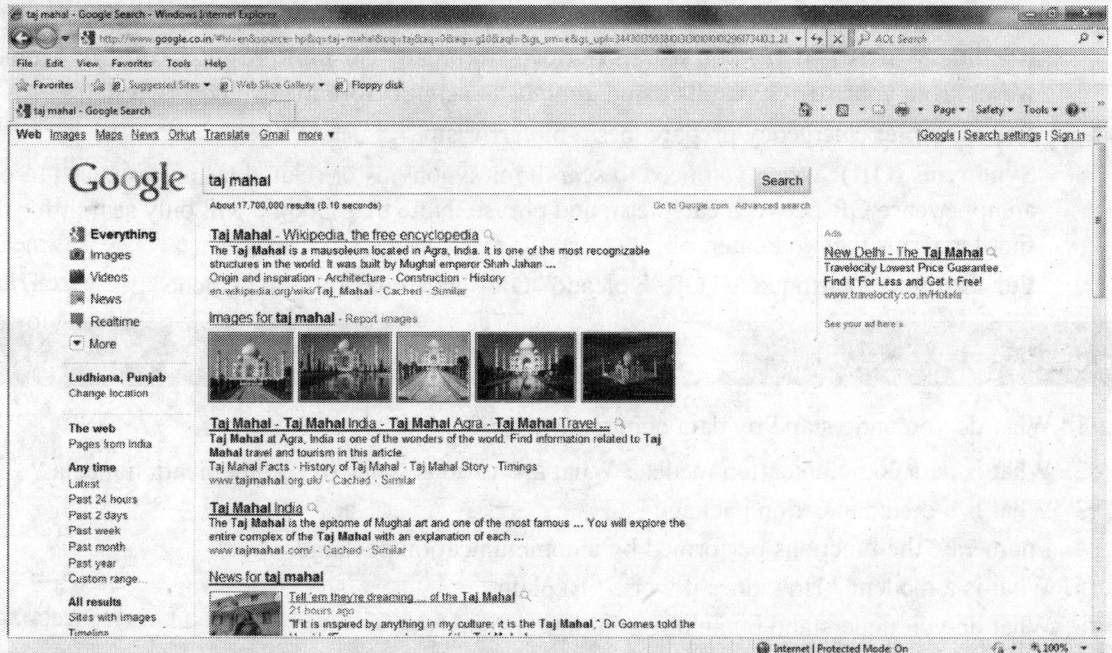

Figure 7.40

3. By clicking on any hyperlink that seems relevant, the searcher can jump to the webpage instantly. There may be hundreds to thousands of matches for a particular keyword. The webpage that lists these results contains link to the next pages at the bottom, clicking on which one can view the next pages in the list.

One should keep the following points in mind before searching for any information:

Automatic AND Between Words: When one enters multiple terms into Google, the search engine will return pages which include all of the terms entered.

For example: anthrax smallpox botulism plague preparedness

Word Variations: At times, Google will search for variations on the terms you have entered. While helpful, this feature works inconsistently and you need to look at your results in order to determine exactly which terms Google has searched. You can turn off this feature by using a plus (+) sign before each term.

For example: If a user needs to search for 'Healthy Food', Google automatically considers the variations of 'Health Food', 'Healthier Food' etc. If the user needs to turn off these variations, just search for '+Healthy Food'.

Common Words (where, how, you, etc.): There are a number of common words that Google will ignore. In order to include common words in your search, you can use a plus (+) sign before each term.

For example: On searching for 'How do you write official letters', Google searches for 'write official letters' only. If one needs to include such words in the search too, adding a + sign before them is a good practice.

Phrase Searching ("Quotes"): In order to search for phrases in Google, you need to place quotation marks around your phrase. Phrase searching will also turn off the exclusion of common words.

For example: "How do you" catch tuberculosis

Exclude Words (–): If your search retrieves too many off-topic results, you can exclude words from your search results using a minus (–) sign before the excluded word.

For example: emergency preparedness -bioterrorism

Synonyms (OR): When you need to search for synonyms or related terms, you need to use an upper case OR between each term and phrase. Note that Google will only search for the first ten terms that you enter.

For example: "earthquake" OR "volcano" OR "landslide" OR "avalanche"

PROBLEMS

1. What do you understand by data communication ?
2. What is data communication media ? What are various types of communication media ?
3. What is a communication package ?
4. Enumerate the functions performed by a communication package.
5. What is a modem ? How does it work ? Explain.
6. What do you understand by analog and digital signals ?
7. What are microwave systems ?
8. What is a RADAR ? How does it work ?

9. What are communication satellites and how do they function ?
10. What is fibre-optics ? State the importance if fibre-optics in communication systems.
11. What are the advantages and disadvantages of fibre-optic cables ?
12. What is an Electronic Mail/Message System (EMMS) ? Enumerate the services rendered by an EMMS.
13. What is a Voice Mail System ? How does it function ?
14. What is message distribution system ? What are its functions.
15. What is microwave and how it can be used for computer communication ? What are their advantages and disadvantages ?
16. What is a FAX system ? Explain its working.
17. What do you means by Information Retrieval Systems ? State their importance.
18. What components are typically found in a simple data communication system ?
19. Enumerate the facilities offered by Bank-at-home and On-line-brokerage information services.
20. Illustrate a microwave communication link used for point-to-point data transfer.
21. What are commercial database services ? Explain any two important commercial database services of your choice.
22. Which type of communication channel can transmit data in digital form ?
23. Why are computing and communication technologies merging ?
24. What is a front-end-processor ? State its function.
25. What is a multiplexer ? What is the purpose of a multiplexer ?
26. Describe and sketch how a point-to-point configuration works.
27. What is polling ? State its usage.
28. Illustrate the difference between bit-rate and baud-rate ?
29. "Coaxial cable has smaller bandwidth than optical fibre". Explain it.
30. What is twisted-pair cable ? In what situations are they suitable for use in data communication?
31. Describe the process of concentration.
32. What are the benefits of internal and external modems ?
33. Differentiate between narrow-band, voice-band and broad-band communication channels.
34. List and describe the various types of modem.
35. What do you understand by modulation and demodulation ? Why is modulation used in signal transmission ?
36. What purpose do modems serve in data communication systems ?
37. What is the normal speed of transmission of digital signals on a telephone line ?
38. Give a brief description of the transmission characteristics of coaxial cable and optical fibre.
39. Describe the various modes in which the transfer of data can occur.
40. When are public telephone lines used to connect a terminal to a computer ?
41. How are data transmission speeds measured ? What are some typical speeds ?
42. What facts must be known in order to communicate with a large computer system ?
43. What is an intelligent modem ?
44. What are the advantages of using fibre-optic as compared to copper wires for data communication ?

45. Explain the various types of communication channels.
46. What is meant by file-transfer protocols? Explain.
47. What are serial and parallel data transmission ? When are they used in data communication?
48. Why is earth to satellite transmission frequency different from satellite to earth transmission frequency ?
49. What is channel-sharing ? How can it be accomplished ?
50. When is RS2332-C standard interconnection used ? Explain the characteristics of the RS232-C interface.
51. What are the various methods of data transmission ?
52. What do you understand by Gateway Services ?
53. How does Videotext Service differ from Teletext Service ?
54. What is video-conferencing ? What is the infrastructure required for video-conferencing ?
55. How does laser beam work as a communication media ?
56. What are the common media used in data transmission ? Also give their advantages and disadvantages.
57. Outline the application of laser beam communication media.
58. What is teleconferencing ? Outline its benefits and limitations.
59. What are the components required for a communication package ?
60. What is the difference between analog and digital transmission ? Give their relative advantages and disadvantages ?
61. What is a microwave media ? Explain its utility in data transmission.
62. What is a communication protocol ? Why are they required in creating networks ?
63. What is packet switching ? Why is this method used for digital communication between computers ?
64. What do you understand by multiplexing ?
65. What is meant by computerised conferencing ?
66. What is meant by bandwidth of a channel ? State its importance.
67. Why are channels multiplexed for signal processing ?
68. What is an E-Mail service ? What are various E-Mail types ?
69. What is a acoustic-coupler ? How is it different from normal modem ?
70. Explain the terms Simplex, Half-duplex and Full-duplex.
71. What is the capacity of coax for digital transmission ? What is its typical bandwidth ?
72. What do you understand by the term broadband and baseband ? How do they differ ?
73. What is the purpose Xmodem and Kermit Protocols ?
74. What are the main advantages of satellite communications ?
75. What is a Bulletin Board System (BBS) ? State its types.
76. Differentiate between synchronous and asynchronous data transmission modes.
77. Why is modulation used in signal transmission ?
78. What are the benefits and limitations of BBSs ?
79. What are the benefits and limitations of E-Mail ?
80. What is computer conferencing ? What are its benefits ?

81. What do you mean by internet?
82. Explain the evolution of internet?
83. Explain the various application of internet?
84. Explain the various ways to connect the internet?
85. What do you mean by e-mail?
86. What are the advantages and disadvantages of email?
87. What do you mean by search engine?
88. Explain the components of Search engine?
89. What do you mean by data communications?
90. Explain the various types of transmission media?
91. What is multiplexing? Explain the types of multiplexing?
92. Explain the various types of network topologies?
93. What are communication protocols?

Basic Concepts of Software and its Types

8.1 INTRODUCTION

The hardware alone can not perform any particular calculation, computation or manipulation without being instructed exactly what to do, when to do and how to do it. These instructions are very important and are called software.

The software acts as an interface between the user and the computer or a software can be defined as a complete set of instructions written by the programmer which enables the computer to obtain the solution to a problem. These programs give life to the circuitry of computer hardware. It consists of a sequence of instructions and decision rules that direct the computer in performing a given task. The CPU must be told:

What data is to be processed?

What manipulation is to be performed on the data?

What must be the sequence of computation to be performed?

What must be the format of the output to be produced?

Software may be viewed as a general term that is used to describe any single program or a group of programs.

In its most general form, software is a term used in contrast to hardware to refer to all programs which can be used on a particular computer system i.e. the term software is used to describe program sets needed to operate an information processing system.

8.2 SOFTWARE TYPES

Software is the means by which computer systems speak with computer users. Software forms the heart of computer systems.

Figure 8.1

Software, by definition, is the collection of computer programs, procedures and documentation that performs different tasks on a computer system. The term 'software' was first used by John Tukey in 1958. At the very basic level, computer software consists of a machine language that consists of groups of binary values, which specify processor instructions. The processor instructions change the state of computer hardware in a predefined sequence. Briefly, computer software is the language in which a computer speaks. There are different types of computer software.

8.2.1 Programming Software

This is one of the most commonly known and popularly used forms of computer software. These software come in forms of tools that assist a programmer in writing computer programs. Computer programs are sets of logical instructions that make a computer system perform certain tasks. The tools that help the programmers in instructing a computer system include text editors, compilers and interpreters.

8.2.2 System Software

It helps in running the computer hardware and the computer system. System software is a collection of system programs; device drivers, servers, windowing systems and utilities. System software helps an application programmer in abstracting away from hardware, memory and other internal complexities of a computer.

8.2.3 Application Software

It enables the end users to accomplish certain specific tasks. Business software, databases and educational software are some forms of application software. Different word processors, which are dedicated for specialized tasks to be performed by the user, are other examples of application software.

8.2.4 Other Software Types

Apart from these three basic types of software, there are some other well-known forms of computer software like inventory management software, ERP, utility software, accounting software and others. Take a look at some of them.

8.2.4.1 Inventory Management Software

This type of software helps an organization in tracking its goods and materials on the basis of quality as well as quantity. Warehouse inventory management functions encompass the internal warehouse movements and storage. Inventory software helps a company in organizing inventory and optimizing the flow of goods in the organization, thus leading to an improved customer service.

8.2.4.2 Utility Software

Also known as service routine, utility software helps in the management of computer hardware and application software. It performs a small range of tasks.

Utility software may be considered as an application software or system software which is used quite often in the development of a program. In other words, these are the programs that support the operations, management, and users of a computer system by providing a variety of support services. These may include:

File Conversions
Data Transfer Utility Software
Data Compression
Sort and Merge Utility Software
Software Guides
Data Communication within a network
Disk Optimization
Calculator utility
Screen Savers
Text Editors
Real time clock utility,
Disk defragmenters,
Systems utilities,
Virus scanners,
and so on.

8.2.4.3 Data Backup and Recovery Software

An ideal data backup and recovery software provides functionalities beyond simple copying of data files. This software often supports user needs of specifying what is to be backed up and when. Backup and recovery software preserve the original organization of files and allow an easy retrieval of the backed up data.

8.2.5 Miscellaneous Software Types

So far we come across mainly two types of wares, namely, hardware and software. Besides there have been a long list of ware which also requires a brief mention. These are given as under.

Firmware: It is a set of micro-programs stored in ROM for the purpose of implementing user's instructions related to their applications. It is named so because these are firmly associated with the hardware by manufacturers.

Humanware (or Liveware): It is nothing but a group of users, end-users, programmers, and other professionals who work with hardware and software of Computer System for an intended application.

Shareware: As the programmers want to share the software with us so it gets name shareware. It is a fully functional and will probably include messages called anonymous screens, reminding us that we haven't yet paid for the program we are running. When we make the payment, we will get the latest version of the program.

Public Domain Software: It is the most free, most unsupported, and most popular software for people with small budgets. Public domain software is released to anyone to use, copy, include in his or her own programs, or to do whatever seems appropriate. As opposed to freeware, it does not carry a copyright, and there is never any payment expected by the original programmer or author.

Begware: It is a type of shareware that uses an extensive number of messages to remind us to pay for our copy.

Postcardware: Few programmers producing shareware simply ask for a postcard from your local venue. This is their way to travel the world, since many programmers won't do it in person. The better the response the programmer gets, the more inspired the software that will be produced.

Retail Software: It is a software that we buy from the company or its dealers and pay for it. Nowadays you can purchase retail software through Internet also using the on-line ordering facility.

Crippleware: It is slightly different from shareware and with crippleware, we receive a program that has one of its major functions absent. Many companies float the idea behind such software that crippled versions of their software make excellent demonstrations. For example, a Word Processor without print feature is crippled.

Bannerware: It is a software that is released to advertise other software. Bannerware is like the lure to catch us and make us really want other software the authors sell. For example, game programs available through shareware web sites offer additional games when we register.

Donorware: It is software that if one wants to continue to use company's software, then company make a donation of that software. Some developers ask a certain amount while others don't set any amount.

Freeware: It is one of the popular ware for which we are normally excited. No charge, no registration, but also no support. Freeware authors release their programs for our use, without expecting or requesting any payment. The authors, however, usually retain their copyright on the software, so we can't start selling it under our name, raking in profit for something we didn't develop.

8.3 LANGUAGE TRANSLATORS

These are the programs that help the users in developing programs, procedures and to prepare user programs for computer processing. Language translators translate other programs to machine language. There are mainly three types of language translators:

Compilers
Interpreters
Assemblers

8.3.1 Compiler

The compiler is a program that resides on a disk or other mass-storage media. When the compiler is needed, it is called by the computer and loaded into RAM. The user enters his source program on the terminal and too is stored in RAM. The compute then performs the translation. It translates the various statements and expressions into the machine code known as the object program. This is illustrated in Fig. 8.2.

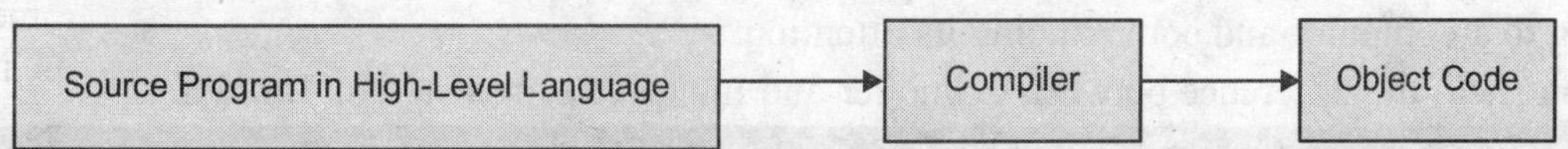

Fig. 8.2: Compilation Process

Once the user's program has been translated into object code, the compiler is no longer needed. The object code may also be output to magnetic tape or disk for storage at the same time when it is stored in RAM. The object program can then be executed. It has to be noted that compilers are not needed to run the program and are needed only to translate it. One more point to be remembered is that one compiler is capable of translating source program written in only one high-level language.

The main purpose of high-level languages is to enable the programmer to write programs more easily by being able to concentrate on the problem being solved, rather than on the machine level features of the computer. But, the process of translating high-level language source program into object code will be more lengthy and complex. Hence compiler tend to be longer and more complex programs than assemblers, and hence occupy more central space.

8.3.2 Interpreter

An interpreter is a program residing in computer's memory that interprets and executes the high-level language source program. Interpretative higher-level languages use statements, expressions, and commands similar to those used in compiler languages. The user preparing a program writes these expressions line by line using the unique syntax of that language to solve the problem. The problem is usually entered into the computer through a terminal. The interpreter can be stored on some type of external media such as magnetic tape or floppy disk and then brought into RAM when it is needed. In some computers, the interpreter is stored in ROM. In this way, it is always available when needed. The main difference between interpreter and compiler is that the interpreter must reside in memory along with the user's source program.

Unlike a computer, which translates an entire program into object code at one time an interpreter evaluates and translates program statements as the program is executed, one instruction at a time. Thus the interpreter takes one source program instruction, translates it into object code, and executes it. It then takes the next instruction, translates it and so on. Using an interpreter can save space since the interpreter program itself can be quite small, and it eliminates the need to store the program's translated object code in the computer.

On the other hand, it has drawbacks :

i) Program statements that are used multiple times must be translated each time they are executed.

ii) Another big disadvantage is of an interpreter is its slow speed. interpreters execute programs at a speed, 10 to 20 times slower than equivalent machine code generated by an assembler or compiler.

Despite of these disadvantages, interpreter are widely used. They are convenient and easy to use because they are totally interactive. The user can literally sit in front of the computer terminal and converse with the computer and solve problems directly through the interpreter. When a compiler language is used, the source program must first be entered and then compiled. The object code generated by the compiler is then loaded and executed. If a programmer wishes to change something in the program, adding features, correcting errors, or the like, the entire process must be repeated. The program changes are made and then entered. The new source program is then recompiled. Finally the new program is executed. With an interpreter, changes and additions can be made interactively. As soon as we discover that we need to modify or add something, we can do it immediately through the interpreter. When using an interpreter, a programmer gets the feeling that he is directly speaking to a computer and commanding its attention.

In nutshell, the difference between Compiler and Interpreter are listed in **Table 8.1.**

Table 8.1: Compiler Vs. Interpreter

S.No.	Compiler	Interpreter
1.	Entire program is scanned first and then gets translated into machine-code.	The program is translated line by line
2.	Debugging of programs is quite slow in Compilers.	Debugging is ver fast in case of Interpreters.
3.	Only after all the syntax errors are removed from the program, the program is translated in machine-language code.	Each line of program is checked for syntax errors first and is then converted to its equivalent machine code
4.	Changes can't be made due to non-interactive nature of compilers.	Changes can be made quite easily and immediately due to interactive nature of interpreters.
5.	After program is translated into machine code, compilers are no more required for running the program.	Interpreter is required for running the translated machine code equivalent of the program.
6.	Compilers occupy more space in memory during program compilation.	Interpreters occupy lesser space in memory during program translation.
7.	Time for execution is lesser.	Time for execution is larger.

8.3.3 Assemblers

Assembler is that class of language translators which are used to translate an assembly language program into a machine language program. This is illustrated in **Fig. 8.3.**

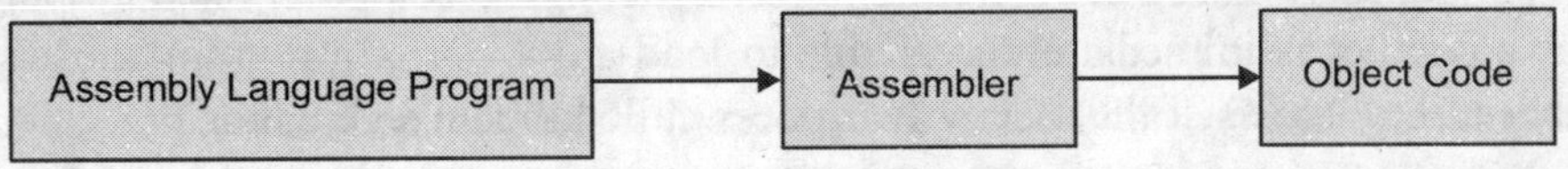

Fig. 8.3: Assembly Process

Some good assemblers for Intel 8086/8088 Assembly include MASM (Macro Assembler) 5.0/ 6.0, TASM (Turbo Assembler), etc.

8.4 SYSTEM UTILITY SOFTWARE

System utilities are a wide variety of general purpose programs that greatly speed up and simplify the use of the computer. They are written to enhance man-machine communications and improve programming efficiency. The exact type of systems program used depend greatly upon the specific computer. Typically however, most microcomputers have the following types of system programs :

Editor
Loader
Monitor
File Manager
Linker
BIOS

Besides these, there are also a wide variety of other programs available. We will consider these most commonly used systems programs only.

8.4.1 Editor

The most often used systems program is the editor. Editors are interactive programs that are stored in the memory and allow the user to write a program, generate text, or to make a wide variety of changes and additions to either of these. The editor is a systems program that is typically stored on some external mass-storage media. When it is needed, the editor is called into RAM. The programmer then communicates with the editor through the video or hard-copy terminal. Like an interpreter, the editor is interactive. All source programs for assemblers and compilers are typically written with the editor.

Since the editor can be used for creating any type of written material, it is useful for writing letters or preparing manuscripts and reports. It can be used for many other word-processing applications. Once a program or a block of text is created, it can then be edited as required. Lines, words, or single characters can be added, deleted, or otherwise modified. Once the final program or text is complete and error free, and editor stores the final text in a file in RAM. The final text can also be stored on external tape or disk or output to a printer.

8.4.2 Loader

Another widely used systems program is the loader. a loader is a short, simple program that is used to load a program into computer's memory. Often, the program resulting from the assembly or compilation process is stored on some external secondary storage media such as floppy diskette. To run that program, it must be loaded into RAM. The loader program is the sequence of instruction that transfers the program from the external media to main memory.

In early minicomputers and some early microcomputers, the loader program actually had to be loaded into RAM manually, an instruction at a time by using the front panel switches. Loading the loader was usually a difficult task since it was time consuming and error prone. Nowadays the loader is permanently stored in ROM and is fixed part of the computer itself. With the loader into ROM, the computer is immediately available to load any external program. closely related to loader is another utility to assist the assembly process called the linkage editor.

The linkage editor allows independently written assembly language programs to share data and variables, by linking them together when they are to be loaded into computer memory and run.

8.4.3 Monitor

Another frequently used systems program is the monitor. Almost all microcomputer use some form of monitor. Typically it is stored in ROM and performs all basic functions required in a microcomputer. For example, most monitors perform the same functions typically performed by a hardware front panel. Older microcomputers and many minicomputers used a hardware from panel containing either binary lights and switches or octal or hex keyboards and displays. These hardware front panels were used for entering programs and data and for displaying contents of memory or registers. Using the front panel controls, the user could enter program, execute them, and also perform a variety of editing and debugging functions, all in machine language. The monitor in a microcomputer performs these functions through the video or hard-copy terminal connected to the computer rather than with a hardware front panel.

Some of the functions that can be performed by a monitor are as follows :

1. Enter or load instructions and data
2. Display contents of memory locations or registers
3. Change contents of memory locations or registers
4. Execute programs

All of these functions are usually performed in machine language. Most monitors use either octal or hexadecimal designations when entering or displaying memory or register information. addresses are also expressed in octal or hex notation. Thus the monitor is a program that essentially permits convenient entry, display, debugging and execution of machine language programs.

Monitor programs are widely used for machine language program debugging. The monitor provides a convenient means of sequencing a program, finding the error and then correcting it.

Finally most monitors contain load and store routines that allow programs to be loaded from some external media or stored on external media. In effect, the monitor contains a loader. However, it also allows a machine language program generated under the monitor to be stored on some external media.

8.4.4 File Manager

A file manager is a program which permits programmers to create, copy, update or delete files on the disks. A file is a collection of information supplied by the programmer which is stored on the disk as a single entity and is accessible by a name. A directory of files stored on the disk as also maintained by the file manager. The directory itself is also stored on the disk. The directory includes file name, size of the file, date and time, and unused memory capacity of the disk, etc.

8.4.5 Locator and Linker

A locator is a program that assigns specific memory addresses for each machine code of a program which is to be loaded into the system memory.

Usually a longer program is divided into a number of smaller subprograms called modules. It is easier to develop, test and debug smaller programs. a linker is a program that links smaller programs to form a single program. While developing a program subroutines are frequently used. The subroutines are stored in a library file. The linker also links subroutines with the main program. The linker links machine codes of the program. Therefore, it accepts user's program after editor has edited the program and compiler has produced machine codes of the program.

8.4.6 BIOS

The abbreviation BIOS stands for Basic Input Output System. Some system programs that manage the computer's operations are stored in ROM as firmware. These programs perform the most fundamental types of supervisory and support work. They provide essential services that all programmers need. These service programs (or subroutines) are called Basic Input/Output Services. They are referred to as BIOS or ROM-BIOS. Each program performs one specific task such as writing some characters to the CRT, reading some data from disk memory or reading a character from the keyboard etc. All these are done using software interrupt instruction.

The services provided by ROM-BIOS are:

Print screen
Video services
Disk services
Serial port (RS-232) services
Cassette port services
Keyboard services
Parallel port (printer) services
Bootstrap services
and so on.

Other system programs are built on the foundation of ROM-BIOS programs and provide higher-level support services. Operating Systems are examples of higher-level system programs. MS-DOS and UNIX are important operating systems.

There are two important differences between ROM-BIOS and DOS :

1. ROM-BIOS provides system services to users at very low-level, while DOS provides at higher-level.
2. DOS does much services to users directly, which the ROM-BIOS does not.

8.5 APPLICATION SOFTWARE

An application package or application program is the software that has been written to process or perform specific job. The term application indicates that the software is applied to the job at hand. application packages are available for all types of tasks. These programs are called Application Packages because they accomplish the processing required for a particular application. They may be for business applications, engineering designs, home applications, teaching aids etc.

An end-user wishing to use an application package has to define his own requirements by means of parameters, which are employed by the programs in the system to produce the specific results required. These are usually written in high-level languages. Of course, the application packages run under the control of the operating system.

Application software is developed to aid in any task that benefits from computation. It is a broad category, and encompasses software of many kinds, including the internet browser being used to display this page. This category includes:

Business software
Computer-aided design
Databases
Decision making software
Educational software
Image editing
Industrial automation
Mathematical software
Medical software
Molecular modeling software
Quantum chemistry and solid state physics software
Simulation software
Spreadsheets
Telecommunications (i.e., the Internet and everything that flows on it)
Video editing software
Video games
Word processing
and so on.

Application packages can be classified as:

General-purpose Application Packages
Application-specific Packages
Customised Application Packages

8.5.1 General-purpose Application Packages

It is that class of application packages that perform quite commonly used day-to-day tasks and also increase the productivity very significantly and that's why these are also known as productivity packages.

Some important examples of this category include:

Word processing packages for processing and manipulating text
Spreadsheet packages for calculating finances and data analysis
CAD for designing or drafting
Database packages for management of files, database, storage and retrieval of information
Engineering design packages
Communication packages
Integrated packages, etc.

Some integrated packages have been developed which combine the functions of word processing, spreadsheets, graphics, database management and communication into a single software. MS-Office, Framework and Symphony are good examples of Integrated Packages.

8.5.2 Application-specific Packages

It is the type of application packages specifically meant for accomplishing a uncommon application. Few important examples include :

General Application Packages

Payroll
Personnel Management
Attendance Management
and so on.

Business Application Packages

Inventory Control
Finance and Accounting
Marketing Analysis
MRP (Material Requirements Planning)
Human-resource Management
and so on

Scientific Application Packages

Computer-Aided Designing and Drafting (CADD)
SPSS (Statistical Package For Social Sciences)
Computer-Aided Manufacturing (CAM)
Statistical Analysis Software (SAS)
and so on.

Miscellaneous Application Packages

Computer-Based Learning (CBL)
MIDI (Musical Instrument Digital Interface) Package
Computer-Based Training (CBT)
and so on

8.5.3 Customised Application Packages

It is a kind of application packages developed by the professional programmers. It has become the trend of the present day Software Industry to develop such kind of packages. Natural Language Processing (NLP) is getting world-wide attention because these are non-procedural and are more closer to human conversation. This is trend has been geared up probably due to the development of the non-procedural 4GLs (4th Generation Languages). This trend will continue to grow as the development in multimedia, graphics, artificial intelligence, networking solutions enhance.

8.6 OPERATING SYSTEM

"Operating System (OS) is a collection of software written to provide the fundamental instructions that a computer needs to manage resources, such as memory, the file system, and processes".

In other words, OS is a master program that controls a computer's basic functions and allows other programs to access the computer's resources such as disk drive, printer, keyboard, and screen.

There are several definitions of operating system. Few of these are:

"Operating system is a set of system programs which controls all the computer's resources and provides the base upon which application programs can be written".

OR

"An operating system may be viewed as an organised collection of software extensions of hardware, consisting of control routines for operating a computer and for providing an environment for execution of programs".

OR

"An operating system is a set of procedures (manual and/or automatic) that enables people or group of people to share a computer installation efficiently".

OR

"An operating system is a program that act as an intermediary between a user of a computer and the computer hardware. The primary goals of an operating system are:

To make the computer system convenient to use and

To use the computer hardware in an efficient manner"

OR

"An operating system is an integrated collection of subsystems and further each subsystem consists of programs that perform specific duties. Just as the processor is the nucleus of the computer system, the operating system is the nucleus of all types software activities".

Examples of operating systems: Linux, MS Windows 95, MS Windows NT, Windows XP, UNIX, DOS and OS/2.

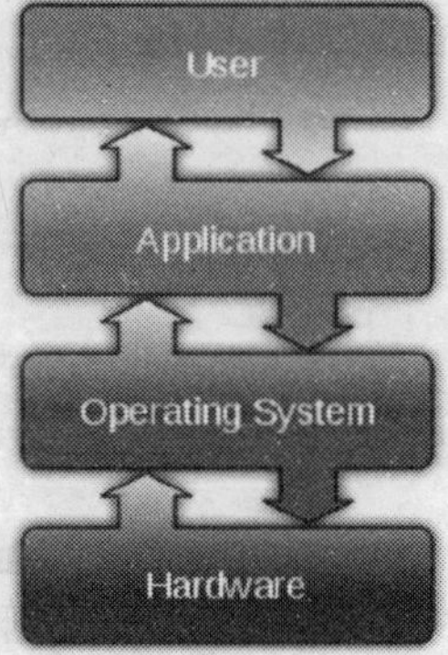

Fig. 8.4: Layers of Computer System

It co-ordinates all the hardware and software components of a computer

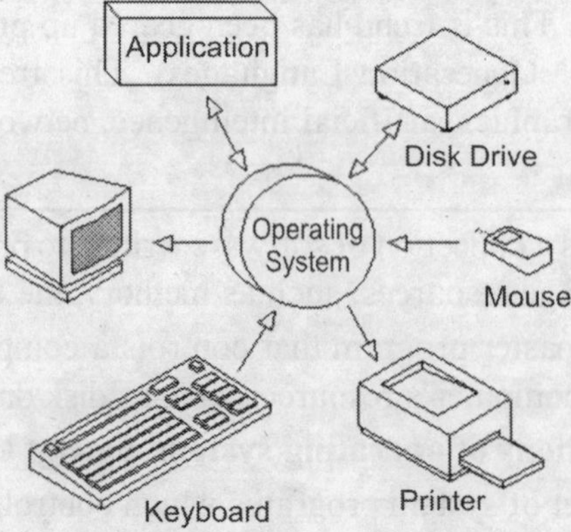

Fig. 8.5: OS as Co-ordinator

The following two types of programs make up the operating system:

i) Control programs and

ii) Processing programs

8.6.1 Control Programs

These programs oversee system operations and performs tasks such as input/output, scheduling, handling interrupts, and communication with computer operator or programmer. The control programs consist of the following :

a) Supervisor Programs

b) Job Control Programs

c) Input/Output Management Program

8.6.2 Processing Programs

These are executed under the supervision of control programs and are used by the programmer to simplify program operation for the computer system. They include language translator programs, link editors, library programs and a set of utility programs. These programs collectively automate the management of all the computing resources available in a computer system including CPU, all peripherals, and software. This integrated collection of programs provides more efficient computer operation. Improved operating convenience is another benefit of an operating system.

Typically, operating systems (OSs) are used in microcomputer systems. They require mass storage media such as magnetic tape or floppy disk. most microcomputers systems use operating systems only with floppy disk mass storage. For this reason, these operating systems are referred to as disk operating systems (DOS). The most commonly used operating systems on personal computers are MS-DOS and PC-DOS.

8.6.3 Characteristics of Operating System

Sharing

Concurrency

Long-term Storage

Non-determinacy

8.6.4 Desirable Features of Operating System

Efficiency

Reliability

Small-Size

Maintainability

Thus the operating system is responsible for directing a given computer into a batch mono-programming system, a multi-programmed system, a time-sharing system or a real-time system. Many operating systems can handle both batch and real-time applications simultaneously.

8.6.5 Booting (or Bootstrapping)

The process of loading the operating system into memory is known as booting. When a computer is turned on the operating system must be brought into the memory of computer from the hard-disk storage. The process is normally started by a small program called bootstrap loader. This program resides in a ROM as a firmware. A computer is designed to fetch its very first instruction from the ROM when power is turned on. The first instruction is bootstrap loader. It is very simple program sufficient only to direct the CPU to look for specific file on the disk memory, and executes the instructions stored in the file. The file contains machine codes to direct the CPU to continue loading the rest of the operating system into the memory. When the operating system is fully loaded into the memory, the computer is ready to accept user's commands.

8.6.7 Family of operating systems

The family of operating systems have evolved over the years:

(a) Windows family of OS:

Windows 1.0
Windows 2.0
Windows 3.0 (the first version to make substantial commercial impact)
Windows 3.1x
Windows 95 (aka Windows 4.0)
Windows 98 (aka Windows 4.1)
Windows Me (aka Windows 4.2)
OS/2 (developed jointly with IBM)
Windows NT
Windows 2000 (aka Windows NT 5.0)
Windows XP (aka Windows NT 5.1)
Windows Server 2003 (aka Windows NT 5.2)
Windows Vista (to be released August 2006)
Windows Longhorn Server (to be released shortly after Windows Vista)
Microsoft Codename Blackcomb (to follow Vista)

(b) Apple/Macintosh

Apple DOS
ProDOS
GS/OS
Lisa OS
A/UX
Mac OS
System 6
System 7 (code-named "Big Bang")
Mac OS 8
Mac OS 9
Mac OS X
Mac OS X v10.0 (aka Mac OS X 10.0 "Cheetah")
Mac OS X v10.1 (aka Mac OS X 10.1 "Puma")
Mac OS X v10.2 (aka Mac OS X 10.2 "Jaguar")
Mac OS X v10.3 (aka Mac OS X 10.3 "Panther")
Mac OS X v10.4 (aka Mac OS X 10.4 "Tiger")
Mac OS X v10.5 (aka Mac OS X 10.5 "Leopard")
Mac OS X Server
Darwin

(c) Unix
(d) Linux
(e) Solaris.

8.7 FUNCTIONS OF OPERATING SYSTEM

The main functions of OS are:

1. It manages the hardware and software resources of the system. In a desktop computer, these resources include such things as the processor, memory, disk, etc.
2. It provides a stable, consistent way for applications to deal with the hardware without having to know all the details of the hardware.

8.7.1 Main Functions

OS acts as an interface between hardware and users. It controls overall operations of computers. It is mainly used for job management, data management, virtual memory management, input/output management, process management, security etc.

(a) **Job Management:** OS manages the job waiting to be processed. It recognizes the jobs, identifies their priorities, allocates the memory for the job, schedules and finally runs each job at the appropriate moment.

(b) **Data Management:** Data management keeps track of the data on disk, tape and optical storage devices. The operating system's file system knows where that data are physically stored.

(c) **Virtual Storage Management:** OS is used for virtual memory management. OS makes possible to increase the capacity of main memory with out actually increasing its size.

(d) **Input/output Management**: OS manages the input and output operation of computer. This applies to the flow of data among the different devices of computer and application programs.

(e) **Process Management:** The main activities of process management are job queuing, job scheduling, keeping track of the status of each process etc.

(f) **Protection and Security:** OS job is to secure data inside the memory of computer. Operating systems provide password protection to keep unauthorized users out of the system.

(g) **User Interface:** OS acts as an interface between a user of a computer and the computer hardware.

8.7.2 Basic Roles of Operating System

(a) Easy interaction between human and computer.
(b) Starting computer operation automatically.
(c) Loading and scheduling users' programs/processes.
(d) Controlling I/O devices
(e) Managing various types of memories such as primary, secondary, cache etc.
(f) Providing security to users' jobs and files.
(g) Accounting hardware resources and handling network communication.
(h) Allowing users to share data and software among themselves.
(i) Preventing the system from unauthorized user, programs etc.

8.7.3 OS as an Extended Machine

The OS effectively isolates the hardware from the user. The user communicates only with the OS and it links the various languages and the systems and applications programs available. The OS fields all requests for services and totally eliminates the need for the user to deal with the hardware or related problems. Thus the operating system allows the user to concentrate on his application and prevents him for having to spend a lot of time determining how things are to be specifically accomplished by the hardware.

In this view, the function of an operating system is to prevent the user with the equivalent of an Extended Machine or Virtual Machine that is easier to program than the underlying hardware.

8.7.4 OS a Resource Manager

An operating system's major function is to manage the resources of the computer system. It allocates the resources on the basis of the user need and system capability. The four major functions of an operating system are:

(i) File and Software Management
(ii) Input/Output and Peripheral Management
(iii) Memory Management
(iv) Processor (or CPU) Management

As a Resource Manager, the operating system must perform the following functions for each resource viz. processor, memory, I/O, files :

(a) Keep track of status of each resource
(b) Decide which job should get the resource and for how much time, according to some policy
(c) Allocate the resource to the job decided
(d) After the resource is used by the job for the allocated time, make the resource free

8.8 OS RELATED COMMON GLOSSARY

Buffering

A buffer is a region of memory used to temporarily hold data while it is being moved from one place to another. Typically, the data is stored in a buffer as it is retrieved from an input device (such as a keyboard) or just before it is sent to an output device (such as a printer). However, a buffer may be used when moving data between processes within a computer. So, buffering is a process of placing the data in a buffer in order to increase the processing capability of a device.

Spooling (Simultaneous Peripheral Operations On-Line)

In computer science, spooling refers to a process of transferring data by placing it in a temporary working area where another program may access it for processing at a later point in time. The term 'spool' is an acronym of 'Simultaneous Peripheral Operations On-Line'. This temporary working area could be a file or storage device, but probably not a buffer.

For example: By using a process spooling, multiple users can send jobs to a printer simultaneously. When users send documents (known as print jobs) to a networked printer, each job is stored temporarily on the file server. As the printer finishes printing the current job, the file server sends the next job to the printer so that it can be printed).

Virtual Memory

Virtual memory is the use of secondary storage devices as an extension of the primary storage of the computer, thus giving the appearance of a larger main memory than actually exists.

Paging:

In paging system, each process is divided into a number of fixed length blocks called 'pages', typically 4K bytes in length. Memory space is viewed as a series of 'page-frames' of the same size. When a process is to be executed, only the pages that are immediately required are loaded into memory.

Swapping:

In a virtual memory system, Swapping is a technique in which high priority process is swap in main memory and low priority process from main memory is swap out. When high priority process is completed, low priority process is swap in again.

Multiprogramming

It is a form of processing in which a computer holds more than one program in memory and works on them in round-robin fashion that is, by sharing out the processor's time so that each program receives some attention some of the time. This way of working is in contrast to using the processor to run one program at a time.

Multitasking

Multitasking, in an operating system, is allowing a user to perform more than one computer task (such as the operation of an application program) at a time. Microsoft Windows 2000, IBM's OS/390, and Linux are examples of operating systems that can do multitasking (almost all of today's operating systems can). When you open your Web browser and then open word at the same time, you are causing the operating system to do multitasking.

Multi-threading

Multi-threading is the ability of an operating system to execute different parts of a program, called threads, simultaneously. The programmer must carefully design the program in such a way that all the threads can run at the same time without interfering with each other.

Job Scheduling

Job scheduling not only assigns priority to jobs but also admits new jobs for processing at appropriate times. When a user job is submitted, the system takes note of its time of arrival, processing requirement etc. Considering all these factors, the scheduling techniques are chosen. There are two types of scheduling

(a) Non-Preemptive Scheduling: In non-preemptive scheduling, a scheduled job always completes before another scheduling decision is made.

(b) Preemptive Scheduling: In preemptive scheduling, a scheduling decision can be made even while the job is executing.

Some scheduling algorithms are:

(a) FCFS (First Come, First Serve

(b) SJF (Shortest Job First)

(c) Priority Scheduling

(d) Round Robin Scheduling

(e) Multilevel Feedback Queue Scheduling

(f) Multilevel queue Scheduling

Interrupt Handling

An interrupt is a signal generated by an event that alters the sequence in which a processor executes instructions. To handle interrupt Operating System has one special routine called ISR (Interrupt Service Routine).

Hardware interrupt: A signal created and sent to the CPU that is caused by some action taken by a hardware device is called hardware interrupt. For example, keystroke depressions and mouse movements cause hardware interrupts.

Software interrupt: A software interrupt, also called an exception, is an interrupt that is caused by software, usually by a program in user mode. Examples of events that cause them are requests by an application program for certain services from the operating system or the termination of such programs.

8.9 CLASSIFICATION OF OPERATING SYSTEMS

Within the broad family of operating systems, these may be categorized based on the types of computers they control and the sort of applications they support. These may be classified in the following categories:

Single-user, Single-task Operating System
Single-user, Multi-task Operating System
Multi-user Operating System
Multi-access Operating System
Multi-processing Operating System
Multi-tasking and Multi-threading Operating System
Real-time Operating System
Distributed Operating System
Embedded Operating System

8.9.1 Single-user, single task Operating System

As the name implies, this operating system is designed to manage the computer so that one user can effectively do one thing at a time. The Palm OS for Palm handheld computers is a good example of a modern single-user, single-task operating system. Other examples of such operating systems include MS-DOS, PC-DOS, etc.

8.9.2 Single-user, multi tasking Operating System

This operating system allows a computer to perform more than one task at a time. Microsoft's Windows and Apple's Mac OS (Leopard) platforms are both examples of operating systems that will let a single user have several programs in operation at the same time.

8.9.3 Multi-user Operating System

A multi-user operating system allows many different users to take advantage of the computer's resources simultaneously. UNIX, VMS and mainframe operating systems, such as MVS, are examples of multi-user operating systems.

These operating systems allow two or more users to run their respective programs at the same time by making all these programs resident in the memory of computer. Such operating systems are normally made to work on minicomputers and mainframe computers.

The concept of allowing more than one programs in the memory of computer is called multi-programming. All time-sharing systems need to be multi-programmed but not necessarily all the multi-programmed systems to be time-shared.

In these types of systems, all the resources are shared among different users' programs. The processor (or CPU) is made to switch among these users' programs after a fixed quantum of time called time-slice. The time-slice needs to be very small so that the user should need have feeling that processor is not attending well to them.

Examples : VMS (on DEC Mainframes), UNIX, XENIX, MVS, etc.

It's important to differentiate here between multi-user operating systems and single-user operating systems that support networking. Windows 2000 and Novell Netware can each support hundreds or thousands of networked users, but the operating systems themselves aren't true multi-user operating systems. The system administrator is the only "user" for Windows 2000 or Netware. The network support and the entire remote user logins the network enables are, in the overall plan of the operating system, a program being run by the administrative user.

8.9.4 Multi-access Operating System

In a multi-access operating system, a user may submit a job by typing on a terminal and may use the terminal to monitor and control the job as it runs. These operating systems allow simultaneous access of a single application onto a computer system through two or more terminals.

The operating system shares the computing resources among the different jobs so that it appears to each user that he has entire machine to himself.

An example is provided by some dedicated transaction-processing systems, such as Airline Ticket Reservation Systems, that supports hundreds of active terminals under control of a single program.

8.9.5 Multiprocessing Operating System

It is that class of operating systems that have the ability to support more than one process at the same time i.e. allowing more than one programs to run concurrently on the multiple CPUs in a single computer system. These operating systems differ from the time-sharing (or multi-user) operating systems in the manner that these refer to utilisation of multiple CPUs.

In such operating system, the resources are allocated comfortably to the competing processes in a reasonable manner which results in a high throughput.

Examples : OS/2 for high-end PCs, UNIX, MVS, etc.

8.9.6 Multitasking and Multithreading Operating System

These operating systems have the capability to execute more than one task concurrently on a computer system having a single CPU. In these operating systems, CPU switches from one task to another so quickly that it gives the illusion to the user of executing all the programs (or tasks) at the same time.

Multithreading permits different portions of a single program to run concurrently and this it is having the ability of an operating system to execute different parts of a program (called threads) simultaneously. It requires the programmer to design the program so carefully that all the threads can run at the same time without interfering with each other.

Examples : Windows 95/98, Windows NT, OS/2, etc.

8.9.7 Real-time Operating Systems (RTOS)

Real-time operating systems are used to control machinery, scientific instruments and industrial systems.

Real-time operating systems are used in environments where a large number of events, most external to the computer, must be accepted and processed in a short-time or within certain deadlines.

These operating systems have the following peculiar characteristics:

Fast response time

Feedback mechanism

Reliability

A primary objective of real-time operating systems is to provide quick response-times, and thus meet the scheduling deadlines. In the design of these operating systems, user-convenience and resource utilisation are of secondary concern.

These operating systems must be designed in such a manner that response-time to the external-stimulus is very immediate as the same are designed for the purpose of controlling and monitoring of external activities with timing constraints.

Such applications include :

Industrial Control
Telephone Switching Equipments
Flight-Control
Real-time Simulators
Few Military Applications etc.

The traditional operating systems like MS-DOS and UNIX are very different from real-time operating systems because memory management and file-management are of least importance in comparison to processor and input/output management.

Examples:

Some examples of real time operating systems are:

BLMX (Board-Level Multitasking eXecutive)
BSO/RTOS (Boston Systems Office/ Real-time Operating System)
CCP (Communication Control Program) Operating System for IBM System/3
iRMX (Intel's 8086 family Real-time Multitasking Executive) Operating System
DMERT (Duplex Multiple Environment Real-time) Operating System etc.

8.9.8 Distributed Operating Systems

A distributed operating system governs the operation of a distributed computer system and provides a virtual machine abstraction to its users. The key objective of a distributed operating system is transparency. Ideally, component and resource distribution should be hidden from users and application programs unless they explicitly demand otherwise.

These operating systems usually provide the means for system-wide sharing of resources, such as computational capacity, files and I/O devices. In addition to typical operating system services provides at each node for the benefit of local clients, a distributed operating system may facilitate access to remote resources, communication with remote processes, and distribution of computations.

The added services necessary for pooling of shared system resources include:

Global naming
Distributed file system, and
Facilities for distribution of computations, such as inter-node process communication and remote procedure calls.

8.9.9 Embedded Operating System

Embedded operating systems are mainly executed on computers that control devices. These devices are mobile phones, TV sets etc. These systems consist of circuits and 32-bit microprocessors that control the functioning of various operations.

Apart from the above main criterion for classification of operating systems, there will be other criterion as well, like basing on whether it is open code or not and whether it is available for free and similar.

Fig. 8.6 shows widely used operating systems in the market.

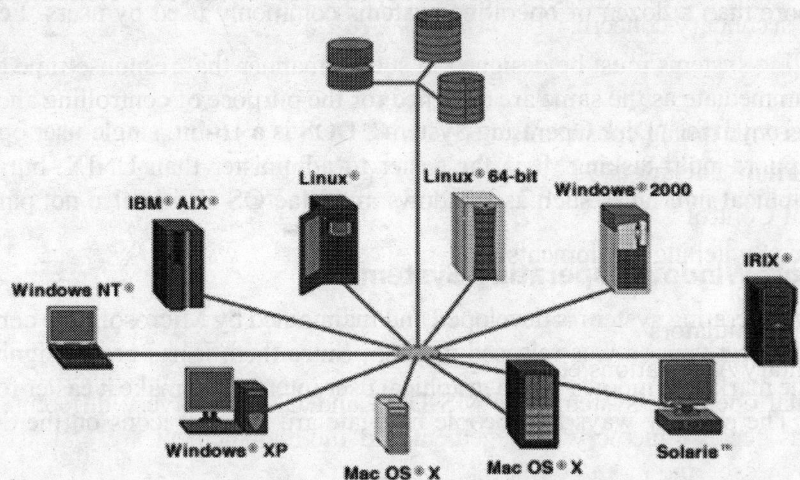

Fig. 8.6 : Widely used OS

8.10 FORMS OF DATA PROCESSING

Data processing is any computer process that converts data into information or knowledge. There are many types of data processing techniques. Some of these are:

8.10.1 Batch Processing

It is also called deferred Processing or off-line processing in which tasks are stored in the form of batches and processed each batches as requirement. It is a slow process of data processing. The purpose of batches is to give full control over the data as it is easier to handle a batch at a time.

Due to turnaround delays and offline debugging, batch is not very convenient for program development. Programs that do not require interaction and programs with long execution times may be served well by a batch operating system. Examples of such programs include:

Payroll
Forecasting
Statistical Analysis, and
Large Scientific Number-crunching Programs.

Serial processing combined with batch-like command files is also found on many PCs.

8.10.2 On-line Processing

The on-line processing is a fast processing in which input device is directly connected to computer. It is also called direct access or random access processing. In this processing result of data processing transaction is available immediately. E.g. ATM (Automated Teller Machine).

8.10.3 Real-time Processing

Real time means immediate response from computer. The essential feature is that the input data must be processed quickly enough so that further action can be promptly taken on the result.

8.10.4 Distributed Data Processing

A data processing system in which processing is decentralized with the computers and storage devices at different geographical locations.

8.11 OPERATING SYSTEM CHOICES

There are more than a dozen of operating systems commonly used by users. Few of these are discussed below:

8.11.1 DOS

DOS is an acronym for "Disk Operating System". DOS is a 16-bit, single-user operating system that does not support multi-tasking. It is far easier to administer than UNIX, but less powerful. Compared to graphical interfaces such as Windows and Mac OS X, it's also not particularly user-friendly.

8.11.2 Microsoft Windows Operating System

The Windows operating system is developed and maintained by Microsoft, the company founded by Bill Gates. The first version was released in 1985. Since then, it has grown significantly, and it now dominates the market. Windows uses a graphical user interface to make it easier for people to use their computers. The primary ways that people navigate are through icons on the desktop and the Start menu.

The Windows operating system, like the Macintosh and Linux, allows people to manage files and run software programs on desktop and laptop computers.

Windows is the most popular PC operating system in the world. A brief outline of few of the popular Windows operating systems is provided below.

8.11.2.1 Windows XP

Windows XP was released in October 2001 and was designed to replace all previous versions of Windows. It is offered in two versions:

Home and

Professional.

Both Home and Professional can be upgraded from Windows 98, Windows 98SE, and Windows ME. Windows NT 4.0, Windows 2000 and Windows XP Home can all be upgraded to Windows XP Professional. Windows 95 and earlier versions of Windows are up gradable to either version.

Main Features

Less crashes than Windows 98 - virtually gone is the infamous 'blue screen of death' that signalled a crashed system.

Error messages are less impersonal and end with 'We are sorry for the inconvenience.'

Installation of peripheral hardware such as printers, scanner and digital cameras is virtually automatic.

Many users can share the same PC. Each can have their own password and individualized desktop, my documents folder and web favourites for example.

With 'Fast User Switching' a user can turn the PC over to another user without logging off. The first user's program continue running and can be resumed when the second user is done.

New look to the desktop with bold greens and blues in places, beige in others. The classic Windows 98 style can be restored without functional loss.

Home networks are automatically recognized and configured. Broadband access can be setup with a few simple steps.

Folders are smarter and have related Task Panes that contains tasks that match the type of files found it. For example, a folder with photos would have a Task Pane containing an instant viewing capability such as a thumbnail viewer.

Files can be dragged and dropped on a CD-RW drive icon. Once you have placed all the files you want on the icon, you tell it burn them an it does it. No special CD writing software is required.

A smarter Start menu lets you keep your favourite programs permanently near the top. A second column contains access to key features like the control Panel and Search.

8.11.2.2 Windows ME

Windows ME is successor to Window 98 appeared late in 2000. It is very similar in look and feel to Windows 98 with a few added features.

Main Features

A more reliable streamlined process that reduces the start up time for the PC.

Automatic restoration of backup version of a file in the event of file corruption.

Protection of files from modification from other software programs.

Windows Media Player 7 was included.

8.11.2.3 Windows 2000

Windows 2000 arrived early in 2000. It is based on the NT operating kernel and targeted toward business users. It is sometimes referred to as Windows NT 5.0 and contains over 29 million lines of code.

It is offered in four versions: Professional, Server, Advanced Server and Datacenter Server

New features of Professional

Support for FAT16, FAT32 and NTFS file systems. Each file is encrypted with a randomly generated key.

A better application installation tracker.

Memory protection for individual applications and processes so that a single application can not lock up the system.

A file encryption system and secure VPN allows a private LAN over the Internet.

Native support is provided for ATM and cable modems.

8.11.2.4 Windows 98

Windows 98 was released in 1998. It retained and refined the desktop look of Windows 95. A second edition called Windows 98SE was released in 1999 and offered some fixes and improvements to the first edition.

Main Features

The biggest advance was the introduction of Internet Explorer, which is a web browser allowing you to view and download web pages from remote servers across the Internet.

An improved File System, FAT32 (File Allocation Table) was introduced. It enabled hard drives bigger than 2G bytes to be used with the OS. By default Windows 98 uses FAT16, which is the file system used on all previous Windows versions and DOS.

In Windows 98 you have the option of using FAT32 when first setting up a hard drive.

Windows 98 is backward compatible with Windows 3.1, Windows 95, and the MS-DOS® operating systems.

8.11.2.5 Windows 95

It was released in 1995 and had the first desktop appearance that has pretty much been retained in all versions of Windows since.

Main Features

The desktop with icons on it first debuted.

A taskbar was added to the bottom of the desktop. Program Manager was replaced with a 'Start' button on the taskbar. It is used to start programs, open documents, customize the system and get help. Toolbars such as quick launch, desktop, address and links can be placed on the taskbar.

Running applications that have been minimized also appear on the taskbar.

Windows Explorer replaced File Manager as the tool to manage folders and files.

Long Filenames (up to 256 characters) were supported which was a tremendous improvement over 8 characters in all earlier versions of Windows as well as DOS.

Plug and Play compatibility was added which meant you could plug in new hardware (expansion cards) which Windows would recognize and set it up for you. This feature wasn't quite there but was a start in the right direction.

Prior to this when you installed new hardware you had to manually insure there were no Interrupts (IRQ) or I/O address conflicts with existing hardware. Failure to do so could produce very strange results or even worse yet, no operation at all.

The Registry appeared, combining what had been multiple configuration files, into two files.

The right mouse click arrived allowing rapid access and text manipulation.

8.11.2.6 Windows NT

It was released in 1994 this was the first Windows OS to support 32 bit programming model of the 386, 486 and Pentium processors. Support for long filenames also appeared for the fist time.

It provided advanced security features, advanced network support and user administration which made it a first choice for many in the business environment.

8.11.2.7 Windows 3.1.1

In 1993 Microsoft released 3.1.1. It was dubbed 'Windows for Workgroups' and provided network support so that multiple PCs could share files and printers.

8.11.2.8 Windows 3.1

In 1992 V3.1 brought True Type fonts, multimedia support, OLE and common dialog boxes. It ran only in protected mode and required a 80286 or better processor.

8.11.2.9 Windows 3.0

Released in 1990 this OS became widespread in both home and office PCs. It supported the protected mode of the 80x86 processors available at the time. A menu bar ran across the top much like the menu bar in all Windows based applications programs.

Main Features

Program Manager provided access to program icons which were kept inside a number of different 'group windows'. A simple mouse click on any icon would start the program it represented.

File Manager allowed easy access and control to all the files on one's hard drive.

Print Manager and the Control Panel appeared.

8.11.2.10 Windows 2.0

Released in April 1987, it had improved windows that could overlap one another. It also included enhancements to the keyboard and mouse interface.

The release of the 80386 processor enabled multitasking of many DOS programs. Windows 2.0 competed with IBM presentation manager of the OS/2 operating system.

8.11.2.11 Windows 1.0

Released November 1985. It ran on DOS and used fixed tiled windows.

8.11.2.13 Windows

The first Microsoft offering was released in the November 1983.

8.11.3 UNIX

UNIX (pronounced as YOO-niks) is a computer operating system originally developed in 1969 by a group of AT&T employees at Bell Labs. UNIX runs on many types of computers, including supercomputers, notebook PCs, mainframes and minicomputers. Its main ability is that it works with so many kinds of hardware.

8.11.4 LINUX

Linux is a generic term that commonly refers to Unix-like computer operating systems that use the Linux kernel. Linux is one of the most prominent examples of free software and open source development; typically all the underlying source code can be used, freely modified, and redistributed by anyone.

Ubuntu, NepaLinux, UserLinux etc are few examples of Linux distributions.

8.12 MOBILE OPERATING SYSTEMS

Like computer operating system a mobile operating system is a software platform on top of which other programs run. When you purchase a mobile device, the manufacturer will have chosen the operating system for that specific device. The operating system is responsible for determining the functions and features available on your device, such as thumb wheel, keyboards, WAP, e-mail, text messaging and more.

Some of the more common and well-known Mobile operating systems include the following:

8.12.1 Symbian OS

Symbian OS has become a standard operating system for smartphones, and is licensed by more than 85 percent of the world's handset manufacturers. The Symbian OS is designed for the specific requirements of 2.5G and 3G mobile phones.

Fig. 8.7 : Symbian OS

Symbian features pre-emptive multitasking and memory protection, like other operating systems (especially those created for use on desktop computers). EPOC's approach to multitasking was inspired by VMS and is based on asynchronous server-based events.

Symbian OS was created with three systems design principles in mind:

the integrity and security of user data is paramount

user time must not be wasted

all resources are scarce

To best follow these principles, Symbian uses a microkernel, has a request-and-callback approach to services, and maintains separation between user interface and engine. The OS is optimised for low-power battery-based devices and for ROM-based systems (e.g. features like XIP and re-entrancy in shared libraries). Applications, and the OS itself, follow an object-oriented design: Model view Controller.

8.12.2 Windows Mobile OS

The Windows Mobile platform is available on a variety of devices from a variety of wireless operators. You will find Windows Mobile software on Dell, HP, Motorola, Palm and i-mate products. Windows Mobile powered devices are available on GSM or CDMA networks

Fig. 8.8 : Windows Mobile 6.5 OS

Windows Mobile 6.5 is based on the Windows CE 5.2 kernel, and features a suite of basic applications developed with the Microsoft Windows API. It is designed to be somewhat similar to desktop versions of Windows, feature-wise and aesthetically. Additionally, third-party software development is available for Windows Mobile, and software applications can be purchased via the Windows Market Place for Mobile.

8.12.3 Palm OS

Since the introduction of the first Palm Pilot in 1996, the Palm OS platform has provided mobile devices with essential business tools, as well as capability to access the Internet or a central corporate database via a wireless connection.

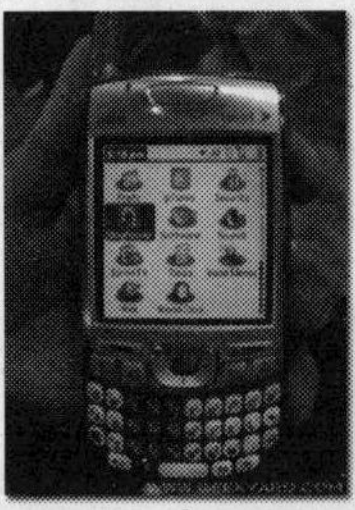

Fig. 8.9 : Palm OS

Palm OS Garnet applications are primarily coded in C/C++. Two officially supported compilers exist: a commercial product, Code warrior Development Studio for Palm OS, and an open source tool chain called prc-tools., based on an old version of gcc. CodeWarrior is criticized for being expensive and is no longer being developed, whereas PRC-Tools lacks several of CodeWarrior's features. A version of PRC-Tools is included in a free Palm OS Developer Suite (PODS).

8.12.4 Mobile Linux

The first company to launch phones with Linux as its OS was Motorola in 2003. Linux is seen as a suitable option for higher-end phones with powerful processors and larger amounts of memory. While not originally designed to be portable,Linux is now one of the most widely ported operating system kernels, running on a diverse range of systems from the iPAO (a handheld computer) to the IBM Z/Architecture (a massive mainframe server that can run hundreds to thousands of concurrent Linux instances). Linux runs as the main operating system on IBM's Blue Gene supercomputers. As of November 2010, **Linux** is the OS on 91.8% of systems on the Top 500 supercomputers list.Linux has also been ported to various handheld devices such as Tuxphone, Apple's ipod and i phone .Some operating systems developed for mobile phones use modified versions of the Linux kernel including Google Android, Hp webOs and Nokia Maemo.

8.12.5 MXI

MXI is a universal mobile operating system that allows existing full-fledged desktop and mobile applications written for Windows, Linux, Java, Palm be enabled immediately on mobile devices without any redevelopment. MXI allows for interoperability between various platforms, networks, software and hardware components.

8.12.6 Android

Android is a software stack for mobile devices that includes an operating system, middle ware and key applications. Google Inc purchased the initial developer of the software, Android Inc., in 2005. Android's mobile operating system is based on the Linux Kernel. Google and other members of the Open Handset Alliance collaborated on Android's development and release. The Android Open Source Project (AOSP) is tasked with the maintenance and further development of Android. The Android operating system is the world's best-selling Smartphone platform.

Fig. 8.10: Android

In May 2011, researchers at University of Ulm publicized a security flaw, present in all Android devices running AndroidOS 2.3.3 and earlier versions (more than 99% of all Android devices worldwide), that affects all Google services using the ClientLogin authentication protocol (such as authentication tokens widely used by eBÁY and other online services) and allows hackers access any personal data available through Android's application programming interfaces (APIs), thus stealing the user's digital credentials over open wireless networks. In response, Google announced a fix that would be rolled out transparently to the use.

8.13 USER INTERFACE

Interface is a common boundary between the user and the computer system. OS provides two types of User interface.

8.13.1 CUI (Command User Interface)

A CUI (command user interface) is a user interface to a computer's operating system or an application in which the user responds to a visual prompt by typing in a command on a specified line, receives a response back from the system, and then enters another command, and so forth. MS-DOS and UNIX are CUI operating systems.

8.13.2 GUI (Graphical User Interface)

GUI is graphical user interface. It is user friendly and easy to understand and use. A GUI uses windows, icons, and menus to carry out commands such as opening files, deleting files, moving files, etc. and although many GUI Operating Systems are operated by using a mouse, the keyboard can also be used by using keyboard shortcuts or arrow keys.

A few examples of a GUI Operating Systems: Microsoft Windows 95, Apple Mac OS etc.

A few examples of a GUI interfaces are: GNOME, KDE etc.

Desktop view of GUI of Windows 7 Home Premium is shown in **Fig. 8.11.**

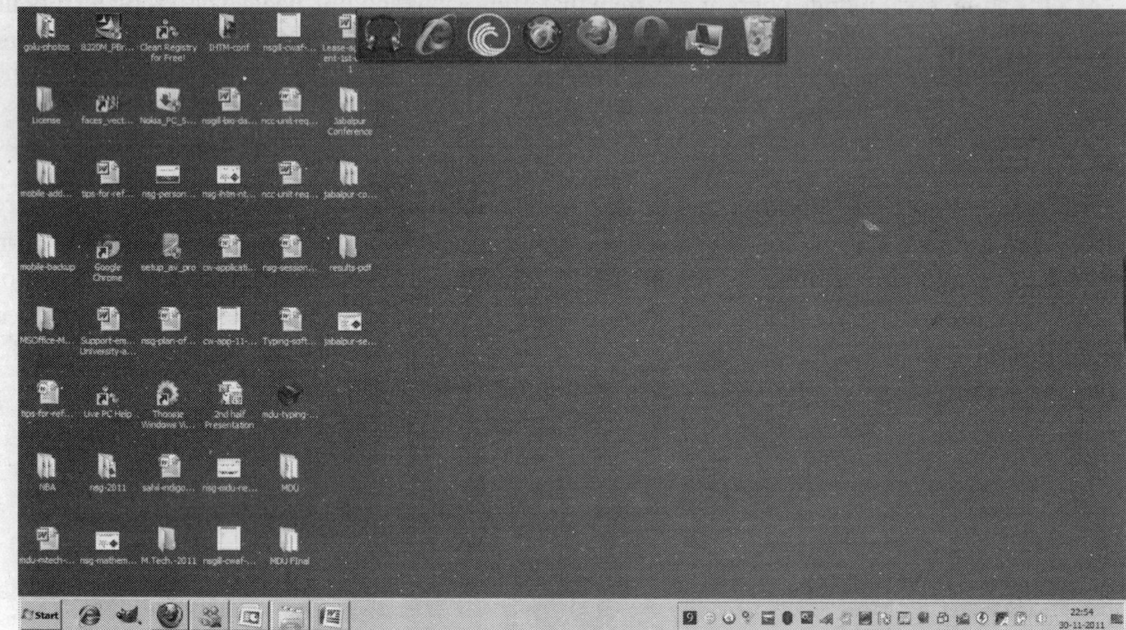

Fig. 8.11: Desktop View of Windows 7 Home Premium

8.13.3 Common Features of GUI

A present day GUI has the following common features:

Pointing device(s): These allow users to point at different parts of the screen as well as can be used to initiate a command. Besides, these can also be used to manipulate objects on the screen by:

selecting objects on the screen

moving objects around the screen, or

merging several objects into another object

Examples: Mouse, light pen, joystick, touch sensitive screen, touch pad and so on.

Windows: It graphically display the progress of the action initiated. When a screen is divided into several independent regions, each one of these is called a window. Each window can highlight results related to the action fired in the respective window.

Switching capability: Windows system offers the switching capability from one application to another or for sharing of data among various applications.

Resizing and Movement: Windows system also support resizing as well as moving around feature of windows.

Graphical Bit-mapped Displays: Bit-mapped display are made up of small pixels and offer a very high resolution. Bit-mapped displays have almost replaced character-based displays. Bit-mapped displays wonderful support graphic manipulation. This feature of these displays is also called WYSIWYG i.e. What You See Is What You Get.

Functionality to support graphics along with height-parameters, color attributes, video-attributes, etc.

Icon: Icons provide a symbolic representation of any system-entity or user-defined object, etc. such as file, folder, address, table, book, applications and so on. A folder icon consists a group of files or other folder icons. Double clicking on the folder icon causes a window to be opened displaying a list of icons and folder icons representing the folder's contents.

Dialog box: Dialog box is used to capture user information or to present information to the user. Normally, a dialog box is displayed to get additional information. Dialog boxes are also used to indicate error messages in the form of alert boxes. Dialog boxes also use a wide range of screen control elements to communicate with the user.

Check box: Such a box is used to capture the information intending confirmation pertaining to any kind of actions desired by the end-user.

Sliders: These are used to show the relative position of the contents or to move to a different position.

Desktop Metaphors: In desktop graphical metaphor, users are not aware of applications and they deal with files, folder, drawers, clipboard and an out-box. For example, merely clicking the mouse on an icon representing the Report cause word processor to get started and to load the report file automatically.

Menus: The functionality on a GUI system must be arranged in the form of structured menus such as horizontal menus, pull-down menus, etc. From the menu, the end-user can select any operation of his choice such as File, Edit, Search, Tool and so on. Rather than remembering commands at each stage, a menu can be used to provide a list of items. Each menu element can be either a word or an icon representing a command or a function. Menu item can be invoked by moving the cursor on the menu item and selecting the item by clicking the mouse.

8.13.4 Components of GUI

GUIs consists of four major components :

Windowing System: It allows to display multiple applications at the same time and it includes programming tools for designing movable and resizable windows, menus, dialog boxes, check boxes, and other items on the display.

Example : Macintosh, X Window, etc.

Imaging Model: It describes how fonts and graphics are designed on the screen and such a model is capable of handling typeface, color, shading, dimension and size of graphical primitives such as simple or complex lines, curves, etc. Some GUIs support more than one imaging model.

API (Application Program Interface): API is a set of programming language functions that allow the programmer to specify how the actual application will control the menus, scroll bars and icons that appear on the screen.

Set of Interface Development Tools: GUI development environments may incorporate toolkits and frameworks. Most of these toolkits are based on object-oriented approach.

8.13.5 CUI Vs GUI Operating Systems

Table 8.2 : CUI Vs GUI OS

GUI	CUI
It is based on graphical user interface mode.	It is based on command user interface mode.
It is graphical and user friendly.	It is more textual and less user friendly.
It is very common.	It is less common.
It uses keyboard and mouse.	It uses only keyboard.
It consists of different components such as text box, icon, desktop, pointing device etc.	It does not consist such components.
E.g. MS-Windows OS	E.g. MS-DOS OS

PROBLEMS

1. Differentiate between assemblers, compilers and interpreters.
2. How is system software different from system utilities ? Explain.
3. What do you understand by an Integrated Software ?
4. Describe two commonly used utility programs.
5. What kind of a program is used to backup from one data storage to another ?
6. What is postcadware ? How is different from bannerware ?
7. Differentiate between application and system software.
8. What is meant by GUI ?
9. What are the important features of GUI ? Explain.
10. Differentiate between shareware and freeware.
11. What do you understand by GUI standards ? Explain.
12. What are various components of GUI ? Explain.
13. What is crippleware ? Give an example.
14. How is freeware different from donorware ? Explain.
15. What is a public domain ware ?
16. What is a computer software ?
17. Is word-processing package a system software ? Justify your answer.
18. What are the functions of an assembler ?
19. What are different types software ? Explain.
20. What are different types of application packages ? Illustrate through suitable examples.
21. What is input to the compiler ?
22. Is Oracle an Application Package ? Justify your answer.
23. Discuss the features of an integrated package.
24. What are advantages of Windows environment ?
25. Enumerate functions of a monitor program.
26. What is the difference between Loader and Linker ?
27. What is the output of the compilers ?
28. What are monitors ? State their significance.
29. What is BIOS ?
30. What do you understand by application-specific package ?

31. What is a bootstrap program ?
32. What is an Editor ? What are the capabilities of an Editor ?
33. What is a firmware ?
34. What is a File Manager ? Outline its responsibilities.
35. What is the purpose of the Loader and Locator ?
36. What is an operating system ?
37. Discuss the important functions of an operating system.
38. Is Windows 95/98 an operating system ? Justify your answer.
39. What are the services provided by ROM-BIOS ?
40. What is a begware ?
41. What is meant by a programming language ?
42. If each new generation of language enhances interaction between programmers and the computer, why not write programs using the most recent generation of languages ?
43. What are the differences between high-level and low-level languages ?
44. Associate each of language with a particular generation of languages.
45. What are various generations of computer programming languages ?
46. What are problem-oriented languages ?
47. What is the difference between machine- and assembly-language ?
48. What are non-procedural languages ? Give few examples.
49. Why are low-level and high-level languages are named so ?
50. What are Application Generators ? Give few examples.
51. What are procedural languages ? Give few examples.
52. What are various types of high-level languages ?
53. State the capabilities of Query Languages ?
54. What are DSSs (Decision Support Systems) ? How are they helpful ?
55. What do you understand by Specialised Languages ? Give few examples.
56. What are Object-Oriented Programming Languages ? Give few examples.
57. What are multi-purpose programming languages ? Name three such languages.
58. What do you understand by Fifth Generation Languages (5GLs) ?
59. What are Report Generators ?
60. What are the differences between 3GLs and 4GLs ?
61. Name a procedure-oriented programming language in each of the three classifications, namely, scientific, business, and specialised.
62. What are query languages ? Give few examples.
63. What are Natural Languages ?
64. What do you understand by Character Codes ?
65. What is a Number System ? State their utility.
66. Why Binary Number System is followed in computer systems ?
67. Differentiate between Octal and Hexa-decimal Number System ?
68. What are BCD Codes ?
69. Differentiate between ASCII and EBCDIC Character Codes.
70. What is the utility of Hexa-decimal Number System ?

Evolution of Programming Languages and Program Development

9.1 INTRODUCTION

A language is a vehicle for communication. In order to communicate with each other, humans need languages like English, Hindi, etc. In the same manner, for communicating with the computer, we use computer language called programming language. A programming language consists of all the symbols, characters and usage rules that permit people to communicate with computers. Learning to program requires learning all these symbols and rules.

There are many programming languages available and each one has its symbols, character set and syntax but each language has an instruction set that permits those familiar operations to be performed.

We know that the computer can neither think nor can make any decision on its own. It needs instructions to understand what to do. A program is a set of logically related instructions that are arranged in a sequence that guides the computer to solve a problem.

The process of writing a program is called programming. If a system is not correctly programmed; it delivers incorrect results.

9.2 HISTORY OF PROGRAMMING LANGUAGES

The first programming languages predate the modern computer. From the first, the languages were codes. Herman Hollerith realized that he could encode information on punch cards when he observed that railroad train conductors would encode the appearance of the ticket holders on the train tickets using the position of punched holes on the tickets. Hollerith then proceeded to encode the 1890 census data on punch cards which he made the same size as the boxes for holding US currency.

The first computer codes were specialized for the applications. In the first decades of the twentieth century, numerical calculations were based on decimal numbers. Eventually it was realized that logic could be represented with numbers, as well as with words. For example, Alonzo Church was able to express the lambda calculus in a formulaic way. The Turing machine was an abstraction of the operation of a tape-marking machine, for example, in use at the telephone companies. However, unlike the lambda calculus, Turing's code does not serve well as a basis for higher-level languages - its principal use is in rigorous analyses of algorithmic complexity.

Like many "firsts" in history, the first modern programming language is hard to identify. From the start, the restrictions of the hardware defined the language. Punch cards allowed 80 columns, but some of the columns had to be used for a sorting number on each card. Fortran included some keywords which were the same as English words, such as "IF", "GOTO" (go to) and "CONTINUE". The use of a magnetic drum for memory meant that computer programs also had to be interleaved with the rotations of the drum. Thus the programs were more hardware dependent than today.

To some people the answer depends on how much power and human-readability is required before the status of "programming language" is granted. Jacquard looms and Charles Babbage's Difference Engine both had simple, extremely limited languages for describing the actions that these machines should perform. One can even regard the punch holes on a player piano scroll as a limited domain-specific programming language, albeit not designed for human consumption.

9.2.1 1940s

In the 1940s the first recognizably modern, electrically powered computers were created. The limited speed and memory capacity forced programmers to write hand tuned assembly language programs. It was soon discovered that programming in assembly language required a great deal of intellectual effort and was error-prone.

In 1945, Konrad Zuse published details of his programming language Plankalkül. However, it was not implemented in his time and his original contributions were isolated from other developments because Germany was isolated during the war.

Some important languages that were developed in this time period include:

1943 - Plankalkül (Konrad Zuse)

1943 - ENIAC coding system

1949 - C-10

9.2.2 1950s and 1960s

In the 1950s the first three modern programming languages whose descendants are still in widespread use today were designed:

FORTRAN, the "FORmula TRANslator", invented by John W. Backus et al.;

LISP, the "LISt Processor", invented by John McCarthy et al.;

COBOL, the COmmon Business Oriented Language, created by the Short Range Committee, heavily influenced by Grace Hopper.

Another milestone in the late 1950s was the publication, by a committee of American and European computer scientists, of "a new language for algorithms"; the Algol 60 Report (the "ALGOrithmic Language"). This report consolidated many ideas circulating at the time and featured two key innovations:

The use of Backus-Naur Form (BNF) for describing the language's syntax. Nearly all subsequent programming languages have used a variant of BNF to describe the context-free portion of their syntax.

The introduction of lexical scoping for names in arbitrarily nested scopes.

Algol 60 was particularly influential in the design of later languages, some of which soon became more popular. The Burroughs B5000 was designed to be programmed in an extended subset of Algol.

Some important languages that were developed in this time period include:

1951 - Regional Assembly Language
1952 - Autocode
1954 - FORTRAN
1958 - LISP
1958 - ALGOL
1959 - COBOL
1962 - APL
1962 - Simula
1964 - BASIC
1964 - PL/I

9.2.3 1967-1978

The period from the late 1960s to the late 1970s brought a major flowering of programming languages. Most of the major language paradigms now in use were invented in this period:

Simula, invented in the late 1960s by Nygaard and Dahl as a superset of Algol 60, was the first language designed to support object-oriented programming. Smalltalk (mid 1970s) provided a complete ground-up design of an object-oriented language.

C, an early systems programming language, was developed by Dennis Ritchie and Ken Thompson at Bell Labs between 1969 and 1973.

Prolog, designed in 1972 by Colmerauer, Roussel, and Kowalski, was the first logic programming language.

ML built a polymorphic type system (invented by Robin Milner in 1978) on top of Lisp, pioneering statically typed functional programming languages.

Each of these languages spawned an entire family of descendants, and most modern languages count at least one of them in their ancestry.

The 1960s and 1970s also saw considerable debate over the merits of "structured programming", which essentially meant programming without the use of GOTO. This debate was closely related to language design: some languages did not include GOTO, which forced structured programming on the programmer.

Some important languages that were developed in this time period include:

1970 - Pascal
1972 - C
1972 - Smalltalk
1972 - Prolog
1973 - ML
1978 - SQL

9.2.4 1980s

The 1980s were years of relative consolidation. C++ combined object-oriented and systems programming. The United States government standardized Ada, a systems programming language intended for use by defense contractors. In Japan and elsewhere, vast sums were spent investigating so-called "fifth generation" languages that incorporated logic programming constructs. The functional languages community moved to standardize ML and Lisp. Rather than inventing new paradigms, all of these movements elaborated upon the ideas invented in the previous decade.

However, one important new trend in language design was an increased focus on programming for large-scale systems through the use of modules, or large-scale organizational units of code. Modula, Ada, and ML all developed notable module systems in the 1980s. Module systems were often wedded to generic programming constructs.

Although major new paradigms for programming languages did not appear, many researchers expanded on the ideas of prior languages and adapted them to new contexts. For example, the languages of the Argus and Emerald systems adapted object-oriented programming to distributed systems.

The 1980s also brought advances in programming language implementation. The RISC movement in computer architecture postulated that hardware should be designed for compilers rather than for human assembly programmers. Aided by processor speed improvements that enabled increasingly aggressive compilation techniques, the RISC movement sparked greater interest in compilation technology for high-level languages.

Language technology continued along these lines well into the 1990s. However, the adoption of languages has always been driven by the adoption of new computer systems, and in the mid-1990s one of the most important new systems in computer history suddenly exploded in popularity.

Some important languages that were developed in this time period include:

1983 - Ada

1983 - C++

1985 - Eiffel

1987 - Perl

1989 - FL (Backus)

9.2.5 1990-2000

The rapid growth of the Internet in the mid-1990s was the next major historic event in programming languages. By opening up a radically new platform for computer systems, the Internet created an opportunity for new languages to be adopted. In particular, the Java programming language rose to popularity because of its early integration with the Netscape Navigator web browser, and various scripting languages achieved widespread use in developing customized applications for web servers. Neither of these developments represented much fundamental novelty in language design; for example, the design of Java was a more conservative version of ideas explored many years earlier in the Smalltalk community, but the widespread adoption of languages that supported features like garbage collection and strong static typing was a major change in programming practice.

Some important languages that were developed in this time period include:

1990 - Haskell

1990 - Python

1991 - Java

1993 - Ruby

1994 - PHP

2000 - C#

9.2.6 Current Trends

Programming language evolution continues, in both industry and research. Some current directions in programming languages include the following:

Mechanisms for adding security and reliability verification to the language: extended static checking, information flow control, static thread safety.

Alternative mechanisms for modularity: mixins, delegates, aspects.

Component-oriented software development.

Increased emphasis on distribution and mobility.

Integration with databases, including XML and relational databases.

Open Source as a developmental philosophy for languages, including recent languages such as Python, Ruby, and Squeak.

Support for Unicode so that source code (program text) is not restricted to those characters contained in the ASCII character set; allowing, for example, use of non-Latin-based scripts or extended punctuation.

9.3 MACHINE LANGUAGE

This is a sequence of instructions written in the form of binary numbers consisting of 1s and 0s to which the computer responds directly. A machine language would have two parts.

The first part is the command or an operation that tells the computer what functions are to be performed. The second part of the instruction is the operand that tells the computer where to find or store the data on which the desired operation is to be performed. The machine language is the only one that computer can understand directly. In the earlier computers programmers had to translate instructions directly into machine language from the computers understood. This task was very difficult and very few programmers could do this job. So, this language was very difficult to understand. But the main advantage of this language is that it is faster in execution as the computer directly starts executing it.

9.4 ASSEMBLY LANGUAGE

To ease the burden of the programmer, mnemonic operation codes and symbolic addresses were developed during the early 1950s. The mnemonic refers to a memory aid. One of the first steps for improving the program preparation process was to substitute letter, symbols and mnemonics for the mnemonic machine-language operation codes. Today every computer has a mnemonic code, though the actual symbols vary among makes and models.

Machine language is still used by the computer as it process data but assembly language software first translates the specified operation code symbol into its machine language equivalent. Symbolic addressing is the practice of expressing an address not in terms of its absolute numeric location but in terms of symbols that are convenient for the programmers. Programmers no longer assign actual address numbers to symbolic data items. Now, they merely specify where they want the first location in the program to be and an assembly language program takes it from there, allocating locations for instructions and data.

A program written by a programmer in an assembly language is called a Source Program. After this source program has been converted into machine code by an assembler, it is referred to as an Object Program. The main advantage of assembly language is that the programs written in it are easy to understand as compared to the programs of machine language. And a big drawback is that they are machine-oriented, depending upon the model of processor being used.

Also, the programs written assembly language are slower to execute as compared to those in the machine language. An assembly language program is not as fast as the machine language. It has to be translated first into machine (binary) language code. A machine cannot execute an assembly language program directly as it is not in a binary form. An assembler is needed in order to translate an assembly language program into the object code executable by the machine.

9.5 HIGH LEVEL LANGUAGE (HLL)

The development of mnemonic technique and macro-instruction led, to the development of high level languages that are often oriented towards a particular class of problem. Unlike assembly programs, HLL programs may be used with different makes of computers with the little modifications. Thus, re-programming expense may be greatly reduced when new equipment is acquired.

The main advantages of HLL are as follows:

Readability Programs written in these languages are more easily readable than those in assembly language and machine language.

Portability Programs could be run on different machines with little or no changes.

Easy debugging Errors are easy to find and remove.

Easy software development Software could easily be developed using the HLL.

The time and cost of creating machine and assembly languages was quite high. And this was the prime motivation for the development of high level languages.

9.6 GENERATION OF PROGRAMMING LANGUAGES

Programming language is a systematic notation by which we describe computational process. Computational process means steps for solving a problem. Programming language consists of symbols, characters and certain rules. There are various programming languages each with a specific purpose. Every language has its own instruction set that permits the operation to be performed.

If we want to make our computer to do something for us, we have to tell the computer what to do in a language that a computer understands called a machine language (language of 0 and 1). Communication with the computer is possible only if we develop a third language that can be understood by both us and the computer. Such a language is called a Programming Language.

Programming languages can be classified broadly in the following four categories :

Low Level Language

High Level Language

Very High Level Language

Natural Language

The programming languages are said to be low or high or very high or natural, depending on how far from the internal architecture of the machine the user is operating at. If we are operating in close proximity of the internal architecture by means of a machine-language or assembly language, then it is called a low-level language. Thus, low-level languages include machine-language and assembly language.

The languages used depending on the relative convenience of the users (like English or more natural way) is referred to as high-level, very high-level or natural language. Movement from machine language towards natural language puts away a user far away from internal details of the computer, thereby increasing the level of the language.

Another categorisation on the basis of the introduction of the programming languages is as follows :

First Generation Language	**:**	**Machine Language**
Second Generation Language	**:**	**Assembly Language**
Third Generation Language	**:**	**High Level Languages**
Fourth Generation Language	**:**	**4 GLs (4th Generation Languages) or Very High Level Language**
Fifth Generation Language	**:**	**Natural Language**

9.6.1 First-Generation Language: Machine Language

Inside a computer, data and program instructions are represented by a series of on-off signals that carry out a system of binary coding. Numbers, letters and other characters are represented by sequences of binary 1 and 0. This method of coding information is called Binary Notation.

The binary notation system for each individual computer is known as its Machine Language. It is the language understood by a computer because it is formed of binary numbers (0 and 1). 0's and 1's are actually the absence and presence of electric pulses. Instruction in machine language is a sequence of 0's and 1's. A computer's machine language establishes the proper electronic states, either on or off, for the recording and processing of instructions and data items.

In a machine language, each number, letter, or other character is represented by a specific combination of 1 or 0 codes. Each position within a coding system is known as a BIT (for Binary digIT). A series of bits, usually 8-bits called Byte, is used to represent a letter, number, or special character.

Instruction consists of two parts :

1. Operation Code (Op-Code)
2. Address or addresses of one or more memory location containing an operand or operands.

Op-Code Operand Addresses

Op-Code	Operand Addresses

Zero Address Instruction

If there is no operand address field in the instruction specified, then it is called a Zero-address instruction. The following is the format of such an instruction:

Op-Code

Example: A stack-organised computer does not use an address field for instruction like ADD, etc.

```
PUSH  X
PUSH  Y
ADD
```

Single Address Instruction

If there is only one address operand of a memory location/register in an instruction, then it is called single address instruction. Its format is :

Op-Code	Address

Example: Instruction requiring an implied accumulator register (AC). For example, ADD instruction in the example given below

LOAD X

ADD Y

Two Address Instruction

If there are addresses of 2 memory locations after the OP code, it is called two address instruction. These instructions are quite common in commercial computers. Its format is :

Op-Code	Address-1	Address-2

Example : The ADD & MOV instructions in the following example are 2-address instruction

MOV R_1, Y

ADD R_1, X

Three Address Instruction

If the instruction has addresses of 3 processor registers/ memory-locations following the OP code, it is called 3 address instruction. Its format is:

Op-Code	Address-1	Address-2	Address-3

The advantage of 3-address instruction format is that the same results in short programs while evaluating arithmetic expressions.

Example : The following example illustrates use of such 3-address instructions :

ADD R_1, X, Y

ADD R_2, U, V

ADD Z, R_1, R_2

Advantages of Writing Machine Language Program

1. Computer understands the machine language.
2. Time taken to execute program is less.

Disadvantages

1. Programmer has to remember the following :
   (a) Binary equivalent of the OP codes
   (b) Binary equivalent of the addresses of the memory locations being used.
2. Machine language are machine dependent and thus the programs written for one machine are of no use for another machine which differs from the former in its internal architecture.
3. It is very difficult to debug machine language programs.
4. Time taken for developing programs in machine language is very consuming.
5. Size of machine language programs is very lengthy.
6. Programs written in machine language are quite sensitive to a minor change i.e. even to a bit change.

9.6.2 Second Generation Language: Assembly Language

To overcome the problems caused by machine language, a major step was the development of 'Symbolic Languages', which permit the use of mnemonic operation codes and symbolic addresses. 'Assembly Language' was developed in the early 1950s and thus it was considered as the second generation language.

Programs used **mnemonic operation codes or symbolic address codes** just similar to that of operation code and operand in machine language respectively. **Mnemonic** refers to memory aid which are extracted from various operators e.g. mnemonic code 'A' may be represented for ADD.

The program which converts assembly language instructions into machine codes are known as Assembler. Assembler converts source program into object-code, where a source program refers to the program written in assembly language and object-code refers to the program converted by the assembler into machine language.

Advantages

(i) Assembly Language is much simpler in understanding, learning and developing in comparison to machine language.
(ii) Mnemonics are far easier to use than op-codes.
(iii) Time taken for developing assembly language programs is comparatively much less than its corresponding machine-language program.
(iv) Symbolic names were assigned to actual storage elements in the operand part.
(v) Chances of committing mistakes while writing assembly language programs are quite less.
(vi) Relieves from remembering all binary op-codes and addresses of memory locations.
(vii) Saves time and the machine may be utilized efficiently with less error in program preparation.

Disadvantages

(i) Assembly language is again 'machine-oriented' language and thus differs from machine to machine which makes it peculiar to architecture.
(ii) Execution of programs takes more time as it has to be converted into machine language.
(iii) Assembly language is still at the machine level and all the rules concerning instructions and input formats have to be scrupulously observed.

9.6.3 Third Generation Languages (3GLs):High-Level Languages (HLLs)

With the languages introduced by the third generation of computer programming, words and commands (instead of just symbols and numbers) were being used. These languages therefore, had syntax that was much easier to understand.

Languages in which instructions are given in English-like text rather than in binary digits that computer understands are known as high-level languages. Instructions used are termed as macro instructions which mean that a single instruction may produce several lines of machine language codes. Mnemonic technique further enhances the power of high level languages.

These languages are also referred to as Procedural Languages because these languages require every step of the task to submit to the computer in the form of a procedure.

High level languages may further be classified into following classes according their areas of application:

Scientific Programming Languages
Business Programming Languages
General or Multipurpose Languages
Specialized Programming Languages
Interactive Programming Languages
Object-Oriented Languages

9.6.3.1 Scientific Programming Languages

High-level programming languages used for scientific applications are known as scientific programming languages.

Examples

(i) FORTRAN (FORmula TRANslation)
(ii) ALGOL (ALOGOrithmic Language)
(iii) IAL (International Algebraic Language) [Later named as ALGOL]
(iv) PL/I (Programming Language I)
(v) COGO (COordinate GeOmetry Language)
(vi) APL (A Programming Language)
(vii) Pascal (Named after a great scientist Blaise Pascal) etc.

9.6.3.2 Business Programming Languages

High-level languages used for business applications are known as Business Programming Languages.

Examples:

(i) COBOL (COmmon Business Oriented Language)
(ii) PL/I (Programming Language I) etc.

9.6.3.3 General or Multipurpose Languages

General or multipurpose languages are equally effective for business, scientific, graphical and other applications. IBM was very much in the forefront of progress at this time and saw the opportunity in providing a computer system for a wide range of users, and following this IBM 360 emerged. To accommodate the new hardware PL/I was the most popular general purpose language. Later on many such languages came into existence.

Examples :

(i) PL/I (Programming Language I)
(ii) Pascal
(iii) BASIC (Beginner's All-purpose Symbolic Instruction Code)
(iv) C
(v) JOVIAL (Jules' own version if International Language)
(vi) Ada etc.

9.6.3.4 Specialized Programming Languages

High-level languages used for specialized applications are known as Specialized Programming Languages.

Examples:

(i) LISP (LISt Processing)
(ii) PROLOG (PROgramming in LOGic)
(iii) Ada (Named after a first lady programmer Augusta Ada)
(iv) LOGO (for teaching geometry, mathematics and programming to children)
(v) RPG (Report Program Generator)
(vi) Modula-2

(vii) APT (Automatic Programming Tool)
(viii) NELIAC (Navy Electronics Laboratory International Algol Compilers)
(ix) CORAL (For Real-time Applications)
(x) FORTH (Originally developed to be used by astronomers & later used for process control applications)
(xi) SIMULA/ SIMULA 67 (Simulation Language)
(xii) GPSS (General Purpose Simulation System) Language
(xiii) SNOBOL (StriNg-Oriented symBOlic Language)
(xiv) SIMSCRIPT (Simulation Script) Language etc.

9.6.3.5 Interactive Programming Languages

High-level programming languages used for real-time and time-sharing applications are known as Interactive Programming Languages.

Example:

(i) BASIC (Beginner's All-purpose Symbolic Instruction Code)
(ii) APL (A Programming Language)
(iii) Interactive FORTRAN
(iv) QUICKTRAN (Subset of FORTRAN and designed for use with multi-access systems) etc.

9.6.3.6 Object-Oriented Languages

It is another category of languages which are object-oriented and these languages must be capable of supporting:

Classes and Objects
Encapsulation of objects
Polymorphism
Inheritance between classes

Examples :

(i) C++
(ii) Smalltalk
(iii) Eiffel
(iv) Simula
(v) Object Pascal
(vi) Object C
(vii) CLOS, etc.

9.6.4 Fourth Generation Languages (4GLs): Very High Level Languages (VHLLs)

The syntax used in 4GL is very close to human language, an improvement from the previous generation of languages. 4GL languages are typically used to access databases and include SQL and ColdFusion, among others.

These languages are also referred to as Non-procedural Languages because these are designed for the end users that matches with application procedure rather than the algorithmic procedure to achieve the desired results. The aim of the 4th generation is to make languages much more problem oriented. The 4GLs are designed to enable users who are not trained programmers to develop applications. Often it is based on a non-procedural language with relational database support.

Moreover, 4GLs are languages that were developed as a result of the dissatisfaction of business users with large conventional languages like COBOL. These users were often not professional programmers who wished to obtain quick results from data stored in a computer.

The term 4GL encompasses:

(a) Presentation Language e.g. Report Generator, Query Language.
(b) Special Languages e.g. language expressions/phrases used in Databases & Spreadsheets.
(c) Application Generator that define, input, update and report data to build applications.
(d) Very high level languages are used to generate application code.

Looking analytically into the wide-perspective of 4GLs, these can be classified mainly into three categories:

Application Generators
Production-Oriented 4GLs
End-User-Oriented 4GLs

9.6.4.1 Application Generator (or Production-Oriented) 4GLs

These languages generate solutions for routine applications. Typical operations include data entry, ideally with full checking, and updating of files or databases.

These languages are designed primarily for computer professionals which help them in creating Information Systems. An application generator consists of a software system with numbers of program modules, pre-programmed for various functions. These languages are aimed at producing higher productivity in comparison to 3GLs for a specified application.

Examples:

(i) AG's Natural 2
(ii) FOCUS
(iii) NATURAL
(iv) PACBASE
(v) ADR's (Application Definition Records) Ideal
(vi) FUSION
(vii) MAPPER System
(viii) UFO
(ix) LIC II
(x) PACBASE, etc.

9.6.4.2 End-User-Oriented (or Query Languages) 4GLs

This type of 4GL is End-user Oriented Language which primarily specifies what the desired output should be instead of stressing the details of how the input or intermediate data should be manipulated. Users write down programs in 4GL to query a database and to create databases.

Examples:

(i) QBE (Query-by-example)
(ii) SQL (Structured Query Language)
(iii) DATATRIEVE
(iv) HAL
(v) EASYTRIEVE PLUS
(vi) INQUIRE

(vii) Honeywell PDQ
(viii) QMF
(ix) INTELLECT

9.6.4.3 Decision-Support and Financial Planning 4GLs

These languages were developed to help the user to make informed and thereafter appropriate decisions. These languages provide the user with facilities to build databases and then to perform statistical calculations, such as an analysis of trends on data.

Decision support systems are interactive software designed to help managers make decisions. Financial planning languages are particular kinds of decision support systems that are employed for mathematical, statistical and forecasting procedures among other uses. Decision-support languages are usually business-oriented and are typically used in the planning stage for analysing projected financial investments. These may include graphics facilities to enhance the display of material. These languages range from simple spreadsheets like Lotus 1-2-3, VisiCalc, etc. to languages with sophisticated statistical and operation research features for decision-making. Most of these languages include some important facilities viz. windowing, data scrolling, etc.

Examples:

(i) Metaphor
(ii) Info Center/1
(iii) FCS
(iv) IFPS
(v) EXPRESS
(vi) Command Center
(vii) SPSS-X
(viii) Application System, etc.

Advantages of 4GLs

(i) These may be easily used by non-programming end-users as well as professional programmers.
(ii) Improves productivity due to easier programming, updation, and maintenance.
(iii) Default alternatives are built-in and thus the end-user need not specify these alternatives thereby reducing the size of instruction(s)
(iv) Hardly requires its staff to undergo a very intensive training.
(v) Result-oriented approach is followed which emphasize on what is to be done rather than how the same is to be done.
(vi) 4GLs are typically database-oriented and thus relieves the user from knowing most of the programming skills.

Disadvantages

(i) Less efficient than 3GLs because 4GLs require larger processor speed to perform operations more efficiently.

9.6.5 Fifth Generation Languages (5GLs): Natural Languages

These are known as 5th generation language and are often called Natural Languages because of their resemblance to the natural spoken English Language. These languages are still in the development stages. Application of these languages will be quite beneficial in the area of Artificial Intelligence (AI) and Expert Systems (ES).

5GLs are currently being used for neural networks. A neural network is a form of artificial intelligence that attempts to imitate how the human mind works.

Natural languages have the following two characteristics:

(i) These are developed to enable the computer to become "intelligent" and "smart".

(ii) These are designed to help a computer establish communication with humans in a more natural way.

Natural languages refer to software that enables computer to accept, interpret, and execute instructions in the 'native' language of the end-user i.e. in English language. These languages are also referred to as Knowledge-based Language because natural languages are used to interact with a base of knowledge on some subject. The use of a natural language to access a Knowledge-base is called a Knowledge-based System.

Example: Two popular natural languages are PROLOG and LISP.

9.7 CLASSIFICATION OF PROGRAMMING LANGUAGES

Every computer programming language is not capable for all kinds of tasks or areas of applications. There are limitations, and actually, different languages are used for different tasks. Depending upon the purpose the language is used primarily for, these can be grouped in the following categories:

Software Languages
Procedural or Procedure-Oriented Languages
GUI-based Languages
Object-Oriented Languages
Web Languages

9.7.1 Software languages

These languages are used for creating executable programs. These can create anything from simple console programs that print some text to the screen to entire operating systems. These vary greatly in terms of power and complexity. Few of these languages are briefly discussed below:

C

It is a general-purpose structured programming language. C is characterized by the ability to write very concise source programs. The compiler of C is commonly available for the computers of all sizes. The compilers are usually compact and they generate object programs that are small and highly efficient as compared to the programs written in any other language. The programs written in the C language are high portable; the program written for one computer with very few changes can run on another computer. The reason for this is that C relegates most computer-dependent features in its library functions. Thus every version of C is accomplished by its own set to library functions.

Dennis Ritchie developed C in 1970s at Bell Telephone laboratories. It was the modified versions of two earlier languages, called BCPL and B, which were also developed at Bell Laboratories.

Originally designed to be a systems programming language but since then has proven itself to be able to be used for various software applications such as business programs, engineering programs, and even games. The UNIX operating system is written in C.

C++

Descendant of the C language. The difference between the two languages is that C++ is object-oriented. C++ was developed by Bjarne Stroustrup at Bell Labs and is a very popular language for graphical applications.

Visual Basic

A language developed by Microsoft based on the BASIC language. Visual Basic is used for creating Windows applications. The VBScript language (also developed by Microsoft) is based on Visual Basic.

Java

Java was developed by James Gosling the chief programmer of Sun Microsystems. Java is an object-oriented programming language that was developed after C++. Java was designed to be small, simple and portable across platforms. James Gosling started a project on controlling consumer electronics devices with a language C++. After some time he found that C++ was not suitable for the project. They faced many problems with the complicated aspects of C++, program bugs and memory leaks. So, Gosling decided to develop a new language that could overcome these problems.

It is a powerful and flexible language that can be used to create applets (a program that is executed from within another program) that run inside web pages as well as software applications. Things you can do with Java include interacting with the user, creating graphical programs, reading from files, and more. Java is often confused with Javascript, but they are two different languages.

As Gosling liked the object oriented features of C++, he decided to take C++ as the base for the new language. He developed a new language, Oak, which was later, called Java.

9.7.2 Procedure-oriented Programming Languages

A type of programming where a structured method of creating programs is used. With procedure-oriented programming, a problem is broken up into parts and each part is then broken up into further parts. All these parts are known as procedures. They are separate but work together when needed. A main program centrally controls them all.

Some of the procedure-oriented languages are discussed below.

LOGO

LOGO was designed by Seymour Papert who was a teacher in the USA. He designed this language so that the children could learn computers by drawing pictures. Most of its commands enable us to draw pictures. This is one of the reasons why LOGO is called a graphic language. The usage of LOGO is based on a friendly little animal called the TURTLE. It is the name given to the LOGO cursor. It looks like a small triangle. The TURTLE has a head which is the upper tip of the triangle. It can be turned around its center in all direction and it can also move forward and backward.

FORTRAN

It is the short form for FORmula TRANslation. As the name suggests it is used extensively in numeric data types such as an integer, real, float and complex. It was the only language developed by the IBM in 1957. Since then, it has been modified into many versions and the latest version FORTRAN 99, is currently available in the markets. The original work on FORTRAN was started in 1954. As the result of this effort, FORTRAN was introduced in 1957 for IBM 704 computer. FORTRAN is very useful for carrying out scientific and mathematical computations.

The main feature of FORTRAN is very useful for carrying out scientific and mathematical computations. The main feature of FORTRAN is that it can handle the complex numbers very easily. But the syntax of FORTRAN is very rigid. FORTRAN language is not suitable for a large amount of data. But, it is not suitable for a large amount of data. So, it is not used for business programming applications.

COBOL

COBOL stands for Common Business Oriented Language and is one of the popular languages used for business applications. The language has provisions that make computerization of business data processing procedures relatively easy. COBOL is suitable for processing large volumes of data and several reports can generate using COBOL based on the stored data. COBOL programs are characterized by their easy readability due to their verbose syntax and good data organizations ad file handling.

COBOL is an English like language with instruction coded using self-documenting English words rather than short abbreviation. Also, the rules of programming in COBOL conform to many of the rules for writing. Due to its similarity with English, COBOL programs are easy to read and write.

Thus people in business, who rely on computer output but have no computer expertise, can understand the programs written in COBOL. That is why COBOL is called a self-documenting language which is self-explanatory. COBOL was initially developed in 1959 by a group called the CODASYL (Conference On DAta SYstems Languages) Committee with the objectives of developing a standard business-oriented language for which all major manufacturers would provide compilers.

The American National Standards Institute (ANSI) then formed an NASO COBOL committee to develop more satisfactory standards for the language. This led to the availability of ANSI COBOL in 1969. This standard was, however, modified and finally, it approved a standard for COBOL in 1985 and is it is also referred to as COBOL 85.

BASIC

Basic stands for Beginners' All-Purpose Symbolic Instruction Code. It is the most popular computer programming language. He main characteristic of BASIC is to handle both mathematical and business problems; this language was developed specifically for the time-sharing environment but can so be used as a standard programming language in batch-processing environment. This language is easy to understand. But the main problem in BASIC is that most versions of this language do not support indexed files.

PROLOG

Prolog stands for PROgramming in LOGic. Prolog was developed in France in 1973. Prolog is very popular in Japan where it is adopted as the official programming language for the fifth generation computers.

As the name suggests, PROLOG lays stress on the usage of logic to solve problems. PROLOG is basically known as a theorem-providing system, using a formal logic technique known as predicate calculus to prove the truth of propositions from a set of axioms.

PROLOG is a conventional language. It waits for us to type in facts and rules that are related to the program that we want to solve. Then, if we ask the right type of questions, PROLOG would work out and display it on the screen.

So, we can say that the computer programming in PROLOG consists of the following steps:

- Declaring some facts about objects and their relationship.
- Defining some rules about objects and relationship.
- Assuming questions about objects and their relationship.

PASCAL

Pascal is a high Level Language that was developed by the Professor Nickalus Wirth at Eidgenossisehe Technisehe Houcheshule (ETH) in Zurich, Switzerland. The first report on the language appeared in the literature in 1971 and revised reports, describing the language with its improvements, appeared in 1972 and 1973. The first Pascal Reference Manual for Pascal programming was produced in 1974.

Pascal is a general-purpose language that can be used for a wide range of numeric and non numeric applications. The primary objectives behind the development of Pascal were as follows:

- The language should be efficient to implement and easy to execute on modern computers.
- The language should be used for teaching the important concept of computer programming.
- The language should be used for the development of well-structured and well organized programs.

The aforementioned features make Pascal a very good introductory programming language.

9.7.3 GUI Based Languages

Few of GUI-based languages are discussed below:

Visual Basic

What is Visual Basic? The "Visual" part refers to the method used to create the graphical user interface (GUI). Rather than writing numerous lines of code to describe the appearance and location of interface elements, you simply add pre-built objects into place on screen. If you've ever used a drawing program such as Paint, you already have most of the skills necessary to create an effective user interface.

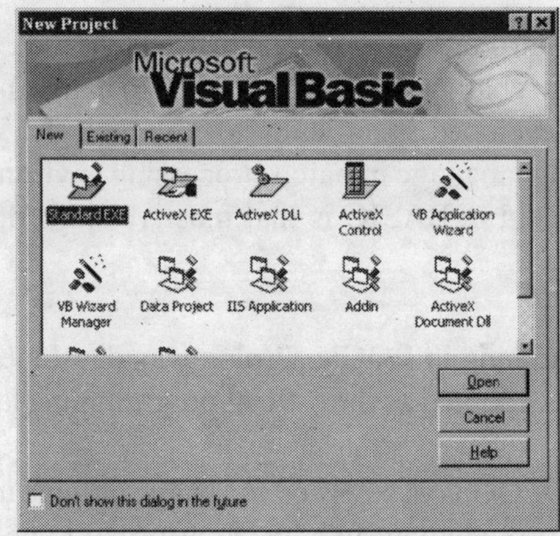

Figure 9.1: Visual Basic

The "Basic" part refers to the BASIC (Beginners All-Purpose Symbolic Instruction Code) language, a language used by more programmers than any other language in the history of computing. Visual Basic has evolved from the original BASIC language and now contains several hundred statements, functions, and keywords, many of which relate directly to the Windows GUI. Beginners can create useful applications by learning just a few of the keywords, yet the power of the language allows professionals to accomplish anything that can be accomplished using any other Windows programming language. The Visual Basic programming language is not unique to Visual Basic. The Visual Basic programming system, Applications Edition included in Microsoft Excel, Microsoft Access, and many other Windows applications uses the same language. The Visual Basic Scripting Edition (VBScript) is a widely used scripting language and a subset of the Visual Basic language. The investment you make in learning Visual Basic will carry over to these other areas.

Visual C++

Since Visual Basic and Visual C++ are similar in nature, you can assume that one is offshoot of Basic and the other is offshoot of C++. If you have graduated from Basic you will use Visual Basic and if you have been using C++, then Visual C++ is for you. However, the similarities end here, both of them are very useful development tools and differ a lot in usage.

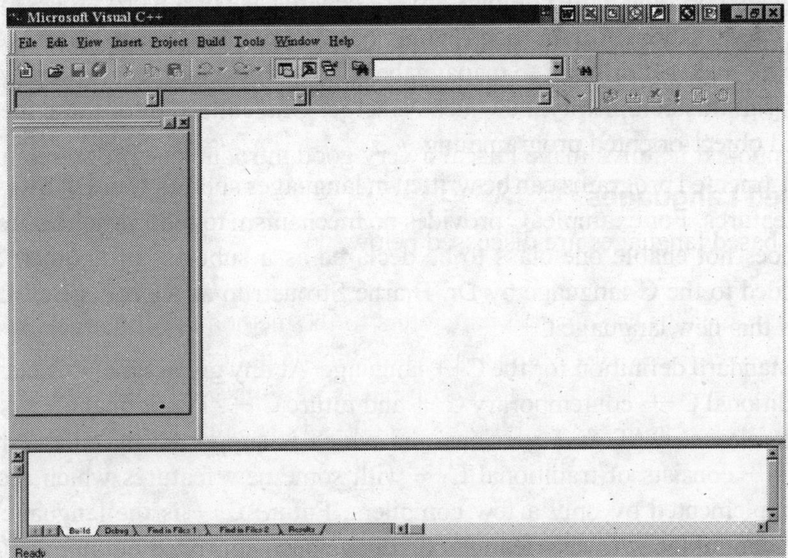

Figure 9.2: Visual C++

C#

It is known as C sharp. Since both C and C++ are DOS based programming languages and do not support Windows and Internet, Microsoft, the producers of C# have decided to produce something which can take care of this problem. So the net result is C#. It enables programmers in quickly building solutions for the Microsoft.net platform. If Visual Basic and Visual C++ were offshoot of Basic and C++, then you can imagine that C# is the offshoot of C.

VB.NET

It is the latest version of Visual Basic for the Internet. It is quite powerful development tool at par with other developing tools. With this you can create projects for Windows and Internet. Visual Basic .Net is a complete development environment; every tool you will need to create your Visual Basic projects is accessed from within Visual Basic.

The Visual Basic environment is called the IDE, short for Integrated Development Environment, and its design framework in which you build applications. To work with Visual Basic projects, you must use Visual Basic IDE.

9.7.4 Object Oriented Programming Languages

A type of programming where data types representing data structures are defined by the programmer as well as their properties and the things that can be done with them. With object-oriented programming, programmers can also create relationships between data structures and create new data types based on existing ones by having one data type inherit characteristics from another one.

In object-oriented programming, data types defined by the programmer are called classes (templates for a real world object to be used in a program). For example, a programmer can create a data type that represents a car - a car class. This class can contain the properties of a car (color, model, year, etc.) and functions that specify what the car does (drive, reverse, stop, etc.)

Some object-oriented languages are C++, Java, and PHP.

C++

C++ is an object-oriented programming language. As software systems develop into more powerful instruments, they also become more complex. Every new release of a word processor, a database, or a spreadsheet program is longer than the previous one and contains more features. This increasing size and complexity makes it difficult to manage the software development process. As programmers struggle to deal with this complexity, new ideas emerge. One collection of these ideas is based on a philosophy called object-oriented programming.

While object-oriented programs can be written in languages such as C or BASIC, these languages lack some vital features. For example, C provides no mechanism to hide variables from unauthorized access. C also does not enable one class to be declared as a subclass of another. These and other features were added to the C language by Dr. Bjarne Stroustrup at AT &T's Bell Labs in the early 1980s. He called this new language C++.

There is no standard definition for the C++ language. At any given time, it is classified into three states-called traditional C++, contemporary C++ and future C++. Traditional C++ is the language as it had existed in release in AT & T versions and which is supported by all the major compilers. Contemporary C++ consists of traditional C++ with some new features which are approved by e committee but implemented by only a few compilers. Future C++ is the language which is under discussion in the committee with new features that have been approved but not yet implemented.

Java

Java was developed by James Gosling the chief programmer of Sun Microsystems. Java is an object-oriented programming language that was developed after C++. Java was designed to be small, simple and portable across platforms. James Gosling started a project on controlling consumer electronics devices with a language C++. After some time he found that C++ was not suitable for the project. They faced many problems with the complicated aspects of C++, program bugs and memory leaks. So, Gosling decided to develop a new language that could overcome these problems.

As Gosling liked the object oriented features of C++, he decided to take C++ as the base for the new language. He developed a new language, Oak, which was later, called Java.

Java Vs C++

Java is most popular because it is used for Internet programming. Previously, only HTML was used for creating web pages. But it is difficult to depend only upon one language for developing the application as a typical diversity exists on Internet in terms of hardware and software. Servers on Internet have to store multiple copies of the same program that has been compiled for different hardware and software environments.

Java is the answer to these problems that exist on the Internet. In java, you can write a single program (called an applet) that is platform-independent. Platform-independent means that the program can be used at any platform with any operating system. The applet can be executed on Internet. Java is an object oriented-language just like C++ but it has some difference as compared to C++. IN Java, the following features are prominent:

- No pointers
- No multiple inheritance

- No goto
- No operator overloading

In C++ we can allocate and deallocate the memory by new and delete. The Java language has an embedded auto garbage collection mechanism. The garbage collector simplifies Java programming by automatically freeing memory area when it is not required.

So, Java is simple as compared to C++. Java code is divided into classes. Java is like any client\server model. Java is reliable. A reliable language is one that allows us to write programs that do not crash when least expected and would also de but-free.

Java is comparable in speed to other languages like C++. Java has sophisticated multitasking features that have been integrated into the language which make it very simple to use and at the same time very robust.

9.7.5 Web Languages

These languages are used for creating and editing pages on the web. These are capable of doing anything from putting plain text on a webpage, to accessing and retrieving data from a database. These vary greatly in terms of power and complexity. Few of these languages are briefly discussed below:

HTML (Hyper Text Markup Language)

HTML is the core language of the world wide web that is used to define the structure and layout of web pages by using various tags and attributes. Although a fundamental language of the web, HTML is static - content created with it does not change. HTML is used to specify the content a webpage will contain, not how the page functions.

XML (Extensible Markup Language)

XML is a language developed by the W3C (World Wide Web Consortium) which works like HTML, but unlike HTML, allows for custom tags that are defined by programmers. XML allows for the transmission of data between applications and organizations through the use of its custom tags.

Javascript

Javascript is a language developed by Netscape used to provide dynamic and interactive contents on web pages. With Javascript, it is possible to communicate with HTML, create animations, create calculators, validate forms, and more. Javascript should not be confused with Java languages.

VBScript

VBScript language a is Scripting Edition of Visual Basic language developed by Microsoft that works only in Microsoft's Internet Explorer web browser and web browsers based on the Internet Explorer engine such as FlashPeak's Slim Browser. VBScript can be used to print dates, make calculations, interact with the user, and more. VBScript is based on Visual Basic, but it is much simpler.

PHP

PHP is a recursive acronym of Hypertext Preprocessor. PHP is a powerful language used for many tasks such as data encryption, database access, and form validation. PHP was originally created in 1994 By Rasmus Lerdorf.

Java

Java is a powerful and flexible language created by Sun MicroSystems that can be used to create applets (a program that is executed from within another program) that run inside web pages as well as software applications. Things you can do with Java include interacting with the user, creating graphical programs, reading from files, and more. Java is often confused with Javascript, but they are two different languages.

9.8 PROBLEM SOLVING WITH COMPUTERS

Problem solving with computers involves following several steps:

1. Clearly define the problem
2. Analyse the problem and formulate a method to solve it
3. Describe the solution in the form of an algorithm
4. Draw a flowchart of the algorithm
5. Write the computer program
6. Compile and run the program (debugging)
7. Test the program (debugging)
8. Interpretation of results

All the above steps are discussed below.

1. Clearly define the problem: This can be trivial for simple problems but solutions to complex problems can be ineffective if the problem is not clearly defined. A great deal of time can be wasted if the problems are not clearly identified and defined at the beginning of a project.

2. Analyse the problem and formulate a method to solve it: Understanding the problem and choosing a correct method to solve it can be difficult especially for the more complex problem. A poorly understood problem or invalid method can lead to a bad solution. Again this becomes important for more complex problems.

3. Describe the solution in the form of an algorithm: At this stage the solution is stated for the first time in the form of a written algorithm. The algorithm gives a step-by-step description of the solution.

4. Draw a flowchart of the algorithm: This gives the logical flow of the solution in a diagrammatic form, and provides a plan from which the computer program can be best written. The logical flow of the algorithm can be seen by tracing through the flowchart and, if necessary, writing down the evolution of numerical values.

5. Write the computer program: Here you use your knowledge of the programming language to convert the logical flow of the solution in the flowchart/algorithm to a set of instructions (the source code) for the computer.

6. Compile and run the program: Program development always involves a cycle of writing-compiling-running the program until it is complete, free of errors, and works in the way the programmer expects it to work. Debugging (removal of errors from a program) usually involves:

correcting compile-time errors
correcting link-time errors
correcting run-time errors
correcting errors that give unexpected or wrong results

7. Test the program: After the initial stage of debugging the program can be tested more rigorously. Various input values can be given and the output checked. If possible, the program should be checked against a problem that has a known solution. Note that the absence of unexpected results does not mean that the program is correct; i.e. the output could still be wrong! For large programs it is usual to check that each section of program does what you intend it to do; this usually involves placing output statements throughout the program, the output statements are removed after each section has been successfully tested.

8. Interpretation of results: If a program simple outputs the mean value of a list of numbers then there is clearly no need for interpretation. However, it is sometimes necessary to make some analysis of the output before you can say you have arrived at the solution. Always think carefully when taking results from a computer - how was the result generated? What assumptions were made? How should the results be applied to solve the problem?

Verification and Validation

If the program has an important application - for example to calculate student grades or guide a rocket then the program MUST be tested properly to make sure it does what the programmer intends it to do and that it is actually a valid solution to the problem. The tests are commonly divided as follows:

Verification - verify that program does what you intended it to do; steps 7(8) above attempt to do this.

Validation - does the program actually solve the original problem i.e. is it valid? This goes back to steps 1 and 2 - if you get these steps wrong then your program is not a valid solution.

9.8.1 Concept of Programming

Computer Programming is the art of making a computer do what you want it to do. At the very simplest level it consists of issuing a sequence of commands to a computer to achieve an objective.

Essentially, a computer (guided by the instructions in programs) performs three basic functions:

1. It receives data (input)
2. It process data by various computations and actions (processing)
3. It emits data (output)

These functions are accomplished by giving the computer a program consisting of a sequence of statements.

The profession or "art" of programming deals with

analyzing a problem
developing a plan for solving the problem (algorithm)
designing and coding a program
testing and debugging
implementation and maintenance

A **programmer** is a person who uses skills in each of these areas to solve problems with computer programs.

There are two aspects to computers. One, you use the computer and the other is to make the computer work for you. This first one is very easy. You run the program which has been designed and created for use. But, it is the second which is very important. This covers the programming part. With programming you design the process where you ask the computer to work according to you. Here the privilege of making any error is not there. Because, you are going to be tested by the computer, which is very accurate.

Programming is one of the step in system development cycle and it starts once the detailed design is over and program specification have been obtained. Flow charts are the first tool developed for design. Flow charts are drawn up as a pictorial guide by programmers for planning the procedure for the solution of a program.

9.8.2 Computer Program

A **computer program** (also **software,** or just a **program**) is a sequence of instructions written to perform a specified task with a computer. A computer requires programs to function, typically executing the program's instructions in a central processor. The program has an executable form that the computer can use directly to execute the instructions. The same program in its human-readable source code form, from which executable programs are derived (e.g., compiled), enables a programmer to study and develop its algorithms.

Computer source code is often written by computer programmers. Source code is written in a programming language that usually follows one of two main paradigms: imperative or declarative programming. Source code may be converted into an executable file (sometimes called an executable program or a binary) by a compiler and later executed by a central processing unit. Alternatively, computer programs may be executed with the aid of an interpreter, or may be embedded directly into hardware.

Computer programs may be categorized along functional lines: system software and application software. Two or more computer programs may run simultaneously on one computer, a process known as multitasking.

Systematic notations for these steps are the computation steps referred to as programming languages. A person engaged in the activity of programming is referred to as programmer.

9.8.3 Characteristics of a Good Program

A good program has to have the following characteristics:

Accuracy	The program must do what it is supposed to do and meet the criteria laid down in its specification.
Reliability	The program must ALWAYS do what it is supposed to do and never crash.
Efficiency	The program must use the available store space and resources in such a way that the system's speed is not wasted.
Robustness	The program should cope with invalid data without stopping with no indication as to the cause and without creating errors.
Usability	The program must be easy to use and well documented.
Maintainability	The program must be easy to amend, having good structuring and documentation.
Readability	The code in the program must be well laid out and explained with comments. Since it is that you are one who is going to read the program always, there will be others too.
Portability	It should be seen that the program is easy to transfer to other machines as well.

9.8.4 Steps in Program Development

The following basic steps are involved in writing computer programs:

1. Problem identification
2. Task analysis and data analysis
3. Output identification
4. Designing the solution

5. Data validation
6. Implementation and debugging
7. Final documentation and maintenance

These steps are mostly performed in sequence mentioned, however, in some cases you can do otherwise too.

9.9 PROGRAMMING PARADIGMS

It is not that there are no rules for writing programs, there are a few of them. We must adhere to these rules to write good programs. Some of these are discussed below.

9.9.1 Unstructured Programming

This type of programming is straight forward programming. Here, everything is in a sequential manner. It does not involve any decision making. A general model of these linear programs is:

1. Read a data value.
2. Compute an intermediate result.
3. Use the intermediate result to compute the desired answer.
4. Print the answer.
5. Stop.

9.9.2 Structured Programming

Structured programs are the ones that are divided into functional modules and arranged in an hierarchical order instead of programs written in a sequence. Structured programming refers to the process in which we break the overall job down into separate piece of modules. These modules, in turn, are broken down into smaller pieces which can also be further subdivided. Modules must be chosen in such a way that we can specify how they have to interact. In effect, there is a contact between each pair of modules.

Advantages of Structured Programming

1. Decreases the complexity of the program by breaking it down into smaller logical units.
2. Allows several programmers to perform coding simultaneously.
3. Allows common functions to be written once and then used in all the programs needing it.
4. Decreases debugging time, because modules make it easier to isolate errors.
5. Amendments to single modules do not affect the rest of the program.
6. It saves time to use modular structures rather than using self made structure. If a job can be done well by using what is already available and known to be well tried and tested then trying out something new for sake of it, is a waste of effort.
7. Standard method; so, less time is required in writing programs.
8. It is easier to name modules in such a way that they are easy to find in the documentation and consistent.

Various characteristics of Structured Programs can be listed out as:

1. Two-way decision statements are based on IF...THEN, IF...THEN...ELSE and nested IF statements.
2. A rule of thumb is that the modules should not be more than one half page long. If they are longer than this, they should preferably be split into two or more sub-modules.

3. The programs are based on top-down modular design. In other words, the problem at hand is analyzed or broken down into major components, each of which is again broken down it necessary. Therefore, the process involves working from the most general down to the most specific. The design of the modules is reflected in hierarchy charts.
4. Loops and not custom designed with the use of the GO TO statement, but are based on the consistent use of WHILE...WEND and FOR...NEXT. In WHILE...WEND, the loop is based on the truth of a condition and in FOR...NEXT, on a counting process and the number of repetitions that can easily be predicted.
5. Each module has one entry point and one exit point. The GOTO statement is never used to jump from one module in the program to another.

9.9.3 Procedural Programming

As the name sounds it is based on certain procedures. A procedure call is used to invoke the procedure. After the execution of statements, flow of control returns to the position from where call was made. Procedures can be further divided into sub procedures. With the help of sub procedures, programs can be written more structured and error free. For example, if the procedure is correct, every time it is used it produces correct results.

9.9.4 Modular Programming

One of the key concepts in the application of programming discipline is the design of a program as a set of units referred to as blocks or modules. A program module is defined as the part of a program that perform a separate function, e.g., input, input validation, processing of one type of input. A program module may be quite large, so that it may be further divided into logical sub modules. The process of subdivision continues until all modules are of manageable size in terms of complexity of logic and numbers of instructions.

Advantages of Modular Programming

1. Program maintenance becomes easier because the affected modules can be quickly identified and changed.
2. If a programmer leaves the the project midway, it is easier for someone else to take over a set of self contained modules.
3. In a very large project, several programmers may be working on a single program. Using a modular approach, each programmer can be given a specific set of modules to work on. This enables the whole program to be finshed sooner.
4. Some modules will be standard procedures used again and again in different programs or parts of the same program.
5. More experienced programmers can be given a more complex module to write and the junior programmers can work on the simpler modules.
6. Since module is small, it is simpler to understand it as a unit of code. It is therefore easier to test and debug, especially if its purpose is clearly defined and documented.
7. A large project becomes easier to monitor and control.
8. Modules can be tested independently, thereby shortening the time taken to get the whole program working.

9.10 SYSTEM DESIGN TECHNIQUES

Following are the main designing techniques called Top Down and Bottom Up.

9.10.1 Top Down Design

Top down design approach is performed in a special way. The main program is written first. It is tested before sub programs are written. To do this, the actual sub programs are replaced with stubs. The stubs simply test to see if the data is passed correctly. After the main program is written and checked each module is written and tested in turn. This should first be done without the main program in order to isolate a stub if an error occurs.

If the module and the main program run properly then the next module is written and checked and so on. To describe the program at its highest level, we use something called the universal program and then by a process of stepwise refinement work out the details of each part of the program.

Advantages of Top Design

1. At each stage, the sub programs are tested by themselves and then the main program is tested. Whenever modules are added, they are tested with the main program so if any error occurs it will probably be in a module only and this will be easy to debut.
2. It is desirable for modules to be kept small in general. As far as possible a module should be less than 100 statement lines long.

Top down implementation

1. Start with a very simple and short statement of what the program does. This is the top level in the design.
2. Go to the next level of details for the whole program, try to describe the program as sequence, selection or repetition of main tasks. Each of these tasks should be complete in itself but will be described in greater detail at the next level of program development. These tasks are called modules. A module should have just one entry point and just one exit point.
3. This process is repeated step by step and at each step all the modules at that levels are refined or developed to the next level of details. This is called step-wise-refinement. The step-wise-refinement stops when there are sufficient details for the procedure to be written in a programming language.
4. At the intermediate steps in the refinement, pseudo code or flowcharts are used to represent the procedure.
5. At every state unnecessary details are left out.
6. It is important that at each state the individual modules are checked to make sure that they perform the correct actions on the appropriate data.

9.10.2 Bottom Up Design

A bottom up approach would be to write the most basic subroutines in the hierarchy first and then use them to make more sophisticated subroutines. The pure bottom approach is generally not recommended because it is difficult to anticipate which low level subroutines will be needed for any particular program. It can often be a useful first step to produce a library of basic functions and procedures before embarking on a major project. In the bottom up approach it is usually assumed that the basic routines created will be general enough to be used more than once.

Using the subroutines, to construct a program, save yourself repeating the same lines of code by reusing it. A routine that is used many times has a very difficult status to those higher in the hierarchy. It is more like a basic instruction in the programming language than a large scale program component.

9.11 COMPUTER PROGRAM LIFE CYCLE

No computer program is ever lasting. Each program overgrows itself. A program is actually the result of your own logic and thought process. If you think something today then it is not possible that you will think the same way a month onwards. If so then probably your mind has struck and is not developing. So once you read your own program, there is every likelihood that you will think of some improvements. The change in program can also occur owing to expansion or changes in the nature of the business, the economic environment, the need to keep up with the new technology or other factors, a program may become inadequate to meet the future needs.

9.11.1 Data Handling and Declaration

Data handling is basically the level of managing data. This can be divided into the following levels.

1. In the first step it is the operating system which handles the data. It manages the physical storage and retrieval of data on floppy disk, CD or other storage device.
2. It refers to the software that allows for the creation, storage, retrieval and manipulation of files interactively at a terminal or personal computer.
3. It is also the management of all data and information within an organization and includes data administration.
4. Lastly it is a function within an organization that manages data. It analyses, classifies and maintains all the data and data relationships. Data handling or administration coordinates the development of data models and data dictionaries which, combined with transaction volume, are the raw materials for database.

9.11.2 Types of Data

Let us see the type of data which can be used for running the program.

Constants

This is the data which is predetermined before a program is used. Values remain unchanged during the execution of a program. It has a fixed range in computer applications.

Variables

Here the data may change or be assigned different values as the program runs. There are limitations imposed by language on maximum number of characters used to form variable names.

9.11.3 ALGORITHM

An algorithm is a finite sequence of instructions, logic, an explicit, step-by-step procedure for solving a problem. An **algorithm** is an effective method expressed as a finite list of well-defined instructions for calculating a function. Algorithms are used for calculation, data processing, and many other fields. An algorithm may be expressed as a pseudo code that is shorthand notation of English sentences.

The computer scientist Niklaus Wirth stated that:

Programs = Algorithms + Data

The algorithm is part of the blueprint or plan for the computer program, an algorithm is:

"An effective procedure for solving a problem in a finite number of steps."

Definition:

"An algorithm is a finite set of instructions which, if followed, accomplish a particular task".

Definition of Algorithm (after Al Kho-war-iz-mi a 9th century Persian mathematician) - an **ordered sequence of unambiguous and well-defined instructions** that **performs some task** and **halts in finite time**

Let's examine the four parts of this definition more closely

1. an ordered sequence means that you can number the steps
2. unambiguous and well-defined instructions means that each instruction is clear, do-able, and can be done without difficulty
3. performs some task
4. halts in finite time (algorithms terminate!)

Algorithms can be executed by a computing agent which is not necessarily a computer.

In addition every algorithm must satisfy the following criteria:

Step 1: Input: There are zero or more quantities which are externally supplied.

Step 2: Output: At least one quantity is produced.

Step 3: Definiteness: Each instruction must be clear and unambiguous.

Step 4: Finiteness: If we trace out the instructions of an algorithm, then for all cases the algorithm will terminate after a finite number of steps.

Step 5: Effectiveness: Every instruction must be sufficiently basic that it can in principle be carried out by a person using only pencil and paper. It is not enough that each operation be definite, but it must also be feasible.

A problem can be solved by using a computer only if an algorithm can be written for it. In addition, the use of algorithm provides many other benefits:-

1. While writing an algorithm, you identify the step-by-step procedure, the major decision points, and the variables necessary to solve the problem. This helps you in the development of the corresponding program.
2. Identification of the procedure and the decision points reduces the problem into a series of smaller problems of more manageable size. Therefore, problems that would be difficult or impossible to solve as a whole can be approached as a series of small solvable sub problems.
3. With the use of an algorithm, decision making becomes a more rational process. This is because algorithms comprise of sub tasks, where each sub task is atomic in nature and is supported by facts.
4. With the use of an algorithm, the same specified steps are used for performing the tasks. This makes the process more consistent and reliable.

Let's follow an example to help get an understanding of the algorithm concept.

Algorithm 1.1: Add Two Numbers

Step 1: Start

Step 2: Enter the value of A and B.

Step 3: A=10, B=5.

Step 4: Perform operation C = A + B.

Step 5: Store the result in C.

Step 6: End

Let us take one more example, to find biggest number between two given numbers. Think the logic, and you'll feel it's very easy to write the steps of an algorithm.

> Algorithm 1.2: Find the Greater number among two numbers.
> Step 1: Start
> Step 2: Read two positive integer numbers 'A' and 'B'
> Step 3: If A is greater than B, then go to step 4 else goto step 5.
> Step 4: Print "A is greater than B" goto step 6.
> Step 5: Print "B is greater than A"
> Step 6: End.

Once these steps are performed on data specified in the problem, the desired result or output is obtained. Whenever an algorithm can be specified it makes sense to wonder about its behavior.

This was realized by Charles Babbage, the father of Computers in 1830. An algorithm is a finite set of instructions, which when followed, perform a particular task.

9.11.3.1 Characteristics of an Algorithm

Let us try to present the scenario of a man brushing his own teeth (natural denture) step-by-step and say it is an algorithm.

Step 1. Take the brush
Step 2. Apply the paste
Step 3. Start brushing
Step 4. Rinse
Step 5. Wash
Step 6. Stop

If one goes through all these steps without being aware of the statement of the problem, he/she could possibly feel that this is the algorithm for cleaning a toilet. This is because of several ambiguities while comprehending every step. The step 1 may imply toothbrush, paintbrush, toilet brush, etc. Such an ambiguity should not be an instruction (step) of an algorithmic. Thus, every step should be made unambiguous. An unambiguous step is called definite instruction. Even if the step 2 is rewritten as apply the toothpaste, to eliminate ambiguities yet the conflicts such as, where to apply the toothpaste and where the source of the toothpaste is, need to be resolved. Hence, the act of applying the toothpaste is not mentioned. Although unambiguous, such unrealizable steps can not be included as an instruction (step) of an algorithmic as they are not effective.

The definiteness and effectiveness of an instruction implies the successful termination with desire output of that instruction. However the above two may not be sufficient to guarantee the termination of the algorithm. Therefore, while designing an algorithm care should be taken to provide a proper termination for algorithm.

Therefore, an algorithm can be defined as a sequence of definite and effective instructions, which terminates with the production of correct output from the given input.

In other words, viewed little more formally, an algorithm is a step-by-step formalization of a mapping function to map input set onto an output set.

Thus, every algorithm should have the following five characteristic features.

Input
Output

Definiteness

Effectiveness

Termination

Algorithm Design and Analysis (ADA) is a branch of Computer Science that consists of designing and analyzing computer algorithms. The **"Design"** pertains to the description of algorithm at an abstract level by means of a pseudo language, and proof of correctness that is, the algorithm solves the given problem in all cases.

9.11.3.2 Algorithmic Notations

The pseudo code uses notations used in common languages like PASCAL and C language. For example, if-else structure, for loop structure, while loop structure, do-while loop structure. A conditional statement of an algorithm has the following form.

(1) If-Else Structure:

If (condition) then

Block 1// Instruction(s)

Else

Block 2// Instruction(s)

// End of Structure

Comments are given with the symbol // for better understanding of the instructions of an algorithm. It is good practice to give comments about the instructions of the algorithm. The above pseudo code executes Block 1 if the condition is true otherwise Block 2 is executed. A block is a set of instructions and it may contain one or more instructions. Sometimes, the If-Else structure is nested and appears as given below.

If (condition) then

Block 1 // Instruction(s)

Else If (condition) then

Block 2 //Instruction(s)

Else

Block 3 //Instruction(s)

// End of Structure

(2) For loop Structure

We use for loop structure to repeat to certain Block (instructions) up to fixed number of times. There is a counter, which keeps track of the number of repetitions. The structure of **for** loop is given below.

For Counter = i to j

{Instruction 1, Instruction 2… Instruction n}

There are three things hidden in the for loop structure.

(a) Counter initialization

(b) Condition checking

(c) Increment of Counter

(3) While loop Structure

When we are not sure about the number of repetitions of a block then we use while loop structure as follows.

while (condition)

{Instruction 1, Instruction 2… Instruction n}

(4) Do-while loop Structure

When we are not sure about the number of repetitions of a block (instructions) and want that the block could execute at least once then we use do-while loop structure as follows.

Do

{Instruction 1, Instruction 2… Instruction n} while (condition)

(5) Conditions and Concatenation of Conditions

We use conditions to make the number of execution of a block finite or infinite, some times as there is need. We use some logical operators like AND, OR, NOT, etc to concatenate the conditions. Conditions are expressions, which give the value TRUE (1) or FALSE (0). When we use the logical operators then we evaluate NOT, AND, and OR in sequence. If conditions are concatenated by AND operator then result is TRUE if and only all conditions are TRUE otherwise FALSE and in case of OR operator, result is TRUE if at least one of the conditions is TRUE and FALSE otherwise.

$C=C_1$ AND C_2 AND…AND C_n =TRUE if and only if $C_1=C_2=\ldots=C_n$=TRUE, otherwise FALSE and $C=C_1$ OR C_2 OR…OR C_n =TRUE if at least one the $C_1, C_2,\ldots,C_n$ is TRUE, otherwise FALSE. The NOT operator reverses the value of the condition. If C_1 is TRUE then NOT C_1 is FALSE.

For example, consider the following conditions and show their values after concatenation.

Condition	Value
C_1	1
C_2	1
C_3	0

(a) $C_4 = C_1$ AND C_2

(b) $C_5 = C_2$ AND C_3

(c) $C_6 = C_1$ AND NOT C_3

Solution

(a) C_4 = 1 AND 1 = 1

(b) C_5 = 1 AND 0 = 0

(c) C_6 = 1 AND NOT 0 = 1 AND 1 = 1

The fundamental knowledge necessary to solve problems using a computer is the notation of an algorithm. For example, suppose we have an array **DATA** of numerical values with size **N** in memory. We want to find the location **K** and the value **MAX** of the largest element of **DATA.** An algorithm for this problem can be constructed as illustrated in Figure 9.3.

The execution of an algorithm begins at **Step1** and continues from there in sequential order unless the result of a condition tested or an unconditional transfer specifies otherwise. In the algorithm given in Figure .3, **Step 1** is executed first if the array **DATA** is empty, the algorithm terminates; otherwise **Step 2** is performed. In this step, **MAX** is initialized to the value of **DATA [I].** Firstly **I** is **1** and variable **I** is incremented by **1. Step 3** leads to termination of this algorithm if we have already tested the last element of the array **DATA;** otherwise **Step 4** is performed. In this step, the value of **MAX** is compared with the value of next element of the array **DATA.** If **MAX** is less than the next element, **MAX** is assigned this new value (by calling Step 2). If the test fails, no reassignment takes place. The completion of **Step 4** is followed by **Step 5** where control returns to the **Step2** when we assign new value to **MAX** and increment the subscript by 1.

It is very much advisable to the readers that before writing a program design an algorithm for a problem. Do not try hit and trial method. Sometimes it may be costly and may result into damaging the system. Keep in mind that C language is middle-level language. So, any bad instruction can damage the system. Designing an algorithm is simple for any problem when we have some solution for that. Derive the solution step by step considering the flow of processing. If some steps are missing or misplaced then result will be undesirable.

```
Step 1: [Initialization]
        I = 1
        K = 1
Step 2: [Increment counter]
        MAX = DATA [I]
        I = I + 1
Step 3: [Test counter]
        If I > N then
        Write K, MAX and Exit
Step 4: [Compare and update]
        If MAX < DATA [I] then
        K = I
Step 5: Go to Step 2:
```

Figure 9.3: Search Algorithm

9.11.3.3 Types of Algorithm

An algorithm is defined as "Step by step approach to solve any problem". There are mainly three types of algorithm exist, which are given as below:

1. Sequential Algorithm
2. Conditional Algorithm
3. Iterative Algorithm

1. Sequential Algorithm: an algorithm whose steps are executed sequentially i.e. execution of algorithm takes place in the same order in which an algorithm is developed. For example consider following algorithm to add two numbers

Read A

Read B

C=A+B

Print "Sum is"

Print C

2. Conditional Algorithm: An algorithm whose execution depends upon certain conditions are called conditional algorithms. For example consider the following algorithm to check whether a given number is positive or negative.

Read A

If A>0 then

Print "A is positive"

Else

Print "A is negative"

End IF

3. Iterative Algorithm: an algorithm that repeat a statement of group of statement for number of times such an algorithm is called iterative algorithm. For example consider the following algorithm that will find the sum of first 100 Natural numbers:

Set S=0

For I=1 to 100

S=S+I

I=I+1

End For

Print "Sum of First 100 Natural numbers is"

Print S

An algorithm can be described in several ways. One way is to give it a graphical form of notation which is known as Flow Chart. This form places each processing step in a "box" and uses arrows to indicate the next step. Different shaped boxes stand for different kinds of operations.

9.11.3.4 Different ways of stating algorithms

There are several ways of stating an algorithm. The following are four different ways of stating algorithms:

1. Step-Form
2. Flowchart
3. Nassi-Schneiderman
4. IPO Chart
5. Pseudocode
6. Hierarchy Chart

9.11.4 Step-Form Algorithms

This form of algorithm is the simplest and consists of a sequence of numbered steps or points. It is the easiest to learn at first since it is rather like a "to-do" list however once you have mastered other ways of stating algorithms you are unlikely to continue using this form.

Example: First of all the problem to solve is:

Design a program which counts all the vowels on a given page of text.

Remember in the second lesson we came up with a strategy for designing algorithms so use this as a starting point:

Step 1: Investigation step

1. Identify the processes
2. Identify the major decisions

3. Identify the loops
4. Identify the variables

Step 2: Preliminary algorithm step

1. Devise a "high level" algorithm
2. Step through the algorithm. Does this "walk-through" reveal any major problems? If it does then correct the problems.

Step 3: Refining the algorithm step

1. Incorporate any refinements indicated in step 2.
2. Group together processes where appropriate
3. Group together variables where appropriate
4. Test the algorithm again by stepping through it

9.11.5 FLOWCHART

A flowchart is a diagrammatic representation that illustrates the sequence of operations to be performed to get the solution of a problem. Flowcharts are generally drawn in the early stages of formulating computer solutions. Flowcharts facilitate communication between programmers and business people. These flowcharts play a vital role in the programming of a problem and are quite helpful in understanding the logic of complicated and lengthy problems. Once the flowchart is drawn, it becomes easy to write the program in any high level language. Often we see how flowcharts are helpful in explaining the program to others. Hence, it is correct to say that a flowchart is a must for the better documentation of a complex program. Flowcharting is a tool for analysing processes. It allows you to break any process down into individual events or activities and to display these in shorthand form showing the logical relationships between them. Constructing flowcharts promotes better understanding of processes, and better understanding of processes is a pre-requisite for improvement.

Flow charts are easy-to-understand diagrams showing how steps in a process fit together. This makes them useful tools for communicating how processes work, and for clearly documenting how a particular job is done. Furthermore, the act of mapping a process out in flow chart format helps you clarify your understanding of the process, and helps you think about where the process can be improved.

A flow chart can therefore be used to:

Define and analyze processes.

Build a step-by-step picture of the process for analysis, discussion, or communication.

Define, standardize or find areas for improvement in a process

Also, by conveying the information or processes in a step-by-step flow, you can then concentrate more intently on each individual step, without feeling overwhelmed by the bigger picture.

9.11.5.1 Flowchart Symbols and Their Usage

Now we define in detail the meaning and significance of each of these symbols. Oval is used for two purposes, to define the starting (START or BEGIN) point of flowchart and to define the ending point (END) of flowchart.

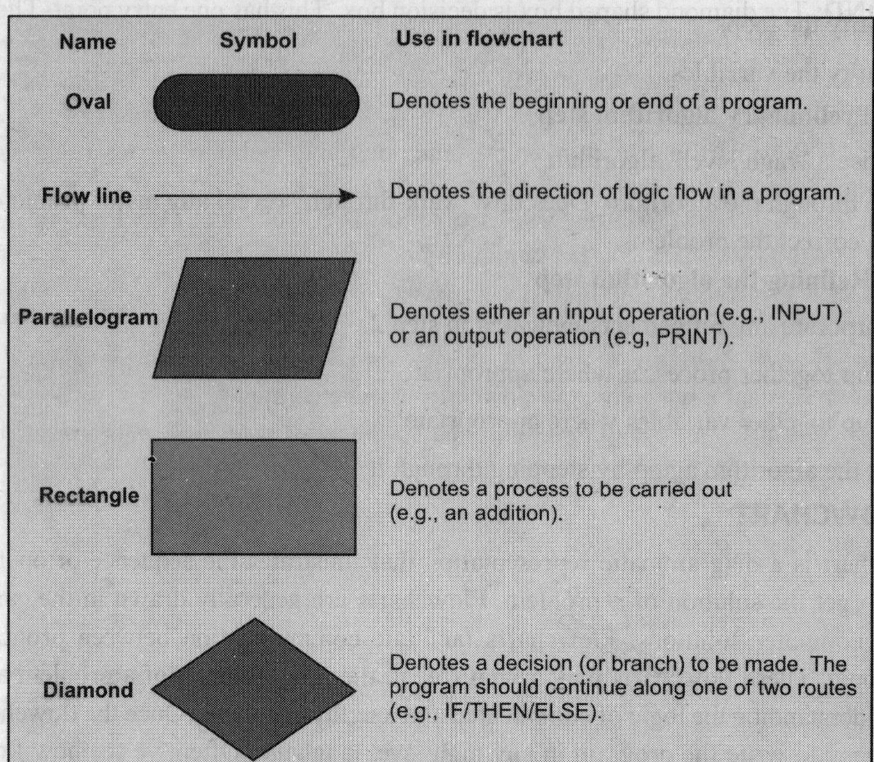

Figure 9.4: General Flowchart Symbols

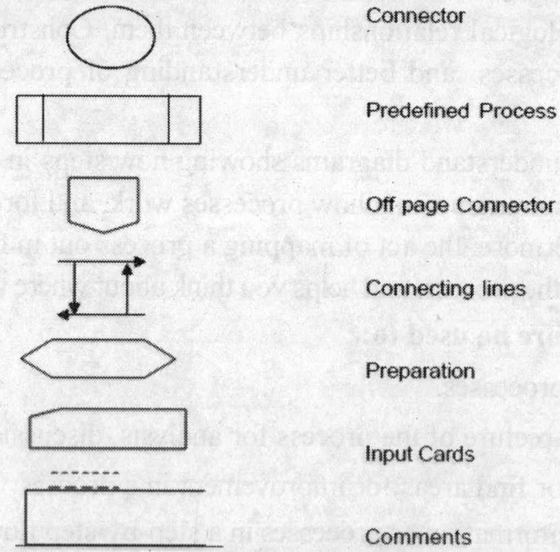

Figure 9.5: Special Flowchart Symbols

PARALLELOGRAM: Parallelogram is used for input-output. This is the input symbol to indicate the input from standard input or output to standard output device.

RECTANGLE: The rectangle is used to indicate the processing. Inside, this processing box statements of processing are specified.

DIAMOND: The diamond shaped box is decision box. This has one entry point. There will be at least two exit points depending upon the decision taken inside the symbol. When a condition is tested, if the condition is true, the path for "yes" is followed. If the condition is false, the path for "no" is followed.

CIRCLE: If flowchart is discontinued at some point and continued again at another place, the connector symbol is used. It is a circle with a number written inside it. If a flowchart is discontinued at some point, a circle is drawn pointing away from the chart. Another circle with same number inside it is placed where the flowchart is to be continued.

SMALL PENTAGON: Sometimes due to spaces limitations or due to some other reasons, it becomes necessary to terminate a flowchart temporarily and continue from the next page. In such situations this off page connector is used. A number is written inside it. Same number is placed in another pentagon on next page where the flowchart is to be continued.

Comment symbol: This symbol contains the comment. These comments are included for the documentation purpose to make the understanding of flowcharts easy.

PENTAGON (rectangle with five corners): The symbol having five corners is used for indicating the input-output. This symbol indicates the input from or output to punched cards.

HEXAGON (flat): This is the preparation box. This box contains the loop setting statement, i.e.

ARROWS These arrows are to indicate the direction of the flow of control. This means these statements indicate the next statement to be executed.

Figures 9.6 and 9.7 show the flowcharting symbols for special processing and input-output purpose. These symbols are rarely used in flowcharting.

Symbol	Meaning
	Internal Storage
	Documents
	Multi-document
	Manual Input
	Manual Operation
	Punched tape
	Or operation
	Sorting of data
	Magnetic Disk
	Collate
	Extract

Figure 9.6: Set of advanced flowchart symbols

Symbol	Meaning
	Merge two data
	Storage data/online storage
	Delay
	Sequential Access Storage/ Magnetic Disk
	Summing Junction
	Direct Access Storage
	Display

Figure 9.7: Set of advanced flowchart symbols

9.11.5.2 Conventions of flowcharts

1. Each symbol of flowchart denotes a particular type of operation.
2. A note is written inside each symbol to indicate the specific function to be performed.
3. Flowcharts are read from top to bottom and left to right.
4. Sequence of operations is performed until a terminate symbol designates the end of the run.
5. Crossed lines do not imply any logical relationship.
6. Where two incoming lines join one outgoing line, they should not join at the same point.
7. Annotation should be included within the symbol to process decision file and input, output giving an indication of the action decision file or document used.
8. Identification of the symbols on a flowchart is aided by numbering the most left top symbols sequentially from 1, so that each symbol can be referred uniquely. Connectors and terminators need to be numbered.
9. Flowcharts are not case-sensitive, so instructions inside the symbols can be written in any case.

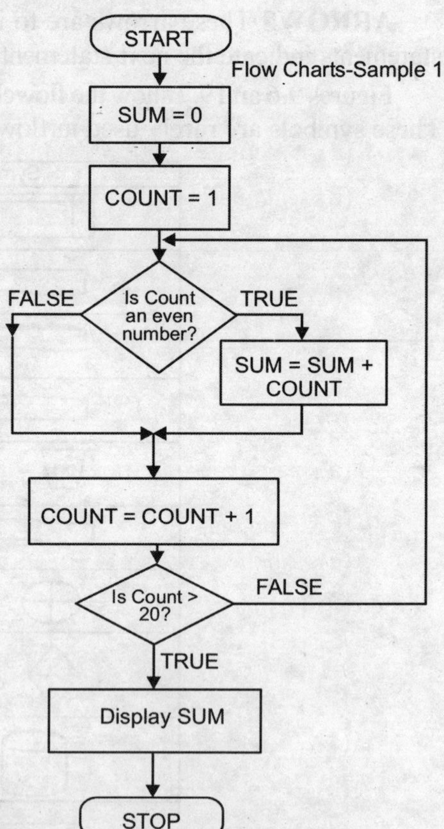

Figure 9.8: A Sample Flowchart

A sample flowchart is given in Fig. 9.8.

9.11.5.3 Advantages of Flowcharts

The benefits of flowcharts are as follows:

1. **Communication:** Flowcharts are better way of communicating the logic of a system to all concerned.

2. **Effective analysis:** With the help of flowchart, problem can be analyzed in more effective way.
3. **Proper documentation:** Program flowcharts serve as a good program documentation, which is needed for various purposes.
4. **Efficient Coding:** The flowcharts act as a guide or blueprint during the systems analysis and program development phase.
5. **Proper Debugging:** The flowchart helps in debugging process.
6. **Efficient Program Maintenance:** The maintenance of operating program becomes easy with the help of flowchart. It helps the programmer to put efforts more efficiently on that part.

Example 1: Write an algorithm for the problem of finding the roots of a quadratic equation $ax^2 + bx + c$ 0. Using the formula $\frac{-b \pm \sqrt{b^2 - 4ac}}{2a}$ or $\frac{-b \pm \sqrt{D}}{2a}$ where $D = b^2 - 4ac$. Draw flowchart for this algorithm

Answer: Algorithm is as follows:

1. Start
2. Read the numeric values for a, b, and c.
3. Calculate the value of D using the formula .
4. if D> 0
   (a) Calculate one root using the formula .
   (b) Calculate another root using the formula .
   (c) Display "roots are real and distinct".
   (d) Display "Root 1 = ", .
   (e) Display "Root 2 = ",
   (f) Exit
5. If D = 0, then
   (a) Calculate one root using the formula.
   (b) Display "roots are real and equal".
   (c) Display "Root 1 = ", .
   (d) Display "Root 2 = ",
   (e) Exit
6. If D = 0, then
   (a) Calculate one term using the formula .
   (b) Calculate another term using the formula or
   (c) Display "roots are imaginary".
   (d) Display "Root 1 = ", +i.
   (e) Display "Root 2 = ", +i.
   (f) Exit

7. Stop

Details of the flowchart are shown in Figure 10.8.

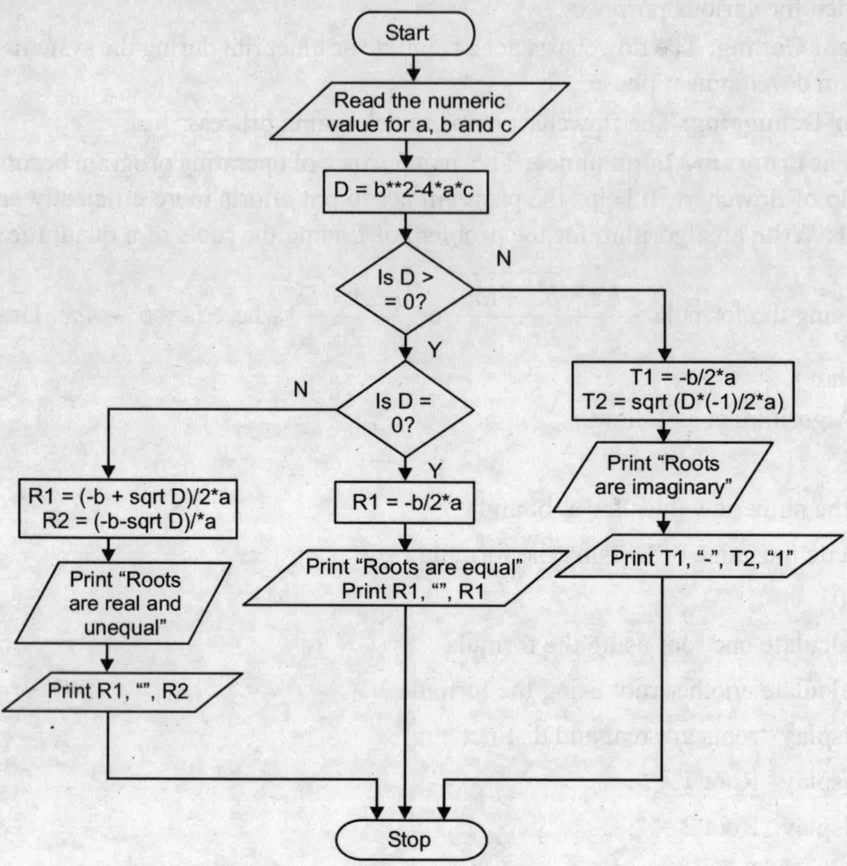

Figure 9.9: Flowchart for quadratic equation

Flowcharts are designed to facilitate encoding. Following section expresses the representation of different mathematical and logical expressions in flowcharts.

9.11.5.4 Limitations of Using Flowcharts

1. **Complex logic:** Sometimes, the program logic is quite complicated. In that case, flowchart becomes complex and clumsy.
2. **Alterations and Modifications:** If alterations are required the flowchart may require re-drawing completely.
3. **Reproduction:** As the flowchart symbols cannot be typed, reproduction of flowchart becomes a problem.
4. The essentials of what is done can easily be lost in the technical details of how it is done.

9.11.6 Basic Control Structures

There are some standard ways of connecting the symbols to represent the three basic structures. Notice that each of the three basic structures has a single entry flow and a single exit flow.

Sequence

Steps that execute in sequence are represented by symbols that follow each other top to bottom or left to right. Top to bottom is the standard. Any one of the processes could be replaced by another structure (for example, a single process "box" could be replaced by a sequence of two process "boxes").

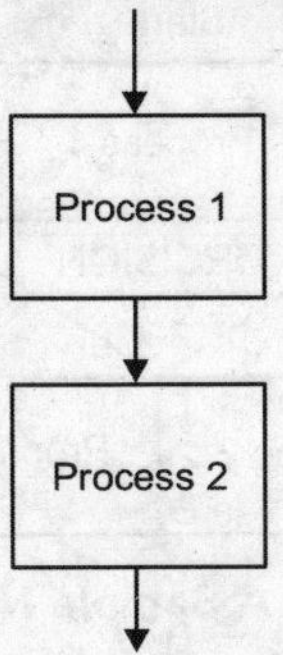

Selection

Once the condition is evaluated, the control flows into one of two paths. Once the conditional execution is finished, the flows rejoin before leaving the structure. Once again the single entry, single exit nature of a structure is evident. Either process could be replaced with any structure (sequence, selection, or repetition) or it could be omitted (for example the process on the "NO" side might not exist).

As an alternative, the "Question" could be replaced with a Boolean expression and the branches labeled "TRUE" and "FALSE".

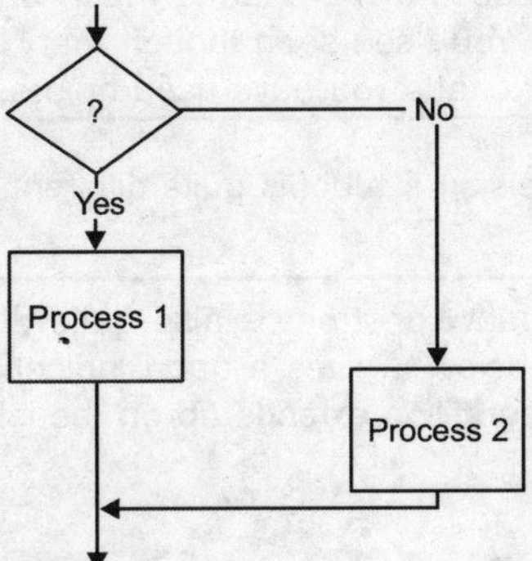

Repetition or Iteration or Looping

Either the processing repeats or the control leaves the structure. (Again, the process could be replace another structure).

Notice that the return line joins the entry line before the question. Never try to insert processing in the entry line between the join and the question.

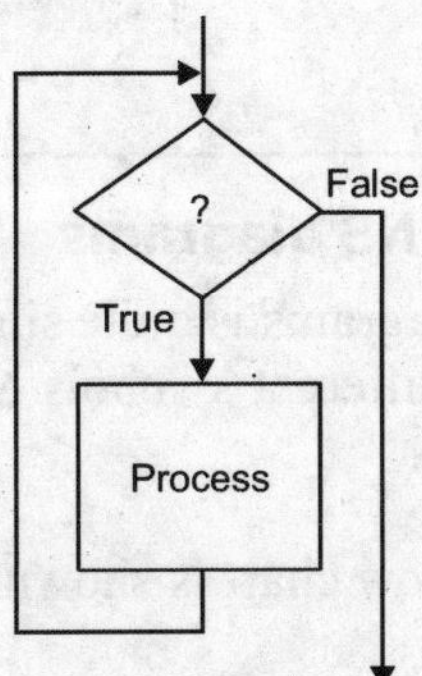

9.11.7 Nassi-Schneiderman Diagram

The Nassi-Schneiderman (NS) diagram is a graphical method of stating algorithms. Many people claim that it is very easy to read, especially for beginners. That is probably true but maintaining NS diagrams can be a problem for the program designer. Here is a simple example of a NS diagram:

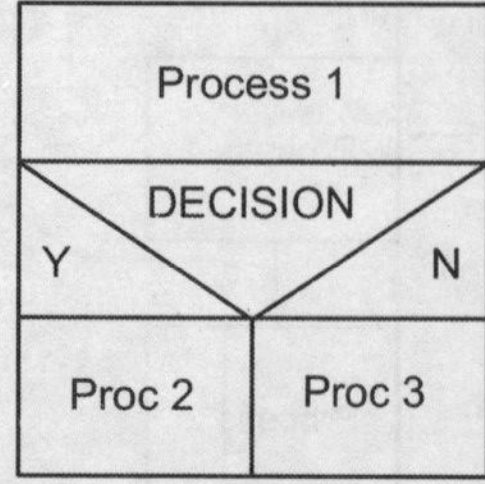

Figure 9.10: A Sample NS Diagram

The diagram indicates an algorithm with a process (Process 1) followed by a decision. Each outcome of the decision has a process associated with it. If the decision evaluates as true then Proc 2 is carried out, if false then Proc 3 is carried out. In the table that follows you will see the symbols that are used in NS diagrams. As with flow charts the symbols are few and easily remembered. The different symbols are "fitted" together like pieces in a jigsaw puzzle.

9.11.7.1 NS Symbols and Constructs

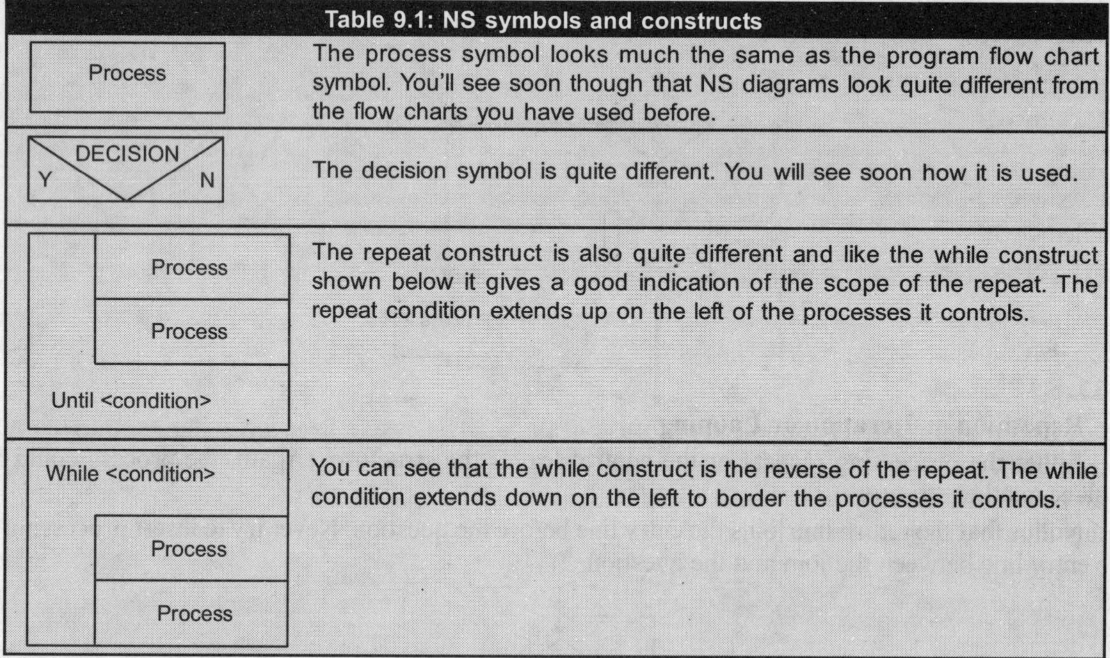

Table 9.1: NS symbols and constructs

Symbol	Description
Process	The process symbol looks much the same as the program flow chart symbol. You'll see soon though that NS diagrams look quite different from the flow charts you have used before.
DECISION Y N	The decision symbol is quite different. You will see soon how it is used.
Process / Process / Until <condition>	The repeat construct is also quite different and like the while construct shown below it gives a good indication of the scope of the repeat. The repeat condition extends up on the left of the processes it controls.
While <condition> / Process / Process	You can see that the while construct is the reverse of the repeat. The while condition extends down on the left to border the processes it controls.

9.11.7.2 Designing programs with NS diagrams

Drawing program designs with NS diagrams is quite simple but the NS method differs from the program flow chart method. Apart from different symbols NS does not use connectors between the symbols.

NS Diagram Vs Flowchart

A comparison of an NS chart and a flow chart is shown below:

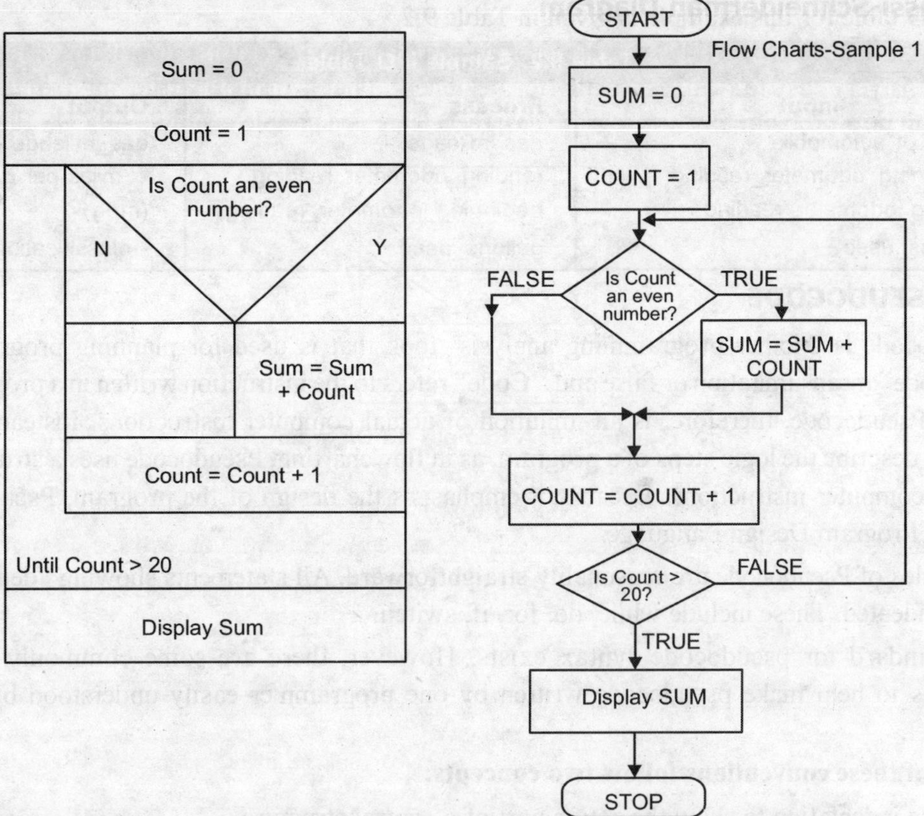

Figure 9.11: Comparison of Sample NS Diagram and Flowchart

As with the flow the direction of sequence in the NS chart is from top to bottom. There are some problems with the NS charts that don't really occur with flow charts:

It is not as easy to stress the process one entry-one exit point rule as it is in flow charts.

The null-else is not really obvious.

Modification of an NS diagram probably requires more work than the equivalent flow chart.

9.11.8 IPO Charts

A useful and relatively simple tool to use in the analysis stage to identify inputs, outputs and corresponding process is the IPO table. An **IPO (Input/Processing/Output) Table** shows the inputs to an object, the required outputs for that object, and the processing that is necessary to convert the inputs into the desired outputs.

Example:

CarRental, Inc., leases automobiles for its salespeople and wishes to create an application that will determine the gas mileage for each type of automobile.

Input should include: the make of the automobile, the beginning odometer reading, the ending odometer reading, and the gallons of gasoline consumed.

Output should include the miles per gallon for the car being tested. (note: gas mileage = (ending odometer reading - beginning odometer reading)/gallons used.).

In addition, the program should classify the car using the following scheme: "gas guzzler" for cars with gas mileage less than 18 mpg, "economy" for cars with gas mileage above 28 mpg, and "average" for cars with gas mileage between 18 and 28 mpg.

An **IPO** table for this example is given in Table 9.2.

Table 9.2: Sample IPO Table

Input	Process	Output
- make of automobile - beginning_odometer_reading - ending_odometer_reading - gallons_used	gas_mileage = (ending_odometer_reading - beginning_odometer_reading)/ gallons_used	gas_mileage in - miles per gallon (mpg) - classification

9.11.9 PSEUDOCODE

Pseudocode is another programming analysis' took that is used for planning program logic. ''Pseudocode'' means imitation or false and ''Code'' refers to the instruction written in a programming language. Pseudocode, therefore, is an imitation of actual computer instructions. Instead of using symbols to describe the logic steps of a program, as in flowcharting, Pseudocode uses a structure that resembles computer instructions. Because it emphasis's the design of the program, Pseudocode is also called Program Design Language.

The rules of Pseudocode are reasonably straightforward. All statements showing "dependency" are to be indented. These include while, do, for, if, switch.

No standard for pseudocode syntax exists. However, there are some commonly followed conventions to help make pseudocode written by one programmer easily understood by another programmer.

Most of these conventions follow two concepts:

Use indentation to show the action part of a control structure

Use an ending phrase word to end a control structure

The sequence control structure simply lists the lines of pseudocode. The concern is not with the sequence category but with selection and two of the iteration control structures.

The following are commonly used ending phrase-words:

Control Structure	Ending Phrase Word
If then Else	Endif
Case	Endcase
While	Endwhile
For	Endfor

The Do While and Repeat Until iteration control structures don't need an ending phrase-word. We simply use the first word, then the action part, followed by the second word with the test expression. **Here is one of the examples.**

Example: Pseudocode for the CarRental, Inc. problem stated above.

```
Begin procedure
    Input make, beginning_odometer, ending_odometer, and gallons_used
        gas_mileage = (ending_odometer - beginning_odometer)/gallons_used
    Output gas_mileage
    If gas_mileage < 18 then
        Output "Gas Guzzler"
```

```
    EndIf
    If gas_mileage > 28 then
        Output "Economy"
    EndIf
    If gas_mileage >= 18 And gas_mileage <= 28 then
        Output "Average"
    EndIf
End procedure
```

9.11.9.1 Types of Pseudocode

Pseudocode is made up of the following basic logic structures that have been proved to be sufficient for writing any computer program.

1. Sequence
2. Selection (IF....THEN....or IF....THEN)
3. Iteration (DO....WHILE or REPEAT.....UNTIL)

1. Sequence Logic: It is used for performing instructions one after another in sequence. Thus, for sequence logic, pseudocode instructions are written in the oper, or sequence, in which they are to be performed. The logic flow of pseudocode is from the top to the bottom.

2. Selection Logic: It is also known as decision logic, is used for making decisions. It is used for selecting the proper path out of the two or more alternative paths in the program.

Logic Selection Logic is depicted as either an IF....THEN or an IF....THEN....ELSE structure.

3. Iteration Logic: It is used to produce loops when one or more instructions may be executed several times depending on some condition. It uses two structures called the DO.....WHILE and the REPEAT....UNTIL. They are illustrated by flowcharts. Their corresponding Pseudocode are also given in DO....WHILE and REPEAT......UNTIL are used for looping. The differences are that in the DO....WHILE, the looping will continue as long as the condition is true. The looping stops when the condition is not true. On the other hand, in case of REPEAT.....UNTIL, the looping continues until the must contain a statement that will change the condition that controls the loop. If it doesn't the looping will continue without end, which of the case of an infinite loop.

Remember that no program should contain an infinite loop. Also note that the condition is tested at the loop of the loop in the DO....WHILE and at the bottom of the loop in the REPEAT....UNTIL. ENDDO marks the end of a DO....WHILE structure and UNTIL followed by some condition marks the end of the REPEAT.....UNTIL structure.

9.11.9.2 Difference between Pseudocode and Flowchart

Pseudocode differs from the flowchart in the following ways:

1. Pseudocode is self-explanatory and does not requires a separate documentation. This is so because it is written in plain English language.
2. Pseudocode has a structure similar to that of a programme written in BASIC or PASCAL language. But flowcharts have a tendency to extend flow lines in all directions and thus their paths of instructions do not parallel the final BASIC code.

9.11.9.3 Advantages and Limitations of Pseudocode

Pseudocode has three main advantages:

Converting a Pseudocode to a programming language is much easier as compared to converting a flowchart or a decision table.

As compared to a flowchart, it is easier to modify the Pseudocode of program logic when program modifications are necessary.

Writing of Pseudocode involves much less time and effort than drawing an equivalent flowchart Pseudocode is easier to write than an actual programming language because it has only a few rules to follow, allowing the programmers to concentrate on the logic of the program.

However, Pseudocode suffers from the following limitations:

In case of Pseudocode, a graphic representation of program logic is not available.

There are no standard rules to follow in using Pseudocode. Different programmers use their own style of writing Pseudocode and hence a communication problem occurs due to lack of standardization.

For a beginner, it is more difficult to follow the logic of or write Pseudocode as compared to flowcharting.

9.11.10 Hierarchy Charts

A hierarchy chart provides a graphical representation about the overall structure of the program. They describe what each module of the program does and how the modules are related to one another.

Example: Hierarchy Chart for the CarRental, Inc. problem is given in Fig. 9.7

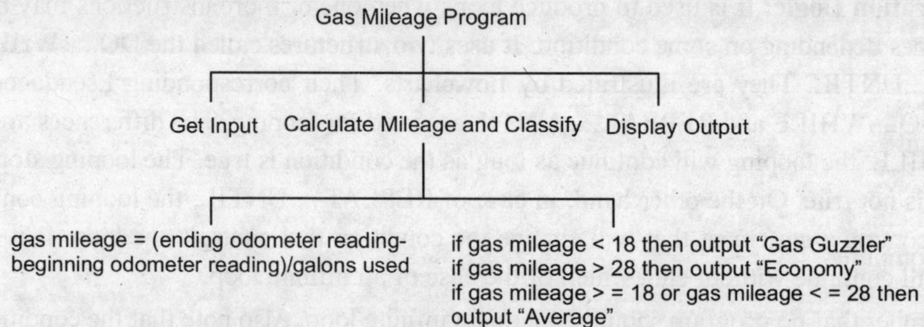

Figure 9.12: Hierarchy Chart Example

9.11.11 Trace Table

After the flowchart has been drawn for the given problem, it is essential to check that the method and plan deployed to solve the problem functions correctly and produces the desired results. There after the flowchart is translated into high level language to be run on the computer. The manual test of the flowchart is called dry run or desk check.

As the name suggests, the trace table traces the sequence, step by step, which leads to the solution of the problem. In the process of tracing, the result of each step and its effect on the next step becomes clear. The logic involved in solving the problem becomes evident. If any error at any stage is discovered while framing the algorithm, or drawing of flowchart, it shows itself at the time of dry run. In presence of any error, the system designed to solve the problem will not function correctly and will produce the incorrect results during dry run. The trace table helps in locating the stage at which the error has occurred and also the nature of error, so that thereafter the error could be eliminated.

How to perform the dry run or desk check?

The dry run or desk check is performed to check each stage of the solution developed to solve the problem. The steps involved in it are as follows:

(a) Draw the table containing as many columns as the number of activities in the flowchart (i.e., one column for each geometrical figure in the flow chart).

(b) Write the activity performed in each vertical columns as the number of activities in the flow chart (i.e., one column for each geometrical figure in the flow chart).

(c) Consider a suitable numerical value, for the variable as required, in the flow chart within the prescribed range.

(d) Keep on writing the values in each column in accordance to the activity mentioned above each column.

(e) Check that the values generated in each column as per the activity mentioned in it are correct and are as expected (this is done by comparing the values generated according to each activity with the values which should occur).

(f) In case of any error locate the stage at which the error was raised and identify the nature of error.

(g) Take adequate measures to eliminate the detected errors.

(h) Recheck the flowchart till it is error free.

How a program is executed?

Following are the necessary steps involved in the execution of the program.

(a) Since the compilers of different high level languages are different hence the compiler for the high level language, in which the program has been written, is loaded in the memory of the computer.

(b) The source program is fed to the computer through some input device. The control unit stores the program in the main memory of computer.

(c) The compiler or interpreter used, not only converts source program in machine code but also check each line for syntax error.

(d) The syntax error message is conveyed to the user by central processing unit through the output devices. The program shall not be executed unless the program is made completely error-free.

(e) Memory locations are allotted to each variable, by the name of each variable itself, in the main memory.

(f) The result of the executed program is communicated to the user, in high level language, through the output devices.

9.11.12 Decision Table

Though earlier discussed flowcharts give a clear idea of direction of flow of data but it has a disadvantage. This is, the flowcharts become more complicated and difficult to understand if there are several decisions to be taken in a program. Also a flowchart may run for more than one page. So at times following and understanding a flowchart becomes more difficult. Because of these disadvantages, in such complex cases instead of flowcharts there is another algorithm development and documentation aid that is the decision table. A *decision table* depicts in a tabular form the set of conditions to be tested and the sequence of actions to be performed to solve a problem. This aid is useful in solving the problems, which require a large number of decisions.

STUB	ENTRY
CONDITION	RULE NUMBER
ACTION	

Figure 9.13: General layout of Decision Table

Decision table is a table defining the problem and the actions to be taken. It is a single representation of conditions and actions. Figure 9.13 shows the general layout of any decision table. A decision table consists of two main partitions- STUB and ENTRY.

The stub part is divided into an upper quadrant called the conditional stub and a lower quadrant called the action stub. The entry part is also divided into two quadrants. The upper quadrant is called the condition entry and a lower quadrant is called the action entry. The condition stub contains in the question form, the condition that may exist. The action stub contains outlines in the narrative form, the action to be taken to meet each condition. The condition entry provides the answers to the questions that are asked in the condition stub quadrant. The action entry indicates the appropriate action resulting from the answers to the conditions in the condition entry quadrant. We now consider an example to understand the way of writing the entries in a decision table.

Example 2: In a marketing firm, commission is given based on the sales. If sales are less than 5000.00, then there is no commission. If sales is more than or equal to 5000. 00 but less than 10000 then commission is 2%. If sales is greater than or equal to 10000 but less than 50000 then commission is 4%. If sales is greater than 50000. 00 the discount is 6%.

Answer: Now we draw a decision table for it. In this case, the conditions are

If sales are less than 5000.00

If sales are less than 10000.00

If sales is less than 50000.00

If sales is greater then 50000.00

From the Figure 9.9, we note certain things. First of all, we see that the answers have been denoted by Y & N and blank column & row denotes that the corresponding condition has not been tested. The check mark (X) denotes the action. Each column indicates a rule. For example rule 3 is, "IF sale is less than 50000 and greater than 10000/- then allow 4% discount".

STUB		ENTRY					
		1	2	3	4	5	6
(Condition)							
IF	Sale >= 50000?	Y	N	N	N	N	N
	Sale < 50000?		Y	Y	Y	Y	Y
	Sale >= 10000?			Y	N	N	N
	Sale < 10000?				Y	Y	Y
	Sale >= 5000?					Y	N
	Sale < 5000?						Y
(Action)							
	Allow 6% discount	X					
THEN	Allow 4% discount		X				
	Allow 2% discount				X		
	No discount allowed						X

Figure 9.14: Decision Table for Example 2

Example 3: Students results are declared using the following rules: There are two subjects in the examination called main and ancillary. If a student gets 50 % or more in the main subject and 40% in the ancillary he/she is passed. If he/she gets less than 50% in the main subject, he/she must get 50% or more in the ancillary to pass. However, the minimum pass marks are 40% in the main subject. If a student gets 60% or more in the main subject, he/she is allowed to repeat ancillary subject if the ancillary subject is less than 40%. However, there are a group of students in the class who are granted special consideration. Their percentage is 40% in main and 40% in ancillary. If they get less than 40% in the ancillary, they are allowed to repeat that subject, if they obtain 40% or more in the main subject.

Answer: The decision table for this problem is shown in Figure 9.10.

Conditions	Rule1	Rule2	Rule3	Rule4	Rule5	Else
Main marks %age	≥50	≥40	≥60	≥40	≥40	
Ancillary marks %age	≥40	≥50	< 40	≥40	< 40	
Special status	No	No	No	Yes	Yes	
Actions						
Pass	x	x	-	x	-	-
Repeat	-	-	x	-	x	-
Fail	-	-	-	-	-	x

Figure 9.15: Decision Table for Example 3.

9.11.12.1 Rules for drawing decision table

The rules that should be following while constructing the decision table are as follows:

1. A decision should have a same.
2. The logic of the table is independent of the sequence in which condition rules are written.
3. Duplication of the terms must be eliminated.

9.11.12.2 Advantages of decision table

Decision tables are best suited for dealing with complex branching routines such as complex links of inventory control or calculating purchasing discounts, sales commissions, etc. These tables are easier to construct than flow charts if several conditions are to be tested and decisions to be taken. Also, it is easier to follow the table when a particular condition is met just by coming down the column.

9.11.13 PROGRAM TESTING

Program testing is an investigation conducted to provide stakeholders with information about the quality of the product or service under test. Software testing can also provide an objective, independent view of the software to allow the business to appreciate and understand the risks of software implementation. Test techniques include, but are not limited to, the process of executing a program or application with the intent of finding software bugs (errors or other defects).

Program testing can be stated as the process of validating and verifying that a software program/application/product:

1. meets the requirements that guided its design and development;
2. works as expected; and
3. can be implemented with the same characteristics.

Program testing, depending on the testing method employed, can be implemented at any time in the development process. However, most of the test effort occurs after the requirements have been defined and the coding process has been completed. As such, the methodology of the test is governed by the software development methodology adopted.

Different software development models will focus the test effort at different points in the development process. Newer development models, such as Agile, often employ test driven development and place an increased portion of the testing in the hands of the developer, before it reaches a formal team of testers. In a more traditional model, most of the test execution occurs after the requirements have been defined and the coding process has been completed.

9.11.13.1 SAMPLE TESTING CYCLE

Although variations exist between organizations, there is a typical cycle for testing. The sample below is common among organizations employing the Waterfall development model.

Requirements analysis: Testing should begin in the requirements phase of the software development life cycle. During the design phase, testers work with developers in determining what aspects of a design are testable and with what parameters those tests work.

Test planning: Test strategy, test plan, testbed creation. Since many activities will be carried out during testing, a plan is needed.

Test development: Test procedures, test scenarios, test cases, test datasets, test scripts to use in testing software.

Test execution: Testers execute the software based on the plans and test documents then report any errors found to the development team.

Test reporting: Once testing is completed, testers generate metrics and make final reports on their test effort and whether or not the software tested is ready for release.

Test result analysis: Or Defect Analysis, is done by the development team usually along with the client, in order to decide what defects should be treated, fixed, rejected (i.e. found software working properly) or deferred to be dealt with later.

Defect Retesting: Once a defect has been dealt with by the development team, it is retested by the testing team.

Regression testing: It is common to have a small test program built of a subset of tests, for each integration of new, modified, or fixed software, in order to ensure that the latest delivery has not ruined anything, and that the software product as a whole is still working correctly.

Test Closure: Once the test meets the exit criteria, the activities such as capturing the key outputs, lessons learned, results, logs, documents related to the project are archived and used as a reference for future projects.

9.11.14 PROGRAM DEBUGGING

Debugging is a methodical process of finding and reducing the number of bugs, or defects, in a computer program or a piece of electronic hardware, thus making it behave as expected. Debugging tends to be harder when various subsystems are tightly coupled, as changes in one may cause bugs to emerge in another.

As software and electronic systems have become generally more complex, the various common debugging techniques have expanded with more methods to detect anomalies, assess impact, and schedule software patches or full updates to a system. The words "anomaly" and "discrepancy" can be used, as being more neutral terms, to avoid the words "error" and "defect" or "bug" where there might be an implication that all so-called errors, defects or bugs must be fixed (at all costs). Instead, an impact assessment can be made to determine if changes to remove an anomaly (or discrepancy) would be cost-effective for the system, or perhaps a scheduled new release might render the change(s) unnecessary. Not all issues are life-critical or mission-critical in a system. Also, it is important to avoid the situation where a change might be more upsetting to users, long-term, than living with the known problem(s) (where the "cure would be worse than the disease"). Basing decisions of the acceptability of some anomalies can avoid a culture of a "zero-defects" mandate, where people might be tempted to deny the existence of problems so that the result would appear as zero defects. Considering the collateral issues, such as the cost-versus-benefit impact assessment, then broader debugging techniques will expand to determine the frequency of anomalies (how often the same "bugs" occur) to help assess their impact to the overall system.

9.11.15 PROGRAM DOCUMENTATION

Program documentation or source code documentation is written text that accompanies computer software. It either explains how it operates or how to use it, or may mean different things to people in different roles.

Role of documentation in software development

Documentation is an important part of software engineering. Types of documentation include:

1. **Requirements**: Statements that identify attributes, capabilities, characteristics, or qualities of a system. This is the foundation for what shall be or has been implemented.
2. **Architecture/Design:** Overview of software. Includes relations to an environment and construction principles to be used in design of software components.
3. **Technical:** Documentation of code, algorithms, interfaces, and APIs.
4. **End User:** Manuals for the end-user, system administrators and support staff.
5. **Marketing:** How to market the product and analysis of the market demand.

9.11.15.1 Report Generation

Commercial applications use formatted outputs. These formatted outputs are known as reports. A formatted report may have the following:

1. Report heading
2. Page heading
3. Page numbering
4. Footers
5. Some remarks
6. Date, month and year of printing

Commercial outputs may also extend over multiple pages. In that case, one will have to keep a provision in his program so that certain details get printed on every page. For example, one may have to print page headings on every page. Report may be of

1. Single page
2. Multiple pages

Multiple page reports in general may consist of following parts:

Report Heading

It represents the title of the report and appears, only on the first page of the report.

Report Sub Heading

It is printed as and when required on each page.

Page Heading

It is printed on the top of each page.

Page Footer

It is printed at the bottom of each page. It is generally the total number of records on the page, sum of the numeric data, etc.

Report Detail

This constitutes the main body of report. The output details or the information of the main consequence are listed in this group.

9.11.15.2 Reports with Control Break

The most important objective of a program is reporting. We need summarized information for decision making. For presenting the summarized information one can use the concept of control break. In control break report, one need to group information based on some common criterion, maybe department, cost centre, etc.

A control break report can have the following:

1. Records of a particular region are grouped together and printed at one page.
2. When the control break occurs, certain procedures are followed. Such as total sales of that region.
3. It may be necessary that performance of each region is printed on each page, i.e., when the control break occurs the report is printed on a fresh page.
4. At the end of the report, it may be necessary to calculate and print the grand totals.

9.11.15.3 Operation on Files

There are some basic operations which can be performed on the files. They are:

Writing on the file

Reading the file for updating or outputting

Deleting the file

Let us discuss each one of these in detail.

Writing to a File: This is the process of making the data permanent on the tape or disk. It can be done with the help of data which has been keyed in either by off-line or by on-line method. Here the data is first stored in the memory and then written on the output medium.

Reading the File for Updating or Outputting: File created in the above step is used here. Once the data from the file comes to the memory, use have the option of making changes or doing calculations based on it or even send the data for printing.

Deleting the File: It is a process in which you delete the file from the storage media making way for some other data to be stored in.

9.11.15.4 File Updation

It is a process in which a data file is processed for changes in the records. These changes can be many to one records or one to many records. You may have to skip various records which do not have any changes or you may have to make several changes in the same record. Updation can be done on both sequential and non-sequential, i.e., random access files.

Sequential File Updation: This process is mostly used in the case of files being on the magnetic tapes. Because of the possibility of record insertions and/or deletions, during an update run, the computer processing creates new master file records. In many applications, some master file records are also deleted from the file. So you need to have one file having the master record before updation and the second having master records after affecting the changes in the master file.

Random File Updation: This process is mostly used in the cases where the file is on floppy disk or hard disk where the data is stored in random. Here a record is added, deleted or modified without affecting any other record in the file. Also when the record is to be accessed the same mapping function, key to address transformation, is used to transform the key to obtain its address. Thus while storing or accessing the record the same mapping function is used to find the address of the record.

Multiple Handling of Updation: Here since you are using more than one file, all the files in use must have the same sequence. Either all of them should be in sequence or all of them in random access mode. The records from all the files are called into the memory and converted into a single stream for updating. Once updated the data is transferred back to the files.

9.12 PROGRAM DEVELOPMENT PROCESS

So far we have discussed about programming concepts and other necessary aspects. Here we will discuss about various steps involved in writing and developing software, which are as under:

9.12.1 Program Definition

Unless you define it how would you know what is to be done. So this is the first step. Various activities involved in this are:

1. Determine objectives of the current system
2. Study the current system
3. Analyse new objectives
4. Prepare design specifications.
5. Identify user's responsibility of data inputs and outputs to other systems
6. Prepare plan for design and implementation phases
7. Produce a report for the user and systems management.

9.12.2 Program Design

We have recently read about the various types of program designs. Choose one of them to design your program. This should envisioned as a step-by-step procedure. The programmer's problem is then to design a process (or algorithm) which, on being given the correct inputs, produced the required outputs. A program specification also includes a description of the constraints which must apply to the solution. This step consists of preparing documents that will guide the actual coding of the program. This step is considered complete when a clean compile walk-through has been held and the program design has been approved.

9.12.3 Coding

This step is the process of transforming the program logic design documents into a computer language format. This stage translates the program design into computer instructions. When the coded program is ready in a high level language, it is entered in a source file using any editor or word processor.

9.12.4 Debugging

Who does not make error? When you type the program and try to run it, you are bound to get errors. This process of correcting errors is called Debugging. Debugging aids the built in the computer which give diagnostic messages about any error in the program language either during coding or during key-punching. The errors are corrected and the program is debugged again to find out further errors, if any. This process is repeated till the program is error free. Debugging does not point out logical or arithmetic errors. Debugging program is an important part of program preparation and may even take more time than the actual program writing.

9.12.4.1 Types of Errors

Once a program has been typed in, different types of errors may show up. These include:

Syntax/Semantic errors

Syntax is a set of rules governing the structure of an relationship between symbols, words and phrases in a language statement. A syntax error occurs when a program cannot understand the command that has been entered. Computer does not have any intelligence. Therefore, it can do what it is made to do provide it known how to do it. For this, a computer has an operating system and the compiler for programming language. These software convert the instructions given to a computer into a machine language equivalent. When we give the same instruction in a high level language, i.e., similar to English, then the computer compiler first translates it into the machine language and then the switches in the microprocessor of the CPU are so set that the computer performs these instructions one by one.

The compiler which translates the high level language instructions will be able to translate into exact machine language instructions, provided it has received the instructions correctly. If not, then the result will be absurd. For example, when we say Mangoes and Man goes, the meaning totally changes in English. Similarly, in computer language also, a little change in the position of comma or semicolon or a gap will make all the differences in the meaning of the entire instruction. This type of error is called syntax error and it is very harmful to the working of the computer. The compiler is able to detect such errors and gives the indication about those locations where the instructions are not understandable. A programmer then correct such instructions and then retypes the syntax errors.

Logic Errors:

Logic refers to a sequence of operations performed by a software or hardware. Software logic or program logic is the sequence of instructions in a program. Logic errors are the errors that have been entered in the instructions created because of the mistake made by a program. Suppose you wanted the sum of A and B and put the result in the variable C. This is accomplished by typing:

C:=A + B

But while typing, the programmer has typed the following expression:

C:= A – B

Such a program will run properly but will give erratic result because the value of C will not be the sum of A and B but it will be the difference of A and B which is quite different. Such errors can only be detected with the help of test data that will give the input values of A and B and the resultant value that should come out of the program as a result of the operation performed on A and B. If the result given by the computer an the result calculated manually with the help of a calculator are the same, then you can say that there is no logical error. Otherwise a logic error may be present in the program.

The logical error given above is very simple. However, all logic errors used not be the result of wrong typing. They could also be the result of wrong definition, as for example. When the sales turnover of a company is checked on the printed price instead of the discounted price. Here if sales are defined as Y and the quantity is defined as X. If we by mistake interpret these two quantities differently, i.e. sales as X instead of Y. Then also the error committed is a logical error. In such a case the result will be logical.

Runtime Error

Runtime errors occur when a program is run on the computer and the results are not achieved due to some misinterpretation of a particular instruction. This could be some thing like dividing a number by zero which results in a very large value of quotient. At the time of executing a program, the runtime error is detected. Because, one of the values for which a program needs to calculate the result may be to divide the quantity by a very small quantity and the resultant value will be so large that it cannot be interpreted by the computer. This will then be shown as a runtime error. For example, the mass of an electron is very small value. If one divides a quantity by the mass of the electron, the result may be so large that it is beyond the capacity of the machine.

To overcome this problem, there is a built-in error detector in the language interpreter or compiler which will give the message and that will reflect the reason for run time error.

9.12.5 Program Testing

It is the job of the program to test, as far as possible, that all parts of the program work correctly. It should be realized that complete testing is not possible except in the case of the most trivial program; one can never be completely certain that all errors have been removed, but sufficient tests can be performed to give a reasonable measure of confidence in the program. The situation is analogous of testing children on multiplication tables; once a child has answered a certain number of multiplication table tests correctly, at some point or other the teacher assume that all other tests will be answered correctly and testing ceases.

9.12.5.1 Designing a Test Plan

Since we cannot test everything because there may be many number of if then else decision and all the test data may not be able to test all the loops. Each test must be carefully planned to provide more information about the program. A major benefit of preparing a comprehensive test plan with expected results is that it forces the programmer to think carefully about the program and often errors are spotted even before running the test.

Testing requires the following:

1. A thorough knowledge and understanding of what the program is supposed to do.
2. Plan out in advance what ought to be tested.
3. To work out expected results for each of the test cases.
4. Writing out the test plan.

9.12.5.2 Methods of Testing

The objectives of testing can be stated in two basic questions:

1. Does the logic work properly? This means, answering the following:
   (i) Does the program work as intended?
   (ii) Can it be made to crash?
2. Is the necessary logic present? This means answering the following:
   (i) Are there any functions missing?
   (ii) Does the program or module do everything specified?

There are two different ways of testing. These are:

1. Functional testing
2. Logical or structural testing

Functional Testing

Functional testing is carried out independently of the code used in the program. It involves looking at the program specification and creating a set of test data that covers all types of inputs and getting outputs and program functions. This type of testing is also known as "black box testing".

Logical (structural) Testing

Logical testing (white box testing) is dependent on the code logic and derives from the program structure rather than its function. In other words, we study the program code and try to test each possible path in the program at least once. The problem with logical testing is that it will not detect the missing functions. One method of devising a test plan is to start with a set of functional test cases and then add additional tests to exercise each statement in the program at least once, making sure that each decision is tested for all outcomes.

9.12.6 Documentation and Program Maintenance

Documentation of a software system involves collecting, organizing, storing and maintaining a complete historical record of programs and other documents used or prepared during different phases of the system development. The documentation of a program is a continuous process. The program specifications, the algorithmic representation and the program itself can all be considered part of the documentation of a program. However, after successfully completing the program, we must ensure that our documentation us complete and it is in a finished, usable form. This includes both technical documentation for the programmers who maybe working with and modifying the completed program and user-level documentation for the users of the program.

One of the mistaken ideas held by too many programmers is that the documentation for a program should be written only after the program is "finished". This is a very dangerous point of view! It will certainly lead to inadequate documentation and might result in an incomplete or incorrect program. Documentation is a continuous process. It starts when we first begin to formulate a clear problem statement and continuous as we device a solution, express the solution algorithmically and code the algorithm as a computer program. The proper point of view is that documentation is an inherent part of a program. It is therefore meaningless to assert that documentation should be written after the program is finished.

Most programs that are written by professional programmers are used in a production environment. This means that once a program is deemed operational it is used on a regular basis, usually by people other than the author(s). For example, programs to process payrolls, maintain inventories, or handles hotel or airline reservations are invariably used by people who did not write them. Moreover, these people are usually not even programmers. In this sort of environment, we can appreciate the need for the following two different kinds of documentation.

9.12.6.1 User Documentation

It provides the information that one needs in order to use a program. This information includes a number of different items. These items are:

1. A description of the application area of the program or what will this program do?
2. A description of the input data that the program requires.
3. A description of the output produced by the program.
4. A description of the commands needed to start the program.
5. A description of the kinds of interactions that are possible with the program.
6. An explanation of all the messages that the program can produce.
7. A discussion (in nontechnical terms) of the performance capabilities and limitations of the program.

9.12.6.2 Technical Documentation

This kind of documentation is addressed to programmers who might be faced with the task of modifying the program at some time. Perhaps a mistake will become apparent after the program has been placed into use, or a decision may be made to enhance the program by adding a new feature. In either case, good technical documentation is a necessity.

9.12.6.3 Uses of Documentation

The uses of documentation are as follows:

1. They facilitate communication about an application between the technical development personnel and the non-technical users.
2. Documents are very helpful in initiating and training not just new employees, but old employees changing jobs or learning to use a computerized version of an old job. Good documentation will provide a self-instructional approach that will allow employees to advance at their own pace.
3. The documents are essential during abnormal maintenance when a new programmer must maintain a system after the original programmer or analyst has left. This is very common and serious problem. There are numerous cases where an application was left undocumented and could not be maintained. When this occurs, the application must be developed all over again.
4. Documents are essential even among technical personnel not only during developing of a system but also during operations and normal maintenance.
5. The provides a package that will contain the information needed to change the system should the environment or management's needs alter.
6. Documentation prevents system dislocation and cost that might otherwise occur if knowledge of the system were centered in a few individuals who resigned, relocated or were subsequently reassigned other duties.

9.12.6.4 Limitations of Documentation

Documentation has the limitations inherent in human communication. The difference in the backgrounds of the user and the documenter and the nature of the high technology that is being documented. This makes the test of a sound documentation more difficult.

Everything cannot be conveyed through the documentation only. It may be difficult for an analyst to convey one's assumptions and one's view of how the system could and should be improved given changed circumstances (of technology or user), interaction which would be invaluable to maintenance and redevelopment.

Points to Remember

1. Programming languages are there to give instructions to the computer.
2. Machine language is the language which a particular computer understands.
3. Assembly language uses the various mmemonic codes.
4. High-level language programs may be used with different makes of computers with the little modifications.
5. LOGO is used for drawing shapes on the monitor.
6. FORTRAN was mainly used in scientific calculations.
7. COBOL is best for business applications.
8. BASIC is the language for the beginners.
9. PROLOG is adopted as the official programming language for the fifth generation computers.
10. PASCAL is a general-purpose language that can be used for a wide range of numeric and non numeric applications.
11. C is a general-purpose structured programming language.
12. C++ is an object-oriented programming language.
13. Visual Basic is Windows based development tool.
14. Visual C++ is Windows version of C++.
15. C# allows you to develop for Internet and Windows both.
16. Java is mostly used for Internet.
17. vb.net is the version of Visual Basic for the Internet.
18. Programming is one of the step in system development cycle.
19. A person engaged in the activity of programming is referred to as programmer.
20. Each program overgrows itself.
21. Data handling is basically the level of manging data.
22. Constant is the data which is predetermined before a program is used.
23. Variables are the data that may change or be assigned different values as the program runs.
24. Pseudocode is self-explanatory and does not requires a separate documentation. This is so because it is written in plain English language.
25. File updation is a process in which a data file is processed for changes in the records.
26. Random file updation is mostly used in the cases where the file is on floppy disk or hard disk where the data is stored in random.
27. Structured programs are the ones that are divided into functional modules and arranged in an hierarchical order instead of programs written in a sequence.

28. Procedural programming is based on certain procedures.
29. Top down design approach is performed in a special way, the main program is written first.
30. Coding is the process of transforming the program logic design documents into a computer language format.
31. The process of correcting errors is called Debugging.
32. A syntax error occurs when a program cannot understand the command that has been entered.
33. Logic errors refers to a sequence of operations performed by a software or hardware.
34. Runtime errors occur when a program is run on the computer and the results are not achieved due to some misinterpretation of a particular instruction.
35. Functional testing is carried out independently of the code used in the program.
36. Documentation of a software system involves collecting, organizing, storing and maintaining a complete historical record of programs and other documents used or prepared during different phases of the system development.

EXERCISES

Multiple Choice Questions

1. Computer understands only one language and that is:
   (a) Source Language (b) Machine Language
   (c) High Level Language
2. Computer language used for scientific calculations are:
   (a) LOGO (b) FORTAN
   (c) BASIC
3. The language used for development of various games is:
   (a) C (b) C++
   (c) Java
4. C# allows you to develop for Windows and :
   (a) DOS (b) Internet
   (c) Both
5. Visual Basic is a development tool:
   (a) Yes (b) No
6. A person engaged in programming is called :
   (a) Operator (b) Programmer
   (c) Analyst
7. Data whose value remains the same thoughout the program is called :
   (a) Variable (b) Constant
   (c) Communicator
8. The process of correcting errors is called:
   (a) programming (b) flow charting
   (c) debugging
9. A syntax error occurs when the system cannot understand a :
   (a) command (b) logic
   (c) flow

10. Pseudocode is written in :
    (a) machine language
    (b) English language
    (c) programming language

Descriptive Type Questions

1. What is meant by a programming language ?
2. If each new generation of language enhances interaction between programmers and the computer, why not write programs using the most recent generation of languages ?
3. What are the differences between high-level and low-level languages ?
4. Associate each of language with a particular generation of languages.
5. What are various generations of computer programming languages ?
6. What are problem-oriented languages ?
7. What is the difference between machine- and assembly-language ?
8. What are non-procedural languages ? Give few examples.
9. Why are low-level and high-level languages are named so ?
10. What are Application Generators ? Give few examples.
11. What are procedural languages ? Give few examples.
12. What do you mean by computer program?
13. What is algorithm?
14. Explain the different types of algorithms in detail?
15. What is flowchart? Explain the types of flowcharts?
16. What do you mean by pseudocode?
17. What do you mean by program testing?
18. Explain the concept of debugging?
19. What do you mean by program documentation?
20. What are various types of high-level languages ?
21. State the capabilities of Query Languages ?
22. What are DSSs (Decision Support Systems) ? How are they helpful ?
23. What do you understand by Specialised Languages ? Give few examples.
24. What are Object-Oriented Programming Languages ? Give few examples.
25. What are multi-purpose programming languages ? Name three such languages.
26. What do you understand by Fifth Generation Languages (5GLs) ?
27. What are Report Generators ?
28. What are the differences between 3GLs and 4GLs ?
29. Name a procedure-oriented programming language in each of the three classifications, namely, scientific, business, and specialised.
30. What are query languages ? Give few examples.
31. What are Natural Languages ?
32. What is programming?
33. What is data handling?
34. What all the steps in program life cycle?
35. What are Pseudocodes?
36. What is the difference between Pseudocode and flow chart?

37. Which are the various parts of reports?
38. What operations you can perform on the files?
39. Which are the different methods of file updation?
40. What do you understand by top down design?
41. How program testing is done?
42. Describe the various type of errors you get when the program is run?
43. What do you understand by documenation of program?
44. What are the usuage and limitations of program documentation?
45. Write a short note on the following:

LOGO	FORTRAN
COBOL	BASIC
PROLOG	PASCAL
C	C++
Java	Visual Basic
Visual C++	C#
VB.NET	

Overview of C Language

10.1 INTRODUCTION

Today we are living in the era of computers and computers are used in almost every walk of life. Can one imagine railway reservation without the use of computers? No, doubt we can do that with computer also but it looks like impossible task. There are various other fields where computers are widely used. When we think of the computer working, we must remember that a computer purchased directly from the manufacturer is like a dead body, i.e., computer system should have programs to execute a job that is very much similar to giving life to it by feeding something to enable it to perform the desired function. As blood circulation is essential for existence of human beings, software is required to run the computers. The software provides the interface between computer and human beings. We have two main categories of software- System software, and Application software which have already been discussed earlier. For development of such software we need some language.

We have many languages; some languages are machine-level, middle-level, and some are high-level; even some languages are similar to natural language like English. But a computer can only understand the binary code so we have translators to convert the high-level code into machine-readable code. We have also see, that when we move from machine-level languages to high-level languages, effort involved in programming decreases but time involved in execution increases.

Now let us see what a language is in general sense. We have so many languages; for example Hindi, English, French, etc. These are natural languages and people using particular languages are very much aware about those languages. For example, let us consider a sentence in English language: "C is middle-level language."

We understand the each character, each word of above sentence. We are also very much aware about the placing of the words in the sentence. The meaning is that we cannot put the words at random to form a sentence. We have well-defined rules and grammar for constructing a sentence. For example,

Present Tense, Past tense, future tense,

Each sentence should be terminated by a dot, etc.

We have categories of words, for example noun, pronoun, verb, adverb, etc. When we use some word in a sentence, we have meaning of that word. So, we can say, "A language has a finite set of characters, characters form words, each word has some meaning, and a well-defined grammar that governs the construction of sentences."

The above facts are also applicable for computer languages; overall we are the designer of computer languages. We know that a computer cannot do any thing without instruction. So, there should be instructions and these instructions should be understand by computer system. If instructions are in machine language, a computer can understand directly and there is no need of any translator (or compiler). For example, consider some pseudo instructions of an assembly language:

Instruction	Meaning
ADD R1 R2	Add contents of registers R1 and R2 and store result into R1 register.
SUB R1 R3	Subtract content of register R3 from content of register R1 and store result into R1 register.

Now, suppose there is an assembler that converts the above instructions into binary code. We have defined the ADD, SUB, R1, R2, and R3 in binary as given below:

Mnemonics	Binary Code
ADD	001
SUB	010
R1	01
R2	10
R3	11

The previous two instructions are converted into binary code as given below:

001 01 10

010 01 11

The binary codes for the mnemonics are stored in system library files and definition of the words or functions are stored in system header files. For example, in C language we use header files like "stdio.h", "math.h", "conio.h", etc and library file "CS.LIB". In this chapter we will discuss overview of C language.

10.2 ORIGIN OF C LANGUAGE

The concept of **C** language was put forward in the early 1970s at Bell Laboratories. The concept of **C** was taken from Algol-60. It was developed in 1972 by **Dennis Ritchie.** It is a successor of B language which is successor of BCPL. This is the reason why it is named as **C**. There is an interesting story behind the development of **C**. Actually it was not the motto to develop a language like **C** before a team lead by Thompson and Ritchie working at AT&T Bell Labs. It came into picture all of a sudden. The final shape of **C** language came into existence in 1973. At this time work on **UNIX** system development was going on and Thompson was writing the first **UNIX** version in assembly language. Thompson found difficulty in debugging a program written in assembly language. So, there was a need to develop higher-level language that may provide interface between computers and humans.

With these concepts, a language B was developed and later on when some problems arose; language B was called by a new name **C.** Then **UNIX** operating system was written in **C** language. One of the most interesting things about the **C** language is that its compiler is written in **C.** Today it is one of the most used languages in system programming.

C is an imperative (procedural) systems implementation language. Its design goals were for it to be compiled using a relatively straightforward compiler, provide low-level access to memory, provide language constructs that map efficiently to machine instructions, and require minimal run-time support. **C** was therefore useful for many applications that had formerly been coded in assembly language. Despite its low-level capabilities, the language was designed to encourage machine-independent programming. A standards-compliant and portably written **C** program can be compiled for a very wide variety of computer platforms and operating systems with minimal change to its source code. The language has become available on a very wide range of platforms, from embedded microcontrollers to supercomputers.

10.3 FEATURES OF C LANGUAGE

C language possesses the features of both low-level and high-level languages and this is the reason why it is called middle-level language.

C language provides facilities for programming at register level. It means we can access some hardware feature directly using C language. A program written in this language is much closer to the hardware and it takes less amount of time in execution as compared to the programs developed in high-level languages.

C language is quite close to English language. So, it is very much convenient for programmers to use and this is the reason why program development is easier and less time consuming as compared to low-level languages.

We can program different types of tasks using C language. It is not limited to one field as some other languages are. It has great impact of system programming and general-purpose programming and this is why it does not loss its applicability even after 36 years of birth. Today many object-oriented and high-level languages can incorporate the program code written in C language. This shows the importance of this language. The place of C language in the spectrum of computer languages is shown in Table 10.1.

Table 10.1 Place of C language in Computer Languages

Level of Programming	Language
High-level	COBOL
	Pascal
	Ada
	FORTRAN
	BASIC
Middle-level	C
	C++
	Other Fourth-generation Language
Low-level	Assembly Language
	Machine Language

C language is distinguished by the following characteristics:

A simple, small core language, with extended functionality such as mathematical functions and file handling provided by library routines.

A procedural programming paradigm, with facilities to support structured programming as well.

Low-level access to computer memory via the use of pointers.

Prevents many operations that are not meaningful.

A standardized C preprocessor for macro definition, source code files inclusion, conditional compilation, etc.

A relatively small set of reserved keywords and easier to remember {Table 10.2}.

Parameters that are passed by value; pass-by-reference semantics may be simulated by explicitly passing pointer values.

Pointer to function and static variables, which allow for a rudimentary form of closures and runtime polymorphism

User-defined aggregate data types (struct, union, etc) which allow related data to be combined and manipulated as a group.

There are 32 keywords in C language. Out of which 27 are given by **Kernighan** and **Retchie de facto** standard and remaining 5 added by **ANSI** standardization committee. The keywords of C are shown in **Table 10.2.** The keywords with bold fonts represent the keywords given by the **ANSI-C** committee.

Table 10.2 Keywords of C

auto	double	int	struct
break	else	long	switch
case	**enum**	register	typedef
char	extern	return	union
const	float	short	unsigned
continue	for	**signed**	**void**
default	goto	sizeof	**volatile**
do	if	static	while

Some features that C language lacks that are found in other languages:

Automatic garbage collection

Object-oriented programming features like inheritance that are provide by language like C++, Java, etc.

Compile-time polymorphism in the form of function overloading and operator overloading

Native support for multithreading and networking, though these facilities are provided by standard libraries today.

10.4 WRITING A C PROGRAM

A computer program consists of two parts: **code** and **data.** The code is the set of instructions for performing a task, and the data is the set of "registers" or "memory locations" which contain the intermediate results which are used as the program performs its calculations.

Note that the code is relatively **static** while the data is **dynamic.** Once we have gotten a program working, its code would not change. But every time we run it, it will typically be working with different data, so the memory locations will take on different values.

Once we have written a program, we have defined a new thing that a computer can do. The applications (text and graphic editors, spreadsheets, games, etc.) which a computer may already have are "just" programs, written by programmers using programming languages such as the one we are about to learn.

It is quite interesting to know *"HOW TO START PROGRAMMING IN C LANGUAGE"*. We have to understand some basic things before getting started. There are several elements which programming languages, and programs written in them, typically contain. These elements are found in all languages, not just in **C.** If we understand these elements and what they are for, not only will we understand **C** better. But we will also find learning other programming languages, and moving between different programming languages, much easier.

1. There are **variables** or **objects,** in which we can store the pieces of data that a program is working on. Variables are the way we talk about memory locations (data), and are analogous to the "registers" in our pocket calculator. Variables may be **global** (i.e., accessible anywhere in a program) or **local** (i.e., private to certain parts of a program).
2. There are expressions which compute new values from old ones.
3. There are assignments which store values (of expressions, or other variables) into variables. In many languages, assignment is indicated by an equal (=) sign; thus, we might have

   b = 3 or c = d + e + 1

   The first sets the variable **b** to 3; the second sets the variable **c** to the sum of the variables **d** plus **e** plus 1.

The use of an equal sign can be mildly confusing at first. In mathematics, an equal sign indicates equality, i.e., two things are stated to be inherently equal, for all time. In programming, there is a time element, and a notion of cause-and-effect: after the assignment, the thing on the left-hand side of the assignment statement is equal to what the stuff on the right-hand side was before. To remind meaning of this, we might want to read the equal sign in an assignment as "gets" or "receives"- a = 3 means "a gets 3" or "a receives 3."

A few programming languages use a left arrow for assignment "a ← 3" to make the "receives" relation obvious. But this notation is not too popular, if for no other reason than that few character sets have left arrows in them, and the left arrow key on the keyboard usually moves the cursor rather than typing a left arrow. If assignment seems natural and non-confusing so far, consider the line

i = i + 1

What can this mean? In algebra, we had subtract i from both sides and end up with

0 = 1

which does not make much sense. In programming, however, lines like

i = i + 1

are extremely common, and as long as we remember how assignment works, they are not too hard to understand: the variable i receives (its new value is), as always, what we get when we evaluate the expression on the right-hand side. The expression says to fetch i's (old) value, and add 1 to it, and this new value is what will get stored into i. So i = i + 1 adds 1 to i; we say that it increments i. We will eventually see that, in C, assignments are just another kind of expression.

4. There are conditionals which can be used to determine whether some condition is true, such as whether one number is greater than another. In some languages, including **C,** conditionals are actually expressions which compare two values and compute a "true" or "false" value.
5. **Variables** and **expressions** may have **types,** indicating the nature of the expected values. For instance, we might declare that one variable is expected to hold a number, and that another is expected to hold a piece of text. In many languages (including C), **declarations** of the names of the variables we plan to use and what types we expect them to hold must be explicit.

There are all sorts of data types handled by various computer languages. There are single characters, integers, and "real" (floating point) numbers. There are text strings (i.e., strings of several characters), and there are arrays of integers, reals, or other types. There are types which reference (point at) values of other types. Finally, there may be user-defined data types, such as structures or records, which allow the programmer to build a more complicated data structure, describing a more complicated object, by accreting together several simpler types (or even other user-defined types).

6. There are statements which contain instructions describing what a program actually does. Statements may compute expressions, perform assignments, or call functions.
7. There are control flow constructs which determine what order statements are performed in. A certain statement might be performed only if a condition is true. A sequence of several statements might be repeated over and over, until some condition is met; this is called a loop.
8. An entire set of statements, declarations, and control flow constructs can be lumped together into a function also called routine, subroutine, or procedure.

When we call a function, we transfer control to it and wait for it to do its job, after which it returns to us. It may also return a value as a result of what it has done. We may also pass values to the function on which it will operate or which otherwise direct its work.

Placing code into functions not only avoids repetition if the same sequence of actions must be performed at several places within a program, but it also makes programs easy to understand, because we can see that some function is being called, and performing some (presumably) well-defined subtask, without always concerning programmer with the details of how that function does its job. If we have ever done any knitting, we know that knitting instructions are often written with little sub-instructions or patterns which describe a sequence of stitches which is to be performed multiple times during the course of the main piece. These sub-instructions are like function calls in programming.

9. A set of functions, global variables, and other elements makes up a program. An additional wrinkle is that the source code for a program may be distributed among one or more source files. In the other direction, it is also common for a suite of related programs to work closely together to perform some larger task, but we will not worry about that "large scale integration" for now.
10. In the process of specifying a program in a form suitable for a compiler, there are usually a few logistical details to keep track of. These details may involve the specification of compiler parameters or interdependencies between different functions and other parts of the program. Specifying these details often involves miscellaneous syntax which does not fall into any of the other categories listed above, and which we might lump together as "boilerplate."

Many of these elements exist in a hierarchy. A program typically consists of functions and global variables. A function is made up of statements and statements usually contain expressions, expressions operate on objects. It is also possible to extend the hierarchy in the other direction; for instance, sometimes several interrelated but distinct programs are assembled into a suite, and used in concert to perform complex tasks. The various "office" packages-integrated word processor, spreadsheet, etc are an example.

As we mentioned, many of the concepts in programming are somewhat arbitrary. This is particularly so for the terms expression, statement, and function. All of these could be defined as "an element of a program that actually does something." The differences are mainly in the level at which the "something" is done, and it is not necessary at this point to define those "levels." We will come to understand them as we begin to write programs.

10.5 STRUCTURE OF C PROGRAM

Just as a book is composed of chapters which are composed of sections which are composed of paragraphs which are composed of sentences which are composed of words which are composed of letters, so is a program composed of functions which are composed of statements which are composed of expressions which are in fact composed of smaller elements which we would not bother to define. Analogies are never perfect, though, and this one is weaker than most; it still does not tell us anything about what expressions, statements, and functions really are. If "expression" and "statement" and "function" seem like totally arbitrary words to us, use the analogy to understand that what they are, is arbitrary words describing arbitrary levels in the hierarchical composition of a program, just as "sentence," "paragraph," and "chapter" are different levels of structure within a book.

In the above section we have presented very general terms, describing features common to most conventional computer languages. If we understand these elements at a relatively abstract level, then learning a new computer language becomes a relatively simple matter of finding out how that language implements each of the elements. Of course, we cannot understand these abstract elements in isolation; it helps to have concrete examples to map them too. If we have never programmed before, most of this section has probably seemed like words without meaning.

Finally, there is no need to overdo the abstraction. For the simple programs we will be writing, in a language like C, the series of calculations and other operations that actually takes place as our program runs is a simpleminded translation (into terms the computer can understand) of the expressions, statements, functions, and other elements of the program. Expressions are evaluated and their results assigned to variables. Statements are executed one after the other, except when the control flow is modified by if/then conditionals and loops. Functions are called to perform subtasks, and return values to their callers which have been waiting for them.

There is one initial file <stdio.h> that is to be included in a program. The system library file "CS.lib" is automatically added to a program when compiler runs. So, we have not to include this into a program but we have to include the necessary header files. One thing noticeable about the header files that these all are ".h" files and included in a program starting with symbol '#' followed by the word "include" and the name of header file is enclosed in < > or " ". For example,

```
#include <stdio.h>
#include <math.h>
#include <conio.h>
```

We include the header files as per need in a program. For example, math.h header file is used when we need some mathematical calculations, but the header file stdio.h (stands for standard input/output) is always there when we develop a program.

Now, the next part is the main function written as main(). This is the main body of a program. When a compiler compiles a program and that program runs, it is always started with the main function. So, we always have a main function while running a program. One cannot think about multiple main functions in a single program. We can have only one main function in a single program. A program written in C language is always saved as ".c" or ".C" file.

Function main() is a part of every C program. C permits different forms of main statement. Following forms are allowed:

```
main()
int main()
```

```
void main()
main(void)
void main(void)
int main(void)
```

Empty pair of parenthesis indicates that the function has no arguments. This may be explicitly indicated by using the keyword void inside the parenthesis. We may also specify the keyword int or void before the word main. The keyword void means that the function does not return any value to the operating system and int means that the function returns an integer value to the operating system. When int is specified, the last statement in the program must be "return 0". For the sake of simplicity, we use the first form in programs.

Now let us see the structure of a C program which is given in Figure 10.1. The document section consists of comment lines giving the name of the program, program author, etc see Example 1. The link section provides instructions to the compiler to link functions from the system library. The definition section defines all symbolic constants. There are some variables which are used in the entire program are also defined here are called global parameters. These parameters declared outside of every function used in the program segment.

Every program has one main() function section. This section having two parts- declaration section and executable code section. These two sections appear between '{' and '}' and there must be at least one executable statement. In the declaration section we define those parameters which have scope within the function main(). The program execution begins at opening brace '{' and ends at closing brace '}'. The closing brace of the function main is being logical end of the program. All the statements in the declaration and execution parts end with a semicolon.

All the sections, except the main function section may be absent when they are not required.

Documentation section	**Main section**

Link section
Definition section
Global declaration section
main ( ) Function Section
{
Declaration section
Executable code section
statement 1;
statement 2;
...
statement n;
}
Subprogram section	

Function 1 Function 2 Function 3 ... Function n	User defined functions

Figure 10.1 An overview of a C Program

We can see that after the main function the opening curly bracket "{" is there and there are n number of statements ending in semicolon (;) and finally the closing curly bracket "}".

10.6 STARTING PROGRAMMING IN C

Let us start with the simplest possible C program and use it to understand the basics of C and the C compilation process. Type the following program into a standard text editor (vi or any other which is convenient). Then save the program to a file named **Test.c.** If we leave off **.c,** we will probably get some sort of error when we compile it. Here is the first Example 1.

Example 1: Write a program which is displaying the information "This is my first program in C Language", on your standard output device.

Answer: This problem is defined as per Figure 10.1 and is containing **documentation** section, **link** section, and the **main** function section.

```
/* Test.c */
#include <stdio.h>

int main()
{
    printf("This is my first program in C Language!\n");
    return 0;
}
```

The first line is practically boilerplate; it will appear in almost all programs we write. It asks that some definitions having to do with the "Standard input/output (I/O) Library" be included in our program; these definitions are needed if we are to call the library function **printf** correctly.

The second line says that we are defining a function named main. Most of the time, we can name our functions anything we want, but the function name main is special: it is the function that will be "called" first when our program starts running. The empty pair of parentheses indicates that our main function accepts no arguments, that is, there is not any information which needs to be passed in when the function is called.

The braces { and } surround a list of statements in C. Here, they surround the list of statements making up the function main(). The line

```
printf("This is my first program in C Language!\n");
```

is the first statement in the program. It asks that the function printf be called; printf is a library function which prints formatted output. The parenthesis surround printf's argument list: the information which is handed to it which it should act on. The semicolon at the end of the line terminates the statement.

printf's first (and, in this case, only) argument is the string which it should print. The string, enclosed in double quotes "", consists of the words "This is my first program in C Language!" followed by a special sequence: \n. In strings, any two-character sequence beginning with the backslash \ represents a single special character. The sequence \n represents the "new line" character, which prints a carriage return or line feed or whatever it takes to end one line of output and move down to the next. This program only prints one line of output, but it is still important to terminate it. The second line in the main function is

```
return 0;
```

In general, a function may return a value to its caller, and main is no exception. When main returns (that is, reaches its end and stops functioning), the program is at its end, and the return value from main tells the operating system (or whatever invoked the program that main is the main function off) whether it succeeded or not. By convention, a return value of 0 indicates success.

Example 2 is of little more practical use than the first, but it introduces a few more programming language elements:

Example 2: Write a program which prints ten numeric digits on your screen in ten different lines.

Answer: The following code is implementing the above discussion.

```
/* Test2.c */
#include <stdio.h>
# define N 10
/* print a few numbers, to illustrate a simple loop */

main()
{
    int i;
    for(i = 0; i < N; i = i + 1)
     printf("i is %d\n", i);

    return 0;
}
```

As before, the line #include <stdio.h> is boilerplate which is necessary since we are calling the printf function, and main() and the pair of braces {} indicate and delineate the function named main we are (again) writing.

Second line after #include <stdio.h> is # define instruction. A #define instruction defines value to a symbolic constant for use in the program. Whenever a symbolic name is encountered, the compiler substitutes the value associated with the name automatically. To change the value we have to simply change the definition. In this example we have defined one symbolic constant N and assigned value 10. A # define is a preprocessor compiler directive and not a statement. Therefore #define lines should not end with a semicolon.

We must note that the defined constants are not variables. We may not change their values the program by using an assignment statement. For example, the statement

N=10;

The first new line is the line

/* print a few numbers, to illustrate a simple loop */

which is a **comment.** Anything between the characters /* and */ is ignored by the compiler, but may be useful to a person trying to read and understand the program. We can add comments anywhere we want to, in the program, to document what the program is, what it does, who wrote it, how it works, what the various functions are for and how they work, what the various variables are for, etc.

The second new line, down within the function main, is

int i;

which declares that our function will use a variable named i. The variable's type is int, which is a plain integer.

Next, we set up a loop:

for(i = 0; i < N; i = i + 1)

The keyword for indicates that we are setting up a "for loop." A for loop is controlled by three expressions, enclosed in parentheses and separated by semicolons. These expressions say that, in this case, the loop starts by setting i to 0, that it continues as long as i is less than 10, and that after each iteration of the loop, i should be incremented by 1 (that is, have 1 added to its value).

Finally, we have a call to the printf function, as before, but with several differences. First, the call to printf is within the body of the for loop. This means that control flow does not pass once through the printf call, but instead that the call is performed as many times as are dictated by the **for** loop. In this case, printf will be called several times: once when i is 0, once when i is 1, once when i is 2, and so on until i is 9, for a total of 10 times.

A second difference in the printf call is that the string to be printed, "i is %d", contains a percent sign. Whenever printf sees a percent sign, it indicates that printf is not supposed to print the exact text of the string, but is instead supposed to read another one of its arguments to decide what to print. The letter after the percent sign tells it what type of argument to expect and how to print it. In this case, the letter d indicates that printf is to expect an int, and to print it in decimal. Finally, we see that printf is in fact being called with another argument, for a total of two, separated by commas. The second argument is the variable i, which is in fact an int, as required by %d. The effect of all of this is that each time it is called, printf will print a line containing the current value of the variable i:

```
i is 0
i is 1
i is 2
...
```

After several trips through the loop, i will eventually equal 9. After that trip through the loop, the third control expression i = i + 1 will increment its value to 10. The condition i < 10 is no longer true, so no more trips through the loop are taken. Instead, control flow jumps down to the statement following the **for** loop, which is the return statement. The main function returns, and the program is finished.

So far, we have used only function that has been provided for us by the C Compiler. Now we will present Example 3 in which we consider user-defined function. See the following program segment:

Example 3: Write a C program which works on the definition of Figure 10.1. The program must perform addition of two integer numbers by using user defined function. This must receive two integers and return an integer. Invoke the function by calling it into function main().

Answer: Following is the implementation code.

```
/** add.c **/
#include<stdio.h>
int add(int , int); /* declaration */
main()
{
    int m, n, result;
     m=20;
     n=15;
     result = add(m, n);
     printf("Result = %d", result);
     return 0;
}

int add(int a, int b)
{
```

```
        int result = 0;
        result = a + b;
        return(result);
    }
```

OUTPUT
Result = 35

In the above program segment we have defined function **add(int, int)** which is equivalent to the function defined in other languages viz., FORTRAN, PASCAL, etc. This function finds summation of two int arguments a and b and assigns the summation to the variable result which is returned to the main() when it is invoked in the statement

result = add(m, n);

The values of m and n are passed onto a and b, respectively when function **add()** is called. Function add() is user defined function. More details about user defined we will consider in later chapters.

10.7 COMPILING C PROGRAMS

Process of processing a program is shown in Figure 10.2. First we need to prepare source code (write a C program) then input to the system, at this stage if required edit the code before submitting it to the translator (compiler/assembler) otherwise forward directly to the compiler/assembler. Translator translates (compiles/assembles) the code as a whole and reports the errors if any with their appropriate type and statement and line number of the code. Translator at this stage reports only syntax errors. When all syntax errors are removed Translator generates object code. Then the linker is called which attaches the library files, required for the used library function (s). After linking the library file(s) it generates executable (binary) codes and forwards to the loader. Loader on receiving the code checks it. If any portion of the code is not properly compiled it compiles the same. Finally loader loads the executable codes into the system memory for the execution. Program during execution may ask for some input data. After getting input data during execution logical (semantic errors) and data errors are checked if data error is there new input data is provided and code is re-executed. If after feeding correct data to the code, result is not correct means there is semantic error in the code, sometimes an appropriate message (s) is displayed regarding semantic errors. Then control is transferred to edit the source code. The above process is repeated till all the existing errors are not removed.

On a UNIX machine, type **cc program file -o object file** (if cc does not work, try gcc). This line invokes the C compiler called cc, asks it to compile **program file** and asks it to place the executable code into the object code file. For example if program file is **test1.c** and object file name is test1. Then the procedure to compile test1.c under UNIX/LINUX is

$ cc test1.c

or

$ cc -o test1 test1.c

or

$ cc test1.c -o test1

There are several options available with the compiler choose as per need of the program. The first option generates an executable file a.out that can be run by giving command:

$a.out

or

$./a.out

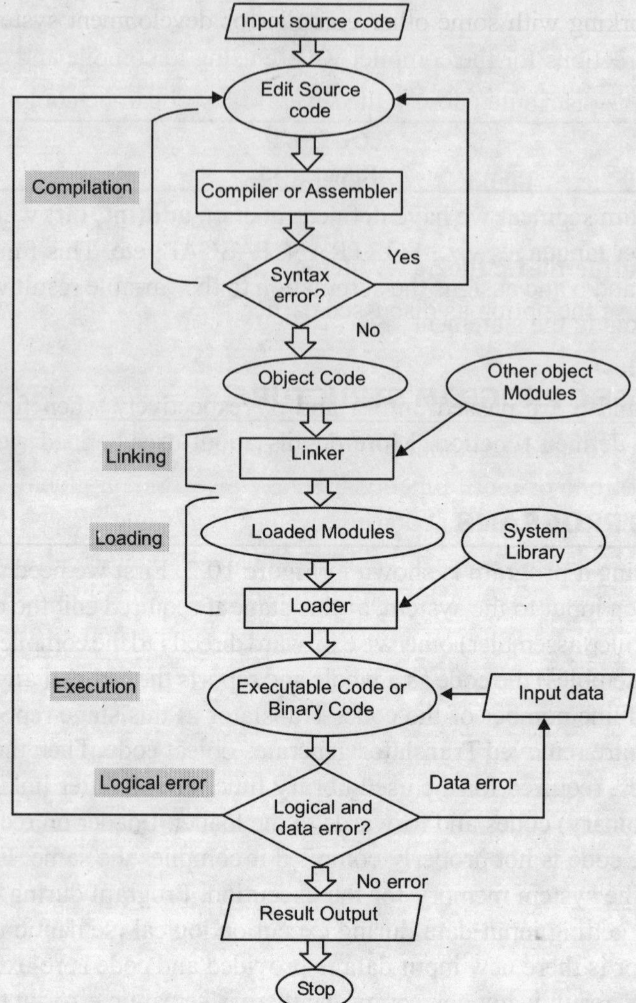

Figure 10.2 Processes of Compiling and Running a C Program

Second and third option generates test1 as an executable file which can be run as

$test1

or

$./test1

On a DOS or Windows machine using TCC, at an MS-DOS prompt type **TCC test1.c -o test1.obj.** This line invokes the C compiler called TCC, asks it to compile **test1.c** and asks it to place the object code in file it creates under the name **test1.obj.** To create executable codes for this object code use **tlink object** code file (here test1.obj) then it will generate an executable file with same name as object code was, i.e., **test1.**exe. To run the program, type test1. There are several options available with the compiler choose as per need of the program.

If we are using Turbo-C compiler and using turbo editor simply press CRTL and F9 keys together to compile and run the code. It will create test1.exe if test1.c is compiled, if test2.c is compiled it will generate test2.exe executable code file. For viewing the result press ALT and F5 keys together to see the result.

If we are working with some other compiler or development system, we need to read and follow the directions for the compiler we are using to compile and executing the program.

If a program is distributed across the several files, it can be compiled and run under UNIX environment as:

$cc file1.c file2.c ... filen.c -o outputfile

or

$cc -o outputfile file1.c file2.c ... filen.c

To run the code use the option as discussed earlier.

$./outputfile

10.8 DISECTION OF C PROGRAM STRUCTURE

We will have more to say later about program structure, but for now let us observe a few basics. A program consists of one or more functions; it may also contain global variables. (Our first two examples so far have contained one function apiece, and no global variables. Third example containing two functions main() and a user defined function add() once again no global declaration). At the top of a source file are typically a few boilerplate lines such as #include <stdio.h>, followed by the definitions (prototype of the function), i.e., code for the functions. It is also possible to split up the several functions making up a larger program into several source files.

Each function is further composed of declarations and statements, in that order. When a sequence of statements should act as one for example, when they should all serve together as the body of a loop, they can be enclosed in braces just as for the outer body of the entire function. The simplest kind of statement is an expression statement, which is an expression (presumably performing some useful operation) followed by a semicolon. Expressions are further composed of operators, objects (variables), and constants.

C source code consists of several lexical elements. Some are words, such as for, return, main, and i, which are either keywords of the language (for, return) or identifiers (names) we have chosen for our own functions and variables (main, i). There are constants such as 1 and 10 which introduce new values into the program. There are operators such as =, +, and >, which manipulate variables and values. There are other punctuation characters (often called delimiters), such as parentheses and squiggly braces {}, which indicate how the other elements of the program are grouped. Finally, all of the preceding elements can be separated by whitespace: spaces, tabs, and the "carriage returns" between lines.

The source code for a C program is, for the most part, "free form." This means that the compiler does not care how the code is arranged: how it is broken into lines, how the lines are indented, or whether whitespace is used between things like variable names and other punctuation. (Lines like #include <stdio.h> are an exception; they must appear alone on their own lines, generally unbroken. Only lines beginning with # are affected by this rule; we will see other examples later.) We can use whitespace, indentation, and appropriate line breaks to make programs more readable for reader (even though the compiler does not care). We can place explanatory comments anywhere in the program- any text between the characters /* and */ is ignored by the compiler. In fact, the compiler pretends that all it saw was whitespace. Though comments are ignored by the compiler, well-chosen comments can make a program much easier to read (for its author, as well as for others).

The usage of whitespace is our first style issue. It is typical to leave a blank line between different parts of the program, to leave a space on either side of operators such as + and =, and to indent the bodies of loops and other control flow constructs. Typically, we arrange the indentation so that the subsidiary statements controlled by a loop statement (the "loop body," such as the printf call in our second example program) are all aligned with each other and placed one tab stop (or some consistent number of spaces) to the right of the controlling statement. This indentation (like all whitespace) is not required by the compiler, but it makes programs much easier to read. However, it can also be misleading, if used incorrectly or in the face of inadvertent mistakes. The compiler will decide what "the body of the loop" is based on its own rules, not the indentation, so if the indentation does not match the compiler's interpretation, confusion is inevitable.

To drive home the point that the compiler does not care about indentation, line breaks, or other whitespace, here are a few (extreme) examples: The fragments

```
for(i = 0; i < 10; i = i + 1)
        printf("%d\n", i);
```

and

```
for(i = 0; i < 10; i = i + 1)
        printf("%d\n", i);
```

and

```
for(i=0;i<10;i=i+1)
        printf("%d\n",i);
```

and

```
  for(i = 0; i < 10; i = i + 1)
        printf("%d\n", i);
```

and

```
for (i=0;i<10;i=i        +1)
        printf("%d\n", i);
```

and

```
for (i=0; i<10;i= i+1)

        printf("%d\n", i);
```

are all treated exactly the same way by the compiler.

Some programmers argue forever over the best set of "rules" for indentation and other aspects of programming style, calling to mind the old philosopher's debates about the number of angels that could dance on the head of a pin. Style issues (such as how a program is laid out) are important, but they are not something to be too dogmatic about, and there are also other, deeper style issues besides mere layout and typography. Although C compilers do not care about how a program looks, proper indentation and spacing are critical in making programs easy for people to read. We recommend writing only one statement per line, and using blanks around operators to clarify grouping. The position of braces is less important, although people hold passionate beliefs. We have chosen one of several popular styles. Pick a style that suits, and then use it consistently.

There is some value in having a reasonably standard style (or a few standard styles) for code layout. Please do not take the above advice to "pick a style that suits" as an invitation to invent own brand-new style. If we have specific objections to specific facets of existing styles, we are welcome to modify them, but if we do not have any particular leanings, we are probably best off copying an existing style at first. If we want to place own stamp of originality on the programs that we write, there are better avenues for creativity than inventing a bizarre layout; we might instead try to make the logic easier to follow, or the user interface easier to use, or the code freer of bugs.

EXERCISES

Multiple Choice Questions

1. Keyword added by ANSI-C
   (a) enum (b) switch
   (c) sizeof (d) none
2. Keywords in 'C' Language are
   (a) 27 (b) 32
   (c) 5 (d) none
3. Keywords added in 'C' by ANSI-C
   (a) 27 (b) 32
   (c) 5 (d) none
4. Place of 'C' in computer language
   (a) middle level (b) high level
   (c) low level (d) none
5. 'C' provides facility for programming at
   (a) register level (b) hardware level
   (c) both (a) and (b) (d) none
6. In strings any two char sequences beginning with represent
   (a) single char (b) two char
   (c) both (a)&(b) (d) none
7. Anything between /* and*/
   (a) ignored by compiler (b) considered by compiler
   (c) both (a) and (b) (d) none

State whether the following statements are true or false

1. Every statement in a C program ends with a comma.
2. In C language lowercase and uppercase letters are significant.
3. Every C program starts with a BEGIN word.
4. main() is the statement from where the program begins its execution.
5. A line in a program may have more than one statement
6. A printf statement can generate only one line of output.
7. The closing brace of the main( ) in a program is the logical end of the program.
8. The purpose of the header file such as stdio.h is to store the source code of a program
9. Comments cause the computer to print the text enclosed between /* and */ when executed
10. Syntax errors will be detected by the compiler.
11. Every C program must have at least one user-defined function.
12. Only one function may be named main().
13. Declaration section contains instructions to the computer.

Which of the following statements about comments are false

1. Use of comments reduces the speed of execution of a program.
2. Comments serve as internal documentation for programmers.
3. A comment can be inserted in the middle of a statement.
4. In C, we can have comments inside comments.

Fill in the blanks with appropriate words in each of the following statements

1. Every statement in a C program must end with a ____________
2. The ________________ function is used to display the output on the standard output device (monitor).
3. The ____________________ header file contains input/output functions.
4. The escape sequence character ____________ causes the cursor to move to the next line on the screen.

Given a set of 100 numbers write an algorithm to find the sum and total number of even and odd numbers in list.

Find errors , if any, in the following progam

```
/* A simple program */
int main( );
{
    /* Does nothing */
}
```

Find errors , if any, in the following progam

```
#include (stdio.h)
void main(void)
{
    print("Hello C");
}
```

Find errors , if any, in the following progam

```
#include <math.h>
void main { }
(
    float X;
    X = 2.5;
    Y = exp(X);
    printf(x, y);
}
```

Descriptive and Programming Problems

1. Design an algorithm to find the summation of the following series:
   (a) n + (n – 1) + (n – 2) +(n – 3)…+1 + 0, where n = 100
   (b) 1 + 2 + 3 +…+ 100
   (c) 1 + 3 + 5 +…+ 101
   (d) 0 + 2 + 4 +…+ 200
   (e) n! + (n – 1)! + (n – 2)! +…+1! + 0!, where n = 10
2. Construct flowchart to find out summation of the following series:
   (a) n + (n – 1) + (n – 2) + (n – 3)…+1+0, where n = 100
   (b) n! + (n – 1)! + (n – 2)! +…+1! + 0!, where n = 10

3. Write an algorithm to find out the value of x^y, where x and y are two positive integers.
4. Draw flowchart to find out the greatest common divisor of two integer numbers.
5. Draw flowchart to find out digits of a number.
6. A Company manufactures three product engines, pumps and fans. It gives a discount of 25 percent on orders for engines, if the order is worth Rs. 10,000 or more. The same discount or more on fan orders of value 5000 or more and on pump orders value Rs. 7000 or more. On all other orders, they do not give any discount. Prepare flowchart for this decision problem.
7. Define the features of C language.
8. Define the algorithm. What is the need of algorithms in computer world?
9. Why flowchart is much expressive as compared to an algorithm?
10. Why and when do we use the #include directive?
11. What does void main(void) mean?
12. Distinguish between the following pairs:
    (a) main() and void main(void)
    (b) int main( ) and void main( )
13. Why the look of a program is important?
14. There are blank spaces permitted in a C program?
15. Describe the structure of a C program.
16. Describe the process of creating and executing a C program under UNIX and DOS system.
17. Given two integers 20 and 10, write a program that uses a function add( ) to add these two numbers and sub( ) to find the difference of these two numbers and then display the sum and difference in the following form: .
    20 + 10 = 30
    20 – 10 = 10
18. How do we implement multiple source program files?
19. Given the values of three variables x, y and z, write a program to compute and display the value of a, where. Execute the program for the following values:
    (a) x = 125, y = 85, z = 25
    (b) x = 150, y = 70, z = 70

Variables, Constants and Data Types

11.1 INTRODUCTION

In the previous chapter we have discussed about how to start programming in C. First we include the necessary header files and then define the main function. Each statement of C terminates by semicolon. If we miss the semicolon, we will get an error message from C compiler. We have not discussed about the type of checking performed by a compiler. There are two types of checking performed by a compiler and based on these we categorize the errors in two categories:

1. **Syntax Error, and**
2. **Semantic Error**

Syntax checking is all about deciding whether a program is grammatically developed or not and semantic checking is about deciding the meaning of the instructions of a program. For example, if we place colon in place of semicolon to end a statement in C language, it result in a syntax error and dividing a number by zero results in semantic error. The missing of semicolon is grammatical error where as the division of a number by zero is illegal operation in C language.

In our general life also, we follow the grammar while using a natural language and we take care of the meaning of the sentences used. If somebody speaks grammatically fine but the meaning of narration is not clear to the listener then this type of speaking does not achieve the objective. Same thing is also true for computer languages. So, a program should be grammatically developed and the instructions of the program should be well defined for a computer system.

11.2 BASIC CHARACTER SET OF C

Characters play a central role in C language. When we write a program, we express C source files as text lines containing characters from the source character set. When a program executes in the target environment, it uses characters from the target character set. These character sets are related, but need not have the same encoding or all the same members. Every character set contains a distinct code value for each character in the basic C character set. A character set can also contain additional characters with other code values. For example,

1. The **character constant** 'x' becomes the value of the code for the character corresponding to x in the target character set.
2. The **string literal** "xyz" becomes a sequence of character constants stored in successive bytes of memory, followed by a byte containing the value zero: {'x', 'y', 'z', '\0'}

A string literal is one way to specify a null-terminated string, an array of zero or more bytes followed by a byte containing the value zero. Visible graphic characters in the basic C character set are shown in Table .1.

Table .1 C Character Set

Form	Members
Alphabet	A B C D E F G H I J K L MN O P Q R S T U V W X Y Za b c d e f g h i j k l mn o p q r s t u v w x y z
Numeric	0 1 2 3 4 5 6 7 8 9
underscore	_
punctuation	! " # % & ' ( ) * + , - . / :; < = > ? [\ ] ^ { | } ~

The code value zero is reserved for the **null character** which is always in the target character set. Code values for the basic C character set are positive when stored in an object of type char. Code values for the digits are contiguous, with increasing value. For example, '0' + 5 equals '5'. Code values for any two letters are not necessarily contiguous.

Escape Sequences: Within character constants and string literals, we can write a variety of escape sequences. Each escape sequence determines the code value for a single character. We use escape sequences to represent character codes:

we cannot otherwise write (such as \n)
that can be difficult to read properly (such as \t)
that might change value in different target character sets (such as \a)
that must not change in value among different target environments (such as \0)

Mnemonic escape sequences help us to remember the characters they represent {Table 11.2}. An escape sequence takes the form as shown in Figure 11.1.

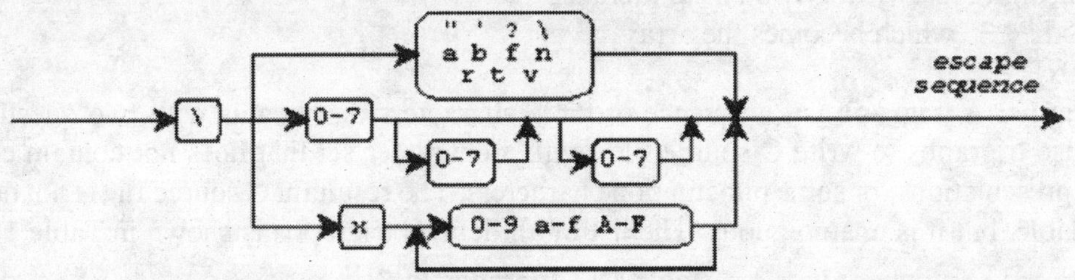

Figure 11.1 Sequence of the escape sequences

Table 11.2 Escape Sequences

Escape Character	Meaning	Short Notation
\n	New Line	NL
\t	Horizontal Tab	HT
\a	Bell	BEL
\b	Back Space	BS
\f	Form Feed	FF
\r	Carriage Return	CR

\v	Vertical Tab	VT
\\	Back Slash	BAS
\?	Question Mark	QM
\'	Single Quote	SQ
\	Double Quote	DQ
\onnn	Octal Number	ON
\xhhh	Hexadecimal Number	HN
\0	Null Character	NC

We can also write **numeric escape sequences** using either octal or hexadecimal digits. An **octal escape sequence** takes one of the forms:

\d **or** \dd **or** \ddd

The escape sequence yields a code value that is the numeric value of the 1, 2, or 3-digit octal number following the backslash (\). Each d can be any digit in the range 0-7.

A **hexadecimal escape sequence** takes one of the forms:

\xh **or** \xhh **or ...**

The escape sequence yields a code value that is the numeric value of the arbitrary-length hexadecimal number following the backslash (\). Each h can be any decimal digit 0-9, or any of the letters a-f or A-F. The letters represent the digit values 10-15, where either a or A has the value 10.

A numeric escape sequence terminates with the first character that does not fit the digit pattern. Here are some examples:

- We can write the null character as '\0'.
- We can write a newline character (NL) within a string literal by writing:
  "hi\n" **which becomes the array**
  {'h', 'i', '\n'}
- We can write a string literal that begins with a specific numeric value:
  "\3abc" **which becomes the array**
  {3, 'a', 'b', 'c', 0}
- We can write a string literal that contains the hexadecimal escape sequence \xF followed by the digit 3 by writing two string literals:
  "\xF" "3" which becomes the array
  {0xF, '3', 0}

Trigraphs: A **trigraph** is a sequence of three characters that begins with two question marks (??). We use trigraphs to write C source files with a character set that does not contain convenient graphic representations for some punctuation characters. The resultant C source file is not necessarily more readable, but it is unambiguous. The list of all defined trigraphs is shown in Table 11.3.

Table 11.3 Trigraphs in C

Character	Trigraph
[	??(
\	??/
]	??)
^	??'
{	??<
|	??!
}	??>
~	??-
#	??=

These are the only trigraphs. The translator does not alter any other sequence that begins with two question marks. For example, the expression statements:

printf("Case ??=3 is done??/n");

printf("You said what????/n");

are equivalent to:

printf("Case #3 is done\n");

printf("You said what??\n");

The translator replaces each trigraph with its equivalent single character representation in an early phase of translation. We can always treat a trigraph as a single source character.

11.3 VARIABLES AND NAMING RULES

We have seen in the previous chapter that we use some variable to hold some data and data has some category such as int, float, string, etc. We use names for other purposes also for example, function's name, data structure name, etc.

Variables play an important role in computer programming because they enable programmers to write flexible programs. Rather than entering data directly into a program, a programmer can use variables to represent the data. Then, when the program is executed, the variables are replaced with real data. This makes it possible for the same program to process different sets of data. The names that are used to reference variables, functions, labels and various user-defined objects, etc are called identifiers (variables), and a data type. A variable's data type indicates what sort of value the variable represents, such as whether it is an integer, a floating-point number, or a character. For example,

- int number;
- float temp1, temp2;
- int age;

The size of an identifier in C language can vary from 1 to 32 characters. The first character must be a letter or an underscore ('_') character with subsequent characters being letters, numbers or underscores. We can define an identifier in lower case letters or in upper case letters or in combination. But, the keywords of C language are always in small letters. For example,

- char Left_right;
- int __date123;
- int year_2006;
- int January_2006;

One can think that what the need of underscore character in identifiers is. It is good practice that we use names (identifiers) such that these reflect some sense or carry some meaning. For example,

- lont int date_of_birth;
- char Company_Name[100];
- char father_name[50];
- char mother_name[40];
- int Flat_no;
- float Square_root_of_integers;

Following are incorrect declarations:

- int 2number; /*Leading character is numeric */
- float; /* Keyword */

```
char .right;              /* Leading character is special character dot */
char father.name[50];     /*In the middle there is a special character dot */
int num&num'              /* In the middle there is a special character & */
float Tem;p;              /* character semicolon is special character */
char My_flat_No_street_no_city_name_country_name[150];
                          /*Invalid identifier name, more than 32 characters are used */
```

If we declare function names according to the above definition, following are valid function names:

```
float _function_square_root( );
int set_xy_value( );
char function1( );
int Finding_date( );
```

Following are invalid function names:

```
int 2fun();
float 2_fun_();
.int integer_to_integer();
int length.calculation();
char !function();
double yes_function_$_function();
char *function_is_a_feature_of_c_language();
```

11.4 PRIMITIVE DATA TYPES

We have discussed that each variable which is used in the program required to be declared first. It means, when we declare a variable within a program, it is required to tell **C** compiler about the variables' name and its data type. A data type defines the set of values the variable can store, as well as the set of operations that can be performed on the data.

For example, integer, character, float, etc. we cannot perform division on characters. So, for each data type variable there are set of permissible operations in **C** language. **C** language supports five primary data types which are shown in Table 11.4.

Table 11.4 Data Types in C

Data Type (Keyword)	Meaning
int	Integer
char	Character or String
float	Floating-point
double	Used with int and float data types for larger numbers.
void	Accept any type of data based on cast operator it returns the value

11.4.1 The int

The keyword **int** in C language is used to define integer data type. **C** uses the type int to store integer data that may be positive or negative. **C** compiler normally allocates 16-bit to store data of the type **int,** but it is compiler dependent and may vary from compiler to compiler, viz., under windows and DOS it allocates 16-bit, Window-NT allocates 32-bit because it is 32-bit Operating System, similarly UNIX and LINUX allocates 32-bit in normal case. A variable of type **int** can store data in the range of -32,768 to 32767. Out of 16-bit the most significant bit (MSB) is used for sign representation. It means 15-bit are used for magnitude representation. The **int** data type always stores integer data and used to operate integer arithmetic operations. For example, following declarations are correct in C language:

```
int number1, number2, Temp=0;
int integer_no = 15;
int first_num, second_num;
```

Following declarations are incorrect:

```
int first_num=15.0;
int temp = harry;
```

We use string "%d" with printf() function to print an integer data type as given below:

```
printf("%d", number1);
printf("number1 = %d", number1);
printf("The first number is: %d", first_number);
```

We can see that we have used printf function differently. Suppose number1 = 20, first_number = 100, then outcome of the above statements are in the following sequence:

20

Number1=20

The first number is: 100

The conclusion is that we can use the *printf* ( ) function as per our convenience with some appropriate message. Go through the Example 1 which is implementing the above discussion.

Example 1: Write a C program which receives a floating point number and prints an integer.

Answer: In the following program segment, the variable num is int type but we have assigned data 50.5 which is real number. The compiler will only allocate the integer part of this data, i.e., num=50.

```
#include<stdio.h>
main( )
{
    int num;
    num = 50.5 ;
    printf("Value of num = %d", num);
}
```

OUTPUT
Value of num = 50

11.4.2 The char

The **char** data type is used to hold **ASCII** (American Standard Code for Information Interchange) characters and there is generally 8-bit or 1 byte memory reservation for it. The compiler normally allocates 8-bits to store data of type **char**. A variable of type **char** can store data in the range –128 to 127, but storage of a character data type is dependent on a compiler. The most significant bit in 8-bit memory is reserved for sign and remaining 7-bit is used for representing binary value of character. The syntax to declare char type variable is given below:

char var1, var2, var3, …, varn;

For example,

- char ch, x, y, z ;
- char str, temp;
- char ch ='Y', x='N'; /* in this declaration we have assigned values to character type variable during declaration, i.e., ch is assigned value 'Y' and x will receive value 'N' */
- char A='a', b='B'; /* A receives 'a' and b receives 'B' */
- char name='Z'; /* name is assigned value 'Z' */

We can print a character using printf( ) function in the similar way as we have for integer type; we put "%c" in place of "%d" as given below:

- printf("%c", x);
- printf(" Entered Character is: %c", ch);
- printf("First character is: %c   and second character is: %c", x, y);

Go through the Example 2 which is implementing the above discussion.

Example 2: Write a 'C' code to print a character and also its ASCI value.

Answer: We will discuss this problem in two steps. In the first part of the code we implement the character printing and in next part ASCI code of the character.

In the following program segment, identifier **ch** is defined as **char** type. In next statement it assigns character 'Y' to **ch** and finally prints the information associated with the variable **ch.**

```
/* The char type data can be processed */
    #include<stdio.h>
    main()
    {
            char ch ;
            ch = 'Y' ;
    printf("Value of ch  = %c", ch);
    }
```

OUTPUT
Value of ch = Y

A character quoted within a single quote is used to assign a character constant value to a parameter. In the above example, we have assigned character Y to variable ch. Here, **ch** will store **ASCII** value of character **c.** Consider the following program segment that outputs the ASCII value of character **c.**

```
/* ASCII value associated with a char type parameter */
    #include<stdio.h>
    void main()
    {
        char ch='c' ;
        printf("ASCII value of ch = %d",ch);
    }
```

OUTPUT
ASCII value of ch = 99

The output 99 is **ASCII** value of character c. From this example, it can be seen that if we change the output format we get the **ASCII** value of a character. It means if we use "%d" in place of "%c" then we can get ASCII value of a character.

11.4.3 The float

C language provides keyword **float** to store floating-point data. An identifier to declare a floating-point data follows the keyword float. **C** compiler normally allocates 32-bits to store floating-point data; it is dependent on a compiler. A variable of type **float** can store data with 6 to 7 of precision in the range of 3.4E-38 to 3.4E+38 (value of E is 10). The MSB is used for sign, next 8-bit is used for exponent and remaining 23-bit is used for mantissa. We declare a float type as follows:

- float real_number;
- float num=12.99;
- float number= 20;

If we assign integer value to a float type variable then C compiler stores it as a floating-point number. We can print the value of a float type variable by using "%f" with the help of printf function. For example,

- printf("The value of real_number is: %f ", real_number);
- printf("Value of num = %f ", num);
- printf("You have entered the value of number = %f ", number);

Go through the Example 3 which is implementing the above discussion.

Example 3: Write a 'C' code which takes input real (floating point) number and prints the same.

Answer: The following program segment prints the value of real_number.

```
/* The float data type declaration */
    #include<stdio.h>
    void main()
    {
        float real_number ;
        real_number = 130.7 ;
        printf("Value of real_number = %f",x);
    }
```

OUTPUT
Value of real_number = 130.7

11.4.4 The double

We have discussed that C compiler allocates 16-bit for **int** data type, 8-bit for char, and 32-bit for float data type. Sometimes in arithmetic operations we need more storage to store larger data. To solve this problem, C provides the type **double** to store floating-point data up to **64-bit storage,** i.e., double storage of what a float data type has. A variable of type double can store data with 14 digits of precision, in the range **-1.7E-308** to **1.7E+308** (value of E is 10). The MSB is used for sign, next 8-bit is used for exponent, and remaining 52-bit is used for mantissa. See Example 4 which is implementing the above discussion.

Example 4: Write a 'C' code which demonstrates double.

Answer: In the following program segment identifier **larger_number** is defined **double** type and is assigned a value 3012345.78888. We can print the value of this identifier in same way as float data is printed.

```
/* The double type declaration of a variable */
   #include<stdio.h>
   main()
   {
        double  larger_number ;
        larger_number = 3012345.78888 ;
        printf("Value of larger_number is %f", larger_number);
   }
```

OUTPUT
Value of larger_number is 3012345.78888

11.4.5 The void (Empty data type)

The keyword void is used in two contexts: function declarations and pointers. The **void** data type is associated with functions in C language. The pointer type void* is a generic pointer type: any pointer can be assigned to a void*, and a void* can be assigned to any pointer. In function definitions and declarations, it is used to indicate either that the function has no return value, or that it takes no arguments. A function is a program segment that solves some specific work. The main () is also a function defined in C language. The function **main()** can also uses void to changes its return type. The data type **void** has three uses:

To declare explicitly a function returning no value.

To declare explicitly a function having no arguments.

To create a generic pointer.

When used as a function return type, void means that the function does not return a value. For example,

```
void hello (char *name)
{
    printf("Hello, %s.", name);
}
```

When found in a function heading, void means the function does not take any parameters. For example,

```
int init (void)
{
    return 1;
}
```

This is not the same as defining

```
int init ()
{
    return 1;
}
```

Because in the second case the compiler will not check whether the function is really called with no arguments at all; instead, a function call with arbitrary number of arguments will be accepted without any warnings (this is implemented only for the compatibility with the old-style function definition syntax).

Pointers can also be declared as **void.** They cannot be de-referenced without explicit casting. This is because the compiler cannot determine the size of the object the pointer points to. See Example 5 which is implementing the above discussion.

Example 5: Write a 'C' code which demonstrates the void pointer type variable.

Answer: Following is the void_pointer() function which is void type and demonstrates the different stage of a **void** pointer data type.

```
void void_pointer()
{
    int x;
    float f;
    void *p = &x;              /* p points to x */
    *(int*)p = 2;              /* p holds 2 */
    p = &r;                            /* p points to r*/
    *(float*)p = 1.1;   /* p holds 1.1 */
}
```

In this program segment we have declared p as void type variable. First it is receiving address of variable x. The p further takes an integer value 2. Then in the next statement p receives address of the r. Finally p holds a float value 1.1.

This section may be a little bit obscure for beginners, but readers are advised to not worry about this. We will discuss this in the coming chapters.

11.5 DATA TYPE MODIFIERS

A type modifier alters the meaning of the basic data type to yield a new type. We have seen so far that **C** provides four basic data types: **int, char, float,** and **double.** As discussed earlier that

int type variable can store data in the range -32,768 to 32,767,
Variable type **char** can store data in the range -128 to 127, and
float type variable can store data in the range 3.4E-38 to 3.4E+38

In **C** language there is facility to change the range of storage of a data type variable. The keywords which are used for this purpose are known as modifiers. Basic data types may have various modifiers. In other words, we can say that **modifiers** alter the meaning of data type to fit the needs of various situations like overflow, etc. **C** supports the following modifiers:

unsigned
long
short
signed

Each of these type modifiers can be applied to the base type int. We simply place the type modifier in front of type name in a variable declaration to change the range of that variable. The modifiers signed and unsigned can be applied to the base type char. In addition long can be applied to data type double. When the base type is omitted from a declaration, int is assumed. For example,

```
long x;                 /* int is implied */
unsigned char ch;
signed int i;           /* signed is default */
unsigned long int l;  /* int is accepted, but not needed */
```

11.5.1 The unsigned

We can use a data type signed or unsigned. If unsigned data type is used then the one bit reserved for sign is used to represent the magnitude along with other bits. The **unsigned** type modifier instructs the compiler not to use the most significant bit (MSB) as a sign bit and to allow the bit to be used to represent larger positive values. A variable of type **unsigned int** can store values in the range from 0 to 65,535.

A **char** type variable can hold the values in the range -128 to 127. Using the unsigned type modifier one can create variables that can store values in the range from 0 to 255. See Example 6 which is implementing the above discussion.

Example 6: Write a 'C' code which demonstrates the unsigned modifier with char and int data types.

Answer: The following program implements the **unsigned int** and **unsigned char** identifiers. We use "%u" to print the unsigned value of a character or integer.

```
/* unsigned int and unsigned char data type declarations */
    #include<stdio.h>
    void main()
    {
        unsigned char  ch  = 'y';
        unsigned int  number  = 6254;
        printf("Unsigned char is: %c", ch);
        printf("\n Unsigned integer value is: %u", number);
    }
```

OUTPUT
Unsigned char is: y Unsigned integer value is: 6254

11.5.2 The long

Variable of type int can store positive or negative values in the range–32,768 to 32767. **C** compiler reserves value of type **int** using 16-bit with the most significant bit indicating sign. In many application programs we need to store larger integer. This can be achieved by using **long** modifier. The **long** type modifier tells the compiler to use 32-bit to represent the integer values in place of 16-bit. A variable of type **long int** can store values in the range of -2,147,483,648 to 2,147,483,647. The MSB is reserved for sign representation. It means remaining 31-bit is used for magnitude representation. We declare long int variable in the following format:

long int variables;

For example,

- long int x;
- long int large_integer, temp;

If a program still needs more range of positive integer values then we can combine **unsigned** and **long** modifiers together to get more storage. The combined **unsigned** and **long** modifier tells the compiler to use 32-bit store values ranging from 0 to 4,292,967,265. The syntax for **unsigned long** int is given below:

unsigned long int num1, num2, num3;

For example,

- unsigned long int large_integer_value;
- unsigned long int number, temp;
- unsigned long int num1, num2, num3=177407059098;

The **long** modifier is useful with **double** data type also. See Example 7 which is implementing the above discussion.

Example 7: Write a 'C' code which demonstrates the long with double.

Answer: The following program that illustrates the idea.

```
/* Use of long double data type*/
#include<stdio.h>
void main()
{
    long double x=234679887 ;
    printf("\n Value of x is %lf", x);
}
```

11.5.3 The short

A C compiler normally represents values of type **int** using 16-bits. If the compiler represents an integer value using 32-bit, then a variable of type **int** could store values in the range –2,147,483,648 to 2,147,483,647. Sometimes it may result in wastage of storage. If we store a value which is outside the range of an **int** variable, an overflow condition occurs and compiler raises error. It is desirable that whenever overflow condition occurs, compiler should automatically assign 32-bit in place of 16-bit. But this facility is not provided by all compilers. Some compilers reserved 32-bit for int type variable. So, whenever there is not need of the 32-bit storage and 16-bit is sufficient for operation, we use short modifier to tell compiler to use 16-bit storage. The syntax to define **short** type **int** is given below:

short int variables;

For example,

- short int x;
- short int number, temp;
- short int num1, num2, num3;

11.5.4 The signed

C compiler normally represents signed variables of type **char** using 8-bit with the most significant bit used to represent the sign value. Such signed variables can store values in the range -128 to 127. Using **unsigned** modifier, we can direct the compiler not to use the sign bit and all 8-bit is used for a character. Using the **unsigned** type modifier, a variable of type **char** can store values in the range 0 to 255.

We face sometimes problem while using different compilers. Suppose a compiler uses unsigned char type and another uses signed char type. If program code of first compiler runs on second compiler then overflow occurs. The reason is that first compiler uses 8-bit for a character and there is no sign bit and second compiler uses 7-bit for a character. To overcome of this type of this situation unsigned char type should be used for second compiler. The syntax to define **signed char** type is given below:

signed char variables;

For example,

```
signed char x;
signed char str, temp;
signed char ch='N';
```

There is a difference between **signed** and **unsigned** data the way the most significant bit (MSB) of the data is interpreted. If a signed data is specified, the compiler will generate code in such a way that the higher order bit of a data is to be used as a **sign flag.**

if **sign flag** = 0 number is positive

if **sign flag** = 1 number is negative

11.6 INPUT FUNCTIONS

We have so far used two functions of C language: main ( ) and printf( ). There are many functions defined in C. We will learn these gradually. But let us see some more functions of C.

scanf( ): It scans a data variable (s) that is input by a user through keyboard. It is used when we want to enter some data types. The syntax of the *scanf ( )* is:

```
scanf (" %d ", &num);              /* For scanning int data type num */
sanf("%c", &ch);                   /* For scanning char data type ch */
scanf("%f", &float_number);              /* For scanning float data type float_number */
scanf("%u", &unsigned_data);       /* For scanning unsigned data type unsigned_data */
scanf("ld", &long_integer);        /* For scanning long int data type long_integer */
scanf("%lf ", &long_float);        /* For scanning long float data type long_float */
```

getch( ) : It takes a character as input. Sometimes the output produced by a program quickly disappears and user cannot see it properly. To avoid this situation we use getch () function, although it is used for other purposes also. This function is generally defined in header file conio.h, i.e., it is window based library function. Now let us see one small program which demonstrates data types and scanf() function.

```
/* Use of the scanf ( ) function*/
#include<stdio.h>
#include<conio.h>
void main( )
{
    int number;
    char ch;
    float float_number;
    printf("Enter  the integer number:");
    scanf("%d", &number);
    printf("Enter  the character:");
    scanf("%c", &ch);
```

```
    printf("Enter the float number:");
    scanf("%f ", &float_number);
    pintf("You have entered the following data:);
    printf("Integer is: %d Character is: %c  Float is: %f ", number, ch, float_number);
    getch( );
}
```

OUTPUT

Enter the integer number: 26

Enter the character: x

Enter the float number: 25.65

You have entered the following data:

Integer is: 26 Character is: x Float is: 25.65

We have seen many small programs and their outputs also. But we have not discussed how to format the output of a program. For example, each message should be appeared in the next line, lines should be equally spaced, etc.

11.7 FORMATTED INPUT/OUTPUT

There are a number of related functions used for formatted input/output (I/O), each one determining the format of the I/O from a format string. For output, the format string consists of plain text, which is output unchanged, and embedded format specifications which call for some special processing of one of the remaining arguments to the function. On input, the plain text must match what is seen in the input stream; the format specifications again specify what the meaning of remaining arguments is? Each format specification is introduced by a % character, followed by the rest of the specification.

11.7.1 Output: the printf family

printf's name comes from **print** formatted. It generates output under the control of a format string (its first argument) which consists of literal characters to be printed and also special character sequences- format specifiers which request that other arguments be fetched, formatted, and inserted into the string. Our very first program was nothing more than a call to printf, printing a constant string. For those functions performing output, the format specification takes the following form, with optional parts enclosed in brackets:

%<flags><field width><precision><length>conversion

The meaning of flags, field width, precision, length, and conversion are given in Table 11.5, although tersely. For example, see the following code:

```
printf("Hello, world!\n");
```

Our second program also featured a call to printf:

```
printf("i is %d\n", i);
```

In this case, whenever printf "printed the string "i is %d", it did not print it verbatim; it replaced the two characters %d with the value of the variable i. There are quite a number of format specifiers for printf which are given in Table 11.6.

It is also possible to specify the width and precision of numbers and strings as they are inserted (somewhat like FORTRAN format statements). A notation like %3d means to print an int in a field at least 3 spaces wide; a notation like %5.2f means to print a float or double in a field at least 5 spaces wide, with two places to the right of the decimal.) To illustrate with a few more examples: the call

```
printf("%c %d %f %e %s %d%%\n", '1', 2, 3.14, 56000000., "eight", 9);
```

would print

1 2 3.140000 5.600000e+07 eight 9%

The call

```
printf("%d %o %x\n", 100, 100, 100);
```

would print

```
100 144 64
```

Successive calls to printf just build up the output a piece at a time, so the calls

```
printf("Hello, ");
printf("world!\n");
```

would also print Hello, world! (on one line of output).

Table 11.5 Format flags

Flags	Meaning
–	Left justify the conversion within its field.
+	A signed conversion will always start with a plus or minus sign.
'' space	If the first character of a signed conversion is not a sign, insert a space. Overridden by + if present.
#	Forces an alternative form of output. The first digit of an octal conversion will always be a 0; inserts 0X in front of a non-zero hexadecimal.
0	Pad d, i, o, u, x, X, e, E, f, F and G conversions on the left with zeros up to the field width. Overridden by the - flag. If a precision is specified for the d, i, o, u, x or X conversions, the flag is ignored. The behaviour is undefined for other conversions.
Flags	**Meaning**
field width	A decimal integer specifying the minimum output field width. This will be exceeded if necessary. If an asterisk is used here, the next argument is converted to an integer and used for the value of the field width; if the value is negative it is treated as a - flag followed by a positive field width. Output that would be less than the field width is padded with spaces (zeros if the field width integer starts with a zero) to fit. The padding is on the left unless the left-adjustment flag is specified.
precision	This starts with a period '.'. It specifies the minimum number of digits for d, i, o, u, x, or X conversions; the number of digits after the decimal point for e, E, f conversions; the maximum number of digits for g and G conversions; the number of characters to be printed from a string for s conversion. The amount of padding overrides the field width. If an asterisk is used here, the next argument is converted to an integer and used for the value of the field width. If the value is negative, it is treated as if it were missing. If only the period is present, the precision is taken to be zero.
length	h preceding a specifier to print an integral type causes it to be treated as if it were a short. (Note that the various sorts of short are always promoted to one of the flavours of int when passed as an argument.) l works like h but applies to a long integral argument. L is used to indicate that a long double argument is to be printed, and only applies to the floating-point specifiers. These are cause undefined behaviour if they are used with the 'wrong' type of conversion see Table 11.6

Earlier we learned that C represents characters internally as small integers corresponding to the characters' values in the machine's character set (typically ASCII). This means that there is not really much difference between a character and an integer in C; most of the difference is in whether we choose to interpret an integer as an integer or a character. printf is one place where we get to make that choice: %d prints an integer value as a string of digits representing its decimal value, while %c prints the character corresponding to a character set value.

Table 11.6 DATA formatters

Specifier	Effect	Default precision
D	signed decimal	1
I	signed decimal	1
U	unsigned decimal	1
O	unsigned octal	1
X	unsigned hexadecimal (0–f)	1
X	unsigned hexadecimal (0–F)	1
Precision	*Precision* specifies minimum number of digits, expanded with leading zeros if necessary. Printing a value of zero with zero precision outputs no characters.	
f	Print a double with *precision* digits (rounded) after the decimal point. To suppress the decimal point use a *precision* of explicitly zero. Otherwise, at least one [illegible]	[illegible]
e, E	Print a double in exponential format, rounded, with one digit before the decimal point, *precision* after it. A *precision* of zero suppresses the decimal point. There will be at least two digits in the exponent, which is printed as 1.23e15 in e format, or 1.23E15 in E format.	6
g,G	Use style f, or e (E with G) depending on the exponent. If the exponent is less than "4 or e" *precision*, f is not used. Trailing zeros are suppressed, a decimal point is only printed if there is a following digit.	unspecified
c	The int argument is converted to an unsigned char and the resultant character printed.	
s	Print a string up to *precision* digits long. If *precision* is not specified, or is greater than the length of the string, the string must be NUL terminated.	infinite
p	Display the value of a (void *) pointer in a system-dependent way.	
n	The argument must be a pointer to an integer. The number of characters output so far by this call will be written into the integer.	
%	A %	—
[ ]	String char []* (character selection)	
%ud	Unsigned integer	
%uc	Unsigned character	
%uf	Unsigned floating point number	
%ld	Long integer	

So the lines

```
char c = 'A';
int i = 65;
printf("c = %c, i = %d\n", c, i);
```

would print c as the character A and i as the number 65. But if, on the other hand, we called

```
printf("c = %d, i = %c\n", c, i);
```

We had see the decimal value (printed by %d) of the character 'A', followed by the character (whatever it is) which happens to have the decimal value 65.

We have to be careful when calling printf. It has no way of knowing how many arguments we have passed it or what their types are other than by looking for the format specifiers in the format string. If there are more format specifiers (that is, more % signs) than there are arguments, or if the arguments have the wrong types for the format specifiers, printf can misbehave badly, often printing nonsense numbers or (even worse) numbers which mislead us into thinking that some other part of a program is broken.

Because of some automatic conversion rules which we have not covered yet, we have a small amount of latitude in the types of the expressions we pass as arguments to printf. The argument for %c may be of type char or int, and the argument for %d may be of type char or int. The string argument for %s may be a string constant, an array of characters, or a pointer to some characters (though we have not really covered strings or pointers yet). Finally, the arguments corresponding to %e, %f, and %g may be of types float or double. But other combinations do not work reliably: %d will not print a long int or a float or a double; %ld will not print an int; %e, %f, and %g will not print an int.

The functions that use these formats are described in Table 11.7. All need the inclusion of <stdio.h>. Their declarations are:

```
#include <stdio.h>

int fprintf(FILE *stream, const char *format, ...);
int printf(const char *format, ...);
int sprintf(char *s, const char *format, ...);

#include <stdarg.h>     /* as well as stdio.h */
int vfprintf(FILE *stream, const char *format, va list arg);
int vprintf(const char *format, va list arg);
int vsprintf(char *s, const char *format, va list arg);
```

All of the above functions return the number of characters output, or a negative value on error. The trailing null is not counted by sprintf and vsprintf.

11.7.2 Input: the scanf family

A number of functions exist analogous to the printf family, but for the purposes of input instead. The most immediate difference between the two families is that the scanf group needs to be passed pointers to their arguments, so that the values read can be assigned to the proper destinations. Forgetting to pass a pointer is a very common error, and one which the compiler cannot detect–the variable argument list prevents it. The format string is used to control interpretation of a stream of input data, which generally contains values to be assigned to the objects pointed to by the remaining arguments to scanf. The contents of the format string may contain:

white space: This causes the input stream to be read up to the next non-white-space character.

ordinary character: Anything except white-space or % characters. The next character in the input stream must match this character.

conversion specification: This is a % character, followed by an optional * character (which suppresses the conversion), followed by an optional nonzero decimal integer specifying the maximum field width, an optional h, l or L to control the length of the conversion and finally a non-optional conversion specifier. Note that use of h, l, or L will affect the type of pointer which must be used.

Table 11.7 Functions performing formatted output

Name	Purpose
fprintf	General formatted output as described. Output is written to the file indicated by stream.
printf	Identical to fprintf with a first argument equal to stdout.
sprintf	Identical to fprintf except that the output is not written to a file, but written into the character array pointed to by s.
vfprintf	Formatted output as for fprintf, but with the variable argument list replaced by arg which must have been initialized by va_start. va_end is not called by this function.
vprintf	Identical to vfprintf with a first argument equal to stdout.
vsprintf	Formatted output as for sprintf, but with the variable argument list replaced by arg which must have been initialized by va_start. va_end is not called by this function. Note (va_start and va_end will discussed later on).

Except for the specifiers c, n and [, a field of input is a sequence of non-space characters starting at the first non-space character in the input. It terminates at the first conflicting character or when the input field width is reached.

The result is put into wherever the corresponding argument points, unless the assignment is suppressed using the * mentioned already. The conversion specifiers shown in Table 11.8 may be used. The size specifiers have the effect shown in Table 11.9. The functions are described below, with the following declarations:

```
#include <stdio.h>
int fscanf(FILE *stream, const char *format, ...);
int sscanf(const char *s, const char *format, ...);
int scanf(const char *format, ...);
```

Table 11.8 Conversion specifiers

Specifier	Effect
d i o u x	Convert a signed integer, a signed integer in a form acceptable to strtol, an octal integer, an unsigned integer and a hexadecimal integer, respectively.
e f g	Convert a float (not a double).
s	Read a string, and add a null at the end. The string is terminated by whitespace on input (which is not read as part of the string).
[	Read a string. A list of characters, called the scan set follows the [. A] delimits the list. Characters are read until (but not including) the first character which is not in the scan set. If the first character in the list is a circumflex ^, then the scan set includes any character not in the list. If the initial sequence is [^] or [], the] is not a delimiter, but part of the list and another] will be needed to end the list. If there is a minus sign (-) in the list, it must be either the first or the last character; otherwise the meaning is implementation defined.
c	Read a single character; white space is significant here. To read the first non-white space character, use %1s. A field width indicates that an array of characters is to be read.
p	Read a (void *) pointer previously written out using the %p of one of the printfs.
%	A % is expected in the input, no assignment is made.
n	Return as an integer the number of characters read by this call so far.

Table 11.9 Size specifiers

Specifier	Modifies	Converts
l	d i o u x	long int
h	d i o u x	short int
l	e f	double
L	e f	long double

fscanf takes its input from the designated stream, scanf is identical to fscanf with a first argument of stdin, and sscanf takes its input from the designated character array. If an input failure occurs before any conversion, EOF is returned. Otherwise, the number of successful conversions is returned: this may be zero if no conversions are performed. An input failure is caused by reading EOF or reaching the end of the input string (as appropriate). A conversion failure is caused by a failure to match the proper pattern for a particular conversion.

11.8 NON-PRIMITIVE DATA TYPES

We have discussed many primitive data types in C like int, float, char, etc. These are used to represent some entity in our real world like salary, roll number of a student, name of a student, etc. There are many entities in real life that are combination of these primitive data types. So, how we represent these entities? C provides luxury to combine the different data types into one. This type of data in C is known as aggregate data type. Following are aggregate data types:

- user Defined Data type: structure
- union
- enumeration:
- bit field

11.8.1 User Defined Data Type

The basic user-defined data type in C is the structure, or struct. C structures are analogous to the records found in some other languages. Defining structures is a two-step process: first we define a template which describes the new type then we declare variables having the new type or functions returning the new type, etc. For example, suppose we want to define a type for representing complex numbers. A complex number consists of a "real and "imaginary part, where the imaginary part is some multiple of the square root of negative 1. We do not have to understand complex numbers to understand this example; we can think of the real and imaginary parts as the x and y coordinates of a point on a plane. How might we add one? Since a complex number consists of a real and imaginary part, we need a way of holding both these quantities in one data type, and a structure will do just the trick. For example, complex type can be declared as:

```
struct complex
{
        double real;
        double imag;
};
```

A structure declaration consists of up to four parts, of which we can see three in the example above. The first part is the keyword struct which indicates that we are talking about a structure. The second part is a name or tag by which this structure (that is, this new data type) will be known. The third part is a list of the structure's members (also called components or fields). This list is enclosed in braces {}, and contains what look like the declarations of ordinary variables. Each member has a name and a type, just like ordinary variables, but here we are not declaring variables; we are setting up the structure of the structure by defining the collection of data types which will make up the structure. Here we see that the complex structure will be made up of two members, both of type double, one named real and one named imag.

It is important to understand that what we have defined here is just the new data type; we have not yet declared any variables of this new type. The name complex is not the name of a variable; it is the name of the structure type. The names real and imag are not the names of variables; they are identifiers for the two components of the structure. For example, we can declare variables of new complex type as:

```
struct complex c1;
or
struct complex c2, c3;
```

These look almost like normal declarations of variables having basic types, except that instead of a type keyword like int or double, we have the two-word type name struct complex. The keyword struct indicates that we are talking about a structure, and the identifier complex is the name for the particular structure we are talking about and c1, c2, and c3 will all be declared as variables of type struct complex; each one of them will have real and imaginary parts buried inside them. The only memory allocated is for two values of type double (the two boxes); all the names are just for our convenience and the compiler's reference; none are typically stored in the program's memory at run time.

Notice that when we define structures in this way we have not defined a new type at par with int or double. We cannot say

```
complex c1;          /* WRONG */
```

The name complex does not become a full-fledged type name like int or double; it is just the name of a particular structure, and we must use the keyword struct and the name of a particular structure (e.g. complex) to talk about that structure type.

A structure definition consisted of up to four parts. We saw the first three of them in the first example; the fourth part of a full structure declaration is simply a list of variables, which are to be declared as having the structure type at the same time as the structure itself is defined. For example, if we write

```
struct complex
{
    double real;
    double imag;
} c1, c2, c3;
```

we would have defined the type struct complex, and right away declared three variables c1, c2, and c3 all of type struct complex.

In fact, three of the four parts of a structure declaration (all but the keyword struct) are optional. If a declaration contains the keyword struct, a structure tag, and a brace-enclosed list of members (as in the first structure definition we saw), it is a definition of the structure itself. If a declaration contains the keyword struct, a structure tag, and a list of variable names (as in the first declarations of c1, c2, and c3 we saw), it is a declaration of those variables having that structure type (the structure type itself must of course typically be declared elsewhere). If a declaration contains all four elements (as in the second declaration of c1, c2, and c3 we saw), it is a definition of the structure type and a declaration of some variables. It is also possible to use the first, third, and fourth parts:

```
struct
{
        double real;
        double imag;
    } c1, c2, c3;
```

Here we declare c1, c2, and c3 as having a structure type with no tag name, which is not usually very useful, because without a tag name we would not be able to declare any other variables or functions of this type for c1, c2, and c3 to play with. Finally, it is also possible to declare just the tag name, leaving both the list of members and any declarations of variables for later, but this is only needed in certain fairly rare and obscure situations. Because a structure definition can also declare variables, it is important not to forget the semicolon at the end of a structure definition. If we accidentally write

```
struct complex
{
        double real;
        double imag;
}
```

Without a semicolon, the compiler will keep looking for something later in the file and try to declare it as being of type struct complex, which will either result in a confusing error message or (if the compiler succeeds) a confusing mis-declaration.

11.8.2 Union

In this group variables share the same storage space. A union is similar to a struct, except it allows us to define variables that share storage space. The syntax for defining unions is:

```
union [tag name]
{
        Data type variable-names;
        ...
} [union variables];
```

For example,

```
union short_or_long
    {
    short i;
    long l;
    } a_number;
```

The compiler will allocate enough storage in a number to accommodate the largest element in the union. Elements of a union are accessed in the same manner as a struct. Unlike a struct, the variables a_number.i and a_number.l occupy the same location in memory. Thus, writing into one will overwrite the other.

11.8.3 Enumeration

It defines a set of constants of type int. The syntax for defining constants using enum is

```
enum [tag] {name [=value], ...};
```

The set can optionally be given a type tag name with tag name is the name of a constant that can optionally be assigned the (constant) value of value, etc. For example,

```
enum Numbers {One = 1, Two = 2, Three = 3, Four = 4, Five = 5};
```

If value is missing, then a value is assumed to be the value of the previous constant in the list + 1. If this is the first constant in the list, the default value is 0. If we give a type tag name, then we can declare variables of enumerated type using enum tag variable-names;

For example,

```
enum Numbers x, y, z;
```

declares three variables x, y and z, all of type Numbers (they are, in fact, integer variables). More precise, 'enum tag' becomes a new type which is equal in rights with any built-in type.

11.8.4 Bit field

A bit field is an element of a structure that is defined in terms of bits. Using a special type of struct definition, we can declare a structure element that can range from 1 to 16 bits in length. For example,

```
struct bit_field
 {
  int bit_1 : 1;
  int bits_2_to_5 : 4;
  int bit_6 : 1;
  int bits_7_to_16 : 10;
 } bit_var;
```

We will discuss these data types in the coming chapters.

11.9 DATA TYPE QUALIFIERS

C language has two data type qualifiers: const and volatile. The idea of const has been borrowed from C++. The concepts of const and volatile are completely independent. A common misconception is to imagine that somehow const is the opposite of volatile and vice versa. They are unrelated and we should remember the fact. Since const declarations are the simpler, we will look at them first, but only after we see where both of these type qualifiers may be used. The complete list of relevant keywords is

char	long	float	volatile
short	signed	double	void
int	unsigned	const	

In the list, const and volatile are type qualifiers, the rest are type specifiers. Various combinations of type specifiers are permitted:

- char, signed char, unsigned char
- int, signed int, unsigned int
- short int, signed short int, unsigned short int
- long int, signed long int, unsigned long int
- float
- double
- long double

A few points should be noted. All declarations to do with an int will be signed anyway, so signed is redundant in that context. If any other type specifier or qualifier is present, then the int part may be dropped, as that is the default.

The keywords const and volatile can be applied to any declaration, including those of structures, unions, enumerated types or typedef names. Applying them to a declaration is called qualifying the declaration-that is why const and volatile are called type qualifiers, rather than type specifiers. Here are a few representative examples:

```
volatile i;
volatile int j;
const long q;
const volatile unsigned long int rt_clk;
struct
{
        const long int li;
        signed char sc;
} volatile vs;
```

Do not be put off; some of them are deliberately complicated: what they mean will be explained later. Remember that they could also be further complicated by introducing storage class specifications as well. In fact, the truly spectacular.

```
extern const volatile unsigned long int rt_clk;
```

is a strong possibility in some real time operating system kernels.

11.9.1 The const

Sometimes we want to keep some data types constant throughout the program. For this purpose we use const keyword in declaration of that identifier. Constant declarations are done with the help of keyword **const.** The values of these types of variables are not altered during program execution. The syntax for **const** is given below:

const data type variables;

For example,

- const ch='Y';
- const float float_constant = 3.17;
- const int num = 256;

See Example 8 which is implementing the above discussion.

Example 8: Write a C code to demonstrate the const.

Answer: The following program illustrates the idea and use of the const data types in C language.

```
#include<stdio.h>
void main()
    {
        const double a = 100000000.2234567;
        const  float b = 1234.56 ;
        const int c = 34234 ;
        const char ch = 'Y' ;
        double d;
        d = a+b+c;
        printf("\n Value of a is: %lf,a);
                printf("\n Value of b is:%f,b);
                printf("\n Value ofc is:%d,c);
        printf("\n Value of ch is:%c,ch);
    }
```

If we write code like:

- a = a + 1;
- c = 256;
- ch = 'N';

Then we will get error message from the compiler because modification of const data type is not permitted in C.

The **const** access modifier does not work with **long double** data type in C. For example, consider the following program:

```
#include<stdio.h>
void main()
{
    const long double num = 15.12345L;
    printf("\n Value of num is: %lf ,num);
}
```

If we run the above program, the output comes -0.000000. In **const** declaration of **float,** character **L** or **l** is used after the last digit of the number. However this is optional.

If we are accessing a hardware port at a fixed memory address and promised only to read from it, then it would be declared to be const but not initialized. Taking the address of a data object of a type which is not const and putting it into a pointer to the const-qualified version of the same type is both safe and explicitly permitted; we will be able to use the pointer to inspect the object, but not modify it. Putting the address of a const type into a pointer to the unqualified type is much more dangerous and consequently prohibited (although we can get around this by using a cast). See Example 9 which is implementing the above discussion.

Example 9: Write a C code which implements const and pointer together and shows their alteration.

Answer: Following program segment implements the idea.

```
#include <stdio.h>
#include <stdlib.h>

main()
{
    int i;
    const int ci = 123;
    /* declare a pointer to a const.. */
    const int *cpi;
    /* ordinary pointer to a non-const */
    int *ncpi;
    cpi = &ci;
    ncpi = &i;
    /* this is allowed      */
    cpi = ncpi;

/* this needs a cast because it is usually a big mistake, see what it permits below */
    ncpi = (int *)cpi;
```

```
/** now to get undefined behaviour modify a const through a pointer */
*ncpi = 0;
exit(0);
}
```

As the example shows, it is possible to take the address of a constant object, generate a pointer to a non-constant, then use the new pointer. This is an error in the program and results in undefined behaviour.

The main intention of introducing const objects was to allow them to be put into read only store, and to permit compilers to do extra consistency checking in a program. Unless we defeat the intent by doing naughty things with pointers, a compiler is able to check that const objects are not modified explicitly by the user. An interesting extra feature pops up now. What does this mean?

```
char c;
char *const cp = &c;
```

It is simple really; cp is a pointer to a char, which is exactly what it would be if the const are not there. The const means that cp is not to be modified, although whatever it points to can be- the pointer is constant, not the thing that it points to. The other way round is

```
const char *cp;
```

which means that now cp is an ordinary, modifiable pointer, but the thing that it points to must not be modified. So, depending on what we choose to do, both the pointer and the thing it points to may be modifiable or not; just choose the appropriate declaration.

11.9.2 The volatile

C provides the luxury to change a constant data type during execution of program. The volatile modifier is used to tell the compiler that a variable value can be changed in the ways which are not explicitly specified by the program. It is also possible to use both (const, volatile) modifiers together. This type of declaration is used when we are writing software for communication purpose and during the software development; the communicating ports do not know it. For example,

const volatile unsigned char *port = 0x2d;

(Where 0x2d is the port address)

The reason for having this type qualifier is mainly to do with the problems that are encountered in real-time or embedded systems programming using C. Imagine that we are writing code that controls a hardware device by placing appropriate values in hardware registers at known absolute addresses.

Let us imagine that the device has two registers, each 16 bits long, at ascending memory addresses; the first one is the control and status register (csr) and the second is a data port. The traditional way of accessing such a device is like this:

```
/* Declare the device registers whether to use int or short is implementation dependent*/
struct devregs
{
    unsigned short csr;   /* control & status */
    unsigned short data;  /* data port */
};

/* bit patterns in the csr */
#define ERROR  0x1
```

```
#define READY   0x2
#define RESET   0x4

/* absolute address of the device */
#define DEVADDR ((struct devregs *)0xffff0004)

/* number of such devices in system */
#define NDEVS  4
/* Busy-wait function to read a byte from device n, check range of device number. Wait until READY or
ERROR if no error, read byte, return it otherwise reset error, return 0xffff */

unsigned int read_dev(unsigned devno)
{
      struct devregs *dvp = DEVADDR + devno;
      if(devno >= NDEVS)
            return(0xffff);
      while((dvp->csr & (READY | ERROR)) == 0)
            ;     /* NULL - wait till done */

      if(dvp->csr & ERROR)
      {
            dvp->csr = RESET;
            return(0xffff);
      }
      return((dvp->data) & 0xff);
}
```

The technique of using a structure declaration to describe the device register layout and names is very common practice. Notice that there are not actually any objects of that type defined, so the declaration simply indicates the structure without using up any store.

To access the device registers, an appropriately cast constant is used as if it is pointing to such a structure, but of course it points to memory addresses instead.

However, a major problem with old C compilers would be in the while loop which tests the status register and waits for the ERROR or READY bit to come on. Any self-respecting optimizing compiler would notice that the loop tests the same memory address over and over again. It would almost certainly arrange to reference memory once only, and copy the value into a hardware register, thus speeding up the loop. This is, of course, exactly what we do not want; this is one of the few places where we must look at the place where the pointer points, every time around the loop.

Because of this problem, most C compilers have been unable to make that sort of optimization in the past. To remove the problem (and other similar ones to do with when to write to where a pointer points), the keyword volatile was introduced. It tells the compiler that the object is subject to sudden change for reasons which cannot be predicted from a study of the program itself, and forces every reference to such an object to be a genuine reference.

Here is how we would rewrite the example, making use of const and volatile to get what we want.

```
/* Declare the device registers whether to use int or short is implementation dependent */
struct devregs
```

```
{
    unsigned short volatile csr;
    unsigned short const volatile data;
};

/* bit patterns in the csr */

#define ERROR   0x1
#define READY   0x2
#define RESET   0x4

/* absolute address of the device */

#define DEVADDR ((struct devregs *)0xffff0004)

/* number of such devices in system */

#define NDEVS   4

/* Busy-wait function to read a byte from device n, check range of device number. Wait until READY or
ERROR if no error, read byte, return it otherwise reset error, return 0xffff */

unsigned int read_dev(unsigned devno)
{
    struct devregs * const dvp = DEVADDR + devno;

    if(devno >= NDEVS)
        return(0xffff);

    while((dvp->csr & (READY | ERROR)) == 0)
        ; /* NULL - wait till done */

    if(dvp->csr & ERROR){
        dvp->csr = RESET;
        return(0xffff);
    }
    return((dvp->data) & 0xff);
}
```

The rules about mixing volatile and regular types resemble those for const. A pointer to a volatile object can be assigned the address of a regular object with safety, but it is dangerous (and needs a cast) to take the address of a volatile object and put it into a pointer to a regular object. It is found that using such a derived pointer results in undefined behaviour.

If an array, union or structure is declared with const or volatile attributes, then all of the members take on that attribute too. This makes sense when we think about it–how could a member of a const structure be modifiable?

That means that an alternative rewrite of the last example would be possible. Instead of declaring the device registers to be volatile in the structure, the pointer could have been declared to point to a volatile structure instead, like this:

```
struct devregs
{
    unsigned short  csr;    /* control & status */
    unsigned short  data;   /* data port */
};
volatile struct devregs *const dvp=DEVADDR+devno;
```

Since dvp points to a volatile object, it is not permitted to optimize references through the pointer. Our feeling is that, although this would work, it is bad style. The volatile declaration belongs in the structure: it is the device registers which are volatile and that is where the information should be kept; it reinforces the fact for a reader.

So, for any object likely to be subject to modification either by hardware or asynchronous interrupt service routines, the volatile type qualifier is important. Now, just when we thought that we understood all that, here comes the final twist. A declaration like this:

```
volatile struct devregs
{
    /* stuff */
}v_decl;
```

The above statement declares the type struct devregs and also a volatile-qualified object of that type, called v_decl. A later declaration like this

```
struct devregs nv_decl;
```

The above statement declares nv_decl which is not qualified with volatile. The qualification is not part of the type of struct devregs but applies only to the declaration of v_decl. Look at the following declaration which is same as previous declaration.

```
struct devregs
{
    /* stuff */
}volatile v_decl;
```

If we do want to get a shorthand way of attaching a qualifier to another type, we can use typedef to do it:

```
struct x
{
    int a;
};

typedef const struct x csx;

csx const_sx;
struct x non_const_sx = {1};

const_sx = non_const_sx;        /* error - attempt to modify a const */
```

Readers are advised reread this section after completion of pointer and arrays.

11.10 CONSTANTS AND ITS TYPES

We have seen data types in C and we know that a variable can hold some data. The data can be assigned while writing a program or inputted through keyboard also. The data can be modified as per need of a programmer. But sometimes we need to make some data constant and it should not be alter during the program execution. A data may be modified knowingly or unknowingly. We have a special feature in C that makes a data constant throughout the execution of a program. For this, we use keyword const defined in C language. We can also make a data constant by using define directive in C. For example, the following directive creates a constant named Size and assigns value 25 to it.

```
#define Size 25
```

This directive (define) is instruction for the C preprocessor; the preprocessor will replace the constant name with its value.

There is a keyword **const** available in **C,** which is also used for the same purpose. With this keyword, one requires to use prefixes/suffixes, which are given in **Table 11.10.** The const ensures that the parameter defined and value associated will not alter during the lifetime of the program. The constants can be classified into five categories:

- Character Constants (also known as Escape sequences given in Table 11.2)
- Integer constants
- Floating-point constants
- Literal constants (Strings, group of characters)
- Enumeration constants

Table 11.10 Constant suffixes/prefixes

Constant suffix/prefix	Example
L, l are used for long integer and double as suffix	6599L, 3547l
F, f are used for float constant as suffix	46578F, 54328f
For hexadecimal constant 0x is used as prefix	0x35536
Single quote is used for character constant	'Y'
For integer constant simply const keyword is placed	const in num =7674

For example, the program constant.c discusses the constant declarations with the help of keyword const.

```
/* constant.c */
#include<stdio.h>
void main()
{
  const int num = 345;
  const long int LONG =999678647L;
  const float Float_num = 1234.30045f;
  const int Octal = 012345;
  const int Hex = 0x1abc;
  const int Unsigned_num = 1236u;
  printf ("\n Integer %d,num);
  printf ("\n Long integer %ld ,LONG);
  printf ("\n Float %f,Float_num);
  printf ("\n Octal %o,Octal);
  printf ("\n Hexadecimal %X,Hex);
  printf ("\nUnsigned integer: %u ,Unsigned_num);
}
```

OUTPUT
Integer 234
Long integer 999678647
Float 1234.30045
Octal 12345
Hexadecimal 1ABC
Unsigned integer 1236

11.10.1 Enumeration Constants

These fall into the category of 'half baked'. They are not proper enumerated types, as in Pascal, and only really serve to help we reduce the number of #define statements in a program. For example,

```
enum e_tag
{
```

```
a, b, c, d=20, e, f, g=20, h
}var;
```

Just as with structures and unions, the e_tag is the tag, and var is the definition of a variable.

The names declared inside the enumeration are constants with int type. Their values are these:

a = 0
b = 1
c = 2
d = 20
e = 21
f = 22
g = 20
h = 21

So we can see that, in the absence of anything to the contrary, the values assigned start at zero and increase. A specific value can be given if we want, when the increase will continue one at a time afterwards; the specific value must be an integral constant that is representable in an int. It is possible for more than one of the names to have the same value. The only use for these things is to give a better-scoped version of this:

```
#define a 0
#define b 1
/* and so on */
```

It is better scoped because the declaration of enumerations follows the standard scope rules for C, whereas #define statements have file scope. Not that we are likely to care, but the C states that enumeration types are of a type that is compatible with an implementation-defined one of the integral types. So what? For interest's sake here is an illustration:

```
enum ee{a,b,c}e_var, *ep;
```

The names a, b, and c all behave as if they were int constants when we use them; e_var has type enum ee and ep is a pointer to enum ee. The compatibility requirement means that (amongst other implications) there will be an integral type whose address can be assigned to ep without violating the type-compatibility requirements for pointers.

EXERCISES

1. Multiple Choice Questions

1. How many bits are reserved for int data type by a C compiler?
   (a) 16-bit (b) 32-bit
   (c) 64-bit (d) Depends on Compiler
2. How many bits are reserved for float data type by a C compiler?
   (a) 16-bit (b) 32-bit
   (c) 64-bit (d) Depends on Compiler
3. How many bits are reserved for char data type by a C compiler?
   (a) 8-bit (b) 16-bit
   (c) 32-bit (d) Depends on Compiler

4. Suppose a C compiler reserves 16-bit for a signed int data type. What is the range of the integer number represented by a signed integer variable?

   (a) –32768 to 32767 (b) –32768 to 32768

   (c) -2^{15} to $2^{15}-1$ (d) None

5. Suppose a C compiler reserves 16-bit for a unsigned int data type. What is the range of the integer number represented by an integer variable?

   (a) 0 to 65536 (b) 0 to 65535

   (c) 0 to 65537 (d) None

6. Suppose a C compiler reserves 16-bit for a char data type. What is the total number of characters that can be represented and stored by compiler?

   (a) 127 (b) 128

   (c) 256 (d) 255

7. Consider the following program:

```
#include<stdio.h>
void main( )
{
int number =16;
printf("The value of number is: %f ", number);
}
```

   What is output of the above program?

   (a) The value of number is: 16

   (b) Syntax error: Opening curly bracket is missing

   (c) Syntax error: number cannot be printed as float

   (d) None

8. Consider the following program:

```
#include<stdio.h>
void main( )
{
const int number =16;
printf("The value of number is: %u ", number);
}
```

   What is output of the above program?

   (a) The value of number is: 16

   (b) Syntax error: Opening curly bracket is missing

   (c) Syntax error: number cannot be printed as unsigned

   (d) None

9. Consider the following program:

```
#include<stdio.h>
void main( )
{
```

```
const int number =16;
number = number +1;
printf("The value of number is: %d ", number);
}
```

What is output of the above program?

(a) The value of number is: 16

(b) Syntax error: Value of number cannot be modified

(c) The value of number is: 17

(d) None

10. Consider the following program:

```
#include<stdio.h>
void main( )
{
    printf(" C is a middle-level
    language");
}
```

What is output of the above program?

(a) C is a middle-level language

(b) Syntax error

(c) C is a middle-level Language

(d) None

11. Consider the following integer type variables in C language:

(i) number (ii) number_132

(iii) ingeter.number (iv) intger_number

(v) data_of_birth

which one is incorrect variable name?

(a) (ii), (iv), (v)

(b) (ii)

(c) (iii)

(d) None

12. Consider the following program:

```
#include<stdio.h>
void main( )
{
    int num1=25, num2=30;
    num1=num1+num2;
    num2=num1- num2;
    num1=num1-num2;
    printf("\n Value of Num1= %  and value of num2= %d", num1, num2);
}
```

What does the above program do?

(a) Swap the value of num1 and num2
(b) Add the num2 with num1
(c) Add num1 with num2
(d) None

13. How many temporary variables are needed to swap two data type?
(a) One (b) Two
(c) Zero (d) At most one

14. Is the following declaration incorrect?

```
char ch= "Y";
```

(a) Yes (b) No
(c) Depends on Compiler (d) Cannot decide

15. How many symbols can be placed in a variable name in C language?
(a) 16 (b) 32
(c) 64 (d) None

16. What is the output of following program?

```
#include<stdio.h>
void main( )
{
    printf("\n C language is middle-level language");
}
```

(a) C language is middle-level language
(b) Syntax error
(c) No output
(d) None

17. What is the output of following program?

```
#include<stdio.h>
void main( )
{
    int number;
    printf("\n number is : %d", number) ;
}
```

(a) 256 (b) 0
(c) Garbage (d) None

18. What is the output of following program?

```
#include<stdio.h>
void main( )
{
    int num1, num2;
    num1=10;  num2=15;
    printf("\n number are : %d", num1, num2) ;
}
```

(a) 10 (b) 10 15
(c) Error (d) None

19. What is the output of following program?

```
#include<stdio.h>
void main( )
{
    int number = 011;
    printf("\n number is : %d", number) ;
}
```

(a) 9 (b) 011
(c) Garbage (d) None

20. What is the output of following program?

```
#include<stdio.h>
void main( )
{
    float number = 7/3;
    printf("\n number is : %f", number) ;
}
```

(a) 2.333333 (b) 2.00000
(c) Garbage (d) None

21. What is the output of following program?

```
#include<stdio.h>
void main( )
{
    float number = 5.0/2;
    printf("\n number is : %f", number) ;
}
```

(a) 2.50000 (b) 2.00000
(c) Garbage (d) None

22. What is the output of following program?

```
#include<stdio.h>
void main( )
{
    int number = 7/3;
    printf("\n number is : %d", number);
}
```

(a) 2.333333 (b) 2
(c) Garbage (d) None

23. What is the output of following program?

```
#include<stdio.h>
void main( )
{
```

```
    float number;
    number = (float) 2+5/2;
    printf("\n number is : %f", number) ;
}
```

(a) 3.555555 (b) 4.00000
(c) Garbage (d) None

24. What is the output of following program?

```
#include<stdio.h>
void main( )
{
    float number;
    number = 2+(float) 5/2;
    printf("\n number is : %f", number) ;
}
```

(a) 3.555555 (b) 4.50000
(c) Garbage (d) None

25. What is the output of following program?

```
#include<stdio.h>
void main( )
{
    float number;
    number = (float) 2+5/2;
    printf( ) ;
}
```

(a) 3.555555 (b) 4.00000
(c) Error (d) None

State whether the following statements are true or false

1. Any valid printable ASCII character can be used in an identifier.
2. All variables must be given a type when they are declared.
3. Declarations can appear anywhere in a program.
4. C treats the variables name and Name to be same.
5. The underscore can be used anywhere in an identifier.
6. The keyword void is a data type in C.
7. Floating point constants, by default, denote float type values.
8. Like variables, constants have a type.
9. Character constants are coded using double quotes.
10. Initialization is the process of assigning a value to a variable at the time of declaration.
11. All static variables are automatically initialized to zero.
12. The scanf function can be used to read only one value at a time.

Fill in the blanks with appropriate words in each of the following statements

1. The keyword__________can be used to create a double data type identifier.
2. ____________is the largest value that an unsigned short int type variable can store.

3. A global variable is also known as _______ variable.
4. A variable can be made constant by declaring it with the qualifier of initialization.

Descriptive Problems

1. What are trigraph characters? How are they useful?
2. Describe the different basic data types available in C. How could we extend the range of values they represent?
3. What is an unsigned integer constant? What is the significance of declaring a constant un-signed?
4. Describe the characteristics and purpose of escape sequence characters.
5. What is a variable and what is meant by the value of a variable?
6. How do variables and symbolic names differ?
7. State the differences between the declaration of a variable and the definition of a symbolic name.
8. What is initialization? Why is it important?
9. What are the modifiers that are used by data types available in whenever required?
10. What are the qualifiers that an int can have at a time?
11. A programmer would like to use the word DPR to declare all the double-precision floating point values in his program. How could he achieve this?
12. What are enumeration variables? How are they declared? What is the advantage of using them in a program?
13. Describe the purpose of the qualifiers const and volatile. When dealing with very small or very large numbers, what steps would programmer take to improve the accuracy of the calculations?
14. Write C program to demonstrate the functionalities of primary data types in C int, char, float, double, void.
15. Write a program to demonstrate the type modifiers in C.
16. Write a program to demonstrate format flags given in Table 11.2.
17. Write C program for demonstrating the data formatters given in Table 11.3.
18. Write a program to demonstrate the conversion specifies given in Tables 11.5 and 11.6.
19. Write a program to determine and print the sum of the following harmonic series for a given value of n: 1 + 1/2 + 1/3 + + l/n. The value of n should be given interactively through the terminal.
20. Write a program to read the price of an item in decimal form (like 15.95) and print the output in paise (like 1595 paise).
21. Write a program that prints the prime numbers from 1 to 100.
22. Write a program that requests two float type numbers from the user and then divides the first number by the second and display the result along with the numbers.
23. The price of one Kg of Milk is Rs. 16.75 and one Kg of Atta is Rs. 15. Write a program to get these values from the user and display the prices as follows:

    *** LIST OF ITEMS ***

Item	Price
Rice	Rs 16.75
Sugar	Rs 15.00

Operator Types in C and Expressions

12.1 INTRODUCTION

In the previous chapter we have discussed about data types used in C language, constants, type modifiers, Formatted Input/Output, aggregation of primitive data types, Type Qualifiers: Const & volatile, and constants, etc. We have operators in C languages for arithmetic, logical operations on different data types used in C. In this chapter we see locality of variables, storage specifiers that are obtained by combining the simple or primitive data types. Main focus of this chapter is different types of operators.

12.2 VARIABLES AND THEIR SCOPE

So far we have discussed many data types provided by C language. Let us see the locality of a variable. We know that a variable is used to represent some data type and that data may be needed local where that variable is declared or outside. We have seen main () function which is necessary to run a program. We can have our own functions that provide some specific computation over data. Data of a function may be declared inside that function or may be declared outside of that function. The variables can be declared:

Inside a function, i.e., local variables of a function

In the definition of the functions, i.e., formal or dummy parameters

Out side all of the functions, i.e., global parameters for all the functions

Actual parameter, i.e., used during the invocation of function.

12.2.1 Local Variables

Variables that are declared within a function are called local variables of that function because scope of these variables exists only inside the function, not outside. So, far we have used only one function, i.e., the main ( ) function. Similar to the main ( ) function we can have other functions also and these functions are called from main ( ) function directly or indirectly. For example,

```
void main ( )
{
    int number=0123;
    float float_num=12.006;
    ...
    ...
}
```

Here variable **number** and **float_num** are local variable and scope of these variables does not identified outside the main ( ) function. See the implementation of the following function.

```
void sum( )
{
    int x=22, y=25, z;
    z = x + y;
}
```

Here sum() is a user defined function and x, y, z are local variables of this function. The local variables are declared at the start of the function body. This makes easier to understand one about the variables that are used in a function block code. However, it is not necessary to do this because local variables can be declared within code block. See Example 1 which is implementing the above discussion.

Example 1: Write a program to define scope of variables in a program segment.

Answer: Following program segment implements the details about scope of the variables.

```
/*scope1.c*/
#include<stdio.h>
void main()
{
    int num1=25, num2=15, sum;
    char ch='y';
    sum = num1+num2;
    printf("\n The sum of 25 and 15 is : %d", sum);
    if(ch= = 'y')
    {
        printf("\n You are in if block .....");
    int num1 = 10, num2=20, sum; /* this declaration is only permitted in C++*/
/* num1, num2, sum are local variables of If block and scope is limited to only If block*/
        sum = num1+num2;
        printf("\n sum= %d", sum);
    }
    printf("Now you are outside the if block....");
    printf(" Sum of two integers is: % d", sum);
}
```

OUTPUT
The sum of 25 and 15 is : 40 You are in If block ..... sum= 30 Now you are outside the If block.... Sum of two integers is: 40

This result is generated after compiling code with C++ compiler.

One can surprise to see the above output? Let us see how we get the above output. First we have declared num1, num2, and sum variables as local variables of main ( ) function and sum hold value 40 (num1+num2). Now, in the if ( ) block we have once again declared variables num1, num2, and sum as local variables of if ( ) block, this declaration is only permitted in C++ not in C. One important point to be noted that local variables of a block (or function) are getting priority over the variables which are existing outside of a block in the program. So, local variables of if ( ) block get priority over the local variables of the main ( ) function and this is why we have sum 30 (num1+num2) in the if ( ) block. We can have the local variables' name same in the different functions as we have above. So, let us conclude the above:

Local variables are declared and used inside a function.

Local variables have existence or scope inside a function.

Names of local variables may be identical in the different functions.

Local variables get priority over outsider local variables.

12.2.2 Dummy Parameters

Sometimes we pass some variables or parameters to a function. The variables which are to be passed to a function are received by that function in form of dummy of formal variables. The parameters defined within the definition of function are called **dummy** or **formal** parameters. The scope of these parameters of the function is same as local variable. The dummy parameters can be accessed anywhere in the function. They behave like any other local variable inside the functions. For example, consider the following program segment:

```
void summation( int x, int y )
{
    int sum ;
    s = x + y ;
}
```

In the above program segment the function summation( ) possesses two dummy parameter x and y. The scope of dummy parameters x and y is same as local parameter sum. As the local parameters are destroyed upon exit from the function in which they are declared it is same for dummy parameters.

12.2.3 Global Variables

We have seen earlier two kinds of variables that are local their scope. C provided another type of variables that are global in their scope and can be used by any function or code in a program. The scope of global variables remains throughout the entire program and these variables can be used by any piece of the code and they hold their values during the entire execution of the program.

The global variables are always declared outside a function. They may be accessed by any expression regardless of the function in which it is expressed. The syntax for a program segment using global variable is:

```
Data Type1 Variables1;      /* Global variables or parameters  */
Data Type2 Variables2;
    ...
Data Typem Variablesm;

void main ( )
{
    ...
    ...
    ...
}
User defined functions are declared here onwards
{
```

```
...
...
...
}
```

See Example 2 which is implementing the above discussion.

Example 2: Write a program to demonstrate the priority of the local and global variables.

Answer: Following implementations (scope2.c and scope3.c) demonstrates the priority of local and global declared variables.

```
/*scope2.c*/
#include<stdio.h>      /* header file */
 /* Global variables */
 int global_num = 20, sum=20 ;
 void main()
 {
        int sum = 100 ;
        /* Variable sum is local to main function */
        printf("\n Variable sum = %d",sum) ;
        printf("\n Variable global_num is: %d", global_num);
        getch();
 }
```

OUTPUT
Variable sum = 100
Variable global_num is: 20

The local variable sum of the main ( ) function gets priority over the global variable and hence the value of the sum in the main ( ) function is output as 100 and value of global_num is 20. Let us see another example.

```
/*scope3.c*/
#include<stdio.h>                          /* header file */
 /* Global variables */
 int global_num = 20, sum=50 ;
 void main()
 {
        int local_sum = 100 ;
        /* Variable local_sum is local to main function */
        printf("\n Variable sum = %d ",sum) ;
        local_sum = sum+global_num;
        printf("\n local_sum = %d ",local_sum) ;
        printf("\n Variable global_num is: %d", global_num);
        getch();
 }
```

OUTPUT
Variable sum = 50
Local_sum = 70
Variable global_num is: 20

The local variable local_sum of the main () function is assigned the addition of two global variables sum and global_sum which is 70.

For better programming practice, one should avoid the use of global variables because if there is large number of global variables, there might be confusion. If there are few global variables declared, the use and type of these can be easily understood. Before defining a variable- local or global, first of all one must find out the scope of these variables. Global variables are very helpful when they are used in many functions.

12.3 STORAGE SPECIFIERS

We have discussed local and global variables in the earlier section. We have also seen that if identical names are used for local and global variables then local variables get priority over global or outsider variables. But one thing is noticeable here that memory is reserved for all the variables. C language provides other types of variables that are intended to use the same memory location as local or global variables used across the different files. One thing should be clear here that sometimes we have more than one file to make a single program. The reason for this is very simple. If a single file becomes large then we have segment of a program in the other files also. This is different from the having multiple functions. Many functions may be declared in a single file or multiple files. All the files that have segments of main program are included in the main file (where main ( ) function is defined) directly or indirectly.

For example, suppose mainfile.c contains main( ) function, and files1.c, file2.c contain the segments of main program then we have code like:

```
/** mainfile.c **/
#include<stdio.h>
#include"file1.c"
#include"file2.c"
void main()
{
    ...
...
...
}
```

Storage specifier type of variables are:

extern
static
register
auto

Further **signed, unsigned, short** or **long** qualifiers may specify more **int, char** and **float.** The **double** only uses **long** specification as we have mentioned in the earlier chapter.

12.3.1 The auto

The keyword "auto" is a storage modifier, and tells C that the variable should be treated as an auto variable. It is important to note, however, this particular storage modifier is completely redundant. By default, variables declared within functions are assumed by C to be auto variables. So we will most likely never see the "auto" keyword in a real C program. When control leaves the block in which the automatic variable was declared (e.g., the function in which it was declared returns), the variable is removed from memory and any value it may have had is lost. We have put the keyword "auto" in front of every variable declaration. An automatic variable is visible throughout the block in which it was declared, but not outside. See Example 3 which is implementing the above discussion.

Example 3: Write a program segment with the help of a user defined function random(). This function is supposed to return a different "random" integer between 0 and N-1, inclusive, every time it is called.

Answer: Go through the following program segment.

```
/* auto.c */
#include <stdio.h>

/* This function is supposed to return a different "random" integer between 0 and N-1, inclusive, every time it is called.  It does not work */

int random (int N)
{
  auto int lastNumber = 1;
  lastNumber = (lastNumber*234721 + 17223) % N;
  return(lastNumber);
}

/* This prints out ten consecutive "random" numbers. */

void main ()
{
  auto int i;
  for (i=1; i <= 10; i++)
    printf("%d\n", random(1000));
}
```

If an initialization is included with the declaration (as is the case with "lastNumber" in "auto.c") the variable is initialized when the variable is allocated-upon block entry. If no initialization is included (as is the case with "i" in "auto.c") the variable is given no particular initial value. The function "random" works by calculating a new random number based upon the last one that was returned. Unfortunately, because "lastNumber" is an automatic variable, it is initialized to 1 every time the function "random" is called. We are not succeeding in saving the last return value. Modify this code segment for getting the desired result.

12.3.2 The extern

This declaration is useful when we design large program and large numbers of global variables are required. In the design of a large program, it is not possible to put complete program in a single file. So the program is divided into segments and these are kept in different files and all variables can be declared in a single file with the help of extern specifier. The variables can be called in different files. When we use extern keyword, the memory requirement is less because the variables declared in different files share the same memory area. See Example 4 which is implementing the above discussion.

Example 4: Write a multiple file program segment for demonstrating the extern specifier.

Answer: Following code segment implements the idea of multiple file programming with the help of extern specifier.

```
/** file1.c **/
# include<stdio.h>
# include "file2.c"
  int x, y, z ;    /*Global variables*/
  void main()
  {
```

```
printf("\n** Address of x , y and z before extern **\n");
printf(" \n Address of x = %x",&x);
printf(" \n Address of y = %x",&y);
printf(" \n Address of z = %x",&z);
}

/** file2.c **/
#include<stdio.h>
extern int x ,y ,z ;
/* Definition of function addition( ) */
void addition( )
{
x = 20 ;
y = 30 ;
z = x +y ;
printf("\n\n\n Address of x , y and z after extern ");
printf(" \n Address of x = %x",&x);
printf(" \n Address of y = %x",&y);
printf(" \n Address of z = %x",&z);
}
```

```
OUTPUT
Address of x , y and z before extern
Address of x = 0x44e
Address of y = 0x450
Address of z = 0x452
Address of x , y and z after extern
Address of x = 0x44e
Address of y = 0x450
Address of z = 0x452
```

In both the cases, we see that the locations of x, y, z are shared. If both the files (**file1.c** and **file2.c**) are compiled together and storage required for x, y, z in **file1.c** would be shared by x, y, z declared in **file2.c.**

The **extern** declaration of variables can also occur inside the same file. For the global declaration and local declarations, the memory area occupied will be same. For example,

```
void main()
{
    extern int x; /*optional use of the extern declaration */
}
```

The static

A static variable is local to particular function. However, it is only initialized once (on the first call to function). Also the value of the variable on leaving the function remains intact. On the next call to the function the static variable has the same value as on leaving. To define a static variable simply prefix the variable declaration with the static keyword. See Example 5 which is implementing the above discussion.

Example 5: Write a program segment for demonstrating the static specifier.

Answer: Following code segment implements the idea of static specifier.

```
void stat(); /* prototype function */
main()
```

```
{
        int i;
         for (i=0;i<5;++i)
    stat();
    }

    void stat()
    {
        int auto_var = 0;
static int static_var = 0;
    printf( "auto_var = %d, static_var = %d \n"', auto_var, static_var);
    ++auto_var;
    ++static_var;
    }
```

OUTPUT

```
auto_var = 0, static_var= 0
auto_var = 0, static_var = 1
auto_var = 0, static_var = 2
auto_var = 0, static_var = 3
auto_var = 0, static_var = 4
```

Clearly the auto_var variable is created each time. The static_var is created once and remembers its value.

The static variables mean permanent variables with in their own functions or files but different from the const data type. These data types are static in nature, i.e., these contain their data static unless until any change. We can modify the static data types and this is advantage over the const data type in C. Another advantage of static data type is its initialization, i.e., the compiler initially assigns zero to static variables if no value is assigned. There are two types of static variables: local and global.

12.3.3 The static local

Sometimes we need to have some variables that retain their values after modifications made to those variables. Suppose we have a function count_people( ) to count the number of people of a city. It's obvious that initially the variable holding the number of people count should be zero and it should reflect the current value not the initial or any other value. For this purpose C provides static local variables.

The static variables mean permanent variables within their own functions or files. When a variable is declared static local in a function, the value of the variable is retained when a call to the function is made. It is contrast to local variables that loss data when a call to a function is completed and when next call to that function is made then local variables holds the initial value is any. See Example 6 which is implementing the above discussion.

Example 6: Write a program segment for demonstrating the static local variable concept.

Answer: Following code segment implements the idea and counts the number of students in a class.

```
/** staticl.c **/
#include<stdio.h>
void count_student();
void main()
{
```

```
    char ch='y';
    while(ch == 'y')
    {
        printf("\n Enter character y if some student is in class..");
        scanf("%c", &ch);
        count_student();        /*Call to function count_student*/
    }
}

/** Function count_student() **/

void count_student()
{
    static int count = 0 ;
    count= count+1;
    printf("\n One more student is added: %d", count);
}
```

When we run the above program, a call to the function count_student ( ) is made every time when character 'y' is entered.

12.3.4 The static global

We can restrict scope of a variable in a single file by using static global variables provided by C language. The static global variables are static in nature and scope of these variables is limited to a single file in which these are declared. The function of storage specifier static is just the reverse of extern specifier. When we define a global variable as static, it is impossible to access this variable in another file. It means, if a program is kept in different files then static global variables of one file cannot be used in other files, which is great flexible provision in C language. See Example 7 which is implementing the above discussion.

Example 7: Write a program segment for demonstrating the static global variable concept using multiple file concepts.

Answer: Following code segment implements the idea using multiple file concept..

```
/** statg1.c **/
# include<stdio.h>
# include "statg2.c" /* calling second file */

 static int x=10, y=20, z;  /* static global variables */
void show( ) ; /* prototype function declaration*/

void main()
{
z=x+y;
printf("\n Sum of x and y is: %d", z);
x=x*x;
y=y*y;
printf("\n Square of x is: %d  and square of y is:
%d", x, y);
display();      /*Call of display() function*/
show();         /* call to show() function in file program26.c*/
}
/*End of main function*/
/* Definition of the function display() */
  void  display()
```

```
{
    printf("\n Values of x, y, and z in display function);
    printf("\n Last value of x = %d",x);
    printf("\n Last value of y = %d",y);
    printf("\n Last value of z = %d",z);
}

/** statg2.c **/

static int x , y, z ;
void show ()
{
        printf("\n Values of x, y, and z in show function:)
    printf("\n Last value of x is: %d",x);
    printf("\n Last value of y is: %d",y);
    printf("\n Last value of z is: %d",z);
}
```

```
OUTPUT
Sum of x and y is: 30
Square of x is: 100 and square of y is: 400
Values of x, y, and z in display function
Last value of x =100
Last value of y = 400
Last value of z = 30
Values of x, y, and z in show function:
Last value of x is:0
Last value of y is:0
Last value of z is:0
```

The output of the above program segment show that the static global integer variables x, y, z retain their values in file statg1.c but when the show( ) function is called then the values of x, y, z no longer exist. The show( ) function is defined in file statg2.c and by default C compiler assigns zero to all three variables x, y, and z.

This shows that static declarations of variables are limited to single file only. The exact use of **static** variables is to hide some portion of program from another. This is a very important advantage when we try to manage a very large and complex program. With the help of **static** specifier, we may create functions that may be put into libraries for later use.

12.3.5 The register

We know that C language is a middle-level language and a programmer can access low-level function of a computer. The word register is borrowed from the world of computer hardware. Each computer has a certain number of registers to hold data and perform arithmetic or logical calculations. Because registers are located within the CPU (central processing unit) chip, it is much quicker to access a register than a memory location. Therefore, storing variables in registers may help to speed up the program. C provides facility to access the registers of a computer. The C language provides with the register specifier. We can apply this specifier to variables when we think it is necessary to put the variables into the computer registers. However, the register specifier only gives the compiler a suggestion. In other words, a variable specified by the register keyword is not guaranteed to be stored in a register. The compiler can ignore the suggestion if there is no register available, or if some other restrictions have to apply. This type of storage specifier is applicable only with the **int** and **char** type variables. The **register** specifier is applicable with local variables only.

When we define a variable with storage specifies register; the value of that variable is stored in the **CPU** registers no memory access is required and this is why the operation is much faster. It is illegal to take the address of a variable that is declared with the register specifier because the variable is intended to be stored in a register, not in the memory. For example, syntax to define a register variable is

register data type variable;

For examples,

register int number;

register char string='y';

In the following portion of code, the integer variable i is declared with the register specifier:

```
int main()
{
   /* block scope with the register specifier */
   register int i;
   . . .
   for (i=0; i<MAX_NUM; i++){
      /* some statements */
   }
   . . .
   return 0;
}
```

The declaration of i suggests that the compiler store the variable in a register. Because i is intensively used in the for loop, storing i in a register may increase the speed of the code shown here.

12.4 TYPES OF OPERATORS

In this section we will discuss about different types of operators such as arithmetic, logical, relational, etc. We know that a computer does only computation. So, whatever problem we have, solution of that problem is based on computations by a computer system. One can think that how word processing, paintbrush, etc applications are based on computation. These all are expressed in the form of some computation. A simple data transfer or data copy is computation for a computer.

Variables and constants can be used in conjunction with C operators to create more complex expressions. In other words operators are used with operands to build expressions. An expression acted on by an operator. A sequence of operators and operands may yield a single value. Table 12.1 presents the set of C operators. For example, the following is an expression containing two operands and one operator.

z = a + b;

a and **b** are both operands of the + operator.

The C operators fall into the following categories:

Postfix operators which follow a single operand.

Unary prefix operators, which precede a single operand.

Binary operators, which take two operands and perform a variety of arithmetic and logical operations.

The conditional operator (a ternary operator), which takes three operands and evaluates either the second or third expression, depending on the evaluation of the first expression.

Assignment operators, which assign a value to a variable.

The comma operator, which guarantees left-to-right evaluation of comma-separated expressions.

The order in which operators are dealt with during the evaluation of an expression is called the precedence. Operator precedence determines the grouping of terms in an expression. This affects how an expression is evaluated. Certain operators have higher precedence than others; for example, the multiplication operator has higher precedence than the addition operator:

```
x = 7 + 3 * 2;      /* x is assigned 13, not 20   */
```

The above statement is equivalent to the following:

```
x = 7 + ( 3 * 2 );
```

Using parenthesis in an expression alters the default precedence. For example,

```
x = (7 + 3) * 2;  /*  (7 + 3) is evaluated first   */
```

In a un-parenthesized expression, operators of higher precedence are evaluated before those of lower precedence. Consider the following expression:

A+B*C

The identifiers B and C are multiplied first because the multiplication operator (*) has higher precedence than the addition operator (+). We detailed precedence of operators in subsequent sections. Let us start with arithmetic operators.

Table 12.1 C Operators

Operator	Example	Description/Meaning
()	f()	Function call
[]	a[10]	Array reference
->	s->a	Structure and union member selection
.	s.a	Structure and union member selection
+ [unary]	+a	Value of a
- [unary]	-a	Negative of a
* [unary]	*a	Reference to object at address a
& [unary]	&a	Address of a
~	~a	One's complement of a
++ [prefix]	++a	The value of a after increment
++ [postfix]	a++	The value of a before increment
- - [prefix]	-a	The value of a after decrement
- - [postfix]	a-	The value of a before decrement
sizeof	sizeof (t1)	Size in bytes of object with type t1
sizeof	sizeof e	Size in bytes of object having the type of expression e
+ [binary]	a + b	a plus b
- [binary]	a - b	a minus b
* [binary]	a * b	a times b
/ %	a / ba	a divided by b
	% b	Remainder of a/b
>>	a >> b	a, right-shifted b bits

<<	a << b	a, left-shifted b bits
<	a < b	1 if a < b; 0 otherwise
>	a > b	1 if a > b; 0 otherwise
<=	a <= b	1 if a <= b; 0 otherwise
>=	a >= b	1 if a >= b; 0 otherwise
==	a == b	1 if a equal to b; 0 otherwise
!=	a != b	1 if a not equal to b; 0 otherwise
& [binary]	a & b	Bitwise AND of a and b
|	a | b	Bitwise OR of a and b
^	a ^ b	Bitwise XOR (exclusive OR) of a and b
&&	a && b	Logical AND of a and b (yields 0 or 1)
||	a || b	Logical OR of a and b (yields 0 or 1)
!	!a	Logical NOT of a (yields 0 or 1)
?:	a ? e1 : e2	Expression e1 if a is nonzero;
		Expression e2 if a is zero
=	a = b	a, after b is assigned to it
+=	a += b	a plus b (assigned to a)
-=	a -= b	a minus b (assigned to a)
*=	a *= b	a times b (assigned to a)
/=	a /= b	a divided by b (assigned to a)
%=	a %= b	Remainder of a/b (assigned to a)
>>=	a >>= b	a, right-shifted b bits (assigned to a)
<<=	a <<= b	a, left-shifted b bits (assigned to a)
&=	a &= b	a AND b (assigned to a)
|=	a |= b	a OR b (assigned to a)
^=	a ^= b	a XOR b (assigned to a)
,	e1,e2	e2 (e1 evaluated first)

12.5 ARITHMETIC OPERATORS

The C language provides +, -, /, *, **%** operators. The % operator is modulus division operator and results the value of the remainder, e.g., **8 % 3** = **2** because the remainder is two and **6%3 = 0,** as the remainder is zero. In case of division operator if both operands are int type we get integer result e.g., **6/3 = 2, 7/3=2**. If one operand is **float,** the division will be float type because **float** data type comes before the **int** data type in hierarchy. The result of the division also depends on the variable to which we assign the result of evaluated expression. If two operands are integer type but variable to which the expression is assigned is **float** type, the result is **float** type. Generally computed value depends on the data type of the recipient variable. For example, see the following,

1. ```
   int x = 30 ;
       int y = 9 ;
   float z = x/y ;
   ```
   Then value of z will be 3.333333
2. ```
   int x  = 30 ;
   int y = 9 ;
   int z = x/y;
   ```
   Then the value of z will be 3

3. float x = 30.04 ;
   int y = 9 ;
   int z = x/y;
   Then the value of z will be 3
4. int x = 30 ;
   float y = 9.2 ;
   int z = x/y;
   Then the value of z will be 3
5. int x = 30 ;
   float y = 9.2 ;
   float z = x/y ;
   Then value of z will be 3.260869

Similar case is for addition, subtraction, and multiplication operations. For examples,

1. int z, w, x=32, y=20;
   z= x-y;
   w=x+y;
   Then values of z and w are 12 and 52, respectively.
2. int z, w, x=32;
   float y=20.22;
   z= x-y;
   w=x+y;
   Then values of z and w are 11 and 42, respectively.
3. float x=32.55, z, w;
   int y=20;
   z=x-y;
   w=x+y;
   Then values of z and w are 12.55 and 42.55, respectively.
4. int x=20, y=32, z;
   z=x-y;
   Then value of z= -12.
5. float y=32.55;
   int x=20, z;
   z=x-y;
   Then value of z is -12.
6. int x=25, y= - 5, z;
   z= x*y;
   Then value of z is -125.
7. int x=25, z;
   float y=10.5;
   z=x*y;
   Then value of z is 262.5.

We can try other combinations also for arithmetic operators. We may get warning from compiler that data types are not compatible, but finally we can run programs. Sometimes we can print the value of an integer variable as float and float variable as integer by placing the appropriate "%d" or "%f". See Example 8 which is implementing the above discussion.

Example 8: Write a program segment for demonstrating the different types of arithmetic operators.

Answer: Following code segment demonstrates different types of arithmetic operators available in C.

For example, let us see the following program segment which demonstrates the arithmetic operators.

```
/* Test of the arithmetic operators */
/*arithopt.c*/
#include<stdio.h>
#include<conio.h>
void main()
{
    int x, y, z;
    float x1 , y1 , zl ;
    printf("\n Division Operator'/' ") ;
    printf("\n---------------");
    x = 100 ;
    y = 30 ;
    z = x / y ;
    printf("\n x = %d",x);
    printf("\n x = %d",y);
    printf("\n x/y(integer value) = %d ",x/y);
    printf("\n x/y (float value) = %f ", (float) a/b);
    x1 = 15.5 ;
    y1 = 5.0 ;
    zl = x1 / y1 ;
    z = x1 / y1 ;
    printf("\n x1 = %f",x1);
    printf("\n y1 = %f",y1);
    printf("\n x1/y1(integer value) = %d ",z);
    printf("\n x1/y1 (float value) = %f ", zl);
    printf("\n Addition Operator '+'") ;
    printf("\n---------------");
    x = 100 ;
    y = 30 ;
    z = x + y ;
    printf("\n x = %d",x);
    printf("\n y = %d",y);
    printf("\n x+y(integer value) = %d ",x+y);
    printf("\n x+y (float value) = %f ", (float) x+y);
    x1 = 15.5 ;
    y1 = 5.0 ;
    zl = x1 + y1 ;
    z = x1 + y1 ;
    printf("\n x1 = %f",x1);
    printf("\n y1 = %f",y1);
    printf("\n x1+y1(integer value) = %d",z);
    printf("\n a1+b1 (float value) = %f ", zl);
    printf("\n Multiplication Operator '*'") ;
    printf("\n---------------");
    x = 100 ;
    y = 30 ;
    z = x * y ;
    printf("\n x = %d",x);
```

```
    printf("\n y = %d",y);
    printf("\n x*y(integer value) = %d ",x*y);
    printf("\n x*y (float value) = %f ", (float) x*y);
    x1 = 15.5 ;
    y1 = 5.0 ;
    zl = x1 * y1 ;
    z = x1 * y1 ;
    printf("\n x1 = %f",x1);
    printf("\n y1 = %f",y1);
    printf("\n x1*y1(integer value) = %d ",z);
    printf("\n x1*y1 (float value) = %f ", zl);
    getch( );
}
```

```
OUTPUT
Division Operator '/ '
x=100
y=30
x/y (integer value) = 3
x/y (float value) = 3.333333
x1=15.500000
y1=5.0000000
x1/y1 (integer value) = 3
x1/y1 (float value) =3.1000000
Addition Operator '+'
x=100
y=30
x+y (integer value) = 130
x+y (float value) = 130.000000
x1=15.5000000
y1=5.0000000
x1+y1 (integer value) = 20
x1+y1 (float value) = 20.500000
Multiplication Operator '*'

x=100
y=30
x*y (integer value) = 3000
x*y (float value) = 3000.00000
x1=15.50000
y1=5.00000
x1*y1 (integer value) = 77
x1*y1 (float value) = 77.50000
```

We have used the printf ( ) as:

printf("\n x*y (float value) = %f ", (float) x*y);

There is escape sequence "\n" and then the message "x*y (float value) =" and then type casting "(float) x*y". Why we need such type of casting? We have two integer variables x and y and we want to print x*y as float value. So, here we need to type cast the x*y to float value. Similarly, we can type cast a float value into integer value to avoid the compiler warning/error message.

Now recall the previous examples of the arithmetic operators {arithopt.c}. We can use type casting as given below to avoid the incompatibility of the operands used:

```
float y=32.55;
        int x=20, z;
        z=(int) x-y;
int x = 30 ;
        float y = 9.2 ;
float z = (float) x/y ;
int x = 30, y=9 ;
        float z = (float) x/y ;
```

See Example 9 which is implementing the above discussion.

Example 9: Following program segment demonstrates the mode '%' operator.

```
#include <stdio.h>
void main()
{
 int i,j;

 /* The modulo is the remainder of after an integer division */
 printf("14 modulo 7 (14%%7) is %i\n", 14%7);            /* answer is 0    */
 printf("15 modulo 7 (15%%7) is %i\n", 15%7);            /* answer is 1    */
 i=10; j=6;
    printf("%i modulo %i (%i%%%i) is %i\n",i,j,i,j,i%j); /* answer is 4    */
}
```

12.6 RELATIONAL OPERATORS

Relational operators are used to compare two operands. Expressions containing relational operators evaluate to true or false in C++. In C, they evaluate to either 0 or 1. The result is not an lvalue.

If the operands have arithmetic types, the usual arithmetic conversions on the operands are performed.

When the operands are pointers, the result is determined by the locations of the objects to which the pointers refer. If the pointers do not refer to objects in the same array, the result is not defined.

A pointer can be compared to a constant expression that evaluates to 0. We can also compare a pointer to a pointer of type void*. The pointer is converted to a pointer of type void*.

If two pointers refer to the same object, they are considered equal. If two pointers refer to non-static members of the same object, the pointer to the object declared later is greater, provided that they are not separated by an access specifier; otherwise the comparison is undefined. If two pointers refer to data members of the same union, they have the same address value.

If two pointers refer to elements of the same array, or to the first element beyond the last element of an array, the pointer to the element with the higher subscript value is greater.

We can only compare members of the same object with relational operators. Relational operators have left-to-right associativity. For example, the expression:

```
a < b <= c
```

is interpreted as:

```
(a < b) <= c
```

If the value of a is less than the value of b, the first relationship yields 1 in C, or true in C++. The compiler then compares the value true (or 1) with the value of c (integral promotions are carried out if needed).

These operators generally used to check some relational conditions like equal to, greater than, less than, etc between two operands. These operators are used when we want to test some relational conditions before executing a group of statements or statement. The relational operators are shown in Table 12.2.

When a statement having a logical expression is evaluated by a compiler, result is either TRUE (in binary 1) or FALSE (in binary 0) logical value. These two logical values are used in statements for setting the conditions true or false. The logical expressions are passed to the if() function defined in C language. Summary of the logical operators are given in Table 12.3. This function returns either true or false value.

Table 12.2 Relational Operators

Operator	Meaning	How to Write	Use
<	Less than	X < Y	Indicates whether the value of the left operand is less than the value of the right operand.
< =	Less than or Equal to	X < = Y	Indicates whether the value of the left operand is less than or equal to the value of the right operand.
>	Greater than	X > Y	Indicates whether the value of the left operand is greater than the value of the right operand.
> =	Greater than or Equal to	X > = Y	Indicates whether the value of the left operand is greater than or equal to the value of the right operand.
= =	Equal to	X= = Y	Indicates whether the value of the left operand is equal to the value of the right operand.
!=	Not Equal to	X != Y	Indicates whether the value of the left operand is not equal to the value of the right operand.

For examples,

1. int x=10, y=10;
   ```
   if ( x = = y)
       printf( "x and y are equal");
   ```
   In this program segment, the if() returns TRUE value because x and y have equal value 10.
2. int x=10, y=10;
   ```
   if ( x != y)
       printf( "x and y are not equal");
   ```
   In this program segment, the if() returns FALSE value because x and y have equal value 10.
3. int x=15, y=10;
   ```
   if ( x > = y)
       printf( "x is greater than  or  equal to y");
   ```

In this program segment, the if() returns TRUE value because x is greater than y. Even if x and y have equal value the return of the if() is TRUE.

4. int x = 10, y=15;
   if(x)
   printf("Have a nice day");

In this program segment, x has integer value 10 which makes the function if() to be evaluated TRUE. If x is zero then if() returns FALSE value.

But do not try the following statements in a program because these make function if() to be evaluated TRUE always and may result in infinite loop and computer may not terminate the running program. So, we should be careful about logical expressions passing to function if(). For example, look into the following which are correct.

```
if(1)
if(TRUE)
if(x+y)         where x or y > 0
if( x)          where x >0
if(ABCD)        where ABCD is a string
```

Table 12.3 Summary of Relational Operators

Operator	Description	Example	Evaluation in C++	Evaluation in C
= =	equal	5 = = 4	FALSE	0
		5 = = 5	TRUE	1
!=	not equal	5 != 4	TRUE	1
		5 != 5	FALSE	0
>	greater than	5 > 4	TRUE	1
		5 > 5	FALSE	0
>=	greater than or equal	5 >= 4	TRUE	1
		5 >= 5	TRUE	1
<	less than	5 < 4	FALSE	0
		5 < 5	FALSE	0
<=	less than or equal	5 <= 4	FALSE	0
		5 <= 5	TRUE	1

For example, consider the following program segment.

```
#include<stdio.h>
void main()
{
    int x, y=6;
    char ch='y';
    if(ch)
    {
        printf("\n Enter an integer number:");
        scanf("%d", &x);
        printf("\n You have entered: %d", x);
    }
    getch();
}
```

Why we have placed a opening curly bracket after function if() and closing curly bracket after function printf()? The reason is very simple, we want to make sure that whenever the function if() returns TRUE then all three statements should be evaluated. Since the condition passed to function if() is true, all three statements will be evaluated. Run the above program and see the output generated. After the first execution change the value of character ch to null, i.e., ch='\0' and run the program. We will not get any message and we are required to press a key to terminate the execution. Now let us see some more examples. See Example 10 which is implementing the above discussion.

Example 10: Write a C program for finding the greatest of three numbers.

Answer: The program segment **great.c** implements the relational operators. In this program segment we find largest of three selected number from the standard input device.

```
/*        great.c        */
/*   To Find greatest of 3 numbers          */
#include<stdio.h>
#include<conio.h>
void main()
{
    int x, y, z ;
    printf("\n Enter value for x, y, z: ") ;
    scanf("%d %d %d", &x,&y,&z) ;
    if ( x > y )
      if ( x > z )
        printf(" \n x is greatest = %d",x) ;
    if ( x < y )
      if ( y > z )
              printf(" \n y is greatest = %d",y) ;
    if ( x < y )
     if( z > y )
       printf(" \n z is greatest = %d",z) ;
           if ( x > y )
             if ( y < z )
              if ( x < z )
      printf(" \n z is greatest = %d",z) ;
    getch();
}
```

OUTPUT
Enter value for x, y, z: 24 10 22
x is greatest =24

The precedence of relational operators is shown in Table 12.3. In this table order of precedence is from top to bottom, at the top operator is of highest precedence and at the bottom of the lowest precedence.

12.7 LOGICAL OPERATORS

We have already discussed about the arithmetic and relational operators that are operated on the operands and operands may be in any number system. Here we will discuss about the logical.

Logical operators are used to combine multiple relational or logical tests. They allow compound conditions to be evaluated. Logical operators are mainly used to control program flow. The logical operators along with their syntax are shown in Table 12.4.

Table 12.4 Logical Operators

Operator	Expression	
&&	Logical AND	exp1 && exp2
||	Logical OR	exp1 || exp2
!	Logical NOT	!exp1

The logical AND operator (&&) and the logical OR (||) operator evaluate the truth or falsehood of pairs of expressions. The AND operator evaluates to 1 if and only if both expressions are true. The OR operator evaluates to 1 if either expression is true. To test whether y is greater than x and less than z, we would write

```
(x < y) && (y < z)
```

The logical negation operator (!) takes only one operand. If the operand is true, the result is false; if the operand is false, the result is true. The operands to the logical operators may be integers or floating-point objects. The expression

```
1 && -5
```

results in 1 because both operands are nonzero. The same is true of the expression

```
0.5 && -5
```

Logical operators (and the comma and conditional operators) are the only operators for which the order of evaluation of the operands is defined. The compiler must evaluate operands from left to right. Moreover, the compiler is guaranteed not to evaluate an operand if it is unnecessary. For example, in the expression

```
if ((a != 0) && (b/a == 6.0))
```

if a equals 0, the expression (b/a == 6) will not be evaluated. This rule can have unexpected consequences when one of the expressions contains side effects.

In C, true is equivalent to any nonzero value, and false is equivalent to 0. Table 12.5 shows the logical tables for each operator, along with the numerical equivalent. All of the operators return 1 for true and 0 for false.

Table 12.6 shows a number of examples that use relational and logical operators. The logical NOT operator has a higher precedence than the others. The AND operator has higher precedence than the OR operator. Both the logical AND and OR operators have lower precedence than the relational and arithmetic operators.

Table 12.5 Truth Table for C's Logical Operators

Operand	Operator	Operand	Result
Zero	&&	zero	0
nonzero	&&	zero	0
Zero	&&	nonzero	0
nonzero	&&	nonzero	1
Zero	||	zero	0
nonzero	||	zero	1
Zero	||	nonzero	1
nonzero	||	nonzero	1
not applicable	!	zero	1
	!	nonzero	0

Logical operators (and the conditional and comma operators) are the only operators for which the order of evaluation of the operands is defined. For these operators, operands must be evaluated from left to right. However, the system evaluates only as much of a logical expression as it needs to determine the result. In many cases, this means that the system does not need to evaluate the entire expression. For instance, consider the following expression:

```
if ((a < b) && (c == d))
```

The system begins by evaluating (a < b). If a is not less than b, the system knows that the entire expression is false, so it will not evaluate (c == d). This can cause problems if some of the expressions contain side effects:

```
if ((a < b) && (c == d++))
```

Table 12.6 Examples of Expressions Using the Logical Operators

Given the following declarations: int j = 0, m = 1, n = -1;float x = 2.5, y = 0.0;

Expression	Equivalent Expression	Result
j && m	(j) && (m)	0
j < m && n < m	(j < m) && (n < m)	1
m + n || ! j	(m + n) || (!j)	1
x * 5 && 5 || m / n	((x * 5) && 5) || (m / n)	1
Expression	**Equivalent Expression**	**Result**
j <= 10 && x >= 1 && m	((j <= 10) && (x >= 1)) && m	1
!x || !n || m+n	((!x) || (!n)) || (m+n)	0
x * y < j + m || n	((x * y) < (j + m)) || n	1
(x > y) + !j || n++	((x > y) + (!j)) || (n++)	1
(j || m) + (x || ++n)	(j || m) + (x || (++n))	2

In this case, d is only incremented when a is less than b. This may or may not be what the programmer intended. In general, we should avoid using side effect operators in logical expressions. See Example 11 which is implementing the above discussion.

Example 11: Write a C program to enjoy your vacation in Europe by winning lottery.

Answer: This program shows how logical operators are used in the implementation of above problem.

```
#include <stdio.h>
int main(void)
{
int won_lottery, enough_vacation, money_saved;
char answer;

won_lottery = enough_vacation = money_saved = 0;


printf("\nThis program determines whether you can ");
printf("take your next vacation in Europe.\n");
printf("Have you won the lottery? y or n: ");
fflush(stdin);
scanf("%c", &answer);
if (answer == 'y')
```

```
won_lottery = 1;

printf(”Do you have enough vacation days saved? y or n: “);
fflush(stdin);
scanf (”%c”, &answer);
if (answer == ‘y’)
enough_vacation = 1;

printf(”Have you saved enough money for the trip? y or n: “);
fflush(stdin);
scanf(”%c”, &answer);
if (answer == ‘y’)
money_saved = 1;

printf(”\n”);

if (won_lottery)
{
   printf(”Why do you need a program to decide if you”);
   printf(” can afford a trip to Europe?\n”);
} /* end if */

if (won_lottery || (enough_vacation &&money_saved))
printf(”Look out Paris!\n”);
else if (enough_vacation &&(!money_saved))
printf(”You’ve got the time, but you haven’t got \the dollars.\n”);
else if (!enough_vacation || (!money_saved))
{
   printf(”Tough luck. Try saving your money and “);
   printf(”vacation days next year.\n”);
} /* end else/if */
}
```

12.8 SPECIAL ARITHMETIC OPERATORS

We have seen many arithmetic operators in the earlier previous sections. There are two special arithmetic operators also. These are known as increment and decrement operators. These are unary operator, i.e., these operate on single operand.

1. Increment operator (++), and
2. Decrement operator (- -)

The assignment operators of the expression v = v op e let us replace with v op= e, so that we did not have to mention v twice. In the most common cases, namely when we are adding or subtracting the constant 1 (that is, when op is + or - and e is 1), C provides another set of shortcuts: the auto-increment and auto-decrement operators. In their simplest forms, they look like this:

++i; *add 1 to* i

–j; *subtract 1 from* j

These correspond to the slightly longer i + = 1; and j -= 1; respectively, and also to the fully "longhand" forms i = i + 1; and j = j - 1;

The ++ and – operators apply to one operand (they are unary operators). The expression ++i adds 1 to i, and stores the incremented result back in i. This means that these operators do not just compute new values; they also modify the value of some variable. They share this property-modifying some variable- with the assignment operators; we can say that these operators all have side effects. That is, they have some effect, on the side, other than just computing a new value. The incremented (or decremented) result is also made available to the rest of the expression, so an expression like

```
k = 2 * ++i;
```

means "add one to i, store the result back in i, multiply it by 2, and store that result in k." This is a pretty meaningless expression; our actual uses of ++ later will make more sense.

Both the ++ and – operators have an unusual property: they can be used in two ways, depending on whether they are written to the left or the right of the variable they are operating on. In either case, they increment or decrement the variable they are operating on; the difference concerns whether it is the old or the new value that is "returned" to the surrounding expression. The prefix form ++i increments i and returns the incremented value. The postfix form i++ increments i, but returns the prior, non-incremented value. Rewriting our previous example slightly, the expression

```
k = 2 * i++;
```

means "take i's old value and multiply it by 2, increment i, store the result of the multiplication in k".

The distinction between the prefix and postfix forms of ++ and - will probably seem strained at first, but it will make more sense once we begin using these operators in more realistic situations. For example, consider the role of these operators on arrays type declaration, see the following statements

```
line[nch] = c;
nch = nch + 1;
```

Using the ++ operator, we could simplify write this to

```
line[nch++] = c;
```

We wanted to increment nch after deciding which element of the line array to store into, so the postfix form nch++ is appropriate. Notice that it only makes sense to apply the ++ and - operators to variables (or to other containers such as a[i]). It would be meaningless to say something like

```
1++;
```

or

```
(2+3)++;
```

The ++ operator does not just mean, "Add one"; it means, "Add one to a variable" or "make a variable's value one more than it was before". But (1+2) is not a variable, it is an expression; so there is no place for ++ to store the incremented result.

Another unfortunate example is

```
i = i++;
```

which some confused programmers sometimes write, presumably because they want to be extra sure that i is incremented by 1. But i++ all by itself is sufficient to increment i by 1; the extra (explicit) assignment to i is unnecessary and in fact counterproductive, meaningless, and incorrect. If we want to increment i (that is, add one to it, and store the result back in i), either use

```
i = i + 1;
```

or

```
i += 1;
```

or

```
++i;
```

or

```
i++;
```

Do not try to use some bizarre combination.

Did it matter whether we used ++i or i++ in this last example? Remember, the difference between the two forms is what value (either the old or the new) is passed on to the surrounding expression. If there is no surrounding expression, if the ++i or i++ appears all by itself, to increment i and do nothing else, we can use either form; it makes no difference. Two ways that an expression can appear "all by itself" with "no surrounding expression" are when it is an expression statement terminated by a semicolon, as above, or when it is one of the controlling expressions of a for loop. For example, both the loops

```
for(i = 0; i < 10; ++i)
        printf("%d\n", i);
```

and

```
for(i = 0; i < 10; i++)
        printf("%d\n", i);
```

will behave exactly the same way and produce exactly the same results. In real code, postfix increment is probably more common, though prefix definitely has its uses too. For example, consider the case

```
a[d1 + d2] = a[d1 + d2] + 1;
```

It can be written as

```
a[d1 + d2] += 1;
```

Using ++, we could simplify it still further to

```
a[d1 + d2]++;
```

or

```
++a[d1 + d2];
```

When we start using the ++ and – operators in larger expressions, we end up with expressions which do several things at once, i.e., they modify several different variables at more or less the same time. When we write such an expression, we must be careful not to have the expression "pull the rüg out from under itself" by assigning two different values to the same variable, or by assigning a new value to a variable at the same time that another part of the expression is trying to use the value of that variable.

There are expressions which did several things at once even before we met the ++ and - operators. The expression

```
(c = getchar()) != EOF
```

assigns getchar's return value to c, and compares it to EOF. The +·- and - operators make it much easier to cram a lot into a small expression: the example

```
line[nch++] = c;
```

This statement assigned c to line[nch], and incremented nch. We will eventually meet expressions which do three things at once, such as

```
a[i++] = b[j++];
```

which assigns b[j] to a[i], and increments i, and increments j.

If we are not careful, though, it is easy for this sort of thing to get out of hand. Can one figure out exactly what the expression

```
a[i++] = b[i++];            /* WRONG */
```

should do? We cannot, and here is the important part: *neither can the compiler.* We know that the definition of postfix ++ is that the former value, before the increment, is what goes on to participate in the rest of the expression, but the expression a[i++] = b[i++] contains two ++ operators. Which of them happens first? Does this expression assign the old ith element of b to the new ith element of a, or vice versa? No one knows.

When the order of evaluation matters but is not well defined (that is, when we cannot say for sure which order the compiler will evaluate the various dependent parts in) we say that the meaning of the expression is undefined, and if we are smart we would not write the expression in the first place. Why would anyone ever write an "undefined" expression? Because sometimes, the compiler happens to evaluate it in the order a programmer wanted, and the programmer assumes that since it works, it must be okay. For example, suppose we carelessly wrote this loop:

```
int i, a[10];
i = 0;
while(i < 10)
        a[i] = i++;            /* WRONG */
```

It looks like we are trying to set a[0] to 0, a[1] to 1, etc. But what if the increment i++ happens before the compiler decides which cell of the array a to store the (un-incremented) result in? We might end up setting a[1] to 0, a[2] to 1, etc., instead. Since, in this case, we cannot be sure which order things would happen in, we simply should not write code like this. In this case, what we are doing matches the pattern of a for loop, anyway, which would be a better choice:

```
for(i = 0; i < 10; i++)
        a[i] = i;
```

Now that the increment i++ is not crammed into the same expression that is setting a[i], the code is perfectly well-defined, and is guaranteed to do what we want. In general, we should be wary of ever trying to second-guess the order an expression will be evaluated in, with two exceptions:

1. We can obviously assume that precedence will dictate the order in which binary operators are applied. This typically says more than just what order things happens in, but also what the expression actually means. In other words, the precedence of * over + says more than that the multiplication "happens first" in 1 + 2 * 3; it says that the answer is 7, not 9.
2. Although we have not mentioned it yet, it is guaranteed that the logical operators && and || are evaluated left-to-right, and that the right-hand side is not evaluated at all if the left-hand side determines the outcome.

To look at one more example, it might seem that the code

```
int i = 7;
printf("%d\n", i++ * i++);
```

would have to print 56, because no matter which order the increments happen in, 7*8 is 8*7 is 56. But ++ just says that the increment happens later, not that it happens immediately, so this code could print 49 (if the compiler chose to perform the multiplication first, and both increments later). And, it turns out that ambiguous expressions like this are such a bad idea that the ANSI C does not require compilers to do anything reasonable with them at all. Theoretically, the above code could end up printing 42, or 8923409342, or 0, or crashing the computer.

Programmers sometimes mistakenly imagine that they can write an expression which tries to do too much at once and then predict exactly how it will behave based on "order of evaluation". For example, we know that multiplication has higher precedence than addition which means that in the expression

```
i + j * k;
```

j will be multiplied by k, and then i will be added to the result. Informally, we often say that the multiplication happens "before" the addition. That is true in this case, but it does not say as much as we might think about a more complicated expression, such as

```
i++ + j++ * k++;
```

In this case, besides the addition and multiplication, i, j, and k are all being incremented. We can not say which of them will be incremented first; it is the compiler's choice. In particular, it is not necessarily the case that j++ or k++ will happen first; the compiler might choose to save i's value somewhere and increment i first, even though it will have to keep the old value around until after it has done the multiplication.

In the preceding example, it probably does not matter which variable is incremented first. It is not too hard, though, to write an expression where it does matter. In fact, we have seen one already: the ambiguous assignment a[i++] = b[i++]. We still do not know which i++ happens first. We can not assume, based on the right-to-left behavior of the = operator, that the right-hand i++ will happen first. But if we had to know what a[i++] = b[i++] really did, we had have to know which i++ happened first.

Finally, note that parentheses do not dictate overall evaluation order any more than precedence does. Parentheses override precedence and say which operands go with which operators and they therefore affect the overall meaning of an expression, but they do not say anything about the order of sub-expressions or side effects. We could not "fix" the evaluation order of any of the expressions we've been discussing by adding parentheses. If we write

```
i++ + (j++ * k++);
```

We still would not know which of the increments would happen first. The parentheses would force the multiplication to happen before the addition, but precedence already would have forced that, anyway. If we write

```
(i++) * (i++)
```

The parentheses would not force the increments to happen before the multiplication or in any well-defined order; this parenthesized version would be just as undefined as i++ * i++ was. The precedence of these operators in comparison to arithmetic operators are given Table 12.7. See few more small examples,

```
int num1=10, num2=5, temp;
        temp= ++num1+num2;
        num2=num2+temp++;
```

Here the final values of num1, num2, and temp are 11, 20, and 16, respectively.

```
    int num1=10, num2=5, temp;
num1= ++num1+num2;
        temp=num2++ - num1;
```

Here the final values of num1, num2, and temp are 16, 6, and -11, respectively.

Table 12.7 Precedence of Arithmetic Operators

Precedence	Operator
Highest	++(Increment), -(Decrement)
	- (Unary minus)
	*(Multiplication), / (Division), % (Modulo)
Lowest	+(Addition), - (Subtraction)

12.9 BITWISE OPERATORS

C Language is rich in bitwise operators. These operators are only applicable to the char and **int** data types and not useful with **float, double, long double, void** or other complex data types. The bitwise operators operate on numbers (always integers) as if they were sequences of binary bits (which, of course, internally to the computer they are). These operators will make the most sense, therefore, if we consider integers as represented in binary, octal, or hexadecimal (bases 2, 8, or 16), not decimal (base 10). Remember, we can use octal constants in C by prefixing them with an extra 0 (zero), and we can use hexadecimal constants by prefixing them with 0x (or 0X). Bit-wise operators and their actions are shown in **Table 12.8.** Bitwise operators fall into two categories: binary bitwise operators and unary bitwise operators. Binary operators take two operands, while unary operators only take one.

Table 12.8 Bitwise Operators

Operator	Action	Example A=0010, B=0011 (in binary)
|	OR	A | B = 0011
&	AND	A&B= 0010
Ù	EX-OR	AÙB = 0001
~	1's complement	~B=1100, ~A=1101
>>	Right Shift	A>>1 = 0001, A>>2=0000, B>>1 = 0001
<<	Left Shift	A<<1 = 0100, A<<2 = 1000,

Bitwise AND (&): It is binary operator and provides TRUE or FALSE value as per the bits of two operands. Each bit in the result is 1 only if both corresponding bits in the two input operands are 1. For example, if operands A = $a_0a_1a_2\ldots a_{n-1}$ and B = $b_0b_1b_2\ldots b_{n-1}$, then X = A&B denotes the AND operation. Bit x_i of X is 1 if and only if corresponding bits of A and B operands are 1, i.e., $a_i = 1$ and $b_i = 1$. The following is a truth table that defines & on individual bits.

Truth Table

a_i	b_i	a_i & b_i
0	0	0
0	1	0
1	0	0
1	1	1

For example, it is easiest to perform & on 4 bit numbers. See the following cases.

Variable	b_3	b_2	b_1	b_0
A	1	1	0	0
B	1	0	1	0
X = A & B	1	0	0	0

Bitwise OR: The | (vertical bar) operator performs a bitwise OR on two integers. If operands $A=a_0a_1a_2...a_{n-1}$ and $B=b_0b_1b_2...b_{n-1}$, then X=A | B denotes the AND operation. Each bit in the result is 1 if either of the corresponding bits in the two input operands is 1. For example, Bit x_i of X is 1 if and only if corresponding bits of A and B operands are 1, 1, or 0, 1, or 1, 0, i.e.,

$a_i = 1$ and $b_i = 1$

$a_i = 0$ and $b_i = 1$

$a_i = 1$ and $b_i = 0$

The following is a truth table that defines |, on individual bits.

Truth Table

a_i	b_i	$a_i \mid b_i$
0	0	0
0	1	1
1	0	1
1	1	1

For example, | operation can be shown easily on 4 bit numbers, and is as follows.

Variable	b_3	b_2	b_1	b_0
A	1	1	0	0
B	1	0	1	0
X = A | B	1	1	1	0

Bitwise XOR: The ^ (caret) operator performs a bitwise exclusive-OR on two integers. Each bit in the result is 1 if one, but not both, of the corresponding bits in the two input operands is 1. The following is a truth table that defines ^, on individual bits.

Truth Table

ai	bi	ai ^ bi
0	0	0
0	1	1
1	0	1
1	1	0

For example ^ operation on 4 bit number is as follows.

Variable	b_3	b_2	b_1	b_0
A	1	1	0	0
B	1	0	1	0
X = A ^ B	0	1	1	0

Bitwise NOT: The ~ (tilde) operator performs a bitwise complement on its single integer operand. The ~ operator is therefore a unary operator, like ! and the unary -, &, and * operators. Bitwise NOT flips all of the bits, i.e., complements all the 0 bits to 1 and all the 1s to 0s of number. It is easiest to do this on 4 bit numbers although only 2 bits are necessary to show the concept. For example see the following.

Variable	b_3	b_2	b_1	b_0
A	1	1	0	0
X = ~A	0	0	1	1

Bitwise Shift Operators: The << operator (left shift) shifts its first operand left by a number of bits given by its second operand, filling in new 0 bits at the right. Similarly, the >> operator (right shift) shifts its first operand right. If the first operand is unsigned, >> fills in 0 bits from the left, but if the first operand is signed, >> might fill in 1 bits if the high-order bit was already 1. (Uncertainty like this is one reason why it is usually a good idea to use all unsigned operands when working with the bitwise operators.) For example, 0x56 << 2 is 0x158:

0 1 0 1 0 1 1 0 << 2

0 1 0 1 0 1 1 0 0 0

And 0x56 >> 1 is 0x2b:

0 1 0 1 0 1 1 0 >> 1

0 1 0 1 0 1 1

For both of the shift operators, bits that scroll "off the end" are discarded; they do not wrap around. Therefore, 0x56 >> 3 is 0x0a. The left shift operator and right shift operator are used for multiplication and division by two, respectively. For examples,

1. Let $x=0100_2 = 4$ then
   $x<<1 = 1000_2 = 8$ (shifting one bit left)
   $x<<2 = 10000_2 =16$ (shifting two bit left)
2. Let $y=100000_2 = 32$ then
   $y>>1 = 10000_2 = 16$ (shifting one bit right)
   $y>>2 = 1000_2 = 8$ (shifting two bit right)

See Example 12 which is implementing the above discussion.

Example 12: Write a program to illustrate operation of bitwise operators.

Answer: Following program segment which demonstrates the bitwise operators.

```
/** bitwise.c **/
# include<stdio.h>
void main()
{
char ch1, ch2, ch3 ;
/* We consider 32-bit based compiler */
/* Hexadecimal in binary is
0000 0000 0000 0000 0000 0000 0000 0011 */
ch1 = 0x03;            /* value is in hexadecimal*/

/* Hexadecimal in binary is
   0000 0000 0000 0000 0000 0000 0000 0110 */
   ch2 = 0x06 ;              /* value is in hexadecimal*/
```

```
        printf("\n 32-Bit compiler Based Output ");
        printf(" **************************************");
        printf("\n Value of ch1 = 0x%x",ch1);
        printf("\n Value of ch2 = 0x%x", ch2);
                    /* AND operator Demo */
        printf("\n The value of ch1&ch2 = 0x%x", ch1&ch2);
        /* OR  Operation Demo*/
        printf("\n The value of ch1|ch2 = 0x%x", ch1|ch2);
        /* EX-OR operator */
        printf("\n The value of ch1^ch2 = 0x%x", ch1^ch2);
        /* 1's complement Demo*/
        printf("\n 1's complement of ch1 = 0x%x ",~ch1);
        /* value print in hex */
        printf("\n 1's complement of ch2 = 0x%x ",~ch2);
        /* value print in hex */
    printf("\n Right shift operator Demo");
    printf("\n Value of ch2 after shifting right one bit ....");
    printf(" ch2>>1 is: %d", ch2>>1);        /*value in integer*/
    printf("\n Left shift operator Demo");
    printf("\n Value of ch1 after shifting left one bit ....");
    printf(" ch1<<1 is: %d", ch1<<1);        /*value in integer*/
    }
```

OUTPUT

```
32-Bit compiler Based Output
**************************************
Value of ch1 = 0x03
Value of ch2 = 0x06
The value of ch1&ch2 = 0x2
The value of ch1|ch2 = 0x7
The value of ch1^ch2 = 0x5
1's complement of ch1 = 0xfffffffc
1's complement of ch2 = 0xfffffff9
Right shift operator Demo
Value of ch2 after shifting right one bit ....
ch2>>1 is:3
Left shift operator Demo
Value of ch1 after shifting left one bit ....
ch1<<1 is:6
```

12.10 THE ? : OPERATOR

So far we have seen unary and binary operators provided in C language. There is one operator which is ternary (? :), i.e., this operator operates on three operands. There is ? : operator in C which supports conditional expression construction. This provides a shorthand way of coding an if...else condition. The difference between the expression notation and an if...else condition is that the ? : Notation is an expression and therefore returns a value, while an if...else condition is a statement and does not return a value. The syntax for this operator is:

```
    expr =  exp1 ? exp2 : exp3 ;
```

This syntax is equivalent to

```
if (exp1)
```

```
expr = exp2;
else
expr = exp3;
```

where **exp1, exp2, exp3** represent expressions.

The meaning of the above statement is that first **exp1** will be evaluated. If it is true then **exp2** is evaluated and assigned to **expr.** If **exp1** is false then **exp3** will be evaluated and its value will be the value of expr. There is no requirement that to put parentheses around the exp1 portion of the conditional expression (in second syntax), but doing so will improve code's readability.

Both *exp2* and *exp3* must be assignment-compatible. If *exp2* and *exp3* are pointers to different types, then the compiler issues a warning. The value of a conditional expression is either *exp2* or *exp3,* whichever is selected. The other expression is not evaluated. The type of the result is the type that would be produced if *exp2* and *exp3* were mixed in an expression. For instance, if *exp2* is a char and *exp3* is a double, the result type will be double regardless of whether *exp2* or *exp3* is selected. For example, consider the following code segment.

```
a = 11 ;
b = a > 100 ? 200 : 300;
```

Here value of a is less than 100 and the condition is false so the value of b becomes 300.

```
a = 101 ;
b = a > 100 ? 200 : 300;
```

Here value of a is greater than 100 and the condition is true so the value of b becomes 200. See Example 13 which is implementing the above discussion.

Example 13: Write a C code without using if statement for selecting one value from two values.

Answer: Following program segment implements idea.

```
/** ternary.c **/
# include<stdio.h>
void main()
{
    int b ;
    int choice ;
    printf("\n Input the choice, an integer number: ") ;
    scanf("%d", &choice) ;
    b = choice > 5 ? choice * choice : choice-10 ;
    printf("\nValue of b = %d", b) ;
}
```

12.11 POINTER OPERATORS

We know that each variable is assigned some data type and stored in memory. C provides facility to access memory location of an identifier. A pointer represents a memory address of a variable. A pointer variable is a variable that holds a pointer to a value of its specified type. To declare a pointer variable, we precede the variable name with an asterisk. The following declaration, for example, makes ptr a variable that can hold addresses of long int variables:

```
long int *ptr;
```

The data type, long in this case, refers to the type of variable that ptr can point to. To assign a pointer variable with the virtual address of a variable, we can use the address-of operator &. For instance, the following is legal:

```
long int *ptr;
long int long_var;
ptr = &long_var; /* Assign the address of long_var to ptr. */
```

But this is illegal:

```
long int *ptr;
float int float_var;
ptr = &float_var; /* Illegal - because ptr can only store the address of a long int. */
```

Go through the Example 14 which is implementing the above discussion.

Example 14: Write a C program which finds difference between a pointer variable and other basic data type variable.

Answer: This problem will be demonstarted in different phases which are implemented, first part illustrates the difference between a pointer variable and an integer variable.

```
/* Program name is ptr1.c */
#include <stdio.h>
int main()
{
int j = 1;
int *pj;
pj = &j; /* Assign the address of j to pj */
printf("The value of j is: %d\n", j);
printf("The address of j is: %p\n", pj);
}
```

OUTPUT (If we run this program on 32-bit mode)
The value of j is: 1
The address of j is: 7b033240

To dereference a pointer (get the value stored at the pointer address), use the * operator. The program below shows how dereferencing works:

```
/* Program name is ptr2.c  */
#include <stdio.h>
int main(void)
{
char *p_ch;
char ch1 = 'A', ch2;
printf("The address of p_ch is %p\n", &p_ch);
p_ch = &ch1;
printf("The value of p_ch is %p\n", p_ch);
printf("The dereferenced value of p_ch is %c\n", *p_ch);
ch2=*p_ch;
}
```

OUTPUT
The address of p_ch is 7b033240
The value of p_ch is 7b033244
The dereferenced value of p_ch is A

This is a roundabout and somewhat contrived example that assigns the character A to both ch1 and ch2. It does, however, illustrate the effect of dereference (*) operator. The variable ch1 is initialized to A. The first printf() call displays the address of the pointer variable p_ch. In the next step, p_ch is assigned the address of ch1, which is also displayed. Finally, the dereferenced value of p_ch is displayed and ch2 is assigned to it.

The expression *p_ch is interpreted as "Take the address value stored in p_ch and get the value stored at that address." This gives us a new way to look at the declaration. The data type in the pointer declaration indicates what type of value results when the pointer is dereferenced. For instance, the declaration

```
float *fp;
```

means that when *fp appears as an expression, the result will be a float value. The expression *fp can also appear on the left side of an expression:

```
*fp = 3.15;
```

In this case, we are storing a value (3.15) at the location designated by the pointer fp. This is different from

```
fp = 3.15;
```

which attempts to store the address 3.15 in fp. This, by the way, is illegal, because addresses are not the same as floating-point values. When we assign a value through a dereferenced pointer, make sure that the data types agree. For example,

```
/* Program name is ptr3.c */
#include <stdio.h>
int main(void)
{
    float f = 1.17e3, g;
    int *ip;
    ip = &f;
    g = *ip;
    printf("The value of f is: %f\n", f);
    printf("The value of g is %f\n", g);
}
```

OUTPUT
The value of f is: 1170.000000
The value of g is: 1150435328.000000

In the above example, instead of getting the value of f, g gets an erroneous value because ip is a pointer to an int, not a float. The C compiler issues a warning message when a pointer type is unmatched. If we compile the preceding program, for instance, we receive error.

Pointer Arithmetic: The following arithmetic operations with pointers are legal, we may add an integer to a pointer or subtract an integer from a pointer, use a pointer as an operand to the ++ and – operators, subtract one pointer from another pointer, if they point to objects of the same type, and compare two pointers. All other arithmetic operations with pointers are illegal. When we add or subtract an integer to or from a pointer, the compiler automatically scales the integer to the pointers' type. In this way, the integer always represents the number of objects to jump, not the number of bytes. For example, consider the following program segment:

```
int x[10], *p1x = x, *p2x;
p2x = p1x + 3;
```

Since pointer p1x points to a variable (x) that is 4 bytes long (in UNIX, LINUX, AIX-L otherwise 2 bytes), then the expression p1x + 3 actually increments p1x by 12 (4 * 3), rather than by 3. It is legal to subtract one pointer value from another, provided that the pointers point to the same type of object. This operation yields an integer value that represents the number of objects between the two pointers.

If the first pointer represents a lower address than the second pointer, the result is negative. For example,

```
&a[3] - &a[0]
```

evaluates to 3, but

```
&a[0] - &a[3]
```

evaluates to -3.

It is also legal to subtract an integral value from a pointer value. This type of expression yields a pointer value. The following examples illustrate some legal and illegal pointer expressions:

```
long *p1, *p2;
int a[5], j;
char *p3;
p1 = a;            /* Same as p1 = &a[0] */
p2 = p1 + 4;       /* legal */
j = p2 - p1;       /* legal - j is assigned 4 */
j = p1 - p2;       /* legal - j is assigned -4 */
p1 = p2 - 2;       /* legal - p2 points to a[2] */
p3 = p1 - 1;       /* ILLEGAL - different pointer types*/
j = p1 - p3;       /* ILLEGAL - different pointer types*/
j = p1 + p2;       /* ILLEGAL - cannot add pointers */
```

The pointer has the following main features:

provides a very fast means for referencing array elements,

in functions for modifying calling parameters,

this is a unary operator and returns the memory address of its operand.

***ptr_exp:** Dereferences a pointer. That is, finds the contents stored at the virtual address that ptr_exp holds.

ptr->member: Dereferences a ptr to a structure or union where member is a member of that structure or union.

&lvalue: Finds the virtual address where the lvalue stored.

Go through the Example 15 which is implementing the above discussion.

Example 15: Write a program using * and &.

Answer: Following code demonstrates the pointer operators (* and &).

```
/** pointopt.c **/
# include<stdio.h>
 void main()
 {
     char ch1 ;  /* ch1 is char type */
 char ch2 = 'a';         /* ch is char type */
 char *address_ch;     /* pointer variable is char type */
 address_ch = &ch2; /* assign address of ch to address variable */
 ch1 = *address_ch; /*value at address_ch is assigned to ch1*/
  printf(" \n Address of ch2 = 0x%x", address_ch) ;          /* print address of ch2 */
 printf(" \nValue  of ch = %c", ch1);  /* print value of ch1*/
  }
```

12.12 COMPILE TIME OPERATORS

There are some operators in C that are operated at the compile time and hence these are known as compile time operators. The **sizeof, malloc()** and **calloc()** operators fall in this category. Syntax for **sizeof** operator is

sizeof ***exp*;**

where **exp** is an expression of any type except function, void, or bit field. If the operand is an expression, **sizeof** returns the number of bytes that the result occupies in memory.

sizeof (type_name)

where **type_name** is the name of a predefined or user-defined data type, or the name of some variable. An example of a predefined data type is int. A user-defined data type could be the tag name of a structure.

The sizeof is an unary operator and it finds the size of an object. The sizeof operator accepts two types of operands: an expression or a data type. If we use an expression operand, the expression itself is not evaluated – the compiler only determines what type the result would be. Any side effects in the expression, therefore, will not have an effect. The result type of the sizeof operator is unsigned int. For example, see the following cases:

```
/* Returns the size of an int (4 if ints are four bytes long) */
sizeof(3 + 5)

/* Returns the size of a double (8 if doubles are eight bytes long) */
sizeof(3.0 + 5)

/* Returns the size of a float (4 if floats are four bytes long) */
float x;
sizeof(x)
```

For expressions, the parentheses are optional, so the following is legal:

```
sizeof x;
```

By convention, however, the parentheses are usually included. The operand can also be a data type, in which case the result is the length in bytes of objects of that type. The parentheses are required if the operand is a data type. For example see the following:

```
sizeof(char);  /* 1 */
sizeof(short);  /* 2 */
sizeof(float); /* 4 */
sizeof(int *);  /* 4 */
```

Major uses of this type of operators are in aggregate data processing. Go through the Example 16 which is implementing the above discussion.

Example 16: Following program segment demonstrates few uses of the sizeof operator.

```
/* sizeof.c */
#include <stdio.h>
int main(void)
{
    printf("TYPE\t\tSIZE\n\n");
    printf("char\t\t%d\n", sizeof(char));
```

```
    printf("short\t\t%d\n", sizeof(short));
    printf("int\t\t%d\n", sizeof(int));
    printf("float\t\t%d\n", sizeof(float));
    printf("double\t\t%d\n", sizeof(double));
}
```

OUTPUT (this run is under fedora 5.0 operating system)
TYPE SIZE
char 1
short 2
int 4
float 4
double 8

12.13 COMMA OPERATOR

Use the comma operator to separate two expressions that are to be evaluated one right after the other. The left-hand side of the comma is always evaluated as void data type. For example,

```
x = (b = 10, b + 5);
```

First **b** is assigned the value 10 and then 5 is added to it and it becomes 15, finally last value of **b** is assigned to **x,** i.e., value of **x** will be 15. Uses of parenthesis are necessary because precedence of this operator is least. Comma causes a sequence of operations to be performed. For example, consider another case

```
int a = 2, x ;
x = ( a = a + 10 , a / 5 ) ;
```

Here, the value of x is 2 because original value of a is 2 and 10 is added to it first and then finally it is divided by 5.

The comma operator is popular within for loops. For example, see the following code segment:

```
for (i = 10, j = 4; i * j < n; i++, j++);
```

In this example, the comma operator allows us to initialize both i and j at the beginning of the loop. The comma operator also allows increment i and j together at the end of each loop iteration.

All expressions return values. When we use a comma operator, the expression returns the value of the rightmost expression. For example, the following statement sets variable j to 2:

```
j = (x = 1, y = 2);
```

Assignments such as these, however, are considered poor programming style. We should confine use of the comma operator to for loops. Let us see the following program that evaluates the above discussion.

```
/** comma.c **/
# include<stdio.h>
void main()
{
    int a , x ;
    a = 2 ;
    x = ( a = a + 10 , a / 5) ;
            /* add 10 to a then divide by 5 */
            /* and result assign to x */
    printf("\n Value of a = %d", a ) ;
    printf(" \n Value of x = %d", x ) ;
    x = (  a / 5 , a = a + 10 ) ;
```

```
            /* a is divided  then 10 is added to a */
            /* And assign result to b */
    printf(" \n Value of a = %d",a ) ;
    printf(" \n Value of b = %d",x ) ;
}
```

12.14 PERIOD (.) AND ARROW (Ò) OPERATORS

A member of a structure or a union can be referenced using either of two operators: the period or the right arrow. General syntax for these operators is:

postfix-expression . identifier

postfix-expression → identifier

Use the period to reference members of structures and unions directly. Use the arrow operator to reference members of structures and unions pointed to by pointers. The arrow operator combines the functions of indirection through a pointer and member selection. If P is a pointer to a structure with a member M, the expression P → M is identical to (*P).M.

The *postfix-expression* in the first alternative must be a structure or a union. The expression is followed by a period (.) and an identifier. The identifier must name a member defined as part of the structure or union referenced in the postfix-expression. The value of the expression is the value of the named member. It is an lvalue if the postfix-expression is an lvalue.

If the *postfix-expression* is a pointer to a structure or a pointer to a union, follow it with an arrow and an identifier. The identifier must name a member of the structure or union which the pointer references. The value of the primary expression is the value of the named member. The resulting expression is an lvalue.

The operator and the → operator are closely related. If S is a structure, M is a member of structure S, and &S is a valid pointer expression, S.M is the same as (&S) → M.

12.15 ARITHMETIC OPERATOR WITH ASSIGNMENT

Consider the expression **x + y.** Do either **x** or **y** get modified? The answer is no. Most built-in binary operators do not modify the values of the arguments. This applies to logical operators too. They do not modify their arguments.

The expressions such as **num = num + 10;** in which the variable on the left-hand side is repeated on the right, can be written as **num + = 10;**. The operator + = is called an assignment operator. Most binary operators have a corresponding assignment operators and having the form "operator=", where operator is one of +, -, *, /, <<, >>, &, ^, |, and %. Thus, when we put operator value get the following assignment operators:

+= -= *= /= %= <<= >>= &= ^= |=

= is the obvious one. It takes the result of the expression on the right and assigns it to the variable on the left (lvalue).

For example, if **num+= 10;** then operator pair + = tells the compiler to assign num, the value of num plus 10, i.e., if initially num=5 then after the evaluation of the above expression num=15.

a* = b + 1; means a = a * (b + 1); rather than a = a * b + 1; .

For example, consider a small code which finds summation of two integer numbers.

```
main ()
{
  int a, b=4, c=10;
  a = b + c;
}
```

We know this is stating the obvious, but:

1. b is assigned the value 4
2. c is assigned the value 10
3. a is assigned the result of b plus C (14).

All the other operators act in a similar way. If we find coding the example on the left, it could be changed to the example on the right.

```
main ()                     main()
{                           {
    int a=4;                    int a=4;
    a = a * 4;                  a *= 4;
}                           }
```

The rule is as follows:

The lvalue is multiplied by the rvalue and the result assigned to the lvalue.

Here is another example.

```
main()                      main()
{                           {
    int a=10, b=2;              int a=10, b=2;
    a /= b * 5;                 a = a / (b*5);
}                           }
```

Again both produce the same answer (1).

Consider another example which counts 1's in an integer number interpreting integer number as binary.

```
int binary_count ( unsigned num)
/* Counts number of 1's in a given number */
{
    int b = 0;
    for ( b; num!=0; num>>1)
    if (num & 1)
    b+ = 1;
    return(b);
}
```

12.16 CAST OPERATORS

We can change an expression to specific type by using cast operators. Most of the time, C performs conversions between related data types automatically. When we assign an int value to a float variable or vice versa, or perform calculations involving mixtures of arithmetic types, the types are converted automatically, as necessary. C even performs some pointer conversions automatically: malloc returns type void * (pointer-to-void), but a void * is automatically converted to whatever pointer type we assign (say) malloc's return value to. Occasionally, we need to request a type conversion explicitly. This operator is unary operator. The syntax for cast operator is:

```
(data type) expression ;
```

For example, consider the following code segment.

```
int i = 1, j = 2;
    float f;
    f = i / j;
```

The division operator / results in an integer division, discarding the remainder, when both operands are integral. It performs a floating-point division, yielding a possibly fractional result, when one or both operands have floating-point types. What happens here? Both operands are int, but the result of the division is assigned to a float, which would be able to hold a fractional result. Is the compiler smart enough to notice, and perform a floating-point division? No, it is not. The rule is, "if both operands are integral, division is integer division and discards any remainder", and this is the rule the compiler follows. In this case, then, we must manually and explicitly force one of the operands to be of floating-point type.

Explicit type conversions are requested in C using a cast operator. The name of the operator comes from the term typecast; "typecasting" is another term for explicit type conversion, and some languages have "typecast operators." Yet another term for type conversion is coercion. A cast operator consists of a type name, in parentheses. One way to fix the example above would be to rewrite it as

```
f = (float)i / j;
```

The construction (float)i involves a cast; it says, "take i's value, and convert it to a float." The only thing being converted is the value fetched from i; we are not changing i's type or anything. Now, one operand of the / operator is floating-point, so we perform a floating-point division, and f receives the value 0.5. Equivalently, we could write

```
f = i / (float)j;
```

or

```
f = (float)i / (float)j;
```

It is sufficient to use a cast on one of the operands, but it certainly does not hurt to cast both. A similar situation is

```
int i = 32000, j = 32000;
long int li;
li = i + j;
```

An int is only guaranteed to hold values up to 32,767. Here, the result i + j is 64,000, which is not guaranteed to fit into an int. Even though the eventual destination is a long int, the compiler does not look ahead to see this. The addition is performed using int arithmetic, and it may overflow. Again, the solution is to use a cast to explicitly convert one of the operands to a long int:

```
li = (long int)i + j;
```

Now, since one of the operands is a long int, the addition is performed using long int arithmetic, and does not overflow.

Cast operators do not have to involve simple types; they can also involve pointer or structure or more complicated types. Once upon a time, before the void * type had been invented, malloc returned a char *, which had to be converted to the type we are using. For example, see the following code segment:

```
int *iarray = (int *)malloc(100 * sizeof(int));
```

and

```
struct list *lp = (struct list *)malloc(sizeof(struct list));
```

These casts are not necessary under an ANSI C compiler because malloc returns void * which the compiler converts automatically. The precedence of this operator is equivalent to the other unary operators.

```
/** castopt.c **/
#include<stdio.h>
  void main()
  {
```

```
int a = 200 ;
int b = 34 ;
printf("\n %f", (float) a/b ) ;
printf("\n %d", (int) a/b ) ;
}
```

12.17 OPERATORS PRECEDENCE AND ASSOCIATIVITY

The data type and the value of an expression depend on the data types of the operands and the order of evaluation of operators which is determined by the precedence, and associativity of operators. Precedence is the order in which the compiler groups operands with operators. The C compiler evaluates certain operators and their operands before others. If operands are not grouped using parentheses, the compiler groups them according to its own rules. Most operators group from the left to the right but some group from the right to the left. The grouping indicates how an expression containing several operators of the same precedence will be evaluated. For example,

Left to right grouping means the expression

```
a/b * c/d;
```

behaves as if it had been written:

```
(((a/b)*c)/d);
```

An operator that groups from the right to the left causes the expression

```
a = b = c;
```

to behave as if it had been written:

```
a = (b = c);
```

means a = (b = c), In other words, first b=c is evaluated and then a=b, that is, right associativity.

```
a + b - c; means (a + b) – c;
```

Here + and – operators have same priority but associativity is left to right and hence first a+b is evaluated and then c is subtracted.

Let us first consider the order of evaluation. When expressions contain more than one operator, the order in which the operators are evaluated depends on their precedence levels. A higher precedence operator is evaluated before a lower precedence operator. When operators of the same precedence level appear in an expression, the order of evaluation is determined by the associativity (or grouping). Except for the assignment operator, associativity of most binary operators is left to right (LTR); associativity of the assignment operator and most unary operators is right to left (RTL).

The unary operators and assignment operators are right associative and the remaining operators are left associative. Table 12.9 shows the precedence levels and associativity of all C operators. In the table, there are 15 precedence levels 0 through 14: higher level implies higher precedence. The precedence levels of operators are separated by solid lines with operators within solid lines having the same precedence level.

For example, binary arithmetic operators, *, / and % have the same precedence level which is higher than binary +, and -. Observe that the precedence of the assignment operator is lower than all but higher than comma operator. This is in accordance with the rule that the expression on the right side of an assignment is evaluated first, and then its value is assigned to the left hand side object. On the other hand, function call has the highest precedence, since a function value is treated like a variable reference in an expression. In any expression, parentheses may be used to over ride the precedence of the operators - innermost parentheses are always evaluated first.

The precedence of binary logical operators is lower than that of binary relational operators; that of binary relational operators is lower than that of binary arithmetic operators, and so forth. The unary NOT operator has a precedence higher than that of all binary operators.

12.18 EXPRESSION AND ITS TYPES

Expressions acted on by operators, i.e., expressions are sequences of operators, operands, and punctuators that specify a computation. The evaluation of expressions is based on the operators that the expressions contain and the context in which they are used. A sequence of operators and operands may yield a single value. An expression is classified as per operands' data type and values used. An expression can result in a value and can produce side effects. A side effect is a change in the state of the execution environment. For example, the following is an expression containing two operands and one operator.

```
z = a + b;
```

a and **b** are both operands of the + operator.

The following are types of expressions:

- Lvalues and rvalues
- Postfix expressions
- Primary expressions
- Conditional expressions
- Assignment expressions
- Comma expressions
- Unary expressions
- Cast expressions
- Binary expressions

Table 12.9 Precedence and Associativity of operators

Operator	Description	Associativity	Precedence
()	Parentheses (grouping)	LTR	14
[]	Brackets (array subscript)		
.	Member selection via object name		
->	Member selection via pointer		
++ -	Unary pre-increment/pre-decrement	RTL	13
+ -	Unary plus/minus		
! ~	Unary logical negation/bitwise complement		
(type)*	Unary cast (change type)		
&	DereferenceAddress		
sizeof	Determine size in bytes		
* / %	Multiplication/division/modulus	LTR	12
+ -	Addition/subtraction	LTR	11
<< >>	Bitwise shift left, Bitwise shift right	LTR	10
< <=	Relational less than/less than or equal to	LTR	9
> >=	Relational greater than/greater than or equal to		
== !=	Relational is equal to/is not equal to	LTR	8
&	Bitwise AND	LTR	7
^	Bitwise exclusive OR	LTR	6

Operator	Description	Associativity	Precedence
|	Bitwise inclusive OR	LTR	5
&&	Logical AND	LTR	4
||	Logical OR	LTR	3
?:	Ternary conditional	RTL	2
=	Assignment		
+= -=	Addition/subtraction assignment	RTL	1
*= /=	Multiplication/division assignment		
%= &=	Modulus/bitwise AND assignment		
^= |=	Bitwise exclusive/inclusive OR assignment		
<<= >>=	Bitwise shift left/right assignment		
,	Comma (separate expressions)	LTR	0

12.19 LVALUES AND RVALUES EXPRESSIONS

An **lvalue** (pronounced "el-value") is an expression that refers to a region of storage that can be manipulated, i.e., an object is a region of storage that can be examined and stored into. An lvalue is an expression that refers to such an object. An lvalue does not necessarily permit modification of the object it designates. For example, a const object is an lvalue that cannot be modified. The term modifiable lvalue is used to emphasize that the lvalue allows the designated object to be changed as well as examined. The following object types are lvalues, but not modifiable lvalues:

An array type

An incomplete type

A const-qualified type

A structure or union type with one of its members qualified as a const type

For example, all simple variables, like ints and floats are lvalues. An element of an array is also an lvalue; however an entire array is not. A member of a structure or union is an lvalue; an entire structure or union is not. Given the following declarations:

```
int *p, a, b;
int arr[4];
int func();
a               /* lvalue */
a + b           /* Not an lvalue */
p               /* lvalue */
*p              /* lvalue */
arr             /* lvalue, but not modifiable */
*(arr + a)      /* lvalue */
arr[a]          /* lvalue, equivalent to *(arr+a) */
func/* Not an lvalue */
func()          /* Not an lvalue */
```

Because these lvalues are not modifiable, they cannot appear on the left side of an assignment statement.

The term rvalue refers to a data value that is stored at some address in memory. An rvalue is an expression that cannot have a value assigned to it. Both a literal constant and a variable can serve as an rvalue. When an lvalue appears in a context that requires an rvalue, the lvalue is implicitly converted to an rvalue. The reverse, however, is not true: an rvalue cannot be converted to an lvalue. Rvalues always have complete types or the void type.

C defines a function designator as an expression that has function type. A function designator is distinct from an object type or an lvalue. It can be the name of a function or the result of dereferencing a function pointer. The C language also differentiates between its treatment of a function pointer and an object pointer. On the other hand, in C++, a function call that returns a reference is an lvalue. Otherwise, a function call is an rvalue expression. In C++, every expression produces an lvalue, an rvalue, or no value. In both C and C++, certain operators require lvalues for some of their operands. Table 12.10 lists these operators and additional constraints on their usage.

Table 12.10 Operators Participating in lvalue and rvalue expression

Operator	Requirement
& (unary)	Operand must be an lvalue.
++ -	Operand must be an lvalue. This applies to both prefix and postfix forms.
= += -= *= %= <<= >>= &= ^= |=	Left operand must be an lvalue.

For example, all assignment operators evaluate their right operand and assign that value to their left operand. The left operand must be a modifiable lvalue or a reference to a modifiable object. The address operator (&) requires an lvalue as an operand while the increment (++) and the decrement (-) operators require a modifiable lvalue as an operand. The following example shows expressions and their corresponding lvalues.

Expression	Lvalue
x = 42	x
*ptr = newvalue	*ptr
a++	a
Int &f()	The function call to f() /* this valid in C++*/

12.20 POSTFIX EXPRESSIONS

Postfix operators are operators that appear after their operands. A postfix expression is a primary expression, or a primary expression that contains a postfix operator. The available postfix operators are:

Function call operator ( )
Array subscripting operator [ ]
Dot operator.
Arrow operator ->
Compound literals

Function call operator ( ): A function call is an expression containing the function name followed by the function call operator, (). If the function has been defined to receive parameters, the values that are to be sent into the function are listed inside the parentheses of the function call operator. The argument list can contain any number of expressions separated by commas. It can also be empty. The type of a function call expression is the return type of the function. This type can either be a complete type, a reference type, or the type void. A function call expression is always an rvalue in C. A function call is an lvalue if and only if the type of the function is a reference in C++. For example, see the following:

```
stub()
overdue(account, date, amount)
notify(name, date + 5)
report(error, time, date, ++num)
```

The order of evaluation for function call arguments is not specified. In the following example:

```
method(sample1, batch.process-, batch.process);
```

The argument batch.process- might be evaluated last, causing the last two arguments to be passed with the same value.

Array subscripting operator [ ]: A postfix expression followed by an expression in [ ] (brackets) specifies an element of an array. The expression within the brackets is referred to as a subscript. The first element of an array has the subscript zero. By definition, the expression a[b] is equivalent to the expression *((a) + (b)), and, because addition is associative, it is also equivalent to b[a]. Between expressions a and b, one must be a pointer to a type T, and the other must have integral or enumeration type. The result of an array subscript is an lvalue. The following example demonstrates this:

```
#include <stdio.h>
int main(void) {
 int a[3] = { 10, 20, 30 };
 printf("a[0] = %d\n", a[0]);
 printf("a[1] = %d\n", 1[a]);
 printf("a[2] = %d\n", *(2 + a));
 return 0;
}
```

OUTPUT
a[0] = 10
a[1] = 20
a[2] = 30

The first element of each array has the subscript 0. The expression contract[35] refers to the 36th element in the array contract. In a multidimensional array, we can reference each element (in the order of increasing storage locations) by incrementing the right-most subscript most frequently. For example, following statement gives the value 100 to each element in the array code[4][3][6]:

```
for (first = 0; first < 4; ++first)
{
for (second = 0; second < 3; ++second)
    {
        for (third = 0; third < 6; ++third)
    {
      code[first][second][third] = 100;
        }
    }
}
```

Dot operator . : The . (dot) operator is used to access class, structure, or union members. The member is specified by a postfix expression, followed by a . (dot) operator, followed by a possibly qualified identifier or a pseudo-destructor name. The postfix expression must be an object of type struct or union. The name must be a member of that object. The value of the expression is the value of the selected member. If the postfix expression and the name are lvalues, the expression value is also an lvalue. If the postfix expression is type-qualified, the same type qualifiers will apply to the designated member in the resulting expression.

Arrow operator -> : The -> (arrow) operator is used to access, structure or union members using a pointer. A postfix expression, followed by an -> (arrow) operator, followed by a possibly qualified identifier or a pseudo-destructor name, designates a member of the object to which the pointer points. The postfix expression must be a pointer to an object of type struct or union. The name must be a member of that object. The value of the expression is the value of the selected member. If the name is an lvalue, the expression value is also an lvalue. If the expression is a pointer to a qualified type, the same type-qualifiers will apply to the designated member in the resulting expression.

Compound literals: A compound literal is a postfix expression that provides an unnamed object whose value is given by an initializer list. The C99 language feature allows us to pass parameters to functions without the need for temporary variables. It is useful for specifying constants of an aggregate type (arrays, structures, and unions) when only one instance of such types is needed. The syntax for a compound literal resembles that of a cast expression. However, a compound literal is an lvalue, while the result of a cast expression is not. Furthermore, a cast can only convert to scalar types or void, whereas a compound literal results in an object of the specified type. Syntax for compound literal is:

```
(type_name){initializer_list};
```

The type_name can be any data type, including vectors, and user-defined types. It can be an array of unknown size, but not a variable length array. If the type is an array of unknown size, the size is determined by the initializer list. The following example passes a constant structure variable of type point containing two integer members to the function drawline:

```
drawline((struct point){6,7});
```

If the compound literal occurs outside the body of a function, the initializer list must consist of constant expressions, and the unnamed object has static storage duration. If the compound literal occurs within the body of a function, the initializer list need not consist of constant expressions, and the unnamed object has automatic storage duration.

12.21 PRIMARY EXPRESSIONS

Primary expressions fall into the following general categories:

Names (identifiers)
Literals (constants)
Integer constant expressions
Parenthesized expressions ( )

Names: The value of a name depends on its type which is determined by how that name is declared. Table 12.11 shows whether a name is an lvalue expression.

Table 12.11 Primary expressions: Names

Name declared as	Evaluates to	Is an lvalue?
Variable of arithmetic,	An object of that type pointer, enumeration, structure, or union type	Yes
Enumeration constant	The associated integer value	No
Array	That array. In contexts subject to conversions, a pointer to the first object in the array, except where the name is used as the argument to the sizeof operator.	In C no but in C++ yes

Name declared as	Evaluates to	Is an lvalue?
Function	That functions. In contexts subject to conversions, a pointer to that function, except where the name is used as the argument to the sizeof operator, or as the function in a function call expression.	In C no but in C++ yes

As an expression, a name may not refer to a label, typedef name, structure member, union member, structure tag, union tag, or enumeration tag. Names used for these purposes reside in a namespace that is separate from that of names used in expressions. However, some of these names may be referred to within expressions by means of special constructs: for example, the dot or arrow operators may be used to refer to structure and union members; typedef names may be used in casts or as an argument to the sizeof operator.

Literals: A literal is a numeric constant or string literal. When a literal is evaluated as an expression, its value is a constant. A lexical constant is never an lvalue. However, a string literal is an lvalue.

Integer constant expressions: An integer compile-time constant is a value that is determined during compilation and cannot be changed at runtime. An integer compile-time constant expression is an expression that is composed of constants and evaluated to a constant. In other words integer expressions are expressions that, after all automatic and explicit type conversions produce a result that has one of the integer types. For example, if j and k are integers, the following are all integral expressions:

j
j * k
j / k + 3
k - 'a'
3 + (int) 5.0

Constant expressions contain only constant values. For example, the following are all constant expressions:

5
5 + 6 * 13 / 3.0
'a'

An integer constant expression is composed of only the following:

literals
enumerators
const variables
static data members of integral or enumeration types
casts to integral types
sizeof expressions, where the operand is not a variable length array

The sizeof operator applied to a variable length array type is evaluated at runtime, and therefore is not a constant expression. We must use an integer constant expression in the following situations:

In the subscript declarator as the description of an array bound.
After the keyword case in a switch statement.
In an enumerator, as the numeric value of an enumeration constant.
In a bit-field width specifier.
In the preprocessor #if statement. (Enumeration constants, address constants, and sizeof cannot be specified in a preprocessor #if statement.)

Parenthesized expressions ( ): Use parentheses to explicitly force the order of expression evaluation. The following expression {Figure 12.1} does not use parentheses to group operands and operators. The parentheses surrounding weight, zipcode are used to form a function call. Note how the compiler groups the operands and operators in the expression according to the rules for operator precedence and associativity.

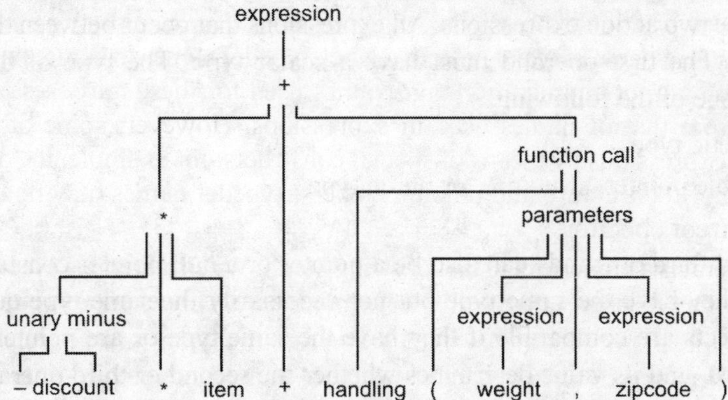

Figure 12.1 Expression does not Using Parenthesis

The following expression {Figure 12.2} is similar to the previous expression, but it contains parentheses that change how the operands and operators are grouped.

In an expression that contains both associative and commutative operators, we can use parentheses to specify the grouping of operands with operators. The parentheses in the following expression guarantee the order of grouping operands with the operators:

x = f + (g + h);

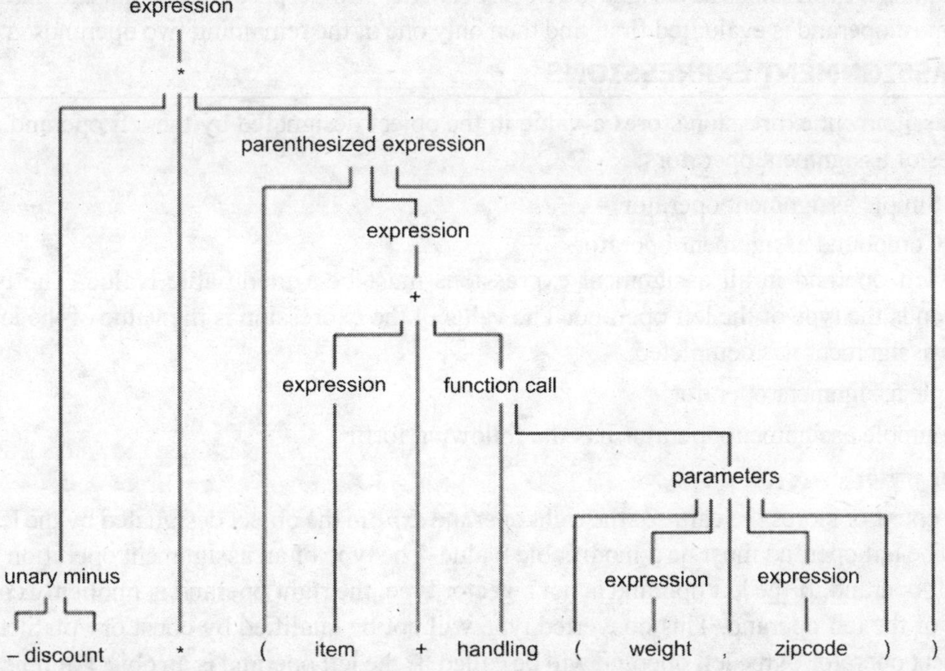

Figure 12.2 Expression Using Parentheses

12.22 CONDITIONAL EXPRESSIONS

A conditional expression is a compound expression that contains a condition that is implicitly converted to type of operand1, an expression to be evaluated if the condition evaluates to true ($operand_2$), and an expression to be evaluated if the condition has the value false ($operand_3$). The conditional expression contains one two-part operator. The ? symbol follows the condition, and the : symbol appears between the two action expressions. All expressions that occur between the ? and : are treated as one expression. The first operand must have a scalar type. The type of the second and third operands must be one of the following:

An arithmetic type

A compatible pointer, structure, or union type

void

The second and third operands can also be a pointer or a null pointer constant. Two objects are compatible when they have the same type but not necessarily the same type qualifiers (volatile or const). Pointer objects are compatible if they have the same type or are pointers to void. The first operand is evaluated, and its value determines whether the second or third operand is evaluated:

If the value is true, the second operand is evaluated.

If the value is false, the third operand is evaluated.

The result is the value of the second or third operand. If the second and third expressions evaluate to arithmetic types, the usual arithmetic conversions are performed on the values. The types of the second and third operands determine the type of the result as shown in the following:

```
a ? b : c ? d : e ? f : g
a ? b : (c ? d : (e ? f : g))
```

Conditional expressions have right-to-left associativity with respect to their first and third operands. The leftmost operand is evaluated first, and then only one of the remaining two operands is evaluated.

12.23 ASSIGNMENT EXPRESSIONS

An assignment expression stores a value in the object designated by the left operand. There are two types of assignment operators:

Simple assignment operator =

Compound assignment operators

The left operand in all assignment expressions must be a modifiable lvalue. The type of the expression is the type of the left operand. The value of the expression is the value of the left operand after the assignment has completed.

Simple assignment operator =

The simple assignment operator has the following form:

```
lvalue = expr
```

The operator stores the value of the right operand *expr* in the object designated by the left operand *lvalue.* The left operand must be a modifiable lvalue. The type of an assignment operation is the type of the left operand. If the left operand is not a vector type, the right operand is implicitly converted to the type of the left operand. This converted type will not be qualified by const or volatile. The copy assignment operator of the left operand will be called. If the left operand is an object of reference type, the compiler will assign the value of the right operand to the object denoted by the reference.

Compound assignment operators: The compound assignment operators consist of a binary operator and the simple assignment operator. They perform the operation of the binary operator on both operands and store the result of that operation into the left operand which must be a modifiable lvalue. The following table shows the operand types of compound assignment expressions:

Operator	Left operand	Right operand
+= or -=	Arithmetic	Arithmetic
+= or -=	Pointer	Integral type
*=, /=, and %=	Arithmetic	Arithmetic
<<=, >>=, &=, ^=, and |=	Integral type	Integral type

Note that the expression

a *= b + c

is equivalent to

a = a * (b + c)

and not

a = a * b + c

Table 12.12 lists the compound assignment operators and shows an expression using each operator:

Table 12.12 Compound Assignment Operators

Operator	Example	Equivalent expression
+=	index += 2	index = index + 2
-=	*(pointer++) -= 1	*pointer = *(pointer++) - 1
*=	bonus *= increase	bonus = bonus * increase
/=	time /= hours	time = time / hours
%=	allowance %= 1000	allowance = allowance % 1000
<<=	result <<= num	result = result << num
>>=	form >>= 1	form = form >> 1
&=	mask &= 2	mask = mask & 2
^=	test ^= pre_test	test = test ^ pre_test
|=	flag |= ON	flag = flag | ON

Although the equivalent expression column shows the left operands (from the example column) twice, it is in effect evaluated only once.

12.24 COMMA EXPRESSIONS

A comma expression contains two operands of any type separated by a comma and has left-to-right associativity. The left operand is fully evaluated, possibly producing side effects, and its value, if there is one, is discarded. The right operand is then evaluated. The type and value of the result of a comma expression are those of its right operand, after the usual unary conversions. The result of a comma expression is not an lvalue. Any number of expressions separated by commas can form a single expression because the comma operator is associative. The use of the comma operator guarantees that the sub-expressions will be evaluated in left-to-right order, and the value of the last becomes the value of the entire expression. In the following example, if omega has the value 11, the expression increments delta and assigns the value 3 to alpha:

```
alpha = (delta++, omega % 4);
```

A sequence point occurs after the evaluation of the first operand. The value of delta is discarded. Similarly, in the following example, the value of the expression:

intensity++, shade * increment, rotate(direction);

is the value of the expression:

rotate(direction)

In some contexts where the comma character is used, parentheses are required to avoid ambiguity. For example, the function

f(a, (t = 3, t + 2), c);

has only three arguments: the value of a, the value 5, and the value of c. Other contexts in which parentheses are required are in field-length expressions in structure and union declarator lists, enumeration value expressions in enumeration declarator lists, and initialization expressions in declarations and initializers.

In the previous example, the comma is used to separate the argument expressions in a function invocation. In this context, its use does not guarantee the order of evaluation (left to right) of the function arguments. Table 12.13 gives some examples of the uses of the comma operator. The primary use of the comma operator is to produce side effects in the following situations:

Calling a function
Entering or repeating an iteration loop
Testing a condition
Other situations where a side effect is required but the result of the expression is not immediately needed.

Table 12.13 Uses of Comma Operator

Statement	Effects
for (i=0; i<2; ++i, f());	A for statement in which i is incremented and f() is called at each iteration.
if (f(), ++i, i>1) { /* ... */ }	An if statement in which function f() is called, variable i is incremented, and variable i is tested against a value. The first two expressions within this comma expression are evaluated before the expression i>1. Regardless of the results of the first two expressions, the third is evaluated and its result determines whether the if statement is processed.
func((++a, f(a)));	A function call to func() in which a is incremented, the resulting value is passed to a function f(), and the return value of f() is passed to func(). The function func() is passed only a single argument, because the comma expression is enclosed in parentheses within the function argument list.

12.25 UNARY EXPRESSIONS

A unary expression contains one operand and a unary operator. The supported standard unary operators are:

Increment operator ++
Decrement operator –
Unary plus operator +
Unary minus operator –
Logical negation operator !
Bitwise negation operator ~
Address operator &
Indirection operator *

Increment operator ++

The ++ (increment) operator adds 1 to the value of a scalar operand, or if the operand is a pointer, increments the operand by the size of the object to which it points. The operand receives the result of the increment operation. The operand must be a modifiable lvalue of arithmetic or pointer type. We can put the ++ before or after the operand. If it appears before the operand, the operand is incremented.

The incremented value is then used in the expression. If we put the ++ after the operand, the value of the operand is used in the expression before the operand is incremented. For example,

```
play = ++play1 + play2++;
```

is similar to the following expressions; play2 is altered before play:

```
int temp, temp1, temp2;
temp1 = play1 + 1;
play1 = temp1;
play2 = play2 + 1;
temp2 = play2;
temp = temp1 + temp2;
play = temp;
```

The result has the same type as the operand after integral promotion. The usual arithmetic conversions on the operand are performed.

Decrement operator –

The – (decrement) operator subtracts 1 from the value of a scalar operand, or if the operand is a pointer, decreases the operand by the size of the object to which it points. The operand receives the result of the decrement operation. The operand must be a modifiable lvalue. We can put the – before or after the operand. If it appears before the operand, the operand is decremented, and the decremented value is used in the expression. If the – appears after the operand, the current value of the operand is used in the expression and the operand is decremented. For example,

```
play = –play1 + play2–;
```

is similar to the following expressions; play2 is altered before play:

```
int temp, temp1, temp2;
temp1 = play1 - 1;
play1 = temp1;
play2 = play2 - 1;
temp2 = play2;
temp = temp1 + temp2;
play = temp;
```

The result has the same type as the operand after integral promotion, but is not an lvalue. The usual arithmetic conversions are performed on the operand.

Unary plus operator +

The + (unary plus) operator maintains the value of the operand. The operand can have any arithmetic type or pointer type. The result is not an lvalue. The result has the same type as the operand after integral promotion. Note-Any plus sign in front of a constant is not part of the constant.

Unary minus operator

The - (unary minus) operator negates the value of the operand. The operand can have any arithmetic type. The result is not an lvalue. For example, if quality has the value 100, -quality has the value -100. The result has the same type as the operand after integral promotion. Note- Any minus sign in front of a constant is not part of the constant.

Logical negation operator !

The ! (logical negation) operator determines whether the operand evaluates to 0 (false) or nonzero (true). The expression yields the value 1 (true) if the operand evaluates to 0, and yields the value 0 (false) if the operand evaluates to a nonzero value. But in C++ expression yields the value true if the operand evaluates to false (0), and yields the value false if the operand evaluates to true (nonzero). The following two expressions are equivalent:

```
!right;
right == 0;
```

Bitwise negation operator ~

The ~ (bitwise negation) operator yields the bitwise complement of the operand. In the binary representation of the result, every bit has the opposite value of the same bit in the binary representation of the operand. The operand must have an integral type. The result has the same type as the operand but is not an lvalue. Suppose x represents the decimal value 5. The 16-bit binary representation of x is:

0000000000000101

The expression ~x yields the following result (represented here as a 16-bit binary number):

1111111111111010

The 16-bit binary representation of ~0 is:

1111111111111111

Address operator &

The & (address) operator yields a pointer to its operand. The operand must be an lvalue, a function designator, or a qualified name. It cannot be a bit field, nor can it have the storage class register. If the operand is an lvalue or function, the resulting type is a pointer to the expression type. For example, if the expression has type int, the result is a pointer to an object having type int. If the operand is a qualified name and the member is not static, the result is a pointer to a member of class and has the same type as the member. The result is not an lvalue. If p_to_y is defined as a pointer to an int and y as an int, the following expression assigns the address of the variable y to the pointer p_to_y :

```
p_to_y = &y;
```

Indirection operator *

The * (indirection) operator determines the value referred to by the pointer-type operand. The operand cannot be a pointer to an incomplete type. If the operand points to an object, the operation yields an lvalue referring to that object. If the operand points to a function, the result is a function designator in C, an lvalue referring to the object to which the operand points. Arrays and functions are converted to pointers. The type of the operand determines the type of the result. For example, if the operand is a pointer to an int, the result has type int. Do not apply the indirection operator to any pointer that contains an address that is not valid, such as NULL. The result is not defined. If p_to_y is defined as a pointer to an int and y as an int, the expressions:

```
p_to_y = &y;
*p_to_y = 3;
```

cause the variable y to receive the value 3.

12.26 CAST EXPRESSIONS

The cast operator is used for explicit type conversions. It converts the value of an expression to a specified type. Syntax for the cast expression is

(type) expression;

The result of this operation is not an lvalue. The following demonstrates the use of the cast operator to dynamically create an integer array of size 10:

```
#include <stdlib.h>
int main(void)
{
  int* myArray = (int*) malloc(10 * sizeof(int));
  free(myArray);
  return 0;
}
```

The malloc library function returns a void pointer that points to memory that will hold an object of the size of its argument. The statement int* myArray = (int*) malloc(10 * sizeof(int)) does the following:

Creates a void pointer that points to memory that can hold ten integers.

Converts that void pointer into an integer pointer with the use of the cast operator.

Assigns that integer pointer to myArray. Because a name of an array is the same as a pointer to the initial element of the array, myArray is an array of ten integers stored in the memory created by the call to malloc().

12.27 BINARY EXPRESSIONS

A binary expression contains two operands separated by one operator. The supported binary operators are:

Multiplication operator *

Division operator /

Remainder operator %

Addition operator +

Subtraction operator -

Bitwise left and right shift operators << >>

Relational operators < > <= >=

Equality and inequality operators == !=

Bitwise AND operator &

Bitwise exclusive OR operator ^

Bitwise inclusive OR operator |

Logical AND operator &&

Logical OR operator ||

All binary operators have left-to-right associativity, but not all binary operators have the same precedence. The ranking and precedence rules for binary operators are summarized in Table 12.9. The order in which the operands of most binary operators are evaluated is not specified. To ensure correct results, avoid creating binary expressions that depend on the order in which the compiler evaluates the operands. As indicated in the descriptions of the operators, the usual arithmetic conversions are performed on the operands of most binary expressions.

Multiplication operator *

The * (multiplication) operator yields the product of its operands. The operands must have an arithmetic or enumeration type. The result is not an lvalue. The usual arithmetic conversions on the operands are performed. Because the multiplication operator has both associative and commutative properties, the compiler can rearrange the operands in an expression that contains more than one multiplication operator. For example, the expression:

```
sites * number * cost
```

can be interpreted in any of the following ways:

```
(sites * number) * cost
sites * (number * cost)
(cost * sites) * number
```

Division operator /

The / (division) operator yields the algebraic quotient of its operands. If both operands are integers, any fractional part (remainder) is discarded. Throwing away the fractional part is often called truncation toward zero. The operands must have an arithmetic or enumeration type. The right operand may not be zero: the result is undefined if the right operand evaluates to 0. For example, expression 7 / 4 yields the value 1 (rather than 1.75 or 2). The result is not an lvalue. The usual arithmetic conversions on the operands are performed.

Remainder operator %

The % (remainder) operator yields the remainder from the division of the left operand by the right operand. For example, the expression 5 % 3 yields 2. The result is not an lvalue. Both operands must have an integral or enumeration type. If the right operand evaluates to 0, the result is undefined. If either operand has a negative value, the result is such that the following expression always yields the value of a if b is not 0 and a/b is representable:

```
( a / b ) * b + a %b;
```

The usual arithmetic conversions on the operands are performed.

Addition operator +

The + (addition) operator yields the sum of its operands. Both operands must have an arithmetic type, or one operand must be a pointer to an object type and the other operand must have an integral or enumeration type. When both operands have an arithmetic type, the usual arithmetic conversions on the operands are performed. The result has the type produced by the conversions on the operands and is not an lvalue. A pointer to an object in an array can be added to a value having integral type. The result is a pointer of the same type as the pointer operand. The result refers to another element in the array, offset from the original element by the amount of the integral value treated as a subscript. If the resulting pointer points to storage outside the array, other than the first location outside the array, the result is undefined. A pointer to one element past the end of an array cannot be used to access the memory content at that address. The compiler does not provide boundary checking on the pointers. For example, after the addition, ptr points to the third element of the array:

```
int array[5];
int *ptr;
ptr = array + 2;
```

Subtraction operator -

The - (subtraction) operator yields the difference of its operands. Both operands must have an arithmetic or enumeration type, or the left operand must have a pointer type and the right operand must have the same pointer type or an integral or enumeration type. We cannot subtract a pointer from an integral value. When both operands have an arithmetic type, the usual arithmetic conversions on the operands are performed. The result has the type produced by the conversions on the operands and is not an lvalue. When the left operand is a pointer and the right operand has an integral type, the compiler converts the value of the right to an address offset. The result is a pointer of the same type as the pointer operand. If both operands are pointers to elements in the same array, the result is the number of objects separating the two addresses. The number is of type ptrdiff_t, which is defined in the header file stddef.h. Behavior is undefined if the pointers do not refer to objects in the same array.

Bitwise left and right shift operators << >>

The bitwise shift operators move the bit values of a binary object. The left operand specifies the value to be shifted. The right operand specifies the number of positions that the bits in the value are to be shifted. The result is not an lvalue. Both operands have the same precedence and are left-to-right associative.

Operator	Usage
<<	Indicates the bits are to be shifted to the left.
>>	Indicates the bits are to be shifted to the right.

Each operand must have an integral or enumeration type. The compiler performs integral promotions on the operands, and then the right operand is converted to type int. The result has the same type as the left operand (after the arithmetic conversions). The right operand should not have a negative value or a value that is greater than or equal to the width in bits of the expression being shifted. The result of bitwise shifts on such values is unpredictable. If the right operand has the value 0, the result is the value of the left operand (after the usual arithmetic conversions). The << operator fills vacated bits with zeros. For example, if left_op has the value 4019, the bit pattern (in 16-bit format) of left_op is:

0000111110110011

The expression left_op << 3 yields:

0111110110011000

The expression left_op >> 3 yields:

0000000111110110

Relational operators < > <= >=

The relational operators compare two operands and determine the validity of a relationship. Table 12.14 describes the four relational operators. Both operands must have arithmetic or enumeration types or be pointers to the same type. The type of the result is int and has the values 1 if the specified relationship is true, and 0 if false. The result is not an lvalue. If the operands have arithmetic types, the usual arithmetic conversions on the operands are performed. When the operands are pointers, the result is determined by the locations of the objects to which the pointers refer. If the pointers do not refer to objects in the same array, the result is not defined. A pointer can be compared to a constant expression that evaluates to 0. We can also compare a pointer to a pointer of type void*. The pointer is converted to a pointer of type void*. If two pointers refer to the same object, they are considered equal. If two pointers refer to nonstatic members of the same object, the pointer to the object declared later is greater, provided that they are not separated by an access specifier; otherwise the comparison is undefined. If two pointers refer to data members of the same union, they have the same address value. If two pointers refer to elements of the same array, or to the first element beyond the last element of an array, the pointer to the element with the higher subscript value is greater. We can only compare members of the same object with relational operators. Relational operators have left-to-right associativity. For example, the expression:

```
a < b <= c
```

is interpreted as:

```
(a < b) <= c
```

If the value of a is less than the value of b, the first relationship yields 1 in C, or true in C++. The compiler then compares the value true (or 1) with the value of c (integral promotions are carried out if needed).

Table 12.14 Relation Operator

Operator	Usage
<	Indicates whether the value of the left operand is less than the value of the right operand.
>	Indicates whether the value of the left operand is greater than the value of the right operand.
<=	Indicates whether the value of the left operand is less than or equal to the value of the right operand.
>=	Indicates whether the value of the left operand is greater than or equal to the value of the right operand.

Equality and inequality operators = = !=

The equality operators, like the relational operators, compare two operands for the validity of a relationship. The equality operators, however, have a lower precedence than the relational operators. Table 12.15 describes the two equality operators.

Both operands must have arithmetic or enumeration types or be pointers to the same type, or one operand must have a pointer type and the other operand must be a pointer to void or a null pointer. The type of the result is int and has the values 1 if the specified relationship is true, and 0 if false. If the operands have arithmetic types, the usual arithmetic conversions on the operands are performed. If the operands are pointers, the result is determined by the locations of the objects to which the pointers refer. If one operand is a pointer and the other operand is an integer having the value 0, the == expression is true only if the pointer operand evaluates to NULL. The != operator evaluates to true if the pointer operand does not evaluate to NULL. We can also use the equality operators to compare pointers to members that are of the same type but do not belong to the same object. The following expressions contain examples of equality and relational operators:

```
time < max_time == status < complete
letter != EOF
```

Table 12.15 Equality Operators

Operator	Usage
==	Indicates whether the value of the left operand is equal to the value of the right operand.
!=	Indicates whether the value of the left operand is not equal to the value of the right operand.

Note: The equality operator (==) should not be confused with the assignment (=) operator. For example,

```
if (x == 3)
```

evaluates to true (or 1) if x is equal to three. Equality tests like this should be coded with spaces between the operator and the operands to prevent unintentional assignments.

while

if (x = 3)

is taken to be true because (x = 3) evaluates to a nonzero value (3). The expression also assigns the value 3 to x.

Bitwise AND operator &

The & (bitwise AND) operator compares each bit of its first operand to the corresponding bit of the second operand. If both bits are 1's, the corresponding bit of the result is set to 1. Otherwise, it sets the corresponding result bit to 0. Both operands must have an integral or enumeration type. The usual arithmetic conversions on each operand are performed. The result has the same type as the converted operands. Because the bitwise AND operator has both associative and commutative properties, the compiler can rearrange the operands in an expression that contains more than one bitwise AND operator. The following example shows the values of a, b, and the result of a & b represented as 16-bit binary numbers:

bit pattern of a	0000000001011100
bit pattern of b	0000000000101110
bit pattern of a & b	0000000000001100

Note: The bitwise AND (&) should not be confused with the logical AND (&&) operator. For example,

1 & 4 evaluates to 0

while

1 && 4 evaluates to true

Bitwise exclusive OR operator ^

The bitwise exclusive OR operator (^)compares each bit of its first operand to the corresponding bit of the second operand. If both bits are 1's or both bits are 0's, the corresponding bit of the result is set to 0. Otherwise, it sets the corresponding result bit to 1. Both operands must have an integral or enumeration type. The usual arithmetic conversions on each operand are performed. The result has the same type as the converted operands and is not an lvalue. Because the bitwise exclusive OR operator has both associative and commutative properties, the compiler can rearrange the operands in an expression that contains more than one bitwise exclusive OR operator. The following example shows the values of a, b, and the result of a ^ b represented as 16-bit binary numbers:

bit pattern of a	0000000001011100
bit pattern of b	0000000000101110
bit pattern of a ^ b	0000000001110010

Bitwise inclusive OR operator |

The | (bitwise inclusive OR) operator compares the values (in binary format) of each operand and yields a value whose bit pattern shows which bits in either of the operands has the value 1. If both of the bits are 0, the result of that bit is 0; otherwise, the result is 1. Both operands must have an integral or enumeration type. The usual arithmetic conversions on each operand are performed. The result has the same type as the converted operands and is not an lvalue. Because the bitwise inclusive OR operator has both associative and commutative properties, the compiler can rearrange the operands in an expression that contains more than one bitwise inclusive OR operator. The following example shows the values of a, b, and the result of a | b represented as 16-bit binary numbers:

bit pattern of a	0000000001011100
bit pattern of b	0000000000101110
bit pattern of a | b	0000000001111110

Note: The bitwise OR (|) should not be confused with the logical OR (||) operator. For example,

1 | 4 evaluates to 5

while

1 || 4 evaluates to true

Logical AND operator &&

The && (logical AND) operator indicates whether both operands are true. If both operands have nonzero values, the result has the value 1. Otherwise, the result has the value 0. The type of the result is int. Both operands must have a arithmetic or pointer type. The usual arithmetic conversions on each operand are performed. Unlike the & (bitwise AND) operator, the && operator guarantees left-to-right evaluation of the operands. If the left operand evaluates to 0 (or false), the right operand is not evaluated. The following examples show how the expressions that contain the logical AND operator are evaluated:

Expression	Result
1 && 0	false or 0
1 && 4	true or 1
0 && 0	false or 0

The following example uses the logical AND operator to avoid division by zero:

```
(y != 0) && (x / y)
```

The expression x / y is not evaluated when y != 0 evaluates to 0 (or false).

Note: The logical AND (&&) should not be confused with the bitwise AND (&) operator. For example,

1 && 4 evaluates to 1 (or true)

while

1 & 4 evaluates to 0

Logical OR operator ||

The || (logical OR) operator indicates whether either operand is true. If either of the operands has a nonzero value, the result has the value 1. Otherwise, the result has the value 0. The type of the result is int. Both operands must have a arithmetic or pointer type. The usual arithmetic conversions on each operand are performed. Unlike the | (bitwise inclusive OR) operator, the || operator guarantees left-to-right evaluation of the operands. If the left operand has a nonzero (or true) value, the right operand is not evaluated. The following examples show how expressions that contain the logical OR operator are evaluated:

Expression	Result
1 || 0	true or 1
1 || 4	true or 1
0 || 0	false or 0

The following example uses the logical OR operator to conditionally increment y:

++x || ++y;

The expression ++y is not evaluated when the expression ++x evaluates to a nonzero (or true) quantity.

Note: The logical OR (||) should not be confused with the bitwise OR (|) operator. For example, 1 || 4 evaluates to 1 (or true) while 1 | 4 evaluates to 5

12.28 TYPE CONVERSIONS AND ITS TYPES

When the variables of one type are mixed with variables of another type in expressions, a type conversion is required. In general, the goal of conversions between arithmetic types is to maintain the same magnitude within the limits of the precisions involved. A value converted from a less precise type to a more precise type and then back to the original type results in the same value.

Integral Conversions: A particular bit pattern, or representation, distinguishes each data object from all others of that type. Data type conversion can involve a change in representation. When signed integer types are converted to unsigned types of the same length, no change in representation occurs. A short int value of -1 is converted to an unsigned short int value of 65535. Likewise, when unsigned integer types are converted to signed types of the same length, no representational change occurs. An unsigned short int value of 65535 converted to a short int has a value of -1.

If a signed int type is converted to an unsigned type that is wider, the conversion takes (conceptually) two steps. First, the source type is converted to a signed type with the same length as the destination type. (This involves sign extension.) Second, the resulting signed type is converted to unsigned. The second step requires no change in representation.

If an unsigned integer type is converted to a signed integer type that is wider, the unsigned source type is padded with zeros on the left and increased to the size of the signed destination type.

When a long long (or long in the 64-bit data model) is converted into another integral data type that is of shorter length, truncation may occur. When a long long is converted into a double type, no overflow will occur, but there may be a loss of precision.

In general, conversions from wide integer types to narrow integer types discard high-order bits. Overflows are not detected. Conversions from narrow integer types to wide integer types pad on the left with either zeros or the sign bit of the source type as described above.

A "plain" char is treated as signed. A "plain" int bit-field is treated as signed.

Floating Point Conversions: When an integer value is converted to a floating type, the result is the equivalent floating-point value. If it cannot be represented exactly, the result is the nearest representable value. If the two nearest representable values are equally near, the result is the one whose least significant bit is zero. When a long long is converted into a floating type no overflow will occur but may result in loss of precision. Converting a long long into a quad precision floating point value should be precise with no overflow.

When a floating type is converted into a long long type, the fractional part is discarded and overflow may occur.

When floating-point types are converted to integral types, the source type value must be in the representable range of the destination type or the result is undefined. The result is the whole number part of the floating-point value with the fractional part discarded as shown in the following examples:

```
int i;
i = 9.99;                    /* i gets the value 9 */
i = -9.99;                   /* i gets the value -9 */

float x1 = 1e38;             /* legal; double is converted to float */
float x2 = 1e39;             /* illegal; value is outside of range for float */
long double x3 = 1.f;   /* legal; float is converted to long double    */
```

When a long double value is converted to a double or float value, or a double value is converted to a float value, if the original value is within the range of values representable in the new type, the result is the nearest representable value (if it cannot be represented exactly). If the two nearest representable values are equally near, the result is the one whose least significant bit is zero. When a float value is converted to a double or long double value, or a double value is converted to a long double value, the value is unchanged.

Arrays, Pointer and Functions: An expression that has function type is called a function designator. For example, a function name is a function designator. With two exceptions, a function designator with type "function returning type" is converted to an expression with type "pointer to function returning type." The exceptions are when the function designator is the operand of sizeof (which is illegal) and when it is the operand of the unary & operator.

In most cases, when an expression with array type is used, it is automatically converted to a pointer to the first element of the array. As a result, array names and pointers are often used interchangeably in C. This automatic conversion is not performed in the following contexts: (1) when the array is the operand of sizeof or the unary &; (2) it is a character string literal initializing an array of characters; or (3) it is a wide string literal initializing an array of wide characters.

For assignment statement, the type conversion rules are very easy. The value of the right hand side of the assignment is converted to the type of the left-hand side identifier. In many expressions involving two operands, the operands are converted according to the following rules, known as the usual arithmetic conversions. The common type resulting from the application of these rules is also the type of the result. These rules are applied in the sequence listed below.

1. If either operand is long double, the other operand is converted to long double.
2. If either operand is double, the other operand is converted to double.
3. If either operand is float, the other operand is converted to float.
4. Integral promotions are performed on both operands, and then the rules listed below are followed. These rules are a strict extension of the ANSI "Usual Arithmetic Conversions" rule. This extension ensures that integral expressions will involve long long only if one of the operands is of type long long. For non-ANSI compilation, the unsigned preserving promotion rule is used.
   (a) If either operand is unsigned long long, the other operand is converted to unsigned long long,
   (b) otherwise, if one operand is long long, the other operand is converted to long long,
   (c) otherwise, if either operand is unsigned long int, the other operand is converted to unsigned long int,
   (d) otherwise, if one operand is long int, and the other is unsigned int, and long int can represent all the values of an unsigned int, then the unsigned int is converted to a long int. (If one operand is long int, and the other is unsigned int, and long int can NOT represent all the values of an unsigned int, then both operands are converted to unsigned long int.)

(e) If either operand is long int, the other operand is converted to long int.

(f) If either operand is unsigned int, the other operand is converted to unsigned int.

(g) Otherwise, both operands have type int.

For example, consider the following code segment which demonstrates little bit about the type conversion.

```
int integer=50;
char ch='y';
float float_num=125.56;
 void conversion_fun ()
{
   ch = integer;
   integer = float_num;
   float_num = ch;
   float_num = integer;
}
```

In expression **ch = integer;** the left high order bits of the integer variable **integer** are lopped off, leaving **ch** with the only lower 8-bit. If **integer** is between 256 and 0, **integer** and ch will have identical values. Otherwise, value of **ch** will reflect only lower order of bits of **integer.** In **integer = float_num; integer** will receive the non-fractional part of the **float_num. If float_num = ch;** the 8-bit value of **float_num from right hand side** will be converted and stored in ch. This also happens in **float_num = integer;** except that **float_num** will hold an integer value into floating point format. Assignment type conversion is considered in the Table 12.16.

Table 12.16 Type conversion on 16-bit Computer

Data Type	Converted in Data Type	Possible Information Loss
int	Char	High order 8-bit
float	Int	Fractional part, possibly more loss
char	signed char	If value > 127, target is negative
short int	Char	High order 8-bit
long int	Char	High order 24-bit
long int	Int	High order 16-bit
double	Float	Precision result rounded
long double	Double	Precision result rounded

EXERCISES

1. Multiple Choice Questions

1. What is the output of the following program? Suppose somebody has entered 25.

```
#include<stdio.h>
void main( )
{
        int number;
        printf("\n Enter the value of number:");
        scanf("%d", number);
        printf("Value of number: %d", number);
}
```

(a) Garbage (b) 25
(c) 26 (d) None

2. What is the output of the following program? Suppose somebody has entered 25.

```
#include<stdio.h>
void main( )
{
    int number;
    printf("\n Enter the value of number:");
    scanf("%d", &number);
    printf("Value of number: %d", number++);
}
```

(a) Garbage (b) 25
(c) 26 (d) None

3. What is the output of the following program?

```
#include<stdio.h>
void main( )
{
    int number=20;
    number=number/++number;
    printf("Value of number: %d", number);
}
```

(a) 1 (b) 2
(c) Garbage (d) None

4. What is the output of the following program?

```
#include<stdio.h>
void main( )
{
    int number=20;
    number=number/number++;
    printf("Value of number: %d", number);
}
```

(a) 1 (b) 2
(c) Garbage (d) None

5. What is the output of the following program?

```
#include<stdio.h>
void main( )
{
    int number;
    number=32760+12;
    printf("Value of number: %d", number);
}
```

(a) 0 (b) -32764
(c) Garbage (d) None

(Hint: whenever value of any integer exceeds 32767 then the value is negative and it is calculated as: -32768+(number-32768)

6. What is the output of the following program?

```
#include<stdio.h>
void main( )
{
        int number;
        number=32767+12;
        printf("Value of number: %d", number);
}
```

(a) -32757 (b) -32764
(c) Garbage (d) None

7. What is the output of the following program?

```
#include<stdio.h>
void main( )
{
        int number=020;                    //Value in octal
        printf("Value of number: %d", number);
}
```

(a) 0 (b) 16
(c) Garbage (d) None
(Hint: Value will be printed in decimal system.)

8. What is the output of the following program?

```
#include<stdio.h>
void main( )
{
        int number=020+0xA+10;             /*Value in octal, hex and decimal*/
        printf("Value of number: %d", number);
}
```

(a) 36 (b) 16
(c) Error (d) None
(Hint: Value will be printed in decimal system.)

9. What is the output of the following program?

```
#include<stdio.h>
void main( )
{
        printf( );
}
```

(a) Error (b) 16
(c) Garbage (d) None

10. Is any error there in the following program?

```
#include<stdio.h>
void main( )
{
        printf("%d %d" );
}
```

(a) Yes (b) No

11. Is any error there in the following program?

```
#include<stdio.h>
void main( )
{
    { }
    { }
}
```

(a) Yes (b) No

12. What is the output of the following program?

```
#include<stdio.h>
void main( )
{
    printf("Prem"
    "Nath");
}
```

(a) Error (b) PremNath (c) Garbage (d) None

13. What is the output of the following program?

```
#include<stdio.h>
void main( )
{
    printf("Prem
    "Nath");
}
```

(a) Error (b) PremNath (c) Garbage (d) None

14. What is the output of the following program?

```
#include<stdio.h>
void main( )
{
    printf("Prem",
"Nath");
 }
```

(a) Error (b) PremNath (c) Prem (d) None What is the

15. What is the output of the following program?

```
#include<stdio.h>
void main( )
{
    printf("Prem", "Nath", "R.B. Patel");
}
```

(a) Error (b) PremNathR.B. Patel (c) Prem (d) None

16. What is the output of the following program?

```
#include<stdio.h>
void main( )
{
    printf("%d", 5||3);
}
```

(a) Error (b) 1 (c) 5 (d) 3

17. What is the output of the following program?

```
#include<stdio.h>
void main( )
{
    printf("%d", 5|3);
}
```

(a) Error (b) 5 (c) 7 (d) 3

18. What is the output of the following program?

```
#include<stdio.h>
void main( )
{
    printf("%d", 5&3);
    getch();
}
```

(a) Error (b)3 (c) 5 (d) 1

19. What is the output of the following program?

```
#include<stdio.h>
void main( )
{
    printf("%d", 5^3);
    getch();
}
```

(a) Error (b) 6 (c) 5 (d) 3

20. What is the output of the following program?

```
#include<stdio.h>
void main( )
{
    printf("%d", 5&&3);
    getch();
}
```

(a) 1 (b) 0 (c) 5 (d) 3

21. What is the output of the following program?

```
#include<stdio.h>
void main( )
{
    printf("%d", 5>3);
    getch();
}
```

(a) Error (b)1 (c) 5 (d) 3

22. What is the output of the following program?

```
#include<stdio.h>
void main( )
{
    printf("%d", 5<3);
    getch();
}
```

(a) 0 (b) 4 (c) 5 (d) 3

23. What is the output of the following program?

```
#include<stdio.h>
void main( )
{
        printf("%d", 5>>3);
        getch();
}
```

(a) 0 (b) (c) 5 (d) 3

24. What is the output of the following program?

```
#include<stdio.h>
void main( )
{
        printf("%d", 5<<3);
        getch();
}
```

(a) 0 (b) 5 (c) 40 (d) 3

25. What is the output of the following program?

```
#include<stdio.h>
void main( )
{
        int number;
        printf("%d", number ^ number);
        getch();
}
```

(a) 0 (b) Garbage (c) 5 (d) Error

26. What is the output of the following program?

```
#include<stdio.h>
void main( )
{
        printf("%d", 5>3?420:500);
        getch();
}
```

(a) 400 (b) 500 (c) 5 (d) 3

27. What is the output of the following program?

```
#include<stdio.h>
void main( )
{
        int number=20;
printf("%d", number= number = = 10);
getch();
}
```

(a) 0 (b) 10 (c) 20 (d) Error

28. What is the output of the following program?

```
#include<stdio.h>
void main( )
{
```

```
int number=20;
printf("%d", number= ++number = = 10);
getch();
}
```

(a) 0 (b)11 (c) 20 (d) 21

29. What is the output of the following program?

```
#include<stdio.h>
void main( )
{
    int number=20;
        printf("%d", number= ++number = = 21);
    getch();
}
```

(a) 1 (b) Error (c) 20 (d) 21

30. What is the output of the following program?

```
#include<stdio.h>
void main( )
{
int number=20;
        printf("%d", number= number++ = = 21);
getch();
}
```

(a) 1 (b) 0 (c) 20 (d) 21

31. What is the output of the following program?

```
#include<stdio.h>
void main( )
{
int number;
number=32767*32767-32767*32766;
printf("%d", number= number++ = = 21);
getch();
}
```

(a) Garbage (b) 0 (c) -32768 (d) 32767

32. What is the output of following program?

```
#include<stdio.h>
void main( )
{
unsigned int number=-40;
        printf("\n Value of number is : %d", number);
getch();
}
```

(a) –40 (b) 40 (c) Error (d) None

33. What is the output of following program?

```
#include<stdio.h>
void main( )
{
unsigned int number=-40;
        printf("\n Value of number is : %u", number);
```

```
    getch();
}
```

(a) –40 (b) 40 (c) 65496 (d) None

(Hint: incase of unsigned print number = 65535-number+1)

34. What is the output of following program?

```
#include<stdio.h>
void main( )
{
        int num1=10, num2=20;
        num1^=num2;
        num2^=num2;
        printf("\n Value of num1 is : %d and num2 is: ", num1, num2);
        getch();
}
```

(a) 30, 400 (b) 30, 40 (c) 10, 20 (d) 30, 0

35. What is the output of following program?

```
#include<stdio.h>
void main()
{
int a = 200 ;
int b = 34 ;
printf("%f", (float) a/b ) ;
printf(" %d", (int) a/b ) ;
}
```

(a) 5.8823535 (b) 55 (c) Error (d) None

36. What will be the output for the following code slice?

```
double Celsius, F = 64;
Celsius = 5/9 * (F - 32);
```

(a) 0 (b) 0.55555 (c) 1 (d) none of these

37. Cast operator is data type provided

(a) In parenthesis after a variable name (b) Before a variable name

(c) After a variable name (d) In parenthesis before a variable name

State whether the following statements are true or false

1. All arithmetic operators have the same level of precedence.
2. The modulus operator % can be used only with integers.
3. The operators <=, >= and != all enjoy the same level of priority.
4. During modulo division, the sign of the result is positive, if both the operands are of the same sign.
5. In C, if a data item is zero, it is considered false.
6. The expression !(x<=y) is same as the expression x>y.
7. A unary expression consists of only one operand with no. operators.
8. Associativity is used to decide which of several different expressions is evaluated first.
9. An expression statement is terminated with a period.
10. During the evaluation of mixed expressions, an implicit cast is generated automatically.

11. An explicit cast can be used to change the expression.
12. Parentheses can be used to change the order of evaluation of expressions.

Fill in the blanks with appropriate words in each of the following statements

1. The expression containing all the float operands is called ____________ expression
2. The operator ________________ cannot be used with real operands.
3. C supports as many as __________ relational operators.
4. An expression that combines two or more relational expressions is termed as expression.
5. The _________ operator returns the number of bytes the operand occupies.
6. The order of evaluation can be changed by us __________ in an expression.
7. The use of ________________ an a variabie can change its type in the memory is used to determine the order in which differen: operators in an expression are evaluated.

Descriptive and Programming Problems

1. Given the statement
   int a = 10, b = 20, c;
   determine whether each of the fallowing statements are true or false.
   (a) The statement a = * 10, is valid.
   (b) The expression a + 4/6 *6/2 evaluates to 11
   (c) The expression b + 3/2 * 2/3 evaluates to 1.
   (d) The statement a -= b; gives the values -10 to a and 20 to b.
   (e) The statement -a-; gives the value 8 to a.
   (f) The statement a = 10/b; assigns the value 0.5 to a
2. Declared a as int and b as float, state whether the following statements are true or false.
   (a) The statement a = 1/3 + 1/3 + 1/3; assigns the value 0 to a.
   (b) The statement b = 1.0/3.0 + 1.0/3.0 + 1.0/3.0; assigns a value 1.0 to b.
   (c) The statement b = 1.0/3.0 * 3.0 gives a value 1.0 to b.
   (d) The statement b = 1.0/3.0 + 2.0/3.0 assigns a value 1.0 to b.
   (e) The statement a = 15/1 0.0 + 3/2; assigns a value 3 to a.
3. Which of the following expressions are true?
   (a) !(5 + 5 >=10)
   (b) 5>101110<20&&3<5
   (c) 10! = 15 && !(10<20) 1115 > 30
4. Which of the following arithmetic expressions are valid? If valid, give the value of the ex-pression; otherwise give reason.

(a) 25/3 % 2	(e) -14 % 3
(b) +9/4 + 5	(f) 15.25 + - 5.0
(c) 7.5 % 3.	(g) (5/3) * 3 + 5 % 3
(d) 14 % 3 + 7 % 2	(h) 21 % (int) 4.5

5. Identify unnecessary parentheses in the following expressions.
   (a) ((x-(y/5)+z)%8)+25
   (b) ((x-y)*p)+q
   (c) (m*n) + (-x/y)
   (d) x/(3*y)
6. Find errors, if any, in the following assignment statements and rectify them.
   (a) x = y = z = 0.5, 2.0. -5~75;
   (b) m = ++a * 5;
   (c) Y = sqrt (100);
   (d) p */= x/y;
   (e) s =+5;
   (f) a = b++ -c*2
7. Determine the value of each of the following logical expressions if a = 5, b = 10 and c =-6
   (a) a > b && a < c
   (b) a < b && a > c
   (c) a == c || b > a
   (d) b>15&&c<0||a>0
   (e) (a/2.0 == 0.0 && b/2.0 != 0.0) || c < 0.0
8. Write a program that assigns the unsigned integer num the value 1. Rotate the variable with a bitwise operator until the value equals 128; print the values before and after the rotation.
9. Why **register** variables are powerful tool? Write a program that multiplies two numbers and stores result in a **register** variable.
10. Evaluate following expressions.
    (a) 5*a+b/c-d++
    (b) a*b + 2 /10
    (c) (~a) + (~b)? c / d
    (d) x = a > b ? 10 * 2 : a * b
    (e) y = (&a) + (&b)
    (f) z = sizeof(a) + sizeof(b)
    (g) x = a && b
    (h) ++a = b++ || c-
    (i) b += 34
    (j) c = float(c)
    Where the values of different variables are following: a = 200, b = 300, c = 20, d = 25.45
11. What is precedence of an operator? Explain with the help of suitable examples.
12. Write a C program, which prints all ASCII values.
13. Given the values of the variables a, b and c, write a program to rotate their values such that a has the value of b, b has then value of c, and c has the value of a.
14. Write a program that reads a floating-point number and then displays the right-most digit of the integral part of the number.

15. Modify the above program to display the two right-most digits of the integral part of the number.
16. Write a program that will obtain the length and width of a rectangle from the user and compute its area and perimeter.
17. The total distance travelled by a vehicle in t seconds is given by

    distance = u*t + (a*t2)/2

    Where u is the initial velocity (meters per second), a is the acceleration (meters per second2). Write a program to evaluate the distance traveled at regular intervals of time, given the val-ues of u and a. The program should provide the flexibility to the user to select his own time intervals and repeat the calculations for different values of u and a.
18. In inventory management, the Economic Order Quantity for a single item is given by

    EOQ = 2 * demand rate * setup costs ______________

    demand rate * holding cost per item per unit time

    and the optimal Time Between Orders

    TBO = 2 * setup costs

    demand rate * holding cost per item per unit time

    Write a program to compute EOQ and TBO, given demand rate (items per unit time), setup costs (per order), and the holding cost (per item per unit time).

Decision Making, Iterative and Control Constructs

13.1 INTRODUCTION

A program consists of a number of statements which are usually executed in sequence. Programs can be much more powerful if we can control the order in which statements are run. Statements fall into three general types:

Assignment, where values, usually the results of calculations, are stored in variables.

Input / Output, data is read in or printed out.

Control, the program makes a decision about what to do next.

Generally, statements of a program are executed one by one starting from the first instruction. This is known as serial or sequential execution. The order in which statements are written and executed in a program is extremely important. In other words when a particular statement is executed, the statements on next line of the program are taken up for the execution and then next and so on. But sometimes it is desirable to skip or jump some statements (block code), which is based on some specified condition. There are some other situations like loops that are not normal sequential execution. So, C language provides looping and jumping facilities also and this makes the C language different from other low-level languages.

13.2 TYPES OF C STATEMENTS

We can categorize the statements of C based on the order of execution. ANSI C standard statements can be grouped into categories as given in **Table 13.1.** This chapter will discuss the use of control statements in C. We will show how they can be used to write powerful programs.

Table 13.1 Category of C statements

Statement Category	Statement Sub-category
Block	Begins with {and ends with}
Expression	All valid C language expressions
Selection/Decision	1. if 2. switch
Iteration	1. for 2. while 3. do-while
Jump or Loop	1. break 2. goto 3. continue 4. return
Labels	1. case 2. default

13.3 DECISION MAKING CONSTRUCTS

We can restrict the flow of execution based on the certain condition what we have. To control the flow of execution of programs, **C** language provides very powerful facilities in the form of selection (conditional) statements. **C** supports two types of selection statements; **if** and **switch.** The **?:** operator is an alternative to **if** statement in certain circumstances as discussed in the previous chapter. The **if** statement can be further classified into two categories:

if

if - else

Now, let us see the both if statements.

13.3.1 The if statement

If a set of statements is executed based on a condition's validity, i.e., **if** the given condition is evaluated true then set of statements is executed otherwise not. The syntax for **if** statement is given below:

```
if (condition )
{
    Statement 1;
    Statement 2;
    ...
    ...
    ...
    Statement n;
}
```

The statements outside if-block do not affected by the validity of condition of if statement, i.e., whether the control enters into the **if** block or not. The condition is opposed in form of expressions like:

```
    if(number > 10)
{
    ...
    ...
}
```

```
if(character = = 'y' || character = = 'Y')
{
    ...
    ...
}
```

Here we have used OR operator to combine two simple conditions; character = = 'y' and character = = 'Y'. If any one of these conditions is evaluated TRUE then statements of if-block are evaluated. We can use other operators also. If condition of if statement is TRUE then control enters into the if-block and statements of if-block are executed and then after the next statement of the if-block is executed. Even if the condition of if statement is found FALSE, the next statement of the if-block is evaluated automatically due to sequential nature of C language. Let us see a simple Example 1 that illustrates the above discussion.

Example 1: Write a C program to find average of five subject marks of a student. Using if statement state whether students has secured more than 50% or not.

Answer: Following is the implementation.

```
#include<stdio.h>
void main()
{
int num1, num2, num3, num4, num5;
float sum;
printf("\n Enter the marks of five subjects:");
scanf("%d%d%d%d%d", &num1, &num2, &num3, &num4, &num5);
sum = (num1+num2+num3+num4+num5)/500;
sum=sum*100;
if(sum >50)
    printf("\n You have scored more than 50% marks");
getch();
}
```

OUTPUT
Enter the marks of five subjects: 56 65 70 45 82
You have scored more than 50% marks

In the above program segment we are taking five input data from the standard device. It finds the summation and divides the summation with 500 and resulting value is multiplied with 100 to get the percentage. This percentage is checked whether it is greater than 50% or not. If greater than 50% then output is displayed otherwise not.

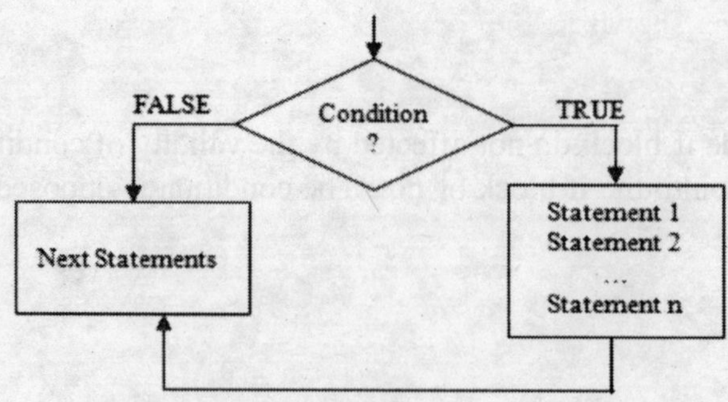

Figure 13.1 Control-flow of if-statement

If the condition is true, the statements enclosed in the braces are executed or if braces are not present after if statement then single statement after if statement is executed. After the if-block statement, next statements to if-block are executed. One thing should be noted here that if there is more than one statement in if-block then we place braces otherwise for single statement there is no need of braces. The control-flow of if-statement is shown in Figure 13.1. This is given below:

```
if(condition)
        {
        Statement1;
        Statement 2;
        ...
        Statement n;
}
if(condition)           /*No need of braces for single statement */
        statement;
```

13.3.2 Nested if statement

We have seen in the previous section that if statement is evaluated if the condition is found TRUE otherwise not. There are certain situations where more than single condition is there. For example, let us consider the previous program. We have printed the marks which is above 50% only. There is no provision of printing other marks that are above or below 50%. We can do it by placing nested if-statements like given below:

```
if ( condition1 )
 if (condition2 )
  if (condition3 )
   if (condition4 )
   ...
   {
        Statement 1;
   Statement 2;
   ...
       Statement n;
   }
```

We can have braces after an if-statement, if more than single statements are there. The first if-statement has one statement that is second if-statement; the second if-statement has one statement that is third if-statement, and so on. We can have many nested if-statements depending on the requirement. In the above syntax 2nd if-statement is an object of 1st **if**-statement and 3rd **if**-statement is an object of 2nd **if**-statement and so on. The main block of code is attached with 4th **if**- statement. The control-flow of nested if-statement is shown in Figure 13.2. The above syntax for nested if-statement is equivalent to the following syntax:

```
if(condition1 && condition2 && condition3 && condition4)
{
  Statement 1;
  Statement 2;
  Statement 3;
  ...
  Statement n;
}
```

Go through the Example 2 and Example 3 which are implementing the above discussion.

Example 2: Let us consider the Example 1 and modify to get first division, second division, third division, and fail. Use the following conditions:

If percentage of marks > = 60 then first division
If percentage of marks > = 50 and marks <60 then second division
If percentage of marks >= 40 and marks <50 then third division
If percentage of marks <40 then fail

Answer: The following program segment implements the above discussion:

```
#include<stdio.h>
void main()
{
int num1, num2, num3, num4, num5;
float sum;
printf("\n Enter the marks of five subjects:");
scanf("%d%d%d%d%d", &num1, &num2, &num3, &num4, &num5);
sum = (num1+num2+num3+num4+num5)/500;
sum=sum*100;
    if(sum >=60)
    printf("\n You secured First Division");
    if(sum >=50 && sum <60)
    printf("\n You secured Second Division");
    if(sum >=40 && sum<50)
    printf("\n You secured Third Division");
    if(sum <40)
    printf("\n Sorry...You are failed");
getch();
}
```

OUTPUT
Enter the marks of five subjects: 56 60 61 45 42
You have secured Second Division

Example 3: Find greatest of three numbers using nested if statement.

Answer: The program **great.c** illustrates the idea.

```
/* great.c **/
/* Finding greatest of 3 integer numbers */
#include<stdio.h>
void main()
{
    int x , y , z ;
    printf("\n Enter value for x , y ,z :") ;
    scanf("%d %d %d", &x, &y, &z) ;
    if ( x >y)
            if(x > z )
                    printf(" \n x is greatest = %d", x) ;
    if ( x < y)
            if( y > z )
                    printf(" \n y is greatest = %d", y) ;
    if ( x < y)
            if(z > y )
                    printf(" \n z is greatest = %d", z) ;
    if ( x >y)
            if( y < z)
                    if(x < z )
                        printf(" \n z is greatest  = %d", z) ;
}
```

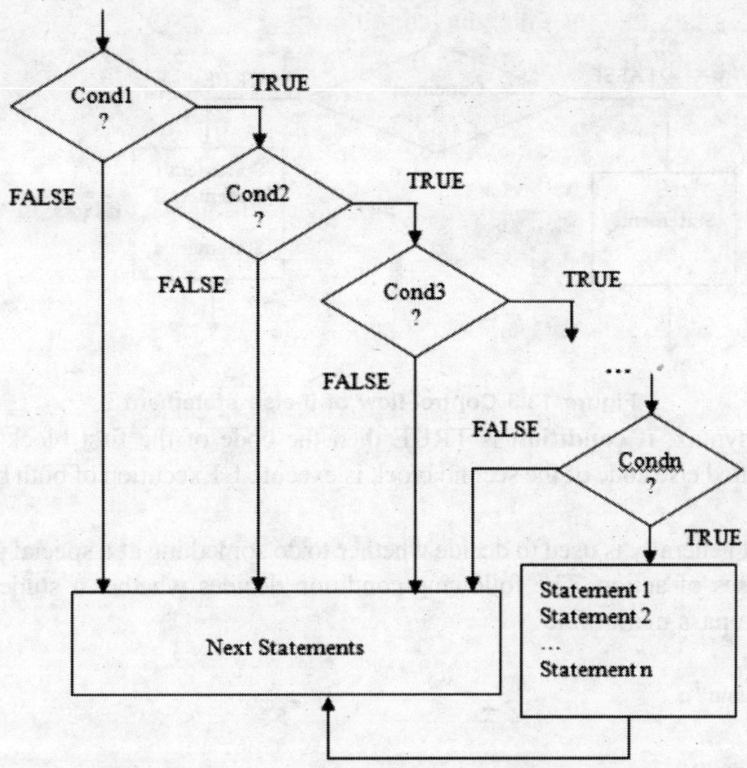

Figure 13.2 Control-flow of Nested if-statement

13.3.3 The if-else statement

Sometimes placing nested if-statements results in a long series of if-statements and it appears complex also. We have seen that statements of a if-block are evaluated if and only if condition is TRUE. But in case of FALSE validity of the condition there is no block such as if-block. C language provides this facility to place else-block after an if-block. If condition of if-statement is found FALSE then statements of else-block are evaluated. So, in this way we use the both values of the opposed condition, i.e., if condition is TRUE then if-block otherwise else-block. The control-flow of if-else statement is shown in Figure 13.3. The syntax for **if-else** statement is given below:

```
if(condition)
{
Statement 1;
Statement 2;
Statement 3;
...
Statement n;
}else
{
Statement 1;
Statement 2;
Statement 3;
...
Statement m;
}
```

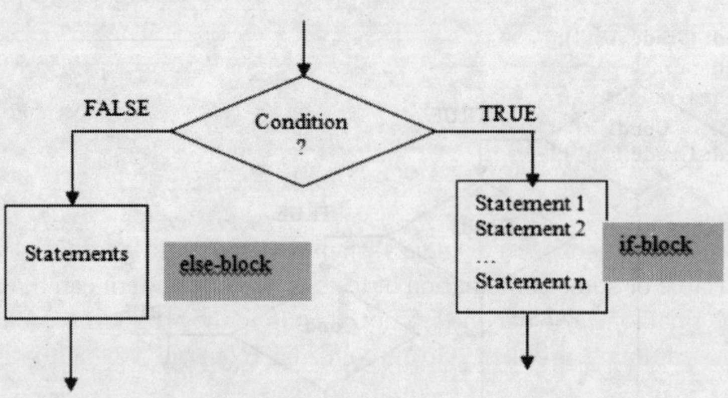

Figure 13.3 Control-flow of if-else statement

In the above syntax, if **condition** is TRUE then the code of the first block (following the if statement) is executed else code of the second block is executed. Execution of both blocks is mutually exclusive.

This statement generally is used to decide whether to do something at a special point, or to decide between two courses of action. The following condition decides whether a student has passed an examination with a pass mark of 45.

```
if (result >= 45)
        printf("Pass\n");
else
        printf("Fail\n");
```

It is possible to use the if part without the else.

```
    if (temperature < 0)
        print("Frozen\n");
```

Each version consists of a condition, this is the bracketed statement following the **if**. If the condition is true then the next statement is obeyed. If is false then the statement following the else is obeyed if present. After this, the rest of the program continues as normal. If we wish to have more than one statement following the **if** or the **else,** they should be grouped together between curly brackets. Such a grouping is called a compound statement or a block. For example, see the following code segment

```
if (result >= 45)
{       printf("Passed\n");                          /* A*/
        printf("Congratulations\n")                  /* B */
}else
{       printf("Failed\n");                          /* C */
        printf("Good luck in the reappear \n");      /* D */
}
```

In the above code segment if the value of result is greater or equal to 45 lines A and B are executed otherwise lines C and D are executed.

Sometimes we wish to make a multi-way decision based on several conditions. The most general way of doing this is by using the **else** if variant on the **if** statement. This works by cascading several comparisons. As soon as one of these gives a true result, the following statement or block is executed, and no further comparisons are performed. In the following example we are awarding grades depending on the examination result.

```
if (result >= 75)
      printf("Passed: Grade A\n");
else if (result >= 60)
      printf("Passed: Grade B\n");
else if (result >= 45)
      printf("Passed: Grade C\n");
else
      printf("Failed\n");
```

In this example, all comparisons test a single variable called **result.** In other cases, each test may involve a different variable or some combination of tests. The same pattern can be used with more or fewer else if's, and the final lone **else** may be left out. It is up to the programmer to devise the correct structure for each programming problem. Go through the Example 4 which is implementing the above discussion.

Example 4: Write a program which computes summation of even and odd numbers between 0 and 100. Put a choice to select whether interest is in even or odd.

Answer: The program segment **ifelse.c** implements the above discussion.

```
/**      ifelse.c      **/
/* Find summation even and odd numbers between 0 and 100 */

# include<stdio.h>
# include<ctype.h>
# include<stdlib.h>
void main()
{
      int even , i ;
      int odd ;
      char choice ;

      /* Initialization section */

      even = 0 ;
      odd  = 0 ;

      /*    end    */

      printf("\nEnter choice O = odd , E = even: ") ;
      choice = getchar() ;
      choice = toupper(choice) ; /* change in upper case */

      /* This section find Summation of even number */

      if ( choice == 'E' )
      {
      for( i = 0 ; i <= 100 ; i += 2 )
      {
            even += i ;
      }
      printf("\n Summation of even number between 0 and 100 = %d", even);
}
      /*    end    */

      /* This section find summation of odd numbers */

      else
      if ( choice == 'O' )
```

```
    {
        for( i = 1 ; i <= 100 ; i += 2 )
        {
                odd += i ;
        }
        printf("\n Summation of odd number between 0 and 100 = %d", odd);
    }
    /*  end */

    else
    {
        printf("\n Wrong Choice ") ;
        exit(0) ;  /* Transfer control to prompt */
    }
}
```

In the above program segment we have defined variable choice which is used to pick choice option from the standard input device (keyboard). If we want to find summation of even number we need to select option 'E' and for odd 'O'. For any other choice it displays "Wrong Choice". In this program segment we have used **for** loop statement, this will be discussed later in this chapter. In for loop we have used increment by 2 in both the case (even and odd). Because whether summation is for even or odd numbers depends on initialization of counter, i.e., value of **i** in the **for** loop. For even numbers summation i=0 and for odd i=1.

13.3.4 The else-if ladder

We have discussed the if-else statement in the previous section. In some situation the else-statement is followed by if-statement and then further else-statement is followed by if-else statement. This looks like a ladder. The syntax for the **else-if** ladder is given below:

```
    if ( condition1 )
    {
    Statement 1;
    Statement 2;
    Statement 3;
    ...
    Statement n;
    }else if ( condition 2 )/* else-statement is corresponding to just above if-statement*/
    {
        Statement 1;
        Statement 2;
        Statement 3;
        ...
        Statement m;
    }else if ( condition 3 ) /* else-statement is corresponding to just above if-statement*/
    {
    Statement 1;
    Statement 2;
    Statement 3;
    ...
    Statement o;
    }else if ( condition 4 ) /* else-statement is corresponding to just above if-statement*/
    {
        Statement 1;
        Statement 2;
        Statement 3;
        ...
```

```
                ...
                ...
                Statement p;
        }else   /* else-statement is corresponding to just above if-statement*/
        {
                Statement 1;
                Statement 2;
                Statement 3;
                ...
                ...
                ...
                Statement q;
        }
```

For example, consider the following algorithm which is used to categories the rank of the students in a class.

```
if marks >=60% then first division
else if marks >40% and marks <=50% then second division
    else if marks >=40% and marks<50% then third division
            else failed
```

Due to the sequential nature of C language, the conditions are evaluated from top to bottom and as soon as a true condition is found, the statements associated with it are executed and rest of the ladder is bypassed. If none of the conditions is true, the code of final **else**-block is executed. Generally this is called **default condition.** If all other conditions are **false** and final else is not present, no action takes place. In the above algorithm if no condition will be true student will be declared failed. Go through the Example 5 and Example 6 which are implementing the above discussion.

Example 5: Write a C code to implement the above algorithm for grading a student.

Answer: The above notion is illustrated in the following program segment.

```
/*** result.c.c  **/
#include<stdio.h>
void main()
{
int num1, num2, num3, num4, num5;
float sum;
printf("\n Enter the marks of five subjects:");
scanf("%d%d%d%d%d", &num1, &num2, &num3, &num4, &num5);
sum = (num1+num2+num3+num4+num5)/500;
sum=sum*100;
    if(sum >=60)
            printf("\n You secured First Division");
    else if(sum >=50 && sum <60)
            printf("\n You secured Second Division");
    else if(sum >=40 && sum<50)
            printf("\n You secured Third Division");
    else
    printf("\n Sorry...You are failed");
getch();
}
```

OUTPUT
Enter the marks of five subjects: 56 60 61 75 52
You have secured First Division

Example 6: Implement a four-function arithmetic calculator for the addition, subtraction, multiplication and division operations.

Answer: Following implementation receives one operand then operator and then second operand for manipulating the said calculator.

```
/* calc2.c */
/* Four-function calculator */
#include <stdio.h>

void main(void)
{
    float num1=1.0, num2=1.0;
    char op;

    while ( !(num1==0.0 && num2==0.0) )
    {
            printf("\n\n Enter expression having number, operator, number\n");
            scanf("%f %c %f", &num1, &op, &num2);
            if ( op == '+')
                    printf(" Summation = %f", num1 + num2);
            else if (op == '-')
                    printf(" Subtraction = %f", num1 - num2);
            else if (op == '*')
                    printf("Multiplication  = %f", num1 * num2);
            else if (op == '/')
                    printf(" Quotient = %f", num1 / num2);
    }
}
```

In the above program segment, there are three **else-if** stairs. The **if-else** statement has only one alternative to be used but it is not always applicable. Simple **if-else** statement has the syntax:

```
    if(condition)
            expression 1 ;   /* must be a single statement */
    else
            expression 2 ;  /* must be a single statement */
```

If both expressions are single statement, it can be represented with the help of ternary operator **(? :)**. Otherwise there is no alternative available in **C** language. The syntax for ternary operator is:

```
    result = condition ? expression 1 : expression 2;
```

For example, consider the following code segment.

```
·   char string ;
int x;
printf("\n enter value of x:");
scanf("%d", &x);
            string =  x < 14 ? 'Y' : 'N' ;
·   int number;
char ch;
printf("\n enter your choice (Y or N:");
scanf("%c", &ch)
    number = ch= = 'Y' ? 400 : 200;
```

In the first example, if value of x is entered less than 14 then **string** is assigned 'Y' otherwise 'N'. In the second example, if character 'Y' is entered then **number** holds 400 otherwise 200.

Let us see one more example,

```
a = 16 ;
b = a < 19 ? a * a : a /4 ;
```

Here, the value of b is 256. If a is greater than or equal to 19, **b** will receive the value 4. The replacement of the same code with the help of **if - else** statement can be written as:

```
a = 16 ;
if ( a < 19 )
    b = a * a ;
else
    b = a / 4 ;
```

The use of **ternary** operator to replace **if-else** statements is not limited to only assignment statement and it can also be used with functions when functions return some values. If functions are declared as void, this operator is not useful.

13.3.5 The switch Statement

We use **if-else** statements if numbers of decisions are small. When number of decision is very large and it is required to select too many decisions, it is not possible with the help of **if-else** statements. **C** language provides a multiple branch selection statement called **switch** statement, which successively tests the value of a condition (expression) against a list of **integer** or **character** constants only. When a match is found, the statements associated with that constant are executed. With the help of **switch** and **case** statements, one may choose any number of decisions. The syntax of switch-case statement is given below:

```
switch ( condition )
    {
        case constant1:
                Statement 1;
                Statement 2;
                Statement 3;
                ...
                Statement p;
        case constant 2:
                Statement 1;
                Statement 2;
                Statement 3;
                ...
                Statement q;
        case constant 3:
                Statement 1;
                Statement 2;
                Statement 3;
                ...
                Statement r;
        default:
                Statement 1;
                Statement 2;
                Statement 3;
                ...
                Statement s;
    }
```

The **switch** statement is well structured, but can only be used in certain cases where;

Only one variable is tested, all branches must depend on the value of that variable. The variable must be an integral type (int, long, short or char).

Each possible value of the variable can control a single branch. A final, catch all default branch may optionally be used to trap all unspecified cases.

Hopefully an example will clarify things. This is a function which converts an integer into a vague description. It is useful where we are only concerned in measuring a quantity when it is quite small.

```
estimate(int number)
/* Estimate a number as none, one, two, several, many */
{   switch(number) {
    case 0 :
          printf("None\n");
          break;
    case 1 :
          printf("One\n");
          break;
    case 2 :
          printf("Two\n");
          break;
    case 3 :
    case 4 :
    case 5 :
          printf("Several\n");
          break;
    default :
          printf("Many\n");
          break;
    }
}
```

Each interesting case is listed with a corresponding action. The break statement prevents any further statements from being executed by leaving the switch. Since case 3 and case 4 have no following break, they continue on allowing the same action for several values of number. Both if and switch constructs allow the programmer to make a selection from a number of possible actions.

The **switch** statement tests whether an expression matches with the integer or character constants specified in the case statements. We label each case or with integers valued constants, constant expression or character constant only. If a case matches the expression value, execution starts from that case. All case expressions, integer constants value or character constant must be different. The case labeled default is executed if none of the case match is found. The default case is optional and if it is not available, control comes out of the switch case statement. Other cases and default case may be placed in any order. The **ANSI-C** standard specifies that a switch can have at most 256 case statements. Go through the Example 7 which is implementing the above discussion.

Example 7: Implement Example 6 using switch and case statement.

Answer: Consider the following program segment which is a five function calculator shows operations performed on two numbers depending on inputting the operators.

```
/** switch1.c **/
# include<stdio.h>
void main()
{
```

```
int x , y, result ;
char choice ;
x = 100 ;
y = 25 ;
printf("\n Enter an arithmetic operator: ") ;
choice = getchar() ;
        switch(choice)
        {
        case '-' :
                printf("\n x = %d", x);
                printf("\n y = %d", y);
                printf("\n Demo of '-' operator");
                result = x - y ;
                printf("\n Difference of two numbers = %d", result);
                getch();
                break ;
        case '+' :
                printf("\n x = %d", x);
                printf("\n y = %d", y);
                printf("\n Demo of '+' operator");
                result = x + y ;
                printf("\n Addition  of two numbers = %d", result);
                getchar();
                break ;
        case '*' :
                printf("\n x = %d", x);
                printf("\n y = %d", y);
                printf("\n Demo of multiplication operator");
                result = x * y ;
                printf("\n Multiplication of two numbers = %d", result);
                break ;

        case '/' :
                printf("\n x = %d", x);
                printf("\n y = %d", y);
                printf("\n Demo of '/' operator ");
                result = x / y ;
                printf("\n Division of two numbers = %d", result);
                getch( );
                break ;

        case '%' :
                printf("\n x = %d", x);
                printf("\n y = %d", y);
                printf("\n Demo of '%; operator ");
                result = x % y ;
                printf("\n Remainder  = %d", result);
                getch( );
                break ;
        default :
                printf(" \n Wrong choice of operator... ");
                getch();
        }
```

OUTPUT
Enter an arithmetic operator: +
Addition of two numbers = 125

When character constants are used, their integer **ASCII** values are automatically obtained. The **break** statement is optional. This is used to terminate the statement sequence associated with each constant. If **break** statement is missing, the execution will continue to next **case** statements until a **break** statement is encountered or the end of switch statement reaches. This type of representation can be implemented with the help of or **case** statement. The syntax for **switch-case** statement without break is given below:

```
switch (condition)
{
    case constant1:  /* No break statement*/
            statements;

    case constant2:  /* No break statement*/
            statements;

    case constant3:  /* No break statement*/
            statements;

    case constant4:  /* No break statement*/
            statements;

    case constant5:  /* No break statement*/
            statements;
            ...
    default: statements;
}
```

Consider the Example 8 in which four case statements case 1, 2, 3 and 4 are combined in one due to absence of **break** statement.

Example 8: switch-case statement with some missing break statement.

Answer: Go through the following code segments for different variants of switch-case statement.

```
/**     switch2.c     **/
# include<stdio.h>
void main()
{
    int choice ;
    printf(" \n Enter your choice (integer value up to 5): ");
    scanf("%d", &choice);

    switch(choice)
    {
    case 1:  printf("\n Your Choice is: %d", choice) ;
    case 2:  printf("\n Your Choice is: %d", choice) ;
    case 3:  printf("\n Your Choice is: %d", choice);
    case 4:  printf("\n Your Choice is: %d", choice);
             break;
    case 5:  printf("\n Your Choice is: %d", choice);
             break ;
    default :  printf("\n Your Choice is invalid"); }
```

In the above program, if we enter **choice = 1,** case **1, 2, 3** and **4** are executed because case 1, case 2 and case 3 have no break statement.

Another form of **switch-case** statement is:

```
switch(choice)      /* Correct declaration */
{
   case 'A' : ...
        char ch ;     /* Valid Declaration of char variable in C++*/
        ...
        statements; /*No break statement*/
   case 'B':
            statements;        /*No break statement*/
   case 'C':
            statements;        /*No break statement*/
   ...
default:
   statements;
}

/* Incorrect declaration of a variable */
   switch(choice)
   {
    char ch ;           /*incorrect declaration*/
    case 'A' : ..
                  statements;
   }
```

Let us see a program that illustrates the above notion.

```
#include<stdio.h>
void main()
 {
   int choice ;
   printf("\n Enter your choice (integer): ");
   scanf("%d",&choice);
   switch(choice)
   {
     case 1 : char ch ;          /* Incorrect declaration and correct for C++*/
              ch = getchar();
                 break ;
     default : break ;
   }
 }
```

In the above program segment **ch** is outside of the block. When one compiles this program segment compiler generates the following errors.

Expression syntax incorrect

ch not defined.

If we define variable **ch** inside a block, this format is correct and does not generate compile time errors. **It should be noted that in block variable's declaration is generally permitted in C++ not in C.** Consider the following syntax that gives correct form of the declaration. The implementation of this syntax is just below the syntax.

```
switch(choice)
 {
  case 'A':
```

```
        if( condition )
        {
                char ch;   /* Correct because declared char ch; in block of if statement */
                ...
        }
    case 'B': statements;
    ...
}
```

Go through the Example 9 which is implementing the above discussion.

Example 9: Write C code for demonstrating block variable declaration.

Answer: Let us see the following program segment that illustrates the above idea.

```
#include<stdio.h>
 void main()
 {
   int choice ;
   printf("\n Enter Your choice (integer): ");
   scanf("%d", &choice);
    switch(choice)
    {
           case 1 :
                       if (choice < 12)
                       {
                               char ch ;
                               ch = getchar();
                               printf("\n No Error in Declaration");
                       }
                     break ;
       default : break ;
    }
 }
```

13.3.6 Nested switch Statement

We can have a **switch**-statement inside a **switch**-statement as a part of the statement sequence and the **case** statements of the inner and outer statement contain common values (integer or character constants) and no conflicts arise. This is known as nested switch-statements. The syntax to declare nested **switch** and **case** statements is given below:

```
    switch(choice)
    {
      case 1 :
       switch(choice1)
       {
          case 'A':
              ...
              break ;
          case 'B':
              ...
              break ;
       }
         break;   /* break of case 1: */

                   case 2:
```

```
        ...
        break;
          ...
                    case n:
        ...
        break;
      default:
        ...
        break;
    }
```

In the nested **switch**-statements one **default** case is used that is with the outer **switch**-statement as given above. The following program segment illustrates the notion of nested **switch**-statements.

```
switch (choice)
{
    case 1:
            printf("\n Input value for choice 2:");
            scanf("&d",&choice2);
            switch (choice2)
            {
                    case 1: printf("\n Hello, You are in nested switch 2");
                            break;
                    case 2: printf("\n Hello, You are in nested switch 2");
                            break;
            }
    case 2: printf("\n Hello, now you are out side of inner switch ");
            break;
    default: printf("\n Have a nice day....");
            break;
}
```

13.4 ITERATIVE CONSTRUCTS

In all programming languages, iteration statements allow a set of instructions to be repeatedly performed until a certain condition is reached. This condition may be predefined or open ended (as in the while and do-while loop), i.e., either we can provide the value of a condition when program is written or when program is executed. C gives us a choice of three types of loop, while, do while and for.

The **while** loop keeps repeating an action until an associated test returns false. This is useful where the programmer does not know in advance how many times the loop will be traversed.

The **do - while** loops is similar, but the test occurs after the loop body is executed. This ensures that the loop body is run at least once.

The **for** loop is frequently used, usually where the loop will be traversed a fixed number of times. It is very flexible and novice programmers should take care not to abuse the power it offers.

13.4.1 The for statement

This looping statement is generally available in every language. **C** language provides more powerful and flexible looping statement. One example of looping statement in **C** is **for** loop. The syntax of **for** statement is given below:

```
for(Initialization; Condition; Increment/Decrement )
{
```

```
        Statement 1;
        Statement 2;
        Statement 3;
        ...
        Statement n;
    }
```

From above syntax, it is clear that there are **n** statements which are controlled by the **for** loop. When number of statements is one then there is no need of curly brackets. The above syntax can be represented with the help of Figure 13.4.

The for loop starts with the initialization of counter that is used to set the condition TRUE or FALSE. Initialization of counter can be done in for-statement or outside before for-statement. After the initialization the condition is checked for its validity and if it is TRUE then statements in for-block are executed in serial order. After this execution counter is modified (generally incremented or decremented). Now, condition is further checked whether it is valid or not; if valid then statements in **for** loop are executed. This is carrying on till the condition is found TRUE (valid). When the condition is found FALSE then **for** loop terminated without executing the statement in **for** loop. It should be noted here that we use for loop in a program when the value of counter is well known in advance.

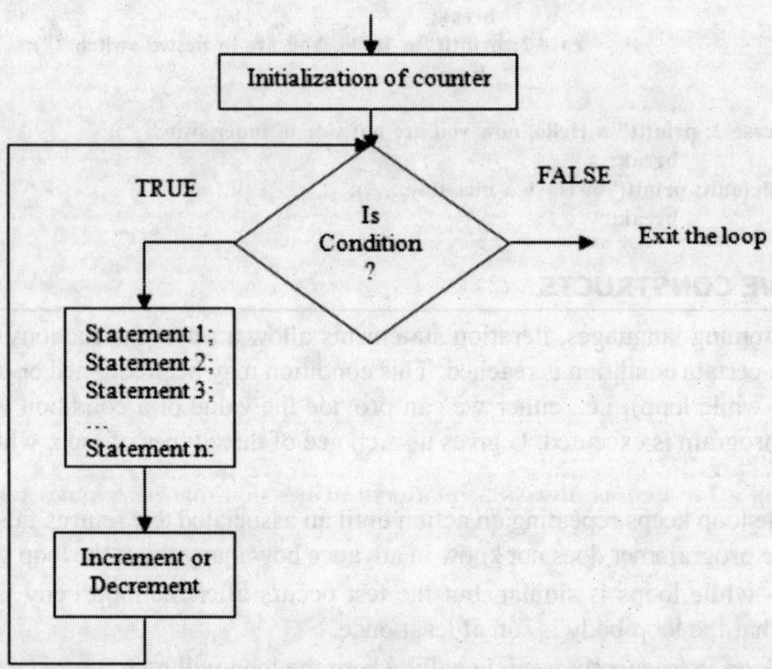

Figure 13.4 Control-flow of for Loop

Go through the Example 10 which is implementing the above discussion.

Example 10: Write C code for implementing simple for loop based program.

Answer: Consider the following program segment which demonstrates for statement.

```
/**  fortest.c **/
# include<stdio.h>
void main()
```

```
{
int counter ;
for (counter = 0 ;  counter < 10 ; counter++ ) /* Initialization inside the loop */
{
 printf("\n It is counter number:   %d time", counter+1 );
}
 printf("\n Have a nice day...... ");
}
```

OUTPUT

```
It is counter number:  1
It is counter number:  2
It is counter number:  3
It is counter number:  4
It is counter number:  5
It is counter number:  6
It is counter number:  7
It is counter number:  8
It is counter number:  9
It is counter number:  10
Have a nice day......
```

The **for**-statement allows many variants in its declaration, but generally there are three:

Initialization is generally an assignment which is used to set the loop control variable that is counter and can be done outside **for** loop. So, **for** loop will also work if initialization is done outside for loop as given below:

```
Initialization of index used in for;
    for( ; condition ; increment/decrement )
    {
        Statement 1;
        Statement 2;
        Statement 3;
        ...
        Statement n;
    }
```

Condition in a **for** loop is always a relational expression that determines when to exit the loop. The relational expression may be a part of arithmetic statements. For example, consider the following **for**-statement:

```
for( i = 0 ; i < ( a + 10 ) ;  i++ )
```

Here, **(a + 10)** is an arithmetic expression where variable a is compatible with variable i, first it is evaluated then the value of this expression is compared with the value of i to check the validity.

The increment/decrement defines how the loop control variable (counter) will be changed each time when loop is repeated. This cannot be done outside the for loop as initialization but it can defined in the for loop any where as given below:

```
for(counter=10, counter>=10; )
{
    Statements;
    counter =counter - 1;
    statements;
}
```

Another thing is to be taken care that the **initialization, condition** and **increment/decrement** must be separated by semicolon (;) otherwise compiler raises error(s). In **C** language semicolon (;) is a statement terminator operator which means for loop may contain many statements. The **for** loop continues to execute as long as the condition is found TRUE. Once the condition becomes FALSE, program execution resumes on the statement following the **for**-statement. Go through the Example 11 which is implementing the above discussion.

Example 11: Write a program to generate table of square of 10-20 integer numbers.

Answer: Following program segment **(fortest2.c)** evaluates square of the numbers 10 to 20 and displays the result in tabular form.

```
/** fortest2.c **/
# include<stdio.h>
void main()
{
    int number ;
    for (number = 10 ; j <= 20 ; number++ )
            /*Single Statement, no need of curly brackets*/
            printf("\n Square %d of %d ", number*number, number );
    printf("\n Have more fun.... ");
}
```

In the above program segment initially the value of number is set to 10. Since number is less than 20, the **printf( )** function is called, number is incremented by 1 and the condition is tested to see if it is still less than or equal to 20. This process is repeated until number is greater than 20 and at this point, the loop is terminated. In this example number is loop control variable that is also known as counter, which controls **for** loop. In the above example, there is a single statement so that opening and closing braces are not required.

In **for** loop, the condition is always tested at the beginning of the loop. It means the code inside the loop block may not be executed at all if the condition is false at the beginning of the loop. Go through the Example 12 which is implementing the above discussion.

Example 12: Write C code using for loop which is not in normal.

Answer: Consider the following program.

```
/** fortest3.c  **/
# include<stdio.h>
void main()
{
    int x=10 ,y;
    y=10;
    for (; y != x ; y++ )
            printf("\n Value of y = %d ", y );
    printf("\n Have a nice day..... ");
}
```

In the above example, **for** loop is never executed because x and y are equal when the condition is initially tested and condition is found FALSE. So, control does not enter the body of for loop, even the counter y does not incremented.

In **for** loop, several variants in its declaration are allowed that increase its power, flexibility and applicability, formally programming situations, e.g., a very powerful facility is achieved with the help of comma (,) operator. With the help of this operator, it is possible to use more than one variable to control the loop. For example, see the following program segment:

```
for( x = 1 , y = 1 ; x*y < 100 ; x++)
{
  printf("\n enter the value of counter y:",);
        scanf("%d", &y);
  othe executable Statements;
}
```

Here in this syntax two-initialization variables are used, viz. x and y. Further, setting of control is done with the help of keyboard by providing the value of y. Conditional expressions may be relational or logical statement. Following example implements many loop control variables:

```
void fun()
{
  int x, y ;
  for( x = 10 , y = 0 ; x != y ; y++, x- - )
  printf("\n WELCOME in era of multiple counters....");
  printf("\n Number of loop computations = %d", j-);
}
```

13.4.2 Infinite Loop

Sometimes misuse of the conditional expression or without conditional statement in **for** loop results in infinite loop. In other words, if the condition of a for loop is not set properly or there is no conditional statement to terminate the for loop, there is infinite loop situation and computer may be in hang situation. So, one should take care about the conditional statement in for loop. The control-flow of infinite for loop is shown in Figure 13.5. Now, let us see the syntaxes of **for** loop that normally causes infinite loop:

- ```
  for( ; ; )            /* Without the conditional expression*/
  {
      Statement 1;
      Statement 2;
      ...
      Statement n;
  }
  ```
- ```
  for( i=0; ;i++ )       /* Without the conditional expression*/
  {
      Statement 1;
      Statement 2;
      ...
      Statement n;
  }
  ```
- ```
  for( i=1 ; i>0  ;i++ )     /* Wrong condition is set*/
  {
      Statement 1;
      Statement 2;
      ...
      Statement n;
  }
  ```
- ```
  for( i=0; i<=10;i- - )     /* Modification of counter variable i is incorrect */
  {
      Statement 1;
      Statement 2;
      ...
      Statement n;
  }
  ```
- ```
  for( i=0;number=5 ;i++ )       /* Without the conditional expression*/
  ```
  ```

```
{
        Statement 1;
        Statement 2;
        ...
        Statement n;
}
```

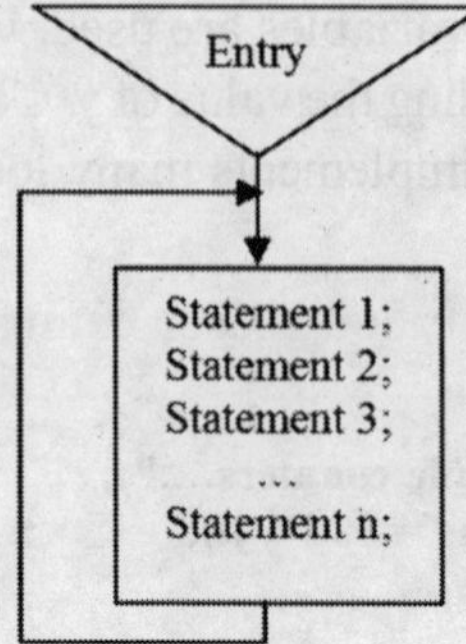

Figure 13.5 Control-flow in Infinite for loop

There are many variations of the above syntax that result in infinite loop. We should be careful about the following:

Which one is the counter variable(s),
What is the condition at which program terminates,
How counter variable(s) is modified (incremented or decremented),
Termination point of **for** loop is well defined or not?

Go through the Example 13 which is implementing the above discussion.

Example 13: Write C code using for loop which is executed for infinite length of time.

Answer: Now, let us see one program that falls in infinite loop:

```
/** fortest4.c **/
# include<stdio.h>
void main()
{
    for ( ; ; )
        printf(" I am in infinite loop");
}
```

When we run the above program, the computer displays string "I am in infinite loop" infinitely. To quit from this program, one is required to press interrupt key, which is **CTRL-BREAK** in **DOS** environment and **DEL in SCO UNIX,** Linux, and **AIX-L** environments.

13.4.3 The for Loop with No body

When we put statement terminator with for-statement, the program body of the loop is executed for infinite length of time and no output is displayed as shown below:

```
#include<stdio.h>
void main()
{
    int number ;
    for ( ; ; );
    {
        printf("Enter Value of number:");
        scanf("%d",&number);
        printf(" Value of x = %d", number);
    }
}
```

The above notion can be used as delay in many programs. Suppose somebody has initialized the counter value 500 or more without for loop body. This provides only the delay, not any other thing. We can use this idea to improve the efficiency of certain algorithms or to construct time delay loops. Removing spaces from an input stream is a common programming task. For example, a database program may allow a query such as "show all balances less than Rs 600.00". The database and to have each word fed to it separately, without spaces. That is, the database input processor recognizes "show" but not "sh   ow". We can remove the spaces between the character 'h' and 'o' using pointer or character array in a **for** loop as given below:

```
for (; *string == ' ' ; string++);
```

Other application is to construct delay loops. For example, following function creates a delay function.

```
Delay_in_display(int counter)
{
    for (; counter; counter- -); // Delay
}
```

The value of variable counter is provided to the function Delay_in_display ( ) and depending on the value function provides delay. Generally, the value of counter is larger like 500 or more.

13.5 JUMPING CONSTRUCTS

So far we have discussed the selection and iterative statements in C language. We know the program behavior in C language is sequential until unless any change is provided by programmer.

In for loop, generally we have some fixed counter value and statements of for loop body are executed till the condition is TRUE. C provides some more flexibility in declaring the value of counter. Sometimes we do not have integer or fixed number value for counter; we have expression that has any non-zero value. Suppose we want to have a loop that can be used, any number of times as user needs. For such a situation, C provides **while** loop facility.

13.5.1 The while statement

The syntax of **while** statement is given below:

```
while( condition )
{
Statement 1;
Statement 2;
...
Statement n;
}
Statement 1;
Statement 2;
...
Statement m;
```

Here, the condition may be any expression having nonzero value. The loop continues until the condition is true else the body of the loop will not be executed any more. Figure 13.6 illustrates the idea. There is no initialization and modification of counter variable as we have in **for** loop. Go through the Example 14 which is implementing the above discussion.

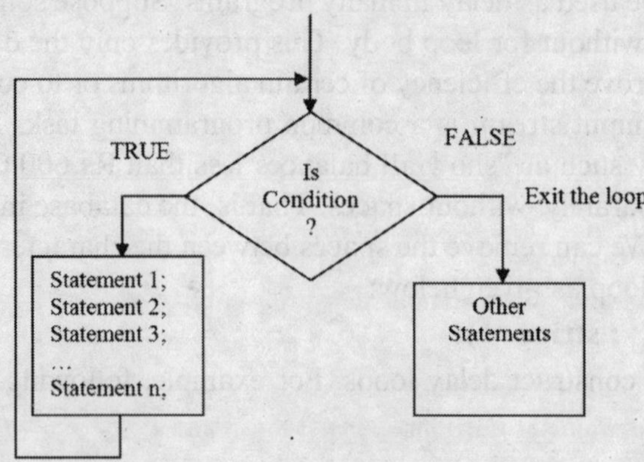

Figure 13.6 Control-flow of while Loop

Example 14: Write C code which is implementing user controlled while loop.

Answer: Consider the following program segment that implements this idea:

```
/**    whiletst1.c       **/
# include<stdio.h>
void main()
{
char choice='\0' ;    /* Initializing choice as NULL*/
while ( choice != 'B' )
 {
 printf("\n Enter choice (B) to break the while loop:");
 choice = getchar();
 printf("\n Your choice is: %c", choice );
 }
}
```

This program run until we input B. When we input B, the condition becomes false and program is terminated.

Like **for** loop, the **while** loop conditions are checked at the beginning. If the condition is true the control is transferred to the program body of the **while** loop otherwise the control is transferred out of the while loop. With **while** loop, it is possible to use several conditions to terminate the loop as illustrated in Example 15.

Example 15: Write C code which is implementing several conditions controlled while loop.

Answer: Consider the following program segment that implements this idea:

```
/**          whiletst2.c            **/
/* Multiple condition checking in while loop*/
#include<stdio.h>
 void demonstration() ;          /* Prototype */
 void main()
 {
    demonstration() ;
 }

/* Definition of the function load() */
void load()
 {
    int condition ;
```

```
condition = 1 ;
  /* any value other than NULL means condition is true */
while(condition)
{
        condition = function1() ;  /* Returned value of function assigned to condition */
        if(condition)
         condition = function2() ;
        /* Returned  value of function assigned to condition */
        if(condition)
                condition = function3() ;
          /* Returned  value of function assigned to condition */
        if (condition)
                condition = function4() ;
          /* Returned  value of function assigned to condition */
    }   /*End of the while loop*/
} /* End of load () function*/

/* Definition of function1() */
int function1()
 {
   int cond1 ;
   printf("\n enter the first condition:");
   scanf("%d", &cond1);
   return(cond1);
 }

/* Definition of function2() */
int function2()
 {
    int cond2 ;
     printf("\n enter the second condition:");
     scanf("%d", &cond2);
     return(cond2);
 }

/* Definition of function3() */
int function3()
 {
    int cond3 ;
     printf("\n enter the third condition:");
     scanf("%d", &cond3);
     return(cond3);
 }
```

```
/* Definition of function4() */
int function4()
 {
        int cond4 ;
        printf("\n enter the fourth condition:");
        scanf("%d", &cond4);
        return(cond4);
 }
```

In the above program, any of the four functions return false value and cause the loop to exit. It is also possible to define **while** loop without program body. In this case, it is possible to include any valid statement of **C** in parenthesis. For example, consider the following statement:

```
while((ch = getchar ()) != '\n' )
```

Here, **ch = getchar** () is a statement which is included the parenthesis of while loop and also the condition is mentioned. This loop continues until we press the enter key.

13.5.2 The do - while statement

We have discussed for loop and while loop that are executed only if the condition is found TRUE. If condition is FALSE, no statement in these loops will be executed. It is look like very much restricted provision in C. But C provides another less restrictive loop also. This is do-while loop. Whatever condition is there, the statements of **do-while** loop are executed at least once. This loop is used when some condition is found valid for its initial value and may or may not valid for other values. The syntax of a **do-while** statement is given below:

```
do
{
Statement 1;
Statement 2;
 ...
Statement n;
} while(condition) ;

  Statement 1;
  Statement 2;
  Statement 3;
  ...
  Statement m;
```

From the above syntax it is clear that the body of the loop will be executed at least once because first the body of the loop is executed and then the condition is checked. Figure 13.7 illustrates the above discussion. Statement 1, statement 2, Statement 3, ..., and Statement n is executed and then condition is checked for its validity. If condition is found valid then Statement 1, statement 2, Statement 3, ..., and Statement n are executed until the invalid condition. It is unique feature of the **do-while** loop that its body is executed at least once as compared to for loop and while loop. Go through the Example 16 which is implementing the above discussion.

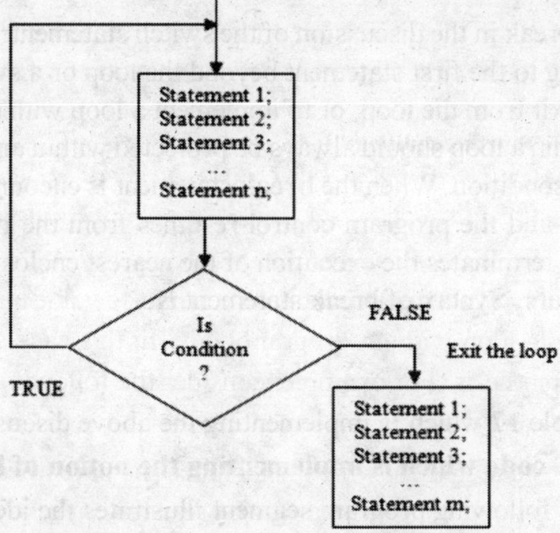

Figure 13.7 Control-flow of do-while Loop

Example 16: Write C code which is implementing the notion of do-while loop.

Answer: Consider the following program segment that implements this idea:

```
/**  dowhile.c**/
# include<stdio.h>
void main()
{
 int number =1;
 char choice='\0';        /*Initially choice =NULL*/
 do
 {
     printf("Enter character y:
     scanf("%c", &choice);
     printf("\n This is %d time...", number++);
 }while(choice=='y'||choice=='Y');          /*end of do-while loop*/
 printf(" You are exit the do-while loop");
}
```

OUTPUT
Enter character y: Y
This is 1 time...
Enter character y: y
This is 2 time...
Enter character y: n
You are exit the do-while loop

13.6 RESUME CONSTRUCTS

We have discussed about condition in for loop, while loop, and do-while loop. These loops have different notion in declaring the condition, checking condition and modifying the condition. Sometimes we need to bypass normal loop condition. C provides this facility. We can terminate a normal loop by using if-statement and break statement.

13.6.1 The break statement

We have already met break in the discussion of the switch statement. It is used to exit from a loop or a switch, control passing to the first statement beyond the loop or a switch. With loops, break can be used to force an early exit from the loop, or to implement a loop with a test to exit in the middle of the loop body. A break within a loop should always be protected within an **if** statement which provides the test to control the exit condition. When the **break** statement is encountered inside a loop, the loop is immediately terminated and the program control resumes from the next statement following the loop. The **break** statement terminates the execution of the nearest enclosing **do, for, switch,** or **while** statement in which it appears. Syntax of break statement is

jump-statement:

break;

Go through the Example 17 which is implementing the above discussion.

Example 17: Write C code which is implementing the notion of break statement.

Answer: Consider the following program segment illustrates the idea of break statement.

```
/**    break1.c  **/
# include<stdio.h>
void main()
{
int num1=420, num2=422, num3=424, num3=426, num4=428, num5=430, num6=432, num7=434, num8=436,
num9=438, num10=440;
    int choice_number, i, flag=0;
    printf("\n Enter a number to be searched:");
    scanf("%d", &choice_number);

    for ( i = 0 ; i <= 10 ; i++ )
    {
            if(choice_number== num1+2*i)
            {
                    printf("\n Number is not found in the list");
                    flag=1;             /*Indicates successful search*/
                    break;
            }
    }       /* end of for loop*/
    if (flag==0)
            printf("\n Search is unsuccessful");
    getch();
}
```

The above program runs successfully, but we will get some warning from compiler that we have not used the value of num2, num3, etc.

The **break** statement is frequently used to terminate the processing of a particular case within a switch statement. Lack of an enclosing iterative or **switch** statement generates an error. Within nested statements, the break statement terminates only the **do-while, while, for,** or **switch-case** statement that immediately encloses it. We can use a return or goto statement to transfer control elsewhere out of the nested structure

In the program break2.c, the nesting of **for** loop is done and the inner **for** loop contains the **break** statement. When the **break** statement is encountered, the control is transferred to the outer for loop. Go through the Example 18 which is implementing the above discussion.

Example 18: Write C code which is implementing the break statement for controlling the execution of loop controlled program.

Answer: Consider the following program segment that implements this idea:

```
/**    break2.c              **/
#include<stdio.h>
void main()
{
    int i , number;
    for( i = 0 ; i < 10 ; i++ )
    {
        number = 10 ;
        for ( ; ; )
        {
            printf(" \n number = %d", number) ;
            number ++;
            if( number == 50)
                break;
        }
    }
}
```

In this program segment value of number is reaches as 50 condition of if statement is satisfied and inner for loop is terminated and control is transferred to outer for loop.

13.6.2 The continue Statement

We have seen in the previous section that a break statement can be used to terminate a normal loop. One must thing that there should be reverse of the break statement, yes there is. C provides the **break** statement. The function of this statement is reverse of **break** statement. The **continue** statement forces the next iteration of the loop to be executed skipping code following the **continue** statement. This is similar to break but is encountered less frequently. It only works within loops where its effect is to force an immediate jump to the loop control statement.

In a while loop, jump to the test statement.

In a do while loop, jump to the test statement.

In a for loop, jump to the test, and perform the iteration.

Like a break, continue should be protected by an if statement. We are unlikely to use it very often.

In continue.c, if any negative number is entered then continue statement forces the control to the previous statements without following the statements after the continue statement. It is very much surprise package in a middle-level language. Go through the Example 19 which is implementing the above discussion.

Example 19: Write C code which is implementing the notion of continue statement for executing code based on some consition.

Answer: Consider the following program segment that implements this idea:

```
/*      continue.c    */
# include<stdio.h>
void main()
{
    int number ;
    do
    {
        printf("\n Input number 101 to break: ");
```

```
        scanf("%d", &number) ;
              if(number < 0 )
                    continue;
                    /* if Condition is true then control back to previous printf( ) statement*/
        printf("\n You Number is = %d", number);
    } while(number !=101) ;
}
```

```
OUTPUT
Input number 101 to break: 400
You Number is = 400
Input number 101 to break: 23
You Number is = 23
Input number 101 to break: -3
Input number 101 to break: 10
You Number is = 10
Input number 101 to break: 101
You Number is = 101
```

The do-while loop runs until the number 101 is entered. Whenever the input number is negative then control is transferred to "printf("\n Input number 101 to break: ");" statement.

13.6.3 The goto Statement

This feature in C language is similar to the **goto** statement in assembly languages. It also indicates that C language is a successor of low-level languages. We have discussed about the continue statement in the previous section that forces the control to the skip the following statements in block and execute the previous statements. The continue statement is equipped with if-statement. C provides the similar functionality of the continue statement. Using a **goto** statement we can make the control to be transferred at any point in a program. It is more powerful than a continue statement but dangerous also. As a good programming style, we must avoid the use of goto statement. A label always follows a goto statement. The label may be an identifier declared, constant, character constant or a string constant. No special characters are allowed in the label but single character is allowed. A label decides the position where the control jumps and be followed by colon (:). A label may be constant as well as a variable. The syntax of goto statement is given below:

```
Label:
        Statement 1;
        Statement 2;
        ...
        Statement n;
if(condition ) goto Label ;
        Statement 1;
        Statement 2;
        Statement 3;
        ...
        Statement p;
```

Consider the program segment **goto.c** which implements the use of **goto** statement given below. Go through the Example 20 which is implementing the above discussion.

Example 20: Write C code which is implementing the notion of goto statement for transferring control of a program from one statement to another whenever required.

Answer: Consider the following program segment that implements this idea:

```
/** goto.c **/
#include<stdio.h>
void main()
{
    int number ;
    do
    {
            printf("\n Input a number 101 to break loop: ");
            scanf("%d",&number) ;
                    if(number < 0 )
                            continue ;
                    /* if Condition is true then control back
                    to previous printf( ) statement*/
            printf(" Your Number is= %d", number);
            goto number ;
    } while(number !=20) ;

    number: /*label */
            printf("\n WELCOME AT SCO UNIX 'C...'");
}
```

OUTPUT
Input number 101 to break: -3
Input number 101 to break: 10
You Number is = 10
WELCOME AT SCO UNIX 'C...'

EXERCISES

1. Multiple Choice Questions

1. How many times will the following program print WELCOME?

```
#include< stdio.h>
void main()
{
    int count;
    for(count=-15; count>=-1; count- -)
    prinft("\n WELCOME");
    getch();
}
```

(a) 1 (b) 0 (c) 14 (d) None

2. How many times will the following program print WELCOME?

```
#include< stdio.h>
void main()
{
    int count;
    for(count=-15; count>=-1; count++)
```

```
        prinft("\n WELCOME");
        getch();
    }
```

(a) Infinite (b) 0 (c) 14 (d) None

3. How many times will the following program print WELCOME?

```
    #include< stdio.h>
    void main()
    {
        int count;
        for(count=-15; count<=-1; count++)
        printf("\n WELCOME");
        getch();
    }
```

(a) 15 (b) 0 (c) 14 (d) None

4. What is the output of following program?

```
    #include< stdio.h>
    void main()
    {
        int i;
        char ch='a';
        for(i=0; i<=25; i++)
        printf("\n %c", ch+i);
        getch();
    }
```

(a) Error (b) a (c) abcd....z (d) None

5. What is the output of following program?

```
    #include< stdio.h>
    void main()
    {
        char ch='a';
        while(ch<='z')
printf("\n %c", ch++);
    getch();
  }
```

(a) Error (b) a (c) abcd....z (d) None

6. What is the output of following program?

```
    #include< stdio.h>
    void main()
    {
        int i=5;
printf("\n %d %d", i++, ++i);
        getch();
    }
```

(a) 5 5 (b) 5 6 (c) 6 5 (d) 6 6

7. What is the output of following program?

```
    #include< stdio.h>
    void main()
    {
        int i;
```

```
for(i=3; i<18; i+=3);
prinft("\n %d", i);
        getch();
    }
```

(a) 15 (b) Error (c) 18 (d) None

8. What is the output of following program?

```
#include<stdio.h>
void main()
{
        int counter=12;
        do
        {
        printf("Its do-while loop..);
} while(count<=12);
```

(a) No output (b) Its do-while loop.. (c) Error (d) None

9. Select the correct statement.
   (a) If condition is missing in for loop, it is assumed to be TRUE
   (b) If condition is missing in for loop, it is assumed to be FALSE
   (c) If condition is missing in for loop, it results in syntax error
   (d) If condition is missing in for loop, it will terminate the program
10. Select the correct statement.
    (a) Body of for loop executed at least once
    (b) Body of while loop executed at least once
    (c) Body of do-while loop executed at least once
    (d) Body of none for, while, and do-while executed without condition
11. If condition is missing in a loop written in C language then infinite loop can be avoided by placing
    (a) break statement (b) goto statement
    (c) return statement (d) All
12. Choose the correct statement(s).
    (a) Any non-zero value represents TRUE condition
    (b) 0 represents FALSE condition
    (c) 0 and negative values represents FALSE condition
    (d) None
13. Select the incorrect statement.
    (a) for loop cannot be nested
    (b) while loop cannot be nested
    (c) switch-case statement can be nested and any value can be supplied to case statement
    (d) do-while loop cannot be bested
14. In case of switch-case statement
    (a) default case must be there
    (b) default case may or may not be there
    (c) if default case is there then it should be last statement
    (d) default case can be placed any where in the body

15. A break-statement in C language can be replaced by
    (a) exit-statement (b) return-statement
    (c) goto-statement (d) Cannot be replaced by any one
16. A switch-case statement can be replaced by
    (a) if-else statement (b) do-while loop
    (c) if-statement (d) None
17. Choose the correct statement a for loop.
    (a) counter can be initialized outside the loop body
    (b) counter cannot be initialized outside the loop body
    (c) counter must be modify inside the loop body
    (d) body of loop cannot be empty
18. Which one of the following is syntactically correct?
    (a) for(;) (b) for(; ;) (c) For(; ;) (d) None
19. What is the output of the following program?

```
#include<stdio.h>
void main()
{
        int number=0;
        printf("\n %d", number+=(number+=3, 10, 25));
        getch();
}
```

(a) 6 (b) 0 (c) 3 (d) Error

20. What is the output of following program?

```
#include<stdio.h>
void main()
{
        int number =25;
        switch(number)
        {
        case 'x':
                if(number>20)
        case 'y':
                number =0;
        printf("\n %d", number);
        }
printf("\n %d", number);
    }
```

(a) Error (b) 25 (c) 0 (d) None

21. What is the output of following program?

```
#include<stdio.h>
void main()
{
        char choice = x;
switch(choice)
{
        case 'x':
                if(choice>20)
```

```
        case 'y':
            choice = 97;
        printf("\n %c", choice);
        }
}
```

(a) c (b) b (c) a (d) None

22. What is the output of following program?

```
#include<stdio.h>
void main()
{
        int number =25;
        switch(number)
        {
            int temp=10;
case 25:
            printf("%d", temp);
            number++;
        case 26:
            printf("\n %d", number);
        }
}
```

(a) Error (b) 25 (c) 0 (d) None

23. What is the output of following program?

```
#include<stdio.h>
void main()
{
        int i, j;
        for(i=0, j=0, i<=2; i++, j++)
        printf(" %d", j);
}
```

(a) Error (b) 012 (c) 0 (d) None

24. What is the output of following program?

```
#include<stdio.h>
void main()
{
        int i, j=0;
        for(i=0, j++, i<=2; i++, printf("%d", j))
}
```

(a) Error (b) 012 (c) 11 (d) None

25. What is the output of following program?

```
#include<stdio.h>
void main()
{
        int i, j=0;
        for(i=0, ++j, i<=2; i++, printf("%d", j))
}
```

(a) Error (b) 012 (c) 11 (d) None

26. What is the output of following program?

```
#include<stdio.h>
```

```
void main()
{
    int i, j=0;
    for(i=0, printf("%d", ++j), i<=2; i++)
}
```

(a) Error (b) 1 (c) 11 (d) 012

27. What is the output of following program?

```
#include<stdio.h>
void main()
{
    int i, j=0;
    for(i=0, printf("%d", j++), i<=2; i++)
}
```

(a) Error (b) 1 (c) 0 (d) 012

28. Choose the correct statement about do-while loop.
    (a) the condition is evaluated first
    (b) body is evaluated first
    (c) condition is initialized first
    (d) None
29. Distinguish between the following pairs:
    (a) getchar and scanf functions.
    (b) %s and %c specifications for reading input from standard input device.
    (c) %s and %[ ] specifications for reading input from standard input device.
    (d) %g and %f specification for printing on standard output device.
    (e) %f and %e specifications for printing on standard output device.
30. Write scanf statements to read the following data lists:
    (a) 78 A 95.89. (b) 123 1.2345 C
    (c) 15-10-2002 (d) 10 TRUE 20
31. State the outputs produced by the following printf statements.
    (a) printf ("%d%c%f", 10, 'x', 1.23);
    (b) printf ("%2d %c %4.2f", 1234 'x', 1.23);
    (c) printf ("%d\t%4.2f", 1234, 456);
    (d) printf ("\"%08.2f\"", 123.4);
    (e) printf ("%d%d %d", 10, 20);
32. State errors, if any, in the following input statements.
    (a) scanf("%c%f%d", city, &price, &year);
    (b) scanf("%s%d", city, amount);
    (c) scanf("%f, %d", &amount, &year);
    (d) scanf(\n"%f", root);
    (e) scanf("%c %d %ld", *code, &count, Root);

33. What will be the values stored in the variables year and code when the data 1988, x is keyed in as a response to the following statements:

    (a) scanf("%d %c", &year, &code); . (b) scanf("%c %d", &year, &code);

    (c) scanf("%d %c", &code, &year); (d) scanf("%s %c", &year, &code);

34. State what (if anything) is wrong with each of the following output statements:
    (a) printf(%d 7.2%f, year, amount};
    (b) printf("%-s, %c"\n, city ,code);
    (c) printf("%f, %d, %s, price, count, city);
    (d) printf("%c%d%f\n", amount, code, year);

Answer the following Questions with justification to your answer.

35. Where the semicolon appears in a for loop with a multi-statement loop body?
    (a) the **for**-statement itself
    (b) the closing brace in a multi-statement loop body
    (c) each statement within the loop body
    (d) the test expression
36. A variable defined within a block is visible:
    (a) from the point of definition onward in the entire program
    (b) from the point of definition onward in the block only
    (c) throughout the function in which it is declared
    (d) from the point of definition onward in the function
37. The **break**-statement causes an exit from
    (a) from the innermost loop only
    (b) from the innermost **switch** only
    (c) from all loops and switches in the program
    (d) from innermost loop or **switch**
38. The goto statement causes control to be transferred to
    (a) an operator
    (b) a label
    (c) a variable
    (d) a function

State whether the following statements are true or false

1. The purpose of the header file <studio.h> is to store the programs created by the users.
2. The C standard function that receives a single character from the keyboard is getchar.
3. The getchar cannot be used to read a line of text from the keyboard.
4. The input list in a scanf statement can contain one or more variables.
5. When an input stream contains more data items than the number of specifications in a scanf statement, the unused items will be used by the next scanf call in the program.
6. Format specifiers for output convert internal representations for data to readable characters.
7. Variables form a legal element of the format control string of a printf statement.

8. The scanf function cannot be used to read a single character from the keyboard.
9. The format specification %+-8d prints an integer left-justified in a field width of 8 with a plus sign, if the number is positive.
10. If the field width of a format specifier is larger than the actual width of the value, the value is printed right-justified in the field.
11. The print list in a printf statement can contain function calls.
12. The format specification %5s will print only the first 5 characters of a given string to be printed.

Fill in the blanks with appropriate words in each of the following statements

1. The use of OPERATOR ? : to replace **if-else** statements is not restricted to ________ only.
2. The operator **?:** is called a ________operator because it requires three operands.
3. A conditional expression evaluates a value that is either ________ or ________ The **switch**-statement defers from **if**-statement in that switch-statement can only test for ________, where as **if**-statement can evaluate ________type of relational or logical expression.
4. The **case** constants in the same **switch**-statement have ________ values.
5. If character constants are used in the **switch**-statement, these are automatically converted to ________by C compiler.
6. The **break**-statements inside the **switch**-statement are ________
7. The________specification is used to read or write a short integer.
8. The conversion specifier________is used to print integers in hexadecimal form.
9. For using character functions, we must include the header file ________ in the program.
10. For reading a double type value, we must use the specification ________
11. The specification________is used to read a data from input list and discard it without assigning it to many variables.
12. The specification________ may be used in scanf to terminate reading at the encounter of a particular character.
13. The specification %[ ] is used for reading strings that contain________.
14. By default, the real numbers are printed with a precision of________decimal places.
15. To print the data left-justified, we must use________ in the field specification.
16. The specifier________prints floating-point values in the scientific notation.

Descriptive and Programming Problems

1. Write a program that counts numerical digits in a given number.
2. Write a program that works like a five-function calculator. The operations are:
   (a) addition (+) (b) subtraction (–)
   (c) multiplication (*) (d) division (\)
   (e) mod (%)
   Use **while** and **if-else** statements only.
3. Write a four-function calculator with the help of **while** and **switch** statements.
4. Write a program that calculates the factorial of an input integer number using **for** and **if** statements only.

5. With the help of while statement, write a program that calculates the factorial of an integer number? Repeat the same with the help of do-while statement.
6. See the beauty of the mathematics in the following series and write programs for generating the series.

   (a) 1*8+1=9
   12*8+2=98
   123*8+3=987
   1234*8+4=9876
   ....
   123456789*8+9=987654321

   (b) 1*9+2=11
   12*9+3=111
   123*9+4=1111
   1234*9+5=11111
   ...
   123456789*9+10=1111111111

   (c) 9*9=7=88
   98*9+6=888
   987*9+5=8888
   9876*9+4=88888
   ...
   987654321*9+0=888888888

   (d) 1*1=1
   11*11=121
   111*111=12321
   1111*1111=1234321
   ...
   111111111 * 111111111=12345678987654321
7. Write a program that splits a number into its constituent digits.
8. Write a program that finds ASCII code for each character inputted by user.
9. Write a program that prints table of ASCII codes.
10. Write a function **itob(n,s,b)** that converts the integer **n** into a base of **b** character representation in the string **s.**
11. Write a program that will read **n** number (integer) from keyboard and display should be in text. For example 113 number entered and can be written as

    (a) One hundred thirteen
    (b) One one three
12. A Government has a particularly simple system of taxation. Income above rupees 60,000 is taxed at 20 percent and income greater than or equal to Rs 1,50,000 is taxed at 33 percent. Write a program that reads incomes and prints the taxes due. The program should read incomes until the user wants. Assume that the income is an integer. Drop the fractional part of the tax, so that it is written as an integer.

13. Read a series of floating point numbers from the keyboard and print a statistical summary of the data that includes

    (a) the largest value input, (b) the smallest value input,

    (c) the sum of all values read, (d) the mean of all values input,

    (d) the population variance and the standard deviation. The population variance measures the spread of the values and given by the formula

    where is the mean of the n values x1, x2, x3 …, xn read. The standard deviation is the square root of the variance.

14. Write a program that prints a calendar for a year. Prompt the user for which day of the week **January 1** is on and whether the year is a leap year. The day that **January 1** is on is coded as given below:

    1 Sunday

    2 Monday

    3 Tuesday

    4 Wednesday

    5 Thursday

    6 Friday

    7 Saturday

    The leap year condition is coded as

    1 leap year

    0 no leap year

User Defined Functions

14.1 INTRODUCTION

We are familiar with several types of functions like **square, square root, exponential** and **trigonometric** functions. These functions and other functions are available to **C** programmer through libraries that are provided by **C** compiler developer. **C** also allows us to define and write our own functions. There are facilities in **C,** to modify the standard libraries or to incorporate new functions in the libraries. In either case, functions provide facilities to transfer a prewritten block of code to perform a specific task. This is very convenient when the same task is to be repeated several times or at different places in a program. The functions relieve us of writing the code for routine tasks different users can also share functions written by one user. This saves time and energy.

Almost all programming languages have some equivalent of the function. We may have met them under the alternative names subroutine or procedure. Some languages distinguish between functions which return variables, and those which do not. C assumes that every function will return a value. If the programmer wants a return value, this is achieved using the return statement. If no return value is required, none should be used when calling the function. In this chapter we will consider every phase of functions used in C.

14.2 CONCEPT OF A FUNCTION AND ITS PROPERTIES

A function is a "black box" that we have locked part of our program into. It is a subprogram which performs a well-defined task. It may be developed separately and tested. We may then name each such subprogram and specify the method of sending data to each of them and getting processed results from them. Once the subprograms are tested, they are linked together to do a specified task. The idea behind a function is that it compartmentalizes part of the program and in particular the code within the function has some useful properties:

1. It performs some well-defined task, which will be useful to other parts of the program.
2. It might be useful to other programs as well, i.e., we might be able to reuse it (and without having to rewrite it).

3. The rest of the program does not have to know the details of how the function is implemented. This can make the rest of the program easier to think about.
4. The function performs its task well. It may be written to do a little more than is required by the first program that calls it, with the anticipation that the calling program or some other program may later need the extra functionality or improved performance. It is important that a finished function does its job well, otherwise there might be a reluctance to call it, and it therefore might not achieve the goal of reusability.
5. By placing the code to perform the useful task into a function, and simply calling the function in the other parts of the program where the task must be performed, the rest of the program becomes clearer: rather than having some large, complicated, difficult-to-understand piece of code repeated wherever the task is being performed, we have a single simple function call, and the name of the function reminds us which task is being performed.
6. Since the rest of the program does not have to know the details of how the function is implemented, the rest of the program does not care if the function is re-implemented later, in some different way as long as it continues to perform its same task, of course. This means that one part of the program can be rewritten, to improve performance or add a new feature without having to rewrite the rest of the program.
7. It is a good idea to break up a big problem into a number of small sub-programs. Divide and conquer is the name given to a method for breaking up a complicated problem into smaller parts and solving each separately and is a well known problem solving method.
8. A program written as sequence of functions with each function carrying out a specified task is easy to understand.
9. It is easy to test small compact functions.
10. Commonly used functions may be generalized, tested and added in the library for future use.
11. Functions developed by others may be used. For example, a larger number of efficient, well-tested programs for common problems like matrix manipulation; statistical computation, sorting and searching, etc are normally available.

The functions are main building blocks of **C** Language. Functions are probably the most important weapon in our battle against software complexity. The syntax for declaring a user defined function is

Data type name of function (Datatype1 parameter1, Datatype2 parameter2,…, Datatypen parameter1n)

```
{
    Data type specifies list of parameters;
    Statement 1;
    Statement 2;
        ...
        ...
        ...
    Statement n;
}
```

14.3 STRUCTURE OF A FUNCTION

Function has a name that is used to call (invoke) it and a list of zero or more arguments or parameters that we hand to it for it to act on or to direct its work; it has a body containing the actual instructions (statements) for carrying out the task the function is supposed to perform; and it may give us back a return value, of a particular type. For example, consider the following code segment which defines a very simple function multibytwo() and accepts one argument, multiplies it by 2, and returns the computed value.

```
int multbytwo(int x)
{
        int retval;
        retval = x * 2;
        return retval;
}
```

On the first line we see the return type of the function (int), the name of the function (multbytwo), and a list of the function's arguments, enclosed in parentheses. Each argument has both a name and a type; multbytwo() accepts one argument, of type int, named x. The name x is arbitrary, and is used only within the definition of multbytwo(). The caller of this function only needs to know that a single argument of type int is expected; the caller does not need to know what name the function will use internally to refer to that argument. In particular, the caller has to pass the value for variable named x.

Next we see, surrounded by the familiar braces, the body of the function itself. This function consists of one declaration of a local variable retval and two statements. The first statement is a conventional expression statement, which computes and assigns a value to retval, and the second statement is a return statement, which causes the function to return to its caller, and also specifies the value which the function returns to its caller. The return statement can return the value of any expression, so we do not really need the local retval variable; the function could be collapsed to

```
int multbytwo(int x)
{
        return x * 2;
}
```

Go through Example 1 which demonstrates above discussion.

Example 1: How do we call a function?

Answer: See the following program segment which is calling to multbytwo() function defined above.

```
#include <stdio.h>
extern int multbytwo(int);
int main()
{
        int i, j;
        i = 3;
        j = multbytwo(i);
        printf("%d\n", j);
        return 0;
}
```

In the above program segment we have defined an external function prototype declaration. It is an external declaration, in that it declares something which is defined somewhere else. We have already seen the defining instance of the function multbytwo, but maybe the compiler has not seen it yet. The function prototype declaration contains the three pieces of information about the function that a caller needs to know: the **function's name, return type, and argument type**(s). Since we do not care what name the multbytwo function will use to refer to its first argument, we do not need to mention it. On the other hand, if a function takes several arguments, giving them names in the prototype may make it easier to remember which are so names may optionally be used in function prototype declarations.

Finally, to remind us that this is an external declaration and not a defining instance, the prototype is preceded by the keyword extern.

The presence of the function prototype declaration lets the compiler know that we intend to call this function, multbytwo. The information in the prototype lets the compiler generate the correct code for calling the function, and also enables the compiler to check up a code segment. Down in the body of main, the action of the function call should be obvious: the line

```
j = multbytwo(i);
```

calls multbytwo, passing it the value of i as its argument. When multbytwo returns, the return value is assigned to the variable j. The value of main's local variable i will become the value of multbytwo's parameter x; this is absolutely not a problem, and is a normal sort of affair. The variable i is not really needed, since we could just as well call

```
j = multbytwo(3);
```

and the variable j is not really needed, either, since we could just as well call

```
printf("%d\n", multbytwo(3));
```

The call to multbytwo is a subexpression which serves as the second argument to printf. The value returned by multbytwo is passed immediately to printf. In general, we see the flexibility and generality of expressions in C. An argument passed to a function may be an arbitrarily complex subexpression, and a function call is itself an expression which may be embedded as a subexpression within arbitrarily complicated surrounding expressions.

We should say a little more about the mechanism by which an argument is passed down from a caller into a function. Formally, C is calling by value, which means that a function receives copies of the values of its arguments. We can illustrate this with an example. Suppose, in implementation of multbytwo, we had gotten rid of the unnecessary retval variable like this:

```
int multbytwo(int x)
{
        x = x * 2;
        return x;
}
```

We might wonder, if we wrote it this way, what would happen to the value of the variable i when we called

```
j = multbytwo(i);
```

When implementation of multbytwo changes the value of x, does that change the value of i up in the caller? The answer is no. x receives a copy of i's value, so when we change x we do not change i. For example, consider the following code segment which is a function that raises a double to the power of an unsigned, and returns the result.

```
double power(double val, unsigned pow)
{    double ret_val = 1.0;
     unsigned i;

     for(i = 0; i < pow; i++)
          ret_val *= val;

     return(ret_val);
}
```

This function power() is multiplying the **val** by itself **pow** times. A for loop is used to control the number of multiplications, and variable ret_val stores the value to be returned. Careful programming has ensured that the boundary condition is correct too, i.e., let us examine the details of this function.

double power(double val, unsigned pow)

This line begins the function definition. It tells us the type of the return value, the name of the function, and a list of arguments used by the function. The arguments and their types are enclosed in parenthesis, each pair separated by commas. The body of the function is bounded by a set of curly brackets. Any variables declared here will be treated as local unless specifically declared as static or extern types.

```
return(ret_val);
```

When execution of a function reaches to a return statement, control of the function returns to the calling function. The bracketed value is the value which is returned from the function. If the final closing curly bracket is reached before any return value, then the function will return automatically, any return value will then be meaningless. The example function can be called by a line in another function which looks like this

```
result = power(val, pow);
```

This calls the function power assigning the return value to variable result. Here is an example of a function which does not return a value.

```
void error_line(int line)
{
    fprintf(stderr, "Error in input data: line %d\n", line);
}
```

The definition uses type void which is optional. It shows that no return value is used. Otherwise the function is much the same as the previous example, except that there is no return statement. Some void type functions might use return, but only to force an early exit from the function, and not to return any value. This is rather like using break to jump out of a loop.

When the argument which is being passed to a function is not a single variable, but is rather an array, the function does not receive a copy of the array, and it therefore can modify the array in the caller. The reason is that it might be too expensive to copy the entire array, and furthermore, it can be useful for the function to write into the caller's array, as a way of handing back more data than would fit in the function's single return value.

14.4 CALLING A FUNCTION

The syntax to activate a function is

Name of function (list of arguments);

where name of the function is any valid variable name and the argument list is to be passed to the function subprogram. The argument list may be **variables, subscripted variable names, array names, constant values, expressions, function names** or NULL. The value of the function is returned through the name of function acting as a variable.

We know that function can return one and only one value at a time and also it can participate in arithmetic operations. Go through Example 2 which demonstrates above discussion.

Example 2: Write a program which multiplies two integer numbers using a user defined function.

Answer: Consider the program segment **FUN_ARTH.C** which computes multiplication of two integer numbers.

```
/* FUN_ARTH.C */
# include<stdio.h>

void main()
{
        int x , y ;
        int result ;
        x = 20 ;
        y = 30 ;
        result = fun ( x, y) * x / y ;  /* Line A */
        printf("\n x = %d",x);
        printf("\n y = %d", y);
        printf("\n Value = %d" result ) ;
}

/* Definition of fun() */
fun(int a , int b )
{
        int result ;
        result =  a*b ;
        return (result) ;
}
```

When we call a function in function **main()** or else where, in other function, the called function is invoked. In the above program segment we have called **fun (x, y)** at **line A** in function main() for invoking it. Return value of **fun (x, y)** is an integer and in function **main (),** it is used as an expression, which is participating in arithmetic operation. We have passed two int argument to **fun(x,y).** Go through Example 3 which demonstrates above discussion.

Example 3: Write a program for computing the factorial of a number using user defined function.

Answer: Consider the program segment **FACT.C** that illustrates the function invocation in some different way. In this code segment we are not using function factorial (int m) in arithmetic operation.

```
/* FACT.C */
/* FIND FACTORIAL OF AN INTEGER NUMBER */
# include<stdio.h>
void main()
{
        int n ;
        long int result ;
        printf("\n Enter a number = ");
        scanf("%d", &n);
        result = factorial(n) ;     /* Invoke function Line A */
        printf("\n Factorial = %ld", result) ;
}
/* Definition of factorial () */
factorial(int m)
{
        int fact  ;
        if ( m == 0 )
                    return ( 1 );
        else
                    fact = m * factorial(m-1) ;
        return (fact);
}
```

Here, in this program segment when we call the function **factorial ()** in the **main()** function at line A, **factorial ()** is invoked. Here, type of function is int and the value passed to it is also an int. This function computes factorial of a non negative integer.

14.5 TERMINATING FUNCTION

A function is terminated in two ways:

When we define a function **void** type, the function is terminated when the last closing brace '}' of that function encountered as illustrated in the function **fun()** in the following codes.

```
/* fun.c */
void fun ( int n , char *s )
{
    int i ;
    for( i = n ; i ; -i)
    {
            printf("\n%s",s) ;
            printf("%d Time ",i) ;
    }
}
```

Here, the above function starts from opening brace '{' and terminates at closing brace '}'.

Second way of termination of function is by using **return** statement. When **return** statement is encountered, control of execution of program exits immediately from the currently executing function to the calling function, optionally returning a value. For example, consider the **find ()** function in the **FIND.C** program segment.

```
/* FIND.C */
find ( int a[3] , int b )
{
    int i ;
    for( i = 0 ;  i < 3 ; i++)
            if(a[i] == 'B' )      /* Line A */
                    return (i) ;
            else
                    return (-1);
}
```

In the above program segment the function can be terminated at two places, firstly at **return (i)** and secondly at statement **return (-1)** depending on the value of the conditions in the line A. If the condition is false, it will terminate at return **(-1),** otherwise at **return (i)** statement.

When a function does not specify its type, it is treated as an integer type. As such, we should define function type according to our requirement. We should define function types before constructing its body. Another way to define a function is:

Data type specified name of function (no arguments)

```
{
        Data type specifies list of parameters;
        Statement 1;
        Statement 2;
            ...
            ...
            ...
        Statement n;
}
```

Go through Example 4 which demonstrates above discussion.

Example 4: Write a program to compute the , where x and y are integer numbers by using user defined function.

Answer: Consider the program segment **FUNC_WP.C** that illustrates the above discussion.

```
/* func_wp.c */
# include<stdio.h>

int x, y;  /* Global  variable */
float xy_power(void) ;  /* Prototype */

void main()
{
     printf("\n Enter value of x, y: ");
     scanf("%d%d",&x,&y);
     printf("\n y power x is: %f", xy_power());
}
/*   Definition of function xy_power() */
float xy_power(void)
{
     float result  ;
     int a , b ;
     a = x ;
     b = y ;
     result = pow1(b,a) ;
     return(result) ;
}

/* Definition of function pow1() */

int pow1( int base, register int exponent)
{
     register int t ;
     t = 1;
     for( ; exponent ; exponent-)
     {
          t *= base ;
     }
     return(t);
}
```

In the above program segment, no arguments were passed to the function **xy_power ().** We have declared the data type global and assign values to them. The values assigned to them remain always in the program. In other words we can say that scope of variables is equal to the total time needed to execute the program.

14.6 FUNCTION OVERHEAD

When we define functions in a program, **C** pushes the return address, parameters and local variables onto the stack. When the function completes, **C** discards (pops) the stack space that contained the local variables then uses the return value to resume the program's execution at the correct location. The use of the stack lets the program invoke and pass information to the functions consumes processing time. The amount of time required pushing and popping stack information is function overhead. Go through Example 5 which demonstrates above discussion.

Example 5: Write a program to compare the computing speed of iterative and function based implementation.

Answer: Go through the program segment **functovr.c,** in this first **for** loop requires approximately 8 seconds to sum 1 to 1,00, 000, 000. The second loop for the same range of data with the help of function takes approximately 54 seconds on 133 MHz machine **SCO UNIX** machine for same number of running processes.

```
/* functovr.c */
#include <stdio.h>
#include <time.h>

float add_em(long int a, float b)
{
    float result;
    result = a + b;
    return(result);
}

void main(void)
{
    long int i;
    float result = 0;
    time_t start_time, stop_time; /* defining system clock struct */
    printf("Working...\n");
    time(&start_time);
    for (i = 1; i <= 100000000L; i++)
        result += i;
    time(&stop_time); /* getting system clock time when execution start */
    printf("Using loop:  %d seconds\n", stop_time - start_time);
    printf("Working...\n");
    time(&start_time);
    for (i = 1; i <= 100000000L; i++)
        result = add_em(i, result);
    time(&stop_time); /* getting system clock time when execution stops */
    printf("Using function:  %d seconds\n", stop_time - start_time); /* find actual computation time. */
}
```

14.7 ARGUMENT PASSING TECHNIQUES

We have already seen how functions can be used to run the same group of statements from multiple places within a program. This works fine where the statements that we want to run and the variables that we want to access are the same in each case but often we will find that the code we want to run for different variables is exactly the same except for the variable (or variables) that we want the code to use. We can solve this problem by defining special variables in our function called arguments that will stand in for the real variables when we define the function. We then tell the function which real variables to use in place of those arguments by passing the required variables as parameters.

Call-by-value and call-by-reference parameters both have merit in given applications and are commonly supported by high level languages. The meaning here is that normally used in C. Call-by-value passes a copy of the value for the actual parameter via the stack from the caller to the callee. Call-by-reference differs in that the offset of the actual parameter is passed via the stack from the caller to the callee.

14.7.1 Call by Value

C language supports mainly call by value technique for parameter passing. We have seemed that functions may have formal parameters associated with them. These formal parameters get assigned **copies** of the actual parameters when the function is called. The **parameter** then acts as a local variable within the called function. A formal parameter behaves like a local variable and can even be modified in the function without affecting the actual **parameter.** This is called call by value parameter passing. Go through Example 6 which demonstrates above discussion.

Example 6: Write a program for demonstrating call by value parameter to a function.

Answer: We will consider this problem in two parts. For first part consider program segment FUNC_VAL.C that illustrates this technique. And for the second part go through noeffect.c.

```
/* FUNC_VAL.C */
# include<stdio.h>

float m_payment(float  , float , int ) ;  /* Prototype */
double pow1( int , register int );

void main()
{
     float A , I ; /* Mortgage amount A , I interest rate */
     int D ;       /* Duration is D */

     printf("\n Enter Mortgage Amount = ");
     scanf("%f", &A);
     printf("\n Enter interest rate = ");
     scanf("%f", &I);
     printf("\n Enter Duration  = " );
     scanf("%d",&D);
     printf("\n Monthly Payment = %f", m_payment(A,I,D) );
}
/* Definition of function */

float m_payment( float a , float i , int d )
{
     float num ;
     float deno ;
     float payment ;
     num = ( a * i /12 ) ;
     deno = pow1( (1/(1+i/12)),d*12);
     payment = num / ( 1 - deno ) ;
     return(payment);
}
/* Definition of function  pow1() */

double pow1( int base, register int exponent)
{
     register int t ;
     t = 1;
     for( ; exponent ; exponent -)
     {
          t *= base ;
     }
     return(t);
}
```

In the above program segment, when function **m_payment ()** is called, the values of **A, D** and **I** are copied into **a, i** and **d.**

Generally, every variable has two-attributes- its current value and its memory address. In the following program segment, let the addresses of variables **x, y** and **z** are as shown in **Figure 14.1.** When we pass parameters to a function, C places the corresponding values on to the stack. In the case of the variable **x, y** and **z,** the stack contains the values 100, 200 and 300, respectively. When the function, accesses the variable's values, the function references the stack locations as illustrated in Figure 14.2. Consider the following example, which demonstrates step-by-step parameter passing by call value method.

```
/* noeffect.c */
#include <stdio.h>
void display_and_change(int first, int second, int third)
{
    printf("Original function parameters values %d %d %d\n", first, second, third);
    first += 100;
    second += 100;
    third += 100;
    printf("Values after adding 100 to each parameter  in function %d, %d, %d\n", first, second, third);
}

void main(void)
{
    int x = 100;
    int y = 200;
    int z = 300;
    printf("Values before function call: %d, %d, %d\n", x, y, z);
    display_and_change(x, y, z);
    printf("Values after function call: %d, %d, %d\n", x, y ,z);
}
```

Changes in the parameter's values actually change the stack values as illustrated in Figure 14.3. When function ends, **C** discards the stack and hence, the changes the function has made to the stack locations. The memory locations that contain each variable's values are never referred by the function. So, using call by value; a function can not make changes to a variable's value that exists after the function ends.

Address	Value	Variable
0x137f0000	100	x
0x137f0002	200	y
0x137f0004	300	z

Figure 14.1 Variables store a value and reside in a specific memory location

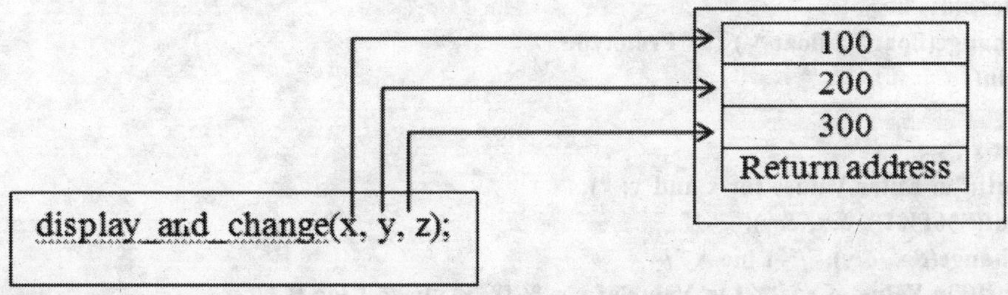

Figure 14.2 Functions reference parameter's values stored on the stack.

(Change made in the content of stack by function **display_and_change(x,y,z)**)

0x137f0000	100
0x137f0002	200
0x137f0004	300

Memory

200
300
400
Return address

Stack

Figure 14.3 Function's reference parameter values stored on the stack.

14.7.2 Call by Reference

Second method, which is used to communicate between arguments via function, is known as call by reference. Call by reference refers to a method of passing the address of an argument in the calling function to a corresponding parameter in the called function. In C, the corresponding parameter in the called function must be declared as a pointer type. In this way, the value of the argument in the calling function can be modified by the called function. Go through Example 7 which demonstrates above discussion.

Example 7: Write a function which demonstrates the parameter pass reference operation.

Answer: Consider the following code segment that illustrates the parameter passing by reference.

```
/* Definition of function */
void exchange (float *x , float *y )
{
    float t ;
    t = *x ;  /* copy x into t */
    *x = *y ; /* copy y into x */
    *y = t ;  /* copy x into y */
}
```

In the above code segment pointer operator '*' is used to access the variable pointed to by its operands. Let we input for **x = 12.25** and **y = 144.75** in the following program segment. The **exchange ()** function is called in function main() at line A with the address of **x and y.** In this line operator (&) is used to produce the addresses of the variables x and y. Hence, the addresses of x and y are passed to the function **exchange ().** Code of line B produces the output. How the pass by reference performs the information exchange between actual and formal parameters is illustrated in Figure 14.4.

```
/* FUNCT_REF.C */
# include<stdio.h>
void exchange(float * , float * ) ; /* Prototype */
void main()
{
    float x , y ;
    printf("\n Enter Values for x and y: ");
    scanf("%f%f", &x, &y);
    exchange(&x, &y);  /* Line A */
    printf("\n Value of x = %f \n Value of y = %f", x, y);  /* Line B */
}
```

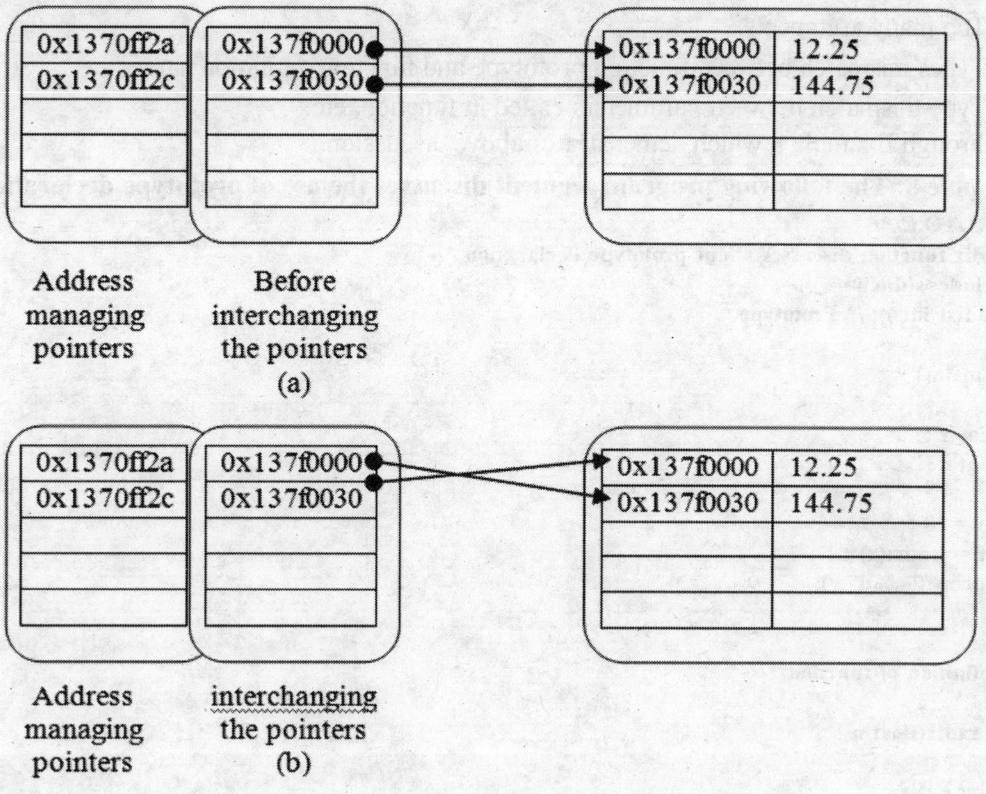

Figure 14.4 Parameters passed by reference

14.8 PROTOTYPES

Before we use a function Compiler must have knowledge about the type it returns and the parameter types the function expects. Generally, the name of the function is placed near the top of the program. When a function is declared before its use, it is known as prototype declaration and the function name is known as prototype name. To declare a function prototype simply state the type the function returns, the function name and in brackets list the type of parameters in the order they appear in the function definition. The prototype allows compiler to find and report any illegal type conversion among the type of arguments used to call the function and the type in the function definition and its parameters. The syntax to define a prototype is

Data type name of function (Data type 1, Date type 2, Data type3, ..., Data typen);

For example, consider the following code slice:

int strlen(char []);

This declaration states that a function called strlen() returns an integer value and accepts an array of characters. This array of characters also may be a single string as a parameter.

It should be noted functions can be prototyped and variables defined on the same line of code.

When we define prototype, the informations about the functions are stored onto the stack during the compilation, starting from the beginning of the program. In subsequent programs the compiler compares the functions with the stack name of the function. If there is a match, there are no errors reported, otherwise errors will be generated. The possible error messages are:

Too few arguments.

Too many arguments.

Types mismatch between function prototype and function definition name.

Type mismatch between parameters called in function, etc.

Go through Example 8 which demonstrates above discussion.

Example 8: The following program segment discusses the use of prototype declaration.

```
/* PROTO.C */
/* radix function discusses about prototype declaration */
# include<stdio.h>
int radix( int ) ; /* Prototype */

void main()
{
    int x ;
    int r ;

    x = 20 ;
    r =  radix(x) ;
    printf(" %d",r);
}

/* Definition of function */

float radix(float n )
{
    int r ;
    r = n % 10 ;
    return(r) ;
}
```

While compiling the above program segment, errors will be generated because in prototype, **radix()** is type integer and the parameter passed to it is also of integer type. However, in function definition, its type is **float** and parameter used in function name is also **float.** Hence, when we compile this program segment, following error will be flashed.

Undefined symbol radix (int) linker error.

The corrected code of **PROTO.C** is:

```
/* PROTO.C (CORRECTED CODE) */
/* radix function discusses about prototype declaration */
# include <stdio.h>
int radix (int ); /* Prototype */
/*Definition of function*/
int radix(int n )
{
    int r ;
    r = n * 10 ;
    return(r) ;
}
void main()
{
    int x ;
```

```
    int r ;
    x = 20 ;
    r =  radix(x) ; /*invoking the function radix() */
    printf("\n %d", r);
}
```

It is also possible to include actual parameters with a prototype, i.e., argument names may like the argument used to invoke a function. The syntax to declare such type of prototypes is

Data type function name (Data type 1 argument 1, Data type 2 argument 2,..., Data type n argument n);

For example, consider the following example that implements the above prototype. In this program segment we have defined **void inter_change(int x , int y)** which is prototype. In this prototype we included name and type of parameters (int x , int y) used in the implementation of the function.

```
/**      argproto.c      **/
# include<stdio.h>
void inter_change(int x , int y ) ; /* Prototype */
void main()
{
    int x ;
    int y ;
    x = 20 ;
    y = 30 ;
    printf("\n\n Values before function call");
    printf("\n\nx = %d \ny = %d", x, y);
    inter_change(x,y);
    printf("\n\n Values after  function call");
    printf("\n\nx = %d \ny = %d", x, y);
}

/*   Definition of function */

void inter_change( int a , int b)
{
    int temp ;
    temp = a;
    a = b;
    b = temp;
}
```

14.8.1 Function Pointers and Prototypes

It is generally a good idea to have a function prototype in scope whenever we call a function. Function prototypes allow the compiler to generate correct code for function calls, and to verify that we have called a function with the correct number and type of arguments. Standard library functions are prototyped by including the relevant standard header files. But what prototype can be used for an indirect function call using a function pointer, such as

(*pfi)(arg1, arg2)

In general, it would not be known until runtime what function pfi actually points to, so there is no way for the compiler to check the call against the prototype of the actually-called function. We have seen that when we declare a function pointer, we must declare what the return value of the pointed-to function will be. It is also possible to specify what the prototype of the pointed-to function will be. Here i's our earlier declaration of pfi, beefed up with a prototype for the arguments:

```
int (*pfi)(int, int);
```

Now we know that pfi is a pointer to a function, this function accepts two int arguments, and returns an int. Having specified this, the compiler will now be able to do some more checking for us. If we call

```
(*pfi)(1, 2, 3)
```

The compiler will complain, because it knows that the function pointed to by pfi is supposed to receive two arguments, but we have passed three. The compiler is also in a position to verify that we actually set pfi to point to function that accept two int arguments. Our examples so far were in terms of functions which we declared as

```
extern int f1();
extern int f2();
extern int f3();
```

that is, as functions taking unspecified arguments and returning int. Remember, empty parentheses in an external function declaration indicate that the function accepts unspecified arguments, while empty parentheses in a function definition indicate that the function accepts no arguments. So the compiler would not be able to check the assignments unless we also provide prototypes:

```
extern int f1(int, int);
extern int f2(int, int);
extern int f3(int, int);
```

Now, when we assign

```
pfi = f1;
```

the compiler can verify that the function pointer being assigned is to a function which accepts two int arguments, as pfi expects. If, on the other hand, we declared and assigned

```
extern int x(int);
pfi = x;
```

the compiler would complain, because pfi is supposed to point to a function which accepts two int arguments, and the eventual call to (*pfi)() is going to be verified to be a call passing two arguments, so assigning pfi to point to x (which accepts a single argument) is incorrect.

14.9 FUNCTION AND ARRAY

We can pass an array to a function. General syntax for this is

Data type function name (Data type 1 array 1, Data type 2 array2, Data type 3 array3... Data type n array n, Data type1argument1, Data type 2 argument 2... Data type n argument n)

```
{
    Data type specifiers list of parameters;
    Statement 1;
    Statement 2;
    ...
    Statement n;
}
```

For example, see the following program segment which defines and implement the above syntax.

```
/**     printn.c     **/
void printf_number(int number[10], int n )
{
    int i ;
    for( i = 0 ; i < n ; i++ )
        printf("\n Index = %d \n Number = %d", i, number[i]);
}
```

Go through Example 9 which demonstrates some use of an array.

Example 9: Write a program to find a data in a given array.

Answer: In program segment **printn.c,** we have defined function **print_number ()** which receives an array of 10 integers. In the following code we have modified the operation performed by **print_number()** and given new name, i.e., **search().**

```
/**  funarray.c     **/
# include<stdlib.h>
# include<stdio.h>

void main()
{
    int data ;
    int least[100] ;
    int number , i ;
    number = 10 ;
    for( i = 0 ; i <= 10 ; i++ )
    {
        least [ i ] = (int) random()/1000 ; /* Generates random number */
    }
    printf(" \n Enter data to which want to see: ");
    scanf("%d",&data);
    printf("\n***********************************");
    printf("\n POSITION NUMBER     VALUE STORED");
    printf("\n***********************************");
    search(least, data, number);
    printf("\n***********************************");
}
/* Definition of function */
search (int l[100] , int data , int number )
{
    int j ;
    j = 0 ;
    while(j <= number )
    {
        system("setcolor 4 15");
        printf("\n %4d     %4d  ",j,l[ j ]);
        if (l[j] == data )
        {
            printf("Found = %d, Position = %d\n", data, j);
            system(" setcolor 5 15 ");
            system ("tput cup 50,24");
            printf("\033[0m Press a key");
            getchar();
            return;
        }
        j++ ;
```

```
    }
    printf("\n Not found “);
    return ;
}
```

Here, in the above program segment, we have used a function **search ()** to which we have passed a list of numbers, number to be searched and the size of the array on which the function **search()** operates. This list contains random numbers which are generated by **random ()** function of **C** library.

Another way to pass an array to a function is with the help of pointers in which a pointer variable receives the base address of the array. The syntax is

Data type function name (Data type *array, Data type 2 arg1, Data type 3 arg2,..., Data type n argn);

```
{
        Data type specifiers list of parameters;
        Statement 1;
        Statement 2;
        ...
        ...
        ...
        Statement n;
}
```

Go through Example 10 which demonstrates above discussion.

Example 10: Implementation of funarray.c is further modified and given new name search.c. The program segment simply implements the above syntax.

```
/**   search.c    **/
# include<stdio.h>
int search (int *list , int el_to_be_search, int i);  /* prototype */
void main()
{
    int el_to_be_search ;
    int i ;
    int list[100] ;
    for( i = 0 ; i <= 10 ; i++ )
            list [ i ] = i*i ;
    printf("\n List is as follows");
    for( i = 0 ; i <= 10 ; i++ )
    printf("\n Index = %d Element = %d", i, list [ i ]);

    printf("\n Enter Element to be search: “);
    scanf("%d",&el_to_be_search);
    search(list , el_to_be_search, i) ;
}

/* Function definition */
int search (int *list , int el_to_be_search, int i)
{
    int j ;
    int l , m , r ;
    int iter = 0 ;
    l = 0 ;
    r = i -1 ;
    do
```

```
{
        iter++ ;
        m = ( l + r ) / 2 ;
        if( el_to_be_search > list[m] )
                l = m + 1 ;
        else
                r = m - 1 ;
} while((list[m] != el_to_be_search) && ( l <= r ));
if( list[m] == el_to_be_search )
        printf("\n Found = %d \n Position = %d",el_to_be_search,m+1 );

else
        printf("\n Not found and total comparison = %d", iter) ;
return ;
}
```

In the above program segment, we have used **'*'** operator with definition of the function because ***list** is same as **list[]**. The **list[]** means an array of unknown length and accepts the maximum size allocated by the C compiler.

Functions and two dimensional arrays are discussed in the next chapter. So, readers are suggested follow the next chapter in which function, arrays and pointer presented together for the clarity.

14.10 FUNCTION AND STRUCTURE

Function can also accept structure type arguments. The syntax is

```
Data type function name (list of arguments)
{
        Local declarations;
        Program body;
}
```

List of arguments may contain any standard data type as well as any aggregate (user defined data types). Here, we are considering the aggregate structure data type which is used to pass **struct** data to the definition of a function. Example 11 implements the idea discussed above.

Example 11: Write a program which implements the concept of struct and function.

Answer: Following code segment demonstrates the idea.

```
/**     struct.c     **/
# include<stdio.h>
struct record
{
     char name[40];
     int age ;
};

void listing( struct record list[10] , int  );
void main()
{
     struct record rec[10] ;
     int i , m ;
     printf("\n Number of record want to read:");
     scanf("%d",&m);
     printf("\n****************");
     printf("\n List of record");
     printf("\n****************\n");
```

```
        listing( rec, m );  /* invoke listing() */

        for( i = 0; i < m ; i++)
        {
                printf("\n Name: ");
                puts(rec[i].name);
                printf("\nAge: %d\n",rec[i].age);
        }
        printf("\n****************\n");
}

/* Definition of function */

void listing ( struct record list[10] , int n )
{
        struct record rec ;
        int i ;

        for( i = 0 ; i < n ; i++)
        {
                printf(" \n Enter Name:");
                scanf("%s", rec.name);
                printf("\nEnter age:");
                scanf("\n%d", &rec.age);
                list[i] = rec ;
        }
}
```

In the above program segment, the function **listing()** accepts structure type data variable list. We have defined a structure which contains two fields **name** and **age.** From this structure we have defined an array of **list** of size 10. With the help of **rec.name** and **rec.age** we input a record and copy it into array type of structure **list.**

It is also possible to define a function of type structure with no argument as the following syntax is

```
        struct tag-name function_name (void)
        {
               Type parameter list;
               Program body;
        }
```

In the above syntax function is defined as structure type. In this type of function declaration the value returned to the function is of structure type. Defined prototype is showing that we are not going provide any input data to this function. For example, consider the following program segment which illustrates the idea.

```
/**   convert.c        **/

# include<stdio.h>
struct gin
{
       int x ;
       int y ;
};
```

```
struct gin  conversion() ; /** prototype **/

void main()
{
      struct gin int_float ;
      int_float = conversion() ;  /* invoking function */
      printf("\n x = %d \n y = %d", int_float.x, int_float.y);
      printf("\n Press a key");
      getchar() ;   /* control screen */
}

/* Definition of function */
struct gin  conversion()
{
      struct gin rec ;
      printf("\n Enter integer part: ");
      scanf("%d",&rec.x);
      printf("\nEnter real part: ");
      scanf("%d",&rec.y);
      return(rec);
}
```

The above program segment contains function **conversion ()** which is defined as structure type. In this function, we input integer and real part of a number to the function. When it is called in the function **main (),** this function **(conversion ())** returns struct and assigned to a struct data type variable.

It is also possible to define a function of type structure and parameters supplied to the function of type structures. In other words, we can say that function accepts structure type parameters and returns structure type. The syntax and its implementation are illustrated below:

```
struct tag_name function_name(struct tag_name new_name 1, struct tag_name new_name 2, ..., struct
tag_name new_name n)
{
      Local declarations;
      Program body;
}
```

Go through Example 12 which demonstrates above discussion.

Example 12: Write a program for adding two complex numbers. Define your own function for adding complex numbers.

Answer: Following code segment implements the Example 12.

```
/**       complex.c      **/
/* complex number addition */
# include<stdio.h>
struct complex1
{
      float x ;
      float y ;
};
typedef struct complex1 com ;
com complex_fun(com  , com ); /* Prototype **/

void main()
{
```

```
    com plex1 , plex2 , plex3 ;
    plex1.x = 40.3 ;
    plex1.y = 30.3 ;

    plex2.x = 0.7 ;
    plex2.y = 0.7 ;
    printf("\n First complex number = ");
    printf("%f + j %f ", plex1.x,plex1.y);
    printf("\n Second complex number = ");
    printf("%f + j %f ", plex2.x,plex2.y);
    plex3 = complex_fun(plex1,plex2) ;
    printf("\n Summation of complex numbers = ");
    printf("%f + j %f ", plex3.x,plex3.y);
    printf("\n Press a key");
    getchar() ;   /* control screen */
}

/* Definition of function */
com complex_fun(com l1 , com l2)
{
    com l3 ;
    l3.x = l1.x + l2.x ;
    l3.y = l1.y + l2.y ;
    return(l3);
}
```

In the above program segment, we have defined function **complex_fun ()** as **complex1** type. The argument passed to it is also of **complex1** type. This function performs addition of two **complex1** type numbers and finally returns **complex1** type value to the function. When this function is called in main program once again, it is assigned to **complex1** type variable **plex3.**

14.11 FUNCTION AND POINTER

Just as for data pointers, we can think of three steps involved in using function pointers. First, we must declare a variable which can hold a pointer to a function, and this ends up being a somewhat complex declaration. A simple function pointer declaration is

```
int (*pfi)();
```

This declares pfi as a pointer to a function which will return an int. As in other declarations, the * indicates that a pointer is involved, and the parentheses () indicate that a function is involved. But what about the extra parentheses we have around (*pfi)? They are needed because there are precedence relationships in declarations just as there are in expressions, and when the default precedence does not give us what we want, we have to override it with explicit parentheses. In declarations, the () indicating functions and the [] indicating arrays "bind" more tightly than the *'s indicating pointers. Without the extra parentheses, the declaration above is

```
int *pfi();                    /* WRONG, for pointer-to-function */
```

and this would declare a function returning a pointer to int. With the explicit parentheses, however, int (*pfi)() tells us that pfi is a pointer first, and that what it's a pointer to is a function, and what that function returns is an int.

It is common to use typedefs with complicated types such as function pointers. For example, after defining

```
typedef int (*funcptr)();
```

The identifier funcptr is now a synonym for the type "pointer to function returning int". This typedef would make declaring pointers such as pfi considerably easier:

```
funcptr pfi;
```

The typedefs are a little bit like preprocessor define directives, but better. Here we see another reason: there is no way we could define a preprocessor macro which would expand to a correct function pointer declaration, but the funcptr type we just defined using typedef will work just fine. Once declared, a function pointer can of course be set to point to some function. If we declare some functions:

```
extern int f1();
extern int f2();
extern int f3();
```

then we can set pointer pfi to point to one of them:

```
pfi = &f1;
```

or to one or another of them depending on some condition:

```
if(condition)
        pfi = &f2;
else    pfi = &f3;
```

Of course, we are not restricted to these two forms; we can assign function pointers under any circumstances we wish. The second example could be rendered more compactly using the conditional operator:

```
pfi = condition ? &f2: &f3;
```

In these examples, we have used the & operator as we always have, to generate a pointer. However, when generating pointers to functions, the & is optional, because when we mention the name of a function but are not calling it, there is nothing else we could possibly be trying to do except generate a pointer to it. So, most programmers write

```
pfi = f1;
```

or

```
if(condition)
        pfi = f2;
else    pfi = f3;
```

or, equivalently, using the conditional operator, pfi = condition ? f2 : f3;

The fact that a function pointer is generated automatically when a function appears in an expression but is not being called is very similar to, and in fact related to, the fact that a pointer to the first element of an array is generated automatically when an array appears in an expression.

Finally, once we have a function pointer variable which does point to a function, we can call the function that it points to. Broken down to a near-microscopic level, this, too, is a three-step procedure. First, we write the name of the function pointer variable:

```
pfi
```

This is a pointer to a function. Then, we put the * operator in front, to "take the contents of the pointer":

```
*pfi
```

Now we have a function. Finally, we append an argument list in parentheses, along with an extra set of parentheses to get the precedence right, and we have a function call:

(*pfi)(arg1, arg2)

The extra parentheses are needed here for almost exactly the same reason as they were in the declaration of pfi. Without them, we had have

***pfi(arg1, arg2) /* WRONG, for pointer-to-function */**

and this would say, "call the function pfi (which had better return a pointer), passing it the arguments arg1 and arg2, and take the contents of the pointer it returns." However, what we want to do is take the contents of pfi (which is a pointer to a function) and call the pointed-to function, passing it the arguments arg1 and arg2. Again, the explicit parentheses override the default precedence, arranging that we apply the * operator to pfi and then do the function call.

Just to confuse things, though, parts of the syntax are optional here as well. There is nothing we can do with a function pointer except assign it to another function pointer, compare it to another function pointer, or call the function that it points to. For example, if we write

pfi(arg1, arg2)

it is obvious, based on the parenthesized argument list, that we are trying to call a function, so the compiler goes ahead and calls the pointed to function, just as if we had written

(*pfi)(arg1, arg2)

When calling the function pointed to by a function pointer, the * operator (and hence the extra set of parentheses) is optional. Example 13 illustrates the idea.

Example 13: Write a program using pointer to function for making comparison of two integer numbers. Repeat the same for the two string comparison.

Answer: Consider the following program segment for the implementation for two integers program code point_f.c implements the idea for two string comparisons.

```
/**          compare.c          **/
# include<stdio.h>
int *compare( int , int * ,  int ) ; /* prototype */
int en ;
void main()
{
    int list[10] = {12,16,18,19,14,20,94,78,30};
    int num ;
    int size ;
    int *ar ;
    printf("\n Enter the size of array: ");
    scanf("%d", &size);
    printf("\n Enter number want to  match: ");
    scanf("%d", &num);

    ar = compare(num, list, size) ; /* invoke */
    if(ar)
    {
            printf("\n Element number = %d", en);
    }
    else
    {
            printf("No Match Found ");
```

```
    }
    getchar();
}
/* Function definition  */

int *compare(int num, int *array , int size)
{
    register int i ;
    i = 0 ;
    en = i ;
    while( (num != array[i]) && (i < size) )
    {
        i++ ;
        en = i;
    }
    return(&array[i-1]) ;
}
```

In the above program, the **compare ()** function returns a pointer to integer array, if the first match with **num** is found. If no match occurs, a **NULL** pointer is returned. In the above program segment **compare.c,** we have called a function **compare ().** We pass a list of 10 numbers and a number, which we want to search in the list. If the match is found, the position in the list is displayed, otherwise message "No Match Found" is displayed.

To obtain address of a function we should use the function's name without any parenthesis or arguments. This is exactly same as array.

int (*point)(); /* function to pointer */

If we want to get address of a function strcmp().

point = strcmp ; /* address of strcmp() is assigned to point function */

Let, function compare (s1, s2, point) is to be constructed which compares two-string s1 and s2. The program segment point_f.c is developed for this purpose.

```
/**         point_f.c           **/
# include<stdio.h>
# include<string.h>
void compare(char * , char * , int(*comp) (char * , char * ) ) ; /* prototype */

void main()
{
    char string1[40],string2[40] ;
    int (*point)() ;

    point = strcmp ; /* get address of strcmp function */

    printf("Enter two strings: ") ;
    gets(string1) ;
    gets(string2) ;
    compare(string1,string2,point) ;
}
/* Definition of function */
void compare(char *s1, char *s2, int (*comp) (char * , char * ))
{
    if( !(*comp)(s1,s2))
    {
        printf("\n Strings are  equal ");
        printf("\n Press a Key ");
```

```
            getchar() ;
        }else
        {
            printf("\n Not equal ");
            printf("\n Press a Key ");
            getchar() ;
        }
}
```

14.12 The main ()

The **main ()** is a function which must be included in every program segment for which we want to generate executable codes. If we do not want to generate executable codes for a program, it is not necessary to include **main ()** function and in this case only object code will be generated. When we forget to include **main ()** function in a program, linker error will be generated as demonstrated below:

```
# include<stdio.h>
void fun()
{
    printf(" I am Emperor of my Heart ");
}
```

When, we compile this program segment, only object code will be generated. To generate executable code also, the program segment should be like this

```
# include <stdio.h>
void fun();  /* Prototype */
void main()
{
    fun() ;
}
/* End of main function */
/* Definition of function */
void fun()
{
    printf(" I am Emperor of my Heart ");
}
/* End of function */
```

14.12.1 Arguments to main

When we write a program which runs in a hosted environment, arguments to main provide a useful opportunity to give parameters to programs. Typically, this facility is used to direct the way the program goes about its task. It is particularly common to provide file names to a program through its arguments. We know that a function accepts arguments but function **main ()** only permits limited numbers of arguments in C. The declaration of main is as follows:

```
int main(int argc, char *argv[]);
```

This indicates that main is a function returning an integer. In hosted environments such as DOS, Windows, Linux, AIX-L, or UNIX, this value or exit status is passed back to the command line interpreter. Under UNIX, for example, the exit status is used to indicate that a program completed successfully (a zero value) or some error occurred (a non-zero value). The Standard has adopted this convention; exit(0) is used to return 'success' to its host environment, any other value is used to indicate failure. If the host environment itself uses a different numbering convention, exit will do the necessary translation. Since the translation is implementation-defined, it is now considered better practice to use the values defined in <stdlib.h>: EXIT_SUCCESS and EXIT_FAILURE.

There are at least two arguments to main: argc and argv. The first of these is a count of the arguments supplied to the program and the second is an array of pointers to the strings which are those arguments-its type is (almost) 'array of pointer to char'. These arguments are passed to the program by the host system's command line interpreter or job control language.

The declaration of the argv argument is often a novice programmer's first encounter with pointers to arrays of pointers and can prove intimidating. However, it is really quite simple to understand. Since argv is used to refer to an array of strings, its declaration is

char *argv[ ]

Remember too that when it is passed to a function, the name of an array is converted to the address of its first element. This means that we can also declare argv as char **argv; the two declarations are equivalent in this context. Indeed, we will often see the declaration of main expressed in these terms. This declaration is exactly equivalent to that shown above:

int main(int argc, char **argv);

When a program starts, the arguments to main will have been initialized to meet the following conditions:

argc is greater than zero.

argv[argc] is a null pointer.

argv[0] through to argv[argc-1] are pointers to strings whose meaning will be determined by the program.

argv[0] will be a string containing the program's name or a null string if that is not available. Remaining elements of argv represent the arguments supplied to the program. In cases where there is only support for single-case characters, the contents of these strings will be supplied to the program in lower-case.

For the illustration of these points, consider the following program segment which writes the arguments supplied to function main() in the program will be displayed on the monitor.

```
/** showargs.c **/
#include <stdio.h>
#include <stdlib.h>
int main(int argc, char **argv)
{
    while(argc-)
        printf("%s\n", *argv++);
    exit(EXIT_SUCCESS);
}
```

If the program name is **showargs** and it has arguments **Don, from,** and **Delhi** when it is run, the state of the arguments and the value of argv can be illustrated as shown in Figure 14.5.

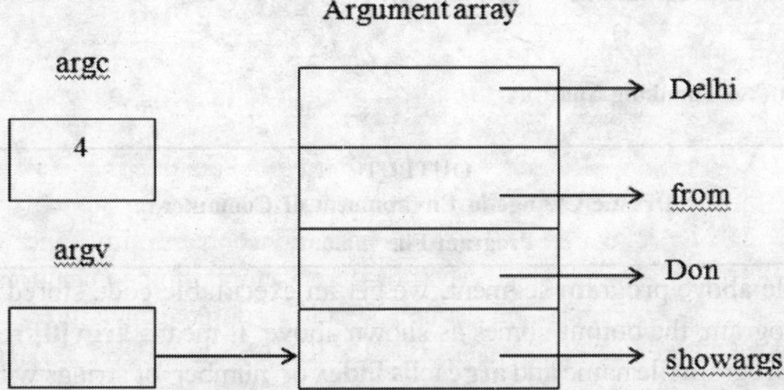

Figure 14.5 Arguments to a program

Each time that argv is incremented; it is stepped one item further along the array of arguments. Thus, after the first iteration of the loop, argv will point to the pointer which in turn points to the Don argument. This is shown in Figure 14.6.

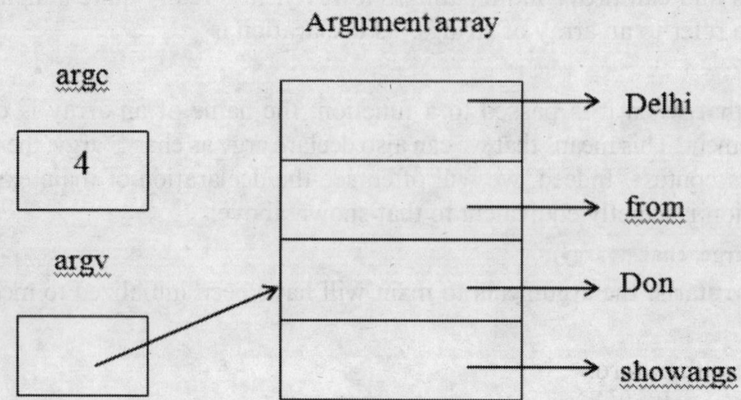

Figure 14.6 Arguments to a program after incrementing argv

On the system where this program was tested, a program is run by typing its name and then the arguments, separated by spaces. This is what happened (the $ is a prompt):

```
$ showargs Don from Delhi
showargs
abcde
text
hello
$
```

The **argc** is used to control the status of **argv.** In other words, we can say that **argc** tells the compiler the number of arguments required for running program.

```
/**    -    main.c    **/
# include<stdio.h>
void main(int argc, char *argv[] )
{
    if(argc == 1 )
    {
        printf("\n Drastic Change in Environment of Computer ");
        printf("\n Program File = %s", argv[0]) ;
    }
    else
        printf("\n Thanking You ");
}
```

OUTPUT
Drastic Change in Environment of Computer
Program File = a.out

When we compile above program segment, we get an executable code stored in the file **a.out.** When we run this program, the output comes as shown above. It means **argv[0]** represents the first argument which is a program file name and **argc** tells **index** or number of strings with argv argument. Go through Example 14 which demonstrates above discussion.

Example 14: Write a C program which is equivalent to copy command of UNIX/LINUX/ WINDOWS/DOS.

Answer: Consider the following program segment which demonstrates more use of argc and argv parameters used in C Language.

```
/**         filecp.c          **/
# include<stdio.h>
# include<stdlib.h>
void main(int argc, char *argv[] )
{
    int ch ;
    FILE *fp ;
    if(argc != 2 )
    {
        printf("\n You Have Missed file ");
        exit(0) ;
    }
    fp = fopen(argv[1], "r") ;
    if(fp == NULL)
    {
        perror("Error") ;
        exit(1);
    }

    ch = getc(fp) ;
    while(ch != EOF)
    {
        putchar(ch) ;
        ch = getc(fp) ;
    }
}
```

If we compile this program, the compiler generates executable code named as **a.out.** To run this program segment type **a.out filecp.c** on the shell prompt ($), i.e.

$ a.out filecp.c

This displays the output, which is complete source code of the a.out executable code on the standard output device. This program segment works like **cat** command in **UNIX** environment and like **type** command in **DOS** and **WINDOWS.** Here, the values of

argv[0] = a.out

argv[1] = filecp.c

argc = 2

There is one more argument, which is some times used with the function **main ().** The name of this argument is **env.** The declaration of this argument is similar to **argv.** The env varies from machine to machine and one can consult manual provided with system for its use.

char *env[];

There is no relationship between env and argc. The env argument is used to find out information about environment string.

```
/**         env.c          **/
# include<stdio.h>
 void main(char *env[])
 {
```

```
int i ;
for( i = 0 ; env[i] ; i++)
{
    printf("\n%s : string number :%d", env[i],i+1);
}
}
```

14.13 RECURSION

This is a complicated idea which we are unlikely to meet frequently. Recursion is the name given to a technique for defining a function in terms of itself. Recursion does not speed up the process of execution rather it defines a process in a simple way to understand. We shall provide some examples to illustrate recursive functions. Recursive functions are useful in evaluating certain types of mathematical function. We may also encounter certain dynamic data structures such as linked lists or binary trees. Recursion is a very useful way of creating and accessing these structures. Here is a recursive version of the Fibonacci function. The recursive definition of the Fibonacci number generator is

$$\text{fibo\_number (num)} = \begin{cases} 0 & \text{If num = 0 or num =1} \\ 1 & \text{If num = 2} \\ \text{fibo\_number(num-1) + fibo\_number(num-2)} & \text{If num > 2} \end{cases}$$

The Fibonacci sequence is as follows, which is generated from the recursive definition Fibonacci generation algorithm mentioned above.

0, 1,1, 2, 3, 5, 8, 13, 21, 21, 34, 55, etc.

If we consider **F0 = 0 and F1 = 1,** then **F2 = F1 + F0 = 1 + 0 = 1,** similarly **F3 = F2 + F1 = 1 + 1 = 2, F4 = F3 + F2** = **2 + 1 = 3** and so on. Thus, it is clear that each succeeding term is the sum of the two preceding terms. The **fibo_number ()** function generates one Fibonacci number at a time. Implementation code of this definition is

```
int fibo_number (int num)
/* Fibonacci value of a number */
{     switch(num) {
    case 0:
        return(0);
        break;
    case 1:
        return(1);
        break;
    case 2:
        return(1);
        break;
    default: /* Including recursive calls */
        return(fib_number(num - 1) + fib_number(num - 2));
        break;
    }
}
```

We met another function earlier called power. Here is an alternative recursive version.

```
double power(double val, unsigned pow)
{
    if(pow == 0) /* pow(x, 0) returns 1 */
        return(1.0);
    else
        return(power(val, pow - 1) * val);
}
```

Notice that each of these definitions incorporates a test. Where an input value gives a trivial result, it is returned directly; otherwise the function calls itself, passing a changed version of the input values. Care must be taken to define functions which will not call themselves indefinitely, otherwise a program will never finish.

The definition of fibo_number() is interesting, because it calls itself twice when recursion is used. Consider the effect on program performance of such a function calculating the fibonacci function of a moderate size number. If such a function is to be called many times, it is likely to have an adverse effect on program performance as shown in Table 14.1. Do not be frightened by the apparent complexity of recursion. Recursive functions are sometimes the simplest answer to a calculation. However there is always an alternative non-recursive solution available too. This will normally involve the use of a loop, and may lack the elegance of the recursive solution.

For example, consider most popular example of recursion used by the mathematician, i.e., factorial of a natural number. The definition of factorial is as follows:

$$\text{Factorial\_num}(n) = \begin{cases} 1 & \text{If } n = 0 \\ n * \text{Factorial\_num}(n-1) & \text{If } n > 0 \end{cases}$$

Here, **Factorial_num(n)** is defined in terms of **Factorial_num(n - 1)** which is again defined in terms of **Factorial_num(n-2)** and so on, until **Factorial_num(0)** is reached. The value of **Factorial_num(0)** is defined as 1.

Table 14.1 Fibonacci number generation

Input value	Number of times fib_number() is called
0	1
1	1
2	3
3	5
4	9
5	15
6	25
7	41
8	67
9	109
10	177

The factorial of 0 is 1. The factorial of 1 is 1. The factorial of 2 is 2*1. The factorial of 3 is 3*2*1. Likewise, the factorial of 4 is 4*3*2*1. This process will continue. If we take a close look on the processing of the factorial, we will find that factorial of 4 is actually 4 times the factorial of 3, i.e., 3*2*1 and the factorial of 3 is 3 times the factorial of 2, i.e., 2*1. The factorial of 2 is 2 times the factorial of 1. Example 15 defines and implements the factorial algorithm discussed above.

Example 15: Write a program for finding the factorial of an integer number.

Answer: The program segment n_fact.c implements the definition of factorial.

```
/**        n_fact.c      **/
# include<stdio.h>
void main()
```

```
{
    int n ;
    long int factorial ;
    printf("\n Enter Number: ");
    scanf("%d", &number);
    factorial = Factorial_num ( n );
    printf("\n Factorial of %d is %ld ", n, factorial);
    printf("\n Press a Key ");
    getchar();
}

/* Definition of function */

int Factorial_num (int n )
{
        int result ;
        if (n == 0 )
        return( 1 ) ;
        result = n * Factorial_num ( n  - 1 );
        return(result);
}
```

When the function **Factorial_num ()** is called it returns **1,** otherwise it returns **n*Factorial_num (n-1).** To calculate the value of the expression, the function **Factorial_num ()** is called with **n-1.** This process continues until n becomes 0.

14.13.1 Types of Recursion

Recursion is of two types

Preemptive recursive function factorial algorithm (discussed above) falls in this category.

Non-preemptive recursive function for example, **Ackermann's** function, a function with two arguments which can be assigned any positive integer such as 0, 1, 2, 3, …, etc. **Ackermann's** function definition is as follows:

$$\text{Ack fun}(M,N) = \begin{cases} N+1 & \text{If } M = 0 \quad \text{(a)} \\ \text{Ack fun}(M-1, 1) & \text{If } N = 0 \quad \text{(b)} \\ \text{Ack fun}(M-1 . \text{Ack fun}(M, N-1)) & \text{Otherwise.} \quad \text{(c)} \end{cases}$$

The following steps show, how one can find the value **Ack_fun(1, 3),** Sequence of function calls and the value returned.

(i) Ack_fun(1,3) = Ack_fun(1-1,Ack_fun(1,3-1)) = Ack_fun(0,Ack_fun(1,2))
(ii) Ack_fun(1,2) = Ack_fun(1-1,Ack_fun(1,2-1)) = Ack_fun(0,Ack_fun(1,1))
(iii) Ack_fun(1,1) = Ack_fun(1-1,Ack_fun(1,1-1)) = Ack_fun(0,Ack_fun(1,0))
(iv) Ack_fun(1,0) = Ack_fun(1-1,1) = Ack_fun(0,1)
(v) Ack_fun(0,1) = N+1 = 1 + 1 = 2 **Here value of N is 1**
(vi) Ack_fun(1,0) = 2
(vii) Ack_fun(1,1) = (0,2) Consider step 3 to 6
(viii) Ack_fun(0,2) = 2 + 1 = 3 **Here value of N is 2**

(ix) Ack_fun(1,1) = Ack_fun(0,2) Consider step 3 to 8

(x) Ack_fun(1,2) = Ack_fun(0,3)

(xi) Ack_fun(0,3) = 3 + 1 = 4 **Here value of N is 3**

(xii) Ack_fun(1,2) = 4

(xiii) Ack_fun(1,3) = Ack_fun(0,4)

(xiv) Ack_fun(0,4_ = 4 + 1 = 5 **Here value of N is 4**

(xv) Ack_fun(1,3) = 5 **Result**

Recursion occurs in **Ackermann's** function because the function **Ack_fun()** becomes an argument in a call to function **Ack_fun().** This is a very typical case of recursion. Preemptive recursive algorithm can easily be implemented with the help of iterative method.

14.13.2 Exponential

In the similar way, one can easily compute the positive (integer) exponential power of a number, i.e., **a b.** The recursive definition is

$$\text{power f(a.b)} = \begin{cases} 1 & \text{If } b = 0 \\ a*\text{power f(a, b} - 1) & \text{If } b > 0 \end{cases}$$

In the similar way one can easily compute the negative (integer) exponential power of a number, i.e., **a-b.** The recursive definition is

$$\text{power f(a.b)} = \begin{cases} 1 & \text{If } b = 0 \\ a*\text{power f(a,-b} + 1) & \text{If } b < 0 \end{cases}$$

Here, the **mantissa = a,** and **exponent = - b.** The power is negative so the returned value of the function is taken as inverse of the returned value of the function.

In the similar way one can easily compute the positive exponential power of a number, i.e., **ab.** The recursive definition is

$$\text{power f(a.b)} = \begin{cases} 1 & \text{If } b = 0.0 \\ a*\text{ power f(a, b - i , i)} & \text{If } b > 0.0 \end{cases}$$

For computing the negative exponential power of a number, i.e., **a-b,** the recursive definition becomes

$$\text{power f(a.b)} = \begin{cases} 1 & \text{If } b = 0.0 \\ a*\text{power f(a, -b + i , i)} & \text{If } b < 0.0 \end{cases}$$

If one wants to program **i** may be taken as a counter and it's value is calculated by passing 10 as **mantissa.** The number of digits after the decimal point is passed as **exponent.** For example, if the digits after the decimal point are four then pass 4 to the recursive function for calculating the value of **i,** after getting the value of **i,** the exponential power of the number is calculated. If the exponent is positive then returned value of the function would be the value of the exponential power the number else take the inverse of the returned value of the function as the exponential power of the number.

14.13.3 Elimination of Recursion

A recursive function is a function that calls itself to perform a specific operation. When a function invokes itself to perform a task, the function is said to perform direct recursion. Indirect recursion occurs when a function (let function X) calls another function (let function Y), which in turn calls the original function (function X). Although, recursive function creates elegant solutions to many problems, yet we should avoid recursion whenever possible. The reasons are:

Recursive functions can be difficult for novice programmers to understand.

Recursive functions are often considerably slower than their non-recursive counterparts.

Consider the following two cases where drawbacks of recursion are explained

```
/* recurs.c */
#include <stdio.h>
#include <time.h>
int Length(const char *str)
{
    if (*str)
            return(1 + Length(str+1));
    else
            return(0);
}
void main(void)
{
    long int counter;
    time_t start_time, end_time;
    time(&start_time);
    printf("\n Processing under progress...");
    for (counter = 0; counter < 100000000L; counter++)
            Length("No alternative of hard work");
    time(&end_time);
    printf("Processing time = %d seconds\n", end_time - start_time);
}
```

OUTPUT
Processing under progress...
Processing time = 423 seconds

```
/* rem_recu.c */
#include <stdio.h>
#include <time.h>
int Length(const char *str)
{
    int length = 0;
    while (*str++)
            length++;
    return(length);
}
```

```
void main(void)
{
    long int counter;
    time_t start_time, end_time;
    time(&start_time);
    printf("\n Processing under progress...");
    for (counter = 0; counter < 100000000L; counter++)
            Length("No alternative of hard work");
    time(&end_time);
    printf("Processing time = %d seconds\n", end_time - start_time);
}
```

```
OUTPUT
Processing under progress...
Processing time = 128 seconds
```

14.14 Working with va_start, va_arg and va_end

All of the functions we have written so far have taken a fixed number of arguments, and we have been careful to call the functions always passing them the correct number of arguments, and we have been tending to use explicit function prototype declarations so that the compiler can verify that we call functions with the correct number of arguments. But what about printf is? Sometimes we call it with one argument, but often we pass it additional arguments. Why does not the compiler complain? How can printf access the extra arguments we pass to it, when it cannot know how many of them there will be or what types they will have, such that it cannot possibly declare conventional function parameters for them? In this section we will discuss the variable-length argument lists **(varargs)** which allow functions such as printf to be written.

14.14.1 Declaring "varargs" Functions

The ANSI C Standard requires that all functions which accept a variable number of arguments be declared explicitly to do so, and also that a function prototype be "in scope" whenever a varargs function is called. Under certain circumstances, unknown functions can be called at will, with the compiler assuming that they take "normal" arguments and return int. However, that exception does not apply here. In other words, for varargs functions, function prototypes are not just a good idea, they are the law. The reason that prototypes are strictly required is that varargs functions may use special calling sequences; that is, the compiler may have to generate special code for these calls.

The presence of a variable-length argument list is indicated by an ellipsis in the prototype. For example, the prototype for printf, as found in <stdio.h>, looks something like this:

```
extern int printf(const char *, ...);
```

Three dots (...) do not mean that we left something out; they are the ellipsis notation; this is the syntax that C uses to indicate the presence of a variable-length argument list. This prototype says that printf's first argument is of type const char *, and that it takes a variable (and hence unspecified) number of additional arguments.

The ellipsis notation must follow the ordinary, fixed arguments, and there must be at least one fixed argument. It is impossible in Standard C to define a function which accepts only variable arguments. In general, this is not too much of a restriction, because the function must always be able to determine, for itself, how many arguments there are in the list, invariably by inspecting the first argument(s) in the list. In other words, the function will generally need at least one well-defined, fixed argument anyway, to get a toehold on the problem of figuring out what the other arguments are.

14.14.2 Writing a "varargs" Function

In ANSI C, the head of a varargs function looks just like its prototype. We will illustrate by writing stripped-down version of printf. The bare outline of the function is

```
void myprintf(const char *fmt, ...)
{
}
```

printf's job, of course, is to print its format string while looking for % characters and treating them specially. So the main loop of printf function is

```
#include <stdio.h>
void myprintf(const char *fmt, ...)
{
const char *p;
for(p = fmt; *p != '\0'; p++)
{
        if(*p != '%')
                putchar(*p);
        else
        {
                handle it specially
        }
}
}
```

In this stripped-down version, we would not worry about width and precision specifiers and other modifiers; we will always look at the very next character after the % and assume that it is the primary format character. Continuing to flesh out our outline, we get

```
#include <stdio.h>
void myprintf(const char *fmt, ...)
{
  const char *p;
  for(p = fmt; *p != '\0'; p++)
  {
        if(*p != '%')
        {
                putchar(*p);
                continue;
        }

        switch(*++p)
        {
                case 'c':
                        fetch and print a character
                        break;
                case 'd':
                        fetch and print an integer
                        break;
                case 's':
                        fetch and print a string
                        break;
                case 'x':
                        print an integer, in hexadecimal
                        break;
```

```
                case '%':
                        print a single %
                        break;
        }
    }
}
```

For clarity, we have rearranged the former if/else statement slightly. If the character we are looking at is not %, we print it out and continue immediately with the next iteration of the for loop. This is a good example of the use of the continue statement. Everything else in the body of the loop then takes care of the case where we are looking at a %.

Printing these various argument types out will be relatively straightforward. The $64,000 question, of course, is how to fetch the actual arguments. The answer involves some specialized macros defined for us by the standard header <stdarg.h>. The macros we will use are va_list, va_start(), va_arg(), and va_end(). va_list is a special "pointer" type which allows us to manipulate a variable-length argument list. va_start() begins the processing of an argument list, va_arg() fetches arguments from it, and va_end() finishes processing. Therefore, va_list is a little bit like the stdio FILE * type, and va_start is a bit like fopen().

Here is the final version of myprintf function, illustrating the fetching, formatting, and printing of the various argument types. Go through Example 16 which demonstrates above discussion.

Example 16: Write C code for printf function.

Answer: For implementation we have used stdarg.h header file which is containing- va_list, va_arg, va_start and va_end. We have implemented various variant of these arguments in arg_add.c and ADD_VARG.C

```
#include <stdio.h>
#include <stdarg.h>
extern char *itoa(int, char *, int);
void myprintf(const char *fmt, ...)
{
const char *p;
va_list argp;
int i;
char *s;
char fmtbuf[256];
va_start(argp, fmt);

for(p = fmt; *p != '\0'; p++)
    {
    if(*p != '%')
    {
            putchar(*p);
            continue;
    }
    switch(*++p)
    {
            case 'c':
                    i = va_arg(argp, int);
                    putchar(i);
                    break;
            case 'd':
                    i = va_arg(argp, int);
```

```
                        s = itoa(i, fmtbuf, 10);
                        fputs(s, stdout);
                        break;
                case 's':
                        s = va_arg(argp, char *);
                        fputs(s, stdout);
                        break;
                case 'x':
                        i = va_arg(argp, int);
                        s = itoa(i, fmtbuf, 16);
                        fputs(s, stdout);
                        break;
                case '%':
                        putchar('%');
                        break;
                }
        }
        va_end(argp);
        }
```

Looking at the new lines, we have:

#include <stdarg.h>

This header file is required in any file which uses the variable argument va_list macros.

va_list argp;

This line declares a variable, argp, which we use while manipulating the variable-length argument list. The type of the variable is va_list, a special type defined in <stdarg.h>.

va_start(argp, fmt);

This line initializes argp and initiates the processing of the argument list. The second argument to va_start() is simply the name of the function's last fixed argument. va_start() uses this to figure out where the variable arguments begin.

i = va_arg(argp, int);

And here is the heart of the matter. va_arg() fetches the next argument from the argument list. The second argument to va_arg() is the type of the argument we expect. Notice carefully that we must supply this argument, which implies that we must somehow know what type of argument to expect next. The variable-length argument list machinery does not know. In this case, we know what the type of the next argument should be because it is supposed to match the format character we are processing. We can see, then, why such havoc results when printf's arguments do not match its format string: printf tells the va_arg machinery to grab an argument of one type, with the type determined by one of the format specifiers, but since the va_arg machinery does not know what the actual argument type is, there is no way for it to do any automatic conversion. If the actual argument has the right type for the va_arg call which grabs it, it works otherwise it does not. It is noticed that we fetched the character to print for %c as an int, not a char. That is deliberate, and is explained in the next section.

s = va_arg(argp, char *);

Here is another invocation of va_arg(), this time fetching a string, represented as a character pointer, or char *.

va_end(argp);

Finally, when we are all finished processing the argument list, we call va_end() which performs any necessary cleanup.

The functions **printf()** or **scanf()** which support a variable number of parameters. For example see the following code segment.

```
printf("\n %d%d%d%f%f", 4, 6, 7, 5.6, 100.125);
printf( "\n %s, %s %f, %s, %c", Name, Address, Salary, State, Grade);
scanf("%d%d%d%f%f", &d1,&d4, &d6, &d7, &f5, &f1);
```

How do these functions work? For this we have considered the built-in macro **va_arg, va_end** and **va_start** defined in the header file **stdarg.h.** Using these macros we have created functions for supporting a variable number of parameters. The macros essentially pull parameters from the stack, one at a time until the last parameter is reached. When we use these macros to get parameters, we must know each parameter's type. In case of **printf()** and **scanf(),** the function uses the format specifiers such as %d, %f, %s, %u …, etc, to track the parameter's types. For example, consider the following program segment in which function **add_values()** that adds up all of the **float** and **int** values, is passed. The last parameter is indicated by the value 0.0 (which does not affect the sum).

```
/* arg_add.c */
#include <stdio.h>
#include <stdarg.h>
double add_values(double value, ...)
{
  va_list argument_ptr;
  double result = 0.0;
  if (value != 0.0)
  {
    result += value;
    va_start(argument_ptr, value);
    while ((value = va_arg(argument_ptr, double)) != 0.0)
          result += value;
    va_end(argument_ptr);
  }
  return(result);
}

void main(void)
{
      double result;
      double x,y;
      double i,j,k;
      printf("\n Input the values for x, y double:");
      scanf("%lf%lf",&x,&y);
      printf("\n Input the values for i, j, k double:");
      scanf("%lf%lf%lf",&i,&j,&k);
      result = add_values(i, x, j, y, k, 0.0);
      printf("\n %lf+%lf+%lf+%lf+%lf = %lf ", i, x, j, y, k, result);
}
```

The function **add_values()** begins by assigning a pointer marker to the first parameter on the stack using the **va_start** macro. Next, using the **va_arg** macro, the function gets the values one at a time. The **va_arg** macro returns a value of the specified type and then increments the pointer to point to the next argument. When the zero terminator is encountered, the function uses the **va_end** macro to assign a value to the argument pointer that will prevent its future use. When we create functions that support a variable number of parameters, the functions must have a way to know the number of parameters and each parameter's type. In the case of **scanf(), printf(),** the format specifier defines the parameters and their types.

Here with the help of pointer variable (argument_ptr in add_arg.c and str in add_varg.c), we examine string character by character. If %s character is found, it goes for the format character. If format character is found corresponding case statement is executed. When the function call is made, the compiler will place the parameters on the stack from right to left, within the function, the **va_start** macro assigns a pointer to the first parameter, as shown in **Figure 14.7.**

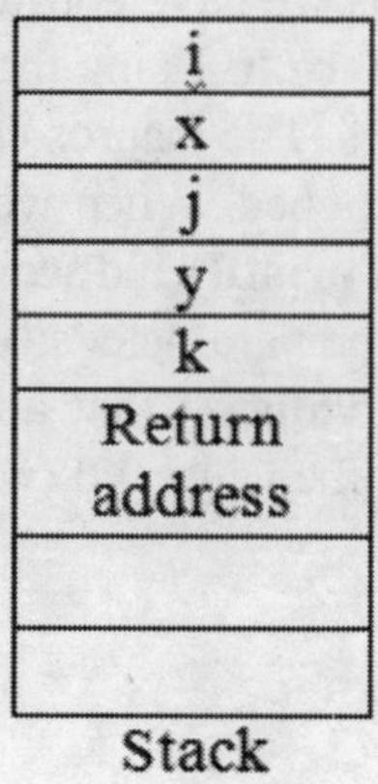

Figure 14.7 Using va_start to assign a pointer to the first parameter

The **va_arg** macro returns the value pointed by the argument pointer. To determine value, the macro must know the parameter's type. A parameter of type **int,** for example, will use 16 bits, whereas a parameter of type **long** will use 32 bits. Similarly, **float** type parameter uses 32 bits, whereas a parameter type **double** will use 64 bits. After the parameter's value is returned, the **va_arg** macro increments the argument pointer so that it points to the next argument. To determine the number of bytes to add to the pointer, va_arg again uses the parameter's type. After the last argument has been retrieved, the va_end macro nullified the argument pointer's value.

The use of the ellipses (…) or three dots within the **add_values()** function header to indicate a variable number of parameters.

In the above program segment, we have seen that 0.0 is used as terminator. In the following program segment, we have used format specifier to eliminate the need of zero terminator.

```
/* Use of va_arg and va_end parameter */
/* ADD_VARG.C */
# include <stdio.h>
# include <stdarg.h>
double add_values(char *str, ...)
{
  va_list marker;
  double result = 0.0;
  va_start(marker, str);  /* mark first additional argument */
  while (*str)          /* examine each character in the string */
  {
    if (*str == '%')    /* if not a %_ format specifier, skip it */
    {
      switch (*(++str))
      {
            case 'd': result += va_arg(marker, int);
                      break;
            case 'f': result += va_arg(marker, double);
                      break;
```

```
            }
        }
        str++;
    }
    va_end(marker);
    return(result);
}

void main(void)
{
        double result;
        int x,y;
        float i,j,k;
        printf("\n Input the values for x, y integer:");
        scanf("%d%d", &x, &y);
        printf("\n Input the values for i, j, k floating:");
        scanf("%f%f%f", &i, &j, &k);
        result = add_values("%f%d%f%d%f", i, x, j, y, k);
        printf("\n %f+%d+%f+%d+%f = %f ", i, x, j, y, k, result);
}
```

14.14.3 Special Issues with Varargs Functions

When a function with a variable-length argument list is called, the variable arguments are passed using C's default argument promotions. These say that types char and short int are automatically promoted to int, and type float is automatically promoted to double. Therefore, varargs functions will never receive arguments of type char, short int, or float. Furthermore, it is an error to "pass" the type names char, short int, or float as the second argument to the va_arg() macro. Finally, for vaguely related reasons, the last fixed argument (the one whose name is passed as the second argument to the va_start() macro) should not be of type char, short int, or float, either.

"How can we determine how many arguments my function was actually called with?" The answer, as discussed above, is that we must figure it out somehow, generally by looking at the arguments themselves (or, in the case of printf, by using clues which are designed into the first, fixed arguments). There is no standard way of asking the compiler or runtime system how many arguments were actually passed, or what their types are.

The macros va_start() and va_arg() are referred to as macros because they cannot possibly be functions. va_start() initializes its first argument, and it uses its second argument not as a value but as a location. Even more unusually, va_arg() accepts a type name as its second argument, which no function in C, indeed no anything in C other than sizeof, can ever do. Finally, va_arg() has no return type, the type it returns is determined by its second argument.

The va_list type, whatever it is, is a mostly normal type. In particular, we can pass it on to other functions, and it is frequently quite useful to do so. For example, suppose that we want to write an error function, which will print nicely annotated error messages complete with filenames, line numbers, severity indicators, and the like. Furthermore, suppose that the rest of the program will find it useful, when calling this error function, to embed % sequences in the string to be printed, requesting that extra arguments be interpolated, just like printf. The obvious question is, will the error function have to duplicate all of printf's code for parsing format strings and formatting variable arguments or can it somehow call on printf or a related function to do most of the work? The outline of the error function is

```
extern char *filename;          /* current input file name */
extern int lineno;          /* current line number */
void error(char *msg, ...)
{
        fprintf(stderr, "%s, line %d: error:", filename, lineno);
        fprintf(stderr, msg, "what goes here? ");
        fprintf(stderr, "\n");
}
```

The tricky line is the second call to fprintf. We have the string, msg, we want to print, possibly containing % characters. How do we pass down to fprintf the extra arguments which our caller passed to us? The answer is that we do not; there is no way to say "call this function with the same arguments we got, however many of them there are." The runtime system simply does not have enough information to do this sort of thing, which is why it cannot tell us how many arguments we got called with, either. However, there is a variant version of fprintf which is designed for just this sort of situation. The variant is called vfprintf, where the v stands for "varargs", and a call to it is

```
void error(char *msg, ...)
{
        va_list argp;
        fprintf(stderr, "%s, line %d: error:", filename, lineno);
        va_start(argp, msg);
        vfprintf(stderr, msg, argp);
        va_end(argp);
        fprintf(stderr, "\n");
}
```

We declare a local variable of type va_list and call va_start(), as before. However, all we do with our argp variable is pass it to vfprintf as its third argument. vfprintf then does all the work-if we could look inside it, it same to version of myprintf function defined earlier, except that vfprintf does not call va_start(), because its caller already has. Notice that vfprintf does not accept a variable number of arguments; it accepts exactly three arguments, the third of which is essentially a "pointer" to the extra arguments it will need.

There are also "varargs" versions of printf and sprintf, namely vprintf and vsprintf. These follow the same pattern, accepting a single last argument of type va_list in lieu of an actual variable-length argument list.

The error function above also called va_end(). This makes sense, since error was the one who called va_start(). The above pattern works, but more complicated ones may not. For example, it is not guaranteed that we can pick a few arguments off of a va_list, pass the va_list to a subfunction to pick a few more off, and then pick the last ones off. Also, there's no direct way to "rewind" a va_list, although it's permissible to call va_end() and then va_start() again, to start over again.

EXERCISES

1. On Library Functions

1. How can I convert numbers to strings (the opposite of atoi)? Is there an itoa function?
2. Why does strncpy not always place a '\0' terminator in the destination string?
3. Does C have anything like the ``substr'' (extract substring) routine present in other languages?

4. How do I convert a string to all upper or lower case?
5. Why do some versions of toupper act strangely if given an upper-case letter?
   Why does some code call islower before toupper?
6. How can I split up a string into whitespace-separated fields?
   How can I duplicate the process by which main() is handed argc and argv?
7. I need some code to do regular expression and wildcard matching.
8. I'm trying to sort an array of strings with qsort, using strcmp as the comparison function, but it's not working.
9. Now I'm trying to sort an array of structures with qsort. My comparison function takes pointers to structures, but the compiler complains that the function is of the wrong type for qsort. How can I cast the function pointer to shut off the warning?
10. How can I sort a linked list?
11. How can I sort more data than will fit in memory?
12. How can I get the current date or time of day in a C program?
13. I know that the library function localtime will convert a time_t into a broken-down struct tm, and that ctime will convert a time_t to a printable string. How can I perform the inverse operations of converting astruct tm or a string into a time_t?
14. How can I add N days to a date? How can I find the difference between two dates?
15. Did C have any Year 2000 problems?
16. I need a random number generator.
17. How can I get random integers in a certain range?
18. Each time I run my program, I get the same sequence of numbers back from rand().
19. I need a random true/false value, so I'm just taking rand() % 2, but it's alternating 0, 1, 0, 1, 0...
20. How can I return a sequence of random numbers which don't repeat at all?
21. How can I generate floating-point random numbers?
22. How can I generate random numbers with a normal or Gaussian distribution?
23. I'm porting this program, and it calls a routine drand48, which my library doesn't have. What is it?
24. Is exit(status) truly equivalent to returning the same status from main?
25. What's the difference between memcpy and memmove?
26. I'm trying to port this old program. Why do I get ``undefined external'' errors for some library functions?
27. I keep getting errors due to library functions being undefined, but I'm #including all the right header files.
28. I'm still getting errors due to library functions being undefined, even though I'm explicitly requesting the right libraries while linking.
29. Why is my simple program, which hardly does more than print ``Hello, world!'' in a window, compiling to such a huge executable (several hundred K)? Should I #include fewer header files?
30. What does it mean when the linker says that _end is undefined?

31. My compiler is complaining that printf is undefined! How can this be? It's the world's most popular C function...

2. Multiple Choice Questions

1. A C program must have a function called
   (a) main() (b) prototype
   (c) definition (d) none of these
2. If a C program has two component functions **main ()** and **funct(),** it is possible that
   (a) **main()** invokes **funct()**
   (b) **funct()** invokes **main()**
   (c) both invoke each other with abnormal program termination
   (d) all of the above
3. An argument and its corresponding parameter must have the
   (a) same names
   (b) different names
   (c) same names but types must be different
   (d) different names but types should be same
4. A function may return
   (a) one value (b) more than one value
   (c) zero value (d) none of these
5. In a function, the parameters are declared in the
   (a) prototype of the function (b) header of the function
   (c) prototype with type only (d) none of these
6. A function's header and body must be defined within the
   (a) same file (b) different file
   (c) header file with extension (.h) (d) none of these
7. A function may contain
   (a) one return statement (b) two return statement
   (c) no return statement (d) none of these
8. Every function returns a value to its
   (a) calling function (b) invoker function
   (c) (a) and (b) are correct (d) none of these
9. A return statement may include an expression that invokes a function.
   (a) True (b) False
10. Every function must be defined in its own separate file.
    (a) True (b) False
11. An involving function must pass arguments to the invoked function.
    (a) True (b) False
12. Is the following statement correct?
    return;
    (a) True (b) False

13. A function is invoked with a call statement as in
    call ckeck (x);
    (a) True (b) False
14. In the following code slice
    A = 10;
    Funct(A++, A++, A++, A++);
    Funct()'s four arguments must evaluate to 11, 12, 13 and 14 in that order.
    (a) True (b) False
15. Call by value ensures that an invoked function cannot change the contents of any variable that occurs as an argument.
    (a) True (b) False
16. The function **exit()** causes an exit from
    (a) The loop in which it occurs (b) The block in which it occurs
    (c) The function in which it occurs (d) The program in which it occurs
17. Function saves return addresses and intermediate values at
    (a) stack (b) secondary storage device
    (c) (a) and (b) (d) none of these
18. What is error in the following code?
    int funct(code char, time float, n int)
19. What is error in the following code slice?

```
int Funct (int, float)
{
int x;
int y = 100;
x = y*y;
return (x);
}
```

20. What is error in the following code?
    return (x, y);
21. Find errors, if any, in each of the following segments:
    (a) if (x + y = z && y > 0)

```
printf (" ");
```

    (b) if (code> 1);

```
a = b + c
    else
a = 0
```

    (c) if (p < 0) II (q < 0)
    printf (" sign is negative");
22. The following is a segment of a program:

```
x = 1;
y = 1;
```

```
if (n > 0)
x = x + 1;
y = y - 1;
printf(" %d %d", x, y);
```

What will be the values of x and y if n assumes a value of (a) 1 and (b) O.

23. Rewrite each of the following without using compound relations:

(a) if (grade <= 59 && grade >= 50)
second = second + 1;

(b) if (number> 100 II number < 0)
printf(" Out of range");
el se.
sum = sum + number;

(c) if ((Ml > 60 && M2 > 60) || T > 200)
printf(" Admitted\n"); else printf(" Not admitted\n");

5.24 Assuming x = 10, state whether the following logical expressions are true or false.

(a) x == 10 && x > 10 && !x   (b) x = = 10 || x> 10&& !x

(c) x==10&&x>1011!x   (d) x= = 10 || X > 10 || !x

25. Find errors, if any, in the following switch related statements. Assume that the variables x and y are of int type and x = land y = 2

(a) switch (y);

(a) case 10;

(b) switch (x + y)

(c) switch (x) {case 2: y = x + y; break};

26. Simplify the following compound logical expressions

(a) !(x <=10)   (b) !(x = = 10) ||! ((y = = 5)|| (z < 0))

(c) !((x+y==z)&&!(z>5)   (d) !((x<=5)&&(y==10)&&(z<5))

27. Assuming that a = 5, b = 0, and c = 1 initially, what will be their values after executing the following code segments?

(i) if (a&& b)
a= 10;
else
b = 10;

(ii) if (a || b || c)
b = 10;
else
c = 0;

(iii) if (a)
if (b)
c = 10;
else
c = 0;

(iv) if (a = = 0 || a& & b)

```
    if (!b)
    c = 0;
        else
    b = 1;
```

28. Assuming that a = 8, b = 9 and c = 0 initially, what will be their values after executing the following code segments?

(i) switch (a)

```
{
    case 2
    a=1;
    b=a+1;
    case 1:
    a=0;
    break;
    default:
    a=1;
    b=0;
}
```

(ii) switch (b)

```
{
    case 0
    a=0;
    b=0;
    case 2:
    a=2;
    c=2;
    default:
    a=1;
    b=2;
}
```

3. State whether the following statements are true or false

1. When if statements are nested, the last else gets associated with the nearest if without an else.
2. One if can have more than one else clause.
3. A switch statement can always be replaced by a series of if-else statements.
4. A switch expression can be of any type.
5. A program stops its execution when a break statement is encountered.
6. Each expression in the else-if must test the same variable.
7. Any expression can be used for the if expression.

8. Each case label can have only one statement.
9. The default case is required in the switch statement.
10. The predicate !((x >= 1O):(y = = 5)) is equivalent to (x < 10) && (Y !=5).

4. Fill in the blanks with appropriate words in each of the following statements

1. The ____________ operator is true only when both the operands are true.
2. Multiway selection can be accomplished using an else if statement or with the ________ statement.
3. The __________________ statement when executed, in a switch statement causes immediate exit from the structure.
4. The ternary conditional expression using the operator ?: could be easily coded using statement __________.
5. The expression! (x ! = Y) can be replaced by the expression __________.

5. Descriptive and Programming Problems

1. Suppose **S** is a string with **N** characters. Let **SUBSTR (S, J, L)** denote the sub-string of **S** beginning at the position J and having length **L.** Let **S1 + S2** denote the concatenation of strings **S1** and **S2.** Suppose **REVERSE (S, N)** is recursively defined by

	S	If N = 1
REVERSE (S, N) =	SUBSTR(S,N,1) + REVERSE(S, 1, N-1), N-1)	Otherwise

   (a) Implement the function **REVERSE (S, N)** and **SUBSTR (S, J, L).** The function **REVERSE (S, N)** reverses a string. For examples, if we have string **PAL,** we will get string **LAP.** The function **SUBSTR (S, J, L)** index a sub-string in a given text.

   (b) Find **REVERSE (S, N)** when

   (i) N = 3 and S = ABC

   (ii) N = 5 and S = ABABC

2. Implement the function **Ackermann(m, n)** having the definition

   (i) If m = 0 then **Ackermann(m, n) = n+1**

   (ii) If m > 0 but n = 0 then **Ackermann(m, n) = Ackermann(m - 1, 1)**

   (iii) If m > 0 and n > 0 then

   Ackermann(m, n) = Ackermann(m- 1, Ackermann(m, n-1))

3. Let **J** and **K** be integers and suppose **Funct (J, K)** is recursively defined by

	5	If J < K
Funct (J, K) =	Funct (J-K, K+2) + J	If J? K

   Implement **Funct (J, K)** and find value of **Funct (2,7)**, **Funct (5, 3)** and **Funct (15, 2)**

4. Let **x** and **y** be non-negative numbers. Suppose a function **GreatestCommonDivisor ()** is recursively defined as

	GreatestCommonDivisor (y, x)	If x < y
GreatestCommonDivisor () =	x	If y = 0
	GreatestCommonDivisor (y, mod(x,y))	Otherwise

Implement the function GreatestCommonDivisor (x, y) and find value of **GreatestCommonDivisor (6, 15), GreatestCommonDivisor (20, 28)** and **GreatestCommonDivisor (540, 168).** Show output generated in each step.

5. Write a nonrecursive-function that computes factorial of an integer number.
6. Write a recursive function that computes summation of the following series:

   S(n) = 1+3+5+ ... + 2*n-1
7. Write a program that prompts the user for two numbers and one operator +, -, * or /. The function **main ()** issues the prompt and user's input in the variable **Operand1** and **Operand2** and Operator. The **main ()** checks the operator and if the operator is +, main () invokes the function **Add ()** with the arguments **Operand1** and **Operand2** and simultaneously for -, * and /. Each of the functions **Add (), Sub (), Multi () and Div ()** invokes function **Display (),** which prints the result of the arithmetic operation.
8. Write a program, which will take input as an integer number and print reverse of the number. Use function to implement it.
9. Write a function, which will take a floating-point number and give output separately for integer part and real part.
10. Write a C program to generate **fibonanci** number, which are lies between 1 and 100. Implement it with the help of recursion.
11. What is Tower of Hanoi? Implement it with the help of recursion.
12. Write an interactive program to determine whether an input number to the program is odd or even and print the message NUMBER IS EVEN or NUMBER IS ODD.

    (a) With using if Option, and (b) with if-else option (c) ternary operator
13. Write a program to find the number of and sum of all integers greater than 1000 and less than 10000 that are divisible by 7.
14. A set of two linear equations with two unknowns xl and x2 is given below:

    ax1 +bx2 = m

    cx1 + dx2 = n

    The set has a unique solution

    $$x_1 = \frac{md - bn}{ad - cb}$$

    $$x_2 = \frac{na - mc}{ad - cb}$$

    provided the denominator ad - cb is not equal to zero. Write a program that will read the values of constants a, b, c, d, m, and n and compute the values of x1 and x2. An appropriate message should be printed if ad - cb =0
15. Given a list of marks ranging from 0 to 100, write a program to prepare result of students:

    (a) who have obtained more than 80 marks, listed as grade A

    (b) who have obtained more than 60 marks, listed as grade B

(c) who have obtained more than 40 marks, listed as grade C
(d) who have obtained 40 or less marks, listed as grade D
(e) in the range 81 to 100,
(f) in the range 61 to 80,
(g) in the range 41 to 60, and
(h) in the range 0 to 40.

The program should use a minimum number of if statements.

16. Admission to a professional course is subject to the following conditions:
    (a) Marks in Mathematics e” 60
    (b) Marks in Physics e”50
    (c) Marks in Chemistry e” 40
    (d) Total in all three subjectse”200

    or

    Total in Mathematics and Physicse”150

    Given the marks in the three subjects, write a program to process the applications to list the eligible candidates.

17. A cloth showroom has announced the following seasonal discounts on purchase of items:

Purchase amount		Discount
	Mill cloth	**Handloom items**
0-100	-	5%
101-200	5%	7.5%
201-300	7.5%	10.0%
Above 300	10.0%	15.0%

    Write a program using **switch** and **if** statements to compute the net amount to be paid by a customer.

18. Write a program that will read the value of a and evaluate the following function

$$b = \begin{cases} 1 \text{ for } a > 0 \\ 0 \text{ for } x = 0 \\ -1 \text{ for } x < 0 \end{cases}$$

    Using
    (a) nested if statements,
    (b) **else if** statements, and
    (c) conditional operator? :

19. Write a program to compute the real roots of a quadratic equation
    $ax^2 + bx + c = 0$

The roots are given by the equations

$$X_1 = -b + \frac{\sqrt{b^2 - 4ac}}{2a}$$

$$X_2 = -b + \frac{\sqrt{b^2 - 4ac}}{2a}$$

The program should request for the values of the constants a, band c and print the values of x_1 and x_2 Use the following rules:

(a) No solution, if both a and b are zero

(b) There is only one root, if a = 0 (x = – c/b)

(c) There are no real roots, if b^2 – 4 ac is negative

(d) Otherwise, there are two real roots

Test the program with appropriate data so that all logical paths are working as per the design. Incorporate appropriate output messages.

Arrays Overview and Its Types

15.1 INTRODUCTION

So far we have used integer, floating point, double, and character data types as well as pointers to them. More details about the pointers will be found in next chapter. These data types are called **base** or **scalar** data types. Such base data types may be used to derive data structures which are organized groupings of instances of these types. The C language provides some widely used **compound** or **derived** data types together with mechanisms which allow the programmer to define variables of these types and access the data stored within them. We have also discussed about the memory allocation for a data type. For example, generally C compiler reserves two bytes for **int** data type, one byte for **char** data type, etc. Let us take one problem here. Suppose we have 50 integer numbers and we have to use these numbers in a program. How these numbers will be identified? For a moment, we can use 50 identifiers of **int** data type to represent these numbers. But declaring and using 50 identifiers are not easy solution. The same problem may be there with char and float data types. To overcome of this type problem, C provides array data structure.

A programmer is concerned with developing and implementing algorithms for a variety of tasks. As tasks become more complex, algorithm development is facilitated by structuring or organizing data in specialized ways. There is no best data structure for all tasks; suitable data structures must be selected for the specific task. Some data structures are provided by programming languages; others must be derived by the programmer from available data types and structures. A **data structure** is a logical or mathematical way of storing data in a computer so that it can be used efficiently. Often a carefully chosen data structure will allow a more efficient operation. There are two types of data structures:

(i) **Linear:** For example, Arrays, Linked Lists, Stacks, Queues, etc, and

(ii) **Non-linear:** For example, Trees (like B Trees, B+ Trees, B* Trees, etc), Graph, etc.

Many tasks require storing and processing a list of data items. For example, we may need to store a list of examination scores and to process it in numerous ways: find the maximum and minimum, average the scores, sort the scores in descending order, search for a specific score, etc. Data items in simple lists are usually of the same scalar type; for example a list of examination scores consists of all integer type items. We naturally think of a list as a data structure that should be referenced as a unit. C provides a derived data type that stores such a list of objects where each object is of the same data type - the array.

The data elements in an array are represented in linear manner, i.e., there is linear relationship among the elements and these elements are stored in consecutive memory locations and this is why an array is known as linear data structure. In other words, an array is a compound data type which allows a collection of data of the same type to be grouped into a single object. As with any data type, to understand how to use an array, one must know how such a structure can be declared, how data may be stored and accessed in the structure, and what operations may be performed using this new type.

15.2 CONCEPT OF ARRAY AND ITS TYPES

In computer programming world, an **array** is a linear data structure also known as a **vector** or **list** (for one-dimensional arrays) or a **matrix** (for two-dimensional arrays). A linear relationship among the elements is represented by means of sequential memory locations. Arrays hold a series of data elements of same data type. We can simply say that an array is a finite list of elements of same data type. Individual elements are accessed by their position in the array. The position is given by an **index,** which is also called a **subscript.** The index usually uses a consecutive range of integers (like 0, 1, 2, 3, …, 50), but the index can have any ordinal set of values. Some arrays are multi-dimensional, meaning they are indexed by a fixed number of integers, for example by a tuple of four integers. Generally, one- and two- dimensional arrays are the most common. For example, let us consider five data elements of integer type.

```
int num1=101;
int num2-201;
int num3=301;
int num4=401;
int num5=501;
```

The list of five integer data elements can be simply represented by an array as given below:

```
integer_number[5]={101, 201, 301, 401, 501};
```

It becomes more difficult to keep track of this as the number of variables increases. Arrays offer a solution to this problem. Arrays, like other variables in C, must be declared before they can be used. The number 5 within the square bracket represents the size of the declared array. This also represents the maximum number of data elements to be stored. We can use an index or subscript to access the elements of an array. In C language **index starts with zero.** In the above example, if i is an index, then

```
integer_number[0]=101,
integer_number[1]=201,
integer_number[2]=301,
integer_number[3]=401, and
integer_number[4]=501
```

The index i varies between 0 to 4.

Two points must be kept in mind while discussing arrays:

The elements of an array are accessed by means of an **index** or **subscript** set consisting of **n** consecutive numbers, where **n** represents the size of array.

The elements of an array exist in consecutive memory locations.

Arrays are of different dimension. Here we are discussing only one and two dimensional arrays other dimensional arrays we see later on.

1. One Dimensional Array

It is also known as vector or list. It is an n-ordered set of n elements. Suppose we have n elements namely a1, a2, a3, …, an of same data type **(homogeneous)** and we have an array named A holds these elements. Mathematically A is represented by:

A=(a1, a2, a3, …, an)   **or**

A(a1, a2, a3, …, an)

Due to the ordering property elements are put in consecutive manner and we can access any element by its index of subscript. For example,

A(1)=a1 or A[1]=a1,

A(3)=a3 or A[3]=a3,

A(i)=ai or A[i]=ai for   **1<=i<=n**

2. Multi-dimensional Array

Two-dimensional, three-dimensional, four-dimensional, etc are known as multi-dimensional array. A two-dimensional array is an array in which each element is itself a one-dimensional array. Two-dimensional array is also known as **table.** A two-dimensional array named X is shown in Figure 15.1. It has m rows and n columns.

We use two subscripts to identify an element of two-dimensional array. For example, in the Figure 15.1 element **X(i, j)** is highlighted. The row number is i and column number is j. The total number of elements in a table of m rows and n columns is **m*n.**

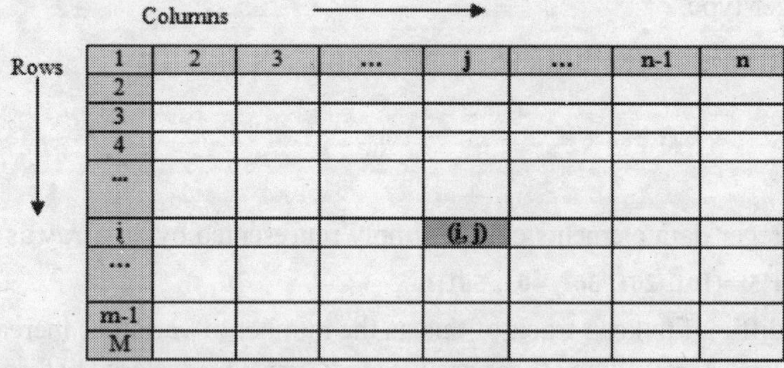

Figure 15.1: Two-dimensional Array

15.3 ONE DIMENSIONAL ARRAY

An array is a collection of objects of the same data type, allocated contiguously in memory. Individual objects in an array, called elements, are accessed by their position in the array. The subscripting operator ([]) provides the mechanics for creating an index to array elements. This form of access is called indexing or subscripting. An array facilitates the coding of repetitive tasks by allowing the statements executed on each element to be put into a loop that iterates through each element in the array.

The C language provides limited built-in support for an array type: reading and writing individual elements. Assignment of one array to another, the comparison of two arrays for equality, returning self-knowledge of size is not supported by this language.

The type of an array is derived from the type of its elements, in what is called array type derivation. If array objects are of incomplete type, the array type is also considered incomplete. Array elements may not be of type void or of function type. However, arrays of pointers to functions are allowed. The syntax to represent subscripted variables of an array in C language is given by:

Data type name_of_array [size of array];

For example, see the following declaration.

```
int number[5];
int list[13] ;
char string[20];
float real_numbers[6];
```

In the above example, **number** is an array of size 5, **list** is an array of size 13. Arrays **number** and list are **int** type. The array **string** is **char** data type of size 20 and **real_number** is an array of size 6 of **float** data type. These all arrays are one-dimensional arrays. We will discuss about the two-dimensional arrays later in this chapter. Example 1 demonstrates simple implementation of an array.

Example 1: Write a program to read into (integer and character) and display the contents of an array.

Answer: See the following program segment (array1.c) that illustrates the above notion fro integer and array2.c explores idea about character array.

```
/** array1.c **/
#include<stdio.h>
void main()
{
        int number[5], counter;
        for(counter=0; counter<5; counter++)
        {
                printf("\n Enter %d Number:", counter+1);
                scanf("%d", &number[i]);
        }
        printf("\n You have entered following numbers:");
        for(counter=0, counter<5;counter++)
        printf("\t %d", number[counter]);
getch();
}       // end of the main
```

OUTPUT

```
Enter 1 Number:25
Enter 2 Number:35
Enter 3 Number:45
Enter 4 Number:55
Enter 5 Number:65
You have entered following numbers:
25 35 45 55 65
```

In the above program, **number** is an **int** data type array of size 5. The **int** variable **counter** is used as index when five numbers are inputted through keyboard. We have used two for loops **for** accepting and displaying five integer numbers in first loop and second loop, respectively.

Let us see another program which takes the name of a person and display it, i.e., it demonstrates char array.

```
/** array2.c **/
#include<stdio.h>
    void main()
    {
        char name[20];
        printf("\n Enter your  good name (not more than 20 characters):");
        scanf("%s", name);
        printf("\n Your good name is: %s", name);
        getch();
    }
```

In the above program, name of a person is taken as input which is not greater than 19 characters, and it is displayed. One thing is noticeable here that when name is scanned the symbol '&' is not used as prefix which has been used through out in scanning any data type so far. This symbol '&' used to get the address of a variable. The name of any char type array itself represents its address (i.e., base address or starting address of an array from where onwards storage reserved for the data elements of the array). So, whenever a char array is scanned, there is no need of using '&' symbol.

15.3.1 Initializing One Dimensional Arrays

The initializer for an array is a comma-separated list of constant expressions enclosed in braces ({ }). The initializer is preceded by an equal sign (=). We do not need to initialize all elements in an array. If an array is partially initialized, elements that are not initialized receive the value 0 of the appropriate type. The same applies to elements of arrays with static storage duration. All file-scope variables and function-scope variables declared with the static keyword have static storage duration. The following definition shows a completely initialized one-dimensional array:

static int number[3] = { 5, 7, 2 };

The array number contains the following values: number[0] is 5, number[1] is 7; number[2] is 2. When we have an expression in the subscript declarator defining the number of elements in this case 3, we cannot have more initializers than the number of elements in the array.

The following definition shows a partially initialized one-dimensional array :

static int number1[3] = { 5, 7 };

The values of number1[0] and number1[1] are the same as in the previous definition, but number1[2] is 0.

A designated initializer, or designator, points out a particular element to be initialized. A designator list is a comma-separated list of one or more designators. A designator list followed by an equal sign constitutes a designation. Designated initializers allow for the following flexibility :

Elements within an aggregate can be initialized in any order.

The initializer list can omit elements that are declared anywhere in the aggregate, rather than only at the end. Elements that are omitted are initialized as if they are static objects: arithmetic types are initialized to 0; pointers are initialized to NULL.

Where inconsistent or incomplete bracketing of initializers for multi-dimensional arrays or nested aggregates may be difficult to understand, designators can more clearly identify the element or member to be initialized.

The following definition shows how we can use designated initializers to skip over elements of the array that we do not want to initialize explicitly. The array number contains the following values: number[0] is 5; number[1] is implicitly initialized to 0; number[2] is 7.

static int number[3] = { [0] = 5, [2] = 7 };

In the following example, the third and second elements of the one-dimensional array aa are initialized to 3 and 6, respectively:

int aa[4] = { [2] = 3, [1] = 6 };

Designated initializers can be combined with regular initializers, as in the following example:

int a[10] = {2, 4, [8]=9, 10};

In this example, a[0] is initialized to 2, a[1] is initialized to 4, a[2] to a[7] are initialized to 0, and a[9] is initialized to 10. In the following example, a single designator is used to "allocate" space from both ends of an array:

int a[MAX] = {1, 3, 5, 7, 9, [MAX-5] = 8, 6, 4, 2, 0};

The designated initializer, [MAX-5] = 8, means that the array element at subscript MAX-5 should be initialized to the value 8. If MAX is 15, a[5] through a[9] will be initialized to zero. If MAX is 7, a[2] through a[4] will first have the values 5, 7, and 9, respectively, which are overridden by the values 8, 6, and 4. In other words, if MAX is 7, the initialization would be the same as if the declaration had been written:

int a[MAX] = {1, 3, 8, 6, 4, 2, 0};

Instead of an expression in the subscript declarator defining the number of elements, the following one-dimensional array definition defines one element for each initializer specified:

static int item[ ] = { 1, 2, 3, 4, 5 };

The compiler gives item the five initialized elements, because no size was specified and there are five initializers.

15.3.2 Initialization of Character Arrays

We can initialize a one-dimensional character array by specifying:

A brace-enclosed comma-separated list of constants, each of which can be contained in a character

A string constant (braces surrounding the constant are optional)

Initializing a string constant places the null character (\0) at the end of the string if there is room or if the array dimensions are not specified. The following definitions show character array initializations:

static char name1[ ] = { 'J', 'a', 'n' };
static char name2[ ] = { "Jan" };
static char name3[4] = "Jan";

These definitions create the following elements:

Element	Value	Element	Value	Element	Value
name1[0]	J	name2[0]	J	name3[0]	J
name1[1]	a	name2[1]	a	name3[1]	a
name1[2]	n	name2[2]	n	name3[2]	n
		name2[3]	\0	name3[3]	\0

Note that the following definition would result in the null character being lost:

static char name3[3]="Jan";

When we initialize an array of characters with a string, the number of characters in the string - including the terminating '\0' - must not exceed the number of elements in the array.

Whenever the initial values are assigned to an array then the size is automatically determined by C compiler. Initializing the size of an array may result in wastage of memory. We will see this later in this chapter.

15.3.3 Memory Allocation For Arrays

We have discussed that when an identifier is declared, C compiler reserves memory for that to hold the data, which is assigned to that identifier. For example, generally C compiler

reserves 2-byte for **int** data type,in windows and DOS, but in UNIX, LINUX, AIX-L it is 4 byte

reserves 1-byte for **char** data type, and

reserves 4-byte for **float** data type, in windows and DOS, but in UNIX, LINUX, AIX-L it is 8 byte

The above memory allocation is totally dependent on the compiler and it may vary as environment, i.e., operating system to operating system.

When we declare an array compiler reserves **continuous memory** for that as per the size of the array. For example, consider the following declaration:

int List[10], 10*2=20 Byte is reserved,

char string[20], 20*1=20 Byte is reserved,

int num[]={1, 2, 3, 4, 5, 6}, 6*2=12 Byte is reserved,

char name[]={"Tom Alter"}, 9*1=9 byte is reserved (including blank space)

int number;

Figure 15.2 shows the memory allocation for int List[10]. The total memory is 10*2=20 bytes for this array. The Cell represents one unit memory allocation, which is 2-byte in this case.

C compiler reserves 10 cells for int List[10] , where each cell is capable to hold one int data type. Generally, one cell is of 2-byte, but it is dependent on the compiler and operating system. We assume that one cell is of 2-byte then total 20-byte is reserved for **int** List[10].

Consider the difference between accessing single cell associated with the variable named **number** and the 10 cells associated with the array **List.** To access one cell associated with the **int** type variable, we simply use the name of the variable. For the array **List,** we must specify an index to indicate exactly which cell among the 10 cells we wish to access. The expression **List [0]** designates the first cell; the expression **List [1]** designates 2nd cell; the expression **List [2]** designates 3rd cell and so on. The integer value enclosed in square brackets is the index, which indicates the offset or distance between the cell to be accessed and the first cell. Thus, the first cell in **List** has index 0, because its distance from the first cell is 0, i.e., it is first cell. The 2nd cell has index 1 because its distance from the first cell is 1. The 3rd cell has index 2 because its distance from the first cell is 2, and so on. An array's first element has index 0, 2nd element has index 1, 3rd element has index 2, and so on.

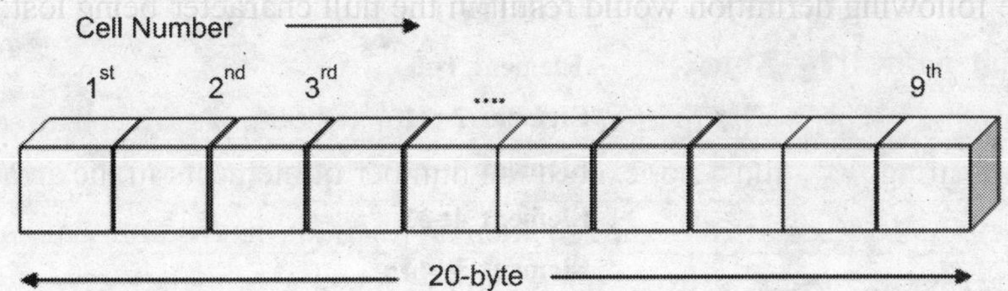

Figure 15.2 Memory Allocation for int List[10]

In dealing with arrays, we use square brackets in two quite different ways. When we define an array, the number of cells is specified in square brackets as shown in Figure 15.2. This declaration defines List to be array consisting of 10 elements of int data types. When we access a specific array element, we use the array's name together with an index enclosed in square brackets or index followed by the name of array in square bracket. It will be seen with pointer and arrays in further Chapters. For example, see the following representation which is same.

List [0] or **0[List]** represents first element,

List [1] or **1[List]** represents second element,

List [2] or **2[List]** represents third element,

...

List [9] or **9[List]** represents tenth element

It should be noted here that **List [10]** is not a legal reference to a cell under the name **List.** The expression **List [10]** attempts to reference a cell at a distance 10 from the first cell, i.e., the 11th cell because there are only 10 cells. In such situations, compiler either issue error message or gives garbage value.

The number of cells in an array is given as a bracketed expression only once in the definition and it does not alter during processing or execution of program. However, the bracketed expression is an index. For example, **List [10]** occurs only once in the definition to indicate that this array has 10 elements. Therefore, expressions such as **List [0], List [2]** and so on identify particular element in the array **List.**

C language is very flexible so that every one can use declarations like array. Size of an array declared in a program depends on the size of memory available on computer on which program is being implemented. In other words, C compiler reserves memory for an array from available memory in a computer. Go through the Example 2 for implementation of this discussion.

Example 2: Write a program for demonstrating the interchange of name and index of an array together.

Answer: Consider the following program (array3.c) that illustrates the above discussion. Further this problem is more highlighted with the help of arrays4.c and array5.c.

```
/* array3.c */
# include<stdio.h>
void main()
{
    int List [10] = {0,11,22,33,44,55,66,77,88,99}, count;
    for (count = 0; count < 10; count++)
    printf("\n Element %d = %d", count+1,count[List]);
}
```

OUTPUT

```
Element 1=0
Element 2=11
Element 3=22
Element 4=33
Element 5=44
Element 6=55
Element 7=66
Element 8=77
Element 9=88
Element 10=99
```

When the above program runs, the C compiler reserves memory for 10 elements of **int** data type for array **List.** Using for loop all the elements are accessed.

The indexing for ten elements of List array is shown in Figure 15.3.

Index	0	1	2	3	4	5	6	7	8	9
Value	0	11	22	33	44	55	66	77	88	99

Figure 15.3: Indexing of List Elements

In the **array3.c,** the array List contains 0, 11, 22, 33, 44, 55, 66, 77, 88, 99 integer values. Arrays of another data type can be also be initialized in another way in the definition discussed later in this.

If in an array definition, fewer initial values are given than the size of the array, the cells beginning with the first are initialized with the given values and remaining cells for which no initial values are there, are initialized zero. It is illustrated in **Figure 15.4.** There is an error if more initial values are supplied than the size of the array. Following program segment illustrates the above discussion:

```
/* array4.c */
# include<stdio.h>
main()
{
    int temp[10] = {11, 22, 33, 44};
    int count;
    for (count = 0; count < 10; count++)
    printf("\n temp[%d] = %d",count, temp[count]);
}
```

In the above program segment we have defined array temp with 10. But in initialization we only supplied 4 elements value and rest are left blank. In this situation C complier assigns 0's to un-initialized cells. The initialization of elements of **temp** array is shown in Figure 15.4.

Index	0	1	2	3	4	5	6	7	8	9
Value	11	22	33	44	0	0	0	0	0	0

Figure 15.4: Initializing temp Array

If we define and initialize arrays, we can omit the size of the array. The C compiler allocates exactly as many cells as are needed to store the given initial values. We can omit the number of cells in a definition only if the array is initialized. For example, see following declaration.

```
int number[] = {12, 134, 22, 65, 65, 77, 88, 99, 110, 210};
char name[]={"WELCOME"};
char city[]={'D','E','L','H','I'};
```

C compiler automatically reserves 10*2=20 bytes for array number and 8*1=8 byte for array **name** (one byte for NULL ('\0') because "" is used to represent a string) and city array is fixed for 5 bytes. But this memory initialization is there if initial value of an array is given, otherwise compiler raises error. Following program illustrates the above discussion.

```
/* array5.c */
# include<stdio.h>
main()
{
    int count[] = {44, 55, 66, 77, 88, 99, 100, 210};
    char name[]={"WELCOME"};
    printf("\n The third element of array count is: %d", count [2]);
    printf("\n The third character of name array is: %c", name[2]);
    getch();
}
```

The above program displays the third element of arrays **count** and **name.**

15.4 ARRAYS AND POINTERS

Using name of the array and relevant index or subscript can access an element of an array. As we know that each identifier is stored at some memory location and this location can be accessed. One thing should be clear here that the location of an identifier is not static, i.e., C compiler allocates memory when a program is compiled and next time when program is compiled then other location is reserved. So, the memory location of an identifier is re-locatable and it is done at compile time by the compiler.

The name of an array provides the address of its first cell that is also known as **base address** and index provides distance from the first cell. The base address is being constant and cannot be modified at any cast. For example, consider the following program:

```
/* array6.c */
# include<stdio.h>
main()
{
    int array_pointer[10] = {11, 22, 33, 44, 55, 66, 77, 88, 99, 100};
    printf("\n %d", array_pointer [4]);
}
```

The output come of the above program is 55, the content of the 5th cell in the array **array_pointer.** The operating system locates the 5th cell by using **array_pointer** as a pointer to base address and the index 4 as a distance from the base address. The above discussion is illustrated in Figure 15.5.

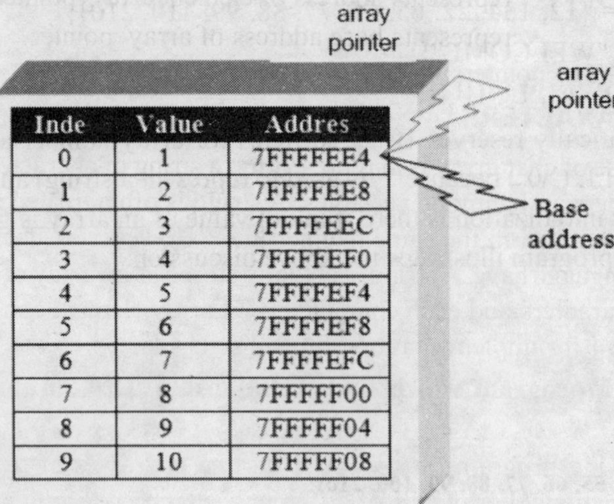

Inde	Value	Addres
0	1	7FFFFEE4
1	2	7FFFFEE8
2	3	7FFFFEEC
3	4	7FFFFEF0
4	5	7FFFFEF4
5	6	7FFFFEF8
6	7	7FFFFEFC
7	8	7FFFFF00
8	9	7FFFFF04
9	10	7FFFFF08

Figure 15.5: Array's name as a pointer to the first cell

Figure 15.5 shows the memory map of the array array_pointer. It is assumed here that compiler reserves 4-byte for one element of array_pointer. The base address is 7FFFFEE4, which is represented by array_pointer. Other addresses are represented as given below:

&array_pointer[0+1] or array_pointer+1 /* represents address of second element */
&array_pointer[0+2] or array_pointer+2 /* represents address of third element */
&array_pointer[0+3] or array_pointer+3 /* represents address of fourth element */
&array_pointer[0+4] or array_pointer++4 /*represents address of fifth element */
&array_pointer[0+5] or array_pointer+5 /*represents address of sixth element */
&array_pointer[0+6] or array_pointer+6 /* represents address of seventh element */
&array_pointer[0+7] or array_pointer+7 /*represents address of eight element */
&array_pointer[0+8] or array_pointer+8 /*represents address of ninth element */
&array_pointer[0+9] or array_pointer+9 /* represents address of tenth element */

Go through the Example 3 for implementation of this discussion.

Example 3: Write a program which finds relationship between pointer and an integer array.

Answer: The following program prints the addresses of the elements of array_pointer.

```
/* array7.c */
# include<stdio.h>
void main()
{
    int array_pointer[10] = {11, 22, 33, 44, 55, 66, 77, 88, 99, 100};
    int count;
    printf("\n Index Address Value");
    for (count =0; count< 10; count++)
    printf("\n %d %X %d", count , &array_pointer[count], array_pointer [count]);
}
```

In the above program, the operator '&' is used to print the address of elements of array_pointer. The operator '&' is read as "Address of" prefix with the followed identifier. For example,

&array_pointer[0] represents address of element array_pointer[0],
&array_pointer[2] represents address of element array_pointer[2],

&array_pointer[3] represents address of element array_pointer[3],
array_pointer represents base address of array_pointer

We will discuss details of pointers in further Chapters.

15.5 ARRAYS OF CHARACTERS

The most common use of char array is in representing a string of characters. Arrays of characters are quite similar to numbers and numeric variables. A string is often treated as a single unit in many languages and it can be handled in the same manner in **C.** However, **C** does not have a true string variable as some other language have. A string is actually stored as an array of characters or individual units. These units are characters and each character is an array element consuming 1-byte memory. Go through the Example 4 for implementation of this discussion.

Example 4: Write a program which finds relationship between pointer and a character array.

Answer: The following program (array8.c) prints the addresses of the elements of character array along with their locations. For details of different scenario go through program code array9.c, array10.c, array11.c and array12.c which gives better details about Example 4.

```
/* array8.c */
#include<stdio.h>
void main()
{
    char name[12] = {"NASIB SINGH"};
    int i = 0;
    printf("\n Index Address Character");
    while(*name[i] != '\0')
    {
        printf("\n %d %X %c",i, name+i,  name[i]);
        i++;
    }
    printf("\n You have entered Name: %s", name);
    getch();
}
```

OUTPUT

Index	Address	Character
0	7FFFFF00	N
1	7FFFFF01	A
2	7FFFFF02	S
3	7FFFFF03	I
4	7FFFFF04	B
5	7FFFFF05	
6	7FFFFF06	S
7	7FFFFF07	I
8	7FFFFF08	N
9	7FFFFF09	G
10	7FFFFFA	H
11	7FFFFFB	\O

You have entered Name: NASIB SINGH

This program segment will display "NASIB SINGH" on the monitor one character in one line with its address. It is illustrated in Figure 15.6. The base address of the name array is 7FFFFF00 and the first character of the name array 'R' is stored at this location. Similarly, the remaining characters of string name are stored in consecutive memory locations. There is a blank character in the string, which is stored at location 7FFFF03. It is noticeable that there are 11 characters (including blank character) in string name but memory allocation of string name represents that the last character at index 11 is null character '\0'. The null character is assigned by the compiler to indicate the termination of the string name and this character is not displayed on the monitor.

What will happen if somebody declare the size of array name 11 or 13? C compiler is smart enough and it reserves 11-byte for 11 characters and then places null character. So, there is no problem in declaring the size 11 or 13. In case of size 13 or more, the compiler leaves the extra bytes uninitialized. But what will be happened if size is 10 or less? It is very simple, how compiler will store 11 characters in place of 10 or less characters. So, compiler raises error that programmer have initialized too many. Let us see the following programs that illustrate the above idea.

```
/** array9.c **/
#include<stdio.h>
void main()
{
    char name[11]={"NASIB SINGH"};
    printf("\n You have initialized following string constant:");
    printf("\n %s", name);
    getch();
}
```

OUTPUT:
You have initialized following string constant:
NASIB SINGH

In the above program segment array size 11 now we have chosen size 10 for array name. The modified code is as follows.

```
/** array10.c **/
#include<stdio.h>
void main()
{
    char name[15]={"NASIB SINGH"};
    printf("\n You have initialized following string constant:");
    printf("\n %s", name);
    getch();
}
```

The C compiler raises error that there are too many initializations. The meaning is that there are 10-byte reserved for string name but there are 11 characters in the given string.

The compiler actually tacks on the **NULL** character although it is never seen in the source code. In this example, string name used without the braces is a pointer to the string contained in the array. The reader may ask why **name** is a pointer to type **char.** The variable was declared a char array and not, specifically, a pointer. This is a valid question since there are no ampersands. The answer lies, in how **C** handles char arrays. The expression **name [0],** for instance is a bonafide variable. It contains the character in the first position (first cell) of array **name.** However, when **name** is used without a subscript, it then becomes a pointer to the address of the first character. Remember the earlier section discussion about the **int** array and memory allocation. Similarly, the name of a char array represents the address of the first character and it is also known as base address.

A name of char array when used without the subscript brackets, is a pointer to the start of the first byte (first cell in memory allocation) that is also the start of the string (base address). It does not return the contents of that byte. It returns the byte's address in memory. It can be safely said that **name[0]** is a variable. It can be reassigned any legal object value. For example,

```
name [0] ='a';
name[1]='B';
It is also possible to assign integer constant as given below:
name [0] =13;
```

Let us consider the following program segment

```
/* array11.c */
# include<stdio.h>
void main()
{
    char name [12];
    name[0] = 'N';
    name[1] = 'A';
    name[2] = 'S';
    name[3] = 'I';
    name[4] = 'B';
    name[5] = ' ';    /* Blank character*/
    name[6] = 'S';
    name[7] = 'I';
    name[8] = 'N';
    name[9] = 'G';
    name[10]= 'H';
    name[11] = '\0';   /*Null character*/
    printf("\n %s", name);
}
```

The above program prints the string constant "NASIB SINGH". We have declared the size of array 12 and last element of the array is assigned null character, i.e., name[11]='\0'. What is the need of this assignment? It is good question here. Since we are assigning the each element of the array, so compiler expects that we will also indicate the termination of the string. If termination is not there, compiler raises no error but output contains garbage. Run the following program segment and see the fact..

```
/** array12.c **/
# include<stdio.h>
void main()
{
    char name [12];
    name[0] = 'N';
    name[1] = 'A';
    name[2] = 'S';
    name[3] = 'I';
    name[4] = 'B';
    name[5] = ' ';    /* Blank character*/
    name[6] = 'S';
    name[7] = 'I';
    name[8] = 'N';
    name[9] = 'G';
    name[10]= 'H';
    /* name[11] = '\0';          */
    printf("\n %s", name);
}
```

15.6 ARRAY BOUNDS CHECKING

We know that C language is used as system programming language due to its variety of features that are very much powerful. But so far we have not discussed any weakness. Since C provides many features that provides low-level features of a computer system. For example, memory and registers can be accessed directly. These features come along with some lacuna also. One of the routed weaknesses of C language is the lack of array bounds checking. This weakness is due to frugal use of memory although it is strength of a language. Lack of bounds checking simply means that no safeguards exist to prevent an array from being overwritten. If a character array is declared with a subscript of 10 sequential bytes, only 10 sequential bytes of memory are reserved for array. However, if a program miscalculates and writes more than 10 characters (including NULL) to this array, the excess characters are written into the memory locations that immediately follow the block that was allocated for the array. The 10-element boundary of the array is exceeded and bytes are written into memory locations not set aside exclusively for this array. When this occurs, what happens? It is programmer responsibility to take care of this.

There is no single answer to this question. If there are a few declared variables in the program, there is a good chance that the unreserved portion of memory that was overwritten by the offending string is not being used anyway and the program may run in a normal fashion. However, if there are many variables, the exclusive storage allocated to these, others may be overwritten by the unwarranted long string. This will certainly cause an improper execution sequence. In a worst-case scenario, those extra string elements may overwrite a management portion of memory or even interact with other variables to do the same thing. The result can be a crash where the computer simply locks up in a continuous loop and must be rebooted/restarted. This is very much dangerous situation if somebody is using C language carelessly. However, there have been cases where hard disk drives have been erased by disastrous overwrites to interrupt addresses (in DOS). Go through the Example 5 for implementation of this discussion.

Example 5: Write a C program for demonstrating the limitation of C in respect to using array without implementing the array checking.

Answer: Following program segment illustrates the above discussion.

```
/** array13.c **/
# include<stdio.h>
# include<string.h>
void main ()
{
    char str1[11] = {"Sahil Gill"};
    char str2[5];
    str2[0]=str1[0];
    str2[1]=str1[1];
    str2[2]=str1[2];
    str2[3]=str1[3];
    str2[4]=str1[4];
    str2[5]=str1[5];
    str2[6]=str1[6];
    str2[7]=str1[7];
    str2[8]=str1[8];
    str2[9]=str1[9];
    str2[10]=str1[10];
    printf("\n The given string is: %s", str1);
    printf("\n Copied string is: %s", str2);
```

```
    getch();
}
```

OUTPUT
The given string is: Sahil Gill
Copied string is: Sahil Gill

We can see here that even the size of array str2 is declared 5; it contains string constant "Sahil Gill" having 11 characters. In the above program, null character is not assigned to indicate the termination of string. This is a weak point of using C language. So, we are required use the memory allocation and initialization very carefully. Pointers add more power and flexibility in memory allocation and data accessing which we will discuss later on.

In the above program the array bounds are exceeded, but there will be no error message or warning when the program compiles. The different types of compilers will generate different type of output. The reason for this aberration lies in the way storage is managed.

15.7 ARRAYS AND FUNCTIONS

We know that an array is a variable capable of storing multiple values of the same data type. Like other variables, arrays can be passed to functions. When a function receives an array as a parameter the compiler does not have to specify the array size in the parameter declaration. Go through the Example 6 for implementation of this discussion. Readers are advised to just understand the concept, although function concept has been discussed in the earlier Chapters.

Example 6: Write a C program which finds summation of elements of an array. Use of function for finding the summation is essential.

Answer: In following program the function **display(),** the square brackets follow the variable name **int_array** inform the compiler that the parameter is an array. Other than knowing that the parameter is an array, the compiler does not care about the size of an array passed to the function.

```
/** array14.c **/
# include<stdio.h>
int display(int integer_array[], int number_of_element)
{
    int count;
    int sum =0;
    for (count =0; count < number_of_element; count++)
    {
        printf("\n   value[%d] = %d", count, integer_array[count]);
        sum += integer_array[count];
    }
    return (sum);
}

void main()
{
    int numbers[5] = {1, 2, 3, 4, 5};
    int result;
    result = display(numbers, 5);
    printf("\n Summation = %d", result);
}
```

In the function **display(),** two parameters are required. They are an array parameter **integer_array** to catch the array passed and a parameter **number_of_element** to catch the index of the last element (information) in the array to be processed.

15.8 CONCEPT OF CHARACTER STRING IN C

Storing a single **ASCII** character requires a byte of memory. We know that a string is a sequence of **ASCII** characters. When we declare a string constant, **C** automatically assigns **NULL ('\0')** character. When we create strings with the help of programs by reading character from standard input device, it is required to assign **NULL** character at the end of the string to indicate the end of the string. The best way to visualize a string is simply a collection of bytes (ASCII characters) terminated by a **NULL.** The above discussion is illustrated in **Figure 15.6.**

When functions work with strings, they normally care about the location at which the string starts (base address). Once the function knows the base address, it can traverse the successive memory locations until it encounters the **NULL** ('\0' end of the string indicators).

In **C,** a character string is a **NULL** or zero terminated arrays of characters. To create a character string, we simply declare a character array to create a character string. We declare a character array such as:

```
char string [15];
Suppose char array string has value "Prit Gupta", i.e.,
char string[12]={"Prit Gupta"};
```

The memory map of the above array string is shown in Figure 15.6.

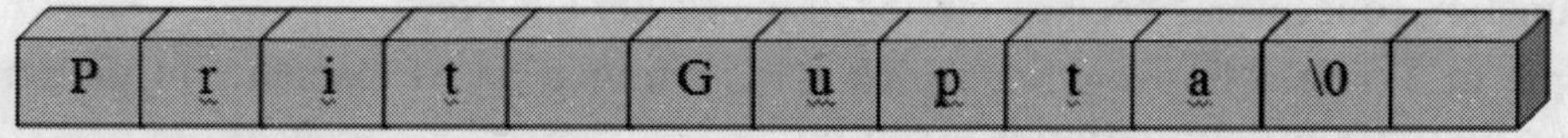

Figure 15.6: Consecutive memory allocation for char array string

In this case **C** compiler will create a string capable of storing 12 characters that is index from string [0] through **string [11]. C** compiler does not typically place the **NULL** character after the last character in the string. Instead, functions such as gets ( ) and fgets ( ) place the **NULL** character at the end of string. When we manipulate strings, it is programmer's responsibility to ensure that the **NULL** character is present. Go through the Example 7 for implementation of this discussion.

Example 7: Write C code which demonstrates the formation of string from character array.

Answer: For example, consider the following program segments (array15.c and array16.c) that manipulate the above discussion:

```
/** array15.c **/
# include<stdio.h>
void main()
{
    char string[27];
    int i;
    for(i =0; i < 26; i++)
            string[i] = 'a'+i;
    string[i] = '\0';    /*assigning null character*/
    printf("\n The string is: %s", string);
    getch();
}
```

The program uses for loop to assign the letter a to z to **string.** The program then places the **NULL** character after the letter z to indicate the string's end. The **printf ()** function then displays each character in the string up to the **NULL** character. As we have discussed, **C** functions that work with strings use the **NULL** character to determine the string's end. For example, consider the following program segment and guess the output.

```
/** array16.c **/
# include<stdio.h>
void main()
{
    char string[27];
    int i;
    for(i =0; i < 26; i++)
    {
        string[i] = 'A'+i;
    }
    string[15] = '\0';
    printf("\n The string is : %s", string);
    getch();
}
```

A character string is a sequence of zero or more characters that is typically terminated by a **NULL** character ('\0'). When we work with characters in **C,** we can use the character's numeric **ASCII** value or we can place the character within single quotes, such as 'x'. When we use the double quotes, on the other hand, such as "x", C creates a character string that contains the letter (or letters) specified and is terminated by **NULL** character.

15.9 OPERATIONS ON VECTORS

One-dimensional arrays are also known as vectors or lists. The operations, which are possible on vectors, are given below:

Addition

Subtraction

Multiplication

Go through the Example 8 for implementation of this discussion.

Example 8: Write C code which demonstrates the operation on one dimensional array.

Answer: In the program segment **array17.c** vector operations on one-dimensional array is given. This program performs above three operations provided in the list on the choice basis given by the user. Following list of characters are used to indicate an operation:

A for addition

S for subtraction

M for Multiplication

```
/** array17.c **/
# include<stdio.h>
void main()
{
    int vector1 [5] = {4, 5, 6, 7, 8};
    int vector2 [5] = {1, 2, 3, 4, 5};
    int result [5 ] ;
    char choice ;
    int i ;
    do
    {
        printf("\n Enter Choice \n A = Addition \n
        S = Subtraction \n M= Multiplication \n Choice is:");
```

```
        choice = getchar() ;         /*receive the characater*/
        choice = toupper(choice) ;   /*convert in upper case*/
        switch(choice)
        {
        case 'A' :
                printf("\n Addition operation:");
                for( i = 0 ; i < 5 ; i++ )
                        result [i] = vector1[i] + vector2[i] ;
                for( i = 0 ; i < 10 ; i++ )
                        printf("\n %d",result [i] );
                        printf("\n Press a key.....");
                        getch() ;
                        break ;

        case 'S' :
                printf("\n Subtraction operation");
                for( i = 0 ; i < 10 ; i++ )
                        result [i] = vector1[i] - vector2[i] ;
                for( i = 0 ; i < 10 ; i++ )
                        printf("\n %d",result [i] );
                        printf("\n Press a key");
                        getch() ;
                        break ;
        case 'M' :
                printf("\n Multiplication operation:");
                for( i = 0 ; i < 10 ; i++ )
                        result [i] = vector1[i] * vector2[i] ;
                for( i = 0 ; i < 10 ; i++ )
                        printf("\n %d",result [i] );
                        printf("\n Press a key");
                        getch() ;
                        break ;
        default :
                printf("\n Choice of operation is wrong....");
                printf("\n Press a key");
                getch() ;
                exit(0);        /*program is terminated here*/
        }
    } while (( choice = = 'A' || choice = = 'S' || choice = = 'M') ;
}   /*End of main function*/
```

The above program segment performs addition, subtraction, and multiplication of two vectors {4, 5, 6, 7, 8} and {1, 2, 3, 4, 5}. The user enters the choice from list {A, S, M} and accordingly operation is performed. If choice is other than the said list then program terminates after raising message "Choice of operation is wrong…"

```
OUTPUT
Enter Choice
A=Addition
S=Subtraction
M=Multiplication
Choice is: M
Multiplication operation:
4
10
18
```

```
28
40
Press a key
Enter Choice
A=Addition
S=Subtraction
M=Multiplication
Choice is: a
Addition operation:
5
7
9
11
13
Press a key
Enter Choice
A=Addition
S=Subtraction
M=Multiplication
Choice is: s
Subtraction operation:
3
3
3
3
3
Press a key
Enter Choice
A=Addition
S=Subtraction
M=Multiplication
Choice is: e
Choice of operation is wrong....
```

15.10 RANDOM ACCESS

Random accessing of the elements in an array is possible. This simple operation is used to find the information stored at any position in the array by using the index. For example, let int **List [10]** be an array. Here, the list contains 10 elements, if one wants to see an element at the 9th position in the array, he/she will simply write the following code:

printf("\n %d", List [8]);

It will show the 9th element of the array List. For the better details, readers are advised to go through the Example 9.

Example 9: Write C code which demonstrates the random operation on an array.

Answer: For example, consider the following program segment that implements the above discussion:

```
/** array19.c **/
# include<stdio.h>
void main()
{
    int choice ;
    char List [ ] = {"ANAMICA"};
```

```
    printf("\n Enter Choice of character(0-6): ") ;
    scanf("%d", &choice) ;
    printf("\n Position : %d Value : %c", choice, List[choice]);
}
```

OUTPUT
Enter Choice of character(0-6): 2
Position: 2 Value: A

This program will randomly display information existing in the **List.** Here the **List** contains 7 characters. If one gives **choice = 6,** it will display **position: 6 Value: A.** Similarly, any choice one may enter as an input.

15.11 TWO DIMENSIONAL ARRAYS

C does not have true multidimensional arrays. However, because of the generality of C's type system, we can have arrays of arrays, which are almost as good. Multi-dimensioned arrays have two or more index values which specify the element in the array. For example, two-dimensional array has two indices; three-dimensional array has three indices, and so on. Two-dimensional arrays are a little more complicated to use than one-dimensional ones. We will use two-dimensional arrays as examples in this section, although the techniques can be extended to three or more dimensions. The syntax for two-dimensional array is as follows:

Data type array_name [size of row] [size of column];

For example, let us consider some declaration given below:

```
int a2[5][7];      /* 5 represent row and 7 represents column*/
char string[3][10];      /* 3 rows and 10 column, i.e., three strings of 10 characters each*/
float real_number[5][4]; /* 5 rows and 4 column */
int temp[5][10][5]       /* Three-dimensional array */
```

In the above declaration, a2 is an array of 5 elements, each of which is an array of 7 ints. We usually think of it as having 5 rows and 7 columns, although this interpretation is not mandatory. Just as we declared a two-dimensional array using two pairs of brackets, we access its individual elements using two pairs of brackets:

```
int i, j;
for(i = 0; i < 5; i++)
{
        for(j = 0; j < 7; j++)
                a2[i][j] = 0;
}
```

Make sure to put each subscript in its own, correct pair of brackets. Neither

```
int a2[5, 7];            /* XXX WRONG */
```

nor

```
a2[i, j] = 0;            /* XXX WRONG */
```

would do anything remotely like what we wanted.

Two-dimensional arrays are used when it is required to process the matrices, tabular data, etc. Go through the Example 10 for implementation of basic concept of two-dimensional array.

Example 10: Write C code which demonstrates the two-dimensional array. You are also required to present memory address of the elements in the array.

Answer: Let us see the following program segment (array19.c) which demonstrates the notion of two-dimensional array. In this program segment we defined number[5][3] a two dimensional array with size 5*3, i.e., 5 rows and 3 columns. We have used two **for** loops to readout data into number[][]. Finally with the help of two for loops we displayed the array **number** contents onto the standard output device. Further we consider **array20.c** which demonstrates how elements of the array are located into the system memory.

```
/** array19.c **/
# include<stdio.h>
void main()
{
    int number[5][3] ;
int i, j;
for( i = 0 ; i < 5 ; i ++ )
{
    for ( j = 0; j < 3 ; j ++ )
    {
        printf("\nEnter row: %d element: %d:", i+1, j+1);
    scanf("%d", &number[i][j]) ;
    }
  }
    printf("\n You have entered:");
    for( i = 0 ; i < 5 ; i ++ )
    {
     printf("\n Row = %d:",i+1);
     for ( j = 0; j < 3 ; j ++ )
        printf("\t     %d ", number[i][j]);
    }
}    /*End of main function*/
```

```
OUTPUT
Enter row: 1 element: 1 :  2
Enter row: 1 element: 2 :  4
Enter row: 1 element: 3 :  6
Enter row: 2 element: 1 :  3
Enter row: 2 element: 2 :  6
Enter row: 2 element: 3 :  9
Enter row: 3 element: 1 :  4
Enter row: 3 element: 2 :  8
Enter row: 3 element: 3 :  12
Enter row: 4 element: 1 :  5
Enter row: 4 element: 2 :  10
Enter row: 4 element: 3 :  15
Enter row: 5 element: 1 :  6
Enter row: 5 element: 2 :  12
Enter row: 5 element: 3 :  18
You have entered:
Row = 1: 2      4       6
Row = 2: 3      6       9
Row = 3: 4      8       12
Row = 4: 5      10      15
Row = 5: 6      12      18
```

Here, a question may arise about the organization of the above data in computer memory and the clarification is given in **Figure 15.7.** We assume that 2-byte is reserved for an int data type.

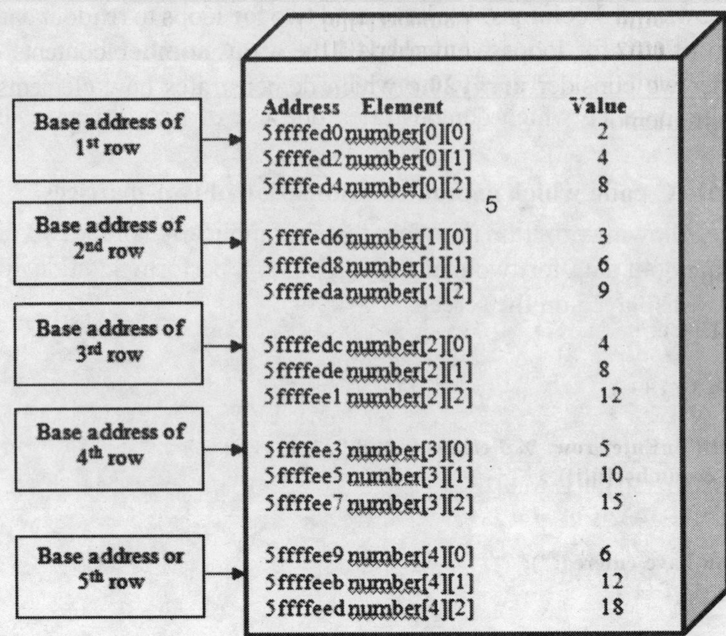

Figure 15.7 Two-dimension arrays in memory

Now let us see another program that prints the addresses of the elements of a two-dimensional array.

```
/**  array20.c **/
# include<stdio.h>
void main( )
{
      int number[5][3] ;
      int i ;
      int j ;
      for( i = 0 ; i < 5 ; i ++ )
         for ( j = 0; j < 3 ; j ++ )
            number[i][j] = i*j ;
      printf("\nAddress  Element  Value \n");
      for( i = 0 ; i < 5 ; i ++ )
      for ( j = 0; j < 3 ; j ++ )
      printf("\n 0%x  | number[%d][%d]  | %d  ", &number[i][j], i,j, number[i][j]);
```

OUTPUT

```
Address     Element              Value
0ffd8       | number[0][0]  |    0
0ffda       | number[0][1]  |    0
0ffdc       | number[0][2]  |    0
0ffde       | number[1][0]  |    0
0ffe0       | number[1][1]  |    1
0ffe2       | number[1][2]  |    2
0ffe4       | number[2][0]  |    0
0ffe6       | number[2][1]  |    2
0ffe8       | number[2][2]  |    4
0ffea       | number[3][0]  |    0
0ffec       | number[3][1]  |    3
0ffee       | number[3][2]  |    6
```

0fff0	| number[4][0] |	0
0fff2	| number[4][1] |	4
0fff4	| number[4][2] |	8

Go through the Example 11 which demonstrates one use of two dimensional arrays, matrix operation.

Example 11: Write C code which computes summation of two-matrices.

Answer: From the following program it is clear that one application of the two dimensional array is the development of random data for two matrices of 3x4 and perform addition operation on these data. The data is finally displayed on the screen.

```
/** array21.c **/
#include<stdio.h>
#include<stdlib.h>
void main()
{
long  matrix1[3][4], matrix2[3][4], result[3][4], i , j ;
 printf("\nGeneration of Matrix of Size 3x4 in Progress");
 printf("\n------------");
    printf("\n MATRIX ONE:");
    for( i = 0 ; i < 3 ; i++ )
    {
          printf("\n") ;
          for ( j = 0 ; j < 4 ; j++ )
          {
                    matrix1[i][j] = rand( )*10/100;
                    printf("%6d   ", matrix1[i][j] ) ;
          }
    }
    printf("\n MATRIX SECOND: ");
    for( i = 0 ; i < 3 ; i++ )
    {
          printf("\n") ;
          for ( j = 0 ; j < 4 ; j++ )
          {
                    matrix2[i][j] = rand( )*10/100;
                    printf("%6d   ", matrix2[i][j] ) ;
          }
    }
    /* Summation Section */
    for( i = 0 ; i < 3 ; i++ )
     for ( j = 0 ; j < 4 ; j++ )
          result[i][j] = matrix1[i][j] + matrix2[i][j];
          /* Output Section*/
    printf("\n\n\n Summation of two  Matrices:");
    printf("\n Output Matrix of Size 3x4");
    for( i = 0 ; i < 3 ; i++ )
    {
          printf("\n") ;
          for ( j = 0 ; j < 4 ; j++ )
          printf("%8d ", result[i][j]) ;
     }
    printf("\n Press a key");
    getch() ;
```

```
OUTPUT
Generation of Matrix of Size 3x4 in Progress
MATRIX ONE:
    34       13      -212      109
  -145       56      -206      -13
  -326     -164       245      145
MATRIX SECOND:
  -298      321      -116      136
  -114       50       280     -116
    90     -132        63       87
Summation of two Matrices:
Output Matrix of Size 3x4
  -264      334      -328      245
  -259      106        74     -129
  -236     -296       308      232
Press a key
```

15.11.1 Initializing Multidimensional Arrays

Like one-dimensional array, two-dimensional arrays can also be initialized. To initialize two-dimensional array, data are provided in set form. The size of each set must be equal to size of the row and each set must be enclosed into braces. We can initialize a multidimensional array using any of the following techniques:

Listing the values of all elements we want to initialize, in the order that the compiler assigns the values. The compiler assigns values by increasing the subscript of the last dimension fastest. This form of a multidimensional array initialization looks like a one-dimensional array initialization. The following definition completely initializes the array month_days:

```
static month_days[2][12] =
{
31, 28, 31, 30, 31, 30, 31, 31, 30, 31, 30, 31,
31, 29, 31, 30, 31, 30, 31, 31, 30, 31, 30, 31
};
```

Using braces to group the values of the elements we want initialized. We can put braces around each element, or around any nesting level of elements. The following definition contains two elements in the first dimension; we can consider these elements as rows. The initialization contains braces around each of these two elements:

```
static int month_days[2][12] =
{
{ 31, 28, 31, 30, 31, 30, 31, 31, 30, 31, 30, 31 },
{ 31, 29, 31, 30, 31, 30, 31, 31, 30, 31, 30, 31 }
};
```

Using nested braces to initialize dimensions and elements in a dimension selectively. In the following example, only the first eight elements of the array grid are explicitly initialized. The remaining four elements that are not explicitly initialized are automatically initialized to zero.

```
static short grid[3] [4] = {8, 6, 4, 1, 9, 3, 1, 1};
```

The initial values of grid are:

Element	Value	Element	Value
grid[0] [0]	8	grid[1] [2]	1
grid[0] [1]	6	grid[1] [3]	1
grid[0] [2]	4	grid[2] [0]	0
grid[0] [3]	1	grid[2] [1]	0
grid[1] [0]	9	grid[2] [2]	0
grid[1] [1]	3	grid[2] [3]	0

Using designated initializers: The following example uses designated initializers to explicitly initialize only the last four elements of the array. The first eight elements that are not explicitly initialized are automatically initialized to zero.

static short grid[3] [4] = { [2][0] = 8, [2][1] = 6, [2][2] = 4, [2][3] = 1 };

The initial values of **grid** are:

Element	Value	Element	Value
grid[0] [0]	0	grid[1] [2]	0
grid[0] [1]	0	grid[1] [3]	0
grid[0] [2]	0	grid[2] [0]	8
grid[0] [3]	0	grid[2] [1]	6
grid[1] [0]	0	grid[2] [2]	4
grid[1] [1]	0	grid[2] [3]	1

Go through the Example 12 which demonstrates initialization of two dimensional arrays.

Example 12: Write C code which initializes two two-dimensional arrays.

Answer: Consider the following program segment, which has initialized two two-dimensional array **matrix1** and **matrix2.** And on the choice basis, perform the addition and subtraction on these arrays.

```
/** array22.c **/
# include<stdio.h>
# include<stdlib.h>
void main()
{
    int matrix1[5][5] = { { 1,1,1,1,1 },
                          { 2,2,2,2,2 },
                          { 3,3,3,3,3 },
                          { 4,4,4,4,4 },
                          { 5,5,5,5,5 } };
    int matrix2[5][5] = { { 0,0,0,0,0 },
                          { 6,6,6,6,6 },
                          { 7,7,7,7,7 },
                          { 8,8,8,8,8 },
                          { 9,9,9,9,9 } };

    int i , j ;
    int result[5][5] ;
    char choice ;
    do
    {
        printf("\nEnter Choice \n A=Addition \n S=Subtraction \n N=Break \n Choice is:");
        choice = getchar() ;
        choice = toupper(choice) ;  /*Convert into Upper case*/
```

```
            if(choice = = 'A')  /*Addition*/
            {
                printf("\n");
                for( i = 0 ; i < 5 ; i++ )
                    for ( j = 0 ; j < 5 ; j++ )
                        result[i][j] = matrix1[i][j] + matrix2[i][j] ;
                /* Output */
                printf("\n Output Matrix Addition of Two Matrices  ");
                printf("\n");
                for( i = 0 ; i < 5 ; i++ )
                {
                    printf("\n") ;
                    for ( j = 0 ; j < 5 ; j++ )
                    printf("%5d", result[i][j]) ;
                }
                printf("\n");
                printf("\n Press a key ");
                getch() ;
            }else   if(choice = = 'S')  /*Subtraction*/
                {
                    printf("\n");
                    for( i = 0 ; i < 5 ; i++ )
                        for ( j = 0 ; j < 5 ; j++ )
                            result[i][j] = matrix1[i][j] - matrix2[i][j] ;

                    /* Output */
                    printf("\n Output Matrix Subtraction of Two Matrices  ");
                    printf("\n");
                    for( i = 0 ; i < 5 ; i++ )
                    {
                        printf("\n") ;
                        for ( j = 0 ; j < 5 ; j++ )
                            printf("%6d", result[i][j]) ;
                    }
                    printf("\n");
                    printf("\n Press a key ");
                    getch() ;
                }else if(choice = = 'N')
                {
                    printf("\n Choice is wrong");
                    printf("\n Press a key to exit");
                    getch() ;
                    exit(0) ; /*Terminates the program*/
                }
        } while (choice !='N');
    }   // End of main function
```

Run the above program segment and perform the desired action.

15.12 DYNAMIC MULTIDIMENSIONAL ARRAYS

It is straightforward to call **malloc** to allocate a block of memory which can simulate an array, but with a size which we get to pick at runtime. Can we do the same sort of thing to simulate multidimensional arrays? We can, but we will end up using pointers to pointers. If we do not know how many columns the array will have, we will clearly allocate memory for each row (as many columns wide as we like) by calling **malloc,** and each row will therefore be represented by a pointer.

How will we keep track of those pointers? There are, after all, many of them, one for each row. So we want to simulate an array of pointers, but we do not know how many rows there will be, either, so we will have to simulate that array (of pointers) with another pointer, and this will be a pointer to a pointer. Go through the Example 13 which demonstrates better illustration.

Example 13: Write C code using pointer to implement two dimensional arrays.

Answer: Following is the implementation.

```
#include <stdlib.h>
int **array;
array = malloc(nrows * sizeof(int *));
if(array == NULL)
{
        fprintf(stderr, "out of memory\n");
        exit or return
}
for(i = 0; i < nrows; i++)
{
        array[i] = malloc(ncolumns * sizeof(int));
        if(array[i] == NULL)
        {
                fprintf(stderr, "out of memory\n");
                exit or return
        }
}
```

The **array** is a pointer-to-pointer-to-int: at the first level, it points to a block of pointers, one for each row. That first-level pointer is the first one we allocate; it has nrows elements, with each element big enough to hold a pointer-to-int, or int *. If we successfully allocate it, we then fill in the pointers (all nrows of them) with a pointer (also obtained from malloc) to ncolumns number of ints, the storage for that row of the array. If this is not quite making sense, Figure 15.8 illustrates the idea.

Once we have done this {as in Figure 15.8}, we can (just as for the one-dimensional case) use array-like syntax to access our simulated multidimensional array. If we write

array[i][j]

We are asking for the ith pointer pointed to by array, and then for the jth int pointed to by that inner pointer. This is a pretty nice result: although some completely different machinery, involving two levels of pointer dereferencing, is going on behind the scenes, the simulated, dynamically-allocated two-dimensional "array" can still be accessed just as if it were an array of arrays, i.e., with the same pair of bracketed subscripts.

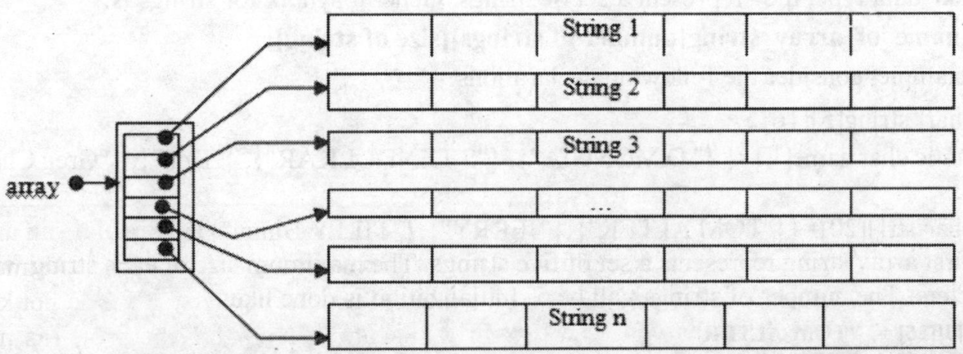

Figure 15.8: Two Dimensional Arrays in memory

If a program uses simulated, dynamically allocated multidimensional arrays, it becomes possible to write "heterogeneous" functions which do not have to know (at compile time) how big the "arrays" are. In other words, one function can operate on "arrays" of various sizes and shapes. The function will look something like

```
func2(int **array, int nrows, int ncolumns)
{
}
```

This function does accept a pointer-to-pointer-to-int, on the assumption that we will only be calling it with simulated, dynamically allocated multidimensional arrays. We must not call this function on arrays like the "true" multidimensional array a2 of the previous sections. The function also accepts the dimensions of the arrays as parameters, so that it will know how many "rows" and "columns" there are, so that it can iterate over them correctly. Here is a function which zeros out a pointer-to-pointer, two-dimensional "array":

```
void zeroit(int **array, int nrows, int ncolumns)
{
        int i, j;
        for(i = 0; i < nrows; i++)
        {
                for(j = 0; j < ncolumns; j++)
                        array[i][j] = 0;
        }
}
```

Finally, when it comes time to free one of these dynamically allocated multidimensional "arrays," we must remember to free each of the chunks of memory that we have allocated. Just freeing the top-level pointer, array, wouldn't cut it; if we did, all the second-level pointers would be lost but not freed, and would waste memory. For example, consider the following code which is used to free memory associated with an array

```
for(i = 0; i < nrows; i++)
        free(array[i]);
free(array);
```

15.13 TWO-DIMENSIONAL ARRAYS AND CHARACTER STRINGS

When we define a two-dimensional character array, the rows give the number of strings and the columns give the maximum size of a string. The declaration syntax is same as two-dimensional arrays are declared for **int, float** or **double** data types. When two-dimensional arrays are declared with the help of **char** data type, they represent a set of strings. General syntax for strings is:

char name_of_array_string[number of strings][size of string];

For example, consider the following declarations:

```
char string[5][16] ;
static char name[][]={ {" D MONGIA"}, {"S TENDULKAR"}, {"Don"}, {"Greg Chappel"}
};
char str[][20]={{"TOM ALTER"},{"JERRY"},{"TILLY Binny"}};
```

The first array string represents a set of five strings. The maximum size of each string will be of 15 characters. The number of strings will be 5. Initialization is done like:

```
string[0][16] = "TOM ALTER"
string[1][16] = "JERRY"
string[2][16] = "TILLY Binny"
```

string[3][16] = "D MONGIA"
string[4][16] = "S TENDULKAR"

The strings are always written in double quotes as discussed previously. The address from where above strings start in computer memory is known as base address of the rows or the strings and it is illustrated in Figure 15.9.

Element	Value	Starting Address
string[0][16]	TOM ALTER	ffa6
string[1][16]	JERRY	ffb6
string[2][16]	TILLY Binny	ffc6
string[3][16]	D MONGIA	ffd6
string[4][16]	S TENDULKAR	ffe6

Figure 15.9: Strings in memory

Go through the Example 14 for the better illustration.

Example 14: Write C code which manipulates the strings shown in Figure 15.9.

Answer: Consider the following code segments array23.c and array24.c.

```
/** array23.c **/
# include<stdio.h>
void main()
{
    char string[5][16] = {
                            "TOM ALTER",
                            "JERRY",
                            "TILLY BINNY",
                            "D MONGIA",
                            "S TENDULKAR"
                         };
    int i ;
    printf("\n Subscripted Variable \t Starting Address \t String");
    for ( i = 0 ; i < 5 ; i++ )
    {
        printf("\n");
        printf("string[%d][6]",i);
        printf("%18x",&string[i]);
        printf(" %12s",string[i]);
    }
    printf("\n Press a key");
    getch() ;
}
```

```
Subscript Variable      Starting        Address String
string[0][6]            ffa6            TOM ALTER
string[1][6]            ffb6            JERRY
string[2][6]            ffc6            TILLY
string[3][6]            ffd6            MONGIA
string[4][6]            ffe6            S TENDULKAR
Press a key
```

The above program prints the subscripted variables, staring address, and string assigned to a particular subscripted variable.

The string is stored in the memory as shown in Figure 15.10. This figure presents how a string constant is stored in computer memory as discussed earlier in this chapter though, we are providing one example given below that tells the storage structure of the string constants. In the string constant's **NULL** character is assigned automatically by the compiler, but when we create a string with the help of program the program must assign this.

	1	2	3	4	5	6	7	8	9	10	12	13	14	15	16
1	T	O	M		A	L	T	E	R	\0					
2	J	E	R	R	Y	\0									
3	T	I	L	L	Y		B	I	N	N	Y	\0			
4	D		M	O	N	G	I	A	\0						
5	S		T	E	N	D	U	L	K	A	R	\0			

Figure 15.10 Memory Allocation of char string [5][16]

```
/** array24.c  **/
# include<stdio.h>
void main()
{
     char string[5][16] ={"TOM ALTER", "JERRY",  "TILLY BINNY",
                          "D MONGIA", "S TENDULKAR"};
     int i ;
     int j ;
     for ( i = 0 ; i < 5 ; i++ )
     {
          printf("\n");
          printf("string[%d][16]     ",i);
          for( j = 0; j < 16 ;  j++)
          {
               printf("%c",string[i][j]);
          }
          printf("\\0");
     }
     printf("\n Press a key");
     getch( ) ;
}
```

15.14 MULTIDIMENSIONAL ARRAYS AND FUNCTIONS

The most straightforward way of passing a multidimensional array to a function is to declare it in exactly the same way in the function as it was declared in the caller. If we want to call

```
     func(a2);
then we might declare
     func(int a[5][7])
     {
          ...
     }
```

and it is clear that the array type which the caller passes is the same as the type which the function func accepts. If we remember what we learned about simple arrays and functions, however, two questions arise. First, in our earlier function definitions, we were able to leave out the (single) array dimension, with the understanding that since the array was really defined in the caller, we did not have to say (or know) how big it is. The situation is the same for multidimensional arrays, although it may not seem so at first. The hypothetical function func above accepts a parameter a, where a is an array of 5 things, where each of the 5 things is itself an array. By the same argument that applies in the single-dimension case, the function does not have to know how big the array a is, overall. However, it certainly does need to know what a is an array of. It is not enough to know that a is an array of "other arrays"; the function must know that a is an array of arrays of 7 ints. The upshot is that although it does not need to know how many "rows" the array has, it does need to know the number of columns, i.e., if we want to leave out any dimensions, we can only leave out the first one:

```
func(int a[][7])
{
...
}
```

The second dimension is still required. (For a three- or more dimensional array, all but the first dimension is required; again, only the first dimension may be omitted.)

The second question we might ask concerns the equivalence between pointers and arrays. We know that when we pass an array to a function, what really gets passed is a pointer to the array's first element. We know that when we declare a function that seems to accept an array as a parameter, the compiler quietly compiles the function as if that parameter were a pointer, since a pointer is what it will actually receive. What about multidimensional arrays? What kind of pointer is passed down to the function?

The answer is, a pointer to the array's first element. And, since the first element of a multidimensional array is another array, what gets passed to the function is a pointer to an array. If we want to declare the function func in a way that explicitly shows the type which it receives, the declaration would be

```
func(int (*a)[7])
{
    ...
}
```

The declaration int (*a)[7] says that a is a pointer to an array of 7 ints. Since declarations like this are hard to write and hard to understand, and since pointers to arrays are generally confusing, we recommend that when a programmer writes functions which accept multidimensional arrays, needs to declare the parameters using array notation, not pointer notation. What if we do not know what the dimensions of the array will be? What if we want to be able to call a function with arrays of different sizes and shapes? Can one say something like

```
func(int x, int y, int a[x][y])
{
    ...
}
```

where the array dimensions are specified by other parameters to the function? Unfortunately, in C, we cannot. Finally, we might explicitly note that if we pass a multidimensional array to a function:

```
int a2[5][7];
func(a2);
```

We cannot declare that function as accepting a pointer-to-pointer:

```
func(int **a)                    /* WRONG */
{
...
}
```

As we said above, the function ends up receiving a pointer to an array, not a pointer to a pointer.

15.15 MULTIDIMENSIONAL ARRAYS

One obvious question here, how many dimensions are supported by a **C** compiler in a definition. This question is accurately answered by the designer of a compiler. So, **C** supports many numbers of subscripted variables to manipulate an array and it is compiler dependent. A multi-dimensional array can be logically converted in one-dimensional arrays. The syntax for multidimensional array is given below:

Data type array name [size1][size2]... [size n];

For example, consider the following three-dimensional array **number.** In this array any expression can be written with the help of three subscript variables:

int number[5][3][4];

The **number** is a three dimensional array declaration. The total number of elements stored in this array will be 5x3x4 = 60 and total memory space required = 60 x 2 = 120 bytes. The following example gives the demonstration of a three dimensional array. This shows representation how any element of array can be accessed by three subscripts. If we want to access the third element of the list, the declaration will be **number[0][0][2].** This array can be logically converted into one-dimensional array that has 60 elements of same data type as multi-dimensional array has. For example, consider the following declarations which have same effect.

```
int num1[3][3][3]={{1, 2, 3}, {4, 5, 6},{7, 8, 9} };
        int num2[3][3]={1, 2, 3, 4, 5, 6, 7, 8, 9};
    char string[2][3][16] = {
                        "TOM ALTER",
                        "JERRY",
                        "TILLY",
                        "MONGIA",
                        "S TENDULKAR"
                        };
char str2[4][10]={ "TOM ALTER", "JERRY", "TILLY", "MONGIA", "S TENDULKAR"};
```

The memory representation for three-dimensional array is similar to one-dimensional and two-dimensional arrays. Go through the Example 15 for the better illustration.

Example 15: Write C code for implementing three-dimensional arrays.

Answer: Following program segment illustrates the above discussion:

```
/* array25.c */
# include<stdio.h>
void main()
{
    char string[2][3][16] = { "TOM ALTER",
                              "JERRY",
                              "TILLY",
                              "MONGIA",
                              "S TENDULKAR"};
    int i , k;
```

```
printf("\n Subscript Variable Starting Address String");
for ( k = 0 ; k < 2 ; k++ )
for ( i = 0 ; i < 3 ; i++ )
{
        printf("\n");
        printf("string[%d][%d][16]",k,i);
        printf("%18x",&string[k][i]);
        printf(" %12s",string[k][i]);
}
printf("\n Press a key");
getchar() ;
}
```

OUTPUT

Subscript Variable	Starting Address	String
string[0][0][16]	ff96	TOM ALTER
string[0][1][16]	ffa6	JERRY
string[0][2][16]	ffb6	TILLY
string[1][0][16]	ffc6	MONGIA
string[1][1][16]	ffd6	S TENDULKAR
string[1][2][16]	ffe6	

Press a key

From the output of the program segment array23.c and array25.c it is clear that output is same, means any dimension of arrays processed as single dimension.

EXERCISES

1. Multiple Choice Questions

1. An array is a

   (a) Collection of homogeneous elements (b) Collection of data types

   (c) Data type (d) None

2. What is the output of following program?

```
#include<stdio.h>
void main()
{
      int array[size], size=5;
      array[0]=1;
      array[1]=2;
      array[2]=3;
      array[3]=4;
      array[4]=5;
      for(size=0; size<5; size++)
      printf("%d", array[size]);
      getch();
}
```

   (a) 1 2 3 4 5 (b) Error (c) 23451 (d) None

3. What is the output of following program?

```
#include<stdio.h>
#define size 5
```

```
void main()
{
        int array[size], i=5;
        array[0]=1;
        array[1]=2;
        array[2]=3;
        array[3]=4;
        array[4]=5;
        for(size=0; size<5; size++)
        printf("%d", array[size]);
        getch();
}
```

(a) 1 2 3 4 5 (b) Error (c) 23451 (d) None

4. What is the output of following program?

```
#include<stdio.h>
#define size 5;
void main()
{
        int array[size], i=5;
        array[0]=1;
        array[1]=2;
        array[2]=3;
        array[3]=4;
        array[4]=5;
        for(size=0; size<5; size++)
        printf("%d", array[size]);
        getch();
}
```

(a) 1 2 3 4 5 (b) Error (c) 23451 (d) None

5. Consider the following program.

```
#include<stdio.h>
void main()
{
        char name[30];
        printf("\n Enter your name:");
        scanf("%s", name);
        printf("\n %s", name);
        getch();
}
```

Suppose you have entered your name as given below:

Enter your name: Prem Nath

What is the output of above program?

(a) Prem Nath (b) PremNath (c) Prem (d) Nath

(Hint: Space from keyboard taken as termination of a string)

6. Consider the following program. What is the output?

```
#include<stdio.h>
void main()
{
```

```
    char name[]="Prem Nath";
    printf("\n %s", name);
    getch();
}
```

(a) Prem Nath (b) Prem (c) Nath (d) Error

7. Consider the following program. What is the output?

```
#include<stdio.h>
void main()
{
    char name[]="Prem Nath";
    name[4]='\0';
    printf("\n %s", name);
    getch();
}
```

(a) Prem Nath (b) Prem (c) Nath (d) Error

8. Consider the following program. What is the output?

```
#include<stdio.h>
void main()
{
    char name[]="Prem Nath";
    printf("\n %s", name[5]);
    getch();
}
```

(a) Prem Nath (b) Prem (c) N (d) Error

9. Consider the following program. What is the output?

```
#include<stdio.h>
void main()
{
    char name[10]="Prem";
    name[4]='N';
    name[5]='a';
    name[6]='t';
    name[7]='h'
    name[8]='\0'
    printf("\n %s", name);
    getch();
}
```

(a) Prem Nath (b) PremNath (c) Prem (d) Error

10. What is the output of following program?

```
#include<stdio.h>
void main()
{
    int number[5];
    number[-3]=3;
    printf("%d", number[-3]);
    getch();
}
```

(a) Error (b) Garbage (c) 3 (d) None

11. What is output of following program?

```
#include<stdio.h>
void main()
{
    int number[5];
    number[-3]=3;
    printf("%d", number[3]++);
    getch();
}
```

(a) Error (b) 4 (c) 3 (d) Garbage

12. What is output of following program?

```
#include<stdio.h>
void main()
{
    int number[5]={1, 2, 3, 4, 5};
    printf("%d", number[5]);
    getch();
}
```

(a) Error (b) 4 (c) 5 (d) Garbage

13. What is output of following program?

```
#include<stdio.h>
void main()
{
    int number[5]={1, 2, 3, 4, 5};
    printf("%d", 4[number]);
    getch();
}
```

(a) Error (b) 4 (c) 5 (d) Garbage

14. What is output of following program?

```
#include<stdio.h>
void main()
{
    int number[5]={a, b, c, d, e};
    printf("%d", 0[number]);
    getch();
}
```

(a) Error (b) 4 (c) 5 (d) Garbage

15. What is output of following program?

```
#include<stdio.h>
void main()
{
    int number[5]={'a', 'b', 'c', 'd', 'e'};
    printf("%d", 0[number]);
    getch();
}
```

(a) Error (b) 4 (c) 5 (d) 97

16. What is output of following program?

```
#include<stdio.h>
void main()
```

```
{
    int number[5]={'a', 'b', 'c', 'd', 'e'};
    printf("%c", 0[number]);
    getch();
}
```

(a) Error (b) Garbage (c) a (d) 97

17. What is output of following program?

```
#include<stdio.h>
void main()
{
    char number[]={'a', 'b', 'c', 'd', 'e'};
    printf("%s", number);
    getch();
}
```

(a) Error (b) Garbage (c) abcde (d) 97

18. What is output of following program?

```
#include<stdio.h>
void main()
{
    char number[]={'a', 'b', 'c', 'd', 'e', '\0'};
    printf("%s", number);
    getch();
}
```

(a) Error (b) Garbage (c) abcde (d) 97

19. What is output of following program?

```
#include<stdio.h>
void main()
{
    char number[]={'1', '+', '3', '=', '4'};
    number[5]='\0';
    printf("%s", number);
    getch();
}
```

(a) Error (b) 1+3=4 (c) 134 (d) None

20. What is output of following program?

```
#include<stdio.h>
void main()
{
    int number[5], i;
    number[0]=printf("");
    number[1]=printf("A");
    number[2]=printf("AB");
    number[3]=printf("ABC");
    number[4]=printf("ABCD");
    for(i=0; i<5; i++)
    printf("%d", number[i]);
    getch();
}
```

(a) Error (b) Garbage (c) AABABCABCD01234 (d) None

21. What is output of following program?

```
#include<stdio.h>
void main()
{
        int number[]={'a', 1, 2, 3, 4}, i;
        number[1]+=number[0];
        number[2]+=number[0];
        number[3]+=number[0];
        number[4]+=number[0];
        for(i=0, i<5; i++)
        printf("%d", number[i]);
        getch();
}
```

(a) Error (b) 979899101102 (c) abcde (d) None

22. What is output of following program?

```
#include<stdio.h>
void main()
{
        int number[]={'a', 1, 2, 3, 4}, i;
        number[1]+=number[0];
        number[2]+=number[0];
        number[3]+=number[0];
        number[4]+=number[0];
        for(i=0, i<5; i++)
        printf("%c", number[i]);
        getch();
}
```

(a) Error (b) 979899101102 (c) abcde (d) None

23. Consider the following program. What is the output?

```
#include<stdio.h>
void main()
{
        char name[]={'P', 'r', 'e', 'm', 0};
        printf("%s", name);
        getch();
}
```

(a) Prem (b) Garbage (c) Prem0 (d) Error

24. Consider the following program. What is the output?

```
#include<stdio.h>
void main()
{
        char name[6];
        name[0]=97;
        name[1]=name[0]+1;
        name[2]=name[1]+1;
        name[3]=name[2]+1;
        name[4]=name[3]+1;
        name[5]=0;
        printf("%s", name);
        getch();
}
```

(a) abcde (b) Garbage (c) Error (d) None

25. The maximum number of dimension of an array supported by C language is
    (a) 6 (b) 3 (c) 4 (d) Compiler dependent
26. What is the output of the following program?

```
#include<stdio.h>
void main()
{
    int number[]={1, 2, 3, 4, 5};
    printf("%d", number[2]+2[number]);
    getch();
}
```

    (a) 6 (b) 4 (c) 8 (d) Error
27. What is the output of the following program?

```
#include<stdio.h>
void main()
{
    int number[2][3]={1, 2, 3, 4, 5, 6};
    printf("%d", number[0][2]+number[1][2]);
    getch();
}
```

    (a) 6 (b) 4 (c) 9 (d) Error
28. Choose the correct statement.
    (a) C provides automatic bounds checking in array definition
    (b) C does not provide automatic bounds checking in array definition
    (c) C provides support up to maximum six dimensional arrays
    (d) None
29. A two-dimensional array is
    (a) Collection of strings
    (b) Collection of rows that contain of same data type
    (c) Collection of columns that contain same data type
    (d) Table
30. Choose the incorrect statement.
    (a) An array element may an array itself
    (b) An array occupies continuous memory
    (c) C provides bound checking in array definition
    (d) Any multi-dimensional array can be logically represented by one-dimensional arrays.
31. Find out incorrect and correct array declarations in the following statements:
    (a) int int [101] ;
    (b) float real [20] ;
    (c) double num [20*10] ;
    (d) int number[SIZE];
    (e) char str1 [2*4/2] ;
    (f) static int count[200] ;
    (g) extern int x [34], y[90*15] ;

32. What is wrong in the following program code?

```
int a[7] = {1,2,3,4,5,6};
int b[15];
int i=0;
b = a;
for (i=0; i <10;i++)
printf("\n %d\n", b[i]);
```

33. Is any difference between program codes **(a)** and **(b)**?

(a)
```
int num[10], I;
for (I =0; I <10; I++)
num1[I] = 0;
```

(b)
```
int num[10];
int I =0;
While (I<10)
num[I++] = 0;
```

34. Explain the operation of each of the following for loops.

(a) for (n = 1; n != 10; n += 2) sum = sum + n;

(b) for (n = 5; n <= m; n -=1) sum = sum + n;

(c) for (11 = 1; n <= 5;) sum = sum + n;

(d) for (n = 1; ; n = n + 1) sum = sum + n;

(e) for (n = 1; n < 5; n ++) n = n -1

35. What would be the output of each of the following code segments?

(a)
```
count = 50;
while (count - > 0)
printf(count);
```

(b)
```
count = 50;
while ( - count> 0)
printf(count);
```

(c)
```
count = 50;
do printf(count);
while (count> 0);
```

(d)
```
for (m = 10; m > 7, m -=2)
printf(m);
```

36. Compare, in terms of their functions, the following pairs of statements:

(a) while and do...while

(b) while and for

(c) break and goto

(d) break and continue

(e) continue and goto

37. Analyze each of the program segments that follow and determine how many times the body of each loop will be executed.

(a)
```
a = 5;
b = 50;
while ( a <= b)
{
a = b/a
```

(b)
```
m=l;
do
{
_______________
_______________
m = m+2;
}
while (m>10);
```

(c)
```
int a;
for (a = 0; a <= 5; a = a+2/3)
{
_______________
_______________
}
```

(d)
```
int m = 10;
int n = 7;
while ( m % n >=0)
{
_______________
m = m + 1;
n = n + 2;
_______________
}
```

38. Find errors, if any, in each of the following looping segments. Assume that all the variables have been declared and assigned values.

(a)
```
while (count != 10);
{
count = 1;
sum = sum + x;
count = count + 1;
}
```

(b)
```
name = 0 ;
do
{
name = name + 1;
printf("My name is John\n");} whil e (name = 1)
```

(c)
```
do;
total = total + value;
scanf("%f", &value);
while (value != 999);
```
(d)
```
for (x = 1, x > 10; x = x + 1)
{
}
```
(e)
```
m = 1;
n = 0;
for ( ; m+n < 10; ++n);
printf("Hello\n");
m = m+lO
```
(f)
```
for (p = 10; p> 0;)
p = p - 1;
printf("%f", p);
```

39. Write a for statement to print each of the following output:
    (a) 1,2,4,8, 16,32
    (b) 1,3,9,27,81,243
    (c) – 4, –2,0,2,4
    (d) –10, –12, –14, –18, –26, – 42
40. Change the following for loops to while loops:
    (a) for (m = 1; m < 10; m = m + 1) printf(m);
    (b) for (; scanf("%d", & m) != -1;) printf(m);

State whether the following statements are true or false

1. The do-while statement first executes the loop body and then evaluates the loop control expression.
2. In a pretest loop, if the body is executed n times, the test expression is executed n + 1 times.
3. The number of times a control variable is updated always equals the number of loop iterations.
4. Both the pretest loops include initialization within the statement.
5. In a for loop expression, the starting value of the control variable must be less than its ending value.
6. The initialization, test condition and increment parts may be missing in a for statement.
7. while loops can be used to replace for loops without any change in the body of the loop.
8. An exit-controlled loop is executed a minimum of one time.
9. The use of continue statement is considered as unstructured programming.
10. The three loop expressions used in a for loop header must be separated by commas.

Fill in the blanks with appropriate words in each of the following statements

(a) In an exit-controlled loop, if the body is executed n times, the test condition is evaluated__________________ times.
(b) The __________________ statement is used to skip a part of the statements in a loop.
(c) A for loop with the no test condition is known as ____________ loop.
(d) The sentinel-controlled loop is also known as __________ loop.
(e) In a counter-controlled loop, variable known as __________ is used to count the loop operations.

Descriptive and Programming Problems

1. Can we change the value of the control variable in for statements? If yes, explain its conse-quences.
2. What is a null statement? Explain a typical use of it.
3. Use of go to should be avoided. Explain a typical example where we find the application of goto becomes necessary.
4. How would you decide the use of one of the three loops in C for a given problem?
5. How can we use for loops when the number of iterations are not known?
6. How would we search a word in a given text? Write a program to search a word of five characters in a text of 100 characters.
7. Write a program to delete an element at position p in a given array.
8. Write a program to fill in a two-dimensional array of Boolean values by setting mat[i][j] to 1 if the greatest common divisor of i and j is 1 and to 0 otherwise.
9. Why do array subscripts start at 0 instead of 1 in C language?
10. Is it possible to use a character as an array subscript? Explain your answer.
11. First load an array numbers with 10 integers between 1 and 100 and then write the code to perform a frequency distribution on the numbers in the array numbers. The output should list the numbers in ascending order and their corresponding frequency as follows:

Numbers	2	13	17	33	56	62	66	70	80	90
Frequency	2	1	4	5	1	3	1	4	2	1

12. Write programs, which will generate the following output:

(a)
```
9 8 7 6 5 4 3 2 1
9 8 7 6 5 4 3 2
9 8 7 6 5 4 3
9 8 7 6 5 4
9 8 7 6 5
9 8 7 6
9 8 7
9 8
9
```

(b)
```
1 2 3 4 5 4 3 2 1
1 2 3 4   4 3 2 1
1 2 3       3 2 1
1 2           2 1
1 1
```

(c)
```
1 2 3 4 5
1 2 3 4
1 2 3
1 2
1
```

(d)
```
1 2 3 4 5 6 7 8 9
1 2 3 4 5 6 7 8
1 2 3 4 5 6 7
1 2 3 4 5 6
1 2 3 4 5
1 2 3 4
1 2 3
1 2
```

Pointers and Applications

16.1 INTRODUCTION

Pointers are often thought to be the most difficult aspect of C. It is true that many people have various problems with pointers. If a programmer wants to be proficient in the writing of code in the C programming language, he/she must have a thorough working knowledge of how to use pointers. Unfortunately, C pointers appear to represent a stumbling block to newcomers, particularly those coming from other computer languages such as FORTRAN, Pascal or Basic. To aid those newcomers in the understanding of pointers we have written this chapter.

The purpose of this chapter is to provide an introduction to pointers and their use to these beginners. One of those things beginners in C find difficult is the concept of pointers. We have found that often the main reason beginners have a problem with pointers is that they have a weak or minimal feeling for variables, (as they are used in C). Thus, we start with a discussion of C variables in general.

16.2 SIZE OF VARIABLE TYPES

A variable in a program is something with a name, the value of which can vary. The way the compiler and linker handles this is that it assigns a specific block of memory within the computer to hold the value of that variable. The size of that block depends on the range over which the variable is allowed to vary. For example, on 32-bit PC's the size of an integer variable is 4 bytes. On older 16 bit PCs integers were 2 bytes. In C the size of a variable type such as an integer need not be the same on all types of machines. Further more there is more than one type of integer variable in C. We have integers, long integers and short integers. In this chapter we have assumed the use of a 32-bit system with 4 byte integers. If a user wants to know the size of the various types of integers on any system, running the following code will give that information.

```
/** Pointer1.C   **/
#include <stdio.h>
int main()
{
```

```
printf("size of a short is %d\n", sizeof(short));
printf("size of a int is %d\n", sizeof(int));
printf("size of a long is %d\n", sizeof(long));
}
```

OUTPUT

```
size of a short is 2
size of a int is 2
size of a long is 4
```

When we declare a variable we inform the compiler two things, the name and type of the variable. For example, we declare a variable of int type with the name k by writing:

int k;

On seeing the **int** part of this statement the compiler sets aside 4 bytes of memory (on a PC in case of UNIX, Linux, AIX-L and 2 bytes in case Windows) to hold the value of the integer. It also sets up a symbol table. In that table it adds the symbol k and the relative address in memory where those 4 bytes were set aside. If we write:

k = 2;

We expect that, at runtime when this statement is executed, the value 2 will be placed in that memory location reserved for the storage of the value of k. In C we refer to a variable such as the integer k as an "object". In a sense there are two "values" associated with the object k. One is the value of the integer stored there (2 in the above example) and the other the "value" of the memory location, i.e., the address of k. We refer to these two values with the nomenclature **rvalue** (right value, pronounced "are value") and **lvalue** (left value, pronounced "el value"), respectively.

In some languages, the **lvalue** is the value permitted on the left side of the assignment operator '=' (i.e., the address where the result of evaluation of the right side ends up). The **rvalue** is that which is on the right side of the assignment statement, the 2 above. **Rvalues** cannot be used on the left side of the assignment statement. Thus: 2 = k; is illegal. Actually the above definition of lvalue is somewhat modified forC. "An **object** is a named region of storage; an **lvalue** is an expression referring to an object." However, at this point, the definition originally cited above is sufficient. As we become more familiar with pointers we will go into more detail on this. Now consider:

```
int j, k;
k = 2;
j = 7;    ← line 1
k=j;      ← line 2
```

In the above, the compiler interprets the **j** in line 1 as the address of the variable **j** (its lvalue) and creates code to copy the value 7 to that address. In line 2, however, the **j** is interpreted as its rvalue (since it is on the right hand side of the assignment operator '='). That is, here the **j** refers to the value stored at the memory location set aside for **j**, in this case 20. So, the 7 is copied to the address designated by the **lvalue** of **k.** In all of these examples, we are using 4 byte integers so all copying of rvalues from one storage location to the other is done by copying 4 bytes. Had we been using two byte integers, we would be copying 2 bytes.

We have a reason for wanting a variable designed to hold an **lvalue** (an address). The size required to hold such a value depends on the system. On older desktop computers with 64K of memory total, the address of any point in memory can be contained in 2 bytes. Computers with more memory would require more bytes to hold an address. The actual size required is not too important so long as we have a way of informing the compiler that what we want to store is an address.

16.3 CONCEPT OF POINTER AND ITS FEATURES

In C pointers may be treated as standard variable in many ways and may behave a bit differently in some operations. They can be used in high-powered constructs for which no other standard variable can be used. There are many aspects of pointers and several programmers are not accustomed to using them. Careless use of pointers can easily result in a program enigma that is nearly impossible to understand.

A pointer is a variable that points at, or refers to, another variable. A pointer is a special variable that holds a memory address. In C when we define a pointer variable we do so by preceding its name with an asterisk. We also give pointer a type which, in this case, refers to the type of data stored at the address we will be storing in pointer. For example, consider the variable declaration:

int*ptr;

ptr is the name of a variable (just as k is the name of int variable shown in the earlier section). The '*' informs the compiler that we want a pointer variable, i.e., to set aside however many bytes is required to store an address in memory. The **int** says that we intend to use a pointer variable to store the address of an integer. Such a pointer is said to "point to" an integer. However, note that when we wrote **int k;** we did not give k a value. If this definition is made outside of any function ANSI compliant compilers will initialize it to zero. Similarly, **ptr** has no value that is we have not stored an address in it in the above declaration. In this case, again if the declaration is outside of any function, it is initialized to a value guaranteed in such a way that it is guaranteed to not point to any C object or function. A pointer initialized in this manner is called a "null" pointer.

The actual bit pattern used for a null pointer may or may not evaluate to zero since it depends on the specific system on which the code is developed. To make the source code compatible between various compilers on various systems, a macro is used to represent a null pointer. That macro goes under the name NULL. Thus, setting the value of a pointer using the NULL macro, as with an assignment statement such as ptr = NULL, guarantees that the pointer has become a null pointer. Similarly, just as one can test for an integer value of zero, as in if (k == 0), we can test for a null pointer using if **(ptr == NULL)**, but, back to using our new variable ptr. Suppose now that we want to store in **ptr** the address of int variable k. To do this we use the unary & operator and write:

ptr = &k;

What the & operator does is retrieve the lvalue (address) of **k,** even though **k** is on the right hand side of the assignment operator '=', and copies that to the contents of pointer ptr. Now, **ptr** is said to "point to" **k** There is only one more operator we need to discuss. The "dereferencing operator" is the asterisk and it is used as follows:

***ptr = 7;**

will copy 7 to the address pointed to by **ptr.** Thus, if **ptr** "points to" (contains the address of) **k,** the above statement will set the value of k to 20. That is, when we use the '*' this way we are referring to the value of that which ptr is pointing to, not the value of the pointer itself. Similarly, we can write:

```
printf("%d\n",*ptr);
```

to print on the screen the integer value stored at the address pointed to by **ptr;.** One way to see how all this stuff fits together see Example 1.

Example 1: Write C code for demonstrating the *, & and void.

Answer: Run the following program and then review the code and the output carefully.

```
/** Pointer2.C   **/
    #include <stdio.h> intj, k; int*ptr;
main(void) {
j = 1;
k = 2;
ptr = &k;
printf("\n");
printf("j has the value %d and is stored at %p\n", j, (void *)&j);
printf("k has the value %d and is stored at %p\n", k, (void *)&k);
printf("ptr has the value %p and is stored at %p\n", ptr,(void *)&ptr);
printf("The value of the integer pointed to by ptr is %d\n", *ptr);
return 0;
}
```

OUTPUT

```
j has the value 1 and is stored at 06F4:041E
k has the value 2 and is stored at 06F4:041C
ptr has the value 06F4:041C and is stored at 06F4:0418
The value of the integer pointed to by ptr is 2
```

Pointers provide two main features

It provides a very fast means of referencing array elements.

In functions it is used to modify calling parameters.

16.4 DECLARING POINTERS

Of course, just like other variables, we have to declare pointers before we can use them. Pointer declarations look much like other declarations: but do not be misled. When pointers are declared, the keyword at the beginning (int, char and so on) declares the type of variable that the pointer will point to. The pointer itself is not of that type, it is of type pointer to that type. A given pointer only points to one particular type, not to all possible types. A pointer represents a memory address of a variable. A pointer variable is one that holds a pointer to a value of its specified type. The syntax to declare a pointer type variable is

Data type pointer operator variable name;

For example, the declaration of an array and three pointers (one char two other are ints) are

```
char *ch ; /* here address of char data type is kept with variable ch */
int *i, *ip; /* here address of int data type is kept with variables i and ip*/
int list[5]:
```

The '*' in front of **ip** in the declaration shows that it is a pointer not an ordinary variable. It is of type pointer to int, and can only be used to refer to variables of type int. It is still uninitialized, so to do anything useful with it, it has to be made to point to something. We cannot just stick some integer value into it, because integer values have the type int, not pointer to int, which is what we want. For example, in any case, what would it means if the following code is:

ip = 6;

What would ip be pointing to? In fact it could be construed to have a number of meanings, but the simple fact is that, in C is just wrong. The operator & is a unary operator and returns the memory address of its operand. The syntax to declare or to assign is

Data type variable name = &variable name;

For example, see the following code slice int **x = 234** ; int *point = &x ; int **list[5],** *ip; ip = **&list[3];**

In this example, the **point** will hold the address of variable x, actually address is a **RAM** memory location where operating system saves program and data during running time. Let **x** exist in memory location **OxffOO** and its value be 234 then after the statement

point = &x ;

the value of **point** will be the address of x, i.e., is **OxffOO** rather than 234, Figure 16.1 illustrates the idea.

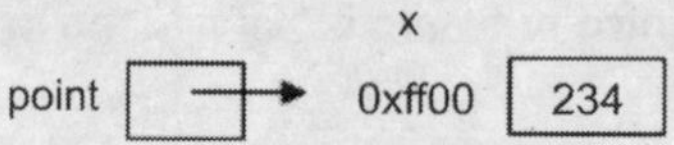

Figure 16.1 Point points to x

The pointer *ip is made to point to the member of the array **list** whose index is 3, i.e., the fourth member. This is important. We can assign values to pointers just like ordinary variables; the difference is simply in what the value means. The values of the variables that we have now are shown in Figure 16.2 (? means un-initialized).

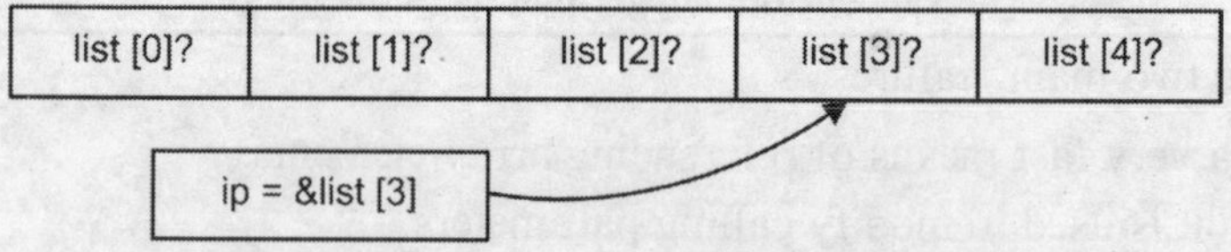

Figure 16.2 Array and initialized pointer

We can see that the variable ip has the value of the expression &list[3]. The arrow indicates that, when used as a pointer, ip points to the variable list[3].

What is this new unary &? It is usually described as the 'address-of operator, since on many systems the pointer will hold the store address of the thing that it points to. If we understand what addresses are, then we will probably have more trouble than those who do not: thinking about pointers as if they were addresses generally leads to grief. What seems a perfectly reasonable address manipulation on processor X can almost always be shown to be impossible on manufacturer Y's washing machine controller which uses 17-bit addressing when it is on the spin cycle, and reverses the order of odd and even bits when it is out of bleach. We will continue to use the term 'address of though, because to invent a different one would be even worse. Applying the & operator to an operand returns a pointer to the operand:

```
int i;
float f;
int *ip;
float *fp;
ip = &i;      /* '&i' would be of type pointer to int */
fp = &f;      /* '&f would be of type pointer to float */
```

In the above declaration each case the pointer would point to the object named in the expression.

A pointer is only useful if there is some way of getting at the thing that it points to. C uses the unary * operator for this job. If p is of type 'pointer to something', then *p refers to the thing that is being pointed to. The operator '*' is the complement of &. This gives the value of the location. The syntax is

Data type *variable name;

For example consider the following code segment:

```
int *a;
int c;
int m = 100; a = &m;
c = *a;
```

In the above example, the value of **m** is 100, value of a is location of **m** and value of c is value of a, a points to m, so that the value of c will be the value of m, i.e., 100. The discussion is illustrated in Figure 16.3. Example 2 implements this discussion.

Example 2: Write C code for finding the relationship between * and &.

Answer: See the following program segment (Pointer3.C) that demonstrates functionality of * and &. Further in program segment Pointer4.C and Pointer5. C relationship of * and & implemented more precisely.

```
/** Pointer3.C **/
# include<stdio.h>
void main()
{
    char value; /* value is char type */
    char ch = 'A'; /* ch is char type */
    char* address; /* pointer variable address is char type */
    address = &ch; /* assign address of ch to pointer variable address */
    value = "address;
    printf("\n Address of ch:0x%X", address); /* prints address of ch */
    printf("\n Value of ch: %d", value ); /* prints integer value of 'A */
    printf("\n Value of ch: %c", value); /* prints value of ch */
}
```

OUTPUT
Address of ch: 0x7FFFFF0A
Value of ch: 65
Value of Ch: A

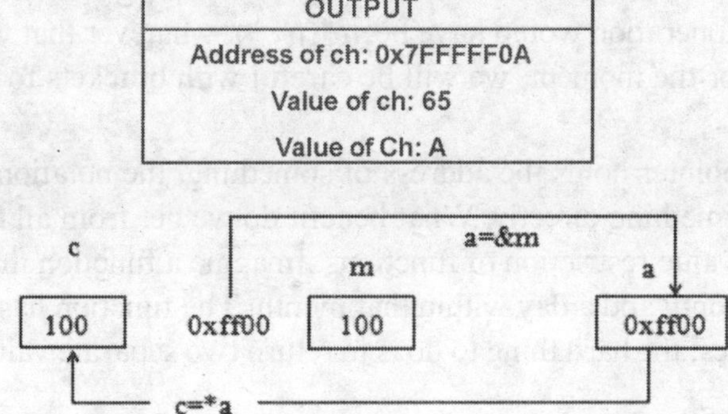

Figure 16.3 Accessing Value of variable via an indirect pointer

In the following example we are accessing the variable x via the pointer variable p.

```
/** Pointer4.C **/
#include <stdio.h>
#include <stdlib.h>
main()
{
intx, *p;
p = &x;        /* initialize pointer */
*p = 0;        /* set x to zero */
printf("x is %d\n", x);
```

```
printf("*p is %d\n", *p);
*p += 1;        /* increment what p points to */
printf("x is %d\n", x);
(*p)++;         /* increment what p points to */
printf("x is %d\n", x);
exit(0);
}
```

OUTPUT
x is 0
*p is 0
x is 1
x is 2

It should be noted that, since & takes the address of an object, returning a pointer to it, and since * means 'the thing pointed to by the pointer', the & and * in the combination *& effectively cancel each other out. But some things, constants for example, do not have addresses and the & operator cannot be applied to them; e.g., &1.5 is not a pointer to anything, it is an error. It is also interesting to see that C is one of the few languages that allow an expression on the left-hand side of an assignment operator. In the above example: the expression *p occurs twice in that position, and then the amazing (*p)++; statement. That last one is a great puzzle to most beginners-even if we have managed to wrap mind around the concept that *p = 0 writes zero into the thing pointed to by p, and that *p += 1 adds one to where p points, it still seems a bit much to apply the ++ operator to *p.

The precedence of (*p)++ deserves some thought. It will be given more later, but for the moment let us work out what happens. The brackets ensure that the * applies to p, so what we have is "post-increment the thing pointed to by p". Looking at **Table 16.9,** it turns out that ++ and * have equal precedence (or just ++ is just one above the *), but they associate right to left; in other words, without the brackets, the implied operation would have been *(p++), whatever that would mean. Later on we will be more used to it-for the moment, we will be careful with brackets to show the way that those expressions work.

So, provided that a pointer holds the address of something, the notation 'pointer is equivalent to giving the name of the something directly. What benefit do we get from all this? Well, straight away it gets round the call-by-value restriction of functions. Imagine a function that has to return, say, two integers representing a month and a day within that month. The function has some (unspecified) way of determining these values; the hard thing to do is to return two separate values. For example, see the following:

```
/** Pointer5.C   **/
#include <stdio.h>
#include <stdlib.h>
void date(int *, int *);     /* declare the function */
main() {
    int month, day;
    date (&day, &month);
    printf("day is %d, month is %d\n", day, month);
    exit(O); }
void date(int*day_p, int*month_p) {
    int day_ret, month_ret;
    printf("input day and month");
    scanf("%d%d",&day_ret,&month_ret);
```

```
    /* At this point, calculate the day and month values in day_ret and month_ret
respectively. */
        *day_p = day_ret;
        *month_p = month_ret;
    }
```

Notice carefully the advance declaration of date showing that it takes two arguments of type 'pointer to inf. It returns void, because the values are passed back via the pointers, not he usual return value. The main function passes pointers as arguments to date, which first uses the internal variables day_ret and month_ret for its calculations, then takes those values and assigns them to the places pointed to by its arguments. When date is called, the situation looks like Figure 16.4.

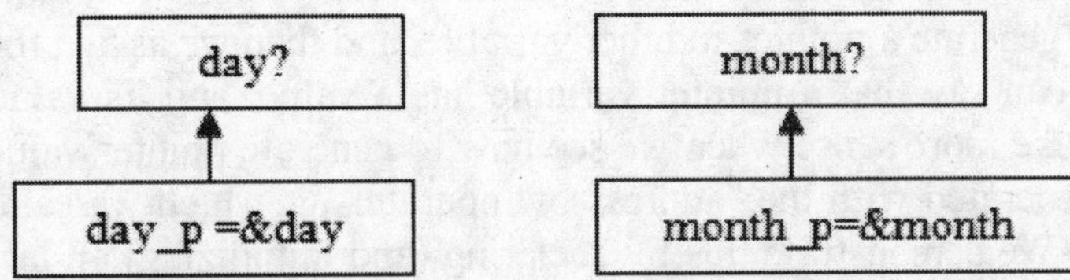

Figure 16.4 Just as date is called

The arguments have been passed to date, but in main, day and month are un-initialized. When date reaches the return statement, the situation is as shown in Figure 16.5 (assuming that the values for day and month are 12 and 5, respectively).

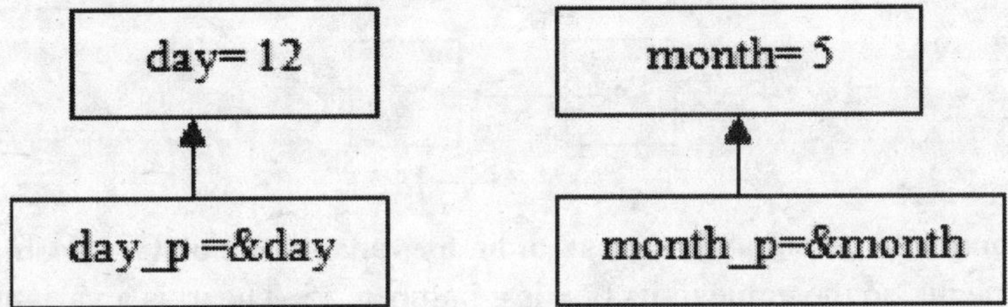

Figure 16.5 Just as date is about to return

One of the great benefits introduced in C is that it allows the types of the arguments to date to be declared in advance. A great favorite (and disastrous) mistake in C is to forget that a function expects pointers as its arguments, and to pass something else instead. Imagine what would have happened if the call of date above had read.

date(day, month);

and no previous declaration of date had been visible. The compiler would not have known that date expects pointers as arguments, so it would pass the int values of day and month as the arguments. On a large number of computers, pointers and integers can be passed in the same way, so the function would execute, then pass back its return values by putting them into wherever day and month would point if their contents were pointers. This is very unlikely to give any sensible results, and in general causes unexpected corruption of data elsewhere in the computer's store.

Fortunately, by declaring date in advance, the compiler has enough information to warn that a mistake has almost certainly been made. Perhaps surprisingly, it is not all that common to see pointers used to give this call-by-reference functionality. In the majority of cases, call-by-value and a single return value are adequate. What is much more common is to use pointers to 'walk' along arrays.

16.5 POINTER OPERATIONS

The first things to do with pointers are to declare a pointer variable, set it to point somewhere, and finally manipulate the value that it points to. Syntax for simple pointer declaration is

Data type 'variable:

For example, consider the following declaration

int*ip;

This declaration looks like earlier declarations, with one obvious difference: that asterisk. The asterisk means that ip, the variable we are declaring, is not of type int, but rather of type pointer-to-int. Another way of looking at it is that *ip, which as we will see is the value pointed to by ip, will be an int. Thus, we are forced to think of setting a pointer variable to point to another variable as a two-step process: first we generate a pointer to other variable, and then we assign this new pointer to the pointer variable. We can say that a pointer variable has a value, and its value is pointer to other variable. This will make more sense when we see how to generate pointer values. Pointers (that is, pointer values) are generated with the "address-of" operator &, which we can also think of as the "pointer-to" operator. We demonstrate this by declaring (and initializing) an int variable i, and then setting ip to point to it:

int i = 55;

ip = &i;

The assignment expression ip = &i; contains both parts of the "two-step process": &i generates a pointer to i, and the assignment operator assigns the new pointer to (that is, places it "in") the variable ip. Now ip "points to" i, which is illustrated in Figure 16.6.

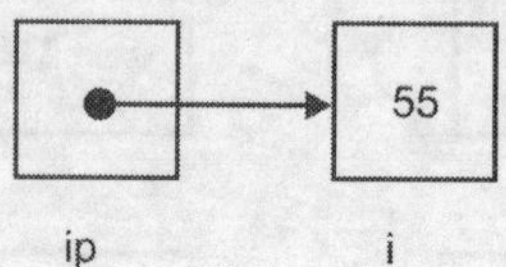

Figure 16.6 Assigning address of an int variable to pointer variable

i is a variable of type int, so the value in its box is a number, 55. The ip is a variable of type pointer-to-int, so the "value" in its box is an arrow pointing at another box. Referring once again back to the "two-step process" for setting a pointer variable: the & operator draws us the arrowhead pointing at i's box, and the assignment operator =, with the pointer variable ip on its left, anchors the other end of the arrow in ip's box.

We discover the value pointed to by a pointer using the "contents-of" operator, *. Placed in front of a pointer, the * operator accesses the value pointed to by that pointer. In other words, if ip is a pointer, then the expression *ip gives us whatever it is that's in the variable or location pointed to by ip. For example, consider the following line of code:

printf("%d\n",*ip);

which would print 55, since ip points to i, and i is containing pointing to 55.

One may wonder how the asterisk * can be the pointer contents-of operator when it is also the multiplication operator. There is no ambiguity here: it is the multiplication operator when it sits between two variables, and it is the contents-of operator when it sits in front of a single variable. The situation is analogous to the minus sign: between two variables or expressions it is the subtraction operator, but in front of a single operator or expression it is the negation operator. Technical terms we may hear for these distinct roles are unary and binary: a binary operator applies to two operands, usually on either side of it, while a unary operator applies to a single operand.

The contents-of operator * does not merely fetch values through pointers; it can also set values through pointers. For example, see the following statement.

***ip = 77;**

which means "set whatever ip points to 720." Again, the * tells us to go to the location pointed to by ip, but this time, the location is not the one to fetch from- we are on the left-hand sign of an assignment operator, so *ip tells us the location to store to. The situation is no different from array subscripting expressions such as list [3] which we have already seen appearing on both sides of assignments. The result of the assignment *ip = 77 is that i's value is changed to 77, and Figure 16.7 illustrates the idea.

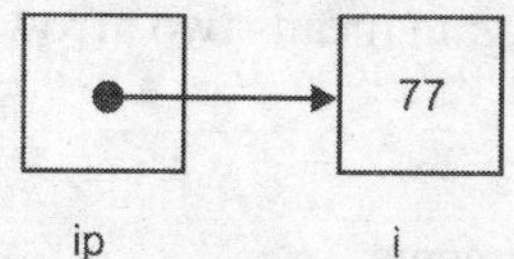

Figure 16.7 Changing contents of a variable using Pointer

If we called printf("%d\n", *ip) again, it would now print 720. At this point, we may be wondering why we are going through this rigmarole- if we wanted to set i to 77, why did not we do it directly? We will begin to explore that next, but first let us notice the difference between changing a pointer (that is, changing what variable it points to) and changing the value at the location it points to. When we write *ip = 77, we are changing the value pointed to by ip, but if we declare another variable j:

int j = 88;

and write

ip = &j;

We have changed ip itself. Illustration of statement is given in Figure 16.8.

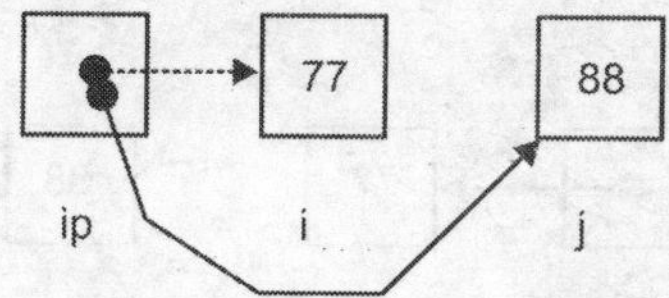

Figure 16.8 Changing pointer variable value to some other value at some different location

We have to be careful when we say that a pointer assignment changes "what the pointer points to." Earlier assignment

***ip = 77;**

changed the value pointed to by ip, but this more recent assignment ip = &j;

has changed what variable ip points to. It is true that "what ip points to" has changed, but this time, it has changed for a different reason. Neither i (which is still 77) nor j (which is still 88) has changed. What has changed is ip's value. If we again call

printf("%d\n", *ip);

this time it will print 88.

We can also assign pointer values to other pointer variables. If we declare a second pointer variable:

int*ip2;

then we can say ip2 = **ip;**

Now ip2 points where ip does; we have essentially made a "copy" of the arrow which is illustrated in Figure 16.9.

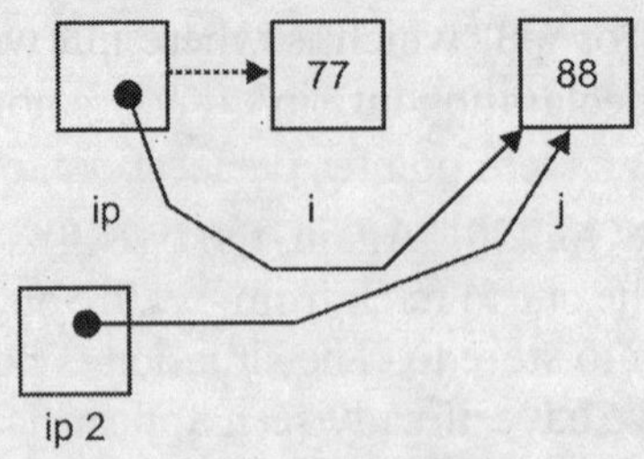

Figure 16.9 Duplicating Pointer

Now, if we set ip to point back to i again means two arrows point to different places as illustrated in Figure 16.10.

ip = &i;

We can now see that the two assignments

ip2 = ip; and

***ip2 = *ip;**

Do two very different things. The first would make ip2 again point to where ip points, i.e., back to i again. The second would store, at the location pointed to by ip2, a copy of the value pointed to by ip; in other words (if ip and ip2 still point to i and j, respectively) it would set j to i's value, or 720.

It is important to keep very clear in mind the distinction between a pointer and what it points to. We cannot mix them. We cannot "set ip to 55" by writing something like

ip = 55;   /* WRONG */

55 is an integer, but ip is a pointer. We probably wanted to "set the value pointed to by ip to 55," which we express by writing

***ip = 55;**

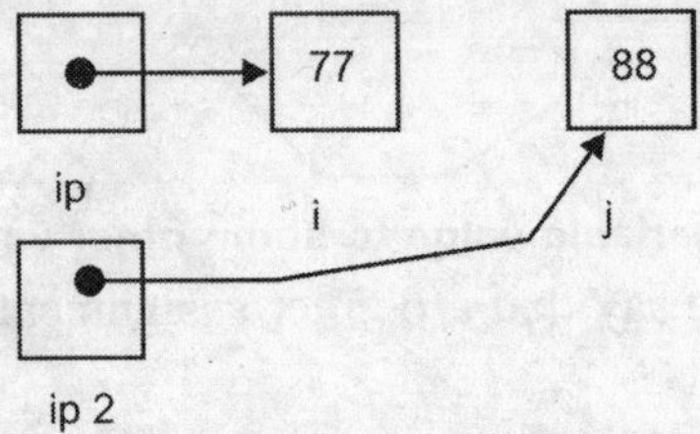

Figure 16.10 Two Pointers pointing at two different locations

Similarly, we cannot "see what ip is" by writing

printf("%d\n", ip); /* WRONG */

Again, ip is a pointer-to-int, but %d expects an int. To print what ip points to, use

printf("%d\n",*ip);

Finally, a few more notes about pointer declarations. The * in a pointer declaration is related to, but different from, the contents-of operator *. After we declare a pointer variable

int*ip;

The expression **ip = &i;**

sets what ip points to, i.e., to which location it points to, while the expression ***ip** = 55;

sets the value of the location pointed to by ip. On the other hand, if we declare a pointer variable and include an initializer:

int*ip3 = &i;

We are setting the initial value for ip3, which is where ip3 will point, so that initial value is a pointer. In other words, the * in the declaration int *ip3 = &i; is not the contents-of operator, it is the indicator that ip3 is a pointer. If we have a pointer declaration containing an initialization, and we ever have occasion to break it up into a simple declaration and a conventional assignment then it can be done as:

int*ip3;

ip3 = &i;

Do not write

int*ip3; *ip3 = &i;

Also, when we write int*ip;

although the asterisk affects ip's type, it goes with the identifier name ip, not with the type int on the left. To declare two pointers at once, the declaration is done as

int*ip1,*ip2;

Some programmer write pointer declarations as

int* ip; This works for one pointer, because C essentially ignores white space. But if we ever write

int* ip1, ip2; /* PROBABLY WRONG*/

It will declare one pointer-to-int ip1 and one plain int ip2, which is probably not what we meant.

What is all of this good for? If it is just for changing variables like i from 55 to 77, it would not be good for much. What it is good for, among other things, is when for various reasons we do not know exactly which variable we want to change, just like the bank did not know exactly which club member it wanted to send the statement to.

16.6 POINTER AND ARRAYS

Let us consider why we need to identify the type of variable that a pointer points to, as in:

int *ptr; One reason for doing this is so that later, once ptr "points to" something, if we write:

***ptr = 2;**

The compiler will know how many bytes to copy into that memory location pointed to by ptr. If ptr was declared as pointing to an integer, 4 bytes would be copied. Similarly for floats and doubles the appropriate number will be copied. But, defining the type that the pointer points to permit a number of other interesting ways a compiler can interpret the code. For example, consider a block in memory consisting if 10 integers in a row. That is, 40 bytes of memory are set aside to hold 10 integers.

Now, let us say int pointer ptr points at the first of these integers. Furthermore let us say that integer is located at memory location OxffOO (decimal). What happens when we write?

ptr + 1;

Because the compiler "knows" this is a pointer (i.e., its value is an address) and that it points to an integer (its current address, OxffOO, is the address of an integer), it adds 4 to ptr instead of 1, so the pointer "points to" the next integer, at memory location 0xff04. Similarly were the ptr declared as a pointer to a short, it would add 2 to it instead of 1. The same goes for other data types such as floats, doubles, or even user defined data types such as structures. This is obviously not the same kind of "addition" that we normally think of. In C it is referred to as addition using "pointer arithmetic", a term which we will come back to later.

Similarly, since ++ptr and ptr++ are both equivalent to ptr + 1 (though the point in the program when ptr is incremented may be different), incrementing a pointer using the unary ++ operator, either pre- or post-, increments the address it stores by the amount sizeof (type) where "type" is the type of the object pointed to (i.e., 4 for an integer).

Since a block of 10 integers located contiguously in memory is, by definition, an array of integers, this brings up an interesting relationship between arrays and pointers. For example, consider the following code segment

int my_array[] = {1,23,17,4,-5,100};

Here we have an array containing 6 integers. We refer to each of these integers by means of a subscript to my_array, i.e., using my_array[0] through my_array[5]. But, we could alternatively access them via a pointer as follows:

```
int *ptr;
ptr = &my_array[0];      /* point at the first integer in the array */
```

And then we could print out elements of array either using the array notation or by dereferencing pointer. Go through the Example 16.3 which demonstrates the relationship of pointer and array.

Example 16.3: Write C code that implements the pointer and array.

Answer: The following program segment illustrates the discussion:

```
/** Pointer6.C  **/
#include <stdio.h>
int my_arrayQ = {1,23,17,4,-5,100};
int*ptr;
int main(void)
{
    inti;
    ptr = &my_array[0];    /* point our pointer to the first element of the array */
    printf("\n\n");
    for(i = 0; i < 6; i++)
    {
        printf("my_array[%d] = %d   ",i,my_array[i]);   /*<- A*/
        printf("ptr + %d = %d\n",i, *(ptr + i));        /*<- B */
    }
    return 0; }
```

```
                         OUTPUT
my_array[0] = 1          ptr + 0 = 1
my_array[1] = 23         ptr + 1 = 23
my_array[2] = 17         ptr + 2 = 17
my_array[3] = 4          ptr + 3 = 4
my_array[4] = -5         ptr + 4 = -5
my_array[5] = 100        ptr + 5 = 100
```

Compile and run the above program and carefully note lines A and B and that the program prints out the same values in either case. Also observe how we de-referenced pointer in line B, i.e., we first added i to it and then de-referenced the new pointer. Change line B to read:

```
printf("ptr + %d = %d\n",i, *ptr++);
```

and run it again then change it to:

```
printf("ptr + %d = %d\n",i, *(++ptr));
```

and try once more. Each time try and predict the outcome and carefully look at the actual outcome.

In C, the standard states that wherever we might use **&var_name[0]** we can replace that with **var_name,** thus in the program segment where we wrote:

```
ptr = &my_array[0];
```

we can write:

```
ptr = my_array;
```

to achieve the same result.

We prefer to mentally think "the name of the array is the address of first element in the array". Many beginners have a tendency to become confused by thinking of it as a pointer. For example, while we can write

```
ptr = my_array;
```

we cannot write

```
my_array = ptr;
```

The reason is that while **ptr** is a variable, **my_array** is a constant. That is, the location at which the first element of **my_array** will be stored cannot be changed once **my_arrayD** has been declared.

Earlier when discussing the term "lvalue" where it stated: "An **object** is a named region of storage; an **lvalue** is an expression referring to an object". This raises an interesting problem. Since **my_array** is a named region of storage, why is **my_array** in the above assignment statement not an lvalue? To resolve this problem, some refer to **my_array** as an "unmodifiable lvalue". Modify the example program segment above by changing

```
ptr = &my_array[0];
```

to

```
ptr = my_array;
```

and run it again to verify the results are identical.

Now, let us delve a little further into the difference between the names **ptr** and **my_array** as used above. We refer to an array's name as a **constant** pointer. What do we mean by that? Well, to understand the term "constant" in this sense, let us go back to definition of the term "variable". When we declare a variable we set aside a spot in memory to hold the value of the appropriate type. Once that is done the name of the variable can be interpreted in one of two ways. When used on the left side of the assignment operator, the compiler interprets it as the memory location to which to move that value resulting from evaluation of the right side of the assignment operator. But, when used on the right side of the assignment operator, the name of a variable is interpreted to mean the contents stored at that memory address set aside to hold the value of that variable. Let us now consider the simplest of constants, as in:

```
int i, k;
i = 2;
```

Here, while i is a variable and then occupies space in the data portion of memory, 2 is a constant and, as such, instead of setting aside memory in the data segment, it is embedded directly in the code segment of memory. That is, while writing something like k = i; tells the compiler to create code which at run time will look at memory location &i to determine the value to be moved to k, code created by i = 2; simply puts the 2 in the code and there is no referencing of the data segment. That is, both k and i are objects, but 2 is not an object.

Similarly, in the above, since my_array is a constant, once the compiler establishes where the array itself is to be stored, it "knows" the address of my_array[0]. For example, look into the following statement.

```
ptr = my_array;
```

It simply uses this address as a constant in the code segment and there is no referencing of the data segment beyond that.

16.6.1 Pointer Arithmetic

Pointers do not have to point to single variables. They can also point at the cells of an array. For example, see the following code segment

```
int*ip;
intlist[10];
ip = &list[3];
```

and we would end up with ip pointing at the fourth cell of the array list (remember, arrays are 0-based, so list[0] is the first cell) Figure 16.11 illustrates the idea.

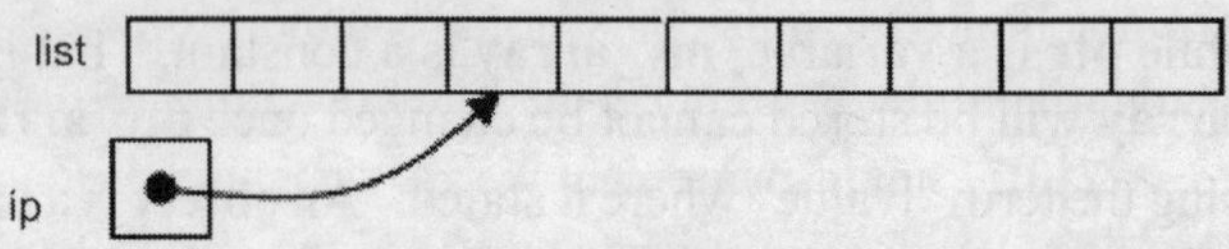

Figure 16.11 Relation of one dimensional array and pointer

We use this ip just like the one in the previous section: *ip gives us what ip points to, which in this case will be the value in list[3]. Once we have a pointer pointing into an array, we can start doing pointer arithmetic. Given that ip is a pointer to list[3], we can add 1 to ip:

```
ip + 1
```

What does it mean to add one to a pointer? In C, it gives a pointer to the cell one farther on, which in this case is list[4]. To make this clear, let us assign this new pointer to another pointer variable {Figure 16.12}:

```
ip2 = ip + 1;
```

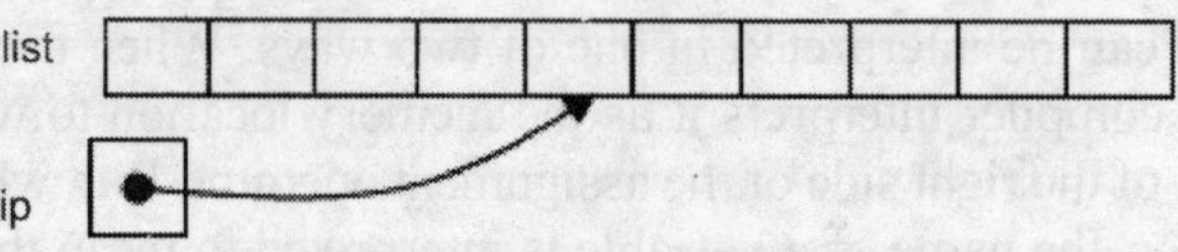

Figure 16.12 Pointer Arithmetic

If we now do

```
*ip2 = 4;
```

We have set list[4] to 4. But it is not necessary to assign a new pointer value to a pointer variable in order to use it; we could also compute a new pointer value and use it immediately:

```
*(ip + 1) = 5;
```

In this example, we have changed list[4] again, setting it to 5. The parentheses are needed because the unary "contents of" operator* has higher precedence (i.e., binds more tightly than) the addition operator. If we write *ip + 1, without the parentheses, we can fetch the value pointed to by ip, and adding 1 to that value. The expression *(ip + 1), on the other hand, accesses the value one past the one pointed to by ip. Given that we can add 1 to a pointer, it is not surprising that we can add and subtract other numbers as well. If ip still points to list[3], then

***(ip + 3) = 7;**

sets list[6] to 7, and

***(ip-2) = 4;**

setslist[1]to4.

Up above, we added 1 to ip and assigned the new pointer to ip2, but there is no reason we cannot add one to a pointer, and change the same pointer:

```
ip = ip + 1;
```

Now ip points one past where it used to (to list[4], if we had not changed it in the meantime). We can increment a pointer using

```
ip+=1;
```

or

```
ip++;
```

Of course, pointers are not limited to ints. It is quite common to use pointers to other types, especially char. Here is the innards of the strcmp(). This function compares two strings char by char. char **p1 = &str1[0], p2 = &str2[0];** /*in this statement we are assigning the base address of the string one to pointer variable p1 an dbase address of the string to pointer variable p2.

```
while(1)
{
    if(*p1 !=*p2)
        return *p1 -*p2;
    if(*p1 =='\0'||*p2=='\0')
        return 0;
    p1++;
    p2++;
}
```

The auto increment operator ++ (like its companion, -) makes it easy to do two things at once. We have seen idioms like list[i++] which accesses listfi] and simultaneously increments i, leaving it referencing the next cell of the array list. We can do the same thing with pointers: an expression like *ip++ lets us access what ip points to, while simultaneously incrementing ip so that it points to the next element. The pre-increment form works, too: *++ip increments ip, then accesses what it points to. Similarly, we can use notations like *ip- and *-ip.

As another example, here we are looking into the skeleton of strcpy() function. It can be rewritten to use pointers:

```
char*dp = &dest[0], *sp = &src[0];
while(*sp != '\0')
    *dp++ = *sp++;
*dp = '\0';
```

One question that comes up is whether the expression *p++ increments p or what it points to. The answer is that it increments p. To increment what p points to, we can use (*p)++.

When we are doing pointer arithmetic, we have to remember how big the array the pointer points into is, so that we don not ever point outside it. If the array list has 10 elements, we cannot access list[50] or list[-1] or even list[10] (remember, the valid subscripts for a 10-element array run from 0 to 9). Similarly, if array list has 10 elements and ip points to list[3], we cannot compute or access ip + 10 or ip - 5. (There is one special case: we can, in this case, compute, but not access, a pointer to the nonexistent element just beyond the end of the array, which in this case is & list[10]. This becomes useful when we are doing pointer comparisons, which we will look at next.

16.6.2 Pointers and Increment Operators

We said that we have eventually revisit expressions like

(*p)++;

and now it is time. Pointers are used so often to walk down arrays that it just seems natural to use the ++ and - operators on them. Here we write zeros into an array:

```
#defineLEN10
int list[LEN], *ip;
ip = list;
while(ip <
      &list[LEN])
      *(ip++) = 0;
```

The pointer ip is set to the start of the array. While it remains inside the array, the place that it points to have zero written into it, then the increment takes effect and the pointer is stepped one element along the array. The postfix form of ++ is particularly useful here.

This is very common stuff indeed. In most programs we will find pointers and increment operators used together like that, not just once or twice, but on almost every line. What is happening, and what combinations can we get? Well, the * means indirection, and ++ or- mean increment/decrement; either pre- or post-increment/decrement. The combinations can be pre- or post-increment/decrement of either the pointer or the thing it points to, depending on where the brackets are put. Table 16.1 gives a list.

Table 16.1 Pointer notation

++(*p)	pre-increment thing pointed to
(*p)++	post-increment thing pointed to
*(p++)	access via pointer, post-increment pointer
*(++p)	access via pointer which has already been incremented

The expressions in the list Table 16.1 can usually be understood after a bit of head scratching. Now, given that the precedence of*, ++ and – is the same in all three cases and that they associate right to left, can we work out what happens if the brackets are removed? Nasty is not it? There is only one case where the brackets have to be there {Table 16.2}.

Table 16.2 More pointer notation

With parentheses	Without, if possible
++(*p)	++*p
(*p)++	(*p)++
*(p++)	*p++
*(++p)	*++p

The usual reaction to that horrible sight is to decide that we do not care that the parentheses can be removed; we will always use them in a code. That is all very well but the problem is that most C programmers have learnt the important precedence rules (or at least learnt the table above) and they very rarely put the parentheses in. Like them, we do not-so if we want to be able to read the rest of the examples, we had better learn to read those expressions with or without parentheses. It will be worth the effort in the end.

Note: procedure for decrement - is same as for increment ++, readers are advised to prepare operation table for decrement -.

16.6.3 Pointer Subtraction and Comparison

As we have seen, we can add an integer to a pointer to get a new pointer, pointing somewhere beyond the original as long as it is in the same array. For example, see the following code segment:

```
ip2 = ip1 +3;
```

Applying a little algebra, we might wonder whether

```
ip2-ip1 =3;
```

and the answer is, yes. When we subtract two pointers, as long as they point into the same array, the result is the number of elements separating them. We can also ask (again, as long as they point into the same array) whether one pointer is greater or less than another: one pointer is "greater than" another if it points beyond where the other one points. We can also compare pointers for equality and inequality: two pointers are equal if they point to the same variable or to the same cell in an array, and are unequal if they do not. When testing for equality or inequality, the two pointers do not have to point into the same array.

One common use of pointer comparisons is when copying arrays using pointers. Here is a code fragment which copies 10 elements from arrayl to array2, using pointers. It uses an end pointer, ep, to keep track of when it should stop copying.

```
int arrayl [10], array2[10];
int*ip1,*ip2 = &array2[0];
int*ep = &array1[10];
for(ip1 =&array1[0]; ip1 < ep; ip1++)
*ip2++ = *ip1;
```

As we mentioned, there is no element arrayl [10], but it is legal to compute a pointer to this (nonexistent) element, as long as we only use it in pointer comparisons like this.

16.7 NULL POINTERS

We said that the value of a pointer variable is a pointer to some other variable. There is one other value a pointer may have: it may be set to a null pointer. A null pointer is a special pointer value that is known not to point anywhere. What this means that no other valid pointer, to any other variable or array cell or anything else, will ever compare equal to a null pointer.

The most straightforward way to "get" a null pointer in a program is by using the predefined constant NULL, which is defined for by several standard header files, including stdio.h, stdlib.h, and string.h. To initialize a pointerto a null pointer, see the following code segment:

```
#include <stdio.h>
int *ip = NULL;
```

and to test it for a null pointer before inspecting the value pointed to using the code segment:

```
if(ip != NULL)
  printf("%d\n", *ip);
```

It is also possible to refer to the null pointer by using a constant 0, and we will discuss some code that sets null pointers by simply doing

```
int*ip = 0;
```

In fact, NULL is a preprocessor macro which typically has the value, or replacement text, '\0'. Furthermore, since the definition of "true" in C is a value that is not equal to 0, we will see code that tests for non-null pointers with abbreviated code like

```
if(ip)
    printf("%d\n",*ip);
```

This has the same meaning as our previous example; if(ip) is equivalent to if(ip != 0) and to if(ip != NULL).

All of these uses are legal, and although we recommend that use the constant NULL for clarity, we will come across the other forms, so we should be able to recognize them.

We can use a null pointer as a placeholder to remind (or, more importantly, to help a program remember) that a pointer variable does not point anywhere at the moment and that we should not use the "contents of" operator on it that is, we should not try to inspect what it points to, since it does not point to anything. A function that returns pointer values can return a null pointer when it is unable to perform its task. A null pointer used in this way is analogous to the EOF value that functions like getchar() return. Go through the Example 16.4 which shows usabilty of pointer operator.

Example 16.4: Write C code which search a pattern in a given text or string.

Answer: See code of the standard library function strstr(), which looks for one string within another, returning a pointer to the string if it can, or a null pointer if it cannot. Here is the function, using the obvious brute-force algorithm: at every character of the input string, the code checks for a match there of the pattern string:

```
#include <stddef.h>
char*mystrstr(char inputQ, char patQ)
{
    char*start,*p1,*p2;
    for(start = &input[0]; *start != '\0'; start++)
    {  /* for each position in input string */
        p1 = pat;   /* prepare to check for pattern string there */
        p2 = start;
        while(*p1 != '\0')
    {
        if(*p1 != *p2)    /* characters differ */
            break;
        p1++;
        p2++;
    }
    if(*p1 == '\0')     /* found match */
        return
    start; }
    return NULL;
}
```

The start pointer steps over each character position in the input string. At each character, the inner loop checks for a match there, by using p1 to step over the pattern string (pat), and p2 to step over the input string (starting at start). We compare successive characters until either

(a) We reach the end of the pattern string (*p1 == '\0'), or

(b) We find two characters which differ. When we are done with the inner loop, if we reached the end of the pattern string (*p1 == '\0'), it means that all preceding characters matched, and we found a complete match for the pattern starting at start, so we return start. Otherwise, we go around the outer loop again, to try another starting position. If we run out of those (if *start == '\0'), without finding a match, we return a null pointer.

Notice that the function is declared as returning a pointer-to-char. We can use mystrstr() (or its standard library counterpart strstr()) to determine whether one string contains another:

```
if(mystrstr("Hello, world!", "lo") == NULL)
        printf("no\n");
else    printf("yes\n");
```

In general, C does not initialize pointers to null, and it never tests pointers to see if they are null before using them. If one of the pointers in programs points somewhere some of the time but not all of the time, an excellent convention to use is to set it to a null pointer when it does not point anywhere valid, and to test to see if it is a null pointer before using it. But we must use explicit code to set it to NULL, and to test it against NULL. In other words, just setting an unused pointer variable to NULL does not guarantee safety; we also have to check for the null value before using the pointer. On the other hand, if we know that a particular pointer variable is always valid, we do not have to insert a paranoid test against NULL before using it.

16.8 SIMILARITY BETWEEN POINTERS AND ARRAYS

There are a number of similarities between arrays and pointers in C. If we have an array

```
int list[10];
```

We can refer to list[0], list[1], list[2], etc, or to listfi] where i is an int. If we declare a pointer variable ip and set it to point to the beginning of an array:

```
int*ip = &list[0];
```

We can refer to *ip, *(ip+1), *(ip+2), etc, or to *(ip+i) where i is an int.

There are also differences, of course. We cannot assign two arrays. For example see the following code slice.

```
int list[10],b[10];
list = b;        /* WRONG */
```

is illegal. As we have seen, though, we can assign two pointer variables:

```
int*ip1,*ip2;
ip1=&list[0];
ip2 = ip1;
```

Pointer assignment is straightforward; the pointer on the left is simply made to point wherever the pointer on the right does. We have not copied the data pointed to (there is still just one copy, in the same place); we have just made two pointers point to that one place. The similarities between arrays and pointers end up being quite useful- in fact C builds on the similarities, leading to what is called "the equivalence of arrays and pointers in C." When we speak of this "equivalence" we do not mean that arrays and pointers are the same thing (they are in fact quite different), but rather that they can be used in related ways, and that certain operations may be used between them. For example, first such operation is that it is possible to (apparently) assign an array to a pointer:

```
int  list[10];
int *ip;
ip = list;
```

C defines the result of ip = list; to be that ip receives a pointer to the first element of list. In other words, it is

```
ip = &list[0];
```

The second facet of the equivalence is that we can use the "array subscripting" notation [i] on pointers, too. If we write

```
ip[3]
```

it is just as if we have written

```
*(ip + 3)
```

So when we have a pointer that point to a block of memory, such as an array or a part of an array, we can treat that pointer "as if" it were an array, using the convenient [i] notation. For example *ip, *(ip+1), *(ip+2), and *(ip+i), can be written ip[0], ip[1], ip[2], and ip[i]. As we will see, this can be quite useful (or at least convenient).

The third facet of the equivalence which is actually a more general version of the first one we mentioned is that whenever we mention the name of an array in a context where the "value" of the array would be needed, C automatically generates a pointer to the first element of the array, as if we have written &list[0]. For example, consider the following code segment:

```
int list[10];
int *ip;
ip = list + 3; /*Line-A*/
```

In the above code segment Line -A is similar to the following code segment

```
ip = &list[0] + 3;
```

which gives the same result as if we had written

ip = &list[3]; For example, if

the character array

char string[100]; contains some string, here is

another way to find its length:

```
int len;
char*p;
for(p = string; *p != '\0'; p++) ;
    /* Null statement */
len = p-string;
```

After the loop, p points to the '\0' terminating the string. The expression p - string is equivalent to p - &string [0], and 0 gives the length of the string.

16.9 POINTER VOID

As we have seen we can have pointers of various types. So far we have discussed pointer to int and pointer to char, pointer to float, and pointer to double. In coming section we will see about pointers to structures and even pointer to pointers. Also we have seen that on different systems the size of a pointer can vary. As it turns out it is also possible that the size of a pointer can vary depending on the data type of the object to which it points. Thus, as with integers where we can run into trouble attempting to assign a long integer to a variable of type short integer, we can run into trouble attempting to assign the values of pointers of various types to pointer variables of other types. To minimize this problem, C provides for a pointer of type void. A pointer's type declaration must be same as the data types used to access. If data type is int, the pointer type must be of int type. For example, consider the following declaration:

```
Int ch;
int *ich;
```

We assign address of the variable ch to pointer variable ich with the help of following statement

```
ich = &ch ;   /* is a correct assignment, similarly */
float f;
int *pf;
pf = &f; /* is incorrect assignment because f is float and pointer variable pf is int type. */
```

A void pointer is sort of a generic pointer. For example, while C will not permit the comparison of a pointer to type integer with a pointer to type character, for example, either of these can be compared to a void pointer. Of course, as with other variables, casts can be used to convert from one type of pointer to another under the proper circumstances. In program Pointer2.c we cast the pointers to integers into void pointers to make them compatible with the %p conversion specification. So, we use straightforward type definition, i.e., void. The syntax for such type declaration is:

void pointer operator variable name;

For example, consider the following declaration, **void**

***ch ;**

Here, **ch** may hold any type of data regardless of type of data we are providing to it. For example, see the following assignment to void type pointer variable **fie** declared in line -A. In line B, C, and D we assigning float, int and char data type to **fie.**

```
float fp ;
int inv ;
char ctype ;
void *fic ;   /* void pointer variable declaration */ /* Line -A */
fie = &fp ;   /* correct */ /* Line -B */
fie = &inv ; /* correct */ /* Line -C */
fie = &ctype; /* correct */ /* Line -D */
```

Go through the example 16.5 for the implementation of the above discussion.

Example 16.5: Write C code which demonstrates the void pointer.

Answer: Consider the following program segments (pointer7.c and pointer8.c) which demonstrate the void pointer implementation.

```
/* pointer7.c */
#include<stdio.h>
void main()
{
    float x;
    int y;
    charch;
    void *pointer;
void *pointer1 ;
void *pointer2;
x = 200.5 ;
y = 10;
ch = 'a' ;
printf(" \n STACK ADDRESS\n");
printf("Location of x in memory: 0x%X \n", &x);
printf("Location of y in memory: 0x%X \n", &y);
printf("Location of ch in memory: 0x%X\n", &ch);
pointer = &x ;
printf("Location of x in memory: 0x%X\n", pointer);
pointer1 = &y;
printf("Location of y in memory: 0x%X\n", pointe1);
pointer2 = &ch;
printf("Location of ch in memory: 0x%X\n", pointer2);
}
```

OUTPUT
STACK ADDRESS
Location of x in memory: 0xFFF2
Location of y in memory: 0xFFF0

```
Location of ch in memory: 0xFFEF
Location of x in memory: 0xFFF2
Location of y in memory: 0xFFF0
Location of ch in memory: 0xFFEF
```

To access values attached to void data type variables, the cast operators are used. The type of cast operator will be the same as the data stored in the pointer void. For example:

```
int i = 20 ;
intj;
void "pointer;
pointer = &i ;   /* assigning address of i to void pointer variable pointer */
j = *(int * ) pointer; /* applying cast operator int as data type of i */
```

In the above example, j holds the value of i as pointed by the void pointer variable pointer. The discussion is implemented in the following program segment:

```
/* pointer8.c */
 # include<stdio.h> void main() {
float x;
int y;
charch;
void "pointer;
void *pointer1 ;
void *pointer2;
x = 7200.725 ;
y = 1110 ;
ch = 'A';
printf("\n STACK ADDRESS\n");
printf("\nl_ocation of x in memory: 0x%X ", &x);
printf("\nLocation of y in memory: 0x%X ", &y);
printf("\nLocation of ch in memory: 0x%X ", &ch);
pointer = &x ;
printf("\n \n Value of x: %6.4f \n", -(float *)pointer);
pointer! = &y;
printf(" Value of y: %d \n", *(int *)pointer1 );
pointer2 = &ch;
printf(" Value of ch: %c\n",*(char*)pointer2 );
}
```

```
OUTPUT
STACK ADDRESS
Location of x in memory: OxFFC
Location of y in memory: OxFFA
Location of ch in memory: 0xFF9
Value of x: 7200.7251
Value of y: 1110
Value of ch: A
```

16.10 LEVEL OF INDIRECTION

When a pointer points to another pointer that points to another pointer or points to the target value is called multiple indirection or pointers to pointers. Figure 16.13 illustrates the multiple indirections. The value of a normal pointer is the address of the object that contains the value desired.

In case of a pointer to a pointer (two level indirection), the first pointer contains the address of the second pointer, which points to the object that contains the value desired.

Multiple indirections can be carried onto whatever extension desired, but more than a pointer to a pointer is rarely needed. A variable, that is a pointer to a pointer, must be declared as such. We do this by placing an additional asterisk in front of the variable name. For example, consider the following declaration, which tells the compiler that **double_ptr,** is a pointer to a pointer of type **int.**

intdouble_ptr;**

is not a pointer to a **int** but rather a pointer to an **int** pointer. To access the target value indirectly pointed to by a pointer, we must apply the asterisk operator twice as illustrated in Example 16.6.

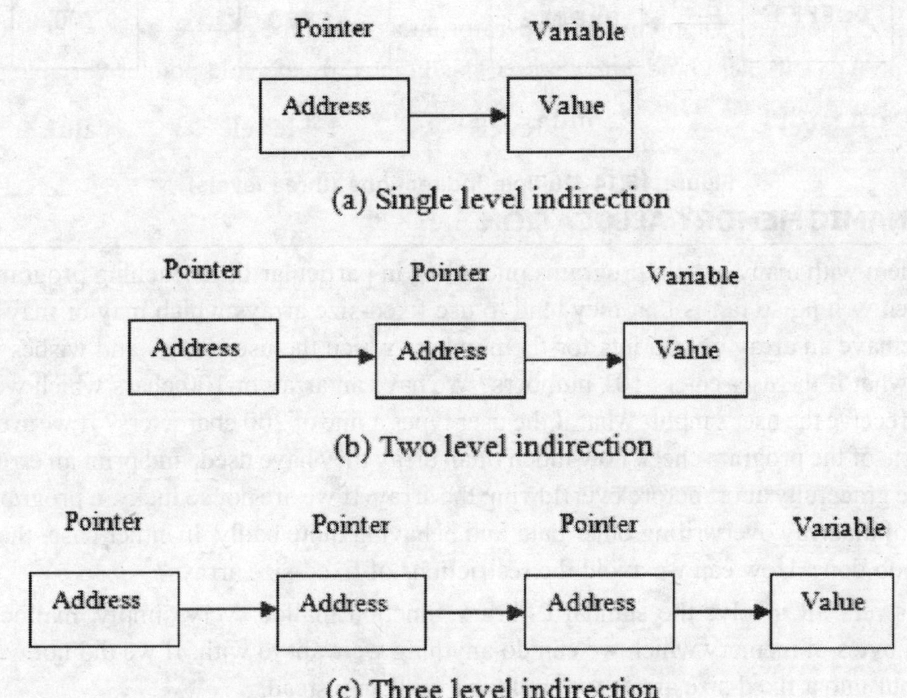

Figure 16.13 Single and Multiple Indirection

Example 16.6: Write C code using multi-stage pointers for accessing the same information.

Answer: Following program segment implements the discussion.

```
/* pointer9.c */ # include<stdio.h>
void main()
{
    int x, *sptr, **dptr, ***tptr;
    x = 200;
    sptr = &x;
    dptr = &sptr;
    tptr = &dptr;
    printf("\n Single level pointer indirection: address: 0x%X Value: %d",sptr, *sptr);
    printf("\n Two level pointer indirection: address: 0x%X Value: %d",dptr, **dptr);
    printf("\n Three level pointer indirection: address: 0x%X Value: %d",tptr,***tptr);
```

OUTPUT
Single level pointer indirection: address: 0xFFF4 Value: 200
Two level pointer indirection: address: 0xFFF2 Value: 200
Three level pointer indirection: address: 0xFFF0 Value: 200

In the above program segment, **sptr** is declared as a pointer to an **int, dptr** as a pointer to pointer to an **int** and **tptr** as a pointer to a pointer to a pointer to an **int.** The pointers point to each other as shown in Figure 16.14.

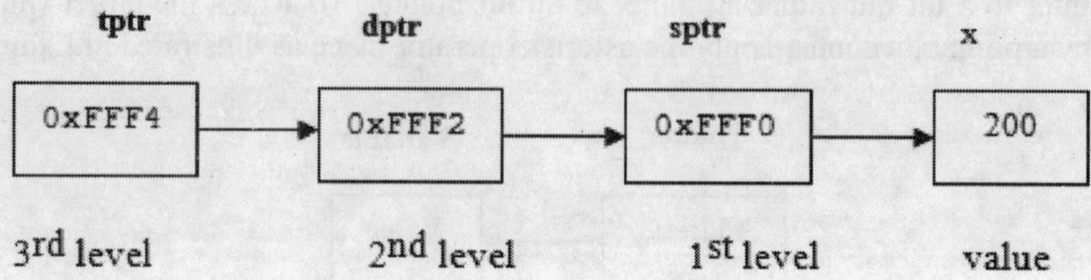

Figure 16.14 Multiple indirections (three levels)

16.11 DYNAMIC MEMORY ALLOCATION

A problem with many simple programs, including in particular little teaching programs such as we have been writing so far, is that they tend to use fixed-size arrays which may or may not be big enough. We have an array of 100 ints for the numbers which the user enters and wishes to find the average of what if the user enters 101 numbers? We have an array of 100 chars which we pass to a function to receive the user's input- what if the user types a line of 200 characters? If we are lucky, the relevant parts of the program check how much of an array they have used, and print an error message or otherwise gracefully abort before overflowing the array. If we are not so lucky, a program may sail off the end of an array overwriting other data and behaving quite badly. In either case, the user does not get his job done. How can we avoid the restrictions of fixed-size arrays?

The answers all involve the standard library function malloc. Very simply, malloc returns a pointer to n bytes of memory which we can do anything we want to with. If we did not want to read a line of input into a fixed-size array, we could use malloc, instead.

Allocating Memory With malloc

It is convenient to allocate memory at runtime using malloc(), calloc(), or other allocation functions. Using this approach permits postponing the decision on the size of the memory block need to store an array, for example, until runtime. Or it permits using a section of memory for the storage of an array of integers at one point in time, and then when that memory is no longer needed it can be freed up for other uses, such as the storage of an array of structures, malloc is declared in stdlib.h, so we #include that header in any program that calls malloc. A "byte" in C is, by definition, an amount of storage suitable for storing one character. For example char* line; line = malloc(100), invocation of malloc gives us exactly as many chars as we ask for. Figure 16.15 illustrates the resulting pointer.

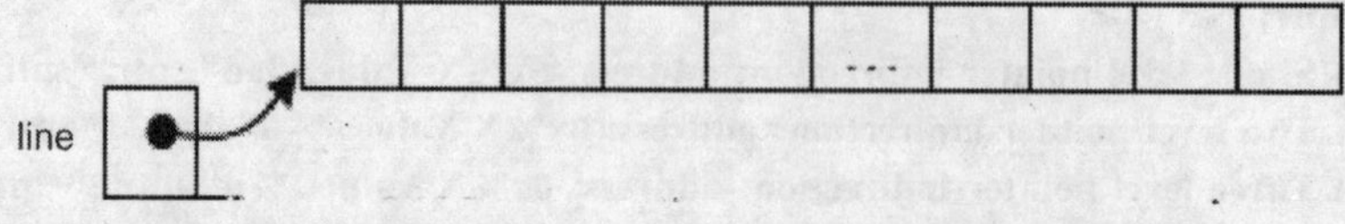

Figure 16.15 Allocating memory space using malloc

The 100 bytes of memory pointed to by line are those allocated by malloc. They are brand-new memory, conceptually a bit different from the memory which the compiler arranges to have allocated automatically for our conventional variables. The 100 boxes in the figure do not have a name next to them, because they are not storage for a variable we have declared.

When memory is allocated, the allocating function (such as malloc(), calloc(), etc.) returns a pointer. The type of this pointer depends on whether we are using an older C compiler or the newer ANSI type compiler. With the older compiler the type of the returned pointer is char, with the ANSI compiler it is void.

If we are using an older compiler, and we want to allocate memory for an array of integers we will have to cast the char pointer returned to an integer pointer. For example, to allocate space for 10 integers syntax is

```
int *iptr;
iptr = (int *)malloc(10 * sizeof(int));
if (iptr == NULL)
{ .. ERROR ROUTINE GOES HERE .. }
```

If we are using an ANSI compliant compiler, malloc() returns a void pointer and since a void pointer can be assigned to a pointer variable of any object type, the (int *) cast shown above is not needed. The array dimension can be determined at runtime and is not needed at compile time. That is, the **10** above could be a variable read in from a data file or keyboard, or calculated based on some need, at runtime. Because of the equivalence between array and pointer notation, once **iptr** has been assigned as above, one can use the array notation. For example,

```
intk;
for(k = 0; k<10; k++)
iptr[k] = 2;
```

to set the values of all elements to 2.

Note: When copying strings, all the strings have a terminating '\0' character. If we use strlen to count the characters in a string that count will not include the trailing '\Q\ so we must add one before calling malloc:

```
char*somestring,*copy;
copy = malloc(strlen(somestring) + 1);     /* +1 for \0 */
/* incomplete - malloc's return value not checked */
strcpy(copy, somestring);
```

What if we are not allocating characters, but integers? If we want to allocate 100 ints, how many bytes is that? If we know how big ints are on our machine (i.e., depending on whether we are using a 16- or 32-bit machine) we could try to compute it ourselves, but it is much safer and more portable to let C compute it for us. C has a sizeof operator, which computes the size, in bytes, of a variable or type. It is just what we need when calling malloc. To allocate space for 100 ints, we could call

```
int *ip = malloc(100 * sizeof(int));
```

The use of the sizeof operator tends to look like a function call, but it is really an operator, and it does its work at compile time.

Since we can use array-indexing syntax on pointers, we can treat a pointer variable after a call to malloc almost exactly as if it were an array. In particular, after the above call to malloc initializes ip to point at storage for 100 ints, we can access ip[0], ip[1],... up to ip[99]. This way, we can get the effect of an array even if we do not know until runtime how big the "array" should be.

Our examples so far have all had a significant omission: they have not checked malloc's return value. Obviously, no real computer has an infinite amount of memory available, so there is no guarantee that malloc will be able to give us as much memory as we ask for. If we call malloc(100000000), or if we call malloc(10) 10,000,000 times, we are probably going to run out of memory.

When malloc is unable to allocate the requested memory, it returns a null pointer. A null pointer, remember, points definitively nowhere. It is a "not a pointer" marker; it is not a pointer we can use. A null pointer can be used as a failure return from a function that returns pointers, and malloc is a perfect. Therefore, whenever we call malloc, it is vital to check the returned pointer before using it. If we call malloc, and it returns a null pointer, and we go off and use that null pointer as if it pointed somewhere, program probably would not last long. Instead, a program should immediately check for a null pointer, and if it receives one, it should at the very least print an error message and exit, or perhaps figure out some way of proceeding without the memory it asked for. But it cannot go on to use the null pointer it got back from malloc in any way, because that null pointer by definition points nowhere. "It cannot use a null pointer in any way" means that the program cannot use the * or [ ] operators on such a pointer value, or pass it to any function that expects a valid pointer.

A call to malloc, with an error check, typically has the form:

```
int *ip = malloc(100 * sizeof(int));
if(ip == NULL)
{
    printf("out of memory\n");
    exit or return
}
```

After printing the error message, this code should return to its caller, or exit from the program entirely; it cannot proceed with the code that would have used ip.

Of course, in our examples so far, we have still limited ourselves to "fixed size" regions of memory, because we have been calling malloc with fixed arguments like 10 or 100. However, since the sizes are now values which can in principle be determined at runtime, we have at least moved beyond having to recompile the program (with a bigger array) to accommodate longer lines, and with a little more work, we could arrange that the "arrays" automatically grew to be as large as required.

Even with a reasonably good understanding of pointers and arrays, one place the newcomer to C is likely to stumble at first is in the dynamic allocation of multi-dimensional arrays. In general, we would like to be able to access elements of such arrays using array notation, not pointer notation, wherever possible. Depending on the application we may or may not know both dimensions at compile time. This leads to a variety of ways to the task.

We have seen that when dynamically allocating a one-dimensional array its dimension can be determined at runtime. Now, when using dynamic allocation of higher order arrays, we never need to know the first dimension at compile time. Whether we need to know the higher dimensions depends on how we go about writing the code. Here we will discuss various methods of dynamically allocating room for two dimensional arrays of integers. First we will consider cases where the 2nd dimension is known at compile time.

Method 1

One way of dealing with the problem is through the use of the typedef keyword. To allocate a two dimensional array of integer's recall that the following two notations result in the same object code being generated:

multi[row][col] = 1;   *(*(multi + row) + col) = 1; It is also true that the

following two notations generate the same code:

multi[row]   and   *(multi + row)

Since the one on the right must evaluate to a pointer, the array notation on the left must also evaluate to a pointer. In fact **multi[0]** will return a pointer to the first integer in the first row, **multi[1]** a pointer to the first integer of the second row, etc. Actually, **multi[n]** evaluates to a pointer to that array of integers that make up the n-th row of two dimensional array. That is, multi can be thought of as an array of arrays and **multi[n]** as a pointer to the n-th array of this array of arrays. Here the word **pointer** is being used to represent an address value. While such usage is common in the literature, when reading such statements one must be careful to distinguish between the constant address of an array and a variable pointer which is a data object in itself. Go through the Example 16.7 which implements the multidimensional dynamic arrays.

Example 16.7: Write C codes which implements multi-dimensional dynamic array.

Answer: Consider the following program segments (Pointer10.C, Pointer11.C, Pointer12.C, and Pointer13.C) which are demonstrating different scenario of the dynamic arrays implementation in C.

```
/* Pointer10.C*/
#include <stdio.h>
#include <stdlib.h>
#define COLS 5
typedef int RowArray[COLS];
RowArray*rptr;
Int main(void) {
intnrows = 10; int row, col;
rptr = malloc(nrows * COLS * sizeof(int));
for (row = 0; row < nrows; row++)
{ for (col = 0; col < COLS; col++)
{
rptr[row][col] = 17; }
}
return 0; }
```

Here we have assumed an ANSI compiler so a cast on the void pointer returned by **malloc()** is not required. If we are using an older C compiler we will have to cast using:

rptr = (RowArray *)malloc(...etc);

Using this approach, **rptr** has all the characteristics of an array name **name,** (except that rptr is modifiable), and array notation may be used throughout the rest of the program. That also means that if we intend to write a function to modify the array contents, we must use COLS as a part of the formal parameter in that function, just as we did when discussing the passing of two dimensional arrays to a function.

Method 2

In the METHOD 1 above, rptr turned out to be a pointer to type "one dimensional array of COLS integers". It turns out that there is syntax which can be used for this type without the need of **typedef.** If we write:

int (*xptr)[COLS];

the variable **xptr** will have all the same characteristics as the variable **rptr** in METHOD 1 above, and we need not use the **typedef** keyword. Here **xptr** is a pointer to an array of integers and the size of array is given by the **#defined COLS.** The parenthesis placement makes the pointer notation predominate, even though the array notation has higher precedence, i.e., had we written

int*xptr[COLS];

We would have defined **xptr** as an array of pointers holding the number of pointers equal to that#defined by COLS. That is not the same thing at all. However, arrays of pointers have their use in the dynamic allocation of two-dimensional arrays, as will be seen in the next 2 methods.

Method 3

Consider the case where we do not know the number of elements in each row at compile time, i.e., both the number of rows and number of columns must be determined at runtime. One way of doing this would be to create an array of pointers to type **int** and then allocate space for each row and point these pointers at each row. For example, consider the following program segment.

```
/**Pointer11.C**/
#include <stdio.h>
#include <stdlib.h>
int main(void)
{
int nrows = 5;     /* Both nrows and ncols could be evaluated */
int ncols = 10;    /* or read in at run time */
int row;
int **rowptr;
rowptr = malloc(nrows * sizeof(int *));
if (rowptr == NULL)
{
    puts("\nFailure to allocate room for row pointersAn");
    exit(0); }
    printf("\n\n\nlndex   Pointer(hex)   Pointer(dec)   Diff.(dec)"); for (row
    = 0; row < nrows; row++)
{
    rowptr[row] = malloc(ncols * sizeof(int));
    if (rowptr[row] == NULL)
    { printf("\nFailure to allocate for row[%d]\n",row); exit(0);
}
    printf("\n%d   %p %d", row, rowptr[row], rowptr[row]);
    if (row > 0)
    printf("%15d",(int)(rowptr[row] - rowptr[row-1])); }
    return 0;
  }
```

OUTPUT

Index	Pointer(hex)	Pointer(dec)	Diff.(dec)
0	0898:0004	4	
1	089A:0004	4	0
2	089C:0004	4	0
3	089E:0004	4	0
4	08A0:0004	4	0

In the above program segment rowptr is a pointer to pointer to type int. In this case it points to the first element of an array of pointers to type int. Consider the number of calls to malloc():

To get the array of pointers	1 call
To get space for the rows	5 calls
Total	6 calls

If we choose to use this approach note that while we can use the array notation to access individual elements of the array, e.g. rowptr[row][col] = 17;, it does not mean that the data in the "two dimensional array" is contiguous in memory. We can, however, use the array notation just as if it were a continuous block of memory. For example, we can write:

rowptr[row][col] = 176;

just as if rowptr were the name of a two dimensional array created at compile time. Of course row and col must be within the bounds of the array we have created, just as with an array created at compile time. If we want to have a contiguous block of memory dedicated to the storage of the elements in the array we can do it as in Method 4.

Method 4

In this method we allocate a block of memory to hold the whole array first. We then create an array of pointers to point to each row. Thus even though the array of pointers is being used, the actual array in memory is contiguous. For example, see the following program segment.

```
/**Pointer12.C**/
#include <stdio.h>
#include <stdlib.h>
int main(void) {
int **rptr;
    int *aptr;
    int *testptr;
    intk;
    int nrows = 5;    /* Both nrows and ncols could be evaluated */
    int ncols = 8;   /* or read in at runtime */
    int row, col;
    /* we now allocate the memory for the array */
    aptr = malloc(nrows * ncols * sizeof(int));
    if (aptr == NULL)
    {
        puts("\nFailure to allocate room for the array"); exit(O);
    }
/* next we allocate room for the pointers to the rows */
rptr = malloc(nrows * sizeof(int *));
if (rptr == NULL)
{
    puts("\nFailure to allocate room for pointers");
    exit(O); }
/* and now we 'point' the pointers */
for (k = 0; k < nrows; k++) {
    rptr[k] = aptr + (k * ncols); }
/* Now we illustrate how the row pointers are incremented */ printf("\n\nlllustrating how row pointers are
incremented"); printf("\n\nlndex   Pointer(hex) Diff.(dec)");
for (row = 0; row < nrows; row++) {
    printf("\n%d        %p", row, rptr[row]);
    if (row > 0)
    printf(" %d",(rptr[row] - rptr[row-1]));
}
```

```
printf("\n\nAnd now we print out the array\n"); for (row = 0; row < nrows; row++) {
        for (col = 0; col < ncols; col++)
        { rptr[row][col] = row + col;
        printf("%d ", rptr[row][col]);
        }
        putchar('\n'); }
    puts("\n");
    /* and here we illustrate that we are, in fact, dealing with a 2 dimensional array in a contiguous block of
memory. */
    printf("And now we demonstrate that they are contiguous in memory\n");
    testptr = aptr;
    for (row = 0; row < nrows; row++)
    {
        for (col = 0; col < ncols; col++)
        { printf("%d ", *(testptr++));
        }
        putchar('\n'); } return 0;
    }
```

OUTPUT		
Illustrating how row pointers are incremented		
Index	Pointer(hex)	Diff.(dec)
0	08B0:0004	
1	08B0:0014	8
2	08B0:0024	8
3	08B0:0034	8
4	08B0:0044	8

```
And now we print out the array
    0      1      2      3      4      5      6      7
    1      2      3      4      5      6      7      8
    2      3      4      5      6      7      8      9
    3      4      5      6      7      8      9      10
And now we demonstrate that they are contiguous in memory
    0      1      2      3      4      5      6      7
    1      2      3      4      5      6      7      8
    2      3      4      5      6      7      8      9
    3      4      5      6      7      8      9      10
    4      5      6      7      8      9      10     11
Consider again, the number of calls to malloc()
    To get room for the array itself          1 call
    To get room for the array of ptrs         1 call
    Total                                     2 calls
```

Now, each call to **malloc()** creates additional space overhead since **malloc()** is generally implemented by the operating system forming a linked list which contains data concerning the size of the block. But, more importantly, with large arrays (several hundred rows) keeping track of what needs to be freed when the time comes can be more cumbersome. This, combined with the contiguousness of the data block that permits initialization to all zeroes using **memset()** would seem to make the second alternative the preferred one. As a final example on multidimensional arrays we will illustrate the dynamic allocation of a three dimensional array. This example will illustrate one more thing to watch when doing this kind of allocation. For reasons cited above we will use the approach outlined in alternative two. Consider the following code:

```
/**Pointer13.C**/
#include <stdio.h>
#include <stdlib.h>
#include <stddef.h>
intX_DIM=16;
intY_DIM=5;
intZ_DIM=3;
int main(void) {
char*space;
char***Arr3D;
int y, z;
ptrdiffj diff;
/* first we set aside space for the array itself */
space = malloc(X_DIM * Y_DIM * Z_DIM * sizeof(char));
/* next we allocate space of an array of pointers, each to eventually point to the first element of a 2 dimensional array of pointers to pointers */
Arr3D = malloc(Z_DIM * sizeof(char**));
/* and for each of these we assign a pointer to a newly allocated array of pointers to a row */
for(z = 0;z<Z_DIM;z++) { Arr3D[z] = malloc(Y_DIM * sizeof(char*));
/* and for each space in this array we put a pointer to the first element of each row in the array space originally allocated */
for(y = 0;y<Y_DIM;y++) {
Arr3D[z][y] = space + (z*(X_DIM * Y_DIM) + y*X_DIM); } }
/* And, now we check each address in our 3D array to see if the indexing of the Arr3d pointer leads through in a continuous manner*/
for(z = 0;z<Z_DIM;z++) {
printf("Location of array %d is %p\n", z, *Arr3D[z]);
for(y = 0;y<Y_DIM;y++)
{ printf(" Array %d and Row %d starts at %p", z, y, Arr3D[z][y]);
                    diff = Arr3D[z][y] - space;
          printf("    diff = %d ",diff);
     printf(" z= %d y = %d\n", z, y); } } return
   0;
}
```

OUTPUT

```
Location of array 0 is 0885:0004
Array 0 and Row 0 starts at 0885:0004        diff = 0 z= 0 y = 0
Array 0 and Row 1 starts at 0885:0014        diff = 16 z= 0 y = 1
Array 0 and Row 2 starts at 0885:0024        diff = 32 z= 0 y = 2
Array 0 and Row 3 starts at 0885:0034        diff = 48 z= 0 y = 3
Array 0 and Row 4 starts at 0885:0044        diff = 64  z= 0  y = 4
```

Location of array 1 is 0885:0054	
Array 1 and Row 0 starts at 0885:0054	diff = 80 z = 1 y = 0
Array 1 and Row 1 starts at 0885:0064	diff = 96 z = 1 y = 1
Array 1 and Row 2 starts at 0885:0074	diff = 112 z = 1 y = 2
Array 1 and Row3 starts at0885:0084	diff =128 z=1 y = 3
Array 1 and Row 4 starts at 0885:0094	diff = 144 z =1 y = 4
Location of array 2 is 0885:00A4	
Array 2 and Row 0 starts at 0885:00A4	diff = 160 z = 2 y = 0
Array 2 and Row 1 starts at 0885:00B4	diff = 176 z = 2 y = 1
Array 2 and Row 2 starts at 0885:00C4	diff = 192 z = 2 y = 2
Array 2 and Row 3 starts at 0885:00D4	diff= 208 z=2 y=3
Array2 and Row4 starts at 0885:00E4	diff = 224 z = 2y = 4

There are a couple of points that should be making clear. Let us start with the line which reads:

Arr3D[z][y] = space + (z*(X_DIM * Y_DIM) + y*X_DIM);

Note that here space is a character pointer, which is the same type as **Arr3D[z][y].** It is important that when adding an integer, such as that obtained by evaluation of the expression **(z*(X_DIM * Y_DIM) + y*X_DIM),** to a pointer, the result is a new pointer value. And when assigning pointer values to pointer variables the data types of the value and variable must match.

Freeing Memory

Memory allocated with malloc lasts as long as we want it to. It does not automatically disappear when a function returns, as automatic-duration variables do, but it does not have to remain for the entire duration of a program, either. Just as we can use malloc to control exactly when and how much memory we allocate, we can also control exactly when we deallocate it.

In fact, many programs use memory on a transient basis. They allocate some memory, use it for a while, but then reach a point where they do not need that particular piece any more. Because memory is not inexhaustible, it is a good idea to deallocate (i.e., release or free) memory programs are no longer using.

Dynamically allocated memory is deallocated with the free function. If p contains a pointer previously returned by malloc, we can call

free(p);

which will "give the memory back" to the stock of memory (sometimes called the "arena" or "pool") from which malloc requests are satisfied. Calling free is sort of the ultimate in recycling: it costs us almost nothing, and the memory we give back is immediately usable by other parts of a program. Theoretically, it may even be usable by other programs.

Freeing unused memory is a good idea, but it's not mandatory. When a program exits, any memory which it has allocated but not freed should be automatically released. If a computer is to somehow "lose" memory just because a program forgot to free it, that would indicate a problem or deficiency in the operating system.

Naturally, once we have freed some memory we must remember not to use it any more. After calling

free(p);

It is probably the case that p still points at the same memory. However, since we have given it back, it is now "available," and a later call to malloc might give that memory to some other part of a program. If the variable p is a global variable or will otherwise stick around for a while, one good way to record the fact that it is not to be used any more would be to set it to a null pointer:

```
free(p);
p = NULL;
```

Now we do not even have the pointer to the freed memory any more, and (as long as we check to see that p is non-NULL before using it), we would not misuse any memory via the pointer p.

When thinking about malloc, free, and dynamically allocated memory in general, remember again the distinction between a pointer and what it points to. If we call malloc to allocate some memory, and store the pointer which malloc gives in a local pointer variable, what happens when the function containing the local pointer variable returns? If the local pointer variable has automatic duration (which is the default, unless the variable is declared static), it will disappear when the function returns. But for the pointer variable to disappear says nothing about the memory pointed to. That memory still exists and, as far as malloc and free are concerned, is still allocated. The only thing that has disappeared is the pointer variable which pointed at the allocated memory. Furthermore, if it contained the only copy of the pointer once it disappears, we will have no way of freeing the memory, and no way of using it, either. Using memory and freeing memory both require that we have at least one pointer to the memory.

Reallocating Memory Blocks

Sometimes we are not sure at first how much memory will need. For example, if we need to store a series of items, programmer read and if the only way to know how many there are is to read them until the user types some "end" signal, we will have noway of knowing, as we begin reading and storing the first few, how many we will have seen by the time we do see that "end" marker. We might want to allocate room for, say, 100 items, and if the user enters a 101st item before entering the "end" marker, we might wish for a way to say "uh, malloc, remember those 100 items we asked for? Could one change his/her mind and have 200 instead?"

In fact, we can do exactly this, with the realloc function. We hand realloc an old pointer (such as we received from an initial call to malloc) and a new size, and realloc does what it can to give a chunk of memory big enough to hold the new size. For example, if we wanted the ip variable from an earlier example to point at 200 ints instead of 100, we could try calling

```
ip = realloc(ip, 200 * sizeof(int));
```

Since we always want each block of dynamically-allocated memory to be contiguous (so that we can treat it as if it were an array), and realloc have to worry about the case where realloc cannot make the old block of memory bigger "in place," but rather has to relocate it elsewhere in order to find enough contiguous space for the new requested size. The realloc does this by returning a new pointer. If realloc was able to make the old block of memory bigger, it returns the same pointer. If realloc has to go elsewhere to get enough contiguous memory, it returns a pointer to the new memory, after copying a old data there. In this case, after it makes the copy, it frees the old block. Finally, if realloc cannot find enough memory to satisfy the new request at all, it returns a null pointer. Therefore, we usually do not want to overwrite a old pointer with realloc's return value until we have tested it to make sure it is not a null pointer. For example, see the following code segment:

```
int *newp;
newp = realloc(ip, 200 * sizeof(int));
if(newp != NULL)
```

```
ip = newp; else{
printf("out of memory\n");
I* exit or return */
/* but ip still points at 100 ints */ }
```

If realloc returns something other than a null pointer, it succeeded, and we set ip to what it returned. We have either set ip to what it used to be or to a new pointer, but in either case, it points to where our data is now. If realloc returns a null pointer, however, we hang on to our old pointer in ip which still points at original 100 values.

Putting this all together, here is a piece of code segment which reads lines of text from the user, treats each line as an integer by calling atoi(), and stores each integer in a dynamically-allocated "array":

```
#defineMAXLINE100
charline[MAXLINE];
int*ip;
int nalloc, nitems;
nalloc = 100;
ip = malloc(nalloc * sizeof(int)); /* initial allocation */
if(ip == NULL)
{
    printf("out of memory\n");
    exit(1); }
nitems = 0;
while(getline(line, MAXLINE) != EOF) {
    if(nitems >= nalloc)    /* increase allocation */ int *newp;
            nalloc+=100;
            newp = realloc(ip, nalloc * sizeof(int)); if(newp ==
            NULL) {
printf("out of memory\n");
exit(1);
}
            ip = newp; }
        ip[nitems++] = atoi(line); }
```

We use two different variables to keep track of the "array" pointed to by ip. The nalloc is how many elements we have allocated, and nitems is how many of them are in use. Whenever we are about to store another item in the "array," if nitems >= nalloc, the old "array" is full, and it is time to call realloc to make it bigger.

Finally, we might ask what the return type of malloc and realloc is, if they are able to return pointers to char or pointers to int or pointers to any other type. The answer is that both of these functions are declared in stdlib.h as returning a type we have not seen, void * (that is, pointer to void).

16.12 The sizeof and Storage Allocation

The sizeof operator returns the size in bytes of its operand. Whether the result of sizeof is unsigned int or unsigned long is implementation defined-which is why the declaration of malloc above ducked the issue by omitting any parameter information; normally we use the stdlib.h header file to declare malloc correctly. Here is the last example done portably:

```
#include <stdlib.h>    /* declares malloc() */
float *fp;
fp = (float *)malloc(sizeof(float));
```

The operand of sizeof only has to be parenthesized if it is a type name, as it was in the example. If we are using the name of a data object instead, then the parentheses can be omitted, but they rarely are.

```
#include <stdlib.h>
Int *ip, ar[100];
ip = (int *)malloc(sizeof  ar);
```

In this example, the array ar is an array of 100 ints; after the call to malloc (assuming that it was successful), ip will point to a region of store that can also be treated as an array of 100 ints. The fundamental unit of storage in C is the char, and by definition sizeof(char); is equal to 1, so we could allocate space for an array of ten chars with malloc(10); while to allocate room for an array of ten ints, we would have to use malloc(sizeof(int[10])); If malloc cannot find enough free space to satisfy a request it returns a null pointer to indicate failure. For historical reasons, the stdio.h header file contains a defined constant called NULL which is traditionally used to check the return value from malloc and some other library functions. An explicit 0 or (void *) 0 could equally well be used.

As a first illustration of the use of malloc, here is a program which reads up to MAXSTRING strings from its input and sort them into alphabetical order using the library strcmp() function. The strings are terminated by a YT character. The sort is done by keeping an array of pointers to the strings and simply exchanging the pointers until the order is correct. This saves having to copy the strings themselves, which improves the efficiency somewhat.

The example is done first using fixed size arrays, then another version uses malloc and allocates space for the strings at runtime. Unfortunately, the array of pointers is still fixed in size: a better solution would use a linked list or similar data structure to store the pointers and would have no fixed arrays at all. At the moment, we have not seen how to do that. The steps for the above discussion is:

```
while(number of strings read < MAXSTRING && input still remains)
{
read next string;
}
sort array of pointers; print array
of pointers; exit;
```

A number of functions are used to implement the above steps.

char*next_string(char *destination)

Read a line of characters terminated by YT from the program's input. The first MAXLEN-1 characters are written into the array pointed to by destination. If the first character read is EOF, return a null pointer, otherwise return the address of the start of the string (destination). On return, destination always points to a null-terminated string.

void sort_arr(const char *p_array[])

p_array[] is an array of pointers to characters. The array can be arbitrarily long; its end is indicated by the first element containing a null pointer.

sort_arr sorts the pointers so that the pointers point to strings which are in alphabetical order when the array is traversed in index order.

void print_arr(const char*p_array[])

It is like sort_arr, but prints the strings in index order.

It will help to understand the examples if we remember that in an expression, an array's name is converted to the address of its first element. Similarly, for a two-dimensional array (such as strings below), then the expression strings [1][2] has type char, but strings [1] has type "array of char" which is therefore converted to the address of the first element: it is equivalent to &strings [1][0]. Go through the Example 16.8 which demonstrates the above discussion.

Example 16.8: Write C code which demonstrates how type of array changes as the dimension changes.

Answer: Following the codes (Pointer14.c, Pointer15.c, Pointer16.c, and Pointer17.c) for the above discussion and other scenarios which will be assumed before writing the code.

```
/* Pointer14.c*/
#include <stdio.h>
#include <stdlib.h>
#include <string.h>
#define MAXSTRING 50     /* max no. of strings */
#define MAXLEN     80     /* max length, of strings */
void print_arr(const char*p_arrayQ); void
sort_arr(const char*p_arrayQ);
char*next_string(char*destination);
main() {
I* leave room for null at end */
char *p_array[MAXSTRING+1];
/* storage for strings*/
charstrings[MAXSTRING][MAXLEN];
/* count of strings read */ int
nstrings;
nstrings = 0; while(nstrings < MAXSTRING && next_string(strings[nstrings]) != 0){
p_array[nstrings] = strings[nstrings]; nstrings++; }
I* terminate p_array */ p_array[nstrings] = 0;
sort_arr(p_array);
print_arr(p_array);
    exit(1);
}
void print_arr(const char*p_arrayQ)
{
    int index;
    for(index = 0; p_array[index] != 0; index++)
            printf("%s\n", p_array[index]);
}
void sort_arr(const char*p_arrayQ) {
    int comp_val, low_index, hi_index; const
    char *tmp;
for(low_index=0;p_array[low_index]!=0&&p_array[low_index+1]!=0; low_index++) {
    for(hi_index = low_index+1;  p_array[hi_index] != 0; hi_index++) {
        comp_val=strcmp(p_array[hi_index], p_array[low_index]);
       if(comp_val >= 0)
            continue; I* swap strings */ tmp =
        p_array[hi_index]; p_array[hi_index] =
        p_array[low_index]; p_array[low_index] =
       tmp;
    }
}
}
char*next_string(char*destination)
{
    char*cp;
    intc;
cp = destination;
while((c = getchar()) != '\n' && c != EOF) {
if(cp-destination < MAXLEN-1) *cp++ = c; }
```

```
*cp = 0; if(c == EOF && cp == destination)
    return(O);
return(destination); }
```

It is no accident that next_string returns a pointer. We can now dispense with the strings array by getting next_string to allocate its own storage.

```
/* Pointer15.c*/
#include <stdio.h>
#include <stdlib.h>
#include <string.h>
#define MAXSTRING       50     /* max no. of strings */
#define MAXLEN                 80        /* max length, of strings */
void print_arr(const char*p_arrayQ); void sort_arr(const char*p_arrayQ); char*next_string(void);
main() {
    char *p_array[MAXSTRING+1];
    int nstrings;
    nstrings = 0;
    while(nstrings < MAXSTRING && (p_array[nstrings] = next_string()) != 0) {
            nstrings++; } /* terminate p_array */
    p_array[nstrings] = 0;
sort_arr(p_array);
print_arr(p_array);
exit(0); }

void print_arr(const char*p_arrayQ) {
    int index;
for(index = 0; p_array[index] != 0; index++)
printf("%s\n", p_array[index]); }
void sort_arr(const char*p_arrayQ) {
    int comp_val, low_index, hi_index;
    const char *tmp;
for(low_index = 0; p_array[low_index] != 0 && p_array[low_index+1] != 0;
low_index++)
{
            for(hi_index = low_index+1; p_array[hi_index] != 0; hi_index++)
    {
            comp_val=strcmp(p_array[hi_index],
            p_array[low_index]);
            if(comp_val >= 0)
                    continue;
            I* swap strings */
            tmp = p_array[hi_index];
            p_array[hi_index] = p_array[low_index];
            p_array[low_index] = tmp;
    }
}
}
char*next_string(void) {
    char*cp, "destination;
    intc;
destination = (char*)malloc(MAXLEN); if(destination != 0)
{
    cp = destination;
    while((c = getchar()) != '\n' && c != EOF) {
    if(cp-destination < MAXLEN-1) *cp++ = c; }
    *cp = 0;
if(c == EOF && cp == destination) return(O); }
return(destination); }
```

Finally, for the extremely brave, here is the whole thing with even p_array allocated using malloc. Further, most of the array indexing is rewritten to use pointer notation. If readers are feeling queasy, skip this example. It is hard. One word of explanation: char**p means a pointer to a pointer to a character. Many C programmers find this hard to deal with.

```
/* Pointer16.c*/
#include <stdio.h>
#include <stdlib.hi>
#include <string.h>
#define MAXSTRING 50       /* max no. of strings */
#define MAXLEN             80     /* max length, of strings */
void print_arr(const char**p_array); void
sort_arr(const char**p_array);
char*next_string(void);

main()
{
    char**p_array;
    int nstrings;  /* count of strings read */
    p_array = (char**)malloc(sizeof(char*[MAXSTRING+1]));
    if(p_array == 0){
            printf("No memory\n");
            exit(O); }
    nstrings = 0;
while(nstrings < MAXSTRING && (p_array[nstrings] = next_string()) != 0) {
    nstrings++; }
/* terminate p_array */ p_array[nstrings] = 0;
sort_arr(p_array); print_arr(p_array); exit(EXIT_SUCCESS); }
void print_arr(const char**p_array)
{
while(*p_array)
    printf("%s\n", *p_array++); }
void sort_arr(const char**p_array) {
    const char**lo_p, **hi_p, *tmp;
    for(lo_p = p_array; *lo_p != 0 && *(lo_p+1) != 0; lo_p++) {
            for(hi_p = lo_p+1; *hi_p != 0; hi_p++) {
                    if(strcmp(*hi_p, *lo_p) >= 0)
    continue; /* swap strings */ tmp
    = *hi_p; *hi_p = *lo_p; *lo_p =
    tmp; } } }
    char*next_string(void) {
    char*cp, "destination; intc;
    destination = (char*)malloc(MAXLEN);
    if(destination != 0){ cp = destination;
        while((c = getchar()) != '\n' && c != EOF) {
        if(cp-destination < MAXLEN-1) *cp++ =
        c; }
        *cp = 0;
if(c == EOF && cp == destination) return(O); }
return(destination); }
```

To further illustrate the use of malloc, another example program follows which can cope with arbitrarily long strings. It simply reads strings from its standard input, looking for a newline character to mark the end of the string, and then prints the string on its standard output. It stops when it detects end-of-file. The characters are put into an array, the end of the string being indicated by a zero. The newline is not stored, but used to detect when a full line of input should be printed on the output. The program does not know how long the string will be, so it starts by allocating ten characters which are enough for a short string.

If the string is more than ten characters long, malloc is called to allocate room for the current string plus ten more characters. The current characters are copied into the new space, the old storage previously allocated is released and the program continues using the new storage.

To release storage allocated by malloc, the library function free() is used. If we do not release storage when it is not needed any more, it just hangs around taking up space. Using free allows it to be "given away", or at least re-used later.

The program reports errors by using fprintf, a close cousin of printf. The only difference between them is that fprintf takes an additional first argument which indicates where its output should go. There are two constants of the right type for this purpose defined in stdio.h. Using stdout indicates that the program's standard output is to be used; stderr refers to the program's standard error stream. On some systems both may be the same, but other systems do make the distinction.

```
/* Pointer17.c*/
#include <stdio.h>
#include <stdlib.h>
#include <string.h>
#define GROW_BY 10     /* string grows by 10 chars */
main() {
    char*str_p, *next_p, *tmp_p;
    int ch, need, chars_read;
    if(GROW_BY < 2) {
    fprintf(stderr, "Growth constant too small\n"); exit(O); }
    str_p = (char*)malloc(GROW_BY);
    if(str_p == NULL)
    {
    fprintf(stderr,"No initial store\n"); exit(O); }
    next_p = str_p; chars_read = 0;
    while((ch = getchar()) != EOF) {
        /* Completely restart at each new line. There will always be room for the
        * terminating zero in the string, because of the check further down,
        * unless GROW_BY is less than 2, and that has already been checked. */ if(ch == '\n')
        {
        /* indicate end of line */ *next_p = 0;
        printf("%s\n", str_p); free(str_p);
        chars_read = 0;
        str_p = (char*)malloc(GROW_BY); if(str_p ==
        NULL) {
            fprintf(stderr,"No initial store\n"); exit(0); }
        next_p = str_p; continue; }
    /* Have we reached the end of the current allocation ? */
    if(chars_read == GROW_BY-1) {
  *next_p = 0;    /* mark end of string */ /* use pointer subtraction to find length of current string. */ need =
next_p - str_p +1; tmp_p = (char*)malloc(need+GROW_BY); if(tmp_p == NULL) {
  fprintf(stderr,"No more store\n");
  exit(0);
  }
  /* Copy the string using library. */
  strcpy(tmp_p, str_p);
  free(str_p);
```

```
str_p = tmp_p;
    I* and reset next_p, character count */
    next_p = str_p + need-1;
    chars_read = 0; }
/* Put character at end of current string. */
*next_p++ = ch; chars_read++; }
/* EOF - but do unprinted characters exist?   */
if(str_p - next_p)
{
    *next_p = 0;
    fprintf(stderr,"Incomplete last line\n");
    printf("%s\n",str_p);
}
    exit(0); }
```

This may not be a particularly realistic example of how to handle arbitrarily long strings; for one thing, the maximum storage demand is twice the amount needed for the longest string-but it does actually work. It also costs rather a lot in terms of copying around. Both problems could be reduced by using the library realloc function instead.

A more sophisticated method might use a linked list, implemented with the use of structures. That would have its drawbacks too though, because then the standard library routines would not work for a different method of storing strings.

The type of sizeof

Now the question arise just what this does:

sizeof (sizeof (anything legal))

That is to say, what type does the result of sizeof have? The answer is that it is implementation defined, and will be either unsigned long or unsigned int, depending on an implementation. There are two safe things to do: either always cast the return value to unsigned long, as the examples have done, or to use the defined type sizej provided in the stddef.h header file. For example,

```
/*Pointer18.c*/
 #include <stddef.h> #include <stdio.h>
#include <stdlib.h>
main() {
    size_t sz;
    sz = sizeof(sz);
    printf("size of sizeof is %lu\n", (unsigned long)sz);
    exit(O); }
```

What sizeof cannot do?

One common mistake made by beginners is shown below: /*Pointer19.c*/

```
 #include <stdio.h>
#include <stdlib.h>
const char arrQ = "hello";
const char *cp = arr;
main() {
    printf("Size of arr%lu\n", (unsigned long) sizeof(arr));
    printf("Size of *cp %lu\n", (unsigned long) sizeof(*cp));
    exit(O); }
```

The numbers printed will not be the same. The first will, correctly, identify the size of arr as 6; five characters followed by a null. The second one will always, on every system, print 1. That is because the type of *cp is const char, which can only have a size of 1, whereas the type of arr is different: array of const char. The confusion arises because this is the one place that the use of an array is not converted into a pointer first. It is never possible, using sizeof, to find out how long an array a pointer points to; we must have a genuine array name instead.

16.13 POINTERS AND STRINGS

The study of strings is useful to further tie in the relationship between pointers and arrays. It also makes it easy to illustrate how some of the C string functions can be implemented. Finally it illustrates how and when pointers can and should be passed to functions.

In C, strings are arrays of characters. This is not necessarily true in other languages. In BASIC, Pascal, FORTRAN and various other languages, a string has its own data type. But in C it does not. In C a string is an array of characters terminated with a binary zero character ('\0'). For example, consider the following code segment,

```
charstring1[40];
string1[0] = 'R';
string1[1] = 'e';
string1[2] = 'd';
string1[3] = '\0';
```

While one would never build a string like this, the end result is a string in that it is an array of characters terminated with a '\0' character. By definition, in C, a string is an array of characters terminated with the null character ('\0'). Be aware that '\0' is not the same as "NULL". It occupies one byte of memory. NULL, on the other hand, is the name of the macro used to initialize null pointers. NULL is #defined in a header file in C compiler, \0 may notbe#definedatall.

Since writing the above code would be very time consuming, C permits two alternate ways of achieving the same thing as

```
charstring1[40] = {'R', 'e', 'd', '\0',};
```

But this also takes more typing than is convenient. So, C permits:

```
charstring1[40] = "Red";
```

When the double quotes are used, instead of the single quotes the '\0' is automatically appended to the end of the string. In all of the above cases, the same thing happens. The compiler sets aside a contiguous block of memory 40 bytes long to hold characters and initialized it such that the first 4 characters are Red\0. Go through the Example 16.9 which demonstrates the implementation.

Example 16.9: Write C code which duplicates a string with the help of pointer.

Answer: Consider the following program segment which demonstrates the real implementation of a string on the computer.

```
/* Pointer20.C */
#include <stdio.h>
char string1[80] = "A string to be used for demonstration purposes";
charstring2[80];
int main(void)
{
    char *pA;    /* a pointer to type character */
    char *pB;    /* another pointer to type character */
    puts(string1); /* show string A*/
    pA = string1;   /* point pA at string A */
    puts(pA);/* show what pA is pointing to */
    pB = string2;   /* point pB at string B */
    putchar('\n');       /* move down one line on the screen */
    while(*pA != '\0')   /* line A (see text) */
{
```

```
*pB++ = *pA++;   /* line B (see text) */ }
*pB = '\0';      /* line C (see text) */
puts(string2);   /* show string2 on screen */
return 0; }
```

OUTPUT
A string to be used for demonstration purposes
A string to be used for demonstration purposes
A string to be used for demonstration purposes

In the above program segment we defined two character arrays of 80 characters each. Since these are globally defined, they are initialized to all '\0's first. Then, string1 has the first 42 characters initialized to the string in quotes. We have declared two character pointers (*pA and *pB) to show the string on the screen. We have shown output on the screen using function puts(stringl) statement. We then point the pointer pA at string1. That is, by means of the assignment statement we copy the address of string1 [0] into variable pA. Now with the help of while loop copying the contents of pA to pB one character at time. Finally we have associated '\0'character to pB and puts(pB) displays the string. Consider here that the function prototype for puts() is:

intputs(constchar*s);

For the moment, ignore the const. The parameter passed to puts() is a pointer, that is the value of a pointer (since all parameters in C are passed by value), and the value of a pointer is the address to which it points, or, simply, an address. Thus, when we write puts(string1); as we have seen, we are passing the address of string1 [0]. Similarly when we write puts(pA); we are passing the same address, since we have set pA = string1;

Given that, follow the code down to the while() statement on line A.

Line A states: While the character pointed to by pA (i.e., *pA) is not a \0 character (i.e., the terminating '\0'), do the following:

Line B states: copy the character pointed to by pA to the space pointed to by pB, then increment pA so it points to the next character and pB so it points to the next space.

When we have copied the last character, pA now points to the terminating \0 character and the loop ends. However, we have not copied the \0 character. And, by definition a string in C **must** be \0 terminated. So, we add the \0 character with line C.

It is very educational to run this program with C debugger while watching string1, string2 **pA** and **pB** and single stepping through the program. It is even more educational if instead of simply defining **string2D** as has been done above, initialize it also with something like:

string2[80]="12345678901234567890123456789012345678901234567890"

where the number of digits used is greater than the length of string1 and then repeat the single stepping procedure while watching the above variables.

Getting back to the prototype for **puts()** for a moment, the "const" used as a parameter modifier informs the user that the function will not modify the string pointed to by s, i.e., it will treat that string as a constant. Of course, what the above program illustrates is a simple way of copying a string. After playing with the above until we have a good understanding of what is happening, we can proceed to creating replacement for the standard **strcpy()** that comes with C is

```
char *my_strcpy(char*destination, char*source)
{
    char*p = destination;
    while ("source != '\0')
```

```
    {
        *p++ = *source++;
    }
    *p = '\0';
    return
  destination; }
```

In this case, we have followed the practice used in the standard routine of returning a pointer to the destination. Again, the function is designed to accept the values of two character pointers, i.e., addresses, and thus in the previous program we could write:

```
int main(void)
{
    puts(string2);
}
```

We have deviated slightly from the form used in C which would have the prototype:

char*my_strcpy(char*destination, const char*source);

Here the "const" modifier is used to assure the user that the function will not modify the contents pointed to by the source pointer. We can prove this by modifying the function above, and its prototype, to include the "const" modifier as shown. Then, within the function we can add a statement which attempts to change the contents of that which is pointed to by source, such as:

***source = 'X';**

which would normally change the first character of the string to an X. The const modifier should cause compiler to catch this as an error.

Now, let us consider some of the things the above examples have shown us. First, consider the fact that *ptr++ is to be interpreted as returning the value pointed to by **ptr** and then incrementing the pointer value. This has to do with the precedence of the operators. Were we to write **(*ptr)++** we would increment, not the pointer, but that which the pointer points to, i.e., if used on the first character of the above example string the T would be incremented to 'U'.

Recall again that a string is nothing more than an array of characters, with the last character being a '\0'. What we have done above is deal with copying an array. It happens to be an array of characters but the technique could be applied to an array of integers, doubles, etc. In those cases, however, we would not be dealing with strings and hence the end of the array would not be marked with a special value like the '\0' character. We could implement a version that relied on a special value to identify the end. For example, we could copy an array of positive integers by marking the end with a negative integer. On the other hand, it is more usual that when we write a function to copy an array of items other than strings we pass the function the number of items to be copied as well as the address of the array, e.g. something like the following prototype might indicate:

void int_copy(int *ptrA, int*ptrB, int nbr);

where **nbr** is the number of integers to be copied. We might want to play with this idea and create an array of integers and see if we can write the function **int_copy()** and make it work.

This permits using functions to manipulate large arrays. For example, if we have an array of 5000 integers that we want to manipulate with a function, we need only pass to that function the address of the array (and any auxiliary information such as **nbr** above, depending on what we are doing). The array itself does not get passed, i.e., the whole array is not copied and put on the stack before calling the function, only its address is sent.

This is different from passing, say an integer, to a function. When we pass an integer we make a copy of the integer, i.e., get its value and put it on the stack. Within the function any manipulation of the value passed can in no way effect the original integer. But, with arrays and pointers we can pass the address of the variable and hence manipulate the values of the original variables. For example, see the next form of the my_strcpy() function defined earlier.

```
char *my_strcpy(char dest[], char sourceQ) {
    int i = 0;
    while (source[i] != '\0')
    { destfi] = sourcefi]:
    i++; }
dest[i] = '\0';
return dest; }
```

Recall that strings are arrays of characters. Here we have chosen to use array notation instead of pointer notation to do the actual copying. The results are the same, i.e., the string gets copied using this notation just as accurately as it did before. This raises some interesting points which we will discuss.

Since parameters are passed by value, in both the passing of a character pointer or the name of the array as above, what actually gets passed is the address of the first element of each array. Thus, the numerical value of the parameter passed is the same whether we use a character pointer or an array name as a parameter. This would tend to imply that somehow source[i] is the same as *(source+i). In fact, this is true, i.e., wherever one writes source[i] it can be replaced with "(source + i) without any problems. In fact, the compiler will create the same code in either case. Thus we see that pointer arithmetic is the same thing as array indexing. Either syntax produces the same result.

This is not saying that pointers and arrays are the same thing, they are not. We are only saying that to identify a given element of an array we have the choice of two syntaxes, one using array indexing and the other using pointer arithmetic, which yield identical results. Now, looking at this last expression, part of it, (source + i), is a simple addition using the + operator and the rules of C state that such an expression is commutative. That is (source + i) is identical to (i + source). Thus we could write *(i + source) just as easily as "(source + i). But *(i + source) could have come from i[source]. From above discussion it is concluded that following code slices are valid.

```
    char source[20]:
    int i;
writing
    source[3] = 'x';
is the same as writing
    3[source] = 'x';
```

Setup an array of characters, integers or longs, etc and assigned the 3rd or 4th element a value using the conventional approach and then print out that value. Then reverse the array notation as we have done above. A good compiler will not balk and the results will be identical. Now, looking at function above, when we write:

dest[i] = source[i]:

due to the fact that array indexing and pointer arithmetic yield identical results, we can write this as:

***(dest + i) = *(source + i);**

But, this takes 2 additions for each value taken on by i. Additions, generally speaking, take more time than increment (such as those done using the ++ operator as in i++). This may not be true in modern optimizing compilers, but one can never be sure. Thus, the pointer version may be a bit faster than the array version. Another way to speed up the pointer version would be to change:

```
while (*source != '\0')
```

to simply

```
while (*source)
```

Since the value within the parenthesis will go to zero (FALSE) at the same time in either case.

16.14 POINTER & STRINGS AND ARRAYS OF STRINGS

Let us go back to strings for a bit. In the following all assignments are to be understood as being global, i.e., made outside of any function, including main(). We pointed out earlier that we could write:

charstring1[40] = "Red";

which would allocate space for a 40 byte array and put the string in the first 4 bytes (three for the characters in the quotes and a 4th to handle the terminating '\0'). Actually, if all we wanted to do was store the name "Red" we could write:

char my_name[] = "Red";

and the compiler would count the characters, leave room for the \0 character and store the total of the four characters in memory the location of which would be returned by the array name, in this case my_name. In some code, instead of the above, we might see:

char*my_name = "Red";

which is an alternate approach. Is there a difference between these? The answer is yes. Using the array notation 4 bytes of storage in the static memory block are taken up, one for each character and one for the terminating \0 character. But, in the pointer notation the same 4 bytes required, plus N bytes to store the pointer variable my_name (where N depends on the system but is usually a minimum of 2 bytes and can be 4 or more).

In the array notation, my_name is short for &my_name[0] which is the address of the first element of the array. Since the location of the array is fixed during run time, this is a constant (not a variable). In the pointer notation **my_name** is a variable. As to which is the better method, that depends on what one is going to do within the rest of the program. Let us now go one step further and consider what happens if each of these declarations are done within a function as opposed to globally outside the bounds of any function.

```
void my_function_A(char *ptr)
{
    Char a[] = "ABCDE"
}
void my_function_B(char *ptr)
{
    char *cp = "FGHIJ"
}
```

In the case of **my_function_A,** the content, orvalue(s), of the array aQ is considered to be the data. The array is said to be initialized to the values ABCDE. In the case of **my_function_B,** the value of the pointer cp is considered to be the data. The pointer has been initialized to point to the string **FGHIJ.** In both **my_function_A** and **my_function_B** the definitions are local variables and thus the string **ABCDE** is stored on the stack, as is the value of the pointer cp. The string **FGHIJ** can be stored anywhere. On my system it gets stored in the data segment. By the way, array initialization of automatic variables as we have done in **my_function_A** was illegal in the older C and only "came of age" in the newer **ANSI C.** A fact that may be important when one is considering portability and backwards compatibility. As long as we are discussing the relationship/differences between pointers and arrays, let us move on to multi-dimensional arrays. For example,

char mu Iti [5] [10]:

Just what does this mean? Well, let us consider it in the following light.

char multi[5][10];

Let us take the underlined part to be the "name" of an array. Then prepending the **char** and appending the **[10]** we have an array of 10 characters. But, the name **multi[5]** is itself an array indicating that there are 5 elements each being an array of 10 characters. Hence we have an array of 5 arrays of 10 characters each.

Assume we have filled this two dimensional array with data of some kind. In memory, it might look as if it had been formed by initializing 5 separate arrays using something like:

multi[0] = {'0','V,'2','3','4','S','6','T,'8','9')
multi[1] = {'a','b','c','d','e','f','g','h','i','j'}
multi[2] = {'A','B','C','D','E','F','G','H','I','J'}
multi[3] = {'9787776757473727170'}
multi[4] = {'J','I','H','G','F','E','D','C','B','A'}

At the same time, individual elements might be addressable using syntax such as:

multi[0][3] = '3'
multi[1][7] = 'h'
multi[4][0] = 'J'

Since arrays are contiguous in memory, our actual memory block for the above should look like:

0123456789abcdefghijABCDEFGHIJ9876543210JIHGFEDCBA

Starting at the address multi[0][0]

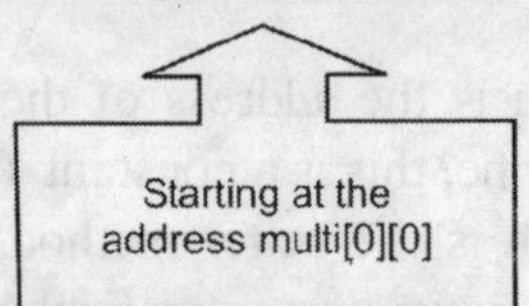

Note that we did not write **multi[0] = "0123456789".** Had we done so a terminating '\0' would have been implied since whenever double quotes are used a '\0' character is appended to the characters contained within those quotes. Had that been the case we would have had to set aside room for 11 characters per row instead of 10.

Goal in the above is to illustrate how memory is laid out for two dimensional arrays. That is, this is a two dimensional array of characters, not an array of "strings". Now, the compiler knows how many columns are present in the array so it can interpret **multi + 1** as the address of the 'a' in the 2nd row above. That is, it adds 10, the number of columns, to get this location. If we were dealing with integers and an array with the same dimension the compiler would add **10*sizeof(int)** which, on a machine may be 20. Thus, the address of the 9 in the 4th row above would be **&multi[3][0] or *(multi + 3)** in pointer notation. To get to the content of the 2nd element in the 4th row we add 1 to this address and dereference the result as in

***(*(multi + 3) + 1)**

With a little thought we can see that: *(*(multi + row) + col) and multi[row][col] yield the same results.

Go through the Example 16.10 which is implementing the above discussion.

Example 16.10: Following program illustrates this using integer arrays instead of character arrays.

```
/**Pointer21.C**/ #include <stdio.h>
#define ROWS 5 #defineCOLS10
int multi[ROWS][COLS];
int main(void) {
int row, col;
for (row = 0; row < ROWS; row++)
{
    for (col = 0; col < COLS; col++) {
    multi[row][col] = row*col; } }
for (row = 0; row < ROWS; row++) {
for (col = 0; col < COLS; col++) { printf("\n%d
",multi[row][col]); printf("%d ",*(*(multi + row) +
col)); } }
return 0; }
```

Because of the double de-referencing required in the pointer version, the name of a two dimensional array is often said to be equivalent to a **pointer to a pointer.** With a three dimensional array we would be dealing with an array of arrays of arrays and some might say its name would be equivalent to a **pointer to a pointer to a pointer.** However, here we have initially set aside the block of memory for the array by defining it using array notation. Hence, we are dealing with a constant, not a variable. That is we are talking about a fixed address not a variable pointer. The dereferencing function used above permits us to access any element in the array of arrays without the need of changing the value of that address, the address of **multi [0][0]** as given by the symbol **multi.** We can access individual elements of the array multi using either:

```
multi[row][col]
```

or

```
*(*(multi + row) + col)
```

To understand more fully what is going on, let us replace

```
*(multi + row) with X
```

as in:

```
*(X + col)
```

Now, from this we see that X is like a pointer since the expression is de-referenced and we know that **col** is an integer. Here the arithmetic being used is of a special kind called "pointer arithmetic" is being used. That means that, since we are talking about an integer array, the address pointed to by (i.e., value of) **X + col + 1** must be greater than the address X + **col** by and amount equal to **sizeof(int).**

Since we know the memory layout for two dimensional arrays, we can determine that in the expression **multi + row** as used above, **multi + row + 1** must increase by value an amount equal to that needed to "point to" the next row, which in this case would be an amount equal to **COLS * sizeof(int).** If the expression ***(*(multi + row) + col)** is to be evaluated correctly at run time, the compiler must generate code which takes into consideration the value of **COLS,** i.e., the 2nd dimension. Because of the equivalence of the two forms of expression, this is true whether we are using the pointer expression as here or the array expression **multi[row][col].** Thus, to evaluate either expression, a total of 5 values must be known:

1. The address of the first element of the array, which is returned by the expression **multi,** i.e., the name of the array.
2. The size of the type of the elements of the array, in this case **sizeof(int).**

3. The 2nd dimension of the array.
4. The specific index value for the first dimension, **row** in this case.
5. The specific index value for the second dimension, **col** in this case.

For example, consider the following program segment which illustrates the above discussion. In the program segment we are assigning all the cell of the array **multi to 1.**

```
void set_value(int m_arrayD[COLS])
{
    int row, col;
    for (row = 0; row < ROWS; row++)
    {
    for (col = 0; col < COLS; col++)
    {
    m_array[row][col] = 1;
    }
  }
}
```

And to call this function we would then use:

```
set_value(multi);
```

Now, within the function we have used the values #defined by ROWS and COLS that set the limits on the for loops. But, these #defines are just constants as far as the compiler is concerned, i.e., there is nothing to connect them to the array size within the function. The row and **col** are local variables, of course. The formal parameter definition permits the compiler to determine the characteristics associated with the pointer value that will be passed at run time. There are occasions where we would prefer not to define it within the parameter definition, out of habit or consistency, we have not used it here. But, the second dimension must be used as has been shown in the expression for the parameter. The reason is that we need this in the evaluation of **m_array[row][col]** as has been described. While the parameter defines the data type (**int** in this case) and the automatic variables for row and column are defined in the for loops, only one value can be passed using a single parameter. In this case, that is the value of **multi** as noted in the call statement, i.e., the address of the first element, often referred to as a pointer to the array. Thus, the only way we have of informing the compiler of the 2nd dimension is by explicitly including it in the parameter definition.

In fact, in general all dimensions of higher order than one are needed when dealing with multi-dimensional arrays. That is if we are talking about 3 dimensional arrays, the 2nd **and** 3rd dimension must be specified in the parameter definition.

16.15 POINTERS TO ARRAYS: TYPEDEF APPROACH

Pointers, of course, can be "pointed at" any type of data object, including arrays. We have discussed earlier that an array of integers points an integer pointer at that array. For example,

```
int *ptr;
ptr = &my_array[0]; /* ptr is a pointer and points at the first integer in my_array */
```

As we have mentioned earlier that the type of the pointer variable must match the type of the first element of the array. In addition, we can use a pointer as a formal parameter of a function which is designed to manipulate an array. For example,

```
intarray[3] = {'1', '5','7'};
voida_func(int*p);
```

Some programmers prefer to write the function prototype as: void

```
a_func(int pQ);
```

which would tend to inform others who might use this function that the function is designed to manipulate the elements of an array. Of course, in either case, what actually gets passed is the value of a pointer to the first element of the array, independent of which notation is used in the function prototype or definition. Note that if the array notation is used, there is no need to pass the actual dimension of the array since we are not passing the whole array, only the address of the first element.

We now turn to the problem of the two dimensional arrays. C interprets a two dimensional array as an array of one-dimensional arrays. That being the case, the first element of a two dimensional array of integers is a one-dimensional array of integers. And a pointer to a two dimensional array of integers must be a pointer to that data type. One way of accomplishing this is through the use of the keyword "typedef". The typedef assigns a new name to a specified data type. For example,

typedef unsigned char byte;

causes the name **byte** to mean type **unsigned char.** Hence

byte b[10]; **would be an array of unsigned characters.**

Note that in the typedef declaration, the word **byte** has replaced that which would normally be the name of **unsigned char.** The rule for using **typedef** is that the new name for the data type is the name used in the definition of the data type. Thus, in the following declaration

typedef int Array[10];

Array becomes a data type for an array of 10 integers, i.e., **Array my_arr;** declares **my_arr** as an array of 10 integers and **Array arr2d[5];** makes **arr2d** an array of 5 arrays of 10 integers each. Also note that **Array *p1 d;** makes **p1 d** a pointer to an array of 10 integers. Because ***p1d** points to the same type as **arr2d,** assigning the address of the two dimensional array arr2d to p1d, the pointer to a one dimensional array of 10 integers is acceptable, i.e**., p1d = &arr2d[0];** or **p1d = arr2d;** are both correct. Since the data type we use for our pointer is an array of 10 integers we would expect that incrementing p1d by 1 would change its value by **10*sizeof(int),** which it does. That is, **sizeof(*p1 d)** is 20. Reader can prove this by writing and running a simple short program. Now, while using typedef makes things clearer for the reader and easier to the programmer, it is not really necessary. What we need is a way of declaring a pointer like **p1d** without the need of the **typedef** keyword. It turns out that this can be done and that

int(*p1d)[10];

is the proper declaration, i.e. **p1** d, here is a pointer to an array of 10 integers just as it was under the declaration using the Array type. Note that this is different from

int*p1d[10];

which would make **p1d** the name of an array of 10 pointers to type **int.**

16.16 POINTERS AND STRUCTURES

As we may know, we can declare the form of a block of data containing different data types by means of a structure declaration. For example, a personnel file might contain structures which may contain:

```
struct tag {
    char lname[20];      /* last name */
    char fname[20];      /* first name */
    int age;   /* age */
    float rate;          /* viz., 5.75 per hour */
    };
```

Let us say we have a bunch of these structures in a disk file and we want to read each one out and print out the first and last name of each one so that we can have a list of the people in a file. The remaining information will not be printed out. We want to do this printing with a function call and pass to that function a pointer to the structure at hand. For demonstration purposes we will use only one structure for now. But realize the goal is the writing of the function, not the reading of the file which, presumably, we know how to do. For review, recall that we can access structure members with the dot operator as in:

```
/**Pointer22.C**/
#include <stdio.h>
#include <string.h>
struct tag {
    char lname[20];      /* last name */
    char fname[20];      /* first name */
    int age;   /* age */
    float rate;          /* viz., 5.75 per hour */
};
struct tag my_struct;      /* declare the structure my_struct */
int main(void)
{
    strcpy(my_struct.lname,"Jensen");
    strcpy(my_struct.fname,"Red");
    printf("\n%s ",my_struct.fname);
    printf("%s\n",my_struct.lname);
    return 0;
}
```

```
OUTPUT
Red Jensen
```

Now, this particular structure is rather small compared to many used in C programs. To the above we might want to add:

```
date_of_hire; (data types not shown)
date_of_last_raise;
last_percent_increase;
emergency_phone;
medical_plan;
Social_S_Nbr;
etc
```

If we have a large number of employees, what we want to do is manipulate the data in these structures by means of functions. For example, we might want a function print out the name of the employee listed in any structure passed to it. However, in the old C it was not possible to pass a structure, only a pointer to a structure could be passed. In ANSI C, it is now permissible to pass the complete structure.

Anyway, if we pass the whole structure it means that we must copy the contents of the structure from the calling function to the called function. In systems using stacks, this is done by pushing the contents of the structure on the stack. With large structures this could prove to be a problem. However, passing a pointer uses a minimum amount of stack space.

We want a function that will accept as a parameter a pointer to a structure and from within that function we want to access members of the structure. For example we want to print out the name of the employee in the structure. So we know that pointer is going to point to a structure declared using struct tag. We declare such a pointer with the declaration:

struct tag *st_ptr;

and we point it to our example structure with: **st_ptr = &my_struct;**

Now, we can access a given member by de-referencing the pointer. But, how do we de-reference the pointer to a structure? Well, consider the fact that we might want to use the pointer to set the age of the employee. We would write:

(*st_ptr).age = 63;

Above statement says, replace that within the parenthesis with that which **st_ptr** points to, which is the structure **my_struct.** Thus, this breaks down to the same as **my_struct.age**. However, this is a fairly often-used expression and the designers of C have created an alternate syntax with the same meaning which is:

st_ptr->age = 63;

Go through the Example 16.11 for better understabnding the above discussion.

Example16.11: Write C code using pointer and structure

Answer: Consider the following program segment which implements the discussion

```
/* Pointer23.C */
#include <stdio.h> #include <string.h>
struct tag{    /* the structure type */
    char lname[20];              /* last name */
    char fname[20];              /* first name */
    int age;  /* age * /
    float rate;                  /* e.g. 12.75 per hour */
};
struct tag my_struct;  /* define the structure */
void show_name(struct tag *p); /* function prototype */
int main(void) {
    struct tag *st_ptr;        /* a pointer to a structure */
    st_ptr = &my_struct;       /* point the pointer to my_struct */
    strcpy(my_struct.lname,"Jensen");
    strcpy(my_struct.fname,"Red");
    printf("\n%s ",my_struct.fname);
    printf("%s\n",my_struct.lname);
    my_struct.age = 63;
    show_name(st_ptr);           /* pass the pointer */
    return 0; }
    void show_name(struct tag *p) {
    printf("\n%s ", p->fname); /* p points to a structure */
    printf("%s ", p->lname);
    printf("%d\n", p->age); }
```

OUTPUT

Red Jensen

Red Jensen 63

Again, this is a lot of information to absorb at one time. The reader should compile and run the various code snippets and using a debugger monitor things like **my_struct** and **p** while single stepping through the main and following the code down into the function to see what is happening.

16.17 POINTERS AND FUNCTIONS

It has been already discussed that arguments are passed to, from function by value. It is not possible to change the value of a calling program variable within a function, unless we have the address of a variable in the calling program. C functions have the capability of returning values that can be, in turn, assigned to variables within the calling program. However, through pointer operations, we can write specialized functions that will return a value to the calling program and change the values in other variables whose memory addresses are handed over to the function. In this fashion, it is possible to write a function that figuratively, returns many values in a single operation. While pointers are indispensable throughout all phases of C programming, their capabilities yield high-powered program performance, especially, when dealing with programmed functions. Go through the Example 16.12 which is implementing **by value** and **by reference.**

Example 16.12: Write C code to compute the cube of two numbers by using by value and by reference parameter technique in a function.

Answer: Consider the following program segment that illustrates the idea of parameter passing **by value** and **by reference.**

```
/* pointer24.c */
# include<stdio.h>
float cube(float a, float *b)
{
    *b = *b * *b * * b ; / rewrite memory */
    return (a * a * a); }
void main() {
    float x = 2.5;
    float y = 5.5;
    printf("\n cube of 2.5 is %f \n", cube(x, &y));
    printf("\n cube of 5.5 is %f", y);
}
```

OUTPUT
cube of 2.5 is 15.625000
cube of 5.5 is 166.375000

In the function **cude(), a** is an auto variable of type **float** and **b** is a pointertype of **float.** The address of y in the calling program was passed to the function **cube ().** The value of this address was assigned to pointer **b** in the function. Figure 16.16 illustrates the status of the parameter x and y before and after the call made to the function **cube ().**

The meaning of the expression

*b = *b**b**b;

is given in Figure 16.17.

If **b** was a standard variable, the above code slice can be written as: b = b * b* b;

The use of a single symbol to name several operators that perform differently in C is a very good reason to stick to established source code formatting conversions. All arithmetic operators should be separated from their variable names by a space. For example,

c = b * a;

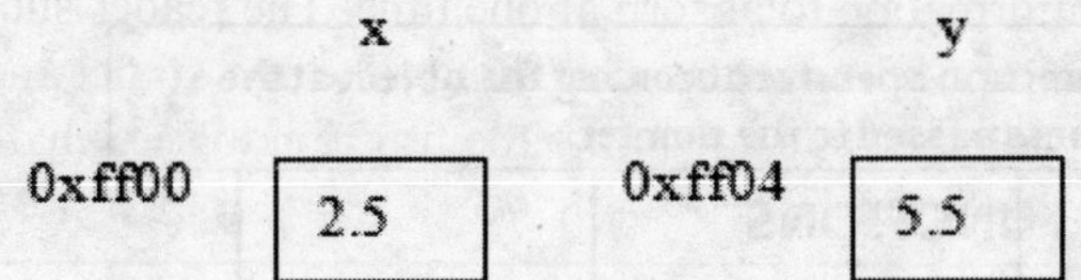

(a) x and y in memory a function call is made

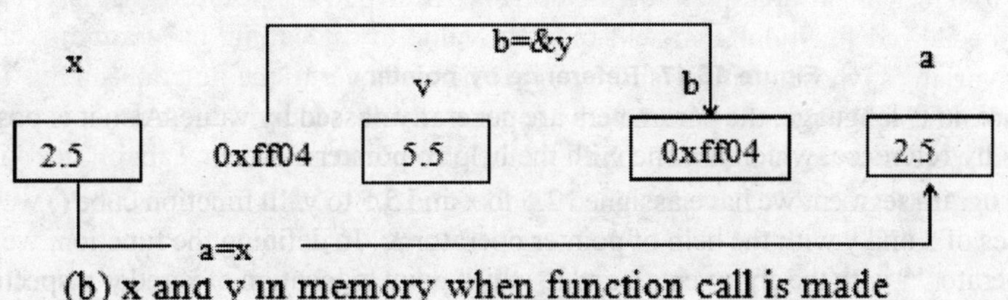

(b) x and y in memory when function call is made

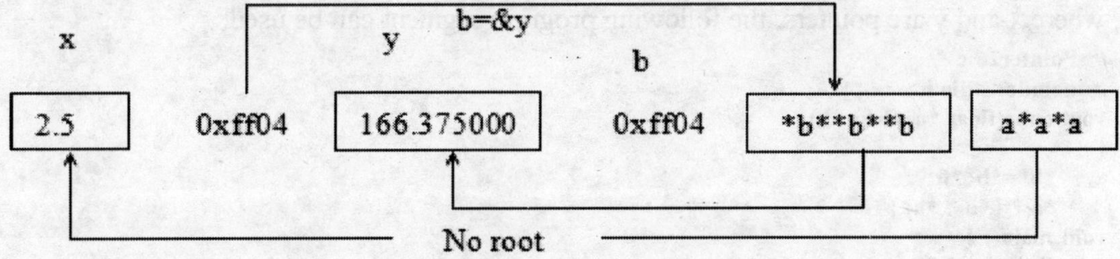

(c) x and y in memory after function call is completed

Figure 16.16 POINTERS and functions

This expression is far easier to decipher than the one that follows:

c = b*a; The multiplication of pointer could also be written in C shorthand.

***b *= *b * * b; /* cube of b */ The above program segment could also be written as follows: /* Pointer25.c */ # include<stdio.h>**

```
void cube(float *a, float *b) {
    *b*=*b**b;
    *a *= *a * *a; }
void main() {
    float x = 2.5;
    float y = 5.5;
    cube(&x, &y);
    printf("\n cube of 2.5 is %f \n", x);
    printf("\n cube of 5.5 is %f", y); }
```

OUTPUT
cube of 2.5 is 15.625000
cube of 5.5 is 166.375000

Indirection operator accessing the object at the address passed to the pointer

*b = *b *   *b *   *b Multiplicative operator

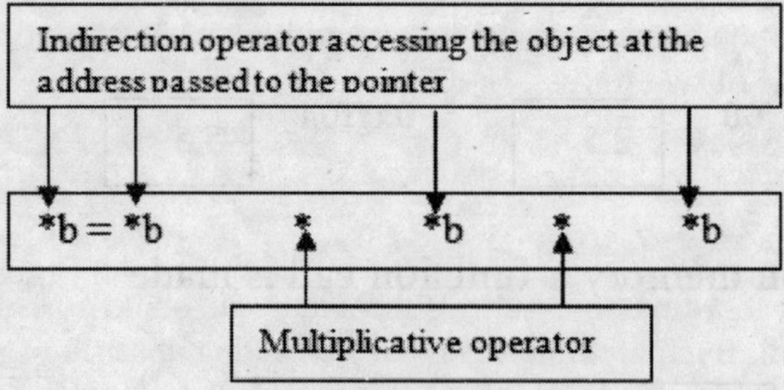

Figure 16.17 Reference by pointer

As we are aware, in C language, the parameters are generally passed by value. Also it is possible to pass parameters by reference, which is done with the help of pointers.

In the above program segment we have assigned 2.5 to x and 5.5 to y. In function cube () we have passed the addresses of x and y with the help of pointer operator &. In defining the function, we have used indirection operator '*' with the arguments a and b, which point to location of x and y, respectively. In the definition of cube () function, a and b are dummy parameters. For getting address of x and y, i.e., where x and y are pointers, the following program segment can be used:

```
/* Pointer26.c */
# include<stdio.h>
void cube(float *a, float *b)
{
    *b*=*b**b;
    *a *= *a * *a; }
void main() {
    float x = 2.5;
    float y = 5.5;
    cube(&x, &y);
    printf("\n Address of x is Ox%X",&x);
    printf("\n Address of y is Ox%X \n",&y);
    printf("\n cube of 2.5 is %f \n", x);
    printf("\n cube of 5.5 is %f", y); }
```

```
OUTPUT
Address of x is 0xFFF2
Address of y is OxFFEE
cube of 2.5 is 15.625000
cube of 5.5 is 166.375000
```

16.18 POINTERS TO FUNCTIONS

A useful technique is the ability to have pointers to functions. A C function is not a variable but we can declare pointers to functions that can then be used in manner in which other parameters are used, such as, placing them in arrays, passing them to other functions, etc. Their declaration is easy: write the declaration, as it would be for the function, say

int func(int a, float b);

and simply put brackets around the name and a * in front of it: that declares the pointer. Because of precedence, if we do not parenthesize the name, we declare a function returning a pointer:

```
/* function returning pointer to int */
int *func(int a, float b);
/* pointer to function returning int */ int
(*func)(int a, float b);
```

Once we have got the pointer, we can assign the address of the right sort of function just by using its name: like an array, a function name is turned into an address when it' used in an expression. We can call the function using one of two forms:

```
(*func)(1,2);
/* or */
func(1,2);
```

The second form has been newly blessed by the C standards.

One rarely sees a pointer to a function, but this technique can some times be useful, such as in hiding the intent of a program. Such a pointer tends to be making absence of the name and source code of that function. For example, consider the following program segment that implements the above idea:

```
/* Pointer27.c */
# include<stdio.h>
#include<string.h>
int hide(char*c, int (*spider)(char*c)) {
    return((*spider)(c)); }
intlength(char*s) {
    int x = 0;
    while(*s++) ++x;
    return(x); }
    void main()
    {
        intx;
char *s = "POINTERS"; x = hide(s,
length); printf("\n Length of %s is %d",s,
 x); }
```

OUTPUT

Length of POINTERS is 8

The process may look a little ridiculous but it effectively demonstrates a pointer to a function. In this case the function **length ()** returns the length of a string argument, as an **int** in the same fashion the intrinsic function **strlen ()** does.

Within the calling program, the arbitrary named function **hide ()** is invoked, which requires two parameters (arguments), a char pointer and a function name. In this usage, **length** without the parenthesis is the address of the function **length ().** Just as the name of an array without the subscripting brackets is a pointer to the memory location of the array, a C function without the parenthesis is pointer to the memory location of that function.

In the function **hide ()**, the address of s assigned to **char *c** and the address of **length** is passed to a pointer to this function **spider().** The declaration of this entity within the function is

```
int (*spider) (char *c)
```

This code slice states that **spider** is a pointer to a function that returns an **int** value and **char c** is the argument to the function. The expression **(*spider)** may be used exactly as we have used function length (). The following code segment:

```
return ((*spider)(c);
```

means the same thing as the following code segment.

```
return (c);
```

(*spider) (c) points to the storage address set aside for **length()** when it is declared within the program.

16.19 FUNCTIONS RETURNING POINTERS

It was shown how pointer arguments to functions could be used to alter values in the calling program. In such cases, no pointer values were returned from the function. The address value passed to the function was used for accessing a variable's address to make changes in memory. These discussions involve functions that return pointers to the calling program. The following program segment calls a function that returns a pointer of type **char.**

```
/* Pointer28.c */
# include<stdio.h>
char*combine(char*s, char*t)
{
    int x = 0; charstr[100];
    while(*s) {
    str[x] = *s++; x++; } while(*t)
    {
        str[x] = *t++; x++; }
    str[x] = '\0';
    return(str); }
main() {
charstr[100] = "Butter", str1[100] = "fly", *ptr; ptr = combine(str, stM);
printf("\n Combined string is %s", ptr);
}
```

OUTPUT
Combined string Butterfly

The function combine () which is nothing but it a version of function strcat () that returns a pointer to the combined string and does not alter the value of any of its argument objects.

The program declares two char arrays and a char pointer. The function "combine () accepts two char pointers as its arguments and returns a char pointer. Two string constants, "Butter" and "fly" are copied into the two arrays str and strl, respectively.

The function combine () is invoked with two arguments and the returned pointer is assigned to a pointer variable, such as

ptr = combine(str,str1);

ptr is a pointer of type **char.** Therefore, the address of a **char** type object must be passed to it, leading to the return from **combine ()** a **char** pointer.

Within the function body, x is declared **int** and **str** is declared a **char** array of 100 bytes. The subscript value should be enough to store the combined strings of **s** and **t.** The following code slice copies the string pointed by **s** into **str** and simultaneously it finds the length of the string pointed by s.

```
while(*s)
{
    str[x] = *s++;
    x++;
}
```

Since x is equal to the number of bytes in **str** and **str** presently holds the contents of the string pointed by s, this means that x will start its count from a value that is equal to the position of the **NULL** byte in **str.** We know that **s** point to "Butter, a string containing 6 characters. When "Butter is copied into **str** and when loop exits from while statement the value of x will be 6. The character in **str at the 6th offset str[6]** is the **NULL.** When the while loop of the following code slice starts the initial value of x is 6. On the first pass, the **NULL** byte in **str** is overwritten by the first byte referenced by t.

```
while(*t)
    {
        str[x] = *t++;
        x++;
    }
```

Again the pointer **t** is incremented by 1 and the loop is repeated again. On the next pass, x is equal to 20. So byte **str[7]** receives the next byte in *t. On each pass of the loop, the exit clause (*t != '\0') is tested.

Since we know that **t** point to "flf, so the loop cycles for three times. After the 3rd pass, the loop terminates. However, the loop variable has already been incremented in readiness for the next pass. Even though this pass never came about, x is set the next logical byte in **str.**

Since the termination of the loop occurred when the **NULL** character referenced by t was encountered, this **NULL** was not written to the end of **str.** Therefore, the contents of **str** encompass a series of discrete characters and not a string. **ANULL** terminator is required to make this string so the contents of **str** are made into an official C string by the following assignment:

```
str[x] = '\0';
```

This puts the finishing touch on the whole of the operation and array str now stores the string. The following statement

```
return(str);
```

returns the address of the first character in the string str. In other words, we can say that it returns the base address of the array str back to the calling program and assigns it to pointer ptr. When ptr is returned to the printf(), it displays "Butterfly as a result.

16.20 POINTERS, FUNCTIONS AND ARRAYS

We have already emphasized that in most cases, the name of an array is converted into the address of its first element; one notable exception being when it is the operand of sizeof, which is essential if the stuff to do with malloc is to work. Another case is when an array name is the operand of the & address-of operator. Here, it is converted into the address of the whole array. What is the difference? Even if we think that addresses would be in some way 'the same', the critical difference is that they have different types. For an array of n elements of type T, then the address of the first element has type 'pointer to T; the address of the whole array has type 'pointer to array of n elements of type T; clearly very different. For example,

```
intar[10];
int*ip;
int(*ar10i)[10];        /* pointer to array of 10 ints */
ip = ar;                /* address of first element */
ip = &ar[0];            /* address of first element */
art Oi = &ar; /* address of whole array */
```

Where do pointers to arrays matter? Not often, in truth, although of course we know that declarations that look like multidimensional arrays are really arrays of arrays. Here is an example which uses that fact, but we will have to work out what it does. It is not common to do this sort of thing in practice:

```
intar2d[5][4];
int (*ar4i)[4]; /* pointer to array of 4 ints */
for(ar4i= ar2d; ar4i < &(ar2d[5]); ar4i++)
    (*ar4i)[2] = 0; /* ar2d[n][2] = 0 */
```

More important than addresses of arrays is what happens when we declare a function that takes an array as an argument. Because of the 'conversion to the address of its first element' rule, even if we do try to pass an array to a function by giving its name as an argument, we actually end up passing a pointer to its first element. The usual rule really does apply in this case. But what happens if we declare a function, does have an argument whose type is 'array of something' like this:

voidf(intar[10]);

What happens? The answer may suprise us slightly. The compiler looks at that and says to itself 'Ho ho. That is going to be a pointer when the function is called' and then rewrites the parameter type to be a pointer. As a result, all three of these declarations are identical:

```
voidf(intar[10]);
voidf(int*ar);
void f(int arQ);   I* since the size of the array is irrelevant! */
```

For the implementation of the discussion go theough the Example 16.13.

Example 16.13: Write C code which demonsterates pointers, functions and arrays together.

Answer: Consider the following program segment:

```
/* Pointer29.c */
/* Pointer and function with array */
#include<stdio.h> /* Prototype */ void
pointer_fun( int*); void main() {
    int p[10] = {12,13,14,15,16,18,19,234,100,400};
int *pointer;
pointer = p; /* assign starting address of array p this same as pointer = &p[0]*/
pointer_fun(pointer); /* invoke function */ }
/* Definition of function*/ void pointer_fun(int*ptr) {
    int i=0;
    while(i<10)
    {
printf(" value = %d\n", *ptr); /* gives value */ i++; ptr++; } }
```

OUTPUT
value = 12
value = 13
value = 14
value = 15
value = 16
value = 18
value = 19
value = 234
value = 100
value = 400

In the above program segment, we have used an array p and a pointer variable **pointer.** The **pointer** stores starting address (base address or address of the first cell) of p with the help of following code segment: pointer = p;

Also the **pointer** is passed to the function **pointer_fun()** where it works as a pointer variable. The access mechanism of the above program segment is same as the program segment **pointer30.c.** In other words, we can say that program segment **pointer29.c** and **pointer30.c** are equivalent. In the program segment **pointer29.c,** we have used a temporary variable i that works like a counter and its value is used for termination condition. In this program segment, the size of the array must be known in advance but in the function **pointer_fun() of pointer30.c,** we have used only pointer variable ptr. Applying indirection operator, we retrieve information associated with **ptr** as illustrated in Figure 16.18.

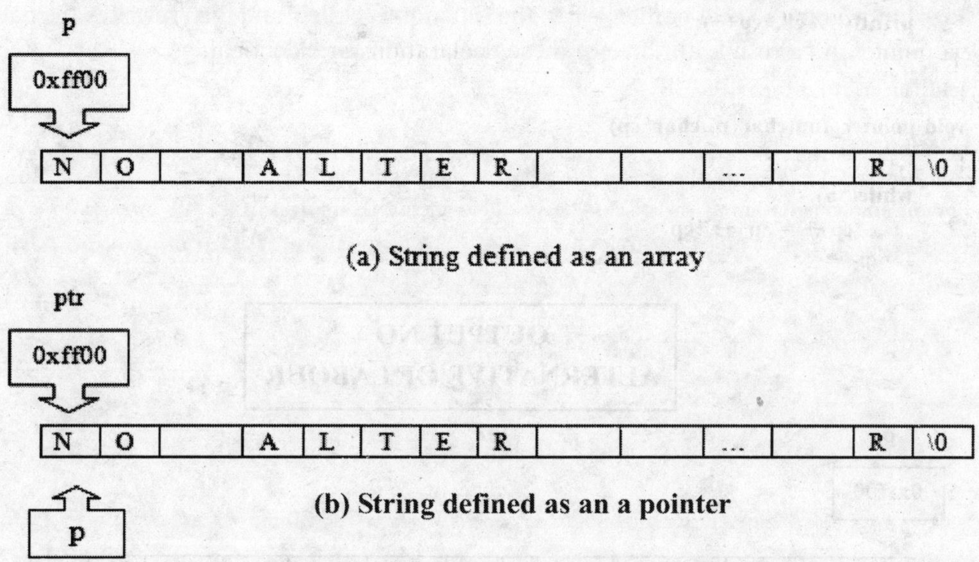

Figure 16.18 Accessing string with help of pointer /* pointer30.c */
/* pointer and function with string */

```
# include<stdio.h>
/* prototype */
void pointer_fun( char*);
void main()
{
    char p[60] = { "NO ALTERNATIVE OF LABOUR"};
    pointer_fun( p);
    printf("\n Press a key");
    getchar(); }
void pointer_fun(char*p) {
    whilefp)
    {
        printf(" value = %c\n", *p); /* give value */ p++;
}}
```

Run and see the output

Consider the following program segment in which we have implemented the standard C library function strcpy () with the help of pointer_fun () function. The discussion is given in Figure 16.19.

```
/*pointer31.c*/
/* pointer and function with string */
#include<stdio.h>
void pointer_fun( char*, char*); /* prototype */
void main() {
    char p[60] = {"NO ALTERNATIVE OF LABOUR"};
    char*cp;
    pointer_fun(p, cp); whilefcp) {
        printf("%c",*cp++);
    }
    }
    void pointer_fun(char*p, char*cp)
    {
        while(*p)
            *cp++ = *p++; *cp
        = '\0';
}
```

OUTPUT NO ALTERNATIVE OF LABOUR

p: 0xff00												
N	O		A	L	T	E	R			...	R	\0

(b) String defined as an array

ptr: 0xff00												
N	O		A	L	T	E	R			...	R	\0

*cp = *p; [strcpy()]

(b) String defined as an a pointer

16.19 Duplicating string

EXERCISES

Descriptive and Programming Problems

1. A text T and patterns P and Q are in memory. Write a program for replacing every occurrence of P in T by Q.
2. Write a function **Div** Q, k) where j and k are positive integers such that **Div** (j, k) = 1, if j divides k, otherwise **Div** Q, k) = 0.
3. Write a function, which finds the location of the largest element and the location of the 2nd largest elements in a list of numbers with the help of pointer.

4. Let W be the string formed by **ABCD.** Write functions for
   (a) Find the length of W. (b)List all sub-strings of W.
   (c) List all the initial sub-strings of W.
5. Write a function that counts the number **NUM** of paragraphs in the short story S.
6. Write a program that interchanges the jth and kth paragraph in text T.
7. Write a function **compare** () that compares two strings.
8. Write a function **strcpy ()** that copies the **stringl** into **string2** using pointers.
9. Most time-sharing computers require the userto login by giving a user name and password. Write a program that simulates this activity. The program begins by giving user a list of available computers (e.g., AS/400, SUN ULTRA, HP-9000, etc). After the user selects a given computer, the program prompts for a user name and checks to see whether such a user is valid. If not, it issues an error message and the program terminates. If the name is found, the program asks for a password. If the password is valid a welcome message is displayed; otherwise an error message is displayed and program terminates. During the password checking it should take three trials.
10. Write a program to find the sum of squares of elements on diagonal of square matrix.
11. A factory has 6 divisions and stocks 8 categories of products. An inventory table is updated for each division and for each product as there is received. There are three independent suppliers of products to the factory.
    (a) Design a data format to represent each transaction
    (b) Write a function to take a transaction and update the inventory.
    (c) If cost per item is also given write a function to calculate the total inventory value.
12. Write a function that will reverse a string. Use **for** loop that swaps the first and **last** character, then **second** and **next to last** characters and so on. The string should be passed to function as an argument. Take following sentences as input: "Able was I eve I saw Elba"
13. Write a program that will read a text file and creates another file that is identical except that the sequence of consecutive blank spaces are replaced by a single space and size of each line should be of 40 characters and should be left and right justified.
14. What does ***p++** increment **p** or what it points to? Write a C code to justify your answer.
15. Write a program for fitting a straight line through a set of points (xi, yi) where i = 1, 2, 3, ...n. The straight line equation is y=mx+c and the values of m and c are given by

    m = nOfr^WOx/KOv/)

    n(6xjy-(6x^

    All summations are from 1 to n.
16. An election is contested by 5 candidates. The candidates are numbered 1 to 5 and the voting is done by marking the candidate number on the ballot paper. Write a program to read the ballots and count the votes cast for each candidate using an array variable count. In case, a number read is outside the range 1 to 5, the ballot should be considered as a 'spoilt ballot' and the program should also count the number of spoilt ballots.

17. The annual examination results of 100 students are tabulated as follows:

Roll No.	Course 1	Course 2	Course 3	Course 4	Course5

Write a program to read the data and determine the following:

(a) Total marks obtained by each student.

(b) The highest marks in each subject and the Roll No. of the student who secured it.

(c) The student who obtained the highest total marks.

18. Given are two one-dimensional arrays A and B which are sorted in ascending order. Write a program to merge them into a single sorted array C that contains every item from arrays A and B, in ascending order. Compare the visiting time of the both the arrays.

19. Write a program to multiple two matrices that have the same number of rows and columns can be multiplied to produce a third matrix.

20. Write a program using pointer that fills a five-by-five matrix as follows.

    Upper left triangle: with + 1s

    Lower right triangle with-1s

    Right to left diagonal with 0s

    Display the contents of the matrix using not more than two printf statements

21. Selection sort is based on the following idea- "Selecting the, largest array element and swapping it with the last array element leaves an unsorted list whose size is 1 less than the size of the original list. If we repeat this step again on the unsorted list we will have an ordered list of size 2 and an unordered list size n-2. When we repeat this until the size of the unsorted list becomes one, the result will be a sorted list." Write a program to implement this algorithm.

22. Develop a program to implement the binary search algorithm. This technique compares the search key value with the value of the element that is midway in a "sorted" list. Then;

(a) If they match, the search is over.

(b) If the search key value is less than the middle value, then the first half of the list contains the key value.

(c) If the search key value is greater than the middle value, then the second half contains the key value.

Multiple Choice Questions

1. What is printed?

```
# include<stdio.h>
void main()
{
```

```
int*p1 ;
int*p2;
int r = 4 ;
p2 = p1 = &r ;
*p1 =4.0*(*P1 + *p2)/r*3.0;
printf("%d", *p1); }
```

(a) 9 (b)10 (c) 4 (d) none

2. What is printed?

```
#include<stdio.h>
#include<string.h>
void main()
{
charstrlQ = "POINTER TO FUNCTION";
charstr2Q = "POINTER TO FUNCTION";
int (*comp)(char*, char*); comp =
strcmp ;
if(! comp(str1, str2))   printf("\n STRINGS ARE NOT EQUAL"); else
printf("\n STRINGS ARE NOT EQUAL"); }
```

(a) STRINGS ARE NOT EQUAL (b) STRINGS ARE NOT EQUAL

(c) none (d) both (a) and (b)

3. What is printed?

```
void main()
{
    char strQ = {"Pointers are powerful tool of C"};
    printf("\n %s",str);
    printf("\n %s", &str[0]);
    printf("\n %s", str+3); }
```

(a) base address of str and n (b) n and base address of str

(c) base address of str and t (d) none

4. What is printed?

```
# include<stdio.h>
void main()
{
float y, *point; y = 20.7 ; *point = y ;
printf("\n %4.3f", *point); }
```

(a) 20.7 (b) 20.70 (c) 20.700 (d) none

5. What is printed?

```
#include<stdio.h>
void main() {
    inta[10] ;
    inti ;
    int *int_ptr;
    for(i = 0 ; i < 10 ; i++)
    {
        a[i] = i * i ; }
    int_ptr = a ;
printf("%d", *(int_ptr + 3 * sizeof(int))); }
```

(a) 36 (b) 25 (c) 49 (d) none

6. What is printed?

```
#include<stdio.h>
int*fun();
void main() {
     printf("\n Ox%x %d",fun(), *fun()); }
int*fun() {
     int p = 4 ;
return(&p); }
```

(a) address of p and 4 (b) 4 (c) both (a) and (b) (d) none

7. What is printed?

```
# include<stdio.h>
void main()
{
     void *point;
     int n[10] = {2,8,7,6,7,8,5,4,2,10};
     inti ;
     point = &n[0];
          point = &n[i] ;
          printf("\nOx%x : %2d", (int *)point, *(int *) point); }
```

(a) 2 and base address (b) 2 and address of the first element

(c) both (a) and (b) (d) None

8. If int spread[]={11,22,33,44,55,66,77,88,99}; then what is printed by the following statement?

printf("\n %d", *(spread+2));

(a) 33 (b) 44 (c) 22 (d) none

9. What is wrong in the following code slice?

char*ptr; *ptr = malloc(100);

(a) *ptr= malloc(100); (b) char*ptr; (c) none

10. What is wrong with the following code?

```
void main()
{
     int aQ = {11,22,33,44};
     int*ptr; ptr = &a;
     printf("\n %d",
*ptr); }
```

(a) ptr = &a; (b) printf("\n %d", *ptr);

(c) int *ptr; (d)none

11. Find error in the following code:

```
int a, ptr;
a = 11;
ptr = &a;
```

(a) ptr=&a; (b)a = 11; (c) int a, ptr; (d) none

12. Find error in the following code:

int i = 11;

int*ptr;

ptr=i;

(a) ptr = i; (b) int *ptr; (c) inti=11; (d) none

13. An expression with the asterisk operator, such as *ptr, cannot occur on the left-hand side of an assignment statement.

(a) True (b) False (c) None

14. A function's name is a pointer constant.

(a) True (b) False (c) None

15. An array's name is

(a) Pointer constant (b) Array's constant

(c) Pointer variable (d) Keep the address of first cell

16. Identify errors, if any, in each of the following array declaration statements, assuming that ROW and COLUMN are declared as symbolic constants:

(a) int scoreboard (100);

(b) double matrix [10,15];

(c) void average_value[ROW],[COLUMN]; (d)voidcharname[15];

(e) f loatsum[];

(f) double emp_salary [i + ROW]

(g) long int list [ROW]

(h)intarray_x[COLUMN];

17. Identify errors, if any, in each of the following initialization statements.

(a) float number[ ] = {0,0,0,0,0};

(b) double item[3][2] = {0,1,2,3,4,5};

(c) charword[] = {'A.,'R', 'R', 'A, Y'};

(d) int m[2,4] = {{0,0,0,0}, {1,1,1,1}};

(e) float result[10] = 0;

18. Assume that the arrays M and N are declared as follows:

int M [5] [4]:
float N [4]:

Find the errors (if any) in the following code segments.

(a) for(i=l;i<=10;i++)

for(j=l;j<=8;j++) M[i] [j] = 0;

(b) for (i=l; i<8; i++) scanf("%f", N[;]);

(c) for (i=0; i<=8; i++) N[i] = N[i]+i;

(d) for (i=4; i>=0; i-) for(j=0;j<8;j++)

M [i] [j] = N [j] + 1.0 ;

19. We want to declare a two-dimensional double type array called matrix for 3 rows and 5 columns. State which of the following declarations are correct in respect to C?
    (a) double matrix [3], [5];
    (b) double matrix [5] [3];
    (c) double matrix [1+2] [2+3];
    (d) double matrix [3,5];
    (e) double matrix [3] [5];
20. Which of the following initialization statements are correct?
    (a) charstr1[4] = "GOOD";
    (b) charstr2[] = "C"; (c)charstr3[5] = "Moon"; (d) char str4[ ] = {'S', 'IT, 'N'}; (e)charstr5[10] = "Sun";

State whether the following statements are true or false

1. The type of all elements in an array must be the same.
2. When an array is declared static, C automatically initializes its elements to zero.
3. An expression that evaluates to an integral value may be used as a subscript.
4. Accessing an array outside its range is a compile time error.
5. A char type variable cannot be used as a subscript in an array.
6. An unsigned long int type can be used as a subscript in an array.
7. In C, by default, the first subscript is zero.
8. When initializing a multidimensional array, not specifying all its dimensions is an error.
9. When we use expressions as a subscript, its result should be always greater than zero.
10. In C, we can use a maximum of n dimensions for an array, where n is any valid greater than 10.
11. In declaring an array, the array size can be a constant or variable or an expression.
12. The declaration int A[5] = {1, 2,3, 4, 5, 6}; is illegal.

Fill in the blanks with appropriate words in each of the following statements

1. The variable used as a subscript in an array is popularly known as ____________ variable.
2. An array can be initialized either at compile time or at ____________.
3. An array created using malloc function at run time is referred to as ____________ array.
4. An array that uses more than two subscript is referred to as ____________ array.
5. ____________ is the process of arranging the elements of an array in order.

Structures and Union

17.1 INTRODUCTION

C provides a method of grouping of information elements into one name called **structure or struct.** It is often convenient to think of several pieces of information as being logically related. For example, if we want to generate a mailing address list of MMEC Company then following information is required to maintain the list in computer or input is required for mailing address program:

1. **Name**
2. **House/Street**
3. **Town/City/District**
4. **State**
5. **PIN**
6. **Country**

A structure is similar to a record, which is a data structure. Other high-level languages also use data structure (record) to store related pieces of information within one name. Once we have created the mailing list structure, we can refer all of the information it contains as a group, rather than having to refer it by six different names. In this chapter we will look on strcut and union.

17.2 CONCEPT OF STRUCTURE

Structure is a part of C which provides a means of defining a single variable that is actually comprised of many different data types. In more technical terms, we can say that a **struct** is a derived data type comprised of a collection of intrinsic (primary) data types. The specific collection of these intrinsic types actually forms the derived data type. In some ways, a **struct** can be compared to an array. The latter also provides a means of combining several variable storage areas into one accessed unit.

In more specific way we can say that a structure is a collection of variables under a single name. These variables can be of different types, and each has a name which is used to select it from the structure.

A structure is a convenient way of grouping several pieces of related information together. It can be defined as a new named typc, thus extending the number of available types. It can use other structures, arrays or pointers as some of its members, though this can get complicated unless we are careful.

In a struct, however, data elements need not be of the same type as is the case of an array. The syntax to declare a struct is

```
struct Tag name
{
    Data typel fielch;
    Data type2 field2:
    Data type3 field3:
    .
    .
    Data typen fieldn ; };
```

For example, consider the following code: struct Record

```
{
char Name[30];
int AccountNumber; double Amount;
};
```

This is a template for a struct named Record which is collection of variables of different data types. The first struct element is a char array named Name. The 2nd and 3rd are numeric types named AccountNumber and Amount of data types int and double, respectively.

The collection of variables may be accessed via the struct tag name Record as implemented in Example 17.1.

Example 17.1: Write C code for implementing simple struct definition.

Answer: Go through the following code.

```
/** struct1 .c**/
#include<stdio.h>
void main() {
    struct Record Rec; printf("\n Input Name: ");
    gets(Rec.Name);
    printf("\n Input Account Number: ");
    scanf("\n %d", &Rec.AccountNumber);
    printf("\n Input Amount:");
    scanf("\n %lf", &Rec.Amount);
    printf("\n Record is as follows");
    printf("\n Name:");
    puts(Rec.Name);
    printf("\n Account Number: %d",Rec.AccountNumber);
    printf("\n Amount: %lf", Rec.Amount);
    }
```

Each member of a structure can be used just like a normal variable, but its name will be a bit longer. To return to the examples above, member Name of structure Rec will behave just like a normal array of char, however we refer to it by the Name.

Rec.Name

Here the dot is an operator which selects a member from a structure. Where we have a pointer to a structure we could dereference the pointer and then use dot as a member selector. This method is a little clumsy to type. Since selecting a member from a structure pointer happens frequently, it has its own operator ? which acts as follows. Assume that Rec_ptr is a pointer to a structure of type Record. We would refer to the name member as

Rec_ptr → Name

Now question arises as to what is the actual meaning of a structure. Consider the declaration shown in Figure 17.1.

Opening and closing braces with semicolon means a structure works like a single statement. When we declare structure type variables, keyword **struct,** tag name and list of variables are required. In the list of variables, the tag name should not be repeated. The syntax for declaring a structure type variable is

struct tag name list of variables;

For example,

```
struct Record Rec;
struct Record {
char Name[30];
int AccountNumber;
double Amount;
};
```

Keyword → struct Record ← TagName
{
char Name[30];
int AccountNumber;
double Amount;
} ← Members
Opening brace
Closing brace → }; ← Statement terminator

Figure 17.1: Structure Declaration

In the Example 17.1 (structlc), the structure member operator (.) connects the structure name (Rec) and the member **Name.** Therefore, **Rec.Name** accesses the structure element **Name** and the value of **Name** is read into by **Rec.Name** with the help of function **gets().** The values of **int** and **double** member are read by using the same operator.

When a structure variable such as **Rec** is declared, C compiler automatically allocates sufficient memory to accommodate all of its members. **Figure 17.2** illustrates how **Rec** appears by assigning memory to 1-byte **char** and 2-bytes int and 8-bytes **double.**

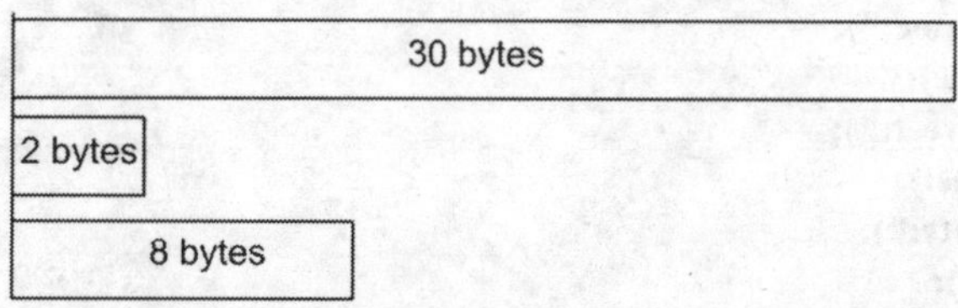

Figure 17.2: Rec structure in memory

We can also declare one or more structure variables as in the following code segment: **struct Address {**

```
char Name[30];
char Street[60];
char  City[100];
char State[20];
unsigned long int Pin;
} Address1, Address2, Address3;
```

Here, a structure type called **Address** declares **Addressl, Address2** and **Address3** variables of that type. If we need only one structure variable, the structure tag name is not required that is:

```
struct
{
    charName[30];
    charStreet[60];
    charCity[100];
    charState[20];
    unsigned long int Pin;
    } Address;
```

The general form for declaring structure is

```
struct tag name
{
    Data type1 Member1;
    Data type2 Member2;
    Data type3 Member3;
    .
    .
    .
    Data typen Membern;
} List of structure variables;
```

All the members may be of different type or of the same type depending upon the requirement. The list of variables may contain zero, one or more variables as illustrated in the following program segment:

```
/* struct2.c */
#include<stdio.h>
struct Address {
    char Name[30]; /* Member 1 */
    char Street[60]; /* Member 2 */
    char City[100]; /* Member 3 */
    char State[20]; /* Member 4*/
    unsigned long int Pin; /* Member 5*/
} Address1;
void main()
{
    printf("\n Input Name:");
    gets(Address1.Name);
    printf("\n Input Street:");
    gets( Address1.Street):
    printf("\n Input City:");
    gets(Address1.City);
    printf("\n Input State:");
    gets(Address1.State);
    printf("\nInputZIP:");
    scanf("\n %ld", &Address1.Pin);
    printf("\n Name: %s", Address1.Name);
    printf("\n Street: %s", Address1.Street);
    printf("\n City: %s", Address1.City);
    printf("\n State: %s", Address1.State);
    printf("\n ZIP: %ld", Address1 .Pin);
```

17.2.1 Structure Definition

A structure type is usually defined near to the start of a file using a typedef statement. typedef defines and names a new type, allowing its use throughout the program, typedefs usually occur just after the #define and #include statements in a file. Here is an example structure definition.

```
typedef struct
{
    char name[64]:
    char course[128];
    int age;
    int year;
} student;
```

This defines a new type student variables of type student can be declared as follows.

```
student st_rec;
```

Notice how similar this is to declaring an int or float. The variable name is st_rec, it has members called name, course, age and year.

17.2.2 Structure Initialization

Providing the values of fields (members) as a set does the initialization, i.e., an initializer for a structure is a brace-enclosed comma-separated list of values. The initializer is preceded by an equal sign (=). For example,

```
struct Address
{
    char Name[30];   /* member 1 */
    char Street[60];   /* member 2 */
    char City[100];   /*member3*/
    char State[20];   /* member 4 */
    unsigned long int Pin; /* member 5 */ };
```

Initialization is done like

```
struct Address Address1 =
{
    "Tom Alter", "B-3 Dong
    Street", "Valley Town",
    "New York", 95136
};
```

This declaration contains five fields the first four are **char** type and 5th is of type **long int.** We know that **char** takes 1 -byte and **long int** takes 4 bytes and here the compiler allocates 214 bytes of memory space for the structure variable **Addressl.** The initialization done as illustrated in Figure 17.3. Go through the Example 17.2 which implements the above discussion.

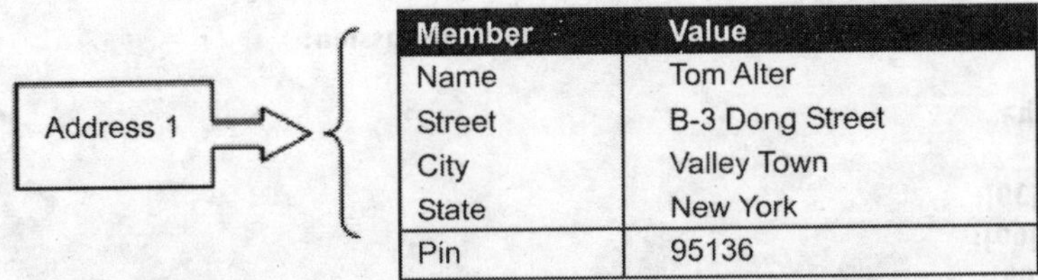

Figure 17.3 INITIALIZATION of structure variable

Example 17.2: Write C code which initializes a struct variable.

Answer: The following program segments (struct3, struct4.c and strcu5.c) implement the above discussion and presents different intermediate scenarios hidden behind the initialization and assignment.

```
/** struct3.c **/
# include<stdio.h>
struct Address {
    charName[30];
    charStreet[60];
    char City[100];
    charState[20];
    unsigned long
    int Pin;
    };
void main() {
    struct Address Addressl = {
    "Tom Alter", "B-3 Dong Street", "Valley Town", "New York", 95136 };

struct Address Address 2 = {
    "Holkar",
    "4-C/3 College Campus",
    "Daught Mouth College, Send Diego",
    "New Jersey",
    94001
 };
printf("\n Name: %s", Address1.Name); printf("\n Street: %s", Address1.Street);
printf("\n City: %s", Address1.City);
 printf("\n State: %s", Address1.State);
printf("\n ZIP: %ld", Address1.Pin);
printf("\n Name: %s", Address2.Name);
printf("\n Street: %s", Address2.Street); printf("\n City: %s", Address2.City);
printf("\n State: %s", Address2.State); printf("\n ZIP: %ld", Address2.Pin);
}
```

It is also possible to initialize structure as follows:

```
struct Address
{
    char Name[30];
    char Street[60];
    char City[100];
    char State[20];
    unsigned long int Pin;
} Address1 ={
    "Tom Alter", "B-3 Dong Street",
    "Valley Town", "New York",
    95136
};
```

The following program segment implements the above discussion:

```
/* struct4.c */
#include<stdio.h>
struct Address {
    char Name[30];
    char Street[60]:
    char City[100];
    char State[20]:
    unsigned long int Pin;
} Addressl ={
"Tom Alter", "B-3 Dong Street", "Valley Town", "New York", 95136
};
```

```
void main() {
    printf("\n Name: %s", Address1.Name);
    printf("\n Street: %s", Address1.Street);
    printf("\n City: %s", Address1.City);
    printf("\n State: %s", Address1.State);
    printf("\n ZIP: %ld", Address1.Pin);
}
```

Further if we already initialized a struct variable and want to initialize another struct variable of the same type this can be done by assigning the initialized struct variable to new one. In words we can say that we making duplicate copy of the existing struct members. For example, if we define as bilM and bill2 as structure Payment variable and definition of the Payment is

```
struct Payment
{
    char Name[40];
    float Cost_of_Item;
    char Code_of_Item[20];
    int Number_of_Item;
};
```

Following statement initialize the struct Payment variable Bill1

struct Payment Bill1 = {"LASER", 23500.75, "S/124/1999",10}; Then Bill2 will be initialized with the following statement

Bill2 = Bill1;

Bill2 will hold the value of Bill1 that is

Bill2 = Bill1 = {"LASER", 23500.75, "S/124/1999", 10};

This idea is explained further with the help of following program segment:

```
/** struct5.c **/
# include<stdio.h>
struct Payment
{
    char Name_of_Item [40];
    float Cost_of_Item;
    char Code_of_Item[20];
    int Number_of_Item;
};
struct Payment Bill1= {"LASER",23500.75,"S/124/1999",10};
struct Payment Bill2;
void main()
{
    double Total_cost;
    Total_cost = Bill1.Number_of_Item * Bill1.Cost_of_Item;
    printf("\n Detail of item sold");
    printf(nn********************************");
    printf("\n Item code   : %s",Bill1.Code_of_Item );
    printf("\n Name of item : %s",Bill1.Name_of_Item);
    printf("\n No.of Item    : %d",Bill1.Number_of_Item);
    printf("\n Cost of item : %f", Bill1.Cost_of_Item);
    printf("\n Total Cost  : %f", Total_cost);
    printf("\n********************************");
    printf("\n Press a key");
    getchar();
    Bill2 = Bill1 ;
    printf("\n Detail of item sold");
    printf("\n********************************");
```

```
printf("\n Item code   : %s",Bill2.Code_of_Item );
printf("\n Name of item : %s",Bill2.Name_of_Item);
printf("\n No.of Item    : %d",Bill2.Number_of_Item);
printf("\n Cost of item : %f", Bill2.Cost_of_Item);
printf("\n Total Cost  : %f",Total_cost);
printf("\n********************************");
printf("\n Press A Key");
getchar();
}
```

Unnamed structure members do not participate in initialization and have indeterminate value after initialization. Therefore, in the following example, the bit field is not initialized, and the initializer 3 is applied to member b:

```
struct {
    inta;
    int:10;
    intb;
    } w = {2, 3};
```

We do not have to initialize all members of a structure; the initial value of uninitialized structure members depends on the storage class associated with the structure variable. In a structure declared as static, any members that are not initialized are implicitly initialized to zero of the appropriate type; the members of a structure with automatic storage have no default initialization. The following definition shows a partially initialized structure:

```
struct address
{
    int street_no;
    char *street_name;
    char *city;
    char *prov;
    char *postal_code;
};

struct address temp_address = { 44, "Knyvet Ave.", "Hamilton", "Ontario" };
```

The values of temp_address are:

Member	Value
temp_address.street_no	44
temp_address.street_name	address of string "Knyvet Ave."
temp_address.city	address of string "Hamilton"
temp_address.prov	address of string "Ontario-
temp_address.postal_code	Depends on the storage class of the temp address variable; if it is static, the value would be NULL.

To initialize only the third and fourth members of the temp_address variable, we could use a designated initializer list, as follows:

```
struct address
{
    int street_no;
    char *street_name;
    char *city;
    char *prov;
```

```
    char *postal_code;
};
struct address temp_address = { .city = "Hamilton", .prov = "Ontario" };
```

Notice that only ANSI C compiler supports this property.

17.3 NESTED STRUCTURES

When a structure is called within another structure, it is called nesting of structure. For example, consider the following syntax:

```
struct X
{
Data type1 Member1;
Data type2 Member2;
Data type3 Member3;
.
.
Data typen Membern;
};
struct Y
{
Data type1 Member1;
Data type2 Member2;
Data type3 Member3;
.
.
Data typep Memberp;
};
struct Z
{
Datatype1 Member1;
Data type2 Member2;
Data type3 Member3;
.
.
Data typem Memberm;
};
    struct R {
    struct X Member1;
    struct Y Member1;
    struct Z Member1;
    ......
};
```

In the above syntax, the structures X, Y and Z are nested in structure R. Figure 17.4 describe the general form of the nested structure.

Nesting one kind of structure inside another is often useful. For example, suppose we have declared the following structure, which can store a person's first name, middle name and last name:

```
struct Person_Name
{
charFirst[20];
char Middle[20];
char Last[20];
};
```

We use the Person_Name structure as a part of another structure as shown below: struct Student {

```
        struct Person_Name Name;
        charSSN[10];
        int Age;
        charBdate[10];
        char
    Sex; }Student1,Student2;
```

Accessing Studentl's first name, middle name or last name requires two applications of the dot (.) operator. For example,

strcpy (Studentl.Name.First, "Ram");

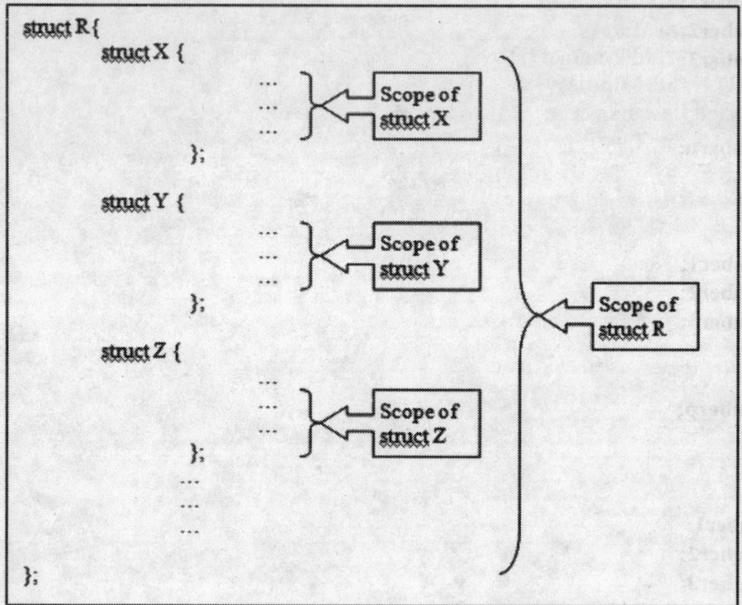

Figure 17.4 Nested structures

In this statement strcpy() function copies "Ram" into variable First. One advantage of making Name a structure instead of having first, middle and last be the members of the **Student** structure is that we can more easily treat names as units of data. For example, if we want to write a function that displays a name, we can pass it with just one argument to **Person_Name** structure instead of three arguments. For example,

Output_Name(Student1 .Name);

Likewise, copying the information from a **Person_Name** structure would take one assignment instead of three. For example:

struct Person_Name New_Name;

Studentl.Name = New_Name;

Go through the Example 17.3 for implementation of the above discussion.

Example 17.3: Write C code and show how it saves number of assignment operator in the computation/operation done by struct based implementation.

Answer: Consider the following program segment that implements the above discussion. /*

```
struct6.c */ #include<stdio.h>
struct Person_Name {
```

```
        charFirst[20];
        char Middle[20];
        char Last[20]: };
    struct Student {
        struct Person_Name Name;
        charSSN[10];
        int Age;
        charBdate[10];
        char Sex; }Student1,Student2;
    void main() {
        I* Input section */
        printf("\n Enter First name:");
        gets(Student1 .Name.First):
        printf("\n Enter Middle name:");
        gets(Student1 .Name.Middle):
        printf("\n Enter Last name:");
        gets(Student1 .Name.Last):
        printf("\nEnter Social Security Number:");
        gets(Studentl.SSN);
        printf("\nEnter Birth date:");
        gets(Studentl.Bdate);
        printf("\n Enter Age:");
        scanf("%d", &Student1.Age);
        printf("\n Enter Sex:");
        scanf("%c", Studentl.Sex);
        printf("\nREPORT GENERATION");
        printf("\n**********************");
        printf("\n First name:");
        puts(Student1 .Name.First);
        printf("\n Middle name:");
        puts(Student1 .Name.Middle);
        printf("\n Last name:");
        puts(Student1 .Name.Last);
        printf("\n Social Security Number:");
        puts(Studentl.SSN);
        printf("\n Birth date:");
        puts(Studentl.Bdate);
        printf("\n Age:");
        printf("%d", Studentl.Age);
        printf("\n Sex:");
        printf("%c", Studentl.Sex);
        }
```

In the above program segment, **struct Student calls struct Person_Name. The fields of struct Person_Name** are accessed by the use of two dots as shown in Figure 17.5.

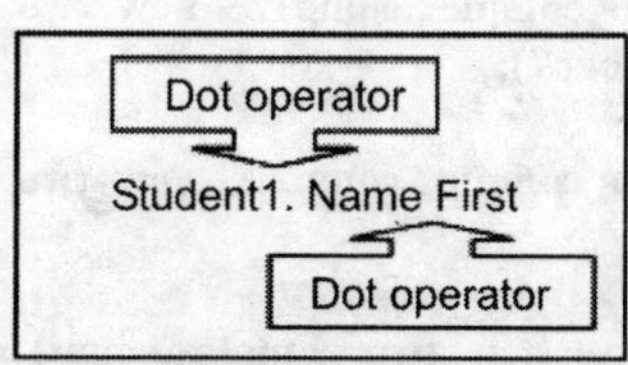

Figure 17.5 Accessing nested structure (one level nesting)

Number of dots depends on level of nesting. If it is three levels nesting, four dots are required to access a field (member) from the first level of structure as illustrated in **Figure 17.6.**

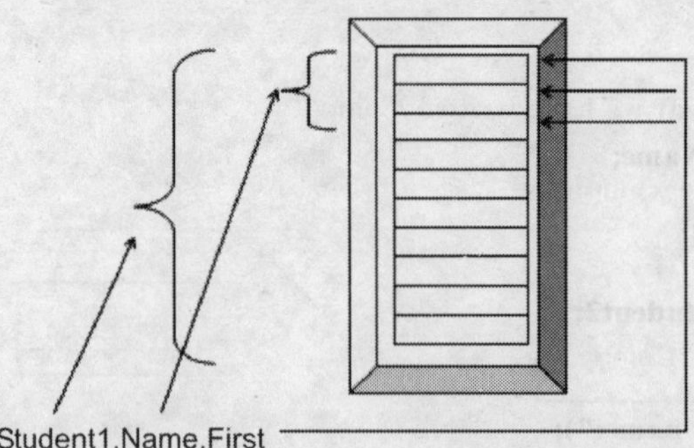

Figure 17.6 Nested structures and dot operator

17.4 IMPLEMENTATION OF NESTED STRUCTURES

Providing values of fields as a set does the initialization, i.e., an initialization for a struct is a brace enclosed comma separated list of values. Go through the Example 17.4 which implements complex number and discusses uses of the nested structure.

Example 17.4: Write C code for adding two complex number without using library function.

Answer: See the following program segment which initializes a nested structure and finds their summation also.

```
/** struct7.c */
I* Two complex numbers addition    */
#include<stdio.h>
struct complexl
{
    float x ;
    float y ;
};
struct two_complex
{
    struct complexl compl ;
    struct complexl comp2 ; };
void main() {
    struct complexl comp;
    struct   two_complex new_two_complex = {
                                    {2.5,4.5},
                                    {3.5,6.5}};
printf("\nFirst Complex Number");

printf("\n*******************");
printf("\n%4.1f + j4.1%f",new_two_complex.comp1.x, new_two_complex.comp1.y);
printf("\n\n\nSecond Complex Number");
printf(nn********************");
printf("\n%4.1f + j%4.1f",new_two_complex.comp2.x, new_two_complex.comp2.y);


comp.x = new_two_complex.comp2.x + new_two_complex.comp1.x ;
comp.y = new_two_complex.comp1.y + new_two_complex.comp2.y;
printf("\n\n\n\nSummation of two complex number");
printf(nn********************************"); printf("\n%4.1f + j%4.1f",comp.x,comp.y);
printf(nn********************************");
```

```
printf("\n Press a key");
getchar();
}
```

In the above program segment we have written $Comp_I$
$Comp_P$

```
struct two_complex new_two_complex =
        { {2.5,4.5}, {3.5,6.5}};
```

Comp$_2$ ⇨ {2.5,4.5}, {3.5,6.5}}; ⇦ Comp$_1$

In other words, we can say that new_two_complex is a set organized with subset of Compl and Comp2. In the declaration, we have used braces to differentiate subset; we have used to initialize a structure. These braces are optional. If we do not use braces, compiler automatically recognizes the size of structures nested in a structure. For example, consider the following program segment, where we have used only values required for the structure without braces:

```
/**struct17.c**/
/* Complex number subtraction */
# include<stdio.h>
struct complexl
{
    float x ;
    float y ; };
struct complex2 {
struct complexl compl ; struct complexl comp2 ; };

void main() {
    struct complexl complex;
    struct complex2 cp = {10,20,30,40};

    printf("\n Complex Number");
    printf("\n **************");
    printf("\n%4.1f + %4.1fj",cp.comp1.x , cp.compl.y);
    printf("\n%4.1f + %4.1fj",cp.comp2.x , cp.comp2.y);
    printf("\n Press a key");
    getchar();
complex.x = cp.compl.x - cp.comp2.x; complex.y =
cp.compl.y - cp.comp2.y; printf("\n %4.1f + %4.1jf",
complex.x, complex.y); }
```

17.5 STRUCTURES AND ARRAYS

When it is required to represent same type of records more than once, it is done through an array representation. Suppose we want to keep information of all the employees in an organization. It is possible through an array or file or through both. If we want to keep information of employees of the following fields:

1. Name
2. Dept
3. Status
4. Basic salary
5. Address of an organization

Then aggregate type declaration of above information can be done as follows: struct

```
Emp {
    char Name [40] ; char
    Dept [120]; char
    Status ; int
    Basic_salary ; char
    Address [120];
};
    struct EmpRec[100];
```

In the above declaration, Rec **[100]** represents storage space for 100 records of type **Emp.** It will require 282 bytes of memory space to keep information of one employee. So, total space required will be 282x100 = 282100 bytes. From this result, it is clear that before defining an array of structure, one must determine the memory space available on the machine. If memory space is less, one can use files. Example 17.5 demonstrates the idea of arrays of structures.

Example 17.5: Write C code for maintaining employee records of an organization using array of structures.

Answer:

```
See the following code. /*
struct9.c */ #include<stdio.h>
struct Emp {
    char Name [40] ;
    char Dept [120];
    char Status ;
    int Basic_salary ;
    char Address [120]; };
struct Emp Rec [100];
void main() {
    int no_of_record ;
    inti ;
    printf("\n Enter number of record want to process:");
    scanf("%d",&no_of_record);

/* Input section */
for( i = 0 ; i < no_of_record ; i++ ) {
    printf("\n Record number: %d",i+1);
    printf("\nEnter employee name:");
    gets(Rec[i].Name);
    printf("\nEnter Deptt:");
    gets(Rec[i].Dept);
    printf("\nEnter class:");
    Recfi].Status = getchar();
    printf("\n Enter basic salary:");
    scanf("%d",&Rec[i].Basic_salary);
    printf("\nEnter address of employee:");
    gets(Rec[i].Address): }
for( i = 0 ; i < no_of_record ; i++ ) {
    printf("\n Record Number: %d",i+1);
    printf("\n Employee Name: ");
    puts(Rec[i].Name);
```

```
        printf("\n Deptt:");
        puts(Rec[i].Dept);
        printf("\n Class:");
        printf("%c",Rec[i].Status);
        printf("\n Basic salary:");
        printf("%d",Rec[i].Basic_salary);
        printf("\n Address:");
        puts(Rec[i].Address):
        printf("\n Press a key");
    getchar() ;
    }
}
```

17.6 INITIALISATION OF ARRAY OF SRUCTURES

Initializing an array of structures is done in the same way as initializing a multidimensional array. Each structure has its own brace- enclosed initializer. The initializer for the array simply wraps another set of braces around the structure initializers.

One application, where initializing of an array of structures is done, is where we treat it as database that would not change during program execution. For example, if we are working on a program (software) that needs access to the country name and codes for international calls (ISD), we setup structure as below:

```
struct ISDCODEDIARY
{
    char Country_Name[40];
    int
ISDNUMBER;
};
```

Now we declare an array of this structure and initialize it to contain the codes, some of the world's most popular nations.

```
const struct ISDCODEDIARY ISD[200] = {
{"Argentina", 54}, {"Australia", 61},
{"Bangladesh" 880}, {"Iraq", 984},
{"New Zealand", 64}, {"China", 86"},
{"Cuba", 53}, {"Hong Kong", 852},
{"Kenya", 254}, {"Jordan", 962},
{"Oman", 968"}, {"Spain", 34},
{"Pakistan", 92}, {"India", 91}, {"U.K.", 44},
{"USA", 01}, {"South Korea", 27},
{"Singapore", 65}, {"UAE", 9711},
{"Qatar", 974} };
```

The inner braces around each structure value are optional but often used for clarity and readability.

17.7 POINTERS TO STRUCTURES

To change the structure member within a function, the function must pass a pointer to the structure. Within the function, the pointer is de-referenced using the asterisk indirection operator, i.e.,

```
(*pointer).member = Info;
```

Here, C starts from the parenthesis by obtaining the location of the structure. Next, C adds to the address the offset of the specified member {Figure 17.7}. If the parenthesis are omitted such that the statement becomes

***pointer.member = Info;**

C assumes that the member itself is pointer and uses the asterisk indirection operator to resolve it. This syntax would be correct for a structure having a member a pointer, such as the following:

```
struct Address
{
      charName[40];
      int*pointer; }
Address;
```

In the above declaration, the 2nd member is a pointer to **int.** Assuming that the pointer has been assigned to a memory location, the following statement places the value 50 in memory location

***Address.pointer = 50;**

To de-reference the pointerwithin the function, C provides two formats. First we have seen it is like

***Address.pointer = 50;**

and other we can refer to a structure member in the following form.

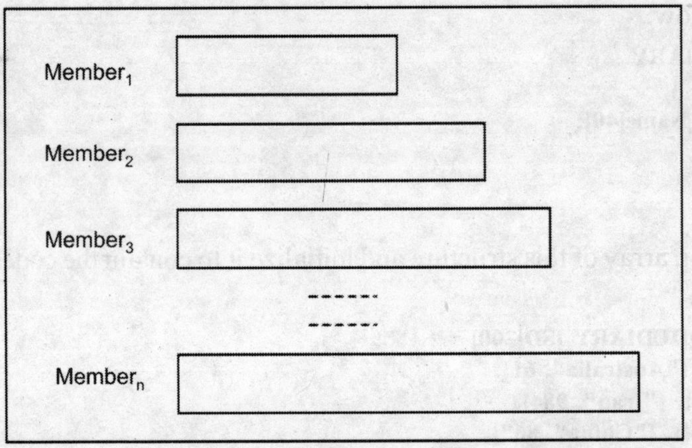

Figure 17.7 Accessing a member of structure using pointer

Consider the Example 17.6 which is implementing the above discussion.

Example 17.6: Write C code using pointer to access the member of a struct.

Answer: See the following program segments struct10.c and struct11.c).

```
/**struct10.c**/
#    include<stdio.h>
#    include<malloc.h> struct Address
{
char Name[40]: charAddr[140]; long int Zip; };
void Update (struct Address *Ref) {
     struct Address Reference=
                              { "Don",
"4-C/3 Mangal Town, Sanjose, California", 95136}; *Ref =
```

```
Reference; }
void main() {
    struct Address Add;
    Update (&Add):
    puts(Add.Name);
    puts(Add.Addr);
    printf("\n Pin Code: %ld", Add.Zip); }
```

Summary of pointer to structure is given in **Table 17.1.** The summary given in **Table 17.1** can be discussed with the help of the following example. In this example, we have defined two structure variables and two pointers to structures.

Table 17.1 Summary Pointer to Structure

*pointer.member is equivalent to *(pointer, member) is meaningful only when pointer is a structure with a pointer member.

(*pointer).member is equivalent to pointer'lmember

Pointer.member[5] is equivalent to (pointer.member)[5]

pointer → member+5 is equivalent to (pointer?member)+5 the expression pointer → member +5 gives the address of the 5th element when we de-reference pointer → member+5, get the information stored at location pointed by pt → member +5, i.e., *(pointer → member+5).

*pointer.member is equivalent to *pointer!member and is equivalent to *(pointer → member)

```
/**struct11.c**/ #
include<stdio.h> struct
Mailing {
    char Name[40]:
    char Father[40];
    int Age;
    float Salary; };
struct Mailing RecorcM = {"TOM ALTER","WANT WATER", 32,48000.75}; struct Mailing Record2 =
{"JORG COOK", "MORTIN COOK", 50, 32000.25};
void main() {
    struct Mailing *ptr1,*ptr2;
    ptrl =&Record1;
    ptr2 = &Record2;
    printf("\n Detail of record 1 is as follows \n");
    printf("\n Name:"");
    puts(Recordl.Name);
    printf(" Father:");
    puts(Record1.Father);
    printf(" Age: %d", Recordl.Age);
    printf("\n Salary: %f", Recordl.Salary);
    printf("\n");
    printf("\n Detail of record 1 with the help of pointer is as follows \n");
    printf("\n Name:");
    puts((*ptr1).Name);
    printf(" Father:");
    puts((*ptr1).Father);
    printf(" Age: %d", (*ptr1).Age);
    printf("\n Salary: %f", (*ptr1).Salary);
    printf("\n");
    printf("\n Detail of record 2 is as follows \n");
```

```
printf("\n Name:");
puts(Record2.Name);
printf(" Father: ");
puts(Record2.Father);
printf(" Age: %d", Record2.Age);
printf("\n Salary: %f", Record2.Salary);
printf("\n");
printf("\n Detail of record 2 with the help of pointer is as follows \n");
printf("\n Name:");
puts((*ptr2).Name);
printf(" Father:");
puts((*ptr2).Father);
printf(" Age: %d", (*ptr2).Age);
printf("\n Salary: %f", (*ptr2).Salary);
printf("\n");

/* Different pointer operation */

printf("\n Output through different pointer operation \n");
puts((*ptr1).Name); puts(ptr1->Name);
printf(" %d",Record1.Age);
printf("\n %d",(*ptr1).Age);
printf("\n %d", ptr1->Age);
printf("\n Byte level operation \n");
printf("\n %c", Record1.Name[2]);
printf("\n %c", (Record1.Name)[2]);
printf("\n %s", ptr1->Name+2); printf("\n %s",
(ptr1->Name)+2);

printf("\n %c", *(ptr1->Name+2));
printf("\n %c", ptr1->Name[2]); printf("\n %c",
(ptr1->Name)[2]);
printf("\n %c", *Record2.Name);
printf("\n %c", *ptr2->Name); printf("\n %c",
*(ptr2->Name));
printf("\n %c", Record2.Name); printf("\n %c",
*(Record2.Name));

printf("\n %c", *Record2.Name+1); printf("\n %c",
*ptr2->Name+1); printf("\n %c",
*(ptr2->Name)+1); }
```

In the above program segment following expressions contain the address of the string "TOM ALTER".

(*ptr1).Name

ptr1->Name

The value of the each of the following expressions is 32: Recordl.Age

(*ptr1).Age ptr1->Age

The member dot (.) operator and the brackets [] have equal precedence and also have LTR associativity. Thus, we can say that the expression

Record1.Name[2]

is equivalent to

(Record 1.Name)[2]

The value of RecorcM.Name is the address of the string "TOM ALTER" and the value of Record 1.Name[2] is 3rd character M.

The pointer operator (*) has a higher precedence than +, so the expression

ptr1->Name+2

is equivalent to

(ptr1->Name)+2

The value of ptrl ->Name is the address of the string "TOM ALTER", and the value of ptrl ->Name+2 is the address of the 3rd character. De-referencing ptr1->Name+2 yields character M. Thus, the value of the expression

***(ptr1->Name+2)**

is again M.

The pointer operator -> and the brackets [] have the same precedence and have LTR associativity. Thus, the expression

ptr1->Name[2]

is equivalent to

(ptr1->Name)[2]

Because the value of the ptrl ->Name is the address of the string "TOM ALTER", the value of the ptr1->Name[2] is again M. We have shown that each of

Record1.Name[2]
***(ptr1->Name+2)**
ptr1->Name[2]

is equal to M.

The value of each of the following expression is J because dot (.) operator has a higher precedence than *.

***Record2.Name**
***ptr2->Name**
***(ptr2->Name)**

The expression

*Record2.Name is equivalent to
*(Record2.Name)

The value of Record2.Name is the address of the string "JORG COOK". When we dereference Record2.Name, we obtain the first character J. Again because -" has a higher precedence than *, the last two expressions

***ptr2->Name**

and

***(ptr2->Name)**

are equivalent.

The value of the **ptr2->Name** is the address of the string "JORG COOK". When we dereference **ptr2->Name,** we again obtain the first character J.

The value of each of the following expressions

***Record2.Name+1 *ptr2->Name+1**
***(ptr2-Name)+1**

is K.

For example, because * and dot (.) have a higher precedence than +, the expression ***Record2.Name+1** is equivalent to

(*Record2.Name)+1

Thus, we first evaluate ***Record2.Name** to obtain J. When we add 1 to J, we get K.

17.8 STRUCTURES AND FUNCTIONS

Structure variable can be used as return values from functions and passed to functions as arguments, just as simple variable can. This is powerful feature that greatly simplifies the use of structures and then the writing of well-constructed modular programs that use structures.

When we pass a member of a structure to a function, we are actually passing the value of that member to the function. Therefore, we are passing a simple variable. For example, consider the following syntax of structure:

```
struct MailingAddress
{
    char Name[40]; /* First member*/
    char Father_Name[40]; /* Second member*/
    char City[40]; /* Third member */
    long int Zip; /* Fourth member */ }
Address;
```

Suppose, we have defined function **pass_struct()** that accepts (receives) **char** type (string), the individual member can be passed like:

```
pass_struct(Address1 .Name)
```

will accept structure member Name (first member). Similarly

```
    pass_struct (Addressl .FatherJMame); pass_struct
    (Addressl .City);
```

will accept second and third member namely **Father_Name** and **City,** respectively. If we want to pass location of an individual structure member, we use & operator before the structure name. For example, to pass the address of the member of the structure **Addressl,**

we write

```
    pass_struct (&Address1 .Name[0]); /* Passed base address of the array member Name */
    pass_struct (&Address1.Father_Name[0]); /* Passed base address of the array member
    FatherJMame */
```

Go through the Example 17.7 for the implementation of the discussion.

Example 17.7: Write C code which defines user function. This function receives a struct as an argument.

Answer: For example, consider the following program segment (struct/I 2.c) that implements the simple struct member acceptance. In the next two strcut13.c and strucH.c finally we have implemented the complete code.

```
/*struct12.c*/
#include<stdio.h>
struct MailingAddress
{
    char Name[40]; /* First member*/
    char Father_Name[40]; /* Second member*/
    char City[40]; /* Third member*/
    long int Zip; /* Fourth member*/ } Address;
void pass_struct(charstrQ);
void main()
{
    struct MailingAddress Addressl = {"Tom Alter", "Tom Cook", "California", 93561 };
pass_struct(Address1 .Name);
pass_struct(Address1.Father_Name);
```

```
pass_struct(&Address1 .Name[0]);
pass_struct(&Address1.Father_Name[0]); }
void pass_struct(charstrQ) {
        puts(str);
}
```

When a structure is used as an argument to a function, the entire structure is passed using the standard call-by-value method. Of course, this means that any changes made to the contents of the structure inside the function, to which it is passed, do not affect the structure used as an argument.

When using a structure as a parameter, we must keep in mind that the type of the argument must match the type of the parameter passed. For example, consider the following program segment where both the argument Act and Ref are declared as the same type of structure:

```
/**struct13.c**/
# include<stdio.h>
struct Tag_Name
{
        inta;
        charb;
        float f; };
void fun (struct Tag_Name Ref) {
        printf("\n Value of a is %d", Ref.a);
        printf("\n Value of b is %c", Ref.b);
        printf("\n Value of f is %f", Ref.f); }
void main() {
        struct Tag_Name Act;
        Act.a = 200;
        Act.b = 'C;
        Act.f = 875.75;
        fun (Act); }
```

As the above program segment illustrates, if we are declaring structure parameters, we must make the declaration of the structure type global, so that all parts of the program can use them. For example, Tag_Name been declared inside the function main (), it would not have been visible to fun().

As just stated, when passing structures, the type of the argument must match the type of the parameter. It is not sufficient for them to simply be physically similar, and then type names must match. For example, consider the following program segment that is similar to previous one and it does not compile because the type name of the argument used to call fun () differs from the type name of its parameters.

```
/**struct14.c**/
# include<stdio.h>
struct Tag_Name
{
        inta;
        charb;
        float f; };
struct Tag_Name1 {
        inta;
        charb;
        float f; };
void fun (struct Tag_Name1 Ref) {
        printf("\n Value of a is %d", Ref.a);
```

```
        printf("\n Value of b is %c", Ref.b);
        printf("\n Value of f is %f", Ref.f); }
    void main() {
        struct Tag_Name Act;
        Act.a = 200;
        Act.b = 'C';
         Act.f = 875.75;
         fun (Act);
    }
```

17.9 BIT-FIELDS

While we are on the subject of structures, we might as well look at bitfields. They can only be declared inside a structure or a union, and allow to specify some very small objects of a given number of bits in length. Their usefulness is limited and they are not seen in many programs, but we will deal with them anyway. C has built-in feature called bit-field that allows one to access a single bit. Bit-fields are useful because

If storage is limited, one can store several Boolean (True/False) variables in a single byte.

Certain devices transmit information encoded into bits.

Certain encryption routines need to access the bits within a byte.

Although these tasks can be performed using the bitwise operators, a bit-field can add more flexibility to programs. To access bits, C uses a method based on the structure. In fact, a bit-field is a special type of structure member that defines how long, in bits, the field is to be. The syntax is

```
    struct Tag_Name
    {
        Datatypel Member1: Length;
        Datatype2 Member2: Length;
        Datatype3 Member3: Length;
        Datatypen Membern: Length; } List
    of variables;
```

In the above syntax, data type specifies the type of the bit-field, which must be either **int, unsigned** or **signed.** Bit-fields of size 1 should be declared as unsigned because a single bit cannot have a sign. The number of bits in the bit-field is specified by **Length.** This example should help to make things clear:

```
    struct
    {
        /* field 4 bits wide */
        unsigned fieldl :4;
        /*
        * unnamed 3 bit field
        * unnamed fields allow for padding */
        unsigned : 3; /*
        * one-bit field
        * can only be 0 or -1 in two's complement! */
    signed field2   :1;
    /* align next field on a storage unit */
    unsigned       :0;
    unsigned field3 :6;
    }full_of_fields;
```

Each field is accessed and manipulated as if it is an ordinary member of a structure. The keywords signed and unsigned mean what we would expect, except that it is interesting to note that a 1-bit signed field on a two's complement machine can only take the values 0 or -1. The declarations are permitted to include the const and volatile qualifiers. The main use of bitfields is either to allow tight packing of data or to be able to specify the fields within some externally produced data files. C gives no guarantee of the ordering of fields within machine words, so if we do use them for the latter reason, a program will not only be nonportable, it will be compiler-dependent too. In C fields are packed into 'storage units', which are typically machine words. The packing order, and whether or not a bitfield may cross a storage unit boundary, is implementation defined. To force alignment to a storage unit boundary, a zero width field is used before the one that we want to have aligned. Be careful using them. It can require a surprising amount of runtime code to manipulate these things and we can end up using more space than they save. Bit fields do not have addresses- we cannot have pointers to them or arrays of them. Bit-fields are frequently used when analyzing input from a hardware device. For example, the status port of a serial communications adapter might return a status byte organized as shown in Table 17.2.

Using the following bit-field, declaration can set the information in a status byte:

```
struct Status
{
    unsigned delta_act:1;
    unsigned delta_dsr:1;
    unsignedtr_edge:1;
    unsigned delta_rec:1;
    unsigned cts:1;
    unsigned dsr:1;
    unsigned ring :1;
    unsigned rec_line:1; } Status;
```

Table 17.2 Meaning of 8 bit code

Bit	Meaning
0	Change in clear to send
1	Change in data set ready
2	Training edge ring detector
3	Change in receive line signal detector
4	Clear to send
5	Data set ready
6	Ring indication
7	Received line signal detect

We might use a routine similar to shown below to enable a program to determine when it can send or receive data:

```
Status = get_port_status ();
if(Status.cts)
    printf("\n Clear to send");
if(Status.dsr)
    printf("\n Data ready");
```

Go though the Example 17.8 which impiements a real system for list devices in computer system.

Example 17.8: Write C code which lists the equipments available in a computer system.

Answer: Consider the following program segment that checks the list of equipment's attached with a computer system.

```
/* showequp.c */
```

```
#include <stdio.h>
#include <bios.h>
void main(void)
{
struct Equip
{
    unsigned floppy_available:1;
    unsigned coprocessor_available:1;
    unsigned system_memory:2; unsigned
    video_memory:2; unsigned
    floppy_disk_count:2; unsigned
    unused_1:1; unsigned
    serial_port_count:3; unsigned
    game_adapter_available:1; unsigned
    unused_2:1; unsigned printer_count:2; };
    union Equipment {
    unsigned list; struct Equip list_bits; } equip;
    equip.list = _bios_equiplist(); if
    (equip.list_bits.coprocessor_available)
              printf("Math coprocessor available\n");
 else
    printf("No math coprocessor\n");
 printf("System board memory %d\n", (equip.list_bits.system_memory + 1)* 16);
    printf("Number of floppies %d\n", equip.list_bits.floppy_disk_count + 1);
    printf("Number of printers %d\n", equip.list_bits.printer_count);
    printf("Number of serial ports %d\n",
    equip.list_bits.serial_port_count); }
```

Case Study: Usually the printing features of dot matrix printers can be divided into two categories:

Text mode

Graphics mode

The dot matrix printers have several different printing modes. When the printer is turned on, it is, by default, in text mode, that uses six lines per inch and the size of computer paper is 12 inches so that 72 lines per page are printed. By default, option selected is of pica type. If we want to print in other fonts and modes, it is required to set the mode of the printer. Sending control characters to the printer before starting the printing does the mode setting. Before sending the control character, first of all ESC character is sent. The ASCII value of this character is 27.

C language defines standard library function to output a character to printer. But this library function varies from compiler to compiler.

biosprintO is defined in TURBO-C

_bios_printer() is defined in MICROSOFT-C

In **ANSI C,** no such type of function is defined, to set the mode of printer. In **UNIX** operating system, we use function **putc()** and open device "/dev/lpO" in write mode and set the mode ofthefile(executable) like

```
#    chmod g+s file name
#    chown bin file name
```

After this setting, file is allowed to execute. For example, suppose we want to set printer in wide mode, then the required setting will be

putc(27,fp1);

putc(14,fp1);

and

putc(20, fp1); is used to reset the mode.

Here, we are providing details for **DOS/WINDOWS.** If one is interested in print function, one can write his/her own function for printing purposes. The syntax for the **biosprint()** function is

biosprint(int cmd, int byte, int port);

where

port: 0 it represents LPT1 port
1 it represents LPT2 port
2 it represents LPT3 port
and so on.

The exact function performed is contingent upon the value of **cmd.** The legal values of **cmd** are given in Table 17.3.

Table 17.3 Macro of printer

Value	Macro	Meaning
0	_PRINTER_WRITE	Print the character in byte
1	_PRINTER_INIT	Initialize the printer port
2	_PRINTER_STATUS	Return the status of the port

Table 17.4 Printer status returned code bits information

Bit	Meaning
1	Device timeout
3	I/O error
4	Device selected (printer)
5	Out of paper
6	Acknowledgement
7	Printer is not busy

This function returns printer port status as encoded into the low order byte of the return value and is given in Table 17.4. These bits are tested as defined below.

```
status = biosprint(2, ch, 0);
if(status & 0x01)
    printf("\n device time out");
    if( status & 0x08)
        printf("\n I/O error");
if(status&0x10)
printf(" \n device selected");
if( status & 0x20) printf("\n
out of paper");

if(status & 0x40)
  printf(" \n acknowledge");

if( status & 0x80)
printf("\n not busy");
```

The syntax for _bios_printer() function is

_bios_printer(int cmd, int port, int byte);

The meaning of cmd, port and byte are same as in the biosprint() function of TURBO-C.

We have earlier discussed that the printer type functions depend on the compiler. When

Structures and Union 39

we write a print routine, we should take care of the types of compiler. The following discussion checks for both **TURBO-C** and **MICROSOFT-C.**

```
#ifdefTURBOC
    status = biosprint(2, ch, 0);

    if(status & 0x01 ) printf("\ndevice
    time out");

    if( status & 0x08)
printf("\n I/O error");
    if(status& 0x10 )
    printf(" \n device selected");

if( status & 0x20)
   printf("\n out of paper");

if(status & 0x40)
   printf(" \n acknowledge");
    if( status & 0x80)
printf("\n not busy");
#endif
# ifdef MICROSOFTC
     _bios_printer(0, 0, ch);
#endif
```

The lists of commands are given in **Appendix-A.** For example, if one wants to print in wide **font,** it is required to send following decimal values to printer port.

27 (ESC)

14 (Control code)

Printer command changes its mode of operation. The new modes remain in effect until the next command arrives. It is also possible to combine different modes to get the combined effect. For example, the printer can be instructed to print text in **boldface** as well as **doublewide** character. Implementation of the above discussion is left as an exercise to the readers.

To assign a value to a bit-field, simply use the syntax/format, for any other type of structure element. For example, following code slice clears the ring field (consider the very first bitfield structure declared earlier):

Status.ring = 0;

Each bit-field can be accessed with the help of dot operator. However, if the structure value is referenced through a pointer, we use the arrow (-") operator.

If we do not want to name each bit-field, this makes it easy to reach the bit we want by passing unused ones. For example, if we care only about the **cts** and **dsr** bits, we could declare the **Status** structure (defined earlier) such as

```
struct Status
{
    unsigned: 4;
    unsigned cts :1;
    unsigned dsr :1; }
Status;
```

It is valid to mix normal structure members with bit-fields. For example, consider the following declaration:

```
struct Address
{
    char Name[40]:
    charStreat[40];
    charCity[20];
    charState[20];
    long int Zip; };
```

The declaration defines an Employee record that uses only 1 byte to hold three pieces of information: the employee status, whether the employee is salaried and the number of deductions. Without bit-field, this information would have taken 3 bytes. Bit-field variables have certain limitations. One cannot take the address of a bit-field and bit-field variables can not be arrayed. It is also not possible to know, from machine to machine, whether the fields will run from right to left or left to right. Thus, we can say that any code that uses bitfields may have some machine dependency.

17.10 STRUCTURES AND FILES

There is very close relationship between structures and files. The structure keeps all information about a record. We can easily process one record at a time with the help of structures and files. The files may be defined as collection of structures or records. We will read/write one record from/into file at a time.

Structure fields exist in memory in contiguous locations. As such, it is possible to access a record from memory by providing starting address of a structure. For example, consider the following declaration of structure:

```
struct person
{
    char ch ;
    int i_num ;
    float f_num ;
    };
```

This structure exists in memory. From Figure 17.8 it is clear that total space required for storing record or structure person is 7 bytes. If we process a file, 7 bytes of data can be read/written from/into file, which is one record at a time. The syntax for write operation is as follows:

fwrite (&struct name , sizeof (struct name), no of struct, file pointer);

char	int	float
1 byte	2 byte	4 byte

Figure 17.8 Structure in memory

Meaning of (&) operator is that we will be given the starting address of the structure for operation. In the other words, before writing structure, one should determine the starting address of it in memory. The **sizeof** operator tells number of bytes to be written into the file, starting from the given address. The actual number of operations performed is shown in Figure 17.9. Go though the Example 17.9 which implements Figure 17.9.

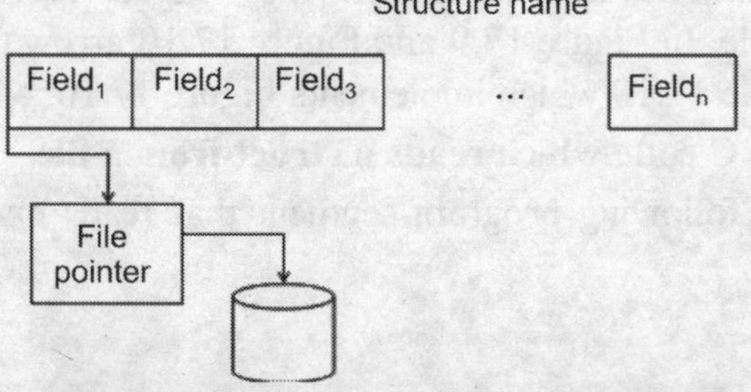

Figure 17.9 Write operations into file

Example 17.9: Write C code which writes a struct into a file.

Answer: Consider the following program segment that reads one record and writes it into a file rec.dat.

```
/**struct12.c**/
#include<stdio.h>
struct Info
{
    char Name[40]:
    charStreet[120];
    char Dist[40]:
    char State[40]:
    long int Pin_code; };
void main() {
    struct Info Play ={
        "Tom Alter", "IV-C-III, Model Town", "New Port City", "San Francisco", 246001};
    FILE *fp;
    fp = fopen("rec.dat","w");
    if(fp == NULL)
    {
    perror("ERROR");
    exit(0);
    }
fwrite(&Play, sizeof(Play), 1, fp); printf("\n
Record is as follows \n\n"); puts(Play.Name);
puts(Play.Street); printf("%s",Play.Dist);
printf("\n%s",Play.State);
printf("\n%ld",Play.Pin_code); printf("\nPress
a key"); getchar(); }
```

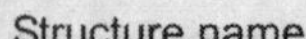

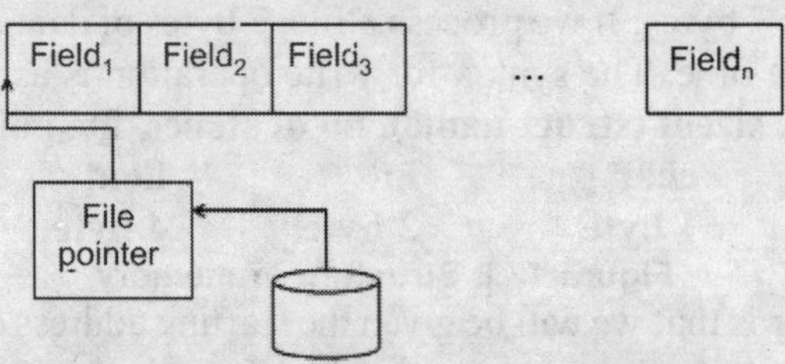

Figure 17.10 Read operation from file

Consider the following syntax that is for read operation:

fread(&struct name , sizeof (struct name), no of struct, file pointer);

How the structure fields are accessed from disk files? Figure 17.10 illustrates the accessing of structure fields from disk file. In Figure 17.9 and Figure 17.10 arrow (-") shows motion of flow of data. Go though the Example 17.10 which implements Figure 17.10.

Example 17.10: Write C code which reads a struct from a file.

Answer: Consider the following program segment that reads one record from a file rec.dat **maintained in Example 17.9.**

```
/**struct13.c**/
#include<stdio.h>
struct Info
{
```

```
        char Name[40]:
        charStreet[120];
        char Dist[40]:
        char State[40]:
        long int Pin_code; };
    void main() {
        struct Info Play ;
        FILE *fp ;
        fp = fopen("rec.dat","rb+");
        if(fp == NULL)
        {
        perror("ERROR");
        exit(O);
        }
fread(&Play, sizeof(Play), 1, fp);
    printf("\n Record is as follows \n\n");
    puts(Play.Name); puts(Play.Street);
    printf("%s",Play.Dist);
    printf("\n%s",Play.State);
    printf("\n%ld",Play.Pin_code);
    printf("\nPress a key"); getchar(); }
```

With the help of above program segment we readout the record which was lying in the file rec.dat, written by struct12.c program segment.

17.11 THE UNION

Unions are used in C Language to save storage space when we need to store anyone of a variety of C language data types in a location. Unions are declared in the same fashion as structs, but have a fundamental difference. Only one item within the union can be used at any time, because the memory allocated for each item inside the union is in a shared memory location. The syntax is

```
    union Tag name
    {
    Datatypel fieldl; Datatype2 field2; Datatype3 field3:
    Datatypen fieldn; };
        For example, consider the following declaration of union:
    union Data_Types {
        charCh;
        int IntegerJMumber;
        long int lnt_l_ong_Number;
        float Float_Number;
        double Double_Number; };
```

The above declaration does not create any variables. We can declare a variable by either placing its name at the end of the declaration or by using a separate declaration statement. To declare a union variable data of type **Data_Types,** we use the definition such that: **union Data_Types Data;**

In Data, character **Ch,** integer **lnteger_Number,** long integer **lnteger_l_ong_Number,** floating point number **Float_Number** and double **Double_Number** share the same memory locations. To access a member of union, same syntax is used as we have used for the structures. The dot (.), arrow (-"), and pointer (*) operators will work in the case of union. If we want to operate directly on the union, we use dot operator. If the union is accessed through a pointer we use arrow operator or use pointer and dot operators. For example, assign **char c** to the field variable **Ch** of **Data we** use:

```
    Data.Ch = 'c'; If a pointer to Data is passed to a function,
we use: Data_Type Fun (Data_Type *Member) {
Member->Ch = 'c';
    Member->Integer_Number= 100;
    Member->Float_Number = 20.50;
    (*Member).Double_Number = 30.5;
    return (Member); }
```

Union helps in production of machine independent (portable) codes. Because the compiler keeps track of the actual size of the union members, no machine dependencies are produced, which means that one should not worry about the size of an **int, long, char, float, double** or whatsoever it is. Go through Example 17.11 which is implementing above discussion.

Example 17.11: Write C code which is demonstrating union operation.

Answer: Consider the following program segment that illustrates how the union shares the common memory area in different variables:

```
/**struct14.c**/
# include<stdio.h>
union demo
{
    charch;
    int i_num;
    float f_num;
    };
void main() {
    union demo info;
    info.ch = 'A';
    info.i_num = 1234;
    info.f_num = 345.23;
    printf("\nOx %x <= address of ch \n", &info.ch);
    printf("\nOx %x <= address of i_num \n", &info.i_num);
    printf("\nOx %x <= address of f_num \n", &info.f_num);
    printf(" \n Output result ");
    printf("\n %c <= value of ch \n", info.ch);
    printf("\n %d <= value of i_num \n", info.i_num);
    printf("\n %f <= value of f_num \n", info.f_num);
    printf("\n Press a key");
    getchar(); }
```

OUTPUT
Ox fff2 <= address of ch
Ox fff2 <= address of i_num
Ox fff2 <= address of f_num
Output result
q <= value of ch
-25231 <= value of i_num
345.230011 <= value of f_num
Press a key

From the output of the above program segment, it is clear that different data types are mapped on the longest size of data.

The unions are generally used with **register** type of variables to save time and space. The union can also be assigned to another union of same type like structure. See Example 17.12 for the implementation.

Example 17.12: Consider the following program segment that implements the above discussion.

```
/**struct15.c**/ #
include<stdio.h> union
data {
    char name[30];
    int age ;
    float salary ; };
void main() {
    union data d;
    union data *d1;
    d.age = 30 ;
    d.salary = 7500;
    d1 = &d; /* assign address of the d to d1 */
    printf("\n%d",d1->age);
    printf("\n%f",d1 ->salary);
    printf("\n Press a key");
    getchar(); }
```

Initialization of Union

An initializer for a union is a brace-enclosed single value. The initializer is preceded by an equal sign (=). The default initializer for a union with static storage is the default for the first component; a union with automatic storage has no default initialization. There are two ways to specify initializers for unions:

1. With C89-style initializers, only the first member of a union can be initialized.
2. Using *designated* initializers, a C99 feature which allows us to name members to be initialized, any (single) member of a union can be initialized.

Using C89-style initialization, the following example shows how we would initialize the first union member birthday of the union variable people:

```
union
{
char birthday[9]: int age;
float weight; } people =
{"23/07/57"};
```

Using a designated initializer in the same example, the following initializes the second union member age:

```
union
{
char birthday[9]:
int age;
float weight; } people = {.age = 14}; /* few C compiler does permit such type of initialization */
```

17.12 Typedef

Although typedef is thought of **as being a storage** class, it is not **really. A typedef** declaration lets us define our own identifiers that can be used in place of type specifiers such as **int, float,** and **double. A typedef** declaration does not reserve storage. The names we define using typedef are not new data types, but synonyms for the data types or combinations of data types they represent. The name space for a **typedef** name is the same as other identifiers. The exception to this rule is if the **typedef** name specifies a variably modified type. In this case, it has block scope. When an object is defined using a **typedef** identifier, the properties of the defined object are exactly the same as if the object were defined by explicitly listing the data type associated with the identifier. The following statements declare LENGTH as a synonym for **int** and then use this **typedef** to declare length, width, and height as integer variables:

typedef int LENGTH;

LENGTH length, width, height;

The following declarations are equivalent to the above declaration:

int length, width, height;

Following code segment discusses other level of typedef used in the declaration.

```
typedef int aaa, bbb, ccc; typedef int ar[15], arr[9][6]; typedef chare, *cp, carr[100];
/* Now declare some objects */
/* all ints */
aaa   intl;
bbb   int2;
ccc      int3;
ar       yyy;   /* array of 15 ints */
arr      xxx;   /* 9*6 array of int */
c        ch;    /*achar*/
cp       pnt;   /* pointer to char*/
carr     chry;  /* array of 100 char*/
```

The general rule with the use of typedef is to write out a declaration as if we are declaring variables of the types that we want. Where a declaration would have introduced names with particular types, prefixing the whole thing with typedef means that, instead of getting variables declared, we declare new type names instead. Those new type names can then be used as the prefix to the declaration of variables of the new type.

The use of typedef is not a particularly common sight in most programs; it is typically found only in header files and is rarely the province of day-to-day coding.

It is sometimes found in applications requiring very high portability: there, new types will be defined for the basic variables of the program and appropriate typedefs used to tailor the program to the target machine. This can lead to code which C programmers from other environments will find difficult to interpret if it is used to excess. The flavour of it is shown below:

```
/* file 'mytype.h' */
typedef short  SMALLINT      /* range *******30000 */
typedef int    BIGINT /* range ******* 2E9 */
/* program */ #include "mytype.h"
SMALLINT      i;
BIGINT        loop_count;
```

On some machines, the range of an int would not be adequate for a BIGINT which would have to be re- typedefed to be long. To reuse a name already declared as a typedef, its declaration must include at least one type specifier, which removes any ambiguity:

```
typedef int newjhing;
func(new_thing x)
{
    float newjhing;
    newjhing = x;
}
```

As a word of warning, typedef can only be used to declare the type of return value from a function, not the overall type of the function. The overall type includes information about the function's parameters as well as the type of its return value.

```
/* Using typedef, declare func to have type 'function taking two int arguments, returning int*/
typedef int func(int, int);

/* ERROR*/
func func_name{ /*....*/}

/* Correct. Returns pointer to a type 'func'
*/ func *func_name(){ /*....*/}

/* Correct if functions could return functions, but C cannot.*/ func
func_name(){ /*....*/}
```

If a typedef of a particular identifier is in scope, that identifier may not be used as the formal parameter of a function. This is because something like the following declaration causes a problem:

```
typedef int i1_t, i2_t, i3_t, i4_t;
int f(i1_t, i2_t, i3_t, i4_t) fTHIS IS POINT 'X'*/
```

A compiler reading the function declaration reaches point X and still does not knowwhether it is looking at a function declaration, essentially similar to

```
int f(int, int, int, int) /* prototype */
```

or

```
int f(a, b, c, d) /* not a prototype */
```

The problem is only resolvable (in the worst case) by looking at what follows point X; if it is a semicolon, then that was a declaration, if it is a '{' then that was a definition. The rule forbidding typedef names to be formal parameters means that a compiler can always tell whether it is processing a declaration or a definition by looking at the first identifier following the function name.

The use of typedef is also valuable when we want to declare things whose declaration syntax is painfully impenetrable, like "array of ten pointers to array of five integers", which tends to cause panic even amongst the hardy. Hiding it in a typedef means we only have to read it once and can also help to break it up into manageable pieces:

```
typedef int (*a10ptoa5i[10])[5];
/* or */
typedef int a5i[5];
typedef a5i *atenptoa5i[10];
```

Points to Remember

Structures can store non-homogenous data types into a single collection, much like an array does for common data (except it is not accessed in the same manner).

Pointers to structs have a special infix operator: -" for dereferencing the pointer.

typedef can help to provide clarity to code up and can help save some keystrokes.

Enumerated types allow having a series of constants much like a series of #define statements.

We can create arrays of structs.

Structs can be copied or assigned.

The & operator may be used with structs to show addresses.

Structs can be passed into functions. Structs can also be returned from functions.

Structs cannot be compared.

EXERCISES

Brief Exercises

1. What's the difference between these two declarations?

```
struct x1 { ... };
typedef struct { ... } x2;
```

2. Why doesn't

```
struct x { ... };
x thestruct;
```

work?

3. Can a structure contain a pointer to itself?
4. How can I implement opaque (abstract) data types in C?
5. Is there a good way of simulating OOP-style inheritance, or other OOP features, in C?
6. Why does the declaration

   extern int f(struct x *p);

   give me an obscure warning message about ``struct x declared inside parameter list''?
7. I came across some code that declared a structure like this:

```
struct name {
  int namelen;
  char namestr[1];
};
```

   and then did some tricky allocation to make the namestr array act like it had several elements, with the number recorded by namelen. How does this work? Is it legal or portable?
8. Is there a way to compare structures automatically?
9. How are structure passing and returning implemented?
10. How can I pass constant values to functions which accept structure arguments? How can I create nameless, immediate, constant structure values?
11. How can I read/write structures from/to data files?
12. Why is my compiler leaving holes in structures, wasting space and preventing ``binary'' I/O to external data files? Can I turn this off, or otherwise control the alignment of structure fields?
13. Why does sizeof report a larger size than I expect for a structure type, as if there were padding at the end?
14. How can I determine the byte offset of a field within a structure?
15. How can I access structure fields by name at run time?
16. Does C have an equivalent to Pascal's with statement?
17. If an array name acts like a pointer to the base of an array, why isn't the same thing true of a structure?
18. This program works correctly, but it dumps core after it finishes. Why?

```
struct list {
      char *item;
```

```
        struct list *next;
    }
    /* Here is the main program. */
    main(argc, argv)
    { ... }
```

19. What's the difference between a structure and a union, anyway?
20. Can I initialize unions?
21. Is there an automatic way to keep track of which field of a union is in use?
22. What's the difference between an enumeration and a set of preprocessor #defines?
23. Are enumerations really portable?
24. Is there an easy way to print enumeration values symbolically?
25. I came across some structure declarations with colons and numbers next to certain fields, like this:

```
    struct record {
    char *name;
    int refcount : 4;
    unsigned dirty : 1;
    };
```

    What gives?
26. Why do people use explicit masks and bit-twiddling code so much, instead of declaring bit-fields?

Multiple Choice Questions

1. A structure is
   (a) Grouping of variables under one name
   (b) Compound data type
   (c) Conglomerate (d)AII of the above
2. The variables that make up the structure are called
   (a) Members (b) Elements
   (c) Fields (d) AII of the above
3. When accessing a structure member, the identifier to the left of the dot (period) operator is the name of
   (a) A structure name (b) A structure tag name
   (c) A structure variable (d) The keyword struct
4. An enumeration data type brings together a group of
   (a) Items of different data types (b) Related data variables
   (c) Integers with user defined names (d) Constant values
5. If one defines
   (i) enum boolean {False, True};
   (ii) enum boolean {True, False};

(a) (i) is correct (b) (ii) is correct
(c) (i) and (ii) both are correct (d) none of these

6. Before one can access a member of structure, one must
   (a) Declare the structure (b) Define a structure
   (c) Give the item in (b) and (a) (d) None of these
7. Array elements must all be of the_________________, whereas structure member may be of _________________.
   (a) same data type, different data types (b) different data types, different data types,
   (c) none of these
8. The closing brace of a structure is followed by a_________________.
   (a); (b),
   (c): (c) none of these
9. The four members of an **enum** type are normally represented by the values ___________, ___________, ___________ and ___________.
   (a) 0,1,2,3 (b) 1,2,3,4
   (c) none of these
10. It is possible to pass a structure to a function in the same way as a simple variable is passed.
    (a) True (b) False
11. An appropriate use for a structure is to store a list of information. (a) True (b) False
12. **A typedef** may be used only with a tagged structure.
    (a) True (b) False
13. When using a **typedef** to declare a structure, the **typedef** name may be the same as a structure is tagged
    (a) True (b) False
14. Can a structure have both a tag and a type name?
    (a) True (b) False

Descriptive and Programming Problems

1. What errors, if any, do occur in the following code?

```
struct Jams_Bond {
      charging;
      char*Jang;
      long ZIP;
 } Jams_Bond;
Jing = "Jing lives in California";
Jang = "Jang lives in New Delhi";
```

2. Find error in the following declaration of structure and write the correct code.

```
struct Link
{
char Nodejnfol [20]; /* Member 1 */
char Node_lnfo2[20]; /* Member 2 */
struct Link next; };
```

3. What is the error in the following declaration of a structure with a pair of bit-field members?

```
struct Saving
{
    signed int Member1 3;
    unsigned int Member2 16; }
Variable;
```

Correct the error and write the error free code for the said code and assign values to the variable **Variable.Memberl** and **Variable.Member2**

4. Is there any error in the following program segment? If there is no error, find output of the

program segment?

```
#include<stdio.h>
enum Player {Ramesh = 1, Saurabh, Dravid, Sachin, Azharuddin, Mongia};
enum One, Two;
One = 12;
Two = 14;
void main()
{
    printf("\n %d", One, Two); }
```

5. Why is it not legal to use == to test whether two structures are equal?
6. Why does C provide two ways to name structure types **Tags** and **typedef** names?
7. When one tried using sizeof to determine the number of bytes in a structure, one got a numberthat was largerthan the sizes of the members added together. How can this be?
8. What is difference between structure and array?
9. Discuss the difference between an array of structure variable that has an array as a member.
10. What is structure Tag?
11. Does any member variables of two different structures have the same name? If 'yes', how is it differentiated by the compiler?
12. What is main difference between a structure and a union?
13. Can a structure be nested in a union?
14. Can one union be nested in another?
15. Under what circumstances would one prefer a union to a structure?
16. What is the main difference between a bit-field and other members of a structure?
17. Can a structure be declared with a mix of bit-field and regular members?
18. In the following code identify the Tag, the members and the structure variable: **struct Mailing_List**

```
{
    charl\lame[40];
    charFather_Name[40];
    charStreet[70];
    charCity[20];
    charState[20];
    long int ZIP; } Ram, Bahadur, Eishita, Rachita;
```

19. Are the following statements equivalent? printf("\n %s",
    ***(pointer).Name); printf("\n %s", pointers Name);**
20. Are the following statements equivalent?

```
scanf( %s", *(pointer).Name); scanf(" %s",
pointer->Name);
```

21. Consider the following program segment:

```
struct Scooter
{
        int Wheels;
        int Brakes;
float BHP; } Scooter;
        struct Automobile {
        char Make[40]:
        charModel[40];
        int Year;
        struct Scooter Scoot, *Scoot_Ptr;
} Car, *Ptr;
Ptr*&Car;
Car.Scoot_Ptr = &Car.Scoot;
Ptr->Make= "Bajaj";
Car.Scoot.Wheels = 3;
```

(a) In how many ways the string *"Bajaf* can be accessed?

(b) In how many ways the integer 3 can be accessed.

22. Is the following structuring self-referential? Discuss.

```
struct Node {
int Info;
struct Node *Next, "Previous, "Last; };
```

23. Consider the following code

```
typedef struct Teaching
{
charName[40]; char Post
[15]; charSSN[10]; char
Grade; float Salary; }
Profession;
Profession Professor, Reader, Lecturer, "Pointer;
```

Assume in the above "Tom Alter Don" has been to the array **Reader.Name** and Pointer points to Reader. Explain the error in the following code slice and write the correct form of the code. puts((*Pointer.Name);

Write a statement that assigns to **Pointer** the address of **Reader.**

24. Declare structure that represents an employee record including the following information:

Name, SSN (social security number), Age, Address, Dependents, Relationship with dependent

25. Define an array of 1000 variables of the structure type of above problem.

26. (a) Declare structures **College** and **Department** nest structure **Department** in structure **College.** Where structure **Department** contains the following information:

1. Computer Science & Engineering

2. Electronics & Communication Engineering

3. Electrical Engineering
4. Mechanical Engineering
5. Applied Science

(b) Consider the declaration in (a) and define a variable of type structure **Department** and assign values to all its members, including the members of the nested structure.

27. Consider the following list of records given in Figure 17.11. Implement the list with the help of structure and find
    (a) The number of elements that must be moved if Brown, Johnson and Peters are inserted into Record at three different times.
    (b) How many elements are moved if three names are inserted at the same time?
    (c) How does the Telephone Company handle insertions in a telephone directory?

28. A college uses the following structure for grading a class

Student Name
  First
  Last
  Middle Initial
Examination
Sessional Subject
  Subject1
  Subject 2
  Subject 3
GPA (4) CGPA

Index	Name	Telephone	City
1.	Allen	6176732	Bombay
2.	Clark	7232156	Delhi
3.	Dickens	6432158	Chennai
4.	Edwords	7562312	Bangalore
5.	Goodmann	3214632	Hyderabad
6.	Hobbs	222855	Pauri
7.	Irwis	2391337	Lucknow
8.	Klien	2632255	Varanasi
9.	Lewis	2351245	Varanasi
10.	Morgan	2354892	Allahabad
11.	Richard	500566	Allahabad
12.	Scot	547717	Bareilly
13.	Tacker	656565	Dehradun
14.	Walton	3245678	Jaipur
15.			
16.			

Figure 17.11 Records

Here, **GPA [k]** refers to the grade points average during the kth year and **CGPA** refers to the cumulative grade point average. Consider the above structure and write following functions.
(a) Update function (b) Insertion (c) Deletion
Implement the above structure for 1000 **Student** and generate transcript as shown in Figure 17.12.

29. The following is a list of entries, with level numbers in a file of employee records. The level numbers also represent level number of the nesting in the **Employee** structure.

    1 Employee
    2 SSN (social security number)
    2 Name
    3 Last
    3 First
    3 Ml (middle initial)
    2 Address
    3 Street
    3 Area
    4 City
    4 State
    4 ZIP
    2 Age
    2 Salary 2 Dependents Implement the above structure.

30. Assume that you have been asked to develop an on-line course registration system (OLCRS) for your university. Define a set of basic requirement and then develop a data model for the system and finally implement the developed data model.

31. Develop software that handles leave sanctioning procedure adopted by some universities and having the following criteria.
    (a) Keeps the record of previously sanctioned leaves from date to date.
    (b) Leave asked by the students from date to date.
    (c) If leaves asked and date lies in past sanctioned date then leave can not be granted.
    (d) If sum of leave previously sanctioned and currently asked is more than 40%age, leaves can not be granted.
    (e) Type of leave forwhich a student is applying.

32. To be eligible for the promotion, teachers at MMME College must have at least 5 years experience in the same college or at least 7 years experience somewhere else. Teachers are not eligible for promotion after 25 years of teaching. To be eligible for promotion to the following ranks, teachers must meet the requirements as given in Figure 17.13.

    In addition, no teacher is eligible for promotion if he/she has not served three full years in his/her rank. The rank below assistant professor is instructor; only four ranks exist at MME College. Design a record layout form for personnel to record all faculty data and write a program to identify the faculty eligible for promotion.

33. Each record of data file contains the following information
    (a) Name
    (b) Sex code
    (c) Salary

    Write a program to print the earning and the names of females earning between ten and twenty thousand dollars. Also print the lowest earning and indicate whether a male or a female earned it. Specify male or female on throughput.

Transcript

Examination:

Date:

Name: Father's Name:

Students ID: Year: Branch:

Subject Code	Subject Name	Sessional	Examination	Grade	Remarks

Result: Cumulative grade point average:

Remarks: Signature

Figure 17.12 Transcript Format

Rank	Requirement
Assistant Professor	Master Degree 5 Year Teaching
Associate Professor	Master's degree **plus** 10 years **in** Teaching
Full Professor	PhD **plus** 8 years **in** Teaching
Senior Professor	PhD: PDF: **plus** 12 years **in** Teaching

Figure 17.13 Qualification Requirements for a Position

File Management in C

18.1 INTRODUCTION

Many applications of computers particularly in business environments require the storage and processing of large amount of data. Typically there is a large amount of data to store in memory at a time, so the data is stored externally. The earliest computers had used punched cards and magnetic tapes for storage of data. Modern computers use magnetic disks and drums as external storage devices.

Data is organized into records containing related data items. Groups of related records compose a file. For example, personnel file might contain one record for each employee in a company. Each record would be composed of such data items as the employee's name, social security number, age, date of birth, date hired and so on. The file might be organized sequentially, randomly or in any other scheme.

C language is very powerful for this type of application purposes as well as for system purposes. Today computers are widely used for data processing. During processing the data is kept in main memory (RAM). When data is quantitatively small, it is possible to keep all data in an array. But there are some drawbacks with array. When data is small and size of array is large, then it causes wastage of memory space, because when we define an array, its size is fixed in computer memory. Another problem of array is, when size of array is small and data is large then it is not possible to load all data into the array. For this problem it is possible to load data, equal to the size of array and after processing, the data is back to the user, but this is not the solution of our problem. Another way to process small amounts of the data is pointers, with help of pointers we can save unused memory space. This technique is limited to memory space of the machine.

Here, we have seen that bulk amount of data processing, requires another technique for storage, (before the processing as well as after the processing), i.e., file. The file processing is main part of any programming language. C language is very powerful in file handling. For example:

Mr. Y wishes to use a computer to maintain data on the number of parts in hand at his store. He has just taken inventory and knows the number of parts in hand. The part numbers and corresponding quantities are entered into the computer system and retained on a disk file. Later on, as parts are sold or as parts are added to the inventory, the parts file is updated. Then either on daily or on weekly basis, reports are produced to list the contents of the inventory file to identify those parts that are needed to be order. Such an information processing system inevitably leads to the following file processing:

Create file
Merging files, i.e., combine records of two or more files into one
Adding records
Deleting records
Update records
Generate reports

C language supports different level of file processing according to the environment used, the details are given in Figure 18.1.

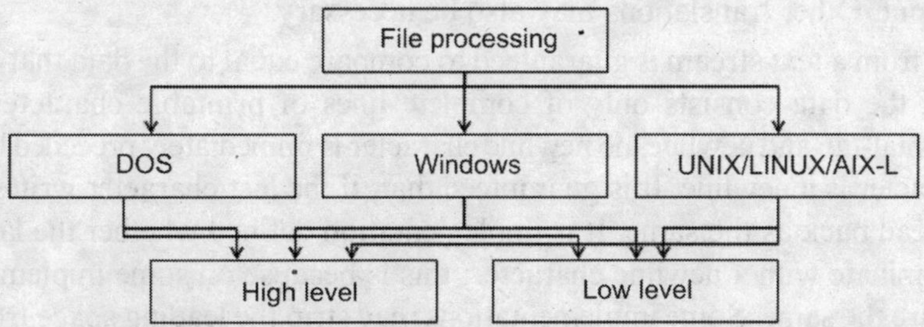

Figure 18.1 FILE operations in different environment

18.2 FILE MANAGEMENT FUNCTIONS

One of the reasons that have prevented many programming languages from becoming widely used for 'real programming' is their poor support for input/output (I/O), a subject which has never seemed to excite language designers. C has avoided this problem, oddly enough, by having no I/O at all. The C language approach has always been to do I/O using library functions, which ensures that system designers can provide tailored I/O instead of being forced to change the language itself.

As C has evolved a library package known as the 'Standard I/O Library' or stdio, has evolved with it and has proved to be both flexible and portable. This package has now become part of the Standard. The old stdio package relied heavily on the UNIX model of file access, in particular the assumption that there is no distinction between unstructured binary files and files containing readable text. Many operating systems do maintain a distinction between the two, and to ensure that C programs can be written portably to run on both types of file model, the stdio package has been modified. There are changes in this area which affect many existing programs, although strenuous efforts were taken to limit the amount of damage.

18.2.1 The I/O model

The I/O model does not distinguish between the types of physical devices supporting the I/O. Each source or sink of data (file) is treated in the same way, and is viewed as a stream of bytes. Since the smallest object that can be represented in C is the character, access to a file is permitted at any character boundary. Any number of characters can be read or written from a movable point, known as the file position indicator. The characters will be read, or written, in sequence from this point, and the position indicator moved accordingly. The position indicator is initially set to the beginning of a file when it is opened, but can also be moved by means of positioning requests. When random access is not possible, the file position indicator is ignored. Opening a file in append mode has an implementation defined effect on the stream's file position indicator. The overall effect is to provide sequential reads or writes unless the stream was opened in append mode, or the file position indicator is explicitly moved.

There are two types of file, text files and binary files, which, within a program, are manipulated as text streams and binary streams once they have been opened for I/O. The stdio package does not permit operations on the contents of files 'directly', but only by viewing them as streams.

Text streams: What is meant by the term text stream? It is essentially considered as file which contains lines of text. A line is a sequence of zero or more characters terminated by a newline character. It is quite possible that the actual representation of lines in the external environment is different from this and there may be transformations of the data stream on the way in and out of the program; a common requirement is to translate the '\n' line-terminator into the sequence '\r\n' on output, and do the reverse on input. Other translations may also be necessary.

Data read in from a text stream is guaranteed to compare equal to the data that was earlier written out to the file if the data consists only of complete lines of printable characters and the control characters horizontal-tab and newline, no newline character is immediately preceded by space characters and the last character is a newline. It is guaranteed that, if the last character written to a text file is a newline, it will read back as the same. It is implementation defined whether the last line written to a text file must terminate with a newline character; this is because on some implementations text files and binary files are the same. Some implementations may strip the leading space from lines consisting only of a space followed by a newline, or strip trailing spaces at the end of a line. An implementation must support text files with lines containing at least 254 characters, including the terminating newline. Opening a text stream in update mode may result in a binary stream in some implementations. Writing on a text stream may cause some implementations to truncate the file at that point-any data beyond the last byte of the current write being discarded.

Binary streams: A binary stream is a sequence of characters that can be used to record a program's internal data, such as the contents of structures or arrays in binary form. Data read in from a binary stream will always compare equal to data written out earlier to the same stream, under the same implementation. In some circumstances, an implementation-defined number of NULL characters may be appended to a binary stream. The contents of binary files are exceedingly machine specific, and not, in general, portable. Other stream types may exist, but are implementation defined.

18.2.2 The stdio.h header file

To provide support for streams of the various kinds, a number of functions and macros exist. The <stdio.h> header file contains the various declarations necessary for the functions, together with the following macro and type declarations:

1. **FILE:** The type of an object used to contain stream control information. Users of stdio never need to know the contents of these objects, but simply manipulate pointers to them. It is not safe to copy these objects within the program; sometimes their addresses may be 'magic'.
2. **fpos_t:** A type of object that can be used to record unique values of a stream's file position indicator.

3. **_IOFBF _IOLBF _IONBF:** Values used to control the buffering of a stream in conjunction with the setvbuf function.
4. **BUFSIZ:** The size of the buffer used by the setbuf function. An integral constant expression whose value is at least 256.
5. **EOF:** A negative integral constant expression, indicating the end-of-file condition on a stream, i.e., that there is no more input.
6. **FILENAME_MAX:** The maximum length which a filename can have, if there is a limit, or otherwise the recommended size of an array intended to hold a file name.
7. **FOPEN_MAX:** The minimum number of files that the implementation guarantees may be held open concurrently; at least eight are guaranteed. Note that three predefined streams exist and may need to be closed if a program needs to open more than five files explicitly.
8. **L_tmpnam:** The maximum length of the string generated by tmpnam; an integral constant expression.
9. **SEEK_CUR SEEK_END SEEK_SET:** Integral constant expressions used to control the actions of fseek.
10. **TMP_MAX:** The minimum number of unique filenames generated by tmpnam; an integral constant expression with a value of at least 25.
11. stdin stdout stderr

Predefined objects of type (FILE *) referring to the standard input, output and error streams, respectively. These streams are automatically opened when a program starts execution.

The standard library functions for file handling are accessible through systems calls. These functions are generally preferred for system calls, as they are less dependent on the implementation and are thus more portable. Losses in program performance are to be expected while using the library functions.

The function for file handling offers an extended buffering of the input and output as well as a better error-check. For this purpose, the library functions work on a special structure, i.e., upon opening or creating a file, the routines return a pointer on the structure of type **FILE** (only in high level processing). Instead of the file descriptor, the library functions need this pointer to access the corresponding structure. Most of these functions are given in **Table 18.1** through **Table 18.7.**

Table 18.1 Block input and output functions

Function	Meaning
fread()	Read a specific number of characters
fwrite	Write a specific number of characters

Table 18.2 Character input and output functions

Functions	Meaning
fgetc()	Read a character
getc()	Read a character
fputc()	Write a character
putc()	Write a character
getchar()	Read a character from stdio
putchar()	Write a character to stdout
ungetc()	Store a character in buffer

Table 18.3 General functions for file operations

Function	Meaning
fopen()	Open a file
fdopen()	Open a file for the prescribed file descriptor
freopen()	Open other file for given file structure
fclose()	Close a file
fflush()	Empty the buffer
flushall()	Empty all buffers
fileno()	Determine the file descriptor for specified file
setbuf()	Set a new file buffer
setvbuf()	Set the buffer address and size

Table 18.4 String input output functions

Function	Meaning
fgets()	Read a string from a file
gets()	Read a string from stdin
fputs()	Write a string into the file
puts()	Write a string to stdout

Table 18.5 formatted input and output functions

Functions	Meaning
fprintf()	Formatted output to a file
printf	Formatted output to stdout
fsacnf()	Formatted input from a file
scanf()	Formatted input from stdin

Table 18.6 Error handling functions

Functions	Meaning
feof()	Check whether end of file is reached
ferror()	Check whether error has been occurred
clearror()	Reset the file error flag

Table 18.7 Random access functions

Functions	Meaning
fseek()	Set the position of the file pointer
fgetspos()	Determine the current position of file pointer
fsetpos()	Set the position of the file pointer
ftell()	Tell the current positions of the file pointer
rewind()	Set the position of the file pointer to 0 (beginning of the file)

18.3 OPENING A FILE

Before we write a file to a disk or read it, we must open it. Opening a file establishes an understanding between a program and the operating system about the file we are going to access and how we are going to do it. We provide the operating system with the name of the file and other information, such as whether we plan to read or write to it. Communication areas are then setup between the file and the program; one of these areas is a **C** structure that holds information about the file. The structure, which is defined to be of type **FILE,** is a contact point. When we make a request to open a file, what we receive back (if the request is granted) is a pointer to a particular **FILE** structure. Each file we open will have its own **FILE** structure with a pointer to it; the discussion is shown in **Figure 18.2.** The **FILE** structure contains information about the file being used, such as its current size and the location of its data buffers. The **FILE** structure is declared in the header file **stdio.h.**

A stream is connected to a file by means of the **fopen, freopen** or **tmpfile** functions. These functions will, if successful, return a pointer to a FILE object. Three streams are available without any special action; they are normally all connected to the physical device associated with the executing program: usually computer terminal. They are referred to by the names stdin (standard input), stdout (standard output), and stderr (standard error) streams. Normal keyboard input is from stdin, normal terminal output is to stdout, and error messages are directed to stderr. The separation of error messages from normal output messages allows the stdout stream to be connected to something other than the terminal device, and still to have error messages appear on the screen, rather than to be redirected to this file. These files are only fully buffered if they do not refer to interactive devices.

As mentioned earlier, the file position indicator may or may not be movable, depending on the underlying device. It is not possible, for example, to move the file position indicator on stdin if that is connected to a terminal, as it usually is.

All non-temporary files must have a filename, which is a string. The rules for what constitutes valid filenames are implementation defined. Whether a file can be simultaneously open multiple times is also implementation defined. Opening a new file may involve creating the file. Creating an existing file causes its previous contents to be discarded.

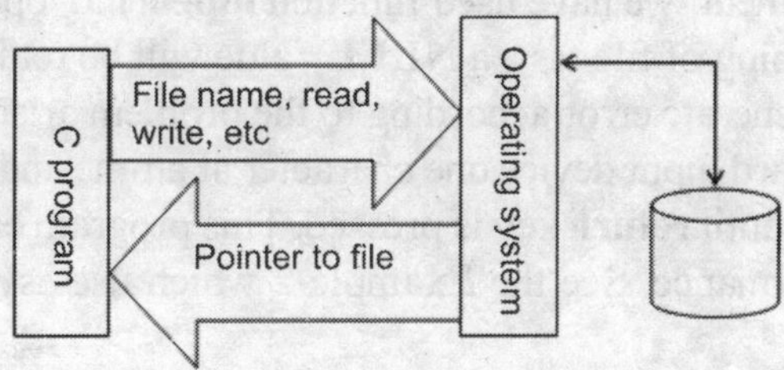

Figure 18.2 Opening a file

Main function which is used to start the above given functions is **fopen ().** To open a file, to create a file, to restart with an existing file, etc, are the main functions, which are performed by it. The syntax for the function **fopen()** is

File_pointer = fopen (file name, mode);

If a file is successfully opened it returns a pointer to the newly opened stream, otherwise it returns **NULL.** This function opens one file at a time. The syntax of structure **FILE** is

FILE *file_pointer;

For example,

FILE *fp;

Mode parameter of the function **fopen ()** tells about the type of operations that can be performed on an opened file. The modes, which are supported by high level file processing, are given in **Table 18.8.** Go thorugh the Example 1 which is opening a file in write mode.

Example 1: Write C code which opens a file in write mode and write characters into it till we have not pressed the enter key.

Answer: The following program segment implements the above discussion:

```
/** file1.c **/

# include<stdio.h>
# include<stdlib.h>

void main()
{
        char ch ;
        FILE *fp ;
        fp = fopen ("test","w");
        if ( fp == NULL )
        {
                perror("ERROR");
                exit(1);
        }
        ch = getchar() ;
        while(ch != '\n' )
        {
                putc(ch,fp);
                ch = getchar();
        }
        fclose(fp);
}
```

In the above program segment, we have used function **fopen()** to open a file **test** in write mode. If there is any problem in opening of file **test,** a **NULL** value will be returned. If **NULL** value arises then function **perror ()** will generate error according to the problem arises. In this program segment, we will read a text from standard input device one character at a time and simultaneously write it into the file **test,** this will continue until **return** key is pressed. This program can be written in another way in which it gives better performance. See the Example 2 which uses system buffer for reading the information.

Table 18.8 File opening modes

Mode	Type of file	Read	Write	Create	Truncate
"r"	text	yes	no	no	no
"rb"	binary	yes	no	no	no
"r+"	text	yes	yes	no	no
"r+b"	binary	yes	yes	no	no
"rb+"	binary	yes	yes	no	no
"w"	text	no	yes	yes	yes
"wb"	binary	no	yes	yes	yes
"w+"	text	yes	yes	yes	yes
"w+b"	binary	yes	yes	yes	yes
"wb+"	binary	yes	yes	yes	yes

"a"	text	no	yes	yes	no
"ab"	binary	no	yes	yes	no
"a+"	text	yes	yes	yes	no
"a+b"	binary	no	yes	yes	no
"ab+"	binary	no	yes	yes	no

Example 2: Write C code which uses system buffer(s) for file operation.

Answer: Go through the following code for the details.

```
/** file2.c **/
# include<stdio.h>
# include<stdlib.h>

void main()
{
     char ch ;
     FILE *fp ;   /* File pointer FILE macro  */
     fp = fopen ("test","w");
     if ( fp == NULL )
     {
          perror("ERROR");
          exit(1);
     }
     ch = getc(stdin) ;

     while(ch !='\n')  /* new line character accept */
     {
          putc(ch,fp);
          ch = getc(stdin);
     }
     fclose(stdin);
     fclose(fp);
}
```

In the above program segment we have used standard input file pointer **stdin.** The **stdin** directly interacts with keyboard buffer. When we open a file, a buffer is created in the system memory and data is transferred from/into the file with help of it. When we close the file, the residual data contained in this buffer are transferred to the opened file. If we do not close the file then there may be some losses of data but it may not happen every time. When we press a key, value of that key goes into standard input buffer, i.e., **stdin.** The **getc ()** function reads data from there and assign this data to the variable ch and finally, it is written into file **test.** When we use **stdin** file pointer then keyboard buffer flushes and closing of destination file is safe. Consider the next example in continuation to the function **fopen ().**

```
/** file3.c **/
# include<stdio.h>
void main()
{
     char ch ;
     ch = getchar();
```

```
/* If we replace getchar() with getche(), we get two time same character on screen. This is valid in DOS environment only but the same operation is performed using the getchar() and putchar () functions */
        putchar(ch);
        getchar();
    }
```

The above program segment reads a character and writes it on the screen (monitor). An equivalent of the above program can be written using standard input output file pointers. Consider the Example 3 which is equivalent to the Example 2.

Example 3: Write C code which uses system buffers (stdin and stdout) for file operation.

Answer: Go through the following code for the details.

```
/** file4.c **/
# include<stdio.h>

void main()
{
    char ch ;
/* It continuously read a charcter and puts on the screen when we press return key it terminates the program */
    ch = getc(stdin);

    while(ch != '\n')  /* new line character only accepts */
    {
        putc(ch,stdout);
        ch = getc(stdin);
    }
}
```

Now see how the contents of a file are read and written directly from/on to the screen (or computer display device VDU). Go through the Example 4 which implements the case.

Example 4: Write C code which uses output system buffer for displaying the contents of a file.

Answer: Go through the following code for the details.

```
/** file5.c **/
# include<stdio.h>
void main()
{
    char ch ;
    FILE *fp ;
    fp = fopen ("DATA.DAT","r");
    if ( fp == NULL )
    {
        perror("ERROR");
        exit(1);
    }
    printf("\n");
    ch = getc(fp) ;
    while(!feof(fp) )
    {
```

```
        putc(ch, stdout); /* This also may be putchar(ch) */
        ch = getc(fp);
    }
    fclose(fp);
}
```

The function **feof ()** is used to find the end of file. When we open a file in read mode the operation which is performed on the file is illustrated in **Figure 18.3.** Go through the Example 5 which implements this concept.

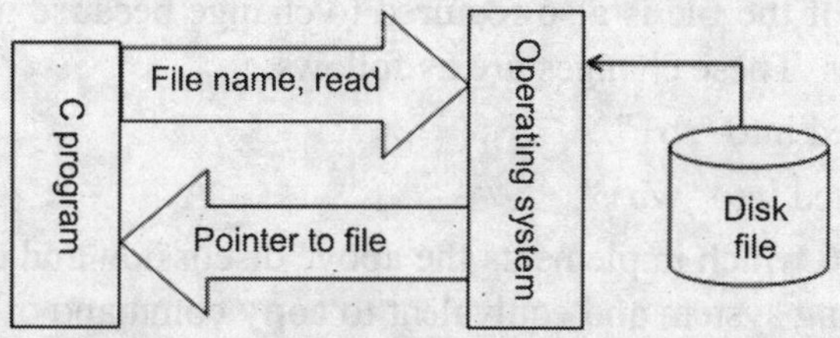

Figure 18.3 Opening a file in read mode

Example 5: Write a program which opens a file in read mode and make backup of the file with new name and extension of the file will be ".bak".

Answer: See the following code.

```
/** file6.c **/
# include<stdio.h>
# include<string.h>
# include<stdlib.h>

void main()
{
    char infile[13], outfile[13];
    char ch ;
    FILE *input,*output ;
    printf("\n Input Source File:");
    gets(infile);
    input = fopen(infile,"r");
    if ( input == NULL )
    {
        printf("\n File %s", infile);
        perror("Error:");
        exit(1);
    }
    printf("\n Input Destination file:");
    gets(outfile);
    strcat(outfile,".bak");
    output = fopen(outfile,"w");
    if ( output == NULL )
    {
        printf("\n File %s", outfile);
        perror("Error: ");
        exit(1);
    }
    ch = getc(input) ;
    while(!feof(input))
```

```
    {
        putc(ch,output);
        ch = getc(input);
    }
    fclose(input);
    fclose(output);
}
```

This program is very near to the **cp** or **copy** command of **UNIX.** This is different from **copy** as it asks to enter a destination file. The equivalent of **copy** command will be obtained by slight modification in the program. The mode of the file is also required to change because the **copy** command can be used with every type of files. These changes are as follows:

The "r" must be changed into "rb+".

The "w" must be changed into "wb+".

Consider the Example 6 which implements the above discussion and equivalent to **cp** and **copy** command of **UNIX** operating system and equivalent to **copy** command of the Windows/DOS.

Example 6: Write C code for cp/copy command of UNIX/Linux and Windows/DOS.

Answer: This is equivalent to **cp** and **copy** command of **UNIX** operating system and equivalent to copy command of the Windows/DOS.

```
/** file7.c **/
# include<stdio.h>
void main(int argc, char *argv[])
{
    char ch ;
    FILE *input,*output ;
    if(argc != 3)
    {
        printf("\n Missing source or destination file ");
        exit(1);
    }
    input = fopen(argv[1],"rb+");
    if ( input == NULL )
    {
        printf("\n File %s",argv[1]);
        perror("Error: ");
        exit(1);
    }
    output = fopen(argv[2],"wb+");
    if ( output == NULL )
    {
        printf("\n File %s",argv[2]);
        perror("Error: ");
        exit(1);
    }
    ch = getc(input) ;
    while(!feof(input) )
    {
        putc(ch,output);
        ch = getc(input);
    }
    fflush(input);
    fflush(output);
```

```
    fclose(input);
    fclose(output);
}
```

After compilation, compiler will generate an executable code file with the name **a.out.** When we will run this program, the syntax will be similar to shown in **Figure 18.4.** But when we are using this code in Windows or DOS in that case in place of **a.out** we have to write **file7** (this will be executable code in the name of source code file).

Here, in the above program a new function **fflush ()** is introduced. The role of this function is same as lavatory **flush.** When we open a file in write mode actual setting of pointer will be as shown in Figure 18.5.

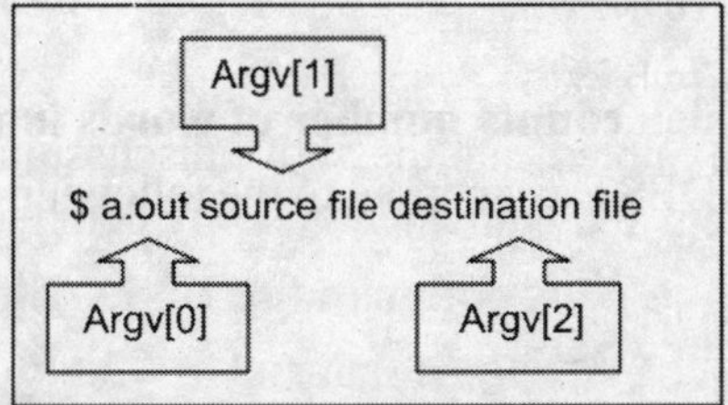

Figure 18.4 Running a C executable file

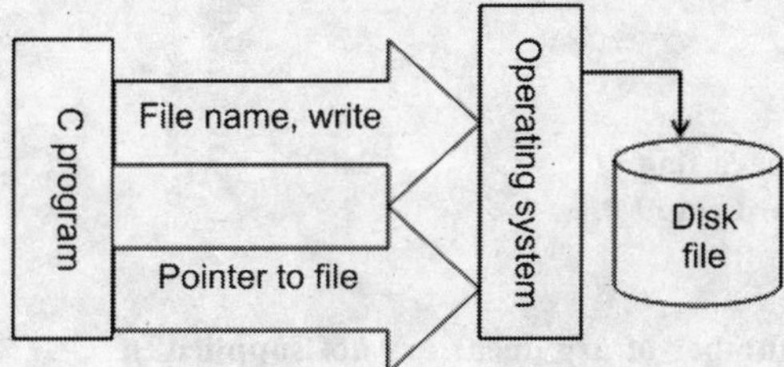

Figure 18.5 Opening a file in write mode

The capability of reading and writing from/to files on a character-by-character basis has many useful applications. Go through the Example 7 which finds size of a given file.

Example 7: Write C code for finding the size of a file.

Answer: Consider the following program segment that opens a file in read mode. It reads one character at a time from the file and checks the condition and then goes for the next character if the condition is true, otherwise, break and exit from the program and finally, display the size of the file.

```
/* filesize.c */
# include<stdio.h>
# include<stdlib.h>

void main(int argc, char *argv[])
{
    FILE *fp;
    int count = 0;
    if (argc != 2)
    {
        printf("\n Proper number of arguments are not supplied");
        exit(1);
    }
    fp = fopen (argv[1], "r");
```

```
    if(fp == NULL)
    {
        printf ("\n Can not open file %s", argv[1]);
        perror("Error: ");
        exit(1);
    }
    while(getc(fp) != EOF)
        count++;
    fclose(fp);
    printf("\n %s contains %d", argv[1], count);
}
```

If one is interested in the number of words that lies in a file then one can write the following program segment that counts the number of words in a file. See Example 8 which is word count command in UNIX/LINUX.

Example 8: Write C code which counts number of words in a given file.

Answer: If we provide the file DEST as an input to the following program segment and it displays 28 words in the file DEST.

```
/* wordcnt.c */
# include<stdio.h>
# include<stdlib.h>

void main(int argc, char *argv[])
{
    FILE *fp;
    char ch;
    int white = 1; /* white space flag */
    int count = 0;      /* word count */
    if (argc != 2)
    {
        printf("\n Proper number of argument are not supplied");
        exit(1);
    }
    fp = fopen (argv[1], "r");

    if( fp == NULL)
    {
        printf("\n Can not be open %s file", argv[1]);
        perror("Error:");
        exit(1);
    }

    while ((ch = getc(fp)) != EOF)
    {
        switch(ch)
        {
        case '':
        case '\t':
        case '\n':
            white ++;
            break;
        default:
            if (white)
            {
```

```
                white = 0;
                count++;
            }
        }
    }
    fclose (fp);
    printf("\n File %s contains %d words", argv[1], count);
}
```

18.4 FORMATTED FILE OPERATION

There are a number of related functions used for formatted I/O, each one determining the format of the I/O from a format string. For output, the format string consists of plain text, which is output unchanged, and embedded format specifications which call for some special processing of one of the remaining arguments to the function. On input, the plain text must match what is seen in the input stream; the format specifications again specify what the meaning of remaining arguments is. Each format specification is introduced by a % character, followed by the rest of the specification. In this mode the data formats are required before performing any operation on the file. The syntax is:

File_Handling _Function(file pointer, data formats, list of variables);

For example, the file handling functions are:

fscanf () **(It is input function)**

fprintf () **(It is output function)**

The syntax for the function **fprintf ()** (output function) is:

int fprintf (file_ pointer, format, arguments);

where

FILE *file_pointer;

char format; /* as given in Table 10.2 */

This is most powerful library function; it is extremely flexible and formats the output data. The argument **file_pointer** specifies the output file and the string formats the **format.** The second argument (format) it is a string, which can also contain special character and wildcards. Instead of a wild card the value of the corresponding argument is printed in the output file. The wildcards consists of the character "%" followed by the format specification. Further arguments must be specified for wildcards. The format specification can also contain many other portions such as flags like:

A decimal number to specify the size of the output field

A decimal number to specify the accuracy

The alphabet l for long integer

An alphabet for specifying the data and output type

The set of flags is given in Table 10.2 and Zero or more flags are used for presenting the format of the output.

A decimal number to specify the size of the output field: This decimal number specifies the minimum length of the field in which the argument is to be printed. Depending upon whether the flag "-" is set or not, the output is done. In this field left or right shift of this decimal number begins with '0'. The rest of the field left is filled with zeros, else with blanks.

A decimal number to specify the accuracy: The number of places to be printed after the decimal point is determined by a period, followed by a decimal number. In the case of strings, the maximum number of characters to be printed is also specified.

The alphabet for specifying the data and output type: This alphabet determines two aspects. On one hand it specifies the data type of the corresponding argument while on the other hand it also specifies the number system and the format of the output.

Another special feature is the possibility of setting a star "*" instead of the number for specifying field size and the accuracy. In this case **fprintf()** expects an additional argument before the actual argument, which determines this value. The function **fprintf()** returns the number of the characters printed. The file pointer is defined with help of macro **FILE** (structure FILE). The data formatters are given in Table 10.3. The functions that use these formats are described in Table 10.4. All need the inclusion of <stdio.h>. Their declarations are as shown.

```
#include <stdio.h>
int fprintf(FILE *stream, const char *format, ...);
int printf(const char *format, ...);
int sprintf(char *s, const char *format, ...);

#include <stdarg.h>     /* as well as stdio.h */
int vfprintf(FILE *stream, const char *format, va list arg);
int vprintf(const char *format, va list arg);
int vsprintf(char *s, const char *format, va list arg);
```

All of the above functions return the number of characters output, or a negative value on error. The trailing null is not counted by sprintf and vsprintf. Implementations must permit at least 509 characters to be produced by any single conversion. The number of data formats must be equal to the number of variables used in the function.

```
fscanf (fp, "%d%f%c%s",&i, &f, ch, string);
fprintf (fp, "%d%f%c%s",i, f, ch, string);
fscanf (fp, "%d%f%c",&i, &f, ch, string); /* incorrect */
fprintf (fp, "%d%f%c%s", i, f, ch); /* incorrect but compiler will  not generate any error */
```

Consider the Example 9 which implements the above discussion.

Example 9: Write C code which is storing information in tabular form on the standard output device.

Answer: See the following code.

```
/* format.c */
# include<stdio.h>
# include<stdlib.h>
void main()
{
    FILE *fp;
    int ivalue = 125;
    float fvalue = 125.125;
    char *string = "Enjoy with C";
    fp = fopen("form.dat", "w");
    if (fp == NULL)
    {
        printf("\n File can not be created \n");
        perror("Error:");
        exit(1);
    }
    printf("\nInteger value: %0d \n Hexdecimal value: %x \n", ivalue, ivalue);
    printf("\n Integer value: %6d\n", ivalue);
    printf("\nOctal value: %o \n General value: %#o\n" , ivalue, ivalue);
    printf("\n %f, \n %22.4f \n %*.*f \n %E \n", fvalue, fvalue,8, 1,  fvalue, fvalue);
```

```
    printf("\n %s \n %20s \n %-20s \n %c \n", string, string, string, string);
    fprintf(fp,"\nInteger value: %0d \n Hexdecimal value: %x \n", ivalue, ivalue);
    fprintf(fp,"\n Integer value: %6d\n", ivalue);
    fprintf(fp,"\nOctal value: %o \n General value: %#o\n" , ivalue, ivalue);
    fprintf(fp,"\n %f, \n %22.4f \n %*.*f \n %E \n", fvalue, fvalue, 8, 1, fvalue, fvalue);
    fprintf(fp, "\n %s \n %20s \n %-20s \n %c \n", string, string, string, string);
    fclose(fp);
}
```

In the above program segment, we have used data formatters for the screen output as well as for file output. This program segment display the formatted result on the screen, simultaneously output being written into the file **form.dat.** See the Example 10 which uses the function **fprintf()**.

Example 10: Write C code which is storing information in tabular form in a given file.

Answer: See the following code.

```
/* fprintf.c */
#include <stdio.h>
void main (void)
{
    FILE *fp;
    int pages = 655;
    float price = 250.0;

    if (fp = fopen("FPRINTF.DAT", "w"))
    {
        fprintf(fp, "Book Title: Expert Data Structures With C++ \n");
        fprintf(fp, "Pages:  %d\n", pages);
        fprintf(fp, "Price: Rs %6.25f\n", price);
        fclose(fp);
    }
    else
        printf("Error opening FPRINTF.DAT\n");
}
```

The above program segment writes the following information into the file **FPRINTF.DAT.**

```
Book Title: Expert Data Structures With C++
Pages: 655
Price: Rs 250.000
```

The function **fscanf()** is an input function and its syntax is

```
    int fscanf (file_pointer, format, arguments);
where
    FILE *file_pointer;
    char *format;
```

The function **fscanf()** reads data from the **file_pointer,** interprets it according to the specifications in the argument format and assigns the resulting values to the variables referred by the arguments. Similar to **fprintf(), fscanf()** also works with wildcards. If the number of wildcards does not confirm the number of the arguments, the behaviour of this function is undefined. The string format can contain various elements or so called "white space characters" (blanks, tabs, LF and FF) cause. This data is read till the appearance of the next such character. Normal characters in this string must confirm the ones read from the file. Wildcards begin again with the character '%'. The actual specification of the input format and the data type can be lead by the alphabets **"i"** or **"h"**, the character "*" and a number specifying the max-field length. Every wildcard serves for the convention of the field. The field is a sequence of characters, which are limited by a white space character or a character not fitting this data type. Leading white space characters are ignored. The **fscanf ()** has "*" if this character is set, the next object is read from the file but not assigned to a variable. No argument may be given for this wildcard.

"l" this is necessary, when a **long** or a **double** value is to be assigned instead of an int or float value.

"h" this alphabet treats the opposite case. An **"h"** must be set, if a short value is to be assigned instead of an **int** value.

Alphabets or wildcards to specify the input format and the data type- it is determined in which number system and with which formatting an object is to be read from a file. Besides this, it also specifies the data type of the variable to which the result of the interpretation is to be assigned. List of various alphabets is given in **Table 10.3.** The wildcard ("[]") a character set can be declared for input. This wildcard has following possibilities:

List all the permissible characters specify area- the wildcard **"%[0123456789]"** defines a character set which allows only the specified characters. During input all the characters up to the first character, not present in this character set are read. It is also possible to define characters in the range form like **"%[a-f]".**

Define negative characters- if the opening square bracket is followed by the character "^", a character set is defined, which permits all the characters with the exception of the character given after that. The wildcard **"%[^0-9]"** reads all the characters till the first occurrence of a digit.

The function **fscanf ()** returns the number of fields processed as value. See the Example 11 for the details.

Example 11: Write C code which is storing information in a given file and finally it is reading them.

Answer: Consider the following program segment that implements the above discussion:

```
/* fscanf.c */
#include <stdio.h>
void main(void)
{
    FILE *fp;
    int age;
    float salary;
    char name[64];

    if ((fp = fopen("DATA.DAT", "w")) == NULL)
        printf("Error opening DATA.DAT for output\n");
    else
    {
        fprintf(fp, "21 11125.75 Rachita");
        fclose(fp);

        if ((fp = fopen("DATA.DAT", "r")) == NULL)
            printf("Error opening DATA.DAT for input\n");
        else
        {
            fscanf(fp, "%d %f %s", &age, &salary, name);
            printf("\n Age: %d \n Salary: %f \n Name: %s\n", age, salary, name);
            fclose(fp);
```

```
        }
    }
}
```

The above program segment, first opens the file **DATA.DAT,** in write mode and writes **"21 11125.75 Rachita"** into it and after completion of write operation, the function **fclose(fp)** closes the file. After closing the file **DATA.DAT** once again is opened but this time in read mode and read operation is performed with the help of function **fscanf ().** And finally it display read information from the file on the screen. Consider the Example 12 in continuation of formatted file operation.

Example 12: Write C code to open a file in binary write and read mode.

Answer: Following code is implementation.

```
/** file8.c **/
# include<stdio.h>

void main()
{
    char name[30] ;
    int age ;
    FILE  *output ;
    output = fopen("DATA","wb+");
    if ( output == NULL )
    {
        printf("\n%DATA");
        perror("Error:");
        exit(1);
    }
    printf("\n Input name:");
    scanf("%s",name);
    printf("\n Input age:");
    scanf("%d",&age);
    fprintf(output,"%s",name);
    fprintf(output," %d",age);
    fflush(output);
    fclose(output);
}
```

This program segment opens file **DATA** in write mode and takes two inputs from keyboard namely **name** and **age** and writes these into file in two steps. If we want to create database of employee of any company or students of any institution in formatted form, there is a very easy way to do so. The drawback/advantage of this type of database is that the list always will be in readable form and the records can be read, modified and written back. Drawback in this mode is that some one will open database file in any editor, modify it and save. Now we will get a changed database. If security is applied, no body can change/modify the database and it can only be read. Consider the Example 13 which is implementing the above discussion.

Example 13: Write C code which maintains text database in a flat file.

Answer: Following is target code.

```
/** file22.c **/
# include<stdio.h>
# include<string.h>
# include<stdlib.h>
void main()
```

```
{
    char file[13];
    int count = 0 ;
    char ch ;
    char name[40];
    char father_name[40];
    char roll_number[8];
    char branch[20];
    int age ;
    FILE *fp;
    printf("\nInput destination file: ");
    gets(file);
    fp = fopen(file,"w");
    if( fp == NULL )
    {
        printf("\n Destination file: %s\n",file);
        perror("Error: ");
        exit(1);
    }
    printf("\n Enter choice (y/n): ");
    ch = getchar();
    ch = toupper(ch);
    getchar();
    while(ch == 'Y')
    {
        count ++ ;
        printf("\n Input  name: ");
        gets(name);
        printf("\n Input father's name: ");
        gets(father_name);
        printf("\n Input roll number: ");
        gets(roll_number);
        printf("\n Input branch: ");
        gets(branch);
        printf("\n Input age: ");
        scanf("%d",&age);

        /* Output section */

        fprintf(fp,"\n %d \n ",count);
        fputs (name, fp);
        fprintf(fp, "\n");
        fputs(father_name, fp);
        fprintf(fp, "\n");
        fputs(roll_number, fp);
        fprintf(fp, "\n");
        fputs(branch, fp);
        fprintf(fp,"\n %d \n",age);
        getchar();
        printf("\n Enter choice (y/n): ");
        ch = getchar();
        ch = toupper(ch);
        getchar();
    }
    fclose(fp);
    printf(" File successfully written");

}
```

This is a program segment creates a text database file **dest.** Suppose we want to see one record at a time from **dest** file. This can be done with the help of Example 14.

Example 14: Write code to see the contents of the database maintained in Example 13.

Answer: Following program segment reads records and displays on the standard output device.

```
/** file10.c **/
# include<stdio.h>
# include<string.h>
# include<stdlib.h>
void main()
{
    char file[13];
    int count = 0 ;
    char ch ;
    char name[40];
    char father_name[40];
    char roll_number[8];
    char branch[20];
    int age ;
    FILE *fp;
    printf("\n Enter Database File: ");
    scanf("%s",file);
    fp = fopen(file,"r");

    if( fp == NULL )
    {
        printf("\nFile %s\n",file);
        perror("Error: ");
        exit(1);
    }
    printf("\n Enter choice (y/n): ");
    ch = getchar();
    ch = toupper(ch);

    /* Read section */

label1:
    while(ch == 'Y')
    {
        fscanf(fp,"\n %d",&count);

        /*    use fgets() function for satisfaction */
        /*    or fscanf(fp,"[\^]",name)  this  type */
        /*    read operation required with   string */
        /*  type data only                   */
        fscanf(fp, "%d", &count);
        fgets(name, 40, fp);
        fscanf(fp, "\n ");
        fgets(father_name, 40, fp);
        fscanf(fp,"\n ");
        fgets(roll_number, 8, fp );
        fscanf(fp,"\n ");
        fgets(branch, 20, fp);
        fscanf(fp, "\n %d",&age);
        /* Output section */
```

```
        printf("\n %d",count);
        puts(name);
        puts(father_name);
        puts(roll_number);
        puts(branch);
        printf("\n %d",age);
        printf("\n Enter choice (y/n):");
        ch = getchar();
        ch = toupper(ch);
    }
    printf("\n Once again want to display data (y/n):");
    ch = getchar ();
    ch = toupper(ch);
    if(ch == 'Y')
    {
        rewind(fp) ;
  /* Return the file pointer to beginning of file if we want to see next data remove rewind () function and then
we will get next record if it exists in the file */

        goto label1 ;
    }else
    {
        printf("\n Thanking You \n");
    }
    fclose(fp);
    printf(" Successfully work on file is done  ");
}
```

18.5 FILES AND STRUCTURES

When we want to crate real database then the structures are used with files. For this purpose we should know about few functions. Some functions are

fread () (input function)

fwrite () (output function)

With the help of these functions, one can perform read/write operations on files for one record at a time, not a single field of the record. First of all we will discuss the function **fread ().** The syntax of the function **fread ()** is

```
int fread (buffer, size, number, file_pointer);
where
    char *buffer;
    size_t size;
    int number;
    FILE file_pointer;
```

This function reads **number** of elements of the **size, size** from the file specified by the **file_pointer** and copies them in the memory area referred to by the **buffer.** The function terminates if an attempt is made to read beyond the **EOF.** The data type **size_t** is defined in the **file.h** and mostly corresponds to the type **unsigned int.** The function **fread ()** returns the number of bytes read as value.

Other syntax of the function **fread ()** in respect of structure is

fread(&name of struct,sizeof(struct name),1, file pointer);

For example,

```
struct Address
{
```

```
        char Name[40];
        char Street[120];
        char  City[20];
        long int Zip;
        char Country[20];
    };

    struct Address per ;

    fread(&per, sizeof(per),1,fp);
```

In the above declaration the function **fread ()** can read 204 bytes of information from the file pointed by file pointer **fp.** If some one asks why we have used pointer operator (&) with structure variable, answer of this question is obtained by looking into Figure 18.6.

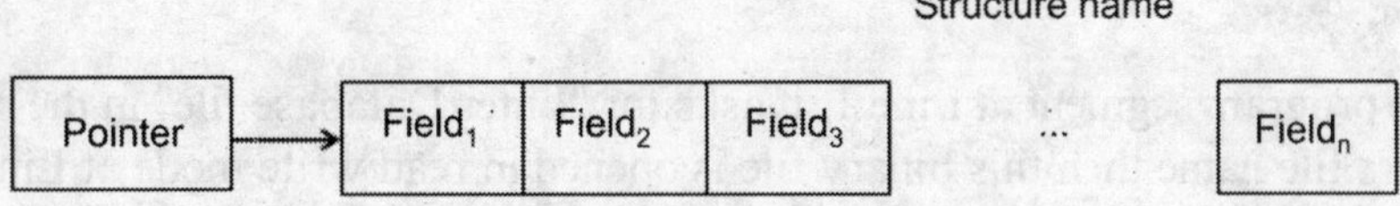

Figure 18.6 Structure in memory

In Figure 18.6 we find that all memory locations are continuous. So, that we provide base address (i.e., starting address of the structure) to the function **fread ().** After finding base address it reads information for all 204 bytes of memory locations. See the Example 15, which is implementing the above discussion.

Example 15: Write C code which reads a record from a given file using fread statement.

Answer: Consider the following program segment that implements the above discussion.

```
/** file11.c **/
# include<stdio.h>

struct Address
{
    char Name[40];
    char Street[120];
    char    City[20];
    long int Zip;
    char Country[20];
};

void main()
{
    struct Address per ;
    char file[13];
    FILE *fp;
    printf("\nEnter Database file:");          /* Line 1 */
    scanf("%s",file);                           /* Line 2 */
    fp = fopen (file,"rb+");                    /* Line  3 opens binary file in read/write mode*/

    if(fp == NULL)
    {
        printf("\n File %s",file);
        perror("Error");
        exit(1);
```

```
    }
    fread(&per, sizeof(per) , 1, fp);               /* Line 4 `raed the first record from the file*/
    while(!feof(fp))                                /* Line 5 */
    {
        /* put information associated with per on the screen */
        puts(per.Name);
        puts(per.Street);
        puts(per.City);
        puts(per.Country);
        printf("%ld",per.Zip);
        fread(&per, sizeof(per) , 1, fp); /* Line 6 read next record from the file*/
        printf("\n Press a key ");
        getchar();     /* wait for press a key */
    }
}
```

In the above program segment at Line 1, it asks for "Enter Database file" in the next statement at Line 2 user enters file name then this binary file is opened in read/write mode at Line 3. If the file is opened successfully, at Line 4 function fread() reads first record (number of bytes equal to the struct Address this size return by the sizeof(per) function) from the file pointer (fp) and assigns it to the struct variable per. Before entering into the while loop at Line 5 we check for the end of file. Under opening and closing braces of while loop first time we display the record readout in the Line 4, then we read next record and check for end of file once again. If not end of file display this readout record again and read next record and this process is continued till the end of file.

Now we will consider the function **fwrite ().** The syntax of this function is

```
int fwrite((buffer, size, number, file_pointer);
where
    char *buffer;
    size_t size;
    int number;
    FILE file_pointer;
```

Analogous to **fread ()** function, this unites **number** of elements of the **size, size** in the file specified by the **file_pointer.** The **buffer** specifies the starting address of the memory area with the output data. The function **fwrite ()** returns the number of bytes transferred as value.

Other syntax of the function **fwrite ()** in respect of structure is

```
fwrite (&name  of struct,sizeof(struct name),1, file pointer);
For example,
    struct Address
    {
        char Name[40];
        char Street[120];
        char    City[20];
        long int Zip;
        char Country[20];
    };
        struct Address add ;
        fwrite(&add, sizeof(add),1,fp);
```

In the above declaration the function **fwrite ()** writes all 204 bytes of information into the file pointed by file pointer **fp.** The function **fwrite ()** returns a value equal to the size of record written into the file. The returned value of function tells about success or failure of write operation that was performed on the file. It is good programming style to check the status of the function **fwrite ()** before any further operation. See the Example 16, which is implementing the above discussion.

Example 16: Write C code which writes a record into a given file using fwrite statement.

Answer: Consider the following program segment that implements the above discussion:

```
/** file12.c **/
    /* Writing structures into file */
    # include<stdio.h>
    # include<stdlib.h>

    struct Address
    {
        char Name[40];
        char Street[120];
        char    City[20];
        long int Zip;
        char Country[20];
    };
/* Prototype */
void gets1( char * ) ;

void main()
{
    struct Address add ;
    int size ;
    char file[13];
    FILE *fp;
    printf("\nEnter Database file: ");  /* Line 1 */
    scanf("%s",file);                   /* Line 2 read a file name from input device */
    fp = fopen (file,"wb+");            /* Line 3 open a file into binary write/read mode */
    if(fp == NULL)                  /* Line 4 check for the existence and device status */
    {
        printf("\n File %s",file);
        perror("Error");
        exit(1);
    }
    getchar();

    /* Here on wards reading of individual fields of the record is done */

    printf("\n Input Name: ");          /* Line 5 */
    gets1(add.Name);
    printf("\n Input Street: ");
    gets1(add.Street);
    printf("\n Input City Name: ");
    gets1(add.City);
    printf("\n Enter Country Name: ");
    gets1(add.Country);
    printf("\n Enter Pin Code: ");
    scanf("%ld", &add.Zip);
    size = sizeof(add);
    fwrite(&add,size,1,fp); /* Line 6 writes complete record into the file pointed by file pointer fp */
}
```

```
/* Definition of function */
/* This function is equivalent to library gets() function */
void   gets1(char *s)
{
     int i ;
     char ch ;
     i = 0 ;
     ch = getchar() ;
     while(ch != '\n')
     {
          s[i] = ch ;
          i ++ ;
          ch = getchar() ;
     }
     s[i] = '\0' ; /* marking array of character as string */
}
```

In the above program segment at Line 1, it asks for "Enter Database file" in the next statement at Line 2 user enters file name then this binary file is opened in write/ read mode at Line 3. If the file is opened successfully it is checked at Line 4 for unsuccessful state program is terminated with exit(1). At Line 5 onwards individual fields of the record (struct add is read from the keyboard and at Line 6 record is written into the file with function fwrite().

18.6 STRINGS AND FILES

To perform read/write operation from/to file for the strings, there are many library functions available in the standard **C** library. The file-oriented functions are

fgets()
fputs()
fwrite()
fread()

First of all, we will discuss about function **fgets ().** The syntax of this function is

```
     fgets(string, size , file_ pointer) ;
where
     char *string;
     int size;
     FILE file_pointer;
```

This function read characters (group) from the file pointed by **file_pointer** and copies them in the memory area indicated by **string.** The function terminates, when **size-1** characters have been read, the end -of- file (EOF) is reached or the character '\n' is also copied. The character '\0' is appended at the end of a string. The function **fgets()** returns a pointer on a string after it is successful. If an error occurs, it returns a **NULL** pointer. Let, we want to read strings from a file, see the Example 17.

Example 17: Write C code which reads a string from a given file.

Answer: For this discussion consider the following program segment.

```
/** file13.c **/
/* Strings and files */
# include<stdio.h>

void main()
{
```

```
    char file[13];
    FILE *fp ;
    char buffer[100];
    printf("\n Enter File Name: ");
    scanf("%s",file); /* read file name which want to open */
    fp = fopen ( file , "r"); /* open file in read mode */
    if( fp == NULL )  /* check for the file status */
    {
        printf("\n File %s ",file );
        perror("Error");
        exit(1);
    }

    /* while not end of file read 100 bytes from the file and writes on screen */
    while(!feof(fp))
    {
        if(fgets(buffer,100,fp))  /* reads 100 bytes into buffer and writes via file pointer fp */
            printf("\n%s",buffer); /* display buffer contents on the screen */
    }
}
```

In the above example, the program segment opens file provided by the programmer and reads one complete buffer 100 bytes specified here at a time and displays on screen. The process is continues till the end of the file.

Now we will consider the function **fputs(),** the syntax for this function is

```
    fputs(string, file_pointer) ;
where
    char *string;
    FILE *file_pointer;
```

The function **fwrite ()** writes **string** in the file pointed by **file_pointer.** The character is '\0' is not written in the file. If the file is not opened for writing, the function **fputs ()** returns the value **EOF,** else the value **0** is returned. For example, suppose we want to write a string into the file see the Example 18.

Example 18: Write C code which writes a string into a given file.

Answer: For this discussion consider the following program segment.

```
/** file14.c **/
/* Strings and file */
# include<stdio.h>

void main()
{
    char file[13];
    FILE *fp ;
    char buffer[200]=  "C is a powerful language";
    printf("\n Enter File Name: ");
    scanf("%s",file);           /* read file name from stdin */

    fp = fopen ( file , "w");   /* open file in write mode */
    if( fp == NULL )            /* check for the file status */
    {
        printf("\n File %s",file );
        perror("Error");
        exit(1);
```

```
    }
    if(fputs(buffer,fp))                /* writes buffer contents into file */
        printf("\n Successful Writing ");
}
```

The above program segment writes a string into a file pointed by file pointer **fp** (that is file provided by programmer). If we want to write more than one string into a file then we have to modify it.

If we use file operation functions **fgetc()** and **fputc()** then end of file position is find out with help of macro EOF. See the Example 19 which implements this discussion.

Example 19: Write C code which uses EOF for checking end of file.

Answer: For this discussion consider the following program segment.

```
/** file15.c **/
/* Strings and file */
# include<stdio.h>
# include<dirent.h>
void main()
{
    char file[13];
    char ch ;
    FILE *fp ;
    char buffer[200]= "C language very powerful and useful keep with it ";
    printf("\n Enter File Name: "); /* line 1 */
    scanf("%s",file); /* line 2 */
    fp = fopen ( file , "r+w");  /* line 3 */
    if( fp == NULL )             /* line 4 */
    {
        printf("\n File %s ",file );
        perror("Error");
        exit(1);
    }
    fputs(buffer,fp);  /* line 5, write contents of the buffer into the file */
    printf("\nSuccessfully reading from file is completed \n ");
    rewind(fp) ; /* line 6, return the file pointer to start of file */
    ch = fgetc(fp);     /* line 7, read first character  from the file */

    /* while not end of file read and display each character on the screen */
    while(ch != EOF )/* line 8 */
    {
        putchar(ch) ; /* line 9, put character on the screen */
        ch = fgetc(fp);          /* line 10, read one character */
    }
    fclose(fp);
}
```

In the above prpgram segment at line 1 it asks for the file name to be entered. In line 2 it reads file name from stdin, at line 3 entered file is opned and in next statement file pointer status is checked. If is successful further operation is successful otherwise program is terminated with statement exit(1). At line 5 buffer contents are written into the file pointed by the file pointer fp with the help of function fputs(). At function rewind() return file pointer at the beginning of the file. In line 7 we are reading first charcter from the file. Line 8 verifies for the end of file with macro EOF, at line 9 putchar() function writes the value of ch variable on screen and in line 10 next character is readout. Process from line 8 to line 10 is repeated till the last character is readout and displayed on screen.

18.7 RANDOM ACCESS FILE OPERATION

So for our entire file reading writing has been sequential. That is, when writing a file we have taken a group of items whether character, strings or more complexes structures and placed them on the disk file one at time. Likewise, when reading, we have started at the beginning of the file and traversed until we come to the end.

It is also possible to access files randomly. This means directly accessing a particular data item, even though it may in the middle of the file. The file pointer points to the byte in the file where the next access will take place. The function **fseek ()** sets the file position indicator associated with file pointer according to the values of the offset and **origin** {Figure 18.7}. The syntax of the function **fseek ()** is:

```
int fseek(file_pointer, offset, origin);
```

where

```
FILE *file_pointer;
long int offset;
int origin;
```

The first argument of the function **fseek ()** is the pointer to the **FILE** structure for the file. This is also referred as a file pointer, but it is something quite different from the file pointer that indicates where we are in the file.

The second argument in **fseek ()** is called the **offset.** This is the number of the bytes from a particular place to start reading. Often, this place is the beginning of the file. For example, in the program segment (file16.c), the offset is calculated by multiplying the size of one record-the structure-**add** by the number of the records we want to access. The **offset** should be **long.** If the **offset** is **long**, only then, it is possible to move more than 64 KB, otherwise not. For example, see Figure 18.7.

The last argument of the function **fseek()** is called the origin. There are three possible values of the origin and they determine from where the offset will be measured. The possible values of third argument are given in **Table 18.9.** In this table we have also given the macro names of the origin.

Table 18.9 values of third argument of fseek()

Macro	Integer value	Meaning
SEEK_SET	0	File pointer at beginning of file
SEEK_CUR	1	Current position of file represented by file pointer
SEEK_END	2	File pointer at end of the file

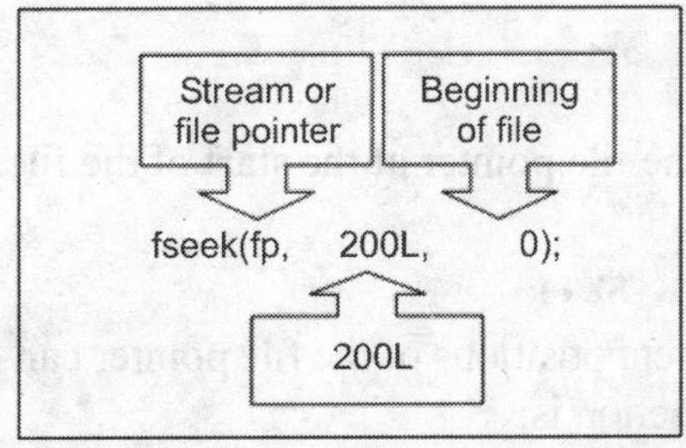

Figure 18.7 Position of file pointer

Another function **ftell ()** returns the current position of the file pointer in the file. We can use it to tell the file size by setting the file pointer to the end of the file with **fseek ()** and then reading its position. See the Example 20 which is implementing the following syntax of the function **ftell ():**

```
long ftell (file_pointer);
```

where

```
FILE *file_pointer;
```

Example 20: Write C code which uses ftell() function for finding the current position of the file pointer of file.

Answer: Consider the following program segment, which implements the properties of the file pointer position indicator. This program segment displays every byte position which is indicated by the file pointer position indicator. This program segment opens the file **dest** in read mode and prints size of the file first. In while statement it reads character by character the file and displays position of every character.

```
/* ftell.c */
#include <stdio.h>
# include<stdlib.h>

void main(void)
{
    FILE *input;
    int letter;
    if ((input = fopen("dest", "r")) == NULL)
        printf("Error opening DEST \n");
    else
    {
        printf("Current position is byte %ld\n\n", ftell(input));

        /* Read and write each character in the file standard output device */
        while ((letter = fgetc(input)) != EOF)
        {
            fputc(letter, stdout);
            printf("\nCurrent position is byte %d\n", ftell(input));
        }
        fclose(input);    /* Close the input file */
    }
}
```

The function **rewind ()** is very useful in the random operation on the file. The syntax for the function **rewind()** is

```
void rewind(file_pointer);
```

where

```
FILE *file_pointer;
```

The function **rewind()** sets the file pointer at the start of the file. This function is the same as the call

```
fseek(file_pointer, 0L, SEEK_SET);
```

If one is interested in the current positions of the file pointer can get directly by using the function fgetpos (). The syntax of this function is:

```
int fgetpos(file_pointer, position);
```

where

```
FILE *file_pointer;
fpos_t  *position;
```

This function tells the value of the **file_pointer** and saves this in the object referred to by **position** with the function **fsetpos ()**, the file pointer can be later reset to the buffered position, after it has been changed by read and write operations. The advantage of the function is that it can be used on extremely big files; which can not be handled with the help of **ftell ()** and **fseek(),** as the position values cannot be represented any more as the data type **long.** The syntax of the function **fsetpos ()** is

```
int fsetpos(file_pointer, position);
```

where

```
FILE *file_pointer;
const fpos_t *position;
```

The function **fsetpos ()** resets the pointer position determined with the help of **fgetpos().** See the Example 21 which is used to maintain database in structured flat file.

Example 21: Write C code which is used to keep records of people of a city.

Answer: See the following code.

```
/** file16.c **/
# include<stdio.h>
# include<stdlib.h>

struct Address
{
    char Name[40];
    char Street[120];
    char    City[20];
    long int Zip;
    char Country[20];
};

/* Prototype */
void gets1( char * ) ;

void main()
{
    struct Address add ;
    int size ;
    int no_record ;
    int position ;
    int n ;
    char ch ;
    char file[13];
    FILE *fp;
    printf("\nEnter Database file: ");
    gets(file);
    fp = fopen (file,"a+"); /* opens file in binary raed/write mode */

    if(fp == NULL)
    {
        printf("\n File %s",file);
        perror("Error");
        exit(1);
    }
    printf("\n Enter choice (y/n) want to add more record: ");
    ch = getchar();
    ch = toupper(ch) ;
    size = sizeof(add);
```

```
while(ch == 'Y')
{
        printf("\n Input Name: ");
        gets1(add.Name);
        printf("\n Input Street: ");
        gets1(add.Street);
        printf("\n Input City Name: ");
        gets1(add.City);
        printf("\n Enter Country Name: ");
        gets1(add.Country);
        printf("\n Enter Pin Code: ");
        scanf("%ld", &add.Zip);

        /* Writining structures into file */

        fwrite(&add,size,1,fp); /* write a record into the file */
        getchar();
        printf("\n Enter choice (y/n) want to add more record: ");
        ch = getchar();
        ch = toupper(ch) ;
}

/* Here we want to find number of record in the file */

rewind(fp);
fseek(fp,0L,2);    /* set file pointer at end of file */
size = ftell(fp);   /* size of file in byte */
no_record = size / (sizeof(add) );  /* sizeof(add) gves the size of a record */
printf("\n Number of record in the file ->%d",no_record);
/* records are stored on the file */
/* random access of any record from the file */
printf("\n Enter Record Number want to seach: ");
scanf("%d", &n);

/* total bytes to be skipped for setting the current position of the file pointer */
position = (n-1)*(sizeof(add)) ;
fseek(fp,position,0);
/* Ths function read out the desired record from the file */
fread(&add,sizeof(add),1,fp);

/* Output section */

puts(add.Name);
puts(add.Street);
puts(add.City);
puts(add.Country);
printf("%ld",add.Zip);
printf("\n Press a key ");
getchar();
}

/* This function is equivalent to gest library function gets() */
/* Definition of function */

void    gets1(char *s)
```

```
{
    int i ;
    char ch ;
    i = 0 ;
    ch = getchar() ;
    while(ch != '\n')
    {
        s[i] = ch ;
        i ++ ;
        ch = getchar() ;
    }
    s[i] = '\0' ;
}
```

Here, first of all, this program segment writes records into a file and then program rewinds the file and gets back file pointer to the end of file. In the next section we will find number of records in the file. In last section asks for choice of the record we want to access randomly. It finds that record and finally after getting that record it will display the record.

18.8 DIRECT FILE MANIPULATION

A number of functions exist to operate on files directly.

```
#include <stdio.h>
int remove(const char *filename);
int rename(const char *old, const char *new);
char *tmpnam(char *s);
FILE *tmpfile(void);
```

The remove() function causes a file to be removed. Subsequent attempts to open the file will fail, unless it is first created again. If the file is already open, the operation of remove is implementation defined. The return value is zero for success, any other value for failure, and assigns the global value **errno** as one of the following: (a) **EACCES** Access denied (b) **ENOENT** File not found. Consider the Example 22 which implements the above discussion.

Example 22: Write C code which delete a given file.

Answer: Following program segment do the task.

```
/* remove.c */
#include <stdio.h>
void main(int argc, char *argv[])
{
    while (*++argv)
    {
        printf("\n Removing file %s", *argv);
        if (remove(*argv))
            printf("Error removing %s\n", *argv);
    }
}
```

The rename() function changes the name of the file identified by old to new. Subsequent attempts to open the original name will fail, unless another file is created with the old name. As with remove, rename returns zero for a successful operation, any other value indicating a failure. If a file with the new name exists prior to calling rename, the behaviour is implementation defined. If rename fails for any reason, the original file is unaffected.

The tmpnam() function generates a string that may be used as a filename and is guaranteed to be different from any existing filename. It may be called repeatedly, each time generating a new name.

The constant TMP_MAX is used to specify how many times tmpnam may be called before it can no longer find a unique name. TMP_MAX will be at least 25. If tmpnam is called more than this number of times, its behaviour is undefined by the Standard, but many implementations offer no practical limit. If the argument s is set to NULL, then tmpnam uses an internal buffer to build the name, and returns a pointer to that. Subsequent calls may alter the same internal buffer. The argument may instead point to an array of at least L_tmpnam characters, in which case the name will be filled into the supplied buffer. Such a filename may then be created, and used as a temporary file. Since the name is generated by the function, it is unlikely to be very useful in any other context. Temporary files of this nature are not removed, except by direct calls to the remove function. They are most often used to pass temporary data between two separate programs.

The function tmpfile() creates a temporary binary file, opened for update, and returns a pointer to the stream of that file. The file will be removed when the stream is closed. If no file could be opened, tmpfile returns a NULL pointer.

The ferror()

When programs perform the file I/O operations, the program should always test the return values of the functions such as **fopen(), fputs(), fgets()** and so on to verify that the operations were successful. To help programs to perform such testing **C** provides the **ferror()** function which examines an I/O stream for a read and write error. If an error has occurred, **ferror()** returns a true value. If no error has occurred, **ferror()** returns false values. The syntax for this function is

```
int ferror(filename);
```

where

```
const char *filename;
```

Once a file I/O error occurs, the function **ferror()** will remain true until programs invoke the **clearrer()** function for the given stream. . Consider the Example 23 which implements the above discussion.

Example 23: Write C code which demonstrates standard errors generated during problem arising when operating on a file.

Answer: Consider the following program segment that reads and display a file's contents on to the screen. After each I/O operation, the program segment tests for an error. If an error occurs, the program ends displaying an error message to **stderr.**

```
/* ferror.c */
#include <stdio.h>
#include <stdlib.h>
void main (int argc, char *argv[])
{
    FILE *fp;
    char line[256];
    if (fp = fopen(argv[1], "r"))
    {
        while (fgets(line, sizeof(line), fp))
        {
            if (ferror(fp))
            {
                    fprintf(stderr, "Error reading from %s\n", argv[1]);
                    exit(1);
            }else
            {
```

```
                    fputs(line, stdout);
                    if (ferror(fp))
                    {
                            fprintf(stderr, "Error writing to stdout\n");
                            exit(1);
                    }
            }
        }
    }else
        printf("Error opening %s\n", argv[1]);
}
```

Why we prefer binary mode over text mode? In the text mode when a text character is written into a file, it requires two bytes of memory space, for some characters one byte for text and other byte for attribute of a character. But in the binary mode it will require only one byte of space for all characters. Text type of files can be displayed by the use of **UNIX** command like **cat.** But in binary file these types of operations are not possible.

18.9 BUFFERED FILE PROCESSING

This is also called system-level input/output (I/O), in this data cannot be written as individual characters or strings or as formatted data, as is possible using standard I/O. There is only one way that data can be written as a buffer full of bytes. Writing a buffer full of data resembles record I/O in the standard I/O package. However, unlike standard I/O, the programmer must set up the buffer for the data, place the appropriate values in it before writing and take them out after reading. The buffer is the part of the program rather than being invisible as in standard I/O. **Figure 18.8** illustrates the discussion.

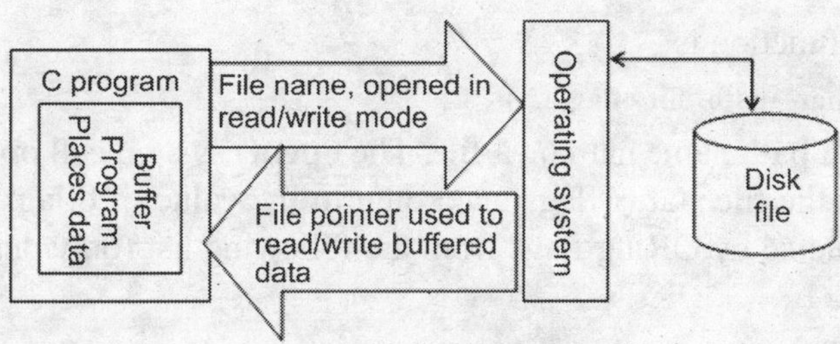

Figure 18.8 Visible buffer

There are advantages to system-level I/O because the amount of code used by **C** library routines is less than with standard I/O, so programs can be smaller. Because there are fewer layers of routines to go through, system I/O can also operate faster. Because it's a more basic system, many compiler writers create the standard I/O package using system I/O routines. The list of functions, which are available with most of compilers, is given in **Table 18.10.**

Table 18.10 Low level file processing functions

Function	Meaning
read()	Reads a buffer of data
write()	Writes a buffer of data
open()	Opens a disk file
creat()	Create a new file on disk
close()	Closes an opened a file
lseek()	Move file pointer to a specified byte in a file
unlink	Remove a file from the disk
tell()	Get the position of current file pointer

The function **creat()** creates a new file or overwrites an existing one. This function lies in **fcntl.h** header file. The syntax for this function is

int creat(const char *path, mode_t mode);

The function **creat()** system call creates a new ordinary file or prepares to rewrite an existing file named by the path name pointed to by **path.** If the file exists, the length is truncated to 0 and the mode and owner are unchanged. Otherwise, the file's owner ID is set to the effective user ID of the process; the group ID of the process is set to the effective group ID of the process and the low-order 12 bits of the file mode are set to the value of mode modified as follows:

- All bits set in the process's file mode creation mask are cleared.
- The "save text image after execution bit" of the mode is cleared.

Upon successful completion, a write-only file descriptor is returned and the file is open for writing, even if the mode does not permit writing. The file pointer is set to the beginning of the file. The file descriptor is set to remain open across **exec()** system calls. No process may have more than **FOPEN_MAX** files open simultaneously. A new file may be created with a mode that forbids writing.

Symbolic constants defining the access permission bits are specified in the **<sys/stat.h>** header file and should be used to construct mode.

The call **creat(path, mode)** is equivalent to the following

open(path, O_WRONLY | O_CREAT | O_TRUNC, mode);

Upon successful completion, a non-negative integer, namely the file descriptor, is returned. Otherwise, a value of -1 is returned, and **errno** is set to indicate the error.

The open()

The syntax for the function is

int open (const char *path, int oflag, ...);

The **path** points to a path name naming a file. The **open()** system call opens a file descriptor for the named file and sets the file status flags according to the value of oflag. For non-**streams** files, **oflag** values are constructed by ORing flags from the following list (only one of the first three flags below can be used):

- **O_RDONLY** Open for reading only.
- **O_WRONLY** Open for writing only.
- **O_RDWR** Open for reading and writing.
- **O_APPEND** If set, the file pointer is set to the end of the file prior to each write.
- **O_CREAT** If the file exists, this flag has no effect. Otherwise, the user ID of the file is set to the effective user ID of the process; the group ID of the file is set to the effective group ID of the process or to the group ID of the file's parent directory and the low-order 12 bits of the file mode are set to the value of mode, modified as follows:

All bits set in the file mode creation mask of the process are cleared. Upon successful completion, the file descriptor is returned. Otherwise, a value of -1 is returned and **errno** is set to indicate the **error.** Consider the Example 24 which implements the above discussion. The "save text image after execution bit" of the mode is cleared. The setting of files is discussed with function **chmod ().**

Example 24: Write C code which performs bufferful reading from a given file.

Answer: Consider the **file17.c** program segment that opens a file and reads, **"C is a charming language"** from the file.

```
/** file17.c **/
# include<stdio.h>
# include<fcntl.h>
# include<string.h>

void main()
{
    int fp ;        /* file pointer */
    char buffer[80] ;

    fp = open("TEST",O_RDONLY);

    if( fp == -1 )
    {
        perror("Error");
        exit(1);
    }

    while(feof)
    {
        read(fp, buffer, 80 ) ;
        printf("\n%s",buffer);
        printf("\n Press a key");
        getchar();
    }
    close(fp);
}
```

This program segment opens a file in read mode and reads a string into the **buffer** from the file **TEST.** The returned value of function **open ()** always being positive integer. If any error arise the returned value becomes -1. For example, if we are trying to open a file but the file does not exist, in that case the returned value of **open()** function will be -1. To construct access we should use mode plus access modifiers together.

Now we will discuss the function **write ().** The syntax of this function is:

```
    int write (fd, buffer, no_bytes);
where
    int fd;
    char buffer;
    unsigned no_bytes;
```

The function **write()** writes **no_bytes** in the file present in the **buffer** and specified by **fd.** The buffer is a pointer on the start of the data to be written. The number of bytes actually written moves the pointer further. The function only writes the data in continuous memory areas. If the file opened with set **O_APPEND** flag, every write operation is done at the end of the file. In case of set **O_SYNC** flag, the write call returns only when the write operation is carried out physically. The function **write ()** returns the number of bytes actually written. The value -1 indicates an error. See the Example 25 for implementation of the above discussion.

Example 25: Write C code which writes a bufferful information on a given file.

Answer: Consider the following program segment that opens a file in write mode, and writes **"C is a charming language"** into the file.

```
/** file18.c **/
# include<stdio.h>
```

```
# include<fcntl.h>
# include<string.h>

void main()
{
    char buffer[] = " C is a charming language ";
    int fp ;  /* file pointer */
    fp = open("TEST",O_CREAT);
    if( fp == -1 )
    {
        perror("Error");
        exit(1);
    }
    write(fp,buffer,strlen(buffer)) ;
    close(fp);
}
```

Now we will discuss about the function **read().** The syntax of this function is:

```
int bytes =read (handle, buffer, no_bytes);
```

where

```
int handle;
char *buffer; /* buffer to read data in */
int no_bytes  /* represents the size of buffer */
```

The function **read ()** takes three argument. The first is the file handle. The second is the address of the **buffer** and the third argument being the maximum number of bytes we want to read. The function **read ()** returns the number of bytes actually read. This is an important number, because it may be less than the buffer size and we shall need to know just how full the buffer is, before we can do any thing with its contents. We assign this number to the variable **bytes.** Once the buffer is full we can display it. We should do this with the help of **for** loop running from 0 to **bytes,** printing one character at a time.

The function **close ()** is used to close an opened file. The syntax for this function is

```
close(fd);
```

where

```
int fd;
```

Putting the contents of a file in a buffer has certain advantages. We can perform various operations on the contents of the buffer without having to access the file again. There are several functions that can speed up operations on buffered data as our next program segment demonstrates. Example 26 searches a text file for a word or phrase typed by the user.

Example 26: Write C code which searches a text file for a word or phrase typed by the user.

Answer: Following code implements this problem.

```
/* search.c */
/* searches file for phrase */
#include <fcntl.h>
#include <stdio.h>
#include <string.h>
#include <stdlib.h>
#define BUFFSIZE 1024                /* buffer size */

char buff[BUFFSIZE];                 /* buffer */
void search(char *, int);            /* prototype */
```

```
int main( int argc, char *argv[] )
{
    int inhandle, bytes;

    if(argc != 3)              /* check arguments */
    {
        printf("\n $ search filename phrase");
        exit(1);
    }
    /*  open file */
    if( (inhandle = open(argv[1], O_RDONLY )) < 0)
    {
        printf("\nCan't open file %s.", argv[1]);
        exit(1);
    }
    /* read file */
    while( (bytes = read(inhandle,buff,BUFFSIZE)) > 0)
        search(argv[2],bytes);          /*  search for phrase */
    close(inhandle);               /*  close file */
    printf("\nPhrase not found");
    return(0);
}

/* search() */

/* Searches buffer for phrase */

void search(char *phrase, int buflen)
{
    char *ptr, *p;
    ptr = buff;
    while( (ptr=memchr(ptr,phrase[0],buflen)) != NULL)
        if( memcmp(ptr,phrase,strlen(phrase)) == 0)  /* if match */
        {
            printf("First occurrence of phrase: \n");
            for(p=ptr-100; p<ptr+100; p++)          /*  display it */
                putchar(*p);
            exit(0);
        }
        else
            ptr++;
}
```

The tell ()

This function is similar to ftell() and sets the file descriptor at the end of the file. The syntax for this function is:

```
int tell(handle)
where
    int handle;
```

In other words we can say that it returns the position of the file descriptor. So it can be used to find the size of a file. Example 27 demonstrates tell function.

Example 27: Write C code which finds end of file.

Answer: Consider the following program segment that displays the size of file and position of every character in the file as an input to the program. Tis program can be run at the prompt with one argument, i.e., program code and filename on which we want to perform the operation.

```
/* tell.c */
#include <stdio.h>
#include <fcntl.h>

void main(int argc, char *argv[])
{
    int handle;
    char buffer[512];
    int bytes_read;
    if ((handle = open(argv[1], O_RDONLY)) == -1)
        printf("Error opening %s\n", argv[1]);
    else
    {
        printf("Current file position %ld\n", tell(handle));

        while (bytes_read = read(handle, buffer, sizeof(buffer)))
            write(1, buffer, bytes_read);

        printf("Current file position %ld\n", tell(handle));
        close(handle);
    }
}
```

Readers/Programmers are advised to run his code and see the output.

The unlink ()

When we want to delete some files from the system, we require the function **unlink ().** The syntax for this function is

```
    int unlink (filename);
where
    const char *filename;
```

If the function successfully removes the file, it returns the value 0. If an error occurs it returns the value -1 and assigns the global value **errno** one of the following: **EACCES** Access denied or **ENOENT** File not found. See Example 28 which deletes a file from the system.

Example 28: Consider the following program segment that deletes.

```
/* unlink.c */
#include <stdio.h>

void main(int argc, char *argv[])
{
    while (*++argv)
    {
        printf("\n Removing %s", *argv);
        if (unlink(*argv))
            printf("Error removing %s\n", *argv);
    }
}
```

18.10 FILE HANDLE

Instead of returning a pointer, as **fopen ()** did in standard I/O, **open** returns an integer value called a file handle. This is number assigned to a particular file, which is used thereafter to refer to the file. If **open ()** returns a value of -1 rather than a valid file handle (which is greater than 0), an error has occurred.

When we work with a file handle, there may be times when we need to know specifics about the corresponding file, such as the disk drive on which the file is stored. In such cases in program we can use the function **stat().** The syntax of this function is:

```
    int stat(path, info)
where
    char *path;
    struct *info;
```

The function **stat()** assigns specifics about the file to a structure of type **stat,** which is defined in the header file **<sys/stat.h>.**

There are two **stat ()** call families, returning different **stat** structures. The old (or traditional) **stat** is compatible with previous **SCO UNIX** systems and **XENIX** system. It is, however, limited to 65,535 (or 16 bits-worth) i-nodes per filesystem and so may return an incorrect (truncated) i-node number on **CD-ROMs.** The **stat ()** routine in **libc** is the old 16-bit version and is provided for backwards compatibility with existing libraries and object modules.

The new **stat** structure is currently unique to **SCO UNIX.** It supports up to 32 bits-worth of i-nodes per filesystem. This 32-bit **stat** support is in two parts. The high level, called "st_stat32", if used on an older system that only supports the old 16-bit stat, automatically converts the old 16-bit stat structure into the desired new 32-bit format. At a lower level the new system call **xstat ()** which we should avoid calling directly takes a third parameter (a version id) and returns whichever format is requested. Both **stat's** conform to ANSI C standards. By default, merely by including this header (<sys/stat.h>), the new 32-bit stat is automatically used.

Always-defined routines to access new 32-bit or old 16-bit **stat** structure formats as desired. **Default case:** The **stat** (structure and function) is the new 32-bit format. On older 16-bit-only-stat systems, the 16-bit format is automatically converted into the new 32-bit format.

```
    struct stat {                         /* 32 bit  struct stata          */
    dev_t    st_dev;                      /* id of device containing dir entry */
    long st_pad1[3];
    ino32_t  st_ino;                      /* i-node number (32 bits-worth)    */
    mode_t   st_mode;/* file mode (permissions and type)  */
    nlink_t  st_nlink;/* number of links */
    uid_t    st_uid;                      /* user id of the file's owner */
    gid_t    st_gid;                      /* group id of the file's owner */
    dev_t    st_rdev; /* id of block/character special file   */
    long st_pad2[2];
    off_tst_size;                         /* file size in bytes */
    long st_pad3;
    time_t   st_atime;                    /* time of last access */
    time_t   st_mtime;                    /* time of last data modification */
    time_t   st_ctime;/* time of last file status change */
    long st_blksize;     /* preferred I/O block size in bytes   */
    long st_blocks;      /* number st_blksize blocks allocated */
    charst_fstype[_ST_FSTYPSZ]; /* containing filesystem's type */
    long st_pad4[8];
 };
```

Backwards-compatibility case: The 16-bit **stat** structure is:

```
struct stat {                          /* 16 bit struct stat*/
    dev_t   st_dev;            /* id of device containing dir entry   */
    ino_t   st_ino;            /* i-node number (16 bits-worth)       */
    mode_t  st_mode;/* file mode (permissions and type)  */
    nlink_t st_nlink; /* number of links */
    uid_t   st_uid;            /* user id of the file's owner */
    gid_t   st_gid;            /* group id of the file's owner */
    dev_t   st_rdev; /* id of block/character special file   */
    off_tst_size;              /* file size in bytes */
    time_t  st_atime;          /* time of last access */
    time_t  st_mtime;          /* time of last data modification */
    time_t  st_ctime;/* time of last file status change */
};
```

If the **stat ()** is successful, it returns the value 0. If an error occurs, **stat ()** returns the value -1 and sets the global variable **errno** to EBADF (for a bad file handle). The file modes and permissions are set according to the value of **st_mode.** The values of st_mode are given in **Table 18.11** and access permissions are given in Table 18.12. See the Example 22.29 which is demonstrating states of a file available on the system.

Table 18.11 Values of st_mode

Macro	Octal	Meaning
S_IFMT	0170000	Type of file
S_IFREG	0100000	Regular
S_IFBLK	0060000	Block special
S_IFDIR	0040000	Directory
S_IFCHR	0020000	Character special
S_IFIFO	0010000	FIFO
S_IFNAM	0050000	Special named file
S_IFLNK	0120000	Symbolic link

Table 18.12 Access Permissions

Macro	Octal values	Meaning
S_IXOTH	00001	Execution permission: Other
S_IREAD	00400	Read permission owner
S_IWRITE	00200	Write permission owner
S_IEXEC	00100	Execute/search permission, owner
S_ISUID	04000	Set user id on execution
S_ISGID	02000	Set group id on execution
S_ISVTX	01000	Save swapped text even after use
S_IRWXU	00700	Read, write, execute: owner
S_IRUSR	00400	Read permission owner
S_IWUSR	00200	Write permission owner
S_IXUSR	00100	Execute permission owner
S_IRWXG	00070	Read, write, execute: group
S_IRGRP	00040	Read permission group
S_IWGRP	00020	Write permission group
S_IXGRP	00010	Execute permission group
S_IRWXO	00007	Read, Write, Execute permission group
S_IROTH	00004	Read permission other
S_IWOTH	00002	Write permission other

Example 29: Write C code which demonstrates states of a file available on the system.

Answer: Consider the following program segment that implements the above discussion.

```
/* filestat.c */
# include<stdio.h>
# include<sys/types.h>
# include<sys/stat.h>

/* Prototypes */

int show_stat( struct stat *);
int show_access(unsigned short);

void main(int argc, char *argv[])
{
    struct stat status;
    int i;
    for(i = 0; i <argc; i++)
    {
        if (stat(argv[i], &status)== -1)
        {
            printf("\n No status information for %s", argv[i]);
        }
        else
        {
            printf("\n Status information for %s", argv[i]);
            show_stat(&status);
        }
    }
}

/* Function show_stat() */
/* Display the information associated with a file */
int show_stat(struct stat *info)
{
    printf("\n File type: ");
    switch(info->st_mode & S_IFMT)
    {
    case S_IFDIR:
        printf("\n Directory ");
        break;
    case S_IFREG:
        printf("\n Normal file ");
        break;
    case S_IFCHR:
        printf("\n Character device ");
        break;
    case S_IFBLK:
        printf("\n Block  device ");
        break;
    case S_IFIFO:
        printf("\n FIFO");
        break;
    }
    printf("\n i-node number: %d", info->st_ino);
```

```
	printf("\n Access permission for User: ");
	show_access(info->st_mode>>6);
	printf("\n Access permission for Group: ");
	show_access(info->st_mode>>3);
	printf("\n Number of references %d",info->st_nlink);
	printf("\n User number: %d ", info->st_uid);
	printf("\n Group number: %d ", info->st_gid);
	printf("\n File size: %ld bytes", info->st_size);
	printf("\n Last access: %s", ctime(&(info->st_atime)));

	printf("\n Last editing: %s ", ctime (&(info->st_mtime)));
	printf("\n Last status change: %s ", ctime (&(info->st_ctime)));
}
/* Show the access permission *//* Function show_access() */

int show_access(unsigned short mode)
{
	if(mode & 04)
		printf("\n Read");
	if(mode & 02)
		printf("\n Write ");
	if(mode & 01)
		printf("\n Execute ");
}
```

```
OUTPUT
Status information for C:\TC\WORK\FILESTAT.EXE
File type:
Normal file
i-node number: 0
Access permission for User:
Read
Write
Access permission for Group:
Number of references 1
User number: 0
Group number: 0
File size: 16797 bytes
Last access: Tue Aug 29 05:27:44 2006
Last editing: Tue Aug 29 05:27:44 2006
Last status change: Tue Aug 29 05:27:44 2006
No status information for filestat
```

18.11 FILE SERVICES

The chmod ()

The function **chmod ()** changes the attributes of a file. The syntax of the function **chmod ()** is:

```
	int chmod(path, mode);
where
	char *path;
	int mode;
```

The function **chmod ()** allows the superuser and the file owner to change the file attributes (access permission of a file). The path specifies the file, mode and the new attributes. It is recommended to specify the file attributes through symbolic constant (MACRO) defined in **<sys/stat.h>** or through an octal number. These values are given in **Table 18.13.** The function **chmod()** also works like system command and it changes the access permissions of a file or directory.

Table 18.13 Absolute Mode

Octal value	Meaning
1000	Set the sticky bit
0400	Read by owner
0200	Write by owner
0100	Execute (search in directory) byowner
0040	Read by group
0020	Write by group
0010	Execute (search in directory) by group
0004	Read by others
0002	Write by others
0001	Execute (search in directory) by others
0000	No permission

To apply a combination of permissions to a single file using absolute mode, combine the permissions by adding the digits in each character position. For example, to combine read by owner permission (0400) and write by owner permission (0200), add the digits in each column to obtain the combined absolute mode 0600. This is equivalent to the logical OR operation. When used to change the permissions of a symbolic link, chmod() automatically follows the link and tries to change the permissions of the linked file. It makes no sense for symbolic links to have their own permissions and ownership. Go through the Example 30 which demonstares the chmod.

Example 30: Write code for chmod roputine.

Answer: Consider the following program segment that implements chmod() routine and set the mode of the input as read only because we have used S_IREAD. If one wants to set in write mode needs to set the flag S_IWRITE and both read and write set the flag using the flag S_IWRITE|S_IREAD?

```
/* chmod.c */
#include <stdio.h>
#include <sys/stat.h>

void main(int argc, char *argv[])
{
    if (chmod(argv[1], S_IREAD)) /* set flag in read mode only */
    {                            /* if one want set in write set the flag */
        /* S_IWRITE */
        /* if we interested in read/write then set the flag S_IWRITE|S_IREAD */
        printf("Error setting %s\n", argv[1]);
        perror("Error:");
        exit(1);
    }
}
```

The chown ()

The function **chown ()** changes the owner ID of group and files. The syntax for this function is:

int chown(path, own_id, grp_id)

where

```
char *path;
int own_id;
int grp_id;
```

This system call is available only to superuser. User and groups number entries in the I-node of the file path are set to the values specified by **own_id** and **grp_id.** This function returns value 0 which indicates that the entries have been successfully altered else returns the value -1. When the function **chown ()** returns -1, it indicates that calling process is not that of superuser (EOERM).

When used to change the ownership of a symbolic link, **chown ()** automatically follows the link and tries to change the ownership of the linked file. It makes no sense for symbolic links to have their own permissions and ownership. Use of this utility is governed by the chown kernel privilege. If one has chown kernel privilege, he/she can change the owner and group of files that he/she has initially owned. If we do not have chown privilege, we cannot change the ownership of files; one can change his/her group, but only if the files are initially owned by he/she and the new group is his/her effective group ID or is listed in his/her supplemental group list.

The fcntl ()

The function **fcntl ()** enables control functions on open files. The syntax of the function fcntl() is:

```
int fcntl ( fd , cmd, arg)
```

where

```
int fd ;
int cmd;
```

The **fcntl** system call provides for control over open files. The **fd** argument is an open file descriptor obtained from a **creat(), open(), dup(), fcntl() or pipe()** (for details about **pipe()** see in system manual) system call. The data type and value of **arg** are specific to the type of command specified by **cmd**. The **<fcntl.h>** header file defines the symbolic names for commands and file status flags.

The structure **flock** defined in the **<fcntl.h>** header file describes a lock. It describes the type (l_type), starting offset (l_whence), relative offset (l_start), size (l_len) and process-ID (l_pid):

```
short l_type;          /* F_RDLCK, F_WRLCK, F_UNLCK */
short l_whence;        /* flag for starting offset */
long l_start;          /* relative offset in bytes */
long l_len;            /* if 0 then until EOF */
short l_pid;           /* returned with F_GETLK */
```

The value of **l_whence** is 0, 1 or 2 to indicate that the relative offset, **l_start** bytes, is measured from the start of the file, current position or end of file, respectively. The value of **l_len** is the number of consecutive bytes to be locked. The process id is used only with the **F_GETLK** cmd to return the values for a blocking lock. Locks may start and extend beyond the current end of a file, but may not be negative relative to the beginning of the file. A lock may be set to always extend to the end of file by setting l_len to zero (0). If such a lock also has l_whence and **l_start** set to zero (0), the whole file is locked. Changing or unlocking a segment from the middle of a larger locked segment leaves two smaller segments for either end. Locking a segment that is already locked by the calling process causes the old lock type to be removed and the new lock type to take effect. All locks associated with a file for a given process are removed when that process closes a file descriptor for that file or the process holding that file descriptor terminates. A child process in a **fork () (for Details see system manual)** system call does not inherit locks. When mandatory file and record locking is active on a file, read and the record affects **write ()** system calls issued on the file locks in effect. Upon successful completion, the value returned depends on **cmd** is as follows:

F_DUPFD A new file descriptor.
F_GETFD Value of flag (only the low-order bit is defined).
F_GETFL Value of file flags.
F_GETLK Value other than -1.
F_SETFD Value other than -1.
F_SETFL Value other than -1.
F_SETLK Value other than -1.
F_SETLKW Value other than -1.

Otherwise, a value of -1 is returned and **errno** is set to indicate the error. Because in the future the variable errno will be set to **EAGAIN** rather than **EACCES** when a section of a file is already locked by another process portable application programs should expect and test for either value.

The access () and eaccess ()

When we write program that works with files, there may be times when we need to determine if program can access a specific file as required. **C** function **access ()** checks whether a file exists as specified and if program can open the file as required. The function **access ()** and function **eaccess ()** determine accessibility of a file. The function **access ()** checks the file accessibility using **RUID** and the function **eaccess ()** checks file accessibility using **EUID.** The syntax of these functions is:

```
int access (path, amode)
where
char *path;
int amode;
int eaccess (path, amode)
where
char *path;
int amode;
```

The **access()** function checks the file named by path for accessibility according to the bit pattern contained in **amode,** using the real user ID in place of the effective user ID and the real group ID in place of the effective group ID. The **access()** should only be used by set-UID and set-GID programs; **access()** is not equivalent to **eaccess()** even when the program is not being used by set-UID and set-GID. The **eaccess()** is similar to **access()** except that the effective user ID and group ID are used.

The value of amode is either the bit-wise inclusive OR of the access permissions to be checked or the existence test is given in **Table 18.14.**

Table 18.14 Access Permission

Macro	Meaning
R_OK	Test for read permission
W_OK	Test for write permission
X_OK	Test for execute (search) permission
F_OK	Test for existence of file

These values are defined in the **unistd.h** header file. If any access permission is to be checked, each is checked individually. The owner of a file has permission checked with respect to the **owner** read, write and execute mode bits. Members of the file's **group** other than the owner have permissions checked with respect to the **group** mode bits and all others have permissions checked with respect to the other mode bits. If the requested access is permitted, a value of 0 is returned. Otherwise, a value of -1 is returned and **errno** is set to indicate the error. Example 31 implements the above discussion.

Example 31: Write C code which finds access modes of a given file.

Answer: Consider the following program segment that implements the function access() and the access permission for a given file.

```
/* access.c */
/* This program segment checks access permission of the file */
#include <stdio.h>
#include <unistd.h>

void main (int argc, char *argv[])
{
    int access_mode;
    int i;
    for(i =0; i< argc; i++)
    {
        access_mode = access(argv[i], 0);
        if (access_mode)
            printf("File %s does not exist\n", argv[i]);
        else
        {
            access_mode = access(argv[i], 2);
            if (access_mode)
                    printf("File %s cannot be written\n", argv[i]);
            else
                    printf("File %s can be written\n", argv[i]);

            access_mode = access(argv[i], 4);
            if (access_mode)
                    printf("File %s cannot be read\n", argv[i]);
            else
                    printf("File %s can be read\n", argv[i]);
            access_mode = access(argv[i], 6);
            if (access_mode)
                    printf("File %s cannot be read/write\n", argv[i]);
            else
                    printf("File %s can be read/write\n", argv[i]);
        }
    }
}
```

The umask ()

The function **umask ()** inquires and changes the file attribute mask. The syntax of this function is:

int umask(mode);

where

int mode

As already we have described in case of **creat(),** the file mode determined during file creation is modified through a negative mask. The mask influences the lower 9-bit of mode (access permission). The access permissions of a new file result from the BIT-AND connection of the specified file mode with the bitwise negative mark. With the system call umask(), the mark is determined, umask() returns the old mask as value. An inquiry of the mask without a simultaneous editing is not possible. Example 32 demonstrates umask function.

Example 32: Write code for the umask function.

Answer: Consider the following program segment that implements the above discussion.

```
/* umask.c */
#include <stdio.h>
#include <fcntl.h>
#include <sys/stat.h>
#include <stdlib.h>
# include<sys/types.h>
# include<string.h>

void main(void)
{
    int output;
    int old_setting;
    char * buffer = "Enjoy with C language: Have you nice day";

    old_setting = umask(S_IWRITE);

    if ((output = creat("OUTPUT.DAT", S_IWRITE)) == -1)
    {
        fprintf(stderr, "Error creating OUTPUT.DAT \n");
        exit(1);
    }else
    {
        if (write(output, buffer, strlen(buffer)) == -1)
            fprintf(stderr, "Cannot write to file opened for write access \n");
        else
            printf("File successfully written to \n");
        close(output);
    }

    if ((output = open("OUTPUT.DAT", O_WRONLY)) == -1)
        fprintf(stderr, "Error opening OUTPUT.DAT for output \n");
    else
        printf("File successfully opened for write access \n");
}
```

The utime ()

When we want to set a file's date and time stamp to the current date and time, a quick way to do so is with the function **utime()**. The syntax of this function is:

```
int utime(path, date_time)
```

where

```
char *path;
struct utimebuf *date_time;
```

The **path** parameter is a character string that specifies the name and directory of the desired file. The **date_time** parameter is a structure that contains the **date** and **time** the file was last changed and last accessed.

```
struct utimebuf
{
    time_t actime; /* Last access */
    time_t modtime; /* Last modification */
};
```

If we are working in the **DOS** environment only modification time is used. When we are working in **UNIX** both last access and last modification times are used. If we have the utime() function with the times set to NULL, the function sets the date and time stamp to the current date and time. If the function is successful, it returns 0. If an error occurs, the function returns -1 and sets global variable **errno.** For example, consider the following program segments (utime.c and newtime.c) that uses the **utime ()** function to set the **date** and **time** stamp of the file specified to current **date** and time. See the Example 33.

Example 33: Sets the date and time of a file.

Answer: See the utime.c and newtime.c programs for this purpose.

```
/* utime.c */
#include <stdio.h>
#include <utime.h>

void main(int argc, char **argv)
{
    int i;
    for (i =0; i <argc; i++)
    {
        if (utime(argv[i], (struct utimbuf *) NULL))
            printf("Error setting date and time\n");
        else
            printf("Date and time stamp set of the file %s\n", argv[i]);
    }
}

/* newtime.c */

# include<stdio.h>
# include<utime.h>
# include<sys/stat.h>
# include<sys/types.h>

struct utimebuf
{
    time_t actime ; /* last read time */
    time_t modtime; /* last edinting time */
};

void main(int argc, char *argv[])
{
    struct stat status; /* file status information */
    struct utimebuf ftime; /* new access time */
    while(-argc)
    {
        printf("\n %s \n ", argv[argc]);
        if(stat(argv[argc], &status) == -1 )
            printf("\n No status for the file %s", argv[argc]);
        else
        {
            printf("\n Last read for the file: %s : %s", argv[argc], ctime(&(status.st_atime)));
            printf("\n Last editing for the file: %s : %s",argv[argc], ctime(&(status.st_mtime)));
            if(status.st_atime>status.st_mtime)
                    ftime.actime = ftime.modtime= status.st_atime;
            else
                    ftime.actime = ftime.modtime = status.st_atime;
```

```
            if(utime(argv[argc], &ftime) == -1)
                        printf("\n %s not edited \n", argv[argc]);
            else
                        printf("\n New time: %s", ctime(&(ftime.actime)));
        }
    }
}
```

18.12 DIRECTORY SERVICES

The mkdir ()

The function **mkdir()** is used to create a valid directory. The syntax for this function is:

```
int status = mkdir(dirname)
```

where

```
char *dirname;
```

The function **mkdir()** creates the directories named in **dirname.** Their permissions are initially set to 0777 (possibly altered by umask()). Creation of a directory requires write permission in the parent directory.

When a directory is created, the standard entries (for example, the files ".", for the directory itself and "..", for its parent) are made automatically. The function **mkdir ()** cannot create these entries by name.

The user and group IDs of a newly created directory are set to the real user and group IDs of the creating process, unless the set group ID (SGID) bit is set on the current directory (see chmod()). If a directory is created in a directory that has the **SGID** bit set its group ID is set to that of the directory? Directories inherit the SGID bit setting of the parent directory in which they are created.

The function mkdir() returns 0 if all directories given in the command line were created successfully; otherwise, it prints a diagnostic and returns a non-zero value and the directory dirname cannot be created. Example 34 used to create a directory on the secondary storage device.

Example 34: Write C code which is creating a directory on the secondary storage device.

Answer: Consider the following program segment that implements the above discussion:

```
/* creatdir.c */
# include<stdio.h>
# include<sys/types.h>
# include<sys/stat.h>
void main(int argc, char *argv[])
{
     if(argc != 2)
     {
          printf("\n File parameters not provided properly ");
          perror("\n Error: ");
          exit(1);
     }

     if(mkdir(argv[1], 0777) == -1)
     {
          printf("\n %s directory not created \n ", argv[1]);
          perror("Error: ");
          exit(2);
     }
     if(chdir(argv[1]) == -1)
```

```
        printf("\n Directory %s not changed ", argv[1]);
}
```

The rmdir()

The function **rmdir()** is used to remove the current directory. The syntax of this function is:

```
int status = rmdir(dirname)
```

where

```
const char *dirname;
```

The function **rmdir()** returns an exit code of 0, if all the specified directories are removed successfully. Otherwise, it returns a non-zero exit code. For example, to remove the directory **tmpdir** from the current directory:

rmdir tmpdir

Go through the Example 35 which implements the removal of directory.

Example 35: Write C code which is removing a directory from the secondary storage device.

Answer: Consider the following program segment that implements the rmdir function and remove the direcoty supplied at the command prompt, when we execute this code.

```
/* rmdir.c */
# include <stdio.h>
# include <stdlib.h>
# include <errno.h>
# include<limits.h>
void main (int argc, char *argv[])
{
    char directory[_POSIX_PATH_MAX];
    if (argc == 1)  /* Display the current directory */
    {
        getcwd(directory, _POSIX_PATH_MAX);
        puts(directory);
    }
    else if ((rmdir(argv[1])) && (errno == ENOENT))
        puts("Invalid directory");
}
```

The chdir ()

The function **chdir ()** is used to change the current directory. There is one more function **fchdir ()** in **UNIX** that performs the same operation as **chdir ().** These functions lie in the **<unistd.h>** header file. The syntax of these functions is

```
int chdir(path);
```

where

```
const char *path;
int fchdir(int fd);
```

where

```
int fd;
```

The function **chdir()** change working directory using pathname. The function **fchdir()** change working directory using file descriptor. The **chdir()** and **fchdir()** cause a directory pointed to by **path** or **fd** to become the current working directory. The starting point for path searches for pathnames not beginning with **/.path** points to the pathname of a directory. The **fd** argument to **fchdir()** is an open file descriptor of a directory. In order for a directory to become the current directory, a process must be executed (search) to access to the directory. On success, the function **chdir()** returns 0. On failure, **chdir()** returns -1, sets errno to identify the error and the currant directory remains unchanged. When we do not want to change the directory using existing routine we can use Example 36.

Example 36: Write C code which is changing a directory.

Answer: Consider the following program segment that implements the above discussion:

```
/* chdir.c */
# include <stdio.h>
# include <stdlib.h>
# include <errno.h>
# include<limits.h>
void main (int argc, char *argv[])
{
    char directory[_POSIX_PATH_MAX];
    if (argc == 1)  /* Display the current directory */
    {
        getcwd(directory, _POSIX_PATH_MAX);
        puts(directory);
    }
    else if ((chdir(argv[1])) && (errno == ENOENT))
        puts("Invalid directory");
}
```

The mount()

The syntax for the function **mount ()** is:

```
int mount (spec, dir, mflag, fstyp, dataptr, datalen)
```

where

```
char *spec, *dir;  int mflag, fstyp;  char *dataptr;  int datalen;
```

The function **mount ()** requests that a removable filesystem contained on the block special file identified by spec be mounted on the directory identified by **dir.** The **spec** and dir are pointers to path names. The **fstyp** is the filesystem type number. The **sysfs ()** system call can be used to determine the filesystem type number. Note: if both the **MS_DATA** and **MS_FS** flag bits of **mflag** are off, the filesystem type defaults to the root filesystem type. Only if either flag is on is **fstyp** used to indicate the filesystem type.

If the **MS_DATA** flag is set in **mflag,** the system expects the **dataptr** and **datalen** arguments to be present. Together they describe a block of file-system specific data at address **dataptr** of length **datalen**. This is interpreted by file-system specific code within the operating system and its format depends upon the filesystem type. A particular filesystem type may not require this data, in such a case dataptr and datalen should both be zero. Note that **MS_FS** is obsolete and is ignored if **MS_DATA** is also set, but if **MS_FS** is set and **MS_DATA** is not, **dataptr** and **datalen** both are assumed to be zero. Upon successful completion, references to the file dir refer to the root directory on the mounted filesystem.

The **MS_RDONLY** bit of **mflag** is used to control write permission on the mounted filesystem. If it is set, writing is forbidden, otherwise writing is permitted according to individual file accessibility. Only the super-user may invoke the **mount().** It is intended for use only by the **mount ()** utility.

Upon successful completion a value of 0 is returned. Otherwise, a value of -1 is returned and errno is set to indicate the error. See the Example 37 for the implementation of mount system routine.

Example 37: Write C code which is mounting a file system.

Answer: Consider the following program segment that demonstrates simple implementation of the function **mount ().**

```
/* mount.c */
# include<stdio.h>
```

```
# include<sys/mount.h>
# include<limits.h>

void main()
{
    char direc[_POSIX_PATH_MAX];
    char device[_POSIX_PATH_MAX];
    printf("\n Mounting a file system: \n");
    printf("\n Directory: > ");
    scanf("%s", direc);
    if(mount(device, direc, 0) == -1)
        printf("\n Error during mounting: \n");
    else
        printf("\n <%s> mounted in the directory <%s> \n ", device, direc);
}
```

The umount()

The syntax of the function **umount ()** is:

```
    int umount (file)
where
    char *file;
```

The **umount()** system call requests that a previously mounted file system contained on the block special device or directory identified by **file** be unmounted. The **file** is a pointer to a path name. After unmounting the file system, the directory upon which the file system was mounted reverts to its ordinary interpretation. Only the super-user may invoke the umount() system call.

Upon successful completion a value of 0 is returned. Otherwise, a value of -1 is returned and **errno** is set to indicate the error.

The fileno ()

It finds the file descriptor for the given file. The syntax for this is:

```
    int fileno(file_pointer);
where
    FILE *file_pointer;
```

This function returns the file descriptor for the file specified by **file_pointer**. This also enables the user call the file through system calls. The access to the file should be done either through library function or through system calls. The **errno** can easily arise, if both methods are used. Example 38 implements the discussion.

Example 38: Consider the following program segment that implements the fileno function.

```
/* fileno.c */
#include <stdio.h>

void main (int argc, char *argv[])
{
    FILE *stream1, *stream2;
    int handle1, handle2;
    int size = 128;
    char buffer[128];

    if (stream1 = fopen(argv[1], "r"))
        if (stream2 = fopen(argv[2], "w"))
        {
            /* Finding handle of opened file argv[1] and  argv[2] */
```

```
            handle1 = fileno(stream1);
            handle2 = fileno(stream2);

            read(handle1, buffer, size);
            write(handle2, buffer, size);

            fclose(stream1);
            fclose(stream2);
        }
        else
            printf("Error opening %s\n", argv[2]);
    else
        printf("Error opening %s\n", argv[1]);
}
```

The above program segment opens two files **dest.bak** in write mode and file **DEST** in read mode. The program reads one buffer from the file **DEST** with the help of file descriptor handle1 and finally writes into the file **dest.bak** with the help of file descriptor handle2 and operation are continued until the end of the file.

The freopen()

This function opens another file for the given **FILE** descriptor. The syntax of this function is:

```
FILE *freopen (fname, access, file_pointer);
```

where

```
char *fname;
char *access;
FILE *file_pointer;
```

The function closes the file-associated with the structure **stream** and opens the new file **fname.** The old file is closed in every case, even if the new file cannot be opened. The most important job of this function is to redirect the substitution of standard input, output and error channels to the data transfer. Example 39 shows implementation of the abobe discussion.

Example 39: Consider the following program segments that are implementing the freopen function.

```
/* freopen.c */
# include<stdio.h>
# include<stdlib.h>

void main()
{
    int ch;
    FILE *fp;

    if((fp = freopen ("freopen.dat", "w", stdout)) == (FILE *) NULL)
    {
        printf("\n File FDOPEN.DAT open error");
        perror("Error: ");
        exit(1);
    }

    while(( ch = getchar()) != '\n')
    {
```

```
            putchar(ch);
        }
    }

    /** file122.c **/
    # include<stdio.h>
    # include<fcntl.h>
    # include<string.h>
    # include<sys/stat.h>

    void main()
    {
        int fp ;        /* file pointer */

        char buffer[80] =" Enjoy with C language " ;
        fp = creat ("test",S_IREAD | S_IWRITE );
        if( fp == -1 )
        {
            perror("Error");
            exit(1);
        }
        write(fp, buffer, strlen(buffer) ) ;
        printf("\n Press a key");
        getchar();
        close(fp);  /* close opened file */
    }

    /** file20.c **/
    # include<stdio.h>
    # include<fcntl.h>
    # include<string.h>
    # include<sys/stat.h>

    void main(int argc , char *argv[])
    {
        int fp ;        /* file pointer */
        int fp1 ;       /* file pointer */
        int  ength ;
        char buffer[80] ;

        if( argc != 3)
        {
            printf("\n Missing some file ");
            exit(1);
        }

        fp = open( argv[1] , O_RDONLY);
        if( fp == -1 )
        {
            printf("\n%s",argv[1]);
            perror("Error");
            exit(1);
        }

        fp1 = open(argv[2] ,O_CREAT);
```

```
        if( fp1 == -1 )
        {
              printf("\n%s",argv[2]);
              perror("Error");
              exit(1);
        }
        read(fp, buffer, 80 ) ;
        while(!feof)
        {
               ength = strlen(buffer);
              write(fp1,buffer, ength);
              read(fp, buffer, 80 ) ;
        }
        close(fp);     /* close file */
        close(fp1);   /* close file */
}
```

EXERCISES

1. Multiple Choice Questions

1. The stdout is a pointer variable.

   (a) True (b) False

2. Fill in the black with EOF or NULL to check correctly for end of file.

   while (fgets(buffer, 100, fp) != _______________)

   (a) EOF (b) NULL

3. Is the following code slice correct?

```
char stock[100];
while(fgets(stock, 100, stdin) != NULL)
puts(stock);
```

   (a) True (b) False

4. Is the following code slice correct?

```
FILE *fp;
char stock[100];
fp = stdin ;
while(fgets(stock, 100, fp) != NULL)
puts(stock);
```

   (a) True (b) False

5. Is the following code slice is correct?

```
# include<stdio.h>
# include<stdlib.h>

void main()
{
FILE *fp;
char stock[100];
fp = fopen("Data.Dat", "r");
if (fp == NULL)
{
```

```
    printf("\n File Data.Dat open error);
    perror("Error:");
    exit(1);
    }else
        stdin = fp;

    while(fgets(stock, 100, stdin) != NULL)
        puts(stock);
}
```

(a) True (b) False

6. A file must be opened, so that
   (a) The program knows how to access the file
   (b) The operating system knows what file to access
   (c) The operating system knows if the file should be read from or written to
   (d) Communication areas are established for communicating with the file
7. The function **fopen()** can specify which of the following
   (a) The file may be opened for appending
   (b) The file may be opened in binary mode
   (c) The file may be given in read-only mode
   (d) Numbers in the file will be written in binary format (e) none
8. When a program has to read one character at a time, which of the following library functions is appropriate?
   (a) fread () (b) read () (c) fgetc() (d) getc()
9. Closing a file after write operation is an option.
   (a) True(b) False
10. To write a small number of mixed strings and integer variables to a file, the appropriate function is:
    (a) fputs() (b) fgets() (c) fprintf() (d) fwrite()
11. To read a small number of mixed strings and integer variables from a file, the appropriate function is
    (a) fscanf() (b) fgets() (c) read() (d) fread()
12. The function **fseek ()**
    (a) finds a given word or phrase in a file
    (b) finds the correct file
    (c) helps to access records in the middle of a file
    (d) moves the file pointer to the desired location
13. The function **ftell()**
    (a) moves the file handle at the end of the file
    (b) tells the size of file
    (c) helps access records in the middle of a file
    (d) moves the file handle to the desired location
    (e) none of these

14. An **oflag** can
    (a) signal when a file is unreachable (b)specify if a file should be read or written
    (c) signal when EOF is detected (d) specify binary mode

State whether the following statements are true or false

1. A file must be opened before it can be used.
2. All files must be explicitly closed.
3. Files are always referred to by name in C programs.
4. Using fseek to position a file beyond the end of the file is an error.
5. Function fseek may be used to seek from the beginning of the file only.

Fill in the blanks with appropriate words in each of the following statements

1. The mode________________ is used for opening a file for updating.
2. The function __________ may be used to position a file at the beginning.
3. The function ________ gives the current position in the file.
4. The function ________ is used to write data to randomly accessed file.

Descriptive and Programming Problems

1. Find Errors in the following code segments

   (a) What is the error in the following declaration?

```
FILE fp;
fp = fopen("Data.Dat", "r");
if (fp == NULL)
{
printf("\n File Data.Dat open error);
perror("Error:");
exit(1);
}
```

   (b) What is error in the following code slice?

```
FILE  *fp;
fp = fopen("Data.Dat", "r");
fclose(*fp);
```

   (c) Find errors in the following program segment.

```
# include<stdio.h>
# include<stdlib.h>
void main()
{
    FILE *fp;
    int n;
    fp = fopen("REC.DAT", "rb");
    while((n = getchar()) != EOF)
        fputc(fp, n);
    fclose("REC.DAT");
}
```

2. Discuss the differences between

   Mode "r" and the mode "r+"

   Mode "w" and the mode "w+"

Mode "a" and the mode "a+"

Mode "a+b" and the mode "ab"

3. What is represented by the following declaration? Discuss.

FILE (*fp) (void);

4. What operation does the following program segment perform? Discuss.

```
# include<stdio.h>
void main()
{
int num ;
int ch ;
printf("\n Input a text with number : \n");
do
{
    if ( ch == EOF)
        printf("\n No Number Found");
    else
        ungetc((char ) ch , stdin );
    scanf("%d",&num);
    printf("\n The number : %d\n", num);

} while((ch !=EOF) && (ch < '0' || ch > '9' ));
}
```

5. What output does the following program segment generate? Discuss.

```
# include<stdio.h>

void main()
{
 printf("\n Hello Sir");
 fclose(stdout);
 printf("\n Good Bye Sir");
}
```

6. What operation does the following program segment perform? Discuss.

```
# include<stdio.h>

void main()
{
    char str1[80], str2[80];
    printf("\n Input the text :");
    scanf("%[0-9' ']%[a-z' ' A-Z' ']",str1,str2);
    printf("\nSTR1 %s", str1);
    printf("\nSTR2 %s", str2);
}
```

7. What operation does the following program segment perform? Discuss.

```
# include<stdio.h>
void main()
{
char str1[80], str2[80];
printf("\n Input the text :");
scanf("%[^0-9]%[^a-z ^A-Z]",str1,str2);
printf("\nSTR1 %s", str1);
printf("\nSTR2 %s", str2);
}
```

8. Describe the use and limitations of the functions getc and putc.
9. What is the significance of EOF?
10. When a program is terminated, all the files used by it are automatically closed. Why is it then necessary to close a file during execution of the program?
11. Distinguish between the following functions:
    (a) getc and getchar
    (b) printf and fprintf
    (c) feof and terror
12. How does an append mode differ from a write mode?
13. What are the common uses of rewind and ftell functions?
14. Explain the general format of fseek function?
15. What is the difference between the statements rewind(fp); and fseek(fp,0L,0);?
16. Suppose that the standard input is
    R A M
    (Each of R, A and M is immediately followed by a new line). Write a function that echoes these characters, so that the standard output is 'RAM'
17. If one declares
    while (fgets(buffer, 100, fp) != EOF)
    then how many bytes are placed in buffer by the function **fgets()?** Write your fgets().
18. Develop the function **fgetstr()** with the help of function **fgetc().**
19. Develop the function **getstr()** with the help of function **getchar().**
20. Develop the function **fputstr()** with the help of function **fputc().**
21. Develop the function **puts ()** with the help of function **putchar().**
22. Develop a function **read_block()** with the help of function **fgetc()** which is equivalent to the function **fread()** except for error checking.
23. Develop a function **write_block ()** with the help of function **fputc()** which is equivalent to the function **fwrite()** except for error checking.
24. Write a program to find five-digit numbers **d1 d2 d3 d4 d5** that when multiplied by a digit **k** between 2 and 9 will give a result of **d5 d4 d3 d2 d1** that is

    d1 d2 d3 d4 d5

    x **k**

    d5 d4 d3 d2 d1

    How many such numbers lie between 11111 and 999922. Save them in a file.
25. A perfect number is a number that is equal to the sum of its entire divisor except itself. Six is the first perfect number, the only numbers that divide 6 evenly are 1, 2, 3, 6 and 6 = 1 + 2 + 3. An abundant number is one that is less than the sum of its divisors (e.g. 12 < 1 + 2 + 3 + 4 + 6); a deficient number is greater than the sum of its divisors (e.g. 9 > 1 + 3). Write a program to generate a table of first **N** integers where **N** is read from a record (file), and classifies each perfect, abandoned or deficient numbers.
26. Write a program, which will generate random numbers between 0 and 100. Store these numbers in a file, after completion of generation, sort the numbers in ascending order in the file. The generated number must be in the interval of 47 and 53.

27. Write a program for inventory control, which should contain the following options.

    Add record

    Delete record

    Update record

    Print record

    List records (Random access mode)

28. Write a program for the MMEC Company sales information systems. A sales file is to be created with records in the following format

    Sales person Id number

    Amount of sales

    A master file must also be created with records in the format

    Sales person id number

    Name

    Amount of sales to that date

    Program is needed to

    (a) Create the file.

    (b) Update the master file from the data in the sales file.

    (c) Produce a report showing each sales person's total sale up to that date.

    (d) Produce hard copy of report.

29. Describe a structure definition for a student-grading program. Associated with each student in respect to his/her name, student ID number, homework and test grades.

    (a) Can be defined structure handle a student name with 35 characters?

    (b) Rework defined structure so that any number of homework assignments and test grades can be entered.

    (c) Write a student grading function-using structure defined above. The student should be organized into classes. It should also be able to print a report for each class. There should be menu displayed showing the user the commands available and function should be called depending upon the menu item chosen. If it is feasible, organize the program to use pointers to function.

PROBLEMS & SOLUTIONS ON C PROGRAMMING

1. How can I find the day of the week of a given date?

Ans. The following code snippet shows how to get the day of week from the given date.

```
dayofweek ( int yy, int mm, int dd )
{
/*Monday = 1 and Sunday = 0 */
/* month number >= 1 and <= 12, yy > 1752 or so */
static int arr[ ] = { 0, 3, 2, 5, 0, 3, 5, 1, 4, 6, 2, 4 } ;
yy = yy - mm < 3 ;
return ( yy + yy / 4 - yy / 100 + yy / 400 + arr[ mm - 1] + dd ) % 7 ;
}
void main( )
{
printf ( "\n\n\nDay of week : %d ", dayofweek ( 2012, 3, 21 ) ) ;
}
```

2. What's the difference between these two declarations?

```
struct str1 { ... } ;
typedef struct { ... } str2 ;
```

Ans. The first form declares a structure tag whereas the second declares a typedef. The main difference is that the second declaration is of a slightly more abstract type -- its users don't necessarily know that it is a structure, and the keyword struct is not used when declaring instances of it.

3. How do I print the contents of environment variables?

Ans. The following program shows how to achieve this:

```
main( int argc, char *argv[ ], char *env[ ] )
{
int i = 0 ;
clrscr( ) ;
while ( env[ i ] )
printf ( "\n%s", env[ i++ ] ) ;
}
```

main( ) has the third command line argument env, which is an array of pointers to the strings. Each pointer points to an environment variable from the list of environment variables.

4. What would the second and the third printf( ) output the following program?

```
main( )
{
char *str[ ] = {
"Good Morning"
"Good Evening"
"Good Afternoon"
} ;
printf ( "\nFirst string = %s", str[0] ) ;
printf ( "\nSecond string = %s", str[1] ) ;
printf ( "\nThird string = %s", str[2] ) ;
}
```

Ans: For the above given program, we expect the output as Good Evening and Good Afternoon, for the second and third printf( ). However, the output would be as shown below.

```
First string = Good MorningGood EveningGood Afternoon
Second string = ( null )
Third string =
```

What is missing in the above given code snippet is a comma separator which should separate the strings Good Morning, Good Evening and Good Afternoon. On adding comma, we would get the output as shown below.

```
First string = Good Morning
Second string = Good Evening
Third string = Good Afternoon
```

5. How do I use scanf( ) to read the date in the form 'dd-mm-yy' ?

Ans. There are two ways to read the date in the form of 'dd-mm-yy' one possible way is...

```
int dd, mm, yy ;
char ch ; /* for char '-' */
printf ( "\nEnter the date in the form of dd-mm-yy : " ) ;
scanf( "%d%c%d%c%d", &dd, &ch, &mm, &ch, &yy ) ;
```

And another best way is to use suppression character * as...

```
int dd, mm, yy ;
scanf( "%d%*c%d%*c%d", &dd, &mm, &yy ) ;
```

The suppression character * suppresses the input read from the standard input buffer for the assigned control character.

6. How do I print a floating-point number with higher precision say 23.34568734 with only precision up to two decimal places?

Ans. This can be achieved through the use of suppression char '*' in the format string of printf( ) as shown in the following program.

```
main( )
{
```

```
int i = 2 ;
float f = 23.34568734 ;
printf ( "%.*f", i, f ) ;
}
```

The output of the above program would be 23.35.

7. Are the expressions *ptr++ and ++*ptr same?

Ans. No. *ptr++ increments the pointer and not the value pointed by it, whereas ++*ptr increments the value being pointed to by ptr.

8. What is strpbrk( ) meant for? Demonstrate its use.

Ans. The function strpbrk( ) takes two strings as parameters. It scans the first string, to find, the first occurrence of any character appearing in the second string. The function returns a pointer to the first occurrence of the character it found in the first string. The following program demonstrates the use of string function strpbrk( ).

```
#include <string.h>
main( )
{
char *str1 = "Hello!" ;
char *str2 = "Better" ;
char *p ;
p = strpbrk ( str1, str2 ) ;
if ( p )
printf ( "The first character found in str1 is %c", *p ) ;
else
printf ( "The character not found" ) ;
}
```

The output of the above program would be the first character found in str1 is e

9. What is div( ) function meant for? Illustrate its use.

Ans. The function div( ) divides two integers and returns the quotient and remainder. This function takes two integer values as arguments; divides first integer with the second one and returns the answer of division of type div_t. The data type div_t is a structure that contains two long ints, namely quot and rem, which store quotient and remainder of division respectively. The following example shows the use of div( ) function.

```
#include <stdlib.h>
void main( )
{
div_t res ;
res = div ( 32, 5 ) ;
printf ( "\nThe quotient = %d and remainder = %d ", res.quot, res.rem ) ;
```

10. Can we convert an unsigned long integer value to a string?

Ans. The function ultoa( ) can be used to convert an unsigned long integer value to a string. This function takes three arguments, first the value that is to be converted, second the base address of the buffer in which the converted number has to be stored (with a string terminating null character '\0') and the last argument specifies the base to be used in converting the value. Following example demonstrates the use of this function.

```
#include <stdlib.h>
void main( )
{
unsigned long ul = 3234567231L ;
char str[25] ;

ultoa ( ul, str, 10 ) ;
printf ( "str = %s unsigned long = %lu\n", str, ul ) ;
}
```

11. What is a local block?

Ans. A local block is any portion of a C program that is enclosed by the left brace ({) and the right brace (}). A C function contains left and right braces, and therefore anything between the two braces is contained in a local block. An if statement or a switch statement can also contain braces, so the portion of code between these two braces would be considered a local block.

Additionally, you might want to create your own local block without the aid of a C function or keyword construct. This is perfectly legal. Variables can be declared within local blocks, but they must be declared only at the beginning of a local block. Variables declared in this manner are visible only within the local block. Duplicate variable names declared within a local block take precedence over variables with the same name declared outside the local block. Here is an example of a program that uses local blocks:

```
#include <stdio.h>
void main(void);
void main()
{
    /* Begin local block for function main() */
    int test_var = 10;
    printf("Test variable before the if statement: %d\n", test_var);
    if (test_var > 5)
    {
        /* Begin local block for "if" statement */
        int test_var = 5;
        printf("Test variable within the if statement: %d\n",
            test_var);
        {
            /* Begin independent local block (not tied to
              any function or keyword) */
            int test_var = 0;
            printf(
            "Test variable within the independent local block:%d\n",
            test_var);
        }
        /* End independent local block */
    }
    /* End local block for "if" statement */
    printf("Test variable after the if statement: %d\n", test_var);
}
/* End local block for function main() */
```

This example program produces the following output:

Test variable before the if statement: 10

Test variable within the if statement: 5

Test variable within the independent local block: 0

Test variable after the if statement: 10

Notice that as each test_var was defined, it took precedence over the previously defined test_var. Also notice that when the if statement local block had ended, the program had reentered the scope of the originaltest_var, and its value was 10.

12. Should variables be stored in local blocks?

Ans. The use of local blocks for storing variables is unusual and therefore should be avoided, with only rare exceptions. One of these exceptions would be for debugging purposes, when you might want to declare a local instance of a global variable to test within your function. You also might want to use a local block when you want to make your program more readable in the current context.

Sometimes having the variable declared closer to where it is used makes your program more readable. However, well-written programs usually do not have to resort to declaring variables in this manner, and you should avoid using local blocks.

13. When is a switch statement better than multiple if statements?

Ans. A switch statement is generally best to use when you have more than two conditional expressions based on a single variable of numeric type. For instance, rather than the code

```
if (x == 1)
    printf("x is equal to one.\n");
else if (x == 2)
    printf("x is equal to two.\n");
else if (x == 3)
    printf("x is equal to three.\n");
else
    printf("x is not equal to one, two, or three.\n");
```

the following code is easier to read and maintain:

```
switch (x)
{
    case 1:  printf("x is equal to one.\n");
             break;
    case 2:  printf("x is equal to two.\n");
             break;
    case 3:  printf("x is equal to three.\n");
             break;
    default: printf("x is not equal to one, two, or three.\n");
             break;
}
```

Notice that for this method to work, the conditional expression must be based on a variable of numeric type in order to use the switch statement. Also, the conditional expression must be based on a single variable. For instance, even though the following if statement contains more than two conditions, it is not a candidate for using a switch statement because it is based on string comparisons and not numeric comparisons:

```
char* name = "Lupto";
if (!stricmp(name, "Isaac"))
    printf("Your name means 'Laughter'.\n");
else if (!stricmp(name, "Amy"))
    printf("Your name means 'Beloved'.\n ");
else if (!stricmp(name, "Lloyd"))
    printf("Your name means 'Mysterious'.\n ");
else
    printf("I haven't a clue as to what your name means.\n");
```

14. Is a default case necessary in a switch statement?

Ans. No, but it is not a bad idea to put default statements in switch statements for error- or logic-checking purposes. For instance, the following switch statement is perfectly normal:

```
switch (char_code)
{
    case 'Y':
    case 'y': printf("You answered YES!\n");
            break;
    case 'N':
    case 'n': printf("You answered NO!\n");
            break;
}
```

Consider, however, what would happen if an unknown character code were passed to this switch statement. The program would not print anything. It would be a good idea, therefore, to insert a default case where this condition would be taken care of:

```
...
    default:  printf("Unknown response: %d\n", char_code);
            break;
...
```

Additionally, default cases come in handy for logic checking. For instance, if your switch statement handled a fixed number of conditions and you considered any value outside those conditions to be a logic error, you could insert a default case which would flag that condition. Consider the following example:

```
void move_cursor(int direction)
{
    switch (direction)
    {
        case UP:    cursor_up();
                break;
        case DOWN:  cursor_down();
                break;
        case LEFT:  cursor_left();
                break;
        case RIGHT: cursor_right();
                break;
```

```
        default:    printf("Logic error on line number %ld!!!\n",
                         __LINE__);
                break;
    }
}
```

15. Can the last case of a switch statement skip including the break?

Ans. Even though the last case of a switch statement does not require a break statement at the end, you should addbreak statements to all cases of the switch statement, including the last case. You should do so primarily because your program has a strong chance of being maintained by someone other than you who might add cases but neglect to notice that the last case has no break statement.

This oversight would cause what would formerly be the last case statement to "fall through" to the new statements added to the bottom of the switch statement. Putting a break after each case statement would prevent this possible mishap and make your program more "bulletproof." Besides, most of today's optimizing compilers will optimize out the last break, so there will be no performance degradation if you add it.

16. Other than in a for statement, when is the comma operator used?

Ans. The comma operator is commonly used to separate variable declarations, function arguments, and expressions, as well as the elements of a for statement. Look closely at the following program, which shows some of the many ways a comma can be used:

```
#include <stdio.h>
#include <stdlib.h>
void main(void);
void main()
{
   /* Here, the comma operator is used to separate
      three variable declarations. */
   int i, j, k;
   /* Notice how you can use the comma operator to perform
      multiple initializations on the same line. */
   i = 0, j = 1, k = 2;
   printf("i = %d, j = %d, k = %d\n", i, j, k);
   /* Here, the comma operator is used to execute three expressions
      in one line: assign k to i, increment j, and increment k.
      The value that i receives is always the rightmost expression. */
   i = (j++, k++);
   printf("i = %d, j = %d, k = %d\n", i, j, k);
   /* Here, the while statement uses the comma operator to
      assign the value of i as well as test it. */
   while (i = (rand() % 100), i != 50)
     printf("i is %d, trying again...\n", i);
   printf("\nGuess what? i is 50!\n");
}
```

Notice the line that reads

```
i = (j++, k++);
```

This line actually performs three actions at once. These are the three actions, in order:

1. Assigns the value of k to i. This happens because the left value (lvalue) always evaluates to the rightmost argument. In this case, it evaluates to k. Notice that it does not evaluate to k++, because k++ is a postfix incremental expression, and k is not incremented until the assignment of k to i is made. If the expression had read ++k, the value of ++k would be assigned to i because it is a prefix incremental expression, and it is incremented before the assignment is made.

2. Increments j.

3. Increments k.

Also, notice the strange-looking while statement:

```
while (i = (rand() % 100), i != 50)
    printf("i is %d, trying again...\n");
```

Here, the comma operator separates two expressions, each of which is evaluated for each iteration of the whilestatement. The first expression, to the left of the comma, assigns i to a random number from 0 to 99.

The second expression, which is more commonly found in a while statement, is a conditional expression that tests to see whether i is not equal to 50. For each iteration of the while statement, i is assigned a new random number, and the value of i is checked to see that it is not 50. Eventually, i is randomly assigned the value 50, and the while statement terminates.

17. How can you tell whether a loop ended prematurely?

Ans. Generally, loops are dependent on one or more variables. Your program can check those variables outside the loop to ensure that the loop executed properly. For instance, consider the following example:

```
#define REQUESTED_BLOCKS 512
int x;
char* cp[REQUESTED_BLOCKS];
/* Attempt (in vain, I must add...) to
  allocate 512 10KB blocks in memory. */
for (x=0; x< REQUESTED_BLOCKS; x++)
{
   cp[x] = (char*) malloc(10000, 1);
   if (cp[x] == (char*) NULL)
      break;
}
/* If x is less than REQUESTED_BLOCKS,
  the loop has ended prematurely. */
if (x < REQUESTED_BLOCKS)
    printf("Bummer! My loop ended prematurely!\n");
```

Notice that for the loop to execute successfully, it would have had to iterate through 512 times. Immediately following the loop, this condition is tested to see whether the loop ended prematurely. If the variable x is anything less than 512, some error has occurred.

18. What is the difference between goto and long jmp( ) and setjmp()?

Ans. A goto statement implements a local jump of program execution, and the longjmp() and setjmp() functions implement a nonlocal, or far, jump of program execution. Generally, a jump in execution of any kind should be avoided because it is not considered good programming practice to use such statements as goto and longjmpin your program.

A goto statement simply bypasses code in your program and jumps to a predefined position. To use the gotostatement, you give it a labeled position to jump to. This predefined position must be within the same function. You cannot implement gotos between functions. Here is an example of a goto statement:

```
void bad_programmers_function(void)
{
    int x;
    printf("Excuse me while I count to 5000...\n");
    x = 1;
    while (1)
    {
        printf("%d\n", x);
        if (x == 5000)
            goto all_done;
        else
            x = x + 1;
    }
all_done:
    printf("Whew! That wasn't so bad, was it?\n");
}
```

This example could have been written much better, avoiding the use of a goto statement. Here is an example of an improved implementation:

```
void better_function(void)
{
    int x;
    printf("Excuse me while I count to 5000...\n");
    for (x=1; x<=5000; x++)
        printf("%d\n", x);
    printf("Whew! That wasn't so bad, was it?\n");
}
```

As previously mentioned, the longjmp() and setjmp() functions implement a nonlocal goto. When your program calls setjmp(), the current state of your program is saved in a structure of type jmp_buf. Later, your program can call the longjmp() function to restore the program's state as it was when you called setjmp(). Unlike the goto statement, the longjmp() and setjmp() functions do not need to be implemented in the same function.

However, there is a major drawback to using these functions: your program, when restored to its previously saved state, will lose its references to any dynamically allocated memory between the longjmp() and thesetjmp(). This means you will waste memory for every malloc() or calloc() you have implemented between your longjmp() and setjmp(), and your program will be horribly inefficient. It is highly recommended that you avoid using functions such as longjmp() and setjmp() because they, like the goto statement, are quite often an indication of poor programming practice.

Here is an example of the longjmp() and setjmp() functions:

```
#include <stdio.h>
#include <setjmp.h>
jmp_buf saved_state;
void main(void);
void call_longjmp(void);
void main(void)
{
    int ret_code;
    printf("The current state of the program is being saved...\n");
    ret_code = setjmp(saved_state);
    if (ret_code == 1)
    {
        printf("The longjmp function has been called.\n");
        printf("The program's previous state has been restored.\n");
        exit(0);
    }
    printf("I am about to call longjmp and\n");
    printf("return to the previous program state...\n");
    call_longjmp();
}
void call_longjmp(void)
{
    longjmp(saved_state, 1);
}
```

19. What is an lvalue?

Ans. An lvalue is an expression to which a value can be assigned. The lvalue expression is located on the left side of an assignment statement, whereas an rvalue is located on the right side of ar. assignment statement. Each assignment statement must have an lvalue and an rvalue. The lvalue expression must reference a storable variable in memory. It cannot be a constant. For instance, the following lines show a few examples of lvalues:

```
int x;
int* p_int;
x = 1;
*p_int = 5;
```

The variable x is an integer, which is a storable location in memory. Therefore, the statement x = 1 qualifies xto be an lvalue. Notice the second assignment statement, *p_int = 5. By using the * modifier to reference the area of memory that p_int points to, *p_int is qualified as an lvalue. In contrast, here are a few examples of what would not be considered lvalues:

```
#define CONST_VAL 10
int x;
/* example 1 */
1 = x;
/* example 2 */
CONST_VAL = 5;
```

In both statements, the left side of the statement evaluates to a constant value that cannot be changed because constants do not represent storable locations in memory. Therefore, these two assignment statements do not contain lvalues and will be flagged by your compiler as errors.

20. Can an array be an lvalue?

Ans. Is an array an expression to which we can assign a value? The answer to this question is no, because an array is composed of several separate array elements that cannot be treated as a whole for assignment purposes. The following statement is therefore illegal:

```
int x[5], y[5];
x = y;
```

You could, however, use a for loop to iterate through each element of the array and assign values individually, such as in this example:

```
int i;
int x[5];
int y[5];
...
for (i=0; i<5; i++)
    x[i] = y[i]
...
```

Additionally, you might want to copy the whole array all at once. You can do so using a library function such as the memcpy() function, which is shown here:

```
memcpy(x, y, sizeof(y));
```

It should be noted here that unlike arrays, structures can be treated as lvalues. Thus, you can assign one structure variable to another structure variable of the same type, such as this:

```
typedef struct t_name
{
   char last_name[25];
   char first_name[15];
   char middle_init[2];
} NAME;
...
NAME my_name, your_name;
...
your_name = my_name;
...
```

In the preceding example, the entire contents of the my_name structure were copied into the your_namestructure. This is essentially the same as the following line:

```
memcpy(your_name, my_name, sizeof(your_name));
```

21. What will be the output of the following code?

```
void main ()
{ int i = 0 , a[3] ;
a[i] = i++;
printf ("%d",a[i]) ;
}
```

Ans. The output for the above code would be a garbage value. In the statement a[i] = i++; the value of the variable i would get assigned first to a[i] i.e. a[0] and then the value of i would get incremented by 1. Since a[i] i.e. a[1] has not been initialized, a[i] will have a garbage value.

22. Why doesn't the following code give the desired result?

```
int x = 3000, y = 2000 ;
long int z = x * y ;
```

Ans. Here the multiplication is carried out between two ints x and y, and the result that would overflow would be truncated before being assigned to the variable z of type long int. However, to get the correct output, we should use an explicit cast to force long arithmetic as shown below:

```
long int z = ( long int ) x * y ;
```

Note that (long int)(x * y) would not give the desired effect.

23. Why doesn't the following statement work?

```
char str[ ] = "Hello" ;
strcat ( str, '!' ) ;
```

Ans. The string function strcat( ) concatenates strings and not a character. The basic difference between a string and a character is that a string is a collection of characters, represented by an array of characters whereas a character is a single character. To make the above statement work writes the statement as shown below:

```
strcat ( str, "!" ) ;
```

24. How do I know how many elements an array can hold?

Ans. The amount of memory an array can consume depends on the data type of an array. In DOS environment, the amount of memory an array can consume depends on the current memory model (i.e. Tiny, Small, Large, Huge, etc.). In general an array cannot consume more than 64 kb. Consider following program, which shows the maximum number of elements an array of type int, float and char can have in case of Small memory model.

```
main( )
{
int i[32767] ;
float f[16383] ;
char s[65535] ;
}
```

25. How do I write code that reads data at memory location specified by segment and offset?

Ans. Use peekb( ) function. This function returns byte(s) read from specific segment and offset locations in memory. The following program illustrates use of this function. In this program from VDU memory we have read characters and its attributes of the first row. The information stored in file is then further read and displayed using peek( ) function.

```
#include <stdio.h>
#include <dos.h>
main( )
{
char far *scr = 0xB8000000 ;
FILE *fp ;
int offset ;
char ch ;
```

```
if ( ( fp = fopen ( "scr.dat", "wb" ) ) == NULL )
{
printf ( "\nUnable to open file" ) ;
exit( ) ;
}

// reads and writes to file
for ( offset = 0 ; offset < 160 ; offset++ )
fprintf ( fp, "%c", peekb ( scr, offset ) ) ;
fclose ( fp ) ;

if ( ( fp = fopen ( "scr.dat", "rb" ) ) == NULL )
{

printf ( "\nUnable to open file" ) ;
exit( ) ;
}

// reads and writes to file
for ( offset = 0 ; offset < 160 ; offset++ )
{
fscanf ( fp, "%c", &ch ) ;
printf ( "%c", ch ) ;
}
fclose ( fp ) ;
}
```

26. How do I compare character data stored at two different memory locations?

Ans. Sometimes in a program we require to compare memory ranges containing strings. In such a situation we can use functions like memcmp( ) or memicmp( ). The basic difference between two functions is that memcmp( ) does a case-sensitive comparison whereas memicmp( ) ignores case of characters. Following program illustrates the use of both the functions.

```
#include <mem.h>
main( )
{
char *arr1 = "Kicit" ;
char *arr2 = "kicitNagpur" ;
int c ;
c = memcmp ( arr1, arr2, sizeof ( arr1 ) ) ;
if ( c == 0 )
printf ( "\nStrings arr1 and arr2 compared using memcmp are identical" ) ;

else
printf ( "\nStrings arr1 and arr2 compared using memcmp are not identical"
) ;
c = memicmp ( arr1, arr2, sizeof ( arr1 ) ) ;
```

```
if ( c == 0 )
printf ( "\nStrings arr1 and arr2 compared using memicmp are identical" )
;
else
printf ( "\nStrings arr1 and arr2 compared using memicmp are not
identical" ) ;
}
```

27. Differentiate between Fixed-size objects and variable size data objects.

Ans. Fixed-size objects are more appropriate as compared to variable size data objects. Using variable-size data objects saves very little space. Variable size data objects usually have some overhead. Manipulation of fixed-size data objects is usually faster and easier. Use fixed size when maximum size is clearly bounded and close to average. And use variable-size data objects when a few of the data items are bigger than the average size. For example,

```
char *num[10] = { "One", "Two", "Three", "Four", "Five", "Six", "Seven", "Eight", "Nine", "Ten" }
;
```

Instead of using the above, use

```
char num[10][6] = { "One", "Two", "Three", "Four","Five", "Six", "Seven", "Eight", "Nine", "Ten" }
;
```

The first form uses variable-size data objects. It allocates 10 pointers, which are pointing to 10 string constants of variable size. Assuming each pointer is of 4 bytes, it requires 90 bytes. On the other hand, the second form uses fixed size data objects. It allocates 10 arrays of 6 characters each. It requires only 60 bytes of space. So, the variable-size in this case does not offer any advantage over fixed size.

28. What is the purpose of Spawnl( ) function? Illustrate its use.

Ans. DOS is a single tasking operating system, thus only one program runs at a time. The Spawnl ( ) function provides us with the capability of starting the execution of one program from within another program. The first program is called the parent process and the second program that gets called from within the first program is called a child process. Once the second program starts execution, the first is put on hold until the second program completes execution. The first program is then restarted. The following program demonstrates use of spawnl( ) function.

```
/* Mult.c */
int main ( int argc, char* argv[ ] )
{
int a[3], i, ret ;
if ( argc < 3 || argc > 3 )
{
printf ( "Too many or Too few arguments..." ) ;
exit ( 0 ) ;
}

for ( i = 1 ; i < argc ; i++ )
a[i] = atoi ( argv[i] ) ;
ret = a[1] * a[2] ;
```

```
return ret ;
}
/* Spawn.c */
#include <process.h>
#include <stdio.h>

main( )
{
int val ;
val = spawnl ( P_WAIT, "C:\\Mult.exe", "3", "10", "20", NULL ) ;
printf ( "\nReturned value is: %d", val ) ;
}
```

Here, there are two programs. The program 'Mult.exe' works as a child process whereas 'Spawn.exe' works as a parent process. On execution of 'Spawn.exe' it invokes 'Mult.exe' and passes the command-line arguments to it. 'Mult.exe' in turn on execution, calculates the product of 10 and 20 and returns the value to val in 'Spawn.exe'. In our call to spawnl( ) function, we have passed 6 parameters, P_WAIT as the mode of execution, path of '.exe' file to run as child process, total number of arguments to be passed to the child process, list of command line arguments and NULL. P_WAIT will cause our application to freeze execution until the child process has completed its execution. This parameter needs to be passed as the default parameter if you are working under DOS. under other operating systems that support multitasking, this parameter can be P_NOWAIT or P_OVERLAY. P_NOWAIT will cause the parent process to execute along with the child process, P_OVERLAY will load the child process on top of the parent process in the memory.

29. Are the following two statements identical?

```
char str[6] = "Kicit" ;
char *str = "Kicit" ;
```

Ans. No! Arrays are not pointers. An array is a single, pre-allocated chunk of contiguous elements (all of the same type), fixed in size and location. A pointer on the other hand, is a reference to any data element (of a particular type) located anywhere. A pointer must be assigned to point to space allocated elsewhere, but it can be reassigned any time. The array declaration char str[6] ; requests that space for 6 characters be set aside, to be known by name str. In other words there is a location named str at which six characters are stored. The pointer declaration char *str ; on the other hand, requests a place that holds a pointer, to be known by the name str. This pointer can point almost anywhere to any char, to any contiguous array of chars, or nowhere.

30. Is the following code fragment correct?

```
const int x = 10 ;
int arr[x] ;
```

Ans. No! Here, the variable x is first declared as an int so memory is reserved for it. Then it is qualified by a const qualifier. Hence, const qualified object is not a constant fully. It is an object with read only attribute, and in C, an object associated with memory cannot be used in array dimensions.

31. How do I write code to retrieve current date and time from the system and display it as a string?

Ans. Use time( ) function to get current date and time and then ctime( ) function to display it as a string. This is shown in following code snippet.

```
#include <sys\types.h>
```

```
void main( )
{
time_t curtime ;
char ctm[50] ;

time ( &curtime ) ; //retrieves current time & stores in curtime
printf ( "\nCurrent Date & Time: %s", ctime (&curtime ) ) ;
}
```

32. How do I change the type of cursor and hide a cursor?

Ans. We can change the cursor type by using function _setcursortype( ). This function can change the cursor type to solid cursor and can even hide a cursor. Following code shows how to change the cursor type and hide cursor.

```
#include <conio.h>
main( )
{
/* Hide cursor */
_setcursortype ( _NOCURSOR ) ;
/* Change cursor to a solid cursor */
_setcursortype ( _SOLIDCURSOR ) ;

/* Change back to the normal cursor */
_setcursortype ( _NORMALCURSOR ) ;
}
```

33. How do I write code that would get error number and display error message if any standard error occurs?

Ans. Following code demonstrates this.

```
#include <stdio.h>
#include <stdlib.h>
#include <errno.h>

main( )
{
char *errmsg ;
FILE *fp ;
fp = fopen ( "C:\file.txt", "r" ) ;
if ( fp == NULL )
{
errmsg = strerror ( errno ) ;
printf ( "\n%s", errmsg ) ;
}
}
```

Here, we are trying to open 'file.txt' file. However, if the file does not exist, then it would cause an error. As a result, a value (in this case 2) related to the error generated would get set in errno. errno is an external int variable declared in 'stdlib.h' and also in 'errno.h'. Next, we have called sterror( ) function which takes an error number and returns a pointer to standard error message related to the given error number.

34. How do I write code to get the current drive as well as set the current drive?

Ans. The function getdisk( ) returns the drive number of current drive. The drive number 0 indicates 'A' as the current drive, 1 as 'B' and so on. The Setdisk( ) function sets the current drive. This function takes one argument which is an integer indicating the drive to be set. Following program demonstrates use of both the functions.

```
#include <dir.h>
main( )
{
int dno, maxdr ;

dno = getdisk( ) ;
printf ( "\nThe current drive is: %c\n", 65 + dno) ;

maxdr = setdisk ( 3 ) ;
dno = getdisk( ) ;
printf ( "\nNow the current drive is: %c\n", 65 +dno ) ;
}
```

35. Illustrate the use of the functions memcmp( ) and memicmp( ).

Ans. The functions memcmp( ) and memicmp( ) compares first n bytes of given two blocks of memory or strings. However, memcmp( ) performs comparison as unsigned chars whereas memicmp( ) performs comparison as chars but ignores case (i.e. upper or lower case). Both the functions return an integer value where 0 indicates that two memory buffers compared are identical. If the value returned is greater than 0 then it indicates that the first buffer is bigger than the second one. The value less than 0 indicate that the first buffer is less than the second buffer. The following code snippet demonstrates use of both

```
#include <stdio.h>
#include <mem.h>

main( )
{
char str1[] = "This string contains some characters" ;
char str2[] = "this string contains" ;
int result ;

result = memcmp ( str1, str2, strlen ( str2 ) ) ;
printf ( "\nResult after comapring buffer using memcmp( )" ) ;
show ( result ) ;

result = memicmp ( str1, str2, strlen ( str2 ) ) ;
printf ( "\nResult after comapring buffer using memicmp( )" ) ;
show ( result ) ;
}
show ( int r )
```

```
{
if ( r == 0 )
printf ( "\nThe buffer str1 and str2 hold identical data" ) ;
if ( r > 0 )
printf ( "\nThe buffer str1 is bigger than buffer str2" ) ;
if ( r < 0 )
printf ( "\nThe buffer str1 is less than buffer str2" ) ;
}
```

36. How do I write code to find an amount of free disk space available on current drive?

Ans. Use getdfree( ) function as shown in follow code.

```
#include <stdio.h>
#include <stdlib.h>
#include <dir.h>
#include <dos.h>

main( )
{
int dr ; struct dfree disk ;
long freesp ;

dr = getdisk( ) ;
getdfree ( dr + 1 , &disk ) ;

if ( disk.df_sclus == 0xFFFF )
{
printf ( "\ngetdfree( ) function failed\n");
exit ( 1 ) ;
}

freesp = ( long ) disk.df_avail
* ( long ) disk.df_bsec
* ( long ) disk.df_sclus ;
printf ( "\nThe current drive %c: has %ld bytes available as free space\n", 'A' + dr, freesp ) ;
}
```

37. Illustrate the use of array indices.

Ans. If we wish to store a character in a char variable ch and the character to be stored depends on the value of another variable say color (of type int), then the code would be as shown below:

```
switch ( color )
{
case 0 :
ch = 'R' ;
break ;
case 1 :
```

```
ch = 'G' ;
break ;
case 2 :
ch = 'B' ;
break ;
}
```

In place of switch-case we can make use of the value in color as an index for a character array. How to do this is shown in following code snippet.

```
char *str = "RGB' ;
char ch ;
int color ;
// code
ch = str[ color ] ;
```

38. What is the use of atexit( )?

Ans. Function atexit( ) recevies parameter as the address of function of the type void fun (void). The function whose address is passed to atexit( ) gets called before the termination of program. If atexit( ) is called for more than one function then the functions are called in "first in last out" order. You can verify that from the output.

```
#include <stdio.h>
#include <stdlib.h>
void fun1( )
{
printf("Inside fun1\n");
}
void fun2( )
{
printf("Inside fun2\n");
}
main( )
{
atexit ( fun1 ) ;
/* some code */
atexit ( fun2 ) ;
printf ( "This is the last statement of program?\n" );
}
```

39. How do I write a user-defined function, which deletes each character in a string str1, which matches any character in string str2?

Ans. The function is as shown below:

```
Compress ( char str1[], char str2[] )
{
int i, j, k ;

for ( i = k = 0 ; str1[i] != '\0' ; i++ )
{
```

```
for ( j = 0 ; str2[j] != '\0' && str2[j] !=str1[i] ; j++ )
;
if ( str2[j] == '\0' )
str1[k++] = str1[I] ;
}
str1[k] = '\0'
}
```

40. How does free( ) know how many bytes to free?

Ans. The malloc( ) / free( ) implementation remembers the size of each block allocated and returned, so it is not necessary to remind it of the size when freeing.

41. What is the use of randomize( ) and srand( ) function?

Ans. While generating random numbers in a program, sometimes we require to control the series of numbers that random number generator creates. The process of assigning the random number generators starting number is called seeding the generator. The randomize( ) and srand( ) functions are used to seed the random number generators. The randomize( ) function uses PC's clock to produce a random seed, whereas the srand( ) function allows us to specify the random number generator's starting value.

42. How do I determine amount of memory currently available for allocating?

Ans. We can use function coreleft( ) to get the amount of memory available for allocation. However, this function does not give an exact amount of unused memory. If, we are using a small memory model, coreleft( ) returns the amount of unused memory between the top of the heap and stack. If we are using a larger model, this function returns the amount of memory between the highest allocated memory and the end of conventional memory. The function returns amount of memory in terms of bytes.

43. How does a C program come to know about command line arguments?

Ans. When we execute our C program, operating system loads the program into memory. In case of DOS, it first loads 256 bytes into memory, called program segment prefix. This contains file table, environment segment, and command line information. When we compile the C program the compiler inserts additional code that parses the command, assigning it to the argv array, making the arguments easily accessible within our C program.

44. When we open a file, how does functions like fread( )/fwrite( ), etc. get to know from where to read or to write the data?

Ans. When we open a file for read/write operation using function like fopen( ), it returns a pointer to the structure of type FILE. This structure stores the file pointer called position pointer, which keeps track of current location within the file. On opening file for read/write operation, the file pointer is set to the start of the file. Each time we read/write a character, the position pointer advances one character. If we read one line of text at a step from the file, then file pointer advances to the start of the next line. If the file is opened in append mode, the file pointer is placed at the very end of the file. Using fseek ( ) function we can set the file pointer to some other place within the file.

45. The sizeof( ) function doesn't return the size of the block of memory pointed to by a pointer. Why?

Ans. The sizeof( ) operator does not know that malloc( ) has been used to allocate a pointer. sizeof( ) gives us the size of pointer itself. There is no handy way to find out the size of a block allocated by malloc( ).

46. Illustrate the use of FP_SEG And FP_OFF.

Ans. Sometimes while working with far pointers we need to break a far address into its segment and offset. In such situations we can use FP_SEG and FP_OFF macros. Following program illustrates the use of these two macros.

```
#include <dos.h>
```

```
main( )
{
unsigned s, o ;
char far *ptr = "Hello!" ;

s = FP_SEG ( ptr ) ;
o = FP_OFF ( ptr ) ;
printf ( "\n%u %u", s, o ) ;
}
```

47. How do I write a program to convert a string containing number in a hexadecimal form to its equivalent decimal?

Ans. The following program demonstrates this:

```
main( )
{
char str[] = "0AB" ;
int h, hex, i, n ;
n = 0 ; h = 1 ;
for ( i = 0 ; h == 1 ; i++ )
{
if ( str[i] >= '0' && str[i] <= '9' )
hex = str[i] - '0' ;
else
{
if ( str[i] >= 'a' && str[i] <= 'f' )
hex = str[i] - 'a' + 10 ;
else
if ( str[i] >= 'A' && str[i] <= 'F' )
hex = str[i] - 'A' + 10 ;
else
h = 0 ;
}
if ( h == 1 )
n = 16 * n + hex ;
}
printf ( "\nThe decimal equivalent of %s is %d", str, n ) ;
}
```

The output of this program would be the decimal equivalent of 0AB is 171.

48. How do I write code that reads the segment register settings?

Ans. We can use segread( ) function to read segment register settings. There are four segment registers-code segment, data segment, stack segment and extra segment. Sometimes when we use DOS and BIOS services in a program we need to know the segment register's value. In such a situation we can use segread( ) function. The following program illustrates the use of this function.

```
#include <dos.h>
main( )
{
```

```
struct SREGS s ;
segread ( &s ) ;
printf ( "\nCS: %X DS: %X SS: %X ES: %X",s.cs, s.ds, s.ss, s.es ) ;
}
```

49. What is environment and how do I get environment for a specific entry?

Ans. While working in DOS, it stores information in a memory region called environment. In this region we can place configuration settings such as command path, system prompt, etc. Sometimes in a program we need to access the information contained in environment. The function getenv( ) can be used when we want to access environment for a specific entry. Following program demonstrates the use of this function.

```
#include <stdio.h>
#include <stdlib.h>

main( )
{
char *path = NULL ;

path = getenv ( "PATH" ) ;
if ( *path != NULL )
printf ( "\nPath: %s", path ) ;
else
printf ( "\nPath is not set" ) ;
}
```

50. What does static variable mean?

Ans. Static variables are the variables which retain their values between the function calls. They are initialized only once their scope is within the function in which they are defined.

51. What is a pointer?

Ans. Pointers are variables which stores the address of another variable. That variable may be a scalar (including another pointer), or an aggregate (array or structure). The pointed-to object may be part of a larger object, such as a field of a structure or an element in an array.

52. What are the uses of a pointer?

Ans. Pointer is used in the following cases

i) It is used to access array elements
ii) It is used for dynamic memory allocation.
iii) It is used in Call by reference
iv) It is used in data structures like trees, graph, linked list etc.

53. What is a structure?

Ans. Structure constitutes a super data type which represents several different data types in a single unit. A structure can be initialized if it is static or global.

54. What is a union?

Ans. Union is a collection of heterogeneous data type but it uses efficient memory utilization technique by allocating enough memory to hold the largest member. Here a single area of memory contains values of different types at different time. A union can never be initialized.

55. What are the differences between structures and union?

Ans. A structure variable contains each of the named members, and its size is large enough to hold all the members. Structure elements are of same size.

A union contains one of the named members at a given time and is large enough to hold the largest member. Union element can be of different sizes.

56. What are the differences between structures and arrays?

Ans. Structure is a collection of heterogeneous data type but array is a collection of homogeneous data types.

Array

1-It is a collection of data items of same data type.

2-It has declaration only

3-.There is no keyword.

4- array name represent the address of the starting element.

Structure

1-It is a collection of data items of different data type.

2- It has declaration and definition

3- keyword struct is used

4-Structure name is known as tag it is the short hand notation of the declaration.

57. In header files whether functions are declared or defined?

Ans. Functions are declared within header file. That is function prototypes exist in a header file,not function bodies. They are defined in library (lib).

58. What are the differences between malloc () and calloc ()?

Ans. Malloc Calloc 1-Malloc takes one argument Malloc(a);where a number of bytes 2-memory allocated contains garbage values

1-Calloc takes two arguments Calloc(b,c) where b no of object and c size of object

2-It initializes the contains of block of memory to zerosMalloc takes one argument, memory allocated contains garbage values.

It allocates contiguous memory locations. Calloc takes two arguments, memory allocated contains all zeros, and the memory allocated is not contiguous.

59. What are macros? What are its advantages and disadvantages?

Ans. Macros are abbreviations for lengthy and frequently used statements. When a macro is called the entire code is substituted by a single line though the macro definition is of several lines. The advantage of macro is that it reduces the time taken for control transfer as in case of function.

The disadvantage of it is here the entire code is substituted so the program becomes lengthy if a macro is called several times.

60. Difference between pass by reference and pass by value?

Ans. Pass by reference passes a pointer to the value. This allows the callee to modify the variable directly.Pass by value gives a copy of the value to the callee. This allows the callee to modify the value without modifying the variable. (In other words, the callee simply cannot modify the variable, since it lacks a reference to it.)

61. What is static identifier?

Ans. A file-scope variable that is declared static is visible only to functions within that file. A function-scope or block-scope variable that is declared as static is visible only within that scope. Furthermore, static variables only have a single instance. In the case of function- or block-scope variables, this means that the variable is not "automatic" and thus retains its value across function invocations.

62. Where is the auto variables stored?

Ans. Auto variables can be stored anywhere, so long as recursion works. Practically, they're stored on the stack. It is not necessary that always a stack exist. You could theoretically allocate function invocation records from the heap.

63. Where does global, static, and local, register variables, free memory and C Program instructions get stored?

Ans. Global: Wherever the linker puts them. Typically the "BSS segment" on many platforms.

Static: Again, wherever the linker puts them. Often, they're intermixed with the globals. The only difference between globals and statics is whether the linker will resolve the symbols across compilation units.Local: Typically on the stack, unless the variable gets register allocated and never spills.Register: Nowadays, these are equivalent to "Local" variables. They live on the stack unless they get register-allocated.

64. Difference between arrays and linked list?

Ans. An array is a repeated pattern of variables in contiguous storage. A linked list is a set of structures scattered through memory, held together by pointers in each element that point to the next element. With an array, we can (on most architectures) move from one element to the next by adding a fixed constant to the integer value of the pointer. With a linked list, there is a "next" pointer in each structure which says what element comes next.

65. What are enumerations?

Ans. They are a list of named integer-valued constants. Example:enum color { black , orange=4, yellow, green, blue, violet };This declaration defines the symbols "black", "orange", "yellow", etc. to have the values "1," "4," "5," … etc. The difference between an enumeration and a macro is that the enum actually declares a type, and therefore can be type checked.

66. Describe about storage allocation and scope of global, extern, static, local and register variables?

Ans. Globals have application-scope. They're available in any compilation unit that includes an appropriate declaration (usually brought from a header file). They're stored wherever the linker puts them, usually a place called the "BSS segment."

Extern? This is essentially "global."

Static: Stored the same place as globals, typically, but only available to the compilation unit that contains them. If they are block-scope global, only available within that block and its subblocks.

Local: Stored on the stack, typically. Only available in that block and its subblocks. (Although pointers to locals can be passed to functions invoked from within a scope where that local is valid.)

Register: See tirade above on "local" vs. "register." The only difference is that the C compiler will not let you take the address of something you've declared as "register."

67. What are register variables? What are the advantages of using register variables?

Ans. If a variable is declared with a register storage class,it is known as register variable.The register variable is stored in the cpu register instead of main memory.Frequently used variables are declared as register variable as it's access time is faster.

68. What is the use of typedef?

Ans. The typedef help in easier modification when the programs are ported to another machine.

A descriptive new name given to the existing data type may be easier to understand the code.

69. Can we specify variable field width in a scanf() format string? If possible how?

Ans. All field widths are variable with scanf(). You can specify a maximum field width for a given field by placing an integer value between the '%' and the field type specifier. (e.g. %64s). Such a specifier will still accept a narrower field width.

The one exception is %#c (where # is an integer). This reads EXACTLY # characters, and it is the only way to specify a fixed field width with scanf().

70. Out of fgets() and gets() which function is safe to use and why?

Ans. fgets() is safer than gets(), because we can specify a maximum input length. Neither one is completely safe, because the compiler can't prove that programmer won't overflow the buffer he pass to fgets ().

71. Difference between strdup and strcpy?

Ans. Both copy a string. strcpy wants a buffer to copy into. strdup allocates a buffer using malloc(). Unlike strcpy(), strdup() is not specified by ANSI .

72. What is recursion?

Ans. A recursion function is one which calls itself either directly or indirectly it must halt at a definite point to avoid infinite recursion.

73. Differentiate between for loop and a while loop? What are it uses?

Ans. For executing a set of statements fixed number of times we use for loop while when the number of iterations to be performed is not known in advance we use while loop.

74. What is storage class? What are the different storage classes in C?

Ans. Storage class is an attribute that changes the behavior of a variable. It controls the lifetime, scope and linkage. The storage classes in c are auto, register, and extern, static, typedef.

75. What the advantages of using Unions?

Ans. When the C compiler is allocating memory for unions it will always reserve enough room for the largest member.

76. What is the difference between Strings and Arrays?

Ans. String is a sequence of characters ending with NULL .it can be treated as a one dimensional array of characters terminated by a NULL character.

77. What is a far pointer? Where we use it?

Ans. In large data model (compact, large, huge) the address B0008000 is acceptable because in these model all pointers to data are 32bits long. If we use small data model(tiny, small, medium) the above address won't work since in these model each pointer is 16bits long. If we are working in a small data model and want to access the address B0008000 then we use far pointer. Far pointer is always treated as a 32bit pointer and contains a segment address and offset address both of 16bits each. Thus the address is represented using

segment : offset format B000h:8000h.

For any given memory address there are many possible far address segment : offset pair. The segment register contains the address where the segment begins and offset register contains the offset of data/code from where segment begins.

78. What is a huge pointer?

Ans. Huge pointer is 32bit long containing segment address and offset address. Huge pointers are normalized pointers so for any given memory address there is only one possible huge address segment: offset pair. Huge pointer arithmetic is doe with calls to special subroutines so its arithmetic slower than any other pointers.

79. What is a normalized pointer, how do we normalize a pointer?

Ans. It is a 32bit pointer, which has as much of its value in the segment register as possible. Since a segment can start every 16bytes so the offset will have a value from 0 to F. for normalization convert the address into 20bit address then use the 16bit for segment address and 4bit for the offset address. Given a pointer 500D: 9407,we convert it to a 20bitabsolute address 549D7,Which then normalized to 549D:0007.

80. What is near pointer?

Ans. A near pointer is 16 bits long. It uses the current content of the CS (code segment) register (if the pointer is pointing to code) or current contents of DS (data segment) register (if the pointer is pointing to data) for the segment part, the offset part is stored in a 16 bit near pointer. Using near pointer limits the data/code to 64kb segment.

81. In C, why is the void pointer useful? When would you use it?

Ans. The void pointer is useful because it is a generic pointer that any pointer can be cast into and back again without loss of information.

82. What is a NULL Pointer? Whether it is same as an uninitialized pointer?

Ans. Null pointer is a pointer which points to nothing but uninitialized pointer may point to anywhere.

83. Are pointers integer?

Ans. No, pointers are not integers. A pointer is an address. It is a positive number.

84. What does the error 'Null Pointer Assignment' means and what causes this error?

Ans. As null pointer points to nothing so accessing a uninitialized pointer or invalid location may cause an error.

85. What is generic pointer in C?

Ans. In C void* acts as a generic pointer. When other pointer types are assigned to generic pointer, conversions are applied automatically (implicit conversion).

86. Are the expressions arr and &arr same for an array of integers?

Ans. Yes for array of integers they are same.

87. How pointer variables are initialized?

Ans. Pointer variables are initialized by one of the following ways.

I. Static memory allocation

II. Dynamic memory allocation

88. What is static memory allocation?

Ans. Compiler allocates memory space for a declared variable. By using the address of operator, the reserved address is obtained and this address is assigned to a pointer variable. This way of assigning pointer value to a pointer variable at compilation time is known as static memory allocation.

89. What is dynamic memory allocation?

Ans. A dynamic memory allocation uses functions such as malloc() or calloc() to get memory dynamically. If these functions are used to get memory dynamically and the values returned by these function are assigned to pointer variables, such a way of allocating memory at run time is known as dynamic memory allocation.

90. What is the purpose of realloc?

Ans. It increases or decreases the size of dynamically allocated array. The function realloc (ptr,n) uses two arguments. The first argument ptr is a pointer to a block of memory for which the size is to be altered. The second argument specifies the new size. The size may be increased or decreased. If sufficient space is not available to the old region the function may create a new region.

91. What is pointer to a pointer?

Ans. If a pointer variable points another pointer value. Such a situation is known as a pointer to a pointer.

Example:

```
int *p1,**p2,v=10;
P1=&v; p2=&p1;
```

Here p2 is a pointer to a pointer.

92. What is an array of pointers?

Ans. if the elements of an array are addresses, such an array is called an array of pointers.

93. Difference between linker and linkage?

Ans. Linker converts an object code into an executable code by linking together the necessary built in functions. The form and place of declaration where the variable is declared in a program determine the linkage of variable.

94. Is it possible to have negative index in an array?

Ans. Yes it is possible to index with negative value provided there are data stored in this location. Even if it is illegal to refer to the elements that are out of array bounds, the compiler will not produce error because C has no check on the bounds of an array.

95. Why is it necessary to give the size of an array in an array declaration?

Ans. When an array is declared, the compiler allocates a base address and reserves enough space in memory for all the elements of the array. The size is required to allocate the required space and hence size must be mentioned.

96. What modular programming?

Ans. If a program is large, it is subdivided into a number of smaller programs that are called modules or subprograms. If a complex problem is solved using more modules, this approach is known as modular programming.

97. What is a function?

Ans. A large program is subdivided into a number of smaller programs or subprograms. Each subprogram specifies one or more actions to be performed for the larger program. Such sub programs are called functions.

98. What is an argument?

Ans. An argument is an entity used to pass data from the calling to a called function.

99. What are built in functions?

Ans. The functions that are predefined and supplied along with the compiler are known as built-in functions. They are also known as library functions.

100. What do the 'c' and 'v' in argc and argv stand for?

Ans. The c in argc(argument count) stands for the number of command line argument the program is invoked with and v in argv(argument vector) is a pointer to an array of character string that contain the arguments.

101. What are C tokens?

Ans. There are six classes of tokens: identifier, keywords, constants, string literals, operators and other separators.

102. What C identifiers?

Ans. These are names given to various programming element such as variables, function, arrays.It is a combination of letter, digit and underscore.It should begin with letter. Backspace is not allowed.

103. Difference between syntax vs logical error?

Ans:

Syntax Error

1-These involves validation of syntax of language.

2-compiler prints diagnostic message.

Logical Error

1-logical error are caused by an incorrect algorithm or by a statement mistyped in such a way that it doesn't violet syntax of language.

2-difficult to find.

104. What is preincrement and post increment?

Ans. ++n (pre increment) increments n before its value is used in an assignment operation or any expression containing it. n++ (post increment) does increment after the value of n is used.

105. Write a program to interchange 2 variables without using the third one.

Ans.

```
a ^= b; ie a=a^b
b ^= a; ie b=b^a;
a ^= b ie a=a^b;
```

here the numbers are converted into binary and then xor operation is performed. You know, you're just asking "have you seen this overly clever trick that's not worth applying on modern architectures and only really applies to integer variables?"

106. What is the maximum combined length of command line arguments including the space between adjacent arguments?

Ans. It depends on the operating system.

107. What are bit fields? What is the use of bit fields in a Structure declaration?

Ans. A bit field is a set of adjacent bits within a single implementation based storage unit that we will call a "word".

The syntax of field definition and access is based on structure.

```
Struct {
unsigned int k :1;
unsigned int l :1;
unsigned int m :1;
}flags;
```

the number following the colon represents the field width in bits.Flag is a variable that contains three bit fields.

108. What is a preprocessor, what are the advantages of preprocessor?

Ans. A preprocessor processes the source code program before it passes through the compiler.

1- a preprocessor involves the readability of program

2- It facilitates easier modification

3- It helps in writing portable programs

4- It enables easier debugging

5- It enables testing a part of program

6- It helps in developing generalized program

109. What are the facilities provided by preprocessor?

Ans.

1-file inclusion

2-substitution facility

3-conditional compilation

110. What are the two forms of #include directive?

Ans.

1.#include"filename"

2.#include

the first form is used to search the directory that contains the source file.If the search fails in the home directory it searches the implementation defined locations.In the second form ,the preprocessor searches the file only in the implementation defined locations.

111. How would you use the functions randomize() and random()?

Ans.

Randomize() initiates random number generation with a random value.

Random() generates random number between 0 and n-1;

112. What do the functions atoi(), itoa() and gcvt() do?

Ans.

atoi() is a macro that converts integer to character.

itoa() It converts an integer to string

gcvt() It converts a floating point number to string

113. How would you use the functions fseek(), freed(), fwrite() and ftell()?

Ans.

fseek(f,1,i) Move the pointer for file f a distance 1 byte from location i.

fread(s,i1,i2,f) Enter i2 dataitems,each of size i1 bytes,from file f to string s.

fwrite(s,i1,i2,f) send i2 data items,each of size i1 bytes from string s to file f.

ftell(f) Return the current pointer position within file f.

The data type returned for functions fread, fseek and fwrite is int and ftell is long int.

114. What is the difference between the functions memmove() and memcpy()?

Ans. The arguments of memmove() can overlap in memory. The arguments of memcpy() cannot.

115. What is a file?

Ans. A file is a region of storage in hard disks or in auxiliary storage devices.It contains bytes of information .It is not a data type.

116. What are the types of file?

Ans. Files are of two types

1-high level files (stream oriented files) :These files are accessed using library functions

2-low level files(system oriented files) :These files are accessed using system calls

117. What is a stream?

Ans. A stream is a source of data or destination of data that may be associated with a disk or other I/O device. The source stream provides data to a program and it is known as input stream. The destination stream eceives the output from the program and is known as output stream.

118. What is meant by file opening?

Ans. The action of connecting a program to a file is called opening of a file. This requires creating an I/O stream before reading or writing the data.

119. What is FILE?

Ans. FILE is a predefined data type. It is defined in stdio.h file.

120. What is a file pointer?

Ans. The pointer to a FILE data type is called as a stream pointer or a file pointer. A file pointer points to the block of information of the stream that had just been opened.

121. How is fopen()used ?

Ans. The function fopen() returns a file pointer. Hence a file pointer is declared and it is assigned as

FILE *fp;

fp= fopen(filename,mode);

filename is a string representing the name of the file and the mode represents:

"r" for read operation

"w" for write operation

"a" for append operation
"r+","w+","a+" for update operation

122. How is a file closed ?

Ans. A file is closed using fclose() function
Eg. fclose(fp);
Where fp is a file pointer.

123. What is a random access file?

Ans.
A file can be accessed at random using fseek() function
fseek(fp,position,origin);
fp file pointer
position number of bytes offset from origin
origin 0,1 or 2 denote the beginning ,current position or end of file respectively.

124. What is the purpose of ftell ?

Ans. The function ftell() is used to get the current file represented by the file pointer.
ftell(fp);
returns a long integer value representing the current file position of the file pointed by the file pointer fp.If an error occurs ,-1 is returned.

125. What is the purpose of rewind() ?

Ans. The function rewind is used to bring the file pointer to the beginning of the file.
Rewind(fp);
Where fp is a file pointer.Also we can get the same effect by
feek(fp,0,0);

126. Difference between a array name and a pointer variable?

Ans. A pointer variable is a variable where as an array name is a fixed address and is not a variable. A pointer variable must be initialized but an array name cannot be initialized. An array name being a constant value , ++ and - operators cannot be applied to it.

127. Represent a two-dimensional array using pointer?

Ans.
Address of a[I][j] Value of a[I][j]
&a[I][j]
or
a[I] + j
or
*(a+I) + j
*&a[I][j] or a[I][j]
or
*(a[I] + j)
or
*(* (a+I) +j)

128. Difference between an array of pointers and a pointer to an array?

Ans.

Array of pointers

1- Declaration is: data_type *array_name[size];
2-Size represents the row size.
3- The space for columns may be dynamically

Pointers to an array

1-Declaration is data_type (*array_name)[size];

2-Size represents the column size.

129. Can we use any name in place of argv and argc as command line arguments ?

Ans. yes we can use any user defined name in place of argc and argv;

130. What are the pointer declarations used in C?

Ans.

1- Array of pointers, e.g , int *a[10]; Array of pointers to integer

2-Pointers to an array,e.g , int (*a)[10]; Pointer to an array of into

3-Function returning a pointer,e.g, float *f( ) ; Function returning a pointer to float

4-Pointer to a pointer ,e.g, int **x; Pointer to apointer to int

5-pointer to a data type ,e.g, char *p; pointer to char

131. Differentiate between a constant pointer and pointer to a constant?

Ans.

const char *p; //pointer to a const character.

char const *p; //pointer to a const character.

char * const p; //const pointer to a char variable.

const char * const p; // const pointer to a const character.

132. Is the allocated space within a function automatically deallocated when the function returns?

Ans. No pointer is different from what it points to .Local variables including local pointers variables in a function are deallocated automatically when function returns.,But in case of a local pointer variable ,deallocation means that the pointer is deallocated and not the block of memory allocated to it. Memory dynamically allocated always persists until the allocation is freed or the program terminates.

133. Discuss on pointer arithmetic?

Ans.

1- Assignment of pointers to the same type of pointers.

2- Adding or subtracting a pointer and an integer.

3-subtracting or comparing two pointer.

4-incrementing or decrementing the pointers pointing to the elements of an array. When a pointer to an integer is incremented by one , the address is incremented by two. It is done automatically by the compiler.

5-Assigning the value 0 to the pointer variable and comparing 0 with the pointer. The pointer having address 0 points to nowhere at all.

134. What is the invalid pointer arithmetic?

Ans.

i) adding ,multiplying and dividing two pointers.

ii) Shifting or masking pointer.

iii) Addition of float or double to pointer.

iv) Assignment of a pointer of one type to a pointer of another type ?

135. What are the advantages of using array of pointers to string instead of an array of strings?

Ans.

i) Efficient use of memory.

ii) Easier to exchange the strings by moving their pointers while sorting.

136. Are the expressions *ptr ++ and ++ *ptr same?

Ans. No,*ptr ++ increments pointer and not the value pointed by it. Whereas ++ *ptr increments the value being pointed to by ptr.

137. What would be the equivalent pointer expression foe referring the same element as a[p][q][r][s] ?

Ans. *(* (* (* (a+p) + q) + r) + s)

138. Are the variables argc and argv are always local to main?

Ans. Yes they are local to main.

139. Can main () be called recursively?

Ans. Yes any function including main () can be called recursively.

140. How do I display current date in the format given below?

Saturday October 12, 2002

Ans. Following program illustrates how we can display date in above given format.

```
#include <stdio.h>
#include <time.h>

main( )
{
struct tm *curtime ;
time_t dtime ;

char str[30] ;

time ( &dtime ) ;
curtime = localtime ( &dtime ) ;
strftime ( str, 30, "%A %B %d, %Y", curtime ) ;

printf ( "\n%s", str ) ;
}
```

Here we have called time( ) function which returns current time. This time is returned in terms of seconds, elapsed since 00:00:00 GMT, January 1, 1970. To extract the week day, day of month, etc. from this value we need to break down the value to a tm structure. This is done by the function localtime( ). Then we have called strftime( ) function to format the time and store it in a string str.

141. If we have declared an array as global in one file and we are using it in another file then why doesn't the sizeof operator works on an extern array?

Ans. An extern array is of incomplete type as it does not contain the size. Hence we cannot use sizeof operator, as it cannot get the size of the array declared in another file. To resolve this use any of one the following two solutions:

1. In the same file declare one more variable that holds the size of array. For example,

```
array.c
int arr[5] ;
int arrsz = sizeof ( arr ) ;
myprog.c
extern int arr[] ;
extern int arrsz ;
```

2. Define a macro which can be used in an array
declaration. For example,

```
myheader.h
```

```
#define SZ 5
array.c
#include "myheader.h"
int arr[SZ] ;
myprog.c
#include "myheader.h"
extern int arr[SZ] ;
```

142. How do I write printf( ) so that the width of a field can be specified at runtime?

Ans. This is shown in following code snippet.

```
main( )
{
int w, no ;
printf ( "Enter number and the width for the
number field:" ) ;
scanf ( "%d%d", &no, &w ) ;
printf ( "%*d", w, no ) ;
}
```

Here, an '*' in the format specifier in printf( ) indicates that an int value from the argument list should be used for the field width.

143. How to find the row and column dimension of a given 2-D array?

Ans. Whenever we initialize a 2-D array at the same place where it has been declared, it is not necessary to mention the row dimension of an array. The row and column dimensions of such an array can be determined programmatically as shown in following program.

```
void main( )
{
int a[][3] = { 0, 1, 2,
9,-6, 8,
7, 5, 44,
23, 11,15 } ;

int c = sizeof ( a[0] ) / sizeof ( int ) ;
int r = ( sizeof ( a ) / sizeof ( int ) ) / c ;
int i, j ;

printf ( "\nRow: %d\nCol: %d\n", r, c ) ;
for ( i = 0 ; i < r ; i++ )
{
for ( j = 0 ; j < c ; j++ )
printf ( "%d ", a[i][j] ) ;
printf ( "\n" ) ;
}
}
```

144. What is the use of the access( ) function?

Ans. The access( ) function checks for the existence of a file and also determines whether it can be read, written to or executed. This function takes two arguments the filename and an integer indicating the access mode. The values 6, 4, 2, and 1 checks for read/write, read, write and execute permission of a given file, whereas value 0 checks whether the file exists or not. Following program demonstrates how we can use access( ) function to check if a given file exists.

```
#include <io.h>

main( )
{
char fname[67] ;

printf ( "\nEnter name of file to open" ) ;
gets ( fname ) ;

if ( access ( fname, 0 ) != 0 )
{
printf ( "\nFile does not exist." ) ;
return ;
}
}
```

145. How do I convert a floating-point number to a string?

Ans. Use function gcvt( ) to convert a floating-point number to a string. Following program demonstrates the use of this function.

```
#include <stdlib.h>
main( )
{
char str[25] ;
float no ;
int dg = 5 ; /* significant digits */

no = 14.3216 ;
gcvt ( no, dg, str ) ;
printf ( "String: %s\n", str ) ;
}
```

146. What is a stack?

Ans. The stack is a region of memory within which our programs temporarily store data as they execute. For example, when a program passes parameters to functions, C places the parameters on the stack. When the function completes, C removes the items from the stack. Similarly, when a function declares local variables, C stores the variable's values on the stack during the function's execution. Depending on the program's use of functions and parameters, the amount of stack space that a program requires will differ.

147. How memory is allocated for a 3-D array?

Ans.

```
#include "alloc.h"
#define MAXX 3
#define MAXY 4
```

```
#define MAXZ 5
main( )
{
int ***p, i, j, k ;
p = ( int *** ) malloc ( MAXX * sizeof ( int ** ) ) ;
for ( i = 0 ; i < MAXX ; i++ )
{
p[i] = ( int ** ) malloc ( MAXY * sizeof ( int * ) ) ;
for ( j = 0 ; j < MAXY ; j++ )
p[i][j] = ( int * ) malloc ( MAXZ * sizeof ( int ) ) ;
}
for ( k = 0 ; k < MAXZ ; k++ )
{
for ( i = 0 ; i < MAXX ; i++ )
{
for ( j = 0 ; j < MAXY ; j++ )
{
p[i][j][k] = i + j + k ;
printf ( "%d ", p[i][j][k] ) ;
}
printf ( "\n" ) ;
}
printf ( "\n\n" ) ;
}
}
```

148. How do I use the function ldexp( ) in a program?

Ans. The math function ldexp( ) is used while solving the complex mathematical equations. This function takes two arguments, a double value and an int respectively. The order in which ldexp( ) function performs calculations is (n * pow (2, exp)) where n is the double value and exp is the integer. The following program demonstrates the use of this function.

```
#include <stdio.h>
#include <math.h>
void main( )
{
double ans ;
double n = 4 ;
ans = ldexp ( n, 2 ) ;
printf ( "\nThe ldexp value is : %lf\n", ans ) ;
}
```

Here, ldexp( ) function would get expanded as (4 * 2 * 2), and the output would be the ldexp value is : 16.000000

149. How to extract the integer part and a fractional part of a floating point number?

Ans. C function modf( ) can be used to get the integer and fractional part of a floating point.

```
#include "math.h"
main( )
```

```
{
double val, i, f ;
val = 5.15 ;
f = modf ( val, &i ) ;
printf ( "\nFor the value %f integer part = %f and fractional part = %f",
val, i, f ) ;
}
```

The output of the above program will be:

For the value 5.150000 integer part = 5.000000 and fractional part = 0.150000

150. How do I define a pointer to a function which returns a char pointer?

Ans.

```
char * ( *p )( ) ;
or
typedef char * ( * ptrtofun )( ) ;
ptrtofun p ;
```

Here is a sample program which uses this definition.

```
main( )
{
typedef char * ( * ptrtofun ) ( ) ;
char * fun( ) ;
ptrtofun fptr ;
char *cptr ;
fptr = fun ;
cptr = (*fptr) ( ) ;
printf ( "\nReturned string is \"%s\"", cptr ) ;
}
char * fun( )
{
static char s[ ] = "Hello!" ;
printf ( "\n%s", s ) ;
return s ;
}
```

151. What's wrong with the following declaration: char* ptr1, ptr2 ; get errors when I try to use ptr2 as a pointer.

Ans. char * applies only to ptr1 and not to ptr2. Hence ptr1 is getting declared as a char pointer, whereas, ptr2 is being declared merely as a char. This can be rectified in two ways :

```
char *ptr1, *ptr2 ;
typedef char* CHARPTR ; CHARPTR ptr1, ptr2 ;
```

152. How to use scanf( ) to read the date in the form of dd-mm-yy?

Ans. To read the date in the form of dd-mm-yy one possible way is,

```
int dd, mm, yy ;
char ch ; /* for char '-' */
printf ( "\nEnter the date in the form of dd-mm-yy : " ) ;
scanf( "%d%c%d%c%d", &dd, &ch, &mm, &ch, &yy ) ;
```

Another way is to use suppression character * is as follows:

```
int dd, mm, yy ;
scanf( "%d%*c%d%*c%d", &dd, &mm, &yy ) ;
```

The suppression character '*' suppresses the input read from the standard input buffer for the assigned control character.

153. Why the output of sizeof ('a') is 2 and not 1 ?

Ans. Character constants in C are of type int, hence sizeof ('a') is equivalent to sizeof (int), i.e. 2. Hence the output comes out to be 2 bytes.

154. Can we use scanf( ) function to scan a multiple words string through keyboard?

Ans. Yes. Although we usually use scanf( ) function to receive a single word string and gets( ) to receive a multi-word string from keyboard we can also use scanf( ) function for scanning a multi-word string from keyboard. Following program shows how to achieve this.

```
main( )
{
char buff[15] ;
scanf ( "%[^\n]s", buff ) ;
puts ( buff ) ;
}
```

In the scanf( ) function we can specify the delimiter in brackets after the ^ character. We have specified '\n' as the delimiter. Hence scanf( ) terminates only when the user hits Enter key.

155. How to set the system date through a C program ?

Ans. We can set the system date using the setdate( ) function as shown in the following program. The function assigns the current time to a

structure date.

```
#include "stdio.h"
#include "dos.h"
main( )
{
struct date new_date ;
new_date.da_mon = 12 ;
new_date.da_day = 27;
new_date.da_year = 2011 ;
setdate ( &new_date ) ;
}
```

156. How can I write a general-purpose swap without using templates?

Ans. Given below is the program which uses the stringizing preprocessor directive ## for building a general purpose swap macro which can swap two integers, two floats, two chars, etc.

```
#define swap( a, b, t ) ( g ## t = ( a ), ( a ) = ( b ), ( b ) = g ## t )
int gint;
char gchar;
float gfloat ;
main( )
{
int a = 10, b = 20 ;
char ch1 = 'a' , ch2 = 'b' ;
float f1 = 1.12, f2 = 3.14 ;
```

```
swap ( a, b, int ) ;
printf ( "\na = %d b = %d", a, b ) ;
swap ( ch1, ch2, char ) ;
printf ( "\nch1 = %c ch2 = %c", ch1, ch2 ) ;
swap ( f1, f2, float ) ;
printf ( "\nf1 = %4.2f f2 = %4.2f", f1, f2 ) ;
}
```

swap (a, b, int) would expand to,

(gint = (a), (a) = (b), (b) = gint)

157. What is a heap ?

Ans. Heap is a chunk of memory. When in a program memory is allocated dynamically, the C run-time library gets the memory from a collection of unused memory called the heap. The heap resides in a program's data segment. Therefore, the amount of heap space available to the program is fixed, and can vary from one program to another.

158. How to obtain a path of the given file?

Ans. The function searchpath( ) searches for the specified file in the subdirectories of the current path. Following program shows how to make use of the searchpath( ) function.

```
#include "dir.h"
void main ( int argc, char *argv[] )
{
char *path ;
if ( path = searchpath ( argv[ 1 ] ) )
printf ( "Pathname : %s\n", path ) ;
else
printf ( "File not found\n" ) ;
}
```

159. Can we get the process identification number of the current program?

Ans. Yes! The macro getpid( ) gives us the process identification number of the program currently running. The process id. uniquely identifies a program. Under DOS, the getpid( ) returns the Program Segment Prefix as the process id. Following program illustrates the use of this macro.

```
#include <stdio.h>
#include <process.h>
void main( )
{
printf ( "The process identification number of this program is %X\n", getpid( ) ) ;
}
```

160. How do I write a function that takes variable number of arguments?

Ans. The following program demonstrates this.

```
#include <stdio.h>
#include <stdarg.h>
void main( )
{
int i = 10 ;
float f = 2.5 ;
char *str = "Hello!" ;
```

```
vfpf ( "%d %f %s\n", i, f, str ) ;
vfpf ( "%s %s", str, "Hi!" ) ;
}
void vfpf ( char *fmt, ... )
{
va_list argptr ;
va_start ( argptr, fmt ) ;
vfprintf ( stdout, fmt, argptr ) ;
va_end ( argptr ) ;
}
```

Here, the function vfpf( ) has called vfprintf( ) that take variable argument lists. va_list is an array that holds information required for the macros va_start and va_end. The macros va_start and va_end provide a portable way to access the variable argument lists. va_start would set up a pointer argptr to point to the first of the variable arguments being passed to the function. The macro va_end helps the called function to perform a normal return.

161. Can we change the system date to some other date?

Ans. Yes, We can! The function stime( ) sets the system date to the specified date. It also sets the system time. The time and date is measured in seconds from the 00:00:00 GMT, January 1, 1970. The following program shows how to use this function.

```
#include <stdio.h>
#include <time.h>
void main( )
{
time_t tm ;
int d ;
tm = time ( NULL ) ;
printf ( "The System Date : %s", ctime ( &tm ) ) ;
printf ( "\nHow many days ahead you want to set the date : " ) ;
scanf ( "%d", &d ) ;
tm += ( 24L * d ) * 60L * 60L ;
stime ( &tm ) ;
printf ( "\nNow the new date is : %s", ctime ( &tm ) ) ;
}
```

In this program we have used function ctime( ) in addition to function stime( ). The ctime( ) function converts time value to a 26-character long string that contains date and time.

162. How to use function strdup( ) in a program?

Ans. The string function strdup( ) copies the given string to a new location. The function uses malloc( ) function to allocate space required for the duplicated string. It takes one argument a pointer to the string to be duplicated. The total number of characters present in the given string plus one bytes get allocated for the new string. As this function uses malloc( ) to allocate memory, it is the programmer's responsibility to deallocate the memory using free( ).

```
#include <stdio.h>
#include <string.h>
#include <alloc.h>
void main( )
```

```
{
char *str1, *str2 = "double";

str1 = strdup ( str2 ) ;
printf ( "%s\n", str1 ) ;
free ( str1 ) ;
}
```

163. On including a file twice I get errors reporting redefinition of function. How can I avoid duplicate inclusion?

Ans. Redefinition errors can be avoided by using the following macro definition. Include this definition in the header file.

```
#if !defined filename_h
#define filename_h
/* function definitions */
#endif
```

Replace filename_h with the actual header file name. For example, if name of file to be included is 'goto.h' then replace filename_h with 'goto_h'.

164. How to write a swap( ) function which swaps the values of the variables using bitwise operators.

Ans. Here is the swap( ) function.

```
swap ( int *x, int *y )
{
*x ^= *y ;
*y ^= *x ;
*x ^= *y ;
}
```

The swap( ) function uses the bitwise XOR operator and does not require any temporary variable for swapping.

165. Can we get the mantissa and exponent form of a given number?

Ans. The function frexp( ) splits the given number into a mantissa and exponent form. The function takes two arguments, the number to be converted as a double value and an int to store the exponent form. The function returns the mantissa part as a double value. Following example demonstrates the use of this function.

```
#include <math.h>
#include <stdio.h>

void main( )
{
double mantissa, number ;
int exponent ;

number = 8.0 ;
mantissa = frexp ( number, &exponent ) ;

printf ( "The number %lf is ", number ) ;
```

```
printf ( "%lf times two to the ", mantissa ) ;
printf ( "power of %d\n", exponent ) ;

return 0 ;
}
```

166. How do I write code that executes certain function only at program termination?

Ans. Use atexit( ) function as shown in following program.

```
#include <stdlib.h>
main( )
{
int ch ;
void fun ( void ) ;
atexit ( fun ) ;
// code
}
void fun( void )
{
printf ( "\nTerminate program......" ) ;
getch( ) ;
}
```

167. What are memory models?

Ans. The compiler uses a memory model to determine how much memory is allocated to the program. The PC divides memory into blocks called segments of size 64 KB. Usually, program uses one segment for code and a second segment for data. A memory model defines the number of segments the compiler can use for each. It is important to know which memory model can be used for a program. If we use wrong memory model, the program might not have enough memory to execute. The problem can be solved using larger memory model. However, larger the memory model, slower is your program execution. So we must choose the smallest memory model that satisfies our program needs. Most of the compilers support memory models like tiny, small, medium, compact, large and huge.

168. How does C compiler store elements in a multi-dimensional array?

Ans. The compiler maps multi-dimensional arrays in two ways-Row major order and Column order. When the compiler places elements in columns of an array first then it is called column-major order. When the compiler places elements in rows of an array first then it is called row-major order. C compilers store multidimensional arrays in row-major order. For example, if there is a multi-dimensional array a[2][3], then according row-major order, the elements would get stored in memory following order:

a[0][0], a[0][1], a[0][2], a[1][0], a[1][1], a[1][2]

169. If the result of an _expression has to be stored to one of two variables, depending on a condition, can we use conditional operators as shown below?

```
( ( i < 10 ) ? j : k ) = l * 2 + p ;
```

Ans: No! The above statement is invalid. We cannot use the conditional operators in this fashion. The conditional operators like most operators, yields a value, and we cannot assign the value of an _expression to a value. However, we can use conditional operators as shown in following code snippet.

```
main( )
{
int i, j, k, l ;
i = 5 ; j = 10 ; k = 12, l = 1 ;
```

```
* ( ( i < 10 ) ? &j : &k ) = 1 * 2 + 14 ;
printf ( "i = %d j = %d k = %d l = %d", i, j, k, l ) ;
}
```

The output of the above program would be as given below:

i = 5 j = 16 k = 12 l = 1

170. Illustrate the use of ceil( ) and floor( ).

Ans. The math function ceil( ) takes a double value as an argument. This function finds the smallest possible integer to which the given number can be rounded up. Similarly, floor( ) being a math function, takes a double value as an argument and returns the largest possible integer to which the given double value can be rounded down. The following program demonstrates the use of both the functions.

```
#include <math.h>
void main( )
{
double no = 1437.23167 ;
double down, up ;
down = floor ( no ) ;
up = ceil ( no ) ;

printf ( "The original number %7.5lf\n", no ) ;
printf ( "The number rounded down %7.5lf\n", down ) ;
printf ( "The number rounded up %7.5lf\n", up ) ;
}
```

The output of this program would be,

The original number 1437.23167
The number rounded down 1437.00000
The number rounded up 1438.00000

171. How do I use function ecvt( ) in a program?

Ans. The function ecvt( ) converts a floating-point value to a null terminated string. This function takes four arguments, such as, the value to be converted to string, the number of digits to be converted to string, and two integer pointers. The two-integer pointer stores the position of the decimal point (relative to the string) and the sign of the number, respectively. If the value in a variable, used to store sign is 0, then the number is positive and, if it is non-zero, then the number is negative. The function returns a pointer to the string containing digits. Following program demonstrates the use of this function.

```
#include <stdlib.h>
main( )
{
char *str ;
double val ;
int dec, sign ;
int ndig = 4 ;
val = 22 ;
str = ecvt ( val, ndig, &dec, &sign ) ;
printf ( "string = %s dec = %d sign = %d\n", str, dec, sign ) ;
val = -345.67 ;
```

```
ndig = 8 ;
str = ecvt ( val, ndig, &dec, &sign ) ;
printf ( "string = %s dec = %d sign = %d\n", str, dec, sign ) ;

// number with a scientific notation
val = 3.546712e5 ;
ndig = 5 ;
str = ecvt ( val, ndig, &dec, &sign ) ;
printf ( "string = %s dec = %d sign = %d\n", str, dec, sign ) ;
}
```

The output of this program would be

```
string = 2200 dec = 2 sign = 0
string = 34567000 dec = 3 sign = 1
string = 35467 dec = 6 sign = 0
```

172. How to run DIR command programmatically?

Ans. We can use the system( ) function to execute the DIR command along with its options. Following program shows how this can be achieved:

```
// mydir.c
main ( int argc, char *argv[ ])
{
char str[30] ;

if ( argc < 2 )
exit ( 0 ) ;

sprintf ( str, "dir %s %s", argv[1], argv[2] ) ;
system ( str ) ;
}
```

If we run the executable file of this program at command prompt passing the command line arguments as follows:

```
> mydir abc.c /s
```

This will search the file 'abc.c' in the current directory.

173. Suppose I have a structure having fields name, age, salary and have passed address of age to a function fun( ). How I can access the other member of the structure using the address of age?

Ans.

```
struct emp
{
char name[20] ;
int age ;
float salary ;
} ;
main( )
{
struct emp e ;
```

```
printf ( "\nEnter name: " ) ;
scanf ( "%s", e.name ) ;
printf ( "\nEnter age: " ) ;
scanf ( "%d", &e.age ) ;
printf ( "\nEnter salary: " ) ;
scanf ( "%f", &e.salary ) ;
fun ( &e.age ) ;
}
fun ( int *p )
{
struct emp *q ;
int offset ;
offset = ( char * ) ( & ( ( struct emp * ) 0 ) -> age ) - ( char * ) ( (
struct emp* ) 0 ) ;
q = ( struct emp * ) ( ( char * ) p - offset ) ;
printf ( "\nname: %s", q -> name ) ;
printf ( "\nage: %d", q -> age ) ;
printf ( "\nsalary: %f", q -> salary ) ;
}
```

174. How to restrict the program's output to a specific screen region?

Ans. A C function window( ) can be used to restrict the screen output to a specific region. The window( ) function defines a text-mode window. The parameters passed to this function defines the upper-left and lower-right corner of the region within which you want the output. In the following program, the string 'Hello!' gets printed within the specified region. To print the string we must use cprintf( ) function which prints directly on the text-mode window.

```
#include <conio.h>
main( )
{
int i, j ;

window ( 20, 8, 60, 17 ) ;
for ( i = 0 ; i < 8 ; i++ )
for ( j = 0 ; j < 10 ; j++ )
cprintf ( "Hello!" ) ;
}
```

175. Sometimes you need to prompt the user for a password. When the user types in the password, the characters the user enters should not appear on the screen. How will you achieve it?

Ans. A standard library function getpass( ) can be used to perform such function. Maximum number of characters that can be entered as password is 8.

```
main( )
{
char *pwd ;
pwd = getpass ( "Enter Password" ) ;
if ( strcmp ( pwd, "orgcity" ) )
```

```
printf ( "\nPassword %s is incorrect", pwd ) ;
else
printf ( "\nCorrect Password" ) ;
}
```

176. How to obtain the current drive through C ?

Ans. We can use the function _getdrive( ) to obtain the current drive. The _getdrive( ) function uses DOS function 0X19 to get the current drive number

```
#include <direct.h>
main( )
{
int disk ;
disk = _getdrive( ) + 'A' - 1 ;
printf ( "The current drive is: %c\n", disk ) ;
}
```

177. How come the output for both the programs is different when the logic is same?

Ans.

```
main( )
{
int i, j ;

for ( i = 1, j = 1 ; i <= 5, j <= 100 ; i++, j++ )
{
gotoxy ( 1, 1, ) ;
printf ( "%d %d", i, j ) ;
}
}
main( )
{
int i, j ;

for ( i =1, j = 1; j <= 100, i <= 5; i++, j++ )
{
gotoxy ( 1, 1 ) ;
printf ( "%d %d", i, j ) ;
}
}
```

Output -> 5 5

Even if logic of both the programs is same the output of the first program comes out to be 100, 100, but of the second program it is 5, 5. The comma operator plays a vital role inside the for loop. It always considers the value of the latest variable. So, at the time of testing the condition in for loop, the value of j will be considered in the first program and value of i in the second.

178. Can we get the x and y coordinate of the current cursor position ?

Ans. The function wherex( ) and wherey( ) returns the x-coordinate and y-coordinate of the current cursor position respectively. Both the functions return an integer value. The value returned by wherex( ) is the horizontal position of cursor and the value returned by wherey( ) is the vertical position of the cursor. Following program shows how to use the wherex( ) and wherey( ) functions.

```
#include <conio.h>
main( )
{
printf ( "Just\n To\n Test\n Where\n the cursor\n goes" ) ;
printf ( "Current location is X: %d Y: %d\n", wherex( ), wherey( ) ) ;
}
```

179. How do I programmatically delete lines in the text window?

Ans. While writing programs that perform screen-based I/O, you may want to-delete the current line's contents, moving one line up, all of the output that follows. In such cases a function called delline( ) can be used. Following code snippet illustrates the use of function delline( ).

```
#include <conio.h>
main( )
{
int i ;
clrscr( ) ;

for ( i = 0; i <= 23; i++ )
printf ( "Line %d\r\n", i ) ;

printf ( "Press a key to continue : " ) ;
getch( ) ;

gotoxy ( 2, 6 ) ;

for ( i = 6; i <= 12; i++ )
delline( ) ;

getch( ) ;
}
```

180. How do I get the time elapsed between two function calls ?

Ans. The function difftime( ) finds the difference between two times. It calculates the elapsed time in seconds and returns the difference between two times as a double value.

```
#include <time.h>
#include <stdio.h>
#include <dos.h>
main( )
{
int a[] = { 2, -34, 56, 78, 112, 33, -7, 11, 45, 29, 6 } ;
int s ;
time_t t1, t2 ; // time_t defines the value used for time function
s = sizeof ( a ) / 2 ;
t1 = time ( NULL ) ;
sel_sort ( a, s ) ; // sort array by selection sort
bub_sort ( a, s ) ; // sort array by bubble sort method
t2 = time ( NULL ) ;
```

```
printf ( "\nThe difference between two function calls is %f", difftime (
t2, t1 ) ) ;
}
```

In the above program we have called difftime( ) function that returns the time elapsed from t1 to t2.

181. How do I use swab( ) in my program ?

Ans. The function swab( ) swaps the adjacent bytes of memory. It copies the bytes from source string to the target string, provided that the number of characters in the source string is even. While copying, it swaps the bytes which are then assigned to the target string.

```
#include <stdlib.h>
#include <stdio.h>
#include <string.h>
main ( )
{
char *str1 = "hS eesll snsiasl not eh es as oher " ;
char *str2 ;
clrscr( ) ;
swab ( str1, str2, strlen ( str1 ) ) ;
printf ( "The target string is : %s\n", str2 ) ; // output -- She sells
snails on the sea shore
getch( ) ;
}
```

182. I have an array declared in file 'F1.C' as,

```
int a[ ] = { 1, 2, 3, 4, 5, 6 } ;
```

and used in the file 'F2.C' as,

```
extern int  a[ ] ;
```

In the file F2.C, why sizeof doesn't work on the array a[ ]?

Ans. An extern array of unspecified size is an incomplete type. You cannot apply sizeof to it, because sizeof operates during compile time and it is unable to learn the size of an array that is defined in another file. You have three ways to resolve this problem:

1. In file 'F1.C' define as,

```
int a[ ] = { 1, 2, 3, 4, 5, 6 } ;
int size_a = sizeof ( a ) ;
```

and in file F2.C declare as,

```
extern int a[ ] ;
extern int size_a ;
```

2. In file 'F1.H' define,

```
#define ARR_SIZ 6
```

In file F1.C declare as,

```
#include "F1.H"
int a[ ARR_SIZ ] ;
```

and in file F2.C declare as,

```
#include "F1.H"
extern int a[ ARR_SIZ ] ;
```

3. In file 'F1.C' define as,
int a[ ] = { 1, 2, 3, 4, 5, 6, -1 } ;
and in file 'F2.C' declare as,
extern int a[ ] ;
Here the element -1 is used as a sentinel value, so the code can understand the end without any explicit size.

183. How to delete a line from text displayed on the screen?

Ans. Sometimes, specially when we are creating a text editor like program we may wish to allow user to delete a line. We can do so by using two functions namely clreol( ) and delline( ). The clreol( ) function deletes the line from the current cursor position to the end of line. The delline() function deletes the entire line at the current cursor position and moves up the following line. Following program shows how to use these functions.

```
#include <conio.h>
main( )
{
int i ;
for ( i = 1 ; i <= 20 ; i++ )
printf ( "This is Line %d\n", i ) ;
getch( ) ;
gotoxy ( 1, 7 ) ;
clreol( ) ;
getch( ) ;
gotoxy ( 1, 12 ) ;
delline( ) ;
getch( ) ;
}
```

184. How do I programmatically insert lines in the text window?

Ans. We can insert a blank line in the text window using the insline( ) function. This function inserts line at current cursor position. While doing so, it shifts down the lines that are below the newly inserted line.

```
#include <conio.h>
void main( )
{
printf ( "The little snail was slowly moving up. She wanted\r\n" ) ;
printf ( "to reach the top of the tree. It was chilly\r\n" ) ;
printf ( "winter season. Most of the animals were resting in\r\n" ) ;
printf ( "their nests as there was a heavy snow fall.\r\n" ) ;
printf ( "\r\nPress any key to continue:" ) ;

gotoxy ( 10, 2 ) ;
getch( ) ;
insline( ) ;
getch( ) ;
}
```

185. What will be the output of the following program?

```
main( )
{
unsigned int num ;
int i ;

printf ( "\nEnter any number" ) ;
scanf ( "%u", &num ) ;

for ( i = 0 ; i < 16 ; i++ )
printf ( "%d", ( num << i & 1 << 15 ) ? 1 : 0 ) ;
}
```

Ans. The output of this program is the binary equivalent of the given number. We have used bitwise operators to get the binary number.

186. Towers of Hanoi

Ans. Suppose there are three pegs labeled A, B and C. Four disks are placed on peg A. The bottom-most disk is largest, and disks go on decreasing in size with the topmost disk being smallest. The objective of the game is to move the disks from peg A to peg C, using peg B as an auxiliary peg. The rules of the game are as follows:

Only one disk may be moved at a time, and it must be the top disk on one of the pegs. A larger disk should never be placed on the top of a smaller disk. Suppose we are to write a program to print out the sequence in which the disks should be moved such that all disks on peg A are finally transferred to peg C. Here it is...

```
main( )
{
int n = 4 ;
move ( n, 'A', 'B', 'C' ) ;
}

move ( n, sp, ap, ep )
int n ;
char sp, ap, ep ;
{
if ( n == 1 )
printf ( "\n Move from %c to %c ", sp, ep ) ;
else
{
move ( n - 1, sp, ep, ap ) ;
move ( 1, sp, ' ', ep ) ;
move ( n - 1, ap, sp, ep ) ;
}
}
```

And here is the output...

Move from A to B
Move from A to C

Move from B to C
Move from A to B
Move from C to A
Move from C to B
Move from A to B
Move from A to C
Move from B to C
Move from B to A
Move from C to A
Move from B to C
Move from A to B
Move from A to C
Move from B to C

This problem is the famous Towers of Hanoi problem, wherein three pegs are to be employed for transferring the disks with the given criteria. Here's how we go about it. We have three pegs: the starting peg, sp, the auxiliary peg ap, and the ending peg, ep, where the disks must finally be. First, using the ending peg as an auxiliary or supporting peg, we transfer all but the last disk to ap. Next the last disk is moved from sp to ep. Now, using sp as the supporting peg, all the disks are moved from ap to ep. 'A', B and C denote the three pegs. The recursive function move( ) is called with different combinations of these pegs as starting, auxiliary and ending pegs.

187. What would be the output of following program?

```
struct syntax
{
int i ;
float g ;
char c ;
}
main( )
{
printf ( "I won't give you any error" ) ;
}
```

Ans. The above program would get compiled successfully and on execution it would print the message given in printf(). What strikes in the above code snippet is the structure syntax which is declared but not terminated with the statement terminator, the semicolon. The compiler would not give any error message for it, as it assumes that main( ) function have a return type of struct syntax and hence would successfully compile and execute the program.

188. How to get the memory size ?

Ans. Consider the following program

```
#include <stdio.h>
#include <bios.h>
main( )
{
int memsize;
memsize = biosmemory( ) ;
printf ( "RAM size = %dK\n",memsize ) ;
```

```
return 0 ;
}
```

The function biosmemory uses BIOS interrupt 0x12 to return the size of memory.

189. What is Float Format? How does C compiler stores float values?

Ans. In C, the float values are stored in a mantissa and exponent form. While writing a number we specify the exponent part in the form of base 10. But, in case of C compiler, the exponent for floats is stored in the form of base 2. Obviously, because, computer stores the numbers in binary form. The C compiler follows an IEEE standard to store a float. The IEEE format expresses a floating-point number in a binary form known as `normalized' form. Normalization involves adjusting the exponent so that the "binary point" (the binary analog of the decimal point) in the mantissa always lies to the right of most significant nonzero digit. In binary representation, this means that the most significant digit of the mantissa is always a 1. This property of the normalized representation is exploited by the IEEE format when storing the mantissa. Let us consider an example of generating the normalized form of a floating point number. Suppose we want to represent the decimal number 5.375. Its binary equivalent can be obtained as shown below:

```
2 | 5
.375 x 2 = 0.750 0
|------
.750 x 2 = 1.500 1
2 | 2 1
.500 x 2 = 1.000 1
|------
2 | 1 0
|------
| 0 1
```

Writing remainders in reverse writing whole parts in the same order we get 101 order in which they are obtained we get 011 thus the binary equivalent of 5.375 would be 101.011. The normalized form of this binary number is obtained by adjusting the exponent until the decimal point is to the right of most significant 1. In this case the result is 1.01011 x 22. The IEEE format for floating point storage uses a sign bit, a mantissa and an exponent for representing the power of 2. The sign bit denotes the sign of the number: a 0 represents a positive value and a 1 denotes a negative value. The mantissa is represented in binary. Converting the floating-point number to its normalized form results in a mantissa whose most significant digit is always 1. The IEEE format takes advantage of this by not storing this bit at all. The exponent is an integer stored in unsigned binary format after adding a positive integer bias. This ensures that the stored exponent is always positive. The value of the bias is 127 for floats and 1023 for doubles. Thus, 1.01011 x 22 is represented as shown below:

```
--- ---------------- ---------------------------------------------
| 0 | 100 0000 1 | 010 1100 0000 0000 0000 0000 |
--- ---------------- ---------------------------------------------
```

sign bit exponent- mantissa stored in normalized form obtained after adding a bias 127 to exponent 2

190. Which is the best sorting method?

Ans. There is no sorting method that is universally superior to all others. The programmer must carefully examine the problem and the desired results before deciding the particular sorting method. Some of the sorting methods are given below:

Bubble sort : When a file containing records is to be sorted then Bubble sort is the best sorting method when sorting by address is used.

Bsort : It can be recommended if the input to the file is known to be nearly sorted.

Meansort : It can be recommended only for input known to be very nearly sorted.

Quick Sort : In the virtual memory environment, where pages of data are constantly being swapped back and forth between external and internal storage. In practical situations, quick sort is often the fastest available because of its low overhead and its average behavior.

Heap sort : Generally used for sorting of complete binary tree. Simple insertion sort and straight selection sort : Both are more efficient than bubble sort. Selection sort is recommended for small files when records are large and for reverse situation insertion sort is recommended. The heap sort and quick sort are both more efficient than insertion or selection for large number of data.

Shell sort : It is recommended for moderately sized files of several hundred elements.

Radix sort : It is reasonably efficient if the number of digits in the keys is not too large.

191. Suppose we have a floating-point number with higher precision say 12.126487687 and we wish it to be printed with only precision up to two decimal places. How can I do this?

Ans. This can achieved through the use of suppression char '*' in the format string of printf( ) which is shown in the following program.

```
main( )
{
int p = 2 ;
float n = 12.126487687 ;
printf ( "%.*f",p, n ) ;
}
```

192. What is an rvalue?

Ans. rvalue can be defined as an expression that can be assigned to an lvalue. The rvalue appears on the right side of an assignment statement.

Unlike an lvalue, an rvalue can be a constant or an expression, as shown here:

```
int x, y;
x = 1;          /* 1 is an rvalue; x is an lvalue */
y = (x + 1);        /* (x + 1) is an rvalue; y is an lvalue */
```

An assignment statement must have both an lvalue and an rvalue. Therefore, the following statement would not compile because it is missing an rvalue:

```
int x; x = void_function_call() /* the function void_function_call() returns nothing */
```

If the function had returned an integer, it would be considered an rvalue because it evaluates into something that the lvalue, x, can store.

193. Is left-to-right or right-to-left order guaranteed for operator precedence?

Ans. The simple answer to this question is neither. The C language does not always evaluate left-to-right or right-to-left. Generally, function calls are evaluated first, followed by complex expressions and then simple expressions.

Additionally, most of today's popular C compilers often rearrange the order in which the expression is evaluated in order to get better optimized code. You therefore should always implicitly define your operator precedence by using parentheses.

For example, consider the following expression:

```
a = b + c/d / function_call() * 5
```

The way this expression is to be evaluated is totally ambiguous, and you probably will not get the results you want. Instead, try writing it by using implicit operator precedence:

```
a = b + (((c/d) / function_call()) * 5)
```

Using this method, you can be assured that your expression will be evaluated properly and that the compiler will not rearrange operators for optimization purposes.

194. What is the difference between ++var and var++?

Ans. The ++ operator is called the increment operator. When the operator is placed before the variable (++var), the variable is incremented by 1 before it is used in the expression. When the operator is placed after the variable (var++), the expression is evaluated, and then the variable is incremented by 1.

The same holds true for the decrement operator (--). When the operator is placed before the variable, you are said to have a prefix operation. When the operator is placed after the variable, you are said to have a postfix operation.

For instance, consider the following example of postfix incrementation:

```
int x, y;
x = 1;
y = (x++ * 5);
```

In this example, postfix incrementation is used, and x is not incremented until after the evaluation of the expression is done. Therefore, y evaluates to 1 times 5, or 5. After the evaluation, x is incremented to 2.

Now look at an example using prefix incrementation:

```
int x, y;
x = 1;
y = (++x * 5);
```

This example is the same as the first one, except that this example uses prefix incrementation rather than postfix. Therefore, x is incremented before the expression is evaluated, making it 2. Hence, y evaluates to 2 times 5, or 10.

195. What does the modulus operator do?

Ans. The modulus operator (%) gives the remainder of two divided numbers. For instance, consider the following portion of code:

x = 15/7

If x were an integer, the resulting value of x would be 2. However, consider what would happen if you were to apply the modulus operator to the same equation:

x = 15%7

The result of this expression would be the remainder of 15 divided by 7, or 1. This is to say that 15 divided by 7 is 2 with a remainder of 1.

The modulus operator is commonly used to determine whether one number is evenly divisible into another. For instance, if you wanted to print every third letter of the alphabet, you would use the following code:

```
int x;
for (x=1; x<=26; x++)
    if ((x%3) == 0)
        printf("%c", x+64);
```

The preceding example would output the string "cfilorux", which represents every third letter in the alphabet.

196. Unique combinations for a given number

Ans. How do I write a program which can generate all possible combinations of numbers from 1 to one less than the given number?

```
main( )
{
long steps, fval, bstp, cnt1 ;
int num, unit, box[2][13], cnt2, cnt3, cnt4 ;
printf ( "Enter Number " ) ;
scanf ( "%d", &num ) ;
num = num < 1 ? 1 : num > 12 ? 12 : num ;
for ( steps = 1, cnt1 = 2 ; cnt1 <= num ; steps *= cnt1++ ) ;
for ( cnt1 = 1 ; cnt1 <= steps ; cnt1++ )
{
for ( cnt2 = 1 ; cnt2 <= num ; cnt2++ )
box[0][cnt2] = cnt2 ;
for ( fval = steps, bstp = cnt1, cnt2 = 1 ; cnt2 <= num ; cnt2++ )
{
if ( bstp == 0 )
{
cnt4=num ;
while ( box[0][cnt4] == 0 )
cnt4-- ;
}
else
{
fval /= num - cnt2 + 1 ;
unit = ( bstp + fval - 1 ) / fval ;
bstp %= fval ;
for ( cnt4 = 0, cnt3 = 1 ; cnt3 <= unit ; cnt3++ )
while ( box[0][++cnt4] == 0 ) ;
}
box[1][cnt2] = box[0][cnt4] ;
box[0][cnt4] = 0 ;
}
printf ( "\nSeq.No.%ld:", cnt1 ) ;
for ( cnt2 = 1 ; cnt2 <= num ; cnt2++ )
printf ( " %d", box[1][cnt2] ) ;
}
}
```

This program computes the total number of steps. But instead of entering into the loop of the first and last combination to be generated it uses a loop of 1 to number of combinations. For example, in case of input being 5 the number of possible combinations would be factorial 5, i.e. 120. The program suffers from the limitation that it cannot generate combinations for input beyond 12 since a long int cannot handle the resulting combinations.

197. Write a program that demonstrates how to get input from the user in graphics mode, echoed in the current colors and font size and font style.

Ans.

```
#define ON 1
#define OFF 0
#include <graphics.h>
main( )
{
char nameString[80], ageString[80] ;
int age, gd = DETECT, gm ;
initgraph ( &gd, &gm, "c:\\tc\\bgi" ) ;
setbkcolor ( BLUE ) ;
setcolor ( YELLOW ) ;
settextstyle ( GOTHIC_FONT, HORIZ_DIR, 0 ) ;
moveto ( 0, 0 ) ;
outtext ( "Enter your name: " ) ;
getGrString ( nameString ) ;
moveto ( 0, gety( ) + textheight ( "A" ) ) ;
outtext ( "Name: " ) ;
outtext ( nameString ) ;
moveto ( 0, gety( ) + textheight ( "A" ) ) ;
outtext ( "Press key to exit! " ) ;
getch( ) ;
closegraph( ) ;
restorecrtmode( ) ;
}
getGrString ( char *inputString )
{
int stringIndex = 0, oldColor ;
char ch, outString[2] ;
/* xVal will store the screen position for each char */
int xVal[255] ;
outString[1] = 0 ;
xVal[0] = getx( ) ;
do
{
cursor ( ON ) ;
ch = getch( ) ;
cursor ( OFF ) ;
if ( ch == 0 ) /* avoid dealing with all special keys */
getch( ) ;
else
{
```

```
if ( ch == 8 ) /* backspace */
{
oldColor = getcolor( ) ;
--stringIndex ;
if ( stringIndex < 0 )
stringIndex = 0 ;
/* move to ( old horz position, current vert position ) */
moveto ( xVal[stringIndex], gety( ) ) ;
setcolor ( getbkcolor( ) ) ;
outString[0] = inputString[stringIndex] ;
outtext ( outString ) ;
moveto ( xVal [stringIndex], gety( ) ) ;
setcolor ( oldColor ) ;
}
else
{
inputString[stringIndex] = ch ;
outString[0] = ch ;
outtext ( outString ) ;
++stringIndex ;
xVal[stringIndex] = getx( ) ;
}
}
} while ( ch != 13 && ch != 10 ) ;
inputString[stringIndex] = 0 ;
}
cursor ( int on )
{
int curX, oldColor ;
/* we'll use an underscore as a cursor */
char uBarStr[2] = { '_', 0 } ;
if ( !on )
{
oldColor = getcolor( ) ;
setcolor ( getbkcolor( ) ) ;
}
/* save horizontal position before drawing cursor */
curX = getx( ) ;
outtext ( uBarStr ) ;
moveto ( curX, gety( ) ) ;
/* if we changed the color to erase cursor, change it back */
if ( !on )
setcolor ( oldColor ) ;
```

```
}
```

The function getGrString( ) echoes graphically the user input and stores it in a buffer, and the function cursor( ) handles the cursor position.

198. How do I get the time elapsed between two function calls?

Ans. The function difftime( ) finds the difference between two times. It calculates the elapsed time in seconds and returns the difference between two times as a double value.

```
#include <time.h>
#include <stdio.h>
#include <dos.h>
main( )
{
int a[] = { 2, -34, 56, 78, 112, 33, -7, 11, 45, 29, 6 } ;
int s ;
time_t t1, t2 ; // time_t defines the value used for time function
s = sizeof ( a ) / 2 ;
t1 = time ( NULL ) ;
sel_sort ( a, s ) ; // sort array by selection sort
bub_sort ( a, s ) ; // sort array by bubble sort method
t2 = time ( NULL ) ;
printf ( "\nThe difference between two function calls is %f", difftime (
t2, t1 ) ) ;
}
```

In the above program we have called difftime( ) function that returns the time elapsed from t1 to t2.

199. Develop a general program to convert a number to binary, octal and hexadecimal equivalent. Implement it for converting the number 128 to the binary.

Ans.

General

```
main( )
{
char *s ;
s = fun ( 128, 2 ) ;
printf ( "\n%s", s ) ;
}
fun ( unsigned int num, int base )
{
static char buff[33] ;
char *ptr ;
ptr = &buff [ sizeof ( buff ) - 1 ] ;
*ptr = '\0' ;
do
{
*--ptr = "0123456789abcdef"[ num % base ] ;
num /= base ;
```

```
} while ( num != 0 ) ;
return ptr ;
}
```

The above program would convert the number 128 to the base 2. You can convert a number to a hexadecimal or octal form by passing the number and the base, to the function fun( ).

200. Can we get the remainder of a floating point division?

Ans. Yes. Although the % operator fails to work on float numbers we can still get the remainder of floating point division by using a function fmod( ). The fmod( ) function divides the two float numbers passed to it as parameters and returns the remainder as a floating-point value. Following program shows fmod( ) function at work.

```
#include <math.h>

main( )
{
printf ( "%f", fmod ( 5.15, 3.0 ) ) ;
}
```

The above code snippet would give the output as 2.150000.

ADDITIONAL DESCRIPTIVE QUESTIONS ON C

1. Describe about storage allocation and scope of global, extern, static, local and register variables?
2. What are register variables? What are the advantage of using register variables?
3. What is the use of typedef?
4. Can we specify variable field width in a scanf() format string? If possible how?
5. Out of fgets() and gets() which function is safe to use and why?
6. Difference between strdup and strcpy?
7. What is recursion?
8. Differentiate between a for loop and a while loop? What are it uses?
9. What are the different storage classes in C?
10. Write down the equivalent pointer expression for referring the same element a[i][j][k][l]?
11. What is difference between Structure and Unions?
12. What the advantages of using Unions?
13. What are the advantages of using pointers in a program?
14. What is the difference between Strings and Arrays?
15. In a header file whether functions are declared or defined?
16. What does static variable mean?
17. What is a pointer?
18. What are the uses of a pointer?
19. What is a structure?
20. What is a union?
21. What are the differences between structures and union?
22. What are the differences between structures and arrays?
23. In header files whether functions are declared or defined?
24. What are the differences between malloc () and calloc ()?
25. What are macros? What are its advantages and disadvantages?
26. Difference between pass by reference and pass by value.
27. What is static identifier?
28. Where is the auto variables stored?
29. Where does global, static, and local, register
30. Difference between arrays and linked list?
31. What are enumerations?
32. What are register variables? What are the advantages?
33. What is the use of typedef?

34. Can we specify variable field width in a scanf()
35. Out of fgets() and gets() which function is safe to use and why?
36. Difference between strdup and strcpy?
37. What is recursion?
38. Differentiate between a for loop and a while loop? What are it uses?
39. What is storage class.What are the different storage classes in C?
40. What the advantages of using Unions?
41. What is the difference between Strings and Arrays?
42. What is a far pointer? where we use it?
43. What is a huge pointer?
44. What is a normalized pointer ,how do we normalize a pointer?
45. What is near pointer.
46. In C, why is the void pointer useful? When would you use it?
47. What is a NULL Pointer? Whether it is same as an uninitialized pointer?
48. Are pointers integer ?
49. What does the error 'Null Pointer Assignment' means and what causes this error?
50. What is generic pointer in C?
51. Are the expressions arr and &arr same for an array of integers?
52. How pointer variables are initialized ?
53. What is static memory allocation ?
54. What is dynamic memory allocation?
55. What is the purpose of realloc ?
56. What is pointer to a pointer?
57. What is an array of pointers ?
58. Difference between linker and linkage ?
59. Is it possible to have negative index in an array?
60. Why is it necessary to give the size of an array in an array declaration ?
61. What modular programming ?
62. What is a function ?
63. What is an argument ?
64. What are built in functions ?
65. Difference between formal argument and actual argument ?
66. Is it possible to have more than one main() function in a C program ?
67. What is the difference between an enumeration and a set of pre-processor # defines?
68. How are Structure passing and returning implemented by the complier?
69. What is the similarity between a Structure, Union and enumeration?
70. Can a Structure contain a Pointer to itself?
71. How can we read/write Structures from/to data files?
72. Write a program which employs Recursion ?
73. Write a program which uses Command Line Arguments?
74. Difference between array and pointer ?
75. What do the 'c' and 'v' in argc and argv stand for?
76. What are C tokens ?
77. What are C identifiers?
78. Difference between syntax vs logical error?

79. What is preincrement and post increment ?
80. Write a program to interchange 2 variables without using the third one.
81. What is the maximum combined length of command line arguments including the space between adjacent arguments?
82. What are bit fields? What is the use of bit fields in a Structure declaration?
83. What is a preprocessor, What are the advantages of preprocessor ?
84. What are the facilities provided by preprocessor ?
85. What are the two forms of #include directive ?
86. How would you use the functions randomize() and random()?
87. What do the functions atoi(), itoa() and gcvt() do?
88. How would you use the functions fseek(), freed(), fwrite() and ftell()?
89. What is the difference between the functions memmove() and memcpy()?
90. What is a file ?
91. What are the types of file?
92. What is a stream ?
93. What is meant by file opening ?
94. What is a file pointer ?
95. How is fopen()used ?
96. How is a file closed ?
97. What is a random access file ?
98. What is the purpose of ftell ?
99. What is the purpose of rewind() ?
100. Difference between a array name and a pointer variable ?
101. Represent a two-dimensional array using pointer ?
102. Difference between an array of pointers and a pointer to an array ?
103. Can we use any name in place of argv and argc as command line arguments ?
104. What are the pointer declarations used in C?
105. Differentiate between a constant pointer and pointer to a constant ?
106. Is the allocated space within a function automatically deallocated when the function returns?
107. Discuss on pointer arithmetic?
108. What are the invalid pointer arithmetic ?
109. What are the advantages of using array of pointers to string instead of an array of strings?
110. Are the expressions *ptr ++ and ++ *ptr same ?
111. What would be the equivalent pointer expression foe referring the same element as a[p][q][r][s]?
112. Are the variables argc and argv are always local to main ?
113. Can main () be called recursively?
114. Can we initialize unions?
115. What's the difference between these two declarations?
116. Why doesn't this code: a[i] = i++; work?
117. Why doesn't struct x { … };x thestruct; work?
118. Why can't we compare structures?
119. How are structure passing and returning implemented?
120. What are the differences between structures and arrays?
121. In header files whether functions are declared or defined?
122. What are the differences between malloc() and calloc()?

123. What are macros? what are its advantages and disadvantages?
124. Difference between pass by reference and pass by value?
125. What is static identifier?
126. Where are the auto variables stored?
127. Where does global, static, local, register variables, free memory and C Program instructions get stored?
128. Difference between arrays and linked list?
129. What are enumerations?
130. What is a far pointer? where we use it?
131. How will you declare an array of three function pointers where each function receives two ints and returns a float?
132. What is a NULL Pointer? Whether it is same as an uninitialized pointer? What is a NULL Macro? What is the difference between a NULL Pointer and a NULL Macro?
133. What does the error 'Null Pointer Assignment' mean and what causes this error?
134. What is near, far and huge pointers? How many bytes are occupied by them?
135. How would you obtain segment and offset addresses from a far address of a memory location?
136. Are the expressions arr and &arr same for an array of integers?
137. Does mentioning the array name gives the base address in all the contexts?
138. Explain one method to process an entire string as one unit?
139. What is the similarity between a Structure, Union and enumeration?
140. Can a Structure contain a Pointer to itself?
141. How can we check whether the contents of two structure variables are same or not?
142. How are Structure passing and returning implemented by the complier?
143. How can we read/write Structures from/to data files?
144. What is the difference between an enumeration and a set of pre-processor # defines?
145. What do the 'c' and 'v' in argc and argv stand for?
146. Are the variables argc and argv are local to main?
147. What is the maximum combined length of command line arguments including the space between adjacent arguments?
148. If we want that any wildcard characters in the command line arguments should be appropriately expanded, are we required to make any special provision? If yes, which?
149. Does there exist any way to make the command line arguments available to other functions without passing them as arguments to the function?
150. What are bit fields? What is the use of bit fields in a Structure declaration?
151. To which numbering system can the binary number 1101100100111100 be easily converted to?
152. Which bit wise operator is suitable for checking whether a particular bit is on or off?
153. Which bit wise operator is suitable for turning off a particular bit in a number?
154. Which bit wise operator is suitable for putting on a particular bit in a number?
155. Which bit wise operator is suitable for checking whether a particular bit is on or off?
156. Which one is equivalent to multiplying by 2:Left shifting a number by 1 or Left shifting an unsigned int or char by 1?
157. Write a program to compare two strings without using the strcmp() function.
158. Write a program to concatenate two strings.
159. Write a program to interchange 2 variables without using the third one.
160. Write programs for String Reversal & Palindrome check

161. Write a program to find the Factorial of a number
162. Write a program to generate the Fibinocci Series
163. Write a program which employs Recursion
164. Write a program which uses Command Line Arguments
165. Write a program which uses functions like strcmp(), strcpy()? etc
166. What are the advantages of using typedef in a program?
167. How would you dynamically allocate a one-dimensional and two-dimensional array of integers?
168. How can you increase the size of a dynamically allocated array?
169. How can you increase the size of a statically allocated array?
170. When reallocating memory if any other pointers point into the same piece of memory do you have to readjust these other pointers or do they get readjusted automatically?
171. Which function should be used to free the memory allocated by calloc()?
172. How much maximum can you allocate in a single call to malloc()?
173. Can you dynamically allocate arrays in expanded memory?
174. What is object file? How can you access object file?
175. Which header file should you include if you are to develop a function which can accept variable number of arguments?
176. Can you write a function similar to printf()?
177. How can a called function determine the number of arguments that have been passed to it?
178. Can there be at least some solution to determine the number of arguments passed to a variable argument list function?
179. How do you declare the following:
    i. An array of three pointers to chars
    ii. An array of three char pointers
    iii. A pointer to array of three chars
    iv. A pointer to function which receives an int pointer and returns a float pointer
    v. A pointer to a function which receives nothing and returns nothing
180. What do the functions atoi(), itoa() and gcvt() do?
181. Does there exist any other function which can be used to convert an integer or a float to a string?
182. How would you use qsort() function to sort an array of structures?
183. How would you use qsort() function to sort the name stored in an array of pointers to string?
184. How would you use bsearch() function to search a name stored in array of pointers to string?
185. How would you use the functions sin(), pow(), sqrt()?
186. How would you use the functions memcpy(), memset(), memmove()?
187. How would you use the functions fseek(), freed(), fwrite() and ftell()?
188. How would you obtain the current time and difference between two times?
189. How would you use the functions randomize() and random()?
190. How would you implement a substr() function that extracts a sub string from a given string?
191. What is the difference between the functions rand(), random(), srand() and randomize()?
192. What is the difference between the functions memmove() and memcpy()?
193. How do you print a string on the printer?
194. Can you use the function fprintf() to display the output on the screen?
195. What is C language ?
196. What are the different storage classes in C ?
197. What is hashing ?

198. Can static variables be declared in a header file ?
199. Can a variable be both constant and volatile ?
200. Can include files be nested?
201. What is a null pointer ?
202. What is the output of printf("%d") ?
203. What is the difference between calloc() and malloc() ?
204. What is the difference between printf() and sprintf() ?
205. How to reduce a final size of executable ?
206. Can you tell me how to check whether a linked list is circular ?
207. Advantages of a macro over a function ?
208. What is the difference between strings and character arrays ?
209. Write down the equivalent pointer expression for referring the same element a[i][j][k][l] ?
210. Which bit wise operator is suitable for checking whether a particular bit is on or off ?
211. Which bit wise operator is suitable for turning off a particular bit in a number ?
212. Which bit wise operator is suitable for putting on a particular bit in a number ?
213. Does there exist any other function which can be used to convert an integer or a float to a string?
214. Why does malloc(0) return valid memory address ? What's the use ?
215. Difference between const char* p and char const* p
216. What is the result of using Option Explicit ?
217. What is the benefit of using an enum rather than a #define constant ?
218. What is the quickest sorting method to use ?
219. When should the volatile modifier be used ?
220. When should the register modifier be used? Does it really help ?
221. How can you determine the size of an allocated portion of memory ?
222. What is page thrashing ?
223. When does the compiler not implicitly generate the address of the first element of an array ?
224. What is the benefit of using #define to declare a constant ?
225. How can I search for data in a linked list ?
226. Why should we assign NULL to the elements (pointer) after freeing them ?
227. What is a null pointer assignment error ? What are bus errors, memory faults, and core dumps ?
228. When should a type cast be used ?
229. What is the difference between a string copy (strcpy) and a memory copy (memcpy)? When should each be used?
230. How can I convert a string to a number ?
231. How can I convert a number to a string ?
232. Is it possible to execute code even after the program exits the main() function?
233. What is the stack ?
234. How do you print an address ?
235. Can a file other than a .h file be included with #include ?
236. What is Preprocessor ?
237. How can you restore a redirected standard stream ?

238. What is the purpose of realloc( ) ?
239. What is the heap ?
240. How do you use a pointer to a function ?
241. What is the purpose of main( ) function ?
242. Why n++ executes faster than n+1 ?
243. What will the preprocessor do for a program ?
244. What is the benefit of using const for declaring constants ?
245. What is the easiest sorting method to use ?
246. Is it better to use a macro or a function ?
247. What are the standard predefined macros ?
248. How can I get the numeric value (i.e. ASCII or other character set code) corresponding to a character, or vice versa?
249. Does C have anything like the ``substr'' (extract substring) routine present in other languages?
250. I'm reading strings typed by the user into an array, and then printing them out later. When the user types a sequence like \n, why isn't it being handled properly?

REFERENCES

1. Bartee T C., *"Digital Computer Fundamentals"*, Tata Mc-Graw Hill Education Private Limited.
2. Nishit Mathur, *"Fundamentals Of Computers"*, Aph Publishing Corporation. 2010.
3. Amal Shankar Shukla, Navneet K Gaur, Madhu Gaur, *"Computer Fundamental And C Programming"*, A. B. Publication. 2010.
4. Gill Nasib Singh, *"Essentials of Computer and Network Technology", Khanna Book Publishing Co.(P) Ltd., N. Delhi.*
5. Satish Jain, *"Computer Fundamental & Data Processing"*, BPB Publications.
6. Manoj Wadhwa, *"Fundamental Of Computers"*, International Book House Pvt. Ltd. 2011.
7. Mandeep Bhatia Singh, *"Fundamentals Of Computer Hardware"*, Khanna Books Pub. Co.(P) Ltd. N Delhi, 2006.
8. Bhaskar Reddy Muvva Vijay, Jhansi P,Venu M., *"Fundamentals Of Computers And Information Technology",* Vdm Verlag. 2010.
9. William S. Davis, *"Computing Fundamentals: Concepts (the Computing Fundamentals Series)"*, Addison-wesley.
10. R B Patel, *"Fundamentals Of Computers And Programming In C",* Khanna Books Pub. Co.(P) Ltd. N Delhi.
11. Gill Nasib Singh and Dixit J.B., *"Digital Design and Computer Organisation", University Science Press (An Imprint of Laxmi Publications),* New Delhi
12. Amal Shankar Shukla, Navneet K Gaur, Madhu Gaur, *"Computer Fundamental And C Programming",* A. B. Publication, 2010.
13. Saroj Singh, *"Fundamentals Of Computer Programing In C",* Arihant Prakashan.
14. M.C. Govil, P.K. Agarwal, A.P. Mathur, Vibhakar Pathak, *"Computer Fundamentals And Programming In C",* Jaipur Publishing House.
15. Chanchal Mittal, *"Fundamentals Of Computer And Programming With C"*, Pragati Prakashan, 2003.
16. Dixit J B., *"Computer Fundamentals And Programming In C 1/e",* Laxmi Publications. 2006.
17. Leon, *"Fundamentals Of Computing C Programming & MS Office"*, Tata Mcgraw Hill Education Private Limited. 2004.
18. Gupta, *"Computer Fundamentals And C Programming",* Excel Books-new Delhi
19. Rizwan Khan, Rizwan Khan, *"Computer Fundamentals And C Programming MADE EASY"*, Cengage Learning India, 2010.
20. A K Sharma, *"Fundamentals Of Computers & Programming With C"*, Dhanpat Rai Publications (p) Ltd.
21. Pradeep Sinha, Priti Sinha. *"Computer Fundamentals"*. BPB publications.
22. Anita Goel, *"Computer Fundamentals"*, Pearson Education.

23. Wilson L.B., Clark R.G., *"Comparative Programming Languages"*, Addison-Wesley Publishing Company.
24. Rajaraman V, Radhakrishnan T, *"An Introduction to Digital Computer Design"*, Prentice-Hall of India Pvt. Ltd.
25. Grauer R.T., Sugrue P.K., *"Microcomputer Applications"*, McGraw-Hill.
26. Turley James L., *"PC Made Easy"*, McGraw-Hill.
27. Malvino A.P., *"Digital Computer Electronics : An Introduction to Microcomputers"*, 2bd Edition, Tata McGraw-Hill.
28. Helms H.L., *"The McGraw Hill Computer Handbook"*, McGraw-Hill.
29. Wright G.G.L., *"Mastering Computers"*, Macmillan.
30. *"386 PC Applications"*, Computers Today, New Delhi.
31. Hussain, *"Computers: Technology, Applications and Social Implications"*, Prentice Hall of India.
32. Malvino A.P., Leach D.P., *"Digital Principles and Applications"*, 2nd Edition, Tata McGraw-Hill.
33. Rajaraman V., *"Elements of Parallel Processing"*, Prentice-Hall of India.
34. Ram B., *"Fundamentals of Microprocessors and Microcomputers"*, 4th Edition, Dnahpat Rai & Sons, Delhi.
35. Hayes J.P., *"Computer Architecture And Organisation"*, McGraw-Hill.
36. Hall D.V., *"Microprocessors and Digital Systems"*, McGraw-Hill.
37. Tannenbaum A.S., *"Structured Computer Organisation"*, Prentice-Hall.
38. Bose Sanjay K., *"Digital Systems : From Gates to Microprocessors"*, New Age International Ltd., Wiley Eastern Limited.
39. Mandell S.L., *"Computers and Data Processing Today"*, West Publishing Company.
40. Spencer W.R., *"A Dictionary of Computer"*, CBS Publishers & Distributors.
41. Leeds H.D., Weingberg G.M., *"Computer Programming Fundamentals"*, McGraw Hill.
42. *"Sams' Teach Yourself The Internet Starter Kit in 24 Hours"*, Techmedia.
43. Leon Alexis, Leon Mathews, *"Fundamentals of Computer Science and Communication Engineering"*, Leon TECHWorld.
44. Mukherjee D.P., *"Fundamentals of Computer Graphics and Multimedia"*, Prentice-Hall India Pvt. Ltd.
45. Hunt R., Shrlly J., *"Computers and Commonsense"*, 4th Editiona, Prentice Hall.
46. Donald H. Sanders, *"Computer Concepts And Applications"*, McGraw-Hill International Editions.
47. Batree, T.C., *"Digital Computer Fundamentals"*, 5th Edition, McGraw-Hill.
48. Rajaraman V., *"Fundamental of Computers"*, Prentice-Hall of India Pvt. Ltd.
49. Lipschutz M.M., Lipschutz S., *"Theory and Problems of Data Processing"*, McGraw-Hill.
50. Rajagopalan R., *"Understanding Computers"*, Tata McGraw-Hill Publishing Company Limited.
51. Rozera, *"Computer Fundamentals"*, Vayu, 2011.
52. Juneja, Seth, *"Computer Fundamentals And C Programming"*, Cl India, 2011.
53. Rohit Khurana, *"Computer Fundamentals And Internet Basics"*, Aph Publishing Corporation, 2010.
54. Sudakshina Kundu, *"Fundamentals Of Computer Networks"*, Phi Learning Pvt Ltd, 2010.
55. Prof. Satish Jain, Shashi Singh, *"Digital Computer Fundamentals"*, BPB, 2008.
56. P N Basu, *"Computer Fundamentals And C Programming"*, Vikas Publishing House, 2011.
57. P Dey, M Ghosh, *"Computer Fundamentals And Programming In C"*, Oxford University Press India, 2006.
58. E Balagurusamy, *"Computing Fundamentals And C Programming"*, Tata McGraw Hill Education Private Limited. 2008.

59. Rajiv Khanna, *"Computer Fundamentals And Programming"*, New Age International. 2011
60. Bright Siaw Afriyie, *"Introduction To Computer Fundamentals"*, Trafford Publishing. 2006.
61. O. P. Nagpal, *"Computer Fundamental"*, 2004.
62. Brian W. Kernighan, Dennis M. Ritchie, *"The C Programming Language (ANSI C Version)"*, PHI Learning, 2009.
63. Yashavant Kanetkar, *"Understanding Pointers In C 4th Revised & Updated Edn."*, BPB Publications, 2003.
64. E Balagurusamy, *"Programming In ANSI C"*, Tata Mcgraw Hill Education Private. 2010.
65. Peter Van, Der Linden, "*Expert C Programming: Deep C Secrets"*, Pearson. 1994.
66. Yashavant Kanetkar, Asang Dani, *"Interview Questions In C Programming"*, BPB. 2008.
67. T Jeyapoovan, *"A First Course In Programming With C"*, Vikas Publishing House. 2002.
68. Stephen Kochan, *"Programming In C"*, Pearson, 2005.
69. Gottfried B S., *"Programming With C (Special Indian Edition) (Schaums Outline Series)"*, Tata McGraw Hill Education Private Limited, 2010.
70. Ashok N. Kamthane, *"Programming With ANSI And Turbo C"*, Pearson, 2002.
71. V Rajaraman, *"Computer Programming In C"*, PHI Learning. 2009.
72. Chhabra J K, *"C Programming Concepts: With Problems & Solutions"*, Tata McGraw Hill Education Private Limited.
73. Yashavant Kanetkar, *"ANSI C Programming"*, BPB Publications, 2009.
74. Susant K Rout, *"C Programming Test Your Knowledge"*, Vikas Publishing House. 2011.
75. Ghosh P. Dey M., *"Programming In C"*, Oxford University Press, 2007.
76. Schneider G.M., Bruell S., *"Advanced Programming and Problem Solving with Pascal"*, Wiley.
77. Ram B., *"Computer Fundamentals: Architecture And Organization"*, Wiley Eastern Limited, New Age International Ltd.
78. Bhujade M.R., *"Parallel Computing"*, New Age international Publishers.
79. James Martin, *"Computer Networks And Distributed Processing"*, Prentice-Hall of India Pvt. Ltd.
80. John Freer, *"Computer Communication and Networks"*, Affiliated East-West Press Pvt. Ltd.
81. Vikas Gupta, *"Computer Concepts And C Programming"*, Dreamtech Press, 2009.
82. Byron Gottfried, *"Schaum's Outline Of Programming With C"*, Mcgraw-Hill, 1996.
83. Donald H. Sanders, *"Computers Today"*, McGraw-Hill International Editions.
84. Schield F., *"Theory and Problems of Computers and Programming"*, Schaum's Outline Series, McGraw-Hill International Editions.
85. Rosch W.L., *"The Winn Rosch Hardware Bible"*, BPB Publications.
86. Gore M.R., Stubbe J.W., *"Computers and Information Systems"*, 2nd Edition, McGraw-Hill.
87. Bhujade M.R., *"Digital Computer Design Principles With Introduction to Microprocessor"*, Pitambar Publishing Company Pvt. Ltd.
88. Subramanian N, *"Introduction to Computers : Fundamentals of Computer Science"*, Tata McGraw Hill.
89. Hayes J.P., *"Digital System Design and Microprocessors"*, McGraw-Hill.
90. Bawankar Hemant, *"Principles of Computer Science"*, Upkar Prakashan.
91. Saxena Sanjay, *"A First Course In Computers"*, Vikas Publishing House.
92. Leon Alexis, Leon Mathews, *"Internet For Everyone"*, Leon TECHWorld.
93. Dickery, L.W., *"Introduction to Computer Concepts : Hardware and Software"*, Prentice-Hall.
94. N. Subramanian, S. Chithra, *"Computers"*, Wheeler Publishing Company.
95. V. B. Aggarwal, *"Principles of Computer Science"*, Pitambar Publishing Company.

96. Stallings William, *"Computer Organization And Architecture"*, Maxwell Macmillan International Editions.
97. Glee Harrah Cady, Pat McGregor, *"Mastering The Internet"*, BPB Publications.
98. Lacy M., *"Understanding Computer Systems Architecture"*, BPB Publications.
99. Hamcher, Vranesic, Zaky, *"Computer Organisation"*, 3rd Edition, McGraw-Hill.
100. Hahn Harley, *"The Internet Complete Reference"*, Osborne McGraw-Hill.
101. Cavanagh J., *"Digital Computer Architecture"*, McGraw-Hill.
102. Mischoff Henry C., *"Understanding Artificial Intelligence"*, BPB Publications.
103. Leon Alexis, Leon Mathews, *"Internet In A Nutshell"*, Leon TECHWorld.
104. Ghezii, Jazayeri, Mandrioli, *"Fundamentals of Software Engineering"*, Prentice-Hall of India Pvt. Ltd.
105. R. Szymanski, D. Szymanski, N. Morris, D. Pulschen, *"Introduction To Computers And Information Systems"*, Merrill Publishing Company, Ohio.
106. Board of Directors, *"Jaico Dictionary of Computers"*, Jaico Publishing House.
107. Singh S., *"Fundamental of Computers"*, Khanna Publications.
108. Mandell S.L., Hopper G.M., *"Understanding Computers"*, West Publishing Company.
109. Tannenbaum A.S., *"Operating Systems: Design and Implementation"*, Prentice Hall.
110. Milenkovic Milan, *"Operating Systems: Concepts and Design"*, McGraw-Hill.
111. Siegel P., *"Understanding Digital Computers"*, Wiley.
112. Delores M. Etter, *"Introduction To C"*, Prentice Hall. 1999.
113. Herbert Schildt, Schildt Herbert, *"C: The Complete Reference"*, McGraw-Hill/Osborne Media, 2004.
114. Jean Corriveau, *"A Step-By-Step Guide To C Programming"*, Prentice Hall, 1997.
115. Amit Verma, "*Fundamentals And C Programming,* Khanna Books Pub. Co.(P) Ltd. N. Delhi.
116. Dromey R.G., *"How to Solve it by Computer"*, Prentice-Hall of India Pvt. Ltd.
117. Dasgupta S., *"Computer Architecture : A Modern Synthesis"*, Vol.1-2, John Wiley and Sons.
118. Carter Roger, *"The Information Technology Handbook"*, Heinemann Professional Publishing Ltd.
119. Luce Thom, *"Computer Hardware, System Software, and Architecture"*, McGraw-Hill.
120. Leventhal L.A., *"Introduction to Microprocessors: Software, Hardware, Programming"*, Prentice-Hall.
121. Donna, Norma, Donald, Robert, *"Introduction to Computers And Information Systems"*, Merrill Publishing Company.
122. Chapra S.C., Canale R.P., *"Introduction to Computing for Engineers"*, McGraw-Hill.
123. Taube, Shilling, *"Principles of Communication Systems"*, McGraw-Hill.
124. Martin James, *"Telecommunications and the Computer"*, Prentice-Hall of India Pvt. Ltd.
125. Mano M. Morris, *"Computer System Architecture"*, Prentice-Hall of India Private Ltd.
126. Davies, G.B., *"Introduction to Computers"*, 3rd Edition, McGraw-Hill.
127. http://www.scribd.com/doc/19677666/Chronology-of-Computer-History
128. http://tomjamieson.wordpress.com/2011/02/14/the-history-of-computers-a-chronological-timeline-infographic/

INDEX